gem

Collins

German

Dictionary

HarperCollins Publishers
Westerhill Road
Bishopbriggs
Glasgow
G64 2QT

Eleventh Edition 2012

10 9 8 7 6 5 4

ISBN 978-0-00-743792-4

www.collins.co.uk

A catalogue record for this book is
available from the British Library

Typeset by RefineCatch Ltd,
Bungay, Suffolk

Supplement typeset by
Davidson Publishing Solutions,
Glasgow

Printed and bound in Italy by
LEGO SpA, Lavis (Trento)

Acknowledgements
We would like to thank those
authors and publishers who
kindly gave permission for
copyright material to be used in
the Collins Word Web. We would
also like to thank Times
Newspapers Ltd for providing
valuable data.

INHALT

CONTENTS

WARENZEICHEN

Warenzeichen, die unseres Wissens eingetragene Warenzeichen darstellen, sind als solche gekennzeichnet. Es ist jedoch zu beachten, dass weder das Vorhandensein noch das Fehlen derartiger Kennzeichnungen die Rechtslage hinsichtlich eingetragener Warenzeichen berührt.

NOTE ON TRADEMARKS

Words which we have reason to believe constitute trademarks have been designated as such. However, neither the presence nor the absence of such designation should be regarded as affecting the legal status of any trademark.

PROJECT MANAGEMENT
Gaëlle Amiot-Cadey
Ruth O'Donovan

EDITOR
Susie Beattie

CONTRIBUTORS
Marianne Noble
Maggie Seaton
Christine Bahr
Stuart Fortey
Helen Galloway
Horst Kopleck
Silke Probst
Robin Sawers
Veronika Schnorr

COMPUTING
Thomas Callan

FOR THE PUBLISHER
Lucy Cooper
Kerry Ferguson
Susanne Reichert

PUBLISHING DIRECTOR
Elaine Higgleton

EINFÜHRUNG

Wir freuen uns sehr, dass Sie sich zum Kauf eines Collins Wörterbuchs Deutsch entschlossen haben. Wir wünschen Ihnen viel Spaß beim Gebrauch in der Schule, zu Hause, im Urlaub und im Beruf.

Diese Einführung wird Ihnen einige nützliche Hinweise dazu geben, wie Sie am besten von Ihrem neuen Wörterbuch profitieren. Schließlich bietet Ihnen das Wörterbuch nicht nur Stichwörter und Übersetzungen, sondern auch zahlreiche Zusatzinformationen in jedem einzelnen Eintrag. Mit Hilfe all dieser Informationen können Sie zum einen ein modernes Deutsch lesen und verstehen, zum anderen auch aktiv auf Deutsch kommunizieren.

Das Collins Wörterbuch Deutsch gibt Ihnen vor dem eigentlichen Wörterbuchtextteil selbst eine Liste aller verwendeten Abkürzungen sowie eine Übersicht zu Aussprache und Gebrauch phonetischer Umschrift. Darüber hinaus finden Sie noch eine Auflistung zu den regelmäßigen deutschen Substantivendungen sowie zu unregelmäßigen englischen und deutschen Verben. Auf den letzten Seiten Ihres Wörterbuchs finden Sie in einem „kleinen Reise-ABC" zahlreiche nützliche Phrasen für verschiedenste Situationen am Urlaubsort.

WIE FINDE ICH WAS?

Die verschiedenen Schriftarten, Schriftgrößen, Symbole, Abkürzungen und Klammern helfen Ihnen dabei, sich innerhalb der Informationen, die das Wörterbuch bietet, zurechtzufinden. Die Konventionen, die diesem Wörterbuch zugrunde liegen, sowie auch der Gebrauch verschiedener Symbole werden im Folgenden näher erläutert.

STICHWÖRTER

Die Wörter, die Sie in Ihrem Wörterbuch nachschlagen, die Stichwörter, sind in alphabetischer Reihenfolge angeordnet. Sie sind **fett** gedruckt und in blauer Farbe, sodass Sie sie schnell finden. Die Stichwörter, die rechts und links oben auf jeder Seite erscheinen, sind das jeweils erste Stichwort einer Seite, wenn es sich dabei um eine linke Seite handelt, bzw. das letzte Stichwort einer Seite, wenn es sich um eine rechte Seite handelt.

Informationen zu Form und Gebrauch des jeweiligen Stichworts werden im Anschluss an die Lautschrift in Klammern angegeben. Normalerweise sind diese Angaben in abgekürzter Form und *kursiver Schrift* (z.B. *(fam)* für umgangssprachlich oder *(Comm)* als Sachgebietsangabe für Wirtschaft).

Wo es sich anbietet, werden zusammengehörige Wörter und Wortgruppen in einem Eintrag zusammengefasst (z.B. gather, **gathering**; höflich, **Höflichkeit**). Hierbei sind die Stichwörter innerhalb des Nests von der Schriftgröße etwas kleiner als das erste Stichwort. Geläufige Ausdrücke, in denen das Stichwort vorkommt, erscheinen ebenfalls **fett**, aber in einer anderen Schriftgröße. Die Tilde (~) steht hierbei für das Hauptstichwort am Anfang eines Eintrags. So steht beispielsweise im Eintrag ‚Mitte' der Ausdruck ‚~ **Juni**' für ‚**Mitte Juni**'.

PHONETISCHE UMSCHRIFT

Die Aussprache jedes Stichworts findet sich in phonetischer Umschrift in eckigen Klammern jeweils direkt hinter dem Stichwort selbst (z.B. mountain ['mauntɪn]). Eine Liste der Lautschriftzeichen mit Erklärungen finden Sie auf S. xi.

BEDEUTUNGEN

Die Übersetzung der Stichwörter ist in Normalschrift angegeben. Gibt es mehrere Bedeutungen oder Gebrauchsmöglichkeiten, so sind diese durch einen Strichpunkt voneinander zu unterscheiden. Sie finden oft weitere Angaben in Klammern vor den jeweiligen Übersetzungen. Diese zeigen Ihnen typische Kontexte auf, in denen das Stichwort verwendet werden kann (z.B. breakup (*of meeting, organisation*)), oder sie liefern Synonyme (z.B. fit (*suitable*)).

GRAMMATISCHE HINWEISE

Die Wortartangabe finden Sie als Abkürzung und in *kursiver Schrift* direkt hinter der Ausspracheinformation zum jeweiligen Stichwort (z.B. *vt*, *adj*, *n*).

Die Genusangaben zu deutschen Substantiven werden wie folgt angegeben: *m* für Maskulinum, *f* für Femininum und *nt* für Neutrum. Darüber hinaus finden Sie neben dem Stichwort in Klammern Genitiv- und Pluralform (Abenteuer (-s, -)).

Die Genusangabe zur deutschen Übersetzung findet sich ebenfalls in *kursiver Schrift* direkt hinter dem Hauptbestandteil der Übersetzung.

INTRODUCTION

We are delighted you have decided to buy the Collins German Dictionary and hope you will enjoy and benefit from using it at school, at home, on holiday or at work.

This introduction gives you a few tips on how to get the most out of your dictionary – not simply from its comprehensive wordlist but also from the information provided in each entry. This will help you to read and understand modern German, as well as to communicate and express yourself in the language.

The Collins German Dictionary begins by listing the abbreviations used in the text and illustrating the sounds shown by the phonetic symbols. Next you will find regular German noun endings and English irregular verbs followed by a section on German irregular verbs. Finally, the new Phrasefinder supplement gives you hundreds of useful phrases which are intended to give you practical help in everyday situations when travelling.

USING YOUR COLLINS DICTIONARY

A wealth of information is presented in the dictionary, using various typefaces, sizes of type, symbols, abbreviations and brackets. The conventions and symbols used are explained in the following sections.

HEADWORDS

The words you look up in the dictionary – 'headwords' – are listed alphabetically. They are printed in **colour** for rapid identification. The headwords appearing at the top of each page indicate the first (if it appears on a left-hand page) and last word (if it appears on a right-hand page) dealt with on the page in question.

Information about the usage or form of certain headwords is given in brackets after the phonetic spelling. This usually appears in abbreviated form and in italics (e.g. (fam), (Comm)).

Where appropriate, words related to headwords are grouped in the same entry (gather, gathering; höflich, Höflichkeit) in a slightly smaller bold type than the headword. Common expressions in which the headword appears are shown in a different size of bold roman type. The swung dash, ~, represents the main headword at the start of each entry. For example, in the entry for 'Mitte' the phrase '~ Juni' should be read 'Mitte Juni'.

PHONETIC SPELLINGS

The phonetic spelling of each headword (indicating its pronunciation) is given in square brackets immediately after the headword (e.g. **mountain** ['maʊntɪn]). A list of these spellings is given on page xi.

MEANINGS

Headword translations are given in ordinary type and, where more than one meaning or usage exists, they are separated by a semicolon. You will often find other words in italics in brackets before the translations. These offer suggested contexts in which the headword might appear (e.g. **breakup** (*of meeting, organisation*)) or provide synonyms (e.g. **fit** (*suitable*)).

GRAMMATICAL INFORMATION

Parts of speech are given in abbreviated form in italics after the phonetic spellings of headwords (e.g. *vt*, *adj*, *n*).

Genders of German nouns are indicated as follows: *m* for a masculine, *f* for a feminine, and *nt* for a neuter noun. Genitive and plural forms of nouns are also shown next to the headword (**Abenteuer** (*-s, -*)).

The gender of the German translation appears in *italics* immediately following the key element of the translation.

ABKÜRZUNGEN

ABBREVIATIONS

auch	*a.*	also
Abkürzung	*abk, abbr*	abbreviation
Akronym	*acr*	acronym
Adjektiv	*adj*	adjective
Adverb	*adv*	adverb
Landwirtschaft	*Agr*	agriculture
Akkusativ	*akk*	accusative
Akronym	*akr*	acronym
Anatomie	*Anat*	anatomy
Artikel	*art*	article
Bildende Künste	*Art*	fine arts
Astronomie, Astrologie	*Astr*	astronomy, astrology
Auto, Verkehr	*Auto*	automobiles, traffic
Luftfahrt	*Aviat*	aviation
Biologie	*Bio*	biology
Botanik	*Bot*	botany
britisch	*BRIT*	British
schweizerisch	*CH*	Swiss
Chemie	*Chem*	chemistry
Film	*Cine*	cinema
Wirtschaft	*Comm*	commerce
Konjunktion	*conj*	conjunction
Dativ	*dat*	dative
Eisenbahn	*Eisenb*	railways
Elektrizität	*Elek, Elec*	electricity
besonders	*esp*	especially
und so weiter	*etc*	et cetera
etwas	*etw*	something
Femininum	*f*	feminine
umgangssprachlich	*fam*	familiar, informal
übertragen	*fig*	figurative
Finanzen, Börse	*Fin*	finance
Fotografie	*Foto*	photography
Gastronomie	*Gastr*	cooking, gastronomy
Genitiv	*gen*	genitive
Geographie, Geologie	*Geo*	geography, geology
Geschichte	*Hist*	history
Imperativ	*imper*	imperative
Imperfekt	*imperf*	past tense
Informatik und Computer	*Inform*	computing
Interjektion, Ausruf	*interj*	interjection
unveränderlich	*inv*	invariable
unregelmäßig	*irr*	irregular
jemand, jemandem	*jd, jdm*	someone, somebody
jemanden, jemandes	*jdn, jds*	
Rechtsprechung	*Jur*	law

Konjunktion	konj	conjunction
Bildende Künste	Kunst	fine arts
Sprachwissenschaft, Grammatik	Ling	linguistics, grammar
Maskulinum	m	masculine
Mathematik	Math	mathematics
Medizin	Med	medicine
Meteorologie	Met	meteorology
Maskulinum und Femininum	mf	masculine and feminine
Militär	Mil	military
Musik	Mus	music
Substantiv	n	noun
Seefahrt	Naut	nautical, naval
Neutrum	nt	neuter
Zahlwort	num	numeral
oder	o	or
pejorativ, abwertend	pej	pejorative
Physik	Phys	physics
Plural	pl	plural
Politik	Pol	politics
Partizip Perfekt	pp	past participle
Präfix	pref	prefix
Präposition	prep	preposition
Pronomen	pron	pronoun
1. Vergangenheit	pt	past tense
Eisenbahn	Rail	railways
Religion	Rel	religion
siehe	s.	see
	sb	someone, somebody
schottisch	Scot	Scottish
Singular	sing	singular
Skisport	Ski	skiing
	sth	something
Technik	Tech	technology
Nachrichtentechnik	Tel	telecommunications
Theater	Theat	theatre
Fernsehen	TV	television
Typographie, Buchdruck	Typo	printing
unpersönlich	unpers	impersonal
(nord)amerikanisch	US	(North) American
Verb	vb	verb
Hilfsverb	vb aux	auxiliary verb
intransitives Verb	vi	intransitive verb
reflexives Verb	vr	reflexive verb
transitives Verb	vt	transitive verb
vulgär	vulg	vulgar
Zoologie	Zool	zoology
ungefähre Entsprechung	≈	cultural equivalent
abtrennbares Präfix	|	separable prefix

LAUTSCHRIFT

PHONETICS SYMBOLS

[:] Längezeichen, length mark
['] Betonung, stress mark
[*] Bindungs-R, 'r' pronounced before a vowel

alle Vokallaute sind nur ungefähre Entsprechungen
all vowel sounds are approximate only

VOKALE UND DIPHTHONGE

plant, arm, father	[ɑ:]	Bahn
fiancé	[ɑ̃:]	Ensemble
life	[aɪ]	weit
house	[au]	Haut
man, sad	[æ]	
but, son	[ʌ]	Butler
get, bed	[e]	Metall
name, lame	[eɪ]	
ago, better	[ə]	bitte
bird, her	[ɜ:]	
there, care	[ɛə]	mehr
it, wish	[ɪ]	Bischof
bee, me, beat, belief	[i:]	viel
here	[ɪə]	Bier
no, low	[əʊ]	
not, long	[ɒ]	Post
law, all	[ɔ:]	Mond
boy, oil	[ɔɪ]	Heu
push, look	[ʊ]	Pult
you, do	[u:]	Hut
poor, sure	[ʊə]	

KONSONANTEN

been, blind	[b]	Ball
do, had	[d]	dann
jam, object	[dʒ]	
father, wolf	[f]	Fass
go, beg	[g]	Gast

xi

house	[h]	Herr
youth, Indian	[j]	ja
keep, milk	[k]	kalt
lamp, oil, ill	[l]	Last
man, am	[m]	Mast
no, manner	[n]	Nuss
long, sing	[ŋ]	lang
El Niño	[ɲ]	El Niño
paper, happy	[p]	Pakt
red, dry	[r]	rot
stand, sand, yes	[s]	Rasse
ship, station	[ʃ]	Schal
tell, fat	[t]	Tal
thank, death	[θ]	
this, father	[ð]	
church, catch	[tʃ]	Rutsch
voice, live	[v]	was
water, we, which	[w]	
loch	[x]	Bach
zeal, these, gaze	[z]	Hase
pleasure	[ʒ]	Genie

REGULAR GERMAN NOUN ENDINGS

nominative		genitive	plural	nominative		genitive	plural
-ade	f	-ade	-aden	-ist	m	-isten	-isten
-ant	m	-anten	-anten	-ium	nt	-iums	-ien
-anz	f	-anz	-anzen	-ius	m	-ius	-iusse
-ar	m	-ars	-are	-ive	f	-ive	-iven
-är	m	-ärs	-äre	-keit	f	-keit	-keiten
-at	nt	-at(e)s	-ate	-lein	nt	-leins	-lein
-atte	f	-atte	-atten	-ling	m	-lings	-linge
-chen	nt	-chens	-chen	-ment	nt	-ments	-mente
-ei	f	-ei	-eien	-mus	m	-mus	-men
-elle	f	-elle	-ellen	-nis	f	-nis	-nisse
-ent	m	-enten	-enten	-nis	nt	-nisses	-nisse
-enz	f	-enz	-enzen	-nom	m	-nomen	-nomen
-ette	f	-ette	-etten	-rich	m	-richs	-riche
-eur	m	-eurs	-eure	-schaft	f	-schaft	-schaften
-euse	f	-euse	-eusen	-sel	nt	-sels	-sel
-heit	f	-heit	-heiten	-tät	f	-tät	-täten
-ie	f	-ie	-ien	-tiv	nt, m	-tivs	-tive
-ik	f	-ik	-iken	-tor	m	-tors	-toren
-in	f	-in	-innen	-tum	m, nt	-tums	-tümer
-ine	f	-ine	-inen	-ung	f	-ung	-ungen
-ion	f	-ion	-ionen	-ur	f	-ur	-uren

Substantive, die mit einem geklammerten 'r' oder 's' enden (z.B. **Angestellte(r)** mf, **Beamte(r)** m, **Gute(s)** nt) werden wie Adjektive dekliniert:

Nouns listed with an 'r' or an 's' in brackets (eg **Angestellte(r)** mf, **Beamte(r)** m, **Gute(s)** nt) take the same endings as adjectives:

der Angestellte m	die Angestellte f	die Angestellten pl
ein Angestellter m	eine Angestellte f	Angestellte pl
der Beamte m		die Beamten pl
ein Beamter m		Beamte pl
das Gute nt		
ein Gutes nt		

UNREGELMÄSSIGE ENGLISCHE VERBEN

present	past tense	past participle	present	past tense	past participle
arise (arising)	arose	arisen	deal	dealt	dealt
			dig (digging)	dug	dug
awake (awaking)	awoke	awaked	do (does)	did	done
			draw	drew	drawn
be (am, is, are; being)	was, were	been	dream	dreamed (o dreamt)	dreamed (o dreamt)
bear	bore	born(e)	drink	drank	drunk
beat	beat	beaten	drive (driving)	drove	driven
become (becoming)	became	become	eat	ate	eaten
begin (beginning)	began	begun	fall	fell	fallen
bend	bent	bent	feed	fed	fed
bet (betting)	bet	bet	feel	felt	felt
bid (bidding)	bid	bid	fight	fought	fought
bind	bound	bound	find	found	found
bite (biting)	bit	bitten	flee	fled	fled
bleed	bled	bled	fling	flung	flung
blow	blew	blown	fly (flies)	flew	flown
break	broke	broken	forbid (forbidding)	forbade	forbidden
breed	bred	bred	foresee	foresaw	foreseen
bring	brought	brought	forget (forgetting)	forgot	forgotten
build	built	built			
burn	burnt (o burned)	burnt (o burned)	forgive (forgiving)	forgave	forgiven
burst	burst	burst	freeze (freezing)	froze	frozen
buy	bought	bought	get (getting)	got	got, (US) gotten
can	could	(been able)			
cast	cast	cast	give (giving)	gave	given
catch	caught	caught	go (goes)	went	gone
choose (choosing)	chose	chosen	grind	ground	ground
cling	clung	clung	grow	grew	grown
come (coming)	came	come	hang	hung (o hanged)	hung (o hanged)
cost	cost	cost	have (has; having)	had	had
creep	crept	crept	hear	heard	heard
cut (cutting)	cut	cut			

xiv

present	past tense	past participle	present	past tense	past participle
hide (hiding)	hid	hidden	ring	rang	rung
hit (hitting)	hit	hit	rise (rising)	rose	risen
hold	held	held	run (running)	ran	run
hurt	hurt	hurt			
keep	kept	kept	saw	sawed	sawn
kneel	knelt (o kneeled)	knelt (o kneeled)	say	said	said
			seek	sought	sought
know	knew	known	see	saw	seen
lay	laid	laid	sell	sold	sold
lead	led	led	send	sent	sent
lean	leant (o leaned)	leant (o leaned)	set (setting)	set	set
			shake (shaking)	shook	shaken
leap	leapt (o leaped)	leapt (o leaped)	shall	should	–
learn	learnt (o learned)	learnt (o learned)	shine (shining)	shone	shone
leave (leaving)	left	left	shoot	shot	shot
lend	lent	lent	show	showed	shown
let (letting)	let	let	shrink	shrank	shrunk
lie (lying)	lay	lain	shut (shutting)	shut	shut
light	lit (o lighted)	lit (o lighted)	sing	sang	sung
			sink	sank	sunk
lose (losing)	lost	lost	sit (sitting)	sat	sat
make (making)	made	made	sleep	slept	slept
			slide (sliding)	slid	slid
may	might	–	sling	slung	slung
mean	meant	meant	slit (slitting)	slit	slit
meet	met	met	smell	smelt (o smelled)	smelt (o smelled)
mow	mowed	mown (o mowed)	sow	sowed	sown (o sowed)
must	(had to)	(had to)			
pay	paid	paid	speak	spoke	spoken
put (putting)	put	put	speed	sped (o speeded)	sped (o speeded)
quit (quitting)	quit (o quitted)	quit (o quitted)	spell	spelt (o spelled)	spelt (o spelled)
read	read	read	spend	spent	spent
rid (ridding)	rid	rid	spin (spinning)	spun	spun
ride (riding)	rode	ridden			

present	past tense	past participle	present	past tense	past participle
spit (spitting)	spat	spat	**swim** (swimming)	swam	swum
split (splitting)	split	split	**swing**	swung	swung
spoil	spoiled (*o* spoilt)	spoiled (*o* spoilt)	**take** (taking)	took	taken
			teach	taught	taught
spread	spread	spread	**tear**	tore	torn
spring	sprang	sprung	**tell**	told	told
stand	stood	stood	**think**	thought	thought
steal	stole	stolen	**throw**	threw	thrown
stick	stuck	stuck	**thrust**	thrust	thrust
sting	stung	stung	**wake** (waking)	woke (*o* waked)	woken (*o* waked)
stink	stank	stunk	**wear**	wore	worn
strike (striking)	struck	struck	**weave** (weaving)	wove (*o* weaved)	woven (*o* weaved)
strive (striving)	strove	striven	**weep**	wept	wept
swear	swore	sworn	**win** (winning)	won	won
sweep	swept	swept	**wind**	wound	wound
swell	swelled	swollen (*o* swelled)	**write** (writing)	wrote	written

IRREGULAR GERMAN VERBS

Infinitiv	Präsens 2., 3. Singular	Imperfekt	Partizip Perfekt
backen	bäckst, bäckt	backte o buk	gebacken
befehlen	befiehlst, befiehlt	befahl	befohlen
beginnen	beginnst, beginnt	begann	begonnen
beißen	beißt, beißt	biss	gebissen
bergen	birgst, birgt	barg	geborgen
betrügen	betrügst, betrügt	betrog	betrogen
biegen	biegst, biegt	bog	gebogen
bieten	bietest, bietet	bot	geboten
binden	bindest, bindet	band	gebunden
bitten	bittest, bittet	bat	gebeten
blasen	bläst, bläst	blies	geblasen
bleiben	bleibst, bleibt	blieb	geblieben
braten	brätst, brät	briet	gebraten
brechen	brichst, bricht	brach	gebrochen
brennen	brennst, brennt	brannte	gebrannt
bringen	bringst, bringt	brachte	gebracht
denken	denkst, denkt	dachte	gedacht
dringen	dringst, dringt	drang	gedrungen
dürfen	darfst, darf	durfte	gedurft
erschrecken	erschrickst, erschrickt	erschrak	erschrocken
essen	isst, isst	aß	gegessen
fahren	fährst, fährt	fuhr	gefahren
fallen	fällst, fällt	fiel	gefallen
fangen	fängst, fängt	fing	gefangen
finden	findest, findet	fand	gefunden
fliegen	fliegst, fliegt	flog	geflogen
fließen	fließt, fließt	floss	geflossen
fressen	frisst, frisst	fraß	gefressen
frieren	frierst, friert	fror	gefroren
geben	gibst, gibt	gab	gegeben
gehen	gehst, geht	ging	gegangen
gelingen	–, gelingt	gelang	gelungen
gelten	giltst, gilt	galt	gegolten
genießen	genießt, genießt	genoss	genossen
geschehen	–, geschieht	geschah	geschehen
gewinnen	gewinnst, gewinnt	gewann	gewonnen
gießen	gießt, gießt	goss	gegossen
gleichen	gleichst, gleicht	glich	geglichen

Infinitiv	Präsens 2., 3. Singular	Imperfekt	Partizip Perfekt
gleiten	gleitest, gleitet	glitt	geglitten
graben	gräbst, gräbt	grub	gegraben
greifen	greifst, greift	griff	gegriffen
haben	hast, hat	hatte	gehabt
halten	hältst, hält	hielt	gehalten
hängen	hängst, hängt	hing	gehangen
heben	hebst, hebt	hob	gehoben
heßmen	heißt, heißt	hieß	geheißen
helfen	hilfst, hilft	half	geholfen
kennen	kennst, kennt	kannte	gekannt
klingen	klingst, klingt	klang	geklungen
kommen	kommst, kommt	kam	gekommen
können	kannst, kann	konnte	gekonnt
kriechen	kriechst, kriecht	kroch	gekrochen
laden	lädst, lädt	lud	geladen
lassen	lässt, lässt	ließ	gelassen
laufen	läufst, läuft	lief	gelaufen
leiden	leidest, leidet	litt	gelitten
leihen	leihst, leiht	lieh	geliehen
lesen	liest, liest	las	gelesen
liegen	liegst, liegt	lag	gelegen
lügen	lügst, lügt	log	gelogen
mahlen	mahlst, mahlt	mahlte	gemahlen
meiden	meidest, meidet	mied	gemieden
messen	misst, misst	maß	gemessen
mögen	magst, mag	mochte	gemocht
müssen	musst, muss	musste	gemusst
nehmen	nimmst, nimmt	nahm	genommen
nennen	nennst, nennt	nannte	genannt
pfeifen	pfeifst, pfeift	pfiff	gepfiffen
raten	rätst, rät	riet	geraten
reiben	reibst, reibt	rieb	gerieben
reißen	reißt, reißt	riss	gerissen
reiten	reitest, reitet	ritt	geritten
rennen	rennst, rennt	rannte	gerannt
riechen	riechst, riecht	roch	gerochen
rufen	rufst, ruft	rief	gerufen
saufen	säufst, säuft	soff	gesoffen
saugen	saugst, saugt	sog o saugte	gesogen o gesaugt

Infinitiv	Präsens 2., 3. Singular	Imperfekt	Partizip Perfekt
schaffen	schaffst, schafft	schuf	geschaffen
scheiden	scheidest, scheidet	schied	geschieden
scheinen	scheinst, scheint	schien	geschienen
schieben	schiebst, schiebt	schob	geschoben
schießen	schießt, schießt	schoss	geschossen
schlafen	schläfst, schläft	schlief	geschlafen
schlagen	schlägst, schlägt	schlug	geschlagen
schleichen	schleichst, schleicht	schlich	geschlichen
schließen	schließt, schließt	schloss	geschlossen
schmeißen	schmeißt, schmeißt	schmiss	geschmissen
schmelzen	schmilzt, schmilzt	schmolz	geschmolzen
schneiden	schneidest, schneidet	schnitt	geschnitten
schreiben	schreibst, schreibt	schrieb	geschrieben
schreien	schreist, schreit	schrie	geschrie(e)n
schweigen	schweigst, schweigt	schwieg	geschwiegen
schwellen	schwillst, schwillt	schwoll	geschwollen
schwimmen	schwimmst, schwimmt	schwamm	geschwommen
schwören	schwörst, schwört	schwor	geschworen
sehen	siehst, sieht	sah	gesehen
sein	bist, ist	war	gewesen
senden	sendest, sendet	sandte	gesandt
singen	singst, singt	sang	gesungen
sinken	sinkst, sinkt	sank	gesunken
sitzen	sitzt, sitzt	saß	gesessen
sollen	sollst, soll	sollte	gesollt
sprechen	sprichst, spricht	sprach	gesprochen
springen	springst, springt	sprang	gesprungen
stechen	stichst, sticht	stach	gestochen
stehen	stehst, steht	stand	gestanden
stehlen	stiehlst, stiehlt	stahl	gestohlen
steigen	steigst, steigt	stieg	gestiegen
sterben	stirbst, stirbt	starb	gestorben
stinken	stinkst, stinkt	stank	gestunken
stoßen	stößt, stößt	stieß	gestoßen
streichen	streichst, streicht	strich	gestrichen
streiten	streitest, streitet	stritt	gestritten
tragen	trägst, trägt	trug	getragen
treffen	triffst, trifft	traf	getroffen
treiben	treibst, treibt	trieb	getrieben

Infinitiv	Präsens 2., 3. Singular	Imperfekt	Partizip Perfekt
treten	trittst, tritt	trat	getreten
trinken	trinkst, trinkt	trank	getrunken
tun	tust, tut	tat	getan
verderben	verdirbst, verdirbt	verdarb	verdorben
vergessen	vergisst, vergisst	vergaß	vergessen
verlieren	verlierst, verliert	verlor	verloren
verschwinden	verschwindest, verschwindet	verschwand	verschwunden
verzeihen	verzeihst, verzeiht	verzieh	verziehen
wachsen	wächst, wächst	wuchs	gewachsen
wenden	wendest, wendet	wandte	gewandt
werben	wirbst, wirbt	warb	geworben
werden	wirst, wird	wurde	geworden
werfen	wirfst, wirft	warf	geworfen
wiegen	wiegst, wiegt	wog	gewogen
wissen	weißt, weiß	wusste	gewusst
wollen	willst, will	wollte	gewollt
ziehen	ziehst, zieht	zog	gezogen
zwingen	zwingst, zwingt	zwang	gezwungen

a

à prep +akk at ... each; **4 Tickets ~ 8 Euro** 4 tickets at 8 euros each

A abk = **Autobahn** ≈ M (Brit), ≈ I (US)

Aal (-(e)s, -e) m eel

 SCHLÜSSELWORT

ab prep +dat from; **Kinder ab 12 Jahren** children from the age of 12; **ab morgen** from tomorrow; **ab sofort** as of now

▷ adv **1** off; **links ab** to the left; **der Knopf ist ab** the button has come off; **ab nach Hause!** off you go home

2 (zeitlich) **von da ab** from then on; **von heute ab** from today, as of today

3 (auf Fahrplänen) **München ab 12.20** leaving Munich 12.20

4 ab und zu o **an** now and then o again

ab|**bauen** vt (Zelt) to take down; (verringern) to reduce

ab|**beißen** irr vt to bite off

ab|**bestellen** vt to cancel

ab|**biegen** irr vi to turn off; (Straße) to bend; **nach links/rechts ~** to turn left/right

Abbildung f illustration

ab|**blasen** irr vt (fig) to call off

ab|**blenden** vt, vi (Auto) (**die Scheinwerfer**) **~** to dip (Brit) (o to dim (US)) one's headlights; **Abblendlicht** nt dipped (Brit) (o dimmed (US)) headlights pl

ab|**brechen** irr vt to break off; (Gebäude) to pull down; (aufhören) to stop; (Computerprogramm) to abort

ab|**bremsen** vi to brake, to slow down

ab|**bringen** irr vt: **jdn von einer Idee ~** to talk sb out of an idea; **jdn vom Thema ~** to get sb away from the subject; **davon lasse ich mich nicht ~** nothing will make me change my mind about it

ab|**buchen** vt to debit (von to)

ab|**danken** vi to resign

ab|**drehen** vt (Gas, Wasser) to turn off; (Licht) to switch off ▷ vi (Schiff, Flugzeug) to change course

Abend (-s, -e) m evening; **am ~** in the evening; **zu ~ essen** to have dinner; **heute/morgen/gestern ~** this/tomorrow/yesterday evening; **guten ~!** good evening; **Abendbrot** nt supper; **Abendessen** nt dinner; **Abendgarderobe** f evening dress (o gown); **Abendkasse** f box office; **Abendkleid** nt evening dress (o gown); **Abendmahl** nt: **das ~** (Holy) Communion; **abends** adv in the evening; **montags ~** on Monday evenings

Abenteuer (-s, -) nt adventure; **Abenteuerurlaub** m adventure holiday

aber *conj* but; (*jedoch*) however; **oder ~** alternatively; **~ ja!** (but) of course; **das ist ~ nett von Ihnen** that's really nice of you

abergläubisch *adj* superstitious

ab|fahren *irr vi* to leave (*o* to depart); (*nach for*); (Ski) to ski down; **Abfahrt** *f* departure; (von Autobahn) exit; (Ski) descent; (Piste) run; **Abfahrtslauf** *m* (Ski) downhill; **Abfahrtszeit** *f* departure time

Abfall *m* waste; (*Müll*) rubbish (Brit), garbage (US); **Abfalleimer** *m* rubbish bin (Brit), garbage can (US)

abfällig *adj* disparaging; **~ von jdm sprechen** to make disparaging remarks about sb

ab|färben *vi* (Wäsche) to run; (fig) to rub off

ab|fertigen *vt* (Pakete) to prepare for dispatch; (an der Grenze) to clear; **Abfertigungsschalter** *m* (am Flughafen) check-in desk

ab|finden *irr vt* to pay off ▷ *vr*: **sich mit etw ~** to come to terms with sth; **Abfindung** *f* (Entschädigung) compensation; (von Angestellten) redundancy payment

ab|fliegen *irr vi* (Flugzeug) to take off; (Passagier a.) to fly off; **Abflug** *m* departure; (Start) takeoff; **Abflughalle** *f* departure lounge; **Abflugzeit** *f* departure time

Abfluss *m* drain; (am Waschbecken) plughole (Brit); **Abflussrohr** *nt* waste pipe; (außen) drainpipe

ab|fragen *vt* (esp Tel; Inform) to call up

ab|führen *vi* (Med) to have a laxative effect ▷ *vt* (Steuern, Gebühren) to pay; **jdn ~ lassen** to take sb into custody; **Abführmittel** *nt* laxative

Abgabe *f* handing in; (von Ball) pass; (Steuer) tax; (einer Erklärung) making; **abgabenfrei** *adj* tax-free; **abgabenpflichtig** *adj* liable to tax

Abgase *pl* (Auto) exhaust fumes *pl*; **Abgas(sonder)untersuchung** *f* exhaust emission test

ab|geben *irr vt* (Gepäck, Schlüssel) to leave (bei with); (Schularbeit etc) to hand in; (Wärme) to give off; (Erklärung, Urteil) to make ▷ *vr*: **sich mit jdm ~** to associate with sb; **sich mit etw ~** to bother with sth

abgebildet *adj*: **wie oben ~** as shown above

ab|gehen *irr vi* (Post) to go; (Knopf etc) to come off; (abgezogen werden) to be taken off; (Straße) to branch off; **von der Schule ~** to leave school; **sie geht mir ab** I really miss her; **was geht denn hier ab?** (fam) what's going on here?

abgehetzt *adj* exhausted, shattered

abgelaufen *adj* (Pass) expired; (Zeit, Frist) up; **die Milch ist ~** the milk is past its sell-by date

abgelegen *adj* remote

abgemacht *interj* OK, it's a deal, that's settled, fine

abgeneigt *adj einer Sache* (dat) **~ sein** to be averse to sth; **ich wäre nicht ~, das zu tun** I wouldn't mind doing that

Abgeordnete(r) *mf* Member of Parliament

abgepackt *adj* prepacked

abgerissen *adj*: **der Knopf ist ~** the button has come off

abgesehen *adj*: **es auf jdn/etw ~ haben** to be after sb/sth; **~ von** apart from

abgespannt *adj* (Person) exhausted, worn out

abgestanden adj stale; (Bier) flat

abgestorben adj (Pflanze) dead; (Finger) numb

abgestumpft adj (Person) insensitive

abgetragen adj (Kleidung) worn

ab|gewöhnen vt: **jdm etw ~** to cure sb of sth; **sich etw ~** to give sth up

ab|haken vt to tick off; **das (Thema) ist schon abgehakt** that's been dealt with

ab|halten irr vt (Versammlung) to hold; **jdn von etw ~** (fernhalten) to keep sb away from sth; (hindern) to keep sb from sth

abhanden adj: **~ kommen** to get lost

Abhang m slope

ab|hängen vt (Bild) to take down; (Anhänger) to uncouple; (Verfolger) to shake off ▷ irr vi: **von jdm/etw ~** to depend on sb/sth; **das hängt davon ab, ob ...** it depends (on) whether ...;

abhängig adj dependent (von on)

ab|hauen irr vt (abschlagen) to cut off ▷ vi (fam: verschwinden) to clear off; **hau ab!** get lost!, beat it!

ab|heben irr vt (Geld) to withdraw; (Telefonhörer, Spielkarte) to pick up ▷ vi (Flugzeug) to take off; (Rakete) to lift off; (Karten) to cut

ab|holen vt to collect; (am Bahnhof etc) to meet; (mit dem Auto) to pick up; **Abholmarkt** m cash and carry

ab|horchen vt (Med) to listen to

ab|hören vt (Vokabeln) to test; (Telefongespräch) to tap; (Tonband etc) to listen to

Abitur (-s, -e) nt German school-leaving examination, ≈ A-levels (Brit), ≈ High School Diploma (US)

ab|kaufen vt: **jdm etw ~** to buy sth from sb; **das kauf ich dir nicht ab!** (fam: glauben) I don't believe you

ab|klingen irr vi (Schmerz) to ease; (Wirkung) to wear off

ab|kommen irr vi to get away; **von der Straße ~** to leave the road; **von einem Plan ~** to give up a plan; **vom Thema ~** to stray from the point

Abkommen (-s, -) nt agreement

ab|koppeln vt (Anhänger) to unhitch

ab|kratzen vt to scrape off ▷ vi (fam: sterben) to kick the bucket, to croak

ab|kühlen vi, vt to cool down ▷ vr: **sich ~** to cool down

ab|kürzen vt (Wort) to abbreviate; **den Weg ~** to take a short cut; **Abkürzung** f (Wort) abbreviation; (Weg) short cut

ab|laden irr vt to unload

Ablage f (für Akten) tray; (Aktenordnung) filing system

Ablauf m (Abfluss) drain; (von Ereignissen) course; (einer Frist, Zeit) expiry; **ab|laufen** irr vi (ablaufen) to drain away; (Ereignisse) to happen; (Frist, Zeit, Pass) to expire

ab|legen vt to put down; (Kleider) to take off; (Gewohnheit) to get out of; (Prüfung) to take, to sit; (Akten) to file away ▷ vi (Schiff) to cast off

ab|lehnen vt to reject; (Einladung) to decline; (missbilligen) to disapprove of; (*Bewerber*) to turn down ▷ *vi* to decline

ab|lenken *vt* to distract; **jdn von der Arbeit ~** to distract sb from their work; **vom Thema ~** to change the subject; **Ablenkung** f distraction

ab|lesen *vt* (*Text, Rede*) to read; **das Gas/den Strom ~** to read the gas/electricity meter

ab|liefern *vt* to deliver

ab|machen *vt* (*entfernen*) to take off; (*vereinbaren*) to agree; **Abmachung** f agreement

ab|melden *vt* (*Zeitung*) to cancel; (*Auto*) to take off the road ▷ *vt*: **sich ~** to give notice of one's departure; (*im Hotel*) to check out; (*vom Verein*) to cancel one's membership

ab|messen *irr vt* to measure

ab|nehmen *irr vt* to take off, to remove; (*Hörer*) to pick up; (*Führerschein*) to take away; (*Geld*) to get (*jdm von* of sb); (*kaufen, umg: glauben*) to buy (*jdm from* sb) ▷ *vi* to decrease; (*schlanker werden*) to lose weight; (*Tel*) to pick up the phone; **fünf Kilo ~** to lose five kilos

Abneigung f dislike (*gegen* of); (*stärker*) aversion (*gegen* to)

ab|nutzen *vt* to wear out ▷ *vr*: **sich ~** to wear out

Abonnement (-s, -s) *nt* subscription; **Abonnent(in)** *m(f)* subscriber; **abonnieren** *vt* to subscribe to

ab|raten *irr vi*: **jdm von etw ~** to advise sb against sth

ab|räumen *vt*: **den Tisch ~** to clear the table; **das Geschirr ~** to clear away the dishes; (*Preis etc*) to walk off with

Abrechnung f settlement; (*Rechnung*) bill

ab|regen *vr*: **sich ~** (*fam*) to calm

(*o to* cool) down; **reg dich ab!** take it easy

Abreise f departure; **ab|reisen** *vi* to leave (*nach* for); **Abreisetag** *m* day of departure

ab|reißen *irr vt* (*Haus*) to pull down; (*Blatt*) to tear off; **den Kontakt nicht ~ lassen** to stay in touch ▷ *vi* (*Knopf etc*) to come off

ab|runden *vt*: **eine Zahl nach oben/unten ~** to round a number up/down

abrupt *adj* abrupt

ABS *nt abk* = **Antiblockiersystem** (*Auto*) ABS

Abs. *abk* = **Absender** from

ab|sagen *vt* to cancel, to call off; (*Einladung*) to turn down ▷ *vi* (*ablehnen*) to decline; **ich muss leider ~** I'm afraid I can't come

Absatz *m* (*Comm*) sales *pl*; (*neuer Abschnitt*) paragraph; (*Schuh*) heel

ab|schaffen *vt* to abolish, to do away with

ab|schalten *vt, vi* (*a. fig*) to switch off

ab|schätzen *vt* to estimate; (*Lage*) to assess

abscheulich *adj* disgusting

ab|schicken *vt* to send off

ab|schieben *irr vt* (*ausweisen*) to deport

Abschied (-(e)s, -e) *m* parting; **~ nehmen** to say good-bye (*von* jdm *to* sb); **Abschiedsfeier** f farewell party

Abschlagszahlung f interim payment

Abschleppdienst *m* (*Auto*) breakdown service; **ab|schleppen** *vt* to tow; **Abschleppseil** *nt* towrope; **Abschleppwagen** *m* breakdown truck (*Brit*), tow truck (*US*)

ab|schließen *irr vt* (*Tür*) to lock; (*beenden*) to conclude, to finish; (*Vertrag, Handel*) to conclude;

Abschluss m (Beendigung) close, conclusion; (von Vertrag, Handel) conclusion

ab|schmecken vt (kosten) to taste; (würzen) to season

ab|schminken vr: **sich ~** to take one's make-up off ▷ vt (fam) **sich** (dat) **etw ~** to get sth out of one's mind

ab|schnallen vr: **sich ~** to undo one's seatbelt

ab|schneiden irr vt to cut off ▷ vi: **gut/schlecht ~** to do well/badly

Abschnitt m (von Buch, Text) section; (Kontrollabschnitt) stub

ab|schrauben vt to unscrew

ab|schrecken vt to deter, to put off

ab|schreiben irr vt to copy (bei, von from, off); (verloren geben) to write off; (Comm: absetzen) to deduct

abschüssig adj steep

ab|schwächen vt to lessen; (Behauptung, Kritik) to tone down

ab|schwellen irr vi (Entzündung) to go down; (Lärm) to die down

absehbar adj foreseeable; **in ~er Zeit** in the foreseeable future;

ab|sehen irr vt (Ende, Folgen) to foresee ▷ vi: **von etw ~** to refrain from sth

abseits adv out of the way; (Sport) offside ▷ prep +gen away from; **Abseits** nt (Sport) offside;

Abseitsfalle f (Sport) offside trap

ab|senden irr vt to send off; (Post) to post; **Absender(in)** (-s, -) m(f) sender

ab|setzen vt (Glas, Brille etc) to put down; (aussteigen lassen) to drop (off); (Comm) to sell; (Fin) to deduct; (streichen) to drop ▷ vr: **sich ~** (sich entfernen) to clear off; (sich ablagern) to be deposited

Absicht f intention; **mit ~** on

purpose; **absichtlich** adj intentional, deliberate

absolut adj absolute

ab|specken vi (fam) to lose weight

ab|speichern vt (Inform) to save

ab|sperren vt to block (o to close) off; (Tür) to lock;

Absperrung f (Vorgang) blocking (o closing) off; (Sperre) barricade

ab|spielen vt (CD etc) to play ▷ vr: **sich ~** to happen

ab|springen irr vi to jump down/off; (von etw Geplantem) to drop out (von of)

ab|spülen vt to rinse; (Geschirr) to wash (up)

Abstand m distance; (zeitlich) interval; **~ halten** to keep one's distance

ab|stauben vt, vi to dust; (fam: stehlen) to pinch

Abstecher (-s, -) m detour

ab|steigen irr vi (vom Rad etc) to get off, to dismount; (in Gasthof) to stay (in +dat at)

ab|stellen vt (niederstellen) to put down; (Auto) to park; (ausschalten) to turn (o to switch) off; (Missstand, Unsitte) to stop; **Abstellraum** m store room

Abstieg (-(e)s, -e) m (vom Berg) descent; (Sport) relegation

ab|stimmen vi to vote ▷ vt (Termine, Ziele) to fit in (auf +akk with); **Dinge aufeinander ~** to coordinate things ▷ vr: **sich ~** to come to an agreement (o arrangement)

abstoßend adj repulsive

abstrakt adj abstract

ab|streiten irr vt to deny

Abstrich m (Med) smear; **~e machen** to cut back (an +dat on); (weniger erwarten) to lower one's sights

Absturz m fall; (Aviat, Inform)

crash; **ab|stürzen** vi to fall;
(Aviat, Inform) to crash

absurd adj absurd

Abszess (-es, -e) m abscess

ab|tauen vt, vi to thaw;
(Kühlschrank) to defrost

Abtei (-, -en) f abbey

Abteil (-(e)s, -e) nt compartment

Abteilung f (in Firma, Kaufhaus)
department; (in Krankenhaus)
section

ab|treiben irr vt (Kind) to abort
▷ vi to be driven off course; (Med:
Abtreibung vornehmen) to carry out
an abortion; (Abtreibung vornehmen
lassen) to have an abortion;
Abtreibung f abortion

ab|trocknen vt to dry

ab|warten vt to wait for; **das
bleibt abzuwarten** that remains
to be seen ▷ vi to wait

abwärts adv down

Abwasch (-(e)s) m washing-up;
ab|waschen irr vt (Schmutz) to
wash off; (Geschirr) to wash (up)

Abwasser (-s, Abwässer) nt
sewage

ab|wechseln vr: **sich ~ to
alternate; sich mit jdm ~ to take
turns with sb; **abwechselnd** adv
alternately; **Abwechslung** f
change; **zur ~ for a change

ab|weisen irr vt to turn away;
(Antrag) to turn down; **abweisend**
adj unfriendly

abwesend adj absent;
Abwesenheit f absence

ab|wiegen irr vt to weigh (out)

ab|wimmeln vt (fam) **jdn ~ to
get rid of sb, to give sb the elbow

ab|wischen vt (Gesicht, Tisch etc)
to wipe; (Schmutz) to wipe off

ab|zählen vt to count; (Geld) to
count out

Abzeichen nt badge

ab|zeichnen vt to draw, to copy;
(Dokument) to initial ▷ vr: **sich
~ to stand out; (fig: bevorstehen) to
loom

ab|ziehen irr vt to take off; (Bett)
to strip; (Schlüssel) to take out;
(subtrahieren) to take away, to
subtract ▷ vi to go away

Abzug m (Foto) print; (Öffnung)
vent; (Truppen) withdrawal;
(Betrag) deduction; **nach ~ der
Kosten** charges deducted;
abzüglich prep +gen minus;
~ 20% Rabatt less 20% discount

ab|zweigen vi to branch off ▷ vt
to set aside; **Abzweigung** f
junction

Accessoires pl accessories pl

ach interj oh; **~ so!** oh, I see;
~ was! (Überraschung) really?;
(Ärger) don't talk nonsense

Achse (-, -n) f axis; (Auto) axle

Achsel (-, -n) f shoulder;
(Achselhöhle) f armpit

Achsenbruch m (Auto) broken
axle

acht num eight; **heute in ~ Tagen**
in a week('s time), a week from
today

Acht (-) f: **sich in ~ nehmen** to be
careful (vor +dat of), to watch out
(vor +dat for); **etw außer ~ lassen**
to disregard sth

achte(r, s) adj eighth; siehe auch
dritte; **Achtel** (-s, -) nt (Bruchteil)
eighth; (Wein etc) eighth of a litre;
(Glas Wein) = small glass

achten vt to respect ▷ vi to pay
attention (auf +akk to)

Achterbahn f big dipper, roller
coaster

acht|geben irr vi to take care
(auf +akk of)

achthundert num eight
hundred; **achtmal** adv eight
times

Achtung f attention; (Ehrfurcht)
respect ▷ interj look out

achtzehn num eighteen;

achtzehnte(r, s) adj eighteenth; siehe auch **dritte**; **achtzig** num eighty; **in den ~er Jahren** in the eighties; **achtzigste(r, s)** adj eightieth

Acker (-s, Äcker) m field

Action (-, -s) f (fam) action; **Actionfilm** m action film

Adapter (-s, -) m adapter

addieren vt to add (up)

Adel (-s) m nobility; **adelig** adj noble

Ader (-, -n) f vein

Adjektiv nt adjective

Adler (-s, -) m eagle

adoptieren vt to adopt; **Adoption** f adoption; **Adoptiveltern** pl adoptive parents pl; **Adoptivkind** nt adopted child

Adrenalin (-s) nt adrenalin

Adressbuch nt directory; (persönliches) address book; **Adresse** (-, -n) f address; **adressieren** vt to address (an +akk to)

ADSL f ADSL

Advent (-s, -e) m Advent; **Adventskranz** m Advent wreath

Adverb nt adverb

Aerobic (-s) nt aerobics sing

Affäre (-, -n) f affair

Affe (-n, -n) m monkey

Afghanistan (-s) nt Afghanistan

Afrika (-s) nt Africa; **Afrikaner(in)** (-s, -) m(f) African; **afrikanisch** adj African

After (-s, -) m anus

Aftershave (-(s), -s) nt aftershave

AG (-, -s) f abk = **Aktiengesellschaft** plc (Brit), corp. (US)

Agent(in) m(f) agent; **Agentur** f agency

aggressiv adj aggressive

Ägypten (-s) nt Egypt

ah interj ah, ooh

aha interj I see, aha

ähneln vi +dat to be like, to resemble ▷ vr: **sich ~** to be alike (o similar)

ahnen vt to suspect; **du ahnst es nicht!** would you believe it?

ähnlich adj similar (dat to); **jdm ~ sehen** to look like sb; **Ähnlichkeit** f similarity

Ahnung f idea; (Vermutung) suspicion; **keine ~!** no idea; **ahnungslos** adj unsuspecting

Ahorn (-s, -e) m maple

Aids (-) nt Aids; **aidskrank** adj suffering from Aids; **Aidstest** m Aids test

Airbag (-s, -s) m (Auto) airbag; **Airbus** m airbus

Akademie (-, -n) f academy; **Akademiker(in)** (-s, -) m(f) (university) graduate

akklimatisieren vr: **sich ~** to acclimatize oneself

Akkordeon (-s, -s) nt accordion

Akku (-s, -s) m (storage) battery

Akkusativ m accusative (case)

Akne (-, -) f acne

Akrobat(in) (-s, -en) m(f) acrobat

Akt (-(e)s, -e) m act; (Kunst) nude

Akte (-, -n) f file; **etw zu den ~n legen** (a. fig) to file sth away; **Aktenkoffer** m briefcase

Aktie (-, -n) f share; **Aktiengesellschaft** f public limited company (Brit), corporation (US)

Aktion f (Kampagne) campaign; (Einsatz) operation

Aktionär(in) (-s, -e) m(f) shareholder

aktiv adj active; **aktivieren** vt to activate

aktualisieren vt to update; **aktuell** adj (Thema) topical;

(*modern*) up-to-date; (*Problem*) current; **nicht mehr ~** no longer relevant

Akupunktur f acupuncture

akustisch adj acoustic; **Akustik** f acoustics *sing*

akut adj acute

AKW (-s, -s) nt abk = **Atomkraftwerk** nuclear power station

Akzent (-(e)s, -e) m accent; (*Betonung*) stress; **mit starkem schottischen ~** with a strong Scottish accent

akzeptieren vt to accept

Alarm (-(e)s, -e) m alarm; **Alarmanlage** f alarm system; **alarmieren** vt to alarm; **die Polizei ~** to call the police

Albanien (-s) nt Albania

Albatros (-ses, -se) m albatross

albern adj silly

Albtraum m nightmare

Album (-s, Alben) nt album

Algen (pl) algae pl; (*Meeresalgen*) seaweed *sing*

Algerien (-s) nt Algeria

Alibi (-s, -s) nt alibi

Alimente pl maintenance *sing*

Alkohol (-s, -e) m alcohol; **alkoholfrei** adj non-alcoholic; **~es Getränk** soft drink; **Alkoholiker(in)** (-s, -) m(f) alcoholic; **alkoholisch** adj alcoholic; **Alkoholtest** m breathalyser® test (*Brit*), alcohol test

All (-s) nt universe

O **SCHLÜSSELWORT**

alle(r, s) adj 1 (*sämtliche*) all; **wir alle** all of us; **alle Kinder waren da** all the children were there; **alle Kinder mögen ...** all children like ...; **alle beide** both of us/them; **sie kamen alle** they all came; **alles Gute** all the best; **alles**

in allem all in all
2 (*mit Zeit- oder Maßangaben*) every; **alle vier Jahre** every four years; **alle fünf Meter** every five metres

▷ pron everything; **alles, was er sagt** everything he says, all that he says

▷ adv (*zu Ende, aufgebraucht*) finished; **die Milch ist alle** the milk's all gone, there's no milk left; **etw alle machen** to finish sth up

Allee (-, -n) f avenue

allein adj, adv alone; (*ohne Hilfe*) on one's own, by oneself; **nicht ~** (*nicht nur*) not only; **alleinerziehend** adj; **~e Mutter** single mother; **Alleinerziehende(r)** mf single mother/father/parent; **alleinstehend** adj single, unmarried

allerbeste(r, s) adj very best

allerdings adv (*zwar*) admittedly; (*gewiss*) certainly, sure (US)

allererste(r, s) adj very first; **zu allererst** first of all

Allergie f allergy; **Allergiker(in)** (-s, -) m(f) allergy sufferer; **allergisch** adj allergic (*gegen* to)

allerhand adj inv (fam) all sorts of; **das ist doch ~!** (*Vorwurf*) that's the limit

Allerheiligen (-) nt All Saints' Day

allerhöchste(r, s) adj very highest; **allerhöchstens** adv at the very most; **allerlei** adj inv all sorts of; **allerletzte(r, s)** adj very last; **allerwenigste(r, s)** adj very least

alles pron everything; **~ in allem** all in all; *siehe auch* **alle**

Alleskleber (-s, -) m all-purpose glue

allgemein adj general; **im Allgemeinen** in general;

Allgemeinarzt m,

Allgemeinärztin f GP (Brit), family practitioner (US)
Alligator (-s, -en) m alligator
alljährlich adj annual
allmählich adj gradual ▷ adv gradually
Allradantrieb m all-wheel drive
Alltag m everyday life; **alltäglich** adj everyday; (gewöhnlich) ordinary; (tagtäglich) daily
allzu adv all too
Allzweckreiniger (-s, -) m multi-purpose cleaner
Alpen pl: **die ~** the Alps pl
Alphabet (-(e)s, -e) nt alphabet; **alphabetisch** adj alphabetical
Alptraum m siehe Albtraum

SCHLÜSSELWORT

als konj **1** (zeitlich) when; (gleichzeitig) as; **damals, als ...** (in the days) when ...; **gerade, als ...** just as ...
2 (in der Eigenschaft) than; **als Antwort** as an answer; **als Kind** as a child
3 (bei Vergleichen) than; **ich kam später als er** I came later than he (did) o later than him; **lieber ...** **als ...** rather ... than ...; **nichts als Ärger** nothing but trouble
4 als ob/wenn as if

also conj (folglich) so, therefore ▷ adv, interj so; **~ gut** (o **schön**)! okay then
alt adj old; **wie ~ sind Sie?** how old are you?; **28 Jahre ~** 28 years old; **vier Jahre älter** four years older
Altar (-(e)s, Altäre) m altar
Alter (-s, -) nt age; (hohes) old age; **im ~ von** at the age of; **er ist in meinem ~** he's my age
alternativ adj alternative; (umweltbewusst) ecologically minded; (Landwirtschaft) organic; **Alternative** f alternative
Altersheim nt old people's home
Altglas nt used glass; **Altglascontainer** m bottle bank; **altmodisch** adj old-fashioned; **Altpapier** nt waste paper; **Altstadt** f old town
Alt-Taste f Alt key
Alufolie f tin (o kitchen) foil
Aluminium (-s) nt aluminium (Brit), aluminum (US)
Alzheimerkrankheit f Alzheimer's (disease)
am kontr von an dem: **~ 2. Januar** on January 2(nd); **~ Morgen** in the morning; **~ Strand** on the beach; **~ Bahnhof** at the station; **was gefällt Ihnen ~ besten?** what do you like best?; **~ besten bleiben wir hier** it would be best if we stayed here
Amateur(in) m(f) amateur
ambulant adj outpatient; **kann ich ~ behandelt werden?** can I have it done as an outpatient?; **Ambulanz** f (Krankenwagen) ambulance; (in der Klinik) outpatients' department
Ameise (-, -n) f ant
amen interj amen
Amerika (-s) nt America; **Amerikaner(in)** (-s, -) m(f) American; **amerikanisch** adj American
Ampel (-, -n) f traffic lights pl
Amphitheater nt amphitheatre
Amsel (-, -n) f blackbird
Amt (-(e)s, Ämter) nt office, department; (Posten) post; **amtlich** adj official; **Amtszeichen** nt (Tel) dialling tone (Brit), dial tone (US)
amüsant adj amusing; **amüsieren** vt to amuse ▷ vr: **sich ~** to enjoy oneself, to have a good time

SCHLÜSSELWORT

an prep +dat 1 (räumlich) (wo?) at; (auf, bei) on; (nahe bei) near; **an diesem Ort** at this place; **an der Wand** on the wall; **zu nahe an etw** near to sth; **unten am Fluss** down by the river; **Köln liegt am Rhein** Cologne is on the Rhine

2 (zeitlich: wann?) on; **an diesem Tag** on this day; **an Ostern** at Easter

3 **arm an Fett** low in fat; **an etw sterben** to die of sth; **an (und für) sich** actually

▷ prep +akk 1 (räumlich: wohin?) to; **er ging ans Fenster** he went (over) to the window; **etw an die Wand hängen/schreiben** to hang/write sth on the wall

2 (woran?) **an etw denken** to think of sth

3 (gerichtet an) to; **ein Gruß/eine Frage an dich** greetings/a question to you

▷ adv 1 (ungefähr) about; **an die hundert** about a hundred

2 (auf Fahrplänen) Frankfurt an 18.30 arriving Frankfurt 18.30

3 (ab) von dort/heute an from there/today onwards

4 (angeschaltet, angezogen) on; **das Licht ist an** the light is on; **ohne etwas an** with nothing on; siehe auch **am**

anal adj anal

analog adj analogous; (Inform) analog

Analyse (-, -n) f analysis; **analysieren** vt to analyse

Ananas (-, - o -se) f pineapple

an|baggern vt (fam) to chat up (Brit), to come on to (US)

Anbau m (Agr) cultivation; (Gebäude) extension; **an|bauen** vt (Agr) to cultivate; (Gebäudeteil) to build on

an|behalten irr vt to keep on

anbei adv enclosed; **~ sende ich ...** please find enclosed ...

an|beten vt to worship

an|bieten irr vt to offer ▷ vr: **sich ~** to volunteer

an|binden irr vt to tie up

Anblick m sight

an|braten irr vt to brown

an|brechen irr vt to start; (Vorräte, Ersparnisse) to break into; (Flasche, Packung) to open ▷ vi to start; (Tag) to break; (Nacht) to fall

an|brennen irr vt, vi to burn; **das Fleisch schmeckt angebrannt** the meat tastes burnt

an|bringen irr vt (herbeibringen) to bring; (befestigen) to fix, to attach

Andacht (-, -en) f devotion; (Gottesdienst) prayers pl

an|dauern vi to continue, to go on; **andauernd** adj continual

Andenken (-s, -) nt memory; (Gegenstand) souvenir

andere(r, s) adj (weitere) other; (verschieden) different; (folgend) next; **am ~n Tag** the next day; **von etw/jmd ~m sprechen** to talk about sth/sb else; **unter ~m** among other things; **andererseits** adv on the other hand

ändern vt to alter, to change ▷ vr: **sich ~** to change

andernfalls adv otherwise

anders adv differently (als from); **jemand/irgendwo ~** someone/somewhere else; **sie ist ~ als ihre Schwester** she's not like her sister; **es geht nicht ~** there's no other way; **anders(he)rum** adv the other way round; **anderswo** adv somewhere else

anderthalb num one and a half

Änderung f change, alteration
an|deuten vt to indicate; (Wink geben) to hint at
Andorra (-s) nt Andorra
Andrang m: **es herrschte großer ~** there was a huge crowd
an|drohen vt: **jdm etw ~** to threaten sb with sth
aneinander adv at/on/to one another (o each other); **~ denken** think of each other; **sich ~ gewöhnen** to get used to each other; **aneinander|geraten** irr vi to clash; **aneinander|legen** vt to put together
an|erkennen irr vt (Staat, Zeugnis etc) to recognize; (würdigen) to appreciate; **Anerkennung** f recognition; (Würdigung) appreciation
an|fahren irr vt (fahren gegen) to run into; (Ort, Hafen) to stop (o call) at; (liefern) to deliver; **jdn ~** (fig: schimpfen) to jump on sb ▷ vi to start; (losfahren) to drive off
Anfall m (Med) attack; **anfällig** adj delicate; (Maschine) temperamental; **~ für** prone to
Anfang (-(e)s, Anfänge) m beginning, start; **zu/am ~** to start with; **~ Mai** at the beginning of May; **sie ist ~ 20** she's in her early twenties; **an|fangen** irr vt, vi to begin, to start; **damit kann ich nichts ~** that's no use to me; **Anfänger(in)** (-s, -) m(f) beginner; **anfangs** adv at first; **Anfangsbuchstabe** m first (o initial) letter
an|fassen vt (berühren) to touch ▷ vi: **kannst du mal mit ~?** can you give me a hand?
Anflug m (Aviat) approach; (Hauch) trace
an|fordern vt to demand; **Anforderung** f request (von for); (Anspruch) demand

Anfrage f inquiry
an|freunden vr: **sich mit jdm ~** to make (o to become) friends with sb
an|fühlen vr: **sich ~** to feel; **es fühlt sich gut an** it feels good
Anführungszeichen pl quotation marks pl
Angabe f (Tech) specification; (fam: Prahlerei) showing off; (Tennis) serve; **~n** pl (Auskunft) particulars pl; **die ~n waren falsch** (Info) the information was wrong; **an|geben** irr vt (Name, Grund) to give; (zeigen) to indicate; (bestimmen) to set ▷ vi (fam: prahlen) to boast; (Sport) to serve; **Angeber(in)** (-s, -) m(f) (fam) show-off; **angeberisch** adj alleged
angeboren adj inborn
Angebot nt offer; (Comm) supply (an +dat of); **~ und Nachfrage** supply and demand
angebracht adj appropriate
angebunden adj: **kurz ~** curt
angeheitert adj tipsy
an|gehen irr vt to concern; **das geht dich nichts an** that's none of your business; **ein Problem ~** to tackle a problem; **was ihn angeht** as far as he's concerned, as for him ▷ vi (Feuer) to catch; (fam: beginnen) to begin; **angehend** adj prospective
Angehörige(r) mf relative
Angeklagte(r) mf accused, defendant
Angel (-, -n) f fishing rod; (an der Tür) hinge
Angelegenheit f affair, matter
Angelhaken m fish hook; **angeln** vt to catch ▷ vi to fish; **Angeln** (-s) nt angling, fishing; **Angelrute** (-, -n) f fishing rod
angemessen adj appropriate, suitable

angenehm adj pleasant; ~! (bei Vorstellung) pleased to meet you

angenommen adj assumed ▷ conj: ~, es regnet, was machen wir dann? suppose it rains, what do we do then?

angesehen adj respected

angesichts prep +gen in view of, considering

Angestellte(r) mf employee

angetan adj: von jdm/etw ~ sein to be impressed by (o taken with) sb/sth

angewiesen adj: auf jdn/etw ~ sein to be dependent on sb/sth

an|gewöhnen vt: sich etw ~ to get used to doing sth; **Angewohnheit** f habit

Angina (-, Anginen) f tonsillitis; **Angina Pectoris** (-) f angina

Angler(in) (-s, -) m(f) angler

Angora (-s) nt angora

an|greifen irr vt to attack; (anfassen) to touch; (beschädigen) to damage; **Angriff** m attack; **etw in ~ nehmen** to get started on sth

Angst (-, Ängste) f fear; ~ haben to be afraid (o scared) (vor +dat of); jdm ~ machen to scare sb; **ängstigen** vt to frighten ▷ vr: sich ~ to worry (um, wegen +dat about); **ängstlich** adj nervous; (besorgt) worried

an|haben irr vt (Kleidung) to have on, to wear; (Licht) to have on

an|halten irr vi to stop; (andauern) to continue; **anhaltend** adj continuous; **Anhalter(in)** (-s, -) m(f) hitch-hiker; per ~ fahren to hitch-hike

anhand prep +gen with; ~ von by means of

an|hängen vt to hang up; (Eisenb: Wagen) to couple; (Zusatz) to add (on); jdm etw ~ (fam: unterschieben) to pin sth on sb;

eine Datei an eine E-Mail ~ (Inform) to attach a file to an email; **Anhänger** (-s, -) m (Auto) trailer; (am Koffer) tag; (Schmuck) pendant; **Anhänger(in)** (-s, -) m(f) supporter; **Anhängerkupplung** f towbar; **anhänglich** adj affectionate; (pej) clinging

Anhieb m: auf ~ straight away; das kann ich nicht auf ~ sagen I can't say offhand

an|himmeln vt to idolize

an|hören vt to listen to ▷ vr: sich ~ to sound; das hört sich gut an that sounds good

Animateur(in) m(f) host/hostess

Anis (-es, -e) m aniseed

Anker (-s, -) m anchor; **ankern** vt, vi to anchor; **Ankerplatz** m anchorage

an|klicken vt (Inform) to click on

an|klopfen vi to knock (an +akk on)

an|kommen irr vi to arrive; bei jdm gut~ to go down well with sb; es kommt darauf an it depends (ob on whether); darauf kommt es nicht an that doesn't matter

an|kotzen vt (vulg) es kotzt mich an it makes me sick

an|kreuzen vt to mark with a cross

an|kündigen vt to announce

Ankunft (-, Ankünfte) f arrival; **Ankunftszeit** f arrival time

Anlage f (Veranlagung) disposition; (Begabung) talent; (Park) gardens pl; (zu Brief etc) enclosure; (Stereoanlage) stereo; (Tech) plant; (Fin) investment

Anlass (-es, Anlässe) m cause (zu for); (Ereignis) occasion; aus diesem ~ for this reason; **an|lassen** irr vt (Motor) to start; (Licht, Kleidung) to leave on;

Anlasser (-s, -) m (Auto) starter; **anlässlich** prep +gen on the occasion of

Anlauf m run-up; **anlaufen** irr vi to begin; (Film) to open; (Fenster) to mist up; (Metall) to tarnish

anlegen vt to put (an +akk against/on); (Schmuck) to put on; (Garten) to lay out; (Geld) to invest; (Gewehr) to aim (auf +akk at); **es auf etw** (akk) **~ to be out for sth** ▷ vi (Schiff) to berth, to dock ▷ vr: **sich mit jdm ~** (fam) to pick a quarrel with sb; **Anlegestelle** f moorings pl

anlehnen vt to lean (an +akk against); (Tür) to leave ajar ▷ vr: **sich ~** to lean (an +akk against)

anleiern vt: **etw ~** (fam) to get sth going

Anleitung f instructions pl

Anliegen (-s, -) nt matter; (Wunsch) request

Anlieger(in) (-s, -) m(f) resident; **~ frei** residents only

anlügen irr vt to lie to

anmachen vt (befestigen) to attach; (einschalten) to switch on; (Salat) to dress; (fam: aufreizen) to turn on; (fam: ansprechen) to chat up (Brit), to come on to (US); (fam: beschimpfen) to have a go at

Anmeldeformular nt application form; (bei Amt) registration form; **anmelden** vt (Besuch etc) to announce ▷ vr: **sich ~** (beim Arzt etc) to make an appointment; (bei Amt, für Kurs etc) to register; **Anmeldeschluss** m deadline for applications, registration deadline; **Anmeldung** f registration; (Antrag) application

annähen vt: **einen Knopf (an den Mantel) ~** to sew a button on (one's coat)

annähernd adv roughly; **nicht ~** nowhere near

Annahme (-, -n) f acceptance; (Vermutung) assumption; **annehmbar** adj acceptable; **annehmen** irr vt to accept; (Namen) to take; (Kind) to adopt; (vermuten) to suppose, to assume

Annonce (-, -n) f advertisement

anöden vt (fam) to bore stiff (o silly)

annullieren vt to cancel

anonym adj anonymous

Anorak (-s, -s) m anorak

anpacken vt (Problem, Aufgabe) to tackle; **mit ~** to lend a hand

anpassen vt (fig) to adapt (dat to) ▷ vr: **sich ~** to adapt (an +akk to)

anpfeifen irr vt (Fußballspiel) **das Spiel ~** to start the game; **Anpfiff** m (Sport) (starting) whistle; (Beginn) kick-off; (fam: Tadel) roasting

anprobieren vt to try on

Anrede f form of address; **anreden** vt to address

anregen vt to stimulate; **Anregung** f stimulation; (Vorschlag) suggestion

Anreise f journey; **anreisen** vi to arrive; **Anreisetag** m day of arrival

Anreiz m incentive

anrichten vt (Speisen) to prepare; (Schaden) to cause

Anruf m call; **Anrufbeantworter** (-s, -) m answering machine, answerphone; **anrufen** irr vt (Tel) to call, to phone, to ring (Brit)

ans kontr von **an das**

Ansage f announcement; (auf Anrufbeantworter) recorded message; **ansagen** vt to announce; **angesagt sein** to be recommended; (modisch sein) to be the in thing

an|schaffen vt to buy
an|schauen vt to look at
Anschein m appearance; **dem** (o **allem**) ~ **nach ...** it looks as if ...; **den ~ erwecken, hart zu arbeiten** to give the impression of working hard; **anscheinend** adj apparent ▷ adv apparently
an|schieben irr vt: **könnten Sie mich mal ~?** (Auto) could you give me a push?
Anschlag m notice; (Attentat) attack; **an|schlagen** irr vt (Plakat) to put up; (beschädigen) to chip ▷ vi (wirken) to take effect; **mit etw an etw** (akk) ~ to bang sth against sth
an|schließen irr vt (Elek, Tech) to connect (an +akk to); (mit Stecker) to plug in ▷ vi, vr (**sich**) **an etw** (akk) ~ (Gebäude etc) to adjoin sth; (zeitlich) to follow sth ▷ vr: **sich** ~ to join (jdm/einer Gruppe sb/a group); **anschließend** adj adjacent; (zeitlich) subsequent ▷ adv afterwards; ~ **an** (+akk) following; **Anschluss** m (Elek, Eisenb) connection; (von Wasser, Gas etc) supply; **im** ~ **an** (+akk) following; **kein** ~ **unter dieser Nummer** (Tel) the number you have dialled has not been recognized; **Anschlussflug** m connecting flight
an|schnallen vt (Skier) to put on ▷ vr: **sich** ~ to fasten one's seat belt
Anschrift f address
an|schwellen irr vi to swell (up)
an|sehen irr vt to look at; (bei etw zuschauen) to watch; **jdm/etw als etw** ~ to look on sb/sth as sth; **das sieht man ihm an** he looks it
an sein vi siehe **an**
an|setzen vt (Termin) to fix; (zubereiten) to prepare ▷ vi (anfangen) to start, to begin; **zu**

etw ~ to prepare to do sth
Ansicht f (Meinung) view, opinion; (Anblick) sight; **meiner** ~ **nach** in my opinion; **zur** ~ on approval; **Ansichtskarte** f postcard
ansonsten adv otherwise
an|spielen vi **auf etw** (akk) ~ to allude to sth; **Anspielung** f allusion (auf +akk to)
an|sprechen irr vt to speak to; (gefallen) to appeal to ▷ vi **auf etw** (akk) ~ (Patient) to respond to sth; **ansprechend** adj attractive; **Ansprechpartner(in)** m(f) contact
an|springen irr vi (Auto) to start
Anspruch m claim; (Recht) right (auf +akk to); **etw in** ~ **nehmen** to take advantage of sth; ~ **auf etw haben** to be entitled to sth; **anspruchslos** adj undemanding; (bescheiden) modest; **anspruchsvoll** adj demanding
Anstalt (-, -en) f institution
Anstand m decency; **anständig** adj decent; (fig, fam) proper; (groß) considerable
an|starren vt to stare at
anstatt prep +gen instead of
an|stecken vt to pin on; (Med) to infect; **jdn mit einer Erkältung** ~ to pass one's cold on to sb ▷ vr: **ich habe mich bei ihm angesteckt** I caught it from him ▷ vi (fig) to be infectious; **ansteckend** adj infectious; **Ansteckungsgefahr** f danger of infection
an|stehen irr vi (in Warteschlange) to queue (Brit), to stand in line (US); (erledigt werden müssen) to be on the agenda
anstelle prep +gen instead of
an|stellen vt (einschalten) to turn on; (Arbeit geben) to employ; (machen) to do; **was hast du**

wieder angestellt? what have you been up to now? ▷ vr: **sich ~ to** queue (Brit), to stand in line (US); (fam) **stell dich nicht so an!** stop making such a fuss

Anstoß m impetus; (Sport) kick-off; **an|stoßen** irr vt to push; (mit Fuß) to kick ▷ vi to knock, to bump; (mit Gläsern) to drink (a toast) (auf +akk to); **anstößig** adj offensive; (Kleidung etc) indecent

an|strengen vt to strain ▷ vr: **sich ~** to make an effort; **anstrengend** adj tiring

Antarktis f Antarctic

Anteil m share (an +dat in); **~ nehmen an** (+dat) (mitleidig) to sympathize with; (sich interessieren) to take an interest in

Antenne (-, -n) f aerial

Antibabypille f: **die ~** the pill; **Antibiotikum** (-s, Antibiotika) nt (Med) antibiotic

antik adj antique

Antilope (-, -n) f antelope

Antiquariat nt (für Bücher) second-hand bookshop

Antiquitäten pl antiques pl; **Antiquitätenhändler(in)** m(f) antique dealer

Antiviren- adj (Inform) antivirus; **Antivirensoftware** f antivirus software

an|törnen vt (fam) to turn on

Antrag (-(e)s, Anträge) m proposal; (Pol) motion; (Formular) application form; **einen ~ stellen auf** (+akk) to apply for

an|treffen irr vt to find

an|treiben irr vt (Tech) to drive; (anschwemmen) to wash up; **jdn zur Arbeit ~** to make sb work

an|treten irr vt: **eine Reise ~** to set off on a journey

Antrieb m (Tech) drive; (Motivation) impetus

an|tun irr vt: **jdm etwas ~** to do

sth to sb; **sich** (dat) **etwas ~** (Selbstmord begehen) to kill oneself

Antwort (-, -en) f answer, reply; **um ~ wird gebeten** RSVP (répondez s'il vous plaît); **antworten** vi to answer, to reply; **jdm ~** to answer sb; **auf etwas** (akk) **~** to answer sth

an|vertrauen vt: **jdm etw ~** to entrust sb with sth

Anwalt (-s, Anwälte) m, **Anwältin** f lawyer

an|weisen vt (anleiten) to instruct; (zuteilen) to allocate (jdm etw sth to sb); **Anweisung** f instruction; (von Geld) money order

an|wenden vt to use; (Gesetz, Regel) to apply; **Anwender(in)** (-s, -) m(f) user; **Anwendung** f use; (Inform) application

anwesend adj present; **Anwesenheit** f presence

an|widern vt to disgust

Anwohner(in) (-s, -) m(f) resident

Anzahl f number (an +dat of); **an|zahlen** vt to pay a deposit on; **100 Euro ~** to pay 100 euros as a deposit; **Anzahlung** f deposit

Anzeichen nt sign; (Med) symptom

Anzeige (-, -n) f (Werbung) advertisement; (elektronisch) display; (bei Polizei) report; **an|zeigen** vt (Temperatur, Zeit) to indicate, to show; (elektronisch) to display; (bekannt geben) to announce; **einen Autodiebstahl bei der Polizei ~** to report a stolen car to the police

an|ziehen irr vt to attract; (Kleidung) to put on; (Schraube, Seil) to tighten ▷ vr: **sich ~** to get dressed; **anziehend** adj attractive

Anzug m suit

anzüglich adj suggestive

an|zünden vt to light; (Haus etc)

to set fire to

an|zweifeln vt to doubt

Aperitif (-s, -s (o -e)) m aperitif

Apfel (-s, Äpfel) m apple;
Apfelbaum m apple tree;
Apfelkuchen m apple cake;
Apfelmus nt apple purée;
Apfelsaft m apple juice; **Apfelsine** f orange; **Apfelwein** m cider

Apostroph (-s, -e) m apostrophe

Apotheke (-, -n) f chemist's
(shop) (Brit), pharmacy (US);
apothekenpflichtig adj only
available at the chemist's;
Apotheker(in) (-s, -) m(f)
chemist (Brit), pharmacist (US)

App (-s) f app

Apparat (-(e)s, -e) m (piece of)
apparatus; (Tel) telephone; (Radio,
TV) set; **am ~!** (Tel) speaking; **am
~ bleiben** (Tel) to hold the line

Appartement (-s, -s) nt studio
flat (Brit) (o apartment (US))

Appetit (-(e)s, -e) m appetite;
guten ~! bon appétit; **appetitlich**
adj appetizing

Applaus (-es, -e) m applause

Aprikose (-, -n) f apricot

April (-(s), -e) m April; siehe auch
Juni; **~, ~!** April fool!; **Aprilscherz**
(-es, -e) m April fool's joke

apropos adv by the way;
~ Urlaub ... while we're on the
subject of holidays ...

Aquaplaning (-(s)) nt
aquaplaning

Aquarell (-s, -e) nt watercolour

Aquarium (-s, Aquarien) nt
aquarium

Äquator (-s, -) m equator

Araber(in) (-s, -) m(f) Arab;
arabisch adj Arab; (Ziffer, Sprache)
Arabic; (Meer, Wüste) Arabian

Arbeit (-, -en) f work; (Stelle) job;
(Erzeugnis) piece of work; **arbeiten**
vi to work; **Arbeiter(in)** (-s, -) m(f)
worker; (ungelernt) labourer;

Arbeitgeber(in) (-s, -) m(f) employer;

Arbeitnehmer(in) (-s, -) m(f) employee;

Arbeitsagentur f job agency
(Brit), unemployment agency (US);

Arbeitsamt nt job centre (Brit),
employment office (US);

Arbeitserlaubnis f work permit;
arbeitslos adj unemployed;

Arbeitslose(r) mf unemployed
person; **Arbeitslosengeld** nt
(income-related) unemployment
benefit, job-seeker's allowance
(Brit); **Arbeitslosenhilfe** f
(non-income related)
unemployment benefit;

Arbeitslosigkeit f unemployment; **Arbeitsplatz** m job; (Ort)
workplace; **Arbeitsspeicher** m
(Inform) main memory;
Arbeitszeit f working hours pl;
Arbeitszimmer nt study

Archäologe (-n, -n) m,
Archäologin f archaeologist

Architekt(in) (-en, -en) m(f)
architect; **Architektur** f
architecture

Archiv (-s, -e) nt archives pl

ARD f = Arbeitsgemeinschaft
der öffentlich-rechtlichen
Rundfunkanstalten der
Bundesrepublik Deutschland
German broadcasting corporation

arg adj bad; (schrecklich) awful
▷ adv (sehr) terribly

Argentinien (-s) nt Argentina

Ärger (-s) m annoyance;
(stärker) anger; (Unannehmlichkeiten)
trouble; **ärgerlich** adj annoying;
(zornig) angry; **ärgern** vt to annoy
▷ vr: **sich ~** to get annoyed

Argument (-s, -e) nt argument

Arktis (-) f Arctic

arm adj poor

Arm (-(e)s, -e) m arm; (Fluss) branch

Armaturenbrett nt instrument
panel; (Auto) dashboard

Armband nt bracelet;

Armbanduhr f (wrist)watch

Armee (-, -n) f army

Ärmel (-s, -) m sleeve; **Ärmelkanal** m (English) Channel

Armut (-) f poverty

Aroma (-s, Aromen) nt aroma

arrogant adj arrogant

Arsch (-es, Ärsche) m (vulg) arse (Brit), ass (US); **Arschloch** nt (vulg: Person) arsehole (Brit), asshole (US)

Art (-, -en) f (Weise) way; (Sorte) kind, sort; (bei Tieren) species; **nach ~ des Hauses** à la maison; **auf diese ~ (und Weise)** in this way; **das ist nicht seine ~** that's not like him

Arterie (-, -n) f artery

artig adj good, well-behaved

Artikel (-s, -) m (Ware) article, item; (Zeitung) article

Artischocke (-, -n) f artichoke

Artist(in) (-en, -en) m(f) (circus) performer

Arznei f medicine; **Arzt** (-es, Ärzte) m doctor; **Arzthelfer(in)** m(f) doctor's assistant; **Ärztin** f (female) doctor; **ärztlich** adj medical; **sich ~ behandeln lassen** to undergo medical treatment

Asche (-, -n) f ashes pl; (von Zigarette) ash; **Aschenbecher** m ashtray; **Aschermittwoch** m Ash Wednesday

Asiat(in) (-en, -en) m(f) Asian; **asiatisch** adj Asian; **Asien** (-s) nt Asia

Aspekt (-(e)s, -e) m aspect

Asphalt (-(e)s, -e) m asphalt

Aspirin® (-s, -e) nt aspirin

aß imperf von **essen**

Ass (-es, -e) nt (Karten, Tennis) ace

Assistent(in) m(f) assistant

Ast (-(e)s, Äste) m branch

Asthma (-s) nt asthma

Astrologie f astrology

Astronaut(in) (-en, -en) m(f)

astronaut; **Astronomie** f astronomy

ASU (-, -s) f abk = **Abgassonderuntersuchung** exhaust emission test

Asyl (-s, -e) nt asylum; (Heim) home; (für Obdachlose) shelter; **Asylant(in)** m(f), **Asylbewerber(in)** m(f) asylum seeker

Atelier (-s, -s) nt studio

Atem (-s) m breath; **atemberaubend** adj breathtaking; **Atembeschwerden** pl breathing difficulties pl; **atemlos** adj breathless; **Atempause** f breather

Athen nt Athens

Äthiopien (-s) nt Ethiopia

Athlet(in) (-en, -en) m(f) athlete; **Athletik** f athletics sing

Atlantik (-s) m Atlantic (Ocean)

Atlas (- o Atlasses, Atlanten) m atlas

atmen vt, vi to breathe; **Atmung** f breathing

Atom (-s) nt atom; **Atombombe** f atom bomb; **Atomkraftwerk** nt nuclear power station; **Atommüll** m nuclear waste; **Atomwaffen** pl nuclear weapons pl

Attentat (-(e)s, -e) nt assassination (auf +akk of); (Versuch) assassination attempt

Attest (-(e)s, -e) nt certificate

attraktiv adj attractive

Attrappe (-, -n) f dummy

ätzend adj (fam) revolting; (schlecht) lousy

au interj ouch; **~ ja!** yeah

Aubergine (-, -n) f aubergine, eggplant (US)

SCHLÜSSELWORT

auch adv 1 (ebenfalls) also, too, as well; **das ist auch schön** that's nice too o as well; **er kommt – ich**

auch he's coming — so am I, me too; **auch nicht** not ... either; **ich auch nicht** nor I, me neither; **oder auch** or; **auch das noch!** not that as well!

2 (*selbst, sogar*) even; **auch wenn das Wetter schlecht ist** even if the weather is bad; **ohne auch nur zu fragen** without even asking

3 (*wirklich*) really; **du siehst müde aus—bin ich auch** you look tired—(so I am); **so sieht es auch aus** it looks like it too

4 (*auch immer*) **wer auch** whoever; **was auch** whatever; **wie dem auch sei** be that as it may; **wie sehr er sich auch bemühte** however much he had tried

audiovisuell *adj* audiovisual

⬤ SCHLÜSSELWORT

auf *prep +dat* (*wo?*) on; **auf dem Tisch** on the table; **auf der Reise** on the way; **auf der Post/dem Fest** at the post office/party; **auf der Straße** on the road; **auf dem Land/der ganzen Welt** in the country/the whole world

▷ *prep +akk* **1** (*wohin?*) on(to); **auf den Tisch** on(to) the table; **auf die Post gehen** to go to the post office; **auf das Land** into the country; **etw auf einen Zettel schreiben** to write sth on a piece of paper

2 (*zeitlich*) **auf Deutsch** in German; **auf Lebenszeit** for my/his lifetime; **bis auf ihn** except for him; **auf einmal** at once; **auf seinen Vorschlag (hin)** at his suggestion

▷ *adv* **1** (*offen*) open; **auf sein** (*fam*) (*Tür, Geschäft*) to be open; **das Fenster ist auf** the window is open

2 (*hinauf*) up; **auf und ab** up and down; **auf und davon** up and away; **auf!** (*los!*) come on!

3 (*aufgestanden*) up; **auf sein** to be up; **ist er schon auf?** is he up yet?

▷ *konj:* **auf dass** (so) that

auf|atmen *vi* to breathe a sigh of relief

auf|bauen *vt* (*errichten*) to put up; (*schaffen*) to build up; (*gestalten*) to construct; (*gründen*) to found, to base (*auf +akk* on); **sich eine Existenz ~** to make a life for oneself

auf|bewahren *vt* to keep, to store

auf|bleiben *irr vi* (*Tür, Laden etc*) to stay open; (*Mensch*) to stay up

auf|blenden *vi, vt:* (*die Scheinwerfer*) **~** to put one's headlights on full beam

auf|brechen *irr vt* to break open ▷ *vi* to burst open; (*gehen*) to leave; (*abreisen*) to set off

auf|drängen *vt:* **jdm etw ~** to force sth on sb ▷ *vr:* **sich ~** to intrude (*jdm* on sb); **aufdringlich** *adj* pushy

aufeinander *adv* (*übereinander*) on top of each other; **~ achten** to look after each other; **~ vertrauen** to trust each other; **aufeinan-der|folgen** *vi* to follow one another; **aufeinander|prallen** *vi* to crash into one another

Aufenthalt *m* stay; (*Zug*) stop; **Aufenthaltsgenehmigung** *f* residence permit; **Aufenthaltsraum** *m* lounge

auf|essen *irr vt* to eat up

auf|fahren *irr vi* (*Auto*) to run (*o* to crash) (*auf +akk* into); (*herankommen*) to drive up; **Auffahrt** *f* (*am Haus*) drive; (*Autobahn*) slip road (*Brit*), ramp (*US*); **Auffahrunfall** *m* rear-end collision; *(mehrere Fahrzeuge)* pile-up

auf|fallen *irr vi* to stand out; **jdm ~** to strike sb; **das fällt gar nicht auf** nobody will notice; **auffallend** *adj* striking; **auffällig** *adj* conspicuous; *(Kleidung)* striking

auf|fangen *vt* to catch; *(Ball)* to catch; *(Stoß)* to cushion

auf|fassen *vt* to understand; **Auffassung** *f* view; *(Meinung)* opinion; *(Auslegung)* concept; *(Auffassungsgabe)* grasp

auf|fordern *vt (befehlen)* to call upon; *(bitten)* to ask

auf|frischen *vt* to brush up

auf|führen *vt (Theat)* to perform; *(in einem Verzeichnis)* to list; *(Beispiel)* to give ▷ *vr* **sich ~** *(sich benehmen)* to behave; **Aufführung** *f (Theat)* performance

Aufgabe *f* job, task; *(Schule)* exercise; *(Hausaufgabe)* homework

Aufgang *m (Treppe)* staircase

auf|geben *irr vt (verzichten auf)* to give up; *(Paket)* to post; *(Gepäck)* to check in; *(Bestellung)* to place; *(Inserat)* to insert; *(Rätsel, Problem)* to set ▷ *vi* to give up

auf|gehen *irr vi (Sonne, Teig)* to rise; *(sich öffnen)* to open; *(klar werden)* to dawn *(jdm* on sb)

aufgelegt *adj:* **gut/schlecht ~** in a good/bad mood

aufgeregt *adj* excited

aufgeschlossen *adj* open(minded)

aufgeschmissen *adj (fam)* in a fix

aufgrund, auf Grund *prep +gen* on the basis of; *(wegen)* because of

auf|haben *irr vt (Hut etc)* to have on; **viel ~** *(Schule)* to have a lot of homework to do ▷ *vi (Geschäft)* to be open

auf|halten *irr vt (jdn)* to detain; *(Entwicklung)* to stop; *(Tür, Hand)* to

hold open; *(Augen)* to keep open ▷ *vr:* **sich ~** *(wohnen)* to live; *(vorübergehend)* to stay

auf|hängen *irr vt* to hang up

auf|heben *irr vt (vom Boden etc)* to pick up; *(aufbewahren)* to keep

Aufheiterungen *pl (Meteo)* bright periods *pl*

auf|holen *vt (Zeit)* to make up ▷ *vi* to catch up

auf|hören *vi* to stop; **~, etw zu tun** to stop doing sth

auf|klären *vt (Geheimnis etc)* to clear up; **jdn ~** to enlighten sb; *(sexuell)* to tell sb the facts of life

Aufkleber *(-s, -) m* sticker

auf|kommen *irr vi (Wind)* to come up; *(Zweifel, Gefühl)* to arise; *(Mode etc)* to appear on the scene; **für den Schaden ~** to pay for the damage

auf|laden *irr vt* to load; *(Handy etc)* to charge; *(Phonkarte etc)* to top up; **Aufladegerät** *nt* charger

Auflage *f* edition; *(von Zeitung)* circulation; *(Bedingung)* condition

auf|lassen *vt (Hut, Brille)* to keep on; *(Tür)* to leave open

Auflauf *m (Menschen)* crowd; *(Speise)* bake

auf|legen *vt (CD, Schminke etc)* to put on; *(Hörer)* to put down ▷ *vi (Tel)* to hang up

auf|leuchten *vi* to light up

auf|lösen *vt (in Flüssigkeit)* to dissolve ▷ *vr:* **sich ~** *(in Flüssigkeit)* to dissolve; **der Stau hat sich aufgelöst** traffic is back to normal; **Auflösung** *f (von Rätsel)* solution; *(von Bildschirm)* resolution

auf|machen *vt* to open; *(Kleidung)* to undo ▷ *vr:* **sich ~** to set out *(nach* for)

aufmerksam *adj* attentive; **jdn auf etw** *(akk)* **~ machen** to draw sb's attention to sth;

Aufmerksamkeit f attention; (Konzentration) attentiveness; (Geschenk) small token

auf|muntern vt (ermutigen) to encourage; (aufheitern) to cheer up

Aufnahme (-, -n) f (Foto) photo(graph); (einzelne) shot; (in Verein, Krankenhaus etc) admission; (Beginn) beginning; (auf Tonband etc) recording; **Aufnahmeprüfung** f entrance exam; **auf|nehmen** irr vt (in Krankenhaus, Verein etc) to admit; (Musik) to record; (beginnen) to take up; (in Liste) to include; (begreifen) to take in; **mit jdm Kontakt ~** to get in touch with sb

auf|passen vi (aufmerksam sein) to pay attention; (vorsichtig sein) to take care; **auf jdn/etw ~** to keep an eye on sb/sth

Aufprall (-s, -e) m impact; **auf|prallen** vi **auf etw** (akk) **~** to hit sth, to crash into sth

Aufpreis m extra charge

auf|pumpen vt to pump up

Aufputschmittel nt stimulant

auf|räumen vt, vi (Dinge) to clear away; (Zimmer) to tidy up

aufrecht adj upright

auf|regen vt to excite; (ärgern) to annoy ▷ vr: **sich ~** to get worked up; **aufregend** adj exciting; **Aufregung** f excitement

auf|reißen irr vt (Tüte) to tear open; (Tür) to fling open; (fam: Person) to pick up

Aufruf m (Aviat, Inform) call; (öffentlicher) appeal; **auf|rufen** irr vt (auffordern) to call upon (zu for); (Namen) to call out; (Aviat) to call; (Inform) to call up

auf|runden vt (Summe) to round up

aufs kontr von **auf das**

Aufsatz m essay

auf|schieben irr vt (verschieben)

to postpone; (verzögern) to put off; (Tür) to slide open

Aufschlag m (auf Preis) extra charge; (Tennis) service; **auf|schlagen** irr vt (öffnen) to open; (verletzen) to cut open; (Zelt) to pitch, to put up; (Lager) to set up ▷ vi (Tennis) to serve; **auf etw** (+akk) **~** (aufprallen) to hit sth

auf|schließen irr vt to unlock, to open up ▷ vi (aufrücken) to close up

auf|schneiden irr vt to cut open; (in Scheiben) to slice ▷ vi (angeben) to boast, to show off

Aufschnitt m (slices pl of) cold meat; (bei Käse) (assorted) sliced cheeses pl

auf|schreiben irr vt to write down

Aufschrift f inscription; (Etikett) label

Aufschub m (Verzögerung) delay; (Vertagung) postponement

Aufsehen (-s) nt stir; **großes ~ erregen** to cause a sensation; **Aufseher(in)** (-s, -) m(f) guard; (im Betrieb) supervisor; (im Museum) attendant; (im Park) keeper

auf sein irr vi siehe **auf**

auf|setzen vt to put on; (Dokument) to draw up ▷ vi (Flugzeug) to touch down

Aufsicht f supervision; (bei Prüfung) invigilation; **die ~ haben** to be in charge

auf|spannen vt (Schirm) to put up

auf|sperren vt (Mund) to open wide; (aufschließen) to unlock

auf|springen irr vi to jump (auf +akk onto); (hochspringen) to jump up; (sich öffnen) to spring open

auf|stehen irr vi to get up; (Tür) to be open

auf|stellen vt (aufrecht stellen) to

put up; (aufreihen) to line up; (nominieren) to put up; (Liste, Programm) to draw up; (Rekord) to set up

Aufstieg (-(e)s, -e) m (auf Berg) ascent; (Fortschritt) rise; (beruflich, im Sport) promotion

Aufstrich m spread

auf|tanken vt, vi (Auto) to tank up; (Flugzeug) to refuel

auf|tauchen vi to turn up; (aus Wasser etc) to surface; (Frage, Problem) to come up

auf|tauen vt (Speisen) to defrost ▷ vi to thaw; (fig: Person) to unbend

Auftrag (-(e)s, Aufträge) m (Comm) order; (Arbeit) job; (Anweisung) instructions pl; (Aufgabe) task; **im ~ von** on behalf of; **auf|tragen** irr vt (Salbe etc) to apply; (Essen) to serve

auf|treten irr vi to appear; (Problem) to come up; (sich verhalten) to behave; **Auftritt** m (des Schauspielers) entrance; (fig: Szene) scene

auf|wachen vi to wake up

auf|wachsen irr vi to grow up

Aufwand (-(e)s) m expenditure; (Kosten a.) expense; (Anstrengung) effort; **aufwändig** adj costly; **das ist zu ~** that's too much trouble

auf|wärmen vt to warm up ▷ vr: **sich ~** to warm up

aufwärts adv upwards; **mit etw geht es ~** things are looking up for sth

auf|wecken vt to wake up

aufwendig adj siehe **aufwändig**

auf|wischen vt to wipe up; (Fußboden) to wipe

auf|zählen vt to list

auf|zeichnen vt to sketch; (schriftlich) to jot down; (auf Band etc) to record; **Aufzeichnung** f

(schriftlich) note; (Tonband etc) recording; (Film) record

auf|ziehen irr vt (öffnen) to pull open; (Uhr) to wind (up); (fam: necken) to tease; (Kinder) to bring up; (Tiere) to rear ▷ vi (Gewitter) to come up

Aufzug m (Fahrstuhl) lift (Brit), elevator (US); (Kleidung) get-up; (Theat) act

Auge (-s, -n) nt eye; **jdm etw aufs ~ drücken** (fam) to force sth on sb; **ins ~ gehen** (fam) to go wrong; **unter vier ~n** in private; **etw im ~ behalten** to keep sth in mind; **Augenarzt** m, **Augenärztin** f eye specialist, eye doctor (US); **Augenblick** m moment; **im ~** at the moment; **Augenbraue** (-, -n) f eyebrow; **Augenbrauenstift** m eyebrow pencil; **Augenfarbe** f eye colour; **seine ~** the colour of his eyes; **Augenlid** nt eyelid; **Augenoptiker(in)** (-s, -) m(f) optician; **Augentropfen** pl eyedrops pl; **Augenzeuge** m, **Augenzeugin** f eyewitness

August (-(e)s o -, -e) m August; siehe auch **Juni**

Auktion f auction

aus prep +dat 1 (räumlich) out of; (von ... her) from; **er ist aus Berlin** he's from Berlin; **aus dem Fenster** out of the window

2 (gemacht/hergestellt aus) made of; **ein Herz aus Stein** a heart of stone

3 (auf Ursache deutend) out of; **aus Mitleid** out of sympathy; **aus Erfahrung** from experience; **aus Spaß** for fun

4 **aus ihr wird nie etwas** she'll never get anywhere

▷ *adv* **1** (*zu Ende*) finished, over; **aus sein** to be over; **aus und vorbei** over and done with **2** (*ausgeschaltet, ausgezogen*) out; (*Aufschrift an Geräten*) off; **aus sein** (*nicht brennen*) to be out; (*abgeschaltet sein: Radio, Herd*) to be off; **Licht aus!** lights out! **3** (*nicht zu Hause*) **aus sein** to be out **4** (*in Verbindung mit von*) **von Rom aus** from Rome; **vom Fenster aus** out of the window; **von sich aus** (*selbstständig*) of one's own accord; **von ihm aus** as far as he's concerned

Aus (-) *nt* (*Sport*) touch; (*fig*) end **aus|atmen** *vi* to breathe out **aus|bauen** *vt* (*Haus, Straße*) to extend; (*Motor etc*) to remove **aus|bessern** *vt* to repair; (*Kleidung*) to mend **aus|bilden** *vt* to educate; (*Lehrling etc*) to train; (*Fähigkeiten*) to develop; **Ausbildung** *f* education; (*von Lehrling etc*) training; (*von Fähigkeiten*) development

Ausblick *m* view; (*fig*) outlook **aus|brechen** *irr vi* to break out; **in Tränen ~** to burst into tears; **in Gelächter ~** to burst out laughing **aus|breiten** *vt* to spread (out); (*Arme*) to stretch out ▷ *vr*: **sich ~** to spread

Ausbruch *m* (*Krieg, Seuche etc*) outbreak; (*Vulkan*) eruption; (*Gefühle*) outburst; (*von Gefangenen*) escape **aus|buhen** *vt* to boo **Ausdauer** *f* perseverance; (*Sport*) stamina **aus|dehnen** *vt* to stretch; (*fig: Macht*) to extend **aus|denken** *irr vt* **sich** (*dat*) **etw ~** to come up with sth

Ausdruck *m* (*Ausdrücke*) expression ▷ *m* (*Ausdrucke, Computerausdruck*) print-out; **aus|drucken** *vt* (*Inform*) to print (out) **aus|drücken** *vt* (*formulieren*) to express; (*Zigarette*) to put out; (*Zitrone etc*) to squeeze ▷ *vr*: **sich ~** to express oneself; **ausdrücklich** *adj* express ▷ *adv* expressly **auseinander** *adv* (*getrennt*) apart; **~ schreiben** to write as separate words; **auseinander|gehen** *irr vi* (*Menschen*) to separate; (*Meinungen*) to differ; (*Gegenstand*) to fall apart; **auseinander|halten** *irr vt* to tell apart; **auseinander|setzen** *vt* (*erklären*) to explain; **auseinander|setzen** *vr*: **sich ~** (*sich beschäftigen*) to look (*mit* at); (*sich streiten*) to argue (*mit* with); **Auseinandersetzung** *f* (*Streit*) argument; (*Diskussion*) debate

Ausfahrt *f* (*des Zuges etc*) departure; (*Autobahn, Garage etc*) exit **aus|fallen** *irr vi* (*Haare*) to fall out; (*nicht stattfinden*) to be cancelled; (*nicht funktionieren*) to break down; (*Strom*) to be cut off; (*Resultat haben*) to turn out; **groß/klein ~** (*Kleidung, Schuhe*) to be too big/too small **ausfindig machen** *vt* to discover **aus|flippen** *vi* (*fam*) to freak out **Ausflug** *m* excursion, outing; **Ausflugsziel** *nt* destination **Ausfluss** *m* (*Med*) discharge **aus|fragen** *vt* to question **Ausfuhr** (-, -en) *f* export **aus|führen** *vt* (*verwirklichen*) to carry out; (*Person*) to take out; (*Comm*) to export; (*darlegen*) to explain

ausführlich adj detailed ⊳ adv in detail

ausfüllen vt to fill up; (Fragebogen etc) to fill in (o out)

Ausgabe f (Geld) expenditure; (Inform) output; (Buch) edition; (Nummer) issue

Ausgang m way out, exit; (Flugsteig) gate; (Ende) end; (Ergebnis) result; **„kein ~"** "no exit"

ausgeben irr vt (Geld) to spend; (austeilen) to distribute; **jdm etw ~** (spendieren) to buy sb sth ⊳ vr: **sich für etw/jdn ~** to pass oneself off as sth/sb

ausgebucht adj fully booked

ausgefallen adj (ungewöhnlich) unusual

ausgehen irr vi (abends etc) to go out; (Benzin, Kaffee etc) to run out; (Haare) to fall out; (Feuer, Licht etc) to go out; (Resultat haben) to turn out; **davon ~, dass** to assume that; **ihm ging das Geld aus** he ran out of money

ausgelassen adj exuberant

ausgeleiert adj worn out

ausgenommen conj, prep +gen o dat except

ausgerechnet adv: **~ du** you of all people; **~ heute** today of all days

ausgeschildert adj signposted

ausgeschlafen adj: **bist du ~?** have you had enough sleep?

ausgeschlossen adj (unmöglich) impossible, out of the question

ausgesprochen adj (absolut) out-and-out; (unverkennbar) marked ⊳ adv extremely; **~ gut** really good

ausgezeichnet adj excellent

ausgiebig adj (Gebrauch) thorough; (Essen) substantial

ausgießen irr vt (Getränk) to pour out; (Gefäß) to empty

ausgleichen irr vt to even out ⊳ vi (Sport) to equalize

Ausguss m (Spüle) sink; (Abfluss) outlet

aushalten irr vt to bear, to stand; **nicht auszuhalten sein** to be unbearable ⊳ vi to hold out

aushändigen vt: **jdm etw ~** to hand sth over to sb

Aushang m notice

Aushilfe f temporary help; (im Büro) temp

auskennen irr vr: **sich ~** to know a lot (bei, mit about); (an einem Ort) to know one's way around

auskommen irr vi: **gut/schlecht mit jdm ~** to get on well/badly with sb; **mit etw ~** to get by with sth

Auskunft f (-, Auskünfte) information; (nähere) details pl; (Schalter) information desk; (Tel) (directory) enquiries sing (kein Artikel, Brit), information (US)

auslachen vt to laugh at

ausladen irr vt (Gepäck etc) to unload; **jdn ~** (Gast) to tell sb not to come

Auslage f window display; **~n** pl (Kosten) expenses

Ausland nt foreign countries pl; **im/ins ~** abroad; **Ausländer(in)** (-s, -) m(f) foreigner; **ausländerfeindlich** adj hostile to foreigners, xenophobic; **ausländisch** adj foreign; **Auslandsgespräch** nt international call; **Auslandskrankenschein** m health insurance certificate for foreign countries, ≈ E111 (Brit); **Auslandsschutzbrief** m international (motor) insurance cover (documents pl)

auslassen irr vt to leave out; (Wort etc a.) to omit; (überspringen) to skip; (*Wut, Ärger*) to vent (*an +dat on*) ▷ *vr* **sich über etw** (*akk*) ~ to speak one's mind about sth

aus|laufen *irr vi* (*Flüssigkeit*) to run out; (*Tank etc*) to leak; (*Schiff*) to leave port; (*Vertrag*) to expire

aus|legen *vt* (*Waren*) to display; (*Geld*) to lend; (*Text etc*) to interpret; (*technisch ausstatten*) to design (*für, auf +akk* for)

aus|leihen *irr vt* (*verleihen*) to lend; **sich** (*dat*) **etw** ~ to borrow sth

aus|loggen *vi* (*Inform*) to log out (*o off*)

aus|lösen *vt* (*Explosion, Alarm*) to set off; (*hervorrufen*) to cause; **Auslöser** (*-s, -*) *m* (*Foto*) shutter release

aus|machen *vt* (*Licht, Radio*) to turn off; (*Feuer etc*) to put out; (*Termin, Preis*) to fix; (*vereinbaren*) to agree; (*Anteil darstellen, betragen*) to represent; (*bedeuten*) to matter; **macht es Ihnen etwas aus, wenn ...?** would you mind if ...?; **das macht mir nichts aus** I don't mind

Ausmaß *nt* extent

Ausnahme (*-, -n*) *f* exception; **ausnahmsweise** *adv* as an exception, just this once

aus|nutzen *vt* (*Zeit, Gelegenheit, Einfluss*) to use; (*jdn, Gutmütigkeit*) to take advantage of

aus|packen *vt* to unpack

aus|probieren *vt* to try (out)

Auspuff (*-(e)s, -e*) *m* (*Tech*) exhaust; **Auspuffrohr** *nt* exhaust (pipe); **Auspufftopf** *m* (*Auto*) silencer (*Brit*), muffler (*US*)

aus|rauben *vt* to rob

aus|räumen *vt* (*Dinge*) to clear away; (*Schrank, Zimmer*) to empty; (*Bedenken*) to put aside

aus|rechnen *vt* to calculate, to work out

Ausrede *f* excuse

aus|reden *vi* to finish speaking ▷ *vt*: **jdm etw** ~ to talk sb out of sth

ausreichend *adj* sufficient, satisfactory; (*Schulnote*) ≈ D

Ausreise *f* departure; **bei der** ~ on leaving the country; **Ausreiseerlaubnis** *f* exit visa; **aus|reisen** *vi* to leave the country

aus|reißen *irr vt* to tear out ▷ *vi* to come off; (*fam: davonlaufen*) to run away

aus|renken *vr* **sich** (*dat*) **den Arm** ~ to dislocate one's arm

aus|richten *vt* (*Botschaft*) to deliver; (*Gruß*) to pass on; (*erreichen*) **ich konnte bei ihr nichts** ~ I couldn't get anywhere with her; **jdm etw** ~ to tell sb sth

aus|rufen *irr vt* (*über Lautsprecher*) to announce; **jdn** ~ **lassen** to page sb; **Ausrufezeichen** *nt* exclamation mark

aus|ruhen *vi* to rest ▷ *vr*: **sich** ~ to rest

Ausrüstung *f* equipment

aus|rutschen *vi* to slip

aus|schalten *vt* to switch off; (*fig*) to eliminate

Ausschau *f*: ~ **halten** to look out (*nach* for)

aus|scheiden *irr vt* (*Med*) to give off, to secrete ▷ *vi* to leave (*aus etw* sth); (*Sport*) to be eliminated

aus|schlafen *irr vi* to have a lie-in ▷ *vr*: **sich** ~ to have a lie-in ▷ *vt* to sleep off

Ausschlag *m* (*Med*) rash; **den** ~ **geben** (*fig*) to tip the balance; **aus|schlagen** *irr vt* (*Zahn*) to knock out; (*Einladung*) to turn down ▷ *vi* (*Pferd*) to kick out; **ausschlaggebend** *adj* decisive

aus|schließen *irr vt* to lock out; (*fig*) to exclude; **ausschließlich**

adv exclusively ▷ prep +gen excluding

Ausschnitt m (Teil) section; (von Kleid) neckline; (aus Zeitung) cutting

Ausschreitungen pl riots pl

aus|schütten vt (Flüssigkeit) to pour out; (Gefäß) to empty

aus|sehen irr vi to look; **krank ~** to look ill; **gut ~** (Person) to be good-looking; (Sache) to be looking good; **es sieht nach Regen aus** it looks like rain; **es sieht schlecht aus** things look bad

aus sein irr vi siehe **aus**

außen adv outside; **nach ~** outwards; **von ~** from (the) outside; **Außenbordmotor** m outboard motor; **Außenminister(in)** m(f) foreign minister, Foreign Secretary (Brit); **Außenseite** f outside; **Außenseiter(in)** m(f) outsider; **Außenspiegel** m wing mirror (Brit), side mirror (US)

außer prep +dat (abgesehen von) except (for); **nichts ~** nothing but; **~ Betrieb** out of order; **~ sich sein** to be beside oneself (vor with); **~ Atem** out of breath ▷ conj (ausgenommen) except; **~ wenn** unless; **~ dass** except; **außerdem** conj besides

äußere(r, s) adj outer, external

außergewöhnlich adj unusual ▷ adv exceptionally; **~ kalt** exceptionally cold; **außerhalb** prep +gen outside

äußerlich adj external

äußern vt to express; (zeigen) to show ▷ vr: **sich ~** to give one's opinion; (sich zeigen) to show itself

außerordentlich adj extraordinary; **außerplanmäßig** adj unscheduled

äußerst adv extremely;

äußerste(r, s) adj utmost; (räumlich) farthest; (Termin) last possible

Äußerung f remark

aus|setzen vt (Kind, Tier) to abandon; (Belohnung) to offer; **ich habe nichts daran auszusetzen** I have no objection to it ▷ vi (aufhören) to stop; (Pause machen) to drop out; (beim Spiel) to miss a turn

Aussicht f (Blick) view; (Chance) prospect; **aussichtslos** adj hopeless; **Aussichtsplattform** f observation platform; **Aussichtsturm** m observation tower

Aussiedler(in) (-s, -) m(f) émigré (person of German descent from Eastern Europe)

aus|spannen vi (erholen) to relax ▷ vt: **er hat ihm die Freundin ausgespannt** (fam) he's nicked his girlfriend

aus|sperren vt to lock out ▷ vr: **sich ~** to lock oneself out

Aussprache f (von Wörtern) pronunciation; (Gespräch) (frank) discussion; **aus|sprechen** irr vt to pronounce; (äußern) to express ▷ vr: **sich ~** to talk (über +akk about) ▷ vi (zu Ende sprechen) to finish speaking

aus|spülen vt to rinse (out)

Ausstattung f (Ausrüstung) equipment; (Einrichtung) furnishings pl; (von Auto) fittings pl

aus|stehen irr vt to endure; **ich kann ihn nicht ~** I can't stand him ▷ vi (noch nicht da sein) to be outstanding

aus|steigen irr vi to get out (aus of); **aus dem Bus/Zug ~** to get off the bus/train; **Aussteiger(in)** m(f) dropout

aus|stellen vt to display; (auf Messe, in Museum etc) to exhibit;

(*fam: ausschalten*) to switch off; (*Scheck etc*) to make out; (*Pass etc*) to issue; **Ausstellung** *f* exhibition

aus|sterben *irr vi* to die out

aus|strahlen *vt* to radiate; (*Programm*) to broadcast; **Ausstrahlung** *f* (*Radio, TV*) broadcast; (*fig: von Person*) charisma

aus|strecken *vr:* **sich ~** to stretch out ▷ *vt* (*Hand*) to reach out (*nach für*)

aus|suchen *vt* to choose

Austausch *m* exchange; **aus|tauschen** *vt* to exchange (*gegen* for)

aus|teilen *vt* to distribute; (*aushändigen*) to hand out

Auster (*-, -n*) *f* oyster; **Austernpilz** *m* oyster mushroom

aus|tragen *irr vt* (*Post*) to deliver; (*Wettkampf*) to hold

Australien (*-s*) *nt* Australia; **Australier(in)** (*-s, -*) *m(f)* Australian; **australisch** *adj* Australian

aus|trinken *irr vt* (*Glas*) to drain; (*Getränk*) to drink up ▷ *vi* to finish one's drink

aus|trocknen *vi* to dry out; (*Fluss*) to dry up

aus|üben *vt* (*Beruf, Sport*) to practise; (*Einfluss*) to exert

Ausverkauf *m* sale; **ausverkauft** *adj* (*Karten, Artikel*) sold out

Auswahl *f* selection, choice (*an* +*dat* of); **aus|wählen** *vt* to select, to choose

aus|wandern *vi* to emigrate

auswärtig *adj* (*nicht am/vom Ort*) not local; (*ausländisch*) foreign; **auswärts** *adv* (*außerhalb der Stadt*) out of town; (*Sport*) **~ spielen** to play away; **Auswärtsspiel** *nt* away match

aus|wechseln *vt* to replace; (*Sport*) to substitute

Ausweg *m* way out

aus|weichen *irr vi* to get out of the way; **jdm/einer Sache ~** to move aside for sb/sth; (*fig*) to avoid sb/sth

Ausweis (*-es, -e*) *m* (*Personalausweis*) identity card, ID; (*für Bibliothek etc*) card; **aus|weisen** *irr vt* to expel ▷ *vr:* **sich ~** to prove one's identity; **Ausweiskontrolle** *f* ID check; **Ausweispapiere** *pl* identification documents *pl*

auswendig *adv* by heart

aus|wuchten *vt* (*Auto: Räder*) to balance

aus|zahlen *vt* (*Summe*) to pay (out); (*Person*) to pay off ▷ *vr:* **sich ~** to be worth it

aus|zeichnen *vt* (*ehren*) to honour; (*Comm*) to price ▷ *vr:* **sich ~** to distinguish oneself

aus|ziehen *irr vt* (*Kleidung*) to take off ▷ *vr:* **sich ~** to undress ▷ *vi* (*aus Wohnung*) to move out

Auszubildende(r) *mf* trainee

authentisch *adj* authentic, genuine

Auto (*-s, -s*) *nt* car; **~ fahren** to drive; **Autoatlas** *m* road atlas; **Autobahn** *f* motorway (*Brit*), freeway (*US*); **Autobahnauffahrt** *f* motorway access road (*Brit*), on-ramp (*US*); **Autobahnausfahrt** *f* motorway exit (*Brit*), off-ramp (*US*); **Autobahngebühr** *f* toll; **Autobahnkreuz** *nt* motorway interchange; **Autobahnring** *m* motorway ring (*Brit*), beltway (*US*); **Autobombe** *f* car bomb; **Autofähre** *f* car ferry; **Autofahrer(in)** *m(f)* driver, motorist; **Autofahrt** *f* drive

Autogramm (*-s, -e*) *nt* autograph

Automarke f make of car
Automat (-en, -en) m vending machine
Automatik (-, -en) f (Auto) automatic transmission; **Automatikschaltung** f automatic gear change (Brit) (o shift (US)); **Automatikwagen** m automatic
automatisch adj automatic ▷ adv automatically
Automechaniker(in) m(f) car mechanic; **Autonummer** f registration (Brit) (o license (US)) number
Autor (-s, -en) m author
Autoradio nt car radio; **Autoreifen** m car tyre; **Autoreisezug** m Motorail train® (Brit), auto train (US); **Autorennen** nt motor racing; (einzelnes Rennen) motor race
Autorin f author(ess)
Autoschlüssel m car key; **Autotelefon** nt car phone; **Autounfall** m car accident; **Autoverleih** m, **Autovermietung** f car hire (Brit) (o rental (US)); (Firma) car hire (Brit) (o rental (US)) company; **Autowaschanlage** f car wash; **Autowerkstatt** f car repair shop, garage; **Autozubehör** nt car accessories pl
Avocado (-, -s) f avocado
Axt · (-, Äxte) f axe
Azubi (-s, -s) m (-, -s) f akr = **Auszubildende** trainee

B abk = **Bundesstraße**
Baby (-s, -s) nt baby; **Babybett** nt cot (Brit), crib (US); **Babyfläschchen** nt baby's bottle; **Babynahrung** f baby food; **Babysitter(in)** m(f) babysitter; **Babysitz** m child seat; **Babywickelraum** m baby-changing room
Bach (-(e)s, Bäche) m stream
Backblech nt baking tray (Brit), cookie sheet (US)
Backbord nt port (side)
Backe (-, -n) f cheek
backen (backte, gebacken) vt, vi to bake
Backenzahn m molar
Bäcker(in) (-s, -) m(f) baker; **Bäckerei** f bakery; (Laden) baker's (shop)
Backofen m oven; **Backpulver** nt baking powder
Backspace-Taste f (Inform)

backspace key
Backstein m brick
Backwaren pl bread, cakes and pastries pl
Bad (-(e)s, Bäder) nt bath; (Schwimmen) swim; (Ort) spa; **ein ~ nehmen** to have (o take) a bath;
Badeanzug m swimsuit, swimming costume (Brit);
Badehose f swimming trunks pl;
Badekappe f swimming cap;
Bademantel m bathrobe;
Bademeister(in) m(f) pool attendant; **Bademütze** f swimming cap
baden vi to have a bath; (schwimmen) to swim, to bathe (Brit) ▷ vt to bath (Brit), to bathe (US)
Baden-Württemberg (-s) nt Baden-Württemberg
Badeort m spa; **Badesachen** pl swimming things pl;
Badeschaum m bubble bath, bath foam; **Badetuch** nt bath towel; **Badewanne** f bath (tub);
Badezeug nt swimming gear;
Badezimmer nt bathroom
Badminton nt badminton
baff adj: **~ sein** (fam) to be flabbergasted (o gobsmacked)
Bagger (-s, -) m excavator;
Baggersee m artificial lake in quarry etc, used for bathing
Bahamas pl: **die ~** the Bahamas pl
Bahn (-, -en) f (Eisenbahn) railway (Brit), railroad (US); (Rennbahn) track; (für Läufer) lane; (Astr) orbit;
Deutsche ~ Germany's main railway operator; **bahnbrechend** adj groundbreaking; **BahnCard®** (-, -s) f rail card (allowing 50% or 25% reduction on tickets); **Bahnfahrt** f railway (Brit) (o railroad (US)) journey; **Bahnhof** m station; **am** (o **auf dem**) **~** at the station;

Bahnlinie f railway (Brit) (o railroad (US)) line; **Bahnpolizei** f railway (Brit) (o railroad (US)) police; **Bahnsteig** (-(e)s, -e) m platform; **Bahnstrecke** f railway (Brit) (o railroad (US)) line;
Bahnübergang m level crossing (Brit), grade crossing (US)
Bakterien pl bacteria pl, germs pl
bald adv (zeitlich) soon; (beinahe) almost; **bis ~!** see you soon (o later); **baldig** adj quick, speedy
Balkan (-s) m: **der ~** the Balkans pl
Balken (-s, -) m beam
Balkon (-s, -s o -e) m balcony
Ball (-(e)s, Bälle) m ball; (Tanz) dance, ball
Ballett (-s) nt ballet
Ballon (-s, -s) m balloon
Ballspiel nt ball game
Ballungsgebiet nt conurbation
Baltikum (-s) nt: **das ~** the Baltic States pl
Bambus (-ses, -se) m bamboo;
Bambussprossen pl bamboo shoots pl
banal adj banal; (Frage, Bemerkung) trite
Banane (-, -n) f banana
band imperf von **binden**
Band (-(e)s, Bände) m (Buch) volume ▷ (-(e)s, Bänder) nt (aus Stoff) ribbon, tape; (Fließband) production line; (Tonband) tape; (Anat) ligament; **etw auf ~ aufnehmen** to tape sth ▷ (-, -s) f (Musikgruppe) band
Bandage (-, -n) f bandage;
bandagieren vt to bandage
Bande (-, -n) f (Gruppe) gang
Bänderriss m (Med) torn ligament
Bandscheibe f (Anat) disc;
Bandwurm m tapeworm
Bank (-, Bänke) f (Sitzbank) bench ▷ (-, -en) f (Fin) bank

Bankautomat m cash dispenser; **Bankkarte** f bank card; **Bankkonto** nt bank account; **Bankleitzahl** f bank sort code; **Banknote** f banknote; **Bankverbindung** f banking (o account) details pl

bar adj: **~es Geld** cash; **etw (in) ~ bezahlen** to pay sth (in) cash

Bar (-, -s) f bar

Bär (-en, -en) m bear

barfuß adj barefoot

barg imperf von **bergen**

Bargeld nt cash; **bargeldlos** adj non-cash

Barkeeper (-s, -) m, **Barmann** m barman, bartender (US)

barock adj baroque

Barometer (-s, -) nt barometer

barsch adj brusque

Barsch (-(e)s, -e) m perch

Barscheck m open (o uncrossed) cheque

Bart (-(e)s, Bärte) m beard; **bärtig** adj bearded

Barzahlung f cash payment

Basar (-s, -e) m bazaar

Baseballmütze f baseball cap

Basel (-s) nt Basle

Basilikum (-s) nt basil

Basis (-, Basen) f basis

Baskenland nt Basque region

Basketball m basketball

Bass (-es, Bässe) m bass

basta interj: **und damit ~!** and that's that

basteln vt to make ▷ vi to make things, to do handicrafts; **Bastler** (-s, -) m do-it-yourselfer

bat imperf von **bitten**

Batterie (-, -n) f battery; **batteriebetrieben** adj battery-powered

Bau (-(e)s) m (Bauen) building, construction; (Aufbau) structure; (Baustelle) building site ▷ m (Baue) (Tier) burrow ▷ m (Bauten)

(Gebäude) building; **Bauarbeiten** pl construction work sing; (Straßenbau) roadworks pl (Brit), roadwork (US); **Bauarbeiter(in)** m(f) construction worker

Bauch (-(e)s, Bäuche) m stomach; **Bauchnabel** m navel; **Bauchredner(in)** m(f) ventriloquist; **Bauchschmerzen** pl stomach-ache sing; **Bauchspeicheldrüse** f pancreas; **Bauchtanz** m belly dance; (das Tanzen) belly dancing; **Bauchweh** (-s) nt stomach-ache

bauen vt, vi to build; (Tech) to construct

Bauer (-n o -s, -n) m farmer; (Schach) pawn; **Bäuerin** f farmer; (Frau des Bauern) farmer's wife; **Bauernhof** m farm

baufällig adj dilapidated; **Baujahr** adj year of construction; **der Wagen ist ~ 2002** the car is a 2002 model, the car was made in 2002

Baum (-(e)s, Bäume) m tree

Baumarkt m DIY centre

Baumwolle f cotton

Bauplatz m building site; **Baustein** m (für Haus) stone; (Spielzeug) brick; (fig) element; **elektronischer ~** chip; **Baustelle** f building site; (bei Straßenbau) roadworks pl (Brit), roadwork (US); **Bauteil** nt prefabricated part; **Bauunternehmer(in)** m(f) building contractor; **Bauwerk** nt building

Bayern (-s) nt Bavaria

beabsichtigen vt to intend

beachten vt (Aufmerksamkeit schenken) to pay attention to; (Vorschrift etc) to observe; **nicht ~** to ignore; **beachtlich** adj considerable

Beachvolleyball nt beach volleyball

Beamte(r) (-n, -n) m, **Beamtin** f official; (Staatsbeamter) civil servant

beanspruchen vt to claim; (Zeit, Platz) to take up; **jdn ~** to keep sb busy

beanstanden vt to complain about; **Beanstandung** f complaint

beantragen vt to apply for

beantworten vt to answer

bearbeiten vt to work; (Material, Daten) to process; (Chem) to treat; (Fall etc) to deal with; (Buch etc) to revise; (fam: beeinflussen wollen) to work on; **Bearbeitungsgebühr** f handling (o service) charge

beatmen vt **jdn ~** to give sb artificial respiration

beaufsichtigen vt to supervise; (bei Prüfung) to invigilate

beauftragen vt to instruct; **jdn mit etw ~** to give sb the job of doing sth

Becher (-s, -) m mug; (ohne Henkel) tumbler; (für Joghurt) pot; (aus Pappe) tub

Becken (-s, -) nt basin; (Spüle) sink; (zum Schwimmen) pool; (Mus) cymbal; (Anat) pelvis

bedanken vr: **sich ~** to say thank you; **sich bei jdm für etw ~** to thank sb for sth

Bedarf (-(e)s) m need (an +dat for); (Comm) demand (an +dat for); **je nach ~** according to demand; **bei ~** if necessary; **Bedarfshaltestelle** f request stop

bedauerlich adj regrettable; **bedauern** vt to regret; (bemitleiden) to feel sorry for; **bedauernswert** adj (Zustände) regrettable; (Mensch) unfortunate

bedeckt adj covered; (Himmel) overcast

bedenken irr vt to consider; **Bedenken** (-s, -) nt (Überlegen)

consideration; (Zweifel) doubt; (Skrupel) scruples pl; **bedenklich** adj dubious; (Zustand) serious

bedeuten vt to mean; **jdm nichts/viel ~** to mean nothing/a lot to sb; **bedeutend** adj important; (beträchtlich) considerable; **Bedeutung** f meaning; (Wichtigkeit) importance

bedienen vt to serve; (Maschine) to operate ▷ vr: **sich ~** (beim Essen) to help oneself; **Bedienung** f service; (Kellner/Kellnerin) waiter/waitress; (Verkäufer(in)) shop assistant; (Zuschlag) service (charge); **Bedienungsanleitung** f operating instructions pl; **Bedienungshandbuch** nt instruction manual

Bedingung f condition; **unter der ~, dass** on condition that; **unter diesen ~en** under these circumstances

bedrohen vt to threaten

Bedürfnis nt need

Beefsteak (-s, -s) nt steak

beeilen vr: **sich ~** to hurry

beeindrucken vt to impress

beeinflussen vt to influence

beeinträchtigen vt to affect

beenden vt to end; (fertigstellen) to finish

beerdigen vt to bury; **Beerdigung** f burial; (Feier) funeral

Beere (-, -n) f berry; (Traubenbeere) grape

Beet (-(e)s, -e) nt bed

befahl imperf von **befehlen**

befahrbar adj passable; (Naut) navigable; **befahren** irr vt (Straße) to use; (Pass) to drive over; (Fluss etc) to navigate ▷ adj: **stark/wenig ~** busy/quiet

Befehl (-(e)s, -e) m order; (Inform) command; **befehlen** (befahl, befohlen) vt to order; **jdm ~, etw zu tun** to order sb to do sth ▷ vi to give orders

befestigen vt to fix; (mit Schnur, Seil) to attach; (mit Klebestoff) to stick

befeuchten vt to moisten

befinden irr vr: **sich ~** to be

befohlen pp von **befehlen**

befolgen vt (Rat etc) to follow

befördern vt (transportieren) to transport; (beruflich) to promote; **Beförderung** f transport; (beruflich) promotion; **Beförderungsbedingungen** pl conditions pl of carriage

Befragung f questioning; (Umfrage) opinion poll

befreundet adj friendly; **~ sein** to be friends (mit jdm with sb)

befriedigen vt to satisfy; **befriedigend** adj satisfactory; (Schulnote) ≈ C; **Befriedigung** f satisfaction

befristet adj limited (auf +akk to)

befruchten vt to fertilize; (fig) to stimulate

Befund (-(e)s, -e) m findings pl; (Med) diagnosis

befürchten vt to fear

befürworten vt to support

begabt adj gifted, talented; **Begabung** f talent, gift

begann imperf von **beginnen**

begegnen vi to meet (jdm sb), to meet with (einer Sache dat sth)

begehen irr vt (Straftat) to commit; (Jubiläum etc) to celebrate

begehrt adj sought-after; (Junggeselle) eligible

begeistern vt to fill with enthusiasm; (inspirieren) to inspire ▷ vr: **sich für etw ~** to be/get enthusiastic about sth; **begeistert** adj enthusiastic

Beginn (-(e)s) m beginning; **zu ~** at the beginning; **beginnen** (begann, begonnen) vt, vi to start, to begin

beglaubigen vt to certify; **Beglaubigung** f certification

begleiten vt to accompany; **Begleiter(in)** m(f) companion; **Begleitung** f company; (Mus) accompaniment

beglückwünschen vt to congratulate (zu on)

begonnen pp von **beginnen**

begraben irr vt to bury; **Begräbnis** nt burial; (Feier) funeral

begreifen irr vt to understand

Begrenzung f boundary; (fig) restriction

Begriff (-(e)s, -e) m concept; (Vorstellung) idea; **im ~ sein, etw zu tun** to be on the point of doing sth; **schwer von ~ sein** to be slow on the uptake

begründen vt (rechtfertigen) to justify; **Begründung** f explanation; (Rechtfertigung) justification

begrüßen vt to greet; (willkommen heißen) to welcome; **Begrüßung** f greeting; (Empfang) welcome

behaart adj hairy

behalten irr vt to keep; (im Gedächtnis) to remember; **etw für sich ~** to keep sth to oneself

Behälter (-s, -) m container

behandeln vt to treat; **Behandlung** f treatment

behaupten vt to claim, to maintain ▷ vr: **sich ~** to assert oneself; **Behauptung** f claim

beheizen vt to heat

behelfen irr vr: **sich mit/ohne etw ~** to make do with/without sth

beherbergen vt to accommodate

beherrschen vt (Situation, Gefühle) to control; (Instrument) to master ▷ vr: **sich ~** to control oneself; **Beherrschung** f control (*über +akk* of); **die ~ verlieren** to lose one's self-control

behilflich adj helpful; **jdm ~ sein** to help sb (*bei* with)

behindern vt to hinder; (*Verkehr, Sicht*) to obstruct; **Behinderte(r)** mf disabled person; **behindertengerecht** adj suitable for disabled people

Behörde (-, -n) f authority; **die ~n** pl the authorities pl

○ SCHLÜSSELWORT

bei prep +*dat* 1 (*nahe bei*) near; (*zum Aufenthalt*) at, with; (*unter, zwischen*) among; **bei München** near Munich; **bei uns** at our place; **beim Friseur** at the hairdresser's; **bei seinen Eltern wohnen** to live with one's parents; **bei einer Firma arbeiten** to work for a firm; **etw bei sich haben** to have sth on one; **jdn bei sich haben** to have sb with one; **bei Goethe** in Goethe; **beim Militär** in the army 2 (*zeitlich*) at, on; (*während*) during; (*Zustand, Umstand*) in; **bei Nacht** at night; **bei Nebel** in fog; **bei Regen** if it rains; **bei solcher Hitze** in such heat; **bei meiner Ankunft** on my arrival; **bei der Arbeit** when I'm *etc* working; **beim Fahren** while driving

bei|behalten irr vt to keep
Beiboot nt dinghy
bei|bringen irr vt: **jdm etw ~** (*mitteilen*) to break sth to sb; (*lehren*) to teach sb sth
beide(s) pron both; **meine ~n Brüder** my two brothers, both my brothers; **wir ~** both (*o* the two) of us; **keiner von ~n** neither of them; **alle ~** both (of them); **~s ist sehr schön** both are very nice; **30**

~ (*beim Tennis*) 30 all
beieinander adv together
Beifahrer(in) m(f) passenger; **Beifahrerairbag** m passenger airbag; **Beifahrersitz** m passenger seat
Beifall (-(e)s) m applause
beige adj inv beige
Beigeschmack m aftertaste
Beil (-(e)s, -e) nt axe
Beilage f (*Gastr*) side dish; (*Gemüse*) vegetables pl; (*zu Buch etc*) supplement
beiläufig adj casual ▷ adv casually
Beileid nt condolences pl; (**mein**) **herzliches ~** please accept my sincere condolences
beiliegend adj enclosed
beim kontr von **bei dem**
Bein (-(e)s, -e) nt leg
beinah(e) adv almost, nearly
beinhalten vt to contain
Beipackzettel m instruction leaflet
beisammen adv together; **Beisammensein** (-s) nt get-together
beiseite adv aside; **beiseite|legen** vt: **etw ~** (*sparen*) to put sth by
Beispiel (-(e)s, -e) nt example; **sich** (*dat*) **an jdm/etw ein ~ nehmen** to take sb/sth as an example; **zum ~** for example
beißen (*biss, gebissen*) vt to bite ▷ vi to bite; (*stechen: Rauch, Säure*) to sting ▷ vr: **sich ~** (*Farben*) to clash
Beitrag (-(e)s, *Beiträge*) m contribution; (*für Mitgliedschaft*) subscription; (*Versicherung*) premium; **bei|tragen** irr vt, vi to contribute (*zu* to)
bekannt adj well-known; (*nicht fremd*) familiar; **mit jdm ~ sein** to know sb; **~ geben** to announce;

jdn mit jdm ~ machen to introduce sb to sb; **Bekannte(r)** mf friend; (entfernter) acquaintance; **bekanntlich** adv as everyone knows; **Bekanntschaft** f acquaintance

bekiffen vr: **sich ~** (fam) to get stoned

beklagen vr: **sich ~** to complain

Bekleidung f clothing

bekommen irr vt to get; (erhalten) to receive; (Kind) to have; (Zug, Grippe) to catch, to get; **wie viel ~ Sie dafür?** how much is that? ▷ vi: **jdm ~** (Essen) to agree with sb; **wir ~ schon** (bedient werden) we're being served

beladen irr vt to load

Belag (-(e)s, Beläge) m coating; (auf Zähnen) plaque; (auf Zunge) fur

belasten vt to load; (Körper) to strain; (Umwelt) to pollute; (fig: mit Sorgen etc) to burden; (Comm: Konto) to debit; (Jur) to incriminate

belästigen vt to bother; (stärker) to pester; (sexuell) to harass; **Belästigung** f annoyance; **sexuelle ~** sexual harassment

belebt adj (Straße etc) busy

Beleg (-(e)s, -e) m (Comm) receipt; (Beweis) proof; **belegen** vt (Brot) to spread; (Platz) to reserve; (Kurs, Vorlesung) to register for; (beweisen) to prove

belegt adj (Tel) engaged (Brit), busy (US); (Hotel) full; (Zunge) coated; **~es Brötchen** sandwich; **der Platz ist ~** this seat is taken; **Belegzeichen** nt (Tel) engaged tone (Brit), busy tone (US)

beleidigen vt to insult; (kränken) to offend; **Beleidigung** f insult; (Jur) slander; (schriftliche) libel

beleuchten vt to light; (bestrahlen) to illuminate; (fig) to examine; **Beleuchtung** f lighting; (Bestrahlung) illumination

Belgien (-s) nt Belgium; **Belgier(in)** (-s, -) m(f) Belgian; **belgisch** adj Belgian

belichten vt to expose; **Belichtung** f exposure; **Belichtungsmesser** (-s, -) m light meter

Belieben nt: **(ganz) nach ~** (just) as you wish

beliebig adj: **jedes ~e Muster** any pattern; **jeder ~e** anyone ▷ adv: **~ lange** as long as you like; **~ viel** as many (o much) as you like

beliebt adj popular; **sich bei jdm ~ machen** to make oneself popular with sb

beliefern vt to supply

bellen vi to bark

Belohnung f reward

Belüftung f ventilation

belügen irr vt to lie to

bemerkbar adj noticeable; **sich ~ machen** (Mensch) to attract attention; (Zustand) to become noticeable; **bemerken** vt (wahrnehmen) to notice; (sagen) to remark; **bemerkenswert** adj remarkable; **Bemerkung** f remark

bemitleiden vt to pity

bemühen vr: **sich ~** to try (hard), to make an effort; **Bemühung** f effort

bemuttern vt to mother

benachbart adj neighbouring

benachrichtigen vt to inform; **Benachrichtigung** f notification

benachteiligen vt to (put at a) disadvantage; (wegen Rasse etc) to discriminate against

benehmen irr vr: **sich ~** to behave; **Benehmen** (-s) nt behaviour

beneiden vt to envy; **jdn um etw ~** to envy sb sth

Beneluxländer pl Benelux countries pl

benommen adj dazed

benötigen vt to need

benutzen vt to use;
Benutzer(in) (-s, -) m(f) user;
benutzerfreundlich adj user-friendly; **Benutzerhandbuch** nt
user's guide; **Benutzerkennung** f
user ID; **Benutzerkonto** nt
(Inform) user account;
Benutzername m (Inform) user-name; **Benutzeroberfläche** f
(Inform) user/system interface;
Benutzung f use;
Benutzungsgebühr f (hire)
charge

Benzin (-s, -e) nt (Auto) petrol
(Brit), gas (US); **Benzinkanister** m
petrol (Brit) (o gas (US)) can;
Benzinpumpe f petrol (Brit) (o
gas (US)) pump; **Benzintank** m
petrol (Brit) (o gas (US)) tank;
Benzinuhr f fuel gauge

beobachten vt to observe;
Beobachtung f observation

bequem adj comfortable;
(Ausrede) convenient; (faul) lazy;
machen Sie es sich ~ make
yourself at home; **Bequemlichkeit**
f comfort; (Faulheit) laziness

beraten irr vt to advise;
(besprechen) to discuss ▷ vr: **sich**
~ to consult; **Beratung** f advice;
(bei Arzt etc) consultation

berauben vt to rob

berechnen vt to calculate;
(Comm) to charge

berechtigen vt to entitle (zu to);
(fig) to justify; **berechtigt** adj
justified; **zu etw ~ sein** to be
entitled to sth

bereden vt (besprechen) to discuss

Bereich (-(e)s, -e) m area;
(Ressort, Gebiet) field

bereisen vt to travel through

bereit adj ready; **zu etw ~ sein** to
be ready for sth; **sich ~ erklären,**
etw zu tun to agree to do sth

bereiten vt to prepare; (Kummer)
to cause; (Freude) to give
bereitlegen vt to lay out
bereit machen vr: **sich ~** to get
ready
bereits adv already
Bereitschaft f readiness;
~ haben (Arzt) to be on call
bereitstehen vi to be ready
bereuen vt to regret
Berg (-(e)s, -e) m mountain;
(kleiner) hill; **in die ~e fahren** to go
to the mountains; **bergab** adv
downhill; **bergauf** adv uphill;
Bergbahn f mountain railway
(Brit) (o railroad (US))
bergen (barg, geborgen) vt
(retten) to rescue; (enthalten) to
contain
Bergführer(in) m(f) mountain
guide; **Berghütte** f mountain hut;
bergig adj mountainous;
Bergschuh m climbing boot;
Bergsteigen (-s) nt
mountaineering; **Bergsteiger(in)**
(-s, -) m(f) mountaineer;
Bergtour f mountain hike
Bergung f (Rettung) rescue; (von
Toten, Fahrzeugen) recovery
Bergwacht (-, -en) f mountain
rescue service; **Bergwerk** nt
mine
Bericht (-(e)s, -e) m report;
berichten vt, vi to report
berichtigen vt to correct
Bermudadreieck nt Bermuda
triangle; **Bermudainseln** pl
Bermuda sing
Bernstein m amber
berüchtigt adj notorious,
infamous
berücksichtigen vt to take into
account; (Antrag, Bewerber) to
consider
Beruf (-(e)s, -e) m occupation;
(akademischer) profession;
(Gewerbe) trade; **was sind Sie von**

~? what do you do (for a living)?;
beruflich adj professional
Berufsausbildung f vocational
training; **Berufsschule** f
vocational college; **berufstätig**
adj employed; **Berufsverkehr** m
commuter traffic
beruhigen vt to calm ▷ vr: **sich**
~ (Mensch, Situation) to calm down;
beruhigend adj reassuring;
Beruhigungsmittel nt sedative
berühmt adj famous
berühren vt to touch;
(gefühlsmäßig bewegen) to move;
(betreffen) to affect; (flüchtig
erwähnen) to mention, to touch on
▷ vr: **sich ~** to touch
besaufen irr vr: **sich ~** (fam) to
get plastered
beschädigen vt to damage
beschäftigen vt to occupy;
(beruflich) to employ ▷ vr: **sich mit**
etw ~ to occupy oneself with sth;
(sich befassen) to deal with sth;
beschäftigt adj busy, occupied;
Beschäftigung f (Beruf)
employment; (Tätigkeit)
occupation; (geistige)
preoccupation (mit with)
Bescheid (-(e)s, -e) m
information; **~ wissen** to be
informed (o know) (über +akk
about); **ich weiß ~** I know; **jdm**
~ geben (o sagen) to let sb know
bescheiden adj modest
bescheinigen vt to certify;
(bestätigen) to acknowledge;
Bescheinigung f certificate;
(Quittung) receipt
bescheißen irr vt (vulg) to cheat
(um out of)
bescheuert adj (fam, pej) crazy
beschimpfen vt (mit
Kraftausdrücken) to swear at
Beschiss (-es) m: **das ist ~** (vulg)
that's a rip-off!; **beschissen** adj
(vulg) shitty

beschlagnahmen vt to
confiscate
Beschleunigung f acceleration;
Beschleunigungsspur f
acceleration lane
beschließen irr vt to decide on;
(beenden) to end; **Beschluss** m
decision
beschränken vt to limit, to
restrict (auf +akk to) ▷ vr: **sich ~** to
restrict oneself (auf +akk to);
Beschränkung f limitation,
restriction
beschreiben irr vt to describe;
(Papier) to write on; **Beschreibung**
f description
beschuldigen vt to accuse (gen
of); **Beschuldigung** f
accusation
beschummeln vt, vi (fam) to
cheat (um out of)
beschützen vt to protect (vor
+dat from)
Beschwerde (-, -n) f complaint;
~n pl (Leiden) trouble sing;
beschweren vt to weight down;
(fig) to burden ▷ vr: **sich ~** to
complain
beschwipst adj tipsy
beseitigen vt to remove;
(Problem) to get rid of; (Müll) to
dispose of; **Beseitigung** f
removal; (von Müll) disposal
Besen (-s, -) m broom
besetzen vt (Haus, Land) to
occupy; (Platz) to take; (Posten) to
fill; (Rolle) to cast; **besetzt** adj
full; (Tel) engaged (Brit), busy (US);
(Platz) taken; (WC) engaged;
Besetztzeichen nt engaged tone
(Brit), busy tone (US)
besichtigen vt (Museum) to visit;
(Sehenswürdigkeit) to have a look at;
(Stadt) to tour
besiegen vt to defeat
Besitz (-es) m possession;
(Eigentum) property; **besitzen** irr

vt to own; (*Eigenschaft*) to have;
Besitzer(in) (-s, -) m(f) owner
besoffen adj (fam) plastered
besondere(r, s) adj special;
(*bestimmt*) particular;
(*eigentümlich*) peculiar; **nichts ~s**
nothing special; **Besonderheit** f
special feature; (*besondere*
Eigenschaft) peculiarity; **besonders**
adv especially, particularly; (*getrennt*) separately
besorgen vt (*beschaffen*) to get;
(*jdm for sb*) (*kaufen a.*) to purchase;
(*erledigen: Geschäfte*) to deal with
besprechen irr vt to discuss;
Besprechung f discussion;
(*Konferenz*) meeting; **Besprechungsraum** m consultation
room
besser adj better; **es geht ihm
~** he feels better; **~ gesagt** or
rather; **~ werden** to improve;
bessern vt to improve ▷ vr: **sich
~** to improve; (*Mensch*) to mend
one's ways; **Besserung** f
improvement; **gute ~!** get well
soon
beständig adj constant; (*Wetter*)
settled
Bestandteil m component
bestätigen vt to confirm;
(*Empfang, Brief*) to acknowledge;
Bestätigung f confirmation; (*von
Brief*) acknowledgement
beste(r, s) adj best; **das ~ wäre,
wir ...** it would be better if we ...
▷ adv: **sie singt am ~n** she sings
best; **so ist es am ~n** it's best that
way; **am ~n gehst du gleich** you'd
better go at once
bestechen irr vt to bribe;
Bestechung f bribery
Besteck (-(e)s, -e) nt cutlery
bestehen irr vi to be, to exist;
(*andauern*) to last; **~ auf** (+*dat*) to
insist on; **~ aus** to consist of ▷ vt
(*Probe, Prüfung*) to pass; (*Kampf*) to

win
bestehlen irr vt to rob
bestellen vt to order; (*reservieren*)
to book; (*Grüße, Auftrag*) to pass on
(*jdm to sb*); (*kommen lassen*) to send
for; **Bestellnummer** f order
number; **Bestellung** f (*Comm*)
order; (*das Bestellen*) ordering
bestens adv very well
bestimmen vt to determine;
(*Regeln*) to lay down; (*Tag, Ort*) to
fix; (*ernennen*) to appoint;
(*vorsehen*) to mean (*für for*);
bestimmt adj definite; (*gewiss*)
certain; (*entschlossen*) firm ▷ adv
definitely; (*wissen*) for sure;
Bestimmung f (*Verordnung*)
regulation; (*Zweck*) purpose
Best.-Nr. abk = **Bestellnummer**
order number
bestrafen vt to punish
bestrahlen vt to illuminate;
(*Med*) to treat with radiotherapy
bestreiten irr vt (*leugnen*) to
deny
Bestseller (-s, -) m bestseller
bestürzt adj dismayed
Besuch (-(e)s, -e) m visit; (*Mensch*)
visitor; **~ haben** to have visitors/a
visitor; **besuchen** vt to visit;
(*Schule, Kino etc*) to go to;
Besucher(in) (-s, -) m(f) visitor;
Besuchszeit f visiting hours pl
betäuben vt (*Med*) to
anaesthetize; **Betäubung** f
anaesthetic; **örtliche ~** local
anaesthetic; **Betäubungsmittel**
nt anaesthetic
Bete (-, -n) f: **Rote ~** beetroot
beteiligen vr: **sich an etw** (*dat*)
~ to take part in sth, to participate
in sth ▷ vt: **jdn an etw** (*dat*) **~** to
involve sb in sth; **Beteiligung** f
participation; (*Anteil*) share;
(*Besucherzahl*) attendance
beten vi to pray
Beton (-s, -s) m concrete

betonen vt to stress; (hervorheben) to emphasize; **Betonung** f stress; (fig) emphasis

Betr. abk = **Betreff** re

Betracht m: **in ~ ziehen** to take into consideration; **in ~ kommen** to be a possibility; **nicht in ~ kommen** to be out of the question; **betrachten** vt to look at; **~ als** to regard as; **beträchtlich** adj considerable

Betrag (-(e)s, Beträge) m amount, sum; **betragen** irr vt to amount (o come) to ▷ vr: **sich ~** to behave

betreffen irr vt to concern; (Regelung etc) to affect; **was mich betrifft** as for me; **betreffend** adj relevant, in question

betreten irr vt to enter; (Bühne etc) to step onto; **„Betreten verboten"** keep off/out"

betreuen vt to look after; (Reisegruppe, Abteilung) to be in charge of; **Betreuer(in)** (-s, -) m(f) (Pfleger) carer; (von Kind) child minder; (von Reisegruppe) groupleader

Betrieb (-(e)s, -e) m (Firma) firm; (Anlage) plant; (Tätigkeit) operation; (Treiben) bustle; **außer ~ sein** to be out of order; **in ~ sein** to be in operation; **betriebsbereit** adj operational; **Betriebsrat** m (Gremium) works council; **Betriebssystem** nt (Inform) operating system

betrinken irr vr: **sich ~** to get drunk

betroffen adj (bestürzt) shaken; **von etw ~ werden/sein** to be affected by sth

betrog imperf von **betrügen**; **betrogen** pp von **betrügen**

Betrug (-(e)s) m deception; (Jur) fraud; **betrügen** (betrog, betrogen) vt to deceive; (Jur) to defraud;

(Partner) to cheat on; **Betrüger(in)** (-s, -) m(f) cheat

betrunken adj drunk

Bett (-(e)s, -en) nt bed; **ins** (o **zu**) **~ gehen** to go to bed; **das ~ machen** to make the bed; **Bettbezug** m duvet cover; **Bettdecke** f blanket

betteln vi to beg

Bettlaken nt sheet

Bettler(in) (-s, -) m(f) beggar

Bettsofa nt sofa bed; **Betttuch** nt sheet; **Bettwäsche** f bed linen; **Bettzeug** m bedding

beugen vt to bend ▷ vr: **sich ~** to bend; (sich fügen) to submit (dat to)

Beule (-, -n) f (Schwellung) bump; (Delle) dent

beunruhigen vt to worry ▷ vr: **sich ~** to worry

beurteilen vt to judge

Beute (-) f (von Dieb) booty, loot; (von Tier) prey

Beutel (-s, -) m bag

Bevölkerung f population

bevollmächtigt adj authorized (zu etw to do sth)

bevor conj before; **bevorstehen** irr vi (Schwierigkeiten) to lie ahead; (Gefahr) to be imminent; **jdm ~** (Überraschung etc) to be in store for sb; **bevorstehend** adj forthcoming; **bevorzugen** vt to prefer

bewachen vt to guard; **bewacht** adj: **~er Parkplatz** supervised car park (Brit), guarded parking lot (US)

bewegen vt to move; **jdn dazu ~, etw zu tun** to get sb to do sth ▷ vr: **sich ~** to move; **es bewegt sich etwas** (fig) things are beginning to happen; **Bewegung** f movement; (Phys) motion; (innere) emotion; (körperlich) exercise; **Bewegungsmelder** (-s, -) m sensor (which reacts to *movement)*

Beweis (-es, -e) m proof; *(Zeugnis)* evidence; **beweisen** *irr vt* to prove; *(zeigen)* to show

bewerben *irr vr*: **sich ~** to apply *(um* for); **Bewerbung** f application; **Bewerbungsunterlagen** *pl* application documents *pl*

bewilligen *vt* to allow; *(Geld)* to grant

bewirken *vt* to cause, to bring about

bewohnen *vt* to live in; **Bewohner(in)** (-s, -) *m(f)* inhabitant; *(von Haus)* resident

bewölkt *adj* cloudy, overcast; **Bewölkung** f clouds *pl*

bewundern *vt* to admire; **bewundernswert** *adj* admirable

bewusst *adj* conscious; *(absichtlich)* deliberate; **sich** (dat) **einer Sache** (gen) **~ sein** to be aware of sth ▷ *adv* consciously; *(absichtlich)* deliberately; **bewusstlos** *adj* unconscious; **Bewusstlosigkeit** f unconsciousness; **Bewusstsein** (-s) *nt* consciousness; **bei ~** conscious

bezahlen *vt* to pay; *(Ware, Leistung)* to pay for; **kann ich bar/mit Kreditkarte ~?** can I pay cash/by credit card?; **sich bezahlt machen** to be worth it; **Bezahlung** f payment

bezeichnen *vt* (kennzeichnen) to mark; *(nennen)* to call; *(beschreiben)* to describe; **Bezeichnung** f *(Name)* name; *(Begriff)* term

beziehen *irr vt* (Bett) to change; *(Haus, Position)* to move into; *(erhalten)* to receive; *(Zeitung)* to take; **einen Standpunkt ~** to take up a position ▷ *vr*: **sich ~** to refer *(auf* +akk to); **Beziehung** f *(Verbindung)* connection; *(Verhältnis)* relationship; **~en**

haben *(vorteilhaft)* to have connections *(o* contacts); **in dieser ~** in this respect; **beziehungsweise** *adv* or; *(genauer gesagt)* or rather

Bezirk (-(e)s, -e) *m* district

Bezug (-(e)s, Bezüge) *m* (Überzug) cover; *(von Kopfkissen)* pillowcase; **in ~ auf** (+akk) with regard to; **bezüglich** *prep* +gen concerning

bezweifeln *vt* to doubt

BH (-s, -s) *m* bra

Bhf. *abk* = **Bahnhof** station

Biathlon (-s, -s) *m* biathlon

Bibel (-, -n) f Bible

Biber (-s, -) *m* beaver

Bibliothek (-, -en) f library

biegen (bog, gebogen) *vt* to bend ▷ *vr*: **sich ~** to bend ▷ *vi* to turn *(in* +akk into); **Biegung** f bend

Biene (-, -n) f bee

Bier (-(e)s, -e) *nt* beer; **helles ~** = lager (Brit), beer (US); **dunkles ~** = brown ale (Brit), dark beer (US); **zwei ~, bitte!** two beers, please; **Biergarten** *m* beer garden; **Bierzelt** *nt* beer tent

bieten (bot, geboten) *vt* to offer; *(bei Versteigerung)* bid; **sich** (dat) **etw ~ lassen** to put up with sth ▷ *vr*: **sich ~** (Gelegenheit) to present itself (dat) to

Bikini (-s, -s) *m* bikini

Bild (-(e)s, -er) *nt* picture; *(gedankliches)* image; *(Foto)* photo

bilden *vt* to form; *(geistig)* to educate; *(ausmachen)* to constitute ▷ *vr*: **sich ~** (entstehen) to form; *(lernen)* to educate oneself

Bilderbuch *nt* picture book

Bildhauer(in) (-s, -) *m(f)* sculptor

Bildschirm *m* screen; **Bildschirmschoner** (-s, -) *m* screensaver; **Bildschirmtext** *m* viewdata, videotext

Bildung f formation; *(Wissen,*

Benehmen) education;
Bildungsurlaub m educational holiday; (von Firma) study leave
Billard nt billiards sing
billig adj cheap; (gerecht) fair
Billigflieger m budget airline
Billigflug m cheap flight
Binde (-, -n) f bandage; (Armbinde) band; (Damenbinde) sanitary towel (Brit), sanitary napkin (US)
Bindehautentzündung f conjunctivitis
binden (band, gebunden) vt to tie; (Buch) to bind; (Soße) to thicken
Bindestrich m hyphen
Bindfaden m string
Bindung f bond, tie; (Skibindung) binding
Bio- in zW bio-; **Biokost** f health food; **Biokraftstoff** m biofuel

○ **BIOLADEN**

- A **Bioladen** is a shop which
- specializes in selling
- environmentally friendly
- products such as
- phosphate-free washing
- powders, recycled paper and
- organically grown vegetables.

Biologie f biology; **biologisch** adj biological; (Anbau) organic
Birke (-, -n) f birch
Birne (-, -n) f (Obst) pear; (Elek) (light) bulb

○ **SCHLÜSSELWORT**

bis prep +akk, adv **1** (zeitlich) till, until; (bis spätestens) by; **Sie haben bis Dienstag Zeit** you have until o till Tuesday; **bis Dienstag muss es fertig sein** it must be ready by Tuesday; **bis auf Weiteres** until further notice; **bis in die Nacht**

into the night; **bis bald/gleich** see you later/soon
2 (räumlich) (up) to; **ich fahre bis Köln** I'm going to o I'm going as far as Cologne; **bis an unser Grundstück** (right o up) to our plot; **bis hierher** this far
3 (bei Zahlen) up to; **bis zu** up to
4 **bis auf etw** akk (außer) except sth; (einschließlich) including sth
▷ konj **1** (mit Zahlen) to; **10 bis 20** 10 to 20
2 (zeitlich) till, until; **bis es dunkel wird** till o until it gets dark; **von ... bis ...** from ... to ...

Bischof (-s, Bischöfe) m bishop
bisher adv up to now, so far
Biskuit (-(e)s, -s o -e) nt sponge
biss imperf von **beißen**
Biss (-es, -e) m bite
bisschen adj: **ein ~ a bit of; ein ~ Salz/Liebe** a bit of salt/love; **ich habe kein ~ Hunger** I'm not a bit hungry ▷ adv: **ein ~ a bit; kein ~ not at all**
bissig adj (Hund) vicious; (Bemerkung) cutting
Bit (-s, -s) nt (Inform) bit
bitte interj please; (wie) **~?** (I beg your) pardon?; **~ (schön o sehr)!** (als Antwort auf Dank) you're welcome; **hier, ~** here you are;
Bitte (-, -n) f request; **bitten** (bat, gebeten) vt, vi to ask (um for)
bitter adj bitter
Blähungen pl (Med) wind sing
blamieren vr: **sich ~** to make a fool of oneself ▷ vt: **jdn ~** to make sb look a fool
Blankoscheck m blank cheque
Blase (-, -n) f bubble; (Med) blister; (Anat) bladder
blasen (blies, geblasen) vi to blow; **jdm einen ~** (vulg) to give sb a blow job
Blasenentzündung f cystitis

blass adj pale

Blatt (-(e)s, Blätter) nt leaf; (von Papier) sheet; **blättern** vi (Inform) to scroll; **in etw** (dat) ~ **to leaf through sth**; **Blätterteig** m puff pastry; **Blattsalat** m green salad; **Blattspinat** m spinach

blau adj blue; (fam: betrunken) plastered; (Gastr) boiled; **~es Auge** black eye; **~er Fleck** bruise; **Blaubeere** f bilberry, blueberry; **Blaulicht** nt flashing blue light; **blau|machen** vi to skip work o school; **Blauschimmelkäse** m blue cheese

Blazer (-s, -) m blazer

Blech (-(e)s, -e) nt sheet metal; (Backblech) baking tray (Brit), cookie sheet (US); **Blechschaden** m (Auto) damage to the bodywork

Blei (-(e)s, -e) nt lead

bleiben (blieb, geblieben) vi to stay; **lass das ~!** stop it; **das bleibt unter uns** that's (just) between ourselves; **mir bleibt keine andere Wahl** I have no other choice

bleich adj pale; **bleichen** vt to bleach

bleifrei adj (Benzin) unleaded; **bleihaltig** adj (Benzin) leaded

Bleistift m pencil

Blende (-, -n) f (Foto) aperture

Blick (-(e)s, -e) m look; (kurz) glance; (Aussicht) view; **auf den ersten ~** at first sight; **einen ~ auf etw** (akk) **werfen** to have a look at sth; **blicken** vi to look; **sich ~ lassen** to show up

blieb imperf von bleiben

blies imperf von blasen

blind adj blind; (Glas etc) dull; **Blinddarm** m appendix; **Blinddarmentzündung** f appendicitis; **Blinde(r)** mf blind person/man/woman; **die ~n** pl the blind pl; **Blindenhund** m guide dog; **Blindenschrift** f braille

blinken vi (Stern, Lichter) to twinkle; (aufleuchten) to flash; (Auto) to indicate; **Blinker** (-s, -) m (Auto) indicator (Brit), turn signal (US)

blinzeln vi (mit beiden Augen) to blink; (mit einem Auge) to wink

Blitz (-es, -e) m (flash of) lightning; (Foto) flash; **blitzen** vi (Foto) to use a/the flash; **es blitzte und donnerte** there was thunder and lightning; **Blitzlicht** nt flash

Block (-(e)s, Blöcke) m (a. fig) block; (von Papier) pad; **Blockflöte** f recorder; **Blockhaus** nt log cabin; **blockieren** vt to block ▷ vi to jam; (Räder) to lock; **Blockschrift** f block letters pl

blöd adj stupid; **blödeln** vi (fam) to fool around

Blog (-s, -s) nt (Inform) blog; **bloggen** vi to blog

blond adj blond; (Frau) blonde

SCHLÜSSELWORT

bloß adj 1 (unbedeckt) bare; (nackt) naked; **mit der bloßen Hand** with one's bare hand; **mit bloßem Auge** with the naked eye 2 (alleinig, nur) mere; **der bloße Gedanke** the very thought; **bloßer Neid** sheer envy
▷ adv only, merely; **lass das bloß!** just don't do that!; **wie ist das bloß passiert?** how on earth did that happen?

blühen vi to bloom; (fig) to flourish

Blume (-, -n) f flower; (von Wein) bouquet; **Blumenbeet** nt flower bed; **Blumengeschäft** nt florist's (shop); **Blumenkohl** m cauliflower; **Blumenladen** m flower shop; **Blumenstrauß** m

bunch of flowers; **Blumentopf** m
flowerpot; **Blumenvase** f vase
Bluse (-, -n) f blouse
Blut (-(e)s) nt blood; **Blutbild** nt
blood count; **Blutdruck** m blood
pressure; **Blutorange** f blood
orange
Blüte (-, -n) f (Pflanzenteil) flower,
bloom; (Baumblüte) blossom; (fig)
prime
bluten vi to bleed
Blütenstaub m pollen
Bluter (-s, -) m (Med)
haemophiliac; **Bluterguss** m
haematoma; (blauer Fleck) bruise;
Blutgruppe f blood group; **blutig**
adj bloody; **Blutkonserve** f unit
of stored blood; **Blutprobe** f
blood sample; **Blutspende** f
blood donation; **Bluttransfusion**
f blood transfusion; **Blutung** f
bleeding; **Blutvergiftung** f
blood poisoning; **Blutwurst** f
black pudding (Brit), blood
sausage (US)
BLZ abk = **Bankleitzahl**
Bob (-s, -s) m bob(sleigh)
Bock (-(e)s, Böcke) m (Reh) buck;
(Schaf) ram; (Gestell) trestle; (Sport)
vaulting horse; **ich hab keinen
~ (drauf)** (fam) I don't feel like it
Boden (-s, Böden) m ground;
(Fußboden) floor; (von Meer, Fass)
bottom; (Speicher) attic;
Bodennebel m ground mist;
Bodenpersonal nt ground staff;
Bodenschätze pl mineral
resources pl
Bodensee m: **der ~** Lake
Constance
Body (-s, -s) m body;
Bodybuilding (-s) nt
bodybuilding
bog imperf von **biegen**
Bogen (-s, -) m (Biegung) curve;
(in der Architektur) arch; (Waffe,
Instrument) bow; (Papier) sheet

Bohne (-, -n) f bean; **grüne ~n** pl
green (o French (Brit)) beans pl;
weiße ~n pl haricot beans pl;
Bohnenkaffee m real coffee;
Bohnensprosse f bean sprout
bohren vt to drill; **Bohrer** (-s, -)
m drill
Boiler (-s, -) m water heater
Boje (-, -n) f buoy
Bolivien (-s) nt Bolivia
Bombe (-, -n) f bomb
Bon (-s, -s) m (Kassenzettel)
receipt; (Gutschein) voucher,
coupon
Bonbon (-s, -s) nt sweet (Brit),
candy (US)
Bonus (- o -ses, -se o Boni) m
bonus; (Punktwertung) bonus points
pl; (Schadenfreiheitsrabatt)
no-claims bonus
Boot (-(e)s, -e) nt boat;
Bootsverleih m boat hire (Brit) (o
rental (US)
Bord (-(e)s, -e) m: **an ~ (eines
Schiffes)** on board (a ship); **an
~ gehen** (Schiff) to go on board;
(Flugzeug) to board; **von ~ gehen**
to disembark; **Bordcomputer** m
dashboard computer
Bordell (-s, -e) nt brothel
Bordkarte f boarding card
Bordstein m kerb (Brit), curb (US)
borgen vt to borrow; **jdm etw
~** to lend sb sth; **sich** (dat) **etw ~** to
borrow sth
Börse (-, -n) f stock exchange;
(Geldbörse) purse
bös adj siehe **böse**; **bösartig** adj
malicious; (Med) malignant
Böschung f slope; (Uferböschung)
embankment
böse adj bad; (stärker) evil;
(Wunde) nasty; (zornig) angry; **bist
du mir ~?** are you angry with me?
boshaft adj malicious
Bosnien (-s) nt Bosnia;
Bosnien-Herzegowina (-s) nt

Bosnia-Herzegovina
böswillig adj malicious
bot imperf von **bieten**
botanisch adj: **~er Garten**
botanical gardens pl
Botschaft f message; (Pol)
embassy; **Botschafter(in)** m(f)
ambassador
Botsuana (-s) nt Botswana
Bouillon (-, -s) f stock
Boutique (-, -n) f boutique
Bowle (-, -n) f punch
Box (-, -en) f (Behälter, Pferdebox)
box; (Lautsprecher) speaker; (bei
Autorennen) pit
boxen vi to box; **Boxer** (-s, -) m
(Hund, Sportler) boxer;
Boxershorts pl boxer shorts pl;
Boxkampf m boxing match
Boykott (-s, -e) m boycott
brach imperf von **brechen**
brachte imperf von **bringen**
Brainstorming (-s) nt
brainstorming
Branchenverzeichnis nt
yellow pages® pl
Brand (-(e)s, Brände) m fire; **einen
~ haben** (fam) to be parched
Brandenburg (-s) nt
Brandenburg
Brandsalbe f ointment for burns
Brandung f surf
Brandwunde f burn
brannte imperf von **brennen**
Brasilien (-s) nt Brazil
braten (briet, gebraten) vt to
roast; (auf dem Rost) to grill; (in der
Pfanne) to fry; **Braten** (-s, -) m
roast; (roher) joint; **Bratensoße** f
gravy; **Brathähnchen** nt roast
chicken; **Bratkartoffeln** pl fried
potatoes pl; **Bratpfanne** f frying
pan; **Bratspieß** m spit;
Bratwurst f fried sausage;
(gegrillte) grilled sausage
Brauch (-s, Bräuche) m custom
brauchen vt (nötig haben) to need

(für, zu for); (erfordern) to require;
(Zeit) to take; (gebrauchen) to use;
wie lange wird er ~? how long will
it take him?; **du brauchst es nur
zu sagen** you only need to say;
das braucht (seine) Zeit it takes
time; **ihr braucht es nicht zu tun**
you don't have (o need) to do it; **sie
hätte nicht zu kommen ~** she
needn't have come
brauen vt to brew; **Brauerei** f
brewery
braun adj brown; (von Sonne)
tanned; **Bräune** (-, -n) f
brownness; (von Sonne) tan;
Bräunungsstudio nt tanning
studio
Brause (-, -n) f (Dusche) shower;
(Getränk) fizzy drink (Brit), soda
(US)
Braut (-, Bräute) f bride;
Bräutigam (-s, -e) m bridegroom
brav adj (artig) good,
well-behaved
bravo interj well done
BRD (-) f abk = **Bundesrepublik
Deutschland** FRG

● **BRD**
●
● The **BRD** is the official name for
● the Federal Republic of
● Germany. It comprises 16
● **Länder** (see **Land**). It was the
● name given to the former West
● Germany as opposed to East
● Germany (the **DDR**). The two
● Germanies were reunited on 3rd
● October 1990.

brechen (brach, gebrochen) vt to
break; (erbrechen) to bring up; **sich
(dat) den Arm ~** to break one's arm
▷ vi to break; (erbrechen) to vomit,
to be sick; **Brechreiz** m nausea
Brei (-(e)s, -e) m (Breimasse) mush,
pulp; (Haferbrei) porridge; (für

Kinder) pap
breit *adj* wide; *(Schultern)* broad;
zwei Meter ~ two metres wide;
Breite (-, -*n*) *f* breadth; *(bei
Maßangaben)* width; *(Geo)* latitude;
der ~ nach widthways;
Breitengrad *m* (degree of)
latitude
Bremen (-s) *nt* Bremen
Bremsbelag *m* brake lining;
Bremse (-, -*n*) *f* brake; *(Zool)*
horsefly; **bremsen** *vi* to brake
▷ *vt (Auto)* to brake; *(fig)* to slow
down; **Bremsflüssigkeit** *f* brake
fluid; **Bremslicht** *nt* brake light;
Bremspedal *nt* brake pedal;
Bremsspur *f* tyre marks *pl*;
Bremsweg *m* braking distance
brennen *(brannte, gebrannt)* *vi* to
burn; *(in Flammen stehen)* to be on
fire; **es brennt!** fire!; **mir ~ die
Augen** my eyes are smarting; **das
Licht ~ lassen** to leave the light
on; **Brennholz** *nt* firewood;
Brennnessel *f* stinging nettle;
Brennspiritus *m* methylated
spirits *pl*; **Brennstab** *m* fuel rod;
Brennstoff *m* fuel
Brett (-*(e)s*, -*er*) *nt* board; *(länger)*
plank; *(Regal)* shelf; *(Spielbrett)*
board; **Schwarzes ~** notice board,
bulletin board *(US)*; **~er** *pl (ski)* skis
pl; **Brettspiel** *nt* board game
Brezel (-, -*n*) *f* pretzel
Brief (-*(e)s*, -*e*) *m* letter;
Briefbombe *f* letter bomb;
Brieffreund(in) *m(f)* penfriend,
pen pal; **Briefkasten** *m* letterbox
(Brit), mailbox *(US)*;
elektronischer ~ electronic
mailbox; **Briefmarke** *f* stamp;
Briefpapier *nt* writing paper;
Brieftasche *f* wallet;
Briefträger(in) *m(f)* post-
man/-woman; **Briefumschlag** *m*
envelope; **Briefwaage** *f* letter
scales *pl*

briet *imperf von* **braten**
Brille (-, -*n*) *f* glasses *pl*;
(Schutzbrille) goggles *pl*; **Brillenetui**
nt glasses case
bringen *(brachte, gebracht)* *vt*
(herbringen) to bring; *(mitnehmen,
vom Sprecher weg)* to take; *(holen,
herbringen)* to get, to fetch; *(Theat,
Cine)* to show; *(Radio, TV)* to
broadcast; **~ Sie mir bitte noch
ein Bier** could you bring me
another beer, please?; **jdn nach
Hause ~** to take sb home; **jdn
dazu ~, etw zu tun** to make sb do
sth; **jdn auf eine Idee ~** to give sb
an idea
Brise (-, -*n*) *f* breeze
Brite (-*n*, -*n*) *m*, **Britin** *f* British
person, Briton; **er ist ~** he is
British; **die ~n** the British; **britisch**
adj British
Brocken (-s, -) *m* bit; *(größer)*
lump, chunk
Brokkoli *m* broccoli
Brombeere *f* blackberry
Bronchitis (-) *f* bronchitis
Bronze (-, -*n*) *f* bronze
Brosche (-, -*n*) *f* brooch
Brot (-*(e)s*, -*e*) *nt* bread; *(Laib)* loaf;
Brotaufstrich *m* spread;
Brötchen *nt* roll; **Brotzeit** *f*
(Pause) break; *(Essen)* snack;
~ machen to have a snack
Browser (-s, -) *m (Inform)*
browser
Bruch (-*(e)s*, Brüche) *m (Brechen)*
breaking; *(Bruchstelle; mit Partei,
Tradition etc)* break; *(Med:
Eingeweidebruch)* rupture, hernia;
(Knochenbruch) fracture; *(Math)*
fraction; **brüchig** *adj* brittle
Brücke (-, -*n*) *f* bridge
Bruder (-s, Brüder) *m* brother
Brühe (-, -*n*) *f (Suppe)* (clear)
soup; *(Grundlage)* stock; *(pej:
Getränk)* muck; **Brühwürfel** *m*
stock cube

brüllen vi to roar; (Stier) to bellow; (vor Schmerzen) to scream (with pain)

brummen vi (Bär, Mensch) to growl; (brummeln) to mutter; (Insekt) to buzz; (Motor, Radio) to drone ▷ vt to growl

brünett adj brunette

Brunnen (-s, -) m fountain; (tief) well; (natürlich) spring

Brust (-, Brüste) f breast; (beim Mann) chest; **Brustschwimmen** (-s) nt breaststroke; **Brustwarze** f nipple

brutal adj brutal

brutto adv gross

BSE (-) nt abk = **bovine spongiforme Enzephalopathie** BSE

Bube (-n, -n) m boy, lad; (Karten) jack

Buch (-(e)s, Bücher) nt book

Buche (-, -n) f beech (tree)

buchen vt to book; (Betrag) to enter

Bücherei f library

Buchfink m chaffinch

Buchhalter(in) m(f) accountant

Buchhandlung f bookshop

Büchse (-, -n) f tin (Brit), can

Buchstabe (-ns, -n) m letter; **buchstabieren** vt to spell

Bucht (-, -en) f bay

Buchung f booking; (Comm) entry

Buckel (-s, -) m hump

bücken vr: **sich ~** to bend down

Buddhismus (-) m Buddhism

Bude (-, -en) f (auf Markt) stall; (fam: Wohnung) pad, place

Büfett (-s, -s) nt sideboard; **kaltes ~** cold buffet

Büffel (-s, -) m buffalo

Bügel (-s, -) m (Kleidung) hanger; (Steigbügel) stirrup; (Brille) sidepiece; (von Skilift) T-bar; **Bügelbrett** nt ironing board;

Bügeleisen nt iron; **Bügelfalte** f crease; **bügelfrei** adj non-iron; **bügeln** vt, vi to iron

buh interj boo

Bühne (-, -n) f stage; **Bühnenbild** nt set

Bulgare (-n, -n) m, **Bulgarin** f Bulgarian; **Bulgarien** (-s) nt Bulgaria; **bulgarisch** adj Bulgarian; **Bulgarisch** nt Bulgarian

Bulimie f bulimia

Bulle (-n, -n) m bull; (fam: Polizist) cop

Bummel (-s, -) m stroll; **bummeln** vi (to stroll; (trödeln) to dawdle; (faulenzen) to loaf around; **Bummelzug** m slow train

bums interj bang

bumsen vi (vulg) to screw

Bund[1] (-(e)s, Bünde) m (von Hose, Rock) waistband; (Freundschaftsbund) bond; (Organisation) association; (Pol) confederation; **der ~** (fam: Bundeswehr) the army ▷ (-(e)s, -e) nt bunch; (von Stroh etc) bundle

Bundes- in zW Federal; (auf Deutschland bezogen a.) German; **Bundeskanzler(in)** m(f) Chancellor; **Bundesland** nt state, Land; **Bundesliga** f **erste/zweite ~** First/Second Division; **Bundespräsident(in)** m(f) President; **Bundesrat** m (in Deutschland) Upper House (of the German Parliament); (in der Schweiz) Council of Ministers; **Bundesregierung** f Federal Government; **Bundesrepublik** f Federal Republic; **~ Deutschland** Federal Republic of Germany; **Bundesstraße** f A road (Brit), = state highway (US); **Bundestag** m Lower House of the German Parliament); **Bundeswehr** f (German) armed forces pl

● **BUNDESWEHR**

● The **Bundeswehr** is the name
● for the German armed forces. It
● was established in 1955, first of
● all for volunteers, but since 1956
● there has been compulsory
● military service for all
● able-bodied young men of 18. In
● peacetime the Defence Minister
● is the head of the 'Bundeswehr',
● but in wartime the
● **Bundeskanzler** takes over. The
● 'Bundeswehr' comes under the
● jurisdiction of NATO.

Bündnis nt alliance
Bungalow (-s, -s) m bungalow
Bungeejumping (-s) nt bungee jumping
bunt adj colourful; (von Programm etc) varied; **~e Farben** bright colours ▷ adv (anstreichen) in bright colours; **Buntstift** m crayon, coloured pencil
Burg (-, -en) f castle
Bürger(in) (-s, -) m(f) citizen; **bürgerlich** adj (Rechte, Ehe etc) civil; (vom Mittelstand) middle-class; (pej) bourgeois; **Bürgermeister(in)** m(f) mayor; **Bürgersteig** (-(e)s, -e) m pavement (Brit), sidewalk (US)
Büro (-s, -s) nt office; **Büroklammer** f paper clip
Bürokratie f bureaucracy
Bursche (-n, -n) m lad; (Typ) guy
Bürste (-, -n) f brush; **bürsten** vt to brush
Bus (-ses, -se) m bus; (Reisebus) coach (Brit), bus; **Busbahnhof** m bus station
Busch (-(e)s, Büsche) m bush; (Strauch) shrub
Busen (-s, -) m breasts pl, bosom
Busfahrer(in) m(f) bus driver; **Bushaltestelle** f bus stop

Businessclass (-) f business class
Buslinie f bus route; **Busreise** f coach tour (Brit); bus tour
Bußgeld nt fine
Büstenhalter (-s, -) m bra
Busverbindung f bus connection
Butter (-) f butter; **Butterbrot** nt slice of bread and butter; **Butterkäse** m type of mild, full-fat cheese; **Buttermilch** f buttermilk; **Butterschmalz** nt clarified butter
Button (-s, -s) m badge (Brit), button (US)
b. w. abk = bitte wenden pto
Byte (-s, -s) nt byte
bzw. adv abk = beziehungsweise

C

ca. adv abk = **circa** approx
Cabrio (-s, -s) nt convertible
Café (-s, -s) nt café
Cafeteria (-, -s) f cafeteria
Call-Center (-s, -) nt call centre
campen vi to camp; **Camping** (-s) nt camping; **Campingbus** m camper; **Campingplatz** m campsite, camping ground (US)
Cappuccino (-s, -) m cappuccino
Carving (-s) nt (Ski) carving; **Carvingski** m carving ski
CD (-, -s) f abk = **Compact Disc** CD; **CD-Brenner** (-s, -) m CD burner, CD writer; **CD-Player** (-s, -) m CD player; **CD-ROM** (-, -s) f abk = **Compact Disc Read Only Memory** CD-ROM; **CD-ROM-Laufwerk** nt CD-ROM drive; **CD-Spieler** m CD player
Cello (-s, -s o Celli) nt cello
Celsius nt celsius; **20 Grad ~** 20

degrees Celsius, 68 degrees Fahrenheit
Cent (-, -s) m (von Dollar und Euro) cent
Chamäleon (-s, -s) nt chameleon
Champagner (-s, -) m champagne
Champignon (-s, -s) m mushroom
Champions League (-, -) f Champions League
Chance (-, -n) f chance; **die ~n stehen gut** the prospects are good
Chaos (-) nt chaos; **Chaot(in)** (-en, -en) m(f) (fam) disorganized person, scatterbrain; **chaotisch** adj chaotic
Charakter (-s, -e) m character; **charakteristisch** adj characteristic (für of)
Charisma (-s, Charismen o Charismata) nt charisma
charmant adj charming
Charterflug m charter flight; **chartern** vt to charter
Chat (-s, -s) m (Inform) chat; **chatten** vi (Inform) to chat
checken vt (überprüfen) to check; (fam: verstehen) to get
Check-in (-s, -s) m check-in; **Check-in-Schalter** m check-in desk
Chef(in) (-s, -s) m(f) boss; **Chefarzt** m, **Chefärztin** f senior consultant (Brit), medical director (US)
Chemie (-) f chemistry; **chemisch** adj chemical; **~e Reinigung** dry cleaning
Chemotherapie f chemotherapy
Chicoree (-s) m chicory
Chiffre (-, -n) f (Geheimzeichen) cipher; (in Zeitung) box number
Chile (-s) nt Chile
Chili (-s, -s) m chilli

China (-s) nt China; **Chinakohl** m Chinese leaves pl (Brit), bok choy (US); **Chinarestaurant** nt Chinese restaurant; **Chinese** (-n, -n) m Chinese; **Chinesin** (-, -nen) f Chinese (woman); **sie ist ~** she's Chinese; **chinesisch** adj Chinese; **Chinesisch** nt Chinese

Chip (-s, -s) m (Inform) chip; **Chipkarte** f smart card

Chips pl (Kartoffelchips) crisps pl (Brit), chips pl (US)

Chirurg(in) (-en, -en) m(f) surgeon

Chlor (-s) nt chlorine

Choke (-s, -s) m choke

Cholera (-) f cholera

Cholesterin (-s) nt cholesterol

Chor (-(e), Chöre) m choir; (Theat) chorus

Choreografie f choreography

Christ(in) (-en, -en) m(f) Christian; **Christbaum** m Christmas tree; **Christi Himmelfahrt** f the Ascension (of Christ); **Christkind** nt baby Jesus; (das Geschenke bringt) ≈ Father Christmas, Santa Claus; **christlich** adj Christian

Chrom (-s) nt chrome; (Chem) chromium

chronisch adj chronic

chronologisch adj chronological ▷ adv in chronological order

Chrysantheme (-, -n) f chrysanthemum

circa adv about, approximately

City (-) f city centre, downtown (US)

Clementine (-, -n) f clementine

clever adj clever, smart

Clique (-, -n) f group; (pej) clique; **David und seine ~** David and his lot o crowd

Clown (-s, -s) m clown

Club (-s, -s) m club; **Cluburlaub**

m club holiday (Brit), club vacation (US)

Cocktail (-s, -s) m cocktail; **Cocktailtomate** f cherry tomato

Cognac (-s) m cognac

Cola (-, -s) f Coke®, cola

Comic (-s, -s) m comic strip; (Heft) comic

Compact Disc (-, -s) f compact disc

Computer (-s, -) m computer; **Computerfreak** m computer nerd; **computergesteuert** adj computer-controlled; **Computergrafik** f computer graphics pl; **computerlesbar** adj machine-readable; **Computerspiel** nt computer game; **Computertomografie** f computer tomography, scan; **Computervirus** m computer virus

Container (-s, -) m (zum Transport) container; (für Bauschutt etc) skip

Control-Taste f control key

Cookie (-s, -s) nt (Inform) cookie

cool adj (fam) cool

Cornflakes pl cornflakes pl

Couch (-, -en) f couch; **Couchtisch** m coffee table

Coupé (-s, -s) nt coupé

Coupon (-s, -s) m coupon

Cousin (-s, -s) m cousin; **Cousine** f cousin

Crack (-s) nt (Droge) crack

Creme (-, -s) f cream; (Gastr) mousse

Creutzfeld-Jakob-Krankheit f Creutzfeld-Jakob disease, CJD

Croissant (-s, -s) nt croissant

Curry (-s) m curry powder ▷ (-s) nt (indisches Gericht) curry; **Currywurst** f fried sausage with ketchup and curry powder

Cursor (-s, -) m (Inform) cursor

Cybercafé nt cybercafé; **Cyberspace** (-) m cyberspace

d

da _adv_ **1** (örtlich) there; (hier) here; **da draußen** out there; **da sein** to be there; **da bin ich** here I am; **da, wo** where; **ist noch Milch da?** is there any milk left?
2 (zeitlich) then; (folglich) so
3 da haben wir Glück gehabt we were lucky there; **da kann man nichts machen** nothing can be done about it
▷ _konj_ (weil) as, since

dabei _adv_ (räumlich) close to it; (zeitlich) at the same time; (obwohl, doch) though; **sie hörte Radio und rauchte ~** she was listening to the radio and smoking (at the same time); **~ fällt mir ein ...** that reminds me ...; **~ kam es zu einem Unfall** this led to an accident; **... und ~ hat er gar keine Ahnung ...**

even though he has no idea; **ich finde nichts ~** I don't see anything wrong with it; **es bleibt ~** that's settled; **~ sein** (anwesend) to be present; (beteiligt) to be involved; **ich bin ~** I count me in; **er war gerade ~ zu gehen** he was just (o on the point of) leaving
dabei|bleiben _irr vi_ to stick with it; **ich bleibe dabei** I'm not changing my mind
dabei|haben _irr vt:_ **er hat seine Schwester dabei** he's brought his sister; **ich habe kein Geld dabei** I haven't got any money on me
Dach (-(e)s, Dächer) _nt_ roof; **Dachboden** _m_ attic, loft; **Dachgepäckträger** _m_ roofrack; **Dachrinne** _f_ gutter
Dachs (-es, -e) _m_ badger
dachte _imperf von_ **denken**
Dackel (-s, -) _m_ dachshund
dadurch _adv_ (räumlich) through it; (durch diesen Umstand) in that way; (deshalb) because of that, for that reason ▷ _conj:_ **~, dass** because; **~, dass er hart arbeitete** (indem) by working hard
dafür _adv_ for it; (anstatt) instead; **~ habe ich 50 Euro bezahlt** I paid 50 euros for it; **ich bin ~ zu bleiben** I'm for (o in favour of) staying; **~ ist er ja da** that's what he's there for; **er kann nichts ~** he can't help it
dagegen _adv_ against it; (im Vergleich damit) in comparison; (bei Tausch) for it; **ich habe nichts ~** I don't mind
daheim _adv_ at home
daher _adv_ (räumlich) from there; (Ursache) that's why ▷ _conj_ (deshalb) that's why
dahin _adv_ (räumlich) there; (zeitlich) (vergangen) gone; **bis ~** (zeitlich) till then; (örtlich) up to there; **bis ~ muss die Arbeit fertig**

sein the work must be finished by then

dahinter adv behind it; **~ kommen** to find out

Dahlie f dahlia

Dalmatiner (-s, -) m dalmatian

damals adv at that time, then

Dame (-, -n) f lady; (Karten) queen; (Spiel) draughts sing (Brit), checkers sing (US); **Damenbinde** f sanitary towel (Brit), sanitary napkin (US); **Damenkleidung** f ladies' wear; **Damentoilette** f ladies' toilet (o restroom (US))

damit adv with it; (begründend) by that; **was meint er ~?** what does he mean by that?; **genug ~!** that's enough o conj so that

Damm (-(e)s, Dämme) m dyke; (Staudamm) dam; (am Hafen) mole; (Bahn-, Straßendamm) embankment

Dämmerung f twilight; (am Morgen) dawn; (am Abend) dusk

Dampf (-(e)s, Dämpfe) m steam; (Dunst) vapour; **Dampfbad** nt Turkish bath; **Dampfbügeleisen** nt steam iron; **dampfen** vi to steam

dämpfen vt (Gastr) to steam; (Geräusch) to deaden; (Begeisterung) to dampen

Dampfer (-s, -) m steamer

Dampfkochtopf m pressure cooker

danach adv after that; (zeitlich a.) afterwards; (demgemäß) accordingly; **mir ist nicht ~** I don't feel like it; **~ sieht es aus** that's what it looks like

Däne (-n, -n) m Dane

daneben adv beside it; (im Vergleich) in comparison

Dänemark (-s) nt Denmark; **Dänin** f Dane, Danish woman/girl; **dänisch** adj Danish; **Dänisch** nt Danish

dank prep +dat o gen thanks to; **Dank** (-(e)s) m thanks pl; **vielen ~!** thank you very much; **jdm ~ sagen** to thank sb; **dankbar** adj grateful; (Aufgabe) rewarding; **danke** interj thank you, thanks; **~ schön** (o sehr) thank you very much; **nein ~!** no, thank you; **~, gern!** yes, please; **~, gleichfalls!** thanks, and the same to you; **danken** vi: **jdm für etw ~** to thank sb for sth; **nichts zu ~!** you're welcome

dann adv then; **bis ~!** see you (later); **~ eben nicht** okay, forget it, suit yourself

daran adv (räumlich) on it; (befestigen) to it; (stoßen) against it; **es liegt ~, dass ...** it's because ...

darauf adv (räumlich) on it; (zielgerichtet) towards it; (danach) afterwards; **es kommt ganz ~ an, ob ...** it all depends whether ...; **ich freue mich ~** I'm looking forward to it; **am Tag ~** the next day; **~ folgend** (Tag, Jahr) next, following

darauffolgend adj (Tag, Jahr) next, following

daraus adv from it; **was ist ~ geworden?** what became of it?

darin adv in it; **das Problem liegt ~, dass ...** the basic problem is that ...

Darlehen (-s, -) nt loan

Darm (-(e)s, Därme) m intestine; (Wurstdarm) skin; **Darmgrippe** f gastroenteritis

dar|stellen vt to represent; (Theat) to play; (beschreiben) to describe; **Darsteller(in)** m(f) actor/actress; **Darstellung** f representation; (Beschreibung) description

darüber adv (räumlich) above it, over it; (fahren) over it; (mehr) more; (*währenddessen*) meanwhile; (*sprechen, streiten, sich freuen*) about it

darum adv (*deshalb*) that's why; **es geht ~, dass ...** the point (o thing) is that ...

darunter adv (*räumlich*) under it; (*dazwischen*) among them; (*weniger*) less; **was verstehen Sie ~?** what do you understand by that?; **~ fallen** to be included

darunterfallen vi to be included

das art the; **~ Auto da** that car; **er hat sich ~ Bein gebrochen** he's broken his leg; **vier Euro ~ Kilo** four euros a kilo ▷ pron that (one), this (one); (*relativ, Sache*) that, which; (*relativ, Person*) who, that; (*demonstrativ*) this/that one; **~ Auto da** that car; **ich nehme ~ da** I'll take that one; **~ Auto, ~ er kaufte** the car (that (o which) he bought); **~ Mädchen, ~ nebenan wohnt** the girl who (o that) lives next door; **~ heißt** that is; **~ sind Amerikaner** they're American

da sein irr vi siehe **da**

dass conj that; **so ~** so that; **es sei denn, ~** unless; **ohne ~ er grüßte** without saying hello

dasselbe pron the same

Datei f (*Inform*) file; **Dateimanager** m file manager

Daten pl data pl; **Datenbank** f database; **Datenmissbrauch** m misuse of data; **Datenschutz** m data protection; **Datenträger** m data carrier; **Datenverarbeitung** f data processing

datieren vt to date

Dativ m dative (case)

Dattel (-, -n) f date

Datum (-s, *Daten*) nt date

Dauer (-, -n) f duration; (*Länge*) length; **auf die ~** in the long run; **für die ~ von zwei Jahren** for (a

period of) two years; **Dauerauftrag** m (*Fin*) standing order; **dauerhaft** adj lasting; (*Material*) durable; **Dauerkarte** f season ticket; **dauern** vi to last; (*Zeit benötigen*) to take; **es hat sehr lange gedauert, bis er ...** it took him a long time to ...; **wie lange dauert es denn noch?** how much longer will it be?; **das dauert mir zu lange** I can't wait that long; **dauernd** adj lasting; (*ständig*) constant ▷ adv always, constantly; **er lachte ~** he kept laughing; **unterbrich mich nicht ~** stop interrupting me; **Dauerwelle** f perm (*Brit*), permanent (US)

Daumen (-s, -) m thumb

Daunendecke f eiderdown

davon adv (*räumlich*) away; (*weg von*) from it; (*Grund*) because of it; **ich hätte gerne ein Kilo ~** I'd like one kilo of that; **~ habe ich gehört** I've heard of it; (*Geschehen*) I've heard about it; **das kommt ~, wenn ...** that's what happens when ...; **was habe ich ~?** what's the point?; **auf und ~** up and away; **davon|laufen** irr vi to run away

davor adv (*räumlich*) in front of it; (*zeitlich*) before; **ich habe Angst ~** I'm afraid of it

dazu adv (*zusätzlich*) on top of that, as well; (*zu diesem Zweck*) for it, for that purpose; **ich möchte Reis ~** I'd like rice with it; **und ~ noch** and in addition; **~ fähig sein, etw zu tun** to be capable of doing sth; **wie kam es ~?** how did it happen?; **dazu|gehören** vi to belong to it; **dazu|kommen** irr vi (*zu jdm* ~) to join sb; **kommt noch etwas dazu?** anything else?

dazwischen adv in between; (*Unterschied etc*) between them; (*in einer Gruppe*) among them

dazwischen|kommen irr vi: **wenn nichts dazwischenkommt** if all goes well; **mir ist etwas dazwischengekommen** something has cropped up

DDR (-) f abk = **Deutsche Demokratische Republik** (Hist) GDR

dealen vi (fam: mit Drogen) to deal in drugs; **Dealer(in)** (-s, -) m(f) (fam) dealer, pusher

Deck (-(e)s, -s o -e) nt deck

Decke (-, -n) f cover; (für Bett) blanket; (für Tisch) tablecloth; (von Zimmer) ceiling

Deckel (-s, -) m lid

decken vt to cover; (Tisch) to lay, to set ▷ vr: **sich ~** (Interessen) to coincide; (Aussagen) to correspond ▷ vi (den Tisch decken) to lay (o set) the table

Decoder (-s, -) m decoder

defekt adj faulty; **Defekt** (-(e)s, -e) m fault, defect

definieren vt to define; **Definition** (-, -en) f definition

deftig adj (Preise) steep; **ein ~es Essen** a good solid meal

dehnbar adj flexible, elastic; **dehnen** vt to stretch ▷ vr: **sich ~** to stretch

Deich (-(e)s, -e) m dyke

dein pron (adjektivisch) your; **deine(r, s)** pron (substantivisch) yours, of you; **deiner** pron gen von **du**; **deinetwegen** adv (wegen dir) because of you; (dir zuliebe) for your sake; (um dich) about you

deinstallieren vt (Programm) to uninstall

Dekolleté (-s, -s) nt low neckline

Dekoration f decoration; (in Laden) window dressing; **dekorativ** adj decorative; **dekorieren** vt to decorate; (Schaufenster) to dress

Delfin (-s, -e) m dolphin

delikat adj (lecker) delicious; (heikel) delicate

Delikatesse (-, -n) f delicacy

Delle (-, -n) f (fam) dent

Delphin (-s, -e) m dolphin

dem dat sing von **der/das**; **wie ~ auch sein mag** be that as it may

demnächst adv shortly, soon

Demo (-, -s) f (fam) demo

Demokratie (-, -n) f democracy; **demokratisch** adj democratic

demolieren vt to demolish

Demonstration f demonstration; **demonstrieren** vt, vi to demonstrate

den art akk sing, dat pl von **der**; **sie hat sich ~ Arm gebrochen** she's broken her arm ▷ pron him; (Sache) that one; (relativ: Person) who, that, whom; (relativ: Sache) which, that; **~ hab ich schon ewig nicht mehr gesehen** I haven't seen him in ages ▷ pron (Person) who, that, whom; (Sache) which, that; **der Typ, auf ~ sie steht** the guy (who) she fancies; **der Berg, auf ~ wir geklettert sind** the mountain (that) we climbed

denkbar adj: **das ist ~** that's possible ▷ adv: **~ einfach** extremely simple; **denken** (dachte, gedacht) vt, vi to think (über +akk about); **an jdn/etw ~** to think of sb/sth; (sich erinnern, berücksichtigen) to remember sb/sth; **woran denkst Du?** what are you thinking about?; **denk an den Kaffee** don't forget the coffee ▷ vr: **sich ~** (sich vorstellen) to imagine; **das kann ich mir ~** I can (well) imagine

Denkmal (-s, Denkmäler) nt monument; **Denkmalschutz** m monument preservation; **unter ~ stehen** to be listed

denn conj for, because ▷ adv

then; (nach Komparativ) than; **was ist ~?** what's wrong?; **ist das ~ so schwierig?** is it really that difficult?

dennoch conj still, nevertheless

Deo (-s, -s) nt, **Deodorant** (-s, -s) nt deodorant; **Deoroller** m roll-on deodorant; **Deospray** m o nt deodorant spray

Deponie (-, -n) f waste disposal site, tip

Depressionen pl: **an ~ leiden** to suffer from depression sing; **deprimieren** vt to depress

🅾 **SCHLÜSSELWORT**

der (f die, nt das, gen des, der, des, dat dem, der, dem, akk den, die, das, pl die) def art the; **der Rhein** the Rhine; **der Klaus** (fam) Klaus; **die Frau** (im Allgemeinen) women; **der Tod/das Leben** death/life; **der Fuß des Berges** the foot of the hill; **gib es der Frau** give it to the woman; **er hat sich die Hand verletzt** he has hurt his hand

▷ relativ pron (bei Menschen) who, that; (bei Tieren, Sachen) which, that; **der Mann, den ich gesehen habe** the man who o whom that I saw

▷ demonstrativ pron he/she/it (jener, dieser) that; (pl) those; **der/die war es** it was him/her; **der mit der Brille** the one with glasses; **ich will den (da)** I want that one

derart adv so; (solcher Art) such; **derartig** adj: **ein ~er Fehler** such a mistake, a mistake like that

deren gen von die ▷ pron (Person) her; (Sache) its; (Plural) their ▷ pron (Person) whose; (Sache) of which; **meine Freundin und ~ Mutter** my

friend and her mother; **das sind ~ Sachen** that's their stuff; **die Frau, ~ Tochter ...** the woman whose daughter ...; **ich bin mir ~ bewusst** that's why I'm asking

dergleichen pron: **und ~ mehr** and the like, and so on; **nichts ~** no such thing

derjenige pron the one; **~, der** (relativ) the one who (o that)

dermaßen adv so much; (mit Adj) so

derselbe pron the same (person/thing)

deshalb adv therefore; **~ frage ich ja** that's why I'm asking

Design (-s, -s) nt design; **Designer(in)** (-s, -) m(f) designer

Desinfektionsmittel nt disinfectant; **desinfizieren** vt to disinfect

dessen gen von der, das ▷ pron (Person) his; (Sache) its; (bin mir ~ bewusst) I'm aware of that ▷ pron (Person) whose; (Sache) of which; **mein Freund und ~ Mutter** my friend and his mother; **der Mann, ~ Tochter ...** the man whose daughter ...; **ich bin mir ~ bewusst** I'm aware of that

Dessert (-s, -s) nt dessert; **zum (o als) ~** for dessert

destilliert adj distilled

desto adv: **je eher, ~ besser** the sooner, the better

deswegen conj therefore

Detail (-s, -s) nt detail; **ins ~ gehen** to go into detail

Detektiv(in) (-s, -e) m(f) detective

deutlich adj clear; (Unterschied) distinct

deutsch adj German; **Deutsch** nt German; **auf ~** in German; **ins ~e übersetzen** to translate into German; **Deutsche(r)** mf

German; **Deutschland** nt Germany

Devise (-, -n) f motto; **~n** pl (Fin) foreign currency sing; **Devisenkurs** m exchange rate

Dezember (-(s), -) m December; siehe auch **Juni**

dezent adj discreet

d.h. abk von **das heißt** i.e. (gesprochen: i.e. oder that is)

Dia (-s, -s) nt slide

Diabetes (-, -) m (Med) diabetes; **Diabetiker(in)** (-s, -) m(f) diabetic

Diagnose (-, -n) f diagnosis

diagonal adj diagonal

Dialekt (-(e)s, -e) m dialect

Dialog (-(e)s, -e) m dialogue; (Inform) dialog

Dialyse (-, -n) f (Med) dialysis

Diamant m diamond

Diaprojektor m slide projector

Diät (-, -en) f diet; **eine ~ machen** to be on a diet; (anfangen) to go on a diet

dich pron akk von **du** you; **~ (selbst)** (reflexiv) yourself; **pass auf ~ auf** look after yourself; **reg ~ nicht auf** don't get upset

dicht adj dense; (Nebel) thick; (Gewebe) close; (wasserdicht) watertight; (Verkehr) heavy ▷ adv: **~ an/bei** close to; **~ bevölkert** densely populated

Dichter(in) (-s, -) m(f) poet; (Autor) writer

Dichtung f (Auto) gasket; (Dichtungsring) washer; (Gedichte) poetry

Dichtungsring m (Tech) washer

dick adj thick; (Person) fat; **jdn ~ haben** to be sick of sb; **Dickdarm** m large intestine; **Dickkopf** m stubborn (o pig-headed) person; **Dickmilch** f sour milk

die art the; **~ arme Sarah** poor Sarah ▷ pron (sing, Person, als

Subjekt) she; (Person, als Subjekt, Plural) they; (Person, als Objekt) her; (Person, als Objekt, Plural) them; (Sache) that (one), this (one); (Plural) those (ones); (Sache, Plural) those (ones); (relativ, auf Person) who, that; (relativ, auf Sache) which, that; **~ mit den langen Haaren** the one (o her) with the long hair; **sie war ~ erste**, **~ es erfuhr** she was the first to know; **ich nehme ~ da** I'll take that one/those ▷ pl von **der, die, das**

Dieb(in) (-(e)s, -e) m(f) thief; **Diebstahl** (-(e)s, Diebstähle) m theft; **Diebstahlsicherung** f burglar alarm

diejenige pron the one; **~, die** (relativ) the one who (o that); **~n** pl those pl, the ones

Diele (-, -n) f hall

Dienst (-(e)s, -e) m service; **außer ~** retired; **~ haben** to be on duty

Dienstag m Tuesday; siehe auch **Mittwoch**; **dienstags** adv on Tuesdays; siehe auch **mittwochs**

Dienstbereitschaft f: **~ haben** (Arzt) to be on call; **diensthabend** adj: **der ~e Arzt** the doctor on duty; **Dienstleistung** f service; **dienstlich** adj official; **er ist ~ unterwegs** he's away on business; **Dienstreise** f business trip; **Dienststelle** f department; **Dienstwagen** m company car; **Dienstzeit** f office hours pl; (Mil) period of service

diesbezüglich adj (formell) on this matter

diese(r, s) pron this (one); pl these; **~ Frau** this woman; **~r Mann** this man; **~s Mädchen** this girl; **~ Leute** these people; **ich nehme ~/~n/~s** (hier) I'll take this one; (dort) I'll take that one; **ich nehme ~** pl (hier) I'll take these (ones); (dort) I'll take those (ones)

Diesel (-s, -) m (Auto) diesel
dieselbe pron the same; **es sind immer ~n** it's always the same people
Dieselmotor m diesel engine; **Dieselöl** nt diesel (oil)
diesig adj hazy, misty
diesmal adv this time
Dietrich (-s, -e) m skeleton key
Differenz (-, -en) f difference
digital adj digital; **Digital-** in zW (Anzeige etc) digital; **Digitalfernsehen** nt digital television, digital TV; **Digitalkamera** f digital camera
Diktat (-(e)s, -e) nt dictation
Diktatur f dictatorship
Dill (-s) m dill
DIN abk = **Deutsche Industrienorm** DIN; **~ A4** A4
Ding (-(e)s, -e) nt thing; **vor allen ~en** above all; **der Stand der ~e** the state of affairs; **das ist nicht mein ~** (fam) it's not my sort of thing (o cup of tea); **Dingsbums** (-) nt (fam) thingy, thingummybob
Dinkel (-s, -) m (Bot) spelt
Dinosaurier (-s, -) m dinosaur
Diphtherie (-, -n) f diphtheria
Diplom (-(e)s, -e) nt diploma
Diplomat(in) (-en, -en) m(f) diplomat
dir pron dat von **du** (to) you; **hat er ~ geholfen?** did he help you?; **ich werde es ~ erklären** I'll explain it to you; (reflexiv) **wasch ~ die Hände** go and wash your hands; **ein Freund von ~** a friend of yours
direkt adj direct; (Frage) straight; **~e Verbindung** through service ▷ adv directly; (sofort) immediately; **~ am Bahnhof** right next to the station; **Direktflug** m direct flight
Direktor(in) m(f) director; (Schule) headmaster/-mistress

(Brit), principal (US)
Direktübertragung f live broadcast
Dirigent(in) m(f) conductor;
dirigieren vt to direct; (Mus) to conduct
Discman® (-s, -s) m Discman®
Diskette f disk, diskette;
Diskettenlaufwerk nt disk drive
Diskjockey (-s, -s) m disc jockey;
Disko (-, -s) f (fam) disco, club;
Diskothek (-, -en) f discotheque, club
diskret adj discreet
diskriminieren vt to discriminate against
Diskussion f discussion;
diskutieren vt, vi to discuss
Display (-s, -s) nt display
disqualifizieren vt to disqualify
Distanz f distance
Distel (-, -n) f thistle
Disziplin (-, -en) f discipline
divers adj various
dividieren vt to divide (durch by);
8 dividiert durch 2 ist 4 8 divided by 2 is 4
DJ (-s, -s) m abk = **Diskjockey** DJ

SCHLÜSSELWORT

doch adv **1** (dennoch) after all; (sowieso) anyway; **er kam doch noch** he came after all; **du weißt es ja doch besser** you know better than I do anyway; **und doch ...** and yet ...
2 (als bejahende Antwort) yes I do/it does etc; **das ist nicht wahr — doch!** that's not true — yes it is!
3 (auffordernd) **komm doch** do come; **lass ihn doch** just leave him; **nicht doch!** oh no!
4 **sie ist doch noch so jung** but she's still so young; **Sie wissen doch, wie das ist** you know how

it is(, don't you?); **wenn doch** if
only
▷ *konj (aber)* but; *(trotzdem)* all the
same; **und doch hat er es getan**
but still he did it

Doktor(in) *m(f)* doctor

Dokument *nt* document;
Dokumentarfilm *m* documentary (film); **dokumentieren**
vt to document;
Dokumentvorlage *f (Inform)*
document template

Dolch (-(e)s, -e) *m* dagger

Dollar (-(s), -s) *m* dollar

dolmetschen *vt, vi* to interpret;
Dolmetscher(in) (-s, -) *m(f)*
interpreter

Dolomiten *pl* Dolomites *pl*

Dom (-(e)s, -e) *m* cathedral

Domäne (-, -n) *f* domain,
province; *(Inform: Domain)* domain

Dominikanische Republik *f*
Dominican Republic

Domino (-s, -s) *nt* dominoes *sing*

Donau (-) *f* Danube

Döner (-s, -) *m*, **Döner Kebab**
(-(s), -s) *m* doner kebab

Donner (-s, -) *m* thunder;
donnern *vi*: **es donnert** it's
thundering

Donnerstag *m* Thursday; *siehe
auch* **Mittwoch**; **donnerstags**
adv on Thursdays; *siehe auch*
mittwochs

doof *adj (fam)* stupid

dopen *vt* to dope; **Doping** (-s) *nt*
doping; **Dopingkontrolle** *f*
drugs test

Doppel (-s, -) *nt* duplicate; *(Sport)*
doubles *sing*; **Doppelbett** *nt*
double bed; **Doppeldecker** *m*
double-decker; **Doppelhaushälfte** *f* semi-detached house
(Brit), duplex (US); **doppelklicken**
vi to double-click; **Doppelname**
m double-barrelled name;

Doppelpunkt *m* colon;
Doppelstecker *m* two-way
adaptor; **doppelt** *adj* double; **in
~er Ausführung** in duplicate;
Doppelzimmer *nt* double room

Dorf (-(e)s, Dörfer) *nt* village

Dorn (-(e)s, -en) *m (Bot)* thorn

Dörrobst *nt* dried fruit

Dorsch (-(e)s, -e) *m* cod

dort *adv* there; **~ drüben** over
there; **dorther** *adv* from there

Dose (-, -n) *f* box; *(Blechdose)* tin
(Brit), can; *(Bierdose)* can

dösen *vi* to doze

Dosenbier *nt* canned beer;
Dosenöffner *m* tin opener (Brit),
can opener

Dotter (-s, -) *m* (egg) yolk

downloaden *vt* to download

Downsyndrom (-(e)s, -e) *nt*
(Med) Down's syndrome

Dozent(in) *m(f)* lecturer

Dr. *abk* = **Doktor**

Drache (-n, -n) *m* dragon;
Drachen (-s, -) *m (Spielzeug)* kite;
(Sport) hang-glider;
Drachenfliegen (-s) *nt*
hang-gliding; **Drachenflieger(in)**
(-s, -) *m(f)* hang-glider

Draht (-(e)s, Drähte) *m* wire;
drahtlos *adj* wireless;
Drahtseilbahn *f* cable railway

Drama (-s, Dramen) *nt* drama;
dramatisch *adj* dramatic

dran *adv (fam) kontr von* **daran**;
gut ~ sein *(reich)* to be well-off;
(glücklich) to be fortunate;
(gesundheitlich) to be well;
schlecht ~ sein to be in a bad way;
wer ist ~? whose turn is it?; **ich
bin ~** it's my turn; **bleib ~!** *(Tel)*
hang on

drang *imperf von* **dringen**

Drang (-(e)s, Dränge) *m (Trieb)*
urge *(nach for)*; *(Druck)* pressure

drängeln *vt, vi* to push

drängen *vt (schieben)* to push;

drankommen | 56

(antreiben) to urge ▷ *vi (eilig sein)* to be urgent; *(Zeit)* to press; **auf etw** *(akk)* ~ to press for sth

dran|kommen *irr vi:* **wer kommt dran?** who's turn is it?, who's next?

drauf *(fam)* kontr von **darauf**; **gut/schlecht ~ sein** to be in a good/bad mood

Draufgänger(in) *(-s, -)* *m(f)* daredevil

drauf|kommen *irr vi* to remember; **ich komme nicht drauf** I can't think of it

drauf|machen *vi (fam)* **einen ~** to go on a binge

draußen *adv* outside

Dreck *(-(e)s)* *m* dirt, filth; **dreckig** *adj* dirty, filthy

drehen *vt, vi* to turn; *(Zigaretten)* to roll; *(Film)* to shoot ▷ *vr:* **sich ~** to turn; *(um Achse)* to rotate; **sich ~ um** *(handeln von)* to be about

Drehstrom *m* three-phase current; **Drehtür** *f* revolving door; **Drehzahlmesser** *m* rev counter

drei *num* three; **~ viertel voll** three-quarters full; **es ist ~ viertel neun** it's a quarter to nine; **Drei** *(-, -en)* *f* three; *(Schulnote)* ≈ C; **Dreieck** *nt* triangle; **dreieckig** *adj* triangular; **dreifach** *adj* triple ▷ *adv* three times; **dreihundert** *num* three hundred; **Dreikönigstag** *m* Epiphany; **dreimal** *adv* three times; **Dreirad** *nt* tricycle; **dreispurig** *adj* three-lane

dreißig *num* thirty; **dreißigste(r, s)** *adj* thirtieth; *siehe auch* **dritte**

Dreiviertelstunde *f:* **eine ~** three quarters of an hour

dreizehn *num* thirteen; **dreizehnte(r, s)** *adj* thirteenth; *siehe auch* **dritte**

dressieren *vt* to train

Dressing *(-s, -s)* *nt (salad)* dressing

Dressman *(-s, Dressmen)* *m (male)* model

Dressur *(-, -en)* *f* training

drin *(fam)* kontr von **darin** in it; **mehr war nicht ~** that was the best I could do

dringen *(drang, gedrungen)* *vi (Wasser, Licht, Kälte)* to penetrate *(durch* through, *in +akk* into); **auf etw** *(akk)* ~ to insist on sth; **dringend, dringlich** *adj* urgent

drinnen *adv* inside

dritt *adv:* **wir sind zu ~** there are three of us; **dritte(r, s)** *adj* third; **die Dritte Welt** the Third World; **3. Juni** *3(rd)* June *(gesprochen: the third of June)*; **am 3. Juni** on *3(rd)* June, on June 3(rd) *(gesprochen: the third of June)*; **München, den 3. Juni** Munich, June 3(rd); **Drittel** *(-s, -)* *nt (Bruchteil)* third; **drittens** *adv* thirdly

Droge *(-, -n)* *f* drug; **drogenabhängig, drogensüchtig** *adj* addicted to drugs

Drogerie *f* chemist's *(Brit)*, drugstore *(US)*; **Drogeriemarkt** *m* discount chemist's *(Brit)* (o drugstore *(US)*)

● **DROGERIE**
●
● The **Drogerie** as opposed to the
● **Apotheke** sells medicines not
● requiring a prescription. It
● tends to be cheaper and also
● sells cosmetics, perfume and
● toiletries.

drohen *vi* to threaten *(jdm* sb); **mit etw** ~ to threaten to do sth

dröhnen *vi (Motor)* to roar; *(Stimme, Musik)* to boom; *(Raum)* to resound

Drohung *f* threat

Drossel (-, -n) f thrush

drüben adv over there; (auf der anderen Seite) on the other side

drüber (fam) kontr von **darüber**

Druck (-(e)s, Drücke) m (Phys) pressure; (fig: Belastung) stress; **jdn unter ~ setzen** to put sb under pressure ▷ (-(e)s, -e) m (Typo: Vorgang) printing; (Produkt, Schriftart) print; **Druckbuchstabe** m block letter; **in ~n schreiben** to print; **drucken** vt, vi to print

drücken vt, vi (Knopf, Hand) to press; (zu eng sein) to pinch; (fig: Preise) to keep down; **jdm etw in die Hand ~** to press sth into sb's hand ▷ vr **sich vor etw** (dat) **~** to get out of sth; **drückend** adj oppressive

Drucker (-s, -) m (Inform) printer; **Druckertreiber** m printer driver

Druckknopf m press stud (Brit), snap fastener (US); **Drucksache** f printed matter; **Druckschrift** f block letters pl

drunten adv down there

drunter (fam) kontr von **darunter**

Drüse (-, -n) f gland

Dschungel (-s, -) m jungle

du pron you; **bist ~ es?** is it you?; **wir sind per ~** we're on first-name terms

Dübel (-s, -) m Rawlplug®

ducken vt to duck ▷ vr: **sich ~** to duck

Dudelsack m bagpipes pl

Duett (-(e)s, -e) nt duet

Duft (-(e)s, Düfte) m scent; **duften** vi to smell nice; **es duftet nach ...** it smells of ...

dulden vt to tolerate

dumm adj stupid; **Dummheit** f stupidity; (Tat) stupid thing; **Dummkopf** m idiot

dumpf adj (Ton) muffled; (Erinnerung) vague; (Schmerz) dull

Düne (-, -n) f dune

Dünger (-s, -) m fertilizer

dunkel adj dark; (Stimme) deep; (Ahnung) vague; (rätselhaft) obscure; (verdächtig) dubious; **im Dunkeln tappen** (fig) to be in the dark; **dunkelblau** adj dark blue; **dunkelblond** adj light brown; **dunkelhaarig** adj dark-haired; **Dunkelheit** f darkness

dünn adj thin; (Kaffee) weak

Dunst (-es, Dünste) m haze; (leichter Nebel) mist; (Chem) vapour

dünsten vt (Gastr) to steam

Duo (-s, -s) nt duo

Dur (-) nt (Mus) major (key); **in G-~** in G major

 SCHLÜSSELWORT

durch prep +akk **1** (hindurch) through; **durch den Urwald** through the jungle; **durch die ganze Welt reisen** to travel all over the world

2 (mittels) through, by (means of); (aufgrund) due to, owing to; **Tod durch Herzschlag/den Strang** death from a heart attack/by hanging; **durch die Post** by post; **durch seine Bemühungen** through his efforts

▷ adv **1** (hindurch) through; **die ganze Nacht durch** all through the night; **den Sommer durch** during the summer; **8 Uhr durch** past 8 o'clock; **durch und durch** completely

2 (durchgebraten etc) **(gut) durch** well-done

durchaus adv absolutely; **~ nicht** not at all

Durchblick m view; **den ~ haben** (fig) to know what's going on; **durch|blicken** vi to look through; (fam: verstehen) to understand (bei etw sth); **etw**

~ lassen (fig) to hint at sth
Durchblutung f circulation
durch|brennen irr vi (Sicherung) to blow; (Draht) to burn through; (fam: davonlaufen) to run away
durchdacht adv: **gut ~** well thought-out
durch|drehen vt (Fleisch) to mince ▷ vi (Räder) to spin; (fam: nervlich) to crack up
durcheinander adv in a mess; (fam: verwirrt) confused;
Durcheinander (-s) nt (Verwirrung) confusion; (Unordnung) mess;
durcheinander|bringen irr vt to mess up; (verwirren) to confuse;
durcheinander|reden vi to talk all at the same time;
durcheinander|trinken irr vi to mix one's drinks
Durchfahrt f way through;
„~ verboten!" "no thoroughfare"
Durchfall m (Med) diarrhoea
durch|fallen irr vi to fall through; (in Prüfung) to fail
durch|fragen vr: **sich ~** to ask one's way
durch|führen vt to carry out
Durchgang m passage; (Sport) round; (bei Wahl) ballot;
Durchgangsverkehr m through traffic
durchgebraten adj well done
durchgefroren adj frozen to the bone
durch|gehen irr vi to go through (durch etw sth); (ausreißen: Pferd) to break loose; (Mensch) to run away; **durchgehend** adj (Zug) through; **~ geöffnet** open all day
durch|halten irr vi to hold out ▷ vt (Tempo) to keep up; **etw ~** (bis zum Schluss) to see sth through
durch|kommen irr vi to get through; (Patient) to pull through

durch|lassen irr vt (jdn) to let through; (Wasser) to let in
durch|lesen irr vt to read through
durchleuchten vt to X-ray
durch|machen vt to go through; (Entwicklung) to undergo; **die Nacht ~** to make a night of it, to have an all-nighter
Durchmesser (-s, -) m diameter
Durchreise f journey through; **auf der ~** passing through; (Güter) in transit; **Durchreisevisum** nt transit visa
durch|reißen irr vt, vi to tear (in two)
durchs kontr von durch das
Durchsage (-, -n) f announcement
durchschauen vt (jdn, Lüge) to see through
durch|schlagen irr vr: **sich ~** to struggle through
durch|schneiden irr vt to cut (in two)
Durchschnitt m (Mittelwert) average; **im ~** on average; **durchschnittlich** adj average ▷ adv (im Durchschnitt) on average; **Durchschnittsgeschwindigkeit** f average speed
durch|setzen vt to get through ▷ vr: **sich ~** (Erfolg haben) to succeed; (sich behaupten) to get one's way
durchsichtig adj transparent, see-through
durch|stellen vt (Tel) to put through
durch|streichen irr vt to cross out
durchsuchen vt to search (nach for); **Durchsuchung** f search
durchwachsen adj (Speck) streaky; (fig: mittelmäßig) so-so
Durchwahl f direct dialling; (Nummer) extension

durch|ziehen *irr vt (Plan)* to carry through
Durchzug *m* draught

○ **SCHLÜSSELWORT**

dürfen *unreg vi* **1** *(Erlaubnis haben)* to be allowed to; **ich darf das** I'm allowed to (do that); **darf ich?** may I?; **darf ich ins Kino?** can o may I go to the cinema?; **es darf geraucht werden** you may smoke **2** *(in Verneinungen)* **er darf das nicht** he's not allowed to (do that); **das darf nicht geschehen** that must not happen; **da darf sie sich nicht wundern** that shouldn't surprise her
3 *(in Höflichkeitsformeln)* **darf ich Sie bitten, das zu tun?** may o could I ask you to do that?; **was darf es sein?** what can I do for you?
4 *(können)* **das dürfen Sie mir glauben** you can believe me
5 *(Möglichkeit)* **das dürfte genug sein** that should be enough; **es dürfte Ihnen bekannt sein, dass ...** as you will probably know ...

dürftig *adj (ärmlich)* poor; *(unzulänglich)* inadequate
dürr *adj* dried-up; *(Land)* arid; *(mager)* skinny
Durst *(-(e)s) m* thirst; **~ haben** to be thirsty; **durstig** *adj* thirsty
Dusche *(-, -n) f* shower; **duschen** *vi* to have a shower ▷ *vr*: **sich ~** to have a shower; **Duschgel** *nt* shower gel; **Duschvorhang** *m* shower curtain
Düse *(-, -n) f* nozzle; *(Tech)* jet; **Düsenflugzeug** *nt* jet (aircraft)
Dussel *(-s, -) m (fam)* dope; **duss(e)lig** *adj (fam)* stupid

düster *adj* dark; *(Gedanken, Zukunft)* gloomy
Dutyfreeshop *(-s, -s) m* duty-free shop
Dutzend *(-s, -e) nt* dozen
duzen *vt* to address as "du" ▷ *vr*: **sich ~ (mit jdm)** to address each other as "du", to be on first-name terms
DVD *(-, -s) f abk =* **Digital Versatile Disk** DVD; **DVD-Player** *(-s, -) m* DVD player; **DVD-Rekorder** *(-s, -) m* DVD recorder
dynamisch *adj* dynamic
Dynamo *(-s, -s) m* dynamo
D-Zug *m* fast train

e

precious stone

EDV (-) f abk = **elektronische Datenverarbeitung** EDP

Efeu (-s) m ivy

Effekt (-s, -e) m effect

egal adj: **das ist ~** it doesn't matter; **das ist mir ~** I don't care, it's all the same to me; **~ wie teuer** no matter how expensive

egoistisch adj selfish

ehe conj before

Ehe (-, -n) f marriage; **Ehefrau** f wife; (verheiratete Frau) married woman; **Eheleute** pl married couple sing

ehemalig adj former; **ehemals** adv formerly

Ehemann m husband; (verheirateter Mann) married man; **Ehepaar** nt married couple

eher adv (früher) sooner; (lieber) rather, sooner; (mehr) more; **je ~, desto besser** the sooner the better

Ehering m wedding ring

eheste(r, s) adj (früheste) first ⊳ adv: **am ~n** (am wahrscheinlichsten) most likely

Ehre (-, -n) f honour; **ehren** vt to honour; **ehrenamtlich** adj voluntary; **Ehrengast** m guest of honour; **Ehrenwort** nt word of honour; **~! I** promise; **ich gebe dir mein ~** I give you my word

ehrgeizig adj ambitious

ehrlich adj honest

Ei (-(e)s, -er) nt egg; **hart gekochtes/weiches ~** hard-boiled/soft-boiled egg

Eiche (-, -n) f oak (tree); **Eichel** (-, -n) f acorn

Eichhörnchen nt squirrel

Eid (-(e)s, -e) m oath

Eidechse (-, -n) f lizard

Eierbecher m eggcup; **Eierstock** m ovary; **Eieruhr** f egg timer

Eifersucht f jealousy;

Ebbe (-, -n) f low tide

eben adj level; (glatt) smooth ⊳ adv just; (bestätigend) exactly

Ebene (-, -n) f plain; (fig) level

ebenfalls adv also, as well; (Antwort: gleichfalls!) you too; **ebenso** adv just as; **~ gut** just as well; **~ viel** just as much

Eber (-s, -) m boar

EC (-, -s) m abk = **Eurocityzug**

Echo (-s, -s) nt echo

echt adj (Leder, Gold) real, genuine; **ein ~er Verlust** a real loss

EC-Karte f debit card

Ecke (-, -n) f corner; (Math) angle; **an der ~** at the corner; **gleich um die ~** just round the corner; **eckig** adj rectangular; **Eckzahn** m canine

Economyclass (-) f coach (class), economy class

Ecstasy (-) f (Droge) ecstasy

edel adj noble; **Edelstein** m

eifersüchtig adj jealous (auf +akk of)

Eigelb (-(e)s, -) nt egg yolk

eigen adj own; (typisch) characteristic (jdm of sb); (eigenartig) peculiar; **eigenartig** adj peculiar; **Eigenschaft** f quality; (Chem, Phys) property; (Merkmal) characteristic

eigentlich adj actual, real ▷ adv actually, really; **was denken Sie sich ~ dabei?** what on earth do you think you're doing?

Eigentum nt property; **Eigentümer(in)** m(f) owner; **Eigentumswohnung** f owner-occupied flat (Brit), condominium (US)

eignen vr: **sich ~ für** to be suited for; **er würde sich als Lehrer ~** he'd make a good teacher

Eilbrief m express letter, special-delivery letter; **Eile** (-) f hurry; **eilen** vi (dringend sein) to be urgent; **es eilt nicht** there's no hurry; **eilig** adj hurried; (dringlich) urgent; **es ~ haben** to be in a hurry

Eimer (-s, -) m bucket

ein adv: **nicht ~ noch aus wissen** not to know what to do; **~ - aus** (Schalter) on - off

ein(e) art a; (vor gesprochenem Vokal) an; **~ Mann** a man; **~ Apfel** an apple; **~e Stunde** an hour; **~ Haus** a house; **~ (gewisser) Herr Miller** a (certain) Mr Miller; **~es Tages** one day

einander pron one another, each other

ein|arbeiten vt to train ▷ vr: **sich ~** to get used to the work

ein|atmen vt, vi to breathe in

Einbahnstraße f one-way street

ein|bauen vt to build in; (Motor etc) to install, to fit; **Einbauküche**

f fitted kitchen

ein|biegen irr vi to turn (in +akk into)

ein|bilden vt **sich** (dat) **etw ~** to imagine sth

ein|brechen irr vi (in Haus) to break in; (Dach etc) to fall in, to collapse; **Einbrecher(in)** (-s, -) m(f) burglar

ein|bringen irr vt (Ernte) to bring in; (Gewinn) to yield; **jdm etw ~** to bring (o earn) sb sth ▷ vr **sich in** (akk) **etw ~** to make a contribution to sth

Einbruch m (Haus) break-in, burglary; **bei ~ der Nacht** at nightfall

Einbürgerung f naturalization

ein|checken vt to check in

ein|cremen vt to put some cream on ▷ vr: **sich ~** to put some cream on

eindeutig adj clear, obvious ▷ adv clearly; **~ falsch** clearly wrong

ein|dringen irr vi (gewaltsam) to force one's way in (in +akk -to); (in Haus) to break in (in +akk -to); (Gas, Wasser) to get in (in +akk -to)

Eindruck m impression; **großen ~ auf jdn machen** to make a big impression on sb

eine(r, s) pron one; (jemand) someone; **~r meiner Freunde** one of my friends; **~r nach dem andern** one after the other

eineiig adj (Zwillinge) identical

eineinhalb num one and a half

einerseits adv on the one hand

einfach adj (nicht kompliziert) simple; (Mensch) ordinary; (Essen) plain; (nicht mehrfach) single; **~e Fahrkarte** single ticket (Brit), one-way ticket (US) ▷ adv simply; (nicht mehrfach) single

Einfahrt f (Vorgang) driving in; (eines Zuges) arrival; (Ort) entrance

Einfall m (Idee) idea; **ein|fallen** irr
vi (Licht etc) to fall in; (einstürzen)
to collapse; **ihm fiel ein, dass ...** it
occurred to him that ...; **ich werde
mir etwas ~ lassen** I'll think of
something; **was fällt Ihnen ein!**
what do you think you're doing?

Einfamilienhaus nt detached
house

einfarbig adj all one colour; (Stoff
etc) self-coloured

Einfluss m influence

ein|frieren irr vt, vi to freeze

ein|fügen irr vt to fit in; (zusätzlich)
to add; (Inform) to insert;
Einfügetaste f (Inform) insert key

Einfuhr (-, -en) f import;
Einfuhrbestimmungen pl import
regulations pl

ein|führen vt to introduce;
(Ware) to import; **Einführung** f
introduction

Eingabe f (Dateneingabe) input;
Eingabetaste f (Inform) return (o
enter) key

Eingang m entrance;
Eingangshalle f entrance hall,
lobby (US)

ein|geben irr vt (Daten etc) to
enter, to key in

eingebildet adj imaginary; (eitel)
arrogant

Eingeborene(r) mf native

ein|gehen irr vi (Sendung, Geld) to
come in, to arrive; (Tier, Pflanze) to
die; (Stoff) to shrink; **auf etw** (akk)
~ to agree to sth; **auf jdn ~** to
respond to sb > vt (Vertrag) to
enter into; (Wette) to make; (Risiko)
to take

eingelegt adj (in Essig) pickled

eingeschaltet adj (switched) on

eingeschlossen adj locked in;
(inklusive) included

ein|gewöhnen vr: **sich ~** to
settle in

ein|gießen irr vt to pour

ein|greifen irr vi to intervene;
Eingriff m intervention;
(Operation) operation

ein|halten irr vt (Versprechen etc)
to keep

einheimisch adj (Produkt,
Mannschaft) local; **Einheimische(r)**
mf local

Einheit f (Geschlossenheit) unity;
(Maß) unit; **einheitlich** adj
uniform

ein|holen vt (Vorsprung aufholen)
to catch up with; (Verspätung) to
make up for; (Rat, Erlaubnis) to ask
for

Einhorn nt unicorn

einhundert num one (o a)
hundred

einig adj (vereint) united; **sich**
(dat) **~ sein** to agree

einige pron pl some; (mehrere)
several > adj some; **nach ~er Zeit**
after some time; **~e hundert Euro**
some hundred euros

einigen vr: **sich ~** to agree (auf
+akk on)

einigermaßen adv fairly, quite;
(leidlich) reasonably

einiges pron something; (ziemlich
viel) quite a bit; (mehreres) a few
things; **es gibt noch ~ zu tun**
there's still a fair bit to do

Einkauf m purchase; **Einkäufe**
(machen) (to do one's) shopping;
ein|kaufen vt to buy > vi to go
shopping; **Einkaufsbummel** m
shopping trip; **Einkaufstasche** f,
Einkaufstüte f shopping bag;
Einkaufswagen m shopping
trolley (Brit) (o cart US);
Einkaufszentrum nt shopping
centre (Brit) (o mall US)

ein|klemmen vt to jam; **er hat**
sich (dat) **den Finger**
eingeklemmt he got his finger
caught

Einkommen (-s, -) nt income

ein|laden irr vt (jdn) to invite; (Gegenstände) to load; **jdn zum Essen ~** to take sb out for a meal; **ich lade dich ein** (bezahle) it's my treat; **Einladung** f invitation

Einlass (-es, Einlässe) m admittance; **~ ab 18 Uhr** doors open at 6 pm; **ein|lassen** irr vr **sich mit jdm/auf etw** (akk) **~** to get involved with sb/sth

ein|leben vr: **sich ~** to settle down

ein|legen vt (Film etc) to put in; (marinieren) to marinate; **eine Pause ~** to take a break

ein|leiten vt to start; (Maßnahmen) to introduce; (Geburt) to induce; **Einleitung** f introduction; (von Geburt) induction

ein|leuchten vi: **jdm ~** to be (o become) clear to sb; **einleuchtend** adj clear

ein|loggen vi (Inform) to log on (o in)

ein|lösen vt (Scheck) to cash; (Gutschein) to redeem; (Versprechen) to keep

einmal adv once; (früher) before; (in Zukunft) some day; (erstens) first; **~ im Jahr** once a year; **noch ~** once more, again; **ich war schon ~ hier** I've been here before; **warst du schon ~ in London?** have you ever been to London?; **nicht ~** not even; **auf ~** suddenly; (gleichzeitig) at once; **einmalig** adj unique; (einmal geschehend) single; (prima) fantastic

ein|mischen vr: **sich ~** to interfere (in +akk with)

Einnahme (-, -n) f (Geld) takings pl; (von Medizin) taking; **ein|nehmen** irr vt (Medizin) to take; (Geld) to take in; (Standpunkt, Raum) to take up; **jdn für sich ~** to win sb over

ein|ordnen vt to put in order; (klassifizieren) to classify; (Akten) to file ▷ vr: **sich ~** (Auto) to get in lane; **sich rechts/links ~** to get into the right/left lane

ein|packen vt to pack (up)

ein|parken vt, vi to park

ein|planen vt to allow for

ein|prägen vt: **sich** (dat) **etw ~** to remember (o memorize) sth

ein|räumen vt (Bücher, Geschirr) to put away; (Schrank) to put things in

ein|reden vt: **jdm/sich etw ~** to talk sb/oneself into (believing) sth

ein|reiben irr vt: **sich mit etw ~** to rub sth into one's skin

ein|reichen vt to hand in; (Antrag) to submit

Einreise f entry; **Einreisebestimmungen** pl entry regulations pl; **Einreiseerlaubnis** f, **Einreisegenehmigung** f entry permit; **ein|reisen** vi to enter (in ein Land a country); **Einreisevisum** nt entry visa

ein|renken vt (Arm, Bein) to set

ein|richten vt (Wohnung) to furnish; (gründen) to establish, to set up; (arrangieren) to arrange ▷ vr: **sich ~** (in Haus) to furnish one's home; (sich vorbereiten) to prepare oneself (auf +akk for); (sich anpassen) to adapt (auf +akk to); **Einrichtung** f (Wohnung) furnishings pl; (öffentliche Anstalt) institution; (Schwimmbad etc) facility

eins num one; **Eins** (-, -en) f one; (Schulnote) ≈ A

einsam adj lonely

ein|sammeln vt to collect

Einsatz m (Teil) insert; (Verwendung) use; (Spieleinsatz) stake; (Risiko) risk; (Mus) entry

ein|schalten vt (Elek) to switch on

ein|schätzen vt to estimate, to assess

ein|schenken vt to pour

ein|schiffen vr: **sich ~** to embark (nach for)

ein|schlafen irr vi to fall asleep, to drop off; **mir ist der Arm eingeschlafen** my arm's gone to sleep

ein|schlagen irr vt (Fenster) to smash; (Zähne, Schädel) to smash in; (Weg, Richtung) to take ▷ vi to hit (in etw akk sth, auf jdn sb); (Blitz) to strike; (Anklang finden) to be a success

ein|schließen irr vt (jdn) to lock in; (Gegenstand) to lock away; (umgeben) to surround; (fig: beinhalten) to include; **einschließlich** adv inclusive ▷ prep +gen including; **von Montag bis ~ Freitag** from Monday up to and including Friday, Monday through Friday (US)

ein|schränken vt to limit, to restrict; (verringern) to cut down on ▷ vr: **sich ~** to cut down (on expenditure)

ein|schreiben irr vr: **sich ~** to register; (Schule) to enrol; **Einschreiben** (-s, -) nt registered letter; **etw per ~ schicken** to send sth by special delivery

ein|schüchtern vt to intimidate

ein|sehen irr vt (verstehen) to see; (Fehler) to recognize; (Akten) to have a look at

einseitig adj one-sided

ein|senden irr vt to send in

ein|setzen vt to put in; (in Amt) to appoint; (Geld) to stake; (verwenden) to use ▷ vi (beginnen) to set in; (Mus) to enter, to come in ▷ vr: **sich ~** to work hard; **sich für jdn/etw ~** to support sb/sth

Einsicht f insight; **zu der**

~ kommen, dass ... to come to realize that ...

ein|sperren vt to lock up

ein|spielen vt (Geld) to bring in

ein|springen vi (aushelfen) to step in (für for)

Einspruch m objection (gegen to)

einspurig adj single-lane

Einstand m (Tennis) deuce

ein|stecken vt to pocket; (Elek: Stecker) to plug in; (Brief) to post, to mail (US); (mitnehmen) to take; (hinnehmen) to swallow

ein|steigen irr vi (in Auto) to get in; (in Bus, Zug, Flugzeug) to get on; (sich beteiligen) to get involved

ein|stellen vt (beenden) to stop; (Geräte) to adjust; (Kamera) to focus; (Sender, Radio) to tune in; (unterstellen) to put; (in Firma) to employ, to take on ▷ vr: **sich auf jdn/etw ~** to adapt to sb/prepare oneself for sth; **Einstellung** f (von Gerät) adjustment; (von Kamera) focusing; (von Arbeiter) taking on; (Meinung) attitude

ein|stürzen vi to collapse

eintägig adj one-day

ein|tauschen vt to exchange (gegen for)

eintausend num one (o a) thousand

ein|teilen vt (in Teile) to divide (up) (in +akk into); (Zeit) to organize

eintönig adj monotonous

Eintopf m stew

ein|tragen irr vt (in eine Liste) to put down, to enter ▷ vr: **sich ~** to put one's name down, to register

ein|treffen irr vi to happen; (ankommen) to arrive

ein|treten irr vi (hineingehen) to enter (in etw akk sth); (in Klub, Partei) to join (in etw akk sth); (sich ereignen) to occur; **~ für** to support; **Eintritt** m admission; **„~ frei"**

"admission free"; **Eintrittskarte** f (entrance) ticket; **Eintrittspreis** m admission charge

einverstanden interj okay, all right ▷ adj: **mit etwas ~ sein** to agree to sth, to accept sth

Einwanderer m, **Einwanderin** f immigrant; **ein|wandern** vi to immigrate

einwandfrei adj perfect, flawless

Einwegflasche f non-returnable bottle

ein|weichen vt to soak

ein|weihen vt (Gebäude) to inaugurate, to open; **jdn in etw** (akk) **~** to let sb in on sth; **Einweihungsparty** f house-warming party

ein|werfen irr vt (Ball, Bemerkung etc) to throw in; (Brief) to post, to mail (US); (Geld) to put in, to insert; (Fenster) to smash

ein|wickeln vt to wrap up; (fig) **jdn ~** to take sb in

Einwohner(in) (-s, -) m(f) inhabitant; **Einwohnermeldeamt** nt registration office for residents

Einwurf m (Öffnung) slot; (Sport) throw-in

Einzahl f singular

ein|zahlen vt to pay in (auf ein Konto -to an account)

Einzel (-s, -) nt (Tennis) singles sing; **Einzelbett** nt single bed; **Einzelfahrschein** m single ticket (Brit), one-way ticket (US); **Einzelgänger(in)** m(f) loner; **Einzelhandel** m retail trade; **Einzelkind** nt only child

einzeln adj individual; (getrennt) separate; (einzig) single; **~e ...** several ..., some ...; **der/die Einzelne** the individual; **im Einzelnen** in detail ▷ adv separately; (verpacken, aufführen) individually; **~ angeben** to specify; **~ eintreten** to enter one

by one

Einzelzimmer nt single room; **Einzelzimmerzuschlag** m single-room supplement

ein|ziehen irr vt: **den Kopf ~** to duck ▷ vi (in ein Haus) to move in

einzig adj only; (einzeln) single; (einzigartig) unique; **kein ~er Fehler** not a single mistake; **das Einzige** the only thing; **der/die Einzige** the only person ▷ adv only; **die ~ richtige Lösung** the only correct solution; **einzigartig** adj unique

Eis (-es, -) nt ice; (Speiseeis) ice-cream; **Eisbahn** f ice(skating) rink; **Eisbär** m polar bear; **Eisbecher** m (ice-cream) sundae; **Eisberg** m iceberg; **Eisbergsalat** m iceberg lettuce; **Eiscafé** nt, **Eisdiele** f ice-cream parlour

Eisen (-s, -) nt iron; **Eisenbahn** f railway (Brit), railroad (US); **eisern** adj iron

eisgekühlt adj chilled; **Eishockey** nt ice hockey; **Eiskaffee** m iced coffee; **eiskalt** adj ice-cold; (Temperatur) freezing; **Eiskunstlauf** m figure skating; **eis|laufen** irr vi to skate; **Eisschokolade** f iced chocolate; **Eisschrank** m fridge, ice-box (US); **Eistee** m iced tea; **Eiswürfel** m ice cube; **Eiszapfen** m icicle

eitel adj vain

Eiter (-s) m pus

Eiweiß (-es, -e) nt egg white; (Chem, Bio) protein

ekelhaft adj, **ek(e)lig** adj disgusting, revolting; **ekeln** vr: **sich ~** to be disgusted (vor +dat at)

EKG (-s, -s) nt abk = **Elektrokardiogramm** ECG

Ekzem (-s, -e) nt (Med) eczema

elastisch adj elastic

Elch (-(e)s, -e) m elk; (nordamerikanischer) moose

Elefant m elephant

elegant adj elegant

Elektriker(in) (-s, -) m(f) electrician; **elektrisch** adj electric; **Elektrizität** f electricity; **Elektroauto** nt electric car; **Elektrogerät** nt electrical appliance; **Elektrogeschäft** nt electrical shop; **Elektroherd** m electric cooker; **Elektromotor** m electric motor; **Elektronik** f electronics sing; **elektronisch** adj electronic; **Elektrorasierer** (-s, -) m electric razor

Element (-s, -e) nt element

elend adj miserable; **Elend** (-(e)s) nt misery

elf num eleven; **Elf** (-, -en) f (Sport) eleven

Elfenbein nt ivory

Elfmeter m (Sport) penalty (kick)

elfte(r, s) adj eleventh; siehe auch **dritte**

Ell(en)bogen m elbow

Elster (-, -n) f magpie

Eltern pl parents pl; **Elternteil** m parent

EM f abk = **Europameisterschaft** European Championship(s)

E-Mail (-, -s) f (Inform) e-mail; **jdm eine ~ schicken** to e-mail sb, to send sb an e-mail; **jdm etwas per ~ schicken** to e-mail sth to sb; **E-Mail-Adresse** f e-mail address; **e-mailen** vt to e-mail

Emoticon (-s, -s) nt emoticon

emotional adj emotional

empfahl imperf von **empfehlen**

empfand imperf von **empfinden**

Empfang (-(e)s, Empfänge) m reception; (Erhalten) receipt; **in ~ nehmen** to receive; **empfangen** (empfing, empfangen) vt to receive; **Empfänger(in)** (-s, -) m(f) recipient; (Adressat) addressee ▷ m

(Tech) receiver; **Empfängnisverhütung** f contraception; **Empfangshalle** f reception area

empfehlen (empfahl, empfohlen) vt to recommend; **Empfehlung** f recommendation

empfinden (empfand, empfunden) vt to feel; **empfindlich** adj (Mensch) sensitive; (Stelle) sore; (reizbar) touchy; (Material) delicate

empfing imperf von **empfangen**

empfohlen pp von **empfehlen**

empfunden pp von **empfinden**

empört adj indignant (über +akk at)

Ende (-s, -n) nt end; (Film, Roman) ending; **am ~** at the end; (schließlich) in the end; **~ Mai** at the end of May; **~ der Achtzigerjahre** in the late eighties; **sie ist ~ zwanzig** she's in her late twenties; **zu ~** over, finished; **enden** vi to end; **der Zug endet hier** this service (o train) terminates here; **endgültig** adj final; (Beweis) conclusive

Endivie f endive

endlich adv at last, finally; (am Ende) eventually; **Endspiel** nt final; (Endrunde) finals pl; **Endstation** f terminus; **Endung** f ending

Energie f energy; **~ sparend** energy-saving; **Energiebedarf** m energy requirement; **Energieverbrauch** m energy consumption

energisch adj (entschlossen) forceful

eng adj narrow; (Kleidung) tight; (fig: Freundschaft, Verhältnis) close; **das wird ~** (fam: zeitlich) we're running out of time, it's getting tight ▷ adv: **~ befreundet sein** to be close friends

engagieren vt to engage ▷ vr: **sich ~** to commit oneself, to be committed (für to)

Engel (-s, -) m angel

England nt England; **Engländer(in)** (-s, -) m(f) Englishman/ -woman; **die ~** pl the English pl; **englisch** adj English; (Gastr) rare; **Englisch** nt English; **ins ~e übersetzen** to translate into English

Enkel (-s, -) m grandson; **Enkelin** f granddaughter

enorm adj enormous; (fig) tremendous

Entbindung f (Med) delivery

entdecken vt to discover; **Entdeckung** f discovery

Ente (-, -n) f duck

Enter-Taste f (Inform) enter (o return) key

entfernen vt to remove; (Inform) to delete ▷ vr: **sich ~** to go away; **entfernt** adj distant; **15 km von X ~** 15 km away from X; **20 km voneinander ~** 20 km apart; **Entfernung** f distance; **aus der ~** from a distance

entführen vt to kidnap; **Entführer(in)** m(f) kidnapper; **Entführung** f kidnapping

entgegen prep +dat contrary to ▷ adv towards; **dem Wind ~** against the wind; **entgegengesetzt** adj (Richtung) opposite; (Meinung) opposing; **entgegen|kommen** irr vi: **jdm ~** to come to meet sb; (fig) to accommodate sb; **entgegenkommend** adj (Verkehr) oncoming; (fig) obliging

entgegnen vt to reply (auf +akk to)

entgehen irr vi: **jdm ~** to escape sb's notice; **sich** (dat) **etw ~ lassen** to miss sth

entgleisen vi (Eisenb) to be derailed; (fig: Mensch) to misbehave

Enthaarungscreme f hair remover

enthalten irr vt (Behälter) to contain; (Preis) to include ▷ vr: **sich ~** to abstain (gen from)

entkoffeiniert adj decaffeinated

entkommen irr vi to escape

entkorken vt to uncork

entlang prep +akk o dat **~ dem Fluss, den Fluss ~** along the river; **entlang|gehen** irr vi to walk along

entlassen irr vt (Patient) to discharge; (Arbeiter) to dismiss

entlasten vt: **jdm ~** (Arbeit abnehmen) to relieve sb of some of his/her work

entmutigen vt to discourage

entnehmen irr vt to take (dat from)

entrahmt adj (Milch) skimmed

entschädigen vt to compensate; **Entschädigung** f compensation

entscheiden irr vt, vi to decide ▷ vr: **sich ~** to decide; **sich für/gegen etw ~** to decide on/against sth; **wir haben uns entschieden, nicht zu gehen** we decided not to go; **das entscheidet sich morgen** that'll be decided tomorrow; **entscheidend** adj decisive; (Stimme) casting; (Frage, Problem) crucial; **Entscheidung** f decision

entschließen irr vr: **sich ~** to decide (zu, für on), to make up one's mind; **Entschluss** m decision

entschuldigen vt to excuse ▷ vr: **sich ~** to apologize; **sich bei jdm für etw ~** to apologize to sb for sth ▷ vi: **entschuldige!, ~ Sie!** (vor einer Frage) excuse me; (Verzeihung!) (I'm) sorry, excuse me (US); **Entschuldigung** f apology;

(*Grund*) excuse: **jdn um ~ bitten** to apologize to sb; **~!** (*bei Zusammenstoß*) (I'm) sorry, excuse me (*US*); (*vor einer Frage*) excuse me; (*wenn man etw nicht verstanden hat*) (I beg your) pardon?

entsetzlich *adj* dreadful, appalling

entsorgen *vt* to dispose of

entspannen *vt* (*Körper*) to relax; (*Pol: Lage*) to ease ▷ *vr:* **sich ~** to relax; (*fam*) to chill out; **Entspannung** *f* relaxation

entsprechen *irr vi* +*dat* to correspond to; (*Anforderungen, Wünschen etc*) to comply with; **entsprechend** *adj* appropriate ▷ *adv* accordingly ▷ *prep* +*dat* according to, in accordance with

entstehen *vi* (*Schwierigkeiten*) to arise; (*gebaut werden*) to be built; (*hergestellt werden*) to be created

enttäuschen *vt* to disappoint; **Enttäuschung** *f* disappointment

entweder *conj:* **~ ... oder ...** either ... or ...; **~ oder!** take it or leave it

entwerfen *irr vt* (*Möbel, Kleider*) to design; (*Plan, Vertrag*) to draft

entwerten *vt* to devalue; (*Fahrschein*) to cancel; **Entwerter** (-s, -) *m* ticket-cancelling machine

entwickeln *vt* (*a. Foto*) to develop; (*Mut, Energie*) to show, to display ▷ *vr:* **sich ~** to develop; **Entwicklung** *f* development; (*Foto*) developing; **Entwicklungshelfer(in)** (-s, -) *m(f)* development worker; **Entwicklungsland** *nt* developing country

Entwurf *m* outline; (*Design*) design; (*Vertragsentwurf*) draft

entzückend *adj* delightful, charming

Entzug *m* withdrawal; (*Behandlung*) detox;

Entzugserscheinung *f* withdrawal symptom

entzünden *vr:* **sich ~** to catch fire; (*Med*) to become inflamed; **Entzündung** *f* (*Med*) inflammation

Epidemie (-, -*n*) *f* epidemic

Epilepsie (-, -*n*) *f* epilepsy

epilieren *vt* to remove body hair, to depilate; **Epiliergerät** *nt* Ladyshave®

er *pron* (*Person*) he; (*Sache*) it; **er ist's** it's him; **wo ist mein Mantel? — ~ ist ...** where's my coat? — it's ...

Erbe (-*n*, -*n*) *m* heir ▷ (-*s*) *nt* inheritance; (*fig*) heritage; **erben** *vt* to inherit; **Erbin** *f* heiress; **erblich** *adj* hereditary

erblicken *vt* to catch sight of

erbrechen *irr vt* to vomit ▷ *vr:* **sich ~** to vomit; **Erbrechen** *nt* vomiting

Erbschaft *f* inheritance

Erbse (-, -*n*) *f* pea

Erdapfel *m* potato; **Erdbeben** *nt* earthquake; **Erdbeere** *f* strawberry; **Erde** (-, -*n*) *f* (*Planet*) earth; (*Boden*) ground; **Erdgas** *nt* natural gas; **Erdgeschoss** *nt* ground floor (*Brit*), first floor (*US*); **Erdkunde** *f* geography; **Erdnuss** *f* peanut; **Erdöl** *nt* (mineral) oil; **Erdrutsch** *m* landslide; **Erdteil** *m* continent

ereignen *vr:* **sich ~** to happen, to take place; **Ereignis** *nt* event

erfahren *irr vt* to learn, to find out; (*erleben*) to experience ▷ *adj* experienced; **Erfahrung** *f* experience

erfinden *irr vt* to invent; **erfinderisch** *adj* inventive, creative; **Erfindung** *f* invention

Erfolg (-(*e*)*s*, -*e*) *m* success; (*Folge*) result; **~ versprechend** promising; **viel ~!** good luck;

erfolglos adj unsuccessful; **erfolgreich** adj successful

erforderlich adj necessary

erforschen vt to explore; (untersuchen) investigate

erfreulich adj pleasing, pleasant; (Nachricht) good; **erfreulicherweise** adv fortunately

erfrieren irr vi to freeze to death; (Pflanzen) to be killed by frost

Erfrischung f refreshment

erfüllen vt (Raum) to fill; (Bitte, Wunsch etc) to fulfil ▷ vr: **sich ~** to come true

ergänzen vt (hinzufügen) to add; (vervollständigen) to complete ▷ vr: **sich ~** to complement one another; **Ergänzung** f completion; (Zusatz) supplement

ergeben irr vt (Betrag) to come to; (zum Ergebnis haben) to result in ▷ irr vr: **sich ~** to surrender; (folgen) to result (aus from) ▷ adj devoted; (demütig) humble

Ergebnis nt result

ergreifen irr vt to seize; (Beruf) to take up; (Maßnahme, Gelegenheit) to take; (rühren) to move

erhalten irr vt (bekommen) to receive; (bewahren) to preserve; **gut ~ sein** to be in good condition; **erhältlich** adj available

erheblich adj considerable

erhitzen vt to heat (up)

erhöhen vt to raise; (verstärken) to increase ▷ vr: **sich ~** to increase

erholen vr: **sich ~** to recover; (sich ausruhen) to have a rest; **erholsam** adj restful; **Erholung** f recovery; (Entspannung) relaxation, rest

erinnern vt to remind (an +akk of) ▷ vr: **sich ~** to remember (an etw akk sth); **Erinnerung** f memory; (Andenken) souvenir;

(Mahnung) reminder

erkälten vr: **sich ~** to catch a cold; **erkältet** adj: (stark) **~ sein** to have a (bad) cold; **Erkältung** f cold

erkennen irr vt to recognize; (sehen, verstehen) to see; **~, dass ...** to realize that ...; **erkenntlich** adj: **sich ~ zeigen** to show one's appreciation

Erker (-s, -) m bay

erklären vt to explain; (kundtun) to declare; **Erklärung** f explanation; (Aussage) declaration

erkundigen vr: **sich ~** to enquire (nach about)

erlauben vt to allow, to permit; **jdm ~, etw zu tun** to allow (o permit) sb to do sth; **sich** (dat) **etw ~** to permit oneself sth; **~ Sie(, dass ich rauche)?** do you mind (if I smoke)?; **was ~ Sie sich?** what do you think you're doing?; **Erlaubnis** f permission

Erläuterung f explanation; (zu Text) comment

erleben vt to experience; (schöne Tage etc) to have; (Schlimmes) to go through; (miterleben) to witness; (noch miterleben) to live to see; **Erlebnis** nt experience

erledigen vt (Angelegenheit, Aufgabe) to deal with; (fam: ruinieren) to finish; **erledigt** adj (beendet) finished; (gelöst) dealt with; (fam: erschöpft) whacked, knackered (Brit)

erleichtert adj relieved

Erlös (-es, -e) m proceeds pl

ermahnen vt (warnend) to warn

ermäßigt adj reduced; **Ermäßigung** f reduction

ermitteln vt to find out; (Täter) to trace ▷ vi (Jur) to investigate

ermöglichen vt to make possible (dat for)

ermorden vt to murder

ermüdend adj tiring

ermutigen vt to encourage

ernähren vt to feed; (Familie) to support ▷ vr: **sich ~** to support oneself; **sich ~ von** to live on; **Ernährung** f (Essen) food; **Ernährungsberater(in)** m(f) nutritional (o dietary) adviser

erneuern vt to renew; (restaurieren) to restore; (renovieren) to renovate; (auswechseln) to replace

ernst adj serious ▷ adv: **jdn/etw ~ nehmen** take sb/sth seriously; **Ernst** (-es) m seriousness; **das ist mein ~** I'm quite serious; **im ~?** seriously?; **ernsthaft** adj serious ▷ adv seriously

Ernte (-, -n) f harvest; **Erntedankfest** nt harvest festival (Brit), Thanksgiving (Day) (US: 4. Donnerstag im November); **ernten** vt to harvest; (Lob etc) to earn

erobern vt to conquer

eröffnen vt to open; **Eröffnung** f opening

erogen adj erogenous

erotisch adj erotic

erpressen vt (jdn) to blackmail; (Geld etc) to extort; **Erpressung** f blackmail; (von Geld) extortion

erraten irr vt to guess

erregen vt to excite; (sexuell) to arouse; (ärgern) to annoy; (hervorrufen) to arouse ▷ vr: **sich ~** to get worked up; **Erreger** (-s, -) m (Med) germ; (Virus) virus

erreichbar adj: **~ sein** to be within reach; (Person) to be available; **das Stadtzentrum ist zu Fuß/mit dem Wagen leicht ~** the city centre is within easy walking/driving distance; **erreichen** vt to reach; (Zug etc) to catch

Ersatz (-es) m replacement; (auf

Zeit) substitute; (Ausgleich) compensation; **Ersatzreifen** m (Auto) spare tyre; **Ersatzteil** nt spare (part)

erscheinen irr vi to appear; (wirken) to seem

erschöpft adj exhausted; **Erschöpfung** f exhaustion

erschrecken vt to frighten ▷ (erschrak, erschrocken) vi to get a fright; **erschreckend** adj alarming; **erschrocken** adj frightened

erschwinglich adj affordable

ersetzen vt to replace; (Auslagen) to reimburse

◯ SCHLÜSSELWORT

erst adv **1** first; **mach erst mal die Arbeit fertig** finish your work first; **wenn du das erst mal hinter dir hast** once you've got that behind you

2 (nicht früher als, nur) only; (nicht bis) not till; **erst gestern** only yesterday; **erst morgen** not until tomorrow; **erst als** only when, not until; **wir fahren erst später** we're not going until later; **er ist (gerade) erst angekommen** he's only just arrived

3 **wäre er doch erst zurück!** if only he were back!

erstatten vt (Kosten) to refund; **Bericht ~** to report (über +akk on); **Anzeige gegen jdn ~** to report sb to the police

erstaunlich adj astonishing; **erstaunt** adj surprised

erstbeste(r, s) adj: **das ~ Hotel** any old hotel; **der Erstbeste** just anyone

erste(r, s) adj first; siehe auch **dritte**; **zum ~n Mal** for the first time; **er wurde Erster** he came

first; **auf den ~n Blick** at first sight
erstens adv first(ly), in the first place
ersticken vi (Mensch) to suffocate; **in Arbeit ~** to be snowed under with work
erstklassig adj first-class;
erstmals adv for the first time
erstrecken vr: **sich ~** to extend, to stretch (auf +akk to; über +akk over)
ertappen vt to catch
erteilen vt (Rat, Erlaubnis) to give
Ertrag (-(e)s, Erträge) m yield; (Gewinn) proceeds pl; **ertragen** irr vt (Schmerzen) to bear, to stand; (dulden) to put up with; **erträglich** adj bearable; (nicht zu schlecht) tolerable
ertrinken irr vi to drown
erwachsen adj grown-up; **~ werden** to grow up; **Erwachsene(r)** mf adult, grown-up
erwähnen vt to mention
erwarten vt to expect; (warten auf) to wait for; **ich kann den Sommer kaum ~** I can hardly wait for the summer
erwerbstätig adj employed
erwidern vt to reply; (Gruß, Besuch) to return
erwischen vt (fam) to catch (bei etw doing sth)
erwünscht adj desired; (willkommen) welcome
Erz (-es, -e) nt ore
erzählen vt to tell (jdm etw sb sth); **Erzählung** f story, tale
erzeugen vt to produce; (Strom) to generate; **Erzeugnis** nt product
erziehen irr vt to bring up; (geistig) to educate; (Tier) to train; **Erzieher(in)** (-s, -) m(f) educator; (Kindergarten) (nursery school)

teacher; **Erziehung** f upbringing; (Bildung) education
es pron (Sache, im Nom und Akk) it; (Baby, Tier) he/she; **ich bin ~** it's me; **~ ist kalt** it's cold; **~ gibt ...** there is .../there are ...; **ich hoffe ~** I hope so; **ich kann ~** I can do it
Escape-Taste f (Inform) escape key
Esel (-s, -) m donkey
Espresso (-s, -) m espresso
essbar adj edible; **essen** (aß, gegessen) vt, vi to eat; **zu Mittag/Abend ~** to have lunch/dinner; **was gibt's zu ~?** what's for lunch/dinner?; **~ gehen** to eat out; **gegessen sein** (fig, fam) to be history; **Essen** (-s, -) nt (Mahlzeit) meal; (Nahrung) food
Essig (-s, -e) m vinegar
Esslöffel m dessert spoon; **Esszimmer** nt dining room
Estland nt Estonia
Etage (-, -n) f floor, storey; **in** (o **auf**) **der ersten ~** on the first (Brit) (o second (US)) floor; **Etagenbett** nt bunk bed
Etappe (-, -n) f stage
ethnisch adj ethnic
Etikett (-(e)s, -e) nt label
etliche pron pl several, quite a few; **etliches** pron quite a lot
etwa adv (ungefähr) about; (vielleicht) perhaps; (beispielsweise) for instance
etwas pron something; (verneinend, fragend) anything; (ein wenig) a little; **~ Neues** something/anything new; **~ zu essen** something to eat; **~ Salz** some salt; **wenn ich noch ~ tun kann ...** if I can do anything else ...
▷ adv a bit, a little; **~ mehr** a little more
EU (-) f abk = **Europäische Union** EU
euch pron akk, dat von **ihr**; you, (to)

you; **~ (selbst)** (reflexiv) yourselves; **wo kann ich ~ treffen?** where can I meet you?; **sie schickt es ~** she'll send it to you; **ein Freund von ~** a friend of yours; **setzt ~ bitte** please sit down; **habt ihr ~ amüsiert?** did you enjoy yourselves?

euer pron (adjektivisch) your; **~ David** (am Briefende) Yours, David ▷ pron gen von **ihr**; of you; **euere(r, s)** pron siehe **eure**

Eule (-, -n) f owl

eure(r, s) pron (substantivisch) yours; **das ist ~** that's yours; **euretwegen** adv (wegen euch) because of you; (euch zuliebe) for your sake; (um euch) about you

Euro (-, -) m (Währung) euro; **Eurocent** m eurocent; **Eurocity** (-(s), -s) m, **Eurocityzug** m European Intercity train; **Europa** (-s) nt Europe; **Europäer(in)** (-s, -) m(f) European; **europäisch** adj European; **Europäische Union** European Union; **Europameister(in)** m(f) European champion; (Mannschaft) European champions pl; **Europaparlament** nt European Parliament

Euter (-s, -) nt udder

evangelisch adj Protestant

eventuell adj possible ▷ adv possibly, perhaps

ewig adj eternal; **er hat ~ gebraucht** it took him ages; **Ewigkeit** f eternity

Ex mf ex

Ex- in zW ex-, former; **~frau** ex-wife; **~freund** m ex-boyfriend; **~minister** former minister

exakt adj precise

Examen (-s, -) nt exam

Exemplar (-s, -e) nt specimen; (Buch) copy

Exil (-s, -e) nt exile

Existenz f existence; (Unterhalt) livelihood, living; **existieren** vi to exist

exklusiv adj exclusive; **exklusive** adv, prep +gen excluding

exotisch adj exotic

Experte (-n, -n) m, **Expertin** f expert

explodieren vi to explode; **Explosion** f explosion

Export (-(e)s, -e) m export; **exportieren** vt to export

Express (-es) m, **Expresszug** m express (train)

extra adj inv (fam: gesondert) separate; (zusätzlich) extra ▷ adv (gesondert) separately; (speziell) specially; (absichtlich) on purpose; **Extra** (-s, -s) nt extra

extrem adj extreme ▷ adv extremely; **~ kalt** extremely cold

exzellent adj excellent

Eyeliner (-s, -) m eyeliner

f

fabelhaft adj fabulous, marvellous

Fabrik f factory

Fach (-(e)s, Fächer) nt compartment; (Schulfach, Sachgebiet) subject; **Facharzt** m, **Fachärztin** f specialist; **Fachausdruck** (-s, Fachausdrücke) m technical term

Fächer (-s, -) m fan

Fachfrau f specialist, expert; **Fachmann** (-leute) m specialist, expert; **Fachwerkhaus** nt half-timbered house

Fackel (-, -n) f torch

fad(e) adj (Essen) bland; (langweilig) dull

Faden (-s, Fäden) m thread

fähig adj capable (zu, gen of); **Fähigkeit** f ability

Fahndung f search

Fahne (-, -n) f flag

Fahrausweis m ticket

Fahrbahn f road; (Spur) lane

Fähre (-, -n) f ferry

fahren (fuhr, gefahren) vt to drive; (Rad) to ride; (befördern) to drive, to take; **50 km/h ~** to drive at (o do) 50 kph ▷ vi (sich bewegen) to go; (Autofahrer) to drive; (Schiff) to sail; (abfahren) to leave; **mit dem Auto/Zug ~** to go by car/train; **rechts ~!** keep to the right; **Fahrer(in)** (-s, -) m(f) driver; **Fahrerairbag** m driver airbag; **Fahrerflucht** f: **~ begehen** to fail to stop after an accident; **Fahrersitz** m driver's seat

Fahrgast m passenger; **Fahrgeld** nt fare; **Fahrgemeinschaft** f car pool; **Fahrkarte** f ticket; **Fahrkartenautomat** m ticket machine; **Fahrkartenschalter** m ticket office

fahrlässig adj negligent

Fahrlehrer(in) m(f) driving instructor; **Fahrplan** m timetable; **Fahrplanauszug** m individual timetable; **fahrplanmäßig** adj (Eisenb) scheduled; **Fahrpreis** m fare; **Fahrpreisermäßigung** f fare reduction; **Fahrrad** nt bicycle; **Fahrradschlauch** m bicycle tube; **Fahrradschloss** nt bicycle lock; **Fahrradverleih** m cycle hire (Brit) (o rental (US)); **Fahrradweg** m cycle path; **Fahrschein** m ticket; **Fahrscheinautomat** m ticket machine; **Fahrscheinentwerter** m ticket-cancelling machine; **Fahrschule** f driving school; **Fahrschüler(in)** m(f) learner (driver) (Brit), student driver (US); **Fahrspur** f lane; **Fahrstreifen** m lane; **Fahrstuhl** m lift (Brit), elevator (US)

Fahrt (-, -en) f journey; (kurz) trip; (Auto) drive; **auf der ~ nach London** on the way to London; **nach drei Stunden ~** after travelling for three hours; **gute ~!** have a good trip; **Fahrtkosten** pl travelling expenses pl; **Fahrtrichtung** f direction of travel

fahrtüchtig f (Person) fit to drive; (Fahrzeug) roadworthy

Fahrtunterbrechung f break in the journey, stop

Fahrverbot nt: **~ erhalten/ haben** to be banned from driving; **Fahrzeug** nt vehicle; **Fahrzeugbrief** m (vehicle) registration document; **Fahrzeughalter(in)** m(f) registered owner; **Fahrzeugpapiere** pl vehicle documents pl

fair adj fair

Fakultät f faculty

Falke (-n, -n) m falcon

Fall (-(e)s, Fälle) m (Sturz) fall; (Sachverhalt, juristisch) case; **auf jeden ~, auf alle Fälle** in any case; (bestimmt) definitely; **auf keinen ~** on no account; **für den ~, dass ...** in case ...

Falle (-, -n) f trap

fallen (fiel, gefallen) vi to fall; **etw ~ lassen** to drop sth

fällig adj due

falls adv if; (für den Fall, dass) in case

Fallschirm m parachute; **Fallschirmspringen** nt parachuting, parachute jumping; **Fallschirmspringer(in)** m(f) parachutist

falsch adj (unrichtig) wrong; (unehrlich, unecht) false; (Schmuck) fake; **~ verbunden** sorry, wrong number; **fälschen** vt to forge; **Falschfahrer(in)** m(f) person driving the wrong way on the motorway; **Falschgeld** nt counterfeit money; **Fälschung** f forgery, fake

Faltblatt nt leaflet

Falte (-, -n) f (Knick) fold; (Haut) wrinkle; (Rock) pleat; (Bügel) crease; **falten** vt to fold; **faltig** adj (zerknittert) creased; (Haut, Gesicht) wrinkled

Familie f family; **Familienangehörige(r)** m(f) family member; **Familienname** m surname; **Familienstand** m marital status

Fan (-s, -s) m fan

fand imperf von **finden**

fangen (fing, gefangen) vt to catch ▷ vr: **sich ~** (nicht fallen) to steady oneself; (fig) to compose oneself

Fantasie f imagination

fantastisch adj fantastic

Farbdrucker m colour printer; **Farbe** (-, -n) f colour; (zum Malen etc) paint; (für Stoff) dye; **färben** vt to colour; (Stoff, Haar) to dye; **Farbfernsehen** nt colour television; **Farbfilm** m colour film; **farbig** adj coloured; **Farbkopierer** m colour copier; **farblos** adj colourless; **Farbstoff** m dye; (für Lebensmittel) colouring

Farn (-(e)s, -e) m fern

Fasan (-(e)s, -e(n)) m pheasant

Fasching (-s, -e) m carnival, Mardi Gras (US); **Faschingsdienstag** (-s, -e) m Shrove Tuesday, Mardi Gras (US)

Faschismus m fascism

Faser (-, -n) f fibre

Fass (-es, Fässer) nt barrel; (Öl) drum

fassen vt (ergreifen) to grasp; (enthalten) to hold; (Entschluss) to take; (verstehen) to understand; **nicht zu ~!** unbelievable ▷ vr: **sich ~** to compose oneself; **Fassung** f (Umrahmung) mount; (Brille) frame; (Lampe) socket; (Wortlaut) version; (Beherrschung) composure; **jdn aus der ~ bringen**

to throw sb; **die ~ verlieren** to lose one's cool
fast adv almost, nearly
fasten vi to fast; **Fastenzeit** f: **die ~** (christlich) Lent; (muslimisch) Ramadan
Fast Food (-s) nt fast food
Fastnacht f (Fasching) carnival
fatal adj (verhängnisvoll) disastrous; (peinlich) embarrassing
faul adj (Obst, Gemüse) rotten; (Mensch) lazy; (Ausreden) lame; **faulen** vi to rot
faulenzen vi to do nothing, to hang around; **Faulheit** f laziness
faulig adj rotten; (Geruch, Geschmack) foul
Faust (-, Fäuste) f fist; **Fausthandschuh** m mitten
Fax (-, -(e)) nt fax; **faxen** vi, vt to fax; **Faxgerät** nt fax machine; **Faxnummer** f fax number
FCKW (-, -s) nt abk = **Fluorchlorkohlenwasserstoff** CFC
Februar (-(s), -e) m February; siehe auch **Juni**
Fechten nt fencing
Feder (-, -n) f feather; (Schreibfeder) (pen-)nib; (Tech) spring; **Federball** m (Ball) shuttlecock; (Spiel) badminton; **Federung** f suspension
Fee (-, -n) f fairy
fegen vi, vt to sweep
fehl adj: **~ am Platz** (o Ort) out of place
fehlen vi (abwesend sein) to be absent; **etw fehlt jdm** sb lacks sth; **was fehlt ihm?** what's wrong with him?; **du fehlst mir** I miss you; **es fehlt an ...** there's no...
Fehler (-s, -) m mistake, error; (Mangel, Schwäche) fault; **Fehlerbeseitigung** f (Inform) debugging; **Fehlermeldung** f (Inform) error message

Fehlzündung f (Auto) misfire
Feier (-, -n) f celebration; (Party) party; **Feierabend** m end of the working day; **~ haben** to finish work; **nach ~** after work; **feierlich** adj solemn; **feiern** vt, vi to celebrate, to have a party; **Feiertag** m holiday; **gesetzlicher ~** public holiday
feig(e) adj cowardly
Feige (-, -n) f fig
Feigling m coward
Feile (-, -n) f file
fein adj fine; (vornehm) refined; **~!** great!; **das schmeckt ~** that tastes delicious
Feind(in) (-(e)s, -e) m(f) enemy; **feindlich** adj hostile
Feinkost (-) f delicacies pl; **Feinkostladen** m delicatessen; **Feinschmecker(in)** (-s, -) m(f) gourmet; **Feinstaub** m particulate matter; **Feinwaschmittel** nt washing powder for delicate fabrics
Feld (-(e)s, -er) nt field; (Schach) square; (Sport) pitch; **Feldsalat** m lamb's lettuce; **Feldweg** m path across the fields
Felge (-, -n) f (wheel) rim
Fell (-(e)s, -e) nt fur; (von Schaf) fleece
Fels (-en, -en) m, **Felsen** (-s, -) m rock; (Klippe) cliff; **felsig** adj rocky
feminin adj feminine; **Femininum** (-s, Feminina) nt (Ling) feminine noun
feministisch adj feminist
Fenchel (-s, -) m fennel
Fenster (-s, -) nt window; **Fensterbrett** nt windowsill; **Fensterladen** m shutter; **Fensterplatz** m windowseat; **Fensterscheibe** f windowpane
Ferien pl holidays pl (Brit), vacation sing (US); **~ haben/ machen** to be/go on holiday (Brit)

(o vacation (US)); **Ferienhaus** nt holiday (Brit) (o vacation (US)) home; **Ferienkurs** m holiday (Brit) (o vacation (US)) course; **Ferienlager** nt holiday camp (Brit), vacation camp (US); (für Kinder im Sommer) summer camp; **Ferienort** m holiday (Brit) (o vacation (US)) resort; **Ferienwohnung** f holiday flat (Brit), vacation apartment (US)

Ferkel (-s, -) nt piglet

fern adj distant, far-off; **von ~** from a distance; **Fernabfrage** f remote-control access; **Fernbedienung** f remote control; **Ferne** f distance; **aus der ~** from a distance

ferner adj, adv further; (außerdem) besides

Fernflug m long-distance flight; **Ferngespräch** nt long-distance call; **ferngesteuert** adj remote-controlled; **Fernglas** nt binoculars pl; **Fernlicht** nt full beam (Brit), high beam (US)

Fernsehapparat m TV (set); **fern|sehen** irr vi to watch television; **Fernsehen** nt television; **im ~** on television; **Fernseher** m TV (set); **Fernsehkanal** m TV channel; **Fernsehprogramm** nt (Sendung) TV programme; (Zeitschrift) TV guide; **Fernsehserie** f TV series sing; **Fernsehturm** m TV tower; **Fernsehzeitschrift** f TV guide

Fernstraße f major road; **Ferntourismus** m long-haul tourism; **Fernverkehr** m long-distance traffic

Ferse (-, -n) f heel

fertig adj (bereit) ready; (beendet) finished; (gebrauchsfertig) ready-made; **~ machen** (beenden) to finish; **sich ~ machen** to get ready; **mit etw ~ werden** to be

able to cope with sth; **auf die Plätze, ~, los!** on your marks, get set, go!; **Fertiggericht** nt ready meal; **fertig|machen** vt (jdn kritisieren) to give sb hell; (jdn zur Verzweiflung bringen) to drive sb mad; (jdn deprimieren) to get sb down

fest adj firm; (Nahrung) solid; (Gehalt) regular; (Schuhe) sturdy; (Schlaf) sound

Fest (-(e)s, -e) nt party; (Rel) festival

Festbetrag m fixed amount

fest|binden irr vt to tie (an +dat to); **fest|halten** irr vt to hold onto ▷ vr: **sich ~** to hold on (an +dat to)

Festiger (-s, -) m setting lotion

Festival (-s, -s) nt festival

Festland nt mainland; **das europäische ~** the (European) continent

fest|legen vt to fix ▷ vr: **sich ~** to commit oneself

festlich adj festive

fest|machen vt to fasten; (Termin etc) to fix; **fest|nehmen** irr vt to arrest; **Festnetz** nt (Tel) landline; **Festplatte** f (Inform) hard disk

fest|setzen vt to fix

Festspiele pl festival sing

fest|stehen irr vi to be fixed

fest|stellen vt to establish; (sagen) to remark

Feststelltaste f shift lock

Festung f fortress

Festzelt nt marquee

Fete (-, -n) f party

fett adj (dick) fat; (Essen etc) greasy; (Schrift) bold; **Fett** (-(e)s, -e) nt fat; (Tech) grease; **fettarm** adj low-fat; **fettig** adj fatty; (schmierig) greasy

feucht adj damp; (Luft) humid; **Feuchtigkeit** f dampness;

(*Luftfeuchtigkeit*) humidity;
Feuchtigkeitscreme f
moisturizing cream
Feuer (-s, -) nt fire; **haben Sie ~?**
have you got a light?; **Feueralarm**
m fire alarm; **feuerfest** adj
fireproof; **Feuerlöscher** (-s, -) m
fire extinguisher; **Feuermelder**
(-s, -) m fire alarm; **Feuertreppe**
f fire escape; **Feuerwehr** (-, -en) f
fire brigade; **Feuerwehrfrau** f
firewoman, fire fighter;
Feuerwehrmann m fireman, fire
fighter; **Feuerwerk** nt
fireworks pl; **Feuerzeug** nt
(cigarette) lighter
Fichte (-, -n) f spruce
ficken vt, vi (vulg) to fuck
Fieber (-s, -) nt temperature,
fever; **~ haben** to have a high
temperature; **Fieber-
thermometer** nt
thermometer
fiel imperf von **fallen**
fies adj (fam) nasty
Figur (-, -en) f figure; (im Schach)
piece
Filet (-s, -s) nt fillet; **filetieren**
vt to fillet; **Filetsteak** nt fillet
steak
Filiale (-, -n) f (Comm) branch
Film (-(e)s, -e) m film, movie;
filmen vt, vi to film
Filter (-s, -) m filter; **Filterkaffee**
m filter coffee; **filtern** vt to
filter; **Filterpapier** nt filter
paper
Filz (-es, -e) m felt; **Filzschreiber**
m, **Filzstift** m felt(-tip) pen,
felt-tip
Finale (-s, -s) nt (Sport) final
Finanzamt nt tax office;
finanziell adj financial;
finanzieren vt to finance
finden (fand, gefunden) vt to find;
(*meinen*) to think; **ich finde nichts
dabei, wenn ...** I don't see what's

wrong if ...; **ich finde es
gut/schlecht** I like/don't like it
▷ vr: **es fanden sich nur wenige
Helfer** there were only a few
helpers
fing imperf von **fangen**
Finger (-s, -) m finger;
Fingerabdruck m fingerprint;
Fingerhandschuh m glove;
Fingernagel m fingernail
Fink (-en, -en) m finch
Finne (-n, -n) m, **Finnin** f Finn,
Finnish man/woman; **finnisch**
adj Finnish; **Finnisch** nt
Finnish; **Finnland** nt Finland
finster adj dark; (verdächtig)
dubious; (verdrossen) grim;
(*Gedanke*) dark; **Finsternis** f
darkness
Firewall (-, -s) f (Inform) firewall
Firma (-, Firmen) f firm
Fisch (-(e)s, -e) m fish; **~e** pl (Astr)
Pisces sing; **fischen** vt, vi to fish;
Fischer(in) (-s, -) m(f) fisherman,
-woman; **Fischerboot** nt
fishing boat; **Fischgericht** nt fish
dish; **Fischhändler(in)** m(f)
fishmonger; **Fischstäbchen** nt
fish finger (Brit) (o stick (US))
Fisole (-, -n) f French bean
fit adj fit; **Fitness** (-) f fitness
Fitnesscenter (-s, -) nt fitness
centre; **Fitnesstrainer(in)** m(f)
fitness trainer, personal trainer
fix adj (schnell) quick; **~ und fertig**
exhausted
fixen vi (fam) to shoot up;
Fixer(in) (-s, -) m(f) (fam) junkie
FKK f abk = **Freikörperkultur**
nudism; **FKK-Strand** m nudist
beach
flach adj flat; (Gewässer; Teller)
shallow; **~er Absatz** low heel;
Flachbildschirm m flat screen
Fläche (-, -n) f area; (Oberfläche)
surface
Flagge (-, -n) f flag

flambiert adj flambé(ed)

Flamme (-, -n) f flame

Flanell (-s) m flannel

Flasche (-, -n) f bottle; **eine ~ sein** (fam) to be useless; **Flaschenbier** nt bottled beer; **Flaschenöffner** m bottle opener; **Flaschenpfand** nt deposit; **Flaschentomate** f plum tomato

flatterhaft adj fickle; **flattern** vi to flutter

flauschig adj fluffy

Flausen pl (fam) daft ideas pl

Flaute (-, -n) f calm; (Comm) recession

Flechte (-, -n) f plait; (Med) scab; (Bot) lichen; **flechten** (flocht, geflochten) vt to plait; (Kranz) to bind

Fleck (-(e)s, -e) m, **Flecken** (-s, -) m spot; (Schmutz) stain; (Stoff~) patch; (Makel) blemish; **Fleckentferner** (-s, -) m stain remover; **fleckig** adj spotted; (mit Schmutzflecken) stained

Fledermaus f bat

Fleisch (-(e)s) nt flesh; (Essen) meat; **Fleischbrühe** f meat stock; **Fleischer(in)** (-s, -) m(f) butcher; **Fleischerei** f butcher's (shop); **Fleischtomate** f beef tomato

fleißig adj diligent, hard-working

flennen vi (fam) to cry, to howl

flexibel adj flexible

flicken vt to mend; **Flickzeug** nt repair kit

Flieder (-s, -) m lilac

Fliege (-, -n) f fly; (Krawatte) bow tie

fliegen (flog, geflogen) vt, vi to fly

Fliese (-, -n) f tile

Fließband nt conveyor belt; (als Einrichtung) production (o assembly) line; **fließen** (floss, geflossen) vi to flow; **fließend** adj fluent; (Übergänge) smooth; **~(es) Wasser** running water

Flipper (-s, -) m pinball machine; **flippern** vi to play pinball

flippig adj (fam) eccentric

flirten vi to flirt

Flitterwochen pl honeymoon sing

flocht imperf von **flechten**

Flocke (-, -n) f flake

flog imperf von **fliegen**

Floh (-(e)s, Flöhe) m flea; **Flohmarkt** m flea market

Flop (-s, -s) m flop

Floskel (-, -n) f empty phrase

floss imperf von **fließen**

Floß (-es, Flöße) nt raft

Flosse (-, -n) f fin; (Schwimmflosse) flipper

Flöte (-, -n) f flute; (Blockflöte) recorder

flott adj lively; (elegant) smart; (Naut) afloat

Fluch (-(e)s, Flüche) m curse; **fluchen** vi to swear, to curse

Flucht (-, -en) f flight; **flüchten** vi to flee (vor +dat from); **flüchtig** adj: **ich kenne ihn nur ~** I don't know him very well at all; **Flüchtling** m refugee

Flug (-(e)s, Flüge) m flight; **Flugbegleiter(in)** (-s, -) m(f) flight attendant; **Flugblatt** nt leaflet

Flügel (-s, -) m wing; (Mus) grand piano

Fluggast m passenger (on a plane); **Fluggesellschaft** f airline; **Flughafen** m airport; **Flugkarte** f airline ticket; **Fluglotse** m air-traffic controller; **Flugnummer** f flight number; **Flugplan** m flight schedule; **Flugplatz** m airport; (klein) airfield; **Flugschein** m plane ticket; **Flugschreiber** m flight recorder, black box; **Flugsteig** (-s, -e) m gate; **Flugstrecke** f air route; **Flugticket** nt plane ticket; **Flugverbindung** f flight connection; **Flugverkehr** m air traffic; **Flugzeit** f flying time; **Flugzeug** nt plane; **Flugzeugentführung** f hijacking

Flunder (-, -n) f flounder

Fluor (-s) nt fluorine

Flur (-(e)s, -e) m hall

Fluss (-es, Flüsse) m river; (Fließen) flow

flüssig adj liquid; **Flüssigkeit** (-, -en) f liquid; **Flüssigseife** f liquid soap

flüstern vt, vi to whisper

Flut (-, -en) f (a. fig) flood; (Gezeiten) high tide; **Flutlicht** nt floodlight

Fohlen (-s, -) nt foal

Föhn (-(e)s, -e) m hairdryer; (Wind) foehn; **föhnen** vt to dry; (beim Friseur) to blow-dry

Folge (-, -n) f (Reihe, Serie) series sing; (Aufeinanderfolge) sequence; (Fortsetzung eines Romans) instalment; (Fortsetzung einer Fernsehserie) episode; (Auswirkung) result; **etw zur ~ haben** to result in sth; **~n haben** to have consequences; **folgen** vi to follow (jdm sb); (gehorchen) to obey (jdm sb); **jdm ~ können** (fig) to be able to follow sb; **folgend** adj following; **folgendermaßen** adv as follows; **folglich** adv consequently

Folie f foil; (für Projektor) transparency

Fön® m siehe **Föhn**

Fondue (-s, -s) nt fondue

fönen vt siehe **föhnen**

fordern vt to demand

fördern vt to promote; (unterstützen) to help

Forderung f demand

Forelle f trout

Form (-, -en) f form; (Gestalt) shape; (Gussform) mould; (Backform) baking tin (Brit) (o pan

(US)); **in ~ sein** to be in good form; **Formalität** f formality; **Format** nt format; **von internationalem ~** of international standing; **formatieren** vt (Diskette) to format; (Text) to edit

Formblatt nt form; **formen** vt to form, to shape; **förmlich** adj formal; (buchstäblich) real; **formlos** adj informal; **Formular** (-s, -e) nt form; **formulieren** vt to formulate

forschen vi to search (nach for); (wissenschaftlich) to (do) research; **Forscher(in)** m(f) researcher; **Forschung** f research

Förster(in) (-s, -) m(f) forester; (für Wild) gamekeeper

fort adv away; (verschwunden) gone; **fort|bewegen** vt to move away ▷ vr: **sich ~** to move; **Fortbildung** f further education; (im Beruf) further training; **fort|fahren** irr vi to go away; (weitermachen) to continue; **fort|gehen** irr vi to go away; **fortgeschritten** adj advanced; **Fortpflanzung** f reproduction

Fortschritt m progress; **~e machen** to make progress; **fortschrittlich** adj progressive **fort|setzen** vt to continue; **Fortsetzung** f continuation; (folgender Teil) instalment; **~ folgt** to be continued

Foto (-s, -s) nt photo ▷ (-s, -s) m (Fotoapparat) camera; **Fotograf(in)** (-en, -en) m(f) photographer; **Fotografie** f photography; (Bild) photograph; **fotografieren** vt to photograph ▷ vi to take photographs; **Fotohandy** nt camera phone; **Fotokopie** f photocopy; **fotokopieren** vt to photocopy

Foul (-s, -s) nt foul

Foyer (-s, -s) nt foyer

Fr. f abk = **Frau** Mrs; (unverheiratet, neutral) Ms

Fracht (-, -en) f freight; (Naut) cargo; (Preis) carriage; **Frachter** (-s, -) m freighter

Frack (-(e)s, Fräcke) m tails pl

Frage (-, -n) f question; (das ist) **eine ~ der Zeit** that's a matter (o question) of time; **das kommt nicht in ~** that's out of the question; **Fragebogen** m questionnaire; **fragen** vt, vi to ask; **Fragezeichen** nt question mark; **fragwürdig** adj dubious

Franken (-s, -) m (Schweizer Währung) Swiss franc ▷ (-s) nt (Land) Franconia

frankieren vt to stamp; (maschinell) to frank

Frankreich (-s) nt France; **Franzose** (-n, -n) m, **Französin** f Frenchman/-woman; **die ~n** pl the French pl; **französisch** adj French; **Französisch** nt French

fraß imperf von **fressen**

Frau (-, -en) f woman; (Ehefrau) wife; (Anrede) Mrs; (unverheiratet, neutral) Ms; **Frauenarzt** m, **Frauenärztin** f gynaecologist; **Frauenbewegung** f women's movement; **frauenfeindlich** adj misogynous; **Frauenhaus** nt refuge (for battered women)

Fräulein (-s) nt (junge Dame) young lady; (veraltet als Anrede) Miss

Freak (-s, -s) m (fam) freak

frech adj cheeky; **Frechheit** f cheek; **so eine ~!** what a cheek

Freeclimbing (-s) nt free climbing

frei adj free; (Straße) clear; (Mitarbeiter) freelance; **ein ~er Tag** a day off; **~e Arbeitsstelle** vacancy; **Zimmer ~** room(s) to let (Brit), room(s) for rent (US); **im Freien** in the open air; **Freibad** nt open-air (swimming) pool;

freiberuflich adj freelance; **freig(i)ebig** adj generous; **Freiheit** f freedom; **Freikarte** f free ticket; **frei|lassen** irr vt to (set) free

freilich adv of course

Freilichtbühne f open-air theatre; **frei|machen** vr: **sich ~** to undress; **frei|nehmen** irr vt **sich** (dat) **einen Tag ~** to take a day off; **Freisprechanlage** f hands-free phone; **Freistoß** m free kick

Freitag m Friday; siehe auch **Mittwoch**; **freitags** adv on Fridays; siehe auch **mittwochs**

freiwillig adj voluntary

Freizeichen nt (Tel) ringing tone

Freizeit f spare (o free) time; **Freizeithemd** nt sports shirt; **Freizeitkleidung** f leisure wear; **Freizeitpark** m leisure park

fremd adj (nicht vertraut) strange; (ausländisch) foreign; (nicht eigen) someone else's; **Fremde(r)** mf (Unbekannter) stranger; (Ausländer) foreigner; **fremdenfeindlich** adj anti-foreigner, xenophobic; **Fremdenführer(in)** m(f) (tourist) guide; **Fremdenverkehr** m tourism; **Fremdenverkehrsamt** nt tourist information office; **Fremdzimmer** nt (guest) room; **Fremdsprache** f foreign language; **Fremdsprachenkenntnisse** pl knowledge sing of foreign languages; **Fremdwort** nt foreign word

Frequenz f (Radio) frequency

fressen (fraß, gefressen) vt, vi (Tier) to eat; (Mensch) to guzzle

Freude (-, -n) f joy, delight; **freuen** vt to please; **es freut mich, dass ...** I'm pleased that ... ▷ vr: **sich ~** to be pleased (über +akk about); **sich auf etw** (akk) **~** to look forward to sth

Freund (-(e)s, -e) m friend; (in Beziehung) boyfriend; **Freundin** f friend; (in Beziehung) girlfriend; **freundlich** adj friendly; (liebenswürdig) kind; **freundlicherweise** adv kindly; **Freundlichkeit** f friendliness; (Liebenswürdigkeit) kindness; **Freundschaft** f friendship

Frieden (-s, -) m peace; **Friedhof** m cemetery; **friedlich** adj peaceful

frieren (fror, gefroren) vt, vi to freeze; **ich friere, es friert mich** I'm freezing

Frikadelle (-) f rissole

Frisbee® nt, **Frisbeescheibe®** f frisbee®

frisch adj fresh; (lebhaft) lively; „**~ gestrichen**" "wet paint"; **sich ~ machen** to freshen up; **Frischhaltefolie** f clingfilm® (Brit), plastic wrap (US); **Frischkäse** m cream cheese

Friseur(in) (-s, -e) m(f) hairdresser; **frisieren** vt: **jdn ~** to do sb's hair ▷ vr: **sich ~** to do one's hair

Frist (-, -en) f period; (Zeitpunkt) deadline; **innerhalb einer ~ von zehn Tagen** within a ten-day period; **eine ~ einhalten** to meet a deadline; **die ~ ist abgelaufen** the deadline has expired; **fristgerecht** adj, adv within the specified time; **fristlos** adj: **~e Entlassung** dismissal without notice

Frisur f hairdo, hairstyle

frittieren vt to deep-fry

Frl. f abk = **Fräulein** Miss

froh adj happy; **~e Weihnachten!** Merry Christmas

fröhlich adj happy, cheerful

Fronleichnam (-(e)s) m Corpus Christi

frontal adj frontal

fror imperf von **frieren**

Frosch (-(e)s, Frösche) m frog

Frost (-(e)s, Fröste) m frost; **bei ~** in frosty weather; **Frostschutzmittel** nt anti-freeze

Frottee nt terry(cloth); **Frottier(hand)tuch** nt towel

Frucht (-, Früchte) f (a. fig) fruit; (Getreide) corn; **Fruchteis** nt fruit-flavoured ice-cream; **Früchtetee** m fruit tea; **fruchtig** adj fruity; **Fruchtpresse** f juicer; **Fruchtsaft** m fruit juice; **Fruchtsalat** m fruit salad

früh adj, adv early; **heute ~** this morning; **um fünf Uhr ~** at five (o'clock) in the morning; **~ genug** soon enough; **früher** adj earlier; (ehemalig) former ▷ adv formerly, in the past; **frühestens** adv at the earliest

Frühjahr nt, **Frühling** m spring; **Frühlingsrolle** f spring roll; **Frühlingszwiebel** f spring onion (Brit), scallion (US)

frühmorgens adv early in the morning

Frühstück nt breakfast; **frühstücken** vi to have breakfast; **Frühstücksbüfett** nt breakfast buffet; **Frühstücksfernsehen** nt breakfast television; **Frühstücksspeck** m bacon

frühzeitig adj early

Frust (-s) m (fam) frustration; **frustrieren** vt to frustrate

Fuchs (-es, Füchse) m fox

fühlen vt, vi to feel ▷ vr: **sich ~** to feel

fuhr imperf von **fahren**

führen vt to lead; (Geschäft) to run; (Name) to bear; (Buch) to keep ▷ vi to lead, to be in the lead ▷ vr: **sich ~** to behave; **Führerschein** m driving licence (Brit), driver's license (US); **Führung** f leadership; (eines Unternehmens) management; (*Mil*) command; (*in Museum, Stadt*) guided tour; **in ~ liegen** to be in the lead

füllen vt to fill; (*Gastr*) to stuff ▷ vr: **sich ~** to fill

Füller (-s, -) m, **Füllfederhalter** (-s, -) m fountain pen

Füllung f filling

Fund (-(e)s, -e) m find; **Fundbüro** nt lost property office (*Brit*), lost and found (*US*); **Fundsachen** pl lost property sing

fünf num five; **Fünf** (-, -en) f five; (*Schulnote*) ≈ E; **fünfhundert** num five hundred; **fünfmal** adv five times; **fünfte(r, s)** adj fifth; *siehe auch* **dritte**; **Fünftel** (-s, -) nt (*Bruchteil*) fifth; **fünfzehn** num fifteen; **fünfzehnte(r, s)** adj fifteenth; *siehe auch* **dritte**; **fünfzig** num fifty; **fünfzigste(r, s)** adj fiftieth

Funk (-s) m radio; **über ~** by radio

Funke (-ns, -n) m spark; **funkeln** vi to sparkle

Funkgerät nt radio set; **Funktaxi** nt radio taxi, radio cab

Funktion f function; **funktionieren** vi to work, to function; **Funktionstaste** f (*Inform*) function key

für prep +akk for; **was ~ (ein) ...?** what kind (o sort) of ...?; **Tag ~ Tag** day after day

Furcht (-) f fear; **furchtbar** adj terrible; **fürchten** vt to be afraid of, to fear ▷ vr: **sich ~** to be afraid (*vor +dat* of); **fürchterlich** adj awful

füreinander adv for each other

fürs kontr von **für das**

Fürst(in) (-en, -en) m(f) prince/princess; **Fürstentum** nt principality; **fürstlich** adj (*fig*) splendid

Furunkel (-s, -) nt boil

Furz (-es, -e) m (*vulg*) fart; **furzen** vi (*vulg*) to fart

Fuß (-es, Füße) m foot; (von Glas, Säule etc) base; (von Möbel) leg; **zu ~** on foot; **zu ~ gehen** to walk; **Fußball** m football (*Brit*), soccer; **Fußballmannschaft** f football (*Brit*) (o soccer) team; **Fußballplatz** m football pitch (*Brit*), soccer field (*US*); **Fußballspiel** nt football (*Brit*) (o soccer) match; **Fußballspieler(in)** m(f) footballer (*Brit*), soccer player; **Fußboden** m floor; **Fußgänger(in)** (-s, -) m(f) pedestrian; **Fußgängerüberweg** m pedestrian crossing (*Brit*), crosswalk (*US*); **Fußgängerzone** f pedestrian precinct (*Brit*) (o zone (*US*)); **Fußgelenk** nt ankle; **Fußpilz** m athlete's foot; **Fußtritt** m kick; **jdm einen ~ geben** to give sb a kick, to kick sb; **Fußweg** m footpath

Futon (-s, -s) m futon

Futter (-s, -) nt feed; (Heu etc) fodder; (Stoff) lining; **füttern** vt to feed; (Kleidung) to line

Futur (-s, -e) nt (*Ling*) future (tense)

Fuzzi (-s, -s) m (*fam*) guy

g

gab imperf von **geben**

Gabe (-, -n) f gift

Gabel (-, -n) f fork; **Gabelung** f fork

Gage (-, -n) f fee

gähnen vi to yawn

Galerie f gallery

Galle (-, -n) f gall; (Organ) gall bladder; **Gallenstein** m gallstone

Galopp (-s) m gallop; **galoppieren** vi to gallop

galt imperf von **gelten**

Gameboy® (-s, -s) m Gameboy®

Gamer(in) (-s, -) m(f) (Inform) gamer

Gameshow f game show

gammeln vi to loaf around; **Gammler(in)** (-s, -) m(f) layabout

gang adj: ~ **und gäbe sein** to be quite normal

Gang (-(e)s, Gänge) m walk; (im Flugzeug) aisle; (Essen, Ablauf) course; (Flur etc) corridor; (Durchgang) passage; (Auto) gear; **den zweiten ~ einlegen** to change into second (gear); **etw in ~ bringen** to get sth going; **Gangschaltung** f gears pl; **Gangway** (-, -s) f (Aviat) steps pl; (Naut) gangway

Gans (-, Gänse) f goose; **Gänseblümchen** nt daisy; **Gänsehaut** f goose pimples pl (Brit), goose bumps pl (US)

ganz adj whole; (vollständig) complete; ~ **Europa** all of Europe; **sein ~es Geld** all his money; **den ~en Tag** all day; ▷ adv quite; (völlig) completely; **es hat mir ~ gut gefallen** I quite liked it; ~ **schön viel** quite a lot; ~ **und gar nicht** not at all; **das ist etwas ~ anderes** that's a completely different matter; **ganztägig** adj all-day; (Arbeit, Stelle) full-time; **ganztags** adv (arbeiten) full-time; **Ganztagsschule** f all-day school; **Ganztagsstelle** f full-time job

gar adj done, cooked ▷ adv at all; ~ **nicht/nichts** not/nothing at all; ~ **nicht schlecht** not bad at all

Garage (-, -n) f garage

Garantie f guarantee; **garantieren** vt to guarantee

Garderobe (-, -n) f (Kleidung) wardrobe; (Abgabe) cloakroom

Gardine f curtain

Garn (-(e)s, -e) nt thread

Garnele (-, -n) f shrimp

garnieren vt to decorate; (Speisen) to garnish

Garten (-s, Gärten) m garden; **Gärtner(in)** (-s, -) m(f) gardener; **Gärtnerei** f nursery; (Gemüsegärtnerei) market garden (Brit), truck farm (US)

Gas (-es, -e) nt gas; ~ **geben** (Auto) to accelerate; (fig) to get a move on; **Gasanzünder** m gas lighter; **Gasbrenner** m gas burner;

Gasflasche f gas bottle;
Gasheizung f gas heating;
Gasherd m gas stove, gas cooker
(Brit); **Gaskocher** (-s, -) m
camping stove; **Gaspedal** nt
accelerator, gas pedal (US)
Gasse (-, -n) f alley
Gast (-es, Gäste) m guest; **Gäste
haben** to have guests;
Gastarbeiter(in) m(f) foreign
worker; **Gästebett** nt spare bed;
Gästebuch nt visitors' book;
Gästehaus nt guest house;
Gästezimmer nt guest room;
gastfreundlich adj hospitable;
Gastfreundschaft f hospitality;
Gastgeber(in) (-s, -) m(f) host/
hostess; **Gasthaus** nt, **Gasthof** m
inn; **Gastland** nt host country
Gastritis (-) f gastritis
Gastronomie f catering trade
Gastspiel nt (Sport) away game;
Gaststätte f restaurant;
(Trinklokal) pub (Brit), bar;
Gastwirt(in) m(f) landlord/-lady
GAU (-s, -s) m akr = **größter
anzunehmender Unfall** MCA
Gaumen (-s, -) m palate
Gaze (-, -n) f gauze
geb. adj abk = **geboren** b. ▷ adj
abk = **geborene** née; siehe **geboren**
Gebäck (-(e)s, -e) nt pastries pl;
(Kekse) biscuits pl (Brit), cookies pl
(US)
gebacken pp von **backen**
Gebärdensprache f sign
language
Gebärmutter f womb
Gebäude (-s, -) nt building
geben (gab, gegeben) vt, vi to give
(jdm etw sb sth, sth to sb); (Karten)
to deal; **lass dir eine Quittung
~** ask for a receipt ▷ vt impers: **es
gibt** there is/are; (in Zukunft) there
will be; **das gibt's nicht** I don't
believe it ▷ vr: **sich ~** (sich
verhalten) to behave, to act; **das**

gibt sich wieder it'll sort itself out
Gebet (-(e)s, -e) nt prayer
gebeten pp von **bitten**
Gebiet (-(e)s, -e) nt area;
(Hoheitsgebiet) territory; (fig) field
gebildet adj educated; (belesen)
well-read
Gebirge (-s, -) nt mountains pl;
gebirgig adj mountainous
Gebiss (-es, -e) nt teeth pl;
(künstlich) dentures pl; **gebissen**
pp von **beißen**; **Gebissreiniger** m
denture tablets pl
Gebläse (-s, -) nt fan, blower
geblasen pp von **blasen**
geblieben pp von **bleiben**
gebogen pp von **biegen**
geboren pp von **gebären** ▷ adj
born; **Andrea Jordan, geborene
Christian** Andrea Jordan, née
Christian
geborgen pp von **bergen** ▷ adj
secure, safe
geboten pp von **bieten**
gebracht pp von **bringen**
gebrannt pp von **brennen**
gebraten pp von **braten**
gebrauchen vt to use;
Gebrauchsanweisung f directions pl for use; **gebrauchsfertig**
adj ready to use; **gebraucht** adj
used; **etw ~ kaufen** to buy sth
secondhand; **Gebrauchtwagen**
m secondhand (o used) car
gebräunt adj tanned
gebrochen pp von **brechen**
Gebühr (-, -en) f charge; (Maut)
toll; (Honorar) fee; **Gebühren-
einheit** f (Tel) unit;
gebührenfrei adj free of charge;
(Telefonnummer) freefone® (Brit),
toll-free (US); **gebührenpflichtig**
adj subject to charges; **~e Straße**
toll road
gebunden pp von **binden**
Geburt (-, -en) f birth; **gebürtig**
adj: **er ist ~er Schweizer** he is

Swiss by birth; **Geburtsdatum** nt date of birth; **Geburtsjahr** nt year of birth; **Geburtsname** m birth name; (einer Frau) maiden name; **Geburtsort** m birthplace; **Geburtstag** m birthday; **herzlichen Glückwunsch zum ~!** Happy Birthday; **Geburtsurkunde** f birth certificate

Gebüsch (-(e)s, -e) nt bushes pl

gedacht pp von **denken**

Gedächtnis nt memory; **im ~ behalten** to remember

Gedanke (-ns, -n) m thought; **sich** (dat) **über etw** (akk) **~n machen** to think about sth; (besorgt) to be worried about sth; **Gedankenstrich** m dash

Gedeck (-(e)s, -e) nt place setting; (Speisenfolge) set meal

Gedenkstätte f memorial; **Gedenktafel** f commemorative plaque

Gedicht (-(e)s, -e) nt poem

Gedränge (-s) nt crush, crowd

gedrungen pp von **dringen**

Geduld (-) f patience; **geduldig** adj patient

gedurft pp von **dürfen**

geehrt adj: **Sehr ~er Herr Young** Dear Mr Young

geeignet adj suitable

Gefahr (-, -en) f danger; **auf eigene ~** at one's own risk; **außer ~** out of danger; **gefährden** vt to endanger

gefahren pp von **fahren**

gefährlich adj dangerous

Gefälle (-s, -) nt gradient, slope

gefallen pp von **fallen** ▸ irr vi: **jdm ~** to please sb; **er/es gefällt mir** I like him/it; **sich** (dat) **etw ~ lassen** to put up with sth

Gefallen (-s, -) nt favour; **jdm einen ~ tun** to do sb a favour

gefälligst adv ..., will you!; **sei ~ still!** be quiet, will you!

gefangen pp von **fangen**

Gefängnis nt prison

Gefäß (-es, -e) nt (Behälter) container, receptacle; (Anat, Bot) vessel

gefasst adj composed, calm; **auf etw** (akk) **~ sein** to be prepared (o ready) for sth

geflochten pp von **flechten**

geflogen pp von **fliegen**

geflossen pp von **fließen**

Geflügel (-s) nt poultry

gefragt adj in demand

gefressen pp von **fressen**

Gefrierbeutel m freezer bag; **gefrieren** irr vi to freeze; **Gefrierfach** nt freezer compartment; **Gefrierschrank** m (upright) freezer; **Gefriertruhe** f (chest) freezer

gefroren pp von **frieren**

Gefühl (-(e)s, -e) nt feeling

gefunden pp von **finden**

gegangen pp von **gehen**

gegeben pp von **geben**; **gegebenenfalls** adv if need be

SCHLÜSSELWORT

gegen prep +akk **1** against; **nichts gegen jdn haben** to have nothing against sb; **X gegen Y** (Sport, Jur) X versus Y; **ein Mittel gegen Schnupfen** something for colds

2 (in Richtung auf) towards; **gegen Osten** to(wards) the east; **gegen Abend** towards evening; **gegen einen Baum fahren** to drive into a tree

3 (ungefähr) round about; **gegen 3 Uhr** around 3 o'clock

4 (gegenüber) towards; (ungefähr) around; **gerecht gegen alle** fair to all

5 (im Austausch für) for; **gegen bar** for cash; **gegen Quittung** against

a receipt
6 (*verglichen mit*) compared with

Gegend (-, -en) f area; **hier in der ~** around here
gegeneinander *adv* against one another
Gegenfahrbahn f opposite lane; **Gegenmittel** *nt* remedy (*gegen* for); **Gegenrichtung** f opposite direction; **Gegensatz** m contrast; **im ~ zu** in contrast to; **gegensätzlich** *adj* conflicting; **gegenseitig** *adj* mutual; **sich ~ helfen** to help each other
Gegenstand m object; (*Thema*) subject
Gegenteil *nt* opposite; **im ~** on the contrary; **gegenteilig** *adj* opposite, contrary
gegenüber *prep* +*dat* opposite; (*zu jdm*) to(wards); (*angesichts*) in the face of ▷ *adv* opposite; **gegenüber|stehen** *vt* to face; (*Problemen*) to be faced with; **gegenüber|stellen** *vt* to confront (*dat* with); (*fig*) compare (*dat* with)
Gegenverkehr m oncoming traffic; **Gegenwart** (-) f present (tense)
Gegenwind m headwind
gegessen *pp von* **essen**
geglichen *pp von* **gleichen**
geglitten *pp von* **gleiten**
Gegner(in) (-s, -) m(f) opponent
gegolten *pp von* **gelten**
gegossen *pp von* **gießen**
gegraben *pp von* **graben**
gegriffen *pp von* **greifen**
gehabt *pp von* **haben**
Gehackte(s) *nt* mince(d meat) (*Brit*), ground meat (*US*)
Gehalt (-(e)s, -e) m content ▷ -(e)s, Gehälter) *nt* salary
gehalten *pp von* **halten**
gehangen *pp von* **hängen**

gehässig *adj* spiteful, nasty
gehauen *pp von* **hauen**
gehbehindert *adj*: **sie ist ~** she can't walk properly
geheim *adj* secret; **etw ~ halten** to keep sth secret; **Geheimnis** *nt* secret; (*rätselhaft*) mystery; **geheimnisvoll** *adj* mysterious; **Geheimnummer** f, **Geheimzahl** f (*von Kreditkarte*) PIN number
geheißen *pp von* **heißen**
gehen (*ging, gegangen*) *vt, vi* to go; (*zu Fuß*) to walk; (*funktionieren*) to work; (*die Straße*) **~** to cross the street; **~ nach** (*Fenster*) to face ▷ *vi geht es (dir)?* how are you (*o things*)?; **mir/ihm geht es gut** I'm/he's (doing) fine; **geht das?** is that possible?; **geht's noch?** can you still manage?; **es geht** not too bad, OK; **das geht nicht** that's not on; **es geht um ...** it's about ...
Gehirn (-(e)s, -e) *nt* brain; **Gehirnerschütterung** f concussion
gehoben *pp von* **heben**
geholfen *pp von* **helfen**
Gehör (-(e)s) *nt* hearing
gehorchen *vi* to obey (*jdm sb*)
gehören *vi* to belong (*jdm* to sb); **wem gehört das Buch?** whose book is this?; **gehört es dir?** is it yours? ▷ *vr impers*: **das gehört sich nicht** it's not done
gehörlos *adj* deaf
gehorsam *adj* obedient
Gehsteig m, **Gehweg** (-(e)s, -e) m pavement (*Brit*), sidewalk (*US*)
Geier (-s, -) m vulture
Geige (-, -n) f violin
geil *adj* randy (*Brit*), horny (*US*); (*fam*: *toll*) fantastic
Geisel (-, -n) f hostage
Geist (-(e)s, -er) m spirit; (*Gespenst*) ghost; (*Verstand*) mind; **Geisterbahn** f ghost train, tunnel

of horror (US); **Geisterfahrer(in)**
m(f) *person driving the wrong way on
the motorway*

geizig *adj* stingy

gekannt *pp von* **kennen**

geklungen *pp von* **klingen**

geknickt *adj* (fig) dejected

gekniffen *pp von* **kneifen**

gekommen *pp von* **kommen**

gekonnt *pp von* **können** ▷ *adj*
skilful

gekrochen *pp von* **kriechen**

Gel (-s, -s) *nt* gel

Gelächter (-s, -) *nt* laughter

geladen *pp von* **laden** ▷ *adj*
loaded; (Elek) live; (fig) furious

gelähmt *adj* paralysed

Gelände (-s, -) *nt* land, terrain;
(Fabrik, Sportgelände) grounds pl;
(Baugelände) site

Geländer (-s, -) *nt* railing;
(Treppengeländer) banister

Geländewagen *m* off-road
vehicle

gelang *imperf von* **gelingen**

gelassen *pp von* **lassen** ▷ *adj*
calm, composed

Gelatine *f* gelatine

gelaufen *pp von* **laufen**

gelaunt *adj*: gut/schlecht ~ in a
good/bad mood

gelb *adj* yellow; (Ampel) amber,
yellow (US); **gelblich** *adj*
yellowish; **Gelbsucht** *f* jaundice

Geld (-(e)s, -er) *nt* money;
Geldautomat *m* cash machine (o
dispenser (Brit)), ATM (US);
Geldbeutel m, **Geldbörse** f
purse; **Geldbuße** f fine;
Geldschein m (bank)note (Brit),
bill (US); **Geldstrafe** f fine;
Geldstück nt coin; **Geldwechsel**
m exchange of money; (Ort)
bureau de change;
Geldwechselautomat m,
Geldwechsler (-s, -) m change
machine

Gelee (-s, -s) *nt* jelly

gelegen *pp von* **liegen** ▷ *adj*
situated; (passend) convenient;
etw kommt jdm ~ sth is
convenient for sb

Gelegenheit f opportunity;
(Anlass) occasion

gelegentlich *adj* occasional
▷ *adv* occasionally; (bei
Gelegenheit) some time (or other)

Gelenk (-(e)s, -e) *nt* joint

gelernt *adj* skilled

gelesen *pp von* **lesen**

geliehen *pp von* **leihen**

gelingen (gelang, gelungen) vi to
succeed; **es ist mir gelungen, ihn
zu erreichen** I managed to get
hold of him

gelitten *pp von* **leiden**

gelockt *adj* curly

gelogen *pp von* **lügen**

gelten (galt, gegolten) vt (wert
sein) to be worth; **jdm viel/wenig
~** to mean a lot/not to mean much
to sb ▷ vi (gültig sein) to be valid;
(erlaubt sein) to be allowed; **jdm
~** (gemünzt sein auf) to be meant for
(o aimed at) sb; **etw ~ lassen** to
accept sth; **als etw ~** to be
considered to be sth;
Geltungsdauer f: **eine ~ von
fünf Tagen haben** to be valid for
five days

gelungen *pp von* **gelingen**

gemahlen *pp von* **mahlen**

Gemälde (-s, -) *nt* painting,
picture

gemäß *prep +dat* in accordance
with ▷ *adj* appropriate (dat to)

gemein *adj* (niederträchtig) mean,
nasty; (gewöhnlich) common

Gemeinde (-, -n) f district,
community; (Pfarrgemeinde)
parish; (Kirchengemeinde)
congregation

gemeinsam *adj* joint, common
▷ *adv* together, jointly; **das Haus**

gehört uns beiden ~ the house belongs to both of us

Gemeinschaft f community; **~ Unabhängiger Staaten** Commonwealth of Independent States

gemeint pp von **meinen; das war nicht so ~** I didn't mean it like that

gemessen pp von **messen**

gemieden pp von **meiden**

gemischt adj mixed

gemocht pp von **mögen**

Gemüse (-s, -) nt vegetables pl; **Gemüsehändler(in)** m(f) greengrocer

gemusst pp von **müssen**

gemustert adj patterned

gemütlich adj comfortable, cosy; (Mensch) good-natured, easy-going; **mach es dir ~** make yourself at home

genannt pp von **nennen**

genau adj exact, precise ▷ adv exactly, precisely; **~ in der Mitte** right in the middle; **es mit etw ~ nehmen** to be particular about sth; **~ genommen** strictly speaking; **ich weiß es ~** I know for certain (o for sure); **genauso** adv exactly the same (way); **~ gut/viel/viele Leute** just as well/much/many people (wie as)

genehmigen vt to approve; **sich** (dat) **etw ~** to indulge in sth; **Genehmigung** f approval

Generalkonsulat nt consulate general

Generation f generation

Genf (-s) nt Geneva; **~er See** Lake Geneva

Genforschung f genetic research

genial adj brilliant

Genick (-(e)s, -e) nt (back of the) neck

Genie (-s, -s) nt genius

genieren vr: **sich ~** to feel awkward; **ich geniere mich vor ihm** he makes me feel embarrassed

genießen (genoss, genossen) vt to enjoy

Genitiv m genitive (case)

genmanipuliert adj genetically modified, GM

genommen pp von **nehmen**

genoss imperf von **genießen**

genossen pp von **genießen**

Gentechnik f genetic technology; **gentechnisch** adv: **~ verändert** genetically modified, GM

genug adv enough

genügen vi to be enough (jdm for sb); **danke, das genügt** thanks, that's enough (o that will do)

Genuss (-es, Genüsse) m pleasure; (Zusichnehmen) consumption

geöffnet adj (Geschäft etc) open

Geografie f geography

Geologie f geology

Georgien (-s) nt Georgia

Gepäck (-(e)s) nt luggage (Brit), baggage; **Gepäckabfertigung** f luggage (Brit) (o baggage) check-in; **Gepäckablage** f luggage (Brit) (o baggage) rack; **Gepäckannahme** f (zur Beförderung) luggage (Brit) (o baggage) office; (zur Aufbewahrung) left-luggage office (Brit), baggage checkroom (US); **Gepäckaufbewahrung** f left-luggage office (Brit), baggage checkroom (US); **Gepäckausgabe** f luggage (Brit) (o baggage) office; (am Flughafen) baggage reclaim; **Gepäckband** nt luggage (Brit) (o baggage) conveyor; **Gepäckkontrolle** f luggage (Brit) (o baggage) check; **Gepäckstück** nt item of luggage (Brit) (o baggage (US)); **Gepäckträger** m porter; (an Fahrrad) carrier;

Gepäckversicherung f luggage (Brit) (o baggage) insurance; **Gepäckwagen** m luggage van (Brit), baggage car (US)

gepfiffen pp von **pfeifen**

gepflegt adj well-groomed; (Park) well looked after

gequollen pp von **quellen**

⚪ SCHLÜSSELWORT

gerade adj straight; (aufrecht) upright; **eine gerade Zahl** an even number
▷ adv 1 (genau) just, exactly; (speziell) especially; **gerade deshalb** that's just o exactly why; **das ist es ja gerade!** that's just it!; **gerade du** you especially; **warum gerade ich?** why me (of all people)?; **jetzt gerade nicht!** not now!; **gerade neben** right next to
2 (eben, soeben) just; **er wollte gerade aufstehen** he was just about to get up; **gerade erst** only just; **gerade noch** (only) just

geradeaus adv straight ahead

gerannt pp von **rennen**

geraspelt adj grated

Gerät (-(e)s, -e) nt device, gadget; (Werkzeug) tool; (Radio, Fernseher) set; (Zubehör) equipment

geraten pp von **raten** ▷ irr vi to turn out; **gut/schlecht ~** to turn out well/badly; **an jdn ~** to come across sb; **in etw** (akk) **~** to get into sth

geräuchert adj smoked

geräumig adj roomy

Geräusch (-(e)s, -e) nt sound; (unangenehm) noise

gerecht adj fair; (Strafe, Belohnung) just; **jdm/einer Sache ~ werden** to do justice to sb/sth

gereizt adj irritable

Gericht (-(e)s, -e) nt (Jur) court; (Essen) dish

gerieben pp von **reiben**

gering adj small; (unbedeutend) slight; (niedrig) low; (Zeit) short; **geringfügig** adj slight, minor
▷ adv slightly

gerissen pp von **reißen**

geritten pp von **reiten**

gern(e) adv willingly, gladly; **etw ~ tun** to like doing sth;
~ geschehen you're welcome; **gern|haben, gern mögen** irr vt to like

gerochen pp von **riechen**

Gerste (-, -n) f barley; **Gerstenkorn** nt (im Auge) stye

Geruch (-(e)s, Gerüche) m smell

Gerücht (-(e)s, -e) nt rumour

gerufen pp von **rufen**

Gerümpel (-s) nt junk

gerungen pp von **ringen**

Gerüst (-(e)s, -e) nt (auf Bau) scaffolding; (Gestell) trestle; (fig) framework (zu of)

gesalzen pp von **salzen**

gesamt adj whole, entire; (Kosten) total; (Werke) complete; **Gesamtschule** f ≈ comprehensive school

gesandt pp von **senden**

Gesäß (-es, -e) nt bottom

geschaffen pp von **schaffen**

Geschäft (-(e)s, -e) nt business; (Laden) shop; (Geschäftsabschluss) deal; **geschäftlich** adj commercial
▷ adv on business; **Geschäftsfrau** f businesswoman; **Geschäftsführer(in)** m(f) managing director; (von Laden) manager; **Geschäftsleitung** f executive board; **Geschäftsmann** m businessman; **Geschäftsreise** f business trip; **Geschäftsstraße** f shopping street; **Geschäftszeiten** pl business (o opening) hours pl

geschehen *(geschah, geschehen)* vi to happen

Geschenk *(-(e)s, -e)* nt present, gift; **Geschenkgutschein** m gift voucher; **Geschenkpapier** nt gift-wrapping paper, giftwrap

Geschichte *(-, -n)* f story; *(Sache)* affair; *(Hist)* history

geschickt adj skilful

geschieden pp von **scheiden**
▷ adj divorced

geschienen pp von **scheinen**

Geschirr *(-(e)s, -e)* nt crockery; *(zum Kochen)* pots and pans pl; *(von Pferd)* harness; **~ spülen** to do (o wash) the dishes, to do the washing-up (Brit); **Geschirrspülmaschine** f dishwasher; **Geschirrspülmittel** nt washing-up liquid (Brit), dishwashing liquid (US); **Geschirrtuch** nt tea towel (Brit), dish towel (US)

geschissen pp von **scheißen**

geschlafen pp von **schlafen**

geschlagen pp von **schlagen**

Geschlecht *(-(e)s, -er)* nt sex; *(Ling)* gender; **Geschlechtskrankheit** f sexually transmitted disease, STD; **Geschlechtsorgan** nt sexual organ; **Geschlechtsverkehr** m sexual intercourse

geschlichen pp von **schleichen**

geschliffen pp von **schleifen**

geschlossen adj closed

Geschmack *(-(e)s, Geschmäcke)* m taste; **geschmacklos** adj tasteless; **Geschmack(s)sache** f: **das ist ~** that's a matter of taste; **geschmackvoll** adj tasteful

geschmissen pp von **schmeißen**

geschmolzen pp von **schmelzen**

geschnitten pp von **schneiden**

geschoben pp von **schieben**

Geschoss *(-es, -e)* nt *(Stockwerk)* floor

geschossen pp von **schießen**

Geschrei *(-s)* nt cries pl; *(fig)* fuss

geschrieben pp von **schreiben**

geschrie(e)n pp von **schreien**

geschützt adj protected

Geschwätz *(-es)* nt chatter; *(Klatsch)* gossip; **geschwätzig** adj talkative, gossipy

geschweige adv: **~ (denn)** let alone

geschwiegen pp von **schweigen**

Geschwindigkeit f speed; *(Phys)* velocity; **Geschwindigkeitsbegrenzung** f speed limit

Geschwister pl brothers and sisters pl

geschwollen adj *(angeschwollen)* swollen; *(Rede)* pompous

geschwommen pp von **schwimmen**

geschworen pp von **schwören**

Geschwulst *(-, Geschwülste)* f growth

Geschwür *(-(e)s, -e)* nt ulcer

gesehen pp von **sehen**

gesellig adj sociable; **Gesellschaft** f society; *(Begleitung)* company; *(Abend~)* party; **~ mit beschränkter Haftung** limited company (Brit), limited corporation (US)

gesessen pp von **sitzen**

Gesetz *(-es, -e)* nt law; **gesetzlich** adj legal; **~er Feiertag** public (o bank (Brit) o legal (US)) holiday; **gesetzwidrig** adj illegal

Gesicht *(-(e)s, -er)* nt face; *(Miene)* expression; **mach doch nicht so ein ~!** stop pulling such a face; **Gesichtscreme** f face cream; **Gesichtswasser** nt toner

gesoffen pp von **saufen**

gesogen pp von **saugen**

gespannt adj tense; *(begierig)* eager; **ich bin ~, ob ...** I wonder if ...; **auf etw/jdn ~ sein** to look forward to sth/to seeing sb

Gespenst (-(e)s, -er) nt ghost

gesperrt adj closed

gesponnen pp von **spinnen**

Gespräch (-(e)s, -e) nt talk, conversation; (Diskussion) discussion; (Anruf) call

gesprochen pp von **sprechen**

gesprungen pp von **springen**

Gestalt (-, -en) f form, shape; (Mensch) figure

gestanden pp von **stehen**, **gestehen**

Gestank (-(e)s) m stench

gestatten vt to permit, to allow; ~ **Sie?** may I?

Geste (-, -n) f gesture

gestehen irr vt to confess

gestern adv yesterday; ~ **Abend/Morgen** yesterday evening/morning

gestiegen pp von **steigen**

gestochen pp von **stechen**

gestohlen pp von **stehlen**

gestorben pp von **sterben**

gestört adj disturbed; (Empfang) poor

gestoßen pp von **stoßen**

gestreift adj striped

gestrichen pp von **streichen**

gestritten pp von **streiten**

gestunken pp von **stinken**

gesund adj healthy; **wieder** ~ **werden** to get better; **Gesundheit** f health; ~! bless you!; **gesundheitsschädlich** adj unhealthy

gesungen pp von **singen**

gesunken pp von **sinken**

getan pp von **tun**

getragen pp von **tragen**

Getränk (-(e)s, -e) nt drink; **Getränkeautomat** m drinks machine; **Getränkekarte** f list of drinks

Getreide (-s, -) nt cereals pl, grain

getrennt adj separate; ~ **leben** to live apart; ~ **zahlen** to pay separately

getreten pp von **treten**

Getriebe (-s, -) nt (Auto) gearbox

getrieben pp von **treiben**

Getriebeschaden m gearbox damage

getroffen pp von **treffen**

getrunken pp von **trinken**

Getue nt fuss

geübt adj experienced

gewachsen pp von **wachsen**
▷ adj: **jdm/einer Sache** ~ **sein** to be a match for sb/up to sth

Gewähr (-) f guarantee; **keine** ~ **übernehmen für** to accept no responsibility for

Gewalt (-, -en) f (Macht) power; (Kontrolle) control; (große Kraft) force; (~taten) violence; **mit aller** ~ with all one's might; **gewaltig** adj tremendous; (Irrtum) huge

gewandt pp von **wenden** ▷ adj (flink) nimble; (geschickt) skilful

gewann imperf von **gewinnen**

gewaschen pp von **waschen**

Gewebe (-s, -) nt (Stoff) fabric; (Bio) tissue

Gewehr (-(e)s, -e) nt rifle, gun

Geweih (-(e)s, -e) nt antlers pl

gewellt adj (Haare) wavy

gewendet pp von **wenden**

Gewerbe (-s, -) nt trade; **Gewerbegebiet** nt industrial estate (Brit) (o park (US)); **gewerblich** adj commercial

Gewerkschaft f trade union

gewesen pp von **sein**

Gewicht (-(e)s, -e) nt weight; (fig) importance

gewiesen pp von **weisen**

Gewinn (-(e)s, -e) m profit; (bei Spiel) winnings pl; **gewinnen** (gewann, gewonnen) vt to win; (erwerben) to gain; (Kohle, Öl) to extract ▷ vi to win; (profitieren) to gain; **Gewinner(in)** (-s, -) m(f) winner

gewiss adj certain ▷ adv certainly

Gewissen (-s, -) nt conscience; **ein gutes/schlechtes ~ haben** to have a clear/bad conscience

Gewitter (-s, -) nt thunderstorm; **gewittern** vi impers: **es gewittert** it's thundering

gewogen pp von **wiegen**

gewöhnen vt **jdn an etw** (akk) **~** to accustom sb to sth ▷ vr: **sich an jdn/etw ~** to get used (or accustomed) to sb/sth; **Gewohnheit** f habit; (Brauch) custom; **gewöhnlich** adj usual; (durchschnittlich) ordinary; (pej) common; **wie ~** as usual; **gewohnt** adj usual; **etw ~ sein** to be used to sth

gewonnen pp von **gewinnen**

geworben pp von **werben**

geworden pp von **werden**

geworfen pp von **werfen**

Gewürz (-es, -e) nt spice; **Gewürznelke** f clove; **gewürzt** adj seasoned

gewusst pp von **wissen**

Gezeiten pl tides pl

gezogen pp von **ziehen**

gezwungen pp von **zwingen**

Gibraltar (-s) nt Gibraltar

Gicht (-) f gout

Giebel (-s, -) m gable

gierig adj greedy

gießen (goss, gegossen) vt to pour; (Blumen) to water; (Metall) to cast; **Gießkanne** f watering can

Gift (-(e)s, -e) nt poison; **giftig** adj poisonous

Gigabyte nt gigabyte

Gin (-s, -s) m gin

ging imperf von **gehen**

Gin Tonic (-(s), -s) m gin and tonic

Gipfel (-s, -) m summit, peak; (Pol) summit; (fig: Höhepunkt)

height

Gips (-es, -e) m (a. Med) plaster; **Gipsbein** nt: **sie hat ein ~** she's got her leg in plaster; **Gipsverband** m plaster cast

Giraffe (-, -n) f giraffe

Girokonto nt current account (Brit), checking account (US)

Gitarre (-, -n) f guitar

Gitter (-s, -) nt bars pl

glänzen vi (a. fig) to shine; **glänzend** adj shining; (fig) brilliant

Glas (-es, Gläser) nt glass; (Marmelade) jar; **zwei ~ Wein** two glasses of wine; **Glascontainer** m bottle bank; **Glaser(in)** m(f) glazier; **Glasscheibe** f pane (of glass); **Glassplitter** m splinter of glass

Glasur f glaze; (Gastr) icing

glatt adj smooth; (rutschig) slippery; (Lüge) downright; **Glatteis** nt (black) ice; **Glätteisen** nt hair straighteners pl

Glatze (-, -n) f bald head; (fam: Skinhead) skinhead

glauben vt, vi to believe (an +akk in); (meinen) to think; **jdm ~** to believe sb

gleich adj equal; (identisch) same, identical; **alle Menschen sind ~** all people are the same; **es ist mir ~** it's all the same to me ▷ adv equally; (sofort) straight away; (bald) in a minute; **~ groß/alt** the same size/age; **~ nach/an** right after/at; **Gleichberechtigung** f equal rights pl; **gleichen** (glich, geglichen) vi: **jdm/einer Sache ~** to be like sb/sth ▷ vr: **sich ~** to be alike; **gleichfalls** adv likewise; **danke ~!** thanks, and the same to you; **gleichgültig** adj indifferent; **gleichmäßig** adj regular; (Verteilung) even, equal;

gleichzeitig adj simultaneous ▷ adv at the same time

Gleis (-es, -e) nt track, rails pl; (Bahnsteig) platform

gleiten (glitt, geglitten) vi to glide; (rutschen) to slide; **Gleitschirmfliegen** (-s) nt paragliding

Gletscher (-s, -) m glacier; **Gletscherskifahren** nt glacier skiing; **Gletscherspalte** f crevasse

glich imperf von **gleichen**

Glied (-(e)s, -er) nt (Arm, Bein) limb; (von Kette) link; (Penis) penis; **Gliedmaßen** pl limbs pl

glitschig adj slippery

glitt imperf von **gleiten**

glitzern vi to glitter; (Sterne) to twinkle

Glocke (-, -n) f bell; **Glockenspiel** nt chimes pl

Glotze (-, -n) f (fam: TV) box; **glotzen** vi (fam) to stare

Glück (-(e)s) nt luck; (Freude) happiness; **~ haben** to be lucky; **viel ~!** good luck; **zum ~** fortunately; **glücklich** adj lucky; (froh) happy; **glücklicherweise** adv fortunately; **Glückwunsch** m congratulations pl; **herzlichen ~ zur bestandenen Prüfung** congratulations on passing your exam; **herzlichen ~ zum Geburtstag!** Happy Birthday

Glühbirne f light bulb; **glühen** vi to glow; **Glühwein** m mulled wine

GmbH (-, -s) f abk = **Gesellschaft mit beschränkter Haftung** = Ltd (Brit), ≈ Inc (US)

Gokart (-(s), -s) m go-kart

Gold (-(e)s) nt gold; **golden** adj gold; (fig) golden; **Goldfisch** m goldfish; **Goldmedaille** f gold medal

Golf (-(e)s, -e) m gulf; **der ~ von Biskaya** the Bay of Biscay ▷ (-s) nt golf; **Golfplatz** m golf course; **Golfschläger** m golf club

Gondel (-, -n) f gondola; (Seilbahn) cable-car

gönnen vt: **ich gönne es ihm** I'm really pleased for him; **sich** (dat) **etw ~** to allow oneself sth

googeln vt to google

goss imperf von **gießen**

gotisch adj Gothic

Gott (-es, Götter) m God; (Gottheit) god; **Gottesdienst** m service; **Göttin** f goddess

Grab (-(e)s, Gräber) nt grave

graben (grub, gegraben) vt to dig; **Graben** (-s, Gräben) m ditch

Grabstein m gravestone

Grad (-(e)s, -e) m degree; **wir haben 30 ~ Celsius** it's 30 degrees Celsius, it's 86 degrees Fahrenheit; **bis zu einem gewissen ~** up to a certain extent

Graf (-en, -en) m count; (in Großbritannien) earl

Graffiti pl graffiti sing

Grafik (-, -en) f graph; (Kunstwerk) graphic; (Illustration) diagram; **Grafikkarte** f (Inform) graphics card; **Grafikprogramm** nt (Inform) graphics software

Gräfin (-, -nen) f countess

Gramm (-s) nt gram(me)

Grammatik f grammar

Grapefruit (-, -s) f grapefruit

Graphik f siehe **Grafik**

Gras (-es, Gräser) nt grass

grässlich adj horrible

Gräte (-, -n) f (fish)bone

gratis adj, adv free (of charge)

gratulieren vi: **jdm (zu etw) ~** to congratulate sb (on sth); **(ich) gratuliere!** congratulations!

grau adj grey, gray (US); **grauhaarig** adj grey-haired

grausam adj cruel

gravierend adj (Fehler) serious

greifen (griff, gegriffen) vt to seize; **zu etw ~** (fig) to resort to sth ▷ vi (Regel etc) to have an effect (bei on)

grell adj harsh

Grenze (-, -n) f boundary; (Staat) border; (Schranke) limit; **grenzen** vi to border (an +akk on); **Grenzkontrolle** f border control; **Grenzübergang** m border crossing point; **Grenzverkehr** m border traffic

Grieche (-n, -n) m Greek; **Griechenland** nt Greece; **Griechin** f Greek; **griechisch** adj Greek; **Griechisch** nt Greek

griesgrämig adj grumpy

Grieß (-es, -e) m (Gastr) semolina

Griff (-(e)s, -e) m grip; (Tür etc) handle; **griffbereit** adj handy

Grill (-s, -s) m grill; (im Freien) barbecue

Grille (-, -n) f cricket

grillen vt to grill ▷ vi to have a barbecue; **Grillfest** nt, **Grillfete** f barbecue; **Grillkohle** f charcoal

grinsen vi to grin; (höhnisch) to sneer

Grippe (-, -n) f flu; **Grippeschutzimpfung** f flu vaccination

grob adj coarse; (Fehler, Verstoß) gross; (Einschätzung) rough

Grönland (-s) nt Greenland

groß adj big, large; (hoch) tall; (fig) great; (Buchstabe) capital; (erwachsen) grown-up; **im Großen und Ganzen** on the whole ▷ adv greatly; **großartig** adj wonderful

Großbritannien (-s) nt (Great) Britain

Großbuchstabe m capital letter

Größe (-, -n) f size; (Länge) height; (fig) greatness; **welche**

~ haben Sie? what size do you take?

Großeltern pl grandparents pl; **Großhandel** m wholesale trade; **Großhandel** m hypermarket; **Großmutter** f grandmother; **Großraum** m: **der ~ Manchester** Greater Manchester; **groß|schreiben** irr vt to write with a capital letter; **Großstadt** f city; **Großvater** m grandfather; **großzügig** adj generous; (Planung) on a large scale

Grotte (-, -n) f grotto

grub imperf von **graben**

Grübchen nt dimple

Grube (-, -n) f pit

grüezi interj (schweizerisch) hello

Gruft (-, -¨e) f vault

grün adj green; **~er Salat** lettuce; **~e Bohnen** French beans; **der ~e Punkt** symbol for recyclable packaging; **im ~en Bereich** hunky-dory

○ **GRÜNER PUNKT**
○
○ The **grüner Punkt** is the green
○ spot symbol which appears on
○ packaging, indicating that the
○ packaging should not be
○ thrown into the normal
○ household refuse but kept
○ separate to be recycled through
○ the **DSD** (Duales System
○ Deutschland) system. The
○ recycling is financed by licences
○ bought by the manufacturer
○ from the 'DSD' and the cost of
○ this is often passed on to the
○ consumer.

Grünanlage f park

Grund (-(e)s, Gründe) m (Ursache) reason; (Erdboden) ground; (See, Gefäß) bottom; (Grundbesitz) land, property; **aus gesundheitlichen**

Gründen for health reasons; **im ~e** basically; **aus diesem ~** for this reason

gründen vt to found; **Gründer(in)** m(f) founder

Grundgebühr f basic charge; **Grundgesetz** nt (German) Constitution

gründlich adj thorough

Gründonnerstag m Maundy Thursday

grundsätzlich adj fundamental, basic; **sie kommt ~ zu spät** she's always late; **Grundschule** f primary school; **Grundstück** nt plot; (Anwesen) estate; (Baugrundstück) site; **Grundwasser** nt ground water

Grüne(r) mf (Pol) Green; **die ~n** the Green Party

Gruppe (-, -n) f group; **Gruppenermäßigung** f group discount; **Gruppenreise** f group tour

Gruselfilm m horror film

Gruß (-es, Grüße) m greeting; **viele Grüße** best wishes; **Grüße an** (+akk) regards to; **mit freundlichen Grüßen** Yours sincerely (Brit), Sincerely yours (US); **sag ihm einen schönen ~ von mir** give him my regards; **grüßen** vt to greet; **grüß deine Mutter von mir** give your mother my regards; **Julia lässt (euch) ~** Julia sends (you) her regards

gucken vi to look

Gulasch (-(e)s, -e) nt goulash

gültig adj valid

Gummi (-s, -s) m o nt rubber; **Gummiband** nt rubber (o elastic (Brit)) band; **Gummibärchen** pl gums (o (in the shape of a bear) (Brit), gumdrops pl (in the shape of a bear) (US); **Gummihandschuhe** pl rubber gloves pl; **Gummistiefel** m wellington (boot) (Brit), rubber

boot (US)

günstig adj favourable; (Preis) good

gurgeln vi to gurgle; (im Mund) to gargle

Gurke (-, -n) f cucumber; **saure ~** gherkin

Gurt (-(e)s, -e) m belt

Gürtel (-s, -) m belt; (Geo) zone; **Gürtelrose** f shingles sing

GUS (-) f akr = **Gemeinschaft Unabhängiger Staaten** CIS

○ **SCHLÜSSELWORT**

gut adj good; **alles Gute** all the best; **also gut** all right then ▷ adv well; **gut gehen** to work, to come off; **es geht gut** sb's doing fine; **gut gemeint** well meant; **gut schmecken** to taste good; **jdm guttun** to do sb good; **gut, aber ...** OK, but ...; **(na) gut, ich komme** all right, I'll come; **gut drei Stunden** good three hours; **das kann gut sein** that may well be; **lass es gut sein** that'll do

Gutachten (-s, -) nt report; **Gutachter(in)** (-s, -) m(f) expert

gutartig adj (Med) benign

Güter pl goods pl; **Güterbahnhof** m goods station; **Güterzug** m goods train

gutgläubig adj trusting; **Guthaben** (-s) nt (credit) balance

gutmütig adj good-natured

Gutschein m voucher; **Gutschrift** f credit

Gymnasium nt = grammar school (Brit), = high school (US)

Gymnastik f exercises pl, keep-fit

Gynäkologe m, **Gynäkologin** f gynaecologist

Gyros (-, -) nt doner kebab

h

Haar (-(e)s, -e) nt hair; **um ein ~ nearly**; **sich** (dat) **die ~e schneiden lassen** to have one's hair cut; **Haarbürste** f hairbrush; **Haarfestiger** m setting lotion; **Haargel** nt hair gel; **Haarglätter** m hair straighteners pl; **haarig** adj hairy; (fig) nasty; **Haarschnitt** m haircut; **Haarspange** f hair slide (Brit), barrette (US); **Haarspliss** m split ends pl; **Haarspray** nt hair spray; **Haartrockner** (-s, -) m hairdryer; **Haarwaschmittel** nt shampoo

haben (hatte, gebabt) vt, vaux to have; **Hunger/Angst ~** to be hungry/afraid; **Ferien ~** to be on holiday (Brit) (o vacation (US)); **welches Datum ~ wir heute?** what's the date today?; **ich hätte gerne ...** I'd like ...; **hätten Sie etwas dagegen, wenn ...?** would you mind if ...?; **was hast du denn?** what's the matter (with you)?

Haben nt (Comm) credit

Habicht (-(e)s, -e) m hawk

Hacke (-, -n) f (im Garten) hoe; (Ferse) heel; **hacken** vt to chop; (Loch) to hack; (Erde) to hoe; **Hacker(in)** (-s, -) m(f) (Inform) hacker; **Hackfleisch** nt mince(d meat) (Brit), ground meat (US)

Hafen (-s, Häfen) m harbour; (großer) port; **Hafenstadt** f port

Hafer (-s, -) m oats pl; **Haferflocken** pl rolled oats pl

Haft (-) f custody; **haftbar** adj liable, responsible; **haften** vi to stick; **~ für** to be liable (o responsible) for; **Haftnotiz** f Post-it®; **Haftpflichtversicherung** f third party insurance; **Haftung** f liability

Hagebutte (-, -n) f rose hip

Hagel (-s) m hail; **hageln** vi impers to hail

Hahn (-(e)s, Hähne) m cock; (Wasserhahn) tap (Brit), faucet (US); **Hähnchen** nt cockerel; (Gastr) chicken

Hai(fisch) (-(e)s, -e) m shark

häkeln vi, vt to crochet; **Häkelnadel** f crochet hook

Haken (-s, -) m hook; (Zeichen) tick

halb adj half; **~ eins** half past twelve; (fam) half twelve; **eine ~e Stunde** half an hour; **~ offen** half-open; **Halbfinale** nt semifinal; **halbieren** vt to halve; **Halbinsel** f peninsula; **Halbjahr** nt half-year; **halbjährlich** adj half-yearly; **Halbmond** m (Astr) half-moon; (Symbol) crescent; **Halbpension** f half board; **halbseitig** adj: **~ gelähmt** paralyzed on one side; **halbtags**

adv (*arbeiten*) part-time; **halbwegs** *adv* (*leidlich*) reasonably; **Halbzeit** *f* half; (*Pause*) half-time

half *imperf von* **helfen**; **Hälfte** (-, -n) *f* half

Halle (-, -n) *f* hall; **Hallenbad** *nt* indoor (swimming) pool

hallo *interj* hello, hi

Halogenlampe *f* halogen lamp; **Halogenscheinwerfer** *m* halogen headlight

Hals (-es, Hälse) *m* neck; (*Kehle*) throat; **Halsband** *nt* (*für Tiere*) collar; **Halsentzündung** *f* sore throat; **Halskette** *f* necklace; **Hals-Nasen-Ohren-Arzt** *m*, **Hals-Nasen-Ohren-Ärztin** *f* ear, nose and throat specialist; **Halsschmerzen** *pl* sore throat *sing*; **Halstuch** *nt* scarf

halt *interj* stop ▷ *adv*: **das ist ~ so** that's just the way it is; **Halt** (-(e)s, -e) *m* stop; (*fester*) hold; (*innerer*) stability

haltbar *adj* durable; (*Lebensmittel*) non-perishable; **Haltbarkeitsdatum** *nt* best-before date

halten (hielt, gehalten) *vt* to keep; (*festhalten*) to hold; **~ für** to regard as; **~ von** to think of; **den Elfmeter ~** to save the penalty; **eine Rede ~** to give (*o* make) a speech ▷ *vi* to hold; (*frisch bleiben*) to keep; (*stoppen*) to stop; **zu jdm ~** to stand by sb ▷ *vr*: **sich ~** (*frisch bleiben*) to keep; (*sich behaupten*) to hold out

Haltestelle *f* stop; **Halteverbot** *nt*: **hier ist ~** you can't stop here

Haltung (*Körper*) posture; (*fig*) attitude; (*Selbstbeherrschung*) composure; **~ bewahren** to keep one's composure

Hamburg (-s) *nt* Hamburg; **Hamburger** (-s, -) *m* (*Gastr*) hamburger

Hammelfleisch *nt* mutton

Hammer (-s, Hämmer) *m* hammer; (*fig, fam*) howler; **das ist der ~** (*unerhört*) that's a bit much

Hämorr(ho)iden *pl* haemorrhoids *pl*, piles *pl*

Hamster (-s, -) *m* hamster

Hand (-, Hände) *f* hand; **jdm die ~ geben** to shake hands with sb; **jdn bei der ~ nehmen** to take sb by the hand; **eine ~ voll Reis/Leute** a handful of rice/people; **zu Händen von** attention; **Handarbeit** *f* (*Schulfach*) handicraft; **~ sein** to be handmade; **Handball** *m* handball; **Handbremse** *f* handbrake; **Handbuch** *nt* handbook, manual; **Handcreme** *f* hand cream; **Händedruck** *m* handshake

Handel (-s) *m* trade; (*Geschäft*) transaction; **handeln** *vi* to act; (*Comm*) to trade; **~ von** to be about ▷ *vr impers*: **sich ~ um** to be about; **es handelt sich um ...** it's about ...; **Handelskammer** *f* chamber of commerce; **Handelsschule** *f* business school

Handfeger (-s, -) *m* brush; **Handfläche** *f* palm; **Handgelenk** *nt* wrist; **handgemacht** *adj* handmade; **Handgepäck** *nt* hand luggage (*Brit*) (*o* baggage)

Händler(in) (-s, -) *m(f)* dealer

handlich *adj* handy

Handlung *f* act, action; (*von Roman, Film*) plot

Handschellen *pl* handcuffs *pl*; **Handschrift** *f* handwriting; **Handschuh** *m* glove; **Handschuhfach** *nt* glove compartment; **Handtasche** *f* handbag, purse (US); **Handtuch** *nt* towel; **Handwerk** *nt* trade; (*Kunst~*) craft; **Handwerker** (-s, -)

m workman

Handy (-s, -s) *nt* mobile (phone) (Brit), cell phone (US);
Handynummer *f* mobile number (Brit), cell phone number (US)

Hanf (-(e)s) *m* hemp

Hang (-(e)s, Hänge) *m* (Abhang) slope; (fig) tendency

Hängebrücke *f* suspension bridge; **Hängematte** *f* hammock

hängen (hing, gehangen) *vi* to hang; **an der Wand/an der Decke ~** to hang on the wall/from the ceiling; **an jdm ~** (fig) to be attached to sb; **~ bleiben** to get caught (an +dat on); (fig) to get stuck ▷ *vt* to hang (an +akk on)

Hantel (-, -n) *f* dumbbell

Hardware (-, -s) *f* (Inform) hardware

Harfe (-, -n) *f* harp

harmlos *adj* harmless

harmonisch *adj* harmonious

Harn (-(e)s, -e) *m* urine; **Harnblase** *f* bladder

Harpune (-, -n) *f* harpoon

hart *adj* hard; (fig) harsh; **zu jdm ~ sein** to be hard on sb; **~ gekocht** (Ei) hard-boiled; **hartnäckig** *adj* stubborn

Haschee (-s, -s) *nt* hash

Haschisch (-) *nt* hashish

Hase (-n, -n) *m* hare

Haselnuss *f* hazelnut

Hasenscharte *f* (Med) harelip

Hass (-es) *m* hatred (auf, gegen +akk of), hate; **einen ~ kriegen** (fam) to see red; **hassen** *vt* to hate

hässlich *adj* ugly; (gemein) nasty

Hast (-) *f* haste, hurry; **hastig** *adj* hasty

hatte *imperf von* **haben**

Haube (-, -n) *f* (Mütze) cap; (Auto) bonnet (Brit), hood (US)

Hauch (-(e)s, -e) *m* breath; (Luft~)

breeze; (fig) trace; **hauchdünn** *adj* (Schicht, Scheibe) wafer-thin

hauen (haute, gehauen) *vt* to hit

Haufen (-s, -) *m* pile; **ein ~ Geld** (viel Geld) a lot of money

häufig *adj* frequent ▷ *adv* frequently, often

Haupt- *in zW* main;
Hauptbahnhof *m* central (o main) station; **Hauptdarsteller(in)** *m(f)* leading actor/lady; **Haupteingang** *m* main entrance; **Hauptgericht** *nt* main course;
Hauptgeschäftszeiten *pl* peak shopping hours *pl*; **Hauptgewinn** *m* first prize

Häuptling *m* chief

Hauptquartier *nt* headquarters *pl*; **Hauptreisezeit** *f* peak tourist season; **Hauptrolle** *f* leading role; **Hauptsache** *f* main thing; **hauptsächlich** *adv* mainly, chiefly; **Hauptsaison** *f* high (o peak) season; **Hauptsatz** *m* main clause; **Hauptschule** *f* = secondary school (Brit), = junior high school (US); **Hauptspeicher** *m* (Inform) main storage (o memory); **Hauptstadt** *f* capital; **Hauptstraße** *f* main road; (im Stadtzentrum) main street; **Hauptverkehrszeit** *f* rush hour

Haus (-es, Häuser) *nt* house; **nach ~e** home; **zu ~e** at home; **jdn nach ~e bringen** to take sb home; **bei uns zu ~e** (Heimat) where we come from; (Familie) in my family; (Haus) at our place; **Hausarbeit** *f* housework; **Hausaufgabe** *f* (Schule) homework; **~n** *pl* homework *sing*; **Hausbesitzer(in)** (-s, -) *m(f)* house owner; (Vermieter) landlord/-lady; **Hausbesuch** *m* home visit; **Hausbewohner(in)** (-s, -) *m(f)* occupant; **Hausflur** *m* hall; **Hausfrau** *f*

housewife; hausgemacht adj
homemade; **Haushalt** m
household; (Pol) budget;
Hausherr(in) m(f) host/hostess;
(Vermieter) landlord/-lady

häuslich adj domestic

Hausmann m house-husband;
Hausmannskost f good plain
cooking; **Hausmeister(in)** m(f)
caretaker (Brit), janitor (US);
Hausnummer f house number;
Hausordnung f (house) rules pl;
Hausschlüssel m front-door key;
Hausschuh m slipper; **Haustier**
nt pet; **Haustür** f front door

Haut (-, Häute) f skin; (Tier) hide;
Hautarzt m, **Hautärztin** f
dermatologist; **Hautausschlag**
m skin rash; **Hautcreme** f skin
cream; **Hautfarbe** f skin colour;
Hautkrankheit f skin disease

Hawaii (-s) nt Hawaii

Hbf. abk = **Hauptbahnhof** central
station

Hebamme (-, -n) f midwife

Hebel (-s, -) m lever

heben (hob, gehoben) vt to raise,
to lift

Hebräisch (-) nt Hebrew

Hecht (-(e)s, -e) m pike

Heck (-(e)s, -e) m (von Boot) stern;
(von Auto) rear; **Heckantrieb** m
rear-wheel drive

Hecke (-, -n) f hedge

Heckklappe f tailgate;
Hecklicht nt tail-light;
Heckscheibe f rear window

Hefe (-, -n) f yeast

Heft (-(e)s, -e) nt notebook,
exercise book; (Ausgabe) issue

heftig adj violent; (Kritik, Streit)
fierce

Heftklammer f paper clip;
Heftpflaster nt plaster (Brit),
Band-Aid® (US)

Heide (-, -n) f heath, moor;
Heidekraut nt heather

Heidelbeere f bilberry, blueberry

heidnisch adj (Brauch) pagan

heikel adj (Angelegenheit)
awkward; (wählerisch) fussy

heil adj (Sache) in one piece,
intact; (Person) unhurt; **heilbar**
adj curable

Heilbutt (-(e)s, -e) m halibut

heilen vt to cure ▷ vi to heal

heilig adj holy; **Heiligabend** m
Christmas Eve; **Heilige(r)** mf
saint

Heilmittel nt remedy, cure (gegen
for); **Heilpraktiker(in)** (-s, -) m(f)
non-medical practitioner

heim adv home; **Heim** (-(e)s, -e) nt
home

Heimat (-, -en) f home
(town/country); **Heimatland** nt
home country

heim|fahren irr vi to drive
home; **Heimfahrt** f journey
home; **heimisch** adj
(Bevölkerung, Brauchtum) local;
(Tiere, Pflanzen) native;

heim|kommen irr vi to come (o
return) home

heimlich adj secret

Heimreise f journey home;
Heimspiel nt (Sport) home game;
Heimvorteil m (Sport) home
advantage; **Heimweg** m way
home; **Heimweh** (-s) nt
homesickness; **~ haben** to be
homesick; **Heimwerker(in)** m(f)
DIY enthusiast

Heirat (-, -en) f marriage;
heiraten vi to get married ▷ vt
to marry; **Heiratsantrag** m
proposal; **er hat ihr einen
~ gemacht** he proposed to her

heiser adj hoarse

heiß adj hot; (Diskussion) heated;
mir ist ~ I'm hot

heißen (hieß, geheißen) vi to be
called; (bedeuten) to mean; **ich
heiße Tom** my name is Tom; **wie**

~ Sie? what's your name?; **wie heißt sie mit Nachnamen?** what's her surname?; **wie heißt das auf Englisch?** what's that in English? ▷ vi impers: **es heißt (man sagt)** it is said; **es heißt in dem Brief ...** it says in the letter ...; **das heißt** that is

Heißluftherd m fan-assisted oven

heiter adj cheerful; (Wetter) bright

heizen vt to heat; **Heizkissen** nt (Med) heated pad; **Heizkörper** m radiator; **Heizöl** nt fuel oil; **Heizung** f heating

Hektar (-s, -) nt hectare

Hektik (-, -en) f: **nur keine ~!** take it easy; **hektisch** adj hectic

Held (-en, -en) m hero; **Heldin** f heroine

helfen (half, geholfen) vi to help (jdm bei etw sb with sth); (nützen) to be of use; **sie weiß sich (dat) zu ~** she can manage ▷ vi impers: **es hilft nichts, du musst ...** it's no use, you have to ...; **Helfer(in)** m(f) helper; (Mitarbeiter) assistant

Helikopter-Skiing (-s) nt heliskiing, helicopter skiing

hell adj bright; (Farbe) light; (Hautfarbe) fair; **hellblau** adj light blue; **hellblond** adj ash-blond; **hellgelb** adj pale yellow; **hellgrün** adj light green; **Hellseher(in)** m(f) clairvoyant

Helm (-(e)s, -e) m helmet; **Helmpflicht** f compulsory wearing of helmets

Hemd (-(e)s, -en) nt shirt; (Unter~) vest

hemmen vt to check; (behindern) to hamper; **gehemmt sein** to be inhibited; **Hemmung** f (psychisch) inhibition; **sie hatte keine ~, ihn zu betrügen** she had no scruples about deceiving him; (moralisch) scruple

Henkel (-s, -) m handle

Henna (-s) nt henna

Henne (-, -n) f hen

Hepatitis (-, Hepatitiden) f hepatitis

○ **SCHLÜSSELWORT**

her adv 1 (Richtung) **komm her zu mir** come here (to me); **von England her** from England; **von weit her** from a long way away; **her damit!** hand it over!; **wo hat er das her?** where did he get that from?; **wo bist du her?** where do you come from?
2 (Blickpunkt) **von der Form her** as far as the form is concerned
3 (zeitlich) **das ist 5 Jahre her** that was 5 years ago; **ich kenne ihn von früher her** I know him from before

herab adv down; **herablassend** adj (Bemerkung) condescending; **herab|sehen** irr vi: **auf jdn ~** to look down on sb; **herab|setzen** vt to reduce; (fig) to disparage

heran adv: **näher ~!** come closer; **heran|kommen** irr vi to approach; **~ an** (+akk) to be able to get at; (fig) to be able to get hold of; **heran|wachsen** irr vi to grow up

herauf adv up; **herauf|beschwören** irr vt to evoke; (verursachen) to cause; **herauf|ziehen** irr vt to pull up ▷ vi to approach; (Sturm) to gather

heraus adv out; **heraus|bekommen** irr vt (Geheimnis) to find out; (Rätsel) to solve; **ich bekomme noch zwei Euro heraus** I've got two euros change to come; **heraus|bringen** irr vt to bring out; **heraus|finden**

irr vt to find out; **heraus|fordern** *vt* to challenge; **Herausforderung** *f* challenge; **heraus|geben** *irr vt* (*Buch*) to edit; (*veröffentlichen*) to publish; **jdm zwei Euro ~** to give sb two euros change; **geben Sie mir bitte auf 20 Euro ~** could you give me change for 20 euros, please?; **heraus|holen** *vt* to get out (*aus of*); **heraus|kommen** *irr vi* to come out; **dabei kommt nichts heraus** nothing will come of it; **heraus|stellen** *vr*: **sich ~** to turn out (*als* to be); **heraus|ziehen** *irr vt* to pull out

Herbergseltern *pl* (youth hostel) wardens *pl*

Herbst (-(e)s, -e) *m* autumn, fall (US)

Herd (-(e)s, -e) *m* cooker, stove

Herde (-, -n) *f* herd; (*Schafe*) flock

herein *adv* in; **~!** come in; **herein|fallen** *irr vi*: **wir sind auf einen Betrüger hereingefallen** we were taken in by a swindler; **herein|legen** *vt*: **jdn ~** (*fig*) to take sb for a ride

Herfahrt *f* journey here; **auf der ~** on the way here

Hergang *m* course (of events); **schildern Sie mir den ~** tell me what happened

Hering (-s, -e) *m* herring

her|kommen *irr vi* to come; **wo kommt sie her?** where does she come from?

Heroin (-s) *nt* heroin

Herpes (-) *m* (*Med*) herpes

Herr (-(e)n, -en) *m* (*vor Namen*) Mr; (*Mann*) gentleman; (*Adliger, Gott*) Lord; **mein ~!** sir; **meine ~en!** gentlemen; **Sehr geehrte Damen und ~en** Dear Sir or Madam; **herrenlos** *adj* (*Gepäck*) abandoned; (*Tier*) stray; **Herrentoilette** *f* men's toilet, gents

her|richten *vt* to prepare

herrlich *adj* marvellous, splendid

Herrschaft *f* rule; (*Macht*) power; **meine ~en!** ladies and gentlemen!

herrschen *vi* to rule; (*bestehen*) to be

her|stellen *vt* to make; (*industriell*) to manufacture; **Hersteller(in)** *m(f)* manufacturer; **Herstellung** *f* production

herüber *adv* over

herum *adv* around; (*im Kreis*) round; **um etw ~** around sth; **du hast den Pulli falsch ~ an** your sweater's inside out; **anders ~** the other way round; **herum|fahren** *irr vi* to drive around; **herum| führen** *vi*: **jdn in der Stadt ~** to show sb around the town ▷ *vi*: **die Straße führt um das Zentrum herum** the road goes around the city centre; **herum|kommen** *irr vi*: **sie ist viel in der Welt herumgekommen** she's been around the world; **um etw ~** (*vermeiden*) to get out of sth; **herum|kriegen** *vt* to talk round; **herum|treiben** *irr vr*: **sich ~** to hang around

herunter *adv* down; **heruntergekommen** *adj* (*Gebäude, Gegend*) run-down; (*Person*) down-at-heel; **herunter|handeln** *vt* to get down; **herunter|holen** *vt* to bring down; **herunter|kommen** *irr vi* to come down; **herunterladbar** *adj* (*Inform*) downloadable; **herunter|laden** *irr vt* (*Inform*) to download

hervor *adv* out; **hervor|bringen** *irr vt* to produce; (*Wort*) to utter; **hervor|heben** *irr vt* to emphasize; **hervorragend** *adj* excellent; **hervor|rufen** *irr vt* to cause, to give rise to

Herz (-ens, -en) *nt* heart; (*Karten*)

hearts pl; **von ganzem ~en**
wholeheartedly; **sich** (dat) **etw zu
~ nehmen** to take sth to heart;
Herzanfall m heart attack;
Herzbeschwerden pl heart
trouble sing; **Herzfehler** m heart
defect; **herzhaft** adj (Essen)
substantial; **~ lachen** to have a
good laugh; **Herzinfarkt** m
heart attack; **Herzklopfen** (-s) nt
(Med) palpitations pl; **ich hatte
~** (vor Aufregung) my heart was
pounding (with excitement);
herzkrank adj; **sie ist ~** she's got
a heart condition; **herzlich** adj
(Empfang, Mensch) warm; **~en
Glückwunsch** congratulations

Herzog(in) (-s, Herzöge) m(f)
duke/duchess

Herzschlag m heartbeat;
(Herzversagen) heart failure;
Herzschrittmacher m pacemaker; **Herzstillstand** m
cardiac arrest

Hessen (-s) nt Hessen

heterosexuell adj heterosexual;
Heterosexuelle(r) mf
heterosexual

Hetze (-, -n) f (Eile) rush; **hetzen**
vt to rush ▷ vr: **sich ~** to rush

Heu (-(e)s) nt hay

heuer adv this year

heulen vi to howl; (weinen) to cry

Heuschnupfen m hay fever;
Heuschrecke (-, -n) f grasshopper; (größer) locust

heute adv today; **~ Abend/früh**
this evening/morning; **~ Morgen**
this morning; **~ Nacht** tonight;
(letzte Nacht) last night; **~ in acht
Tagen** a week (from) today; **sie
hat bis ~ nicht bezahlt** she hasn't
paid to this day; **heutig** adj: **die
~e Zeitung/Generation** today's
paper/generation; **heutzutage**
adv nowadays

Hexe (-, -n) f witch;

Hexenschuss m lumbago

hielt imperf von **halten**

hier adv here; **~ entlang** this way;
ich bin auch nicht von ~ I'm a
stranger here myself; **hier|bleiben**
irr vi to stay here; **hier|lassen**
irr vt to leave here; **hierher** adv
here; **das gehört nicht ~** that
doesn't belong here; **hiermit** adv
with this; **hierzulande** adv in
this country

hiesig adj local

hieß imperf von **heißen**

Hi-Fi-Anlage f hi-fi (system)

high adj (fam) high; **Highlife** (-s)
nt high life; **~ machen** to live it
up; **Hightech** (-s) nt high tech

Hilfe (-, -n) f help; (für Notleidende,
finanziell) aid; **~!** help!; **Erste
~ leisten** to give first aid; **um
~ bitten** to ask for help; **hilflos**
adj helpless; **hilfsbereit** adj
helpful; **Hilfsmittel** nt aid

Himbeere f raspberry

Himmel (-s, -) m sky; (Rel)
heaven; **Himmelfahrt** f
Ascension; **Himmelsrichtung** f
direction; **himmlisch** adj
heavenly

○ **SCHLÜSSELWORT**

hin adv 1 (Richtung) **hin und zurück**
there and back; **hin und her** to
and fro; **bis zur Mauer hin** up to
the wall; **wo ist er hin?** where has
he gone?; **Geld hin, Geld her**
money or no money
2 (auf... hin) **auf meine Bitte hin**
at my request; **auf seinen Rat hin**
on the basis of his advice
3 **mein Glück ist hin** my happiness
has gone

hinab adv down; **hinab|gehen** irr
vi to go down

hinauf adv up; **hinauf|gehen** irr

vi, vt to go up; **hinauf|steigen** *irr vi* to climb (up)

hinaus *adv out;* **hinaus|gehen** *irr vi* to go out; **das Zimmer geht auf den See hinaus** the room looks out onto the lake; **~ über** (+*akk*) to exceed; **hinaus|laufen** *irr vi* to run out; **~ auf** (+*akk*) to come to, to amount to; **hinaus|schieben** *irr vt* to put off, to postpone; **hinaus|werfen** *irr vt* to throw out; (*aus Firma*) to fire, to sack (*Brit*); **hinaus|zögern** *vr:* **sich ~** to take longer than expected

Hinblick *m in* (*o* **im**) **~ auf** (+*akk*) with regard to; (*wegen*) in view of

hin|bringen *irr vt:* **ich bringe Sie hin** I'll take you there

hindern *vt* to prevent; **jdn daran ~, etw zu tun** to stop (*o* prevent) sb from doing sth; **Hindernis** *nt* obstacle

Hinduismus *m* Hinduism

hindurch *adv* through; **das ganze Jahr ~** throughout the year, all year round; **die ganze Nacht ~** all night (long)

hinein *adv in;* **hinein|gehen** *vi* to go in; **~ in** (+*akk*) to go into, to enter; **hinein|passen** *vi* to fit in; **~ in** (+*akk*) to fit into

hin|fahren *irr vi* to go there ▷ *vt* to take there; **Hinfahrt** *f* outward journey

hin|fallen *irr vi* to fall (down)

Hinflug *m* outward flight

hing *imperf von* **hängen**

hin|gehen *irr vi* to go there; (*Zeit*) to pass; **hin|halten** *irr vt* to hold out; (*warten lassen*) to put off

hinken *vi* to limp; **der Vergleich hinkt** the comparison doesn't work

hin|knien *vr:* **sich ~** to kneel down; **hin|legen** *vt* to put down ▷ *vr:* **sich ~** to lie down; **hin|nehmen** *irr vt* (*fig*) to put up

with, to take; **Hinreise** *f* outward journey; **hin|setzen** *vr:* **sich ~** to sit down; **hinsichtlich** *prep* +*gen* with regard to; **hin|stellen** *vt* to put (down) ▷ *vr:* **sich ~** to stand

hinten *adv* at the back; (*im Auto*) in the back; (*dahinter*) behind

hinter *prep* +*dat o akk* behind; (*nach*) after; **~ jdm her sein** to be after sb; **etw ~ sich** (*akk*) **bringen** to get sth over (and done) with; **Hinterachse** *f* rear axle; **Hinterausgang** *m* rear exit; **Hinterbein** *nt* hind leg; **Hinterbliebene(r)** *mf* dependant; **hintere(r, s)** *adj* rear, back; **hintereinander** *adv* (*in einer Reihe*) one behind the other; (*hintereinander her*) one after the other; **drei Tage ~** three days running (*o* in a row); **Hintereingang** *m* rear entrance; **Hintergedanke** *m* ulterior motive; **hintergehen** *irr vt* to deceive; **Hintergrund** *m* background; **hinterher** *adv* (*zeitlich*) afterwards; **los, ~!** come on, after him/her/them; **Hinterkopf** *m* back of the head; **hinterlassen** *irr vt* to leave; **jdm eine Nachricht ~** to leave a message for sb; **hinterlegen** *vt* to leave (*bei* with)

Hintern (-, -) *m* (*fam*) backside, bum

Hinterradantrieb *m* (*Auto*) rear-wheel drive; **Hinterteil** *nt* back (part); (*Hintern*) behind; **Hintertür** *f* back door

hinüber *adv* over; **~ sein** (*fam: kaputt*) to be ruined; (*verdorben*) to have gone bad; **hinüber|gehen** *irr vi* to go over

hinunter *adv* down; **hinunter|gehen** *irr vi, vt* to go down; **hinunter|schlucken** *vt* *(a. fig)* to swallow

Hinweg *m* outward journey

hinweg|setzen *vr* **sich über etw** *(akk)* ~ to ignore sth

Hinweis *(-es, -e) m (Andeutung)* hint; *(Anweisung)* instruction; *(Verweis)* reference; **hin|weisen** *vi* **jdn auf etw** *(acc)* ~ to point sth out to sb; **jdn nochmal auf etw** ~ to remind sb of sth

hinzu *adv* in addition; **hinzu|fügen** *vt* to add; **hinzu|kommen** *vi:* **zu jdm** ~ to join sb; **es war kalt, hinzu kam, dass es auch noch regnete** it was cold, and on top of that it was raining

Hirn *(-(e)s, -e) nt* brain; *(Verstand)* brains *pl;* **Hirnhautentzündung** *f* meningitis

Hirsch *(-(e)s, -e) m* deer; *(als Speise)* venison

Hirte *(-n, -n) m* shepherd

historisch *adj* historical

Hit *(-s, -s) m (fig, Mus, Inform)* hit; **Hitliste** *f,* **Hitparade** *f* charts *pl*

Hitze *(-) f* heat; **hitzebeständig** *adj* heat-resistant; **Hitzewelle** *f* heatwave; **hitzig** *adj* hot-tempered; *(Debatte)* heated; **Hitzschlag** *m* heatstroke

HIV *(-(s), -(s)) nt abk =* **Human Immunodeficiency Virus** HIV; **HIV-negativ** *adj* HIV-negative; **HIV-positiv** *adj* HIV-positive

H-Milch *f* long-life milk

hob *imperf von* **heben**

Hobby *(-s, -s) nt* hobby

Hobel *(-s, -) m* plane

hoch *adj* high; *(Baum)* tall; *(Schnee)* deep; **der Zaun ist drei Meter** ~ the fence is three metres high; ~ **auflösend** high-resolution; ~ **begabt** extremely gifted; **das ist mir zu** ~ that's above my head; ~ **soll sie leben!, sie lebe ~!** three cheers for her; **4 ~ 2 ist 16** 4 squared

is 16; **4 ~ 5 4** to the power of 5

Hoch *(-s, -s) nt (Ruf)* cheer; *(Meteo)* high; **hochachtungsvoll** *adv (in Briefen)* Yours faithfully; **Hochbetrieb** *m:* **es herrscht** ~ they/we are extremely busy; **Hochdeutsch** *nt* High German; **Hochgebirge** *nt* high mountains *pl;* **Hochgeschwindigkeitszug** *m* high-speed train; **Hochhaus** *nt* high rise; **hoch|heben** *irr vt* to lift (up); **hoch|laden** *irr vt (Inform)* to upload; **Hochsaison** *f* high season; **Hochschule** *f* college; *(Universität)* university; **Hochschulreife** *f* **er hat (die)** ~ he's got his A-levels *(Brit),* he's graduated from high school *(US);* **Hochsommer** *m* midsummer; **Hochspannung** *f* great tension; *(Elek)* high voltage; **Hochsprung** *m* high jump

höchst *adv* highly, extremely; **höchste(r, s)** *adj* highest; *(äußerste)* extreme; **höchstens** *adv* at the most; **Höchstform** *f (Sport)* top form; **Höchstgeschwindigkeit** *f* maximum speed; **Höchstparkdauer** *f* maximum stay

Hochstuhl *m* high chair

höchstwahrscheinlich *adv* very probably

Hochwasser *nt* high water; *(Überschwemmung)* floods *pl;* **hochwertig** *adj* high-quality

Hochzeit *(-, -en) f* wedding; **Hochzeitsnacht** *f* wedding night; **Hochzeitsreise** *f* honeymoon; **Hochzeitstag** *m* wedding day; *(Jahrestag)* wedding anniversary

hocken *vi* to squat, to crouch

Hocker *(-s, -) m* stool

Hockey *(-s) nt* hockey

Hoden *(-s, -) m* testicle

Hof *(-(e)s, Höfe) m (Hinterhof)* yard;

(Innenhof) courtyard; *(Bauernhof)* farm; *(Königshof)* court

hoffen vi to hope *(auf +akk* for*)*; **ich hoffe es** I hope so; **hoffentlich** adv hopefully; **~ nicht** I hope not; **Hoffnung** f hope; **hoffnungslos** adj hopeless

höflich adj polite; **Höflichkeit** f politeness

hohe(r, s) adj siehe hoch

Höhe (-, -n) f height; *(Anhöhe)* hill; *(einer Summe)* amount; **in einer ~ von 5000 Metern** at an altitude of 5,000 metres; *(Flughöhe)* altitude; **Höhenangst** f vertigo

Höhepunkt m *(einer Reise)* high point; *(einer Veranstaltung)* highlight; *(eines Films; sexuell)* climax

höher adj, adv higher

hohl adj hollow

Höhle (-, -n) f cave

holen vt to get, to fetch; *(abholen)* to pick up; *(Atem)* to catch; **die Polizei ~** to call the police; **jdn/etw ~ lassen** to send for sb/sth

Holland nt Holland; **Holländer(in)** (-s, -) m(f) Dutchman/-woman; **holländisch** adj Dutch

Hölle (-, -n) f hell

Hologramm nt hologram

holperig adj bumpy

Holunder (-s, -) m elder

Holz (-es, Hölzer) nt wood; **Holzboden** m wooden floor; **hölzern** adj wooden; **holzig** adj *(Stängel)* woody; **Holzkohle** f charcoal

Homebanking (-s) nt home banking, online banking; **Homepage** (-, -s) f home page; **Hometrainer** m exercise machine

Homoehe f *(fam)* gay marriage

homöopathisch adj homeopathic

homosexuell adj homosexual; **Homosexuelle(r)** mf homosexual

Honig (-s, -e) m honey; **Honigmelone** f honeydew melon

Honorar (-s, -e) nt fee

Hopfen (-s, -) m *(Bot)* hop; *(beim Brauen)* hops pl

hoppla interj whoops, oops

horchen vi to listen *(auf +akk* to*)*; *(an der Tür)* to eavesdrop

hören vt, vi *(passiv, mitbekommen)* to hear; *(zufällig)* to overhear; *(aufmerksam zuhören; Radio, Musik)* to listen to; **ich habe schon viel von Ihnen gehört** I've heard a lot about you; **Hörer** m *(Tel)* receiver; **Hörer(in)** m(f) listener; **Hörgerät** nt hearing aid

Horizont (-(e)s, -e) m horizon; **das geht über meinen ~** that's beyond me

Hormon (-s, -e) nt hormone

Hornhaut f hard skin; *(des Auges)* cornea

Hornisse (-, -n) f hornet

Horoskop (-s, -e) nt horoscope

Hörsaal m lecture hall; **Hörsturz** m acute hearing loss; **Hörweite** f: **in/außer ~** within/out of earshot

Höschenwindel (-, -n) f nappy *(Brit)*, diaper *(US)*

Hose (-, -n) f trousers pl *(Brit)*, pants pl *(US)*; *(Unterhose)* (under)pants pl; **eine ~** a pair of trousers/pants; **kurze ~** (pair of) shorts pl; **Hosenanzug** m trouser suit *(Brit)*, pantsuit *(US)*; **Hosenschlitz** m fly, flies *(Brit)*; **Hosentasche** f trouser pocket *(Brit)*, pant pocket *(US)*; **Hosenträger** m braces pl *(Brit)*, suspenders pl *(US)*

Hospital (-s, Hospitäler) nt hospital

Hotdog (-s, -s) nt o m hot dog

Hotel (-s, -s) nt hotel; **in
welchem ~ seid ihr?** which hotel
are you staying at?;
Hoteldirektor(in) m(f) hotel
manager; **Hotelkette** f hotel
chain; **Hotelzimmer** nt hotel
room

Hotline (-, -s) f hot line; **Hotspot**
m (wireless) hotspot

Hubraum m cubic capacity

hübsch adj (Mädchen, Kind, Kleid)
pretty; (gutaussehend: Mann, Frau)
good-looking, cute

Hubschrauber (-s, -) m
helicopter

Huf (-(e)s, -e) m hoof; **Hufeisen**
nt horseshoe

Hüfte (-, -n) f hip

Hügel (-s, -) m hill; **hügelig** adj
hilly

Huhn (-(e)s, Hühner) nt hen;
(Gastr) chicken; **Hühnchen** nt
chicken; **Hühnerauge** nt corn;
Hühnerbrühe f chicken
broth

Hülle (-, -n) f cover; (für Ausweis)
case; (Zellophan) wrapping

Hummel (-, -n) f bumblebee

Hummer (-s, -) m lobster;
Hummerkrabbe f king prawn

Humor (-s) m humour; **~ haben**
to have a sense of humour;
humorlos adj humourless;
humorvoll adj humorous

humpeln vi hobble

Hund (-(e)s, -e) m dog;
Hundeleine f dog lead (Brit), dog
leash (US)

hundert num hundred;
Hundertjahrfeier f centenary;
hundertprozentig adj, adv one
hundred per cent; **hundertste(r,
s)** adj hundredth

Hündin f bitch

Hunger (-s) m hunger;
~ haben/bekommen to be/get
hungry; **hungern** vi to go

hungry; (ernsthaft, dauernd) to
starve

Hupe (-, -n) f horn; **hupen** vi to
sound one's horn

Hüpfburg f bouncy castle®;
hüpfen vi to hop; (springen) to
jump

Hürde (-, -n) f hurdle

Hure (-, -n) f whore

hurra interj hooray

husten vi to cough; **Husten** (-s)
m cough; **Hustenbonbon** nt
cough sweet; **Hustensaft** m
cough mixture

Hut (-(e)s, Hüte) m hat

hüten vt to look after ▷ vr: **sich
~** to watch out; **sich ~, etw zu tun**
to take care not to do sth; **sich
~ vor** (+dat) to beware of

Hütte (-, -n) f hut, cottage;
Hüttenkäse m cottage cheese

Hyäne (-, -n) f hyena

Hydrant m hydrant

hygienisch adj hygienic

Hyperlink (-s, -s) m hyperlink

Hypnose (-, -n) f hypnosis;
Hypnotiseur(in) m(f) hypnotist;
hypnotisieren vt to hypnotize

Hypothek (-, -en) f mortgage

hysterisch adj hysterical

I

i. A. abk = **im Auftrag** pp

IC (-, -s) m abk = **Intercityzug**
Intercity (train)

ICE (-, -s) m abk =
Intercityexpresszug German
high-speed train

ich pron I; **~ bin's** it's me; **~ nicht**
not me; **du und ~** you and me; **hier
bin ~!** here I am; **~ Idiot!** stupid me

Icon (-s, -s) nt (Inform) icon

IC-Zuschlag m Intercity
supplement

ideal adj ideal

Idee (-, -n) f idea

identifizieren vt to identify
▷ vr: **sich mit jdm/etw ~** to
identify with sb/sth

identisch adj identical

Identität f identity

Idiot(in) (-en, -en) m(f) idiot;
idiotisch adj idiotic

Idol (-s, -e) nt idol

Idylle f idyll; **idyllisch** adj idyllic

Igel (-s, -) m hedgehog

ignorieren vt to ignore

ihm pron dat sing von **er/es**; (to)
him, (to) it; **wie geht es ~?** how is
he?; **ein Freund von ~** a friend of
his ▷ pron dat von **es**; (to) it

ihn pron akk sing von **er**; (Person)
him; (Sache) it

ihnen pron dat pl von **sie**; (to)
them; **wie geht es ~?** how are
they?; **ein Freund von ~** a friend of
theirs

Ihnen pron dat sing u pl von **Sie**;
(to) you; **wie geht es ~?** how are
you?; **ein Freund von ~** a friend of
yours

⬤ SCHLÜSSELWORT

ihr pron **1** (nom pl) you; **ihr seid es**
it's you
2 (dat von sie) to her; **gib es ihr** give
it to her; **er steht neben ihr** he is
standing beside her
▷ possessiv pron **1** (sg) her; (bei
Tieren, Dingen) its; **ihr Mann** her
husband
2 (pl) their; **die Bäume und ihre
Blätter** the trees and their
leaves

Ihr pron von **Sie**; (adjektivisch) your;
~(e) XY (am Briefende) Yours, XY

ihre(r, s) pron (substantivisch,
sing) hers; (pl) theirs; **das ist
~/~r/ihr(e)s** that's hers; (pl) that's
theirs

Ihre(r, s) pron (substantivisch)
yours; **das ist ~/~r/ihr(e)s** that's
yours

ihretwegen adv (wegen ihr)
because of her; (ihr zuliebe) for her
sake; (um sie) about her; (von ihr
aus) as far as she is concerned
▷ adv (wegen ihnen) because of
them; (ihnen zuliebe) for their sake;
(um sie) about them; (von ihnen aus)

as far as they are concerned; **ihretwegen** adv (wegen ihnen) because of you; (ihnen zuliebe) for your sake; (um Sie) about you; (von ihnen aus) as far as you are concerned

Ikone (-, -n) f icon

illegal adj illegal

Illusion f illusion; **sich** (dat) **~en machen** to delude oneself; **illusorisch** adj illusory

Illustration f illustration

Illustrierte (-n, -n) f (glossy) magazine

im kontr von in dem; **~ Bett** in bed; **~ Fernsehen** on TV; **~ Radio** on the radio; **~ Bus/Zug** on the bus/train; **~ Januar** in January; **~ Stehen** (while) standing up

Imbiss (-es, -e) m snack; **Imbissbude** f, **Imbissstube** f snack bar

Imbusschlüssel m hex key

immer adv always; **~ mehr** more and more; **~ wieder** again and again; **~ noch** still; **~ noch nicht** still not; **für ~** forever; **~ wenn ich ...** every time I ...; **~ schöner/trauriger** more and more beautiful/sadder and sadder; **was/wer/wo/wann (auch) ~** whatever/whoever/wherever/whenever; **immerhin** adv after all; **immerzu** adv all the time

Immigrant(in) m(f) immigrant

Immobilien pl property sing, real estate sing; **Immobilienmakler(in)** m(f) estate agent (Brit), realtor (US)

immun adj immune (gegen to); **Immunschwäche** f immunodeficiency; **Immunschwächekrankheit** f immune deficiency syndrome; **Immunsystem** nt immune system

impfen vt to vaccinate; **ich muss mich gegen Pocken ~ lassen** I've got to get myself vaccinated against smallpox; **Impfpass** m vaccination card; **Impfstoff** m vaccine; **Impfung** f vaccination

imponieren vi to impress (jdm sb)

Import (-(e)s, -e) m import; **importieren** vt to import

impotent adj impotent

imstande adj: **~ sein** to be in a position; (fähig) to be able

SCHLÜSSELWORT

in prep +akk **1** (räumlich: wohin?) in; into; **in die Stadt** into town; **in die Schule gehen** to go to school **2** (zeitlich) **bis ins 20. Jahrhundert** into o up to the 20th century ▷ +dat **1** (räumlich: wo?) in; **in der Stadt** in town; **in der Schule sein** to be at school **2** (zeitlich: wann?) **in diesem Jahr** this year; (in jenem Jahr) in that year; **heute in zwei Wochen** two weeks today

inbegriffen adj included

indem conj: **sie gewann, ~ sie mogelte** she won by cheating

Inder(in) (-s, -) m(f) Indian

Indianer(in) (-s, -) m(f) American Indian, Native American; **indianisch** adj American Indian, Native American

Indien (-s) nt India

indirekt adj indirect

indisch adj Indian

indiskret adj indiscreet

individuell adj individual

Indonesien (-s) nt Indonesia

Industrie f industry; **Industrie-** in zW industrial; **Industriegebiet** nt industrial area; **industriell** adj industrial

ineinander adv in(to) one another (o each other)

Infarkt (-(e)s, -e) m (Herzinfarkt) heart attack

Infektion f infection; **Infektionskrankheit** f infectious disease; **infizieren** vt to infect ▷ vr: **sich ~** to be infected

Info (-, -s) f (fam) info

infolge prep +gen as a result of, owing to; **infolgedessen** adv consequently

Infomaterial nt (fam) bumf, info

Informatik f computer science; **Informatiker(in)** (-s, -) m(f) computer scientist

Information f information; **Informationsschalter** m information desk; **informieren** vt to inform; **falsch ~** to misinform ▷ vr: **sich ~** to find out (über +akk about)

infrage adv: **das kommt nicht ~** that's out of the question; **etw ~ stellen** to question sth

Infrastruktur f infrastructure

Infusion f infusion

Ingenieur(in) (-s, -e) m(f) engineer

Ingwer (-s) m ginger

Inhaber(in) (-s, -) m(f) owner; (Haus~) occupier; (von Lizenz) holder; (Fin) bearer

Inhalt (-(e)s, -e) m contents pl; (eines Buchs etc) content; (Math) volume; (Flächeninhalt) area; **Inhaltsangabe** f summary; **Inhaltsverzeichnis** nt table of contents

Initiative f initiative; **die ~ ergreifen** to take the initiative

Injektion f injection

inklusive adv, prep inclusive (gen of)

inkonsequent adj inconsistent

Inland nt (Pol, Comm) home; **im ~** at home; (Geo) inland;

inländisch adj domestic; **Inlandsflug** m domestic flight; **Inlandsgespräch** nt national call

Inliner pl, **Inlineskates** pl (Sport) Rollerblades® pl, in-line skates pl

innen adv inside; **Innenarchitekt(in)** m(f) interior designer; **Innenhof** m (inner) courtyard; **Innenminister(in)** m(f) minister of the interior, Home Secretary (Brit); **Innenseite** f inside; **Innenspiegel** m rearview mirror; **Innenstadt** f town centre; (von Großstadt) city centre

innere(r, s) adj inner; (im Körper, inländisch) internal; **Innere(s)** nt inside; (Mitte) centre; (fig) heart

Innereien pl innards pl

innerhalb adv, prep +gen within; (räumlich) inside

innerlich adj internal; (geistig) inner

innerste(r, s) adj innermost

Innovation f innovation; **innovativ** adj innovative

inoffiziell adj unofficial; (zwanglos) informal

ins kontr von **in das**

Insasse (-n, -n) m, **Insassin** f (Auto) passenger; (Anstalt) inmate

insbesondere adv particularly, in particular

Inschrift f inscription

Insekt (-(e)s, -en) nt insect, bug (US); **Insektenschutzmittel** nt insect repellent; **Insektenstich** m insect bite

Insel (-, -n) f island

Inserat nt advertisement

insgesamt adv altogether, all in all

Insider(in) (-s, -) m(f) insider

insofern adv in that respect; (deshalb) (and) so ▷ conj if; **~ als** in so far as

Installateur(in) m(f) (Klempner)
plumber; (Elektroinstallateur)
electrician; **installieren** vt
(Inform) to install

Instinkt (-(e)s, -e) m instinct

Institut (-(e)s, -e) nt institute

Institution f institution

Instrument nt instrument

Insulin (-s) nt insulin

Inszenierung f production

intakt adj intact

intellektuell adj intellectual

intelligent adj intelligent;
Intelligenz f intelligence

intensiv adj (gründlich) intensive;
(Gefühl, Schmerz) intense;
Intensivkurs m crash course;
Intensivstation f intensive care
unit

interaktiv adj interactive

Intercityexpress(zug) m German
high-speed train; **Intercityzug** m
Intercity (train); **Intercityzuschlag**
m Intercity supplement

interessant adj interesting;
Interesse (-s, -n) nt interest;
~ haben an (+dat) to be interested
in; **interessieren** vt to interest
▷ vr: **sich ~** to be interested (für in)

Interface (-, -s) nt (Inform)
interface

Internat nt boarding school

international adj international

Internet (-s) nt internet, net; **im
~ on** the internet; **im ~ surfen** to
surf the net; **Internetanschluss**
m internet connection;
Internetauktion f internet
auction; **Internetcafé** nt
internet café, cybercafé;
Internetfirma f dotcom
company; **Internethandel** m
e-commerce; **Internetseite** f
web page; **Internetzugang** m
internet access

interpretieren vt to interpret
(als as)

Interpunktion f punctuation

Interview (-s, -s) nt interview;
interviewen vt to interview

intim adj intimate

intolerant adj intolerant

investieren vt to invest

inwiefern adv in what way; (in
welchem Ausmaß) to what extent;
inwieweit adv to what extent

inzwischen adv meanwhile

iPod® m iPod®

Irak (-(s)) m: **(der) ~** Iraq

Iran (-(s)) m: **(der) ~** Iran

Ire (-n, -n) m Irishman

irgend adv: **~ so ein Idiot** some
idiot; **wenn ~ möglich** if at all
possible; **irgendein** pron,
irgendeine(r, s) adj some;
(fragend, im Bedingungssatz; beliebig)
any; **irgendetwas** pron
something; (fragend, im
Bedingungssatz) anything;
irgendjemand pron somebody;
(fragend, im Bedingungssatz)
anybody; **irgendwann** adv
sometime; (zu beliebiger Zeit) any
time; **irgendwie** adv somehow;
irgendwo adv somewhere;
(fragend, im Bedingungssatz)
anywhere

Irin f Irishwoman; **irisch** adj
Irish; **Irland** nt Ireland

ironisch adj ironic

irre adj crazy, mad; (toll) terrific;
Irre(r) mf lunatic; **irreführen** irr
vt to mislead; **irremachen** vt to
confuse; **irren** vi to be mistaken;
(umherirren) to wander ▷ vr: **sich
~** to be mistaken; **wenn ich mich
nicht irre** if I'm not mistaken; **sich
in der Nummer ~** (Telefon) to get
the wrong number; **irrsinnig** adj
mad, crazy; **Irrtum** (-s, -tümer) m
mistake, error; **irrtümlich** adj
mistaken ▷ adv by mistake

ISBN (-) nt abk = **industrial
standard business network** ISBN

▷ (-) *f abk* = **Internationale Standard Buchnummer** ISBN
Ischias (-) *m* sciatica
ISDN (-) *nt abk* = **integrated services digital network** ISDN
Islam (-s) *m* Islam; **islamisch** *adj* Islamic
Island *nt* Iceland; **Isländer(in)** (-s, -) *m(f)* Icelander; **isländisch** *adj* Icelandic; **Isländisch** *nt* Icelandic
Isolierband *nt* insulating tape; **isolieren** *vt* to isolate; (*Elek*) to insulate
Isomatte *f* thermomat, karrymat®
Israel (-s) *nt* Israel; **Israeli** (-(s), -(s)) *m* (-, -(s)) *f* Israeli; **israelisch** *adj* Israeli
IT (-) *f abk* = **Informationstechnologie** IT
Italien (-s) *nt* Italy; **Italiener(in)** (-s, -) *m(f)* Italian; **italienisch** *adj* Italian; **Italienisch** *nt* Italian

J

ja *adv* 1 yes; **haben Sie das gesehen? — ja** did you see it? — yes(, I did); **ich glaube ja** (yes,) I think so
2 (*fragend*) really?; **ich habe gekündigt — ja?** I've quit — have you?; **du kommst, ja?** you're coming, aren't you?
3 **sei ja vorsichtig** do be careful; **Sie wissen ja, dass ...** as you know, ...; **tu das ja nicht!** don't do that!; **ich habe es ja gewusst** I just knew it; **ja, also ...** well you see ...

Jacht (-, -en) *f* yacht; **Jachthafen** *m* marina
Jacke (-, -n) *f* jacket; (*Wolljacke*) cardigan
Jackett (-s, -s *o* -e) *nt* jacket
Jagd (-, -en) *f* hunt; (*Jagen*) hunting; **jagen** *vi* to hunt ▷ *vt* to

hunt; (*verfolgen*) to chase; **Jäger(in)** *m(f)* hunter

Jaguar (-s, -e) *m* jaguar

Jahr (-(e)s, -e) *nt* year; **ein halbes ~** six months *pl*; **Anfang der neunziger ~e** in the early nineties; **mit sechzehn ~en** at (the age of) sixteen; **Jahrestag** *m* anniversary; **Jahreszahl** *f* date, year; **Jahreszeit** *f* season; **Jahrgang** *m* (*Wein*) year, vintage; **der ~ 1989** (*Personen*) those born in 1989; **Jahrhundert** (-s, -e) *nt* century; **jährlich** *adj* yearly, annual; **Jahrmarkt** *m* fair; **Jahrtausend** *nt* millennium; **Jahrzehnt** *nt* decade

jähzornig *adj* hot-tempered

Jakobsmuschel *f* scallop

Jalousie *f* (venetian) blind

Jamaika (-s) *nt* Jamaica

jämmerlich *adj* pathetic

jammern *vi* to moan

Januar (-(s), -e) *m* January; *siehe auch* **Juni**

Japan (-s) *nt* Japan; **Japaner(in)** (-s, -) *m(f)* Japanese; **japanisch** *adj* Japanese; **Japanisch** *nt* Japanese

jaulen *vi* to howl

jawohl *adv* yes (of course)

Jazz (-) *m* jazz

je *adv* 1 (*jemals*) ever; **hast du so was je gesehen?** did you ever see anything like it?
2 (*jeweils*) every, each; **sie zahlten je 3 Euro** they paid 3 euros each ▷ *präp* 1 **je nach** depending on; **je nachdem** it depends; **je nachdem, ob ...** depending on whether ... 2 **je eher, desto** *o* **umso besser** the sooner the better

Jeans (-, -) *f* jeans *pl*

jede(r, s) *unbest Zahlwort* (*insgesamt gesehen*) every; (*einzeln gesehen*) each; (*jede(r, s) beliebige*) any; **~s Mal** every time, each time; **~n zweiten Tag** every other day; **sie hat an ~m Finger einen Ring** she's got a ring on each finger; **~r Computer reicht aus** any computer will do; **bei ~m Wetter** in any weather ▷ *pron* everybody; (*jeder Einzelne*) each; **~r von euch/uns** each of you/us; **jedenfalls** *adv* in any case; **jederzeit** *adv* at any time; **jedesmal** *adv* every time

jedoch *adv* however

jemals *adv* ever

jemand *pron* somebody; (*in Frage und Verneinung*) anybody

Jemen (-(s)) *m* Yemen

jene(r, s) *adj* that, those *pl* ▷ *pron* that (one), those *pl*

jenseits *adv* on the other side ▷ *präp* +*gen* on the other side of; (*fig*) beyond

Jetlag (-s) *m* jet lag

jetzig *adj* present

jetzt *adv* now; **erst ~** only now; **~ gleich** right now; **bis ~** so far, up to now; **von ~ an** from now on

jeweils *adv*: **~ zwei zusammen** two at a time; **zu ~ 5 Euro** at 5 euros each

Job (-s, -s) *m* job; **jobben** *vi* (*fam*) to work, to have a job

Jod (-(e)s) *nt* iodine

joggen *vi* to jog; **Jogging** (-s) *nt* jogging; **Jogginganzug** *m* jogging suit, tracksuit; **Jogginghose** *f* jogging pants *pl*

Jog(h)urt (-s, -s) *m o nt* yoghurt

Johannisbeere *f*: **Schwarze ~** blackcurrant; **Rote ~** redcurrant

Joint (-s, -s) *m* (*fam*) joint

jonglieren *vi* to juggle

Jordanien (-s) *nt* Jordan

Journalist(in) *m(f)* journalist

Joystick (-s, -s) m (Inform)
joystick

jubeln vi to cheer

Jubiläum (-s, Jubiläen) nt jubilee;
(Jahrestag) anniversary

jucken vi to itch ⊳ vt: **es juckt
mich am Arm** my arm is itching;
das juckt mich nicht (fam) I
couldn't care less; **Juckreiz** m
itch

Jude (-n, -n) m, **Jüdin** f Jew; **sie
ist Jüdin** she's Jewish; **jüdisch** adj
Jewish

Judo (-(s)) nt judo

Jugend (-) f youth; **jugendfrei**
adj: **ein ~er Film** a U-rated film
(Brit), a G-rated film (US); **ein
nicht ~er Film** an X-rated film;
Jugendgruppe f youth group;
Jugendherberge (-, -n) f youth
hostel; **Jugendherbergsausweis**
m youth hostel card; **jugendlich**
adj youthful; **Jugendliche(r)** mf
young person; **Jugendstil** m art
nouveau; **Jugendzentrum** nt
youth centre

Jugoslawien (-s) nt (Hist)
Yugoslavia; **das ehemalige ~** the
former Yugoslavia

Juli (-(s), -s) m July; siehe auch **Juni**

jung adj young

Junge (-n, -n) m boy

Junge(s) (-n, -n) nt young animal;
die ~n pl the young pl

Jungfrau f virgin; (Astr) Virgo

Junggeselle (-n, -n) m bachelor;
Junggesellin f single woman

Juni (-(s), -s) m June; **im ~** in June;
am 4. ~ on 4(th) June, on June
4(th) (gesprochen: on the fourth of
June); **Anfang/Mitte/Ende ~** at
the beginning/in the middle/at
the end of June;
letzten/nächsten ~ last/next
June

Jupiter (-s) m Jupiter

Jura ohne Artikel (Studienfach) law;

~ **studieren** to study law;
Jurist(in) m(f) lawyer; **juristisch**
adj legal

Justiz (-) f justice;
Justizminister(in) m(f) minister
of justice

Juwel (-s, -en) nt jewel;
Juwelier(in) (-s, -e) m(f) jeweller

Kabel (-s, -) nt (Elek) wire; (stark) cable; **Kabelfernsehen** nt cable television
Kabeljau (-s, -e o -s) m cod
kabellos adj wireless
Kabine f cabin; (im Schwimmbad) cubicle
Kabrio (-s, -s) nt convertible
Kachel (-, -n) f tile; **Kachelofen** m tiled stove
Käfer (-s, -) m beetle, bug (US)
Kaff (-s, -s) nt dump, hole
Kaffee (-s, -s) m coffee; ~ **kochen** to make some coffee; **Kaffeefilter** m coffee filter; **Kaffeekanne** f coffeepot; **Kaffeeklatsch** (-(e)s, -e) m chat over coffee and cakes, coffee klatch (US); **Kaffeelöffel** m coffee spoon; **Kaffeemaschine** f coffee maker (o machine); **Kaffeetasse** f coffee cup
Käfig (-s, -e) m cage
kahl adj bald; (Baum, Wand) bare

Kahn (-(e)s, Kähne) m boat; (Lastkahn) barge
Kai (-s, -e o -s) m quay
Kaiser (-s, -) m emperor; **Kaiserin** f empress; **Kaiserschnitt** m (Med) caesarean (section)
Kajak (-s, -s) nt kayak; **Kajakfahren** nt kayaking
Kajüte (-, -n) f cabin
Kakao (-s, -s) m cocoa; (Getränk) (hot) chocolate
Kakerlake (-, -n) f cockroach
Kaki (-, -s) f kaki
Kaktee (-, -n) f, **Kaktus** (-, -se) m cactus
Kalb (-(e)s, Kälber) nt calf; **Kalbfleisch** nt veal; **Kalbsbraten** m roast veal; **Kalbsschnitzel** nt veal cutlet; (paniert) escalope of veal
Kalender (-s, -) m calendar; (Taschenkalender) diary
Kalk (-(e)s, -e) m lime; (in Knochen) calcium
Kalorie f calorie; **kalorienarm** adj low-calorie
kalt adj cold; **mir ist (es)** ~ I'm cold; **kaltblütig** adj cold-blooded; **Kälte** f cold; (fig) coldness
kam imperf von **kommen**
Kambodscha (-s) nt Cambodia
Kamel (-(e)s, -e) nt camel
Kamera (-, -s) f camera
Kamerad(in) (-en, -en) m(f) friend; (als Begleiter) companion
Kamerafrau f camerawoman; **Kamerahandy** nt cameraphone; **Kameramann** m cameraman
Kamille (-, -n) f camomile; **Kamillentee** m camomile tea
Kamin (-s, -e) m (innen) fireplace; (außen) chimney; (innen) fireplace
Kamm (-(e)s, Kämme) m comb; (Berg) ridge; (Hahn) crest; **kämmen** vr **sich** ~, **sich** (dat) **die Haare** ~ to

comb one's hair; **Kammermusik**
f chamber music

Kampf (-(e)s, Kämpfe) m fight;
(Schlacht) battle; (Wettbewerb)
contest; (fig: Anstrengung)
struggle; **kämpfen** vi to fight
(für, um for); **Kampfsport** m
martial art

Kanada (-s) nt Canada;
Kanadier(in) (-s, -) m(f) Canadian; **kanadisch** adj Canadian

Kanal (-s, Kanäle) m (Fluss) canal;
(Rinne, TV) channel; (für Abfluss)
drain; **der ~** (Ärmelkanal) the
(English) Channel; **Kanalinseln**
pl Channel Islands pl;
Kanalisation f sewerage system;
Kanaltunnel m Channel Tunnel

Kanarienvogel m canary

Kandidat(in) (-en, -en) m(f)
candidate

Kandis(zucker) (-) m rock
candy

Känguru (-s, -s) nt kangaroo

Kaninchen nt rabbit

Kanister (-s, -) m can

Kännchen nt pot; **ein
~ Kaffee/Tee** a pot of coffee/tea;

/ **Kanne** (-, -n) f (Krug) jug;
(Kaffeekanne) pot; (Milchkanne)
churn; (Gießkanne) can

kannte imperf von **kennen**

Kante (-, -n) f edge

Kantine f canteen

Kanton (-s, -e) m canton

Kanu (-s, -s) nt canoe

Kanzler(in) (-s, -) m(f)
chancellor

Kap (-s, -s) nt cape

Kapazität f capacity; (Fachmann)
authority

Kapelle f (Gebäude) chapel; (Mus)
band

Kaper (-, -n) f caper

kapieren vt, vi (fam) to
understand; **kapiert?** got it?

Kapital (-s, -e o -ien) nt capital

Kapitän (-s, -e) m captain

Kapitel (-s, -) nt chapter

Kappe (-, -n) f cap

Kapsel (-, -n) f capsule

kaputt adj (fam) broken; (Mensch)
exhausted; **kaputt|gehen** irr vi
to break; (Schuhe) to fall apart;
(Firma) to go bust; (Stoff) to wear
out; **kaputt|machen** vt to
break; (jdn) to wear out

Kapuze (-, -n) f hood

Kap Verde (-s) nt Cape Verde

Karaffe (-, -n) f carafe; (mit
Stöpsel) decanter

Karamell (-s) m caramel, toffee

Karaoke (-(-s)) nt karaoke

Karat (-s, -e) nt carat

Karate (-s) nt karate

Kardinal (-s, Kardinäle) m
cardinal

Karfreitag m Good Friday

kariert adj checked; (Papier)
squared

Karies (-) f (tooth) decay

Karikatur f caricature

Karneval (-s, -e o -s) m carnival

KARNEVAL

Karneval is the name given to
the days immediately before
Lent when people gather to
sing, dance, eat, drink and
generally make merry before the
fasting begins. **Rosenmontag**,
the day before Shrove Tuesday,
is the most important day of
'Karneval' on the Rhine. Most
firms take a day's holiday on
that day to enjoy the parades
and revelry. In South Germany
'Karneval' is called **Fasching**.

Kärnten (-s) nt Carinthia

Karo (-s, -s) nt square; (Karten)
diamonds pl

Karosserie f (Auto) body(work)

Karotte (-, -n) f carrot
Karpfen (-s, -) m carp
Karriere (-, -n) f career
Karte (-, -n) f card; (Landkarte)
map; (Speisekarte) menu;
(Eintrittskarte, Fahrkarte) ticket; **mit
~ bezahlen** to pay by credit card;
~n spielen to play cards; **die ~n
mischen/geben** to shuffle/deal
the cards
Kartei f card index; **Karteikarte**
f index card
Kartenspiel nt card game;
Kartentelefon nt cardphone;
Kartenvorverkauf m advance
booking
Kartoffel (-, -n) f potato;
Kartoffelbrei m mashed
potatoes pl; **Kartoffelchips** pl
crisps pl (Brit), chips pl (US);
Kartoffelpuffer m potato cake
(made from grated potatoes);
Kartoffelpüree m mashed
potatoes pl; **Kartoffelsalat** m
potato salad
Karton (-s, -s) m cardboard;
(Schachtel) (cardboard) box
Kartusche (-, -n) f cartridge
Karussell (-s, -s) nt roundabout
(Brit), merry-go-round
Kaschmir (-s, e) m (Stoff)
cashmere
Käse (-s, -) m cheese;
Käsekuchen m cheesecake;
Käseplatte f cheeseboard
Kasino (-s, -s) nt (Spielkasino)
casino
Kaskoversicherung f com-
prehensive insurance
Kasper(l) (-s, -) m Punch; (fig)
clown; **Kasperl(e)theater** nt
(Vorstellung) Punch and Judy
show; (Gebäude) Punch and Judy
theatre
Kasse (-, -n) f (in Geschäft) till,
cash register; (im Supermarkt)
checkout; (Geldkasten) cashbox;

(Theater) box office; (Kino) ticket
office; (Krankenkasse) health
insurance; (Spar~) savings bank;
Kassenbon (-s, -s) m,
Kassenzettel m receipt
Kassette f (small) box; (Tonband)
cassette; **Kassettenrekorder** m
cassette recorder
kassieren vt to take ▷ vi: **darf
ich ~?** would you like to pay now?;
Kassierer(in) m(f) cashier
Kastanie (-, -n) f chestnut
Kasten (-s, Kästen) m (Behälter)
box; (Getränkekasten) crate
Kat m abk = **Katalysator**
Katalog (-(e)s, -e) m catalogue
Katalysator m (Auto) catalytic
converter; (Phys) catalyst
Katar (-s) nt Qatar
Katarr(h) (-s, -e) m catarrh
Katastrophe (-, -n) f catas-
trophe, disaster
Kategorie (-, -n) f category
Kater (-s, -) m tomcat; (fam: nach
zu viel Alkohol) hangover
Kathedrale (-, -n) f cathedral
Katholik(in) m(f) Catholic;
katholisch adj Catholic
Katze (-, -n) f cat
Kauderwelsch (-(s)) nt (unver-
ständlich) gibberish; (Fachjargon)
jargon
kauen vt, vi to chew
Kauf (-(e)s, Käufe) m purchase;
(Kaufen) buying; **ein guter ~** a
bargain; **etw in ~ nehmen** to put
up with sth; **kaufen** vt to buy;
Käufer(in) m(f) buyer; **Kauffrau**
f businesswoman; **Kaufhaus** nt
department store; **Kaufmann** m
businessman; (im Einzelhandel)
shopkeeper (Brit), storekeeper
(US); **Kaufpreis** m purchase
price; **Kaufvertrag** m purchase
agreement
Kaugummi m chewing gum
Kaulquappe (-, -n) f tadpole

kaum adv hardly, scarcely

Kaution f deposit; (Jur) bail

Kaviar m caviar

KB (-, -) nt, **Kbyte** (-, -) nt abk = **Kilobyte** KB

Kebab (-(s), -s) m kebab

Kegel (-s, -) m skittle; (beim Bowling) pin; (Math) cone; **Kegelbahn** f bowling alley; **kegeln** vi to play skittles; (bowlen) to bowl

Kehle (-, -n) f throat; **Kehlkopf** m larynx

Kehre (-, -n) f sharp bend

kehren vt (fegen) to sweep

Keilriemen m (Auto) fan belt

kein pron no, not ... any; **ich habe ~ Geld** I have no money, I don't have money; **~ Mensch** no one; **du bist ~ Kind mehr** you're not a child any more; **keine(r, s)** pron (Person) no one, nobody; (Sache) not ... any, none; **~r von ihnen** none of them; (bei zwei Personen/Sachen) neither of them; **ich will keins von beiden** I don't want either (of them); **keinesfalls** adv on no account, under no circumstances

Keks (-es, -e) m biscuit (Brit), cookie (US); **jdm auf den ~ gehen** (fam) to get on sb's nerves

Keller (-s, -) m cellar; (Geschoss) basement

Kellner (-s, -) m waiter; **Kellnerin** f waitress

Kenia (-s) nt Kenya

kennen (kannte, gekannt) vt to know; **wir ~ uns seit 1990** we've known each other since 1990; **wir ~ uns schon** we've already met; **kennst du mich noch?** do you remember me?; **kennen|lernen** vt to get to know; **sich ~** to get to know each other; (zum ersten Mal) to meet

Kenntnis f knowledge; **seine ~se** his knowledge

Kennwort nt (a. Inform) password; **Kennzeichen** nt mark, sign; (Auto) number plate (Brit), license plate (US); **besondere ~** distinguishing marks

Kerl (-s, -e) m guy, bloke (Brit)

Kern (-(e)s, -e) m (Obst) pip; (Pfirsich, Kirsche etc) stone; (Nuss) kernel; (Atomkern) nucleus; (fig) heart, core

Kernenergie f nuclear energy; **Kernkraft** f nuclear power; **Kernkraftwerk** nt nuclear power station

Kerze (-, -n) f candle; (Zündkerze) plug

Ket(s)chup (-(s), -s) m o nt ketchup

Kette (-, -n) f chain; (Halskette) necklace

keuchen vi to pant; **Keuchhusten** m whooping cough

Keule (-, -n) f club; (Gastr) leg; (von Hähnchen a.) drumstick

Keyboard (-s, -s) nt (Mus) keyboard

Kfz nt abk = **Kraftfahrzeug**; **Kfz-Brief** m = logbook; **Kfz-Steuer** f = road tax (Brit), vehicle tax (US)

KG (-, -s) f abk = **Kommanditgesellschaft** limited partnership

Kichererbse f chick pea

kichern vi to giggle

Kickboard® (-s, -s) nt micro scooter

Kicker (-s, -) m (Spiel) table football (Brit), foosball (US)

kidnappen vt to kidnap

Kidney-Bohne f kidney bean

Kiefer (-s, -) m jaw ▷ (-, -n) f pine; **Kieferchirurg(in)** m(f) oral surgeon

k

Kieme (-, -n) f gill
Kies (-es, -e) m gravel; **Kiesel** (-s, -) m, **Kieselstein** m pebble
Kilo (-s, -(s)) nt kilo; **Kilobyte** nt kilobyte; **Kilogramm** nt kilogram; **Kilometer** m kilometre; **Kilometerstand** m ≈ mileage; **Kilometerzähler** m ≈ mileometer; **Kilowatt** nt kilowatt
Kind (-(e)s, -er) nt child; **sie bekommt ein ~** she's having a baby; **Kinderarzt** m, **Kinderärztin** f paediatrician; **Kinderbetreuung** f childcare; **Kinderbett** nt cot (Brit), crib (US); **Kinderfahrkarte** f child's ticket; **Kindergarten** m nursery school, kindergarten; **Kindergärtner(in)** m(f) nursery-school teacher; **Kindergeld** nt child benefit; **Kinderkrippe** f crèche (Brit), daycare center (US); **Kinderlähmung** f polio; **Kindermädchen** nt nanny (Brit), nurse(maid); **kindersicher** adj childproof; **Kindersicherung** f childproof safety catch; (an Flasche) childproof cap; **Kindersitz** m child seat; **Kindertagesstätte** nt day nursery; **Kinderteller** m (im Restaurant) children's portion; **Kinderwagen** m pram (Brit), baby carriage (US); **Kinderzimmer** nt children's (bed)room; **Kindheit** f childhood; **kindisch** adj childish; **kindlich** adj childlike
Kinn (-(e)s, -e) nt chin
Kino (-s, -s) nt cinema (Brit), movie theater (US); **ins ~ gehen** to go to the cinema (Brit) (o to the movies (US))
Kiosk (-(e)s, -e) m kiosk
Kippe f (fam: Zigarettenstummel) cigarette end, fag end (Brit)
kippen vi to tip over ▷ vt to tilt; (Regierung, Minister) to topple

Kirche (-, -n) f church; **Kirchturm** m church tower; (mit Spitze) steeple; **Kirchweih** f fair
Kirmes (-, -sen) f fair
Kirsche (-, -n) f cherry; **Kirschtomate** f cherry tomato
Kissen (-s, -) nt cushion; (Kopfkissen) pillow; **Kissenbezug** m cushion cover; (für Kopfkissen) pillowcase
Kiste (-, -n) f box; (Truhe) chest
KITA (-, -s) f abk =
Kindertagesstätte day-care centre (Brit), day-care center (US)
kitschig adj kitschy, cheesy
kitzelig adj (a. fig) ticklish; **kitzeln** vt, vi to tickle
Kiwi (-, -s) f (Frucht) kiwi (fruit)
Klage (-, -n) f complaint; (Jur) lawsuit; **klagen** vi to complain (über +akk about, bei to); **kläglich** adj wretched
Klammer (-, -n) f (in Text) bracket; (Büroklammer) clip; (Wäscheklammer) peg (Brit), clothespin (US); (Zahnklammer) brace; **Klammeraffe** m (fam) at-sign, @; **klammern** vr: **sich ~** to cling (an +akk to)
Klamotten pl (fam: Kleider) clothes pl
klang imperf von **klingen**
Klang (-(e)s, Klänge) m sound
Klappbett nt folding bed
klappen vi impers (gelingen) to work; **es hat gut geklappt** it went well
klappern vi to rattle; (Geschirr) to clatter; **Klapperschlange** f rattlesnake
Klappfahrad nt folding bicycle; **Klappstuhl** m folding chair
klar adj clear; **sich (dat) im Klaren sein** to be clear (über +akk about); **alles ~?** everything okay?
klären vt (Flüssigkeit) to purify; (Probleme, Frage) to clarify ▷ vr:

sich ~ to clear itself up

Klarinette (-, -n) f clarinet

klar|kommen irr vi: **mit etw ~** to cope with something; **kommst du klar?** are you managing all right?; **mit jdm ~** to get along with sb; **klar|machen** vt: **jdm etw ~** to make sth clear to sb; **klar|stellen** vt to clarify

Klärung f (von Frage, Problem) clarification

klasse adj inv (fam) great, brilliant

Klasse (-, -n) f class; (Schuljahr) form (Brit), grade (US); **erster ~ reisen** to travel first class; **in welche ~ gehst du?** which form (Brit) (o grade (US)) are you in?; **Klassenarbeit** f test; **Klassenlehrer(in)** m(f) class teacher; **Klassenzimmer** nt classroom

Klassik f (Zeit) classical period; (Musik) classical music

Klatsch (-(e)s, -e) m (Gerede) gossip; **klatschen** vt (schlagen) to smack; (Beifall) to applaud, to clap; (reden) to gossip; **klatschnass** adj soaking (wet)

Klaue (-, -n) f claw; (fam: Schrift) scrawl; **klauen** vt (fam) to pinch

Klavier (-s, -e) nt piano

Klebeband nt adhesive tape; **kleben** vt to stick (an +akk to) ▸ vi (klebrig sein) to be sticky; **klebrig** adj sticky; **Klebstoff** m glue; **Klebstreifen** m adhesive tape

Klecks (-es, -e) m blob; (Tinte) blot

Klee (-s) m clover

Kleid (-(e)s, -er) nt (Frauen~) dress; **~er** pl (Kleidung) clothes pl; **Kleiderbügel** m coat hanger; **Kleiderschrank** m wardrobe (Brit), closet (US); **Kleidung** f clothing

klein adj small, little; (Finger) little; **mein ~er Bruder** my little (o younger) brother; **als ich noch**

~ war when I was a little boy/girl; **etw ~ schneiden** to chop sth up; **Kleinanzeige** f classified ad; **Kleinbuchstabe** m small letter; **Kleinbus** m minibus; **Kleingeld** nt change; **Kleinigkeit** f trifle; (Zwischenmahlzeit) snack; **Kleinkind** nt toddler; **klein|schreiben** vt (mit kleinem Anfangsbuchstaben) to write with a small letter; **Kleinstadt** f small town

Kleister (-s, -) m paste

Klempner(in) m(f) plumber

klettern vi to climb

Klettverschluss m Velcro® fastening

klicken vi (a. Inform) to click

Klient(in) (-en, -en) m(f) client

Klima (-s, -s) nt climate; **Klimaanlage** f air conditioning; **klimatisiert** adj air-conditioned; **Klimawandel** m climate change

Klinge (-, -n) f blade

Klingel (-, -n) f bell; **klingeln** vi to ring

klingen (klang, geklungen) vi to sound

Klinik f clinic; (Krankenhaus) hospital

Klinke (-, -n) f handle

Klippe (-, -n) f cliff; (im Meer) reef; (fig) hurdle

Klischee (-s, -s) nt (fig) cliché

Klo (-s, -s) nt (fam) loo (Brit), john (US); **Klobrille** f toilet seat; **Klopapier** nt toilet paper

klopfen vt, vi to knock; (Herz) to thump

Kloß (-es, Klöße) m (im Hals) lump; (Gastr) dumpling

Kloster (-s, Klöster) nt (für Männer) monastery; (für Frauen) convent

Klub (-s, -s) m club

klug adj clever

knabbern vt, vi to nibble

k

Knäckebrot nt crispbread
knacken vt, vi to crack
Knall (-(e)s, -e) m bang; **knallen**
vi to bang
knapp adj (kaum ausreichend)
scarce; (Sieg) narrow; **~ bei Kasse
sein** to be short of money; **~ zwei
Stunden** just under two hours
Knauf (-s, Knäufe) m knob
kneifen (kniff, gekniffen) vt, vi to
pinch; (sich drücken) to back out
(vor +dat of); **Kneifzange** f
pincers pl
Kneipe (-, -n) f (fam) pub (Brit),
bar
Knete (-) f (fam: Geld) dough;
kneten vt to knead; (formen) to
mould
knicken vt, vi (brechen) to break;
(Papier) to fold; **geknickt sein** (fig)
to be downcast
Knie (-s, -) nt knee; **in die
~ gehen** to bend one's knees;
Kniebeuge f knee bend;
Kniegelenk nt knee joint;
Kniekehle f back of the knee;
knien vi to kneel; **Kniescheibe** f
kneecap; **Knieschoner** (-s, -) m,
Knieschützer (-s, -) m knee pad;
Kniestrumpf (-(e)s, -) m
knee-length sock
kniff imperf von kneifen
knipsen vt to punch; (Foto) to
snap ▷ vi (Foto) to take snaps
knirschen vi to crunch; **mit den
Zähnen ~** to grind one's teeth
knitterfrei adj non-crease;
knittern vi to crease
Knoblauch m garlic;
Knoblauchbrot nt garlic bread;
Knoblauchzehe f clove of garlic
Knöchel (-s, -) m (Finger)
knuckle; (Fuß) ankle
Knochen (-s, -) m bone;
Knochenbruch m fracture;
Knochenmark nt marrow
Knödel (-s, -) m dumpling
Knollensellerie m celeriac

Knopf (-(e)s, Knöpfe) m button;
Knopfdruck m: **auf ~** at the
touch of a botton; **Knopfloch** nt
buttonhole
Knospe (-, -n) f bud
knoten vt to knot; **Knoten** (-s, -)
m knot; (Med) lump
Know-how (-(s)) nt know-how,
expertise
knurren vi (Hund) to growl;
(Magen) to rumble; (Mensch) to
grumble
knusprig adj crisp; (Keks) crunchy
knutschen vi (fam) to smooch
k. o. adj inv (Sport) knocked out;
(fig) knackered
Koalition f coalition
Koch (-(e)s, Köche) m cook;
Kochbuch nt cookery book,
cookbook; **kochen** vt, vi to cook;
(Wasser) to boil; (Kaffee, Tee) to
make; **Köchin** f cook;
Kochlöffel m wooden spoon;
Kochnische f kitchenette;
Kochplatte f hotplate;
Kochrezept nt recipe; **Kochtopf**
m saucepan
Kode (-s, -s) m code
Köder (-s, -) m bait
Koffein (-s) nt caffeine;
koffeinfrei adj decaffeinated
Koffer (-s, -) m (suit)case;
Kofferraum m (Auto) boot (Brit),
trunk (US)
Kognak (-s, -s) m brandy
Kohl (-(e)s, -e) m cabbage
Kohle (-, -n) f coal; (Holzkohle)
charcoal; (Chem) carbon; (fam:
Geld) cash, dough; **Kohlehydrat**
nt carbohydrate; **Kohlendioxid**
nt carbon dioxide; **Kohlensäure**
f (in Getränken) fizz; **ohne ~** still,
non-carbonated (US); **mit
~** sparkling, carbonated (US);
Kohletablette f charcoal tablet
Kohlrabi (-(s), -(s)) m kohlrabi
Koje (-, -n) f cabin; (Bett) bunk

Kokain (-s) nt cocaine
Kokosnuss f coconut
Kolben (-s, -) m (Tech) piston; (Mais-) cob
Kolik (-, -en) f colic
Kollaps (-es, -e) m collapse
Kollege (-n, -n) m, **Kollegin** f colleague
Köln (-s) nt Cologne; **Kölnischwasser** nt eau du cologne
Kolonne (-, -n) f convoy
Kölsch (-, -) nt (Bier) (strong) lager (from the Cologne region)
Kolumbien (-s) nt Columbia
Koma (-s, -s) nt coma
Kombi (-(s), -s) m estate (car) (Brit), station wagon (US); **Kombination** f combination; (Folgerung) deduction; (Hemdhose) combinations pl; (Aviat) flying suit; **kombinieren** vt to combine ▷ vi to reason; (vermuten) to guess; **Kombizange** f (pair of) pliers pl
Komfort (-s) m conveniences pl; (Bequemlichkeit) comfort
Komiker(in) m(f) comedian, comic; **komisch** adj funny
Komma (-s, -s) nt comma
Kommanditgesellschaft f limited partnership
kommen (kam, gekommen) vi to come; (näher kommen) to approach; (passieren) to happen; (gelangen, geraten) to get; (erscheinen) to appear; (in die Schule, das Gefängnis etc) to go; **~ lassen** to send for; **zu sich ~** to come round (o to); **zu etw ~** (bekommen) to acquire sth; (Zeit dazu finden) to get round to sth; **wer kommt zuerst?** who's first?; **kommend** adj coming; **-e Woche** next week; **in den -en Jahren** in the years to come
Kommentar m commentary; **kein ~** no comment
Kommilitone (-n, -n) m,

Kommilitonin f fellow student
Kommissar(in) m(f) inspector
Kommode (-, -n) f chest of drawers
Kommunikation f communication
Kommunion f (Rel) communion
Kommunismus m communism
Komödie f comedy
kompakt adj compact
Kompass (-es, -e) m compass
kompatibel adj compatible
kompetent adj competent
komplett adj complete
Kompliment nt compliment; **jdm ein ~ machen** to pay sb a compliment; **~!** congratulations
Komplize (-n, -n) m accomplice
kompliziert adj complicated
Komponist(in) m(f) composer
Kompost (-(e)s, -e) m compost; **Komposthaufen** m compost heap; **kompostierbar** adj biodegradable
Kompott (-(e)s, -e) nt stewed fruit
Kompresse (-, -n) f compress
Kompromiss (-es, -e) m compromise
Kondensmilch f condensed milk, evaporated milk
Kondition f (Leistungsfähigkeit) condition; **sie hat eine gute ~** she's in good shape
Konditorei f cake shop; (mit Café) café
Kondom (-s, -e) nt condom
Konfektionsgröße f size
Konferenz f conference
Konfession f religion; (christlich) denomination
Konfetti (-(s)) nt confetti
Konfirmation f (Rel) confirmation
Konfitüre (-, -n) f jam
Konflikt (-(e)s, -e) m conflict
konfrontieren vt to confront

Kongress (-es, -e) m conference;
der ~ (Parlament der USA)
Congress
König (-(e)s, -e) m king; **Königin**
f queen; **königlich** adj royal;
Königreich nt kingdom
Konkurrenz f competition

○ SCHLÜSSELWORT

können (pt **konnte**, pp **gekonnt** o
(als Hilfsverb) **können**) vt, vi 1 to be
able to; **ich kann es machen** I can
do it, I am able to do it; **ich kann
es nicht machen** I can't do it, I'm
not able to do it; **ich kann nicht ...**
I can't ..., I cannot ...; **ich kann
nicht mehr** I can't go on
2 (wissen, beherrschen) to know;
können Sie Deutsch? can you
speak German?; **er kann gut
Englisch** he speaks English well;
sie kann keine Mathematik she
can't do mathematics
3 (dürfen) to be allowed to; **kann
ich gehen?** can I go?; **könnte ich
...?** could I ...?; **kann ich mit?** (fam)
can I come with you?
4 (möglich sein) **Sie könnten recht
haben** you may be right; **das kann
sein** that's possible; **kann sein**
maybe

konsequent adj consistent;
Konsequenz f consequence
konservativ adj conservative
Konserven pl tinned food sing
(Brit), canned food sing;
Konservendose f tin (Brit), can
konservieren vt to preserve;
Konservierungsmittel nt
preservative
Konsonant m consonant
Konsul(in) (-s, -n) m(f) consul;
Konsulat nt consulate
Kontakt (-(e)s, -e) m contact;
kontaktarm adj: **er ist ~** he lacks

contact with other people;
kontaktfreudig adj sociable;
Kontaktlinsen pl contact lenses
pl
Kontinent m continent
Konto (-s, Konten) nt account;
Kontoauszug m (bank)
statement;
Kontoauszugsdrucker m
bank-statement machine;
Kontoinhaber(in) m(f) account
holder; **Kontonummer** f
account number; **Kontostand** m
balance
Kontrabass m double bass
Kontrast (-(e)s, -e) m contrast
Kontrolle (-, -n) f control;
(Aufsicht) supervision;
(Passkontrolle) passport control;
kontrollieren vt to control;
(nachprüfen) to check
Konzentration f concentra-
tion; **Konzentrationslager** nt
(Hist) concentration camp;
konzentrieren vt to concentrate
▷ vr: **sich ~** to concentrate
Konzept (-(e)s, -e) nt rough draft;
jdn aus dem ~ bringen to put sb
off
Konzern (-(e)s, -e) m firm
Konzert (-(e)s, -e) nt concert;
(Stück) concerto; **Konzertsaal** m
concert hall
koordinieren vt to coordinate
Kopf (-(e)s, Köpfe) m head; **pro
~ per** person; **sich den
~ zerbrechen** to rack one's brains;
Kopfhörer m headphones pl;
Kopfkissen nt pillow; **Kopfsalat**
m lettuce; **Kopfschmerzen** pl
headache sing; **Kopfstütze** f
headrest; **Kopftuch** nt
headscarf; **kopfüber** adv
headfirst
Kopie f copy; **kopieren** vt (a.
Inform) to copy; **Kopierer** (-s, -) m,
Kopiergerät nt copier

Kopilot(in) m(f) co-pilot
Koralle (-, -n) f coral
Koran (-s) m (Rel) Koran
Korb (-(e)s, Körbe) m basket; **jdm einen ~ geben** (fig) to turn sb down
Kord (-(e)s, -e) m corduroy
Kordel (-, -n) f cord
Kork (-(e)s, -e) m cork; **Korken** (-s, -) m cork; **Korkenzieher** (-s, -) m corkscrew
Korn (-(e)s, Körner) nt grain; **Kornblume** f cornflower
Körper (-s, -) m body; **Körperbau** m build; **Körpergeruch** m body odour; **Körpergröße** f height; **körperlich** adj physical; **Körperteil** m part of the body; **Körperverletzung** f physical injury
korrekt adj correct
Korrespondent(in) m(f) correspondent; **Korrespondenz** f correspondence
korrigieren vt to correct
Kosmetik f cosmetics pl; **Kosmetikkoffer** m vanity case; **Kosmetiksalon** m beauty parlour; **Kosmetiktuch** nt paper tissue
Kost (-) f (Nahrung) food; (Verpflegung) board
kostbar adj precious; (teuer) costly, expensive
kosten vt to cost ▷ vt, vi (versuchen) to taste; **Kosten** pl costs pl, cost; (Ausgaben) expenses pl; **auf ~ von** at the expense of; **kostenlos** adj free (of charge); **Kostenvoranschlag** m estimate
köstlich adj (Essen) delicious; (Einfall) delightful; **sich ~ amüsieren** to have a marvellous time
Kostprobe f taster; (fig) sample; **kostspielig** adj expensive
Kostüm (-s, -e) nt costume;

(Damenkostüm) suit
Kot (-(e)s) m excrement
Kotelett (-(e)s, -e o -s) nt chop, cutlet
Koteletten pl sideboards pl (Brit), sideburns pl (US)
Kotflügel m (Auto) wing
kotzen vi (vulg) to puke, to throw up
Krabbe (-, -n) f shrimp; (größer) prawn; (Krebs) crab
krabbeln vi to crawl
Krach (-(e)s, -s o -e) m crash; (andauernd) noise; (fam: Streit) row
Kraft (-, Kräfte) f strength; (Pol, Phys) force; (Fähigkeit) power; (Arbeits~) worker; **in ~ treten** to come into effect; **Kraftausdruck** m swearword; **Kraftfahrzeug** nt motor vehicle; **Kraftfahrzeugbrief** m = logbook; **Kraftfahrzeugschein** m vehicle registration document; **Kraftfahrzeugsteuer** f = road tax (Brit), vehicle tax (US); **Kraftfahrzeugversicherung** f car insurance; **kräftig** adj strong; (gesund) healthy; (Farben) intense, strong; **Kraftstoff** m fuel; **Kraftwerk** nt power station
Kragen (-s, -) m collar
Krähe (-, -n) f crow
Kralle (-, -n) f claw; (Parkkralle) wheel clamp
Kram (-(e)s) m stuff
Krampf (-(e)s, Krämpfe) m cramp; (zuckend) spasm; **Krampfader** f varicose vein
Kran (-(e)s, Kräne) m crane
Kranich (-s, -e) m (Zool) crane
krank adj ill, sick
kränken vt to hurt
Krankengymnastik f physiotherapy; **Krankenhaus** nt hospital; **Krankenkasse** f health insurance; **Krankenpfleger** (-s, -) m (male) nurse;

Krankenschein m health insurance certificate; **Krankenschwester** f nurse; **Krankenversicherung** f health insurance; **Krankenwagen** m ambulance; **Krankheit** f illness; (durch Infektion hervorgerufen) disease

Kränkung f insult

Kranz (-es, Kränze) m wreath

krass adj crass; (fam: toll) wicked

kratzen vt, vi to scratch; **Kratzer** (-s, -) m scratch

kraulen vi (schwimmen) to do the crawl ▷ vt (streicheln) to pet

Kraut (-(e)s, Kräuter) nt plant; (Gewürz) herb; (Gemüse) cabbage; **Kräuter** pl herbs pl; **Kräuterbutter** f herb butter; **Kräutertee** m herbal tea; **Krautsalat** m coleslaw

Krawatte f tie

kreativ adj creative

Krebs (-es, -e) m (Zool) crab; (Med) cancer; (Astr) Cancer

Kredit (-(e)s, -e) m credit; **auf ~** on credit; **einen ~ aufnehmen** to take out a loan; **Kreditkarte** f credit card

Kreide (-, -n) f chalk

Kreis (-es, -e) m circle; (Bezirk) district

kreischen vi to shriek; (Bremsen, Säge) to screech

Kreisel (-s, -) m (Spielzeug) top; (Verkehrskreisel) roundabout (Brit), traffic circle (US)

Kreislauf m (Med) circulation; (fig: der Natur etc) cycle; **Kreislaufstörungen** pl (Med) **ich habe ~** I've got problems with my circulation; **Kreisverkehr** m roundabout (Brit), traffic circle (US)

Kren (-s) m horseradish

Kresse (-, -n) f cress

Kreuz (-es, -e) nt cross; (Anat) small of the back; (Karten) clubs pl;

mir tut das ~ weh I've got backache; **Kreuzband** nt cruciate ligament; **kreuzen** vt to cross ▷ vr: **sich ~** to cross ▷ vi (Naut) to cruise; **Kreuzfahrt** f cruise; **Kreuzgang** m cloisters pl; **Kreuzotter** (-, -n) f adder; **Kreuzschlitzschraubenzieher** m Phillips® screwdriver; **Kreuzschlüssel** m (Auto) wheel brace; **Kreuzschmerzen** pl backache sing; **Kreuzung** f (Verkehrskreuzung) crossroads sing, intersection; (Züchtung) cross; **Kreuzworträtsel** nt crossword (puzzle)

kriechen (kroch, gekrochen) vi to crawl; (unauffällig) to creep; (fig, pej) (vor jdm) ~ to crawl (to sb); **Kriechspur** f crawler lane

Krieg (-(e)s, -e) m war

kriegen vt (fam) to get; (erwischen) to catch; **sie kriegt ein Kind** she's having a baby; **ich kriege noch Geld von dir** you still owe me some money

Krimi (-s, -s) m (fam) thriller; **Kriminalität** f criminality; **Kriminalpolizei** f detective force, = CID (Brit), = FBI (US); **Kriminalroman** m detective novel; **kriminell** adj criminal

Krippe (-, -n) f (Futterkrippe) manger; (Weihnachtskrippe) crib (Brit), crèche (US); (Kinderkrippe) crèche (US), daycare center (US)

Krise (-, -n) f crisis

Kristall (-s, -e) m crystal ▷ (-s) nt (Glas) crystal

Kritik f criticism; (Rezension) review; **Kritiker(in)** m(f) critic; **kritisch** adj critical

kritzeln vt, vi to scribble, to scrawl

Kroate (-n, -n) m Croat; **Kroatien** (-s) nt Croatia; **Kroatin** f Croat; **kroatisch** adj Croatian;

Kroatisch nt Croatian
kroch imperf von **kriechen**
Krokodil (-s, -e) nt crocodile
Krokus (-, -o -se) m crocus
Krone (-, -n) f crown;
  Kronleuchter m chandelier
Kropf (-(e)s, Kröpfe) m (Med)
  goitre; (von Vogel) crop
Kröte (-, -n) f toad
Krücke (-, -n) f crutch
Krug (-(e)s, Krüge) m jug;
  (Bierkrug) mug
Krümel (-s, -) m crumb
krumm adj crooked
Krüppel (-s, -) m cripple
Kruste (-, -n) f crust
Kruzifix (-es, -e) nt crucifix
Kuba (-s) nt Cuba
Kübel (-s, -) m tub; (Eimer) bucket
Kubikmeter m cubic metre
Küche (-, -n) f kitchen; (Kochen)
  cooking
Kuchen (-s, -) m cake; (mit
  Teigdeckel) pie; **Kuchengabel** f
  cake fork
Küchenmaschine f food
  processor; **Küchenpapier** nt
  kitchen roll; **Küchenschrank** m
  (kitchen) cupboard
Kuckuck (-s, -e) m cuckoo
Kugel (-, -n) f ball; (Math) sphere;
  (Mil) bullet; (Weihnachtskugel)
  bauble; **Kugellager** nt ball
  bearing; **Kugelschreiber** m
  (ball-point) pen, biro® (Brit);
  Kugelstoßen (-s) nt shot put
Kuh (-, Kühe) f cow
kühl adj cool; **Kühlakku** (-s, -s) m
  ice pack; **Kühlbox** f cool box;
  kühlen vt to cool; **Kühler** (-s, -)
  m (Auto) radiator; **Kühlerhaube**
  f (Auto) bonnet (Brit), hood (US);
  Kühlschrank m fridge,
  refrigerator; **Kühltasche** f cool
  bag; **Kühltruhe** f freezer;
  Kühlwasser nt (Auto) radiator
  water

Kuhstall m cowshed
Küken (-s, -) nt chick
Kuli (-s, -s) m (fam: Kugelschreiber)
  pen, biro® (Brit)
Kulisse (-, -n) f scenery
Kult (-s, -e) m cult; **Kultfigur** f
  cult figure
Kultur f culture; (Lebensform)
  civilization; **Kulturbeutel** m
  toilet bag (Brit), washbag;
  kulturell adj cultural
Kümmel (-s, -) m caraway
  seeds pl
Kummer (-s) m grief, sorrow
kümmern vr: **sich um jdn ~** to
  look after sb; **sich um etw ~** to
  see to sth ▷ vt to concern; **das
  kümmert mich nicht** that doesn't
  worry me
Kumpel (-s, -) m (fam) mate, pal
Kunde (-n, -n) f customer;
  Kundendienst m after-sales (o
  customer) service;
  Kunden(kredit)karte f storecard, chargecard; **Kunden-
  nummer** f customer number
kündigen vi to hand in one's
  notice; (Mieter) to give notice that
  one is moving out; **jdm ~** to give
  sb his/her notice; (Vermieter) to
  give sb notice to quit ▷ vt to
  cancel; (Vertrag) to terminate; **jdm
  die Stellung ~** to give sb his/her
  notice; **jdm die Wohnung ~** to
  give sb notice to quit; **Kündigung**
  f (Arbeitsverhältnis) dismissal;
  (Vertrag) termination;
  (Abonnement) cancellation; (Frist)
  notice; **Kündigungsfrist** f
  period of notice
Kundin f customer; **Kundschaft**
  f customers pl
künftig adj future
Kunst (-, Künste) f art; (Können)
  skill; **Kunstausstellung** f art
  exhibition; **Kunstgewerbe** nt arts
  and crafts pl; **Künstler(in)** (-s, -)

m(f) artist; **künstlerisch** *adj* artistic

künstlich *adj* artificial

Kunststoff *m* synthetic material; **Kunststück** *nt* trick; **Kunstwerk** *nt* work of art

Kupfer (-s, -) *nt* copper

Kuppel (-, -n) *f* dome

kuppeln *vi* (*Auto*) to operate the clutch; **Kupplung** *f* coupling; (*Auto*) clutch

Kur (-, -en) *f* course of treatment; (*am Kurort*) cure

Kür (-, -en) *f* (*Sport*) free programme

Kurbel (-, -n) *f* crank; (*von Rollo, Fenster*) winder

Kürbis (-ses, -se) *m* pumpkin

Kurierdienst *m* courier service

kurieren *vt* to cure

Kurort *m* health resort

Kurs (-es, -e) *m* course; (*Fin*) rate; (*Wechselkurs*) exchange rate

kursiv *adj* italic ▷ *adv* in italics

Kursleiter(in) *m(f)* course tutor; **Kursteilnehmer(in)** *m(f)* (*course*) participant; **Kurswagen** *m* (*Eisenb*) through carriage

Kurve (-, -n) *f* curve; (*Straßenkurve*) bend; **kurvenreich** *adj* (*Straße*) winding

kurz *adj* short; (*zeitlich a.*) brief; **~ vorher/darauf** shortly before/after; **kannst du ~ kommen?** could you come here for a minute?; **~ gesagt** in short; **kurzärmelig** *adj* short-sleeved; **kürzen** *vt* to cut short; (*in der Länge*) to shorten; (*Gehalt*) to reduce; **kurzerhand** *adv* on the spot; **kurzfristig** *adj* short-term; **das Konzert wurde ~ abgesagt** the concert was called off at short notice; **Kurzgeschichte** *f* short story; **kurzhaarig** *adj* short-haired; **kürzlich** *adv* recently; **Kurzparkzone** *f* short-stay (*Brit*) (*o* short-term (*US*)) parking zone; **Kurzschluss** *m* (*Elek*) short circuit; **kurzsichtig** *adj* short-sighted; **Kurztrip** *m* trip, break; **Kurzurlaub** *m* short holiday (*Brit*), short vacation (*US*); **Kurzwelle** *f* short wave

Kusine *f* cousin

Kuss (-es, Küsse) *m* kiss; **küssen** *vt* to kiss ▷ *vr*: **sich ~** to kiss

Küste (-, -n) *f* coast; (*Ufer*) shore; **Küstenwache** *f* coastguard

Kutsche (-, -n) *f* carriage; (*geschlossene*) coach

Kuvert (-s, -s) *nt* envelope

Kuvertüre (-, -n) *f* coating

Kuwait (-s) *nt* Kuwait

KZ (-s, -s) *nt abk* = **Konzentrationslager** (*Hist*) concentration camp

l

cargo; (Jur) summons sing

lag imperf von **liegen**

Lage (-, -n) f position, situation; (Schicht) layer; **in der ~ sein zu** to be in a position to

Lager (-s, -) nt camp; (Comm) warehouse; (Tech) bearing; **Lagerfeuer** nt campfire; **lagern** vi (Dinge) to be stored; (Menschen) to camp ▷ vt to store

Lagune f lagoon

lahm adj lame; (langweilig) dull; **lähmen** vt to paralyse; **Lähmung** f paralysis

Laib (-s, -e) m loaf

Laie (-n, -n) m layman

Laken (-s, -) nt sheet

Lakritze (-, -n) f liquorice

Lamm (-(e)s, Lämmer) nt lamb

Lampe (-, -n) f lamp; (Glühbirne) bulb; **Lampenfieber** nt stage fright; **Lampenschirm** m lampshade

Lampion (-s, -s) m Chinese lantern

Land (-(e)s, Länder) nt (Gelände) land; (Nation) country; (Bundesland) state, Land; **auf dem ~(e)** in the country

● **LAND**

● A **Land** (plural **Länder**) is a
● member state of the **BRD**. There
● are 16 **Länder**, namely
● Baden-Württemberg, Bayern,
● Berlin, Brandenburg, Bremen,
● Hamburg, Hessen,
● Mecklenburg-Vorpommern,
● Niedersachsen,
● Nordrhein-Westfalen,
● Rheinland-Pfalz, Saarland,
● Sachsen, Sachsen-Anhalt,
● Schleswig-Holstein and
● Thüringen. Each "Land" has its
● own parliament and
● constitution.

Labor (-s, -e o -s) nt lab

Labyrinth (-s, -e) nt maze

Lache (-, -n) f (Pfütze) puddle; (Blut~, Öl~) pool

lächeln vi to smile; **Lächeln** (-s) nt smile; **lachen** vi to laugh; **lächerlich** adj ridiculous

Lachs (-es, -e) m salmon

Lack (-(e)s, -e) m varnish; (Farblack) lacquer; (an Auto) paint; **lackieren** vt to varnish; (Auto) to spray; **Lackschaden** m scratch (on the paintwork)

Ladegerät nt (battery) charger; **laden** (lud, geladen) vt (a. Inform) to load; (einladen) to invite; (Handy etc) to charge

Laden (-s, Läden) m shop; (Fensterladen) shutter; **Ladendieb(in)** m(f) shoplifter; **Ladendiebstahl** m shoplifting; **Ladenschluss** m closing time

Ladung f load; (Naut, Aviat)

Landebahn f runway; **landen** vt, vi to land; (Schiff) to dock

Länderspiel nt international (match)

Landesgrenze f national border, frontier; **Landesinnere** nt interior; **landesüblich** adj customary; **Landeswährung** f national currency; **landesweit** adj nationwide

Landhaus nt country house; **Landkarte** f map; **Landkreis** m administrative region, ≈ district

ländlich adj rural

Landschaft f countryside; (schöne) scenery; (Kunst) landscape; **Landstraße** f country road, B road (Brit)

Landung f landing; **Landungsbrücke** f, **Landungssteg** m gangway

Landwirt(in) m(f) farmer; **Landwirtschaft** f agriculture, farming; **landwirtschaftlich** adj agricultural

lang adj long; (Mensch) tall; **ein zwei Meter ~er Tisch** a table two metres long; **den ganzen Tag ~** all day long; **die Straße ~** along the street; **langärmelig** adj long-sleeved; **lange** adv (for) a long time; **ich musste ~ warten** I had to wait (for) a long time; **ich bleibe nicht ~** I won't stay long; **es ist ~ her, dass wir uns gesehen haben** it's a long time since we saw each other; **Länge** (-, -n) f length; (Geo) longitude

langen vi (fam: ausreichen) to be enough; (fam: fassen) to reach (nach for); **mir langt's** I've had enough

Langeweile f boredom

langfristig adj long-term ⊳ adv in the long term

Langlauf m cross-country skiing

längs prep +gen **die Bäume ~ der Straße** the trees along(side) the road ⊳ adv: **die Streifen laufen ~ über das Hemd** the stripes run lengthways down the shirt

langsam adj slow ⊳ adv slowly

Langschläfer(in) (-s, -) m(f) late riser

längst adv: **das ist ~ fertig** that was finished a long time ago; **sie sollte ~ da sein** she should have been here long ago; **als sie kam, waren wir ~ weg** when she arrived we had long since left

Langstreckenflug m long-haul flight

Languste (-, -n) f crayfish, crawfish (US)

langweilen vt to bore; **ich langweile mich** I'm bored; **langweilig** adj boring; **Langwelle** f long wave

Laos (-) nt Laos

Lappen (-s, -) m cloth, rag; (Staublappen) duster

läppisch adj silly; (Summe) ridiculous

Laptop (-s, -s) m laptop

Lärche (-, -n) f larch

Lärm (-(e)s) m noise

las imperf von **lesen**

Lasche (-, -n) f flap

Laser (-s, -) m laser; **Laserdrucker** m laser printer

○ SCHLÜSSELWORT

lassen (pt **ließ**, pp **gelassen** o (als Hilfsverb) **lassen**) vt **1** (unterlassen) to stop; (momentan) to leave; **lass das (sein)!** don't (do it)!; (hör auf!) stop it!; **lass mich!** leave me alone; **lassen wir das!** let's leave it; **er kann das Trinken nicht lassen** he can't stop drinking

2 (zurücklassen) to leave; **etw lassen, wie es ist** to leave sth (just) as it is

3 (*überlassen*) **jdn ins Haus lassen** to let sb into the house
▷ *vi* ; **lass mal, ich mache das schon** leave it, I'll do it
▷ *Hilfsverb* **1** (*veranlassen*) **etw machen lassen** to have o get sth done; **sich** *dat* **etw schicken lassen** to have sth sent (to one)
2 (*zulassen*) **jdn etw wissen lassen** to let sb know sth; **das Licht brennen lassen** to leave the light on; **jdn warten lassen** to keep sb waiting; **das lässt sich machen** that can be done
3 lass uns gehen let's go

lässig *adj* casual
Last (-, -en) *f* load; (*Bürde*) burden; (*Naut, Aviat*) cargo
Laster (-s, -) *nt* vice; (*fam*) truck, lorry (*Brit*)
lästern *vi*: **über jdn/etw ~ to** make nasty remarks about sb/sth
lästig *adj* annoying; (*Person*) tiresome
Last-Minute-Angebot *nt* last-minute offer; **Last-Minute-Flug** *m* last-minute flight; **Last-Minute-Ticket** *nt* last-minute ticket
Lastwagen *m* truck, lorry (*Brit*)
Latein (-s) *nt* Latin
Laterne (-, -n) *f* lantern; (*Straßenlaterne*) streetlight
Latte (-, -n) *f* slat; (*Sport*) bar
Latz (-es, *Lätze*) *m*; **Lätzchen** *nt* bib; **Latzhose** *f* dungarees *pl*
lau *adj* (*Wind, Luft*) mild
Laub (-(e)s) *nt* foliage; **Laubfrosch** *m* tree frog; **Laubsäge** *f* fretsaw
Lauch (-(e)s, -e) *m* leeks *pl*; **eine Stange ~** a leek; **Lauchzwiebel** *f* spring onions *pl* (*Brit*), scallions *pl* (*US*)
Lauf (-(e)s, *Läufe*) *m* run; (*Wettlauf*) race; (*Entwicklung*) course; (*von*

Gewehr*) barrel; **Laufbahn *f* career;
laufen (*lief, gelaufen*) *vi, vt* to run; (*gehen*) to walk; (*funktionieren*) to work; **mir läuft die Nase** my nose is running; **was läuft im Kino?** what's on at the cinema?; **wie läuft's so?** how are things?; **laufend** *adj* running; (*Monat, Ausgaben*) current; **auf dem Laufenden sein/halten** to be/to keep up-to-date; **Läufer** (-s, -) *m* (*Teppich*) rug; (*Schach*) bishop; **Läufer(in)** *m(f)* (*Sport*) runner; **Laufmasche** *f* ladder (*Brit*), run (*US*); **Laufwerk** *nt* (*Inform*) drive
Laune (-, -n) *f* mood; **gute/schlechte ~ haben** to be in a good/bad mood; **launisch** *adj* moody
Laus (-, *Läuse*) *f* louse
lauschen *vi* to listen; (*heimlich*) to eavesdrop
laut *adj* loud ▷ *adv* loudly; (*lesen*) aloud ▷ *prep* +*gen* o *dat* according to
läuten *vt, vi* to ring
lauter *adv* (*fam: nichts als*) nothing but
Lautsprecher *m* loudspeaker; **Lautstärke** *f* loudness; (*Radio, TV*) volume
lauwarm *adj* lukewarm
Lava (-, *Laven*) *f* lava
Lavendel (-s, -) *m* lavender
Lawine *f* avalanche
LCD-Anzeige *f* LCD-display
leasen *vt* to lease; **Leasing** (-s) *nt* leasing
leben *vt, vi* to live; (*am Leben sein*) to be alive; **wie lange ~ Sie schon hier?** how long have you been living here?; **von ... ~** (*Nahrungsmittel etc*) to live on ...; (*Beruf, Beschäftigung*) to make one's living from ...; **Leben** (-s, -) *nt* life; **lebend** *adj* living; **lebendig** *adj* alive; (*lebhaft*) lively;

lebensgefährlich adj very dangerous; (Verletzung) critical;
Lebensgefährte m,
Lebensgefährtin f partner;
Lebenshaltungskosten pl cost sing of living; **lebenslänglich** adj for life; **~ bekommen** to get life;
Lebenslauf m curriculum vitae (Brit), CV (Brit), resumé (US);
Lebensmittel pl food sing;
Lebensmittelgeschäft nt grocer's (shop); **Lebensmittelvergiftung** f food poisoning;
lebensnotwendig adj vital;
Lebensretter(in) m(f) rescuer;
Lebensstandard m standard of living; **Lebensunterhalt** m livelihood; **Lebensversicherung** f life insurance (o assurance (Brit));
Lebenszeichen nt sign of life
Leber (-, -n) f liver; **Leberfleck** m mole; **Leberpastete** f liver pâté
Lebewesen nt living being
lebhaft adj lively; (Erinnerung, Eindruck) vivid; **Lebkuchen** m gingerbread; **ein ~** a piece of gingerbread; **leblos** adj lifeless
Leck nt leak
lecken vi (Loch haben) to leak ▷ vt, vi (schlecken) to lick
lecker adj delicious, tasty
Leder (-s, -) nt leather
ledig adj single
leer adj empty; (Seite) blank; (Batterie) dead; **leeren** vt to empty ▷ vr: **sich ~** to empty;
Leerlauf m (Gang) neutral;
Leertaste f space bar; **Leerung** f emptying; (Briefkasten) collection; **Leerzeichen** nt blank, space
legal adj legal, lawful
legen vt to put, to place; (Eier) to lay ▷ vr: **sich ~** to lie down; (Sturm, Begeisterung) to die down; (Schmerz, Gefühl) to wear off

Legende (-, -n) f legend
leger adj casual
Lehm (-(e)s, -e) m loam; (Ton) clay
Lehne (-, -n) f arm(rest); (Rückenlehne) back(rest); **lehnen** vt to lean ▷ vr: **sich ~** to lean (an/gegen +akk against); **Lehnstuhl** m armchair
Lehrbuch nt textbook; **Lehre** (-, -n) f teaching; (beruflich) apprenticeship; (moralisch) lesson; **lehren** vt to teach; **Lehrer(in)** (-s, -) m(f) teacher; **Lehrgang** m course; **Lehrling** m apprentice; **lehrreich** adj instructive
Leib (-(e)s, -er) m body;
Leibgericht nt, **Leibspeise** f favourite dish; **Leibwächter(in)** m(f) bodyguard
Leiche (-, -n) f corpse;
Leichenhalle f mortuary;
Leichenwagen m hearse
leicht adj light; (einfach) easy, simple; (Erkrankung) slight; **es sich** (dat) **~ machen** to take the easy way out ▷ adv (mühelos, schnell) easily; (geringfügig) slightly;
Leichtathletik f athletics sing; **leichtfallen** irr vi: **jdm ~** to be easy for sb; **leichtsinnig** adj careless; (stärker) reckless
leid adj: **jdn/etw ~ sein** to be tired of sb/sth; **Leid** (-(e)s) nt grief, sorrow; **leiden** (litt, gelitten) vi, vt to suffer (an, unter +dat from); **ich kann ihn/es nicht ~** I can't stand him/it; **Leiden** (-s, -) nt suffering; (Krankheit) illness
Leidenschaft f passion;
leidenschaftlich adj passionate
leider adv unfortunately; **wir müssen jetzt ~ gehen** I'm afraid we have to go now; **~ ja/nein** I'm afraid so/not
leidtun irr vi: **es tut mir/ihm leid** I'm/he's sorry; **er tut mir leid** I'm sorry for him

Leihbücherei f lending library
leihen (lieh, geliehen) vt: **jdm etw ~** to lend sb sth; **sich** (dat) **etw von jdm ~** to borrow sth from sb;
Leihfrist f lending period;
Leihgebühr f hire charge; (für Buch) lending charge; **Leihwagen** m hire car (Brit), rental car (US)
Leim (-(e)s, -e) m glue
Leine (-, -n) f cord; (für Wäsche) line; (Hundeleine) lead (Brit), leash (US)
Leinen (-s, -) nt linen; **Leintuch** nt (für Bett) sheet; **Leinwand** f (Kunst) canvas; (Cine) screen
leise adj quiet; (sanft) soft ▷ adv quietly
Leiste (-, -n) f ledge; (Zierleiste) strip; (Anat) groin
leisten vt (Arbeit) to do; (vollbringen) to achieve; **jdm Gesellschaft ~** to keep sb company; **sich** (dat) **etw ~** (gönnen) to treat oneself to sth; **ich kann es mir nicht ~** I can't afford it
Leistenbruch m hernia
Leistung f performance; (gute) achievement
Leitartikel m leading article (Brit), editorial (US)
leiten vt to lead; (Firma) to run; (in eine Richtung) to direct; (Elek) to conduct
Leiter (-, -n) f ladder
Leiter(in) (-s, -) m(f) (von Geschäft) manager
Leitplanke (-, -n) f crash barrier
Leitung f (Führung) direction; (Tel) line; (von Firma) management; (Wasserleitung) pipe; (Kabel) cable; **eine lange ~ haben** to be slow on the uptake; **Leitungswasser** nt tap water
Lektion f lesson
Lektüre (-, -n) f (Lesen) reading; (Lesestoff) reading matter

Lende (-, -n) f (Speise) loin; (vom Rind) sirloin; **die ~n** pl (Med) the lumbar region sing
lenken vt to steer; (Blick) to direct (auf +akk towards); **jds Aufmerksamkeit auf etw** (akk) **~** to draw sb's attention to sth; **Lenker** m (von Fahrrad, Motorrad) handlebars pl; **Lenkrad** nt steering wheel; **Lenkradschloss** nt steering lock; **Lenkstange** f handlebars pl
Leopard (-en, -en) m leopard
Lepra (-) f leprosy
Lerche (-, -n) f lark
lernen vt, vi to learn; (für eine Prüfung) to study, to revise
lesbisch adj lesbian
Lesebuch nt reader; **lesen** (las, gelesen) vi, vt to read; (ernten) to pick; **Leser(in)** m(f) reader; **Leserbrief** m letter to the editor; **leserlich** adj legible; **Lesezeichen** nt bookmark
Lettland nt Latvia
letzte(r, s) adj last; (neueste) latest; (endgültig) final; **zum ~n Mal** for the last time; **am ~n Montag** last Monday; **in ~r Zeit** lately, recently; **letztens** adv (vor kurzem) recently; **letztere(r, s)** adj the latter
Leuchtanzeige f illuminated display; **Leuchte** (-, -n) f lamp, light; **leuchten** vi to shine; (Feuer, Zifferblatt) to glow; **Leuchter** (-s, -) m candlestick; **Leuchtfarbe** f fluorescent colour; (Anstrichfarbe) luminous paint; **Leuchtreklame** f neon sign; **Leuchtstoffröhre** f strip light; **Leuchtturm** m lighthouse
leugnen vt to deny ▷ vi to deny everything
Leukämie f leukaemia (Brit), leukemia (US)

Leukoplast® (-(e)s, -e) nt
Elastoplast® (Brit), Band-Aid®
(US)

Leute pl people pl

Lexikon (-s, Lexika) nt encyclopaedia (Brit), encyclopedia (US);
(Wörterbuch) dictionary

Libanon (-s) m: **der ~** Lebanon

Libelle f dragonfly

liberal adj liberal

Libyen (-s) nt Libya

Licht (-(e)s, -er) nt light;
Lichtblick m ray of hope;
lichtempfindlich adj sensitive to
light; **Lichtempfindlichkeit** f
(Foto) speed; **Lichthupe** f: **die
~ betätigen** to flash one's lights;
Lichtjahr nt light year;
Lichtmaschine f dynamo;
Lichtschalter m light switch;
Lichtschranke f light barrier;
Lichtschutzfaktor m sun
protection factor, SPF

Lichtung f clearing

Lid (-(e)s, -er) nt eyelid;
Lidschatten m eyeshadow

lieb adj (nett) nice; (teuer, geliebt)
dear; (liebenswert) sweet; **das ist
~ von dir** that's nice of you; **Lieber
Herr X** Dear Mr X; **Liebe** (-, -n) f
love; **lieben** vt to love; (sexuell) to
make love to; **liebenswürdig** adj
kind; **lieber** adv rather; **ich
möchte ~ nicht** I'd rather not;
welches ist dir ~? which one do
you prefer?; siehe auch **gern, lieb**;
Liebesbrief m love letter;
Liebeskummer m: **~ haben** to be
lovesick; **Liebespaar** nt lovers pl;
liebevoll adj loving;
Liebhaber(in) (-s, -) m(f) lover;
lieblich adj lovely; (Wein) sweet;
Liebling m darling; (Günstling)
favourite; **Lieblings-** in zW
favourite; **liebste(r, s)** adj
favourite; **liebsten** adv: **am
~ esse ich ...** my favourite food

is ...; **am ~ würde ich bleiben** I'd
really like to stay

Liechtenstein (-s) nt
Liechtenstein

Lied (-(e)s, -er) nt song; (Rel) hymn

lief imperf von **laufen**

Lieferant(in) m(f) supplier

lieferbar adj available

liefern vt to deliver; (beschaffen)
to supply

Lieferschein m delivery note;
Lieferung f delivery;
Lieferwagen m delivery van

Liege (-, -n) f (beim Arzt) couch;
(Notbett) campbed; (Gartenliege)
lounger; **liegen** (lag, gelegen) vi to
lie; (sich befinden) to be; **mir liegt
nichts/viel daran** it doesn't
matter to me/it matters a lot to
me; **woran liegt es nur, dass ...?**
why is it that ...?; **~ bleiben**
(Mensch) to stay lying down; (im
Bett) to stay in bed; (Ding) to be left
(behind); **~ lassen** (vergessen) to
leave behind; **Liegestuhl** m deck
chair; **Liegestütz** m press-up
(Brit), push-up (US); **Liegewagen**
m (Eisenb) couchette car

lieh imperf von **leihen**

ließ imperf von **lassen**

Lift (-(e)s, -e o -s) m lift, elevator
(US)

Liga (-, Ligen) f league, division

light adj (Cola) diet; (fettarm)
low-fat; (kalorienarm) low-calorie;
(Zigaretten) mild

Likör (-s, -e) m liqueur

lila adj inv purple

Lilie f lily

Limette (-, -n) f lime

Limo (-, -s) f (fam) fizzy drink
(Brit), soda (US); **Limonade** f
fizzy drink (Brit), soda (US); (mit
Zitronengeschmack) lemonade

Limone (-, -n) f lime

Limousine (-, -n) f saloon (car)
(Brit), sedan (US); (fam) limo

Linde (-, -n) f lime tree
lindern vt to relieve, to soothe
Lineal (-s, -e) nt ruler
Linie f line; **Linienflug** m
scheduled flight; **liniert** adj
ruled, lined
Link (-s, -s) m (Inform) link
Linke (-n, -n) f left-hand side;
(Hand) left hand; (Pol) left (wing);
linke(r, s) adj left; **auf der ~n
Seite** on the left, on the left-hand
side; **links** adv on the left;
~ abbiegen to turn left; **~ von**
to the left of; **~ oben** at the top left;
Linkshänder(in) (-s, -) m(f) left-
hander; **linksherum** adv to the
left, anticlockwise; **Linksverkehr**
m driving on the left
Linse (-, -n) f lentil; (optisch) lens
Lippe (-, -n) f lip; **Lipgloss** nt lip
gloss; **Lippenstift** m lipstick
lispeln vi to lisp
List (-, -en) f cunning; (Trick)
trick
Liste (-, -n) f list
Litauen (-s) nt Lithuania
Liter (-s, -) m or nt litre
literarisch adj literary; **Literatur**
f literature
Litschi (-, -s) f lychee, litchi
litt imperf von **leiden**
live adv (Radio, TV) live
Lizenz f licence
Lkw (-(s), -(s)) m abk =
Lastkraftwagen truck, lorry (Brit);
Lkw-Maut f heavy goods vehicle
toll
Lob (-(e)s) nt praise; **loben** vt to
praise
Loch (-(e)s, Löcher) nt hole;
lochen vt to punch; **Locher** (-s, -)
m (hole) punch
Locke (-, -n) f curl; **locken** vt
(anlocken) to lure; (Haare) to curl;
Lockenstab m curling tongs pl
(Brit), curling irons pl (US);
Lockenwickler (-s, -) m curler

locker adj (Schraube, Zahn) loose;
(Haltung) relaxed; (Person)
easy-going; **das schaffe ich
~** (fam) I'll manage it, no problem;
lockern vt to loosen ▷ vr: **sich
~** to loosen
lockig adj curly
Löffel (-s, -) m spoon; **einen
~ Mehl zugeben** add a spoonful of
flour; **Löffelbiskuit** (-s, -s) m
sponge finger
log imperf von **lügen**
Loge (-, -n) f (Theat) box
logisch adj logical
Logo (-s, -s) nt logo
Lohn (-(e)s, Löhne) m reward;
(Arbeitslohn) pay, wages pl
lohnen vr: **sich ~** to be worth it;
es lohnt sich nicht zu warten it's
no use waiting
Lohnerhöhung f pay rise (Brit),
pay raise (US); **Lohnsteuer** f
income tax
Lokal (-(e)s, -e) nt (Gaststätte)
restaurant; (Kneipe) pub (Brit), bar
Lokomotive f locomotive
London (-s) nt London
Lorbeer (-s, -en) m laurel;
Lorbeerblatt nt (Gastr) bay leaf
los adj loose; **~!** go on!; **jdn/etw
~ sein** to be rid of sb/sth; **was ist
~?** what's the matter?, what's up?;
dort ist nicht viel ~ there's
nothing/a lot going on there
Los (-es, -e) nt (Schicksal) lot, fate;
(Lotterie etc) ticket
los|binden irr vt to untie
löschen vt (Feuer, Licht) to put
out, to extinguish; (Durst) to
quench; (Tonband) to erase; (Daten,
Zeile) to delete; **Löschtaste** f
delete key
lose adj loose
Lösegeld nt ransom
losen vi to draw lots
lösen vt (lockern) to loosen;
(Rätsel) to solve; (Chem) to

dissolve; *(Fahrkarte)* to buy ▷ vr: **sich ~** *(abgehen)* to come off; *(Zucker etc)* to dissolve; *(Problem, Schwierigkeit)* to (re)solve itself

los|fahren *irr vi* to leave; **los|gehen** *irr vi* to set out; *(anfangen)* to start; **los|lassen** *irr vt* to let go

löslich *adj* soluble

Lösung *f (eines Rätsels, Problems, Flüssigkeit)* solution

los|werden *irr vt* to get rid of

Lotterie *f* lottery; **Lotto** *(-s) nt* National Lottery; **~ spielen** to play the lottery

Löwe *(-n, -n) m (Zool)* lion; *(Astr)* Leo; **Löwenzahn** *m* dandelion

Luchs *(-es, -e) m* lynx

Lücke *(-, -n) f* gap; **Lückenbüßer(in)** *(-s, -) m(f)* stopgap

lud *imperf von* **laden**

Luft *(-, Lüfte) f* air; *(Atem)* breath; **Luftballon** *m* balloon; **Luftblase** *f* (air) bubble; **luftdicht** *adj* airtight; **Luftdruck** *m (Meteo)* atmospheric pressure; *(in Reifen)* air pressure

lüften *vt* to air; *(Geheimnis)* to reveal

Luftfahrt *f* aviation; **Luftfeuchtigkeit** *f* humidity; **Luftfilter** *m* air filter; **Luftfracht** *f* air freight; **Luftkissenboot** *nt*, **Luftkissenfahrzeug** *nt* hovercraft; **Luftlinie** *f*: **10 km** ~ 10 km as the crow flies; **Luftmatratze** *f* airbed; **Luftpirat(in)** *m(f)* hijacker; **Luftpost** *f* airmail; **Luftpumpe** *f* (bicycle) pump; **Luftröhre** *f* windpipe

Lüftung *f* ventilation

Luftveränderung *f* change of air; **Luftverschmutzung** *f* air pollution; **Luftwaffe** *f* air force; **Luftzug** *m* draught *(Brit)*, draft *(US)*

Lüge *(-, -n) f* lie; **lügen** *(log, gelogen) vi* to lie; **Lügner(in)** *(-s, -) m(f)* liar

Luke *(-, -n) f* hatch

Lumpen *(-s, -) m* rag

Lunchpaket *nt* packed lunch

Lunge *(-, -n) f* lungs *pl*; **Lungenentzündung** *f* pneumonia

Lupe *(-, -n) f* magnifying glass; **etw unter die ~ nehmen** *(fig)* to have a close look at sth

Lust *(-, Lüste) f* joy, delight; *(Neigung)* desire; **~ auf etw** *(akk)* **haben** to feel like sth; **~ haben, etw zu tun** to feel like doing sth

lustig *adj (komisch)* amusing, funny; *(fröhlich)* cheerful

lutschen *vt* to suck ▷ vi: **~ an** *(+dat)* to suck; **Lutscher** *(-s, -) m* lollipop

Luxemburg *(-s) nt* Luxembourg

luxuriös *adj* luxurious

Luxus *(-) m* luxury

Lymphdrüse *f* lymph gland; **Lymphknoten** *m* lymph node

Lyrik *(-) f* poetry

m

machbar adj feasible

🔵 **SCHLÜSSELWORT**

machen vt **1** to do; *(herstellen, zubereiten)* to make; **was machst du da?** what are you doing (there)?; **das ist nicht zu machen** that can't be done; **das Radio leiser machen** to turn the radio down; **aus Holz gemacht** made of wood

2 *(verursachen, bewirken)* to make; **jdm Angst machen** to make sb afraid; **das macht die Kälte** it's the cold that does that

3 *(ausmachen)* to matter; **das macht nichts** that doesn't matter; **die Kälte macht mir nichts** I don't mind the cold

4 *(kosten, ergeben)* to be; **3 und 5 macht 8** 3 and 5 is o are 8; **was o wie viel macht das?** how much

does that make?

5 was macht die Arbeit? how's the work going?; **was macht dein Bruder?** how is your brother doing?; **das Auto machen lassen** to have the car done; **mach's gut!** take care! *(viel Glück)* good luck!

▷ vi: **mach schnell!** hurry up!; **Schluss machen** to finish (off); **mach schon!** come on!; **das macht müde** it makes you tired; **in etw** *dat* **machen** to be o deal in sth

▷ vr to come along (nicely); **sich an etw** *akk* **machen** to set about sth; **sich verständlich machen** to make o.s. understood; **sich viel aus jdm/etw machen** to like sb/sth

Macho (-s, -s) m *(fam)* macho (type)

Macht (-s, *Mächte*) f power; **mächtig** adj powerful; *(fam: ungeheuer)* enormous; **machtlos** adj powerless; **da ist man ~** there's nothing you can do (about it)

Mädchen nt girl; **Mädchenname** m maiden name

Made (-, -n) f maggot

Magazin (-s, -e) nt magazine

Magen (-s, - o Mägen) m stomach; **Magenbeschwerden** pl stomach trouble sing; **Magen-Darm-Infektion** f gastroenteritis; **Magengeschwür** nt stomach ulcer; **Magenschmerzen** pl stomach-ache sing

mager adj *(Fleisch, Wurst)* lean; *(Person)* thin; *(Käse, Joghurt)* low-fat; **Magermilch** f skimmed milk; **Magersucht** f anorexia; **magersüchtig** adj anorexic

magisch adj magical

Magnet (-s o -en, -en) m magnet

mähen vt, vi to mow

mahlen *(mahlte, gemahlen)* vt to grind

Mahlzeit f meal; *(für Baby)* feed ▷ interj *(guten Appetit)* enjoy your meal

Mähne *(-, -n)* f mane

mahnen vt to urge; **jdn schriftlich ~** to send sb a reminder; **Mahngebühr** f fine; **Mahnung** f warning; *(schriftlich)* reminder

Mai *(-(s), -e)* m May; *siehe auch* **Juni; Maifeiertag** m May Day; **Maiglöckchen** nt lily of the valley; **Maikäfer** m cockchafer

Mail *(-, -s)* f e-mail; **jdm eine~ schicken** to mail sb, to e-mail sb; **Mailbox** f *(Inform)* mailbox; **mailen** vi, vt to e-mail

Mais *(-es, -e)* m maize, corn *(US)*; **Maiskolben** m corn cob; *(Gastr)* corn on the cob

Majestät *(-, -en)* f Majesty

Majonäse *(-, -n)* f mayonnaise

Majoran *(-s, -e)* m marjoram

makaber adj macabre

Make-up *(-s, -s)* nt make-up

Makler(in) *(-s, -)* m(f) broker; *(Immobilienmakler)* estate agent *(Brit)*, Realtor® *(US)*

Makrele *(-, -n)* f mackerel

Makro *(-s, -s)* nt *(Inform)* macro

Makrone *(-, -n)* f macaroon

mal adv *(beim Rechnen)* times, multiplied by; *(beim Messen)* by; *(fam: einmal = früher)* once; *(einmal = zukünftig)* some day; **4 ~ 3 ist 12** 4 times 3 is (o equals) twelve; **da habe ich ~ gewohnt** I used to live there; **irgendwann ~ werde ich dort hinfahren** I'll go there one day; **das ist nun ~ so** well, that's just the way it is (o goes); **Mal** *(-(e)s, -e)* nt *(Zeitpunkt)* time; *(Markierung)* mark; **jedes ~** every time; **ein paar ~** a few times; **ein einziges ~** just once

Malaria *(-)* f malaria

Malaysia *(-s)* nt Malaysia

Malbuch nt colouring book

Malediven pl Maldives pl

malen vt, vi to paint; **Maler(in)** *(-s, -)* m(f) painter; **Malerei** f painting; **malerisch** adj picturesque

Mallorca *(-s)* nt Majorca, Mallorca

mal|nehmen irr vt to multiply *(mit by)*

Malta *(-s)* nt Malta

Malventee m mallow tea

Malz *(-es)* nt malt; **Malzbier** nt malt beer

Mama *(-, -s)* f mum(my) *(Brit)*, mom(my) *(US)*

man pron you; *(förmlich)* one; *(jemand)* someone, somebody; *(die Leute)* they, people pl; **wie schreibt ~ das?** how do you spell that?; **~ hat ihr das Fahrrad gestohlen** someone stole her bike; **~ sagt, dass ...** they (o people) say that ...

managen vt *(fam)* to manage; **Manager(in)** *(-s, -)* m(f) manager

manche(r, s) adj many a; *(mit pl)* a number of, some ▷ pron *(einige)* some; *(viele)* many; **~ Politiker** many politicians pl, many a politician; **manchmal** adv sometimes

Mandant(in) m(f) client

Mandarine f mandarin, tangerine

Mandel *(-, -n)* f almond; **~n** *(Anat)* tonsils pl; **Mandelentzündung** f tonsillitis

Manege *(-, -n)* f ring

Mangel *(-s, Mängel)* m *(Fehlen)* lack; *(Knappheit)* shortage *(an +dat* of); *(Fehler)* defect, fault; **mangelhaft** adj *(Ware)* faulty; *(Schulnote)* = E

Mango *(-, -s)* f mango

Mangold *(-s)* m mangel(wurzel)

Manieren pl manners pl

Maniküre (-, -n) f manicure

manipulieren vt to manipulate

Manko (-s, -s) nt deficiency

Mann (-(e)s, Männer) m man; (Ehemann) husband; **Männchen** nt: **es ist ein ~** (Tier) it's a he; **männlich** adj masculine; (Bio) male

Mannschaft f (Sport, fig) team; (Naut, Aviat) crew

Mansarde (-, -n) f attic

Manschettenknopf m cufflink

Mantel (-s, Mäntel) m coat; (Tech) casing, jacket

Mappe (-, -n) f briefcase; (Aktenmappe) folder

Maracuja (-, -s) f passion fruit

Marathon (-s, -s) m marathon

Märchen (-s, -) nt fairy tale

Marder (-s, -) m marten

Margarine f margarine

Marienkäfer m ladybird (Brit), ladybug (US)

Marihuana (-s) nt marijuana

Marille (-, -n) f apricot

Marinade f marinade

Marine f navy

marinieren vt to marinate

Marionette f puppet

Mark (-(e)s) nt (Knochenmark) marrow; (Fruchtmark) pulp

Marke (-, -n) f (Warensorte) brand; (Fabrikat) make; (Briefmarke) stamp; (Essenmarke) voucher, ticket; (aus Metall etc) disc; (Messpunkt) mark; **Markenartikel** m branded item, brand name product; **Markenzeichen** nt trademark

markieren vt to mark; **Markierung** f marking; (Zeichen) mark

Markise (-, -n) f awning

Markt (-(e)s, Märkte) m market; **auf den ~ bringen** to launch; **Markthalle** f covered market;

Marktlücke f gap in the market; **Marktplatz** m market place; **Marktwirtschaft** f market economy

Marmelade f jam; (Orangenmarmelade) marmalade

Marmor (-s) m marble; **Marmorkuchen** m marble cake

Marokko (-s) nt Morocco

Marone (-, -n) f chestnut

Mars (-) m Mars

Marsch (-(e)s, Märsche) m march

Märtyrer(in) (-s, -) m(f) martyr

März (-(es), -e) m March; siehe auch **Juni**

Marzipan (-s, -e) nt marzipan

Maschine f machine; (Motor) engine; **maschinell** adj mechanical, machine-; **Maschinenbau** m mechanical engineering

Masern pl (Med) measles sing

Maske (-, -n) f mask; **Maskenball** m fancy-dress ball; **maskieren** vr: **sich ~** (Maske aufsetzen) to put on a mask; (verkleiden) to dress up

Maskottchen nt mascot

maß imperf von **messen**

Maß (-es, -e) nt measure; (Mäßigung) moderation; (Grad) degree, extent; **~e** (Person) measurements; (Raum) dimensions; **in gewissem/hohem ~e** to a certain/high degree; **in zunehmendem ~e** increasingly

Mass (-, -(en)) f (Bier) litre of beer

Massage (-, -n) f massage

Masse (-, -n) f mass; (von Menschen) crowd; (Großteil) majority; **massenhaft** adv masses (o loads) of; **am See sind ~ Mücken** there are masses of mosquitoes at the lake; **Massenkarambolage** f pile-up; **Massenmedien** pl mass media pl; **Massenproduktion** f mass

production; **Massentourismus**
m mass tourism
Masseur(in) *m(f)*
masseur/masseuse
maßgeschneidert *adj (Kleidung)* made-to-measure
massieren *vt* to massage
mäßig *adj* moderate
massiv *adj* solid; *(fig)* massive
maßlos *adj* extreme
Maßnahme *(-, -n) f* measure,
step
Maßstab *m* rule, measure; *(fig)*
standard; **im ~ von 1:5** on a scale
of 1:5
Mast *(-(e)s, -e(n)) m* mast; *(Elek)*
pylon
Material *(-s, -ien) nt* material;
(Arbeitsmaterial) materials *pl*;
materialistisch *adj* materialistic
Materie *f* matter; **materiell** *adj*
material
Mathe *(-) f (fam)* maths *(Brit)*,
math *(US)*; **Mathematik** *f*
mathematics *sing*; **Mathe-
matiker(in)** *m(f)* mathematician
Matinee *(-, -n) f* ≈ matinee
Matratze *(-, -n) f* mattress
Matrose *(-n, -n) m* sailor
Matsch *(-(e)s) m* mud; *(Schnee)*
slush; **matschig** *adj* muddy;
(Schnee) slushy; *(Obst)* mushy
matt *adj* weak; *(glanzlos)* dull;
(Foto) matt; *(Schach)* mate
Matte *(-, -n) f* mat
Matura *(-) f* Austrian
school-leaving examination; ≈
A-levels *(Brit),* ≈ High School
Diploma *(US)*
Mauer *(-, -n) f* wall
Maul *(-(e)s, Mäuler) nt* mouth;
(fam) gob; **halt's ~!** shut your face
(o gob); **Maulbeere** *f* mulberry;
Maulesel *m* mule; **Maulkorb** *m*
muzzle; **Maul- und Klauenseuche**
f foot-and-mouth disease;
Maulwurf *m* mole

Maurer(in) *(-s, -) m(f)* bricklayer
Mauritius *(-) nt* Mauritius
Maus *(-, Mäuse) f* mouse;
Mausefalle *f* mousetrap;
Mausklick *(-s, -s) m* mouse click;
Mauspad *(-s, -s) nt* mouse mat *(o
pad)*; **Maustaste** *f* mouse key *(o
button)*
Maut *(-, -en) f* toll; **Mautgebühr**
f toll; **mautpflichtig** *adj:* **~e
Straße** toll road, turnpike *(US)*;
Mautstelle *f* tollbooth, tollgate;
Mautstraße *f* toll road, turnpike
(US)
maximal *adv:* **ihr habt ~ zwei
Stunden Zeit** you've got two
hours at (the) most; **~ vier Leute** a
maximum of four people
Mayonnaise *f siehe* **Majonäse**
Mazedonien *(-s) nt* Macedonia
MB *(-, -) nt*, **Mbyte** *(-, -) nt abk =
Megabyte* MB
Mechanik *f* mechanics *sing*;
(Getriebe) mechanics *pl*;
Mechaniker(in) *(-s, -) m(f)* mechanic;
mechanisch *adj* mechanical;
Mechanismus *m* mechanism
meckern *vi (Ziege)* to bleat; *(fam:
schimpfen)* to moan
Mecklenburg-Vorpommern
(-s) nt Mecklenburg-Western
Pomerania
Medaille *(-, -n) f* medal
Medien *pl* media *pl*
Medikament *nt* medicine
Meditation *f* meditation;
meditieren *vi* to meditate
medium *adj (Steak)* medium
Medizin *(-, -en) f* medicine *(gegen
for)*; **medizinisch** *adj* medical
Meer *(-(e)s, -e) nt* sea; **am ~** by
the sea; **Meerenge** *f* straits *pl*;
Meeresfrüchte *pl* seafood *sing*;
Meeresspiegel *m* sea level;
Meerrettich *m* horseradish;
Meerschweinchen *nt* guinea
pig; **Meerwasser** *nt* seawater

Megabyte nt megabyte;
Megahertz nt megahertz

Mehl (-(e)s, -e) nt flour;
Mehlspeise f sweet dish made from
flour, eggs and milk

mehr pron, adv more; **~ will ich
nicht ausgeben** I don't want to
spend any more, that's as much as I
want to spend; **was willst du ~?**
what more do you want? ▷ adv:
immer ~ (Leute) more and more
(people); **~ als fünf Minuten** more
than five minutes; **je ~ ..., desto
besser** the more ..., the better; **ich
kann nicht ~ stehen** I can't stand
any more (o longer); **es ist kein
Brot ~ da** there's no bread left; **nie
~** never again; **mehrdeutig** adj
ambiguous; **mehrere** pron
several; **mehreres** pron several
things; **mehrfach** adj multiple;
(wiederholt) repeated;
Mehrfachstecker m multiple
plug; **Mehrheit** f majority;
mehrmals adv repeatedly;
mehrsprachig adj multilingual;
Mehrwegflasche f returnable
bottle, deposit bottle;
Mehrwertsteuer f value added
tax, VAT; **Mehrzahl** f majority;
(Plural) plural

meiden (mied, gemieden) vt to
avoid

Meile (-, -n) f mile

mein pron (adjektivisch) my;
meine(r, s) pron (substantivisch)
mine

meinen vt, vi (glauben, der Ansicht
sein) to think; (sagen) to say; (sagen
wollen, beabsichtigen) to mean; **das
war nicht so gemeint** I didn't
mean it like that

meinetwegen adv (wegen mir)
because of me; (mir zuliebe) for my
sake; (von mir aus) as far as I'm
concerned

Meinung f opinion; **meiner**
~ nach in my opinion;
Meinungsumfrage f opinion
poll; **Meinungsverschiedenheit**
f disagreement (über +akk about)

Meise (-, -n) f tit; **eine ~ haben**
(fam) to be crazy

Meißel (-s, -) m chisel

meist adv mostly; **meiste(r, s)**
pron (adjektivisch) most; **die ~n**
(Leute) most people; **die ~ Zeit**
most of the time; **das ~ (davon)**
most of it; **die ~n von ihnen** most
of them; (substantivisch) most of
them; **am ~** (the) most;
meistens adv mostly; (zum
größten Teil) for the most part

Meister(in) (-s, -) m(f) master;
(Sport) champion; **Meisterschaft**
f championship; **Meisterwerk**
nt masterpiece

melden vt to report ▷ vr: **sich
~ to report** (bei to); (Schule) to put
one's hand up; (freiwillig) to
volunteer; (auf etw, am Telefon) to
answer; **Meldung** f
announcement; (Bericht) report;
(Inform) message

Melodie f tune, melody

Melone (-, -n) f melon

Memoiren pl memoirs pl

Menge (-, -n) f quantity;
(Menschen) crowd; **eine ~ (große
Anzahl)** a lot (gen of);
Mengenrabatt m bulk discount

Meniskus (-, Menisken) m
meniscus

Mensa (-, Mensen) f canteen,
cafeteria (US)

Mensch (-en, -en) m human
being, man; (Person) person; **kein
~ nobody**; **~! (bewundernd)** wow!;
(verärgert) bloody hell!;
Menschenmenge f crowd;
Menschenrechte pl human
rights pl; **Menschenverstand** m:
gesunder ~ common sense;
Menschheit f humanity,

mankind; **menschlich** adj
human; *(human)* humane
Menstruation f menstruation
Mentalität f mentality, mindset
Menthol (-s) nt menthol
Menü (-s, -s) nt set meal; *(Inform)*
menu; **Menüleiste** f *(Inform)*
menu bar
Merkblatt nt leaflet; **merken** vt
(bemerken) to notice; **sich** *(dat)* **etw**
~ to remember sth; **Merkmal** nt
feature
Merkur (-s) m Mercury
merkwürdig adj odd
Messbecher m measuring jug
Messe (-, -n) f fair; *(Rel)* mass;
Messebesucher(in) m(f) visitor
to a/the fair; **Messegelände** nt
exhibition site
messen *(maß, gemessen)* vt to
measure; *(Temperatur, Puls)* to take
▷ vr: **sich** ~ to compete; **sie kann
sich mit ihm nicht** ~ she's no
match for him
Messer (-s, -) nt knife
Messgerät nt measuring device,
gauge
Messing (-s) nt brass
Metall (-s, -e) nt metal
Meteorologe m, **Meteorologin**
f meteorologist
Meter (-s, -) m o nt metre;
Metermaß nt tape measure
Methode (-, -n) f method
Metzger(in) (-s, -) m(f) butcher;
Metzgerei f butcher's (shop)
Mexiko (-s) nt Mexico
MEZ f abk = **mitteleuropäische
Zeit** CET
miau interj miaow
mich pron akk von **ich** me;
~ **(selbst)** *(reflexiv)* myself; **stell
dich hinter** ~ stand behind me;
ich fühle ~ **wohl** I feel fine
mied imperf von **meiden**
Miene (-, -n) f look, expression
mies adj *(fam)* lousy

Miesmuschel f mussel
Mietauto nt siehe **Mietwagen**;
Miete (-, -n) f rent; **mieten** vt to
rent; *(Auto)* to hire (Brit), to rent
(US); **Mieter(in)** (-s, -) m(f)
tenant; **Mietshaus** nt block of
flats (Brit), apartment house (US);
Mietvertrag m rental
agreement; **Mietwagen** m hire
car (Brit), rental car (US); **sich** *(dat)*
einen ~ **nehmen** to hire (Brit) (o
rent (US)) a car
Migräne (-, -n) f migraine
Migrant(in) (-en, -en) m(f)
migrant (worker)
Mikrofon (-s, -e) nt microphone
Mikrowelle (-, -n) f,
Mikrowellenherd m microwave
(oven)
Milch (-) f milk; **Milcheis** nt
ice-cream *(made with milk)*;
Milchglas nt *(dickes, trübes Glas)*
frosted glass; **Milchkaffee** m
milky coffee; **Milchprodukte** pl
dairy products pl; **Milchpulver** nt
powdered milk; **Milchreis** m rice
pudding; **Milchshake** m milk
shake; **Milchstraße** f Milky Way
mild adj mild; *(Richter)* lenient;
(freundlich) kind
Militär (-s) nt military, army
Milliarde (-, -n) f billion;
Milligramm nt milligram;
Milliliter m millilitre; **Millimeter**
m millimetre; **Million** f million;
Millionär(in) m(f) millionaire
Milz (-) f spleen
Mimik f facial expression(s)
Minderheit f minority
minderjährig adj underage
minderwertig adj inferior;
Minderwertigkeitskomplex m
inferiority complex
Mindest- in zW minimum;
mindeste(r, s) adj least;
mindestens adv at least;
Mindesthaltbarkeitsdatum nt

best-before date, sell-by date (Brit)

Mine (-, -n) f mine; (Bleistift) lead; (Kugelschreiber) refill

Mineralwasser nt mineral water

Minibar f minibar; **Minigolf** m miniature golf, crazy golf (Brit)

minimal adj minimal

Minimum (-s, Minima) nt minimum

Minirock m miniskirt

Minister(in) (-s, -) m(f) minister; **Ministerium** nt ministry; **Ministerpräsident(in)** m(f) (von Bundesland) Minister President (Prime Minister of a Bundesland)

minus adv minus; **Minus** (-, -) nt deficit; **im ~ sein** to be in the red; (Konto) to be overdrawn

Minute (-, -n) f minute

Minze (-, -n) f mint

Mio. nt abk von **Million(en)** m

mir pron dat von **ich** (to) me; **kannst du ~ helfen?** can you help me?; **kannst du es ~ erklären?** can you explain it to me?; **ich habe ~ einen neuen Rechner gekauft** I bought (myself) a new computer; **ein Freund von ~** a friend of mine

Mirabelle (-, -n) f mirabelle (small yellow plum)

mischen vt to mix; (Karten) to shuffle; **Mischmasch** m (fam) hotchpotch; **Mischung** f mixture (aus of)

missachten vt to ignore; **Missbrauch** m abuse; (falscher Gebrauch) misuse; **missbrauchen** vt to misuse (zu for); (sexuell) to abuse; **Misserfolg** m failure; **Missgeschick** nt (Panne) mishap; **misshandeln** vt to ill-treat

Mission f mission

misslingen (misslang, misslungen) vi to fail; **der Versuch ist mir misslungen** my attempt failed;

misstrauen vt +dat to distrust; **Misstrauen** (-s) nt mistrust, suspicion (gegenüber of); **misstrauisch** adj distrustful; (argwöhnisch) suspicious;

Missverständnis nt misunderstanding; **missverstehen** irr vt to misunderstand

Mist (-(e)s) m (fam) rubbish; (von Kühen) dung; (als Dünger) manure

Mistel (-, -n) f mistletoe

mit prep +dat with; (mittels) by; **~ der Bahn** by train; **~ der Kreditkarte bezahlen** to pay by credit card; **~ 10 Jahren** at the age of 10; **wie wärs ~ ...?** how about ...? ▷ adv along, too; **wollen Sie ~?** do you want to come along?

Mitarbeiter(in) m(f) (Angestellter) employee; (an Projekt) collaborator; (freier) freelancer

mit|bekommen irr vt (fam: aufschnappen) to catch; (hören) to hear; (verstehen) to get

mit|benutzen vt to share

Mitbewohner(in) m(f) (in Wohnung) flatmate (Brit), roommate (US)

mit|bringen irr vt to bring along; **Mitbringsel** (-s, -) nt small present

miteinander adv with one another; (gemeinsam) together

mit|erleben vt to see (with one's own eyes)

Mitesser (-s, -) m blackhead

Mitfahrgelegenheit f ~ lift, ride (US); **Mitfahrzentrale** f agency for arranging lifts

mit|geben irr vt: **jdm etw ~** to give sb sth (to take along)

Mitgefühl nt sympathy

mit|gehen irr vi to go/come along

mitgenommen adj worn out, exhausted

Mitglied nt member

mithilfe prep +gen **~ von** with the help of

mit|kommen irr vi to come along; (verstehen) to follow

Mitleid nt pity; **~ haben mit** to feel sorry for

mit|machen vt to take part in ▷ vi to take part

mit|nehmen irr vt to take along; (anstrengen) to wear out, to exhaust

mit|schreiben irr vi to take notes ▷ vt to take down

Mitschüler(in) m(f) schoolmate

mit|spielen vi (in Mannschaft) to play; (bei Spiel) to join in; **in einem Film/Stück ~** to act in a film/play

Mittag m midday; **gestern ~ at** midday yesterday, yesterday lunchtime; **über ~ geschlossen** closed at lunchtime; **zu ~ essen** to have lunch; **Mittagessen** nt lunch; **mittags** adv at lunchtime, at midday; **Mittagspause** f lunch break

Mitte (-, -n) f middle; **~ Juni** in the middle of June; **sie ist ~ zwanzig** she's in her mid-twenties

mit|teilen vt: **jdm etw ~** to inform sb of sth; **Mitteilung** f notification

Mittel (-s -) nt means sing; (Maßnahme, Methode) method; (Med) remedy (gegen for); **das ist ein gutes ~, (um) junge Leute zu erreichen** that's a good way of engaging with young people

Mittelalter nt Middle Ages pl; **mittelalterlich** adj medieval; **Mittelamerika** nt Central America; **Mitteleuropa** nt Central Europe; **Mittelfeld** nt midfield; **Mittelfinger** m middle finger; **mittelmäßig** adj mediocre; **Mittelmeer** nt Mediterranean (Sea);

Mittelohrentzündung f inflammation of the middle ear; **Mittelpunkt** m centre; **im ~ stehen** to be the centre of attention

mittels prep +gen by means of

Mittelstreifen m central reservation (Brit), median (US); **Mittelstürmer(in)** m(f) striker, centre-forward; **Mittelwelle** f medium wave

mitten adv in the middle; **~ auf der Straße/in der Nacht** in the middle of the street/night

Mitternacht f midnight

mittlere(r, s) adj middle; (durchschnittlich) average

mittlerweile adv meanwhile

Mittwoch (-s, -e) m Wednesday; **(am) ~** on Wednesday; (am) **~ Morgen/Nachmittag/Abend** (on) Wednesday morning/ afternoon/evening; **diesen/letzten/nächsten ~** this/last/next Wednesday; **jeden ~** every Wednesday; **~ in einer Woche** a week on Wednesday, Wednesday week; **mittwochs** adv on Wednesdays; **~ abends** (jeden Mittwochabend) on Wednesday evenings

mixen vt to mix; **Mixer** (-s, -) m (Küchengerät) blender

MKS f abk = **Maul- und Klauenseuche** FMD

mobben vt to harass (o to bully) (at work)

Mobbing (-s) nt workplace bullying (o harassment)

Möbel (-s, -) nt piece of furniture; **die ~** pl the furniture sing; **Möbelwagen** m removal van

mobil adj mobile

Mobilfunknetz nt cellular network; **Mobiltelefon** nt mobile phone

möblieren vt to furnish

mochte imperf von **mögen**
Mode (-, -n) f fashion
Model (-s, -s) nt model
Modell (-s, -e) nt model
Modem (-s, -s) nt (Inform) modem
Mode(n)schau f fashion show
Moderator(in) m(f) presenter
modern adj modern; (modisch) fashionable
Modeschmuck m costume jewellery; **modisch** adj fashionable
Modus (-, Modi) m (Inform) mode; (fig) way
Mofa (-s, -s) nt moped
mogeln vi to cheat

🔵 SCHLÜSSELWORT

mögen (pt **mochte**, pp **gemocht** o (als Hilfsverb) **mögen**) vt, vi to like; **magst du/mögen Sie ihn?** do you like him?; **ich möchte ...** I would like ..., I'd like ...; **er möchte in die Stadt** he'd like to go into town; **ich möchte nicht, dass du ...** I wouldn't like you to ...; **ich mag nicht mehr** I've had enough
▷ Hilfsverb to like to; (wollen) to want; **möchtest du etwas essen?** would you like something to eat?; **sie mag nicht bleiben** she doesn't want to stay; **das mag wohl sein** that may well be; **was mag das heißen?** what might that mean?; **Sie möchten zu Hause anrufen** could you please call home?

möglich adj possible; **so bald wie ~** as soon as possible; **möglicherweise** adv possibly; **Möglichkeit** f possibility; **möglichst** adv as ... as possible
Mohn (-(e)s, -e) m (Blume) poppy; (Samen) poppy seed

Möhre (-, -n) f, **Mohrrübe** f carrot
Mokka (-s, -s) m mocha
Moldawien (-s) nt Moldova
Molkerei (-, -en) f dairy
Moll (-) nt minor (key); **a-~** A minor
mollig adj cosy; (dicklich) plump
Moment (-(e)s, -e) m moment; **im ~** at the moment; **einen ~ bitte!** just a minute; **momentan** adj momentary ▷ adv at the moment
Monaco (-s) nt Monaco
Monarchie f monarchy
Monat (-(e)s, -e) m month; **sie ist im dritten ~** (schwanger) she's three months pregnant; **monatlich** adj, adv monthly; **~ 100 Euro zahlen** to pay 100 euros a month (o every month); **Monatskarte** f monthly season ticket
Mönch (-s, -e) m monk
Mond (-(e)s, -e) m moon; **Mondfinsternis** f lunar eclipse
Mongolei (-) f: **die ~** Mongolia
Monitor m (Inform) monitor
monoton adj monotonous
Monsun (-s, -e) m monsoon
Montag m Monday; siehe auch **Mittwoch**; **montags** adv on Mondays; siehe auch **mittwochs**
Montenegro (-s) nt Montenegro
Monteur(in) (-s, -e) m(f) fitter; **montieren** vt to assemble, to set up
Monument nt monument
Moor (-(e)s, -e) nt moor
Moos (-es, -e) nt moss
Moped (-s, -s) nt moped
Moral (-) f (Werte) morals pl; (einer Geschichte) moral; **moralisch** adj moral
Mord (-(e)s, -e) m murder;

m

Mörder(in) (-s, -) m(f) murderer/murderess

morgen adv tomorrow; **~ früh** tomorrow morning

Morgen (-s, -) m morning; **am ~** in the morning; **Morgenmantel** m, **Morgenrock** m dressing gown; **Morgenmuffel** m: **er ist ein ~** he's not a morning person; **morgens** adv in the morning; **um 3 Uhr ~ at** 3 (o'clock) in the morning, at 3 am

Morphium (-s) nt morphine

morsch adj rotten

Mosaik (-s, -e(n)) nt mosaic

Mosambik (-s) nt Mozambique

Moschee (-, -n) f mosque

Moskau (-s) nt Moscow

Moskito (-s, -s) m mosquito; **Moskitonetz** nt mosquito net

Moslem (-s, -s) m, **Moslime** (-, -n) f Muslim

Most (-(e)s, -e) m (unfermented) fruit juice; (Apfelwein) cider

Motel (-s, -s) nt motel

motivieren vt to motivate

Motor m engine; (Elek) motor; **Motorboot** nt motorboat; **Motorenöl** nt engine oil; **Motorhaube** f bonnet (Brit), hood (US); **Motorrad** nt motorbike, motorcycle; **Motorradfahrer(in)** m(f) motorcyclist; **Motorroller** m (motor) scooter; **Motorschaden** m engine trouble

Motte (-, -n) f moth

Motto (-s, -s) nt motto

Mountainbike (-s, -s) nt mountain bike

Möwe (-, -n) f (sea)gull

MP3-Player (-s, -) m MP3 player

Mrd. f abk = **Milliarde(n)**

MS (-) f abk = **multiple Sklerose** MS

Mücke (-, -n) f midge; (tropische) mosquito; **Mückenstich** m mosquito bite

müde adj tired

muffig adj (Geruch) musty; (Gesicht, Mensch) grumpy

Mühe (-, -n) f trouble, pains pl; **sich** (dat) **große ~ geben** to go to a lot of trouble

muhen vi to moo

Mühle (-, -n) f mill; (Kaffeemühle) grinder

Müll (-(e)s) m rubbish (Brit), garbage (US); **Müllabfuhr** f rubbish (Brit) (o garbage (US)) disposal

Mullbinde f gauze bandage

Müllcontainer m waste container; **Mülldeponie** f rubbish (Brit) (o garbage (US)) dump; **Mülleimer** m rubbish bin (Brit), garbage can (US); **Mülltonne** f dustbin (Brit), garbage can (US); **Mülltrennung** f sorting and collecting household waste according to type of material; **Müllverbrennungsanlage** f incineration plant; **Müllwagen** m dustcart (Brit), garbage truck (US)

multikulturell adj multicultural

Multimedia- in zW multimedia

Multiple-Choice-Verfahren nt multiple choice

multiple Sklerose (-n, -n) f multiple sclerosis

Multiplexkino nt multiplex (cinema)

multiplizieren vt to multiply (mit by)

Mumie f mummy

Mumps (-) m mumps sing

München (-s) nt Munich

Mund (-(e)s, Münder) m mouth; **halt den ~!** shut up; **Mundart** f dialect; **Munddusche** f dental water jet

münden vi to flow (in +akk into)

Mundgeruch m bad breath; **Mundharmonika** (-, -s) f mouth organ

mündlich adj oral
Mundschutz m mask;
  Mundwasser nt mouthwash
Munition f ammunition
Münster (-s, -) nt minster,
  cathedral
munter adj lively
Münzautomat m vending
  machine; **Münze** (-, -n) f coin;
  Münzeinwurf m slot;
  Münzrückgabe f coin return;
  Münztelefon nt pay phone;
  Münzwechsler m change
  machine
murmeln vt, vi to murmur, to
  mutter
Murmeltier nt marmot
mürrisch adj sullen, grumpy
Mus (-es, -e) nt puree
Muschel (-, -n) f mussel; (~schale)
  shell
Museum (-s, Museen) nt
  museum
Musical (-s, -s) nt musical
Musik f music; **musikalisch** adj
  musical; **Musiker(in)** (-s, -) m(f)
  musician; **Musikinstrument** nt
  musical instrument; **musizieren**
  vi to play music
Muskat (-(e)s) m nutmeg
Muskel (-s, -n) m muscle;
  Muskelkater m: ~ **haben** to be
  stiff; **Muskelriss** m torn muscle;
  Muskelzerrung f pulled muscle;
  muskulös adj muscular
Müsli (-s, -) nt muesli
Muslim(in) (-s, -s) m(f) Muslim
Muss (-) nt must

○ **SCHLÜSSELWORT**

müssen (pt **musste**, pp **gemusst**
o (als Hilfsverb) **müssen**) vi
1 (Zwang) must; (nur im Präsens) to
  have to; **ich muss es tun** I must do
  it, I have to do it; **ich musste es
  tun** I had to do it; **er muss es**

nicht tun he doesn't have to do it;
muss ich? must I?, do I have to?;
wann müsst ihr zur Schule?
when do you have to go to
school?; **er hat gehen müssen** he
(has) had to go; **muss das sein?** is
that really necessary?; **ich muss
mal** (fam) I need the toilet
2 (sollen) **das musst du nicht tun!**
you oughtn't to o shouldn't do
that; **Sie hätten ihn fragen
müssen** you should have asked
him
3 **es muss geregnet haben** it
must have rained; **es muss nicht
wahr sein** it needn't be true

Muster (-s, -) nt (Dessin) pattern,
  design; (Probe) sample; (Vorbild)
  model; **mustern** vt to have a
  close look at; **jdn ~** to look sb up
  and down
Mut (-(e)s) m courage; **jdm
  ~ machen** to encourage sb; **mutig**
  adj brave, courageous
Mutter (-, Mütter) f mother
  ▷ (-, -n) f (Schraubenmutter) nut;
  Muttersprache f mother
  tongue; **Muttertag** m Mother's
  Day; **Mutti** f mum(my) (Brit),
  mom(my) (US)
mutwillig adj deliberate
Mütze (-, -n) f cap
MwSt. abk = **Mehrwertsteuer**
  VAT
Myanmar (-s) nt Myanmar

m

n

N *abk* = **Nord** N

na *interj*: ~ **also!**, ~ **bitte!** see?, what did I tell you?; ~ **ja** well; ~ **und?** so what?

Nabel (-s, -) *m* navel

 SCHLÜSSELWORT

nach *prep* +*dat* **1** (*örtlich*) to; **nach Berlin** to Berlin; **nach links/rechts** (to the) left/right; **nach oben/hinten** up/back **2** (*zeitlich*) after; **einer nach dem anderen** one after the other; **nach Ihnen!** after you!; **zehn (Minuten) nach drei** ten (minutes) past three **3** (*gemäß*) according to; **nach dem Gesetz** according to the law; **dem Namen nach** judging by his/her name; **nach allem, was ich weiß** as far as I know
▷ *adv*: **ihm nach!** after him!; **nach und nach** gradually, little by little; **nach wie vor** still

nach|ahmen *vt* to imitate

Nachbar(in) (-n, -n) *m(f)* neighbour; **Nachbarschaft** *f* neighbourhood

nach|bestellen *vt* to order some more

nachdem *conj* after; (*weil*) since; **je ~ (ob/wie)** depending on (whether/how)

nach|denken *irr vi* to think (*über* +*akk* about); **nachdenklich** *adj* thoughtful

nacheinander *adv* one after another (o the other)

Nachfolger(in) (-s, -) *m(f)* successor

nach|forschen *vt* to investigate

Nachfrage *f* inquiry; (*Comm*) demand; **nach|fragen** *vi* to inquire

nach|geben *irr vi* to give in (*jdm* to sb)

Nachgebühr *f* surcharge; (*für Briefe etc*) excess postage

nach|gehen *irr vi* to follow (*jdm* sb); (*erforschen*) to inquire (*einer Sache dat* into sth); **die Uhr geht (zehn Minuten) nach** this watch is (ten minutes) slow

nachher *adv* afterwards; **bis ~!** see you later

Nachhilfe *f* extra tuition

nach|holen *vt* to catch up with; (*Versäumtes*) to make up for

nach|kommen *irr vi* to follow; **einer Verpflichtung** (*dat*) ~ **to** fulfil an obligation

nach|lassen *irr vt* (*Summe*) to take off ▷ *vi* to decrease, to ease off; (*schlechter werden*) to deteriorate; **nachlässig** *adj* negligent, careless

nach|laufen *irr vi* to run after, to chase (*jdm* sb)

take sb/sth seriously; **etw zu sich ~** to eat sth; **jdn zu sich ~** to have sb come and live with one; **jdn an die Hand ~** to take sb by the hand

neidisch adj envious

neigen vi: **zu etw ~** to tend towards sth; **Neigung** f (des Geländes) slope; (Tendenz) inclination; (Vorliebe) liking

nein adv no

Nektarine f nectarine

Nelke (-, -n) f carnation; (Gewürz) clove

nennen (nannte, genannt) vt to name; (mit Namen) to call

Neonazi (-s, -s) m neo-Nazi

Nepal (-s) nt Nepal

Neptun (-s) m Neptune

Nerv (-s, -en) m nerve; **jdm auf die ~en gehen** to get on sb's nerves; **nerven** vt: **jdn ~** (fam) to get on sb's nerves; **Nerven-zusammenbruch** m nervous breakdown; **nervös** adj nervous

Nest (-(e)s, -er) nt nest; (pej: Ort) dump

nett adj nice; (freundlich) kind; **sei so ~ und ...** do me a favour and ...

netto adv net

Netz (-es, -e) nt net; (für Einkauf) string bag; (System) network; (Stromnetz) mains, power (US); **Netzanschluss** m mains connection; **Netzbetreiber(in)** m(f) network operator; (Inform) Internet operator; **Netzgerät** nt power pack; **Netzkarte** f season ticket; **Netzwerk** nt (Inform) network; **Netzwerken** nt (social) networking; **Netzwerkkarte** f network card

neu adj new; (Sprache, Geschichte) modern; **die ~esten Nachrichten** the latest news; **Neubau** m new building; **neuerdings** adv recently; **Neueröffnung** f

new business; **Neuerung** f innovation; (Reform) reform

Neugier f curiosity; **neugierig** adj curious (auf +akk about); **ich bin ~, ob ...** I wonder whether (o if) ...; **ich bin ~, was du dazu sagst** I'll be interested to hear what you have to say about it

Neuheit f novelty; **Neuigkeit** f news sing; **eine ~** a piece of news; **Neujahr** nt New Year; **prosit ~!** Happy New Year; **neulich** adv recently, the other day; **Neumond** m new moon

neun num nine; **neunhundert** num nine hundred; **neunmal** adv nine times; **neunte(r, s)** adj ninth; siehe auch **dritte; Neuntel** (-s, -) nt ninth; **neunzehn** num nineteen; **neunzehnte(r, s)** adj nineteenth; siehe auch **dritte; neunzig** num ninety; **in den ~er Jahren** in the nineties; **Neunzigerjahre** pl nineties pl; **neunzigste(r, s)** adj ninetieth

neureich adj nouveau riche

Neurologe m, **Neurologin** f neurologist; **Neurose** (-, -n) f neurosis; **neurotisch** adj neurotic

Neuseeland nt New Zealand

Neustart m (Inform) restart, reboot

neutral adj neutral

neuwertig adj nearly new

Nicaragua (-s) nt Nicaragua

⭕ **SCHLÜSSELWORT**

nicht adv **1** (Verneinung) not; **er ist es nicht** it's not him, it isn't him; **er raucht nicht** (gerade) he isn't smoking; (gewöhnlich) he doesn't smoke; **ich kann das nicht** — I can't do it — neither o nor can I; **es regnet nicht mehr** it's not raining any more; **nicht rostend** stainless

2 (Bitte, Verbot) **nicht!** don't!, no!;
nicht berühren! do not touch!;
nicht doch! don't!
3 (rhetorisch) **du bist müde, nicht
(wahr)?** you're tired, aren't you?;
das ist schön, nicht (wahr)? it's
nice, isn't it?
4 was du nicht sagst! the things
you say!

Nichte (-, -n) f niece
Nichtraucher(in) m(f) non-
smoker; **Nichtraucherzone** f
non-smoking area
nichts pron nothing; **für ~ und
wieder ~** for nothing at all; **ich
habe ~ gesagt** I didn't say
anything; **macht ~** never mind
Nichtschwimmer(in) m(f)
non-swimmer
nichtssagend adj meaningless
Nick (-s) m username
nicken vi to nod
Nickerchen nt nap
Nickname (-ns, -n) m username
nie adv never; **~ wieder** (o mehr)
never again; **fast ~** hardly ever
nieder adj (niedrig) low; (gering)
inferior ▷ adv down;
niedergeschlagen adj depressed;
Niederlage f defeat
Niederlande pl Netherlands pl;
Niederländer(in) m(f) Dutch-
man/Dutchwoman;
niederländisch adj Dutch;
Niederländisch nt Dutch
Niederlassung f branch
Niederösterreich nt Lower
Austria; **Niedersachsen** nt
Lower Saxony
Niederschlag m (Meteo)
precipitation; (Regen) rainfall
niedlich adj sweet, cute
niedrig adj low; (Qualität)
inferior
niemals adv never
niemand pron nobody, no one;

ich habe ~en gesehen I haven't
seen anyone; **~ von ihnen** none of
them
Niere (-, -n) f kidney;
Nierenentzündung f kidney
infection; **Nierensteine** pl
kidney stones pl
nieseln vi impers to drizzle;
Nieselregen m drizzle
niesen vi to sneeze
Niete (-, -n) f (Los) blank; (Reinfall)
flop; (pej: Mensch) failure; (Tech) rivet
Nigeria (-s) nt Nigeria
Nikotin (-s) nt nicotine
Nilpferd nt hippopotamus
nippen vi to sip; **an etw** (dat) **~** to
sip sth
nirgends adv nowhere
Nische (-, -n) f niche
Niveau (-s, -s) nt level; **sie hat
~** she's got class
nobel adj (großzügig) generous;
(fam: luxuriös) classy, posh;
Nobelpreis m Nobel Prize

○ **SCHLÜSSELWORT**

noch adv **1** (weiterhin) still; **noch
nicht** not yet; **noch nie** never
(yet); **noch immer** o **immer noch**
still; **bleiben Sie doch noch** stay a
bit longer
2 (in Zukunft) still, yet; **das kann
noch passieren** that might still
happen; **er wird noch kommen**
he'll come (yet)
3 (nicht später als) **noch vor einer
Woche** only a week ago; **noch am
selben Tag** the very same day;
noch im 19. Jahrhundert as late
as the 19th century; **noch heute**
today
4 (zusätzlich) **wer war noch da?**
who else was there?; **noch einmal**
once more, again; **noch dreimal**
three more times; **noch einer**
another one

5 (bei Vergleichen) **noch größer** even bigger; **das ist noch besser** that's better still; **und wenn es noch so schwer ist** however hard it is
6 Geld noch und noch heaps (and heaps) of money; **sie hat noch und noch versucht, ...** she tried again and again to ...
▷ konj: **weder A noch B** neither A nor B

nochmal(s) adv again, once more
Nominativ m nominative (case)
Nonne (-, -n) f nun
Nonstop-Flug m nonstop flight
Nord north; **Nordamerika** nt North America; **Norddeutschland** nt Northern Germany; **Norden** (-s) m north; **im ~ Deutschlands** in the north of Germany; **Nordeuropa** nt Northern Europe
Nordic Walking nt (Sport) Nordic Walking
Nordirland nt Northern Ireland; **nordisch** adj (Völker, Sprache) Nordic; **Nordkorea** (-s) nt North Korea; **nördlich** adj northern; (Kurs, Richtung) northerly; **Nordost(en)** m northeast; **Nordpol** m North Pole; **Nordrhein-Westfalen** (-s) nt North Rhine-Westphalia; **Nordsee** f North Sea; **nordwärts** adv north, northwards; **Nordwest(en)** m northwest; **Nordwind** m north wind
nörgeln vi to grumble
Norm (-, -en) f norm; (Größenvorschrift) standard
normal adj normal; **Normalbenzin** nt regular (petrol (Brit) o gas (US)); **normalerweise** adv normally
normen vt to standardize
Norwegen (-s) nt Norway;

Norweger(in) m(f) Norwegian; **norwegisch** adj Norwegian; **Norwegisch** nt Norwegian
Not (-, Nöte) f need; (Armut) poverty; (Elend) hardship; (Bedrängnis) trouble; (Mangel) want; (Mühe) trouble; (Zwang) necessity; **zur ~** if necessary; (gerade noch) just about
Notar(in) m(f) public notary; **notariell** adj: **~ beglaubigt** attested by a notary
Notarzt m, **Notärztin** f emergency doctor; **Notarztwagen** m emergency ambulance; **Notaufnahme** f A&E, casualty (Brit), emergency room (US); **Notausgang** m emergency exit; **Notbremse** f emergency brake; **Notdienst** m emergency service, after-hours service; **notdürftig** adj scanty; (behelfsmäßig) makeshift
Note (-, -n) f note; (in Schule) mark, grade (US); (Mus) note
Notebook (-(s), -s) nt (Inform) notebook
Notfall m emergency; **notfalls** adv if necessary
notieren vt to note down
nötig adj necessary; **etw ~ haben** to need sth
Notiz (-, -en) f note; (Zeitungs~) item; **Notizblock** m notepad; **Notizbuch** nt notebook
Notlage f crisis; (Elend) plight; **notlanden** vi to make a forced (o emergency) landing; **Notlandung** f emergency landing; **Notruf** m emergency call; **Notrufnummer** f emergency number; **Notrufsäule** f emergency telephone
notwendig adj necessary
Nougat (-s, -s) m od nt nougat
November (-(s), -) m November; siehe auch **Juni**

Nr. abk = **Nummer** No., no.

Nu m: **im ~** in no time

nüchtern adj sober; (Magen) empty

Nudel (-, -n) f noodle; **~n** pl (italienische) pasta sing

null num zero; (Tel) O (Brit), zero (US); **~ Fehler** no mistakes; **~ Uhr** midnight; **Null** (-, -en) f nought, zero; (pej: Mensch) dead loss; **Nulltarif** m: **zum ~** free of charge

Numerus clausus (-) m restriction on the number of students allowed to study a particular subject

Nummer (-, -n) f number; **nummerieren** vt to number; **Nummernschild** nt (Auto) number plate (Brit), license plate (US)

nun adv now; **von ~ an** from now on ▷ interj well; **~ gut!** all right, then; **es ist ~ mal so** that's the way it is

nur adv only; **nicht ~ ..., sondern auch ...** not only ..., but also ...; **~ Anna nicht** except Anna

Nürnberg (-s) nt Nuremberg

Nuss (-, Nüsse) f nut; **Nussknacker** (-s, -) m nutcracker; **Nuss-Nougat-Creme** f chocolate nut cream

Nutte (-, -n) f (fam) tart

nutz, nütze adj: **zu nichts ~ sein** to be useless; **nutzen, nützen** vt to use (zu etw for sth); **was nützt es?** what use is it? ▷ vi to be of use; **das nützt nicht viel** that doesn't help much; **es nützt nichts(, es zu tun)** it's no use (doing it); **Nutzen** (-s, -) m usefulness; (Gewinn) profit; **nützlich** adj useful

Nylon (-s) nt nylon

O

o interj oh

O abk = **Ost** E

Oase (-, -n) f oasis

ob conj if, whether; **so als ~** as if; **er tut so, als ~ er krank wäre** he's pretending to be sick; **und ~!** you bet

obdachlos adj homeless

oben adv (am oberen Ende) at the top; (obenauf) on (the) top; (im Haus) upstairs; (in einem Text) above; **~ erwähnt** or (**~ genannt**) above-mentioned; **mit dem Gesicht nach ~** face up; **da ~** up there; **von ~ bis unten** from top to bottom; **siehe ~** see above

Ober (-s, -) m waiter

obere(r, s) adj upper, top

Oberfläche f surface; **oberflächlich** adj superficial; **Obergeschoss** nt upper floor

oberhalb adv, prep +gen above

Oberhemd nt shirt; **Oberkörper**

m upper body; **Oberlippe** *f* upper lip; **Oberösterreich** *nt* Upper Austria; **Oberschenkel** *m* thigh

oberste(r, s) *adj* very top, topmost

Oberteil *nt* top

obig *adj* above(-mentioned)

Objekt (-(e)s, -e) *nt* object

objektiv *adj* objective; **Objektiv** *nt* lens

obligatorisch *adj* compulsory, obligatory

Oboe (-, -n) *f* oboe

Observatorium *nt* observatory

Obst (-(e)s) *nt* fruit; **Obstkuchen** *m* fruit tart; **Obstsalat** *m* fruit salad

obszön *adj* obscene

obwohl *conj* although

Ochse (-n, -n) *m* ox; **Ochsenschwanzsuppe** *f* oxtail soup

ocker *adj* ochre

öd(e) *adj* waste; (unbebaut) barren; (fig) dull

oder *conj* or; ~ **aber** or else; **er kommt doch, ~?** he's coming, isn't he?

Ofen (-s, Öfen) *m* oven; (Heizofen) heater; (Kohleofen) stove; (Herd) cooker, stove; **Ofenkartoffel** *f* baked (o jacket) potato

offen *adj* open; (aufrichtig) frank; (Stelle) vacant ▷ *adv* frankly; ~ **gesagt** to be honest

offenbar *adj* obvious; **offensichtlich** *adj* evident, obvious

öffentlich *adj* public; **Öffentlichkeit** *f* (Leute) public; (einer Versammlung etc) public nature

offiziell *adj* official

offline *adv* (Inform) offline

öffnen *vt* to open ▷ *vr*: **sich ~** to open; **Öffner** (-s, -) *m* opener; **Öffnung** *f* opening;

Öffnungszeiten *pl* opening times *pl*

oft *adv* often; **schon ~** many times; **öfter** *adv* more often (o frequently); **öfters** *adv* often, frequently

ohne *conj, prep* +*akk* without; ~ **weiteres** without a second thought; (sofort) immediately; ~ **ein Wort zu sagen** without saying a word; ~ **mich** count me out

Ohnmacht (-machten) *f* unconsciousness; (Hilflosigkeit) helplessness; **in ~ fallen** to faint; **ohnmächtig** *adj* unconscious; **sie ist ~** she has fainted

Ohr (-(e)s, -en) *nt* ear; (Gehör) hearing

Öhr (-(e)s, -e) *nt* eye

Ohrenarzt *m*, **Ohrenärztin** *f* ear specialist; **Ohrenschmerzen** *pl* earache; **Ohrentropfen** *pl* ear drops *pl*; **Ohrfeige** *f* slap (in the face); **Ohrläppchen** *nt* earlobe; **Ohrringe** *pl* earrings *pl*

oje *interj* oh dear

okay *interj* OK, okay

Ökoladen *m* health food store; **ökologisch** *adj* ecological; **~e Landwirtschaft** organic farming

ökonomisch *adj* economic; (sparsam) economical

Ökostrom *m* green electricity; **Ökosystem** *nt* ecosystem

Oktanzahl *f* (bei Benzin) octane rating

Oktober (-(s), -) *m* October; siehe auch **Juni**

OKTOBERFEST

The annual October beer festival, the **Oktoberfest**, takes place in Munich on a huge field where beer tents, roller coasters and many other amusements are set up. People sit at long wooden tables, drink beer from enormous litre beer mugs, eat pretzels and listen to brass bands. It is a great attraction for tourists and locals alike.

Öl (-(e)s, -e) nt oil; **Ölbaum** m olive tree; **ölen** vt to oil; (Tech) to lubricate; **Ölfarbe** f oil paint; **Ölfilter** m oil filter; **Ölgemälde** nt oil painting; **Ölheizung** f oil-fired central heating; **ölig** adj oily

oliv adj inv olive-green; **Olive** (-, -n) f olive; **Olivenöl** nt olive oil

Ölmessstab m dipstick; **Ölofen** m oil stove; **Ölpest** f oil pollution; **Ölsardine** f sardine in oil; **Ölstandanzeiger** m (Auto) oil gauge; **Ölteppich** m oil slick; **Ölwechsel** m oil change

Olympiade f Olympic Games pl; **olympisch** adj Olympic

Oma f, **Omi** (-, -s) f grandma, gran(ny)

Omelett (-(e)s, -s) nt, **Omelette** f omelette

Omnibus m bus

onanieren vi to masturbate

Onkel (-s, -) m uncle

online adv (Inform) online; **Onlinedienst** m (Inform) online service

OP (-s, -s) m abk = **Operationssaal** operating theatre (Brit) (o room (US))

Opa m, **Opi** (-s, -s) m grandpa, grandad

Open-Air-Konzert nt open-air concert

Oper (-, -n) f opera; (Gebäude) opera house

Operation f operation

Operette f operetta

operieren vi to operate ▷ vt to operate on

Opernhaus nt opera house, opera; **Opernsänger(in)** m(f) opera singer

Opfer (-s, -) nt sacrifice; (Mensch) victim; **ein ~ bringen** to make a sacrifice

Opium (-s) nt opium

Opposition f opposition

Optiker(in) (-s, -) m(f) optician

optimal adj optimal, optimum

optimistisch adj optimistic

oral adj oral; **Oralverkehr** m oral sex

orange adj inv orange; **Orange** (-, -n) f orange; **Orangenmarmelade** f marmalade; **Orangensaft** m orange juice

Orchester (-s, -) nt orchestra

Orchidee (-, -n) f orchid

Orden (-s, -) m (Rel) order; (Mil) decoration

ordentlich adj (anständig) respectable; (geordnet) tidy, neat; (fam: annehmbar) not bad; (fam: tüchtig) proper ▷ adv properly

ordinär adj common, vulgar; (Witz) dirty

ordnen vt to sort out; **Ordner** (-s, -) m (bei Veranstaltung) steward; (Aktenordner) file; **Ordnung** f order; (Geordnetsein) tidiness; **(geht) in ~!** (that's) all right; **mit dem Drucker ist etwas nicht in ~** there's something wrong with the printer

Oregano (-s) m oregano

Organ (-s, -e) nt organ; (Stimme) voice

Organisation f organization; **organisieren** vt to organize; (fam: beschaffen) to get hold of ▷ vr: **sich ~** to organize

Organismus m organism

Orgasmus m orgasm

Orgel (-, -n) f organ

Orgie f orgy
orientalisch adj oriental
orientieren vr: **sich ~** to get
one's bearings; **Orientierung** f
orientation; **Orientierungssinn**
m sense of direction
original adj original; (echt)
genuine; **Original** (-s, -e) nt
original
originell adj original; (komisch)
witty
Orkan (-(e)s, -e) m hurricane
Ort (-(e)s, -e) m place; (Dorf)
village; **an ~ und Stelle, vor ~** on
the spot
Orthopäde (-n, -n) m,
Orthopädin f orthopaedist
örtlich adj local; **Ortschaft** f
village, small town; **Ortsgespräch**
nt local call; **Ortstarif** m local
rate; **Ortszeit** f local time

● **OSSI**
●
● **Ossi** is a colloquial and rather
● derogatory word used to
● describe a German from the
● former **DDR**.

Ost east; **Ostdeutschland** nt
(als Landesteil) Eastern Germany;
(Hist) East Germany; **Osten** (-s) m
east
Osterei nt Easter egg;
Osterglocke f daffodil;
Osterhase m Easter bunny;
Ostermontag m Easter Monday;
Ostern (-, -) nt Easter; **an** (o **zu**)
~ at Easter; **frohe ~** Happy Easter
Österreich (-s) nt Austria;
Österreicher(in) (-s, -) m(f) Austrian;
österreichisch adj Austrian
Ostersonntag m Easter Sunday
Osteuropa nt Eastern Europe;
Ostküste f east coast; **östlich**
adj eastern; (Kurs, Richtung)
easterly; **Ostsee** f: **die ~** the

Baltic (Sea); **Ostwind** m
east(erly) wind
OSZE (-) f abk = **Organisation für
Sicherheit und Zusammenarbeit
in Europa** OSCE
Otter (-s, -) m otter
out adj (fam) out; **outen** vt to
out
oval adj oval
Overheadprojektor m overhead projector
Ozean (-s, -e) m ocean; **der Stille
~** the Pacific (Ocean)
Ozon (-s) nt ozone;
Ozonbelastung f ozone level;
Ozonloch nt hole in the ozone
layer; **Ozonschicht** f ozone
layer; **Ozonwerte** pl ozone
levels pl

p

paar *adj inv* **ein ~** a few; **ein ~ Mal** a few times; **ein ~ Äpfel** some apples

Paar (-(e)s, -e) *nt* pair; (*Ehepaar*) couple; **ein ~ Socken** a pair of socks

pachten *vt* to lease

Päckchen *nt* package; (*Zigaretten*) packet; (*zum Verschicken*) small parcel; **packen** *vt* to pack; (*fassen*) to grasp, to seize; (*fam: schaffen*) to manage; (*fig: fesseln*) to grip; **Packpapier** *nt* brown paper; **Packung** *f* packet, pack (*US*); **Packungsbeilage** *f* package insert, patient information leaflet

Pädagoge (-n, -n) *m*, **Pädagogin** *f* teacher; **pädagogisch** *adj* educational; **~e Hochschule** college of education

Paddel (-s, -) *nt* paddle; **Paddelboot** *nt* canoe; **paddeln**

vi to paddle

Paket (-(e)s, -e) *nt* packet; (*Postpaket*) parcel; (*Inform*) package; **Paketbombe** *f* parcel bomb; **Paketkarte** *f* dispatch form (*to be filled in with details of the sender and the addressee when handing in a parcel at the post office*)

Pakistan (-s) *nt* Pakistan

Palast (-es, Paläste) *m* palace

Palästina (-s) *nt* Palestine; **Palästinenser(in)** (-s, -) *m(f)* Palestinian

Palatschinken *pl* filled pancakes *pl*

Palette *f* (*von Maler*) palette; (*Ladepalette*) pallet; (*Vielfalt*) range

Palme (-, -n) *f* palm (tree); **Palmsonntag** *m* Palm Sunday

Pampelmuse (-, -n) *f* grapefruit

pampig *adj* (*fam: frech*) cheeky; (*breiig*) gooey

Panda(bär) (-s, -s) *m* panda

Pandemie (-, -n) *f* pandemic

panieren *vt* (*Gastr*) to coat with breadcrumbs; **paniert** *adj* breaded

Panik *f* panic

Panne (-, -n) *f* (*Auto*) breakdown; (*Missgeschick*) slip; **Pannendienst** *m*, **Pannenhilfe** *f* breakdown (*o* rescue) service

Pant(h)er (-s, -) *m* panther

Pantomime (-, -n) *f* mime

Panzer (-s, -) *m* (*Panzerung*) armour (plating); (*Mil*) tank

Papa (-s, -s) *m* dad(dy), pa (*US*)

Papagei (-s, -en) *m* parrot

Papaya (-, -s) *f* papaya

Papier (-s, -e) *nt* paper; **~e** *pl* (*Ausweispapiere*) papers *pl*; (*Dokumente, Urkunden*) papers *pl*, documents *pl*; **Papiercontainer** *m* paper bank; **Papierformat** *nt* paper size; **Papiergeld** *nt* paper money; **Papierkorb** *m* wastepaper basket; (*Inform*)

recycle bin; **Papiertaschentuch** nt (paper) tissue; **Papiertonne** f paper bank

Pappbecher m paper cup; **Pappe** (-, -n) f cardboard; **Pappkarton** m cardboard box; **Pappteller** m paper plate

Paprika (-s, -s) m (Gewürz) paprika; (Schote) pepper

Papst (-(e)s, Päpste) m pope

Paradeiser (-s, -) m tomato

Paradies (-es, -e) nt paradise

Paragliding (-s) nt paragliding

Paragraph (-en, -en) m paragraph; (Jur) section

parallel adj parallel

Paranuss f Brazil nut

Parasit (-en, -en) m parasite

parat adj ready; **etw ~ haben** to have sth ready

Pärchen nt couple

Parfüm (-s, -s o -e) nt perfume; **Parfümerie** f perfumery; **parfümieren** vt to scent, to perfume

Pariser (-s, -) m (fam: Kondom) rubber

Park (-s, -s) m park

Park-and-ride-System nt park-and-ride system; **Parkbank** f park bench; **Parkdeck** nt parking level; **parken** vt, vi to park

Parkett (-s, -e) nt parquet flooring; (Theat) stalls pl (Brit), parquet (US)

Parkhaus nt multi-storey car park (Brit), parking garage (US)

parkinsonsche Krankheit f Parkinson's disease

Parkkralle f (Auto) wheel clamp; **Parklicht** nt parking light; **Parklücke** f parking space; **Parkplatz** m (für ein Auto) parking space; (für mehrere Autos) car park (Brit), parking lot (US); **Parkscheibe** f parking disc; **Parkscheinautomat** m pay

point; (Parkscheinausgabegerät) ticket machine; **Parkuhr** f parking meter; **Parkverbot** nt (Stelle) no-parking zone; **hier ist ~** you can't park here

Parlament nt parliament

Parmesan (-s) m Parmesan (cheese)

Partei f party

Parterre (-s, -s) nt ground floor (Brit), first floor (US)

Partie f part; (Spiel) game; (Mann, Frau) catch; **mit von der ~ sein** to be in on it

Partitur f (Mus) score

Partizip (-s, -ien) nt participle

Partner(in) (-s, -) m(f) partner; **Partnerschaft** f partnership; **eingetragene ~** civil partnership; **Partnerstadt** f twin town

Party (-, -s) f party; **Partymuffel** (-s, -) m party pooper; **Partyservice** m catering service

Pass (-es, Pässe) m pass; (Ausweis) passport

passabel adj reasonable

Passagier (-s, -e) m passenger

Passamt nt passport office

Passant(in) m(f) passer-by; **Passbild** nt passport photo

passen vi (Größe) to fit; (Farbe, Stil) to go (zu with); (auf Frage) to pass; **passt (es) dir morgen?** does tomorrow suit you?; **das passt mir gut** that suits me fine; **das passend** adj suitable; (zusammenpassend) matching; (angebracht) fitting; (Zeit) convenient; **haben Sie es nicht ~?** (Kleingeld) have you got the right change?

passieren vi to happen

passiv adj passive

Passkontrolle f passport control

Passwort nt password

Paste (-, -n) f paste

Pastellfarbe f pastel colour
Pastete (-, -n) f (warmes Gericht) pie; (Pastetchen) vol-au-vent; (ohne Teig) pâté
Pastor, in (-s, -en) m(f) minister, vicar
Pate (-n, -n) m godfather; **Patenkind** nt godchild
Patient(in) m(f) patient
Patin f godmother
Patrone (-, -n) f cartridge
patsch interj splat; **patschnass** adj soaking wet
pauschal adj (Kosten) inclusive; (Urteil) sweeping; **Pauschale** (-, -n) f, **Pauschalgebühr** f flat rate (charge); **Pauschalpreis** m flat rate; (für Hotel, Reise) all-inclusive price; **Pauschalreise** f package tour
Pause (-, -n) f break; (Theat) interval; (Kino etc) intermission; (Innehalten) pause
Pavian (-s, -e) m baboon
Pavillon (-s, -s) m pavilion
Pay-TV (-s) nt pay-per-view television, pay TV
Pazifik (-s) m Pacific (Ocean)
PC (-s, -s) m abk = **Personal Computer** PC
Pech (-s, -e) nt (fig) bad luck; ~ **haben** to be unlucky; ~ **gehabt!** tough (luck)
Pedal (-s, -e) nt pedal
Pediküre (-, -n) f pedicure
Peeling (-s, -s) nt (facial/body) scrub
peinlich adj (unangenehm) embarrassing, awkward; (genau) painstaking; **es war mir sehr ~** I was totally embarrassed
Peitsche (-, -n) f whip
Pelikan (-s, -e) m pelican
Pellkartoffeln pl potatoes pl boiled in their skins
Pelz (-es, -e) m fur; **pelzig** adj (Zunge) furred

pendeln vi (Zug, Bus) to shuttle; (Mensch) to commute; **Pendelverkehr** m shuttle traffic; (für Pendler) commuter traffic; **Pendler(in)** (-s, -) m(f) commuter
penetrant adj sharp; (Mensch) pushy
Penis (-, -se) m penis
Pension f (Geld) pension; (Ruhestand) retirement; (für Gäste) guesthouse, B&B; **pensioniert** adj retired; **Pensionsgast** m guest (in a guesthouse)
Peperoni (-, -) f chilli
per prep +akk by, per; (pro) per; (bis) by
perfekt adj perfect
Pergamentpapier nt grease-proof paper
Periode (-, -n) f period
Perle (-, -n) f (a. fig) pearl
perplex adj dumbfounded
Person (-, -en) f person; **ein Tisch für drei ~en** a table for three; **Personal** (-s) nt staff, personnel; (Bedienung) servants pl; **Personalausweis** m identity card; **Personalien** pl particulars pl; **Personenschaden** m injury to persons; **Personenwaage** f (bathroom) scales pl; **Personenzug** m passenger train; **persönlich** adj personal; (auf Briefen) private ▷ adv personally; (selbst) in person; **Persönlichkeit** f personality
Peru (-s) nt Peru
Perücke (-, -n) f wig
pervers adj perverted
pessimistisch adj pessimistic
Pest (-) f plague
Petersilie f parsley
Petroleum (-s) nt paraffin (Brit), kerosene (US)
Pfad (-(e)s, -e) m path; **Pfadfinder** (-s, -) m boy scout;

Pfadfinderin f girl guide
Pfahl (-(e)s, Pfähle) m post, stake
Pfand (-(e)s, Pfänder) nt security; (Flaschenpfand) deposit; (im Spiel) forfeit; **Pfandflasche** f returnable bottle
Pfanne (-, -n) f (frying) pan
Pfannkuchen m pancake
Pfarrei f parish; **Pfarrer(in)** (-s, -) m(f) priest
Pfau (-(e)s, -en) m peacock
Pfeffer (-s, -) m pepper; **Pfefferkuchen** m gingerbread; **Pfefferminze** (-e) f peppermint; **Pfefferminztee** m peppermint tea; **Pfeffermühle** f pepper mill; **pfeffern** vt to put pepper on/in; **Pfefferstreuer** (-s, -) m pepper pot
Pfeife (-, -n) f whistle; (für Tabak, von Orgel) pipe; **pfeifen** (pfiff, gepfiffen) vt, vi to whistle
Pfeil (-(e)s, -e) m arrow
Pfeiltaste f (Inform) arrow key
Pferd (-(e)s, -e) nt horse; **Pferdeschwanz** m (Frisur) ponytail; **Pferdestall** m stable; **Pferdestärke** f horsepower
pfiff imperf von **pfeifen**
Pfifferling m chanterelle
Pfingsten (-, -) nt Whitsun, Pentecost (US); **Pfingstmontag** m Whit Monday; **Pfingstsonntag** m Whit Sunday, Pentecost (US)
Pfirsich (-s, -e) m peach
Pflanze (-, -n) f plant; **pflanzen** vt to plant; **Pflanzenfett** nt vegetable fat
Pflaster (-s, -) nt (für Wunde) plaster, Band Aid® (US); (Straßenpflaster) road surface, pavement (US)
Pflaume (-, -n) f plum
Pflege (-, -n) f care; (Krankenpflege) nursing; (von Autos, Maschinen) maintenance; **pflegebedürftig** adj in need of

care; **pflegeleicht** adj easy-care; (fig) easy to handle; **pflegen** vt to look after; (Kranke) to nurse; (Beziehungen) to foster; (Fingernägel, Gesicht) to take care of; (Daten) to maintain; **Pflegepersonal** nt nursing staff; **Pflegeversicherung** f long-term care insurance
Pflicht (-, -en) f duty; (Sport) compulsory section; **pflicht-bewusst** adj conscientious; **Pflichtfach** nt (Schule) compulsory subject; **Pflicht-versicherung** f compulsory insurance
pflücken vt to pick
Pforte (-, -n) f gate; **Pförtner(in)** (-s, -) m(f) porter
Pfosten (-s, -) m post
Pfote (-, -n) f paw
pfui interj ugh
Pfund (-(e)s, -e) nt pound
pfuschen vi (fam) to be sloppy
Pfütze (-, -n) f puddle
Phantasie f siehe **Fantasie**; **phantastisch** adj siehe **fantastisch**
Phase (-, -n) f phase
Philippinen pl Philippines pl
Philosophie f philosophy
Photo nt siehe **Foto**
pH-neutral adj pH-balanced; **pH-Wert** m pH-value
Physalis (-, Physalen) f physalis
Physik f physics sing
physisch adj physical
Pianist(in) (-en, -en) m(f) pianist
Pickel (-s, -) m pimple; (Werkzeug) pickaxe; (Berg~) ice-axe
Picknick (-s, -e o -s) nt picnic; **ein ~ machen** to have a picnic
piepsen vi to chirp
piercen vt: **sich die Nase ~ lassen** to have one's nose pierced; **Piercing** (-s) nt (body) piercing
pieseln vi (fam) to pee

Pik (-, -) nt (Karten) spades pl
pikant adj spicy
Pilates nt (Sport) Pilates
Pilger(in) m(f) pilgrim;
Pilgerfahrt f pilgrimage
Pille (-, -n) f pill; **sie nimmt die ~** she's on the pill
Pilot(in) (-en, -en) m(f) pilot
Pils (-, -) nt (Pilsner) lager
Pilz (-es, -e) m (essbar) mushroom; (giftig) toadstool; (Med) fungus
PIN (-, -s) f PIN (number)
pingelig adj fussy
Pinguin (-s, -e) m penguin
Pinie f pine; **Pinienkern** m pine nut
pink adj shocking pink
pinkeln vi (fam) to pee
Pinsel (-s, -) m (paint)brush
Pinzette f tweezers pl
Pistazie f pistachio
Piste (-, -n) f (Ski) piste; (Aviat) runway
Pistole (-, -n) f pistol
Pixel (-s) nt (Inform) pixel
Pizza (-, -s) f pizza; **Pizzaservice** m pizza delivery service; **Pizzeria** (-, Pizzerien) f pizzeria
Pkw (-(s), -(s)) m abk = **Personenkraftwagen** car
Plakat nt poster
Plakette f (Schildchen) badge; (Aufkleber) sticker
Plan (-(e)s, Pläne) m plan; (Karte) map; **planen** vt to plan
Planet (-en, -en) m planet; **Planetarium** nt planetarium
planmäßig adj scheduled
Plan(t)schbecken nt paddling pool; **plan(t)schen** vi to splash around
Planung f planning
Plastik f sculpture ▷ (-s) nt plastic; **Plastikfolie** f plastic film; **Plastiktüte** f plastic bag
Platin (-s) nt platinum
platsch interj splash

platt adj flat; (fam: überrascht) flabbergasted; (fig: geistlos) flat, boring
Platte (-, -n) f (Foto, Tech, Gastr) plate; (Steinplatte) flag; (Schallplatte) record;
Plattenspieler m record player
Plattform f platform; **Plattfuß** m flat foot; (Reifen) flat (tyre)
Platz (-es, Plätze) m place; (Sitzplatz) seat; (freier Raum) space, room; (in Stadt) square; (Sportplatz) playing field; **nehmen Sie ~** please sit down, take a seat; **ist dieser ~ frei?** is this seat taken?;
Platzanweiser(in) m(f) usher/usherette
Plätzchen nt spot; (Gebäck) biscuit
platzen vi to burst; (Bombe) to explode
Platzkarte f seat reservation; **Platzreservierung** f seat reservation; **Platzverweis** m: **er erhielt einen ~** he was sent off; **Platzwunde** f laceration, cut
plaudern vi to chat, to talk
pleite adj (fam) broke; **Pleite** (-, -n) f (Bankrott) bankruptcy; (fam: Reinfall) flop
Plombe (-, -n) f lead seal; (Zahnplombe) filling; **plombieren** vt (Zahn) to fill
plötzlich adj sudden ▷ adv suddenly, all at once
plump adj clumsy; (Hände) ungainly; (Körper) shapeless
plumps interj thud; (in Flüssigkeit) plop
Plural (-s, -e) m plural
plus adv plus; **fünf ~ sieben ist zwölf** five plus seven is (o are) twelve; **zehn Grad ~** ten degrees above zero; **Plus** (-, -) nt plus; (Fin) profit; (Vorteil) advantage
Plüsch (-(e)s, -e) m plush
Pluto (-) m Pluto

PLZ *abk* = **Postleitzahl** postcode (Brit), zip code (US)

Po (-s, -s) *m* (fam) bottom, bum

Pocken *pl* smallpox *sing*

Podcast (-s, -s) *m* podcast

poetisch *adj* poetic

Pointe (-, -n) *f* punch line

Pokal (-s, -e) *m* goblet; (Sport) cup

pökeln *vt* to pickle

Pol (-s, -e) *m* pole

Pole (-n, -n) *m* Pole; **Polen** (-s) *nt* Poland

Police (-, -n) *f* (insurance) policy

polieren *vt* to polish

Polin *f* Pole, Polish woman

Politik *f* politics *sing*; (eine bestimmte) policy; **Politiker(in)** *m(f)* politician; **politisch** *adj* political

Politur *f* polish

Polizei *f* police *pl*; **Polizeibeamte(r)** *m*, **Polizeibeamtin** *f* police officer; **polizeilich** *adj* police; **sie wird ~ gesucht** the police are looking for her; **Polizeirevier** *nt*, **Polizeiwache** *f* police station; **Polizeistunde** *f* closing time; **Polizeiwache** *f* police station; **Polizist(in)** *m(f)* policeman/-woman

Pollen (-s, -) *m* pollen; **Pollenflug** (-s) *m* pollen count

polnisch *adj* Polish; **Polnisch** *nt* Polish

Polo (-s) *nt* polo; **Polohemd** *nt* polo shirt

Polster (-s, -) *nt* cushion; (Polsterung) upholstery; (in Kleidung) padding; (fig: Geld) reserves *pl*; **polstern** *vt* to upholster; (Kleidung) to pad

Polterabend *m* party prior to a wedding, at which old crockery is smashed to bring good luck

poltern *vi* (Krach machen) to crash; (schimpfen) to rant

Polyester (-s, -) *m* polyester

Polypen *pl* (Med) adenoids *pl*

Pommes frites *pl* chips *pl* (Brit), French fries *pl* (US)

Pony (-s) *m* (Frisur) fringe (Brit), bangs *pl* (US) ▷ (-s, -s) *nt* (Pferd) pony

Popcorn (-s) *nt* popcorn

Popmusik *f* pop (music)

populär *adj* popular

Pore (-, -n) *f* pore

Pornografie *f* pornography

Porree (-s, -s) *m* leeks *pl*; **eine Stange ~** a leek

Portemonnaie, Portmonee (-s, -s) *nt* purse

Portier (-s, -s) *m* porter

Portion *f* portion, helping

Porto (-s, -s) *nt* postage

Portrait, Porträt (-s, -s) *nt* portrait

Portugal (-s) *nt* Portugal; **Portugiese** (-n, -n) *m* Portuguese; **Portugiesin** (-, -nen) *f* Portuguese; **portugiesisch** *adj* Portuguese; **Portugiesisch** *nt* Portuguese

Portwein (-s, -e) *m* port

Porzellan (-s, -e) *nt* china

Posaune (-, -n) *f* trombone

Position *f* position

positiv *adj* positive

Post® (-, -en) *f* post office; (Briefe) post (Brit), mail; **Postamt** *nt* post office; **Postanweisung** *f* postal order (Brit), money order (US); **Postbank** *f* German post office bank; **Postbote** *m*, **-botin** *f* postman/-woman

posten *vt* (auf Forum, Blog) to post

Posten (-s, -) *m* post, position; (Comm) item; (auf Liste) entry

Poster (-s, -) *nt* poster

Postfach *nt* post-office box, PO box; **Postkarte** *f* postcard;

postlagernd adv poste restante;
Postleitzahl f postcode (Brit), zip
code (US)
postmodern adj postmodern
Postsparkasse f post office
savings bank; **Poststempel** m
postmark; **Postweg** m: **auf dem
~ by mail
Potenz f (Math) power; (eines
Mannes) potency
PR (-, -s) f abk = **Public Relations**
PR
prächtig adj splendid
prahlen vi to boast, to brag
Praktikant(in) m(f) trainee;
Praktikum (-s, Praktika) nt prac-
tical training; **praktisch** adj
practical; **~er Arzt** general
practitioner
Praline f chocolate
Prämie f (bei Versicherung)
premium; (Belohnung) reward; (von
Arbeitgeber) bonus
Präparat nt (Med) medicine; (Bio)
preparation
Präservativ nt condom
Präsident(in) m(f) president
Praxis (-, Praxen) f practice;
(Behandlungsraum) surgery; (von
Anwalt) office; **Praxisgebühr** f
surgery surcharge
präzise adj precise, exact
predigen vt, vi to preach; **Predigt**
(-, -en) f sermon
Preis (-es, -e) m (zu zahlen) price;
(bei Sieg) prize; **den ersten
~ gewinnen** to win first prize;
Preisausschreiben nt
competition
Preiselbeere f cranberry
preisgünstig adj inexpensive;
Preislage f price range; **Preisliste**
f price list; **Preisschild** nt price
tag; **Preisträger(in)** m(f)
prizewinner; **preiswert** adj
inexpensive
Prellung f bruise

Premiere (-, -n) f premiere, first
night
Premierminister(in) m(f) prime
minister, premier
Prepaidhandy nt prepaid
mobile (Brit), prepaid cell phone
(US); **Prepaidkarte** f prepaid
card
Presse (-, -n) f press
pressen vt to press
prickeln vi to tingle
Priester(in) (-s, -) m(f) priest/(woman)
priest
Primel (-, -n) f primrose
primitiv adj primitive
Prinz (-en, -en) m prince;
Prinzessin f princess
Prinzip (-s, -ien) nt principle; **im
~ basically; aus ~** on principle
Priorität f priority
privat adj private;
Privatfernsehen nt commercial
television; **Privatgrundstück** nt
private property; **privatisieren**
vt to privatize
pro prep +akk per; **5 Euro
~ Stück/Person** 5 euros each/per
person; **Pro** (-s) nt pro
Probe (-, -n) f test; (Teststück)
sample; (Theat) rehearsal;
Probefahrt f test drive; **eine
~ machen** to go for a test drive;
Probezeit f trial period;
probieren vt, vi to try; (Wein,
Speise) to taste, to sample
Problem (-s, -e) nt problem
Produkt (-(e)s, -e) nt product;
Produktion f production;
(produzierte Menge) output;
produzieren vt to produce
Professor(in) (-s, -en) m(f)
professor
Profi (-s, -s) m pro
Profil (-s, -e) nt profile; (von
Reifen, Schuhsohle) tread
Profit (-(e)s, -e) m profit;
profitieren vi to profit (von from)

Prognose (-, -n) f prediction; (Wetter) forecast

Programm (-s, -e) nt programme; (Inform) program; (TV) channel; **Programmheft** nt programme; **programmieren** vt to program; **Programmierer(in)** (-s, -) m(f) programmer; **Programmkino** nt arts (o repertory (US)) cinema

Projekt (-(e)s, -e) nt project

Projektor m projector

Promenade (-, -n) f promenade

Promille (-(s), -) nt (blood) alcohol level; **0,8 ~** 0,08 per cent; **Promillegrenze** f legal alcohol limit

prominent adj prominent; **Prominenz** f VIPs pl, prominent figures pl; (fam: Stars) the glitterati pl

Propeller (-s, -) m propeller

prosit interj cheers

Prospekt (-(e)s, -e) m leaflet, brochure

prost interj cheers

Prostituierte(r) mf prostitute

Protest (-(e)s, -e) m protest

Protestant(in) m(f) Protestant; **protestantisch** adj Protestant

protestieren vi to protest (gegen against)

Prothese (-, -n) f artificial arm/leg; (Gebiss) dentures pl

Protokoll (-s, -e) nt (bei Sitzung) minutes pl; (diplomatisch, Inform) protocol; (bei Polizei) statement

protzen vi to show off; **protzig** adj flashy

Proviant (-s, -e) m provisions pl

Provider (-s, -) m (Inform) (service) provider

Provinz (-, -en) f province

Provision f (Comm) commission

provisorisch adj provisional; **Provisorium** (-s, Provisorien) nt stopgap; (Zahn) temporary filling

provozieren vt to provoke

Prozent (-(e)s, -e) nt per cent

Prozess (-es, -e) m (Vorgang) process; (Jur) trial; (Rechtsfall) (court) case; **prozessieren** vi to go to law (mit against)

Prozession f procession

Prozessor (-s, -en) m (Inform) processor

prüde adj prudish

prüfen vt to test; (nachprüfen) to check; (Prüfung f (Schule) exam; (Überprüfung) check; **eine ~ machen** (Schule) to take an exam

Prügelei f fight; **prügeln** vt to beat ▷ vr: **sich ~** to fight

PS abk = **Pferdestärke** hp; = **Postskript(um)** PS

pseudo- präf pseudo; **Pseudokrupp** (-s) m (Med) pseudocroup; **Pseudonym** (-s, -e) nt pseudonym

pst interj ssh

Psychiater(in) (-s, -) m(f) psychiatrist; **psychisch** adj psychological; (Krankheit) mental;

Psychoanalyse f psychoanalysis;

Psychologe (-n, -n) m, **Psychologin** f psychologist; **Psychologie** f psychology

Psychopharmaka pl mind-affecting drugs pl, psychotropic drugs pl; **psychosomatisch** adj psychosomatic; **Psychoterror** m psychological intimidation; **Psychotherapie** f psychotherapy

Pubertät f puberty

Publikum (-s) nt audience; (Sport) crowd

Pudding (-s, -e o -s) m blancmange

Pudel (-s, -) m poodle

Puder (-s, -) m powder; **Puderzucker** m icing sugar

Puerto Rico nt Puerto Rico

Pulli (-s, -s) m, **Pullover** (-s, -) m sweater, pullover, jumper (Brit)

Puls (-es, -e) m pulse
Pulver (-s, -) nt powder;
  Pulverkaffee m instant coffee;
  Pulverschnee m powder snow
pummelig adj chubby
Pumpe (-, -n) f pump; **pumpen**
  vt to pump; (fam: verleihen) to lend;
  (fam: sich ausleihen) to borrow
Pumps pl court shoes pl (Brit),
  pumps pl (US)
Punk (-s, -s) m (Musik, Mensch)
  punk
Punkt (-(e)s, -e) m point; (bei
  Muster) dot; (Satzzeichen) full stop
  (Brit), period (US); **~ zwei Uhr** at
  two o'clock sharp
pünktlich adj punctual, on time;
  Pünktlichkeit f punctuality
Punsch (-(e)s, -e) m punch
Pupille (-, -n) f pupil
Puppe (-, -n) f doll
pur adj pure; (völlig) sheer;
  (Whisky) neat
Püree (-s, -s) nt puree;
  (Kartoffelpüree) mashed potatoes pl
Puste (-) f (fam) puff; **außer**
  ~ sein to be puffed
Pustel (-, -n) f pustule; (Pickel)
  pimple; **pusten** vi to blow;
  (keuchen) to puff
Pute (-, -n) f turkey;
  Putenschnitzel nt turkey
  escalope
Putsch (-(e)s, -e) m putsch
Putz (-es) m (Mörtel) plaster
putzen vt to clean; to polish; **die**
  Nase ~ to blow one's nose; **sich**
  (dat) **die Zähne ~** to brush one's
  teeth; **Putzfrau** f cleaner;
  Putzlappen m cloth, **Putzmann**
  m cleaner; **Putzmittel** nt
  cleaning agent, cleaner
Puzzle (-s, -s) nt jigsaw (puzzle)
Pyjama (-s, -s) m pyjamas pl
Pyramide (-, -n) f pyramid
Python (-s, -s) m python

q

Quadrat nt square; **quadratisch**
  adj square; **Quadratmeter** m
  square metre
quaken vi (Frosch) to croak; (Ente)
  to quack
Qual (-, -en) f pain, agony;
  (seelisch) anguish; **quälen** vt to
  torment ▷ vr: **sich ~** to struggle;
  (geistig) to torment oneself;
  Quälerei f torture, torment
qualifizieren vt to qualify;
  (einstufen) to label ▷ vr: **sich ~** to
  qualify
Qualität f quality
Qualle (-, -n) f jellyfish
Qualm (-(e)s) m thick smoke;
  qualmen vt, vi to smoke
Quantität f quantity
Quarantäne (-, -n) f quarantine
Quark (-s) m quark; (fam: Unsinn)
  rubbish
Quartett (-s, -e) nt quartet;
  (Kartenspiel) happy families sing

Quartier (-s, -e) nt accommodation

quasi adv more or less

Quatsch (-es) m (fam) rubbish; **quatschen** vi (fam) to chat

Quecksilber nt mercury

Quelle (-, -n) f spring; (eines Flusses) source

quellen vi to pour

quer adv crossways, diagonally; (rechtwinklig) at right angles; **~ über die Straße** straight across the street; **querfeldein** adv across country; **Querflöte** f flute; **Querschnitt** m cross section; **querschnittsgelähmt** adj paraplegic; **Querstraße** f side street

quetschen vt to squash, to crush; (Med) to bruise; **Quetschung** f bruise

Queue (-s, -s) m (billiard) cue

quietschen vi to squeal; (Tür, Bett) to squeak; (Bremsen) to screech

quitt adj quits, even

Quitte (-, -n) f quince

Quittung f receipt

Quiz (-, -) nt quiz

Quote (-, -n) f rate; (Comm) quota

r

Rabatt (-(e)s, -e) m discount

Rabbi (-(s), -s) m rabbi; **Rabbiner** (-s, -) m rabbi

Rabe (-n, -n) m raven

Rache (-) f revenge, vengeance

Rachen (-s, -) m throat

rächen vt to avenge ▷ vr: **sich ~** to take (one's) revenge (an +dat on)

Rad (-(e)s, Räder) nt wheel; (Fahrrad) bike; **~ fahren** to cycle; **mit dem ~ fahren** to go by bike

Radar (-s) m o nt radar; **Radarfalle** f speed trap; **Radarkontrolle** f radar speed check

radeln vi (fam) to cycle; **Radfahrer(in)** m(f) cyclist; **Radfahrweg** m cycle track (o path)

Radicchio (-s) m (Salatsorte) radicchio

radieren vt to rub out, to erase;
Radiergummi m rubber (Brit),
eraser; **Radierung** f (Kunst)
etching

Radieschen nt radish

radikal adj radical

Radio (-s, -s) nt radio; **im ~** on
the radio

radioaktiv adj radioactive

Radiologe (-n, -n) m, **Radiologin**
f radiologist

Radiorekorder m radio cassette
recorder; **Radiosender** m radio
station; **Radiowecker** m radio
alarm (clock)

Radkappe f (Auto) hub cap

Radler(in) (-s, -) m(f) cyclist

Radler (-s, -) nt ≈ shandy

Radlerhose f cycling shorts pl;
Radrennen nt cycle racing;
(einzelnes Rennen) cycle race;
Radtour f cycling tour; **Radweg**
m cycle track (o path)

raffiniert adj crafty, cunning;
(Zucker) refined

Rafting (-s) nt white water
rafting

Ragout (-s, -s) nt ragout

Rahm (-s) m cream

rahmen vt to frame; **Rahmen**
(-s, -) m frame

Rakete (-, -n) f rocket

rammen vt to ram

Rampe (-, -n) f ramp

ramponieren vt (fam) to
damage, to batter

Ramsch (-(e)s, -e) m junk

ran (fam) kontr von **heran**

Rand (-(e)s, Ränder) m edge; (von
Brille, Tasse etc) rim; (auf Papier)
margin; (Schmutzrand, unter Augen)
ring; (fig) verge, brink

randalieren vi to (go on the)
rampage; **Randalierer(in)** (-s, -)
m(f) hooligan

Randstein m kerb (Brit), curb
(US); **Randstreifen** m shoulder

rang imperf von **ringen**

Rang (-(e)s, Ränge) m rank; (in
Wettbewerb) place; (Theat) circle

rannte imperf von **rennen**

ranzig adj rancid

Rap (-(s), -s) m (Mus) rap; **rappen**
vi (Mus) to rap; **Rapper(in)** (-s, -)
m(f) (Mus) rapper

rar adj rare, scarce

rasant adj quick, rapid

rasch adj quick

rascheln vi to rustle

rasen vi (sich schnell bewegen)
to race; (toben) to rave; **gegen
einen Baum ~** to crash into a
tree

Rasen (-s, -) m lawn

rasend adj (vor Wut) furious

Rasenmäher (-s, -) m
lawnmower

Rasierapparat m razor;
(elektrischer) shaver; **Rasiercreme**
f shaving cream; **rasieren** vt to
shave ▷ vr: **sich ~** to shave;
Rasierer m shaver; **Rasiergel** nt
shaving gel; **Rasierklinge** f
razor blade; **Rasiermesser** nt
(cutthroat) razor; **Rasierpinsel**
m shaving brush; **Rasierschaum**
m shaving foam; **Rasierzeug** nt
shaving tackle, shaving
equipment

Rasse (-, -n) f race; (Tiere) breed

Rassismus m racism;
Rassist(in) m(f) racist;
rassistisch adj racist

Rast (-, -en) f rest, break;
~ machen to have a rest (o break);
rasten vi to rest; **Rastplatz** m
(Auto) rest area; **Raststätte** f
(Auto) service area; (Gaststätte)
motorway (Brit) (o highway (US))
restaurant

Rasur f shave

Rat (-(e)s, Ratschläge) m (piece of)
advice; **sie hat mir einen
~ gegeben** she gave me some

advice; **um ~ fragen** to ask for advice

Rate (-, -n) f instalment; **etw auf ~n kaufen** to buy sth in instalments (Brit), to buy sth on the instalment plan (US)

raten (riet, geraten) vt, vi to guess; (empfehlen) to advise (jdm sb)

Rathaus nt town hall

Ration f ration

ratlos adj at a loss, helpless; **ratsam** adj advisable

Rätsel (-s, -) nt puzzle; (Worträtsel) riddle; **das ist mir ein ~** it's a mystery to me; **rätselhaft** adj mysterious

Ratte (-, -n) f rat

rau adj rough, coarse; (Wetter) harsh

Raub (-(e)s) m robbery; (Beute) loot, booty; **rauben** vt to steal; **jdm etw ~** to rob sb of sth; **Räuber(in)** (-s, -) m(f) robber; **Raubfisch** m predatory fish; **Raubkopie** f pirate copy; **Raubmord** m robbery with murder; **Raubtier** nt predator; **Raubüberfall** m mugging; **Raubvogel** m bird of prey

Rauch (-(e)s) m smoke; (Abgase) fumes pl; **rauchen** vt, vi to smoke; **Raucher(in)** (-s, -) m(f) smoker; **Raucherabteil** nt smoking compartment

Räucherlachs m smoked salmon; **räuchern** vt to smoke

rauchig adj smoky; **Rauchmelder** m smoke detector; **Rauchverbot** nt smoking ban; **hier ist ~** there's no smoking here

rauf (fam) kontr von **herauf**

rauh adj siehe **rau**; **Rauhreif** m siehe **Raureif**

Raum (-(e)s, Räume) m space; (Zimmer, Platz) room; (Gebiet) area

räumen vt to clear; (Wohnung, Platz) to vacate; (wegbringen) to shift, to move; (in Schrank etc) to put away

Raumfähre f space shuttle; **Raumfahrt** f space travel; **Raumschiff** nt spacecraft, spaceship; **Raumsonde** f space probe; **Raumstation** f space station

Raumtemperatur f room temperature

Räumungsverkauf m clearance sale, closing-down sale

Raupe (-, -n) f caterpillar

Raureif m hoarfrost

raus (fam) kontr von **heraus, hinaus**; **~!** (get) out!

Rausch (-(e)s, Räusche) m intoxication; **einen ~ haben/kriegen** to be/get drunk

rauschen vi (Wasser) to rush; (Baum) to rustle; (Radio etc) to hiss; **Rauschgift** nt drug; **Rauschgiftsüchtige(r)** mf drug addict

rausfliegen irr vi (fam) to be kicked out

raushalten irr vr (fam) **halt du dich da raus!** you (just) keep out of it

räuspern vr: **sich ~** to clear one's throat

rausschmeißen irr vt (fam) to throw out

Razzia (-, Razzien) f raid

reagieren vi to react (auf+akk to); **Reaktion** f reaction

real adj real; **realisieren** vt (merken) to realize; (verwirklichen) to implement; **realistisch** adj realistic; **Realität** (-, -en) f reality; **Reality-TV** (-s) nt reality TV

Realschule f ≈ secondary school, junior high (school) (US)

Rebe (-, -n) f vine

rebellieren vi to rebel

Rebhuhn nt partridge

rechnen vt, vi to calculate; **~ mit** to expect; (bauen auf) to count on ▷ vr: **sich ~** to pay off, to turn out to be profitable; **Rechner** (-s, -) m calculator; (Computer) computer; **Rechnung** f calculation(s); (Comm) bill (Brit), check (US); **die ~, bitte!** can I have the bill, please?; **das geht auf meine ~** this is on me

recht adj (richtig, passend) right; **~ haben** to be right; **jdm ~ geben** to agree with sb; **mir soll's ~ sein** it's alright by me; **mir ist es ~** I don't mind ▷ adv really, quite; (richtig) right(ly); **mir ist nicht ~ wohl** I don't know really; **es geschieht ihm ~** it serves him right

Recht (-(e)s, -e) nt right; (Jur) law

Rechte (-n, -n) f right-hand side; (Hand) right hand; (Pol) right (wing); **rechte(r, s)** adj right; **auf der ~n Seite** on the right, on the right-hand side; **Rechte(s)** nt right thing; **etwas/nichts ~s** something/nothing proper

Rechteck (-s, -e) nt rectangle; **rechteckig** adj rectangular

rechtfertigen vt to justify ▷ vr: **sich ~** to justify oneself

rechtlich adj legal; **rechtmäßig** adj legal, lawful

rechts adv on the right; **~ abbiegen** to turn right; **~ von** to the right of; **~ oben** at the top right

Rechtsanwalt m, **-anwältin** f lawyer

Rechtschreibung f spelling

Rechtshänder(in) (-s, -) m(f) right-hander; **rechtsherum** adv to the right, clockwise; **rechtsradikal** adj (Pol) extreme right-wing

Rechtsschutzversicherung f legal costs insurance

Rechtsverkehr m driving on the right

rechtswidrig adj illegal

rechtwinklig adj right-angled; **rechtzeitig** adj timely ▷ adv in time

recycelbar adj recyclable; **recyceln** vt to recycle; **Recycling** (-s) nt recycling; **Recyclingpapier** nt recycled paper

Redakteur(in) m(f) editor; **Redaktion** f editing; (Leute) editorial staff; (Büro) editorial office(s)

Rede (-, -n) f speech; (Gespräch) talk; **eine ~ halten** to make a speech; **reden** vi to talk, to speak ▷ vt to say; (Unsinn etc) to talk; **Redewendung** f idiom; **Redner(in)** m(f) speaker

reduzieren vt to reduce

Referat (-s, -e) nt paper; **ein ~ halten** to give a paper (über +akk on)

reflektieren vt to reflect

Reform (-, -en) f reform; **Reformhaus** nt health food shop; **reformieren** vt to reform

Regal (-s, -e) nt shelf; (Möbelstück) shelves pl

Regel (-, -n) f rule; (Med) period; **regelmäßig** adj regular; **regeln** vt to regulate, to control; (Angelegenheit) to settle ▷ vr: **sich von selbst ~** to sort itself out; **Regelung** f regulation

Regen (-s, -) m rain; **Regenbogen** m rainbow; **Regenmantel** m raincoat; **Regenrinne** f gutter; **Regenschauer** m shower; **Regenschirm** m umbrella; **Regenwald** m rainforest; **Regenwurm** m earthworm

Regie f direction

regieren vt, vi to govern, to rule;

Regierung f government; (von Monarch) reign

Region f region; **regional** adj regional

Regisseur(in) m(f) director

registrieren vt to register; (bemerken) to notice

regnen vi impers to rain; **regnerisch** adj rainy

regulär adj regular; **regulieren** vt to regulate, to adjust

Reh (-(e)s, -e) nt deer; (Fleisch) venison

Rehabilitationszentrum nt (Med) rehabilitation centre

Reibe (-, -n) f, **Reibeisen** nt grater; **reiben** (rieb, gerieben) vt to rub; (Gastr) to grate; **reibungslos** adj smooth

reich adj rich

Reich (-(e)s, -e) nt empire; (eines Königs) kingdom

reichen vi to reach; (genügen) to be enough, to be sufficient (jdm for sb) ▷ vt to hold out; (geben) to pass, to hand; (anbieten) to offer

reichhaltig adj ample, rich; **reichlich** adj (Trinkgeld) generous; (Essen) ample; **~ Zeit** plenty of time; **Reichtum** (-s, -tümer) m wealth

reif adj ripe; (Mensch, Urteil) mature

Reif (-(e)s) m (Raureif) hoarfrost ▷ (-(e)s, -e) m (Ring) ring, hoop

reifen vi to mature; (Obst) to ripen

Reifen (-s, -) m ring, hoop; (von Auto) tyre; **Reifendruck** m tyre pressure; **Reifenpanne** f puncture; **Reifenwechsel** m tyre change

Reihe (-, -n) f row; (von Tagen etc, fam: Anzahl) series sing; **der ~** nach one after the other; **er ist an der ~** it's his turn; **Reihenfolge** f

order, sequence; **Reihenhaus** nt terraced house (Brit), row house (US)

Reiher (-s, -) m heron

rein (fam) kontr von **herein, hinein** ▷ adj pure; (sauber) clean

Reinfall m (fam) letdown; **rein|fallen** irr vi (fam) **auf etw** (akk) ~ to fall for sth

reinigen vt to clean; **Reinigung** f cleaning; (Geschäft) (dry) cleaner's; **Reinigungsmittel** nt cleaning agent, cleaner

rein|legen vt: **jdn ~** to take sb for a ride

Reis (-es, -e) m rice

Reise (-, -n) f journey; (auf Schiff) voyage; **Reiseapotheke** f first-aid kit; **Reisebüro** nt travel agent's; **Reisebus** m coach; **Reiseführer(in)** m(f) (Mensch) courier; (Buch) guide(book); **Reisegepäck** nt luggage (Brit), baggage; **Reisegesellschaft** f (Veranstalter) tour operator; **Reisegruppe** f tourist party; (mit Reisebus) coach party; **Reiseleiter(in)** m(f) courier; **reisen** vi to travel; **~ nach** to go to; **Reisende(r)** mf traveller; **Reisepass** m passport; **Reiseroute** f route, itinerary; **Reiserücktrittversicherung** f holiday cancellation insurance; **Reisescheck** m traveller's cheque; **Reisetasche** f holdall (Brit), carryall (US); **Reiseveranstalter** m tour operator; **Reiseverkehr** m holiday traffic; **Reiseversicherung** f travel insurance; **Reiseziel** nt destination

Reiskocher (-s, -) m rice steamer

reißen (riss, gerissen) vt, vi to tear; (ziehen) to pull, to drag; (Witz) to crack

Reißnagel *m* drawing pin (*Brit*), thumbtack (*US*); **Reißverschluss** *m* zip (*Brit*), zipper (*US*); **Reißzwecke** *f* drawing pin (*Brit*), thumbtack (*US*)

reiten (ritt, geritten) *vt, vi* to ride; **Reiter(in)** *m(f)* rider; **Reithose** *f* riding breeches *pl*; **Reitsport** *m* riding; **Reitstiefel** *m* riding boot

Reiz (-es, -e) *m* stimulus; (*angenehm*) charm; (*Verlockung*) attraction; **reizen** *vt* to stimulate; (*unangenehm*) to annoy; (*verlocken*) to appeal to, to attract; **reizend** *adj* charming; **Reizgas** *nt* irritant gas; **Reizung** *f* irritation

Reklamation *f* complaint

Reklame (-, -n) *f* advertising; (*Einzelwerbung*) advertisement; (*im Fernsehen*) commercial

reklamieren *vi* to complain (*wegen* about)

Rekord (-(e)s, -e) *m* record

relativ *adj* relative ▷ *adv* relatively

relaxen *vi* to relax, to chill out

Religion *f* religion; **religiös** *adj* religious

Remoulade (-, -n) *f* tartar sauce

Renaissance *f* renaissance, revival; (*Hist*) Renaissance

Rennbahn *f* racecourse; (*Auto*) racetrack; **rennen** (rannte, gerannt) *vt, vi* to run; **Rennen** (-s, -) *nt* running; (*Wettbewerb*) race; **Rennfahrer(in)** *m(f)* racing driver; **Rennrad** *nt* racing bike; **Rennwagen** *m* racing car

renommiert *adj* famous, noted (*wegen*, *für* for)

renovieren *vt* to renovate; **Renovierung** *f* renovation

rentabel *adj* profitable

Rente (-, -n) *f* pension; **Rentenversicherung** *f* pension scheme

Rentier *nt* reindeer

rentieren *vr*: **sich ~** to pay, to be profitable

Rentner(in) (-s, -) *m(f)* pensioner, senior citizen

Reparatur *f* repair; **Reparaturwerkstatt** *f* repair shop; (*Auto*) garage; **reparieren** *vt* to repair

Reportage *f* report; **Reporter(in)** (-s, -) *m(f)* reporter

Reptil (-s, -ien) *nt* reptile

Republik *f* republic

Reservat (-s, -e) *nt* nature reserve; (*für Ureinwohner*) reservation; **Reserve** (-, -n) *f* reserve; **Reservekanister** *m* spare can; **Reserverad** *nt* (*Auto*) spare wheel; **reservieren** *vt* to reserve; **Reservierung** *f* reservation

resignieren *vi* to give up; **resigniert** *adj* resigned

Respekt (-(e)s) *m* respect; **respektieren** *vt* to respect

Rest (-(e)s, -e) *m* rest, remainder; (*Überreste*) remains *pl*; **der ~ ist für Sie** keep the change

Restaurant (-s, -s) *nt* restaurant

restaurieren *vt* to restore

Restbetrag *m* balance; **restlich** *adj* remaining; **restlos** *adj* complete; **Restmüll** *m* non-recyclable waste

Resultat *nt* result

retten *vt* to save, to rescue

Rettich (-s, -e) *m* radish (*large white or red variety*)

Rettung *f* rescue; (*Hilfe*) help; (*Rettungsdienst*) ambulance service; **Rettungsboot** *nt* lifeboat; **Rettungshubschrauber** *m* rescue helicopter; **Rettungsring** *m* lifebelt, life preserver (*US*); **Rettungswagen** *m* ambulance

Reue (-) *f* remorse; (*Bedauern*)

regret; **reuen** vt: **es reut ihn** he regrets it

revanchieren vr: **sich ~** (sich rächen) to get one's own back, to get one's revenge; (für Hilfe etc) to return the favour

Revolution f revolution

Rezept (-(e)s, -e) nt (Gastr) recipe; (Med) prescription; **rezeptfrei** adj over-the-counter, non-prescription

Rezeption f (im Hotel) reception

rezeptpflichtig adj available only on prescription

R-Gespräch nt reverse-charge (Brit) o (collect US)) call

Rhabarber (-s) m rhubarb

Rhein (-s) m Rhine; **Rheinland-Pfalz** (-) nt Rhineland-Palatinate

Rheuma (-s) nt rheumatism

Rhythmus m rhythm

richten vt (lenken) to direct (auf +akk to); (Waffe, Kamera) to point (auf +akk at); (Brief, Anfrage) to address (an +akk to); (einstellen) to adjust; (instand setzen) to repair; (zurechtmachen) to prepare ▷ vr: **sich ~ nach** (Regel etc) to keep to; (Mode, Beispiel) to follow; (abhängen von) to depend on

Richter(in) (-s, -) m(f) judge

Richtgeschwindigkeit f recommended speed

richtig adj right, correct; (echt) proper ▷ adv (fam: sehr) really; **richtigstellen** vt: **etw ~** (berichtigen) to correct sth

Richtlinie f guideline

Richtung f direction; (Tendenz) tendency; **Richtungstaste** f arrow key

rieb imperf von **reiben**

riechen (roch, gerochen) vt, vi to smell; **nach etw ~** to smell of sth; **an etw** (dat) **~** to smell sth

rief imperf von **rufen**

Riegel (-s, -) m bolt; (Gastr) bar

Riemen (-s, -) m strap; (Gürtel) belt

Riese (-n, -n) m giant; **Riesengarnele** f king prawn; **riesengroß** adj gigantic, huge; **Riesenrad** nt big wheel; **riesig** adj enormous, huge

riet imperf von **raten**

Riff (-(e)s, -e) nt reef

Rind (-(e)s, -er) nt cow; (Bulle) bull; (Gastr) beef; **~er** pl cattle pl

Rinde (-, -n) f (Baum) bark; (Käse) rind; (Brot) crust

Rinderbraten m roast beef; **Rinderwahn(sinn)** m mad cow disease; **Rindfleisch** nt beef

Ring (-(e)s, -e) m ring; (Straße) ring road; **Ringbuch** nt ring binder

ringen (rang, gerungen) vi to wrestle; **Ringer(in)** m(f) wrestler; **Ringfinger** m ring finger; **Ringkampf** m wrestling match; **ringsherum** adv round about

Rippe (-, -n) f rib; **Rippenfellentzündung** f pleurisy

Risiko (-s, -s o Risiken) nt risk; **auf eigenes ~** at one's own risk; **riskant** adj risky; **riskieren** vt to risk

riss imperf von **reißen**

Riss (-es, -e) m tear; (in Mauer, Tasse etc) crack; **rissig** adj cracked; (Haut) chapped

ritt imperf von **reiten**

Ritter (-s, -) m knight

Rivale (-n, -n) m, **Rivalin** f rival

Rizinusöl nt castor oil

Robbe (-, -n) f seal

Roboter (-s, -) m robot

robust adj robust

roch imperf von **riechen**

Rock (-(e)s, Röcke) m skirt

Rockband (Musikgruppe) rock band; **Rockmusik** f rock (music)

r

Rodelbahn f toboggan run;
  rodeln vi to toboggan

Roggen (-s, -) m rye;
  Roggenbrot nt rye bread

roh adj raw (Mensch) coarse,
  crude; **Rohkost** f raw vegetables
  and fruit pl

Rohr (-(e)s, -e) nt pipe; (Bot) cane;
  (Schilf) reed; **Röhre** (-, -n) f tube;
  (Leitung) pipe; (Elek) valve;
  (Backröhre) oven; **Rohrzucker** m
  cane sugar

Rohstoff m raw material

Rokoko (-s) nt rococo

Rollbrett nt skateboard

Rolle (-, -n) f (etw
  Zusammengerolltes) roll; (Theat) role

rollen vt, vi to roll

Roller (-s, -) m scooter

Rollerblades® pl Rollerblades®
  pl; **Rollerskates** pl roller skates pl

Rollkragenpullover m polo-
  neck (Brit) (o turtleneck (US))
  sweater; **Rollladen** m, **Rollo**
  (-s, -s) m (roller) shutters pl;
  Rollschuh m roller skate;
  Rollstuhl m wheelchair;
  rollstuhlgerecht adj suitable
  for wheelchairs; **Rolltreppe** f
  escalator

Roman (-s, -e) m novel

Romantik f romance;
  romantisch adj romantic

römisch-katholisch adj Roman
  Catholic

röntgen vt to X-ray;
  Röntgenaufnahme f,
  Röntgenbild nt X-ray;
  Röntgenstrahlen pl X-rays pl

rosa adj inv pink

Rose (-, -n) f rose

Rosenkohl m (Brussels) sprouts
  pl

Rosé(wein) m rosé (wine)

rosig adj rosy

Rosine f raisin

Rosmarin (-s) m rosemary

Rosskastanie f horse chestnut

Rost (-(e)s, -e) m rust; (zum Braten)
  grill, gridiron; **Rostbratwurst** f
  grilled sausage; **rosten** vi to
  rust; **rösten** vt to roast, to grill;
  (Brot) to toast; **rostfrei** adj
  rustproof; (Stahl) stainless; **rostig**
  adj rusty; **Rostschutz** m
  rustproofing

rot adj red; **~ werden** to blush;
  Rote Karte red card; **Rote Bete**
  beetroot; **bei Rot über die Ampel
  fahren** to jump the lights; **das
  Rote Kreuz** the Red Cross

Röteln pl German measles sing

röten vt to redden ▷ vr: **sich ~** to
  redden

rothaarig adj red-haired

rotieren vi to rotate; **am
  Rotieren sein** (fam) to be rushing
  around like a mad thing

Rotkehlchen nt robin; **Rotkohl**
  m, **Rotkraut** nt red cabbage;
  Rotlichtviertel nt red-light
  district; **Rotwein** m red wine

Rouge (-s, -s) nt rouge

Route (-, -n) f route

Routine f experience; (Trott)
  routine

Rubbellos nt scratchcard;
  rubbeln vt to rub

Rübe (-, -n) f turnip; **Gelbe
  ~ carrot; Rote ~** beetroot

rüber (fam) kontr von **herüber,
  hinüber**

rückbestätigen vt (Flug etc) to
  reconfirm

rücken vt, vi to move; **könntest
  du ein bisschen ~?** could you
  move over a bit?

Rücken (-s, -) m back;
  Rückenlehne f back(rest);
  Rückenmark nt spinal cord;
  Rückenschmerzen pl backache
  sing; **Rückenschwimmen** (-s) nt
  backstroke; **Rückenwind** m
  tailwind

Rückerstattung f refund;
Rückfahrkarte f return ticket
(Brit), round-trip ticket (US);
Rückfahrt f return journey;
Rückfall m relapse; **Rückflug** m
return flight; **Rückgabe** f return;
rückgängig adj: **etw ~ machen**
to cancel sth; **Rückgrat** (-(e)s, -e)
nt spine, backbone; **Rückkehr**
(-, -en) f return; **Rücklicht** nt
rear light; **Rückreise** f return
journey; **auf der ~** on the way
back

Rucksack m rucksack, backpack;
Rucksacktourist(in) m(f)
backpacker

Rückschritt m step back;
Rückseite f back; (hinterer Teil)
rear; **siehe ~** see overleaf;
Rücksicht f consideration;
~ nehmen auf (+akk) to show
consideration for; **rücksichtslos**
adj inconsiderate; (Fahren)
reckless; (unbarmherzig) ruthless;
rücksichtsvoll adj considerate;
Rücksitz m back seat;
Rückspiegel m (Auto) rear-view
mirror; **Rückstand** m: **sie sind
zwei Tore im ~** they're two goals
down; **im ~ sein mit** (Arbeit, Miete)
to be behind with; **Rücktaste** f
backspace key; **Rückvergütung**
f refund; **rückwärts** adv
backwards, back (US); **Rückwärtsgang** m (Auto) reverse (gear);
Rückweg m return journey, way
back; **Rückzahlung** f repayment

Ruder (-s, -) nt oar; (Steuer)
rudder; **Ruderboot** nt rowing
boat (Brit), rowboat (US); **rudern**
vt, vi to row

Ruf (-(e)s, -e) m call, cry; (Ansehen)
reputation; **rufen** (rief, gerufen) vt,
vi to call; (schreien) to cry;
Rufnummer f telephone number

Ruhe (-) f rest; (Ungestörtheit)
peace, quiet; (Gelassenheit, Stille)

calm; (Schweigen) silence; **lass
mich in ~!** leave me alone; **ruhen**
vi to rest; **Ruhestand** m
retirement; **im ~ sein** to be retired;
Ruhestörung f disturbance of
the peace; **Ruhetag** m closing
day; **montags ~ haben** to be
closed on Mondays

ruhig adj quiet; (bewegungslos)
still; (Hand) steady; (gelassen) calm

Ruhm (-(e)s) m fame, glory

Rührei nt scrambled egg(s);
rühren vt to move; (umrühren) to
stir ▷ vr: **sich ~** to move; (sich
bemerkbar machen) to say
something; **rührend** adj
touching, moving; **Rührung** f
emotion

Ruine (-, -n) f ruin; **ruinieren** vt
to ruin

rülpsen vi to burp, to belch

rum (fam) kontr von **herum**

Rum (-s, -s) m rum

Rumänien (-s) nt Romania

Rummel (-s) m (Trubel) hustle
and bustle; (Jahrmarkt) fair;
(Medienrummel) hype;
Rummelplatz m fairground

rumoren vi: **es rumort in
meinem Bauch/Kopf** my
stomach is rumbling/my head is
spinning

Rumpf (-(e)s, Rümpfe) m (Anat)
trunk; (Aviat) fuselage; (Naut)
hull

rümpfen vt: **die Nase ~** to turn
one's nose up (über at)

Rumpsteak nt rump steak

rund adj round ▷ adv (etwa)
around; **~ um etw** (a)round sth;
Runde (-, -n) f round; (in Rennen)
lap; **Rundfahrt** f tour (durch of);
Rundfunk m broadcasting
service; **im ~** on the radio;
Rundgang m tour (durch of); (von
Wächter) round

rundlich adj plump; **Rundreise** f tour (durch of)

runter (fam) kontr von **herunter, hinunter**; **runterscrollen** vt (Inform) to scroll down

runzeln vt: **die Stirn ~** to frown; **runzelig** adj wrinkled

ruppig adj gruff

Rüsche (-, -n) f frill

Ruß (-es) m soot

Russe (-n, -n) m Russian

Rüssel (-s, -) m (Elefant) trunk; (Schwein) snout

Russin f Russian; **russisch** adj Russian; **Russisch** nt Russian; **Russland** nt Russia

Rüstung f (mit Waffen) arming; (Ritterrüstung) armour; (Waffen) armaments pl

Rutsch (-(e)s, -e) m: **guten ~ (ins neue Jahr)!** Happy New Year; **Rutschbahn** f, **Rutsche** f slide; **rutschen** vi to slide; (ausrutschen) to slip; **rutschig** adj slippery

rütteln vt, vi to shake

S

S abk = **Süd** S

s. abk = **siehe** see; = **Seite** p.

Saal (-(e)s, Säle) m hall; (für Sitzungen) room

Saarland nt Saarland

sabotieren vt to sabotage

Sache (-, -n) f thing; (Angelegenheit) affair, business; (Frage) matter; **bei der ~ bleiben** to keep to the point; **sachkundig** adj competent; **Sachlage** f situation; **sachlich** adj (objektiv) objective; (nüchtern) matter-of-fact; (inhaltlich) factual; **sächlich** adj (Ling) neuter; **Sachschaden** m material damage

Sachsen (-s) nt Saxony; **Sachsen-Anhalt** (-s) nt Saxony-Anhalt

sacht(e) adv softly, gently

Sachverständige(r) mf expert

Sack (-(e)s, Säcke) m sack; (pej:

Mensch) bastard, bugger;
Sackgasse f dead end, cul-de-sac
Safe (-s, -s) m safe
Safer Sex m safe sex
Safran (-s, -e) m saffron
Saft (-(e)s, Säfte) m juice; **saftig** adj juicy
Sage (-, -n) f legend
Säge (-, -n) f saw; **Sägemehl** nt sawdust
sagen vt, vi to say (*jdm* to sb), to tell (*jdm* sb); **wie sagt man ... auf Englisch?** what's ... in English?
sägen vt, vi to saw
sagenhaft adj legendary; (*fam:* großartig) fantastic
sah imperf von **sehen**
Sahne (-) f cream
Saison (-, -s) f season; **außerhalb der ~** out of season
Saite (-, -n) f string
Sakko (-s, -s) nt jacket
Salami (-, -s) f salami
Salat (-(e)s, -e) m salad; (*Kopfsalat*) lettuce; **Salatbar** f salad bar; **Salatschüssel** f salad bowl; **Salatsoße** f salad dressing
Salbe (-, -n) f ointment
Salbei (-s) m sage
Salmonellenvergiftung f salmonella (poisoning)
salopp adj (*Kleidung*) casual; (*Sprache*) slangy
Salsamusik f salsa (music)
Salto (-s, -s) m somersault
Salz (-es, -e) nt salt; **salzarm** adj low-salt; **salzen** (*salzte, gesalzen*) vt to salt; **Salzgurke** f pickled gherkin; **Salzhering** m pickled herring; **salzig** adj salty; **Salzkartoffeln** pl boiled potatoes pl; **Salzstange** f pretzel stick; **Salzstreuer** m salt cellar (Brit) (o shaker (US)); **Salzwasser** nt salt water

Samba (-, -s) f samba
Samen (-s, -) m seed; (*Sperma*) sperm
sammeln vt to collect;
Sammler(in) m(f) collector;
Sammlung f collection;
(*Ansammlung, Konzentration*) concentration
Samstag m Saturday; *siehe auch* **Mittwoch**; **samstags** adv on Saturdays; *siehe auch* **mittwochs**
samt prep +dat (*along*) with, together with
Samt (-(e)s, -e) m velvet
sämtliche(r, s) adj all (the)
Sanatorium (-s, Sanatorien) nt sanatorium (Brit), sanitarium (US)
Sand (-(e)s, -e) m sand
Sandale (-, -n) f sandal
sandig adj sandy; **Sandkasten** m sandpit (Brit), sandbox (US); **Sandpapier** nt sandpaper; **Sandstrand** m sandy beach
sandte imperf von **senden**
sanft adj soft, gentle
sang imperf von **singen**
Sänger(in) (-s, -) m(f) singer
Sangria (-, -s) f sangria
sanieren vt to redevelop; (*Gebäude*) to renovate; (*Betrieb*) to restore to profitability
sanitär adj sanitary; **~e Anlagen** pl sanitation
Sanitäter(in) (-s, -) m(f) ambulance man/woman, paramedic
sank imperf von **sinken**
Sankt Gallen (-s) nt St Gallen
Saphir (-s, -e) m sapphire
Sardelle f anchovy
Sardine f sardine
Sarg (-(e)s, Särge) m coffin
saß imperf von **sitzen**
Satellit (-en, -en) m satellite; **Satellitenfernsehen** nt satellite TV; **Satellitenschüssel** f (*fam*) satellite dish
Satire (-, -n) f satire (*auf+akk* on)

s

satt adj full; (Farbe) rich, deep;
~ **sein** (gesättigt) to be full;
~ **machen** to be filling; **jdn/etw**
~ **sein** to be fed up with sb/sth

Sattel (-s, Sättel) m saddle

satt|haben irr vt: **jdn/etw**
~ (nicht mehr mögen) to be fed up
with sb/sth

Saturn (-s) m Saturn

Satz (-es, Sätze) m (Ling) sentence;
(Mus) movement; (Tennis) set;
(Kaffee) grounds pl; (Comm) rate
(Sprung) jump; (Comm) rate

Satzzeichen nt punctuation
mark

Sau (-, Säue) f sow; (pej: Mensch)
dirty bugger

sauber adj clean; (ironisch) fine;
~ **machen** to clean; **Sauberkeit** f
cleanness; (von Person) cleanliness;
säubern vt to clean

saublöd adj (fam) really stupid,
dumb

Sauce (-, -n) f sauce; (zu Braten)
gravy

Saudi-Arabien (-s) nt Saudi
Arabia

sauer adj sour; (Chem) acid; (fam:
verärgert) cross; **saurer Regen** acid
rain; **Sauerkirsche** f sour
cherry; **Sauerkraut** nt
sauerkraut; **säuerlich** adj
slightly sour; **Sauermilch** f
sour milk; **Sauerrahm** m sour
cream; **Sauerstoff** m oxygen

saufen (soff, gesoffen) vt to drink;
(fam: Mensch) to knock back ▷ vi
to drink; (fam: Mensch) to booze

saugen (sog o saugte, gesogen o
gesaugt) vt, vi to suck; (mit
Staubsauger) to vacuum, to hoover
(Brit); **Sauger** (-s, -) m (auf Flasche)
teat; **Säugetier** nt mammal;
Säugling m infant, baby

Säule (-, -n) f column, pillar

Saum (-s, Säume) m hem; (Naht)
seam

Sauna (-, -s) f sauna

Säure (-, -n) f acid

sausen vi (Ohren) to buzz; (Wind)
to howl; (Mensch) to rush

Saustall m pigsty; **Sauwetter**
nt: **was für ein** ~ (fam) what lousy
weather

Saxophon (-s, -e) nt saxophone

S-Bahn f suburban railway;
S-Bahn-Haltestelle f, **S-Bahnhof**
m suburban (train) station

scannen vt to scan; **Scanner**
(-s, -) m scanner

schäbig adj shabby

Schach (-s, -s) nt chess; (Stellung)
check; **Schachbrett** nt
chessboard; **Schachfigur** f
chess piece; **schachmatt** adj
checkmate

Schacht (-(e)s, Schächte) m shaft

Schachtel (-, -n) f box

schade interj what a pity

Schädel (-s, -) m skull;
Schädelbruch m fractured skull

schaden vi to damage, to harm
(jdm sb); **das schadet nichts** it
won't do any harm; **Schaden**
(-s, Schäden) m damage;
(Verletzung) injury; (Nachteil)
disadvantage; **einen**
~ **verursachen** to cause damage;
Schadenersatz m compensation, damages pl; **schadhaft** adj
faulty; (beschädigt) damaged;
schädigen vt to damage; (jdn) to
do harm to, to harm; **schädlich**
adj harmful (für to); **Schadstoff**
m harmful substance;
schadstoffarm adj low-emission

Schaf (-(e)s, -e) nt sheep;
Schafbock m ram; **Schäfer** (-s, -)
m shepherd; **Schäferhund** m
Alsatian (Brit), German shepherd;
Schäferin f shepherdess

schaffen (schuf, geschaffen) vt to
create; (Platz) to make ▷ vt
(erreichen) to manage, to do;

(erledigen) to finish; (Prüfung) to pass; (transportieren) to take; **jdm ~ machen** to cause sb trouble

Schaffner(in) (-s, -) m(f) (in Bus) conductor/conductress; (Eisenb) guard

Schafskäse m sheep's (milk) cheese

schal adj (Getränk) flat

Schal (-s, -e o -s) m scarf

Schälchen nt (small) bowl

Schale (-, -n) f skin; (abgeschält) peel; (Nuss, Muschel, Ei) shell; (Geschirr) bowl, dish

schälen vt to peel; (Tomate, Mandel) to skin; (Erbsen, Eier, Nüsse) to shell; (Getreide) to husk ▷ vr: **sich ~** to peel

Schall (-(e)s, -e) m sound; **Schalldämpfer** (-s, -) m (Auto) silencer (Brit), muffler (US); **Schallplatte** f record

Schalotte (-, -n) f shallot

schalten vt to switch ▷ vi (Auto) to change gear; (fam: begreifen) to catch on; **Schalter** (-s, -) m (auf Post, Bank) counter; (an Gerät) switch; **Schalterhalle** f main hall; **Schalteröffnungszeiten** pl business hours pl

Schaltfläche f (Inform) button; **Schalthebel** m gear lever (Brit) (o shift (US)); **Schaltjahr** nt leap year; **Schaltknüppel** m gear lever (Brit) (o shift (US)); **Schaltung** f gear change (Brit), gearshift (US)

Scham (-) f shame; (Schamgefühl) modesty; **schämen** vr: **sich ~** to be ashamed

Schande (-) f disgrace

Schanze (-, -n) f ski jump

Schar (-, -en) f (von Vögeln) flock; (Menge) crowd; **in -en** in droves

scharf adj (Messer, Kritik) sharp; (Essen) hot; **auf etw** (akk) **~ sein** (fam) to be keen on sth

Schärfe (-, -n) f sharpness; (Strenge) rigour; (Foto) focus

Scharlach (-s) m (Med) scarlet fever

Scharnier (-s, -e) nt hinge

Schaschlik (-s, -s) m o nt (shish) kebab

Schatten (-s, -) m shadow; **30 Grad im ~** 30 degrees in the shade; **schattig** adj shady

Schatz (-es, Schätze) m treasure; (Mensch) love

schätzen vt (abschätzen) to estimate; (Gegenstand) to value; (würdigen) to value, to esteem; (vermuten) to reckon; **Schätzung** f estimate; (das Schätzen) estimation; (von Wertgegenstand) valuation; **schätzungsweise** adv roughly, approximately

Schau (-, -en) f show; (Ausstellung) exhibition

schauen vi to look; **ich schau mal, ob ...** I'll go and have a look whether ...; **schau, dass ...** see (to it) that ...

Schauer (-s, -) m (Regen) shower; (Schreck) shudder

Schaufel (-, -n) f shovel; **~ und Besen** dustpan and brush; **schaufeln** vt to shovel; **Schnee ~** to clear the snow away

Schaufenster nt shop window; **Schaufensterbummel** m window-shopping expedition

Schaukel (-, -n) f swing; **schaukeln** vi to rock; (mit Schaukel) to swing

Schaulustige(r) mf gawper (Brit), rubbernecker (US)

Schaum (-(e)s, Schäume) m foam; (Seifenschaum) lather; (Bierschaum) froth; **Schaumbad** nt bubble bath; **schäumen** vi to foam; **Schaumfestiger** (-s, -) m styling mousse; **Schaumgummi** m foam (rubber); **Schaumwein** m sparkling wine

Schauplatz m scene; **Schauspiel** nt spectacle; (Theat) play; **Schauspieler(in)** m(f) actor/actress

Scheck (-s, -s) m cheque; **Scheckheft** nt chequebook; **Scheckkarte** f cheque card

Scheibe (-, -n) f disc; (von Brot, Käse etc) slice; (Glasscheibe) pane; **Scheibenbremse** f (Aut) disc brake; **Scheibenwaschanlage** f (Aut) windscreen (Brit) (o windshield (US)) washer unit; **Scheibenwischer** (-s, -) m (Aut) windscreen (Brit) (o windshield (US)) wiper

Scheich (-s, -s) m sheik(h)

Scheide (-, -n) f (Anat) vagina

scheiden (schied, geschieden) vt (trennen) to separate; (Ehe) to dissolve; **sich ~ lassen** to get a divorce; **sie hat sich von ihm ~ lassen** she divorced him; **Scheidung** f divorce

Schein (-(e)s, -e) m light; (Anschein) appearance; (Geld) (bank)note; **scheinbar** adj apparent; **scheinen** (schien, geschienen) vi (Sonne) to shine; (den Anschein haben) to seem; **Scheinwerfer** (-s, -) m floodlight; (Theat) spotlight; (Aut) headlight

Scheiß- in zW (vulg) damned, bloody (Brit); **Scheiße** (-) f (vulg) shit, crap; **scheißegal** adj (vulg) **das ist mir ~** I don't give a damn (o toss); **scheißen** (schiss, geschissen) vi (vulg) to shit

Scheitel (-s, -) m parting (Brit), part (US)

scheitern vi to fail (an +dat because of)

Schellfisch m haddock

Schema (-s, -s o Schemata) nt scheme, plan; (Darstellung) diagram

Schenkel (-s, -) m thigh

schenken vt to give; **er hat es mir geschenkt** he gave it to me (as a present); **sich** (dat) **etw ~** (fam: weglassen) to skip sth

Scherbe (-, -n) f broken piece, fragment

Schere (-, -n) f scissors pl; (groß) shears pl; **eine ~** a pair of scissors/shears

Scherz (-es, -e) m joke

scheu adj shy

scheuen vr **sich ~ vor** (+dat) to be afraid of, to shrink from ▷ vt to shun ▷ vi (Pferd) to shy

scheuern vt to scrub; **jdm eine ~** (fam) to slap sb in the face

Scheune (-, -n) f barn

scheußlich adj dreadful

Schi (-s, -er) m siehe **Ski**

Schicht (-, -en) f layer; (in Gesellschaft) class; (in Fabrik etc) shift

schick adj stylish, chic

schicken vt to send ▷ vr: **sich ~** (sich beeilen) to hurry up

Schickimicki (-(s), -s) m (fam) trendy

Schicksal (-s, -e) nt fate

Schiebedach nt (Aut) sunroof; **schieben** (schob, geschoben) vt, vi to push; **die Schuld auf jdn ~** to put the blame on sb; **Schiebetür** f sliding door

schied imperf von **scheiden**

Schiedsrichter(in) m(f) referee; (Tennis) umpire; (Schlichter) arbitrator

schief adj crooked; (Blick) funny ▷ adv crooked(ly); **schiefgehen** irr vi (fam: misslingen) to go wrong

schielen vi to squint

schien imperf von **scheinen**

Schienbein nt shin

Schiene (-, -n) f rail; (Med) splint

schier adj pure; (fig) sheer ▷ adv nearly, almost

schießen (schoss, geschossen) vt to shoot; (Ball) to kick; (Tor) to score; (Foto) to take ▷ vi to shoot (auf +akk at)

Schiff (-(e)s, -e) nt ship; (in Kirche) nave; **Schifffahrt** f shipping; **Schiffsreise** f voyage

schikanieren vt to harass; (Schule) to bully

Schild (-(e)s, -e) m (Schutz) shield ▷ (-(e)s, -er) nt sign; **was steht auf dem ~?** what does the sign say? **Schilddrüse** f thyroid gland

schildern vt to describe

Schildkröte f tortoise; (Wasserschildkröte) turtle

Schimmel (-s, -) m mould; (Pferd) white horse; **schimmeln** vi to go mouldy

schimpfen vt to tell off ▷ vi (sich beklagen) to complain; **mit jdm ~** to tell sb off; **Schimpfwort** nt swearword

Schinken (-s, -) m ham

Schirm (-(e)s, -e) m (Regenschirm) umbrella; (Sonnenschirm) parasol, sunshade

schiss imperf von **scheißen**

Schlacht (-, -en) f battle; **schlachten** vt to slaughter; **Schlachter(in)** (-s, -) m(f) butcher

Schlaf (-(e)s) m sleep; **Schlafanzug** m pyjamas pl; **Schlafcouch** f bed settee

Schläfe (-, -n) f temple

schlafen (schlief, geschlafen) vi to sleep; **schlaf gut!** sleep well; **hast du gut geschlafen?** did you sleep all right?; **er schläft noch** he's still [...]o; **~ gehen** to go to bed [...] adj slack; (kraftlos) limp; [...]ft) exhausted

[...]elegenheit f place to [...]

[...]hlaflosigkeit f

sleeplessness; **Schlafmittel** nt sleeping pill; **schläfrig** adj sleepy

Schlafsaal m dormitory; **Schlafsack** m sleeping bag; **Schlaftablette** f sleeping pill; **er ist eine richtige ~** (fam: langweilig) he's such a bore; **Schlafwagen** m sleeping car, sleeper; **Schlafzimmer** nt bedroom

Schlag (-(e)s, Schläge) m blow; (Puls) beat; (Elek) shock; (fam: Portion) helping; (Art) kind, type; **Schlagader** f artery; **Schlaganfall** m (Med) stroke; **schlagartig** adj sudden

schlagen (schlug, geschlagen) vt to hit; (besiegen) to beat; (Sahne) to whip; **jdn zu Boden ~** to knock sb down ▷ vi (Herz) to beat; (Uhr) to strike; **mit dem Kopf gegen etw ~** to bang one's head against sth ▷ vr: **sich ~** to fight

Schläger (-s, -) m (Sport) bat; (Tennis) racket; (Golf) (golf) club; (Hockey) hockey stick; (Mensch) brawler; **Schlägerei** f fight, brawl

schlagfertig adj quick-witted; **Schlagloch** nt pothole; **Schlagsahne** f whipping cream; (geschlagen) whipped cream; **Schlagzeile** f headline; **Schlagzeug** nt drums pl; (in Orchester) percussion

Schlamm (-(e)s, -e) m mud

schlampig adj (fam) sloppy

schlang imperf von **schlingen**

Schlange (-, -n) f snake; (von Menschen) queue (Brit), line (US); **~ stehen** to queue (Brit), to stand in line (US); **Schlangenlinie** f wavy line; **in ~n fahren** to swerve about

schlank adj slim

schlapp adj limp; (locker) slack

Schlappe (-, -n) f (fam) setback

schlau adj clever, smart; (raffiniert) crafty, cunning

Schlauch (-(e)s, Schläuche) m hose; (in Reifen) inner tube; **Schlauchboot** nt rubber dinghy

schlecht adj bad; **mir ist ~** I feel sick; **die Milch ist ~** the milk has gone off ▷ adv badly; **es geht ihm ~** he's having a hard time; (gesundheitlich) he's not feeling well; (finanziell) he's pretty hard up; **schlecht|machen** vt: **jdn ~** (herabsetzen) to run sb down

schleichen (schlich, geschlichen) vi to creep

Schleier (-s, -) m veil

Schleife (-, -n) f (Inform, Aviat, Elek) loop; (Band) bow

schleifen vt (ziehen, schleppen) to drag ▷ (schliff, geschliffen) vt (schärfen) to grind; (Edelstein) to cut

Schleim (-(e)s, -e) m slime; (Med) mucus; **Schleimer** (-s, -) m (fam) creep; **Schleimhaut** f mucous membrane

schlendern vi to stroll

schleppen vt to drag; (Auto, Schiff) to tow; (tragen) to lug; **Schlepplift** m ski tow

Schleswig-Holstein (-s) nt Schleswig-Holstein

Schleuder (-, -n) f catapult; (für Wäsche) spin-dryer; **schleudern** vt to hurl; (Wäsche) to spin-dry ▷ vi (Auto) to skid; **Schleudersitz** m ejector seat

schlich imperf von **schleichen**

schlicht adj simple, plain

schlichten vt (Streit) to settle

schlief imperf von **schlafen**

schließen (schloss, geschlossen) vt, vi to close, to shut; (beenden) to close; (Freundschaft, Ehe) to enter into; (folgern) to infer (aus from) ▷ vr: **sich ~** to close, to shut; **Schließfach** nt locker

schließlich adv finally; (schließlich doch) after all

schliff imperf von **schleifen**

schlimm adj bad; **schlimmer** adj worse; **schlimmste(r, s)** adj worst; **schlimmstenfalls** adv at (the) worst

Schlinge (-, -n) f loop; (Med) sling

Schlips (-es, -e) m tie

Schlitten (-s, -) m sledge, toboggan; (mit Pferden) sleigh; **Schlittenfahren** (-s) nt tobogganing

Schlittschuh m ice skate; **~ laufen** to ice-skate

Schlitz (-es, -e) m slit; (für Münze) slot; (an Hose) flies pl

schloss imperf von **schließen**

Schloss (-es, Schlösser) nt lock; (Burg) castle

Schlosser(in) m(f) mechanic

Schlucht (-, -en) f gorge, ravine

schluchzen vi to sob

Schluck (-(e)s, -e) m swallow; **Schluckauf** (-s) m hiccups pl; **schlucken** vt, vi to swallow

schludern vi (fam) to do sloppy work

schlug imperf von **schlagen**

Schlüpfer (-s, -) m panties pl

schlürfen vt, vi to slurp

Schluss (-es, Schlüsse) m end; (Schlussfolgerung) conclusion; **am ~** at the end; **mit jdm ~ machen** to finish (o split up) with sb

Schlüssel (-s, -) m (a. fig) key; **Schlüsselbein** nt collarbone; **Schlüsselbund** m bunch of keys; **Schlüsseldienst** m key-cutting service; **Schlüsselloch** nt keyhole

Schlussfolgerung f conclusion; **Schlusslicht** nt tail-light; (fig) tail-ender; **Schlussverkauf** m clearance sale

schmächtig adj frail

schmal adj narrow; (Mensch, Buch etc) slim; (karg) meagre

Schmalz (-es, -e) nt dripping, lard; (fig: Sentimentalitäten) schmaltz

schmatzen vi to eat noisily

schmecken vt, vi to taste (nach of); **es schmeckt ihm** he likes it; **lass es dir ~!** bon appétit

Schmeichelei f flattery; **schmeichelhaft** adj flattering; **schmeicheln** vi: **jdm ~** to flatter sb

schmeißen (schmiss, geschmissen) vt (fam) to chuck, to throw

schmelzen (schmolz, geschmolzen) vt, vi to melt; (Metall, Erz) to smelt; **Schmelzkäse** m cheese spread

Schmerz (-es, -en) m pain; (Trauer) grief; **~en haben** to be in pain; **~en im Rücken haben** to have a pain in one's back; **schmerzen** vt, vi to hurt; **Schmerzensgeld** nt compensation; **schmerzhaft, schmerzlich** adj painful; **schmerzlos** adj painless; **Schmerzmittel** nt painkiller; **schmerzstillend** adj painkilling; **Schmerztablette** f painkiller

Schmetterling m butterfly

Schmied(in) (-(e)s, -e) m(f) blacksmith; **schmieden** vt to forge; (Pläne) to make

schmieren vt to smear; (ölen) to lubricate, to grease; (bestechen) to bribe ▷ vt, vi (unsauber schreiben) to scrawl; **schmiergeld** nt (fam) bribe; **schmierig** adj greasy; **Schmierseife** f soft soap

Schminke (-, -n) f make-up; **schminken** vr: **sich ~** to put one's make-up on

schmiss imperf von **schmeißen**

schmollen vi to sulk; **schmollend** adj sulky

schmolz imperf von **schmelzen**

Schmuck (-(e)s, -e) m jewellery (Brit), jewelry (US); (Verzierung) decoration; **schmücken** vt to decorate

schmuggeln vt, vi to smuggle

schmunzeln vi to smile

schmusen vi to (kiss and) cuddle

Schmutz (-es) m dirt, filth; **schmutzig** adj dirty

Schnabel (-s, Schnäbel) m beak, bill; (Ausguss) spout

Schnake (-, -n) f mosquito

Schnalle (-, -n) f buckle

Schnäppchen nt (fam) bargain; **schnappen** vt (fangen) to catch ▷ vi: **nach Luft ~** to gasp for breath; **Schnappschuss** m (Foto) snap(shot)

Schnaps (-es, Schnäpse) m schnapps

schnarchen vi to snore

schnaufen vi to puff, to pant

Schnauzbart m moustache; **Schnauze** (-, -n) f snout, muzzle; (Ausguss) spout; (fam: Mund) trap; **die ~ voll haben** to have had enough

schnäuzen vr: **sich ~** to blow one's nose

Schnecke (-, -n) f snail; **Schneckenhaus** nt snail's shell

Schnee (-s) m snow; **Schneeball** m snowball; **Schneebob** m snowmobile; **Schneebrille** f snow goggles pl; **Schneeflocke** f snowflake; **Schneegestöber** (-s, -) nt snow flurry; **Schneeglöckchen** nt snowdrop; **Schneegrenze** f snowline; **Schneekanone** f snow thrower; **Schneekette** f (Auto) snow chain; **Schneemann** m snowman; **Schneepflug** m snowplough; **Schneeregen** m sleet; **Schneeschmelze** f thaw; **Schneesturm** m snowstorm, blizzard; **Schneetreiben** nt light blizzards pl; **Schneewehe** f snowdrift

s

Schneide (-, -n) f edge; (Klinge)
blade; **schneiden** (schnitt,
geschnitten) vt to cut; **sich** (dat) **die
Haare ~ lassen** to have one's hair
cut ▷ vr: **sich ~** to cut oneself;
Schneider(in) (-s, -) m(f) tailor;
(für Damenmode) dressmaker;
Schneiderin f dressmaker;
Schneidezahn m incisor
schneien vi impers to snow
schnell adj quick, fast ▷ adv
quickly, fast; **mach ~!** hurry up;
Schnelldienst m express service;
Schnellhefter m loose-leaf
binder; **Schnellimbiss** m snack
bar; **Schnellkochtopf** m
pressure cooker;
Schnellreinigung f express dry
cleaning; (Geschäft) express (dry)
cleaner's; **Schnellstraße** f
expressway; **Schnellzug** m fast
train
schneuzen vr siehe **schnäuzen**
schnitt imperf von **schneiden**
Schnitt (-(e)s, -e) m cut;
(Schnittpunkt) intersection;
(Querschnitt) (cross) section;
(Durchschnitt) average; (eines
Kleides) style; **Schnitte** (-, -n) f
slice; (belegt) sandwich;
Schnittkäse m cheese slices pl;
Schnittlauch m chives pl;
Schnittmuster nt pattern;
Schnittstelle f (Inform, fig)
interface; **Schnittwunde** f cut,
gash
Schnitzel (-s, -) nt (Papier) scrap;
(Gastr) escalope
schnitzen vt to carve
Schnorchel (-s, -) m snorkel;
schnorcheln vi to go snorkelling,
to snorkel
schnüffeln vi, vt to sniff
Schnuller (-s, -) m dummy (Brit),
pacifier (US)
Schnulze (-, -n) f (Film, Roman)
weepie

Schnupfen (-s, -) m cold
schnuppern vi to sniff
Schnur (-, Schnüre) f string, cord;
(Elek) lead; **schnurlos** adj
(Telefon) cordless
Schnurrbart m moustache
schnurren vi to purr
Schnürsenkel (-s, -) m shoelace
schob imperf von **schieben**
Schock (-(e)s, -e) m shock; **unter
~ stehen** to be in a state of shock;
schockieren vt to shock
Schokolade f chocolate;
Schokoriegel m chocolate bar
Scholle (-, -n) f (Fisch) plaice; (Eis)
ice floe

SCHLÜSSELWORT

schon adv 1 (bereits) already; **er ist
schon da** he's there already, he's
already there; **ist er schon da?** is
he there yet?; **warst du schon
einmal da?** have you ever been
there?; **ich war schon einmal da**
I've been there before; **das war
schon immer so** that has always
been the case; **schon oft** often;
hast du schon gehört? have you
heard?
2 (bestimmt) all right; **du wirst
schon sehen** you'll see (all right);
das wird schon noch gut that'll
be OK
3 (bloß) just; **allein schon das
Gefühl ...** just the very feeling ...;
schon der Gedanke the very
thought; **wenn ich das schon
höre** I only have to hear that
4 (einschränkend) **ja schon, aber ...**
yes (well), but ...
5 **schon möglich** possible; **schon
gut!** OK!; **du weißt schon** you
know; **komm schon!** come on!

schön adj beautiful; (nett) nice;
(Frau) beautiful, pretty; (Mann)

beautiful, handsome; (Wetter) fine;
~e Grüße best wishes; **~es
Wochenende** have a nice
weekend

schonen vt (pfleglich behandeln) to
look after ▷ vr: **sich ~** to take it
easy

Schönheit f beauty

Schonkost f light diet

schöpfen vt to scoop; (mit Kelle)
to ladle; **Schöpfkelle** f,
Schöpflöffel m ladle

Schöpfung f creation

Schoppen (-s, -) m glass (of
wine)

Schorf (-(e)s, -e) m scab

Schorle (-, -n) f spritzer

Schornstein m chimney;
Schornsteinfeger(in) (-s, -) m(f)
chimney sweep

schoss imperf von **schießen**

Schoß (-es, Schöße) m lap

Schotte (-n, -n) m Scot,
Scotsman; **Schottin** f Scot,
Scotswoman; **schottisch** adj
Scottish, Scots; **Schottland** nt
Scotland

schräg adj slanting; (Dach)
sloping; (Linie) diagonal; (fam:
unkonventionell) wacky

Schrank (-(e)s, Schränke) m
cupboard; (Kleiderschrank)
wardrobe (Brit), closet (US)

Schranke (-, -n) f barrier

Schrankwand f wall unit

Schraube (-, -n) f screw;
schrauben vt to screw; **Schrau-
bendreher** (-s, -) m screwdriver;
Schraubenschlüssel m spanner;
Schraubenzieher (-s, -) m screwdriver; **Schraubverschluss** m
screw top, screw cap

Schreck (-(e)s, -e) m, **Schrecken**
(-s, -) m terror; (Angst) fright; **jdm
einen ~ einjagen** to give sb a
fright; **schreckhaft** adj jumpy;
schrecklich adj terrible, dreadful

Schrei (-(e)s, -e) m scream; (Ruf)
shout

Schreibblock m writing pad;
schreiben (schrieb, geschrieben) vt,
vi to write; (buchstabieren) to spell;
wie schreibt man ...? how do you
spell ...?; **Schreiben** (-s, -) nt
writing; (Brief) letter;
Schreibfehler m spelling
mistake; **schreibgeschützt** adj
(Diskette) write-protected;
Schreibtisch m desk;
Schreibwaren pl stationery sing;
Schreibwarenladen m
stationer's

schreien (schrie, geschrie(e)n) vt, vi
to scream; (rufen) to shout

Schreiner(in) m(f) joiner;
Schreinerei f joiner's workshop

schrie imperf von **schreien**

schrieb imperf von **schreiben**

Schrift (-, -en) f writing;
(Handschrift) handwriting;
(Schriftart) typeface; (Schrifttyp)
font; **schriftlich** adj written ▷ adv
in writing; **würden Sie uns das
bitte ~ geben?** could we have
that in writing, please?; **Schrift-
steller(in)** (-s, -) m(f) writer

Schritt (-(e)s, -e) m step; **~ für
~** step by step; **~e gegen etw
unternehmen** to take steps
against sth; **Schrittgeschwind-
igkeit** f walking speed;
Schrittmacher m (Med)
pacemaker

Schrott (-(e)s, -e) m scrap metal;
(fig) rubbish

schrubben vi, vt to scrub;
Schrubber (-s, -) m scrubbing
brush

schrumpfen vi to shrink

Schubkarren (-s, -) m wheelbarrow; **Schublade** f drawer

schubsen vt to shove, to push

schüchtern adj shy

schuf imperf von **schaffen**

Schuh (-(e)s, -e) *m* shoe;
Schuhcreme *f* shoe polish;
Schuhgeschäft *nt* shoe shop;
Schuhgröße *f* shoe size;
Schuhlöffel *m* shoehorn

Schulabschluss *m* school-leaving qualification

schuld *adj*: **wer ist ~ daran?**
whose fault is it?; **er ist ~** it's his fault, he's to blame; **Schuld** (-) *f*
guilt; (*Verschulden*) fault; **~ haben**
to be to blame (*an +dat for*); **er hat ~** it's his fault; **sie gibt mir die ~ an dem Unfall** she blames me for the accident; **schulden** *vt* to owe (*jdm etw jdb sth*); **Schulden** *pl*
debts *pl*; **~ haben** to be in debt;
~ machen to run up debts; **seine ~ bezahlen** to pay off one's debts;
schuldig *adj* guilty (*an +dat of*);
(*gebührend*) due; **jdm etw ~ sein** to owe sb sth

Schule (-, -n) *f* school; **in der ~** at school; **in die ~ gehen** to go to school; **Schüler(in)** (-s, -) *m(f)*
(*jüngerer*) pupil; (*älterer*) student;
Schüleraustausch *m* school exchange; **Schulfach** *nt* subject;
Schulferien *pl* school holidays *pl*
(*Brit*) (*o vacation* (*US*)); **schulfrei**
adj: **morgen ist ~** there's no school tomorrow; **Schulfreund(in)** *m(f)*
schoolmate; **Schuljahr** *nt* school year; **Schulkenntnisse** *pl*: **~ in Französisch** school(-level) French;
Schulklasse *f* class; **Schul-
leiter(in)** *m(f)* headmaster/
headmistress (*Brit*), principal (*US*)

Schulter (-, -n) *f* shoulder;
Schulterblatt *nt* shoulder blade

Schulung *f* training;
(*Veranstaltung*) training course

schummeln *vi* (*fam*) to cheat

Schuppe (-, -n) *f* (*von Fisch*) scale;
schuppen *vt* to scale ▷ *vr*: **sich ~** to peel; **Schuppen** *pl* (*im Haar*)
dandruff *sing*

Schürfwunde *f* graze

Schürze (-, -n) *f* apron

Schuss (-es, Schüsse) *m* shot; **mit einem ~ Wodka** with a dash of vodka

Schüssel (-, -n) *f* bowl

Schuster(in) (-s, -) *m(f)*
shoemaker

Schutt (-(e)s) *m* rubble

Schüttelfrost *m* shivering fit;
schütteln *vt* to shake ▷ *vr*: **sich ~** to shake

schütten *vt* to pour; (*Zucker, Kies etc*) to tip ▷ *vi impers* to pour (down)

Schutz (-es) *m* protection (*gegen, vor against, from*); (*Unterschlupf*)
shelter; **jdn in ~ nehmen** to stand up for sb; **Schutzblech** *nt*
mudguard; **Schutzbrief** *m* travel insurance document for drivers;
Schutzbrille *f* (safety) goggles *pl*

Schütze (-n, -n) *m* (*beim Fußball*)
scorer; (*Astr*) Sagittarius

schützen *vt*: **jdn gegen/vor etw ~** to protect sb against/from sth;
Schutzimpfung *f* inoculation,
vaccination

schwach *adj* weak; **~e Augen**
poor eyesight *sing*; **Schwäche**
(-, -n) *f* weakness; **Schwachstelle**
f weak point; **Schwachstrom** *m*
low-voltage current

Schwager (-s, Schwäger) *m*
brother-in-law; **Schwägerin** *f*
sister-in-law

Schwalbe (-, -n) *f* swallow; (*beim Fußball*) dive

schwamm *imperf von*
schwimmen

Schwamm (-(e)s, Schwämme) *m*
sponge; **~ drüber!** (*fam*) let's forget it!

Schwan (-(e)s, Schwäne) *m* swan

schwanger *adj* pregnant; **im vierten Monat ~ sein** to be four

months pregnant; **Schwangerschaft** f pregnancy; **Schwanger-
schaftsabbruch** m abortion;
Schwangerschaftstest m
pregnancy test
schwanken vi to sway; (Preise,
Zahlen) to fluctuate; (zögern) to
hesitate; (taumeln) to stagger; **ich
schwanke zwischen A und B** I
can't decide between A and B
Schwanz (-es, Schwänze) m tail;
(vulg: Penis) cock
Schwarm (-(e)s, Schwärme) m
swarm; (fam: angehimmelte Person)
heartthrob; **schwärmen** vi to
swarm; **~ für** to be mad about
schwarz adj black; **mir wurde
~ vor Augen** everything went
black; **Schwarzarbeit** f illicit
work; **Schwarzbrot** nt black
bread; **schwarz|fahren** irr vi to
travel without a ticket; (ohne
Führerschein) to drive without a
licence; **Schwarzfahrer(in)** m(f)
fare-dodger; **Schwarzmarkt** m
black market; **schwarz|sehen** irr
vi (fam: pessimistisch sein) to be
pessimistic (für about);
Schwarzwald m Black Forest;
schwarzweiß adj black and
white
schwatzen vi to chatter;
Schwätzer(in) (-s, -) m(f) chat-
terbox; (Schwafler) gasbag;
(Klatschmaul) gossip
Schwebebahn f suspension
railway; **schweben** vi to float;
(hoch) to soar
Schwede (-n, -n) m Swede;
Schweden (-s) nt Sweden;
Schwedin f Swede; **schwedisch**
adj Swedish; **Schwedisch** nt
Swedish
Schwefel (-s) m sulphur
schweigen (schwieg, geschwiegen)
vi to be silent; (nicht mehr reden) to
stop talking; **Schweigen** (-s) nt

silence; **Schweigepflicht** f duty
of confidentiality; **die ärztliche
~** medical confidentiality
Schwein (-(e)s, -e) nt pig; (fam:
Glück) luck; (pej: gemeiner Mensch)
swine; **Schweinebraten** m roast
pork; **Schweinefleisch** nt pork;
Schweinegrippe f swine flu;
Schweinerei f mess; (Gemeinheit)
dirty trick
Schweiß (-es) m sweat
schweißen vt, vi to weld
Schweiz (-) f: **die ~** Switzerland;
Schweizer(in) (-s, -) m(f) Swiss;
Schweizerdeutsch nt Swiss
German; **schweizerisch** adj
Swiss
Schwelle (-, -n) f doorstep; (a.
fig) threshold
schwellen vi to swell (up);
Schwellung f swelling
schwer adj heavy; (schwierig)
difficult, hard; (schlimm) serious,
bad; **er ist ~ zu verstehen** it's
difficult to understand what he's
saying ▷ adv (sehr) really; (verletzt
etc) seriously, badly; **etw
~ nehmen** to take sth hard;
Schwerbehinderte(r) mf severely
disabled person; **schwer|fallen** irr
vi (Schwierigkeiten bereiten) **jdm
~** to be difficult for sb;
schwerhörig adj hard of hearing
Schwert (-(e)s, -er) nt sword;
Schwertlilie f iris
Schwester (-, -n) f sister; (Med)
nurse
schwieg imperf von **schweigen**
Schwiegereltern pl parents-in-
law pl; **Schwiegermutter** f
mother-in-law; **Schwiegersohn**
m son-in-law; **Schwiegertochter**
f daughter-in-law; **Schwiegervater** m father-in-law
schwierig adj difficult, hard;
Schwierigkeit f difficulty; **in ~en
kommen** to get into trouble; **jdm**

~en machen to make things difficult for sb

Schwimmbad nt swimming pool; **Schwimmbecken** nt swimming pool; **schwimmen** (schwamm, geschwommen) vi to swim; (treiben) to float; (fig: unsicher sein) to be at sea; **Schwimmer(in)** m(f) swimmer; **Schwimmflosse** f flipper; **Schwimmflügel** m water wing; **Schwimmreifen** m rubber ring; **Schwimmweste** f life jacket

Schwindel (-s) m dizziness; (Anfall) dizzy spell; (Betrug) swindle; **schwindelfrei** adj: **nicht ~ sein** to suffer from vertigo; **~ sein** to have a head for heights; **schwindlig** adj dizzy; **mir ist ~** I feel dizzy

Schwips m: **einen ~ haben** to be tipsy

schwitzen vi to sweat

schwoll imperf von **schwellen**

schwor imperf von **schwören**

schwören (schwor, geschworen) vt, vi to swear; **einen Eid ~** to take an oath

schwul adj gay

schwül adj close

Schwung (-(e)s, Schwünge) m swing; (Triebkraft) momentum; (fig: Energie) energy; (fam: Menge) batch; **in ~ kommen** to get going

Schwur (-s, Schwüre) m oath

scrollen vi (Inform) to scroll

sechs num six; **Sechs** (-, -en) f six; (Schulnote) = F; **Sechserpack** m sixpack; **sechshundert** num six hundred; **sechsmal** adv six times; **sechste(r, s)** adj sixth; siehe auch **dritte**; **Sechstel** (-s, -) nt sixth; **sechzehn** num sixteen; **sechzehnte(r, s)** adj sixteenth; siehe auch **dritte**; **sechzig** num sixty; **in den ~er Jahren** in the

sixties; **sechzigste(r, s)** adj sixtieth

Secondhandladen m secondhand shop

See (-, -n) f sea; **an der ~** by the sea ▷ (-s, -n) m lake; **am ~** by the lake; **Seegang** m waves; **hoher/schwerer/leichter ~** rough/heavy/calm seas pl; **Seehund** m seal; **Seeigel** m sea urchin; **seekrank** adj seasick

Seele (-, -n) f soul

seelisch adj mental, psychological

Seelöwe m sea lion; **Seemann** m sailor, seaman; **Seemeile** f nautical mile; **Seemöwe** f seagull; **Seenot** f distress (at sea); **Seepferdchen** nt sea horse; **Seerose** f water lily; **Seestern** m starfish; **Seezunge** f sole

Segel (-s, -) nt sail; **Segelboot** nt yacht; **Segelfliegen** (-s) nt gliding; **Segelflugzeug** nt glider; **segeln** vt, vi to sail; **Segelschiff** nt sailing ship

sehbehindert adj partially sighted

sehen (sah, gesehen) vt, vi to see; (in bestimmte Richtung) to look; **gut/schlecht ~** to have good/bad eyesight; **auf die Uhr ~** to look at one's watch; **kann ich das mal ~?** can I have a look at it?; **wir ~ uns morgen!** see you tomorrow!; **ich kenne sie nur vom Sehen** I only know her by sight; **Sehenswürdigkeiten** pl sights pl

Sehne (-, -n) f tendon; (an Bogen) string

sehnen vr: **sich ~** to long (nach for)

Sehnenscheidenentzündung f (Med) tendovaginitis;

Sehnenzerrung f (Med) pulled tendon

Sehnsucht f longing; **sehnsüchtig** adj longing

sehr adv (vor Adjektiv, Adverb) very; (mit Verben) a lot, very much; **zu ~** too much

seicht adj shallow

Seide (-, -n) f silk

Seife (-, -n) f soap; **Seifenoper** f soap (opera); **Seifenschale** f soap dish

Seil (-(e)s, -e) nt rope; (Kabel) cable; **Seilbahn** f cable railway

🔵 SCHLÜSSELWORT

sein¹ (pt war, pp gewesen) vi 1 to be; **ich bin** I am; **du bist** you are; **er/sie/es ist** he/she/it is; **wir sind/ihr seid/sie sind** we/you/they are; **wir waren** we were; **wir sind gewesen** we have been

2 **seien Sie nicht böse** don't be angry; **sei so gut und ...** be so kind as to ...; **das wäre gut** that would o that'd be a good thing; **wenn ich ... wäre** if I were o was you; **das wär's** that's all, that's it; **morgen bin ich in Rom** tomorrow I'll o I will o I shall be in Rome; **waren Sie mal in Rom?** have you ever been to Rome?

3 **wie ist das zu verstehen?** how is that to be understood?; **er ist nicht zu ersetzen** he cannot be replaced; **mit ihr ist nicht zu reden** you can't talk to her

4 **mir ist kalt** I'm cold; **was ist?** what's the matter?, what is it?; **ist was?** is something the matter?; **es sei denn, dass ...** unless ...; **wie dem auch sei** be that as it may; **wie wäre es mit ...?** how o what about ...?; **lass das sein!** stop that!

sein² pron possessiv von **er**; (adjektivisch) his ▷ pron possessiv von **es**; (adjektivisch) its; (adjektivisch, männlich) his; (weiblich) her; (weiblich) its; **das ist ~e Tasche** that's his bag; **jeder hat ~e Sorgen** everyone has their problems; **seine(r, s)** pron possessiv von **er**; (substantivisch) his ▷ pron possessiv von **es**; (substantivisch) its; (substantivisch, männlich) his; (weiblich) hers; **das ist ~r/~/~s** that's his/hers; **seiner** pron gen von **er**; of him ▷ pron gen von **es**; of it; **seinetwegen** adv (wegen ihm) because of him; (ihm zuliebe) for his sake; (um ihn) about him; (von ihm aus) as far as he is concerned

seit conj (bei Zeitpunkt) since; (bei Zeitraum) for; **er ist ~ Montag hier** he's been here since Monday; **er ist ~ einer Woche hier** he's been here for a week; **~ langem** for a long time; **seitdem** adv, conj since

Seite (-, -n) f side; (in Buch) page; **zur ~ gehen** to step aside; **Seitenairbag** m side-impact airbag; **Seitenaufprallschutz** m (Auto) side-impact protection; **Seitensprung** m affair; **Seitenstechen** (-s) nt: **~ haben/bekommen** to have/get a stitch; **Seitenstraße** f side street; **Seitenstreifen** m hard shoulder (Brit), shoulder (US); **Seitenwind** m crosswind

seither adv since (then)

seitlich adj side

Sekretär(in) m(f) secretary; **Sekretariat** (-s, -e) nt secretary's office

Sekt (-(e)s, -e) m sparkling wine (similar to champagne)

Sekte (-, -n) f sect

Sekunde (-, -n) f second;
Sekundenkleber (-s, -) m superglue; **Sekundenschnelle** f: **es
geschah alles in ~** it was all over
in a matter of seconds

○ SCHLÜSSELWORT

selbst pron **1** ich/er/wir selbst I
myself/he himself/we ourselves;
sie ist die Tugend selbst she's
virtue itself; **er braut sein Bier
selbst** he brews his own beer; **wie
geht's? — gut, und selbst?** how
are things? — fine, and yourself?
2 (ohne Hilfe) alone, on
my/his/one's etc own; **von selbst**
by itself; **er kam von selbst** he
came of his own accord; **selbst
gemacht** home-made
▷ adv even; **selbst wenn** even if;
selbst Gott even God (himself)

selbständig adj siehe
selbstständig
Selbstauslöser (-s, -) m (Foto)
self-timer; **Selbstbedienung** f
self-service; **Selbstbefriedigung** f
masturbation;
Selbstbeherrschung f
self-control; **Selbstbeteiligung** f
(einer Versicherung) excess;
selbstbewusst adj
(self-)confident; **Selbstbräuner**
(-s, -) m self-tanning lotion;
selbstgemacht adj self-made;
selbstklebend adj self-adhesive;
Selbstlaut m vowel; **Selbstmord**
m suicide; **Selbstmordattentat**
nt suicide bombing; **Selbstmord-
attentäter(in)** m(f) suicide
bomber; **selbstsicher** adj
self-assured; **selbstständig** adj
independent; (arbeitend)
self-employed; **Selbstverpflegung**
f self-catering;
selbstverständlich adj obvious;

ich halte das für ~ I take that for
granted ▷ adv naturally;
Selbstvertrauen nt
self-confidence

Sellerie (-s, -(s)) m (-, -n) f (Knollensellerie) celeriac; (Stangensellerie)
celery

selten adj rare ▷ adv seldom,
rarely

seltsam adj strange;
~ schmecken/riechen to
taste/smell strange

Semester (-s, -) nt semester;
Semesterferien pl vacation sing

Semikolon (-s, Semikola) nt
semicolon

Seminar (-s, -e) nt seminar;

Semmel (-, -n) f roll;
Semmelbrösel pl breadcrumbs

Senat (-(e)s, -e) m senate

senden (sandte, gesandt) vt to
send ▷ vt, vi (Radio, TV) to
broadcast; **Sender** (-s, -) m (TV)
channel; (Radio) station; (Anlage)
transmitter; **Sendung** f (Radio,
TV) broadcasting; (Programm)
programme

Senf (-(e)s, -e) m mustard

Senior(in) m(f) senior citizen;
Seniorenpass m senior citizen's
travel pass

senken vt to lower ▷ vr: **sich
~** to sink

senkrecht adj vertical

Sensation (-, -en) f sensation

sensibel adj sensitive

sentimental adj sentimental

separat adj separate

September (-(s), -) m
September; siehe auch **Juni**

Serbien (-s) nt Serbia

Serie f series sing

seriös adj (ernsthaft) serious;
(anständig) respectable

Serpentine f hairpin (bend)

Serum (-s, Seren) nt serum

Server (-s, -) m (Inform) server

Service (-(s), -) nt (Geschirr)
service ▷ (-, -s) m service
servieren vt, vi to serve
Serviette f napkin, serviette
Servolenkung f (Auto) power
steering
Sesam (-s, -s) m sesame seeds pl
Sessel (-s, -) m armchair;
Sessellift m chairlift
Set (-s, -s) m o nt (: Tischset)
tablemat
setzen vt to put; (Baum etc) to
plant; (Segel) to set ▷ vr: **sich ~** to
settle; (hinsetzen) to sit down; **~ Sie
sich doch** please sit down
Seuche (-, -n) f epidemic
seufzen vt, vi to sigh
Sex (-(es)) m sex; **Sexismus** m
sexism; **sexistisch** adj sexist;
Sextourismus m sex tourism;
Sexualität f sexuality; **sexuell**
adj sexual
Seychellen pl Seychelles pl
sfr abk = Schweizer Franken Swiss
franc(s)
Shampoo (-s, -s) nt shampoo
Shareware (-, -s) f (Inform)
shareware
Shorts pl shorts pl
Shuttlebus m shuttle bus

⬤ SCHLÜSSELWORT

sich pron 1 (akk) **er/sie/es ... sich**
he/she/it ... himself/herself/itself;
sie pl/man ... sich they/one ...
themselves/oneself; **Sie ... sich**
you ... yourself/yourselves pl; **sich
wiederholen** to repeat
oneself/itself

2 (dat) **er/sie/es ... sich** he/she/it
... to himself/herself/itself; **sie
pl/man ... sich** they/one ... to
themselves/oneself; **Sie ... sich**
you ... to yourself/yourselves pl;
**sie hat sich einen Pullover
gekauft** she bought herself a

jumper; **sich die Haare waschen**
to wash one's hair

3 (mit Präposition) **haben Sie Ihren
Ausweis bei sich?** do you have
your pass on you?; **er hat nichts
bei sich** he's got nothing on him;
sie bleiben gern unter sich they
keep themselves to themselves
4 (einander) each other, one
another; **sie bekämpfen sich** they
fight each other o one another
5 **dieses Auto fährt sich gut** this
car drives well; **hier sitzt es sich
gut** it's good to sit here

sicher adj safe (vor +dat from);
(gewiss) certain (gen of);
(zuverlässig) reliable; (selbstsicher)
confident; **aber ~!** of course, sure;
Sicherheit f safety; (Aufgabe von
Sicherheitsbeamten) (Fin) security;
(Gewissheit) certainty;
(Selbstsicherheit) confidence; **mit
~** definitely; **Sicherheitsabstand**
m safe distance; **Sicherheitsgurt**
m seat belt; **sicherheitshalber**
adv just to be on the safe side;
Sicherheitsnadel f safety pin;
Sicherheitsvorkehrung f safety
precaution; **sicherlich** adv
certainly; (wahrscheinlich) probably

sichern vt to secure (gegen
against); (schützen) to protect;
(Daten) to back up; **Sicherung** f
(Sichern) securing; (Vorrichtung)
safety device; (an Waffen) safety
catch; (Elek) fuse; (Inform) backup;
die ~ ist durchgebrannt the fuse
has blown
Sicht (-) f sight; (Aussicht) view;
sichtbar adj visible; **sichtlich**
adj evident, obvious;
Sichtverhältnisse pl visibility
sing; **Sichtweite** f: **in/außer
~** within/out of sight
sie pron (3. Person sing) she; (3.
Person pl) they; (akk von sing) her;

(akk von pl) them; (für eine Sache) it; **da ist ~ ja** there she is; **da sind ~ ja** there they are; **ich kenne ~** (Frau) I know her; (mehrere Personen) I know them; **~ lag gerade noch hier** (meine Jacke, Uhr) it was here just a minute ago; **ich hab ~ gefunden** (meine Jacke, Uhr) I've found it; **hast du meine Brille/Hose gesehen? — ich kann ~ nirgends finden** have you seen my glasses/trousers? — I can't find them anywhere

Sie pron (Höflichkeitsform, Nom und Akk) you

Sieb (-(e)s, -e) nt sieve; (Teesieb) strainer

sieben num seven; **siebenhundert** num seven hundred; **siebenmal** adv seven times; **siebte(r, s)** adj seventh; siehe auch **dritte**; **Siebtel** (-s, -) nt seventh; **siebzehn** num seventeen; **siebzehnte(r, s)** adj seventeenth; siehe auch **dritte**; **siebzig** num seventy; **in den ~er Jahren** in the seventies; **siebzigste(r, s)** adj seventieth

Siedlung (-, -en) f (Wohngebiet) housing estate (Brit) (o development (US))

Sieg (-(e)s, -e) m victory; **siegen** vi to win; **Sieger(in)** (-s, -) m(f) winner; **Siegerehrung** f presentation ceremony

siehe imper see

siezen vt to address as "Sie"

Signal (-s, -e) nt signal

Silbe (-, -n) f syllable

Silber (-s) nt silver; **Silberhochzeit** f silver wedding; **Silbermedaille** f silver medal

Silikon (-s, -e) nt silicone

Silvester (-s, -) nt, **Silvesterabend** m New Year's Eve, Hogmanay (Scot)

● **Silvester** is the German name
● for New Year's Eve. Although
● not an official holiday, most
● businesses close early and
● shops shut at midday. Most
● Germans celebrate in the
● evening and at midnight they
● let off fireworks and rockets;
● the revelry usually lasts until the
● early hours of the morning.

Simbabwe (-s) nt Zimbabwe

SIM-Karte f SIM card

simpel adj simple

simultan adj simultaneous

simsen vt, vi (fam) to text

Sinfonie (-, -n) f symphony; **Sinfonieorchester** nt symphony orchestra

Singapur (-s) nt Singapore

singen (sang, gesungen) vt, vi to sing; **richtig/falsch ~** to sing in tune/out of tune

Single (-, -s) f (CD) single ▷ (-s, -s) m (Mensch) single

Singular m singular

sinken (sank, gesunken) vi to sink; (Preise etc) to fall, to go down

Sinn (-(e)s, -e) m (Denken) mind; (Wahrnehmung) sense; (Bedeutung) sense, meaning; **~ machen** to make sense; **das hat keinen ~** it's no use; **sinnlich** adj sensuous; (erotisch) sensual; (Wahrnehmung) sensory; **sinnlos** adj (unsinnig) stupid; (Verhalten) senseless; (zwecklos) pointless; (bedeutungslos) meaningless; **sinnvoll** adj meaningful; (vernünftig) sensible

Sirup (-s, -e) m syrup

Sitte (-, -n) f custom

Situation f situation

Sitz (-es, -e) m seat; **sitzen** (saß, gesessen) vi to sit; (Bemerkung, Schlag) to strike home; (Gelerntes) to have sunk in; **der Rock sitzt**

gut the skirt is a good fit;
~ bleiben (Schule) to have to repeat
a year; **Sitzgelegenheit** f place to
sit down; **Sitzplatz** m seat;
Sitzung f meeting

Sizilien (-s) nt Sicily
Skandal (-s, -e) m scandal
Skandinavien (-s) nt
Scandinavia
Skateboard (-s, -s) nt
skateboard: **skateboarden** vi to
skateboard
Skelett (-s, -e) nt skeleton
skeptisch adj sceptical
Ski (-s, -er) m ski: **~ laufen** (o
fahren) to ski; **Skianzug** m ski
suit; **Skibrille** f ski goggles pl;
Skifahren (-s) nt skiing; **Skigebiet**
(-s, -e) nt skiing area; **Skihose** f
skiing trousers pl; **Skikurs** m
skiing course; **Skilanglauf** m
cross-country skiing; **Skiläufer(in)**
m(f) skier; **Skilehrer(in)** m(f) ski
instructor; **Skilift** m ski-lift
Skinhead (-s, -s) m skinhead
Skipiste f ski run; **Skischanze**
(-, -n) f ski jump; **Skischuh** m
ski boot; **Skischule** f ski school;
Skispringen (-s, -n) nt ski jumping;
Skistiefel (-s, -) m ski boot;
Skistock m ski pole; **Skiträger** m
ski rack; **Skiurlaub** m skiing
holiday (Brit) (o vacation (US))
Skizze (-, -n) f sketch
Skonto (-s, -s) m o nt discount
Skorpion (-s, -e) m (Zool)
scorpion; (Astr) Scorpio
Skulptur (-, -en) f sculpture
S-Kurve f double bend
Slalom (-s, -s) m slalom
Slip (-s, -s) m (pair of) briefs pl;
Slipeinlage f panty liner
Slowakei (-) f Slovakia;
slowakisch adj Slovakian;
S~ Republik Slovak Republic;
Slowakisch nt Slovakian
Slowenien (-s) nt Slovenia;

slowenisch adj Slovenian;
Slowenisch nt Slovenian
Smiley (-s, -s) m smiley
Smog (-s, -s) m smog; **Smogalarm**
m smog alert
Smoking (-s, -s) m dinner jacket
(Brit), tuxedo (US)
SMS nt abk = **Short Message
Service** ▷ f (Nachricht) text
message; **ich schicke dir eine ~** I'll
text you, I'll send you a text
Snowboard (-s, -s) nt snow-
board; **snowboarden** vi to
snowboard; **Snowboardfahren**
(-s) nt snowboarding;
Snowboardfahrer(in) m(f)
snowboarder

○ SCHLÜSSELWORT

so adv 1 (so sehr) so; **so groß/schön
etc** so big/nice etc; **so groß/schön
wie ... als** big/nice as ...; **so viel
(wie)** as much as; **rede nicht so
viel** don't talk so much; **so weit
sein** to be ready; **so weit wie** o **als
möglich** as far as possible; **ich bin
so weit zufrieden** by and large I'm
quite satisfied; **so wenig (wie)** as
little (as); **das hat ihn so
geärgert, dass ...** that annoyed
him so much that ...; **so einer wie
ich** somebody like me; **na so was!**
well, well!
2 (auf diese Weise) like this; **mach
es nicht so** don't do it like that; **so
oder so** in one way or the other;
und so weiter and so on; **... oder
so was** ... or something like that;
das ist gut so that's fine
3 (fam) (umsonst) **ich habe es so
bekommen** I got it for nothing
▷ konj: **sodass** so that; **so wie es
jetzt ist** as things are at the
moment
▷ excl: **so?** really?; **so, das wär's**
so, that's it then

s. o. abk = **siehe oben** see above

sobald conj as soon as

Socke (-, -n) f sock

Sodbrennen (-s) nt heartburn

Sofa (-s, -s) nt sofa

sofern conj if, provided (that)

soff imperf von **saufen**

sofort adv immediately, at once; **Sofortbildkamera** f instant camera

Softeis nt soft ice-cream

Software (-, -s) f software

sog imperf von **saugen**

sogar adv even; **kalt, ~ sehr kalt** cold, in fact very cold

sogenannt adj so-called

Sohle (-, -n) f sole

Sohn (-(e)s, Söhne) m son

Soja (-, Sojen) f soya; **Sojasprossen** pl bean sprouts pl

solang(e) conj as long as

Solarium nt solarium

Solarzelle f solar cell

solche(r, s) pron such; **eine ~ Frau, solch eine Frau** such a woman, a woman like that; **~ Sachen** things like that, such things; **ich habe ~ Kopfschmerzen** I've got such a headache; **ich habe ~n Hunger** I'm so hungry

Soldat(in) (-en, -en) m(f) soldier

solidarisch adj showing solidarity; **sich ~ erklären mit** to declare one's solidarity with

solid(e) adj solid; (Leben, Mensch) respectable

Soll (-(s), -(s)) nt (Fin) debit; (Arbeitsmenge) quota, target

⊙ **SCHLÜSSELWORT**

sollen (pt **sollte**, pp **gesollt** o (als Hilfsverb) **sollen**) Hilfsverb **1** (Pflicht, Befehl) to be supposed to; **du hättest nicht gehen sollen** you shouldn't have gone, you oughtn't to have gone; **soll ich?** shall I?; **soll**

ich dir helfen? shall I help you?; **sag ihm, er soll warten** tell him he's to wait; **was soll ich machen?** what should I do?

2 (Vermutung) **sie soll verheiratet sein** she's said to be married; **was soll das heißen?** what's that supposed to mean?; **man sollte glauben, dass ...** you would think that ...; **sollte das passieren, ...** if that should happen ...

▷ vt, vi: **was soll das?** what's all this?; **das sollst du nicht** you shouldn't do that; **was soll's?** what the hell!

Solo (-s, -) nt solo

Sommer (-s, -) m summer; **Sommerfahrplan** m summer timetable; **Sommerferien** pl summer holidays pl (Brit) o vacation sing (US)); **sommerlich** adj summery; (Sommer-) summer; **Sommerreifen** m normal tyre; **Sommersprossen** pl freckles pl; **Sommerzeit** f summertime; (Uhrzeit) daylight saving time

Sonderangebot nt special offer; **sonderbar** adj strange, odd; **Sondermarke** f special stamp; **Sondermaschine** f special plane; **Sondermüll** m hazardous waste

sondern conj but; **nicht nur ..., ~ auch** not only ..., but also

Sonderpreis m special price; **Sonderschule** f special school; **Sonderzeichen** nt (Inform) special character; **Sonderzug** m special train

Song (-s, -s) m song

Sonnabend m Saturday; siehe auch **Mittwoch**; **sonnabends** adv on Saturdays; **~ morgens** on Saturday mornings; siehe auch **mittwochs**

Sonne (-, -n) f sun; **sonnen** vr:
sich ~ to sunbathe;
Sonnenaufgang m sunrise;
Sonnenblume f sunflower;
Sonnenblumenkern m sunflower seed; **Sonnenbrand** m
sunburn; **Sonnenbrille** f
sunglasses pl, shades pl;
Sonnencreme f sun cream;
Sonnendach nt (an Haus)
awning; (Auto) sunroof; **Sonnen-
deck** nt sun deck; **Sonnenmilch** f
suntan lotion; **Sonnenöl** nt
suntan oil; **Sonnenschein** m
sunshine; **Sonnenschirm** m
parasol, sunshade; **Sonnenschutz-
creme** f sunscreen; **Sonnenstich**
m sunstroke; **Sonnenstudio** nt
solarium; **Sonnenuhr** f sundial;
Sonnenuntergang m sunset;
sonnig adj sunny
Sonntag m Sunday; siehe auch
Mittwoch; **sonntags** adv on
Sundays; siehe auch **mittwochs**
sonst adv, conj (außerdem) else;
(andernfalls) otherwise, (or) else;
(mit Pron, in Fragen) else;
(normalerweise) normally, usually;
~ noch etwas? anything else?;
~ nichts nothing else
sooft conj whenever
Sopran (-s, -e) m soprano
Sorge (-, -n) f worry; (Fürsorge)
care; **sich** (dat) **um jdn ~ machen**
to be worried about sb; **sorgen**
vi: **für jdn ~** to look after sb; **für
etw ~** to take care of sth, to see to
sth ▷ vr: **sich ~** to worry (um
about); **sorgfältig** adj careful
sortieren vt to sort (out)
Sortiment nt assortment
sosehr conj however much
Soße (-, -n) f sauce; (zu Braten)
gravy
Soundkarte f (Inform) sound card
Souvenir (-s, -s) nt souvenir
soviel conj as far as

soweit conj as far as
sowie conj (wie auch) as well as;
(sobald) as soon as
sowohl conj: **~ ... als** (o **wie**) **auch**
both ... and
sozial adj social; **~er
Wohnungsbau** public-sector
housing (programme); **~es
Netzwerk** social networking site;
Sozialhilfe f income support
(Brit), welfare (aid) (US);
Sozialismus m socialism;
Sozialkunde f social studies pl;
Sozialversicherung f social
security; **Sozialwohnung** f
council flat (Brit), state-subsidized
apartment (US)
Soziologie f sociology
sozusagen adv so to speak
Spachtel (-s, -) m spatula
Spag(h)etti pl spaghetti sing
Spalte (-, -n) f crack; (Gletscher)
crevasse; (in Text) column
spalten vt to split
Spam (-s, -s) nt (Inform) spam
Spange (-, -n) f clasp; (Haar-
spange) slide (Brit), barrette (US)
Spanien (-s) nt Spain;
Spanier(in) (-s, -) m(f) Spaniard;
spanisch adj Spanish; **Spanisch**
nt Spanish
spann imperf von **spinnen**
spannen vt (straffen) to tighten;
(befestigen) to brace ▷ vi to be tight
spannend adj exciting, gripping;
Spannung f tension; (Elek)
voltage; (fig) suspense
Sparbuch nt savings book;
(Konto) savings account; **sparen**
vt, vi to save
Spargel (-s, -) m asparagus
Sparkasse f savings bank;
Sparkonto nt savings account
spärlich adj meagre; (Bekleidung)
scanty
sparsam adj economical;
Sparschwein nt piggy bank

S

Spaß (-es, Späße) m joke; (Freude)
fun; **es macht mir ~** I enjoy it, it's
(great) fun; **viel ~!** have fun

spät adj, adv late; **zu ~ kommen**
to be late

Spaten (-s, -) m spade

später adj, adv later; **spätestens**
adv at the latest; **Spätvorstellung**
f late-night performance

Spatz (-en, -en) m sparrow

spazieren vi to stroll, to walk;
~ gehen to go for a walk;
Spaziergang m walk

Specht (-(e)s, -e) m woodpecker

Speck (-(e)s, -e) m bacon fat;
(durchwachsen) bacon

Spedition f (für Umzug) removal
firm

Speiche (-, -n) f spoke

Speichel (-s) m saliva

Speicher (-s, -) m storehouse;
(Dachboden) attic; (Inform)
memory; **Speicherkarte** f
memory card; **speichern** vt
(Inform) to store; (sichern) to save

Speise (-, -n) f food; (Gericht)
dish; **Speisekarte** f menu;
Speiseröhre f gullet,
oesophagus; **Speisesaal** m
dining hall; **Speisewagen** m
dining car

Spende (-, -n) f donation;
spenden vt to donate, to give

spendieren vt: **jdm etw ~** to
treat sb to sth

Sperre (-, -n) f barrier; (Verbot)
ban; **sperren** vt to block; (Sport)
to suspend; (verbieten) to ban

Sperrgepäck nt bulky luggage;
Sperrstunde f closing time;
Sperrung f closing

Spesen pl expenses pl

spezialisieren vr: **sich ~** to
specialize (auf+akk in);
Spezialist(in) m(f) specialist;
Spezialität f speciality (Brit),
specialty (US); **speziell** adj

special ▷ adv especially

Spiegel (-s, -) m mirror;
Spiegelei nt fried egg (sunny-side
up (US)); **spiegelglatt** adj very
slippery; **Spiegelreflexkamera** f
reflex camera

Spiel (-(e)s, -e) nt game; (Tätigkeit)
play(ing); (Karten) pack, deck;
(Tech) (free) play; **Spielautomat** m
(ohne Geldgewinn) gaming
machine; (mit Geldgewinn) slot
machine; **spielen** vt, vi to play;
(um Geld) to gamble; (Theat) to
perform, to act; **Klavier ~** to play
the piano; **spielend** adv easily;
Spieler(in) (-s, -) m(f) player; (um
Geld) gambler; **Spielfeld** nt (für
Fußball, Hockey) field; (für
Basketball) court; **Spielfilm** m
feature film; **Spielkasino** nt
casino; **Spielkonsole** f games
console; **Spielplatz** m
playground; **Spielraum** m room
to manoeuvre; **Spielregel** f rule;
sich an die ~n halten to stick to
the rules; **Spielsachen** pl toys pl;
Spielzeug nt toys pl; (einzelnes)
toy

Spieß (-es, -e) m spear; (Bratspieß)
spit; **Spießer(in)** (-s, -) m(f)
square, stuffy type; **spießig** adj
square, uncool

Spikes pl (Sport) spikes pl; (Auto)
studs pl

Spinat (-(e)s, -e) m spinach

Spinne (-, -n) f spider; **spinnen**
(spann, gesponnen) vt, vi to spin;
(fam: Unsinn reden) to talk rubbish;
(verrückt sein) to be crazy; **du
spinnst!** you must be mad;
Spinnwebe (-, -n) f cobweb

Spion(in) (-s, -e) m(f) spy;
spionieren vi to spy; (fig) to
snoop around

Spirale (-, -n) f spiral; (Med) coil

Spirituosen pl spirits pl, liquor
sing (US)

Spiritus (-, -se) m spirit

spitz adj (Nase, Kinn) pointed; (Bleistift, Messer) sharp; (Winkel) acute; **Spitze** (-, -n) f point; (von Finger, Nase) tip; (Bemerkung) taunt, dig; (erster Platz) lead; (Gewebe) lace; **Spitzer** (-s, -) m pencil sharpener; **Spitzname** m nickname

Spliss (-) m split ends pl

sponsern vt to sponsor; **Sponsor(in)** (-s, -en) m(f) sponsor

spontan adj spontaneous

Sport (-(e)s, -e) m sport; **~ treiben** to do sport; **Sportanlage** f sports grounds pl; **Sportart** f sport; **Sportbekleidung** f sportswear; **Sportgeschäft** nt sports shop; **Sporthalle** f gymnasium, gym; **Sportlehrer(in)** (-s, -) m(f) sports instructor; (Schule) PE teacher; **Sportler(in)** (-s, -) m(f) sportsman/-woman; **sportlich** adj sporting; (Mensch) sporty; **Sportplatz** m playing field; **Sporttauchen** nt (skin-)diving; (mit Gerät) scuba-diving; **Sportverein** m sports club; **Sportwagen** m sports car

sprach imperf von **sprechen**

Sprache (-, -n) f language; (Sprechen) speech; **Sprachenschule** f language school; **Sprachführer** m phrasebook; **Sprachkenntnisse** pl knowledge sing of languages; **gute englische ~ haben** to have a good knowledge of English; **Sprachkurs** m language course; **Sprachunterricht** m language teaching

sprang imperf von **springen**

Spray (-s, -s) m o nt spray

Sprechanlage f intercom; **sprechen** (sprach, gesprochen) vt, vi

to speak (jdn, mit jdm to sb); (sich unterhalten) to talk (mit to, über, von about); **~ Sie Deutsch?** do you speak German?; **kann ich bitte mit David ~?** (am Telefon) can I speak to David, please?; **Sprecher(in)** m(f) speaker; (Ansager) announcer; **Sprechstunde** f consultation; (Arzt) surgery hours pl; (Anwalt etc) office hours pl; **Sprechzimmer** nt consulting room

Sprengstoff m explosive

Sprichwort nt proverb

Springbrunnen m fountain

springen (sprang, gesprungen) vi to jump; (Glas) to crack; (mit Kopfsprung) to dive

Sprit (-(e)s, -e) m (fam: Benzin) petrol (Brit), gas (US)

Spritze (-, -n) f (Gegenstand) syringe; (Injektion) injection; (an Schlauch) nozzle; **spritzen** vt to spray; (Med) to inject ▷ vi to splash; (Med) to give injections

Spruch (-(e)s, Sprüche) m saying

Sprudel (-s, -) m sparkling mineral water; (süßer) fizzy drink (Brit), soda (US); **sprudeln** vi to bubble

Sprühdose f aerosol (can); **sprühen** vt, vi to spray; (fig) to sparkle; **Sprühregen** m drizzle

Sprung (-(e)s, Sprünge) m jump; (Riss) crack; **Sprungbrett** nt springboard; **Sprungschanze** f ski jump; **Sprungturm** m diving platforms pl

Spucke (-) f spit; **spucken** vt, vi to spit; (fam: sich erbrechen) to vomit; **Spucktüte** f sick bag

spuken vi (Geist) to walk; **hier spukt es** this place is haunted

Spülbecken nt sink

Spule (-, -n) f spool; (Elek) coil

Spüle (-, -n) f sink; **spülen** vt, vi to rinse; (Geschirr) to wash up;

(Toilette) to flush; **Spülmaschine** f dishwasher; **Spülmittel** nt washing-up liquid *(Brit)*, dishwashing liquid *(US)*; **Spültuch** nt dishcloth; **Spülung** f *(von WC)* flush

Spur (-, -en) f trace; *(Fußspur, Radspur)* track; *(Fährte)* trail; *(Fahrspur)* lane; **die ~ wechseln** to change lanes pl

spüren vt to feel; *(merken)* to notice; **Spürhund** m sniffer dog

Squash (-) nt squash; **Squashschläger** m squash racket

Sri Lanka (-s) nt Sri Lanka

Staat (-(e)s, -en) m state; **staatlich** adj state(-); *(vom Staat betrieben)* state-run; **Staatsangehörigkeit** f nationality; **Staatsanwalt** m, **-anwältin** f prosecuting counsel *(Brit)*, district attorney *(US)*; **Staatsbürger(in)** m(f) citizen; **Staatsbürgerschaft** f nationality; **doppelte ~** dual nationality; **Staatsexamen** nt final exam taken by trainee teachers, medical and law students

Stab (-(e)s, Stäbe) m rod; *(Gitter)* bar; **Stäbchen** nt *(Essstäbchen)* chopstick; **Stabhochsprung** m pole vault

stabil adj stable; *(Möbel)* sturdy

stach imperf von **stechen**

Stachel (-s, -n) m spike; *(von Tier)* spine; *(von Insekten)* sting; **Stachelbeere** f gooseberry; **Stacheldraht** m barbed wire; **stachelig** adj prickly

Stadion (-s, Stadien) nt stadium

Stadt (-, Städte) f town; *(groß)* city; **in der ~** in town; **Stadtautobahn** f urban motorway *(Brit)* (o expressway *(US)*); **Stadtbummel** (-s) m: **einen ~ machen** to go round town; **Stadtführer** m *(Heft)* city

guide; **Stadtführung** f city sightseeing tour; **Stadthalle** f municipal hall; **städtisch** adj municipal; **Stadtmauer** f city wall(s); **Stadtmitte** f town/city centre, downtown *(US)*; **Stadtplan** m *(street)* map; **Stadtrand** m outskirts pl; **Stadtrundfahrt** f city tour; **Stadtteil** m, **Stadtviertel** nt district, part of town; **Stadtzentrum** nt town/city centre, downtown *(US)*

stahl imperf von **stehlen**

Stahl (-(e)s, Stähle) m steel

Stall (-(e)s, Ställe) m stable; *(Kaninchen)* hutch; *(Schweine)* pigsty; *(Hühner)* henhouse

Stamm (-(e)s, Stämme) m *(Baum)* trunk; *(von Menschen)* tribe; **stammen** vi: **~ aus** to come from; **Stammgast** m regular (guest); **Stammkunde** m, **Stammkundin** f regular (customer); **Stammtisch** m table reserved for regulars

stampfen vt, vi to stamp; *(mit Werkzeug)* to pound; *(stapfen)* to tramp

stand imperf von **stehen**

Stand (-(e)s, Stände) m *(Wasser, Benzin)* level; *(Stehen)* standing position; *(Zustand)* state; *(Spielstand)* score; *(auf Messe etc)* stand; *(Klasse)* class; **im ~e sein** to be in a position; *(fähig)* to be able

Stand-by-Betrieb m stand-by; **Stand-by-Ticket** nt stand-by ticket

Ständer (-s, -) m *(Gestell)* stand; *(fam: Erektion)* hard-on

Standesamt nt registry office

ständig adj permanent; *(ununterbrochen)* constant, continual

Standlicht nt sidelights pl *(Brit)*, parking lights pl *(US)*; **Standort** m position; **Standpunkt** m standpoint; **Standspur** f (Auto) hard shoulder (Brit), shoulder (US)

Stange (-, -n) f stick; (Stab) pole; (Metall) bar; (Zigaretten) carton; **Stangenbohne** f runner (Brit) (o string (US)) bean; **Stangenbrot** nt French stick; **Stangensellerie** m celery

stank imperf von **stinken**

Stapel (-s, -) m pile

Star (-(e)s, -e) m (Vogel) starling; (Med) cataract ▷ (-s, -s) m (in Film etc) star

starb imperf von **sterben**

stark adj strong; (heftig, groß) heavy; (Maßangabe) thick; **Stärke** (-, -n) f strength; (Dicke) thickness; (Wäschestärke, Speisestärke) starch; **stärken** vt to strengthen; (Wäsche) to starch; **Starkstrom** m high-voltage current; **Stärkung** f strengthening; (Essen) refreshment

starr adj stiff; (unnachgiebig) rigid; (Blick) staring **starren** vi to stare

Start (-(e)s, -e) m start; (Aviat) takeoff; **Startautomatik** f automatic choke; **Startbahn** f runway; **starten** vt, vi to start; (Aviat) to take off; **Starthilfekabel** nt jump leads pl (Brit), jumper cables pl (US); **Startmenü** nt (Inform) start menu

Station f (Haltestelle) stop; (Bahnhof) station; (im Krankenhaus) ward; **stationär** adj stationary; **~e Behandlung** in-patient treatment; **jdn ~ behandeln** to treat sb as an in-patient

Statistik f statistics pl

Stativ nt tripod

statt conj, prep +gen o dat instead of; **~ zu arbeiten** instead of working

statt|finden irr vi to take place

Statue (-, -n) f statue

Statusleiste f, **Statuszeile** f (Inform) status bar

Stau (-(e)s, -e) m (im Verkehr) (traffic) jam; **im ~ stehen** to be stuck in a traffic jam

Staub (-(e)s) m dust; **~ wischen** to dust; **staubig** adj dusty; **staubsaugen** vt, vi to vacuum, to hoover (Brit); **Staubsauger** m vacuum cleaner, Hoover® (Brit); **Staubtuch** nt duster

Staudamm m dam

staunen vi to be astonished (über +akk at)

Stausee m reservoir; **Stauung** f (von Wasser) damming-up; (von Blut, Verkehr) congestion; **Stauwarnung** f traffic report

Std. abk = **Stunde** h

Steak (-s, -s) nt steak

stechen (stach, gestochen) vt, vi (mit Nadel etc) to prick; (mit Messer) to stab; (mit Finger) to poke; (Biene) to sting; (Mücke) to bite; (Sonne) to burn; (Kartenspiel) to trump; **Stechen** (-s, -) nt sharp pain, stabbing pain; **Stechmücke** f mosquito

Steckdose f socket; **stecken** vt to put; (Nadel) to stick; (beim Nähen) to pin ▷ vi (festsitzen) to be stuck; (Nadeln) to be (sticking); **der Schlüssel steckt** the key is in the door; **Stecker** (-s, -) m plug; **Steckrübe** f swede (Brit), rutabaga (US)

Steg (-s, -e) m bridge

stehen (stand, gestanden) vi to stand (zu by); (sich befinden) to be; (stillstehen) to have stopped; **was steht im Brief?** what does it say in the letter?; **jdm (gut) ~** to suit sb; **~ bleiben** (Uhr) to stop; **~ lassen** to leave ▷ vi impers: **wie steht's?** (Sport) what's the score?

stehlen *(stahl, gestohlen)* vt to steal

Stehplatz m *(im Konzert etc)* standing ticket

Steiermark *(-)* f Styria

steif *adj* stiff

steigen *(stieg, gestiegen)* vi *(Preise, Temperatur)* to rise; *(klettern)* to climb; **~ in/auf** *(+akk)* to get in/on

steigern vt to increase ▷ vr: **sich ~** to increase

Steigung f incline, gradient

steil *adj* steep; **Steilhang** m steep slope; **Steilküste** f steep coast

Stein *(-(e)s, -e)* m stone; **Steinbock** m *(Zool)* ibex; *(Astr)* Capricorn; **steinig** *adj* stony; **Steinschlag** m falling rocks *pl*

Stelle *(-, -n)* f place, spot; *(Arbeit)* post, job; *(Amt)* office; **ich an deiner ~** if I were you; **auf der ~** straightaway; **an deiner ~** if I were you; *(Uhr etc)* to set *(auf +akk to)*; *(zur Verfügung stellen)* to provide ▷ vr: **sich ~** *(bei Polizei)* to give oneself up; **sich schlafend ~** to pretend to be asleep; **Stellenangebot** nt job offer, vacancy; **stellenweise** *adv* in places; **Stellenwert** m *(fig)* status; **einen hohen ~ haben** to play an important role; **Stellplatz** m parking space; **Stellung** f position; **zu etw ~ nehmen** to comment on sth; **Stellvertreter(in)** m(f) representative; *(amtlich)* deputy; *(von Arzt)* locum *(Brit)*, locum tenens *(US)*

Stempel *(-s, -)* m stamp; **stempeln** vt to stamp; *(Briefmarke)* to cancel

sterben *(starb, gestorben)* vi to die

Stereoanlage f stereo (system)

steril *adj* sterile; **sterilisieren** vt to sterilize

Stern *(-(e)s, -e)* m star; **ein Hotel mit vier ~en** a four-star hotel; **Sternbild** nt constellation; *(Sternzeichen)* star sign, sign of the zodiac; **Sternfrucht** f star fruit; **Sternschnuppe** *(-, -n)* f shooting star; **Sternwarte** *(-e, -n)* f observatory; **Sternzeichen** nt star sign, sign of the zodiac; **welches ~ bist du?** what's your star sign?

stets *adv* always

Steuer *(-s, -)* nt *(Auto)* steering wheel ▷ *(-, -n)* f tax; **Steuerberater(in)** m(f) tax adviser; **Steuerbord** nt starboard; **Steuererklärung** f tax declaration; **steuerfrei** *adj* tax-free; *(Waren)* duty-free; **Steuerknüppel** m control column; *(Aviat, Inform)* joystick; **steuern** vt, vi to steer; *(Flugzeug)* to pilot; *(Entwicklung, Tonstärke)* to control; **steuerpflichtig** *adj* taxable; **Steuerung** f *(Auto)* steering; *(Vorrichtung)* controls *pl*; *(Aviat)* piloting; *(fig)* control; **Steuerungstaste** f *(Inform)* control key

Stich *(-(e)s, -e)* m *(von Insekt)* sting; *(von Mücke)* bite; *(durch Messer)* stab; *(beim Nähen)* stitch; *(Färbung)* tinge; *(Kartenspiel)* trick; *(Kunst)* engraving

sticken vt, vi to embroider

Sticker *(-s, -)* m sticker

Stickerei f embroidery

stickig *adj* stuffy, close

Stiefbruder m stepbrother

Stiefel *(-s, -)* m boot

Stiefmutter f stepmother

Stiefmütterchen nt pansy

Stiefschwester f stepsister; **Stiefsohn** m stepson; **Stieftochter** f stepdaughter; **Stiefvater** m stepfather

stieg *imperf von* **steigen**

Stiege (-, -n) f steps pl

Stiel (-(e)s, -e) m handle; (Bot) stalk; **ein Eis am ~** an ice lolly (Brit), a Popsicle® (US)

Stier (-(e)s, -e) m (Zool) bull; (Astr) Taurus; **Stierkampf** m bullfight

stieß imperf von **stoßen**

Stift (-(e)s, -e) m (aus Holz) peg; (Nagel) tack; (zum Schreiben) pen; (Farbstift) crayon; (Bleistift) pencil

Stil (-s, -e) m style

still adj quiet; (unbewegt) still

stillen vt (Säugling) to breast-feed

still|halten irr vi to keep still; **still|stehen** irr vi to stand still

Stimme (-, -n) f voice; (bei Wahl) vote

stimmen vi to be right; **stimmt!** that's right; **hier stimmt was nicht** there's something wrong here; **stimmt so!** (beim Bezahlen) keep the change

Stimmung f mood; (Atmosphäre) atmosphere

Stinkefinger m (fam) **jdm den ~ zeigen** to give sb the finger (o bird (US))

stinken (stank, gestunken) vi to stink (nach of)

Stipendium nt scholarship; (als Unterstützung) grant

Stirn (-, -en) f forehead; **Stirnhöhle** f sinus

Stock (-(e)s, Stöcke) m stick; (Bot) stock ▷ m (Stockwerke) floor, storey; **Stockbett** nt bunk bed; **Stöckelschuhe** pl high-heels; **Stockwerk** nt floor; **im ersten ~** on the first floor (Brit), on the second floor (US)

Stoff (-(e)s, -e) m (Gewebe) material; (Materie) matter; (von Buch etc) subject (matter); (fam: Rauschgift) stuff

stöhnen vi to groan (vor with)

stolpern vi to stumble, to trip

stolz adj proud

stopp interj hold it; (Moment mal!) hang on a minute; **stoppen** vt, vi to stop; (mit Uhr) to time; **Stoppschild** nt stop sign; **Stoppuhr** f stopwatch

Stöpsel (-s, -) m plug; (für Flaschen) stopper

Storch (-(e)s, Störche) m stork

stören vt to disturb; (behindern) to interfere with; **darf ich dich kurz ~?** can I trouble you for a minute?; **stört es dich, wenn ...?** do you mind if ...?

stornieren vt to cancel; **Stornogebühr** f cancellation fee

Störung f disturbance; (in der Leitung) fault

Stoß (-es, Stöße) m (Schub) push; (Schlag) blow; (mit Fuß) kick; (Haufen) pile; **Stoßdämpfer** (-s, -) m shock absorber

stoßen (stieß, gestoßen) vt (mit Druck) to shove, to push; (mit Schlag) to knock; (mit Fuß) to kick; (anstoßen) to bump; (zerkleinern) to pulverize ▷ vr: **sich ~** to bang oneself; **sich ~ an** (+dat) (fig) to take exception to

Stoßstange f (Auto) bumper

stottern vt, vi to stutter

Str. abk von **Straße** St, Rd

Strafe (-, -n) f punishment; (Sport) penalty; (Gefängnisstrafe) sentence; (Geldstrafe) fine; **strafen** vt to punish; **Straftat** f (criminal) offence; **Strafzettel** m ticket

Strahl (-s, -en) m ray, beam; (Wasser) jet; **strahlen** vi to radiate; (fig) to beam

Strähne (-, -n) f strand; (weiß, gefärbt) streak

Strand (-(e)s, Strände) m beach; **am ~** on the beach; **Strandcafé** nt beach café; **Strandkorb** m wicker beach chair with a hood; **Strandpromenade** f promenade

strapazieren vt (Material) to be hard on; (Mensch, Kräfte) to be a strain on

Straße (-, -n) f road; (in der Stadt) street; **Straßenarbeiten** pl roadworks pl (Brit), road repairs pl (US); **Straßenbahn** f tram (Brit), streetcar (US); **Straßencafé** nt pavement café (Brit), sidewalk café (US); **Straßenfest** nt street party; **Straßenglätte** f slippery roads pl; **Straßenkarte** f road map; **Straßenrand** m: **am ~** at the roadside; **Straßenschild** nt street sign; **Straßensperre** f roadblock; **Straßenverhältnisse** pl road conditions pl

Strategie (-, -n) f strategy

Strauch (-(e)s, Sträucher) m bush, shrub; **Strauchtomate** f vine-ripened tomato

Strauß (-es, Sträuße) m bunch; (als Geschenk) bouquet ▷ m (Strauße) (Vogel) ostrich

Strecke (-, -n) f route; (Entfernung) distance; (Eisenb) line

strecken vt to stretch ▷ vr: **sich ~** to stretch

streckenweise adv (teilweise) in parts; (zeitweise) at times

Streich (-(e)s, -e) m trick, prank

streicheln vt to stroke

streichen (strich, gestrichen) vt (anmalen) to paint; (berühren) to stroke; (auftragen) to spread; (durchstreichen) to delete; (nicht genehmigen) to cancel

Streichholz nt match; **Streichholzschachtel** f matchbox; **Streichkäse** m cheese spread

Streifen (-s, -) m (Linie) stripe; (Stück) strip; (Film) film

Streifenwagen m patrol car

Streik (-(e)s, -s) m strike; **streiken** vi to be on strike

Streit (-(e)s, -e) m argument (um, wegen about, over); **streiten** (stritt, gestritten) vi to argue (um, wegen about, over) ▷ vr: **sich ~** to argue (um, wegen about, over)

streng adj (Blick) severe; (Lehrer) strict; (Geruch) sharp

Stress (-es) m stress; **stressen** vt to stress (out); **stressig** adj (fam) stressful

Stretching (-s) nt (Sport) stretching exercises pl

streuen vt to scatter; **die Straßen ~** to grit the roads; (mit Salz) to put salt down on the roads; **Streufahrzeug** nt gritter lorry (Brit), salt truck (US)

strich imperf von **streichen**

Strich (-(e)s, -e) m (Linie) line; **Stricher** m (fam: Strichjunge) rent boy (Brit), boy prostitute; **Strichkode** (-s, -s) m bar code; **Stricherin** f (fam: Strichmädchen) hooker; **Strichpunkt** m semicolon

Strick (-(e)s, -e) m rope

stricken vt, vi to knit; **Strickjacke** f cardigan; **Stricknadel** f knitting needle

String (-s, -s m, **Stringtanga** m G-string

Stripper(in) m(f) stripper; **Striptease** (-) m striptease

stritt imperf von **streiten**

Stroh (-(e)s) nt straw; **Strohdach** nt thatched roof; **Strohhalm** m (drinking) straw

Strom (-(e)s, Ströme) m river; (fig) stream; (Elek) current; **Stromanschluss** m connection; **Stromausfall** m power failure

strömen vi to stream, to pour; **Strömung** f current

Stromverbrauch m power consumption; **Stromzähler** m electricity meter

Strophe (-, -n) f verse

Strudel (-s, -) m (in Fluss) whirlpool; (Gebäck) strudel

Struktur f structure; (von Material) texture

Strumpf (-(e)s, Strümpfe) m (Damenstrumpf) stocking; (Socke) sock; **Strumpfhose** f (pair of) tights pl (Brit), pantyhose (US)

Stück (-(e)s, -e) nt piece; (von Zucker) lump; (etwas) bit; (Zucker) lump; (Theat) play; **ein ~ Käse** a piece of cheese

Student(in) m(f) student; **Studentenausweis** m student card; **Studentenwohnheim** nt hall of residence (Brit), dormitory (US); **Studienabschluss** m qualification (at the end of a course of higher education); **Studienfahrt** f study trip; **Studienplatz** m university/college place; **studieren** vt, vi to study; **Studium** nt studies pl; **während seines ~s** while he is/was studying

Stufe (-, -n) f step; (Entwicklungsstufe) stage

Stuhl (-(e)s, Stühle) m chair

stumm adj silent; (Med) dumb

stumpf adj blunt; (teilnahmslos, glanzlos) dull; **stumpfsinnig** adj dull

Stunde (-, -n) f hour; (Unterricht) lesson; **eine halbe ~** half an hour; **Stundenkilometer** m: **80 ~** 80 kilometres an hour; **stundenlang** adv for hours; **Stundenlohn** m hourly wage; **Stundenplan** m timetable; **stündlich** adj hourly

Stuntman (-s, Stuntmen) m stuntman; **Stuntwoman** (-, Stuntwomen) f stuntwoman

stur adj stubborn; (stärker) pigheaded

Sturm (-(e)s, Stürme) m storm; **stürmen** vi (Wind) to blow hard; (rennen) to storm; **Stürmer(in)**

m(f) striker, forward; **Sturmflut** f storm tide; **stürmisch** adj stormy; (fig) tempestuous; (Zeit) turbulent; (Liebhaber) passionate; (Beifall, Begrüßung) tumultuous; **Sturmwarnung** f gale warning

Sturz (-es, Stürze) m fall; (Pol) overthrow; **stürzen** vt (werfen) to hurl; (Pol) to overthrow; (umkehren) to overturn ▷ vi to fall; (rennen) to dash; **Sturzhelm** m crash helmet

Stute (-, -n) f mare

Stütze (-, -n) f support; (Hilfe) help; (fam: Arbeitslosenunterstützung) dole (Brit), welfare (US)

stützen vt to support; (Ellbogen) to prop

stutzig adj perplexed, puzzled; (misstrauisch) suspicious

Styropor® (-s) nt polystyrene (Brit), styrofoam (US)

subjektiv adj subjective

Substanz (-, -en) f substance

subtrahieren vt to subtract

Subvention f subsidy; **subventionieren** vt to subsidize

Suche f search (nach for); **auf der ~ nach etw sein** to be looking for sth; **suchen** vt to look for; (Inform) to search ▷ vi to look, to search (nach for); **Suchmaschine** f (Inform) search engine

Sucht (-, Süchte) f mania; (Med) addiction; **süchtig** adj addicted; **Süchtige(r)** mf addict

Süd south; **Südafrika** nt South Africa; **Südamerika** nt South America; **Süddeutschland** nt Southern Germany; **Süden** (-s) m south; **im ~ Deutschlands** in the south of Germany; **Südeuropa** nt Southern Europe; **Südkorea** (-s) nt South Korea; **südlich** adj southern; (Kurs, Richtung) southerly; **Verkehr in ~er**

Richtung southbound traffic; **Südost(en)** m southeast; **Südpol** m South Pole; **Südstaaten** pl (der USA) the Southern States pl, the South sing; **südwärts** adv south, southwards; **Südwest(en)** m southwest; **Südwind** m south wind

Sülze (-, -n) f jellied meat

Summe (-, -n) f sum; (Gesamtsumme) total

summen vi, vt to hum; (Insekt) to buzz

Sumpf (-(e)s, Sümpfe) m marsh; (subtropischer) swamp; **sumpfig** adj marshy

Sünde (-, -n) f sin

super adj (fam) super, great; **Super** (-s) nt (Benzin) four star (petrol) (Brit), premium (US); **Supermarkt** m supermarket

Suppe (-, -n) f soup; **Suppengrün** nt bunch of herbs and vegetables for flavouring soup; **Suppenlöffel** m soup spoon; **Suppenschüssel** f soup tureen; **Suppentasse** f soup cup; **Suppenteller** m soup plate; **Suppenwürfel** m stock cube

Surfbrett nt surfboard; **surfen** vi to surf; **im Internet ~** to surf the Internet; **Surfer(in)** (-s, -) m(f) surfer

Surrealismus m surrealism

Sushi (-s, -s) nt sushi

süß adj sweet; **süßen** vt to sweeten; **Süßigkeit** f (Bonbon etc) sweet (Brit), candy (US); **Süßkartoffel** f sweet potato (Brit), yam (US); **süßsauer** adj sweet-and-sour; **Süßspeise** f dessert; **Süßstoff** m sweetener; **Süßwasser** nt fresh water

Sweatshirt (-s, -s) nt sweatshirt

Swimmingpool (-s, -s) m (swimming) pool

Sylvester nt siehe Silvester

Symbol (-s, -e) nt symbol; **Symbolleiste** f (Inform) toolbar

Symmetrie (-, -n) f symmetry; **symmetrisch** adj symmetrical

sympathisch adj nice; **jdn ~ finden** to like sb

Symphonie (-, -n) f symphony

Symptom (-s, -e) nt symptom (für of)

Synagoge (-, -n) f synagogue

synchronisiert adj (Film) dubbed; **Synchronstimme** f dubbing voice

Synthetik (-, -en) f synthetic (fibre); **synthetisch** adj synthetic

Syrien (-s) nt Syria

System (-s, -e) nt system; **systematisch** adj systematic; **Systemsteuerung** f (Inform) control panel

Szene (-, -n) f scene

t

Tabak (-s, -e) m tobacco; **Tabakladen** m tobacconist's

Tabelle f table

Tablett (-s, -s) nt tray

Tablette f tablet, pill

Tabulator m tabulator, tab

Tacho(meter) (-s, -) m (Auto) speedometer

Tafel (-, -n) f (a. Math) table; (Anschlagtafel) board; (Wandtafel) blackboard; (Schiefer-) slate; (Gedenktafel) plaque; **eine ~ Schokolade** a bar of chocolate; **Tafelwasser** nt table water; **Tafelwein** m table wine

Tag (-(e)s, -e) m day; (Tageslicht) daylight; **guten ~!** good morning/afternoon; **am ~** during the day; **sie hat ihre ~e** she's got her period; **eines ~es** one day; **~ der Arbeit** Labour Day; **Tagebuch** nt diary; **tagelang** adj for days (on end);

Tagesanbruch m daybreak; **Tagesausflug** m day trip; **Tagescreme** f day cream; **Tagesdecke** f bedspread; **Tagesgericht** nt dish of the day; **Tageskarte** f (Fahrkarte) day ticket; **die ~** (Speisekarte) today's menu; **Tageslicht** nt daylight; **Tagesmutter** f child minder; **Tagesordnung** f agenda; **Tagestour** f day trip; **Tageszeitung** f daily newspaper; **täglich** adj, adv daily; **tags(über)** adv during the day; **Tagung** f conference

Tai Chi (-) nt tai chi

Taille (-, -n) f waist

Taiwan (-s) nt Taiwan

Takt (-(e)s, -e) m (Taktgefühl) tact; (Mus) time

Taktik (-, -en) f tactics pl

taktlos adj tactless; **taktvoll** adj tactful

Tal (-(e)s, Täler) nt valley

Talent (-(e)s, -e) nt talent; **talentiert** adj talented

Talkmaster(in) (-s, -) m(f) talk-show host; **Talkshow** (-, -s) f talkshow

Tampon (-s, -s) m tampon

Tandem (-s, -s) nt tandem

Tang (-s, -e) m seaweed

Tanga (-s, -s) m thong

Tank (-s, -s) m tank; **Tankanzeige** f fuel gauge; **Tankdeckel** m fuel cap; **tanken** vi to get some petrol (Brit) (o gas (US)); (Aviat) to refuel; **Tanker** (-s, -) m (oil) tanker; **Tankstelle** f petrol station (Brit), gas station (US); **Tankwart(in)** (-s, -e) m(f) petrol pump attendant (Brit), gas station attendant (US)

Tanne (-, -n) f fir; **Tannenzapfen** m fir cone

Tansania (-s) nt Tanzania

Tante (-, -n) f aunt; **Tante-Emma-Laden** m corner

shop (Brit), grocery store (US)

Tanz (-es, Tänze) m dance; **tanzen**
vt, vi to dance; **Tänzer(in)** m(f)
dancer; **Tanzfläche** f dance floor;
Tanzkurs m dancing course;
Tanzlehrer(in) m(f) dancing
instructor; **Tanzstunde** f
dancing lesson

Tapete (-, -n) f wallpaper;
tapezieren vt, vi to wallpaper

Tarantel (-, -n) f tarantula

Tarif (-s, -e) m tariff, (scale of)
fares/charges pl

Tasche (-, -n) f bag; (Hosentasche)
pocket; (Handtasche) bag (Brit),
purse (US)

Taschen- in zW pocket;
Taschenbuch nt paperback;
Taschendieb(in) m(f) pick-
pocket; **Taschengeld** nt pocket
money; **Taschenlampe** f torch
(Brit), flashlight (US);
Taschenmesser nt penknife;
Taschenrechner m pocket
calculator; **Taschentuch** nt
handkerchief

Tasse (-, -n) f cup; **eine ~ Kaffee**
a cup of coffee

Tastatur f keyboard; **Taste**
(-, -n) f button; (von Klavier,
Computer) key; **Tastenkombi-
nation** f (Inform) shortcut

tat imperf von **tun**

Tat (-, -en) f action

Tatar (-s, -s) nt raw minced beef

Täter(in) (-s, -) m(f) culprit

tätig adj active; **in einer Firma
~ sein** to work for a firm;
Tätigkeit f activity; (Beruf)
occupation

tätowieren vt to tattoo;
Tätowierung f tattoo (an +dat
on)

Tatsache f fact; **tatsächlich** adj
actual ▷ adv really

Tau (-(e)s, -e) nt (Seil) rope ▷ (-(e)s)
m dew

taub adj deaf; (Füße etc) numb (vor
Kälte with cold)

Taube (-, -n) f pigeon; (Turtel-,
fig: Friedenssymbol) dove

taubstumm adj deaf-and-dumb;
Taubstumme(r) mf deaf-mute

tauchen vt to dip ▷ vi to dive;
(Naut) to submerge; **Tauchen** (-s)
nt diving; **Taucher(in)** (-s, -) m(f)
diver; **Taucheranzug** m diving
(o wet) suit; **Taucherbrille** f
diving goggles pl; **Tauchermaske**
f diving mask; **Tauchkurs** m
diving course; **Tauchsieder** (-s, -)
m portable immersion coil for heating
water

tauen vi impers to thaw

Taufe (-, -n) f baptism; **taufen**
vt to baptize; (nennen) to christen

taugen vi to be suitable (für for);
nichts ~ to be no good

Tausch (-(e)s, -e) m exchange;
tauschen vt to exchange, to
swap

täuschen vt to deceive ▷ vi to
be deceptive ▷ vr: **sich ~** to be
wrong; **täuschend** adj
deceptive; **Täuschung** f
deception; (optisch) illusion

tausend num a thousand;
vier~ four thousand; **~ Dank!**
thanks a lot; **tausendmal** adv a
thousand times; **tausendste(r, s)**
adj thousandth; **Tausendstel**
(-s, -) nt (Bruchteil) thousandth

Taxi nt taxi; **Taxifahrer(in)** m(f)
taxi driver; **Taxistand** m taxi
rank (Brit), taxi stand (US)

Team (-s, -s) nt team;
Teamarbeit f team work;
teamfähig adj able to work in a
team

Technik f technology;
(angewandte) engineering;
(Methode) technique;
Techniker(in) (-s, -) m(f) engineer; (Sport, Mus) technician;

technisch adj technical

Techno (-s) m (Mus) techno

Teddybär m teddy bear

TEE abk = **Trans-Europ-Express**
Trans-Europe-Express

Tee (-s, -s) m tea; **Teebeutel** m
teabag; **Teekanne** f teapot;
Teelöffel m teaspoon

Teer (-(e)s, -e) m tar

Teesieb nt tea strainer; **Teetasse**
f teacup

Teich (-(e)s, -e) m pond

Teig (-(e)s, -e) m dough;
Teigwaren pl pasta sing

Teil (-(e)s, -e) m part; (Anteil)
share; **zum ~** partly ▷ (-(e)s, -e) nt
part; (Bestandteil) component;
teilen vt to divide; (mit jdm) to
share (mit with); **20 durch 4 ~** to
divide 20 by 4 ▷ vr: **sich ~** to
divide

Teilkaskoversicherung f third
party, fire and theft insurance

teilmöbliert adj partly furnished

Teilnahme (-, -n) f participation
(an +dat in); **teil|nehmen** irr vi to
take part (an +dat in); **Teilneh-
mer(in)** (-s, -) m(f) participant

teils adv partly; **teilweise** adv
partially, in part; **Teilzeit** f:
~ arbeiten to work part-time

Teint (-s, -s) m complexion

Tel. abk von **Telefon** tel.

Telefon (-s, -e) nt telephone;
Telefonanruf m, **Telefonat** nt
(tele)phone call;
Telefonanschluss m telephone
connection; **Telefonauskunft** f
directory enquiries pl (Brit),
directory assistance (US);
Telefonbuch nt telephone
directory; **Telefongebühren** pl
telephone charges pl;
Telefongespräch nt telephone
conversation; **telefonieren** vi:
ich telefoniere gerade (mit ...)
I'm on the phone (to ...);

telefonisch adj telephone;
(Benachrichtigung) by telephone;
Telefonkarte f phonecard;
Telefonnummer f (tele)phone
number; **Telefonrechnung** f
phone bill; **Telefonverbindung** f
telephone connection;
Telefonzelle f phone box (Brit),
phone booth; **Telefonzentrale** f
switchboard; **über die ~** through
the switchboard

Telegramm nt telegram;
Teleobjektiv nt telephoto lens;
Teleshopping (-s) nt teleshopping; **Teleskop** (-s, -e) nt
telescope

Teller (-s, -) m plate

Tempel (-s, -) m temple

Temperament nt temperament; (Schwung) liveliness;
temperamentvoll adj lively

Temperatur f temperature; **bei
~en von 30 Grad** at temperatures
of 30 degrees; **~ haben** to have a
temperature; **~ bei jdm messen** to
take sb's temperature

Tempo (-s, -s) nt (Geschwindigkeit)
speed; **Tempolimit** (-s, -s) nt
speed limit

Tempotaschentuch® nt
(Papiertaschentuch) (paper) tissue

Tendenz f tendency; (Absicht)
intention

Tennis (-) nt tennis; **Tennisball**
m tennis ball; **Tennisplatz** m
tennis court; **Tennisschläger** m
tennis racket; **Tennisspieler(in)**
m(f) tennis player

Tenor (-s, Tenöre) m tenor

Teppich (-s, -e) m carpet;
Teppichboden m (fitted) carpet

Termin (-s, -e) m (Zeitpunkt) date;
(Frist) deadline; (Arzttermin etc)
appointment

Terminal (-s, -s) nt (Inform, Aviat)
terminal

Terminkalender m diary;

Terminplaner m (in Buchform) personal organizer, Filofax®; (Taschencomputer) personal digital assistant, PDA

Terpentin (-s, -e) nt turpentine, turps sing

Terrasse (-, -n) f terrace; (hinter einem Haus) patio

Terror (-s) m terror; **Terroranschlag** m terrorist attack; **terrorisieren** vt to terrorize; **Terrorismus** m terrorism; **Terrorist(in)** m(f) terrorist

Tesafilm® m = sellotape® (Brit), ≈ Scotch tape® (US)

Test (-s, -s) m test

Testament nt will; **das Alte/Neue ~** the Old/New Testament

testen vt to test; **Testergebnis** nt test results pl

Tetanus m tetanus; **Tetanusimpfung** f (anti-)tetanus injection

teuer adj expensive, dear (Brit)

Teufel (-s, -) m devil; **was/wo zum ~** what/where the devil; **Teufelskreis** m vicious circle

Text (-(e)s, -e) m text; (Liedertext) words pl, lyrics pl; **Textmarker** (-s, -) m highlighter; **Textverarbeitung** f word processing; **Textverarbeitungsprogramm** nt word processing program

Thailand nt Thailand

Theater (-s, -) nt theatre; (fam) fuss; **ins ~ gehen** to go to the theatre; **Theaterkasse** f box office; **Theaterstück** nt (stage) play; **Theatervorstellung** f (stage) performance

Theke (-, -n) f (Schanktisch) bar; (Ladentisch) counter

Thema (-s, Themen) nt subject, topic; **kein ~!** no problem

Themse (-) f Thames

Theologie f theology

theoretisch adj theoretical; **~ stimmt das** that's right in theory; **Theorie** f theory

Therapeut(in) m(f) therapist; **Therapie** f therapy; **eine ~ machen** to undergo therapy

Thermalbad nt thermal bath; (Ort) thermal spa; **Thermometer** (-s, -) nt thermometer

Thermosflasche® f, **Thermoskanne®** f Thermos® (flask); **Thermostat** (-(e)s, -e) m thermostat

These (-, -n) f theory

Thron (-(e)s, -e) m throne

Thunfisch m tuna

Thüringen nt Thuringia

Thymian (-s, -e) m thyme

Tick (-(e)s, -e) m tic; (Eigenart) quirk; (Fimmel) craze; **ticken** vi to tick; **er tickt nicht ganz richtig** he's off his rocker

Ticket (-s, -s) nt (plane) ticket

tief adj deep; (Ausschnitt, Ton, Sonne) low; **2 Meter ~** 2 metres deep; **Tief** (-s, -s) nt (Meteo) low; (seelisch) depression; **Tiefdruck** m (Meteo) low pressure; **Tiefe** (-, -n) f depth; **Tiefgarage** f underground car park (Brit) (o garage (US)); **tiefgekühlt** adj frozen; **Tiefkühlfach** nt freezer compartment; **Tiefkühlkost** f frozen food; **Tiefkühltruhe** f freezer; **Tiefpunkt** m low

Tier (-(e)s, -e) nt animal; **Tierarzt** m, **Tierärztin** f vet; **Tiergarten** m zoo; **Tierhandlung** f pet shop; **Tierheim** nt animal shelter; **tierisch** adj animal ▷ adv (fam) really; **~ ernst** deadly serious; **ich hatte ~ Angst** I was dead scared; **Tierkreiszeichen** nt sign of the zodiac; **Tierpark** m zoo; **Tierquälerei** f cruelty to animals;

Tierschützer(in) (-s, -) m(f) animal rights campaigner; **Tierversuch** m animal experiment

Tiger (-s, -) m tiger

timen vt to time; **Timing** (-s) nt timing

Tinte (-, -n) f ink; **Tintenfisch** m cuttlefish; (klein) squid; (achtarmig) octopus; **Tintenfischringe** pl calamari pl; **Tintenstrahldrucker** m ink-jet printer

Tipp (-s, -s) m tip; **tippen** vt, vi to tap; (fam: schreiben) to type; (fam: raten) to guess

Tirol (-s) nt Tyrol

Tisch (-(e)s, -e) m table; **Tischdecke** f tablecloth; **Tischlerei** f joiner's workshop; (Arbeit) joinery; **Tischtennis** nt table tennis; **Tischtennisschläger** m table-tennis bat

Titel (-s, -) m title; **Titelbild** nt cover picture

Toast (-(e)s, -s) m toast; **toasten** vt to toast; **Toaster** (-s, -) m toaster

Tochter (-, Töchter) f daughter

Tod (-(e)s, -e) m death; **Todesopfer** nt casualty; **Todesstrafe** f death penalty; **todkrank** terminally ill; (sehr krank) seriously ill; **tödlich** adj deadly, fatal; **er ist ~ verunglückt** he was killed in an accident; **todmüde** adj (fam) dead tired; **todsicher** adj (fam) dead certain

Tofu (-(s)) m tofu, bean curd

Toilette f toilet, restroom (US); **Toilettenpapier** nt toilet paper

toi, toi, toi interj good luck

tolerant adj tolerant (gegen of)

toll adj mad; (Treiben) wild; (fam: großartig) great; **Tollkirsche** f deadly nightshade; **Tollwut** f rabies sing

Tomate (-, -n) f tomato; **Tomatenmark** nt tomato purée (Brit) (o paste (US)); **Tomatensaft** m tomato juice

Tombola (-, -s) f raffle, tombola (Brit)

Ton (-(e)s, -e) m (Erde) clay ▷ m (Töne; Laut) sound; (Mus) note; (Redeweise) tone; (Farbton, Nuance) shade; **Tonband** nt tape; **Tonbandgerät** nt tape recorder

tönen vi to sound ▷ vt to shade; (Haare) to tint

Toner (-s, -) m toner; **Tonerkassette** f toner cartridge

Tonne (-, -n) f (Fass) barrel; (Gewicht) tonne, metric ton

Tontechniker(in) m(f) sound engineer

Tönung f hue; (für Haar) rinse

Top (-s, -s) nt top

Topf (-(e)s, Töpfe) m pot

Töpfer(in) (-s, -) m(f) potter; **Töpferei** f pottery; (Gegenstand) piece of pottery

Tor (-(e)s, -e) nt gate; (Sport) goal; **ein ~ schießen** to score a goal; **Torhüter(in)** m(f) goalkeeper

torkeln vi to stagger

Tornado (-s, -s) m tornado

Torschütze m, **Torschützin** f (goal)scorer

Torte (-, -n) f (Obsttorte) flan; (Sahnetorte) gateau

Torwart(in) (-s, -e) m(f) goalkeeper

tot adj dead; **~er Winkel** blind spot

total adj total, complete; **Totalschaden** m complete write-off

Tote(r) mf dead man/woman; (Leiche) corpse; **töten** vt, vi to kill; **Totenkopf** m skull

totlachen vr: **sich ~** to kill oneself laughing

Toto (-s, -s) m o nt pools pl

tot|schlagen *irr vt* to beat to death; **die Zeit ~** to kill time
Touchscreen (-s, -s) *m* touch screen
Tour (-, -en) *f* trip; (*Rundfahrt*) tour; **eine ~ nach York machen** to go on a trip to York; **Tourenski** *m* touring ski
Tourismus *m* tourism; **Tourist(in)** *m(f)* tourist; **Touristenklasse** *f* tourist class; **touristisch** *adj* tourist; (*pej*) touristy
traben *vi* to trot
Tournee (-, -n) *f* tour
Tracht (-, -en) *f* (*Kleidung*) traditional costume
Trackball (-s, -s) *m* (*Inform*) trackball
Tradition *f* tradition; **traditionell** *adj* traditional
traf *imperf von* **treffen**
Trafik (-, -en) *f* tobacconist's
Tragbahre (-, -n) *f* stretcher
tragbar *adj* portable
träge *adj* sluggish, slow
tragen (**trug, getragen**) *vt* to carry; (*Kleidung, Brille, Haare*) to wear; (*Namen, Früchte*) to bear; **Träger** (-s, -) *m* (*an Kleidung*) strap; (*Hosen~*) braces *pl* (Brit), suspenders *pl* (US); (*in der Architektur*) beam; (*Stahl~, Eisen~*) girder
Tragfläche *f* wing; **Tragflügelboot** *nt* hydrofoil
tragisch *adj* tragic; **Tragödie** *f* tragedy
Trainer(in) (-s, -) *m(f)* trainer, coach; **trainieren** *vt, vi* to train; (*jdn a.*) to coach; (*Übung*) to practise; **Training** (-s, -s) *nt* training; **Trainingsanzug** *m* tracksuit
Traktor *m* tractor
Trambahn *f* tram (Brit), streetcar (US)

trampen *vi* to hitchhike; **Tramper(in)** *m(f)* hitchhiker
Träne (-, -n) *f* tear; **tränen** *vi* to water; **Tränengas** *nt* teargas
trank *imperf von* **trinken**
Transfusion *f* transfusion
Transit *m* transit; **Transitverkehr** *m* transit traffic; **Transitvisum** *nt* transit visa
Transplantation *f* transplant; (*Hauttransplantation*) graft
Transport (-(e)s, -e) *m* transport; **transportieren** *vt* to transport; **Transportmittel** *nt* means *sing of* transport; **Transportunternehmen** *nt* haulage firm
Transvestit (-en, -en) *m* transvestite
trat *imperf von* **treten**
Traube (-, -n) *f* (*einzelne Beere*) grape; (*ganze Frucht*) bunch of grapes; **Traubensaft** *m* grape juice; **Traubenzucker** *m* glucose
trauen *vi*: **jdm/einer Sache ~** to trust sb/sth; **ich traute meinen Ohren nicht** I couldn't believe my ears ▷ *vr*: **sich ~** to dare ▷ *vt* to marry; **sich ~ lassen** to get married
Trauer (-) *f* sorrow; (*für Verstorbenen*) mourning
Traum (-(e)s, Träume) *m* dream; **träumen** *vt, vi* to dream (*von* about); **traumhaft** *adj* dreamlike; (*fig*) wonderful
traurig *adj* sad (*über +akk* about)
Trauschein *m* marriage certificate; **Trauung** *f* wedding ceremony; **Trauzeuge** *m*, **Trauzeugin** *f* witness (*at wedding ceremony*), ≈ best man/maid of honour
Travellerscheck *m* traveller's cheque
treffen (**traf, getroffen**) *vr*: **sich ~** to meet ▷ *vt, vi* to hit; (*Bemerkung*) to hurt; (*begegnen*) to

meet; (*Entscheidung*) to make; (*Maßnahmen*) to take; **Treffen** (-s, -) *nt* meeting; **Treffer** (-s, -) *m* (*Tor*) goal; **Treffpunkt** *m* meeting place
treiben (*trieb, getrieben*) *vt* to drive; (*Sport*) to do ▷ *vi* (*im Wasser*) to drift; (*Pflanzen*) to sprout; (*Tee, Kaffee*) to be diuretic; **Treiber** (-s, -) *m* (*Inform*) driver
Treibgas *nt* propellant; **Treibhaus** *nt* greenhouse; **Treibstoff** *m* fuel
trennen *vt* to separate; (*teilen*) to divide ▷ *vr*: **sich ~** to separate; **sich von jdm ~** to leave sb; **sich von etw ~** to part with sth; **Trennung** *f* separation
Treppe (-, -n) *f* stairs *pl*; (*im Freien*) steps *pl*; **Treppengeländer** *nt* banister; **Treppenhaus** *nt* staircase
Tresen (-s, -) *m* (*in Kneipe*) bar; (*in Laden*) counter
Tresor (-s, -e) *m* safe
Tretboot *nt* pedal boat; **treten** (*trat, getreten*) *vi* to step; **mit jdm in Verbindung ~** to get in contact with sb ▷ *vt* to kick; (*nieder~*) to tread
treu *adj* (*gegenüber Partner*) faithful; (*Kunde, Fan*) loyal; **Treue** (-) *f* (*eheliche*) faithfulness; (*von Kunde, Fan*) loyalty
Triathlon (-s, -s) *m* triathlon
Tribüne (-, -n) *f* stand; (*Rednertribüne*) platform
Trick (-s, -e o -s) *m* trick; **Trickfilm** *m* cartoon
trieb *imperf von* **treiben**
Trieb (-(e)s, -e) *m* urge; (*Instinkt*) drive; (*Neigung*) inclination; (*an Baum etc*) shoot; **Triebwerk** *nt* engine
Trikot (-s, -s) *nt* shirt, jersey
Trimm-Dich-Pfad *m* fitness trail

trinkbar *adj* drinkable; **trinken** (*trank, getrunken*) *vt, vi* to drink; **einen ~ gehen** to go out for a drink; **Trinkgeld** *nt* tip; **Trinkhalm** *m* (drinking) straw; **Trinkwasser** *nt* drinking water
Trio (-s, -s) *nt* trio
Tripper (-s, -) *m* gonorrhoea
Tritt (-(e)s, -e) *m* (*Schritt*) step; (*Fußtritt*) kick; **Trittbrett** *nt* running board
Triumph (-(e)s, -e) *m* triumph; **triumphieren** *vi* to triumph (*über +akk* over)
trivial *adj* trivial
trocken *adj* dry; **Trockenhaube** *f* hair-dryer; **Trockenheit** *f* dryness; **trocken|legen** *vt* (*Baby*) to change; **trocknen** *vt, vi* to dry; **Trockner** (-s, -) *m* dryer
Trödel (-s) *m* (*fam*) junk; **Trödelmarkt** *m* flea market
trödeln *vi* (*fam*) to dawdle
Trommel (-, -n) *f* drum; **Trommelfell** *nt* eardrum; **trommeln** *vt, vi* to drum
Trompete (-, -n) *f* trumpet
Tropen *pl* tropics *pl*
Tropf (-(e)s, -e) *m* (*Med*) drip; **am ~ hängen** to be on a drip; **tröpfeln** *vi* to drip; **es tröpfelt** it's drizzling; **tropfen** *vt, vi* to drip; **Tropfen** (-s, -) *m* drop; **tropfenweise** *adv* drop by drop; **tropfnass** *adj* dripping wet; **Tropfsteinhöhle** *f* stalactite cave
tropisch *adj* tropical
Trost (-es) *m* consolation, comfort; **trösten** *vt* to console, to comfort; **tröstlich** *adj* bleak; (*Verhältnisse*) wretched; **Trostpreis** *m* consolation prize
Trottoir (-s, -s) *nt* pavement (*Brit*), sidewalk (*US*)
trotz *prep +gen o dat* in spite of; **Trotz** (-es) *m* defiance; **trotzdem** *adv* nevertheless ▷ *conj* although;

trotzig adj defiant

trüb adj dull; (Flüssigkeit, Glas) cloudy; (fig) gloomy

Trüffel (-, -n) f truffle

trug imperf von **tragen**

trügerisch adj deceptive

Truhe (-, -n) f chest

Trümmer pl wreckage sing; (Bau~) ruins pl

Trumpf (-(e)s, Trümpfe) m trump

Trunkenheit f intoxication; **~ am Steuer** drink driving (Brit), drunk driving (US)

Truthahn m turkey

Tscheche (-n, -n) m, **Tschechin** f Czech; **Tschechien** (-s) nt Czech Republic; **tschechisch** adj Czech; **die Tschechische Republik** Czech Republic; **Tschechisch** nt Czech

Tschetschenien (-s) nt Chechnya

tschüs(s) interj bye

T-Shirt (-s, -s) nt T-shirt

Tube (-, -n) f tube

Tuberkulose (-, -n) f tuberculosis, TB

Tuch (-(e)s, Tücher) nt cloth; (Halstuch) scarf; (Kopftuch) headscarf

tüchtig adj competent; (fleißig) efficient; (fam: kräftig) good

Tugend (-, -en) f virtue; **tugendhaft** adj virtuous

Tulpe (-, -n) f tulip

Tumor (-s, -en) m tumour

tun (tat, getan) vt (machen) to do; (legen) to put; **was tust du da?** what are you doing?; **das tut man nicht** you shouldn't do that; **jdm etw ~** (antun) to do sth to sb; **das tut es auch** that'll do ▷ vi to act; **so ~, als ob** to act as if ▷ vr impers: **es tut sich etwas/viel** something/a lot is happening

Tuner (-s, -) m tuner

Tunesien (-s) nt Tunisia

Tunfisch m siehe **Thunfisch** tuna

Tunnel (-s, -s o -) m tunnel

Tunte (-, -n) f (pej, fam) fairy

tupfen vt, vi to dab; (mit Farbe) to dot; **Tupfen** (-s, -) m dot

Tür (-, -en) f door; **vor/an der ~** at the door; **an die ~ gehen** to answer the door

Türke (-n, -n) m Turk; **Türkei** (-) f: **die ~** Turkey; **Türkin** f Turk

Türkis (-es, -e) m turquoise

türkisch adj Turkish; **Türkisch** nt Turkish

Turm (-(e)s, Türme) m tower; (spitzer Kirchturm) steeple; (Sprung~) diving platform; (Schach) rook, castle

turnen vi to do gymnastics; **Turnen** (-s) nt gymnastics sing; (Schule) physical education, PE; **Turner(in)** m(f) gymnast; **Turnhalle** f gym(nasium); **Turnhose** f gym shorts pl

Turnier (-s, -e) nt tournament

Turnschuh m gym shoe, sneaker (US)

Türschild nt doorplate; **Türschloss** nt lock

tuscheln vt, vi to whisper

Tussi (-, -s) f (pej, fam) chick

Tüte (-, -n) f bag

TÜV (-s, -s) m akr = **Technischer Überwachungsverein** = MOT (Brit), vehicle inspection (US)

● **TÜV**
●
● The **TÜV** is the organization
● responsible for checking the
● safety of machinery, particularly
● vehicles. Cars over three years
● old have to be examined every
● two years for their safety and
● for their exhaust emissions.
● **TÜV** is also the name given to
● the test itself.

TÜV-Plakette f badge attached to a vehicle's numberplate, indicating that it has passed the "TÜV"

Tweed (-s, -s) m tweed

twittern vi (auf Twitter) to tweet

Typ (-s, -en) m type; (Auto) model; (Mann) guy, bloke

Typhus (-) m typhoid

typisch adj typical (für of); **ein ~er Fehler** a common mistake; **~ Marcus!** that's just like Marcus!; **~ amerikanisch!** that's so American

u

u. abk = und

u. a. abk = **und andere(s)** and others; = **unter anderem, unter anderen** among other things

u. A. w. g. abk = **um Antwort wird gebeten** RSVP

U-Bahn f underground (Brit), subway (US)

übel adj bad; (moralisch) wicked; **mir ist ~** I feel sick; **diese Bemerkung hat er mir ~ genommen** he took offence at my remark; **Übelkeit** f nausea

üben vt, vi to practise

○ **SCHLÜSSELWORT**

über prep +dat 1 (räumlich) over, above; **zwei Grad über null** two degrees above zero

2 (zeitlich) over; **über der Arbeit einschlafen** to fall asleep over one's work

▷ prep +akk **1** (räumlich) over; (hoch über auch) above; (quer über auch) across

2 (zeitlich) over; **über Weihnachten** over Christmas; **über kurz oder lang** sooner or later

3 (mit Zahlen) **Kinder über 12 Jahren** children over o above 12 years of age; **ein Scheck über 200 Euro** a cheque for 200 euros

4 (auf dem Wege) via; **nach Köln über Aachen** to Cologne via Aachen; **ich habe es über die Auskunft erfahren** I found out from information

5 (betreffend) about; **ein Buch über ...** a book about o on ...; **über jdn/etw lachen** to laugh about o at sb/sth

6 Macht über jdn haben to have power over sb; **sie liebt ihn über alles** she loves him more than everything

▷ adv over; **über und über** over and over; **den ganzen Tag über** all day long; **jdm in etw dat über sein** to be superior to sb in sth

überall adv everywhere
überanstrengen vr: **sich ~** to overexert oneself
überbacken adj: **(mit Käse) ~** au gratin; **überbelichten** vt (Foto) to overexpose; **überbieten** irr vt to outbid; (übertreffen) to surpass; (Rekord) to break
Überbleibsel (-s, -) nt remnant
Überblick m overview; (fig: in Darstellung) survey; (Fähigkeit zu verstehen) grasp (über +akk of)
überbuchen vt to overbook; **Überbuchung** f overbooking
überdurchschnittlich adj above average
übereinander adv on top of each other; (sprechen etc) about

each other
übereinstimmen vi to agree (mit with)
überempfindlich adj hypersensitive
überfahren irr vt (Auto) to run over; **Überfahrt** f crossing
Überfall m (Banküberfall) robbery; (Mil) raid; (auf jdn) assault; **überfallen** irr vt to attack; (Bank) to raid
überfällig adj overdue
überfliegen irr vt to fly over; (Buch) to skim through
Überfluss m overabundance, excess (an +dat of); **überflüssig** adj superfluous
überfordern vt to demand too much of; (Kräfte) to overtax; **da bin ich überfordert** (bei Antwort) you've got me there
Überführung f (Brücke) flyover (Brit), overpass (US)
überfüllt adj overcrowded
Übergabe f handover
Übergang m crossing; (Wandel, Überleitung) transition; **Übergangslösung** f temporary solution, stopgap
übergeben irr vt to hand over
▷ vr: sich ~ to be sick, to vomit
Übergepäck nt excess baggage
Übergewicht nt excess weight; **(10 Kilo) ~ haben** to be (10 kilos) overweight
überglücklich adj overjoyed; (fam) over the moon
Übergröße f outsize
überhaupt adv at all; (im Allgemeinen) in general; (besonders) especially; **was willst du ~?** what is it you want?
überheblich adj arrogant
überholen vt to overtake; (Tech) to overhaul; **Überholspur** f overtaking (Brit) (o passing (US)) lane; **überholt** adj outdated

Überholverbot nt: **hier herrscht ~** you can't overtake here

überhören vt to miss, not to catch; (absichtlich) to ignore;

überladen irr vt to overload ▷ adj (fig) cluttered; **überlassen** irr vt: **jdm etw ~** to leave sth to sb; **über|laufen** irr vi (Flüssigkeit) to overflow

überleben vt, vi to survive; **Überlebende(r)** mf survivor

überlegen vt to consider; **sich** (dat) **etw ~** to think about sth; **er hat es sich** (dat) **anders überlegt** he's changed his mind ▷ adj superior (dat to); **Überlegung** f consideration

überm kontr von **über dem**

übermäßig adj excessive

übermorgen adv the day after tomorrow

übernächste(r, s) adj: **~ Woche** the week after next

übernachten vi to spend the night (bei jdm at sb's place); **übernächtigt** adj bleary-eyed, very tired; **Übernachtung** f overnight stay; **~ mit Frühstück** bed and breakfast

übernehmen irr vt to take on; (Amt, Geschäft) to take over ▷ vr: **sich ~** to take on too much

überprüfen vt to check; **Überprüfung** f check; (Überprüfen) checking

überqueren vt to cross

überraschen vt to surprise; **Überraschung** f surprise

überreden vt to persuade; **er hat mich überredet** he talked me into it

überreichen vt to hand over

übers kontr von **über das**

überschätzen vt to overestimate; **überschlagen** irr vt (berechnen) to estimate; (auslassen: Seite) to skip ▷ vr: **sich**

~ to somersault; (Auto) to overturn; (Stimme) to crack; **überschneiden** irr vr: **sich ~** (Linien etc) to intersect; (Termine) to clash

Überschrift f heading

Überschwemmung f flood

Übersee f: **nach/in ~** overseas

übersehen irr vt (Gelände) to look (out) over; (nicht beachten) to overlook

übersetzen vt to translate (aus from, in +akk into); **Übersetzer(in)** (-s, -) m(f) translator; **Übersetzung** f translation

Übersicht f overall view; (Darstellung) survey; **übersichtlich** adj clear

überstehen irr vt (durchstehen) to get over; (Winter etc) to get through

Überstunden pl overtime sing

überstürzt adj hasty

überteuert adj overpriced

übertragbar adj transferable; (Med) infectious; **übertragen** irr vt to transfer (auf +akk to); (Radio) to broadcast; (Krankheit) to transmit ▷ vr to spread (auf +akk to) ▷ adj figurative; **Übertragung** f (Radio) broadcast; (von Daten) transmission

übertreffen irr vt to surpass

übertreiben irr vt, vi to exaggerate, to overdo; **Übertreibung** f exaggeration; **übertrieben** adj exaggerated, overdone

überwachen vt to supervise; (Verdächtigen) to keep under surveillance

überwand imperf von **überwinden**

überweisen irr vt to transfer; (Patienten) to refer (an +akk to); **Überweisung** f transfer; (von Patienten) referral

u

überwiegend adv mainly
überwinden (überwand,
überwunden) vt to overcome ▷ vr:
sich ~ to make an effort, to force
oneself; **überwunden** pp von
überwinden
Überzelt nt flysheet
überzeugen vt to convince;
Überzeugung f conviction
überziehen irr vt (bedecken)
to cover; (Jacke etc) to put on;
(Konto) to overdraw; **die
Betten frisch ~** to change
the sheets
üblich adj usual
übrig adj remaining; **ist noch
Saft ~?** is there any juice left?; **die
Übrigen** pl the rest pl; **im Übrigen**
besides; **~ bleiben** to be left (over);
**mir blieb nichts anderes ~(, als
zu gehen)** I had no other choice
(but to go); **übrigens** adv
besides; (nebenbei bemerkt) by the
way; **übrig|haben** irr vt: **für jdn
etwas ~** (fam: jdn mögen) to have a
soft spot for sb
Übung f practice; (im Sport,
Aufgabe etc) exercise
Ufer (-s, -) nt (Fluss) bank; (Meer,
See) shore; **am ~** on the
bank/shore
Ufo (-(s), -s) nt akr = **unbekanntes
Flugobjekt** UFO
Uhr (-, -en) f clock; (am Arm)
watch; **wie viel ~ ist es?** what
time is it?; **1 ~ 1** o'clock; **20 ~ 8**
o'clock, 8 pm; **Uhrzeigersinn** m:
im ~ clockwise; **gegen den
~** anticlockwise (Brit),
counterclockwise (US); **Uhrzeit** f
time (of day)
Ukraine (-) f: **die ~** the Ukraine
UKW abk = **Ultrakurzwelle** VHF
Ulme (-, -n) f elm
Ultrakurzwelle f very high
frequency; **Ultraschallaufnahme**
f (Med) scan

○ **SCHLÜSSELWORT**

um prep +akk **1** (um herum)
(a)round; **um Weihnachten**
around Christmas; **er schlug um
sich** he hit about him
2 (mit Zeitangabe) at; **um acht
(Uhr)** at eight (o'clock)
3 (mit Größenangabe) by; **etw um 4
cm kürzen** to shorten sth by 4 cm;
um 10% teurer 10% more
expensive; **um vieles besser**
better by far; **um so besser** so
much the better
4 der Kampf um den Titel the
battle for the title; **um Geld
spielen** to play for money; **Stunde
um Stunde** hour after hour; **Auge
um Auge** an eye for an eye
▷ prep +gen: **um ... willen** for the
sake of ...; **um Gottes willen** for
goodness' o (stärker) God's sake
▷ konj: **um ... zu** (in order) to ...;
zu klug, um zu ... too clever to ...;
siehe **umso**
▷ adv **1** (ungefähr) about; **um (die)
30 Leute** about o around 30
people
2 (vorbei) **die 2 Stunden sind um**
the two hours are up

umarmen vt to embrace
Umbau m rebuilding; (zu etwas)
conversion (zu into); **um|bauen**
vt to rebuild; (zu etwas) to convert
(zu into)
um|blättern vi, vt to turn over
um|bringen irr vt to kill
um|buchen vi to change one's
reservation/flight
um|drehen vt to turn (round);
(obere Seite nach unten) to turn over
▷ vr: **sich ~** to turn (round);
Umdrehung f turn; (Phys, Auto)
revolution
um|fahren irr vt to knock down

um|fallen *irr vi* to fall over
Umfang *m* (*Ausmaß*) extent; (*von Buch*) size; (*Reichweite*) range; (*Math*) circumference;
umfangreich *adj* extensive
Umfeld *nt* environment
Umfrage *f* survey
Umgang *m* company; (*mit jdm*) dealings *pl*; **umgänglich** *adj* sociable; **Umgangssprache** *f* colloquial language, slang
Umgebung *f* surroundings *pl*; (*Milieu*) environment; (*Personen*) people around one
umgehen *irr vi* (*Gerücht*) to go round; **~ (können) mit** (know how to) handle ▷ *irr vt* to avoid; (*Schwierigkeit*, *Verbot*) to get round
um|gehen *irr vi*: **mit etw ~** to handle sth; **Umgehungsstraße** *f* bypass
umgekehrt *adj* reverse; (*gegenteilig*) opposite ▷ *adv* the other way round; **und ~** and vice versa
um|hören *vr*: **sich ~** to ask around; **um|kehren** *vi* to turn back ▷ *vt* to reverse; (*Kleidungsstück*) to turn inside out; **um|kippen** *vt* to tip over ▷ *vi* to overturn; (*fig*) to change one's mind; (*fam*: *ohnmächtig werden*) to pass out
Umkleidekabine *f* changing cubicle (*Brit*), dressing room (*US*); **Umkleideraum** *m* changing room
Umkreis *m* neighbourhood; **im ~ von** within a radius of
um|leiten *vt* to divert; **Umleitung** *f* diversion
um|rechnen *vt* to convert (*in +akk* into); **Umrechnung** *f* conversion; **Umrechnungskurs** *m* rate of exchange
Umriss *m* outline
um|rühren *vi*, *vt* to stir

ums *kontr von* **um das**
Umsatz *m* turnover
um|schalten *vi* to turn over
Umschlag *m* cover; (*Buch*) jacket; (*Med*) compress; (*Brief*) envelope
Umschulung *f* retraining
um|sehen *irr vr*: **sich ~** to look around; (*suchen*) to look out (*nach* for)
umso *adv* all the; **~ mehr** all the more; **~ besser** so much the better
umsonst *adv* (*vergeblich*) in vain; (*gratis*) for nothing
Umstand *m* circumstance; **Umstände** (*pl*) (*fig*) fuss; **in anderen Umständen sein** to be pregnant; **jdm Umstände machen** to cause sb a lot of trouble; **machen Sie bitte keine Umstände** please, don't put yourself out; **unter diesen/keinen Umständen** under these/no circumstances; **unter Umständen** possibly;
umständlich *adj* (*Methode*) complicated; (*Ausdrucksweise*) long-winded; (*Mensch*) ponderous; **Umstandsmode** *f* maternity wear
um|steigen *irr vi* to change (trains/buses)
um|stellen *vt* (*an anderen Ort*) to change round; (*Tech*) to convert ▷ *vr*: **sich ~** to adapt (*auf +akk* to); **Umstellung** *f* change; (*Umgewöhnung*) adjustment; (*Tech*) conversion
Umtausch *m* exchange; **um|tauschen** *vt* to exchange; (*Währung*) to change
Umweg *m* detour
Umwelt *f* environment; **Umweltbelastung** *f* ecological damage; **umweltbewusst** *adj* environmentally aware;

umweltfreundlich adj
environment-friendly;
Umweltpapier nt recycled paper;
umweltschädlich adj harmful to
the environment; **Umweltschutz**
m environmental protection;
Umweltschützer(in) (-s, -) m(f)
environmentalist;
Umweltsteuer f green tax;
Umweltverschmutzung f
pollution; **umweltverträglich** adj
environment-friendly

um|werfen irr vt to knock over;
(fig: ändern) to upset; (fig, fam: jdn)
to flabbergast

um|ziehen irr vt to change ▷ vr:
sich ~ to change ▷ vi to move
(house); **Umzug** m
(Straßenumzug) procession;
(Wohnungsumzug) move

unabhängig adj independent;
Unabhängigkeitstag m
Independence Day, Fourth of July
(US)

unabsichtlich adv
unintentionally

unangenehm adj unpleasant;
Unannehmlichkeit f inconvenience;
~en pl trouble sing

unanständig adj indecent;
unappetitlich adj (Essen)
unappetizing; (abstoßend)
off-putting; **unbeabsichtigt** adj
unintentional; **unbedeutend** adj
insignificant, unimportant;
(Fehler) slight

unbedingt adj unconditional
▷ adv absolutely

unbefriedigend adj unsatis-
factory; **unbegrenzt** adj
unlimited; **unbekannt** adj
unknown; **unbeliebt** adj
unpopular; **unbemerkt** adj
unnoticed; **unbequem** adj
(Stuhl, Mensch) uncomfortable;
(Regelung) inconvenient;
unbeständig adj (Wetter)

unsettled; (Lage) unstable;
(Mensch) unreliable; **unbestimmt**
adj indefinite; **unbeteiligt** adj
(nicht dazugehörig) uninvolved;
(innerlich nicht berührt) indifferent,
unconcerned; **unbewacht** adj
unguarded; **unbewusst** adj
unconscious; **unbezahlt** adj
unpaid; **unbrauchbar** adj
useless

und conj and; **~ so weiter** and so
on; **na ~?** so what?

undankbar adj (Person)
ungrateful; (Aufgabe) thankless;
undenkbar adj inconceivable;
undeutlich adj indistinct;
undicht adj leaky; **uneben** adj
uneven; **unecht** adj (Schmuck etc)
fake; **unehelich** adj (Kind)
illegitimate; **unendlich** adj
endless; (Math) infinite;
unentbehrlich adj indispensable;
unentgeltlich adj free (of charge)

unentschieden adj undecided;
~ enden (Sport) to end in a draw

unerfreulich adj unpleasant
unerhört adj unheard-of; (Bitte)
outrageous; **unerlässlich** adj
indispensable; **unerträglich** adj
unbearable; **unerwartet** adj
unexpected

unerwünscht adj unwelcome;
(Eigenschaften) undesirable;
unfähig adj incompetent; **~ sein,**
etw zu tun to be incapable of
doing sth; **unfair** adj unfair

Unfall m accident; **Unfallflucht** f
failure to stop after an accident;
Unfallhergang m: **den**
~ schildern to give details of the
accident; **Unfallstation** f
casualty ward; **Unfallstelle** f
scene of the accident;
Unfallversicherung f accident
insurance

unfreundlich adj unfriendly
Ungarn (-s) nt Hungary

Breakdowns	Pannen
My car has broken down.	**Ich habe eine Panne.**
Where is the next garage?	Wo ist die nächste Werkstatt?
The exhaust	Der Auspuff
The gearbox	Das Getriebe
The windscreen	Die Windschutzscheibe
... is broken.	... ist kaputt.
The brakes	Die Bremsen
The headlights	Die Scheinwerfer
The windscreen wipers	Die Scheibenwischer
... are not working.	... funktionieren nicht.
The battery is flat.	Die Batterie ist leer.
The car won't start.	Der Motor springt nicht an.
The engine is overheating.	Der Motor wird zu heiß.
I have a flat tyre.	Ich habe einen Platten.
Can you repair it?	Können Sie das reparieren?
When will the car be ready?	Wann ist das Auto fertig?

Parking	Parken
Can I park here?	Kann ich hier parken?
Do I need to buy a (car-parking) ticket?	Muss ich einen Parkschein lösen?
Where is the ticket machine?	Wo ist der Parkschein-automat?
The ticket machine isn't working.	Der Parkscheinautomat funktioniert nicht.

Petrol Station	Tankstelle
Where is the nearest petrol station?	Wo ist die nächste Tankstelle?
Fill it up, please.	Volltanken bitte.

Asking the Way | Erkundigungen

Where is the nearest ...?	Wo ist der/die/das nächste ...?
How do I get to ...?	Wie komme ich zum/zur/ nach ...?
Is it far?	Ist es weit?
How far is it?	Wie weit ist es?
Is this the right way to ...?	Bin ich hier richtig zum/zur/ nach ...?
I'm lost.	Ich habe mich verlaufen/ verfahren.
Can you show me on the map?	Können Sie mir das auf der Karte zeigen?
You have to turn round.	Kehren Sie um.
Go straight on.	Fahren Sie geradeaus.
Turn left/right.	Biegen Sie nach links/rechts ab.
Take the second street on the left/right.	Nehmen Sie die zweite Straße links/rechts.

Car Hire | Autovermietung

I want to hire ...	Ich möchte ... mieten.
a car.	ein Auto
a moped.	ein Moped
How much is it for ...?	Was kostet das für ...?
one day	einen Tag
a week	eine Woche
Is there a kilometre charge?	Verlangen Sie eine Kilometer-gebühr?
What is included in the price?	Was ist alles im Preis inbegriffen?
I'd like a child seat for a ...-year-old child.	Ich möchte einen Kindersitz für ein ... Jahre altes Kind.
What do I do if I have an accident/if I break down?	Was tue ich bei einem Unfall/ einer Panne?

Hello!	Guten Tag!
Good evening!	Guten Abend!
Good night!	Gute Nacht!
Goodbye!	Auf Wiedersehen!
What's your name?	Wie heißen Sie?
My name is …	Mein Name ist …
This is …	Das ist …
my wife.	meine Frau.
my husband.	mein Mann.
my partner.	mein Partner/
	meine Partnerin.
Where are you from?	Wo kommen Sie her?
I come from …	Ich komme aus …
How are you?	Wie geht es Ihnen?
Fine, thanks.	Danke, gut.
And you?	Und Ihnen?
Do you speak English?	Sprechen Sie Englisch?
I don't understand German.	Ich verstehe kein Deutsch.
Thanks very much!	Vielen Dank!

TOPICS | THEMEN

TOPICS		THEMEN

Taxi	Taxi
Where can I get a taxi?	Wo bekomme ich hier ein Taxi?
Call me a taxi, please.	Bitte rufen Sie mir ein Taxi.
Please order me a taxi for ... o'clock.	Bitte bestellen Sie mir ein Taxi für ... Uhr.
To the airport/station, please.	Zum Flughafen/Bahnhof, bitte.
I'm in a hurry.	Ich habe es sehr eilig.
How much is it?	Was kostet die Fahrt?
I need a receipt.	Ich brauche eine Quittung.
Keep the change.	Stimmt so.
Stop here, please.	Bitte halten Sie hier.

Plane | Flugzeug

Where is ...?	Wo ist ...?
the taxi rank	*der Taxistand*
the bus stop	*die Bushaltestelle*
the information office	*die Information*
My luggage hasn't arrived.	Mein Gepäck ist nicht angekommen.
Where do I check in for the flight to ...?	Wo ist das Check-in für den Flug nach ...?
Which gate for the flight to ...?	Von welchem Ausgang geht der Flug nach ...?
When does boarding begin?	Wann beginnt das Einsteigen?
Window/aisle, please.	Fenster/Gang bitte.
I've lost my boarding pass/ my ticket.	Ich habe meine Einsteige-karte/meinen Flugschein verloren.

Local Public Transport | Öffentlicher Nahverkehr

How do I get to ...?	Wie komme ich zum/zur/ nach ...?
Where is the nearest ...?	Wo ist die nächste ...?
bus stop	*Bushaltestelle*
tram stop	*Straßenbahnhaltestelle*
underground station	*U-Bahn-Station*
Where is the bus station?	Wo ist der Busbahnhof?
Is there a reduction ...?	Gibt es eine Ermäßigung ...?
for students	*für Studenten*
for pensioners	*für Rentner*
with this card	*mit diesem Ausweis*
Do you have a map of the rail network?	Haben Sie eine Karte mit dem Streckennetz?
What is the next stop?	Was ist die nächste Halte-stelle?

When is the next train to ...?	Wann geht der nächste Zug nach ...?
Is there a supplement to pay?	Muss ich einen Zuschlag kaufen?
Do I need to change?	Muss ich umsteigen?
Where do I change?	Wo muss ich umsteigen?
Is this the train for ...?	Ist das der Zug nach ...?
I have a reservation.	Ich habe eine Platzkarte/ Reservierung.
Is this seat free?	Ist dieser Platz noch frei?
Where is the buffet car?	Wo ist der Speisewagen?
Where is coach number ...?	Wo ist Wagen Nummer ...?

Ferry — Fähre

Is there a ferry to ...?	Gibt es eine Fähre nach ...?
When is the next ferry to ...?	Wann geht die nächste Fähre nach ...?
When is the first/last ferry to ...?	Wann geht die erste/letzte Fähre nach ...?
How much is ...?	Was kostet ...?
a single	*die einfache Fahrt*
a return	*die Hin- und Rückfahrt*
How much is it for a car/ camper with ... people?	Was kostet es für eine Auto/ Wohnmobil mit ... Personen?
How long does the crossing take?	Wie lange dauert die Überfahrt?
Where is ...?	Wo ist ...?
the restaurant	*das Restaurant*
the duty-free shop	*der Duty-free-Shop*
Where is cabin number ...?	Wo ist Kabine Nummer ...?

| Do you have a road map of this area? | Haben Sie eine Straßenkarte von dieser Gegend? |

Cycling | Fahrrad

Where is the cycle path to ...?	Wo ist der Radwanderweg nach ...?
Can I keep my bike here?	Kann ich hier mein Fahrrad unterstellen?
My bike has been stolen.	Mein Fahrrad ist gestohlen worden.
Where is the nearest bike repair shop?	Wo gibt es hier eine Fahrradwerkstatt?
The brake isn't working.	Die Bremse funktioniert nicht.
The gears aren't working.	Die Gangschaltung funktioniert nicht.
The chain is broken.	Die Kette ist gerissen.
I've got a flat tyre.	Ich habe einen Platten.
I need a puncture repair kit.	Ich brauche Reifenflickzeug.

Train | Eisenbahn

A single to ..., please.	Eine einfache Fahrt nach ... bitte.
Two returns to ..., please.	Zweimal hin und zurück nach ... bitte.
Is there a reduction ...?	Gibt es eine Ermäßigung ...?
for students	*für Studenten*
for pensioners	*für Rentner*
with this pass	*mit diesem Pass*
I'd like to reserve a seat on the train to ..., please.	Eine Platzkarte für den Zug nach ... bitte.
I want to book a couchette/a berth to ...	Ich möchte einen Liegewagenplatz/Schlafwagenplatz nach ... buchen.

40 euros' worth of ..., please.	Für 40 Euro ... bitte.
diesel	*Diesel*
unleaded (economy) petrol	*Normalbenzin*
premium unleaded	*Super*
Pump number ... please.	Säule Nummer ... bitte.
Please check ...	Bitte überprüfen Sie ...
the tyre pressure.	*den Reifendruck.*
the oil.	*das Öl.*
the water.	*das Wasser.*

Accident — Unfall

Please call ...	Bitte rufen Sie ...
the police.	*die Polizei.*
the emergency doctor.	*den Notarzt.*
Here are my insurance details.	Hier sind meine Versicherungsangaben.
Give me your insurance details, please.	Bitte geben Sie mir Ihre Versicherungsangaben.
Can you be a witness for me?	Würden Sie das bezeugen?
You were driving too fast.	Sie sind zu schnell gefahren.
It wasn't your right of way.	Sie haben die Vorfahrt nicht beachtet.

Car Travel — Unterwegs mit dem Auto

What's the best route to ...?	Wie kommt man am besten nach/zu ...?
Where can I pay the toll?	Wo kann ich die Maut bezahlen?
I'd like a motorway tax sticker ...	Ich möchte einen Aufkleber für die Autobahngebühr/ eine Vignette ...
for a week.	*für eine Woche.*
for a month.	*für einen Monat.*

Wales (-) nt Wales; **Waliser(in)** m(f) Welshman/Welshwoman; **walisisch** adj Welsh; **Walisisch** nt Welsh

Walkie-Talkie (-(s), -s) nt walkie-talkie

Walkman® m (-s, -s) m walk-man®; personal stereo

Wall m (-(e)s, Wälle) m embankment

Wallfahrt f pilgrimage

Wallfahrtsort m place of pilgrimage

Walnuss f walnut

Walross (-es, -e) nt walrus

wälzen vt to roll; (Bücher) to pore over; (Probleme) to deliberate on ▶ sich ~ vr to roll about; (im Bett) to toss and turn

Walzer (-s, -) m waltz

Wand f (-, Wände) f (Trenn-) partition; (Berg-) (rock) face

Wandel (-s) m change ▶ vr: sich ~ to change ▶ vt to change

wandern vi to hike; (Blick) to wander; (Gedanken) to stray

Wanderer (-s, -), **Wanderin** f(-, -nen) hiker; **Wanderkarte** f hiking map; **Wanderschuh** m walking shoe; **Wanderstiefel** m walking boot; **Wanderung** f hike; eine ~ **machen** to go on a hike; **Wanderweg** m walking (o hiking) trail

Wandleuchte f wall lamp; **Wandmalerei** f mural; **Wandschrank** m built-in cupboard (Brit), closet (US)

Wange f (-, -n) f cheek

wann adv when; **seit ~ ist sie da?** how long has she been here?; **bis ~ bleibt ihr?** how long are you staying?

Wappen (-s, -) nt coat of arms

war imperf von sein

warb imperf von werben

Ware f (-, -n) f product; **~n** pl goods

Warenhaus nt department store; **Warenprobe** f sample; **Warenzeichen** nt trademark

warm adj (Essen) hot; **– I'm too warm; Wärme** f (-, -n) f warmth; **wärmen** vt to warm; (Essen) to heat up ▶ vi (Kleidung, Sonne) to be warm ▶ vr: **sich ~** to warm up; (gegenseitig) to keep each other warm; **Wärmflasche** f hot-water bottle; **Warmstart** m (Inform) warm start

Warnanlage f (Auto) warning flasher; **Warndreieck** nt (Auto) warning triangle; **warnen** vt to warn (vor +dat about, of); **Warnung** f warning

Warteliste f waiting list; **warten** vi to wait (auf +akk for) ▶ vt (Tech) to service; **warte mal** wait to hang on a minute ▶ vt (Tech) to service; **Wärter(in)** m(f) attendant; **Wartesaal** m, **Wartezimmer** nt waiting room; **Wartung** f service; (das Warten) servicing

warum adv why

Warze f (-, -n) f wart

was pron what; (fam: etwas) something; **~ kostet das?** what does it cost? how much is it?; **– für ein Auto ist das?** what kind of car is that?; **– für eine Farbe/Größe** what colour/size?; **~ gibt's?** what is it? what's up? **du weißt, ~ ich meine** you know what I mean; **– (auch) immer** whatever; **soll ich dir – mitbringen?** do you want me to bring you anything?; **alles, ~ er hat** everything he's got

Waschanlage f (Auto) car wash; **waschbar** adj washable; **Waschbär** m raccoon; **Waschbecken** nt washbasin

Wäsche (-, -n) f washing; (schmutzig) laundry; (Bettwäsche) linen; (Unterwäsche) underwear; **in der ~** in the wash; **Wäscheklammer** f clothes peg (Brit) (o pin (US)); **Wäscheleine** f clothesline

waschen (wusch, gewaschen) vt, vi to wash ▷ vr: **sich ~** to (have a) wash; **sich** (dat) **die Haare ~** to wash one's hair

Wäscherei f laundry; **Wäscheständer** m clothes horse; **Wäschetrockner** m tumble-drier

Waschgelegenheit f washing facilities pl; **Waschlappen** m flannel (Brit), washcloth (US); (fam: Mensch) wet blanket; **Waschmaschine** f washing machine; **Waschmittel** nt, **Waschpulver** nt washing powder; **Waschraum** m washroom; **Waschsalon** (-s, -s) m launderette (Brit), laundromat (US); **Waschstraße** f car wash

Wasser (-s, -) nt water; **fließendes ~** running water; **Wasserball** m (Sport) water polo; **Wasserbob** m jet ski; **wasserdicht** adj watertight; (Uhr etc) waterproof; **Wasserfall** m waterfall; **Wasserfarbe** f watercolour; **wasserfest** adj watertight, waterproof; **Wasserhahn** m tap (Brit), faucet (US); **wässerig** adj watery; **Wasserkessel** (-s, -) m kettle; **Wasserkocher** (-s, -) m electric kettle; **Wasserleitung** f water pipe; **wasserlöslich** adj water-soluble; **Wassermann** m (Astr) Aquarius; **Wassermelone** f water melon; **Wasserrutschbahn** f water chute; **Wasserschaden** m water damage; **wasserscheu** adj scared of water; **Wasserski** nt water-skiing; **Wasserspiegel** m surface of the water; (Wasserstand) water level; **Wassersport** m water sports pl; **wasserundurchlässig** adj watertight, waterproof; **Wasserverbrauch** m water consumption; **Wasserversorgung** f water supply; **Wasserwaage** f spirit level; **Wasserwerk** nt waterworks pl

waten vi to wade

Watt (-(e)s, -en) nt (Geo) mud flats pl ▷ (-s, -) nt (Elek) watt

Watte (-, -n) f cotton wool; **Wattepad** (-s, -s) m cotton pad; **Wattestäbchen** nt cotton bud, Q-tip® (US)

WC (-s, -s) nt toilet, restroom (US); **WC-Reiniger** m toilet cleaner

Web (-s) nt (Inform) Web; **Webadresse** f (Inform) web address; **Webseite** f (Inform) web page

Wechsel (-s, -) m change; (Spieler~: Sport) substitution; **Wechselgeld** nt change; **wechselhaft** adj (Wetter) changeable; **Wechseljahre** pl menopause sing; **Wechselkurs** m exchange rate; **wechseln** vt to change; (Blicke) to exchange; **Geld ~** to change some money; (in Kleingeld) to get some change; **Euro in Pfund ~** to change euros into pounds ▷ vi to change; **kannst du ~?** can you change this?; **Wechselstrom** m alternating current, AC; **Wechselstube** f bureau de change

Weckdienst m wake-up call service; **wecken** vt to wake (up);

w

Wecker (-s, -) m alarm clock; (los, ob) ...
Weckruf m wake-up call
wedeln vi (Ski) to wedel; **mit etw ~** to wave sth; **mit dem Schwanz ~** to wag its tail; **der Hund wedelte mit dem Schwanz** the dog wagged its tail
weder conj: **~ ... noch ...** neither ... nor ...
weg adv (entfernt, verreist) away; (los, ab) off; **er war schon ~** he had already left (o gone); **Hände ~!** hands off; **weit ~** a long way away (o off)
Weg (-(e)s, -e) m way; (Pfad) path; (Route) route; **jdn nach dem ~ fragen** to ask for directions
wegbleiben irr vi to stay away
wegbringen irr vt to take away
wegen prep +gen o dat because of
wegfahren irr vi to drive away; (abfahren) to leave; (in Urlaub) to go away
Wegfahrsperre f (Auto) (engine) immobilizer; **weggehen** irr vi to go away; **wegkommen** irr vi to get away; (fig) **gut/schlecht ~** to come off well/badly; **weglassen** irr vt to leave out; **weglaufen** irr vi to run away; **weglegen** irr vt to put aside; **wegmachen** vt (fam) to get rid of; **wegmüssen** irr vi: **ich muss weg** I've got to go; **wegnehmen** irr vt to take away; **wegräumen** vt to clear away; **wegrennen** irr vi to run away; **wegschicken** vt to send away; **wegschmeißen** irr vt to throw away; **wegtun** irr vt to put away; **Wegweiser** (-s, -) m signpost; **wegwerfen** irr vt to throw away; **wegwischen** vt to wipe away; **wegziehen** irr vt to move off, irr vi to move (away)
weh adj sore; siehe auch **wehtun**

wehen vt, vi to blow; (Fahne) to flutter
Wehen pl labour pains pl
Wehrdienst m military service
wehren vr: **sich ~** to defend oneself
wehtun irr vi to hurt; **jdm/sich ~** to hurt sb/oneself
Weibchen nt: **es ist ein ~** (Tier) it's a she; (Bio) female
weiblich adj feminine
weich adj soft; **~ gekocht** (Ei) soft-boiled
Weichkäse m soft cheese; (Streichkäse) cheese spread
weichlich adj soft; (körperlich) weak
Weichspüler (-s, -) m (für Wäsche) (fabric) softener
Weide (-, -n) f (Baum) willow; (Grasfläche) meadow
weigern vr: **sich ~** to refuse
Weigerung f refusal
Weiher (-s, -) m pond
Weihnachten (-, -) nt Christmas; frohe ~ merry Christmas
Weihnachtsabend m Christmas Eve
Weihnachtsbaum m Christmas tree
Weihnachtsfeier f Christmas party; **Weihnachtsferien** pl Christmas holidays pl (Brit), Christmas vacation sing (US); **Weihnachtsgeld** nt Christmas bonus; **Weihnachtsgeschenk** nt Christmas present; **Weihnachtskarte** f Christmas card; **Weihnachtslied** nt Christmas carol; **Weihnachtsmann** m Father Christmas, Santa (Claus)

WEIHNACHTSMARKT

The **Weihnachtsmarkt** is a market held in most large towns in Germany in the weeks prior to Christmas. People visit it to buy presents, toys and

Christmas decorations, and to enjoy the festive atmosphere. **Weihnachtsmarkt** *m* Christmas market. **Weihnachtsmann** *m* Father Christmas. Food and drink associated with the Christmas festivities can also be eaten and drunk there, for example, gingerbread and mulled wine.

Weihnachtsstern *m* (Bot) poinsettia. **Weihnachtstag** *m*: **erster ~** Christmas Day; **zweiter ~** Boxing Day. **Weihnachtszeit** *f* Christmas season

weil *conj* because

Weile *f* (-) while, short time; **es kann noch eine ~ dauern** it could take some time

Wein *m* (-(e)s, -e) wine; (*Pflanze*) vine; **Weinbeere** *f* grape; **Weinberg** *m* vineyard; **Weinbergschnecke** *f* snail; **Weinbrand** *m* brandy; **weinen** *vt, vi* to cry; **Weinglas** *nt* wine glass; **Weinkarte** *f* wine list; **Weinkeller** *m* wine cellar; **Weinlese** *f* (-, -n) vintage; **Weinprobe** *f* wine tasting; **Weintraube** *f* grape; **weise** *adj* wise; **Weise** *f* (-, -n) manner, way; **auf diese (Art und) ~** this way; **weisen** (**wies, gewiesen**) *vt* to show; **Weisheit** *f* wisdom; **Weisheitszahn** *m* wisdom tooth

weiß *adj* white; **Weißbier** *nt* = wheat beer; **Weißbrot** *nt* white bread; **weißhaarig** *adj* white-haired; **Weißkohl** *m* (white) cabbage; **Weißkraut** *nt* (white) cabbage; **Weißwein** *m* white wine; **Weißwurst** *f* white sausage; **weit** *adj* (*Begriff*) broad; (*Reise, Wurf*) long; (*Kleid*) loose; **wie ~ ist es ...?** how far is it ...?; **so ~ sein** to be ready ▸ *adv* far:

~ verbreitet widespread; **~ gereist** widely travelled; **~ offen** wide open; **das geht zu ~** that's going too far, that's pushing it; **weiter** *adj* wider; **~ (weg)** farther (away); (*zusätzlich*) further; **~e Informationen** further information *sing* ▸ *adv* further: **~!** go on; (*weitergehen*) keep moving; **nichts/niemand ~** nothing/nobody else; **und so ~** and so on; **weiterarbeiten** *vi* to carry on working; **Weiterbildung** *f* further training (*o* education); **weiterempfehlen** *irr vt* to recommend; **weitererzählen** *vt*: **nicht ~!** don't tell anyone; **weiterfahren** *irr vi* to go on (*nach* to, *bis* to, as far as); **weitergeben** *irr vt* to pass on; **weitergehen** *irr vi* to go on; **weiterhelfen** *irr vi*: **jdm ~** to help sb; **weiterhin** *adv*: **etw ~ tun** to carry on doing sth; **weitermachen** *vt, vi* to continue; **weiterreisen** *vi* to continue one's journey

weitgehend *adj* considerable ▸ *adv* largely; **weitsichtig** *adj* (*fig*) far-sighted; **Weitsprung** *m* long jump; **Weitwinkelobjektiv** *nt* (*Foto*) wide-angle lens

Weizen (-s, -) *m* wheat; **Weizenbier** *nt* = wheat beer

○ **SCHLÜSSELWORT**

welche(r, s) *interrogativ pron* which, **welcher von beiden?** which (one) of the two?; **hast du genommen?** which (one) did you take?; **welche eine ...!** **welche Freude!** what a ...!; what joy! ▸ *indef pron* some; (*in Fragen*) any; **ich habe welche** I have some; **haben Sie welcher?** do you have

any? ▷ *relativ pron (bei Menschen)* who; *(bei Sachen)* which, that; **welche(r, s) auch immer** whoever/whichever/whatever

welk *adj* withered; **welken** *vi* to wither

Welle (-, -n) *f* wave; **Wellengang** *m* waves *pl;* **starker ~** heavy seas *pl;* **Wellenlänge** *f (a. fig)* wavelength; **Wellenreiten** *nt* surfing; **Wellensittich** (-s, -e) *m* budgerigar, budgie; **wellig** *adj* wavy

Wellness *f* health and beauty *(Brit)*, wellness *(US)*

Welpe (-n, -n) *m* puppy

Welt (-, -en) *f* world; **auf der ~** in the world; **auf die ~ kommen** to be born; **Weltall** *nt* universe; **weltbekannt, weltberühmt** *adj* world-famous; **Weltkrieg** *m* world war; **Weltmacht** *f* world power; **Weltmeister(in)** *m(f)* world champion; **Weltmeisterschaft** *f* world championship; *(im Fußball)* World Cup; **Weltraum** *m* space; **Weltreise** *f* trip round the world; **Weltrekord** *m* world record; **Weltstadt** *f* metropolis; **weltweit** *adj* worldwide, global

wem *pron dat von* **wer** who ... to, (to) whom; **~ hast du's gegeben?** who did you give it to?; **~ gehört es?** who does it belong to?, whose is it?; **~ auch immer es gehört** whoever it belongs to

wen *pron akk von* **wer** whom, who; **~ hast du besucht?** who did you visit?; **~ möchten Sie sprechen?** who would you like to speak to?

Wende (-, -n) *f* turning point; *(Veränderung)* change; **die ~** *(Hist)* the fall of the Berlin Wall; **Wendekreis** *m (Auto)* turning circle

Wendeltreppe *f* spiral staircase

wenden *(wendete o wandte, gewendet o gewandt) vt, vi* to turn (round); *(um 180°)* to make a U-turn; **sich an jdn ~** to turn to sb; **bitte ~!** please turn over, PTO ▷ *vr:* **sich ~** to turn; **sich an jdn ~** to turn to sb

wenig *pron, adv* little; **~(e)** *pl* few; **(nur) ein (klein) ~** (just) a little (bit); **ein ~ Zucker** a little bit of sugar, a little sugar; **wir haben ~ Zeit** we haven't got much time; **zu ~** too little; *pl* too few; **nur ~ wissen** only a few know ▷ *adv:* **er spricht ~** he doesn't talk much; **~ bekannt** little known; **wenige** *pron pl* few *pl;* **wenigste(r, s)** *adj* least; **wenigstens** *adv* at least

○ **SCHLÜSSELWORT**

wenn *konj* 1 *(falls, bei Wünschen)* if; **wenn auch ..., selbst wenn ...** even if ...; **wenn ich doch ...** if only I ...
2 *(zeitlich)* when; **immer wenn** whenever

wennschon *adv:* **na ~** so what?

wer *pron* who; **~ war das?** who was that?; **~ von euch?** which (one) of you? ▷ *pron* anybody who, anyone who; **~ das glaubt, ist dumm** anyone who believes that is stupid; **~ auch immer** whoever ▷ *pron* somebody, someone; *(in Fragen)* anybody, anyone; **ist da ~?** is (there) anybody there?

Werbefernsehen *nt* TV commercials *pl;* **Werbegeschenk** *nt* promotional gift; **werben** *(warb, geworben) vt* to win; *(Mitglied)* to recruit ▷ *vi* to advertise; **Werbespot** (-s, -s) *m* commercial; **Werbung** *f* advertising

w

SCHLÜSSELWORT

werden (pt **wurde**, pp **geworden** o (bei Passiv **worden**)) vi ○ to become: **was ist aus ihm/aus der Sache geworden?** what became of him/it?; **es ist nichts/gut geworden** it came to nothing/turned out well; **es wird Nacht/Tag** it's getting dark/light; **mir wird kalt** I'm getting cold; **mir wird schlecht** I feel ill; **Erster werden** to come to or be first; **das muss anders werden** that'll have to change; **rot/zu Eis werden** to turn red/to ice; **was willst du (mal) werden?** what do you want to be?; **die Fotos sind gut geworden** the photos have come out nicely

▷ als Hilfsverb 1 (bei Futur) **er wird es tun** he will do it; **er wird das nicht tun** he will not or he won't do it; **es wird gleich regnen** it's going to rain

2 (bei Konjunktiv) **ich würde ...** I would ...; **er würde gern ...** he would like to ...; **ich würde lieber ...** I would or I'd rather ...

3 (bei Vermutung) **sie wird in der Küche sein** she will be in the kitchen

4 (bei Passiv) **gebraucht werden** to be used; **er ist geschossen worden** he has or he's been shot; **mir wurde gesagt, dass ...** I was told that ...

werfen (warf, geworfen) vt to throw

Werft (-, -en) f shipyard, dockyard

Werk (-(e)s, -e) nt (Kunstwerk, Buch etc) work; (Fabrik) factory; (Mechanismus) works pl; **Werkstatt** (-, -stätten) f workshop; (Auto)

garage; **Werktag** m working day; **werktags** adv on weekdays, during the week; **Werkzeug** nt tool; **Werkzeugkasten** m toolbox

wert adj worth; **es ist etwa so** 50 Euro ~ it's worth about 50 euros; **das ist nichts ~** it's worthless; **Wert** (-(e)s, -e) m worth; (Zahlen~) (Fin) value; (+akk) **to legen auf ~** to attach importance to; **es hat doch keinen ~** (Sinn) it's pointless; **Wertangabe** f declaration of value; **Wertbrief** m insured letter; **Wertgegenstand** m valuable object; **wertlos** adj worthless; **Wertmarke** f token, valuable object; **Wertpapiere** pl securities pl; **Wertsachen** pl valuables pl; **Wertstoff** m recyclable waste; **wertvoll** adj valuable

Wesen (-s, -) nt being; (Natur, Charakter) nature

wesentlich adj significant; (beträchtlich) considerable ▷ adv considerably

weshalb adv why

Wespe (-, -n) f wasp; **Wespenstich** m wasp sting

wessen pron gen von **wer** whose

WESSI

- A Wessi is a colloquial and often derogatory word used to describe a German from the former West Germany. The expression 'Besserwessi' is used by East Germans to describe a West German who is considered to be a know-all.

West west; **Westdeutschland** nt (als Landesteil) Western Germany; (Hist) West Germany; **Weste** (-, -n) f waistcoat (Brit), vest (US); (Wollweste) cardigan

Westen (-s) m west; **im ~ Englands** in the west of England; **der Wilde ~** the Wild West; **Westeuropa** nt Western Europe; **Westküste** f west coast; **westlich** adj western; (Kurs, Richtung) westerly; **Westwind** m west(erly) wind

weswegen adv why

Wettbewerb m competition; **Wettbüro** nt betting office; **Wette** (-, -n) f bet; **eine ~ abschließen** to make a bet; **die ~ gilt!** you're on; **wetten** vt, vi to bet (auf +akk on); **ich habe mit ihm gewettet, dass ...** I bet him that ...; **ich wette mit dir um 50 Euro** I'll bet you 50 euros; **~, dass?** wanna bet?

Wetter (-s, -) nt weather; **Wetterbericht** m, **Wettervorhersage** f weather forecast; **Wetterkarte** f weather map; **Wetterlage** f weather situation; **Wettervorhersage** f weather forecast

Wettkampf m contest; **Wettlauf** m race; **Wettrennen** nt race

WG (-, -s) f abk = **Wohngemeinschaft**

Whirlpool® (-s, -s) m jacuzzi®

Whisky (-s, -s) m (schottisch) whisky; (irisch, amerikanisch) whiskey

wichtig adj important

wickeln vt (Schnur) to wind (um round); (Schal, Decke) to wrap (um round); **ein Baby ~** to change a baby's nappy (Brit) (o diaper (US)); **Wickelraum** m baby-changing room; **Wickeltisch** m baby-changing table

Widder (-s, -) m (Zool) ram; (Astr) Aries sing

wider prep +akk against

widerlich adj disgusting

widerrufen irr vt to withdraw; (Auftrag, Befehl etc) to cancel

widersprechen irr vi to contradict (jdm sb); **Widerspruch** m contradiction

Widerstand m resistance; **widerstandsfähig** adj resistant (gegen to)

widerwärtig adj disgusting

widerwillig adj unwilling

widmen vt to dedicate ▷ vr: **sich jdm/etw ~** to devote oneself to sb/sth; **Widmung** f dedication

🔵 **SCHLÜSSELWORT**

wie adv how; **wie groß/schnell?** how big/fast?; **wie wär's?** how about it?; **wie ist er?** what's he like?; **wie gut du das kannst!** you're very good at it; **wie bitte?** pardon?; (entrüstet) I beg your pardon!; **und wie!** and how!; **wie viel** how much; **wie viele Menschen** how many people; **wie weit** to what extent

▷ konj 1 (bei Vergleichen) **so schön wie ...** as beautiful as ...; **wie ich schon sagte** as I said; **wie du** like you; **singen wie ein ...** to sing like a ...; **wie (zum Beispiel)** such as (for example)

2 (zeitlich) **wie er das hörte, ging er** when he heard that he left; **er hörte, wie der Regen fiel** he heard the rain falling

wieder adv again; **~ ein(e) ...** another ...; **~ erkennen** to recognize; **etw ~ gutmachen** to make up for sth; **~ verwerten** to recycle

wieder|bekommen irr vt to get back

wiederbeschreibbar adj (CD, DVD) rewritable

w

wiederholen vt to repeat;
Wiederholung f repetition
wiederhören nt (Tel) **auf ~** goodbye
wiederkommen irr vi to come back
wiedersehen irr vt to see again; (wieder treffen) to meet
Wiedersehen (-s) nt again; **auf ~!** goodbye
Wiedervereinigung f reunification
Wiege (-, -n) f cradle; **wiegen** (wog, gewogen) vt, vi to weigh
Wien (-s) nt Vienna
Wiese (-, -n) f meadow
wies imperf von **weisen**
wieso adv why
Wiesel (-s, -) nt weasel
wievielmal adv how often;
wievielte(r, s) adj: **zum ~n Mal?**
how many times; **den**
Wievielten haben wir heute?
what's the date today?; **am**
Wievielten hast du Geburtstag?
which day is your birthday?
wieweit conj to what extent
WiFi nt WI-FI
wild adj wild
Wild (-(e)s) nt game
wildfremd adj (fam) **ein ~er**
Mensch a complete (o total)
stranger; **Wildleder** nt suede;
Wildpark m game park;
Wildschwein nt (wild) boar;
Wildwasserfahren (-s) nt
whitewater rafting
Wille (-ns, -n) m will
Willen prep gen **um ... for the**
sake of ...; **um Himmels ~!**
(vorwurfsvoll) for heaven's sake;
(betroffen) goodness me
willkommen adj welcome; **jdn**
~ heißen to welcome sb
Wimper (-, -n) f eyelash;
Wimperntusche f mascara
Wind (-(e)s, -e) m wind

Windel (-, -n) f nappy (Brit),
diaper (US)
windgeschützt adj sheltered
from the wind; **windig** adj windy;
(fig) dubious; **Windjacke** f
windcheater; **Windmühle** f
windmill; **Windpark** m wind
farm; **Windpocken** pl chickenpox
sing; **Windschutzscheibe** f (Auto)
windscreen (Brit), windshield (US);
Windstärke f wind force;
windsurfen vi to windsurf;
Windsurfer(in) m(f) windsurfer
Winkel (-s, -) m (Math) angle;
(Gerät) set square; (Raum)
corner; **im rechten ~ zu** at right
angles to
winken vt, vi to wave
Winter (-s, -) m winter;
Winterausrüstung f (Auto)
winter equipment;
Winterfahrplan m winter
timetable; **winterlich** adj
wintry; **Wintermantel** m winter
coat; **Winterreifen** m winter
tyre; **Winterschlussverkauf** m
winter sales pl; **Wintersport** m
winter sports pl; **Winterzeit** f
(Uhrzeit) winter time (Brit), standard
time (US)
winzig adj tiny
wir pron we; **~ selbst** we
ourselves; **~ alle** all of us; **~ drei**
the three of us; **~ sind's** it's us
Wirbel (-s, -) m whirl; (Trubel)
hurly-burly; (Aufsehen) fuss; (Anat)
vertebra; **Wirbelsäule** f spine
wirken vi to be effective;
(erfolgreich sein) to work; (scheinen)
to seem
wirklich adj real; **Wirklichkeit** f
reality
wirksam adj effective; **Wirkung** f
effect
wirr adj confused; **Wirrwarr** (-s)
m confusion

Wirsing (-s) m savoy cabbage
Wirt (-(e)s, -e) m landlord; **Wirtin**
f landlady
Wirtschaft f (Comm) economy;
(Gaststätte) pub; **wirtschaftlich**
adj (Pol, Comm) economic;
(sparsam) economical
Wirtshaus nt pub
wischen vt, vi to wipe; **Wischer**
(-s, -) m wiper
wissen (wusste, gewusst) vt to
know; **weißt du schon, ...?** did
you know ...?; **woher weißt du
das?** how do you know?; **das
musst du selbst ~** that's up to
you; **Wissen** (-s) nt knowledge
Wissenschaft f science;
Wissenschaftler(in) (-s, -) m(f)
scientist; (Geisteswissenschaftler)
academic; **wissenschaftlich** adj
scientific; (geisteswissenschaftlich)
academic
Witwe (-, -n) f widow; **Witwer**
(-s, -) m widower
Witz (-(e)s, -e) m joke; **mach
keine ~e!** you're kidding!; **das soll
wohl ein ~ sein** you've got to be
joking; **witzig** adj funny
wo adv where; **zu einer Zeit, ~ ...**
at a time when ...; **überall, ~ ich
hingehe** wherever I go ▷ conj:
jetzt, ~ du da bist now that you're
here; **~ ich dich gerade spreche**
while I'm talking to you;
woanders adv somewhere else
wobei adv: **~ mir einfällt ...**
which reminds me ...
Woche (-, -n) f week; **während** (o
unter) **der ~** during the week;
einmal die ~ once a week;
Wochenende nt weekend; **am
~** at (Brit) (o on (US)) the weekend;
wir fahren übers ~ weg we're
going away for the weekend;
Wochenendhaus nt weekend
cottage; **Wochenendtrip** m
weekend trip; **Wochenendurlaub**

m weekend break; **Wochenkarte**
f weekly (season) ticket;
wochenlang adv for weeks (on
end); **Wochenmarkt** m weekly
market; **Wochentag** m
weekday; **wöchentlich** adj, adv
weekly
Wodka (-s, -s) m vodka
wodurch adv: **~ unterscheiden
sie sich?** what's the difference
between them?; **~ hast du es
gemerkt?** how did you notice?;
wofür adv (relativ) for which;
(Frage) what ... for; **~ brauchst du
das?** what do you need that for?
wog imperf von **wiegen**
woher adv where ... from; **wohin**
adv where ... to

SCHLÜSSELWORT

wohl adv **1** wohl oder übel
whether one likes it or not
2 (wahrscheinlich) probably; (gewiss)
certainly; (vielleicht) perhaps; **sie
ist wohl zu Hause** she's probably
at home; **das ist doch wohl nicht
dein Ernst!** surely you're not
serious; **das mag wohl sein** that
may well be; **ob das wohl stimmt?**
I wonder if that's true; **er weiß das
sehr wohl** he knows that perfectly
well

Wohl (-(e)s) nt: **zum ~!** cheers;
wohlbehalten adv safe and
sound; **wohl|fühlen** vr: **sich
~** (zufrieden) to feel happy;
(gesundheitlich) to feel well;
Wohlstand m prosperity,
affluence; **wohl|tun** irr vi: **jdm
~** to do sb good; **Wohlwollen** nt
goodwill
Wohnblock m block of flats
(Brit), apartment house (US);
wohnen vi to live;
Wohngemeinschaft f shared flat

w

(Brit) (o apartment (US)); **ich wohne in einer ~** I share a flat (o apartment); **wohnhaft** adj resident; **Wohnküche** f kitchen-cum-living-room; **Wohnmobil** (-s, -e) nt camper, RV (US); **Wohnort** m place of residence; **Wohnsitz** m place of residence; **Wohnung** f flat (Brit), apartment (US); **Wohnungstür** f front door; **Wohnwagen** m caravan, **Wohnzimmer** nt living room

Wolf (-(e)s, Wölfe) m wolf

Wolke (-, -n) f cloud. **Wolkenkratzer** m skyscraper; **wolkenlos** adj cloudless; **wolkig** adj cloudy

Wolldecke (-, -n) f (woollen) blanket; **Wolle** (-, -n) f wool

SCHLÜSSELWORT

wollen (pt **wollte**, pp **gewollt** o (als Hilfsverb) **wollen**) vt, vi to want; **ich will nach Hause** I want to go home; **er will nicht** he doesn't want to; **er will das nicht** he didn't want it; **wenn du willst** if you like; **ich will, dass du mir zuhörst** I want you to listen to me
▷ Hilfsverb: **er will ein Haus kaufen** he wants to buy a house; **ich wollte, ich wäre ...** I wish I were ...; **etw gerade tun wollen** to be going to do sth

Wolljacke f cardigan

womit adv what ... with; **~ habe ich das verdient** what have I done to deserve that?

womöglich adv possibly

woran adv **~ ist er gestorben?** what did he die of?; **~ denkst du?** what are you thinking of?; **~ sieht man das?** how can you tell?

worauf adv **~ wartest du?** what are you waiting for?

woraus adv **~ ist das gemacht** what is it made of?

Workshop (-s, -s) m workshop

World Wide Web nt World Wide Web

Wort (-(e)s, Wörter) nt (Vokabel) word ▷ -(e)s, -e nt (Äußerung) word; **mit anderen ~en** in other words; **jdn beim ~ nehmen** to take sb at his/her word;

Wörterbuch nt dictionary

wörtlich adj literal

worum adv **~ geht's?** what is it about?

worunter adv **~ leidet er** what is he suffering from?

wovon adv (relativ) from which; **~ redest du?** what are you talking about?;

wozu adv (relativ) to/for which; (interrogativ) what ... for/to; (warum) why; **~ brauchst du das?** what do you need it for?; **~ hast du Lust** what do you feel like doing?

Wrack (-(e)s, -s) nt wreck

Wucher (-s) m profiteering; **das ist ~!** that's daylight robbery!

wuchs imperf von **wachsen**

Wühlen vi to rummage; (Tier) to root; (Maulwurf) to burrow

Wühltisch m bargain counter

wund adj sore; **Wunde** (-, -n) f wound

Wunder (-s, -) nt miracle; **es ist kein ~** it's no wonder; **wunderbar** adj wonderful, marvellous; **Wunderkerze** f sparkler; **Wundermittel** nt wonder cure; **wundern** vr: **sich ~** to be surprised ▷ vt to surprise: **wunderschön** adj

beautiful; **wundervoll** *adj* wonderful

Wundsalbe *f* antiseptic ointment; **Wundstarrkrampf** *m* tetanus

Wunsch (-(e)s, Wünsche) *m* wish (*nach* for); **wünschen** *vt* to wish; **sich** (*dat*) **etw ~** to want sth; **ich wünsche dir alles Gute** I wish you all the best; **wünschenswert** *adj* desirable

wurde *imperf von* **werden**

Wurf (-s, Würfe) *m* throw; (*Zool*) litter

Würfel (-s, -) *m* dice; (*Math*) cube; **würfeln** *vi* to throw (the dice); (*Würfel spielen*) to play dice ▷ *vt* (*Zahl*) to throw; (*Gastr*) to dice; **Würfelzucker** *m* lump sugar

Wurm (-(e)s, Würmer) *m* worm

Wurst (-, Würste) *f* sausage; **das ist mir ~** (*fam*) I couldn't care less

Würstchen *nt* frankfurter

Würze (-, -n) *f* seasoning, spice

Wurzel (-, -n) *f* root; **Wurzelbehandlung** *f* root canal treatment

würzen *vt* to season, to spice; **würzig** *adj* spicy

wusch *imperf von* **waschen**

wusste *imperf von* **wissen**

wüst *adj* (*unordentlich*) chaotic; (*ausschweifend*) wild; (*öde*) desolate; (*fam: heftig*) terrible

Wüste (-, -n) *f* desert

Wut (-) *f* rage, fury; **ich habe eine ~ auf ihn** I'm really mad at him; **wütend** *adj* furious

WWW (-) *nt abk =* **World Wide Web** WWW

X-Beine *pl* knock-knees *pl*; **x-beinig** *adj* knock-kneed

x-beliebig *adj:* **ein ~es Buch** any book (you like)

x-mal *adv* umpteen times

Xylophon (-s, -e) *nt* xylophone

Yoga (-(s)) *m o nt* yoga
Yuppie (-s, -s) *m* (-, -s) *f* yuppie

zackig *adj* (*Linie etc*) jagged; (*fam:
Tempo*) brisk
zaghaft *adj* timid
zäh *adj* tough; (*Flüssigkeit*) thick
Zahl (-, -en) *f* number; **zahlbar**
adj payable; **zahlen** *vt, vi* to pay;
~ bitte! could I have the bill (*Brit*)
(o check (*US*)) please?; **bar ~** to pay
cash; **zählen** *vt, vi* to count (*auf
+akk* on); **~ zu** to be one of;
Zahlenschloss *nt* combination
lock; **Zähler** (-s, -) *m* (*Gerät*)
counter; (*für Strom, Wasser*) meter;
zahlreich *adj* numerous;
Zahlung *f* payment;
Zahlungsanweisung *f* money
order; **Zahlungsbedingungen** *pl*
terms *pl* of payment
zahm *adj* tame; **zähmen** *vt* to
tame
Zahn (-(e)s, Zähne) *m* tooth;
Zahnarzt *m*, **Zahnärztin** *f*
dentist; **Zahnbürste** *f*

toothbrush; **Zahncreme** f
toothpaste; **Zahnersatz** m
denture; **Zahnfleisch** nt gums
pl; **Zahnfleischbluten** nt bleeding
gums; **Zahnfüllung** f filling;
Zahnklammer f brace;
toothpaste; **Zahnpasta** f
Zahnradbahn f rack
railway (Brit) or railroad (US));
Zahnschmerzen pl toothache
sing; **Zahnseide** f dental floss;
Zahnspange f brace;
Zahnstocher m (-s, -) m toothpick
Zange f (-, -n) f pliers pl;
(Zuckerzange) tongs pl; (Beißzange,
Zool) pincers pl; (Med) forceps pl
zanken vi to quarrel;
Zäpfchen nt (Anat) uvula; (Med)
suppository
zapfen vt (Bier) to pull; **Zapfsäule** f
petrol (Brit) or gas (US) (pump)
zappeln vi (vor Wut) to wriggle; (unruhig
sein) to fidget
zart adj (weich, leise) soft; (Braten
etc) tender; (fein, zerbrechlich)
delicate; **zartbitter** adj
(Schokolade) plain, dark
zärtlich adj tender, affectionate;
Zärtlichkeit f tenderness; **-en** pl
hugs and kisses pl
Zauber m (-s, -) m magic; (Baam)
spell; **Zauberer** m magic; Zauberer
(-s, -) m magician; (Künstler)
conjuror; **Zauberformel** f (magic)
spell; **zauberhaft** adj enchanting;
Zauberin f sorceress;
Zauberkünstler(in) m(f) magician,
conjuror; **Zaubermittel** nt magic
cure; **zaubern** vt to do magic;
Künstler) to do conjuring tricks;
Zauberspruch m (magic) spell
z. B. abk = zum Beispiel e.g., eg
Zaun m (-(e)s, Zäune) m fence
ZDF nt = Zweites Deutsches
Fernsehen second German television
channel

Zebra nt (-s, -s) nt zebra;
Zebrastreifen pl zebra crossing
(Brit), crosswalk (US)
Zecke f (-, -n) f tick
Zehe f (-, -n) f toe; (Knoblauch)
clove; **Zehennagel** m toenail;
Zehenspitze f tip of the toes
zehn num ten; **Zehnerkarte** f
ticket valid for ten trips; **Zehnkampf**
m (-(e)s) decathlon; **Zehnkämpfer(in)**
m(f) decathlete; **zehntausend** num ten
thousand; **zehnte(r, s)** adj
tenth; siehe auch dritte; **Zehntel**
nt (-s, -) nt tenth; **Zeichen**
(-s, -) nt sign; (Schriftzeichen) character;
Zeichenblock m sketch pad;
Zeichenerklärung f key;
Zeichensetzung f punctuation;
Zeichensprache f sign language;
Zeichentrickfilm m cartoon
zeichnen vt, vi to draw;
Zeichnung f drawing
Zeigefinger m index finger;
zeigen vt to show; **sie zeigte uns
die Stadt** she showed us around
the town; **zeig mir** let me see
▶ vi to point (auf +Akk to); ▶ vr:
sich ~ to show oneself; **es wird
sich ~** time will tell; **Zeiger** m (-s, -)
m pointer; (Uhr) hand
Zeit f (-, -en) f time; **ich habe keine
~** I haven't got time; **lass dir
Zeit** take your time; **das hat ~** there's no
hurry; **von ~ zu ~** from time to
time; **Zeitansage** f (Tel)
speaking clock (Brit), correct time
(US); **Zeitarbeit** f temporary
work; **zeitgenössisch** adj
contemporary, modern; **zeitgleich**
adj simultaneous ▶ adv at exactly
the same time; **zeitig** adj early;
Zeitkarte f season ticket;
zeitlich adj (Reihenfolge)

zeitlich adj chronological; es passt mir ~ nicht it isn't a convenient time; ich schaff es ~ nicht I'm not going to make it; Zeitlupe f slow motion; Zeitplan m schedule; Zeitpunkt m point in time; Zeitraum m period (of time); Zeitschrift f magazine; (wissenschaftliche) periodical

Zeitung f newspaper; es steht in der ~ it's in the paper(s). Zeitungsanzeige f newspaper advertisement; Zeitungsartikel m newspaper article; Zeitungskiosk m, Zeitungsstand m newsstand

Zeitunterschied m time difference; Zeitverschiebung f time lag; Zeitvertreib ‹-(e)s, -e› m; zum ~ to pass the time; zeitweise adv occasionally; Zeitzone f time zone

Zelle ‹-, -n› f cell

Zellophan ‹-s› nt cellophane®

Zelt ‹-(e)s, -e› nt tent; zelten vi to camp, to go camping; Zeltplatz m campsite, camping site

Zement ‹-(e)s, -e› m cement

Zentimeter m or nt centimetre

Zentner ‹-s, -› m (metric) hundredweight; (in Deutschland) fifty kilos; (in Österreich und der Schweiz) one hundred kilos

zentral adj central; Zentrale f ‹-, -n› f central office; (Tel) exchange; Zentralheizung f central heating. Zentralverriegelung f (Auto) central locking; Zentrum ‹-s, Zentren› nt centre

zerbrechen irr v ⊳ vi, vt to break; zerbrechlich adj fragile

Zeremonie ‹-, -n› f ceremony

zergehen vi irr to melt (schmelzen) to dissolve.

zerkleinern vt to cut up; (zerhacken) to chop (up):

zerkratzen vt to scratch;

zerlegen vt to take to pieces; (Fleisch) to carve; (Gerät, Maschine) to dismantle. zerquetschen vt to squash. zerreißen irr v ⊳ vt to tear to pieces ⊳ vi to tear

zerren ⊳ vt to drag; sich (dat) einen Muskel ~ to pull a muscle ⊳ vi to tug (an +dat an). Zerrung f (Med) pulled muscle

zerschlagen irr vt to smash ⊳ vr ▷ sich ~ to come to nothing

zerschneiden vt ... to cut up

zerstören vt to destroy. Zerstörung f destruction

zerstreuen vt to scatter; (Menge) to disperse; (Zweifel etc) to dispel ▷ vr ▷ sich ~ (Menge) to disperse. zerstreut adj scattered; (Mensch) absent-minded; (kurzfristig) distracted

zerteilen vt to split up

Zertifikat ‹-(e)s, -e› nt certificate

Zettel ‹-s, -› m piece of paper; (Notizzettel) note

Zeug ‹-(e)s, -› nt (fam) stuff; (Ausrüstung) gear; dummes ~ - nonsense

Zeuge ‹-n, -n› m, Zeugin f witness

Zeugnis nt certificate; (Schule) report; (Referenz) reference

z.H(d). abk = zu Händen von attn

zickig adj (fam) touchy, bitchy

Zickzack ‹-(e)s, -e› m; im ~ fahren to zigzag (across the road)

Ziege ‹-, -n› f goat

Ziegel ‹-s, -› m brick; (Dach) tile

Ziegenkäse m goat's cheese. Ziegenpeter m mumps

ziehen (zog, gezogen) vt to draw; (zerren) to pull; (Spielfigur) to move; (züchten) to rear ⊳ vi (zerren) to pull; (sich bewegen) to move; (Rauch, Wolke etc) to drift; den Tee

Ziel (-(e)s, -e) nt (Reise) destination; (Sport) finish; (Absicht) goal, aim; **zielen** vi to aim (auf +akk at); **Zielgruppe** f target group; **ziellos** adj aimless; **Zielscheibe** f target

ziemlich adj considerable; **ein -es Durcheinander** quite a mess; ▷ adv (mit Adjektiv) quite, rather; **- er Sicherheit** with some certainty ▷ adv rather, quite; **- viel** quite a lot

zierlich adj dainty, (Frau) petite

Ziffer (-, -n) f figure; **arabische/römische -n** pl Arabic/Roman numerals pl; **Zifferblatt** nt dial; face

zig adj (fam) umpteen

Zigarette f cigarette; **Zigarettenautomat** m cigarette machine; **Zigarettenpapier** nt cigarette paper; **Zigarettenschachtel** f cigarette packet; **Zigarettenstummel** m cigarette end; **Zigarre** (-, -n) f cigar

Zigeuner(in) (-s, -) m(f) gipsy

Zimmer (-s, -) nt room; **haben Sie ein - für zwei Personen** do you have a room for two?; **Zimmerlautstärke** f reasonable volume; **Zimmermädchen** nt chambermaid; **Zimmermann** m carpenter; **Zimmerpflanze** f house plant; **Zimmerschlüssel** m room key; **Zimmerservice** m room service; **Zimmervermittlung** f accommodation agency

Zimt (-(e)s, -e) m cinnamon; **Zimtstange** f cinnamon stick

Zink (-(e)s) nt zinc

Zinn (-(e)s) nt (Element) tin; (legiertes) pewter

Zinsen pl interest sing

Zipfel (-s, -) m corner; (spitz) tip; (Hemd) tail; (Wurst) end.

Zirkumflex m pointed hat

zirka adv about, approximately

Zirkel (-s, -) m (Math) (pair of) compasses; **Zirkus** (-, -se) m circus

zischen vi to hiss

Zitat (-(e)s, -e) nt quotation (aus from); **zitieren** vt to quote (from); **Zitronat** nt candied lemon peel; **Zitrone** (-, -n) f lemon; **Zitronenlimonade** f lemonade; **Zitronensaft** m lemon juice

zittern vi to tremble (vor +dat with)

zivil adj civilian; (Preis) reasonable; **Zivil** (-s) nt plain clothes pl; (Mil) civilian clothes pl; **Zivildienst** m community service (for conscientious objectors); **Zivilist** m civilian

zocken vi (fam) to gamble

Zoff (-s, -) m (fam) trouble

zog imperf von **ziehen**

zögern vi to hesitate; **zögernd** adj hesitant

Zoll (-(e)s, Zölle) m customs pl; (Abgabe) duty; **Zollabfertigung** f customs clearance; **Zollamt** nt customs office; **Zollbeamte(r)** m, **Zollbeamtin** f customs official; **Zollerklärung** f customs declaration; **zollfrei** adj duty-free; **Zollkontrolle** f customs check; **Zöllner(in)** m(f) customs officer; **zollpflichtig** adj liable to duty

Zone (-, -n) f zone

Zoo (-s, -s) m zoo; **Zoom** (-s, -s) nt zoom (shot); (Objektiv) zoom (lens)

Zopf (-(e)s, Zöpfe) m plait (Brit), braid (US)

Zorn (-(e)s) m anger; **zornig** adj angry (über +akk about sth, auf jdn with sb)

SCHLÜSSELWORT

zu prep +dat 1 (örtlich) to; **zum Bahnhof/Arzt gehen** to go to the station/doctor; **zur Schule/Kirche gehen** to go to school/church; **sollen wir zu euch gehen?** shall we go to your place?; **sie sah zu ihm hin** she looked towards him; **zum Fenster herein** through the window; **zu meiner Linken** to o on my left

2 (zeitlich) at; **zu Ostern** at Easter; **bis zum 1. Mai** until May 1st; (nicht später als) by May 1st; **zu meiner Zeit** in my time

3 (Zusatz) with; **Wein zum Essen trinken** to drink wine with one's meal; **sich zu jdm setzen** to sit down beside sb; **setz dich doch zu uns** (come and) sit with us; **Anmerkungen zu etw** notes on sth

4 (Zweck) for; **Wasser zum Waschen** water for washing; **Papier zum Schreiben** paper to write on; **etw zum Geburtstag bekommen** to get sth for one's birthday

5 (Veränderung) into; **zu etw werden** to turn into sth; **jdn zu etw machen** to make sb (into) sth; **zu Asche verbrennen** to burn to ashes

6 (mit Zahlen) **3 zu 2** (Sport) 3-2; **das Stück 5 Euro** at 5 euros each; **zum ersten Mal** for the first time

7 **zu meiner Freude** etc to my joy etc; **zum Glück** luckily; **zu Fuß** on foot; **es ist zum Weinen** it's enough to make you cry

▷ konj to; **etw zu essen** sth to eat; **um besser sehen zu können** in order to see better; **ohne es zu wissen** without knowing it; **noch zu bezahlende Rechnungen** bills

that are still to be paid

▷ adv 1 (allzu) too; **zu sehr** too much; **zu viel** too much; **zu wenig** too little

2 (örtlich) toward(s); **er kam auf mich zu** he came up to me

3 (geschlossen) shut, closed; **die Geschäfte haben zu** the shops are closed; **„auf/zu"** (Wasserhahn etc) "on/off"

4 (fam) (los) **nur zu!** just keep on!; **mach zu!** hurry up!

zuallererst adv first of all; **zuallerletzt** adv last of all

Zubehör (-(e)s, -e) nt accessories pl

zu|bereiten vt to prepare; **Zubereitung** f preparation

zu|binden irr vt to do (o tie) up

Zucchini f courgettes pl (Brit), zucchini pl (US)

züchten vt (Tiere) to breed; (Pflanzen) to grow

zucken vi to jerk; (krampfhaft) to twitch; (Strahl etc) to flicker; **mit den Schultern ~** to shrug (one's shoulders)

Zucker (-s, -) m sugar; (Med) diabetes sing; **Zuckerdose** f sugar bowl; **zuckerkrank** adj diabetic; **Zuckerrohr** nt sugar cane; **Zuckerrübe** f sugar beet; **Zuckerwatte** f candy-floss (Brit), cotton candy (US)

zu|decken vt to cover up

zu|drehen vt to turn off

zueinander adv to one other; (mit Verb) together; **zueinander|halten** irr vi to stick together

zuerst adv first; (zu Anfang) at first; **~ einmal** first of all

Zufahrt f access; (Einfahrt) drive(way); **Zufahrtsstraße** f access road; (Autobahn) slip road (Brit), ramp (US)

Zufall m chance; (Ereignis) coincidence; **durch ~** by accident; **so ein ~!** what a coincidence; **zufällig** adj chance ▷ adv by chance; **weißt du ~, ob ...?** do you happen to know whether ...?

zufrieden adj (befriedigt) satisfied; (zufriedengestellt) content(ed); **lass sie in ~** leave her alone; **sich mit etw ~ geben** to settle for sth; **Zufriedenheit** f contentment; (Befriedigung) satisfaction; **zufriedenstellen** vt: **sie ist schwer zufriedenzustellen** she is hard to please; **zufügen** vt to add (dat to); **jdm Schaden/Schmerzen ~** to cause sb harm/pain

Zug m (-(e)s, Züge) (Eisenb) train; (Luft) draught; (Ziehen) pull; (Zigarette) puff, drag; (Schluck) gulp; (Charakterzug) trait; (an Gesichtszug) feature; (Schach) move; **Zugabe** f extra (in Konzert etc) encore

Zugabteil nt train compartment; **Zugang** m access; **kein ~** "no entry"; **Zugauskunft** f (Stelle) train information office/desk; **Zugbegleiter(in)** m(f) guard (Brit), conductor (US)

zugeben vt to admit; **zugegeben** adv admittedly

zugehen irr vi: **auf jdn/etw ~** to walk towards sb/sth; **dem Ende ~** to be coming to a close ▷ vi impers (sich ereignen) to happen; **es ging lustig zu** we/they had a lot of fun; **dort geht es streng zu** it's strict there

Zügel (-s, -) m rein

zügig adj speedy; **Zugführer(in)** m(f) guard (Brit); conductor (US)

zugleich adv (zur gleichen Zeit) at the same time; (ebenso) both

Zugluft f draught; **Zugpersonal** nt train staff

zugreifen irr vi (fig) to seize the opportunity; (beim Essen) to help oneself; **auf** (+akk) (Inform) to access

Zugrestaurant nt dining car, diner (US)

zugrunde adv: **~ gehen** an (+dat) (sterben) to perish; **~ gehen** access right

Zugschaffner(in) m(f) ticket inspector; **Zugunglück** nt train crash

zugunsten prep +gen o dat in favour of

Zugverbindung f train connection

zuhaben irr vi to be closed

zuhalten irr vt: **sich (dat) die Nase ~** to hold one's nose; **sich (dat) die Ohren ~** to hold one's hands over one's ears; **die Tür ~** hold the door shut

Zuhause (-s) nt home

zuhören irr vi to listen (dat to); **Zuhörer(in)** m(f) listener

zukleben vt to seal

zukommen irr vi to come up (auf +akk to); **jdm etw ~ lassen** to give/send sb sth; **etw auf sich ~ lassen** to take sth as it comes

zukriegen vt: **ich krieg den Koffer nicht zu** I can't shut the case

Zukunft f (-, Zukünfte) future; **zukünftig** adj future ▷ adv in future

zulassen irr vt (hereinlassen) to admit; (erlauben) to permit; (Auto) to license; (fam: nicht öffnen) to keep shut; **zulässig** adj permissible, permitted

zuletzt adv finally, at last
zuliebe adv: ~ **jdm** – for sb's sake
zum kontr von zu dem; ~ **dritten**
Mal for the third time; ~ **Scherz** as
a joke; ~ **Trinken** for drinking
zumachen vt to shut; (Kleidung)
to do up ▸ vi to shut
zumindest adv at least
zumuten vt: **jdm etw** ~ to
expect sth of sb ▸ vr: **sich** (dat) **zu**
viel ~ to overdo things
zunächst adv first of all; ~
einmal to start with
Zunahme (-, -n) f increase
Zuname m surname, last name
zünden vi, vt (Auto) to ignite, to
fire; **Zündkabel** nt (Auto) ignition
cable; **Zündkerze** f (Auto) spark
plug; **Zündschloss** nt ignition
lock; **Zündschlüssel** m ignition
key; **Zündung** f ignition
zunehmen irr vi to increase;
(Mensch) to put on weight ▸ vt: **5**
Kilo ~ to put on 5 kilos
Zunge (-, -n) f tongue
Zungenkuss m French kiss
zunichtemachen vt (zerstören)
to ruin
zunutze adv: **sich** (dat) **etw**
~ **machen** to make use of sth
zu|parken vt to block
zur kontr von zu der
zurechtfinden irr vr: **sich** ~ to
find one's way around;
zurechtkommen irr vi to cope
(mit etw with sth);
zurechtmachen vt to prepare
▸ vr: **sich** ~ to get ready
Zürich nt (-s) Zurich
zurück adv back
zurück|bekommen irr vt to get
back; **zurück|blicken** vi to look
back, (auf +akk at); **zurück|bringen**
irr vt (wiederbringen) to bring back;
zurück|erstatten vt to refund;
(wandern/sth) to take back;
zurück|fahren irr vi to go back;

zurück|geben irr vt to give back;
(antworten) to answer;
zurück|gehen irr vi to go back;
(zeitlich) to date back (auf +akk to);
zurück|halten irr vt to hold
back; (hindern) to prevent ▸ vr:
sich ~ to hold back;
zurück|haltend adj reserved
zurück|holen vt to fetch back;
zurück|kommen irr vi to come
back; **auf etw** (akk) ~ to return (o
get back) to sth; **zurück|lassen** irr
vt to leave behind; **zurück|legen**
vt (zur Seite) (Geld) to put by;
(reservieren) to keep back; (Strecke)
to cover; **zurück|nehmen** irr vt
to take back; **zurück|rufen** irr vt
to call back; **zurück|schicken** vt
to send back; **zurück|stellen** vt
to put back; **zurück|treten** irr vi
to step back; (von Amt) to retire;
zurück|verlangen vt: **etw** ~ to
ask for sth back; **zurück|zahlen**
vt to pay back
zurzeit adv at present
Zusage f (Annahme)
acceptance; **zusagen** vt to
promise; (gefallen) **jdm** ~ to
appeal to sb
zusammen adv together
Zusammenarbeit f collaboration; **zusammen|arbeiten** vi
to work together
zusammen|brechen irr vi to
collapse; (psychisch) to break
down; **Zusammenbruch** m
collapse; (psychischer) breakdown
zusammen|fassen vt to
summarize; (vereinigen) to unite;
zusammenfassend adj
summarizing ▸ adv to
summarize; **Zusammenfassung**
f summary
zusammen|gehören vi to
belong together;
zusammen|halten irr vi to stick
together

Zusammenhang *m* connection; **im/aus dem ~** in/out of context; **zusammen|hängen** *irr vi* to be connected; **zusammenhängend** *adj* coherent; **zusammenhang(s)los** *adj* incoherent

zusammen|klappen *vi, vt* to fold up

zusammen|knüllen *vt* to screw up

zusammen|kommen *irr vi* to meet; *(sich ereignen)* to happen together; **zusammen|legen** *vt* to fold up ▷ *vi (Geld sammeln)* to club together; **zusammen|nehmen** *irr vt* to summon up; **alles zusammengenommen** all in all ▷ *vr:* **sich ~** to pull oneself together; *(fam)* to get a grip, to get one's act together; **zusammen|passen** *vi* to go together; *(Personen)* to be suited; **zusammen|rechnen** *vt* to add up

Zusammensein (-s) *nt* get-together

zusammen|setzen *vt* to put together ▷ *vr:* **sich ~ aus** to be composed of; **Zusammensetzung** *f* composition

Zusammenstoß *m* crash, collision; **zusammen|stoßen** *irr vi* to crash *(mit into)*

zusammen|zählen *vt* to add up

zusammen|ziehen *irr vi (in Wohnung etc)* to move in together

Zusatz *m* addition; **zusätzlich** *adj* additional ▷ *adv* in addition

zu|schauen *vi* to watch; **Zuschauer(in)** (-s, -) *m(f)* spectator; **die ~** *(pl) (Theat)* the audience *sing*; **Zuschauertribüne** *f* stand

zu|schicken *vt* to send

Zuschlag *m* extra charge; *(Fahrkarte)* supplement

zuschlagpflichtig *adj* subject to an extra charge; *(Eisenb)* subject to a supplement

zu|schließen *irr vt* to lock

zu|sehen *irr vi* to watch *(jdm sb)*; **~, dass** *(dafür sorgen)* to make sure that

zu|sichern *vt:* **jdm etw ~** to assure sb of sth

Zustand *m* state, condition; **sie bekommt Zustände, wenn sie das sieht** *(fam)* she'll have a fit if she sees that

zustande *adv:* **~ bringen** to bring about; **~ kommen** to come about

zuständig *adj (Behörde)* relevant; **~ für** responsible for

Zustellung *f* delivery

zu|stimmen *vi* to agree *(einer Sache dat* to sth, *jdm* with sb); **Zustimmung** *f* approval

zu|stoßen *irr vi (fig)* to happen *(jdm* to sb)

Zutaten *pl* ingredients *pl*

zu|trauen *vt:* **jdm etw ~** to think sb is capable of sth; **das hätte ich ihm nie zugetraut** I'd never have thought he was capable of it; **ich würde es ihr ~** *(etw Negatives)* I wouldn't put it past her; **Zutrauen** (-s) *nt* confidence *(zu* in); **zutraulich** *adj* trusting; *(Tier)* friendly

zu|treffen *irr vi* to be correct; **~ auf** *(+akk)* to apply to; **Zutreffendes bitte streichen** please delete as applicable

Zutritt *m* entry; *(Zugang)* access; **~ verboten!** no entry

zuverlässig *adj* reliable; **Zuverlässigkeit** *f* reliability

Zuversicht *f* confidence; **zuversichtlich** *adj* confident

zuvor *adv* before; *(zunächst)* first; **zuvor|kommen** *irr vi:* **jdm ~** to

beat sb to it; **zuvorkommend** adj obliging

Zuwachs (-es, Zuwächse) m increase, growth; (fam: Baby) addition to the family

zuwider vi: **jdm/es ist mir ~** I hate (o detest) it

zuwinken vi: **jdm ~** to wave to sb

zuzüglich prep +gen plus

Zwang (-(e)s, Zwänge) m (innerer) compulsion; (Gewalt) force

zwang imperf von **zwingen**

zwängen vt to squeeze (in +akk into); vr: **sich ~** to squeeze (in +akk into)

zwanglos adj informal

zwanzig num twenty; **zwanzigste(r, s)** adj twentieth; siehe auch **dritte**

zwar adv **und ~ ...** (genauer) ... to be precise; **das ist ~ schön, aber ...** it is nice, but ...; **ich kenne ihn ~, aber ...** I know him all right, but ...

Zweck (-(e)s, -e) m purpose, but ...; **zwecklos** adj pointless

zwei num two; **Zwei** (-, -en) f two (Schulnote) = B; **Zweibettzimmer** nt twin room; **zweideutig** adj ambiguous; (unanständig) suggestive; **zweifach** adj double

Zweifel (-s, -) m doubt; **zweifellos** adv undoubtedly; **zweifeln** vi to doubt (an etw dat sth); **Zweifelsfall** m: **im ~** in case of doubt

Zweig (-(e)s, -e) m branch; **zweihundert** num two hundred; **Zweigstelle** f branch

zweimal adv twice; **zweisprachig** adj bilingual; **zweispurig** adj (Auto) two-lane; **zu zweit** – there are two of us; **zweite(r, s)** adj second; siehe auch **dritte**; eine **Portion a**

second helping; **zweitens** adv secondly; (bei Aufzählungen) second; **zweitgrößte(r, s)** adj second largest; **Zweitschlüssel** m spare key

Zwerchfell (-(e)s, -e) nt (Med) diaphragm

Zwerg(in) (-(e)s, -e, m (f)) m (f) dwarf

zwicken vt to pinch

Zwieback (-(e)s, -e) m rusk

Zwiebel (-, -n) f onion; (von Blume) bulb; **Zwiebelsuppe** f onion soup

Zwilling (-s, -e) m twin; -e (pl) (Astr) Gemini sing

zwingen (zwang, gezwungen) vt to force

zwinkern vi to blink; (absichtlich) to wink

zwischen prep +akk o dat between; **Zwischenablage** f (Inform) clipboard; **zwischendurch** adv in between; **Zwischenfall** m incident; **Zwischenlandung** f stopover; **Zwischenraum** m space; **zwischenmenschlich** adj interpersonal; **Zwischenstopp** m; **Zwischensumme** f subtotal; **Zwischenzeit** f: **in der ~** in the meantime

zwitschern vt, vi to twitter, to chirp

zwölf num twelve; **zwölfte(r, s)** adj twelfth; siehe auch **dritte**

Zylinder (-s, -) m cylinder; (Hut) top hat

zynisch adj cynical

Zypern (-s) nt Cyprus

Zyste (-, -n) f cyst

Phrasefinder

Sprachführer

Camping	Camping
Is there a campsite here?	Gibt es hier einen Camping-platz?
We'd like a site for ...	Wir möchten einen Platz für ...
a tent.	*ein Zelt.*
a camper van.	*ein Wohnmobil.*
a caravan.	*einen Wohnwagen.*
We'd like to stay one night/ ... **nights.**	Wir möchten eine Nacht/ ... Nächte bleiben.
How much is it per night?	Was kostet die Nacht?
Where are ...?	Wo sind ...?
the toilets	*die Toiletten*
the showers	*die Duschen*
Where is ...?	Wo ist ...?
the shop	*der Laden*
the site office	*die Verwaltung*
Can we camp here overnight?	Können wir über Nacht hier zelten?

Self-Catering	Ferienwohnung/-haus
Where do we get the key for the apartment/house?	Wo bekommen wir den Schlüssel für die Wohnung/ das Haus?
Do we have to pay extra for electricity/gas?	Müssen wir Strom/Gas extra bezahlen?
How does ... work?	Wie funktioniert ...?
the washing machine	*die Waschmaschine*
the cooker	*der Herd*
the heating	*die Heizung*
Who do I contact if there are any problems?	An wen kann ich mich bei Problemen wenden?
We need ...	Wir brauchen ...
a second key.	*einen zweiten Schlüssel.*
more sheets.	*mehr Bettwäsche.*

The gas has run out.	Das Gas ist alle.
There is no electricity.	Es gibt keinen Strom.
Where do we hand in the keys when we're leaving?	Wo geben wir die Schlüssel bei der Abreise ab?
Do we have to clean the apartment/the house before we leave?	Müssen wir die Wohnung/ das Haus vor der Abreise sauber machen?

Hotel | Hotel

Do you have a ... for tonight?	Haben Sie ein ... für heute Nacht?
single room	*Einzelzimmer*
double room	*Doppelzimmer*
with bath/shower	mit Bad/Dusche
I want to stay for one night/ ... nights.	Ich möchte eine Nacht/ ... Nächte bleiben.
I booked a room in the name of ...	Ich habe ein Zimmer auf den Namen ... reserviert.
I'd like another room.	Ich möchte ein anderes Zimmer.
What time is breakfast?	Wann gibt es Frühstück?
Where is breakfast served?	Wo gibt es Frühstück?
Can I have breakfast in my room?	Können Sie mir das Frühstück aufs Zimmer bringen?
Where is ...?	Wo ist ...?
the restaurant	*das Restaurant*
the bar	*die Bar*
the gym	*der Fitnessraum*
the swimming pool	*der Swimmingpool*
I'd like an alarm call for tomorrow morning at ...	Bitte wecken Sie mich morgen früh um ...
The key, please.	Den Schlüssel bitte.
Are there any messages for me?	Sind Nachrichten für mich da?

SHOPPING | **EINKAUFEN**

I'm looking for ...	Ich suche ...
I'd like ...	Ich möchte ...
Do you have ...?	Haben Sie ...?
Do you have this ...?	Haben Sie das ...?
in another size	*in einer anderen Größe*
in another colour	*in einer anderen Farbe*
in another design	*mit einem anderen Muster*
I take size ...	Ich trage Größe ...
I'll take it.	Ich nehme das.
Do you have anything else?	Haben Sie noch etwas anderes?
That's too expensive.	Das ist zu teuer.
I'm just looking.	Ich sehe mich nur um.
Do you take credit cards?	Nehmen Sie Kreditkarten?

Food Shopping | Lebensmittel

Where is the nearest ...?	Wo ist hier ...?
supermarket	*ein Supermarkt*
baker's	*eine Bäckerei*
butcher's	*eine Metzgerei*
greengrocer's	*ein Obst- und Gemüseladen*
Where is the market?	Wo ist der Markt?
When is the market on?	Wann ist Markt?
a kilo of ...	ein Kilo ...
a pound of ...	ein Pfund ...
200 grams of ...	200 Gramm ...
... slices ...	... Scheiben ...
a litre of ...	ein Liter ...
a bottle of ...	eine Flasche ...
a packet of ...	ein Päckchen ...

Photos | Foto

A colour film, please.	Einen Farbfilm bitte.
My memory card is full.	Meine Speicherkarte ist voll.
Can I have batteries for this camera, please?	Batterien für diesen Apparat bitte.
Where can I buy a digital camera?	Wo kann ich eine Digitalkamera kaufen?
I'd like the photos ...	Ich hätte die Bilder gern ...
matt.	*matt.*
glossy.	*Hochglanz.*
10 by 15 centimetres.	*im Format 10 mal 15.*
Can I print my digital photos here?	Kann ich meine Digitalfotos hier drucken lassen?
How much do the photos cost?	Wie viel kosten die Bilder?
Are you allowed to take photos here?	Darf man hier fotografieren?
Could you take a photo of us, please?	Könnten Sie bitte ein Foto von uns machen?

Post Office | Post

Where is the nearest post office?	Wo ist die nächste Post?
When does the post office open?	Wann hat die Post geöffnet?
I'd like ... stamps for postcards/letters to Germany/Switzerland.	Ich möchte ... Briefmarken für Postkarten/Briefe nach Deutschland/in die Schweiz.
Where is the nearest postbox?	Wo ist hier ein Briefkasten?

Sightseeing | Besichtigungen

Where is the tourist office?	Wo ist die Touristen-information?
Do you have any leaflets about ...?	Haben Sie Broschüren über ...?
What sights can you visit here?	Welche Sehenswürdigkeiten gibt es hier?
Is there a guided tour in English?	Gibt es eine Stadtrundfahrt/einen Stadtrundgang auf Englisch?
When is ... open?	Wann ist ... geöffnet?
the museum	*das Museum*
the church	*die Kirche*
the castle	*das Schloss*
How much does it cost to get in?	Was kostet der Eintritt?
Are there any reductions ...?	Gibt es eine Ermäßigung ...?
for students	*für Studenten*
for children	*für Kinder*
for pensioners	*für Rentner*
for the unemployed	*für Arbeitslose*
I'd like a catalogue.	Ich möchte einen Katalog.
Can I take photos here?	Kann ich hier fotografieren?
Can I film here?	Kann ich hier filmen?

Entertainment | Unterhaltung

What is there to do here?	Was kann man hier unternehmen?
Do you have a list of events?	Haben Sie einen Veranstaltungskalender?
Where can we ...?	Wo kann man hier ...?
go dancing	*tanzen gehen*
hear live music	*Livemusik hören*

Where is there ...?	Wo gibt es hier ... ?
a nice pub	*eine nette Kneipe*
a good disco	*eine gute Disko*
What's on tonight ...?	Was gibt es heute Abend ...?
at the cinema	*im Kino*
at the theatre	*im Theater*
at the opera	*in der Oper*
at the concert hall	*in der Konzerthalle*
Where can I buy tickets for ...?	Wo kann ich Karten für ... kaufen?
the theatre	*das Theater*
the concert	*das Konzert*
the opera	*die Oper*
the ballet	*das Ballett*
How much is it to get in?	Was kostet der Eintritt?
I'd like a ticket/... tickets for ...	Ich möchte eine Karte/ ... Karten für ...
Are there any reductions for ...?	Gibt es eine Ermäßigung für ...?
children	*Kinder*
pensioners	*Rentner*
students	*Studenten*
the unemployed	*Arbeitslose*

At the Beach | Am Strand

Can you swim here/ in this lake?	Kann man hier/in diesem See baden?
Where is the nearest quiet beach?	Wo gibt es hier einen ruhigen Strand?
Is there a beach with lifeguards?	Gibt es einen bewachten Strand?
How deep is the water?	Wie tief ist das Wasser?

What is the water temperature?	Wie viel Grad hat das Wasser?
Are there currents?	Gibt es hier Strömungen?
Is there a lifeguard?	Gibt es hier einen Rettungsschwimmer?
Where can you ...?	Wo kann man hier ...?
go surfing	*surfen*
go waterskiing	*Wasserski fahren*
go diving	*tauchen*
go paragliding	*Gleitschirm fliegen*
I'd like to hire ...	Ich möchte ... mieten.
a beach chair.	*einen Strandkorb*
a deckchair.	*einen Liegestuhl*
a sunshade.	*einen Sonnenschirm*
I'd like to hire ...	Ich möchte ... ausleihen.
a surfboard.	*ein Surfbrett*
a jet-ski.	*einen Jetski*
a rowing boat.	*ein Ruderboot*
a pedal boat.	*ein Tretboot*

Skiing | Ski

Where can I hire skiing equipment?	Wo kann ich eine Skiausrüstung ausleihen?
I'd like to hire ...	Ich möchte ... ausleihen.
downhill skis.	*Abfahrtski*
cross-country skis.	*Langlaufski*
ski boots.	*Skischuhe*
Where can I buy a ski pass?	Wo kann ich einen Skipass kaufen?
I'd like a ski pass ...	Ich möchte einen Skipass ...
for a day.	*für einen Tag.*
for five days.	*für fünf Tage.*
for a week.	*für sieben Tage.*

How much is a ski pass?	Wie viel kostet der Skipass?
Do you have a map of the ski runs?	Haben Sie eine Pistenkarte?
Where are the beginners' slopes?	Wo sind die Abfahrten für Anfänger?
How difficult is this slope?	Welchen Schwierigkeitsgrad hat diese Abfahrt?
Is there a ski school?	Gibt es eine Skischule?
What's the weather forecast?	Wie ist der Wetterbericht?
What is the snow like?	Wie ist der Schnee?
Is there a danger of avalanches?	Besteht Lawinengefahr?

Sport | Sport

Where can we ...?	Wo kann man hier ...?
play tennis/golf	*Tennis/Golf spielen*
go swimming	*schwimmen*
go riding	*reiten*
How much is it per hour?	Wie viel kostet es pro Stunde?
Where can I book a court?	Wo kann ich einen Platz buchen?
Where can I hire rackets?	Wo kann ich Schläger ausleihen?
Where can I hire a rowing boat/a pedal boat?	Wo kann ich ein Ruderboot/ ein Tretboot mieten?
Do you need a fishing permit?	Braucht man einen Angel- schein?
I'd like to see ...	Ich möchte ... ansehen.
a football match.	*ein Fußballspiel*
a horse race.	*ein Pferderennen*

RESTAURANT	RESTAURANT

A table for ... people, please.	Einen Tisch für ... Personen bitte.
The menu, please.	Die Speisekarte bitte.
The wine list, please.	Die Weinkarte bitte.
What do you recommend?	Was empfehlen Sie?
Do you have ...?	Haben Sie ...?
any vegetarian dishes	*vegetarische Gerichte*
children's portions	*Kinderportionen*
Does that contain ...?	Enthält das ...?
peanuts	*Erdnüsse*
alcohol	*Alkohol*
Can you bring (more) ..., please?	Bitte bringen Sie (noch) ...
I'll have ...	Ich nehme ...
The bill, please.	Zahlen bitte.
All together, please.	Bitte alles zusammen.
Separate bills, please.	Getrennte Rechnungen bitte.
Keep the change.	Stimmt so.
I didn't order this.	Das habe ich nicht bestellt.
The bill is wrong.	Die Rechnung stimmt nicht.
The food is cold/too salty.	Das Essen ist kalt/versalzen.

see also **MENU READER**   *siehe auch* **SPEISEKARTE**

Where can I make a phone call?	Wo kann ich hier telefonieren?
Can I pay for a call using my credit card?	Kann ich für ein Gespräch mit Kreditkarte bezahlen?
I'd like a ten euro phone card.	Ich möchte eine Telefonkarte für zehn Euro.
I'd like some coins for the phone, please.	Ich möchte Münzen für das Telefon bitte.
I'd like to make a reverse charge call.	Ich möchte ein R-Gespräch anmelden.
Hello.	Hallo.
This is ...	Hier ist ...
Who's speaking, please?	Wer spricht dort bitte?
Can I speak to Mr/Ms ..., please?	Kann ich mit Herrn/ Frau ... sprechen?
Extension ..., please.	Apparat ... bitte.
I'll phone back later.	Ich rufe später wieder an.
Where can I charge my mobile (phone)?	Wo kann ich mein Handy aufladen?
I need a new battery.	Ich brauche einen neuen Akku.
I can't get a network.	Hier ist kein Netz.
You're breaking up.	Die Verbindung ist sehr schlecht.

Passport/Customs | Pass/Zoll

Here is ...	Hier ist ...
my passport.	*mein Pass.*
my identity card.	*mein Personalausweis.*
my driving licence.	*mein Führerschein.*
Here are my vehicle documents.	Hier sind meine Fahrzeugpapiere.
The children are on this passport.	Die Kinder stehen in diesem Pass.
Do I have to pay duty on this?	Muss ich das verzollen?
This is ...	Das ist ...
a present.	*ein Geschenk.*
a sample.	*ein Warenmuster.*
This is for my own personal use.	Das ist für meinen persönlichen Gebrauch.
I'm on my way to ...	Ich bin auf der Durchreise nach ...

Changing Money | Bank

Where can I change money?	Wo kann ich hier Geld wechseln?
Is there a bank/bureau de change here?	Gibt es hier eine Bank/eine Wechselstube?
When is the bank/bureau de change open?	Wann ist die Bank/Wechselstube geöffnet?
I'd like to change ... euros into pounds/dollars.	Ich möchte ... Euro in Pfund/Dollar umtauschen.
I'd like to cash these traveller's cheques.	Ich möchte diese Reiseschecks einlösen.
What's the commission?	Wie hoch ist die Gebühr?
Can I use my credit card to get cash?	Kann ich hier mit meiner Kreditkarte Bargeld bekommen?

Where is the nearest cash machine?	Wo gibt es hier einen Geldautomaten?
The cash machine swallowed my card.	Der Geldautomat hat meine Karte geschluckt.
Can you give me some change, please.	Bitte geben Sie mir etwas Kleingeld.

Emergency Services | Notfalldienste

Help!	Hilfe!
Fire!	Feuer!
Please call ...	Bitte rufen Sie ...
the emergency doctor.	den Notarzt.
the fire brigade.	die Feuerwehr.
the police.	die Polizei.
I need to make an urgent phone call.	Ich muss dringend telefonieren.
I need an interpreter.	Ich brauche einen Dolmetscher.
Where is the police station?	Wo ist die Polizeiwache?
Where is the nearest hospital?	Wo ist das nächste Krankenhaus?
I want to report a theft.	Ich möchte einen Diebstahl melden.
... has been stolen.	... ist gestohlen worden.
There's been an accident.	Es ist ein Unfall passiert.
There are ... people injured.	Es gibt ... Verletzte.
My location is ...	Mein Standort ist ...
I've been ...	Ich bin ... worden.
robbed	beraubt
attacked	überfallen
raped	vergewaltigt
I'd like to phone my embassy.	Ich möchte mit meiner Botschaft sprechen.

Pharmacy | Apotheke

Where is the nearest pharmacy?	Wo gibt es hier eine Apotheke?
Which pharmacy provides emergency service?	Welche Apotheke hat Bereitschaft?
I'd like something for ...	Ich möchte etwas gegen ...
diarrhoea.	*Durchfall.*
a temperature.	*Fieber.*
travel sickness.	*Reisekrankheit.*
a headache.	*Kopfschmerzen.*
a cold.	*Erkältung.*
I'd like ...	Ich möchte ...
plasters.	*Pflaster.*
a bandage.	*einen Verband.*
I can't take ...	Ich vertrage kein ...
aspirin.	*Aspirin.*
penicillin.	*Penizillin.*
Is it safe to give to children?	Kann man das Kindern geben?
How should I take it?	Wie soll ich das einnehmen?

At the Doctor's | Beim Arzt

I need a doctor.	Ich brauche einen Arzt.
Where is casualty?	Wo ist die Notaufnahme?
I have a pain here.	Ich habe hier Schmerzen.
I feel ...	Mir ist ...
hot.	*heiß.*
cold.	*kalt.*
sick.	*übel.*
dizzy.	*schwindlig.*

I'm allergic to ...	Ich bin allergisch gegen ...
I am ...	Ich bin ...
pregnant.	*schwanger.*
diabetic.	*Diabetiker.*
HIV-positive.	*HIV-positiv.*
I'm on this medication.	Ich nehme dieses Medikament.
My blood group is ...	Meine Blutgruppe ist ...

At the Hospital | Krankenhaus

Which ward is ... in?	Auf welcher Station liegt ...?
When are visiting hours?	Wann ist die Besuchszeit?
I'd like to speak to ...	Ich möchte mit ... sprechen.
a doctor.	*einem Arzt*
a nurse.	*einer Krankenschwester*
I'd like to hire a phone.	Ich möchte ein Telefon mieten.
I'd like headphones for the TV, please.	Ich möchte Kopfhörer für das Fernsehen, bitte.
When will I be discharged?	Wann werde ich entlassen?

At the Dentist's | Beim Zahnarzt

I need a dentist.	Ich brauche einen Zahnarzt.
This tooth hurts.	Dieser Zahn tut weh.
One of my fillings has fallen out.	Mir ist eine Füllung herausgefallen.
I have an abscess.	Ich habe einen Abszess.
I want/don't want an injection for the pain.	Ich möchte eine/keine Spritze gegen die Schmerzen.
Can you repair my dentures?	Können Sie mein Gebiss reparieren?
I need a receipt for the insurance.	Ich brauche eine Quittung für die Versicherung.

Business Travel | Dienstreisen

I'd like to arrange a meeting with ...	Ich möchte eine Besprechung mit ... ausmachen.
I have an appointment with Mr/Ms ...	Ich haben einen Termin mit Herrn/Frau ...
Here is my card.	Hier ist meine Karte.
I work for ...	Ich arbeite für ...
How do I get to ...?	Wie komme ich ...?
your office	*zu Ihrem Büro*
Mr/Ms ...'s office	*zum Büro von Herrn/Frau ...*
the canteen	*zur Kantine*
I need an interpreter.	Ich brauche einen Dolmetscher.
Can you copy that for me, please?	Bitte kopieren Sie das für mich.
May I use ...?	Darf ich ... benutzen?
your phone	*Ihr Telefon*
your computer	*Ihren Computer*
your desk	*Ihren Schreibtisch*

Disabled Travellers | Behinderte

Where is the wheelchair-accessible entrance?	Wo ist der Eingang für Rollstuhlfahrer?
Is your hotel accessible to wheelchairs?	Ist Ihr Hotel rollstuhlgerecht?
I need a room ...	Ich brauche ein Zimmer ...
on the ground floor.	*im Erdgeschoss.*
with wheelchair access.	*für Rollstuhlfahrer.*
Do you have a lift for wheelchairs?	Haben Sie einen Aufzug für Rollstühle?
Where is the disabled toilet?	Wo ist die Behindertentoilette?
Is the train wheelchair accessible?	Kann ich als Rollstuhlfahrer in diesem Zug mitfahren?

Can you help me get on/off please?	Bitte helfen Sie mir beim Einsteigen/Aussteigen.
Where is the nearest repair shop for wheelchairs?	Wo gibt es hier eine Werkstatt für Rollstühle?
The wheels lock.	Die Räder blockieren.

Travelling with Children — Reisen mit Kindern

Is it OK to bring children here?	Können wir die Kinder mitbringen?
Are children allowed in, too?	Ist der Eintritt auch Kindern gestattet?
Is there a reduction for children?	Gibt es eine Ermäßigung für Kinder?
Do you have children's portions?	Haben Sie Kinderportionen?
Do you have ...?	Haben Sie ...?
a high chair	*einen Kinderstuhl*
a cot	*ein Kinderbett*
a child's seat	*einen Kindersitz*
a baby's changing table	*einen Wickeltisch*
Where can I change the baby?	Wo kann ich das Baby wickeln?
Where can I breast-feed the baby?	Wo kann ich das Baby stillen?
Can you warm this up, please?	Können Sie das bitte aufwärmen?
What is there for children to do?	Was können Kinder hier unternehmen?
Where is the nearest playground?	Wo gibt es hier einen Spielplatz?
Is there a child-minding service?	Gibt es hier eine Kinderbetreuung?
My son/daughter is ill.	Mein Sohn/meine Tochter ist krank.

COMPLAINTS | BESCHWERDEN

I'd like to make a complaint.	Ich möchte mich beschweren.
To whom can I complain?	Bei wem kann ich mich beschweren?
I'd like to speak to the manager, please.	Ich möchte mit dem Geschäftsführer sprechen.
The light	*Das Licht*
The heating	*Die Heizung*
The shower	*Die Dusche*
... doesn't work.	... funktioniert nicht.
The room is ...	Das Zimmer ist ...
dirty.	*schmutzig.*
too small.	*zu klein.*
too cold.	*zu kalt.*
Can you clean the room, please?	Bitte machen Sie das Zimmer sauber.
Can you turn down the TV/the radio, please?	Bitte stellen Sie den Fernseher/das Radio leiser.
The food is ...	Das Essen ist ...
cold.	*kalt.*
too salty.	*versalzen.*
This isn't what I ordered.	Das habe ich nicht bestellt.
We've been waiting for a very long time.	Wir warten schon sehr lange.
The bill is wrong.	Die Rechnung stimmt nicht.
I want my money back.	Ich möchte mein Geld zurück.
I'd like to exchange this.	Ich möchte das umtauschen.
I'm not satisfied with this.	Ich bin damit nicht zufrieden.

Alsterwasser lager shandy

Apfelkorn apple brandy

arme Ritter French toast

Backpflaumen prunes

Bauernfrühstück cooked breakfast of scrambled eggs, bacon, diced potatoes, onions, tomatoes

Berliner doughnut filled with jam

Bierschinken ham sausage

Bierwurst Bavarian boiled sausage

Bockwurst boiled sausage; a popular snack served with a bread roll

Dunkles dark beer

Eierkuchen pancakes

Eisbein boiled pork knuckle, often served with sauerkraut

Eiswein a rich, naturally sweet white wine made from grapes harvested after a period of frost

Fledermaus boiled beef in a horseradish cream

Fünfkornbrot wholemeal bread made with five different cereals

geschmort braised

Gewürzgurken gherkins

Hackbraten meatloaf

Helles light beer

Heuriger new wine

Jägerschnitzel escalope served with mushrooms and a wine sauce

Kasseler smoked pork

Knackwurst hot spicy sausage; a popular snack served with bread

Kraftsuppe consommé

Kroketten croquettes

Leberkäse pork liver meatloaf

Leinsamenbrot wholemeal bread with linseed

Linzer Torte latticed tart with jam topping

Malzbier dark malt beer

Maß a litre of beer

Mischbrot grey bread made with rye and wheat flour

Nockerln small dumplings

Pils, Pilsner a strong, slightly bitter lager

Pumpernickel very dark bread made with coarse wholemeal rye flour

Raclette melted cheese and potatoes

Räucherkäse smoked cheese

Reibekuchen potato cakes

Rösti fried diced potatoes, onions and bacon

Roulade beef olive
Sachertorte rich chocolate gâteau
Sauerbraten braised pickled beef served with dumplings and vegetables
Schwertfisch swordfish
Spanferkel suckling pig
Steinbutt turbot
Steinpilze porcini mushrooms

Stollen spiced loaf with candied peel traditionally eaten at Christmas
Wiener Schnitzel escalope fried in breadcrumbs
Wildbraten roast venison
Zervelatwurst fine beef and pork salami
Zigeunerschnitzel escalope in paprika sauce

apple turnover Apfeltasche

bangers and mash Kartoffelpüree mit Bratwurst, Zwiebeln und Soße

banoffee pie Törtchen mit einer Füllung aus Bananen, Toffee und Sahne

BLT (sandwich) Sandwich mit Schinkenspeck, Salat und Tomaten

bubble and squeak zusammen gebratene Fleischreste und Gemüse

butternut squash Moschuskürbis

Caesar salad Salatgericht aus Kopfsalat, Eiern, Parmesankäse und Vinaigrette

chocolate brownie kleiner Schokoladenkuchen

chicken Kiev Hähnchenbrust, mit Knoblauchbutter gefüllt

chicken nuggets Hähnchen-Nuggets

club sandwich dreilagiges, mit Toastbrot zubereitetes Sandwich

Cornish pasty Gebäckstück aus Blätterteig mit Fleischfüllung

English breakfast englisches Frühstück

filo pastry Blätterteig

haggis mit gehackten Schafsinnereien und Haferschrot gefüllter Schafsmagen

hash browns Rösti-Ecken

hotpot Fleischeintopf mit Kartoffeln

Irish stew Eintopf mit Hammelfleisch, Kartoffeln und Zwiebeln

monkfish Seeteufel

pavlova Baisertorte, mit Sahne und Früchten gefüllt

purée Püree

Quorn® proteinreicher Fleischersatz aus Gemüsesubstanz

savoy cabbage Wirsing

Scotch broth Gemüsesuppe mit Graupen und Hammelfleisch

Scotch egg hart gekochtes Ei in Wurstbrät, paniert und ausgebacken

scrumpy starker Cider aus Südwestengland

sea bass Wolfsbarsch

shortcrust pastry Mürbeteig

spare ribs Schälrippchen

Stilton englischer Blauschimmelkäse

stout Starkbier

sundae Eisbecher mit Nüssen und Sirup

Thousand Island dressing Salatsoße aus Mayonnaise, Ketchup, Paprika und Pickles

toad in the hole in Teig gebackene Bratwürste

turbot Steinbutt

Waldorf salad Waldorfsalat

Welsh rarebit überbackene Käseschnitte

Yorkshire pudding im Backofen ausgebackener Teig als Beilage zu Fleischgerichten

a

abandon [ə'bændən] vt (desert) verlassen; (give up) aufgeben

abbey ['æbi] n Abtei f

abbreviate [ə'bri:vɪ'eɪt] vt abkürzen; **abbreviation** [əbri:vɪ'eɪʃən] n Abkürzung f

ABC ['eɪbi:'si:] n (a. fig) Abc nt

abdicate ['æbdɪkeɪt] vi (king) abdanken; **abdication** [æbdɪ'keɪʃən] n Abdankung f

abdomen ['æbdəmən] n Unterleib m

ability [ə'bɪlɪtɪ] n Fähigkeit f; **able** ['eɪbl] adj fähig; **to be ~ to do sth** etw tun können

abnormal [æb'nɔ:ml] adj anormal

aboard [ə'bɔ:d] adv, prep an Bord +gen

abolish [ə'bɒlɪʃ] vt abschaffen

aborigine [æbə'rɪdʒɪni:] n Ureinwohner(in) m(f) (Australiens)

abort [ə'bɔ:t] vt (Med: foetus) abtreiben; (Space: mission) abbrechen; **abortion** [ə'bɔ:ʃən] n Abtreibung f

---

a [eɪ, ə; æn, ən] (before vowel or silent h: **an**) indef art **1** ein, eine; **a woman** eine Frau; **a book** ein Buch; **an eagle** ein Adler; **she's a doctor** sie ist Ärztin

2 (instead of the number "one") ein, eine; **a year ago** vor einem Jahr; **a hundred/thousand** etc **pounds** (ein) hundert/(ein) tausend etc Pfund

3 (in expressing ratios, prices etc) pro; **3 a day/week** 3 pro Tag/Woche, 3 am Tag/in der Woche; **10 km an hour** 10 km pro Stunde/in der Stunde

AA abbr = **Automobile Association** britischer Automobilklub, ≈ ADAC m

aback adv: **taken ~** erstaunt

---

about [ə'baʊt] adv **1** (approximately) etwa, ungefähr; **about a hundred/thousand** etc etwa hundert/tausend etc; **at about 2 o'clock** etwa um 2 Uhr; **I've just about finished** ich bin gerade fertig

2 (referring to place) herum, umher; **to leave things lying about** Sachen herumliegen lassen; **to run/walk** etc **about** herumrennen/gehen etc

3 to be about to do sth im Begriff sein, etw zu tun; **he was about to go to bed** er wollte gerade ins Bett gehen

▷ *prep* **1** (*relating to*) über +*akk*; **a book about London** ein Buch über London; **what is it about?** worum geht es?; (*book etc*) wovon handelt es?; **we talked about it** wir haben darüber geredet; **what o how about doing this?** wollen wir das machen?
2 (*referring to place*) um (... herum); **to walk about the town** in der Stadt herumgehen; **her clothes were scattered about the room** ihre Kleider waren über das ganze Zimmer verstreut

above [ə'bʌv] *adv* oben; **children aged 8 and ~** Kinder ab 8 Jahren; **on the floor ~** ein Stockwerk höher ▷ *prep* über; **~ 40 degrees** über 40 Grad; **~ all** vor allem ▷ *adj* obig

abroad [ə'brɔːd] *adv* im Ausland; **to go ~** ins Ausland gehen

abrupt [ə'brʌpt] *adj* (*sudden*) plötzlich, abrupt

abscess ['æbsɪs] *n* Geschwür *nt*

absence ['æbsns] *n* Abwesenheit *f*; **absent** ['æbsənt] *adj* abwesend; **to be ~** fehlen; **absent-minded** *adj* zerstreut

absolute ['æbsəluːt] *adj* absolut; (*power*) unumschränkt; (*rubbish*) vollkommen, total; **absolutely** *adv* absolut; (*true, stupid*) vollkommen; **~!** genau!; **you're ~ right** du hast/Sie haben völlig recht

absorb [əb'zɔːb] *vt* absorbieren; (*fig: information*) in sich aufnehmen; **absorbed** *adj*: **~ in sth** in etw vertieft; **absorbent cotton** (*US*) Watte *f*; **absorbing** *adj* (*fig*) faszinierend, fesselnd

abstain [əb'steɪn] *vi*: **to ~ (from voting)** sich (der Stimme) enthalten

abstract ['æbstrækt] *adj* abstrakt

absurd [əb'sɜːd] *adj* absurd

abundance [ə'bʌndəns] *n* Reichtum *m* (*of* an +*dat*)

abuse [ə'bjuːs] *n* (*rude language*) Beschimpfungen *pl*; (*mistreatment*) Missbrauch *m* ▷ [ə'bjuːz] *vt* (*misuse*) missbrauchen; **abusive** [ə'bjuːsɪv] *adj* beleidigend

AC *abbr* = **alternating current** Wechselstrom *m* ▷ *abbr* = **air conditioning** Klimaanlage

a/c *abbr* = **account** Kto.

academic [ækə'demɪk] *n* Wissenschaftler(in) *m(f)* ▷ *adj* akademisch, wissenschaftlich

accelerate [ək'seləreɪt] *vi* (*car etc*) beschleunigen; (*driver*) Gas geben; **acceleration** [əkselə'reɪʃən] *n* Beschleunigung *f*; **accelerator** [ək'seləreɪtə°] *n* Gas(pedal) *nt*

accent ['æksənt] *n* Akzent *m*

accept [ək'sept] *vt* annehmen; (*agree to*) akzeptieren; (*responsibility*) übernehmen; **acceptable** [ək'septəbl] *adj* annehmbar

access ['ækses] *n* Zugang *m*; (*Inform*) Zugriff *m*; **accessible** [æk'sesəbl] *adj* (*leicht*) zugänglich/erreichbar; (*place*) (*leicht*) erreichbar

accessory [æk'sesərɪ] *n* Zubehörteil *nt*

access road *n* Zufahrtsstraße *f*

accident ['æksɪdənt] *n* Unfall *m*; **by ~** zufällig; **accidental** [æksɪ'dentl] *adj* unbeabsichtigt; (*meeting*) zufällig; (*death*) durch Unfall; **~ damage** Unfallschaden *m*; **accident-prone** *adj* vom Pech verfolgt

acclimatize [ə'klaɪmətaɪz] *vt*: **to ~ oneself** sich gewöhnen (*to* an +*akk*)

accommodate [əˈkɒmədeɪt] vt
unterbringen;
accommodation(s)
[əkɒməˈdeɪʃən(z)] n Unterkunft f
accompany [əˈkʌmpənɪ] vt
begleiten
accomplish [əˈkʌmplɪʃ] vt
erreichen
accord [əˈkɔːd] n: **of one's own**
~ freiwillig; **according to** prep
nach, laut +dat
account [əˈkaʊnt] n (in bank etc)
Konto nt; (narrative) Bericht m; **on**
~ **of** wegen; **on no** ~ auf keinen
Fall; **to take into** ~
berücksichtigen, in Betracht
ziehen; **accountant** [əˈkaʊntənt]
n Buchhalter(in) m(f); **account for**
vt (explain) erklären; (expenditure)
Rechenschaft ablegen für;
account number n
Kontonummer f
accumulate [əˈkjuːmjʊleɪt] vt
ansammeln ▷ vi sich ansammeln
accuracy [ˈækjʊrəsɪ] n
Genauigkeit f; **accurate** [ˈækjʊrɪt]
adj genau
accusation [ækjʊˈzeɪʃən] n
Anklage f, Beschuldigung f
accusative [əˈkjuːzətɪv] n
Akkusativ m
accuse [əˈkjuːz] vt beschuldigen;
(Jur) anklagen (of wegen +gen); ~ **sb**
of doing sth jdn beschuldigen,
etw getan zu haben; **accused** n
(Jur) Angeklagte(r) mf
accustom [əˈkʌstəm] vt
gewöhnen (to an +akk);
accustomed adj gewohnt; **to get**
~ **to sth** sich an etw akk gewöhnen
ace [eɪs] n Ass nt ▷ adj Star-
ache [eɪk] n Schmerz m ▷ vi
wehtun
achieve [əˈtʃiːv] vt erreichen;
achievement n Leistung f
acid [ˈæsɪd] n Säure f ▷ adj sauer;
~ **rain** saurer Regen

acknowledge [əkˈnɒlɪdʒ] vt
(recognize) anerkennen; (admit)
zugeben; (receipt of letter etc)
bestätigen; **acknowledgement** n
Anerkennung f; (of letter)
Empfangsbestätigung f
acne [ˈæknɪ] n Akne f
acorn [ˈeɪkɔːn] n Eichel f
acoustic [əˈkuːstɪk] adj akustisch; **acoustics** [əˈkuːstɪks] npl
Akustik f
acquaintance [əˈkweɪntəns] n
(person) Bekannte(r) mf
acquire [əˈkwaɪə*] vt erwerben,
sich aneignen; **acquisition**
[ækwɪˈzɪʃn] n (of skills etc) Erwerb
m; (object) Anschaffung f
acrobat [ˈækrəbæt] n Akrobat(in)
m(f)
across [əˈkrɒs] prep über +akk; **he**
lives ~ **the street** er wohnt auf der
anderen Seite der Straße ▷ adv
hinüber, herüber; **100m** ~ 100m
breit
act [ækt] n (deed) Tat f; (Jur: law)
Gesetz nt; (Theat) Akt m; (fig:
pretence) Schau f; **it's all an** ~ es ist
alles nur Theater; **to be in the** ~ **of**
doing sth gerade dabei sein, etw
zu tun ▷ vi (take action) handeln;
(behave) sich verhalten; (Theat) spielen;
to ~ **as** (person) fungieren als; (thing)
dienen als ▷ vt (a part) spielen
action [ˈækʃən] n (of play, novel
etc) Handlung f; (in film Kino etc)
Action f; (Mil) Kampf m; **to take** ~
unternehmen; **out of** ~ (machine)
außer Betrieb; **to put a plan into**
~ einen Plan in die Tat umsetzen;
action replay n (Sport, TV)
Wiederholung f
activate [ˈæktɪveɪt] vt aktivieren;
active [ˈæktɪv] adj lebhaft; (child)
lebhaft; **activity** [ækˈtɪvɪtɪ] n
Aktivität f; (occupation)
Beschäftigung f; (organized event)
Veranstaltung f

actor ['æktə*] n Schauspieler(in)
m(f); **actress** ['æktrɪs] n
Schauspielerin f

actual ['æktjʊəl] adj wirklich;
actually adv eigentlich; (said in
surprise) tatsächlich

acupuncture ['ækjʊpʌŋktʃə*] n
Akupunktur f

acute [ə'kjuːt] adj (pain) akut;
(sense of smell) fein; (Math: angle)
spitz

ad [æd] abbr = **advertisement**

AD abbr = **Anno Domini** nach
Christi, n. Chr.

adapt [ə'dæpt] vi sich anpassen
(to +dat) ▷ vt anpassen (to +dat);
(rewrite) bearbeiten (for für);
adaptable adj anpassungsfähig;
adaptation n (of book etc)
Bearbeitung f; **adapter**, **adaptor** n (Elec)
Zwischenstecker m, Adapter m

add [æd] vt (ingredient)
hinzufügen; (numbers) addieren;
add up vi (make sense) stimmen
▷ vt (numbers) addieren

addict ['ædɪkt] n Süchtige(r) mf;
addicted [ə'dɪktɪd] adj: **- to**
alcohol/drugs alkohol-/
drogensüchtig

addition [ə'dɪʃən] n Zusatz m; (to
bill) Aufschlag m; (Math) Addition f;
in - außerdem, zusätzlich (to zu);
additional adj zusätzlich, weiter;
additive ['ædɪtɪv] n Zusatz m;
add-on ['ædɒn] n Zusatzgerät nt

address [ə'dres] n Adresse f ▷ vt
(letter) adressieren; (person)
anreden

adequate ['ædɪkwɪt] adj
(appropriate) angemessen;
(sufficient) ausreichend; (time)
genügend

adhesive [əd'hiːsɪv] n Klebstoff
m; **adhesive tape** n Klebstreifen
m

adjacent [ə'dʒeɪsənt] adj
benachbart

adjective ['ædʒəktɪv] n Adjektiv
nt

adjoining [ə'dʒɔɪnɪŋ] adj
benachbart, Neben-

adjust [ə'dʒʌst] vt einstellen;
(put right also) richtig stellen;
(speed, flow) regulieren; (in position)
verstellen ▷ vi sich anpassen (to
+dat); **adjustable** adj verstellbar

admin [əd'mɪn] n (fam)
Verwaltung f; **administration**
[ədmɪnɪs'treɪʃən] n Verwaltung f;
(Pol) Regierung f

admirable ['ædmərəbl] adj
bewundernswert; **admiration**
[ædmɪ'reɪʃən] n Bewunderung f;
admire [əd'maɪə*] vt bewundern

admission [əd'mɪʃən] n (entrance)
Zutritt m; (to university etc)
Zulassung f; (fee) Eintritt m;
(confession) Eingeständnis nt;
admission charge, **admission fee**
n Eintrittspreis m; **admit** [əd'mɪt]
vt (let in) hereinlassen (to in +akk);
(to university etc) zulassen; (confess)
zugeben, gestehen; **to be ~ted to**
hospital ins Krankenhaus
eingeliefert werden

adolescent [ædə'lesnt] n
Jugendliche(r) mf

adopt [ə'dɒpt] vt (child)
adoptieren; (idea) übernehmen;
adoption [ə'dɒpʃn] n (of child)
Adoption f; (of idea) Übernahme f

adorable [ə'dɔːrəbl] adj
entzückend; **adore** [ə'dɔː*] vt
anbeten; (person) über alles lieben,
vergöttern

ADSL abbr = **asymmetric**
digital subscriber line ADSL f

adult ['ædʌlt] adj erwachsen;
(film etc) für Erwachsene ▷ n
Erwachsene(r) mf

adultery [ə'dʌltərɪ] n Ehebruch
m

advance [əd'vɑːns] n (money)
Vorschuss m; (progress) Fortschritt

m; **in ~** im Voraus; **to book in ~**
vorbestellen ▷ *vi* (*move forward*)
vorrücken ▷ *vt* (*money*)
vorschießen; **advance booking** *n*
Reservierung *f*; (*Theat*) Vorverkauf
m; **advanced** *adj* (*modern*)
fortschrittlich; (*course, study*) für
Fortgeschrittene; **advance**
payment *n* Vorauszahlung *f*

advantage [əd'vɑːntɪdʒ] *n*
Vorteil *m*; **to take ~ of** (*exploit*)
ausnutzen; (*profit from*) Nutzen
ziehen aus; **it's to your ~** es ist in
deinem/Ihrem Interesse

adventure [əd'ventʃə*] *n*
Abenteuer *nt*; **adventure holiday**
n Abenteuerurlaub *m*; **adventure**
playground *n* Abenteuerspiel-
platz *m*; **adventurous**
[əd'ventʃərəs] *adj* (*person*)
abenteuerlustig

adverb ['ædvɜːb] *n* Adverb *nt*

adverse ['ædvɜːs] *adj* (*conditions*
etc) ungünstig; (*effect, comment etc*)
negativ

advert ['ædvɜːt] *n* Anzeige *f*;
advertise ['ædvətaɪz] *vt* werben
für; (*in newspaper*) inserieren; (*job*)
ausschreiben ▷ *vi* Reklame
machen; (*in newspaper*)
annoncieren (*for* für);
advertisement [əd'vɜːtɪsmənt]
n Werbung *f*; (*announcement*)
Anzeige *f*; **advertising** *n*
Werbung *f*

advice [əd'vaɪs] *n* Rat(schlag) *m*;
word *o* **piece of ~** Ratschlag *m*;
take my ~ folge mir nach;
advisable [əd'vaɪzəbl] *adj* ratsam; **advise** [əd'vaɪz] *vt* raten
(*sb* jdm); **to ~ sb to do sth/not to**
do sth jdm zuraten/abraten, etw
zu tun

Aegean [iː'dʒiːən] *n*: **the ~ (Sea)**
die Ägäis

aerial ['ɛərɪəl] *n* Antenne *f* ▷ *adj*
Luft-

aerobatics [ɛərəʊ'bætɪks] *npl*
Kunstfliegen *nt*

aerobics [ɛə'rəʊbɪks] *nsing*
Aerobic *nt*

aeroplane ['ɛərəpleɪn] *n*
Flugzeug *nt*

afaik *abbr* = **as far as I know**;
(*SMS*) ≈ soweit ich weiß

affair [ə'fɛə*] *n* (*matter, business*)
Sache *f*, Angelegenheit *f*; (*scandal*)
Affäre *f*; (*love affair*) Verhältnis *nt*

affect [ə'fekt] *vt* (*influence*)
(ein)wirken auf +*akk*; (*health,*
organ) angreifen; (*move deeply*)
berühren; (*concern*) betreffen;
affection [ə'fekʃən] *n* Zuneigung
f; **affectionate** [ə'fekʃənɪt] *adj*
liebevoll

affluent ['æfluənt] *adj*
wohlhabend

afford [ə'fɔːd] *vt* sich leisten; **I**
can't ~ it ich kann es mir nicht
leisten; **affordable** [ə'fɔːdəbl]
adj erschwinglich

Afghanistan [æf'gænɪstæn] *n*
Afghanistan *nt*

aforementioned
[əfɔː'menʃənd] *adj* oben genannt

afraid [ə'freɪd] *adj*: **to be ~** Angst
haben (*of* vor +*dat*); **to be ~ that ...**
fürchten, dass ...; **I'm ~ – I don't**
know das weiß ich leider nicht

Africa ['æfrɪkə] *n* Afrika *nt*;
African *adj* afrikanisch ▷ *n*
Afrikaner(in) *m(f)*; **African**
American, Afro-American ▷ *n*
Afroamerikaner(in) *m(f)*

after ['ɑːftə*] *prep* nach; **ten**
~ five (*US*) zehn nach fünf; **to be**
~ sb/sth (*following, seeking*) hinter
jdm/etw her sein; **~ all**
schließlich; (*in spite of everything*)
(schließlich) doch ▷ *conj*
nachdem ▷ *adv*: **soon ~** bald
danach; **aftercare** *n*
Nachbehandlung *f*; **after-effect** *n*
Nachwirkung *f*

afternoon n Nachmittag m; ~, **good** ~ guten Tag!; **in the** ~ nachmittags

afters npl Nachtisch m; **after-sales service** n Kundendienst m; **after-shave (lotion)** n Rasierwasser nt; **aftersun** n After-Sun-Lotion f; **afterwards** adv nachher; (after that) danach

again [ə'gen] adv wieder; (one more time) noch einmal; **not ~!** (nicht) schon wieder; **~ and ~** immer wieder; **the same ~ please** das Gleiche noch mal bitte

against [ə'genst] prep gegen; **~ my will** gegen meinen Willen; **~ the law** unrechtmäßig, illegal

age [eɪdʒ] n Alter nt; (period of history) Zeitalter nt; **at the ~ of four** im Alter von vier (Jahren); **what ~ is she?, what is her ~?** wie alt ist sie?; **to come of ~** volljährig werden; **under ~** minderjährig ▷ vi altern, alt werden; **aged** adj: **~ thirty** dreißig Jahre alt; **a son ~ twenty** ein zwanzigjähriger Sohn ▷ adj ['eɪdʒɪd] (elderly) betagt; **age group** n Altersgruppe f; **ageism** n Diskriminierung f aufgrund des Alters; **age limit** n Altersgrenze f

agency ['eɪdʒənsɪ] n Agentur f

agenda [ə'dʒendə] n Tagesordnung f

agent ['eɪdʒənt] n (Comm) Vertreter(in) m(f); (for writer, actor etc) Agent(in) m(f)

aggression [ə'greʃn] n Aggression f; **aggressive** [ə'gresɪv] adj aggressiv

agitated adj aufgeregt; **to get ~** sich aufregen

AGM abbr = **Annual General Meeting** JHV f

ago [ə'gəʊ] adv: **two days ~** heute vor zwei Tagen; **not long ~** (erst) vor Kurzem

agonize ['ægənaɪz] vi sich den Kopf zerbrechen (over über dat); **agonizing** adj qualvoll; **agony** ['ægənɪ] n Qual f

agree [ə'griː] vt (date, price etc) vereinbaren; **to ~ to do sth** sich bereit erklären, etw zu tun; **to ~ that ...** sich darauf einig sein, dass ...; (decide) beschließen, dass ...; (admit) zugeben, dass ... ▷ vi (have same opinion, correspond) übereinstimmen (with mit); (consent) zustimmen; (come to an agreement) sich einigen (about, on auf +akk); (food) **not to ~ with sb** jdm nicht bekommen; **agreement** n (agreeing) Übereinstimmung f; (contract) Abkommen nt, Vereinbarung f

agricultural [ægrɪ'kʌltʃərəl] adj landwirtschaftlich, Landwirtschafts-; **agriculture** ['ægrɪkʌltʃə°] n Landwirtschaft f

ahead [ə'hed] adv: **to be ~** führen, vorne liegen; **~ of** vor +dat; **to be ~ of sb** (person) jdm voraus sein; (thing) vor jdm liegen; **to be 3 metres ~** 3 Meter Vorsprung haben

aid [eɪd] n Hilfe f; **in ~ of** zugunsten +gen; **with the ~ of** mithilfe +gen ▷ vt helfen +dat; (support) unterstützen

Aids [eɪdz] n acr = **acquired immune deficiency syndrome** Aids nt

aim [eɪm] vt (gun, camera) richten (at auf +akk) ▷ vi: **to ~ at** (with gun etc) zielen auf +akk; (fig) abzielen auf +akk; **to ~ to do sth** beabsichtigen, etw zu tun ▷ n Ziel nt

air [ɛə°] n Luft f; **in the open ~** im Freien; (Radio, TV) **to be on the ~** (programme) auf Sendung sein;

(station) senden ▷ vt lüften;
airbag n (Auto) Airbag m;
air-conditioned adj mit
Klimaanlage; **air-conditioning** n
Klimaanlage f; **aircraft** n
Flugzeug nt; **airfield** n Flugplatz
m; **air force** n Luftwaffe f;
airgun n Luftgewehr nt;
airline n Fluggesellschaft f;
airmail n Luftpost f; **by ~** mit
Luftpost; **airplane** n (US)
Flugzeug nt; **air pollution** n
Luftverschmutzung f; **airport** n
Flughafen m; **airsick** adj
luftkrank; **airtight** adj luftdicht;
air-traffic controller n Fluglotse
m, Fluglotsin f; **airy** adj luftig;
(manner) lässig
aisle [aɪl] n Gang m; (in church)
Seitenschiff nt; **~ seat** Sitz m am
Gang
ajar [ə'dʒɑː] adj (door) angelehnt
alarm [ə'lɑːm] n (warning) Alarm
m; (bell etc) Alarmanlage f ▷ vt
beunruhigen; **alarm clock** n
Wecker m; **alarmed** adj (protected)
alarmgesichert; **alarming** adj
beunruhigend
Albania [æl'beɪnɪə] n Albanien
nt; **Albanian** adj albanisch ▷ n
(person) Albaner(in) m(f); (language)
Albanisch nt
album ['ælbəm] n Album nt
alcohol ['ælkəhɒl] n Alkohol m;
alcohol-free adj alkoholfrei;
alcoholic [ælkə'hɒlɪk] adj (drink)
alkoholisch ▷ n Alkoholiker(in)
m(f); **alcoholism** n Alkoholismus
m
ale [eɪl] n Ale nt (helles englisches
Bier)
alert [ə'lɜːt] adj wachsam ▷ n
Alarm m ▷ vt warnen (to vor +dat)
algebra ['ældʒɪbrə] n Algebra f
Algeria [æl'dʒɪərɪə] n Algerien nt
alibi ['ælɪbaɪ] n Alibi nt
alien ['eɪlɪən] n (foreigner)

Ausländer(in) m(f); (from space)
Außerirdische(r) mf
align [ə'laɪn] vt ausrichten (with
auf +akk)
alike [ə'laɪk] adj, adv gleich;
(similar) ähnlich
alive [ə'laɪv] adj lebendig; **to
keep sth ~** etw am Leben
erhalten; **he's still ~** er lebt noch

⭕ KEYWORD

all [ɔːl] adj alle(r, s); **all day/night**
den ganzen Tag/die ganze Nacht;
all men are equal alle Menschen
sind gleich; **all five came** alle fünf
kamen; **all the books/food** die
ganzen Bücher/das ganze Essen;
all the time die ganze Zeit (über);
all his life sein ganzes Leben
(lang)
▷ pron **1** alles; **I ate it all, I ate all of
it** ich habe alles gegessen; **all of
us/the boys went** wir gingen
alle/alle Jungen gingen; **we all sat
down** wir setzten uns alle
2 (in phrases) **above all** vor allem;
after all schließlich; **at all: not at
all** (in answer to question)
überhaupt nicht; (in answer to
thanks) gern geschehen; **I'm not at
all tired** ich bin überhaupt nicht
müde; **anything at all will do** es
ist egal, welche(r, s); **all in all** alles
in allem
▷ adv ganz; **all alone** ganz allein;
it's not as hard as all that so
schwer ist es nun auch wieder
nicht; **all the more/the better**
umso mehr/besser; **all but** fast;
the score is 2 all es steht 2 zu 2

allegation [ælɪ'geɪʃən] n
Behauptung f; **alleged** adj
angeblich
allergic [ə'lɜːdʒɪk] adj allergisch

(to gegen); **allergy** ['ælədʒɪ] n
Allergie f

alleviate [ə'li:vɪeɪt] vt (pain)
lindern

alley ['ælɪ] n (enge) Gasse;
(passage) Durchgang m; (bowling)
Bahn f

alliance [ə'laɪəns] n Bündnis nt

alligator ['ælɪgeɪtə°] n Alligator
m

all-night adj (café, cinema) die
ganze Nacht geöffnet

allocate ['æləkeɪt] vt zuweisen,
zuteilen (to dat)

allotment (plot)
Schrebergarten m

allow [ə'laʊ] vt (permit) erlauben
(sb jdm); (grant) bewilligen; (time)
einplanen; **allow for** vt
berücksichtigen; (cost etc)
einkalkulieren; **allowance** n (from
state) Beihilfe f; (from parent)
Unterhaltsgeld nt

all right ['ɔːl'raɪt] adj okay, in
Ordnung; **I'm ~** mir geht's gut
▷ adv (satisfactorily) ganz gut
▷ interj okay

all-time adj (record, high) aller
Zeiten

allusion [ə'luːʒn] n Anspielung f
(to auf +akk)

ally ['ælaɪ] n Verbündete(r) mf;
(Hist) Alliierte(r) mf

almond ['ɑːmənd] n Mandel f

almost ['ɔːlməʊst] adv fast

alone [ə'ləʊn] adj, adv allein

along [ə'lɒŋ] prep entlang
+akk; **~ the river** den Fluss
entlang; (position) am Fluss
entlang ▷ adv (onward) weiter;
~ with zusammen mit; **all ~** die
ganze Zeit, von Anfang an;
alongside prep neben +dat ▷ adv
(walk) nebenher

aloud [ə'laʊd] adv laut

alphabet ['ælfəbet] n Alphabet
nt

alpine ['ælpaɪn] adj alpin; **Alps**
[ælps] npl die **the ~** die Alpen

already [ɔːl'redɪ] adv schon,
bereits

Alsace ['ælsæs] n Elsass nt;
Alsatian [æl'seɪʃən] adj
elsässisch ▷ n Elsässer(in) m(f);
(Brit: dog) Schäferhund m

also ['ɔːlsəʊ] adv auch

altar ['ɔːltə°] n Altar m

alter ['ɔːltə°] vt ändern;
alteration [ɔːltə'reɪʃən] n
Änderung f; **~s** (to building) Umbau
m

alternate [ɔːl'tɜːnət] adj
abwechselnd ▷ ['ɔːltəneɪt] vi
abwechseln (with mit);
alternating current n
Wechselstrom m

alternative [ɔːl'tɜːnətɪv] adj
Alternativ- ▷ n Alternative f

although [ɔːl'ðəʊ] conj obwohl

altitude ['æltɪtjuːd] n Höhe f

altogether [ɔːltə'geðə°] adv (in
total) insgesamt; (entirely) ganz
und gar

aluminium [æljʊ'mɪnɪəm], **aluminum** (US)
[ə'luːmɪnəm] n
Aluminium nt

always ['ɔːlweɪz] adv immer

am [æm] present of **be**; bin

am, a.m. abbr = **ante meridiem**
vormittags, vorm.

amateur ['æmətə°] n Ama-
teur(in) m(f) ▷ adj Amateur-;
(theatre, choir) Laien-

amaze [ə'meɪz] vt erstaunen;
amazed adj erstaunt (at über
+akk); **amazing** adj erstaunlich

Amazon ['æməzən] n: **~ (river)**
Amazonas m

ambassador [æm'bæsədə°] n
Botschafter m

amber ['æmbə°] n Bernstein m

ambiguity [æmbɪ'gjʊɪtɪ] n
Zweideutigkeit f; **ambiguous**
[æm'bɪgjʊəs] adj zweideutig

ambition [æm'bɪʃən] n Ambition f; (ambitious nature) Ehrgeiz m; **ambitious** [æm'bɪʃəs] adj ehrgeizig

ambulance ['æmbjʊləns] n Krankenwagen m

amend [ə'mend] vt (law etc) ändern

America [ə'merɪkə] n Amerika nt; **American** adj amerikanisch ▷ n Amerikaner(in) m(f); **native ~** Indianer(in) m(f)

amiable ['eɪmɪəbl] adj liebenswürdig

amicable ['æmɪkəbl] adj freundlich; (relations) freundschaftlich; (Jur: settlement) gütlich

amnesia [æm'niːzɪə] n Gedächtnisverlust m

among(st) [ə'mʌn(st)] prep unter +dat

amount [ə'maʊnt] n (quantity) Menge f; (of money) Betrag m; **a large/small ~ of ...** ziemlich viel/wenig ... ▷ vi: **to ~ to** (total) sich belaufen auf +akk

amp, ampere [æmp, 'æmpeə°] n Ampere m

amplifier ['æmplɪfaɪə°] n Verstärker m

amputate ['æmpjʊteɪt] vt amputieren

Amtrak® ['æmtræk] n amerikanische Eisenbahngesellschaft

amuse [ə'mjuːz] vt amüsieren; (entertain) unterhalten; **amused** adj: **I'm not ~** das finde ich gar nicht lustig; **amusement** n (enjoyment) Vergnügen nt; (recreation) Unterhaltung f; **amusement arcade** n Spielhalle f; **amusement park** n Vergnügungspark m; **amusing** adj amüsant

an [æn, ən] art ein(e)

anaemic [ə'niːmɪk] adj blutarm

anaesthetic [ænɪs'θetɪk] n

Narkose f; (substance) Narkosemittel nt

analyse, analyze ['ænəlaɪz] vt analysieren; **analysis** [ə'nælɪsɪs] n Analyse f

anatomy [ə'nætəmɪ] n Anatomie f; (structure) Körperbau m

ancestor ['ænsestə°] n Vorfahr m

anchor ['æŋkə°] n Anker m ▷ vt verankern; **anchorage** n Ankerplatz m

anchovy ['æntʃəvɪ] n Sardelle f

ancient ['eɪnʃənt] adj alt; (fam: person, clothes etc) uralt

and [ænd, ənd] conj und

Andorra [æn'dɔːrə] n Andorra nt

anemic adj (US) see **anaemic**

anesthetic n (US) see **anaesthetic**

angel ['eɪndʒəl] n Engel m

anger ['æŋgə°] n Zorn m ▷ vt ärgern

angina, angina pectoris [æn'dʒaɪnə('pektərɪs)] n Angina Pectoris f

angle ['æŋgl] n Winkel m; (fig) Standpunkt m

angler ['æŋglə°] n Angler(in) m(f); **angling** ['æŋglɪŋ] n Angeln nt

angry ['æŋgrɪ] adj verärgert; (stronger) zornig; **to be ~ with sb** auf jdn böse sein

angular ['æŋgjʊlə°] adj eckig; (face) kantig

animal ['ænɪməl] n Tier nt; **animal rights** npl Tierrechte pl

animated ['ænɪmeɪtɪd] adj lebhaft; **~ film** Zeichentrickfilm m

aniseed ['ænɪsiːd] n Anis m

ankle ['æŋkl] n (Fuß)knöchel m

annex ['æneks] n Anbau m

anniversary [ænɪ'vɜːsərɪ] n Jahrestag m

announce [ə'naʊns] vt bekannt geben; (officially) bekannt machen; (on radio, TV etc) (Radio,

TV) ansagen; **announcement** n
Bekanntgabe f; (official)
Bekanntmachung f; (Radio, TV)
Ansage f; **announcer** n (Radio, TV)
Ansager(in) m(f)

annoy [ə'nɔɪ] vt ärgern;
annoyance n Ärger m; **annoyed**
adj ärgerlich; **to be ~ with sb**
(about sth) sich über jdn (über
etw) ärgern; **annoying** adj
ärgerlich; (person) lästig, nervig

annual ['ænjʊəl] adj jährlich
▷ n Jahrbuch nt

anonymous [ə'nɒnɪməs] adj
anonym

anorak ['ænəræk] n Anorak m

anorexia [ænə'rɛksɪə] n Magersucht f; **anorexic** adj
magersüchtig

another [ə'nʌðə°] adj, pron
(different) ein(e) andere(r, s);
(additional) noch eine(r, s); **let me**
put it ~ way lass es mich anders
sagen

answer ['ɑːnsə°] n Antwort f (to
auf +akk); (solution) Lösung f +gen
▷ vi antworten; (on phone) sich
melden ▷ vt (person) antworten
+dat; (letter, question) beantworten;
(telephone) gehen an +akk,
abnehmen; (door) öffnen; **answer**
back vi widersprechen;
answering machine,
answerphone n Anrufbeantworter m

ant [ænt] n Ameise f

Antarctic [ænt'ɑːktɪk] n
Antarktis f; **Antarctic Circle** n
südlicher Polarkreis

antelope ['æntɪləʊp] n Antilope f

antenna ['æntenə] (pl **antennae**)
n (Zool) Fühler m; (Radio) Antenne f

anti- ['æntɪ] pref Anti-, anti-;
antibiotic ['æntɪbaɪ'ɒtɪk] n
Antibiotikum nt

anticipate [æn'tɪsɪpeɪt] vt (expect:
trouble, question) erwarten,

rechnen mit; **anticipation**
[æntɪsɪ'peɪʃən] n Erwartung f

anticlimax [æntɪ'klaɪmæks] n
Enttäuschung f; **anticlockwise**
[æntɪ'klɒkwaɪz] adv entgegen
dem Uhrzeigersinn

antidote ['æntɪdəʊt] n Gegenmittel nt; **antifreeze** n
Frostschutzmittel nt

Antipodes [æn'tɪpədiːz] npl
Australien und Neuseeland

antiquarian [æntɪ'kwɛərɪən]
adj: **~ bookshop** Antiquariat nt

antique [æn'tiːk] n Antiquität f
▷ adj antik; **antique shop** n
Antiquitätengeschäft nt

anti-Semitism [æntɪ'semɪtɪzm]
n Antisemitismus m; **antiseptic**
[æntɪ'septɪk] n Antiseptikum nt
▷ adj antiseptisch; **antisocial** adj
(person) ungesellig; (behaviour)
unsozial, asozial; **antivirus** adj
(Inform) Antiviren-; **antivirus**
software n Antivirensoftware f

antlers ['æntləz] npl Geweih nt

anxiety [æŋ'zaɪətɪ] n Sorge f
(about um); **anxious** ['æŋkʃəs] adj
besorgt (about um); (apprehensive)
ängstlich

◯ **KEYWORD**

any ['enɪ] adj **1** (in questions etc)
have you any butter? haben Sie
(etwas) Butter?; **have you any**
children? haben Sie Kinder?; **if**
there are any tickets left falls
noch Karten da sind
2 (with negative) **I haven't any**
money ich habe kein Geld
3 (no matter which) jede(r, s)
(beliebig); **any colour (at all)**
jede beliebige Farbe; **choose any**
book you like nehmen Sie ein
beliebiges Buch
4 (in phrases) **in any case** in jedem

Fall; **any day now** jeden Tag; **at any moment** jeden Moment; **at any rate** auf jeden Fall
▷ *pron* 1 *(in questions etc)* **have you got any?** haben Sie welche?; **can any of you sing?** kann (irgend)einer von euch singen?
2 *(with negative)* **I haven't any (of them)** ich habe keinen/keine/keins (davon)
3 *(no matter which one(s))*: **take any of those books (you like)** nehmen Sie irgendeines dieser Bücher
▷ *adv* 1 *(in questions etc)* **do you want any more soup/ sandwiches?** möchten Sie noch Suppe/Brote?; **are you feeling any better?** fühlen Sie sich etwas besser?
2 *(with negative)* **I can't hear him any more** ich kann ihn nicht mehr hören

anybody *pron (whoever one likes)* irgendjemand; *(everyone)* jeder; *(in question)* jemand
anyhow *adv:* **I don't want to talk about it, not now ~** ich möchte nicht darüber sprechen, jedenfalls nicht jetzt; **they asked me not to go, but I went ~** sie baten mich, nicht hinzugehen, aber ich bin trotzdem hingegangen; **anyone** *pron (whoever one likes)* irgendjemand; *(everyone)* jeder; *(in question)* jemand; **isn't there ~ you can ask?** gibt es denn niemanden, den du fragen kannst/den Sie fragen können?; **anyplace** *adv (US)* irgendwo; *(direction)* irgendwohin; *(everywhere)* überall

KEYWORD

anything [ˈɛnɪθɪŋ] *pron* 1 *(in questions etc)* (irgend)etwas; **can**

you see anything? können Sie etwas sehen?
2 *(with negative)* **I can't see anything** ich kann nichts sehen
3 *(no matter what)* **you can say anything you like** Sie können sagen, was Sie wollen; **anything will do** irgendetwas (wird genügen), irgendeine(r, s) (wird genügen); **he'll eat anything** er isst alles

anytime *adv* jederzeit; **anyway** *adv:* **I didn't want to go there ~** ich wollte da sowieso nicht hingehen; **thanks ~** trotzdem danke; **~, as I was saying, ...** jedenfalls, wie ich schon sagte, ...; **anywhere** *adv* irgendwo; *(direction)* irgendwohin; *(everywhere)* überall

apart [əˈpɑːt] *adv* auseinander; **~ from** außer; **live ~** getrennt leben
apartment [əˈpɑːtmənt] *n (esp US)* Wohnung *f;* **apartment block** *n (esp US)* Wohnblock *m*
ape [eɪp] *n* (Menschen)affe *m*
aperitif [əˈpɛrɪtɪf] *n* Aperitif *m*
apologize [əˈpɒlədʒaɪz] *vi* sich entschuldigen; **apology** *n* Entschuldigung *f*
apostrophe [əˈpɒstrəfɪ] *n* Apostroph *m*
app [æp] *(for mobile phone)* App *f*
appalled [əˈpɔːld] *adj* entsetzt *(at über +akk);* **appalling** *adj* entsetzlich
apparatus [æpəˈreɪtəs] *n* Apparat *m;* *(piece of apparatus)* Gerät *nt*
apparent [əˈpærənt] *adj (obvious)* offensichtlich *(to für); (seeming)* scheinbar; **apparently** *adv* anscheinend
appeal [əˈpiːl] *vi (dringend)*

bitten (for um, to +akk); (Jur) Berufung einlegen; **to ~ to sb** (be attractive) jdm zusagen ▷ n Aufruf m (to an +akk); (Jur) Berufung f; (attraction) Reiz m; **appealing** adj ansprechend, attraktiv

appear [əˈpɪə*] vi erscheinen; (Theat) auftreten; (seem) scheinen; **appearance** n Erscheinen nt; (Theat) Auftritt m; (look) Aussehen nt

appendicitis [əpendɪˈsaɪtɪs] n Blinddarmentzündung f; **appendix** [əˈpendɪks] n Blinddarm m; (to book) Anhang m

appetite [ˈæpɪtaɪt] n Appetit m; (fig: desire) Verlangen nt; (sexual) Lust f; **appetizing** [ˈæpɪtaɪzɪŋ] adj appetitlich, appetitanregend

applause [əˈplɔːz] n Beifall m, Applaus m

apple [ˈæpl] n Apfel m; **apple crumble** n mit Streuseln bestreutes Apfeldessert; **apple juice** n Apfelsaft m; **apple pie** n gedeckter Apfelkuchen m; **apple puree**, **apple sauce** n Apfelmus nt; **apple tart** n Apfelkuchen m; **apple tree** n Apfelbaum m

appliance [əˈplaɪəns] n Gerät nt; **applicable** [əˈplɪkəbl] adj anwendbar; (on forms) zutreffend; **applicant** [ˈæplɪkənt] n Bewerber(in) m(f); **application** [æplɪˈkeɪʃən] n (request) Antrag m (for auf +akk); (for job) Bewerbung f (for um); **application form** n Anmeldeformular nt; **apply** [əˈplaɪ] vi (be relevant) zutreffen (to auf +akk); (for job etc) sich bewerben (for um) ▷ vt (cream, paint etc) auftragen; (put into practice) anwenden; (brakes) betätigen

appoint [əˈpɔɪnt] vt (to post) ernennen; **appointment** n Verabredung f; (at doctor, hairdresser

etc, in business) Termin m; **by ~** nach Vereinbarung

appreciate [əˈpriːʃɪeɪt] vt (value) zu schätzen wissen; (understand) einsehen; **to be much ~d** richtig gewürdigt werden ▷ vi (increase in value) im Wert steigen; **appreciation** [əpriːʃɪˈeɪʃən] n (esteem) Anerkennung f, Würdigung f; (of person also) Wertschätzung f

apprehensive [æprɪˈhensɪv] adj ängstlich

apprentice [əˈprentɪs] n Lehrling m

approach [əˈprəʊtʃ] vi sich nähern ▷ vt (place) sich nähern +dat; (person) herantreten an +akk; (problem) angehen

appropriate [əˈprəʊprɪət] adj passend; (to occasion) angemessen; (remark) treffend; **appropriately** adv passend; (expressed) treffend

approval [əˈpruːvəl] n (show of satisfaction) Anerkennung f; (permission) Zustimmung f (of zu); **approve** [əˈpruːv] vt billigen ▷ vi: **to ~ of sth/sb** etw billigen/von jdm etwas halten; **I don't ~** ich missbillige das

approx [əˈprɒks] abbr = **approximately** ca.; **approximate** [əˈprɒksɪmɪt] adj ungefähr; **approximately** adv ungefähr, circa

apricot [ˈeɪprɪkɒt] n Aprikose f

April [ˈeɪprəl] n April m; see also **September**

apron [ˈeɪprən] n Schürze f

aptitude [ˈæptɪtjuːd] n Begabung f

aquaplaning [ˈækwəpleɪnɪŋ] n (Auto) Aquaplaning nt

aquarium [əˈkweərɪəm] n Aquarium nt

Aquarius [əˈkweərɪəs] n (Astr) Wassermann m

Arab ['ærəb] n Araber(in) m(f); (horse) Araber m; **Arabian** [ə'reɪbɪən] adj arabisch; **Arabic** ['ærəbɪk] n (language) Arabisch nt ▷ adj arabisch

arbitrary ['ɑːbɪtrərɪ] adj willkürlich

arcade [ɑː'keɪd] n Arkade f; (shopping arcade) Einkaufspassage f

arch [ɑːtʃ] n Bogen m

archaeologist, archeologist (US) [ɑːkɪ'ɒlədʒɪst] n Archäologe m, Archäologin f; **archaeology, archeology** (US) [ɑːkɪ'ɒlədʒɪ] n Archäologie f

archaic [ɑː'keɪɪk] adj veraltet

archbishop [ɑːtʃ'bɪʃəp] n Erzbischof m

archery ['ɑːtʃərɪ] n Bogenschießen nt

architect ['ɑːkɪtekt] n Architekt(in) m(f); **architecture** ['ɑːkɪtektʃə] n Architektur f

archive(s) ['ɑːkaɪv(z)] n(pl) Archiv nt

archway ['ɑːtʃweɪ] n Torbogen m

Arctic ['ɑːktɪk] n Arktis f; **Arctic Circle** n nördlicher Polarkreis

are [ə, unstressed ɑː] present of **be**

area ['ɛərɪə] n (region, district) Gebiet nt, Gegend f; (amount of space) Fläche f; (part of building etc) Bereich m, Zone f; (fig: field) Bereich m; **the London ~** der Londoner Raum; **area code** n (US) Vorwahl f

aren't [ɑːnt] contr of **are not**

Argentina [ɑːdʒən'tiːnə] n Argentinien nt

argue ['ɑːgjuː] vi streiten (about, over über +akk); **to ~ that ...** behaupten, dass ...; **to ~ for/against ...** sprechen für/gegen ...; **argument** n (reasons) Argument nt; (quarrel)

Streit m; **to have an ~** sich streiten

Aries ['ɛəriːz] nsing (Astr) Widder m

arise [ə'raɪz] (arose, arisen) vi sich ergeben, entstehen; (problem, question, wind) auftreten

aristocracy [ærɪs'tɒkrəsɪ] n (class) Adel m; **aristocrat** ['ærɪstəkræt] n Adlige(r) mf; **aristocratic** [ærɪstə'krætɪk] adj aristokratisch, adlig

arm [ɑːm] n Arm m; (sleeve) Ärmel m; (of armchair) Armlehne f ▷ vt bewaffnen; **armchair** n Lehnstuhl m

armed [ɑːmd] adj bewaffnet

armpit ['ɑːmpɪt] n Achselhöhle f

arms [ɑːmz] npl Waffen pl

army ['ɑːmɪ] n Armee f, Heer nt

A road ['eɪrəʊd] n (Brit) = Bundesstraße f

aroma [ə'rəʊmə] n Duft m, Aroma nt; **aromatherapy** [ərəʊmə'θerəpɪ] n Aromatherapie f

arose [ə'rəʊz] pt of **arise**

around [ə'raʊnd] adv herum, umher; (present) hier (irgendwo); (approximately) ungefähr; (with time) gegen; **he's ~ somewhere** ist hier irgendwo in der Nähe ▷ prep (surrounding) um ... (herum); (about in) in ... herum

arr. abbr = **arrival, arrives** Ank.

arrange [ə'reɪndʒ] vt (put in order) (an)ordnen; (alphabetically) ordnen; (artistically) anordnen; (agree to: meeting etc) vereinbaren, festsetzen; (holidays) festlegen; (organize) planen; **to ~ that ...** es so einrichten, dass ...; **we ~d to meet at eight o'clock** wir haben uns für acht Uhr verabredet; **it's all ~d** es ist alles arrangiert; **arrangement** n (layout) Anordnung f; (agreement)

Vereinbarung f, Plan m; **make ~s**
Vorbereitungen treffen

arrest [ə'rest] vt (person)
verhaften ▷ n Verhaftung f;
under ~ verhaftet

arrival [ə'raɪvl] n Ankunft f;
new ~ (person) Neuankömmling m;
arrivals n (airport) Ankunftshalle
f; **arrive** [ə'raɪv] vi ankommen
(at bei, in +dat); **to ~ at a solution**
eine Lösung finden

arrogant ['ærəgənt] adj arrogant

arrow ['ærəʊ] n Pfeil m

arse [ɑːs] n (vulg) Arsch m

art [ɑːt] n Kunst f, **the ~s** (pl)
Geisteswissenschaften f

artery ['ɑːtərɪ] n Schlagader f,
Arterie f

art gallery n Kunstgalerie f,
Kunstmuseum nt

arthritis [ɑː'θraɪtɪs] n Arthritis f

artichoke ['ɑːtɪtʃəʊk] n
Artischocke f

article ['ɑːtɪkl] n Artikel m;
(object) Gegenstand m

artificial [ɑːtɪ'fɪʃəl] adj künstlich,
Kunst-; (smile etc) gekünstelt

artist ['ɑːtɪst] n Künstler(in) m(f);
artistic [ɑː'tɪstɪk] adj
künstlerisch

O **KEYWORD**

as [æz, əz] conj 1 (referring to time)
als; **as the years went by** mit den
Jahren; **he came in as I was
leaving** als er hereinkam, ging ich
gerade; **as from tomorrow** ab
morgen

2 (in comparisons) **as big as** so groß
wie; **twice as big as** zweimal so
groß wie; **as much/many as** so
viel/so viele wie; **as soon as**
sobald

3 (since, because) da; **he left early
as he had to be home by 10** er

ging früher, da er um 10 zu Hause
sein musste

4 (referring to manner, way) wie; **do
as you wish** mach was du willst;
as she said wie sie sagte

5 (concerning) **as for** o **to that** was
das betrifft o angeht

6 **as if** o **though** als ob
▷ prep als; see also **long**; **he
works as a driver** er arbeitet als
Fahrer; see also **such**; **he gave it
to me as a present** er hat es
mir als Geschenk gegeben; see
also **well**

asap [eɪeseɪ'piː, 'eɪsæp] acr = **as
soon as possible** möglichst bald

ascertain [æsə'teɪn] vt
feststellen

ash [æʃ] n (dust) Asche f; (tree)
Esche f

ashamed [ə'ʃeɪmd] adj beschämt;
to be ~ (of sb/sth) sich (für
jdn/etw) schämen

ashore [ə'ʃɔː] adv an Land

ashtray ['æʃtreɪ] n Aschenbecher
m

Asia ['eɪʃə] n Asien nt; **Asian** adj
asiatisch ▷ n Asiat(in) m(f)

aside [ə'saɪd] adv beiseite, zur
Seite; **~ from** (esp US) außer

ask [ɑːsk] vt, vi fragen; (question)
stellen; (request) bitten um; (invite)
einladen; **to ~ sb the way** jdn
nach dem Weg fragen; **to ~ sb to
do sth** jdn darum bitten, etw zu
tun; **ask for** bitten um

asleep [ə'sliːp] adj, adv: **to be
~ schlafen**; **to fall ~** einschlafen

asparagus [əs'pærəgəs] n
Spargel m

aspect ['æspekt] n Aspekt m

aspirin ['æsprɪn] n Aspirin® nt

ass [æs] n (a. fig) Esel m; (US vulg)
Arsch m

assassinate [ə'sæsɪneɪt] vt
ermorden; **assassination**

[əˈsæsɪneɪʃn] *n* Ermordung *f*;
~ attempt Attentat *nt*

assault [əˈsɔːlt] *n* Angriff *m*; (*Jur*)
Körperverletzung *f* ▷ *vt*
überfallen, herfallen über +*akk*

assemble [əˈsembl] *vt* (*parts*)
zusammensetzen; (*people*)
zusammenrufen ▷ *vi* sich
versammeln; **assembly**
[əˈsemblɪ] *n* (*of people*)
Versammlung *f*; (*putting together*)
Zusammensetzen *nt*; **assembly
hall** *n* Aula *f*

assert [əˈsɜːt] *vt* behaupten;
assertion [əˈsɜːʃən] *n* Behauptung *f*

assess [əˈses] *vt* einschätzen;
assessment *n* Einschätzung *f*

asset [ˈæset] *n* Vermögenswert
m; (*fig*) Vorteil *m*; **~s** *pl* Vermögen
nt

assign [əˈsaɪn] *vt* zuweisen;
assignment *n* Aufgabe *f*;
(*mission*) Auftrag *m*

assist [əˈsɪst] *vt* helfen +*dat*;
assistance *n* Hilfe *f*; **assistant** *n*
Assistent(in) *m(f)*, Mitarbeiter(in)
m(f); (*in shop*) Verkäufer(in) *m(f)*;
assistant referee *n* (*Sport*)
Schiedsrichterassistent(in) *m(f)*

associate [əˈsəʊʃɪeɪt] *vt*
verbinden (*with* mit); **association**
[əsəʊsɪˈeɪʃən] *n* (*organization*)
Verband *m*, Vereinigung *f*; **in
~ with ...** in Zusammenarbeit
mit ...

assorted [əˈsɔːtɪd] *adj* gemischt;
assortment *n* Auswahl *f* (*of an*
+*dat*); (*of sweets*) Mischung *f*

assume [əˈsjuːm] *vt* annehmen
(*that ...* dass ...); (*role, responsibility*)
übernehmen; **assumption**
[əˈsʌmpʃən] *n* Annahme *f*

assurance [əˈʃʊərəns] *n* Versicherung *f*; (*confidence*) Zuversicht
f; **assure** [əˈʃʊə] *vt* (*say
confidently*) versichern +*dat*; **to**

~ sb of sth jdm etw zusichern; **to
be ~d of sth** einer Sache sicher
sein

asterisk [ˈæstərɪsk] *n* Sternchen
nt

asthma [ˈæsmə] *n* Asthma *nt*

astonish [əˈstɒnɪʃ] *vt* erstaunen;
astonished *adj* erstaunt (*at*
über); **astonishing** *adj*
erstaunlich; **astonishment** *n*
Erstaunen *nt*

astound [əˈstaʊnd] *vt* sehr
erstaunen; **astounding** *adj*
erstaunlich

astray [əˈstreɪ] *adv*: **to go ~**
(*letter etc*) verloren gehen;
(*person*) vom Weg abkommen; **to
lead ~** irreführen, verführen

astrology [əsˈtrɒlədʒɪ] *n*
Astrologie *f*

astronaut [ˈæstrənɔːt] *n* Astro-
naut(in) *m(f)*

astronomy [əsˈtrɒnəmɪ] *n*
Astronomie *f*

asylum [əˈsaɪləm] *n* (*home*)
Anstalt *f*; (*political asylum*) Asyl *nt*;
asylum seeker *n*
Asylbewerber(in) *m(f)*

O KEYWORD

at [æt] *prep* **1** (*referring to position,
direction*) an +*dat*; bei +*dat*; (*with
place*) in +*dat*; **at the top** an der
Spitze; **at home/school** zu Hause,
zuhause (*österreichisch,
schweizerisch*)/in der Schule; **at the
baker's** beim Bäcker; **to look at
sth** auf etw *akk* blicken; **to throw
sth at sb** etw nach jdm werfen
2 (*referring to time*) um; **at 4 o'clock** um
4 Uhr; **at night** bei Nacht; **at
Christmas** zu Weihnachten; **at
times** manchmal
3 (*referring to rates, speed etc*) at **£1 a
kilo** zu £1 pro Kilo; **two at a time**

zwei auf einmal; **at 50 km/h** mit 50 km/h
4 (*referring to manner*) **at a stroke** mit einem Schlag; **at peace** in Frieden
5 (*referring to activity*) **to be at work** bei der Arbeit sein; **to play at cowboys** Cowboy spielen; **to be good at sth** gut in etw *dat* sein
6 (*referring to cause*) **surprised/annoyed at sth** überrascht/verärgert über etw *akk*; **I went at his suggestion** ich ging auf seinen Vorschlag hin
7 (*@ symbol*) At-Zeichen *nt*

ate [et, eɪt] *pt of* **eat**

athlete ['æθliːt] *n* Athlet(in) *m(f)*; (*track and field*) Leichtathlet(in) *m(f)*; (*sportsman*) Sportler(in) *m(f)*; **~'s foot** Fußpilz *m*; **athletic** [æθ'letɪk] *adj* sportlich; (*build*) athletisch; **athletics** *npl* Leichtathletik *f*

Atlantic [ət'læntɪk] *n*: **the ~ (Ocean)** der Atlantik

atlas ['ætləs] *n* Atlas *m*

ATM *abbr* = **automated teller machine** Geldautomat *m*

atmosphere ['ætməsfɪə] *n* Atmosphäre *f*; (*fig*) Stimmung *f*

atom ['ætəm] *n* Atom *nt*; **atomic** [ə'tɒmɪk] *adj* Atom-; **~ energy** Atomenergie *f*; **~ power** Atomkraft *f*

A to Z® ['eɪtə'zed] *n* Stadtplan *m* (*in Buchform*)

atrocious [ə'trəʊʃəs] *adj* grauenhaft; **atrocity** [ə'trɒsɪtɪ] *n* Grausamkeit *f*; (*deed*) Gräueltat *f*

attach [ə'tætʃ] *vt* befestigen, anheften (*to an +dat*); **to ~ importance to sth** Wert auf etw *akk* legen; **to be ~ed to sb/sth** an jdm/etw hängen; **to ~ a file to an email** eine Datei an eine E-mail anhängen; **attachment** *n*

(*affection*) Zuneigung *f*; (*Inform*) Attachment *nt*, Anhang *m*, Anlage *f*

attack [ə'tæk] *vt*, *vi* angreifen ⊳ *n* Angriff *m* (*on auf +akk*); (*Med*) Anfall *m*

attempt [ə'tempt] *n* Versuch *m*; **to make an ~ to do sth** versuchen, etw zu tun ⊳ *vt* versuchen

attend [ə'tend] *vt* (*go to*) teilnehmen an +dat; (*lectures, school*) besuchen ⊳ *vi* (*be present*) anwesend sein; **attend to** *vt* sich kümmern um; (*customer*) bedienen; **attendance** *n* (*presence*) Anwesenheit *f*; (*people present*) Teilnehmerzahl *f*; **attendant** *n* (*in car park etc*) Wächter(in) *m(f)*; (*in museum*) Aufseher(in) *m*

attention [ə'tenʃən] *n* Aufmerksamkeit *f*; (*your*) **~ please** Achtung!; **to pay ~ to sth** etw beachten; **to pay ~ to sb** jdm aufmerksam zuhören; (*listen*) jdm/etw aufmerksam zuhören; **for the ~ of ...** zu Händen von ...; **attentive** [ə'tentɪv] *adj* aufmerksam

attic ['ætɪk] *n* Dachboden *m*; (*lived in*) Mansarde *f*

attitude ['ætɪtjuːd] *n* (*mental*) Einstellung *f* (*to, towards zu*); (*more general, physical*) Haltung *f*

attorney [ə'tɜːnɪ] *n* (*US: lawyer*) Rechtsanwalt *m*, Rechtsanwältin *f*

attract [ə'trækt] *vt* anziehen; (*attention*) erregen; **to be ~ed to o by sb** sich zu jdm hingezogen fühlen; **attraction** [ə'trækʃən] *n* Anziehungskraft *f*; (*thing*) Attraktion *f*; **attractive** *adj* attraktiv; (*thing, idea*) reizvoll

aubergine ['əʊbəʒiːn] *n* Aubergine *f*

auction ['ɔːkʃən] *n* Versteigerung *f*, Auktion *f* ⊳ *vt* versteigern

audible ['ɔːdɪbl] *adj* hörbar

audience ['ɔːdɪəns] *n* Publikum *nt*; (*Radio*) Zuhörer *pl*; (*TV*) Zuschauer *pl*

audio ['ɔːdɪəʊ] *adj* Ton-

audition [ɔːˈdɪʃən] *n* Probe *f* ▷ *vi* (*Theat*) vorspielen, vorsingen

auditorium [ɔːdɪˈtɔːrɪəm] *n* Zuschauerraum *m*

Aug *abbr* = **August**

August ['ɔːgəst] *n* August *m; see also* **September**

aunt [ɑːnt] *n* Tante *f*

au pair [əʊˈpɛə°] *n* Aupairmädchen *nt*, Aupairjunge *m*

Australia [ɒˈstreɪlɪə] *n* Australien *nt*; **Australian** *adj* australisch ▷ *n* Australier(in) *m(f)*

Austria ['ɒstrɪə] *n* Österreich *nt*; **Austrian** *adj* österreichisch ▷ *n* Österreicher(in) *m(f)*

authentic [ɔːˈθɛntɪk] *adj* echt; (*signature*) authentisch; **authenticity** [ɔːθɛnˈtɪsɪtɪ] *n* Echtheit *f*

author ['ɔːθə°] *n* Autor(in) *m(f)*; (*of report etc*) Verfasser(in) *m(f)*

authority [ɔːˈθɒrɪtɪ] *n* (*power, expert*) Autorität *f*; **an ~ on sth** eine Autorität auf dem Gebiet einer Sache; **the authorities** (*pl*) die Behörden *pl*; **authorize** ['ɔːθəraɪz] *vt* (*permit*) genehmigen; **to be ~d to do sth** offiziell berechtigt sein, etw zu tun

auto ['ɔːtəʊ] (*pl* **-s**) *n* (*US*) Auto *nt*

autobiography [ɔːtəʊbaɪˈɒgrəfɪ] *n* Autobiographie *f*; **autograph** ['ɔːtəgrɑːf] *n* Autogramm *nt*

automatic [ɔːtəˈmætɪk] *adj* automatisch; **~ gear change** (*Brit*), **~ gear shift** (*US*) Automatikschaltung *f* ▷ *n* (*car*) Automatikwagen *m*

automobile ['ɔːtəməbiːl] *n* (*US*) Auto(mobil) *nt*; **autotrain**

['ɔːtəʊtreɪn] *n* (*US*) Autoreisezug *m*

autumn ['ɔːtəm] *n* (*Brit*) Herbst *m*

auxiliary [ɔːgˈzɪlɪərɪ] *adj* Hilfs-; **~ verb** Hilfsverb *nt* ▷ *n* Hilfskraft *f*

availability [əveɪləˈbɪlɪtɪ] *n* (*of product*) Lieferbarkeit *f*; (*of resources*) Verfügbarkeit *f*;

available [əˈveɪləbl] *adj* erhältlich; (*existing*) vorhanden; (*product*) lieferbar; (*person*) erreichbar; **to be/make ~ to sb** jdm zur Verfügung stehen/stellen; **they're only ~ in black** es gibt sie nur in Schwarz, sie sind nur in Schwarz erhältlich

avalanche ['ævəlɑːnʃ] *n* Lawine *f*

Ave *abbr* = **avenue**

avenue ['ævənjuː] *n* Allee *f*

average ['ævərɪdʒ] *n* Durchschnitt *m*; **on ~** im Durchschnitt ▷ *adj* durchschnittlich; **~ speed** Durchschnittsgeschwindigkeit *f*; **~ of ~ height** von mittlerer Größe

avian flu ['eɪvɪənˈfluː] *n* Vogelgrippe *f*

aviation [eɪvɪˈeɪʃən] *n* Luftfahrt *f*

avocado [ævəˈkɑːdəʊ] (*pl* **-s**) *n* Avocado *f*

avoid [əˈvɔɪd] *vt* vermeiden; **to ~ sb** jdm aus dem Weg gehen; **avoidable** *adj* vermeidbar

awake [əˈweɪk] (**awoke, awoken**) *vi* aufwachen ▷ *adj* wach

award [əˈwɔːd] *n* (*prize*) Preis *m*; (*for bravery etc*) Auszeichnung *f* ▷ *vt* zuerkennen (*to sb jdm*); (*present*) verleihen (*to sb jdm*)

aware [əˈwɛə°] *adj* bewusst; **to be ~ of sth** sich *dat* einer Sache *gen* bewusst sein; **I was not ~ that ...** es war mir nicht klar, dass ...

away [əˈweɪ] *adv* weg; **to look ~** wegsehen; **he's ~** er ist nicht da; (*on a trip*) er ist verreist; (*from school, work*) er fehlt; (*Sport*) **they**

are (**playing**) ~ sie spielen
auswärts; (*with distance*) **three
miles** ~ drei Meilen (von hier)
entfernt; **to work** ~ drauflos
arbeiten

awful ['ɔːfʊl] *adj* schrecklich,
furchtbar; **awfully** *adv* furchtbar

awkward ['ɔːkwəd] *adj* (*clumsy*)
ungeschickt; (*embarrassing*)
peinlich; (*difficult*) schwierig

awning ['ɔːnɪŋ] *n* Markise *f*

awoke [ə'wəʊk] *pt of* **awake**;
awoken [ə'wəʊkən] *pp of* **awake**

ax (*US*), **axe** [æks] *n* Axt *f*

axle ['æksl] *n* (*Tech*) Achse *f*

BA *abbr* = **Bachelor of Arts**
BSc *abbr* = **Bachelor of Science**
babe [beɪb] *n* (*fam*) Baby *nt*;
(*fam: affectionate*) Schatz *m*,
Kleine(r) *mf*

baby ['beɪbɪ] *n* Baby *nt*; (*of animal*)
Junge(s) *nt*; (*fam: affectionate*)
Schatz *m*, Kleine(r) *mf*; **to have a**
~ ein Kind bekommen; **it's your**
~ (*fam: responsibility*) das ist dein
Bier; **baby carriage** *n* (*US*)
Kinderwagen *m*; **baby food** *n*
Babynahrung *f*; **babyish** *adj*
kindisch; **baby shower** *n* (*US*)
Party für die werdende Mutter;
baby-sit *irr vi* babysitten;
baby-sitter *n* Babysitter(in) *m(f)*

bachelor ['bætʃələ²] *n* Junggeselle *m*; **Bachelor of**
Arts/Science *erster akademischer*
Grad, ≈ Magister/Diplom;
bachelorette *n* Junggesellin *f*;
bachelorette party *n* (*US*)

Junggesellinnenabschied; **bachelor party** n (US) *Junggesellenabschied*

back [bæk] n *(of person, animal)* Rücken m; *(of house, coin etc)* Rückseite f; *(of chair)* Rückenlehne f; *(of car)* Rücksitz m; *(of train)* Ende nt; *(Sport: defender)* Verteidiger(in) m(f); **at the ~ of ...,** (US) **in ~ of** *(inside)* hinten in ...; *(outside)* hinter ...; **~ to front** verkehrt herum ▷ vt *(support)* unterstützen; *(car)* rückwärtsfahren ▷ vi *(go backwards)* rückwärtsgehen o rückwärtsfahren ▷ adj Hinter-; **~ wheel** Hinterrad nt ▷ adv zurück; **they're ~** sie sind wieder da; **back away** vi sich zurückziehen; **back down** vi nachgeben; **back up** vi *(car etc)* zurücksetzen ▷ vt *(support)* unterstützen; *(Inform)* sichern; *(car)* zurückfahren

backache n Rückenschmerzen pl; **backbone** n Rückgrat nt; **backdate** vt zurückdatieren; **backdoor** n Hintertür f; **backfire** vi *(plan)* fehlschlagen; *(Auto)* fehlzünden; **background** n Hintergrund m; **backhand** n *(Sport)* Rückhand f; **backlog** n *(of work)* Rückstand m; **backpack** n (US) Rucksack m; **backpacker** n Rucksacktourist(in) m(f); **backpacking** n Rucksacktourismus m; **back seat** n Rücksitz m; **backside** n *(fam)* Po m; **back street** n Seitensträßchen nt; **backstroke** n Rückenschwimmen nt; **back-up** n *(support)* Unterstützung f; **~ (copy)** *(Inform)* Sicherungskopie f; **backward** adj *(child)* zurückgeblieben; *(region)* rückständig; **~ movement** Rückwärtsbewegung f; **backwards** adv rückwärts; **backyard** n Hinterhof m

bacon ['beɪkən] n Frühstücksspeck m

bacteria [bæk'tɪərɪə] npl Bakterien pl

bad [bæd] **(worse, worst)** adj schlecht, schlimm; *(smell)* übel; **I have a ~ back** mir tut der Rücken weh; **I'm ~ at maths/sport** ich bin schlecht in Mathe/Sport; **to go ~** schlecht werden, verderben

badge [bædʒ] n Abzeichen nt

badger ['bædʒə°] n Dachs m

badly ['bædlɪ] adv schlecht; **~ wounded** schwer verwundet; **to need sth ~** etw dringend brauchen; **bad-tempered** ['bæd'tempəd] adj schlecht gelaunt

bag [bæg] n *(small)* Tüte f; *(larger)* Beutel m; *(handbag)* Tasche f; **my ~s** *(luggage)* mein Gepäck

baggage ['bægɪdʒ] n Gepäck nt; **baggage allowance** n Freigepäck nt; **baggage (re)claim** n Gepäckrückgabe f

baggy ['bægɪ] adj *(zu)* weit; *(trousers, suit)* ausgebeult

bag lady ['bægleɪdɪ] n Stadtstreicherin f

bagpipes ['bægpaɪps] npl Dudelsack m

Bahamas [bə'hɑːməz] npl: **the ~** die Bahamas pl

bail [beɪl] n *(money)* Kaution f

bait [beɪt] n Köder m

bake [beɪk] vt, vi backen; **baked beans** npl weiße Bohnen in Tomatensoße; **baked potato** (pl **-es**) n die im Schale gebackene Kartoffel, Ofenkartoffel f; **baker** ['beɪkə°] n(f); **bakery** ['beɪkərɪ] n Bäckerei f; **baking powder** n Backpulver nt

balance ['bæləns] n *(equilibrium)* Gleichgewicht nt ▷ vt *(make up for)* ausgleichen; **balanced** adj

ausgeglichen; **balance sheet** n
Bilanz f
balcony ['bælkənɪ] n Balkon m
bald [bɔːld] adj kahl; **to be ~** eine
Glatze haben
Balkans ['bɔːlkənz] npl: **the ~**
der Balkan, die Balkanländer pl
ball [bɔːl] n Ball m; **to have a ~**
(fam) sich prima amüsieren
ballet ['bæleɪ] n Ballett nt; **ballet
dancer** n Balletttänzer(in) m(f)
balloon [bə'luːn] n (Luft)ballon
m
ballot ['bælət] n (geheime)
Abstimmung; **ballot box** n
Wahlurne f; **ballot paper** n
Stimmzettel m
ballpoint (pen) ['bɔːlpɔɪnt] n
Kugelschreiber m
ballroom [bɔːlruːm] n Tanzsaal
m
Baltic ['bɔːltɪk] adj: **~ Sea** Ostsee
f; **the ~ States** die baltischen
Staaten
Baltics ['bɔːltɪks] n: **the ~** das
Baltikum nt
bamboo [bæm'buː] n Bambus m;
bamboo shoots npl
Bambussprossen pl
ban [bæn] n Verbot nt ⊳ vt
verbieten
banana [bə'nɑːnə] n Banane f;
he's ~s er ist völlig durchgeknallt;
banana split n Bananensplit nt
band [bænd] n (group) Gruppe f;
(of criminals) Bande f; (Mus) Kapelle
f; (pop, rock etc) Band f; (strip) Band
nt
bandage ['bændɪdʒ] n Verband
m; (elastic) Bandage f ⊳ vt
verbinden
B & B abbr = **bed and breakfast**
bang [bæŋ] n (noise) Knall m;
(blow) Schlag m ⊳ vt, vi knallen;
(door) zuschlagen, zuknallen;
banger [bæŋə*] n (Brit fam:
firework) Knallkörper m; (sausage)

Würstchen nt; (fam: old car)
Klapperkiste f
bangs [bæŋz] npl (US: of hair)
Pony m
banish ['bænɪʃ] vt verbannen
banister(s) ['bænɪstə*] n (Treppen)geländer nt
bank [bæŋk] n (Fin) Bank f; (of
river etc) Ufer nt; **bank account** n
Bankkonto nt; **bank balance** n
Kontostand m; **bank card** n
Bankkarte f; **bank code** n
Bankleitzahl f; **bank holiday** n
gesetzlicher Feiertag

● **BANK HOLIDAY**
●
● Als **bank holiday** wird in
● Großbritannien ein gesetzlicher
● Feiertag bezeichnet, an dem die
● Banken geschlossen sind. Die
● meisten dieser Feiertage,
● abgesehen von Weihnachten
● und Ostern, fallen auf Montage
● im Mai und August. An diesen
● langen Wochenenden (bank
● holiday weekends) fahren viele
● Briten in Urlaub, sodass dann
● auf den Straßen, Flughäfen und
● bei der Bahn sehr viel Betrieb
● ist.

bank manager n Filialleiter(in)
m(f); **banknote** n Banknote f
bankrupt vt ruinieren; **to go
~** Pleite gehen
bank statement n
Kontoauszug m
baptism ['bæptɪzəm] n Taufe f;
baptize ['bæptaɪz] vt taufen
bar [bɑː*] n (for drinks) Bar f; (less
smart) Lokal nt; (rod) Stange f; (of
chocolate etc) Riegel m, Tafel f; (of
soap) Stück nt; (counter) Theke f
⊳ prep außer; **~ none** ohne
Ausnahme
barbecue ['bɑːbɪkjuː] n (device)

Grill m; (party) Barbecue nt, Grillfete f; **to have a ~** grillen

barbed wire ['bɑ:bd'waɪəˤ] n Stacheldraht m

barber ['bɑ:bəˤ] n (Herren)friseur m

bar code ['bɑ:kəʊd] n Strichkode m

bare [beəˤ] adj nackt; **~ patch** kahle Stelle; **barefoot** adj, adv barfuß; **bareheaded** adj, adv ohne Kopfbedeckung; **barely** adv kaum; (with age) knapp

bargain ['bɑ:gɪn] n (cheap offer) günstiges Angebot, Schnäppchen nt; (transaction) Geschäft nt; **what a ~** das ist aber günstig! ▷ vi (ver)handeln

barge [bɑ:dʒ] n (for freight) Lastkahn m; (unpowered) Schleppkahn m

bark [bɑ:k] n (of tree) Rinde f; (of dog) Bellen nt ▷ vi (dog) bellen

barley ['bɑ:lɪ] n Gerste f

barmaid ['bɑ:meɪd] n Barkeeperin f; **barman** ['bɑ:mən] (pl **-men**) n Barkeeper m

barn [bɑ:n] n Scheune f

barometer [bə'rɒmɪtəˤ] n Barometer nt

baroque [bə'rɒk] adj barock, Barock-

barracks ['bærəks] npl Kaserne f

barrel ['bærəl] n Fass nt; **barrel organ** n Drehorgel f

barricade [bærɪ'keɪd] n Barrikade f

barrier ['bærɪəˤ] n (obstruction) Absperrung f, Barriere f; (across road etc) Schranke f

barrow ['bærəʊ] n (cart) Schubkarren m

bartender ['bɑ:tendəˤ] n (US) Barkeeper(in) m(f)

base [beɪs] n Basis f; (of lamp, pillar etc) Fuß m; (Mil) Stützpunkt m

▷ vt gründen (on auf +akk); **to be ~d on sth** auf etw dat basieren;

baseball n Baseball m; **baseball cap** n Baseballmütze f

basement n Kellergeschoss nt

bash [bæʃ] (fam) n Schlag m; (fam) Party f ▷ vt hauen

basic ['beɪsɪk] adj einfach; (fundamental) Grund-; (importance, difference) grundlegend; (in principle) grundsätzlich; **the accomodation is very ~** die Unterkunft ist sehr bescheiden; **basically** adv im Grunde; **basics** npl: **the ~** das Wesentliche

basil ['bæzl] n Basilikum nt

basin ['beɪsn] n (for washing, valley) (Wasch)becken nt

basis ['beɪsɪs] n Basis f; **on the ~ of** aufgrund +gen; **on a monthly ~** monatlich

basket ['bɑ:skɪt] n Korb m; **basketball** n Basketball m

Basque [bæsk] n (person) Baske m, Baskin f; (language) Baskisch nt ▷ adj baskisch

bass [beɪs] n (Mus) Bass m; (Zool) Barsch m ▷ adj (Mus) Bass-

bastard ['bɑ:stəd] n (vulg: awful person) Arschloch nt

bat [bæt] n (Zool) Fledermaus f; (Sport: cricket, baseball) Schlagholz nt; (table tennis) Schläger m

batch [bætʃ] n Schwung m; (fam: of letters, books etc) Stoß m

bath [bɑ:θ] n Bad nt; (tub) Badewanne f; **to have a ~** baden ▷ vt (child etc) baden

bathe [beɪð] vt, vi (wound etc) baden; **bath foam** ['bɑ:θfəʊm] n Badeschaum m; **bathing cap** n Badekappe f; **bathing costume, bathing suit** (US) n Badeanzug m

bathmat ['bɑ:θmæt] n Badevorleger m; **bathrobe** n Bademantel m; **bathroom** n Bad(ezimmer) nt; **baths** [bɑ:ðz] npl (Schwimm)bad

nt; **bath towel** n Badetuch nt; **bathtub** n Badewanne f
baton ['bætən] n (Mus) Taktstock m; (police) Schlagstock m
batter ['bætə] n Teig m ▷ vt heftig schlagen; **battered** adj übel zugerichtet; (hat, car) verbeult; (wife, baby) misshandelt
battery ['bætəri] n (Elec) Batterie f; **battery charger** n Ladegerät nt
battle ['bætl] n Schlacht f; (fig) Kampf m (for um +akk); **battlefield** n Schlachtfeld nt; **battlements** npl Zinnen pl
Bavaria [bə'vεərɪə] n Bayern nt; **Bavarian** adj bay(e)risch ▷ n Bayer(in) m(f)
bay [beɪ] n (of sea) Bucht f; (on house) Erker m; (tree) Lorbeerbaum m; **bay leaf** n Lorbeerblatt nt; **bay window** n Erkerfenster nt
BBC abbr = **British Broadcasting Corporation** BBC f
BC abbr = **before Christ** vor Christi Geburt, v. Chr.

○ **KEYWORD**

be [bi:] (pt was, were, pp been) vb aux 1 (with present participle: forming continuous tenses): **what are you doing?** was machst du (gerade)?; **it is raining** es regnet; **I've been waiting for you for hours** ich warte schon seit Stunden auf dich
2 (with pp: forming passives): **to be killed** getötet werden; **the thief was nowhere to be seen** der Dieb war nirgendwo zu sehen
3 (in tag questions) **it was fun, wasn't it?** es hat Spaß gemacht, nicht wahr?
4 (+to +infin) **the house is to be sold** das Haus soll verkauft werden; **he's not to open it** er darf es nicht öffnen
▷ vb +complement 1 (usu) sein; **I'm tired** ich bin müde; **I'm hot/cold** mir ist heiß/kalt; **he's a doctor** er ist Arzt; **2 and 2 are 4** 2 und 2 ist o sind 4; **she's tall/pretty** sie ist groß/hübsch; **be careful/quiet** sei vorsichtig/ruhig
2 (of health) **how are you?** wie geht es dir?; **he's very ill** er ist sehr krank; **I'm fine now** jetzt geht es mir gut
3 (of age) **how old are you?** wie alt bist du?; **I'm sixteen (years old)** ich bin sechzehn (Jahre alt)
4 (cost) **how much was the meal?** was o wie viel hat das Essen gekostet?; **that'll be £5.75, please** das macht £5.75, bitte
▷ vi 1 (exist, occur etc) sein; **is there a God?** gibt es einen Gott?; **be that as it may** wie dem auch sei; **so be it** also gut
2 (referring to place) **I won't be here tomorrow** ich werde morgen nicht hier sein
3 (referring to movement) **where have you been?** wo bist du gewesen?; **I've been in the garden** ich war im Garten
▷ impers vb 1 (referring to time, distance, weather) sein; **it's 5 o'clock** es ist 5 Uhr; **it's 10 km to the village** es sind 10 km bis zum Dorf; **it's too hot/cold** es ist zu heiß/kalt
2 (emphatic) **it's me** ich bin's; **it's the postman** es ist der Briefträger

beach [bi:tʃ] n Strand m; **beachwear** n Strandkleidung f
bead [bi:d] n (of glass, wood etc) Perle f; (drop) Tropfen m
beak [bi:k] n Schnabel m
beam [bi:m] n (of wood etc) Balken m; (of light) Strahl m ▷ vi (smile etc) strahlen
bean [bi:n] n Bohne f; **bean curd** n Tofu m

bear [bɛəʳ] (**bore, borne**) vt (carry) tragen; (tolerate) ertragen ▷ n Bär m; **bearable** adj erträglich

beard [bɪəd] n Bart m

beast [biːst] n Tier nt; (brutal person) Bestie f; (disliked person) Biest nt

beat [biːt] (**beat, beaten**) vt schlagen; (as punishment) prügeln; **to ~ sb at tennis** jdn im Tennis schlagen ▷ n (of heart, drum etc) Schlag m; (Mus) Takt m; (type of music) Beat m; **beat up** vt zusammenschlagen

beaten [ˈbiːtn] pp of **beat**; **off the ~ track** abgelegen

beautiful [ˈbjuːtɪful] adj schön; (splendid) herrlich; **beauty** [ˈbjuːtɪ] n Schönheit f; **beauty spot** n (place) lohnendes Ausflugsziel

beaver [ˈbiːvəʳ] n Biber m

became [bɪˈkeɪm] pt of **become**

because [bɪˈkɒz] adv, conj weil ▷ prep: **~ of** wegen +gen o dat

become [bɪˈkʌm] (**became, become**) vi werden; **what's ~ of him?** was ist aus ihm geworden?

bed [bed] n Bett nt; (in garden) Beet nt; **bed and breakfast** n Übernachtung f mit Frühstück; **bedclothes** npl Bettwäsche f; **bedding** n Bettzeug nt; **bed linen** n Bettwäsche f; **bedroom** n Schlafzimmer nt; **bed-sit(ter)** n (fam) möblierte Einzimmerwohnung; **bedspread** n Tagesdecke f; **bedtime** n Schlafenszeit f

bee [biː] n Biene f

beech [biːtʃ] n Buche f

beef [biːf] n Rindfleisch nt; **beefburger** n Hamburger m; **beef tomato** (pl **-es**) n Fleischtomate f

beehive [ˈbiːhaɪv] n Bienenstock m

been [biːn] pp of **be**

beer [bɪəʳ] n Bier nt; **beer garden** n Biergarten m

beetle [ˈbiːtl] n Käfer m

beetroot [ˈbiːtruːt] n Rote Bete f

before [bɪˈfɔːʳ] prep vor; **the year ~ last** vorletztes Jahr; **the day ~ yesterday** vorgestern ▷ conj bevor ▷ adv (of time) vorher; **have you been there ~?** waren Sie/warst du schon einmal dort?; **beforehand** adv vorher

beg [beg] vt: **to ~ sb to do sth** jdn inständig bitten, etw zu tun ▷ vi (beggar) betteln (for um +akk)

began [bɪˈgæn] pt of **begin**

beggar [ˈbegəʳ] n Bettler(in) m(f)

begin [bɪˈgɪn] (**began, begun**) vt, vi anfangen, beginnen; **to ~ to do sth** anfangen, etw zu tun; **beginner** n Anfänger(in) m(f); **beginning** n Anfang m

begun [bɪˈgʌn] pp of **begin**

behalf [bɪˈhɑːf] n: **on ~ of, in ~ of** (US) im Namen/Auftrag von; **on my ~** für mich

behave [bɪˈheɪv] vi sich benehmen; **~ yourself!** benimm dich!; **behaviour** (US), **behavior** [bɪˈheɪvjəʳ] n Benehmen nt

behind [bɪˈhaɪnd] prep hinter; **to be ~ time** Verspätung haben ▷ adv hinten; **to be ~ with one's work** mit seiner Arbeit im Rückstand sein ▷ n (fam) Hinterteil nt

beige [beɪʒ] adj beige

being [ˈbiːɪŋ] n (existence) Dasein nt; (person) Wesen nt

Belarus [belaˈrʊs] n Weißrussland nt

belch [beltʃ] n Rülpser m ▷ vi rülpsen

belfry [ˈbelfrɪ] n Glockenturm m

Belgian [ˈbeldʒən] adj belgisch ▷ n Belgier(in) m(f); **Belgium** [ˈbeldʒəm] n Belgien nt

belief [bɪ'li:f] n Glaube m (in an +akk); (conviction) Überzeugung f; **it's my ~ that ...** ich bin der Überzeugung, dass ...; **believe** [bɪ'li:v] vt glauben; **believe in** vi glauben an +akk; **believer** n (Rel) Gläubige(r) mf

bell [bel] n (church) Glocke f; (bicycle, door) Klingel f; **bellboy** ['belbɔɪ] n (esp US) Page m

bellows ['beləʊz] npl (for fire) Blasebalg m

belly ['belɪ] n Bauch m; **bellyache** n Bauchweh nt ⊳ vi (fam) meckern; **belly button** n (fam) Bauchnabel m; **bellyflop** n (fam) Bauchklatscher m

belong [bɪ'lɒŋ] vi gehören (to sb jdm); (to club) angehören +dat; **belongings** npl Habe f

below [bɪ'ləʊ] prep unter ⊳ adv unten

belt [belt] n (round waist) Gürtel m; (safety belt) Gurt m; **below the ~** unter die Gürtellinie ⊳ vi (fam: go fast) rasen, düsen; **beltway** n (US) Umgehungs-straße f

bench [bentʃ] n Bank f

bend [bend] n Biegung f; (in road) Kurve f ⊳ vt (be, bent, bent) (curve) biegen; (head, arm) beugen ⊳ vi sich biegen; (person) sich beugen; **bend down** vi sich bücken

beneath [bɪ'ni:θ] prep unter ⊳ adv darunter

beneficial [benɪ'fɪʃl] adj gut, nützlich (to für); **benefit** ['benɪfɪt] n (advantage) Vorteil m; (profit) Nutzen m; **for your/his ~** deinetwegen/seinetwegen; **unemployment ~** Arbeitslosengeld nt ⊳ vt guttun +dat ⊳ vi Nutzen ziehen (from aus)

benign [bɪ'naɪn] adj (person) gütig; (climate) mild; (Med) gutartig

bent [bent] pt, pp of **bend** ⊳ adj krumm; (fam) korrupt

beret ['bereɪ] n Baskenmütze f

Bermuda [bə'mju:də] n die ~s pl die Bermudas pl ⊳ adj: **~ shorts** pl Bermudashorts pl; **the ~ triangle** das Bermudadreieck

berry ['berɪ] n Beere f

berth [bɜ:θ] n (for ship) Ankerplatz m; (in ship) Koje f; (in train) Bett nt ⊳ vt am Kai festmachen ⊳ vi anlegen

beside [bɪ'saɪd] prep neben; **~ the sea/lake** am Meer/See; **besides** [bɪ'saɪdz] prep außer ⊳ adv außerdem

besiege [bɪ'si:dʒ] vt belagern

best [best] adj beste(r, s); **my ~ friend** mein bester o engster Freund; **the ~ thing (to do) would be to ...** das Beste wäre zu ...; (on food packaging) **~ before ...** mindestens haltbar bis ... ⊳ n der/die/das Beste; **all the ~** alles Gute; **to make the ~ of it** das Beste daraus machen ⊳ adv am besten; **I like this ~** das mag ich am liebsten; **best-before date** n Mindesthaltbarkeitsdatum nt; **best man** ['best'mæn] (pl **men**) n Trauzeuge m; **bestseller** ['bestselə] n Bestseller m

bet [bet] (**bet, bet**) vt, vi wetten (on auf +akk); **I ~ him £5 that ...** ich habe mit ihm um 5 Pfund gewettet, dass ...; **you ~** (fam) und ob!; **I ~ he'll be late** er kommt mit Sicherheit zu spät ⊳ n Wette f

betray [bɪ'treɪ] vt verraten; **betrayal** n Verrat m

better ['betə] adj, adv besser; **to get ~** (healthwise) sich erholen, wieder gesund werden; (improve) sich verbessern; **I'm much ~ today** es geht mir heute viel besser; **you'd ~ go** du solltest/Sie sollten lieber gehen; **a change for the ~** eine Wendung zum Guten

betting ['betɪŋ] n Wetten nt; **betting shop** n Wettbüro nt

between [bɪ'twiːn] prep zwischen; (among) unter; **~ you and me, ...** unter uns gesagt, ... ▷ adv: **(in) ~** dazwischen

beverage ['bevərɪdʒ] n (formal) Getränk nt

beware [bɪ'weə'] vt: **to ~ of sth** sich vor etw +dat hüten; **"~ of the dog"** "Vorsicht, bissiger Hund!"

bewildered [bɪ'wɪldəd] adj verwirrt

beyond [bɪ'jɒnd] prep (place) jenseits +gen; (time) über ... hinaus; (out of reach) außerhalb +gen; **it's ~ me** da habe ich keine Ahnung, da bin ich überfragt ▷ adv darüber hinaus

bias ['baɪəs] n (prejudice) Vorurteil nt, Voreingenommenheit f

bias(s)ed adj voreingenommen

bib [bɪb] n Latz m

Bible ['baɪbl] n Bibel f

bicycle ['baɪsɪkl] n Fahrrad nt

bid [bɪd] (bid, bid) vt (offer) bieten ▷ n (attempt) Versuch m; (offer) Gebot nt

big [bɪg] adj groß; **it's no ~ deal** (fam) es ist nichts Besonderes; **big-headed** [bɪg'hedɪd] adj eingebildet

bike [baɪk] n (fam) Rad nt

bikini [bɪ'kiːnɪ] n Bikini m

bilingual [baɪ'lɪŋgwəl] adj zweisprachig

bill [bɪl] n (account) Rechnung f; (US: banknote) Banknote f; (Pol) Gesetzentwurf m; (Zool) Schnabel m; **billfold** ['bɪlfəʊld] n (US) Brieftasche f

billiards ['bɪlɪədz] nsing Billard nt; **billiard table** Billardtisch m

billion ['bɪljən] n Milliarde f

bin [bɪn] n Behälter m; (rubbish

bin) (Müll)eimer m; (for paper) Papierkorb m

bind [baɪnd] (**bound, bound**) vt binden; (bind together) zusammenbinden; (wound) verbinden; **binding** n (ski) Bindung f; (book) Einband m

binge [bɪndʒ] n (fam: drinking) Sauferei f; **to go on a ~** auf Sauftour gehen

bingo ['bɪŋgəʊ] n Bingo nt

binoculars [bɪ'nɒkjʊləz] npl Fernglas nt

biodegradable ['baɪəʊdɪ'greɪdəbl] adj biologisch abbaubar

biofuel ['baɪəʊ'fjʊəl] n Biokraftstoff m

biography [baɪ'ɒgrəfɪ] n Biografie f

biological [baɪə'lɒdʒɪkəl] adj biologisch; **biology** [baɪ'ɒlədʒɪ] n Biologie f

birch [bɜːtʃ] n Birke f

bird [bɜːd] n Vogel m; (Brit fam: girl, girlfriend) Tussi f; **bird flu** n Vogelgrippe f; **bird watcher** n Vogelbeobachter(in) m(f)

birth [bɜːθ] n Geburt f; **birth certificate** n Geburtsurkunde f; **birth control** n Geburtenkontrolle f; **birthday** n Geburtstag m; **happy ~** herzlichen Glückwunsch zum Geburtstag; **birthday card** n Geburtstagskarte f; **birthday party** n Geburtstagsfeier f; **birthplace** n Geburtsort m

biscuit ['bɪskɪt] n (Brit) Keks m

bisexual [baɪ'seksjʊəl] adj bisexuell

bishop ['bɪʃəp] n Bischof m; (in chess) Läufer m

bit [bɪt] pt of **bite** ▷ n (piece) Stück(chen) nt; (Inform) Bit nt; **a ~ (of ...)** (small amount) ein bisschen ...; **a ~ tired** etwas müde;

~ by ~ allmählich; (*time*) **for a ~** ein Weilchen; **quite a ~** (*a lot*) ganz schön viel

bitch [bɪtʃ] n (*dog*) Hündin f; (*pej: woman*) Miststück nt, Schlampe f; **son of a ~** (*US: vulg*) Hurensohn m, Scheißkerl m; **bitchy** adj gemein, zickig

bite [baɪt] (**bit, bitten**) vt, vi beißen ▷ n Biss m; (*mouthful*) Bissen m; (*insect*) Stich m; **to have a ~** eine Kleinigkeit essen; **bitten** pp of **bite**

bitter ['bɪtə'] adj bitter; (*memory etc*) schmerzlich ▷ n (*Brit: beer*) halbdunkles Bier; **bitter lemon** n Bitter Lemon nt

bizarre [bɪ'zɑ:'] adj bizarr

black [blæk] adj schwarz; **blackberry** n Brombeere f; **blackbird** n Amsel f; **blackboard** n (Wand)tafel f; **black box** n (*Aviat*) Flugschreiber m; **blackcurrant** n Schwarze Johannisbeere; **black eye** n blaues Auge; **Black Forest** n Schwarzwald m; **Black Forest gateau** n Schwarzwälder Kirschtorte f; **blackmail** n Erpressung f ▷ vt erpressen; **black market** n Schwarzmarkt m; **blackout** n (*Med*) Ohnmacht f; **to have a ~** ohnmächtig werden; **black pudding** n ≈ Blutwurst f; **Black Sea** n: **the ~** das Schwarze Meer; **blacksmith** n Schmied(in) m(f); **black tie** n Abendanzug m, Smoking m; **is it ~?** ist/besteht da Smokingzwang?

bladder ['blædə'] n Blase f

blade [bleɪd] n (*of knife*) Klinge f; (*of propeller*) Blatt nt; (*of grass*) Halm m

blame [bleɪm] n Schuld f ▷ vt: **to ~ sth on sb** jdm die Schuld an etw dat geben; **he is to ~** er ist daran schuld

bland [blænd] adj (*taste*) fade; (*comment*) nichtssagend

blank [blæŋk] adj (*page, space*) leer, unbeschrieben; (*look*) ausdruckslos; **~ cheque** Blankoscheck m

blanket ['blæŋkɪt] n (Woll)decke f

blast [blɑ:st] n (*of wind*) Windstoß m; (*of explosion*) Druckwelle f ▷ vt (*blow up*) sprengen; **~!** (*fam*) Mist!, verdammt!

blatant ['bleɪtənt] adj (*undisguised*) offen; (*obvious*) offensichtlich

blaze [bleɪz] vi lodern; (*sun*) brennen ▷ n (*building*) Brand m; (*other fire*) Feuer nt; **a ~ of colour** eine Farbenpracht

blazer ['bleɪzə'] n Blazer m

bleach [bli:tʃ] n Bleichmittel nt ▷ vt bleichen

bleak [bli:k] adj öde, düster; (*future*) trostlos

bleary ['blɪərɪ] adj (*eyes*) trübe, verschlafen

bleed [bli:d] (**bled, bled**) vi bluten

blend [blend] n Mischung f ▷ vt mischen ▷ vi sich mischen; **blender** n Mixer m

bless [bles] vt segnen; **~ you!** Gesundheit!; **blessing** n Segen m

blew [blu:] pt of **blow**

blind [blaɪnd] adj blind; (*corner*) unübersichtlich; **to turn a ~ eye to sth** bei etw ein Auge zudrücken ▷ n (*for window*) Rollo nt ▷ vt blenden; **blind alley** n Sackgasse f; **blind spot** n (Auto) toter Winkel; (*fig*) schwacher Punkt

blink [blɪŋk] vi blinzeln; (*light*) blinken

bliss [blɪs] n (Glück)seligkeit f

blister ['blɪstə'] n Blase f

blizzard ['blɪzəd] n Schneesturm m

bloated ['bləʊtɪd] adj aufgedunsen

block [blɒk] n (of wood, stone, ice) Block m, Klotz m; (of buildings) Häuserblock m; **~ of flats** (Brit) Wohnblock m ▷ vt (road etc) blockieren; (pipe, nose) verstopfen; **blockage** ['blɒkɪdʒ] n Verstopfung f; **blockbuster** ['blɒkbʌstə°] n Knüller m; **block letters** npl Blockschrift f

blog [blɒg] n (Inform) Blog m, Weblog m ▷ vi bloggen; **blogger** n Blogger(in) m(f)

bloke [bləʊk] n (Brit fam) Kerl m, Typ m

blond(e) [blɒnd] adj blond ▷ n (person) Blondine f, blonder Typ

blood [blʌd] n Blut nt; **blood count** n Blutbild nt; **blood donor** n Blutspender(in) m(f); **blood group** n Blutgruppe f; **blood orange** n Blutorange f; **blood poisoning** n Blutvergiftung f; **blood pressure** n Blutdruck m; **blood sample** n Blutprobe f; **bloodsports** npl Sportarten, bei denen Tiere getötet werden; **bloodthirsty** adj blutrünstig; **bloody** adj (Brit fam) verdammt, Scheiß-; (literal sense) blutig

bloom [bluːm] n Blüte f ▷ vi blühen

blossom ['blɒsəm] n Blüte f ▷ vi blühen

blot [blɒt] n (of ink) Klecks m; (fig) Fleck m

blouse [blaʊz] n Bluse f; **big girl's ~** (fam) Schwächling m

blow [bləʊ] n Schlag m ▷ vi, vt (blew, blown) (wind) wehen, blasen; (person: trumpet etc) blasen; **to ~ one's nose** sich dat die Nase putzen; **blow out** vt (candle etc) ausblasen; **blow up** vi

explodieren ▷ vt sprengen; (balloon, tyre) aufblasen; (Foto: enlarge) vergrößern; **blow-dry** vt föhnen; **blowjob** n (fam) **to give sb a ~** jdm einen blasen; **blown** [bləʊn] pp of **blow**; **blow-out** n (Auto) geplatzter Reifen

BLT n abbr = **bacon, lettuce and tomato sandwich** n Frühstücksspeck, Kopfsalat und Tomaten belegtes Sandwich

blue [bluː] adj blau; (fam: unhappy) trübsinnig, niedergeschlagen; (film) pornografisch; (joke) anzüglich; (language) derb; **bluebell** n Glockenblume f; **blueberry** n Blaubeere f; **blue cheese** n Blauschimmelkäse m; **blues** npl: **the ~** (Mus) der Blues; **to have the ~** (fam) niedergeschlagen sein

blunder ['blʌndə°] n Schnitzer m

blunt [blʌnt] adj (knife) stumpf; (fig) unverblümt; **bluntly** adv geradeheraus

blurred [blɜːd] adj verschwommen, unklar

blush [blʌʃ] vi erröten

board [bɔːd] n (of wood) Brett nt; (committee) Ausschuss m; (of firm) Vorstand m; **~ and lodging** Unterkunft und Verpflegung; **on ~** an Bord ▷ vt (ship) an Bord +gen gehen; (train, bus) einsteigen in +akk; **boarder** n (school) Internatsschüler(in) m(f); **board game** n Brettspiel nt; **boarding card, boarding pass** n Bordkarte f, Einsteigekarte f; **boarding school** n Internat nt; **board meeting** n Vorstandssitzung f; **boardroom** n Sitzungssaal m (des Vorstands)

boast [bəʊst] vi prahlen (about mit) ▷ n Prahlerei f

boat [bəʊt] n Boot nt; (ship) Schiff nt; **boatman** n (hirer)

Bootsverleiher m; **boat race** n
Regatta f; **boat train** n Zug m mit
Schiffsanschluss
bob(sleigh) ['bɒbsleɪ] n Bob m
bodily ['bɒdɪlɪ] adj körperlich
▷ adv (forcibly) gewaltsam; **body**
['bɒdɪ] n Körper m; (of car) Karosserie f; **bodybuilding**
n Bodybuilding nt; **bodyguard** n
Leibwächter m; (group) Leibwache
f; **body jewellery** n
Intimschmuck m; **body odour** n
Körpergeruch m; **body piercing** n
Piercing nt; **bodywork** n
Karosserie f
boil [bɔɪl] n, vi kochen ▷ n (Med)
Geschwür nt; **boiler** n Boiler m;
boiling adj (water etc) kochend
(heiß); **I was ~** (hot) mir war
fürchterlich heiß; (with rage) ich
kochte vor Wut; **boiling point** n
Siedepunkt m
bold [bəʊld] adj kühn, mutig;
(colours) kräftig; (type) fett
Bolivia [bə'lɪvɪə] n Bolivien nt
bolt [bəʊlt] n (lock) Riegel m;
(screw) Bolzen m ▷ vt verriegeln
bomb [bɒm] n Bombe f ▷ vt
bombardieren
bond [bɒnd] n (link) Bindung f;
(Fin) Obligation f
bone [bəʊn] n Knochen m; (of
fish) Gräte f; **boner** n (US fam)
Schnitzer m; (vulg: erection) Ständer
m
bonfire ['bɒnfaɪə*] n Feuer nt
(im Freien)
bonnet ['bɒnɪt] n (Brit Auto)
Haube f; (for baby) Häubchen nt
bonny ['bɒnɪ] adj (esp Scottish)
hübsch
bonus ['bəʊnəs] n Bonus m,
Prämie f
boo [buː] vt auspfeifen,
ausbuhen ▷ vi buhen ▷ n Buhruf
m
book [bʊk] n Buch nt; (of tickets,

stamps) Heft nt ▷ vt (ticket etc)
bestellen; (hotel, flight etc) buchen;
(Sport) verwarnen; **fully ~ed** (up)
ausgebucht; (performance)
ausverkauft; **book** in vt
eintragen; **to be ~ed in at a hotel**
ein Zimmer in einem Hotel
bestellt haben; **bookcase** n
Bücherregal nt; **booking** n
Buchung f; **booking office** n
(Rail) Fahrkartenschalter m; (Theat)
Vorverkaufsstelle f; **book-keeping**
n Buchhaltung f; **booklet** n
Broschüre f; **bookmark** n (a.
Inform) Lesezeichen nt; **bookshelf**
n Bücherbord nt; **bookshelves**
n Bücherregal nt; **bookshop**,
bookstore n (esp US)
Buchhandlung f
boom [buːm] n (of business)
Boom m; (noise) Dröhnen nt ▷ vi
(business) boomen; (fam) florieren;
(voice etc) dröhnen
boomerang ['buːməræŋ] n
Bumerang m
boost [buːst] n Auftrieb m ▷ vt
(production, sales) ankurbeln;
(power, profits etc) steigern;
booster (injection) n
Wiederholungsimpfung f
boot [buːt] n Stiefel m; (Brit Auto)
Kofferraum m ▷ vt (Inform) laden,
booten
booth [buːð] n (at fair etc) Bude f;
(at trade fair etc) Stand m
booze [buːz] n (fam) Alkohol m
▷ vi (fam) saufen
border ['bɔːdə*] n Grenze f; (edge)
Rand m; **north/south of the**
Border in Schottland/England;
borderline n Grenze f
bore [bɔː*] pt of **bear** n (hole
etc) bohren; (person) langweilen
▷ n (person) Langweiler(in) m(f),
langweiliger Mensch; (thing)
langweilige Sache; **bored** adj: **to**
be ~ sich langweilen; **boredom** n

Langeweile f; **boring** adj
langweilig

born [bɔːn] adj: **he was ~ in
London** er ist in London geboren

borne [bɔːn] pp of **bear**

borough ['bʌrə] n Stadtbezirk m

borrow ['bɔrəʊ] vt borgen

Bosnia-Herzegovina
['bɒzniəhɜːtsəgəʊviːnə] n
Bosnien-Herzegowina nt; **Bosnian**
['bɒzniən] adj bosnisch ▷ n
Bosnier(in) m(f)

boss [bɒs] n Chef(in) m(f), Boss
m; **boss around** vt
herumkommandieren; **bossy** adj
herrisch

botanical [bə'tænɪkəl] adj botanisch; **~ garden(s)** botanischer
Garten

both [bəʊθ] adj beide; **~ the
books** beide Bücher ▷ pron
(people) beide; (things) beides;
~ (of) the boys die beiden Jungs; I
like ~ of them ich mag sie (alle)
beide ▷ adv: **~ X and Y** sowohl X
als auch Y

bother ['bɒðə'] vt ärgern,
belästigen; **it doesn't ~ me** das
stört mich nicht; **he can't be ~ed
with details** mit Details gibt er
sich nicht ab; **I'm not ~ed** das ist
mir egal ▷ vi sich kümmern
(about um); **don't ~** (das ist) nicht
nötig, lass es! ▷ n (trouble) Mühe f;
(annoyance) Ärger m

bottle ['bɒtl] n Flasche f ▷ vt (in
Flaschen) abfüllen; **bottle out** vi
(fam) den Mut verlieren, aufgeben;
bottle bank n Altglascontainer
m; **bottled** adj in Flaschen; **~ beer**
Flaschenbier nt; **bottleneck** n
(fig) Engpass m; **bottle opener** n
Flaschenöffner m

bottom ['bɒtəm] n (of container)
Boden m; (bigger) Unterseite f;
(fam: of person) Po m; **at the ~ of
the sea/table/page** auf dem

Meeresgrund/am Tabellen-
ende/unten auf der Seite ▷ adj
unterste(r, s); **to be ~ of the
class/league** Klassen-
letzte(r)/Tabellenletzte(r) sein;
~ gear (Auto) erster Gang

bought [bɔːt] pt, pp of **buy**

bounce [baʊns] vi (ball)
springen, aufprallen; (cheque)
platzen; **~ up and down** (person)
herumhüpfen; **bouncy** adj (ball)
gut springend; (person) munter;
bouncy castle® n Hüpfburg f

bound [baʊnd] pt, pp of **bind**
▷ adj (tied up) gebunden; (obliged)
verpflichtet; **to be ~ to do sth** (sure
to) etw bestimmt tun (werden);
(have to) etw tun müssen; **it's ~ to
happen** es muss so kommen; **to
be ~ for ...** auf den Weg nach ...
sein; **boundary** ['baʊndərɪ] n
Grenze f

bouquet [bu'keɪ] n (flowers)
Strauß m; (of wine) Blume f

boutique [buːˈtiːk] n Boutique f

bow [bəʊ] n (ribbon) Schleife f;
(instrument, weapon) Bogen m
▷ [baʊ] vi sich verbeugen ▷ [baʊ]
n (with head) Verbeugung f; (of
ship) Bug m

bowels ['baʊəlz] npl Darm m

bowl [bəʊl] n (basin) Schüssel f;
(shallow) Schale f; (for animal) Napf
m ▷ vt, vi (in cricket) werfen

bowler ['bəʊlə'] n (in cricket)
Werfer(in) m(f); (hat) Melone f

bowling ['bəʊlɪŋ] n Kegeln nt;
bowling alley n Kegelbahn f;
bowling green n Rasen m zum
Bowling-Spiel; **bowls** [bəʊlz]
nsing (game) Bowling-Spiel nt

bow tie [bəʊˈtaɪ] n Fliege f

box [bɒks] n Schachtel f;
(cardboard) Karton m; (bigger)
Kasten m; (space on form) Kästchen
nt; (Theat) Loge f; **boxer** n
Boxer(in) m(f); **boxers, boxer**

shorts npl Boxershorts pl; **boxing**
n (Sport) Boxen nt; **Boxing Day** n
zweiter Weihnachtsfeiertag

● BOXING DAY
●
● **Boxing Day** ist ein Feiertag in
● Großbritannien. Fällt
● Weihnachten auf ein
● Wochenende, wird der Feiertag
● am nächsten Wochentag
● nachgeholt. Der Name geht auf
● einen alten Brauch zurück:
● früher erhielten Händler und
● Lieferanten an diesem Tag ein
● Geschenk, die sogenannte
● Christmas Box.

boxing gloves npl
Boxhandschuhe pl; **boxing ring** n
Boxring m
box number n Chiffre f
box office n (cinema, theatre)
Kasse f
boy [bɔɪ] n Junge m
boycott ['bɔɪkɒt] n Boykott m
▷ vt boykottieren
boyfriend ['bɔɪfrɛnd] n (fester)
Freund m; **boy scout** n
Pfadfinder m
bra [brɑː] n BH m
brace [breɪs] n (on teeth) Spange f
bracelet ['breɪslɪt] n Armband nt
braces ['breɪsɪz] npl (Brit)
Hosenträger pl
bracket ['brækɪt] n (in text)
Klammer f; (Tech) Träger m ▷ vt
einklammern
brag [bræg] vi angeben
Braille [breɪl] n Blindenschrift f
brain [breɪn] n (Anat) Gehirn nt;
(mind) Verstand m; **~s** (pl)
(intelligence) Grips m;
(intelligence) Geistesblitz m; **brainy** adj schlau,
clever
braise [breɪz] vt schmoren
brake [breɪk] n Bremse f ▷ vi

bremsen; **brake fluid** n
Bremsflüssigkeit f; **brake light** n
Bremslicht nt; **brake pedal** n
Bremspedal nt
branch [brɑːntʃ] n (of tree) Ast m;
(of family, subject) Zweig m; (of firm)
Filiale f, Zweigstelle f; **branch off**
vi (road) abzweigen
brand [brænd] n (Comm) Marke f
brand-new ['brænd'njuː] adj
(funkel)nagelneu
brandy ['brændɪ] n Weinbrand m
brass [brɑːs] n Messing nt; (Brit
fam: money) Knete f; **brass band** n
Blaskapelle f
brat [bræt] n (pej, fam) Gör nt
brave [breɪv] adj tapfer, mutig;
bravery ['breɪvərɪ] n Mut m
brawl [brɔːl] n Schlägerei f
brawn [brɔːn] n (strength)
Muskelkraft f; (Gastr) Sülze f;
brawny adj muskulös
Brazil [brə'zɪl] n Brasilien nt;
Brazilian adj brasilianisch ▷ n
Brasilianer(in) m(f); **brazil nut** n
Paranuss f
bread [brɛd] n Brot nt; **breadbin** n
(Brit), **breadbox** (US) n
Brotkasten m; **breadcrumbs** npl
Brotkrumen pl; (Gastr) Paniermehl
nt; **breaded** adj paniert;
breadknife n Brotmesser nt
breadth [brɛdθ] n Breite f
break [breɪk] n (fracture) Bruch
m; (rest) Pause f; (short holiday)
Kurzurlaub m; **give me a ~** gib mir
eine Chance, hör auf damit! ▷ vt
(**broke, broken**) (fracture) brechen;
(in pieces) zerbrechen; (toy, device)
kaputt machen; (promise) nicht
halten; (silence) brechen; (law)
verletzen; (journey) unterbrechen;
(news) mitteilen (to sb jdm); **I
broke my leg** ich habe mir das
Bein gebrochen; **he broke it to
her gently** er hat es ihr schonend
beigebracht ▷ vi (come apart)

(auseinander)brechen; (in pieces) zerbrechen; (toy, device) kaputtgehen; (person) zusammenbrechen; (day, dawn) anbrechen; (news) bekannt werden; **break down** vi (car) eine Panne haben; (machine) versagen; (person) zusammenbrechen; **break in** vi (burglar) einbrechen; **break into** vt einbrechen in +akk; **break off** vt, vi abbrechen; **break out** vi ausbrechen; **to ~ in a rash** einen Ausschlag bekommen; **break up** vi aufbrechen; (meeting, organisation) sich auflösen; (marriage) in die Brüche gehen; (couple) sich trennen; **school breaks up on Friday** am Freitag beginnen die Ferien ▷ vt aufbrechen; (marriage) zerstören; (meeting) auflösen; **breakable** adj zerbrechlich; **breakage** n Bruch m; **breakdown** n (of car) Panne f; (of machine) Störung f; (of person, relations, system) Zusammenbruch m; **breakdown service** n Pannendienst m; **breakdown truck** n Abschleppwagen m

breakfast ['brɛkfəst] n Frühstück nt; **to have ~** frühstücken; **breakfast cereal** n Cornflakes, Muesli etc; **breakfast television** n Frühstücksfernsehen nt

break-in ['breɪkɪn] n Einbruch m; **breakup** ['breɪkʌp] n (of meeting, organization) Auflösung f; (of marriage) Zerrüttung f

breast [brɛst] n Brust f; **breastfeed** vt stillen; **breaststroke** n Brustschwimmen nt

breath [brɛθ] n Atem m; **out of ~** außer Atem; **breathalyse**, **breathalyze** ['brɛθəlaɪz] vt (ins Röhrchen) blasen lassen; **breathalyser**, **breathalyzer** n Promillemesser m; **breathe** [briːð]

vt, vi atmen; **breathe in** vt, vi einatmen; **breathe out** vt, vi ausatmen; **breathless** ['brɛθlɪs] adj atemlos; **breathtaking** ['brɛθteɪkɪŋ] adj atemberaubend

bred [brɛd] pt, pp of **breed**

breed [briːd] n (race) Rasse f ▷ vi (**bred, bred**) sich vermehren ▷ vt züchten; **breeder** n Züchter(in) m(f); (fam) Hetero m; **breeding** n (of animals) Züchtung f; (of person) (gute) Erziehung

breeze [briːz] n Brise f

brevity ['brɛvɪtɪ] n Kürze f

brew [bruː] vt (beer) brauen; (tea) kochen; **brewery** n Brauerei f

bribe ['braɪb] n Bestechungsgeld nt ▷ vt bestechen; **bribery** ['braɪbərɪ] n Bestechung f

brick [brɪk] n Backstein m; **bricklayer** n Maurer(in) m(f)

bride [braɪd] n Braut f; **bridegroom** n Bräutigam m; **bridesmaid** n Brautjungfer f

bridge [brɪdʒ] n Brücke f; (cards) Bridge nt

brief [briːf] adj kurz ▷ vt instruieren (on über +akk); **briefcase** n Aktentasche f; **briefs** npl Slip m

bright [braɪt] adj hell; (colour) leuchtend; (cheerful) heiter; (intelligent) intelligent; (idea) glänzend; **brighten up** vt aufhellen; (person) aufheitern ▷ vi sich aufheitern; (person) fröhlicher werden

brilliant ['brɪljənt] adj (sunshine, colour) strahlend; (person) brillant; (idea) glänzend; (Brit fam) **it was ~** es war fantastisch

brim [brɪm] n Rand m

bring [brɪŋ] (**brought, brought**) vt bringen; (with one) mitbringen; **bring about** vt herbeiführen, bewirken; **bring back** vt zurückbringen; (memories) wecken; **bring down** vt (reduce) senken; (*government etc*) zu Fall bringen; **bring in** vt hereinbringen; (*introduce*) einführen; **bring out** vt herausbringen; **bring round**, **bring to** vt wieder zu sich bringen; **bring round** (*child*) aufziehen; (*question*) zur Sprache bringen

brisk [brɪsk] adj (*trade*) lebhaft; (*wind*) frisch

bristle ['brɪsl] n Borste f

Brit [brɪt] n (*fam*) Brite m, Britin f; **Britain** ['brɪtn] n Großbritannien nt; **British** ['brɪtɪʃ] adj britisch; **the ~ Isles** (*pl*) die Britischen Inseln pl ▷ n **the ~** (*pl*) die Briten pl

brittle ['brɪtl] adj spröde

broad [brɔːd] adj breit; (*accent*) stark; **in ~ daylight** am helllichten Tag ▷ (*US fam*) Frau f

B road ['biːrəʊd] n (*Brit*) = Landstraße f

broadcast ['brɔːdkɑːst] n Sendung f ▷ irr vt, vi senden; (*event*) übertragen

broaden ['brɔːdn] vt: **to ~ the mind** den Horizont erweitern; **broad-minded** adj tolerant

broccoli ['brɒkəlɪ] n Brokkoli pl

brochure ['brəʊʃjʊə°] n Prospekt m, Broschüre f

broke [brəʊk] pt of **break** ▷ adj (*Brit fam*) pleite; **broken** ['brəʊkən] pp of **break**; **broken-hearted** adj untröstlich

broker ['brəʊkə°] n Makler(in) m(f)

brolly ['brɒlɪ] n (*Brit*) Schirm m

bronchitis [brɒŋ'kaɪtɪs] n Bronchitis f

bronze [brɒnz] n Bronze f

brooch [brəʊtʃ] n Brosche f

broom [bruːm] n Besen m

Bros [brɒs] abbr = **brothers** Gebr.

broth [brɒθ] n Fleischbrühe f

brothel ['brɒθl] n Bordell nt

brother ['brʌðə°] n Bruder m; **~s** (*pl*) (*Comm*) Gebrüder pl; **brother-in-law** (*pl* **brothers-in-law**) n Schwager m

brought [brɔːt] pt, pp of **bring**

brow [braʊ] n (*eyebrow*) (Augen)braue f; (*forehead*) Stirn f

brown [braʊn] adj braun; **brown bread** n Mischbrot nt; (*wholemeal*) Vollkornbrot nt; **brownie** ['braʊnɪ] n (*Gastr*) Brownie m; (*Brit*) junge Pfadfinderin; **brown paper** n Packpapier nt; **brown rice** n Naturreis m; **brown sugar** n brauner Zucker

browse [braʊz] vi (*in book*) blättern; (*in shop*) schmökern, herumschauen; **browser** n (*Inform*) Browser m

bruise [bruːz] n blauer Fleck ▷ vt: **to ~ one's arm** sich dat einen blauen Fleck (am Arm) holen

brunette [bruː'net] n Brünette f

brush [brʌʃ] n Bürste f; (*for sweeping*) Handbesen m; (*for painting*) Pinsel m ▷ vt bürsten; (*sweep*) fegen; **to ~ one's teeth** sich dat die Zähne putzen; **brush up** vt (*French etc*) auffrischen

Brussels sprouts [brʌsl'spraʊts] npl Rosenkohl m, Kohlsprossen pl

brutal ['bruːtl] adj brutal; **brutality** [bruː'tælɪtɪ] n Brutalität f

BSE abbr = **bovine spongiform encephalopathy** BSE f

bubble ['bʌbl] n Blase f; **bubble bath** n Schaumbad nt, Badeschaum m; **bubbly** ['bʌblɪ] adj sprudelnd; (*person*) temperamentvoll ▷ n (*fam*) Schampus m

buck [bʌk] n (*animal*) Bock m; (*US fam*) Dollar m

bucket ['bʌkɪt] n Eimer m

BUCKINGHAM PALACE

Der **Buckingham Palace** ist die offizielle Londoner Residenz der britischen Monarchen und liegt am St James's Park. Der Palast wurde 1703 für den Herzog von Buckingham erbaut, 1762 von George III gekauft, zwischen 1821 und 1836 von John Nash umgebaut und Anfang des 20. Jahrhunderts teilweise neu gestaltet. Teile des Buckingham Palace sind heute der Öffentlichkeit zugänglich.

buckle ['bʌkl] n Schnalle f ▷ vi (Tech) sich verbiegen ▷ vt zuschnallen

bud [bʌd] n Knospe f

Buddhism ['budɪzəm] n Buddhismus m; **Buddhist** adj buddhistisch ▷ n Buddhist(in) m(f)

buddy ['bʌdɪ] n (fam) Kumpel m

budget ['bʌdʒɪt] n Budget nt ▷ adj preisgünstig; **budget airline** n Billigflieger m

budgie ['bʌdʒɪ] n Wellensittich m

buff [bʌf] adj (US) muskulös; **in the ~** nackt ▷ n (enthusiast) Fan m

buffalo ['bʌfələu] (pl **-es**) n Büffel m

buffer ['bʌfə⁰] n (a. Inform) Puffer m

buffet ['bufeɪ] n (food) (kaltes) Büfett nt

bug [bʌg] n (Inform) Bug m, Programmfehler m; (listening device) Wanze f; (US: insect) Insekt nt; (fam: illness) Infektion f ▷ vt (fam) nerven

bugger ['bʌgə⁰] n (vulg) Scheißkerl m ▷ interj (vulg) Scheiße f; **bugger off** vi (vulg) abhauen, Leine ziehen

buggy® ['bʌgɪ] n (for baby) Buggy® m

build [bɪld] (built, built) vt bauen; **build up** vt aufbauen; **builder** n Bauunternehmer(in) m(f); **building** n Gebäude nt; **building site** n Baustelle f; **building society** n Bausparkasse f

built pt, pp of **build**; **built-in** adj (cupboard) Einbau-, eingebaut

bulb [bʌlb] n (Bot) (Blumen)zwiebel f; (Elec) Glühbirne f

Bulgaria [bʌl'gɛərɪə] n Bulgarien nt; **Bulgarian** adj bulgarisch ▷ n (person) Bulgare m, Bulgarin f; (language) Bulgarisch nt

bulimia [bə'lɪmɪə] n Bulimie f

bulk [bʌlk] n (size) Größe f; (greater part) Großteil m (of +gen); **in ~** en gros; **bulky** adj (goods) sperrig; (person) stämmig

bull [bul] n Stier m; **bulldog** n Bulldogge f; **bulldoze** ['buldəuz] vt planieren; **bulldozer** n Planierraupe f

bullet ['bulɪt] n Kugel f

bulletin ['bulɪtɪn] n Bulletin nt; (announcement) Bekanntmachung f; (Med) Krankenbericht m; **bulletin board** n (US: Inform) schwarzes Brett

bullfight ['bulfaɪt] n Stierkampf m; **bullshit** n (fam) Scheiß m

bully ['bulɪ] n Tyrann m

bum [bʌm] n (Brit fam: backside) Po m; (US: vagrant) Penner m; (worthless person) Rumtreiber m; **bum around** vi herumgammeln

bumblebee ['bʌmblbiː] n Hummel f

bumf [bʌmf] n Infomaterial nt, Papierkram m

bump [bʌmp] n (on skin: swelling) Beule f; (road) Unebenheit f; (blow) Stoß m ▷ vt stoßen; **to ~ one's head** sich dat den Kopf anschlagen (on an +dat); **bump into** vt stoßen gegen; (fam: meet)

(zufällig) begegnen +dat; **bumper**
n (Auto) Stoßstange f ▷ adj
(edition etc) Riesen-; (crop etc)
Rekord-; **bumpy** ['bʌmpɪ] adj
holp(e)rig

bun [bʌn] n süßes Brötchen

bunch [bʌntʃ] n (of flowers)
Strauß m; (fam: of people) Haufen m;
~ **of keys** Schlüsselbund m; ~ **of
grapes** Weintraube f

bundle ['bʌndl] n Bündel nt

bungalow ['bʌŋgələʊ] n Bungalow m

bungee jumping ['bʌndʒɪ-
dʒʌmpɪŋ] n Bungeejumping nt

bunk [bʌŋk] n Koje f; **bunk
bed(s)** n(pl) Etagenbett nt

bunker ['bʌŋkə°] n (Mil) Bunker
m

bunny ['bʌnɪ] n Häschen nt

buoy [bɔɪ] n Boje f; **buoyant**
['bɔɪənt] adj (floating)
schwimmend

BUPA ['buːpə] abbr (Brit) private
Krankenkasse

burden ['bɜːdn] n Last f

bureau ['bjʊərəʊ] n Büro nt;
(government department) Amt nt;
bureaucracy [bjʊ'rɒkrəsɪ] n
Bürokratie f; **bureaucratic**
[bjʊərə'krætɪk] adj bürokratisch;
bureau de change ['bjʊərəʊ də
'ʃɑːnʒ] n Wechselstube f

burger ['bɜːgə°] n Hamburger m

burglar ['bɜːglə°] n Einbre-
cher(in) m(f); **burglar alarm** n
Alarmanlage f; **burglarize** vt (US)
einbrechen in +akk; **burglary** n
Einbruch m; **burgle** ['bɜːgl] vt
einbrechen in +akk

burial ['berɪəl] n Beerdigung f

burn [bɜːn] (burnt o burned,
burnt o burned) vt verbrennen;
(food, slightly) anbrennen; **to
~ one's hand** sich dat die Hand
verbrennen ▷ vi brennen ▷ n
(injury) Brandwunde f; (on material)

verbrannte Stelle; **burn down** vt,
vi abbrennen

burp [bɜːp] vi rülpsen ▷ vt (baby)
aufstoßen lassen

bursary ['bɜːsərɪ] n Stipendium nt

burst [bɜːst] (burst, burst) vt
platzen lassen ▷ vi platzen;
to ~ into tears in Tränen
ausbrechen

bury ['berɪ] vt begraben; (in grave)
beerdigen; (hide) vergraben

bus [bʌs] n Bus m; **bus driver** n
Busfahrer(in) m(f)

bush [bʊʃ] n Busch m

business ['bɪznɪs] n Geschäft nt;
(enterprise) Unternehmen nt;
(concern, affair) Sache f; **I'm here on
~** ich bin geschäftlich hier; **it's
none of your ~** das geht dich
nichts an; **business card** n
Visitenkarte f; **business class** n
(Aviat) Businessclass f;
businessman (pl -men) n
Geschäftsmann m; **business
studies** npl Betriebswirtschaft-
slehre f; **businesswoman** (pl
-women) n Geschäftsfrau f

bus service n Busverbindung f;
bus shelter n Wartehäuschen nt;
bus station n Busbahnhof m; **bus
stop** n Bushaltestelle f

bust [bʌst] n Büste f ▷ adj
(broken) kaputt; **to go ~** Pleite
gehen; **bust-up** n (fam) Krach m

busy ['bɪzɪ] adj beschäftigt;
(street, place) belebt; (esp US:
telephone) besetzt; **~ signal** (US)
Besetztzeichen nt

⭕ **KEYWORD**

but [bʌt, bət] conj **1** (yet) aber; **not
X but Y** nicht X sondern Y
2 (however) **I'd love to come, but
I'm busy** ich würde gern kommen,
bin aber beschäftigt
3 (showing disagreement, surprise etc)

but that's fantastic! (aber) das ist ja fantastisch!
▷ prep (apart from, except): **nothing but trouble** nichts als Ärger; **no-one but him can do it** niemand außer ihm kann es machen; **but for you/your help** ohne dich/deine Hilfe; **anything but that** alles, nur das nicht
▷ adv (just, only) **she's but a child** sie ist noch ein Kind; **had I but known** wenn ich es nur gewusst hätte; **I can but try** ich kann es immerhin versuchen; **all but finished** so gut wie fertig

butcher ['bʊtʃə] n Fleischer(in) m(f), Metzger(in) m(f)

butler ['bʌtlə] n Butler m

butt [bʌt] (US fam) n Hintern m

butter ['bʌtə] n Butter f ▷ vt buttern; **buttercup** n Butterblume f; **butterfly** n Schmetterling m

buttocks ['bʌtəks] npl Gesäß nt

button ['bʌtn] n Knopf m; (badge) Button m ▷ vt zuknöpfen; **buttonhole** n Knopfloch m

buy [baɪ] n Kauf m ▷ vt (bought, bought) kaufen (from von); **he bought me a ring** er hat mir einen Ring gekauft; **buyer** n Käufer(in) m(f)

buzz [bʌz] n Summen nt; **to give sb a ~** (fam) jdn anrufen ▷ vi summen; **buzzer** ['bʌzə] n Summer m; **buzz word** n (fam) Modewort nt

KEYWORD

by [baɪ] prep **1** (referring to cause, agent) von, durch; **killed by lightning** vom Blitz getötet; **a painting by Picasso** ein Gemälde von Picasso
2 (referring to method, manner) **by**

bus/car/train mit dem Bus/Auto/Zug; **to pay by cheque** per Scheck bezahlen; **by moonlight** bei Mondschein; **by saving hard, he ...** indem er eisern sparte, ... er ...
3 (via, through) über +akk; **he came in by the back door** er kam durch die Hintertür herein
4 (close to, past) bei, an +dat; **a holiday by the sea** im Urlaub am Meer; **she rushed by me** sie eilte an mir vorbei
5 (not later than) **by 4 o'clock** bis 4 Uhr; **by this time tomorrow** morgen um diese Zeit; **by the time I got here it was too late** als ich hier ankam, war es zu spät
6 (during) **by day** bei Tag
7 (amount) **by the kilo/metre** kiloweise/meterweise; **paid by the hour** stundenweise bezahlt
8 (math, measure) **to divide by 3** durch 3 teilen; **to multiply by 3** mit 3 malnehmen; **a room 3 metres by 4** ein Zimmer 3 mal 4 Meter; **it's broader by a metre** es ist (um) einem Meter breiter
9 (according to) nach; **it's all right by me** von mir aus gern
10 (all) **by oneself** etc ganz allein
11 (by the way) übrigens
▷ adv **1** see go; **pass** etc
2 by and by irgendwann; (with past tenses) nach einiger Zeit; **by and large** (on the whole) im Großen und Ganzen

bye-bye ['baɪ'baɪ] interj (fam) Wiedersehen, tschüss
by-election n Nachwahl f; **bypass** n Umgehungsstraße f; (Med) Bypass m; **byproduct** n Nebenprodukt nt; **byroad** n Nebenstraße f; **bystander** n Zuschauer(in) m(f)
byte [baɪt] n Byte nt

C

C [siː] abbr = **Celsius** C

c abbr = **circa** ca

cab [kæb] n Taxi nt

cabbage ['kæbɪdʒ] n Kohl m

cabin ['kæbɪn] n (Naut) Kajüte f; (Aviat) Passagierraum m; (wooden house) Hütte f; **cabin crew** n Flugbegleitpersonal nt; **cabin cruiser** n Kajütboot nt

cabinet ['kæbɪnɪt] n Schrank m; (for display) Vitrine f; (Pol) Kabinett nt

cable ['keɪbl] n (Elec) Kabel nt; **cable-car** n Seilbahn f; **cable railway** n Drahtseilbahn f; **cable television, cablevision** (US) n Kabelfernsehen nt

cactus ['kæktəs] n Kaktus m

CAD abbr = **computer-aided design** CAD nt

Caesarean [siːˈzɛərɪən] adj: ~ **(section)** Kaiserschnitt m

café ['kæfeɪ] n Café nt; **cafeteria** [kæfɪˈtɪərɪə] n Cafeteria f; **cafetiere** [kæfəˈtjɛə] n Kaffeebereiter m

cage [keɪdʒ] n Käfig m

Cairo ['kaɪərəʊ] n Kairo nt

cake [keɪk] n Kuchen m; **cake shop** n Konditorei f

calamity [kəˈlæmɪtɪ] n Katastrophe f

calculate ['kælkjʊleɪt] vt berechnen; (estimate) kalkulieren; **calculating** adj berechnend; **calculation** [kælkjʊˈleɪʃən] n Berechnung f; (estimate) Kalkulation f; **calculator** ['kælkjʊleɪtə] n Taschenrechner m

calendar ['kælɪndə] n Kalender m

calf [kɑːf] n (pl calves) n Kalb nt; (Anat) Wade f

California [kælɪˈfɔːnɪə] n Kalifornien nt

call [kɔːl] vt rufen; (name, describe as) nennen; (Tel) anrufen; (Inform, Aviat) aufrufen; **what's this ~ed?** wie heißt das?; **that's what I ~ service** das nenne ich guten Service ▷ vi (shout) rufen (for help um Hilfe); (visit) vorbeikommen; **to ~ at the doctor's** beim Arzt vorbeigehen; (of train) **to ~ at …** in … halten ▷ n (shout) Ruf m; (Tel) Anruf; (Inform, Aviat) Aufruf m; **to make a ~** telefonieren; **to give sb a ~** jdn anrufen; **to be on ~** Bereitschaftsdienst haben; **call back** vt, vi zurückrufen; **call for** vt (come to pick up) abholen; (demand, require) verlangen; **call off** vt absagen

call centre n Callcenter nt; **caller** n Besucher(in) m(f); (Tel) Anrufer(in) m(f)

calm [kɑːm] n Stille f; (also of person) Ruhe f; (of sea) Flaute f ▷ vt

beruhigen ▷ *adj* **ruhig; calm down** *vi* sich beruhigen
calorie ['kælərɪ] *n* Kalorie *f*
calves [kɑːvz] *pl of* **calf**
Cambodia [kæm'bəʊdɪə] *n* Kambodscha *nt*
camcorder ['kæmkɔːdə°] *n* Camcorder *m*
came [keɪm] *pt of* **come**
camel ['kæməl] *n* Kamel *nt*
camera ['kæmərə] *n* Fotoapparat *m*, Kamera *f*; **camera phone** ['kæmərəfəʊn] *n* Fotohandy *nt*
camomile ['kæməmaɪl] *n* Kamille *f*
camouflage ['kæməflɑːʒ] *n* Tarnung *f*
camp [kæmp] *n* Lager *nt*; (*camping place*) Zeltplatz *m* ▷ *vi* zelten, campen ▷ *adj* (*fam*) theatralisch, tuntig
campaign [kæm'peɪn] *n* Kampagne *f*; (*Pol*) Wahlkampf *m* ▷ *vi* sich einsetzen (*for/against* für/gegen)
campbed ['kæmpbed] *n* Campingliege *f*; **camper** ['kæmpə°] *n* (*person*) Camper(in) *m(f)*; (*van*) Wohnmobil *nt*; **camping** ['kæmpɪŋ] *n* Zelten *nt*, Camping *nt*; **campsite** ['kæmpsaɪt] *n* Zeltplatz *m*, Campingplatz *m*
campus ['kæmpəs] *n* (*of university*) Universitätsgelände *nt*, Campus *m*

○ **KEYWORD**

can [kæn] (*negative* **cannot, can't**, *conditional* **could**) *vb aux* **1** (*be able to, know how to*) können; **I can see you tomorrow,** if you like ich könnte Sie morgen sehen, wenn Sie wollen; **I can swim** ich kann schwimmen; **you can speak German?** sprechen Sie Deutsch?

2 (*may*) können, dürfen; **could I have a word with you?** könnte ich Sie kurz sprechen?

Canada ['kænədə] *n* Kanada *nt*; **Canadian** [kə'neɪdjən] *adj* kanadisch ▷ *n* Kanadier(in) *m(f)*
canal [kə'næl] *n* Kanal *m*
canary [kə'neərɪ] *n* Kanarienvogel *m*
cancel ['kænsəl] *vt* (*plans*) aufgeben; (*meeting, event*) absagen; (*Comm: order etc*) stornieren; (*contract*) kündigen; (*Inform*) löschen; (*Aviat: flight*) streichen; **to be ~led** (*event, train, bus*) ausfallen; **cancellation** [kænsə'leɪʃən] *n* Absage *f*; (*Comm*) Stornierung *f*; (*Aviat*) gestrichener Flug
cancer ['kænsə°] *n* (*Med*) Krebs *m*; **Cancer** *n* (*Astr*) Krebs *m*
candid ['kændɪd] *adj* (*person, conversation*) offen
candidate ['kændɪdət] *n* (*for post*) Bewerber(in) *m(f)*; (*Pol*) Kandidat(in) *m(f)*
candle ['kændl] *n* Kerze *f*; **candlelight** *n* Kerzenlicht *nt*; **candlestick** *n* Kerzenhalter *m*
candy ['kændɪ] *n* (*US*) Bonbon *nt*; (*quantity*) Süßigkeiten *pl*; **candy-floss** (*Brit*) Zuckerwatte *f*
cane [keɪn] *n* Rohr *nt*; (*stick*) Stock *m*
cannabis ['kænəbɪs] *n* Cannabis *m*
canned [kænd] *adj* Dosen-
cannot ['kænɒt] *contr of* **can not**
canny ['kænɪ] *adj* (*shrewd*) schlau
canoe [kə'nuː] *n* Kanu *nt*; **canoeing** *n* Kanufahren *nt*
can opener ['kænəʊpnə°] *n* Dosenöffner *m*
canopy ['kænəpɪ] *n* Baldachin *m*; (*awning*) Markise *f*; (*over entrance*) Vordach *nt*

can't [kɑːnt] contr of **can not**

canteen [kæn'tiːn] n (in factory) Kantine f; (in university) Mensa f

canvas ['kænvəs] n (for sails, shoes) Segeltuch nt; (for tent) Zeltstoff m; (for painting) Leinwand f

canvass ['kænvəs] vi um Stimmen werben (for für)

canyon ['kænjən] n Felsenschlucht f; **canyoning** ['kænjənıŋ] n Canyoning nt

cap [kæp] n Mütze f; (lid) Verschluss m, Deckel m

capability [keıpə'bılıtı] n Fähigkeit f; **capable** ['keıpəbl] adj fähig; **to be ~ of sth** zu etw fähig (o imstande) sein; **to be ~ of doing sth** etw tun können

capacity [kə'pæsıtı] n (of building, container) Fassungsvermögen nt; (ability) Fähigkeit f; (function) **in his ~ as ...** in seiner Eigenschaft als ...

cape [keıp] n (garment) Cape nt, Umhang m; (Geo) Kap nt

caper ['keıpə°] n (for cooking) Kaper f

capital ['kæpıtl] n (Fin) Kapital nt; (letter) Großbuchstabe m; **~ (city)** Hauptstadt f; **capitalism** n Kapitalismus m; **capital punishment** n die Todesstrafe

Capricorn ['kæprıkɔːn] n (Astr) Steinbock m

capsize [kæp'saız] vi kentern

capsule ['kæpsjuːl] n Kapsel f

captain ['kæptın] n Kapitän m; (army) Hauptmann m

caption ['kæpʃən] n Bildunterschrift f

captive ['kæptıv] n Gefangene(r) mf; **capture** ['kæptʃə°] vt (person) fassen, gefangen nehmen; (town etc) einnehmen; (Inform: data) erfassen ▷ n Gefangennahme f; (Inform) Erfassung f

car [kɑː°] n Auto nt; (US Rail)

Wagen m

carafe [kə'ræf] n Karaffe f

caramel ['kærəmel] n Karamelle f

caravan ['kærəvæn] n Wohnwagen m; **caravan site** n Campingplatz m für Wohnwagen

caraway (seed) ['kærəweɪ] n Kümmel m

carbohydrate [kɑːbəʊ'haɪdreɪt] n Kohle(n)hydrat nt

car bomb n Autobombe f

carbon ['kɑːbən] n Kohlenstoff m; **carbon footprint** n ökologischer Fußabdruck

car boot sale n auf einem Parkplatz stattfindender Flohmarkt

carburettor, carburetor (US) ['kɑːbjʊretə°] n Vergaser m

card [kɑːd] n Karte f; (material) Pappe f; **cardboard** n Pappe f; **~ (box)** n Karton m; (smaller) Pappschachtel f; **card game** n Kartenspiel nt

cardigan ['kɑːdɪɡən] n Strickjacke f

card index n Kartei f; **cardphone** ['kɑːdfəʊn] n Kartentelefon nt

care [keə°] n (worry) Sorge f; (carefulness) Sorgfalt f; (looking after things, people) Pflege f; **with ~** sorgfältig; (cautiously) vorsichtig; **to take ~** (watch out) vorsichtig sein; (in address) **~ of** bei; **to take ~ of** sorgen für, sich kümmern um ▷ vi: **I don't ~** es ist mir egal; **to ~ about sth** Wert auf etw akk legen; **he ~s about her** sie liegt ihm am Herzen; **care for** vt (look after) sorgen für, sich kümmern um; (like) mögen

career [kə'rıə°] n Karriere f, Laufbahn f; **career woman** (pl **women**) n Karrierefrau f; **careers adviser** n Berufsberater(in) m(f)

carefree ['keəfriː] adj sorgenfrei; **careful, carefully** adj, adv sorgfältig; (cautious, cautiously)

vorsichtig; **careless, carelessly**
adj, adv nachlässig; (driving etc)
leichtsinnig; (remark)
unvorsichtig; **carer** ['kɛərə*] n
Betreuer(in) m(f), Pfleger(in) m(f);
caretaker ['kɛəteɪkə*] n Haus-
meister(in) m(f); **careworker** n
Pfleger(in) m(f)

car-ferry ['kɑːferɪ] n Autofähre f
cargo ['kɑːgəʊ] (pl **-(e)s**) n
Ladung f

car hire, car hire company n
Autovermietung f

Caribbean [kærɪˈbiːən] n Karibik
f ▷ adj karibisch

caring ['kɛərɪŋ] adj mitfühlend;
(parent, partner) liebevoll; (looking
after sb) fürsorglich

car insurance n
Kraftfahrzeugversicherung f

carnation [kɑːˈneɪʃən] n Nelke f
carnival ['kɑːnɪvəl] n Volksfest
nt; (before Lent) Karneval m

carol ['kærəl] n Weihnachtslied nt
carp [kɑːp] n (fish) Karpfen m

car park n (Brit) Parkplatz m;
(multi-storey car park) Parkhaus nt

carpenter ['kɑːpəntə*] n Zimmermann m

carpet ['kɑːpɪt] n Teppich m
car phone n Autotelefon nt;
carpool n Fahrgemeinschaft f;
(vehicles) Fuhrpark m ▷ vi eine
Fahrgemeinschaft bilden; **car
rental** n Autovermietung f

carriage ['kærɪdʒ] n (Brit Rail:
coach) Wagen m; (compartment)
Abteil nt; (horse-drawn) Kutsche f;
(transport) Beförderung f;
carriageway n (Brit: on road)
Fahrbahn f

carrier ['kærɪə*] n (Comm)
Spediteur(in) m(f); **carrier bag** n
Tragetasche f

carrot ['kærət] n Karotte f
carry ['kærɪ] vt tragen; (in vehicle)
befördern; (have on one) bei sich

haben; **carry on** vi (continue)
weitermachen; (fam: make a scene)
ein Theater machen ▷ vt
(continue) fortführen; **to ~ on
working** weiter arbeiten; **carry
out** vt (orders, plan) ausführen,
durchführen

carrycot n Babytragetasche f
carsick ['kɑːsɪk] adj: **he gets
~** ihm wird beim Autofahren übel

cart [kɑːt] n Wagen m, Karren m;
(US: shopping trolley)
Einkaufswagen m

carton ['kɑːtən] n (Papp)karton
m; (of cigarettes) Stange f

cartoon [kɑːˈtuːn] n Cartoon m o
nt; (one drawing) Karikatur f; (film)
(Zeichen)trickfilm m

cartridge ['kɑːtrɪdʒ] n (for film)
Kassette f; (for gun, pen, printer)
Patrone f; (for copier) Kartusche f

carve [kɑːv] vt, vi (wood)
schnitzen; (stone) meißeln; (meat)
schneiden, tranchieren; **carving** n
(in wood) Schnitzerei f; (in stone)
Skulptur f; (Ski) Carving nt

car wash n Autowaschanlage f
case [keɪs] n (crate) Kiste f; (box)
Schachtel f; (for jewels) Schatulle f;
(for spectacles) Etui nt; (Jur, matter)
Fall m; in ~ falls; **in that ~** in dem
Fall; **in ~ of fire** bei Brand; **it's a
~ of ...** es handelt sich hier um ...

cash [kæʃ] n Bargeld nt; **in ~ bar**;
~ on delivery per Nachnahme
▷ vt (cheque) einlösen; **cash desk**
n Kasse f; **cash dispenser** n
Geldautomat m; **cashier** [kæˈʃɪə*]
n Kassierer(in) m(f); **cash
machine** n (Brit) Geldautomat m

cashmere ['kæʃmɪə*] n Kasch-
mirwolle f

cash payment n Barzahlung f;
cashpoint n (Brit) Geldautomat m
casing ['keɪsɪŋ] n Gehäuse nt
casino [kəˈsiːnəʊ] (pl **-s**) n
Kasino nt

cask [kɑːsk] n Fass nt

casserole [ˈkæsərəʊl] n Kasserole f; (food) Schmortopf m

cassette [kæˈset] n Kassette f; **cassette recorder** n Kassettenrekorder m

cast [kɑːst] (**cast, cast**) vt (throw) werfen; (Theat, Cine) besetzen; (roles) verteilen ▷ n (Theat, Cine) Besetzung f; (Med) Gipsverband m; **cast off** vi (Naut) losmachen

caster [ˈkɑːstə°] n: ~ **sugar** Streuzucker m

castle [ˈkɑːsl] n Burg f

castrate [kæsˈtreɪt] vt kastrieren

casual [ˈkæʒjʊəl] adj (arrangement, remark) beiläufig; (attitude, manner) (nach)lässig, zwanglos; (dress) leger (work, earnings) Gelegenheits-; (look, glance) flüchtig; ~ **wear** Freizeitkleidung f; ~ **sex** Gelegenheitssex m; **casually** adv (remark, say) beiläufig; (meet) zwanglos; (dressed) leger

casualty [ˈkæʒjʊəltɪ] n Verletzte(r) mf; (dead) Tote(r) mf; (department in hospital) Notaufnahme f

cat [kæt] n Katze f; (male) Kater m

catalog (US), **catalogue** [ˈkætəlɒg] n Katalog m ▷ vt katalogisieren

cataract [ˈkætərækt] n Wasserfall m; (Med) grauer Star

catarrh [kəˈtɑː°] n Katarr(h) m

catastrophe [kəˈtæstrəfɪ] n Katastrophe f

catch [kætʃ] n (fish etc) Fang m ▷ vt (**caught, caught**) fangen; (thief) fassen; (train, bus etc) nehmen; (not miss) erreichen; **to ~ a cold** sich erkälten; **to ~ fire** Feuer fangen; **I didn't ~ that** das habe ich nicht verstanden; **catch on** vi (become popular) Anklang finden; **catch up** vt, vi: **to ~ with** sb jdn einholen; **to ~ on sth** etw nachholen; **catching** adj ansteckend

category [ˈkætɪgərɪ] n Kategorie f

cater [ˈkeɪtə°] vi die Speisen und Getränke liefern (for für); **cater for** vt (have facilities for) eingestellt sein auf +akk; **catering** n Versorgung f mit Speisen und Getränken, Gastronomie f; **catering service** n Partyservice m

caterpillar [ˈkætəpɪlə°] n Raupe f

cathedral [kəˈθiːdrəl] n Kathedrale f, Dom m

Catholic [ˈkæθəlɪk] adj katholisch ▷ Katholik(in) m(f)

cat nap n (Brit) kurzer Schlaf; **cat's eyes** [ˈkætsaɪz] npl (in road) Katzenaugen pl, Reflektoren pl

catsup [ˈkætsəp] n (US) Ketschup nt o m

cattle [ˈkætl] npl Vieh nt

caught [kɔːt] pt, pp of **catch**

cauliflower [ˈkɒlɪflaʊə°] n Blumenkohl m; **cauliflower cheese** n Blumenkohl m in Käsesoße

cause [kɔːz] n (origin) Ursache f (of für); (reason) Grund m (for zu); (purpose) Sache f; **for a good ~** für wohltätige Zwecke; **no ~ for alarm/complaint** kein Grund zur Aufregung/Klage ▷ vt verursachen

causeway [ˈkɔːzweɪ] n Damm m

caution [ˈkɔːʃən] n Vorsicht f; (Jur, Sport) Verwarnung f ▷ vt (ver)warnen; **cautious** [ˈkɔːʃəs] adj vorsichtig

cave [keɪv] n Höhle f; **cave in** vi einstürzen

cavity [ˈkævɪtɪ] n Hohlraum m; (in tooth) Loch nt

cayenne (pepper) [keɪˈen] n Cayennepfeffer m

CCTV *abbr* = **closed circuit television** Videoüberwachungsanlage *f*

CD *abbr* = **Compact Disc** CD *f*; **CD player** *n* CD-Spieler *m*; **CD-ROM** *abbr* = **Compact Disc Read Only Memory** CD-ROM *f*; **CD-RW** *abbr* = **Compact Disc Rewritable** CD-RW *f*

cease [siːs] *vi* aufhören ▷ *vt* beenden; **to ~ doing sth** aufhören, etw zu tun; **cease fire** *n* Waffenstillstand *m*

ceiling ['siːlɪŋ] *n* Decke *f*

celebrate ['selɪbreɪt] *vt*, *vi* feiern; **celebrated** *adj* gefeiert; **celebration** [selɪ'breɪʃən] *n* Feier *f*; **celebrity** [sɪ'lebrɪtɪ] *n* Berühmtheit *f*, Star *m*

celeriac [sə'lerɪæk] *n* (Knollen)sellerie *m* o *f*; **celery** ['selərɪ] *n* (Stangen)sellerie *m* o *f*

cell [sel] *n* Zelle *f*; (US) *see* **cellphone**

cellar ['selə°] *n* Keller *m*

cello ['tʃeləʊ] (*pl* **-s**) *n* Cello *nt*

cellphone ['selfəʊn], **cellular phone** ['seljʊlə° 'fəʊn] *n* Mobiltelefon *nt*, Handy *nt*

Celt [kelt] *n* Kelte *m*, Keltin *f*; **Celtic** ['keltɪk] *adj* keltisch ▷ *n* (*language*) Keltisch *nt*

cement [sɪ'ment] *n* Zement *m*

cemetery ['semɪtrɪ] *n* Friedhof *m*

censorship ['sensəʃɪp] *n* Zensur *f*

cent [sent] *n* (*of dollar, euro etc*) Cent *m*

center *n* (US) *see* **centre**

centiliter (US), **centilitre** ['sentɪliːtə°] *n* Zentiliter *m*; **centimeter** (US), **centimetre** ['sentɪmiːtə°] *n* Zentimeter *m*

central ['sentrəl] *adj* zentral; **Central America** *n* Mittelamerika *nt*; **Central Europe** *n* Mitteleuropa *nt*; **central heating** *n* Zentralheizung *f*; **centralize** *vt* zentralisieren; **central locking** *n* (*Auto*) Zentralverriegelung *f*; **central reservation** *n* (*Brit*) Mittelstreifen *m*; **central station** *n* Hauptbahnhof *m*

centre ['sentə°] *n* Mitte *f*; (*building, of city*) Zentrum *nt* ▷ *vt* zentrieren; **centre forward** *n* (*Sport*) Mittelstürmer *m*

century ['sentjʊrɪ] *n* Jahrhundert *nt*

ceramic [sɪ'ræmɪk] *adj* keramisch

cereal ['sɪərɪəl] *n* (*any grain*) Getreide *nt*; (*breakfast cereal*) Frühstücksflocken *pl*

ceremony ['serɪmənɪ] *n* Feier *f*, Zeremonie *f*

certain ['sɜːtən] *adj* sicher (*of +gen*); (*particular*) bestimmt; **for ~** mit Sicherheit; **certainly** *adv* sicher; (*without doubt*) bestimmt; **~!** aber sicher!; **~ not** ganz bestimmt nicht!

certificate [sə'tɪfɪkɪt] *n* Bescheinigung *f*; (*in school, qualification*) Zeugnis *nt*; **certify** ['sɜːtɪfaɪ] *vt*, *vi* bescheinigen

cervical smear ['sɜːvɪkəl smɪə°] *n* Abstrich *m*

CFC *abbr* = **chlorofluorocarbon** FCKW *m*

chain [tʃeɪn] *n* Kette *f* ▷ *vt*: **to ~ (up)** anketten; **chain reaction** *n* Kettenreaktion *f*; **chain store** *n* Kettenladen *m*

chair [tʃeə°] *n* Stuhl *m*; (*university*) Lehrstuhl *m*; (*armchair*) Sessel *m*; (*chairperson*) Vorsitzende(r) *mf*; **chairlift** *n* Sessellift *m*; **chairman** (*pl* **-men**) *n* Vorsitzende(r) *m*; (*of firm*) Präsident *m*; **chairperson** *n* Vorsitzende(r) *mf*; (*of firm*) Präsident(in) *m(f)*; **chairwoman**

(pl **-women**) n Vorsitzende f; (of firm) Präsidentin f

chalet ['ʃæleɪ] n (in mountains) Berghütte f; (holiday dwelling) Ferienhäuschen nt

chalk ['tʃɔːk] n Kreide f

challenge ['tʃælɪndʒ] n Herausforderung f ▷ vt (person) herausfordern; (statement) bestreiten

chambermaid ['tʃeɪmbə*meɪd] n Zimmermädchen nt

chamois leather ['ʃæmwɑː'leðə*] n (for windows) Fensterleder nt

champagne [ʃæm'peɪn] n Champagner m

champion ['tʃæmpɪən] n (Sport) Meister(in) m(f); **championship** n Meisterschaft f

chance [tʃɑːns] n (fate) Zufall m; (possibility) Möglichkeit f; (opportunity) Gelegenheit f; (risk) Risiko nt; **by ~** zufällig; **he doesn't stand a ~ (of winning)** er hat keinerlei Chance(, zu gewinnen)

chancellor ['tʃɑːnsələ*] n Kanzler(in) m(f)

chandelier [ʃændɪ'lɪə*] n Kronleuchter m

change ['tʃeɪndʒ] vt verändern; (alter) ändern; (money, wheel, nappy) wechseln; (exchange) (um)tauschen; **to ~ one's clothes** sich umziehen; **to ~ trains** umsteigen; **to ~ gear** (Auto) schalten ▷ vi sich ändern; (esp outwardly) sich verändern; (get changed) sich umziehen ▷ n Veränderung f; (alteration) Änderung f; (money) Wechselgeld nt; (coins) Kleingeld nt; **for a ~** zur Abwechslung; **can you give me ~ for £10?** können Sie mir auf 10 Pfund herausgeben?; **change down** vi (Brit Auto) herunterschalten; **change over** vi

sich umstellen (to auf +akk); **change up** vi (Brit Auto) hochschalten

changeable adj (weather) veränderlich, wechselhaft; **change machine** n Geldwechsler m; **changing room** n Umkleideraum m

channel ['tʃænl] n Kanal m; (Radio, TV) Kanal m, Sender m; **the (English) Channel** der Ärmelkanal; **the Channel Islands** die Kanalinseln; **the Channel Tunnel** der Kanaltunnel; **channel-hopping** n Zappen nt

chaos ['keɪɒs] n Chaos nt; **chaotic** [keɪ'ɒtɪk] adj chaotisch

chap [tʃæp] n (Brit fam) Bursche m, Kerl m

chapel ['tʃæpl] n Kapelle f

chapped ['tʃæpt] adj (lips) aufgesprungen

chapter ['tʃæptə*] n Kapitel nt

character ['kærəktə*] n Charakter m, Wesen nt; (in a play, novel etc) Figur f; (Typo) Zeichen nt; **he's a real ~** er ist ein echtes Original; **characteristic** [kærəktə'rɪstɪk] adj typisches Merkmal

charcoal ['tʃɑːkəʊl] n Holzkohle f

charge [tʃɑːdʒ] n (cost) Gebühr f; (Jur) Anklage f; **free of ~** gratis, kostenlos; **to be in ~ of** verantwortlich sein für ▷ vt (money) verlangen; (Jur) anklagen; (battery) laden; **charge card** n Kundenkreditkarte f

charity ['tʃærɪtɪ] n (institution) wohltätige Organisation f; **a collection for ~** eine Sammlung für wohltätige Zwecke; **charity shop** n Geschäft einer 'charity', in dem freiwillige Helfer gebrauchte Kleidung, Bücher etc verkaufen

charm [tʃɑːm] n Charme m ▷ vt bezaubern; **charming** adj reizend, charmant

chart [tʃɑːt] n Diagramm nt; (map) Karte f; **the ~s** pl die Charts, die Hitliste

charter [ˈtʃɑːtə°] n Urkunde f ▷ vt (Naut, Aviat) chartern; **charter flight** n Charterflug m

chase [tʃeɪs] vt jagen, verfolgen ▷ n Verfolgungsjagd f; (hunt) Jagd f

chassis [ˈʃæsɪ] n (Auto) Fahrgestell nt

chat [tʃæt] vi plaudern; (Inform) chatten ▷ n Plauderei f; (Inform) Chat m; **chat up** vt anmachen, anbaggern; **chatroom** n (Inform) Chatroom m; **chat show** n Talkshow f; **chatty** adj geschwätzig

chauffeur [ˈʃəʊfə°] n Chauffeur(in) m(f), Fahrer(in) m(f)

cheap [tʃiːp] adj billig; (of poor quality) minderwertig

cheat [tʃiːt] vt, vi betrügen; (in school, game) mogeln

Chechen [ˈtʃetʃen] adj tschetschenisch ▷ n Tschetschene m, Tschetschenin f

Chechnya [ˈtʃetʃnɪə] n Tschetschenien nt

check [tʃek] vt (examine) überprüfen (for auf +akk); (Tech: adjustment etc) kontrollieren; (US: tick) abhaken; (Aviat: luggage) einchecken; (US: coat) abgeben ▷ n (examination, restraint) Kontrolle f; (US: restaurant bill) Rechnung f; (pattern) Karo(muster) nt; (US) see **cheque**; **check in** vt, vi (Aviat) einchecken; (into hotel) sich anmelden; **check out** vi sich abmelden, auschecken; **check up** vi nachprüfen; **to ~ on sb** Nachforschungen über jdn anstellen

checkers [ˈtʃekəz] nsing (US) Damespiel nt

check-in [ˈtʃekɪn] n (airport) Check-in m; (hotel) Anmeldung f; **check-in desk** n

Abfertigungsschalter m; **checking account** n (US) Scheckkonto nt; **check list** n Kontrollliste f; **checkout** n (supermarket) Kasse f; **checkout time** n (hotel) Abreise(zeit) f; **checkpoint** n Kontrollpunkt m; **checkroom** n (US) Gepäckaufbewahrung f; **checkup** n (Med) (ärztliche) Untersuchung

cheddar [ˈtʃedə°] n Cheddarkäse m

cheek [tʃiːk] n Backe f, Wange f; (insolence) Frechheit f; **what a ~** so eine Frechheit!; **cheekbone** n Backenknochen m; **cheeky** adj frech

cheer [tʃɪə°] n Beifallsruf m; **~s** (when drinking) prost!; (for thanks) danke; (Brit: goodbye) tschüs ▷ vt zujubeln +dat ▷ vi jubeln; **cheer up** vt aufmuntern ▷ vi fröhlicher werden; **~!** Kopf hoch!; **cheerful** [ˈtʃɪəfʊl] adj fröhlich

cheese [tʃiːz] n Käse m; **cheeseboard** n Käsebrett nt; (as course) (gemischte) Käseplatte; **cheesecake** n Käsekuchen m

chef [ʃef] n Koch m; (in charge of kitchen) Küchenchef(in) m(f)

chemical [ˈkemɪkəl] adj chemisch ▷ Chemikalie f; **chemist** [ˈkemɪst] n (pharmacist) Apotheker(in) m(f); (industrial chemist) Chemiker(in) m(f); **~'s** (shop) Apotheke f; **chemistry** n Chemie f

cheque [tʃek] n (Brit) Scheck m; **cheque account** n (Brit) Girokonto nt; **cheque book** n (Brit) Scheckheft nt; **cheque card** n (Brit) Scheckkarte f

chequered [ˈtʃekəd] adj kariert

cherish [ˈtʃerɪʃ] vt (look after) liebevoll sorgen für; (hope) hegen; (memory) bewahren

cherry ['tʃɛrɪ] n Kirsche f; **cherry tomato** (pl **-es**) n Kirschtomate f

chess [tʃɛs] n Schach nt; **chessboard** n Schachbrett nt

chest [tʃɛst] n Brust f; (box) Kiste f; **~ of drawers** Kommode f

chestnut ['tʃɛsnʌt] n Kastanie f

chew [tʃuː] vt, vi kauen; **chewing gum** n Kaugummi m

chick [tʃɪk] n Küken nt; **chicken** n Huhn nt; (food: roast) Hähnchen nt; (coward) Feigling m; **chicken breast** n Hühnerbrust f; **chicken Kiev** n paniertes Hähnchen, mit Knoblauchbutter gefüllt; **chickenpox** n Windpocken pl; **chickpea** n Kichererbse f

chicory ['tʃɪkərɪ] n Chicorée f

chief [tʃiːf] n (of department etc) Leiter(in) m(f); (boss) Chef(in) m(f); (of tribe) Häuptling m ▷ adj Haupt-; **chiefly** adv hauptsächlich

child [tʃaɪld] (pl **children**) n Kind nt; **child abuse** n Kindesmisshandlung f; **child allowance**, **child benefit** (Brit) n Kindergeld nt; **childbirth** n Geburt f, Entbindung f; **childhood** n Kindheit f; **childish** adj kindisch; **child lock** n Kindersicherung f; **childproof** adj kindersicher; **children** ['tʃɪldrən] pl of **child**; **child seat** n Kindersitz m

Chile ['tʃɪlɪ] n Chile nt

chill [tʃɪl] n Kühle f; (Med) Erkältung f ▷ vt (wine) kühlen; **chill out** vi (fam) chillen, relaxen; **chilled** adj gekühlt

chilli ['tʃɪlɪ] n Pepperoni pl; (spice) Chili m; **chilli con carne** ['tʃɪlɪkɔn'kɑːnɪ] n Chili con carne nt

chilly ['tʃɪlɪ] adj kühl, frostig

chimney ['tʃɪmnɪ] n Schornstein m; **chimneysweep** n Schornsteinfeger(in) m(f)

chimpanzee [tʃɪmpæn'ziː] n Schimpanse m

chin [tʃɪn] n Kinn nt

china ['tʃaɪnə] n Porzellan nt

China ['tʃaɪnə] n China nt; **Chinese** [tʃaɪ'niːz] adj chinesisch ▷ n (person) Chinese m, Chinesin f; (language) Chinesisch nt; **Chinese leaves** npl Chinakohl m

chip [tʃɪp] n (of wood etc) Splitter m; (damage) angeschlagene Stelle; (Inform) Chip m; **~s** (Brit: potatoes) Pommes (frites) pl; (US: crisps) Kartoffelchips pl ▷ vt anschlagen, beschädigen; **chippie** (fam), **chip shop** n Frittenbude f

chiropodist [kɪ'rɔpədɪst] n Fußpfleger(in) m(f)

chirp [tʃɜːp] vi zwitschern

chisel ['tʃɪzl] n Meißel m

chitchat ['tʃɪttʃæt] n Gerede nt

chives [tʃaɪvz] npl Schnittlauch m

chlorine ['klɔːriːn] n Chlor nt

chocaholic, chocoholic [tʃɒkə'hɒlɪk] n Schokoladenfreak m; **choc-ice** ['tʃɒkaɪs] n Eis nt mit Schokoladenüberzug; **chocolate** ['tʃɒklɪt] n Schokolade f; (chocolate-coated sweet) Praline f; **a bar of ~** eine Tafel Schokolade; **a box of ~s** eine Schachtel Pralinen; **chocolate cake** n Schokoladenkuchen m; **chocolate sauce** n Schokoladensoße f

choice [tʃɔɪs] n Wahl f; (selection) Auswahl f ▷ adj auserlesen; (product) Qualitäts-

choir ['kwaɪə] n Chor m

choke [tʃəʊk] vi sich verschlucken; (Sport) die Nerven verlieren ▷ vt erdrosseln ▷ n (Auto) Choke m

cholera ['kɒlərə] n Cholera f
cholesterol [kə'lestərəl] n Cholesterin nt
chook [tʃuk] n (Aust, NZ fam) Huhn nt
choose [tʃu:z] (**chose**, **chosen**) vt wählen; (pick out) sich aussuchen; **there are three to ~ from** es stehen drei zur Auswahl
chop [tʃɒp] vt (zer)hacken; (meat etc) klein schneiden ▷ n (meat) Kotelett nt; **to get the ~** gefeuert werden; **chopper** n Hackbeil nt; (fam: helicopter) Hubschrauber m; **chopsticks** npl Essstäbchen pl
chorus ['kɔːrəs] n Chor m; (in song) Refrain m
chose, chosen [tʃəʊz, 'tʃəʊzn] pt, pp of **choose**
chowder ['tʃaʊdəʳ] n (US) dicke Suppe mit Meeresfrüchten
christen ['krɪsn] vt taufen; **christening** n Taufe f; **Christian** ['krɪstɪən] adj christlich ▷ n Christ(in) m(f); **Christian name** n (Brit) Vorname m
Christmas ['krɪsməs] n Weihnachten pl; **Christmas card** n Weihnachtskarte f; **Christmas carol** n Weihnachtslied nt; **Christmas Day** n der erste Weihnachtstag; **Christmas Eve** n Heiligabend m; **Christmas pudding** n Plumpudding m; **Christmas tree** n Weihnachtsbaum m
chronic ['krɒnɪk] adj (Med, fig) chronisch; (fam: very bad) miserabel
chrysanthemum [krɪ'sænθɪməm] n Chrysantheme f
chubby ['tʃʌbɪ] adj (child) pummelig; (adult) rundlich
chuck [tʃʌk] vt (fam) schmeißen; **chuck in** vt (fam: job) hinschmeißen; **chuck out** vt (fam) rausschmeißen; **chuck up** vi (fam) kotzen
chunk [tʃʌŋk] n Klumpen m; (of bread) Brocken m; (of meat) Batzen m; **chunky** adj (person) stämmig
Chunnel ['tʃʌnəl] n (fam) Kanaltunnel m
church [tʃɜːtʃ] n Kirche f; **churchyard** n Kirchhof m
chute [ʃuːt] n Rutsche f
chutney ['tʃʌtnɪ] n Chutney m
CIA abbr = **Central Intelligence Agency** (US) CIA f
CID abbr = **Criminal Investigation Department** (Brit) ≈ Kripo f
cider ['saɪdəʳ] n = Apfelmost m
cigar [sɪ'gɑːʳ] n Zigarre f
cigarette [sɪgə'ret] n Zigarette f
cinema ['sɪnəmə] n Kino nt
cinnamon ['sɪnəmən] n Zimt m
circle ['sɜːkl] n Kreis m ▷ vi kreisen; **circuit** ['sɜːkɪt] n Rundfahrt f; (on foot) Rundgang m; (for racing) Rennstrecke f; (Elec) Stromkreis m; **circular** ['sɜːkjʊləʳ] adj (kreis)rund, kreisförmig ▷ n Rundschreiben nt; **circulation** [sɜːkjʊ'leɪʃən] n (of blood) Kreislauf m; (of newspaper) Auflage f
circumstances ['sɜːkəmstənsəz] npl (facts) Umstände pl; (financial condition) Verhältnisse pl; **in/under the ~** unter den Umständen; **under no ~** auf keinen Fall
circus ['sɜːkəs] n Zirkus m
cissy ['sɪsɪ] n (fam) Weichling m
cistern ['sɪstən] n Zisterne f; (of WC) Spülkasten m
citizen ['sɪtɪzn] n Bürger(in) m(f); (of nation) Staatsangehörige(r) mf; **citizenship** n Staatsangehörigkeit f
city ['sɪtɪ] n Stadt f; (large) Großstadt f; **the ~** (London's financial centre) die (Londoner

City; **city centre** n Innenstadt f, Zentrum nt

civil ['sɪvɪl] adj (of town) Bürger-; (of state) staatsbürgerlich; (not military) zivil; **civil ceremony** n standesamtliche Hochzeit; **civil engineering** n Hoch- und Tiefbau m, Bauingenieurwesen nt; **civilian** [sɪ'vɪljən] n Zivilist(in) m(f); **civilization** [sɪvɪlaɪ'zeɪʃən] n Zivilisation f, Kultur f; **civilized** ['sɪvɪlaɪzd] adj zivilisiert, kultiviert; **civil partnership** n eingetragene Partnerschaft; **civil rights** npl Bürgerrechte pl; **civil servant** n (Staats)beamte(r) m, (Staats)beamtin f; **civil service** n Staatsdienst m; **civil war** n Bürgerkrieg m

CJD abbr = **Creutzfeld-Jakob disease** Creutzfeld-Jakob-Krankheit f

cl abbr = **centilitre(s)** cl

claim [kleɪm] vt beanspruchen; (apply for) beantragen; (demand) fordern; (assert) behaupten (that dass) ▷ n (demand) Forderung f (for für); (right) Anspruch m (to auf +akk); **~ for damages** Schadensersatzforderung f; **to make o put in a ~** (insurance) Ansprüche geltend machen; **claimant** n Antragsteller(in) m(f)

clam [klæm] n Venusmuschel f; **clam chowder** n (US) dicke Muschelsuppe (mit Sellerie, Zwiebeln etc)

clap [klæp] vi (Beifall) klatschen

claret ['klærɪt] n roter Bordeaux(wein)

clarify ['klærɪfaɪ] vt klären

clarinet [klærɪ'net] n Klarinette f

clarity ['klærɪtɪ] n Klarheit f

clash [klæʃ] vi (physically) zusammenstoßen (with mit); (argue) sich auseinandersetzen (with mit); (fig: colours) sich beißen ▷ n Zusammenstoß m; (argument) Auseinandersetzung f

clasp [klɑːsp] n (on belt) Schnalle f

class [klɑːs] n Klasse f ▷ vt einordnen, einstufen

classic ['klæsɪk] adj (mistake, example etc) klassisch ▷ n Klassiker m; **classical** ['klæsɪkəl] adj (music, ballet etc) klassisch

classification [klæsɪfɪ'keɪʃn] n Klassifizierung f; **classify** ['klæsɪfaɪ] vt klassifizieren; **classified advertisement** Kleinanzeige f

classroom ['klɑːsrʊm] n Klassenzimmer nt

classy ['klɑːsɪ] adj (fam) nobel, exklusiv

clatter ['klætə*] vi klappern

clause [klɔːz] n (Ling) Satz m; (Jur) Klausel f

claw [klɔː] n Kralle f

clay [kleɪ] n Lehm m; (for pottery) Ton m

clean [kliːn] adj sauber; **~ driving licence** Führerschein ohne Strafpunkte ▷ vt sauber machen; (carpet etc) reinigen; (window, shoes, vegetables) putzen; (wound) säubern; **clean up** vt sauber machen ▷ vi aufräumen; **cleaner** n (person) Putzmann m, Putzfrau f; (substance) Putzmittel nt; **~'s** (firm) Reinigung f

cleanse [klenz] vt reinigen; (wound) säubern; **cleanser** n Reinigungsmittel nt

clear [klɪə*] adj klar; (distinct) deutlich; (conscience) rein; (free, road etc) frei; **to be ~ about sth** sich über etw im Klaren sein ▷ adv: **to stand ~** zurücktreten ▷ vt (road, room etc) räumen; (table) abräumen; (Jur: find innocent) freisprechen (of von) ▷ vi (fog, mist) sich verziehen; (weather) aufklaren; **clear away** vt

wegräumen; (*dishes*) abräumen;
clear off vi (*fam*) abhauen; **clear
up** vi (*tidy up*) aufräumen;
(*weather*) sich aufklären ▷ vt
(*room*) aufräumen; (*litter*)
wegräumen; (*matter*) klären

clearing n Lichtung f; **clearly**
adv klar; (*speak, remember*)
deutlich; (*obviously*) eindeutig;
clearout n Entrümpelungs-
aktion f; **clearway** n (*Brit*) Straße
f mit Halteverbot nt

clench [klɛntʃ] vt (*fist*) ballen;
(*teeth*) zusammenbeißen

clergyman ['klɜːdʒɪmæn] (*pl
-men*) n Geistliche(r) m;
clergywoman ['klɜːdʒɪwʊmən] (*pl
-women*) n Geistliche f

clerk [klɑːk], (US) [klɜːk] n (*in
office*) Büroangestellte(r) m/f; (*US:
salesperson*) Verkäufer(in) m(f)

clever ['klɛvə°] adj schlau, klug;
(*idea*) clever

cliché ['kliːʃeɪ] n Klischee nt

click [klɪk] n Klicken nt; (*Inform*)
Mausklick m ▷ vi klicken; **to ~ on
sth** (*Inform*) etw anklicken; **it ~ed**
(*fam*) ich hab's/er hat's etc
geschnallt, es hat gefunkt, es hat
Klick gemacht; **they ~ed** sie haben
sich gleich verstanden; **click on** vt
(*Inform*) anklicken

client ['klaɪənt] n Kunde m,
Kundin f; (*Jur*) Mandant(in) m(f)

cliff [klɪf] n Klippe f

climate ['klaɪmɪt] n Klima nt;
climate change n Klimawandel
m

climax ['klaɪmæks] n Höhepunkt
m

climb [klaɪm] vi (*person*) klettern;
(*aircraft, sun*) steigen; (*road*)
ansteigen ▷ vt (*mountain*)
besteigen; (*tree etc*) klettern auf
+akk ▷ n Aufstieg m; **climber** n
(*mountaineer*) Bergsteiger(in) m(f);
climbing n Klettern nt,

Bergsteigen nt; **climbing frame** n
Klettergerüst nt

cling [klɪŋ] (**clung, clung**) vi
sich klammern (*to* an +akk); **cling
film**® n Frischhaltefolie f

clinic ['klɪnɪk] n Klinik f; **clinical**
adj klinisch

clip [klɪp] n Klammer f ▷ vt (*fix*)
anklemmen (*to* an +akk);
(*fingernails*) schneiden; **clipboard**
n Klemmbrett nt; **clippers** npl
Schere f; (*for nails*) Zwicker m

cloak [kləʊk] n Umhang m;
cloakroom n (*for coats*)
Garderobe f

clock [klɒk] n Uhr f; (*Auto: fam*)
Tacho m; **round the ~** rund um die
Uhr; **clockwise** adv im
Uhrzeigersinn

clog [klɒg] n Holzschuh m ▷ vt
verstopfen

cloister ['klɔɪstə°] n Kreuzgang
m

clone [kləʊn] n Klon m ▷ vt
klonen

close [kləʊs] adj nahe (*to* +dat);
(*friend, contact*) eng; (*resemblance*)
groß; **~ to the beach** in der Nähe
des Strandes; **~ win** knapper Sieg;
on ~r examination bei näherer o
genauerer Untersuchung ▷ adv
[kləʊs] dicht; **he lives ~ by** er
wohnt ganz in der Nähe ▷ vt
[kləʊz] schließen; (*road*) sperren;
(*discussion, matter*) abschließen-
▷ vi [kləʊz] schließen
▷ n [kləʊz] Ende nt; **close
down** vi schließen; (*factory*)
stillgelegt werden ▷ vt (*shop*)
schließen; (*factory*) stilllegen;
closed adj (*road*) gesperrt;
(*shop etc*) geschlossen; **closed
circuit television** n
Videoüberwachungsanlage f;
closely adv (*related*) eng, nah;
(*packed, follow*) dicht; (*attentively*)
genau

closet ['klɒzɪt] n (esp US) Schrank m

close-up ['kləʊsʌp] n Nahaufnahme f

closing ['kləʊzɪŋ] adj: ~ **date** letzter Termin; (for competition) Einsendeschluss m; ~ **time** (of shop) Ladenschluss m; (Brit: of pub) Polizeistunde f

closure ['kləʊʒə'] n Schließung f; Abschluss m; **to look for** ~ mit etw abschließen wollen

clot [klɒt] n (blood) ~ Blutgerinnsel nt; (fam: idiot) Trottel m ▷ vi (blood) gerinnen

cloth [klɒθ] n (material) Tuch nt; (for cleaning) Lappen m

clothe [kləʊð] vt kleiden; **clothes** [kləʊðz] npl Kleider pl, Kleidung f; **clothes line** n Wäscheleine f; **clothes peg**, **clothespin** (US) n Wäscheklammer f; **clothing** ['kləʊðɪŋ] n Kleidung f

clotted ['klɒtɪd] adj: ~ **cream** dicke Sahne (aus erhitzter Milch)

cloud [klaʊd] n Wolke f; **cloudy** adj (sky) bewölkt; (liquid) trüb

clove [kləʊv] n Gewürznelke f; ~ **of garlic** Knoblauchzehe f

clover ['kləʊvə'] n Klee m; **cloverleaf** (pl -**leaves**) n Kleeblatt nt

clown [klaʊn] n Clown m

club [klʌb] n (weapon) Knüppel m; (society) Klub m, Verein m; (nightclub) Disko f; (golf club) Golfschläger m; ~**s** (Cards) Kreuz nt; **clubbing** n: **to go** ~ in die Disko gehen; **club class** n (Aviat) Businessclass f

clue [kluː] n Anhaltspunkt m, Hinweis m; **he hasn't a** ~ er hat keine Ahnung

clumsy ['klʌmzɪ] adj unbeholfen, ungeschickt

clung [klʌŋ] pt, pp of **cling**

clutch [klʌtʃ] n (Auto) Kupplung f ▷ vt umklammern; (book etc) an sich akk klammern

cm abbr = **centimetre(s)** cm

c/o abbr = **care of** bei

Co abbr = **company** Co

coach [kəʊtʃ] n (Brit: bus) Reisebus m; (Rail) (Personen)wagen m; (Sport: trainer) Trainer(in) m(f) ▷ vt Nachhilfeunterricht geben +dat; (Sport) trainieren; **coach (class)** n (Aviat) Economyclass f; **coach driver** n Busfahrer(in) m(f); **coach party** n Reisegruppe f (Bus); **coach station** n Busbahnhof m; **coach trip** n Busfahrt f; (tour) Busreise f

coal [kəʊl] n Kohle f

coalition [kəʊə'lɪʃən] n (Pol) Koalition f

coalmine ['kəʊlmaɪn] n Kohlenbergwerk nt; **coalminer** n Bergarbeiter m

coast [kəʊst] n Küste f; **coastguard** n Küstenwache f; **coastline** n Küste f

coat [kəʊt] n Mantel m; (jacket) Jacke f; (on animals) Fell nt, Pelz m; (of paint) Schicht f; ~ **of arms** Wappen nt; **coathanger** n Kleiderbügel m; **coating** n Überzug m; (layer) Schicht f

cobble(stone)s ['kɒbl(stəʊn)z] npl Kopfsteine pl; (surface) Kopfsteinpflaster nt

cobweb ['kɒbweb] n Spinnennetz nt

cocaine [kə'keɪn] n Kokain nt

cock [kɒk] n Hahn m; (vulg: penis) Schwanz m; **cock up** vt (Brit fam) vermasseln, versauen; **cockerel** ['kɒkərəl] n junger Hahn

cockle ['kɒkl] n Herzmuschel f

cockpit ['kɒkpɪt] n (in plane, racing car) Cockpit nt; **cockroach** ['kɒkrəʊtʃ] n Kakerlake f; **cocktail**

['kɒkteɪl] n Cocktail m; **cock-up** n (Brit fam) **to make a ~ of sth** bei etw Mist bauen; **cocky** ['kɒkɪ] adj großspurig, von sich selbst überzeugt

cocoa ['kəʊkəʊ] n Kakao m

coconut ['kəʊkənʌt] n Kokosnuss f

cod [kɒd] n Kabeljau m

COD abbr = **cash on delivery** per Nachnahme

code [kəʊd] n Kode m

coeducational [kəʊedjʊ'keɪʃənl] adj (school) gemischt

coffee ['kɒfɪ] n Kaffee m; **coffee bar** n Café nt; **coffee break** n Kaffeepause f; **coffee machine** n Kaffeemaschine f; **coffee pot** n Kaffeekanne f; **coffee shop** n Café nt; **coffee table** n Couchtisch m

coffin ['kɒfɪn] n Sarg m

coil [kɔɪl] n Rolle f; (Elec) Spule f; (Med) Spirale f

coin [kɔɪn] n Münze f

coincide [kəʊɪn'saɪd] vi (happen together) zusammenfallen (with mit); **coincidence** [kəʊ'ɪnsɪdəns] n Zufall m

coke [kəʊk] n Koks m; **Coke®** Cola f

cola ['kəʊlə] n Cola f

cold [kəʊld] adj kalt; **I'm ~** mir ist kalt, ich friere ▷ n Kälte f; (illness) Erkältung f, Schnupfen m; **to catch a ~** sich erkälten; **cold box** n Kühlbox f; **cold sore** n Herpes m; **cold turkey** n (fam) Totalentzug m; (symptoms) Entzugserscheinungen pl

coleslaw ['kəʊlslɔː] n Krautsalat m

collaborate [kə'læbəreɪt] vi zusammenarbeiten (with mit); **collaboration** [kəlæbə'reɪʃən] n Zusammenarbeit f; (of one party) Mitarbeit f

collapse [kə'læps] vi zusammenbrechen; (building etc) einstürzen ▷ n Zusammenbruch m; (of building) Einsturz m; **collapsible** [kə'læpsəbl] adj zusammenklappbar, Klapp-

collar ['kɒlə°] n Kragen m; (for dog, cat) Halsband nt; **collarbone** n Schlüsselbein nt

colleague ['kɒliːg] n Kollege m, Kollegin f

collect [kə'lekt] vt sammeln; (fetch) abholen ▷ vi sich sammeln; **collect call** n (US) R-Gespräch nt; **collected** adj (works) gesammelt; (person) gefasst; **collector** n Sammler(in) m(f); **collection** [kə'lekʃən] n Sammlung f; (Rel) Kollekte f; (from postbox) Leerung f

college ['kɒlɪdʒ] n (residential) College nt; (specialist) Fachhochschule f; (vocational) Berufsschule f; (US: university) Universität f; **to go to ~** (US) studieren

collide [kə'laɪd] vi zusammenstoßen; **collision** [kə'lɪʒən] n Zusammenstoß m

colloquial [kə'ləʊkwɪəl] adj umgangssprachlich

Cologne [kə'ləʊn] n Köln nt

colon ['kəʊlən] n (punctuation mark) Doppelpunkt m

colonial [kə'ləʊnɪəl] adj Kolonial-; **colonize** ['kɒlənaɪz] vt kolonisieren; **colony** ['kɒlənɪ] n. Kolonie f

color n (US), **colour** ['kʌlə°] n Farbe f; (of skin) Hautfarbe f ▷ vt anmalen; (bias) färben; **colour-blind** adj farbenblind; **coloured** adj farbig; (biased) gefärbt; **colour film** n Farbfilm m; **colourful** adj (lit, fig) bunt; (life, past) bewegt; **colouring** n (in food etc) Farbstoff m; (complexion) Gesichtsfarbe f; **colourless** adj *(lit, fig)* farblos; **colour photo(graph)** n Farbfoto nt; **colour television** n Farbfernsehen nt

column ['kɒləm] n Säule f; *(of print)* Spalte f

comb [kəʊm] n Kamm m ▷ vt kämmen; **to ~ one's hair** sich kämmen

combination [kɒmbɪ'neɪʃən] n Kombination f; *(mixture)* Mischung f *(of aus)*; **combine** [kəm'baɪn] vt verbinden *(with mit)*; *(two things)* kombinieren

come [kʌm] *(came, come)* vi kommen; *(arrive)* ankommen; *(on list, in order)* stehen; *(with adjective: become)* werden; **~ and see us** besuchen Sie uns mal; **coming** ich komm ja schon!; **to ~ first/second** erster/zweiter werden; **to ~ true** wahr werden; **to ~ loose** sich lockern; **the years to ~** die kommenden Jahre; **there's one more to ~** es kommt noch eins/noch einer; **how ~ ...?** *(fam)* wie kommt es, dass ...?; **~ to think of it** *(fam)* wo es mir gerade einfällt; **come across** vt *(find)* stoßen auf +akk; **come back** vi zurückkommen; **I'll ~ to that** ich komme darauf zurück; **come down** vi herunterkommen; *(rain, snow, price)* fallen; **come from** vt *(result)* kommen von; **where do you ~?** ich komme aus London!; **come in** vi hereinkommen; *(arrive)* ankommen; *(in race)* **to ~ fourth** Vierter werden; **come off** vi *(button, handle etc)* abgehen; *(succeed)* gelingen; **~ well/badly** gut/schlecht wegkommen; **come on** vi *(progress)* vorankommen; **~!** komm!; *(hurry)* beeil dich!; *(encouraging)* los!; **come out** vi

herauskommen; *(photo)* was werden; *(homosexual)* sich outen; **come round** vi *(visit)* vorbeikommen; *(regain consciousness)* wieder zu sich kommen; **come to** vi *(regain consciousness)* wieder zu sich kommen ▷ vt *(sum)* sich belaufen auf +akk; **when it comes to ...** wenn es um ... geht; **come up** vi hochkommen; *(sun, moon)* aufgehen; **to ~ (for discussion)** zur Sprache kommen; **come up to** vt *(approach)* zukommen auf +akk; *(water)* reichen bis zu; *(expectations)* entsprechen +dat; **come up with** vt *(idea)* haben; *(solution, answer)* kommen auf +akk; **to ~ a suggestion** einen Vorschlag machen

comedian [kə'miːdɪən] n Komiker(in) m(f)

comedown ['kʌmdaʊn] n Abstieg m

comedy ['kɒmədɪ] n Komödie f, Comedy f

comfort ['kʌmfət] n Komfort m; *(consolation)* Trost m ▷ vt trösten; **comfortable** adj bequem; *(income)* ausreichend; *(temperature, life)* angenehm; **comforting** adj tröstlich

comic ['kɒmɪk] n *(magazine)* Comic(heft) nt; *(comedian)* Komiker(in) m(f) ▷ adj komisch

coming ['kʌmɪŋ] adj kommend; *(event)* bevorstehend

comma ['kɒmə] n Komma nt

command [kə'mɑːnd] n Befehl m; *(control)* Führung f; *(Mil)* Kommando nt ▷ vt befehlen +dat

commemorate [kə'meməreɪt] vt gedenken +gen; **commemoration** [kəmemə'reɪʃən] n: **in ~ of** in Gedenken an +akk

comment ['kɒment] n *(remark)*

Bemerkung f; (note) Anmerkung f; (official) Kommentar m (on zu); **no** ~ kein Kommentar ▷ vi sich äußern (on zu); **commentary** ['kɒməntri] n Kommentar m (on zu); (TV, Sport) Livereportage f; **commentator** ['kɒmənteɪtə°] n Kommentator(in) m(f); (TV, Sport) Reporter(in) m(f)

commerce ['kɒmɜːs] n Handel m; **commercial** [kə'mɜːʃəl] adj kommerziell; (training) kaufmännisch; ~ **break** Werbepause f; ~ **vehicle** Lieferwagen m ▷ n (TV) Werbespot m

commission [kə'mɪʃən] n Auftrag m; (fee) Provision f; (reporting body) Kommission f ▷ vt beauftragen

commit [kə'mɪt] vt (crime) begehen ▷ vr: **to** ~ **oneself** (undertake) sich verpflichten (to zu); **commitment** n Verpflichtung f; (Pol) Engagement nt

committee [kə'mɪtɪ] n Ausschuss m, Komitee nt

commodity [kə'mɒdɪtɪ] n Ware f

common ['kɒmən] adj (experience) allgemein, alltäglich; (shared) gemeinsam; (widespread, frequent) häufig; (pej) gewöhnlich, ordinär; **to have sth in** ~ etw gemein haben ▷ n (Brit: land) Gemeindewiese f; **commonly** adv häufig, allgemein; **commonplace** adj alltäglich; (pej) banal; **commonroom** n Gemeinschaftsraum m; **Commons** n (Brit Pol) **the (House of)** ~ das Unterhaus; **common sense** n gesunder Menschenverstand; **Commonwealth** n Commonwealth nt; ~ **of Independent States** Gemeinschaft f Unabhängiger Staaten

communal ['kɒmjuːnl] adj gemeinsam; (of a community) Gemeinschafts-, Gemeinde-

communicate [kə'mjuːnɪkeɪt] vi kommunizieren (with mit); **communication** [kəmjuːnɪ'keɪʃən] n Kommunikation f, Verständigung f; **communications satellite** n Nachrichtensatellit m; **communications technology** n Nachrichtentechnik f; **communicative** adj gesprächig

communion [kə'mjuːnɪən] n: **(Holy) Communion** Heiliges Abendmahl; (Catholic) Kommunion f

communism ['kɒmjunɪzəm] n Kommunismus m; **communist** ['kɒmjunɪst] adj kommunistisch ▷ n Kommunist(in) m(f)

community [kə'mjuːnɪtɪ] n Gemeinschaft f; **community centre** n Gemeindezentrum nt; **community service** n (Jur) Sozialdienst m

commutation ticket [kɒmjuː'teɪʃəntɪkɪt] n (US) Zeitkarte f; **commute** [kə'mjuːt] vi pendeln; **commuter** n Pendler(in) m(f)

compact [kəm'pækt] adj kompakt ▷ ['kɒmpækt] n (for make-up) Puderdose f; (US: car) ≈ Mittelklassewagen m; **compact camera** n Kompaktkamera f; **compact disc** n Compact Disc f, CD f

companion [kəm'pænɪən] n Begleiter(in) m(f)

company ['kʌmpənɪ] n Gesellschaft f; (Comm) Firma f; **to keep sb** ~ jdm Gesellschaft leisten; **company car** n Firmenauto nt

comparable ['kɒmpərəbl] adj vergleichbar (with, to mit)

comparative [kəm'pærətɪv] adj relativ ▷ n (Ling) Komparativ m; **comparatively** adv verhältnismäßig

compare [kəm'pɛəʳ] vt vergleichen (with, to mit); **~d with** o **to** im Vergleich zu; **beyond ~** unvergleichlich; **comparison** [kəm'pærɪsn] n Vergleich m; **in ~ with** im Vergleich mit (o zu)

compartment [kəm'pɑ:tmənt] n (Rail) Abteil nt; (in desk etc) Fach nt

compass ['kʌmpəs] n Kompass m; **~es** pl Zirkel m

compassion [kəm'pæʃən] n Mitgefühl nt

compatible [kəm'pætɪbl] adj vereinbar (with mit); (Inform) kompatibel; **we're not ~** wir passen nicht zueinander

compensate ['kɒmpenseɪt] vt (person) entschädigen (for für) ▷ vi: **to ~ for sth** Ersatz für etw leisten; (make up for) etw ausgleichen; **compensation** [kɒmpen'seɪʃən] n Entschädigung f; (money) Schadenersatz m; (Jur) Abfindung f

compete [kəm'pi:t] vi konkurrieren (for um); (Sport) kämpfen (for um); (take part) teilnehmen (in an +dat)

competence ['kɒmpɪtəns] n Fähigkeit f; (Jur) Zuständigkeit f; **competent** adj fähig; (Jur) zuständig

competition [kɒmpɪ'tɪʃən] n (contest) Wettbewerb m; (Comm) Konkurrenz f (for um); **competitive** [kəm'petɪtɪv] adj (firm, price, product) konkurrenzfähig; **competitor** [kəm'petɪtəʳ] n (Comm) Konkurrent(in) m(f); (Sport) Teilnehmer(in) m(f)

complain [kəm'pleɪn] vi klagen; (formally) sich beschweren (about über +akk); **complaint** n Klage f; Beanstandung f; (formal) Beschwerde f; (Med) Leiden nt

complement vt ergänzen

complete [kəm'pli:t] adj vollständig; (finished) fertig; (failure, disaster) total; (happiness) vollkommen; **are we ~?** sind wir vollzählig? ▷ vt vervollständigen; (finish) beenden; (form) ausfüllen; **completely** adv völlig; **not ~ ...** nicht ganz ...

complex ['kɒmpleks] adj komplex; (task, theory etc) kompliziert ▷ n Komplex m

complexion [kəm'plekʃən] n Gesichtsfarbe f, Teint m

complicated ['kɒmplɪkeɪtɪd] adj kompliziert; **complication** ['kɒmplɪkeɪʃən] n Komplikation f

compliment ['kɒmplɪmənt] n Kompliment nt; **complimentary** [kɒmplɪ'mentərɪ] adj lobend; (free of charge) Gratis-; **~ ticket** Freikarte f

comply [kəm'plaɪ] vi: **to ~ with the regulations** den Vorschriften entsprechen

component [kəm'pəʊnənt] n Bestandteil m

compose [kəm'pəʊz] vt (music) komponieren; **to ~ oneself** sich zusammennehmen; **composed** adj gefasst; **to be ~ of** bestehen aus; **composer** n Komponist(in) m(f); **composition** [kɒmpə'zɪʃən] n (of a group) Zusammensetzung f; (Mus) Komposition f

comprehend [kɒmprɪ'hend] vt verstehen; **comprehension** [kɒmprɪ'henʃən] n Verständnis nt

comprehensive [kɒmprɪ'hensɪv] adj umfassend; **~ school** Gesamtschule f

compress [kəm'pres] vt
komprimieren

comprise [kəm'praɪz] vt
umfassen, bestehen aus

compromise ['kɒmprəmaɪz] n
Kompromiss m ▷ vi einen
Kompromiss schließen

compulsory [kəm'pʌlsərɪ] adj
obligatorisch; **~ subject**
Pflichtfach nt

computer [kəm'pjuːtə*] n
Computer m; **computer-aided** adj
computergestützt;
computer-controlled adj rech-
nergesteuert; **computer game** n
Computerspiel nt;
computer-literate adj: **to be**
~ mit dem Computer umgehen
können; **computer scientist** n
Informatiker(in) m(f); **computing**
n (subject) Informatik f

con [kɒn] (fam) n Schwindel m
▷ vt betrügen (out of um)

conceal [kən'siːl] vt verbergen
(from vor +dat)

conceivable [kən'siːvəbl] adj
denkbar, vorstellbar; **conceive**
[kən'siːv] vt (imagine) sich
vorstellen; (child) empfangen

concentrate ['kɒnsəntreɪt] vi
sich konzentrieren (on auf +akk);
concentration [kɒnsən'treɪʃən]
n Konzentration f

concept ['kɒnsept] n Begriff m

concern [kən'sɜːn] n (affair)
Angelegenheit f; (worry) Sorge f;
(Comm: firm) Unternehmen nt; **it's**
not my ~ das geht mich nichts an;
there's no cause for ~ kein Grund
zur Beunruhigung ▷ vt (affect)
angehen; (have connection with)
betreffen; (be about) handeln von;
those ~ed die Betroffenen; **as far**
as I'm ~ed was mich betrifft;
concerned adj (anxious) besorgt;
concerning prep bezüglich,
hinsichtlich +gen

concert ['kɒnsət] n Konzert nt;
~ hall Konzertsaal m

concession [kən'seʃən] n Zu-
geständnis nt; (reduction)
Ermäßigung f

concise [kən'saɪs] adj knapp
gefasst, prägnant

conclude [kən'kluːd] vt (end)
beenden, (ab)schließen; (infer)
folgern (from aus); **to ~ that ...** zu
dem Schluss kommen, dass ...;
conclusion [kən'kluːʒən] n
Schluss m, Schlussfolgerung f

concrete ['kɒŋkriːt] n Beton m
▷ adj konkret

concussion [kən'kʌʃən] n
Gehirnerschütterung f

condemn [kən'dem] vt
verdammen; (esp Jur)
verurteilen

condensed milk n
Kondensmilch f, Dosenmilch f

condition [kən'dɪʃən] n (state)
Zustand m; (requirement)
Bedingung f; **on ~ that ...** unter
der Bedingung, dass ...; **~s** pl
(circumstances, weather)
Verhältnisse pl; **conditional** adj
bedingt; (Ling) Konditional-;
conditioner n Weichspüler m; (for
hair) Pflegespülung f

condo ['kɒndəʊ] (pl **-s**) n see
condominium

condolences [kən'dəʊlənsɪz]
npl Beileid nt

condom ['kɒndəm] n Kondom nt

condominium [kɒndə'mɪnɪəm]
n (US: apartment)
Eigentumswohnung f

conduct ['kɒndʌkt] n (behaviour)
Verhalten nt ▷ [kən'dʌkt] vt
führen, leiten; (orchestra)
dirigieren; **conductor**
[kən'dʌktə*] n (of orchestra)
Dirigent(in) m(f); (Brit: in bus)
Schaffner(in) m(f); (US: on train)
Zugführer(in) m(f)

cone [kəʊn] n Kegel m; (for ice cream) Waffeltüte f; (fir cone) (Tannen)zapfen m

conference ['kɒnfərəns] n Konferenz f

confess [kən'fes] vt, vi: **to ~ that ...** gestehen, dass ...; **confession** [kən'feʃən] n Geständnis nt; (Rel) Beichte f

confetti [kən'feti] n Konfetti nt

confidence ['kɒnfɪdəns] n Vertrauen nt (in zu); (assurance) Selbstvertrauen nt; **confident** adj (sure) zuversichtlich (that ... dass ...), überzeugt (of von); (self-assured) selbstsicher; **confidential** [kɒnfɪ'denʃəl] adj vertraulich

confine [kən'faɪn] vt beschränken (to auf +akk)

confirm [kən'fɜːm] vt bestätigen; **confirmation** [kɒnfə'meɪʃən] n Bestätigung f; (Rel) Konfirmation f; **confirmed** adj überzeugt; (bachelor) eingefleischt

confiscate ['kɒnfɪskeɪt] vt beschlagnahmen, konfiszieren

conflict ['kɒnflɪkt] n Konflikt m

confuse [kən'fjuːz] vt verwirren (sth with sth) verwechseln (with mit); (several things) durcheinanderbringen; **confused** adj (person) konfus, verwirrt; (account) verworren; **confusing** adj verwirrend; **confusion** [kən'fjuːʒən] n Verwirrung f; (of two things) Verwechslung f; (muddle) Chaos nt

congested [kən'dʒestɪd] adj verstopft; (overcrowded) überfüllt; **congestion** [kən'dʒestʃən] n Stau m

congratulate [kən'grætjʊleɪt] vt gratulieren (on zu); **congratulations** [kəngrætjʊ'leɪʃənz] npl Glück-

wünsche pl; **~!** gratuliere!, herzlichen Glückwunsch!

congregation [kɒŋgrɪ'geɪʃən] n (Rel) Gemeinde f

congress ['kɒŋgres] n Kongress m; (US) **Congress** der Kongress; **congressman** (pl **-men**), **congresswoman** (pl **-women**) n (US) Mitglied m des Repräsentantenhauses

conifer ['kɒnɪfəʳ] n Nadelbaum m

conjunction [kən'dʒʌŋkʃən] n (Ling) Konjunktion f; **in ~ with** in Verbindung mit

conk out [kɒŋk 'aʊt] vi (fam: appliance, car) den Geist aufgeben, streiken; (person: die) ins Gras beißen

connect [kə'nekt] vt verbinden (with, to mit); (Elec, Tech: appliance etc) anschließen (to an +akk) ▷ vi (train, plane) Anschluss haben (with an +akk); **~ing flight** Anschlussflug m; **~ing train** Anschlusszug m; **connection** [kə'nekʃən] n Verbindung f; (link) Zusammenhang m; (for train, plane, electrical appliance) Anschluss m (with, to an +akk); (business etc) Beziehung f; **in ~ with** in Zusammenhang mit; **bad ~** (Tel) schlechte Verbindung; (Elec) Wackelkontakt m; **connector** n (Inform: computer) Stecker m

conscience ['kɒnʃəns] n Gewissen nt; **conscientious** [kɒnʃɪ'enʃəs] adj gewissenhaft

conscious ['kɒnʃəs] adj (act) bewusst; (Med) bei Bewusstsein; **to be ~** bei Bewusstsein sein; **consciousness** n Bewusstsein nt

consecutive [kən'sekjʊtɪv] adj aufeinanderfolgend

consent [kən'sent] n Zustimmung f ▷ vi zustimmen (to dat)

consequence ['kɒnsɪkwəns] n Folge f, Konsequenz f; **consequently** ['kɒnsɪkwəntlɪ] adv folglich, deshalb

conservation [kɒnsə'veɪʃən] n Erhaltung f; (nature conservation) Naturschutz m; **conservation area** n Naturschutzgebiet nt

conservative (Pol) **Conservative** [kən'sɜːvətɪv] adj konservativ

conservatory [kən'sɜːvətrɪ] n (greenhouse) Gewächshaus nt; (room) Wintergarten m

consider [kən'sɪdə°] vt (reflect on) nachdenken über, sich überlegen; (take into account) in Betracht ziehen; (regard) halten für; **he is ~ed (to be) ...** er gilt als ...; **considerable** [kən'sɪdərəbl] adj beträchtlich; **considerate** [kən'sɪdərɪt] adj aufmerksam, rücksichtsvoll; **consideration** [kənsɪdə'reɪʃən] n (thoughtfulness) Rücksicht f; (thought) Überlegung f; **to take sth into ~** etw in Betracht ziehen; **considering** [kən'sɪdərɪŋ] prep in Anbetracht +gen ▷ conj da

consist [kən'sɪst] vi: **to ~ of ...** bestehen aus ...

consistent [kən'sɪstənt] adj (behaviour, process etc) konsequent; (statements) übereinstimmend; (argument) folgerichtig; (performance, results) beständig

consolation [kɒnsə'leɪʃən] n Trost m; **console** [kən'səʊl] vt trösten

consolidate [kən'sɒlɪdeɪt] vt festigen

consonant ['kɒnsənənt] n Konsonant m

conspicuous [kən'spɪkjuəs] adj auffällig, auffallend

conspiracy [kən'spɪrəsɪ] n Komplott nt; **conspire**

[kən'spaɪə°] vi sich verschwören (against gegen)

constable ['kʌnstəbl] n (Brit) Polizist(in) m(f)

Constance ['kɒnstəns] n Konstanz nt; **Lake ~** der Bodensee

constant ['kɒnstənt] adj (continual) ständig, dauernd; (unchanging: temperature etc) gleichbleibend; **constantly** adv dauernd

consternation [kɒnstə'neɪʃən] n (dismay) Bestürzung f

constituency [kən'stɪtjʊənsɪ] n Wahlkreis m

constitution [kɒnstɪ'tjuːʃən] n Verfassung f; (of person) Konstitution f

construct [kən'strʌkt] vt bauen; **construction** [kən'strʌkʃən] n (process, result) Bau m; (method) Bauweise f; **under ~** im Bau befindlich; **construction site** n Baustelle f; **construction worker** n Bauarbeiter(in) m(f)

consulate ['kɒnsjʊlət] n Konsulat nt

consult [kən'sʌlt] vt um Rat fragen; (doctor) konsultieren; (book) nachschlagen in +dat; **consultant** n (Med) Facharzt m, Fachärztin f; **consultation** [kɒnsəl'teɪʃən] n Beratung f; (Med) Konsultation f; **~ room** n Besprechungsraum; Sprechzimmer

consume [kən'sjuːm] vt verbrauchen; (food) konsumieren; **consumer** n Verbraucher(in) m(f); **consumer-friendly** adj verbraucherfreundlich

contact ['kɒntækt] n (touch) Berührung f; (communication) Kontakt m; (person) Kontaktperson f; **to be/keep in ~ (with sb)** (mit jdm) in Kontakt sein/bleiben ▷ vt sich in Verbindung setzen mit;

contact lenses *npl* Kontaktlinsen *pl*

contagious [kən'teɪdʒəs] *adj* ansteckend

contain [kən'teɪn] *vt* enthalten; **container** *n* Behälter *m*; (for transport) Container *m*

contaminate [kən'tæmɪneɪt] *vt* verunreinigen; (chemically) verseuchen; **~d by radiation** strahlenverseucht, verstrahlt; **contamination** [kəntæmɪ'neɪʃən] *n* Verunreinigung *f*; (by radiation) Verseuchung *f*

contemporary [kən'tempərərɪ] *adj* zeitgenössisch

contempt [kən'tempt] *n* Verachtung *f*; **contemptuous** *adj* verächtlich; **to be ~** voller Verachtung sein (of für)

content [kən'tent] *adj* zufrieden

content(s) ['kɒntent(s)] *n pl* Inhalt *m*

contest ['kɒntest] *n* (Wett)kampf *m* (for um); (competition) Wettbewerb *m* ▷ [kən'test] *vt* kämpfen um +akk; (dispute) bestreiten; **contestant** [kən'testənt] *n* Teilnehmer(in) *m(f)*

context ['kɒntekst] *n* Zusammenhang *m*; **out of ~** aus dem Zusammenhang gerissen

continent ['kɒntɪnənt] *n* Kontinent *m*, Festland *nt*; **the Continent** (Brit) das europäische Festland, der Kontinent; **continental** [kɒntɪ'nentl] *adj* kontinental; **~ breakfast** kleines Frühstück mit Brötchen und Marmelade, Kaffee oder Tee

continual [kən'tɪnjʊəl] *adj* (endless) ununterbrochen; (constant) dauernd, ständig; **continually** *adv* dauernd; (again and again) immer wieder; **continuation** [kəntɪnjʊ'eɪʃən] *n*

Fortsetzung *f*; **continue** [kən'tɪnjuː] *vi* weitermachen (with mit); (esp talking) fortfahren (with mit); (travelling) weiterfahren; (state, conditions) fortdauern, anhalten ▷ *vt* fortsetzen; **to be ~d** Fortsetzung folgt; **continuous** [kən'tɪnjʊəs] *adj* (endless) ununterbrochen; (constant) ständig

contraceptive [kɒntrə'septɪv] *n* Verhütungsmittel *nt*

contract ['kɒntrækt] *n* Vertrag *m*

contradict [kɒntrə'dɪkt] *vt* widersprechen +dat; **contradiction** [kɒntrə'dɪkʃən] *n* Widerspruch *m*

contrary ['kɒntrərɪ] *n* Gegenteil *nt*; **on the ~** im Gegenteil ▷ *adj*: **~ to** entgegen +dat

contrast ['kɒntrɑːst] *n* Kontrast *m*, Gegensatz *m*; **in ~ to** im Gegensatz zu ▷ [kən'trɑːst] *vt* entgegensetzen

contribute [kən'trɪbjuːt] *vt, vi* beitragen (to zu); (money) spenden (to für); **contribution** [kɒntrɪ'bjuːʃən] *n* Beitrag *m*

control [kən'trəʊl] *vt* (master) beherrschen; (temper etc) im Griff haben; (esp Tech) steuern; **to ~ oneself** sich beherrschen ▷ *n* Kontrolle *f*; (mastery) Beherrschung *f*; (esp Tech) Steuerung *f*; **~s** *pl* (knobs, switches etc) Bedienungselemente *pl*; (collectively) Steuerung *f*; **to be out of ~** außer Kontrolle sein; **control knob** *n* Bedienungsknopf *m*; **control panel** *n* Schalttafel *f*

controversial [kɒntrə'vɜːʃəl] *adj* umstritten

convalesce [kɒnvə'les] *vi* gesund werden; **convalescence** *n* Genesung *f*

convenience [kən'viːnɪəns] *n* (quality, thing) Annehmlichkeit *f*; **at**

your ~ wann es Ihnen passt; **with all modern ~s** mit allem Komfort; **convenience food** n Fertiggericht nt; **convenient** adj günstig, passend

convent ['kɒnvənt] n Kloster nt

convention [kən'venʃən] n (custom) Konvention f; (meeting) Konferenz f; **the Geneva Convention** die Genfer Konvention; **conventional** adj herkömmlich, konventionell

conversation [kɒnvə'seɪʃən] n Gespräch nt, Unterhaltung f

conversion [kən'vɜːʃən] n Umwandlung f (into in +akk); (of building) Umbau m (into zu); (calculation) Umrechnung f; **conversion table** n Umrechnungstabelle f; **convert** [kən'vɜːt] vt umwandeln; (person) bekehren; (Inform) konvertieren; **to ~ into euros** in Euro umrechnen; **convertible** n (Auto) Kabrio nt ▷ adj umwandelbar

convey [kən'veɪ] vt (carry) befördern; (feelings) vermitteln; **conveyor belt** n Förderband nt, Fließband nt

convict [kən'vɪkt] vt verurteilen (of wegen) n ['kɒnvɪkt] Strafgefangene(r) mf; **conviction** n (Jur) Verurteilung f; (strong belief) Überzeugung f

convince [kən'vɪns] vt überzeugen (of von); **convincing** adj überzeugend

cook [kʊk] vt, vi kochen ▷ n Koch m, Köchin f; **cookbook** n Kochbuch nt; **cooker** n Herd m; **cookery** n Kochkunst f; **~ book** Kochbuch nt; **cookie** n (US) Keks m; **cooking** n Kochen nt; (style of cooking) Küche f

cool [kuːl] adj kühl, gelassen; (fam: brilliant) cool, stark ▷ vt, vi (ab)kühlen; **~ it** reg dich ab! ▷ n:

to keep/lose one's ~ (fam) ruhig bleiben/durchdrehen; **cool down** vi abkühlen; (calm down) sich beruhigen

cooperate [kəʊ'ɒpəreɪt] vi zusammenarbeiten, kooperieren; **cooperation** [kəʊɒpə'reɪʃən] n Zusammenarbeit f, Kooperation f; **cooperative** [kəʊ'ɒpərətɪv] adj hilfsbereit ▷ n Genossenschaft f

coordinate [kəʊ'ɔːdɪneɪt] vt koordinieren

cop [kɒp] n (fam: policeman) Bulle m

cope [kəʊp] vi zurechtkommen, fertig werden (with mit)

Copenhagen [kəʊpən'heɪgən] n Kopenhagen nt

copier ['kɒpɪə] n Kopierer m

copper ['kɒpə] n Kupfer nt; (Brit fam: policeman) Bulle m; (fam: coin) Kupfermünze f; **~s** Kleingeld nt

copy ['kɒpɪ] n Kopie f; (of book) Exemplar nt ▷ vt kopieren; (imitate) nachahmen; **copyright** n Urheberrecht nt

coral ['kɒrəl] n Koralle f

cord [kɔːd] n Schnur f; (material) Kordsamt m; **cordless** ['kɔːdlɪs] adj (phone) schnurlos

core [kɔː*] n (a. fig) Kern m; (of apple, pear) Kerngehäuse nt; **core business** n Kerngeschäft nt

cork [kɔːk] n (material) Kork m; (stopper) Korken m; **corkscrew** ['kɔːkskruː] n Korkenzieher m

corn [kɔːn] n Getreide nt, Korn nt; (US: maize) Mais m; (on foot) Hühnerauge nt; **~ on the cob** (gekochter) Maiskolben; **corned beef** n Cornedbeef nt

corner ['kɔːnə*] n Ecke f; (on road) Kurve f; (Sport) Eckstoß m ▷ vt in die Enge treiben; **corner shop** n Laden m an der Ecke

cornflakes ['kɔːfleɪks] npl Cornflakes pl

Cornish ['kɔːnɪʃ] adj kornisch; ~ **pasty** mit Fleisch und Kartoffeln gefüllte Pastete; **Cornwall** ['kɔːnwəl] n Cornwall nt

coronation [kɒrə'neɪʃən] n Krönung f

corporation [kɔːpə'reɪʃən] n (US Comm) Aktiengesellschaft f

corpse [kɔːps] n Leiche f

correct [kə'rekt] adj (accurate) richtig; (proper) korrekt ▷ vt korrigieren, verbessern; **correction** n (esp written) Korrektur f

correspond [kɒrɪ'spɒnd] vi entsprechen (to dat); (two things) übereinstimmen; (exchange letters) korrespondieren; **corresponding** adj entsprechend

corridor ['kɒrɪdɔː] n (in building) Flur m; (in train) Gang m

corrupt [kə'rʌpt] adj korrupt

cosmetic [kɒz'metɪk] adj kosmetisch; **cosmetics** npl Kosmetika pl; **cosmetic surgeon** n Schönheitschirurg(in) m(f); **cosmetic surgery** n Schönheitschirurgie f

cosmopolitan [kɒzmə'pɒlɪtən] adj international; (attitude) weltoffen

cost [kɒst] (cost, cost) vt kosten ▷ n Kosten pl; **at all ~s, at any ~** um jeden Preis; **~ of living** Lebenshaltungskosten pl; **costly** adj kostspielig

costume ['kɒstjuːm] n (Theat) Kostüm n

cosy ['kəʊzɪ] adj gemütlich

cot [kɒt] n (Brit) Kinderbett nt; (US) Campingliege f

cottage ['kɒtɪdʒ] n kleines Haus; (country cottage) Landhäuschen nt; **cottage cheese** n Hüttenkäse m; **cottage pie** n Hackfleisch mit Kartoffelbrei überbacken

cotton ['kɒtn] n Baumwolle f;

cotton candy n (US) Zuckerwatte f; **cotton wool** n (Brit) Watte f

couch [kaʊtʃ] n Couch f; (sofa) Sofa nt; **couchette** [kuː'ʃet] n Liegewagen(platz) m

cough [kɒf] vi husten ▷ n Husten m; **cough mixture** n Hustensaft m; **cough sweet** n Hustenbonbon nt

could [kʊd] pt of **can** konnte; conditional könnte; **~ you come earlier?** könntest du/könnten Sie früher kommen?

couldn't contr of **could not**

council ['kaʊnsl] n (Pol) Rat m; (local ~) Gemeinderat m; (town ~) Stadtrat m; **council estate** n Siedlung f des sozialen Wohnungsbaus; **council house** n Sozialwohnung f; **councillor** ['kaʊnsɪlə] n Gemeinderat m, Gemeinderätin f; **council tax** n Gemeindesteuer f

count [kaʊnt] vt, vi zählen; (include) mitrechnen ▷ n Zählung f; (noble) Graf m; **count on** vt (rely on) sich verlassen auf +akk; (expect) rechnen mit

counter ['kaʊntə°] n (in shop) Ladentisch m; (in café) Theke f; (in bank, post office) Schalter m; **counter attack** n Gegenangriff m ▷ vi zurückschlagen; **counter-clockwise** adv (US) entgegen dem Uhrzeigersinn

counterpart ['kaʊntəpɑːt] n Gegenstück nt (of zu)

countess ['kaʊntɪs] n Gräfin f

countless ['kaʊntlɪs] adj zahllos, unzählig

country ['kʌntrɪ] n Land nt; **in the ~** auf dem Land(e); **in this ~** hierzulande; **country cousin** n (fam) Landei nt; **country dancing** n Volkstanz m; **country house** n Landhaus nt; **countryman** n (compatriot) Landsmann m;

country music n Countrymusic f;
country road n Landstraße f;
countryside n Landschaft f; (rural area) Land nt

county ['kaʊntɪ] n (Brit) Grafschaft f; (US) Verwaltungsbezirk m; **county town** n (Brit) = Kreisstadt f

couple ['kʌpl] n Paar nt; **a ~ of** ein paar

coupon ['ku:pɒn] n (voucher) Gutschein m

courage ['kʌrɪdʒ] n Mut m; **courageous** [kə'reɪdʒəs] adj mutig

courgette [kʊə'ʒet] n (Brit) Zucchini f

courier ['kʊrɪə°] n (for tourists) Reiseleiter(in) m(f); (messenger) Kurier m

course [kɔ:s] n (of study) Kurs m; (for race) Strecke f; (Naut, Aviat) Kurs m; (at university) Studiengang m; (in meal) Gang m; **of ~** natürlich; **in the ~ of** während

court [kɔ:t] n (Sport) Platz m; (Jur) Gericht nt

courteous ['kɜ:tɪəs] adj höflich; **courtesy** ['kɜ:təsɪ] n Höflichkeit f; **~ bus/coach** (gebührenfreier) Zubringerbus

courthouse ['kɔ:thaʊs] n (US) Gerichtsgebäude nt; **court order** n Gerichtsbeschluss m; **courtroom** n Gerichtssaal m

courtyard ['kɔ:tjɑ:d] n Hof m

cousin ['kʌzn] n (male) Cousin m; (female) Cousine f

cover ['kʌvə°] vt bedecken (in, with mit); (distance) zurücklegen; (loan, costs) decken ▷ n (for bed etc) Decke f; (of cushion) Bezug m; (lid) Deckel m; (of book) Umschlag m; (**insurance**) ~ Versicherungsschutz m; **cover up** vt zudecken; (error etc) vertuschen; **coverage** n Berichterstattung f (of über +akk);

cover charge n Kosten pl für ein Gedeck; **covering** n Decke f; **covering letter** n Begleitbrief m; **cover story** n (newspaper) Titelgeschichte f

cow [kaʊ] n Kuh f

coward ['kaʊəd] n Feigling m; **cowardly** adj feig(e)

cowboy n Cowboy m

coy [kɔɪ] adj gespielt schüchtern, kokett

cozy ['kəʊzɪ] adj (US) gemütlich

CPU abbr = **central processing unit** Zentraleinheit f

crab [kræb] n Krabbe f

crabby ['kræbɪ] adj mürrisch, reizbar

crack [kræk] n Riss m; (in pottery, glass) Sprung m; (drug) Crack nt; **to have a ~ at sth** etw ausprobieren ▷ vi (pottery, glass) einen Sprung bekommen; (wood, ice etc) einen Riss bekommen; **to get ~ing** (fam) loslegen ▷ vt (bone) anbrechen; (nut, code) knacken

cracker ['krækə°] n (biscuit) Kräcker m; (Christmas ~) Knallbonbon nt; **crackers** adj (fam) verrückt, bekloppt; **he's ~** er hat nicht alle Tassen im Schrank

crackle ['krækl] vi knistern; (telephone, radio) knacken; **crackling** n (Gastr) Kruste f (des Schweinebratens)

cradle ['kreɪdl] n Wiege f

craft [krɑ:ft] n Handwerk nt; (art) Kunsthandwerk nt; (Naut) Boot nt; **craftsman** (pl **-men**) n Handwerker m; **craftsmanship** n Handwerkskunst f; (ability) handwerkliches Können

crafty ['krɑ:ftɪ] adj schlau

cram [kræm] vt stopfen (into in +akk); **to be ~med with** ... mit ... vollgestopft sein ▷ vi (revise for exam) pauken (for für)

cramp [kræmp] n Krampf m

cranberry ['krænbəri] n Preiselbeere f

crane [krein] n (machine) Kran m; (bird) Kranich m

crap [kræp] n (vulg) Scheiße f; (rubbish) Mist m ▷ adj beschissen, Scheiß-

crash [kræʃ] vi einen Unfall haben; (two vehicles) zusammenstoßen; (plane, computer) abstürzen; (economy) zusammenbrechen; **to ~ into sth** gegen etw knallen ▷ vt einen Unfall haben mit ▷ n (car) Unfall m; (train) Unglück nt; (collision) Zusammenstoß m; (Aviat, Inform) Absturz m; (noise) Krachen nt; **crash barrier** n Leitplanke f; **crash course** n Intensivkurs m; **crash helmet** n Sturzhelm m; **crash landing** n Bruchlandung f

crate [kreit] n Kiste f; (of beer) Kasten m

crater ['kreitə'] n Krater m

craving ['kreiviŋ] n starkes Verlangen, Bedürfnis nt

crawl [krɔːl] vi kriechen; (baby) krabbeln ▷ n (swimming) Kraul nt; **crawler lane** n Kriechspur f

crayfish ['kreifiʃ] n Languste f

crayon ['kreiən] n Buntstift m

crazy ['kreizi] adj verrückt (about nach)

cream [kriːm] n (from milk) Sahne f, Rahm m; (polish, cosmetic) Creme f ▷ adj cremefarben; **cream cake** n (small) Sahnetörtchen nt; (big) Sahnetorte f; **cream cheese** n Frischkäse m; **creamer** n Kaffeeweißer m; **cream tea** n (Brit) Nachmittagstee mit Törtchen, Marmelade und Schlagsahne; **creamy** adj sahnig

crease [kriːs] n Falte f ▷ vt falten; (untidy) zerknittern

create [kriːˈeit] vt schaffen; (cause) verursachen; **creative**

[kriːˈeitiv] adj schöpferisch; (person) kreativ; **creature** ['kriːtʃə'] n Geschöpf nt

crèche [kreiʃ] n Kinderkrippe f

credible ['kredibl] adj (person) glaubwürdig; **credibility** n Glaubwürdigkeit f

credit ['kredit] n (Fin: amount allowed) Kredit m; (amount possessed) Guthaben nt; (recognition) Anerkennung f; **~s** (of film) Abspann m; **credit card** n Kreditkarte f; **credit crunch** n Kreditklemme f

creep [kriːp] (crept, crept) vi kriechen; **creeps** n: **he gives me the ~** er ist mir nicht ganz geheuer; **creepy** ['kriːpi] adj (frightening) gruselig, unheimlich

crept [krept] pt, pp of **creep**

cress [kres] n Kresse f

crest [krest] n Kamm m; (coat of arms) Wappen nt

crew [kruː] n Besatzung f, Mannschaft f

crib [krib] n (US) Kinderbett nt

cricket ['krikit] n (insect) Grille f; (game) Cricket nt

crime [kraim] n Verbrechen nt; **criminal** ['kriminl] n Verbrecher(in) m(f) ▷ adj kriminell, strafbar

cripple ['kripl] n Krüppel m ▷ vt verkrüppeln, lähmen

crisis ['kraisis] (pl crises) n Krise f

crisp [krisp] adj knusprig; **crisps** npl (Brit) Chips pl; **crispbread** n Knäckebrot nt

criterion [kraiˈtiəriən] n Kriterium nt

critic ['kritik] n Kritiker(in) m(f); **critical** adj kritisch; **critically** adv kritisch; **~ ill/injured** schwer krank/verletzt; **criticism** ['kritisizəm] n Kritik f; **criticize** ['kritisaiz] vt kritisieren

Croat ['krəuæt] n Kroate m,

Kroatin f; **Croatia** [krəʊˈeɪʃə] n Kroatien nt; **Croatian** [krəʊˈeɪʃən] adj kroatisch

crockery [ˈkrɒkərɪ] n Geschirr nt

crocodile [ˈkrɒkədaɪl] n Krokodil nt

crocus [ˈkrəʊkəs] n Krokus m

crop [krɒp] n (harvest) Ernte f; **crops** npl Getreide nt; **crop up** vi auftauchen

croquette [krəˈket] n Krokette f

cross [krɒs] n Kreuz nt; **to mark sth with a ~** etw ankreuzen ▷ vt (road, river etc) überqueren; (legs) übereinanderschlagen; **it ~ed my mind** es fiel mir ein; **to ~ one's fingers** die Daumen drücken ▷ adj ärgerlich, böse; **cross out** vt durchstreichen

crossbar n (of bicycle) Stange f; (Sport) Querlatte f; **cross-country** adj: **~ running** Geländelauf m; **~ skiing** Langlauf m; **cross-examination** n Kreuzverhör nt; **cross-eyed** adj: **to be ~** schielen; **crossing** n (crossroads) (Straßen)kreuzung f; (for pedestrians) Fußgängerübergang m; (on ship) Überfahrt f; **crossroads** nsing o pl Straßenkreuzung f; **cross section** n Querschnitt m; **crosswalk** n (US) Fußgängerübergang m; **crossword (puzzle)** n Kreuzworträtsel nt

crouch [kraʊtʃ] vi hocken

crouton [ˈkruːtɒn] n Croûton m

crow [krəʊ] n Krähe f

crowbar [ˈkrəʊbɑːʳ] n Brecheisen nt

crowd [kraʊd] n Menge f ▷ vi sich drängen (into n +akk; round um); **crowded** adj überfüllt

crown [kraʊn] n Krone f ▷ vt krönen; (fam) **and to ~ it all ...** und als Krönung ...

crucial [ˈkruːʃəl] adj entscheidend

crude [kruːd] adj primitiv; (humour, behaviour) derb, ordinär ▷ n: **~ (oil)** Rohöl nt

cruel [ˈkrʊəl] adj grausam (to zu, gegen); (unfeeling) gefühllos; **cruelty** n Grausamkeit f; **~ to animals** Tierquälerei f

cruise [kruːz] n Kreuzfahrt f ▷ vi (ship) kreuzen; (car) mit Reisegeschwindigkeit fahren; **cruise liner** n Kreuzfahrtschiff nt; **cruise missile** n Marschflugkörper m; **cruising speed** n Reisegeschwindigkeit f

crumb [krʌm] n Krume f

crumble [ˈkrʌmbl] vt, vi zerbröckeln ▷ n mit Streuseln überbackenes Kompott

crumpet [ˈkrʌmpɪt] n weiches Hefegebäck (zum Toasten; (fam: attractive woman) Schnecke f

crumple [ˈkrʌmpl] vt zerknittern

crunchy [ˈkrʌntʃɪ] adj (Brit) knusprig

crusade [kruːˈseɪd] n Kreuzzug m

crush [krʌʃ] vt zerdrücken; (finger etc) quetschen; (spices, stone) zerstoßen ▷ n: **to have a ~ on sb** in jdn verknallt sein; **crushing** adj (defeat, remark) vernichtend

crust [krʌst] n Kruste f; **crusty** adj knusprig

crutch [krʌtʃ] n Krücke f

cry [kraɪ] vi (call) rufen; (scream) schreien; (weep) weinen ▷ n (call) Ruf m; (louder) Schrei m

crypt [krɪpt] n Krypta f

crystal [ˈkrɪstl] n Kristall m

cu abbr = **see you** (SMS, e-mail) bis bald

Cuba [ˈkjuːbə] n Kuba nt

cube [kjuːb] n Würfel m

cubic [ˈkjuːbɪk] adj Kubik-

cubicle [ˈkjuːbɪkl] n Kabine f

cuckoo ['kʊkuː] n Kuckuck m

cucumber ['kjuːkʌmbə⁰] n Salatgurke f

cuddle ['kʌdl] vt in den Arm nehmen; (amorously) schmusen mit ▷ n Liebkosung f, Umarmung f; **to have a ~** schmusen; **cuddly** adj verschmust; **cuddly toy** n Plüschtier m

cuff [kʌf] n Manschette f; (US: trouser ~) Aufschlag m; **off the ~** aus dem Stegreif; **cufflink** n Manschettenknopf m

cuisine [kwiˈziːn] n Kochkunst f, Küche f

cul-de-sac ['kʌldəsæk] n (Brit) Sackgasse f

culprit ['kʌlprɪt] n Schuldige(r) mf; (fig) Übeltäter(in) m(f)

cult [kʌlt] n Kult m

cultivate ['kʌltɪveɪt] vt (Agr: land) bebauen; (crop) anbauen; **cultivated** adj (person) kultiviert, gebildet

cultural ['kʌltʃərəl] adj kulturell, Kultur-; **culture** ['kʌltʃə⁰] n Kultur f; **cultured** adj gebildet, kultiviert; **culture vulture** (Brit fam) n Kulturfanatiker(in) m(f)

cumbersome ['kʌmbəsəm] adj (object) unhandlich

cumin ['kʌmɪn] n Kreuzkümmel m

cunning ['kʌnɪŋ] adj schlau; (person a.) gerissen

cup [kʌp] n Tasse f; (prize) Pokal m; **it's not his ~ of tea** das ist nicht sein Fall; **cupboard** ['kʌbəd] n Schrank m; **cup final** n Pokalendspiel nt; **cup tie** n Pokalspiel nt

cupola ['kjuːpələ] n Kuppel f

curable ['kjʊərəbl] adj heilbar

curb [kɜːb] n (US) see kerb

curd [kɜːd] n: **~ cheese**, **~s ~** Quark m

cure [kjʊə⁰] n Heilmittel nt (for

gegen); (process) Heilung f ▷ vt heilen; (Gastr) pökeln; (smoke) räuchern

curious ['kjʊərɪəs] adj neugierig; (strange) seltsam

curl [kɜːl] n Locke f ▷ vi sich kräuseln; **curly** adj lockig

currant ['kʌrənt] n (dried) Korinthe f; (red, black) Johannisbeere f

currency ['kʌrənsɪ] n Währung f; **foreign ~** Devisen pl

current ['kʌrənt] n (in water) Strömung f; (electric ~) Strom m ▷ adj (issue, affairs) aktuell, gegenwärtig; (expression) gängig; **current account** n Girokonto nt; **currently** adv zur Zeit

curriculum [kəˈrɪkjələm] n Lehrplan m; **curriculum vitae** [kəˈrɪkjələmˈviːtaɪ] n (Brit) Lebenslauf m

curry ['kʌrɪ] n Currygericht nt; **curry powder** n Curry(pulver) nt

curse [kɜːs] vi (swear) fluchen (at auf +akk) ▷ n Fluch m

cursor ['kɜːsə⁰] n (Inform) Cursor m

curt [kɜːt] adj schroff, kurz angebunden

curtain ['kɜːtn] n Vorhang m; **it was ~s for Benny** für Benny war alles vorbei

curve [kɜːv] n Kurve f ▷ vi einen Bogen machen; **curved** adj gebogen

cushion ['kʊʃən] n Kissen nt

custard ['kʌstəd] n dicke Vanillesoße, die warm oder kalt zu vielen englischen Nachspeisen gegessen wird

custom ['kʌstəm] n Brauch m; (habit) Gewohnheit f; **customary** ['kʌstəmrɪ] adj üblich; **custom-built** adj nach Kundenangaben gefertigt

customer ['kʌstəmə⁰] n Kunde

m, Kundin f; **customer loyalty card** n Kundenkarte f; **customer service** n Kundendienst m

customs ['kʌstəmz] npl (organization, location) Zoll m; **to pass through ~** durch den Zoll gehen; **customs officer** n Zollbeamte(r) m, Zollbeamtin f

cut [kʌt] (**cut, cut**) vt schneiden; (cake) anschneiden; (wages, benefits) kürzen; (prices) heruntersetzen; **I ~ my finger** ich habe mir in den Finger geschnitten ▷ n Schnitt m; (wound) Schnittwunde f; (reduction) Kürzung f (in gen); **price/tax ~** Preissenkung/Steuersenkung f; **to be a ~ above the rest** eine Klasse besser als die anderen sein; **cut back** vt (workforce etc) reduzieren; **cut down** vt (tree) fällen; **to ~ on sth** etwas einschränken; **cut in** vi (Auto) scharf einscheren; **to ~ on sb** jdn schneiden; **cut off** vt abschneiden; (gas, electricity) abdrehen, abstellen; (Tel) **I was ~** ich wurde unterbrochen

cutback n Kürzung f

cute [kjuːt] adj putzig, niedlich; (US: shrewd) clever

cutlery ['kʌtləri] n Besteck nt

cutlet ['kʌtlɪt] n (pork) Kotelett nt; (veal) Schnitzel nt

cut-price adj verbilligt

cutting ['kʌtɪŋ] n (from paper) Ausschnitt m; (of plant) Ableger m ▷ adj (comment) verletzend

CV abbr = **curriculum vitae**

cwt abbr = **hundredweight** = Zentner, Ztr.

cybercafé [saɪbə'kæfeɪ] n Internetcafé nt; **cyberspace** n Cyberspace m

cycle ['saɪkl] n Fahrrad nt ▷ vi Rad fahren; **cycle lane, cycle path** n Radweg m; **cycling**

Radfahren nt; **cyclist** ['saɪklɪst] n Radfahrer(in) m(f)

cylinder ['sɪlɪndə°] n Zylinder m

cynical ['sɪnɪkəl] adj zynisch

cypress ['saɪprɪs] n Zypresse f

Cypriot ['sɪprɪət] adj zypriotisch ▷ n Zypriote m, Zypriotin f; **Cyprus** ['saɪprəs] n Zypern nt

czar [zaː°] n Zar m; **czarina** [zaː'riːnə] n Zarin f

Czech [tʃek] adj tschechisch ▷ n (person) Tscheche m, Tschechin f; (language) Tschechisch nt; **Czech Republic** n Tschechische Republik, Tschechien nt

d

dab [dæb] vt (wound, nose etc) betupfen (with mit)

dachshund ['dækshʊnd] n Dackel m

dad(dy) ['dæd(ɪ)] n Papa m, Vati m; **daddy-longlegs** nsing (Brit) Schnake; (US) Weberknecht m

daffodil ['dæfədɪl] n Osterglocke f

daft [dɑːft] adj (fam) blöd, doof

dahlia ['deɪlɪə] n Dahlie f

daily ['deɪlɪ] adj, adv täglich ▷ n (paper) Tageszeitung f

dairy ['dɛərɪ] n (on farm) Molkerei f; **dairy products** npl Milchprodukte pl

daisy ['deɪzɪ] n Gänseblümchen nt

dam [dæm] n Staudamm m ▷ vt stauen

damage ['dæmɪdʒ] n Schaden m; **~s** pl (Jur) Schadenersatz m ▷ vt beschädigen; (reputation, health) schädigen, schaden +dat

damn [dæm] adj (fam) verdammt ▷ vt (condemn) verurteilen; **~ (it)!** verflucht! ▷ n: **he doesn't give a ~** es ist ihm völlig egal

damp [dæmp] adj feucht ▷ n Feuchtigkeit f; **dampen** ['dæmpən] vt befeuchten

dance [dɑːns] n Tanz m; (event) Tanzveranstaltung f ▷ vi tanzen; **dance floor** n Tanzfläche f; **dancer** n Tänzer(in) m(f); **dancing** n Tanzen nt

dandelion ['dændɪlaɪən] n Löwenzahn m

dandruff ['dændrəf] n Schuppen pl

Dane [deɪn] n Däne m, Dänin f

danger ['deɪndʒə°] n Gefahr f; **~ (sign)** Achtung!; **to be in ~** in Gefahr sein; **dangerous** adj gefährlich

Danish ['deɪnɪʃ] adj dänisch ▷ n (language) Dänisch nt; **the ~** pl die Dänen; **Danish pastry** n Plundergebäck nt

Danube ['dænjuːb] n Donau f

dare [dɛə°] vi: **to ~ (to) do sth** es wagen, etw zu tun; **I didn't ~ ask** ich traute mich nicht, zu fragen; **how ~ you** was fällt dir ein!; **daring** adj (person) mutig; (film, clothes etc) gewagt

dark [dɑːk] adj dunkel; (gloomy) düster, trübe; (sinister) finster; **~ chocolate** Bitterschokolade f; **~ green/blue** dunkelgrün/dunkelblau ▷ n Dunkelheit f; **in the ~** im Dunkeln; **dark glasses** npl Sonnenbrille f; **darkness** n Dunkelheit f

darling ['dɑːlɪŋ] n Schatz m; (also favourite) Liebling m

darts [dɑːts] nsing (game) Darts nt

dash [dæʃ] vi stürzen, rennen

▷ vt: **to ~ hopes** Hoffnungen
zerstören ▷ n (in text)
Gedankenstrich m; (of liquid)
Schuss m; **dashboard** n
Armaturenbrett nt

data ['deɪtə] npl Daten pl; **data
bank, data base** n Datenbank f;
data capture n Datenerfassung
f; **data processing** n
Datenverarbeitung f; **data
protection** n Datenschutz m

date [deɪt] n Datum nt; (for
meeting, delivery etc) Termin m;
(with person) Verabredung f; (with
girlfriend/boyfriend etc) Date nt;
(fruit) Dattel f; **what's the
~ (today)?** der Wievielte ist
heute?; **out of ~** adj veraltet; **up
to ~** adj (news) aktuell; (fashion)
zeitgemäß ▷ vt (letter etc)
datieren; (person) gehen mit;
dated adj altmodisch; **date of
birth** n Geburtsdatum nt; **dating
agency** n Partnervermittlung f

dative ['deɪtɪv] n Dativ m

daughter ['dɔːtəʳ] n Tochter f;
daughter-in-law (pl
daughters-in-law) n Schwiegertochter f

dawn [dɔːn] n Morgendäm-
merung f ▷ vi dämmern; **it ~ed
on me** mir ging ein Licht auf

day [deɪ] n Tag m; **one ~** eines
Tages; **by ~** bei Tage; **~ by
~** Tag für Tag; **the ~ after/
before** am Tag danach/zuvor; **the
~ before yesterday** vorgestern; **the
~ after tomorrow**
übermorgen; **these ~s**
heutzutage; **in those ~s** damals;
let's call it a ~ Schluss für heut!;
daybreak n Tagesanbruch m;
day-care center (US), **day-care
centre** n (Brit) Kita f
(Kindertagesstätte); **daydream** n
Tagtraum m ▷ vi mit offenen
Augen träumen; **daylight** n

Tageslicht nt; **in ~** bei Tage; **day
nursery** n Kita f
(Kindertagesstätte); **day return** n
(Brit Rail) Tagesrückfahrkarte f;
daytime n: **in the ~** bei Tage,
tagsüber; **daytrip** n Tagesausflug
m

dazed [deɪzd] adj benommen

dazzle ['dæzl] vt blenden;
dazzling adj blendend, glänzend

dead [ded] adj tot; (limb)
abgestorben ▷ adv genau; (fam)
total, völlig; **~ tired** adj todmüde;
~ slow (sign) Schritt fahren; **dead
end** n Sackgasse f; **deadline** n
Termin m; (period) Frist f; **~ for
applications** Anmeldeschluss m;
deadly adj tödlich ▷ adv: **~ dull**
todlangweilig

deaf [def] adj taub; **deafen** vt
taub machen; **deafening** adj
ohrenbetäubend

deal [diːl] (**dealt, dealt**) vt, vi
(cards) geben, austeilen ▷ n
(business ~) Geschäft nt; (agreement)
Abmachung f; **it's a ~** abgemacht!;
a good/great ~ of ziemlich/sehr
viel; **deal in** vt handeln mit; **deal
with** vt (matter) sich beschäftigen
mit; (book, film) behandeln;
(successfully: person, problem) fertig
werden mit; (matter) erledigen;
dealer n (Comm) Händler(in) m(f);
(drugs) Dealer(in) m(f); **dealings**
npl (Comm) Geschäfte pl

dealt [delt] pt, pp of **deal**

dear [dɪəʳ] adj lieb, teuer; **Dear
Sir or Madam** Sehr geehrte
Damen und Herren; **Dear David**
Lieber David ▷ n Schatz m; (as
address) mein Schatz, Liebling;
dearly adv (love) (heiß und) innig;
(pay) teuer

death [deθ] n Tod m; (of project,
hopes) Ende nt; (in accident etc)
Todesfall m, Todesopfer nt; **death
certificate** n Totenschein m;

death penalty n Todesstrafe f;
death toll n Zahl f der Todesopfer; **death trap** n Todesfalle f
debatable [dɪˈbeɪtəbl] adj
fraglich; (question) strittig; **debate**
[dɪˈbeɪt] n Debatte f ▷ vt
debattieren
debauched [dɪˈbɔːtʃt] adj
ausschweifend
debit [ˈdebɪt] n Soll nt ▷ vt
(account) belasten; **debit card** n
Geldkarte f
debris [ˈdebriː] n Trümmer pl
debt [det] n Schuld f; **to be in
~** verschuldet sein
debug [diːˈbʌg] vt (Inform) Fehler
beseitigen in +dat
decade [ˈdekeɪd] n Jahrzehnt nt
decadent [ˈdekədənt] adj
dekadent
decaff [ˈdiːkæf] n (fam) koffein-
freier Kaffee; **decaffeinated**
[diːˈkæfɪneɪtɪd] adj koffeinfrei
decanter [dɪˈkæntə°] n Dekanter
m, Karaffe f
decay [dɪˈkeɪ] n Verfall m;
(rotting) Verwesung f; (of tooth)
Karies f ▷ vi verfallen; (rot)
verwesen; (wood) vermodern;
(teeth) faulen; (leaves) verrotten
deceased [dɪˈsiːst] n: **the ~**
der/die Verstorbene
deceit [dɪˈsiːt] n Betrug m;
deceive [dɪˈsiːv] vt täuschen
December [dɪˈsembə°] n
Dezember m; see also **September**
decent [ˈdiːsənt] adj anständig
deception [dɪˈsepʃən] n Betrug
m; **deceptive** [dɪˈseptɪv] adj
täuschend, irreführend
decide [dɪˈsaɪd] vt (question)
entscheiden; (body of people)
beschließen; **I can't ~ what to do**
ich kann mich nicht entscheiden,
was ich tun soll ▷ vi sich
entscheiden; **to ~ on sth** (in favour
of sth) sich für etw entscheiden,

sich zu etw entschließen; **decided**
adj entschieden; (clear) deutlich;
decidedly adv entschieden
decimal [ˈdesɪməl] adj Dezimal-;
decimal system n
Dezimalsystem nt
decipher [dɪˈsaɪfə°] vt entziffern
decision [dɪˈsɪʒən] n Entscheidung f (on über +akk); (of committee,
jury etc) Beschluss m; **to make a
~** eine Entscheidung treffen;
decisive [dɪˈsaɪsɪv] adj entscheidend; (person)
entscheidungsfreudig
deck [dek] n (Naut) Deck nt; (of
cards) Blatt nt; **deckchair** n
Liegestuhl m
declaration [dekləˈreɪʃən] n
Erklärung f; **declare** [dɪˈkleə°] vt
erklären; (state) behaupten (that
dass); (at customs) **have you
anything to ~?** haben Sie etwas
zu verzollen?
decline [dɪˈklaɪn] n Rückgang m
▷ vt (invitation, offer) ablehnen ▷ vi
(become less) sinken, abnehmen;
(health) sich verschlechtern
decode [diːˈkəʊd] vt
entschlüsseln
decompose [diːkəmˈpəʊz] vi sich
zersetzen
decontaminate
[diːkənˈtæmɪneɪt] vt entgiften;
(from radioactivity) entseuchen
decorate [ˈdekəreɪt] vt
(aus)schmücken; (wallpaper)
tapezieren; (paint) anstreichen;
decoration [dekəˈreɪʃən] n
Schmuck m; (process) Schmücken
nt; (wallpapering) Tapezieren nt;
(painting) Anstreichen nt;
Christmas ~s Weihnachts-
schmuck m; **decorator** n
Maler(in) m(f)
decrease [ˈdiːkriːs] n Abnahme f
▷ [diːˈkriːs] vi abnehmen
dedicate [ˈdedɪkeɪt] vt widmen

(to sb jdm); **dedicated** adj (person) engagiert; **dedication** [dedɪˈkeɪʃən] n Widmung f; (commitment) Hingabe f, Engagement nt

deduce [dɪˈdjuːs] vt folgern, schließen (from aus, that dass)

deduct [dɪˈdʌkt] vt abziehen (from von); **deduction** [dɪˈdʌkʃən] n (of money) Abzug m; (conclusion) (Schluss)folgerung f

deed [diːd] n Tat f

deep [diːp] adj tief; **deepen** vt vertiefen; **deep-freeze** n Tiefkühltruhe f; (upright) Gefrierschrank m; **deep-fry** vt frittieren

deer [dɪəˢ] n Reh nt; (with stag) Hirsch m

defeat [dɪˈfiːt] n Niederlage f; **to admit ~** sich geschlagen geben ▷ vt besiegen

defect [ˈdiːfekt] n Defekt m, Fehler m; **defective** [dɪˈfektɪv] adj fehlerhaft

defence [dɪˈfens] n Verteidigung f; **defend** [dɪˈfend] vt verteidigen; **defendant** [dɪˈfendənt] n (Jur) Angeklagte(r) mf; **defender** n (Sport) Verteidiger(in) m(f); **defensive** [dɪˈfensɪv] adj defensiv

deficiency [dɪˈfɪʃənsɪ] n Mangel m; **deficient** adj mangelhaft; **deficit** [ˈdefɪsɪt] n Defizit nt

define [dɪˈfaɪn] vt (word) definieren; (duties, powers) bestimmen; **definite** [ˈdefɪnɪt] adj (clear) klar, eindeutig; (certain) sicher; **it's ~** es steht fest; **definitely** adv bestimmt; **definition** [defɪˈnɪʃən] n Definition f; (Foto) Schärfe f

defrost [diːˈfrɒst] vt (fridge) abtauen; (food) auftauen

degrading [dɪˈgreɪdɪŋ] adj erniedrigend

degree [dɪˈgriː] n Grad m; (at university) akademischer Grad; **a certain/high ~ of** ein gewisses/hohes Maß an +dat; **to a certain ~** einigermaßen; **I have a ~ in chemistry** ~ ich habe einen Abschluss in Chemie

dehydrated [diːhaɪˈdreɪtɪd] adj (food) getrocknet, Trocken-; (person) ausgetrocknet

de-ice [diːˈaɪs] vt enteisen

delay [dɪˈleɪ] vt (postpone) verschieben, aufschieben; **to be ~ed** (event) sich verzögern; **the train/flight was ~ed** der Zug/die Maschine hatte Verspätung ▷ vi warten; (hesitate) zögern ▷ n Verzögerung f; (of train etc) Verspätung f; **without ~** unverzüglich; **delayed** adj (train etc) verspätet

delegate n [ˈdelɪgət] Delegierte(r) mf ▷ [ˈdelɪgeɪt] vt delegieren; **delegation** [delɪˈgeɪʃən] n Abordnung f; (foreign) Delegation f

delete [dɪˈliːt] vt (aus)streichen; (Inform) löschen; **deletion** n Streichung f; (Inform) Löschung f

deli [ˈdelɪ] n (fam) Feinkostgeschäft nt

deliberate [dɪˈlɪbərət] adj (intentional) absichtlich; **deliberately** adv mit Absicht, extra

delicate [ˈdelɪkɪt] adj (fine) fein; (fragile) zart; (a. Med) empfindlich; (situation) heikel

delicatessen [delɪkəˈtesn] nsing Feinkostgeschäft nt

delicious [dɪˈlɪʃəs] adj köstlich, lecker

delight [dɪˈlaɪt] n Freude f ▷ vt entzücken; **delighted** adj sehr erfreut (with über +akk); **delightful** adj entzückend; (weather, meal etc) herrlich

deliver [dɪ'lɪvə°] vt (goods) liefern (to sb jdm); (letter, parcel) zustellen; (speech) halten; (baby) entbinden; **delivery** n Lieferung f; (of letter, parcel) Zustellung f; (of baby) Entbindung f; **delivery van** n Lieferwagen m

delude [dɪ'luːd] vt täuschen; **don't ~ yourself** mach dir nichts vor; **delusion** n Irrglaube m

de luxe [dɪ'lʌks] adj Luxus-

demand [dɪ'mɑːnd] vt verlangen (from von); (time, patience etc) erfordern ▷ n (request) Forderung f, Verlangen nt (for nach); (Comm: for goods) Nachfrage f; **on ~** auf Wunsch; **very much in ~** sehr gefragt; **demanding** adj anspruchsvoll

demented [dɪ'mentɪd] adj wahnsinnig

demerara [demə'reərə] n: ~ **(sugar)** brauner Zucker

demister n Defroster m

demo [deməʊ] (pl -s) n (fam) Demo f

democracy [dɪ'mɒkrəsɪ] n Demokratie f; **democrat** ['deməkræt] Demokrat(in) m(f); **democratic** adj demokratisch; **the Democratic Party** (US Pol) die Demokratische Partei

demolish [dɪ'mɒlɪʃ] vt abreißen; (fig) zerstören; **demolition** [demə'lɪʃən] n Abbruch m

demonstrate ['demənstreɪt] vt, vi demonstrieren, beweisen; **demonstration** n Demonstration f

demoralize [dɪ'mɒrəlaɪz] vt demoralisieren

denial [dɪ'naɪəl] n Leugnung f; (official ~) Dementi nt

denim ['denɪm] n Jeansstoff m; **denim jacket** n Jeansjacke f; **denims** npl Bluejeans pl

Denmark ['denmɑːk] n Dänemark nt

denomination [dɪnɒmɪ'neɪʃən] n (Rel) Konfession f; (Comm) Nennwert m

dense [dens] adj dicht; (fam: stupid) schwer von Begriff; **density** ['densɪtɪ] n Dichte f

dent [dent] n Beule f, Delle f ▷ vt einbeulen

dental ['dentl] adj Zahn-; ~ **care** Zahnpflege f; ~ **floss** Zahnseide f; **dentist** ['dentɪst] n Zahnarzt m, Zahnärztin; **dentures** ['dentʃəz] npl Zahnprothese f; (full) Gebiss nt

deny [dɪ'naɪ] vt leugnen, bestreiten; (refuse) ablehnen

deodorant [diː'əʊdərənt] n Deo(dorant) nt

depart [dɪ'pɑːt] vi abreisen; (bus, train) abfahren (for nach, from von); (plane) abfliegen (for nach, from von)

department [dɪ'pɑːtmənt] n Abteilung f; (at university) Institut nt; (Pol: ministry) Ministerium nt; **department store** n Kaufhaus nt

departure [dɪ'pɑːtʃə°] n (of person) Weggang m; (on journey) Abreise f (for nach); (of train etc) Abfahrt f (for nach); (of plane) Abflug m (for nach); **departure lounge** n (Aviat) Abflughalle f; **departure time** n Abfahrtzeit f; (Aviat) Abflugzeit f

depend [dɪ'pend] vi: **it -s** es kommt darauf an; (whether, if ob); **depend on** vt (thing) abhängen von; (person: rely on) sich verlassen auf +akk; (person, area etc) angewiesen sein auf +akk; **it -s on the weather** es kommt auf das Wetter an; **dependable** adj zuverlässig; **dependence** n Abhängigkeit f (on von); **dependent** adj abhängig (on von)

deport [dɪ'pɔːt] vt ausweisen,

abschieben; **deportation**
[di:pɔ:ˈteɪʃən] n Abschiebung f

deposit [dɪˈpɔzɪt] n (down
payment) Anzahlung f; (security)
Kaution f; (for bottle) Pfand nt; (to
bank account) Einzahlung f; (in river
etc) Ablagerung f ▷ vt (put down)
abstellen, absetzen; (to bank
account) einzahlen; (sth valuable)
deponieren; **deposit account** n
Sparkonto nt

depot [ˈdepəʊ] n Depot nt

depreciate [dɪˈpriːʃɪeɪt] vi an
Wert verlieren

depress [dɪˈpres] vt (in mood)
deprimieren; **depressed** adj
(person) niedergeschlagen,
deprimiert; **~ area**
Notstandsgebiet nt; **depressing**
adj deprimierend; **depression**
[dɪˈpreʃən] n (mood) Depression f;
(Meteo) Tief nt

deprive [dɪˈpraɪv] vt: **to ~ sb of
sth** jdn einer Sache berauben;
deprived adj (child) (sozial)
benachteiligt

dept abbr = **department** Abt.

depth [depθ] n Tiefe f

deputy [ˈdepjʊtɪ] adj stell-
vertretend, Vize- ▷ n
Stellvertreter(in) m(f); (US Pol)
Abgeordnete(r) mf

derail [dɪˈreɪl] vt entgleisen
lassen; **to be ~ed** entgleisen

deranged [dɪˈreɪndʒd] adj
geistesgestört

derivation [derɪˈveɪʃən] n
Ableitung f; **derive** [dɪˈraɪv] vt
ableiten (from von) ▷ abstammen
(from von)

dermatitis [dɜːməˈtaɪtɪs] n
Hautentzündung f

derogatory [dɪˈrɒgətərɪ] adj
abfällig

descend [dɪˈsend] vt, vi
hinabsteigen, hinuntergehen;
(person) **to ~** o **be ~ed from**

abstammen von; **descendant** n
Nachkomme m; **descent** [dɪˈsent]
n (coming down) Abstieg m; (origin)
Abstammung f

describe [dɪsˈkraɪb] vt beschreiben; **description**
[dɪsˈkrɪpʃən] n Beschreibung f

desert [ˈdezət] n Wüste f
▷ [dɪˈzɜːt] vt verlassen; (abandon)
im Stich lassen; **deserted** adj
verlassen; (empty) menschenleer

deserve [dɪˈzɜːv] vt verdienen

design [dɪˈzaɪn] n (plan) Entwurf
m; (of vehicle, machine)
Konstruktion f; (of object) Design
nt; (planning) Gestaltung f ▷ vt
entwerfen; (machine etc)
konstruieren; **~ed for sb/sth**
(intended) für jdn/etw konzipiert

designate [ˈdezɪgneɪt] vt
bestimmen

designer [dɪˈzaɪnəʳ] n
Designer(in) m(f); (Tech)
Konstrukteur(in) m(f); **designer
drug** n Designerdroge f

desirable [dɪˈzaɪərəbl] n
wünschenswert; (person)
begehrenswert; **desire** [dɪˈzaɪəʳ]
n Wunsch m (for nach); (esp sexual)
Begierde f (for auf) ▷ vt
wünschen; (ask for) verlangen; **if
~d** auf Wunsch

desk [desk] n Schreibtisch m;
(reception ~) Empfang m; (at airport
etc) Schalter m; **desktop
publishing** n Desktoppublishing
nt

desolate [ˈdesəlɪt] adj trostlos

despair [dɪsˈpeəʳ] n Verzweiflung f (at über +akk) ▷ vi
verzweifeln (of an +dat)

despatch [dɪsˈpætʃ] see **dispatch**

desperate [ˈdespərɪt] adj
verzweifelt; (situation)
hoffnungslos; **to be ~ for sth** etw
dringend brauchen, unbedingt
wollen; **desperation**

[despə'reɪʃən] n Verzweiflung f

despicable [dɪ'spɪkəbl] adj verachtenswert; **despise** [dɪ'spaɪz] vt verachten

despite [dɪ'spaɪt] prep trotz +gen

dessert [dɪ'zɜːt] n Nachtisch m; **dessert spoon** n Dessertlöffel m

destination [destɪ'neɪʃən] n (of person) (Reise)ziel nt; (of goods) Bestimmungsort m

destiny ['destɪnɪ] n Schicksal nt

destroy [dɪ'strɔɪ] vt zerstören; (completely) vernichten; **destruction** [dɪ'strʌkʃən] n Zerstörung f; (complete) Vernichtung f; **destructive** [dɪ'strʌktɪv] adj zerstörerisch; (esp fig) destruktiv

detach [dɪ'tætʃ] vt abnehmen; (from form etc) abtrennen; (free) lösen (from von); **detachable** adj abnehmbar; (from form etc) abtrennbar; **detached** adj (attitude) distanziert, objektiv; ~ **house** Einzelhaus nt

detail ['diːteɪl, (US) dɪ'teɪl] n Einzelheit f, Detail nt; (further) ~**s from ...** Näheres erfahren Sie bei ...; **to go into** ~ ins Detail gehen; **in** ~ ausführlich; **detailed** adj detailliert, ausführlich

detain [dɪ'teɪn] vt aufhalten; (police) in Haft nehmen

detect [dɪ'tekt] vt entdecken; (notice) wahrnehmen; **detective** [dɪ'tektɪv] n Detektiv(in) m(f); **detective story** n Krimi m

detention [dɪ'tenʃən] n Haft f; (Sch) Nachsitzen nt

deter [dɪ'tɜː] vt abschrecken (from von)

detergent [dɪ'tɜːdʒənt] n Reinigungsmittel nt; (soap powder) Waschmittel nt

deteriorate [dɪ'tɪərɪəreɪt] vi sich verschlechtern

determination [dɪtɜːmɪ'neɪʃən] n Entschlossenheit f; **determine** [dɪ'tɜːmɪn] vt bestimmen; **determined** adj (fest) entschlossen

deterrent [dɪ'terənt] n Abschreckungsmittel nt

detest [dɪ'test] vt verabscheuen; **detestable** adj abscheulich

detour [diː'tuə] n Umweg m; (of traffic) Umleitung f

deuce [djuːs] n (Tennis) Einstand m

devalue [diː'væljuː] vt abwerten

devastate ['devəsteɪt] vt verwüsten; **devastating** ['devəsteɪtɪŋ] adj verheerend

develop [dɪ'veləp] vt entwickeln; (illness) bekommen ▷ vi sich entwickeln; **developing country** n Entwicklungsland nt; **development** n Entwicklung f; (of land) Erschließung f

device [dɪ'vaɪs] n Vorrichtung f, Gerät nt

devil ['devl] n Teufel m; **devilish** adj teuflisch

devote [dɪ'vəut] vt widmen (to dat); **devoted** adj liebend; (servant etc) treu ergeben; **devotion** n Hingabe f

devour [dɪ'vauə] vt verschlingen

dew [djuː] n Tau m

diabetes [daɪə'biːtiːz] n Diabetes m, Zuckerkrankheit f; **diabetic** [daɪə'betɪk] adj zuckerkrank, für Diabetiker ▷ n Diabetiker(in) m(f)

diagnosis (diagnoses) [daɪəg'nəusɪs] (pl **diagnoses**) n Diagnose f

diagonal [daɪ'ægənl] adj diagonal

diagram ['daɪəgræm] n Diagramm nt

dial ['daɪəl] n Skala f; (of clock)

Zifferblatt nt ▷ vt (Tel) wählen;
dial code n (US) Vorwahl f
dialect ['daɪəlɛkt] n Dialekt m
dialling code n (Brit) Vorwahl f;
dialling tone n (Brit) Amtszeichen nt
dialogue, dialog (US) ['daɪəlɒg]
n Dialog m
dial tone n (US) Amtszeichen nt
dialysis [daɪˈælɪsɪs] n (Med)
Dialyse f
diameter [daɪˈæmɪtə°] n
Durchmesser m
diamond ['daɪəmənd] n Diamant m; (Cards) Karo nt
diaper ['daɪpə°] n (US) Windel f
diarrhoea [daɪəˈriːə] n Durchfall
m
diary ['daɪərɪ] n (Taschen)ka-
lender m; (account) Tagebuch nt
dice [daɪs] npl Würfel pl; **diced**
adj in Würfel geschnitten
dictate [dɪkˈteɪt] vt diktieren;
dictation [dɪkˈteɪʃən] n Diktat nt
dictator [dɪkˈteɪtə°] n Dikta-
tor(in) m(f); **dictatorship**
[dɪkˈteɪtəʃɪp] n Diktatur f
dictionary ['dɪkʃənrɪ] n
Wörterbuch nt
did [dɪd] pt of **do**
didn't ['dɪdnt] contr of **did not**
die [daɪ] vi sterben (of an +dat);
(plant, animal) eingehen; (engine)
absterben; **to be dying to do sth**
darauf brennen, etw zu tun; **I'm
dying for a drink** ich brauche
unbedingt was zu trinken; **die
away** vi schwächer werden;
(wind) sich legen; **die down** vi
nachlassen; **die out** vi aussterben
diesel ['diːzəl] n (fuel, car) Diesel
m; ~ **engine** Dieselmotor m
diet ['daɪət] n Kost f; (special food)
Diät f ▷ vi eine Diät machen
differ ['dɪfə°] vi (be different) sich
unterscheiden; (disagree) anderer
Meinung sein; **difference**

['dɪfrəns] n Unterschied m; **it
makes no ~ (to me)** es ist (mir)
egal; **it makes a big ~** es macht
viel aus; **different** adj andere(r, s);
(with pl) verschieden; **to be quite
~** ganz anders sein (from als); (two
people, things) völlig verschieden
sein; **a ~ person** ein anderer
Mensch; **differentiate**
[dɪfəˈrenʃieɪt] vt, vi
unterscheiden; **differently**
['dɪfrəntlɪ] adv anders (from als);
(from one another) unterschiedlich
difficult ['dɪfɪkəlt] adj schwierig; **I find it ~** es fällt mir schwer;
difficulty n Schwierigkeit f; **with
~** nur schwer; **to have ~ in doing
sth** etw nur mit Mühe machen
können
dig [dɪg] (**dug, dug**) vt, vi (hole)
graben; **dig in** vi (fam: to food)
reinhauen; **~I** greif(t) zu!; **dig up** vt
ausgraben
digest [daɪˈdʒest] vt (a. fig)
verdauen; **digestible** [dɪˈdʒestəbl]
adj verdaulich; **digestion**
[dɪˈdʒestʃən] n Verdauung f;
digestive [dɪˈdʒestɪv] adj: **~ biscuit** (Brit) Vollkornkeks m
digit ['dɪdʒɪt] n Ziffer f; **digital**
['dɪdʒɪtəl] adj digital; **~ computer**
Digitalrechner m; **~ watch/clock**
Digitaluhr f; **digital camera** n
Digitalkamera f; **digital
television, digital TV** n
Digitalfernsehen nt
dignified ['dɪgnɪfaɪd] adj
würdevoll; **dignity** ['dɪgnɪtɪ] n
Würde f
dilapidated [dɪˈlæpɪdeɪtɪd] adj
baufällig
dilemma [daɪˈlemə] n Dilemma
nt
dill [dɪl] n Dill m
dilute [daɪˈluːt] vt verdünnen
dim [dɪm] adj (light) schwach;
(outline) undeutlich; (stupid)

schwer von Begriff ▷ vt
verdunkeln; (US Auto) abblenden;
~med headlights (US)
Abblendlicht nt

dime [daɪm] n (US)
Zehncentstück nt

dimension [daɪˈmenʃən] n
Dimension f; **~s** pl Maße pl

diminish [dɪˈmɪnɪʃ] vt
verringern ▷ vi sich verringern

dimple [ˈdɪmpl] n Grübchen nt

dine [daɪn] vi speisen; **dine out**
vi außer Haus essen; **diner** n Gast
m; (Rail) Speisewagen m; (US)
Speiselokal nt

dinghy [ˈdɪŋgɪ] n Ding(h)i nt;
(inflatable) Schlauchboot nt

dingy [ˈdɪndʒɪ] adj düster; (dirty)
schmuddelig

dining car [ˈdaɪnɪŋkɑːˈ] n
Speisewagen m; **dining room** n
Esszimmer nt; (in hotel)
Speiseraum m; **dining table** n
Esstisch m

dinkum [ˈdɪŋkəm] (Aust, NZ
fam): (fair) ~ echt, wirklich;
he's a ~ Aussie er ist ein
waschechter Australier (fam)

dinner [ˈdɪnəˈ] n Abendessen nt;
(lunch) Mittagessen nt; (public)
Diner nt; **to be at ~** beim Essen
sein; **to have ~** zu Abend/Mittag
essen; **dinner jacket** n Smoking
m; **dinner party** n
Abendgesellschaft f (mit Essen);
dinnertime n Essenszeit f

dinosaur [ˈdaɪnəsɔːˈ] n Dinosaurier m

dip [dɪp] n Tauchen (in in +akk);
to ~ (one's headlights) (Brit Auto)
abblenden; **~ped headlights**
Abblendlicht nt ▷ n (in ground)
Bodensenke f; (sauce) Dip m

diploma [dɪˈpləʊmə] n Diplom nt

diplomat [ˈdɪpləmæt] n Diplo-
mat(in) m(f); **diplomatic**
[dɪpləˈmætɪk] adj diplomatisch

dipstick [ˈdɪpstɪk] n Ölmessstab
m

direct [daɪˈrekt] adj direkt;
(cause, consequence) unmittelbar;
~ debit (mandate)
Einzugsermächtigung f;
(transaction) Abbuchung f im
Lastschriftverfahren; **~ train**
durchgehender Zug ▷ vt (aim,
send) richten (at, to an +akk); (film)
die Regie führen bei; (traffic)
regeln; **direct current** n (Elec)
Gleichstrom m

direction [dɪˈrekʃən] n (course)
Richtung f; (Cine) Regie f; **in
the ~ of ...** in Richtung ...; **~s**
pl (to a place) Wegbeschreibung f

directly [dɪˈrektlɪ] adv direkt; (at
once) sofort

director [dɪˈrektəˈ] n Direk-
tor(in) m(f), Leiter(in) m(f); (of film)
Regisseur(in) m(f)

directory [dɪˈrektərɪ] n Adressbuch nt; (Tel) Telefonbuch nt;
~ enquiries o (US) **assistance** (Tel)
Auskunft f

dirt [dɜːt] n Schmutz m, Dreck m;
dirt cheap adj spottbillig; **dirt
road** n unbefestigte Straße; **dirty**
adj schmutzig

disability [dɪsəˈbɪlɪtɪ] n
Behinderung f; **disabled**
[dɪsˈeɪbld] adj behindert,
Behinderten- ▷ npl: **the ~** die
Behinderten

disadvantage [dɪsədˈvɑːntɪdʒ]
n Nachteil m; **at a ~** benachteiligt

disagree [dɪsəˈgriː] vi anderer
Meinung sein; (two people) sich
nicht einig sein; (two reports etc)
nicht übereinstimmen; **to ~ with
sb** mit jdm nicht übereinstimmen;
(food) jdm nicht bekommen;
disagreeable adj unangenehm;
(person) unsympathisch;
disagreement n Meinungsverschiedenheit f

disappear [dɪsə'pɪəʳ] vi verschwinden; **disappearance** n Verschwinden nt

disappoint [dɪsə'pɔɪnt] vt enttäuschen; **disappointing** adj enttäuschend; **disappointment** n Enttäuschung f

disapproval [dɪsə'pruːvl] n Missbilligung f; **disapprove** [dɪsə'pruːv] vi missbilligen (of akk)

disarm [dɪs'ɑːm] vt entwaffnen ▷ vi (Pol) abrüsten; **disarmament** n Abrüstung f; **disarming** adj (smile, look) gewinnend

disaster [dɪ'zɑːstəʳ] n Katastrophe f; **disastrous** [dɪ'zɑːstrəs] adj katastrophal

disbelief [dɪsbə'liːf] n Unglaübigkeit f

disc [dɪsk] n Scheibe f, CD f; see also **disk**; (Anat) Bandscheibe f; **disc brake** n Scheibenbremse f

discharge ['dɪstʃɑːdʒ] n (Med) Ausfluss m ▷ [dɪs'tʃɑːdʒ] vt (person) entlassen; (emit) ausstoßen; (Med) ausscheiden

discipline ['dɪsɪplɪn] n Disziplin f

disc jockey ['dɪskdʒɒkɪ] n Diskjockey m

disclose [dɪs'kləʊz] vt bekannt geben; (secret) enthüllen

disco ['dɪskəʊ] (pl -s) n Disko f, Diskomusik f

discomfort [dɪs'kʌmfət] n (slight pain) leichte Schmerzen pl; (unease) Unbehagen nt

disconnect [dɪskə'nekt] vt (electricity, gas, phone) abstellen; (unplug) **to ~ the TV (from the mains)** den Stecker des Fernsehers herausziehen; (Tel) **I've been ~ed** das Gespräch ist unterbrochen worden

discontent [dɪskən'tent] n Unzufriedenheit f; **discontented** adj unzufrieden

discontinue [dɪskən'tɪnjuː] vt einstellen; (product) auslaufen lassen

discount ['dɪskaʊnt] n Rabatt m

discover [dɪs'kʌvəʳ] vt entdecken; **discovery** n Entdeckung f

discredit [dɪs'kredɪt] vt in Verruf bringen ▷ n Misskredit m

discreet [dɪs'kriːt] adj diskret

discrepancy [dɪs'krepənsɪ] n Unstimmigkeit f, Diskrepanz f

discriminate [dɪs'krɪmɪneɪt] vi unterscheiden; **to ~ against sb** jdn diskriminieren; **discrimination** [dɪskrɪmɪ'neɪʃən] n (different treatment) Diskriminierung f

discus ['dɪskəs] n Diskus m

discuss [dɪs'kʌs] vt diskutieren, besprechen; **discussion** [dɪs'kʌʃən] n Diskussion f

disease [dɪ'ziːz] n Krankheit f

disembark [dɪsɪm'bɑːk] vi von Bord gehen

disentangle [dɪsɪn'tæŋgl] vt entwirren

disgrace [dɪs'greɪs] n Schande f ▷ vt Schande machen +dat; (family etc) Schande bringen über +akk; (less strong) blamieren; **disgraceful** adj skandalös

disguise [dɪs'gaɪz] vt verkleiden; (voice) verstellen ▷ n Verkleidung f; **in ~** verkleidet

disgust [dɪs'gʌst] n Abscheu m; (physical) Ekel m ▷ vt anekeln, anwidern; **disgusting** adj widerlich; (physically) ekelhaft

dish [dɪʃ] n Schüssel f; (food) Gericht nt; **to do/wash the ~es** abwaschen; **dishcloth** n (for washing) Spültuch nt; (for drying) Geschirrtuch nt

dishearten [dɪsˈhɑːtən] vt
entmutigen; **don't be ~ed** lass den
Kopf nicht hängen!

dishonest [dɪsˈɒnɪst] adj
unehrlich

dishonour [dɪsˈɒnə°] n Schande
f

dish towel n (US) Geschirrtuch
nt; **dish washer** n
Geschirrspülmaschine f

dishy [ˈdɪʃɪ] adj (Brit fam) gut
aussehend

disillusioned [dɪsɪˈluːʒənd] adj
desillusioniert

disinfect [dɪsɪnˈfekt] vt desinfizieren; **disinfectant** n
Desinfektionsmittel nt

disintegrate [dɪsˈɪntɪgreɪt]
vi zerfallen; (group) sich
auflösen

disjointed [dɪsˈdʒɔɪntɪd] adj
unzusammenhängend

disk [dɪsk] n (Inform: floppy)
Diskette f; **disk drive** n
Diskettenlaufwerk nt; **diskette**
[dɪsˈket] n Diskette f

dislike [dɪsˈlaɪk] n Abneigung f
▷ vt nicht mögen; **to ~ doing sth**
etw ungern tun

dislocate [ˈdɪsləʊkeɪt] vt (Med)
verrenken, ausrenken

dismal [ˈdɪzməl] adj trostlos

dismantle [dɪsˈmæntl] vt
auseinandernehmen; (machine)
demontieren

dismay [dɪsˈmeɪ] n Bestürzung f;
dismayed adj bestürzt

dismiss [dɪsˈmɪs] vt (employee)
entlassen; **dismissal** n
Entlassung f

disobedience [dɪsəˈbiːdɪəns] n
Ungehorsam m; **disobedient** adj
ungehorsam; **disobey** [dɪsəˈbeɪ]
vt nicht gehorchen +dat

disorder [dɪsˈɔːdə°] n (mess)
Unordnung f; (riot) Aufruhr m;
(Med) Störung f, Leiden nt

disorganized [dɪsˈɔːgənaɪzd] adj
chaotisch

disparaging adj geringschätzig

dispatch [dɪsˈpætʃ] vt abschicken, abfertigen

dispensable [dɪsˈpensəbl] adj
entbehrlich; **dispense** vt
verteilen; **dispense with** vt
verzichten auf +akk; **dispenser** n
Automat m

disperse [dɪsˈpɜːs] vi sich
zerstreuen

display [dɪsˈpleɪ] n (exhibition)
Ausstellung f, Show f; (of goods)
Auslage f; (Tech) Anzeige f, Display
nt ▷ vt zeigen; (goods) ausstellen

disposable [dɪsˈpəʊzəbl] adj
(container, razor etc) Wegwerf-;
~ nappy Wegwerfwindel f;
disposal [dɪsˈpəʊzəl] n Loswerden nt; (of waste) Beseitigung f; **to
be at sb's ~** jdm zur Verfügung
stehen; **to have at one's
~** verfügen über; **dispose of** vt
loswerden; (waste etc) beseitigen

dispute [dɪsˈpjuːt] n Streit m;
(industrial) Auseinandersetzung f
▷ vt bestreiten

disqualification
[dɪskwɒlɪfɪˈkeɪʃən] n Disquali-
fikation f; **disqualify**
[dɪsˈkwɒlɪfaɪ] vt disqualifizieren

disregard [dɪsrɪˈgɑːd] vt nicht
beachten

disreputable [dɪsˈrepjʊtəbl] adj
verrufen

disrespect [dɪsrɪˈspekt] n
Respektlosigkeit f

disrupt [dɪsˈrʌpt] vt stören;
(interrupt) unterbrechen;
disruption [dɪsˈrʌpʃən] n
Störung f; (interruption)
Unterbrechung f

dissatisfied [dɪsˈsætɪsfaɪd] adj
unzufrieden

dissent [dɪsˈsent] n Widerspruch
m

dissolve [dɪˈzɒlv] vt auflösen ▷ vi sich auflösen

dissuade [dɪˈsweɪd] vt (davon abbringen) **to ~ sb from doing sth** jdn davon abbringen, etw zu tun

distance [ˈdɪstəns] n Entfernung f; **in the/from a ~** in/aus der Ferne; **distant** adj (a. in time) fern; (relative etc) entfernt; (person) distanziert

distaste [dɪsˈteɪst] n Abneigung f (for gegen)

distil [dɪsˈtɪl] vt destillieren; **distillery** n Brennerei f

distinct [dɪsˈtɪŋkt] adj verschieden; (clear) klar, deutlich; **distinction** [dɪsˈtɪŋkʃən] n (difference) Unterschied m; (in exam etc) Auszeichnung f; **distinctive** adj unverkennbar; **distinctly** adv deutlich

distinguish [dɪsˈtɪŋgwɪʃ] vt unterscheiden (sth from sth etw von etw)

distort [dɪsˈtɔːt] vt verzerren; (truth) verdrehen

distract [dɪsˈtrækt] vt ablenken; **distraction** [dɪsˈtrækʃən] n Ablenkung f; (diversion) Zerstreuung f

distress [dɪsˈtrɛs] n (need, danger) Not f; (suffering) Leiden nt; (mental) Qual f; (worry) Kummer m ▷ vt mitnehmen, erschüttern; **distressed area** n Notstandsgebiet nt; **distress signal** n Notsignal nt

distribute [dɪsˈtrɪbjuːt] vt verteilen; (Comm: goods) vertreiben; **distribution** [dɪstrɪˈbjuːʃən] n Verteilung f; (Comm: of goods) Vertrieb m; **distributor** [dɪsˈtrɪbjʊtə°] n (Auto) Verteiler m; (Comm) Händler(in) m(f)

district [ˈdɪstrɪkt] n Gegend f; (administrative) Bezirk m; **district attorney** n (US) Staatsanwalt m, Staatsanwältin f

distrust [dɪsˈtrʌst] vt misstrauen +dat ▷ n Misstrauen nt

disturb [dɪsˈtɜːb] vt stören; (worry) beunruhigen; **disturbance** n Störung f; **disturbing** adj beunruhigend

ditch [dɪtʃ] n Graben m ▷ vt (fam: person) den Laufpass geben +dat; (plan etc) verwerfen

ditto [ˈdɪtəʊ] adv dito, ebenfalls

dive [daɪv] n (into water) Kopfsprung m; (Aviat) Sturzflug m; (fam) zwielichtiges Lokal ▷ vi (under water) tauchen; **diver** n Taucher(in) m(f)

diverse [daɪˈvɜːs] adj verschieden; **diversion** [daɪˈvɜːʃən] n (of traffic) Umleitung f; (distraction) Ablenkung f; **divert** [daɪˈvɜːt] vt ablenken; (traffic) umleiten

divide [dɪˈvaɪd] vt teilen; (in several parts, between people) aufteilen ▷ vi sich teilen; **dividend** [ˈdɪvɪdend] n Dividende f

divine [dɪˈvaɪn] adj göttlich

diving [ˈdaɪvɪŋ] n (Sport) tauchen nt; (jumping in) Springen nt; (Sport: from board) Kunstspringen nt; **diving board** n Sprungbrett nt; **diving goggles** npl Taucherbrille f; **diving mask** n Tauchmaske f

division [dɪˈvɪʒən] n Teilung f; (Math) Division f; (department) Abteilung f; (Sport) Liga f

divorce [dɪˈvɔːs] n Scheidung f ▷ vt sich scheiden lassen von; **divorced** adj geschieden; **to get ~** sich scheiden lassen; **divorcee** [dɪvɔːˈsiː] n Geschiedene(r) mf

DIY [diːaɪˈwaɪ] abbr =

do-it-yourself; DIY centre n
Baumarkt m

dizzy ['dɪzɪ] adj schwindlig

DJ [di:'dʒeɪ] abbr = **dinner jacket**
Smoking m ▷ abbr = **disc jockey**
Diskjockey m, DJ m

DNA abbr = **desoxyribonucleic
acid** DNS f

KEYWORD

do [du:] (pt **did**, pp **done**) n (inf)
(party etc) Fete f
▷ vb aux **1** (in negative constructions
and questions) **I don't understand**
ich verstehe nicht; **didn't you
know?** wusstest du das nicht?;
what do you think? was meinen
Sie?
2 (for emphasis, in polite phrases) **she
does seem rather tired** sie
scheint wirklich sehr müde zu
sein; **do sit down/greifen yourself**
setzen Sie sich doch hin/greifen
Sie doch zu
3 (used to avoid repeating vb) **she
swims better than I do** sie
schwimmt besser als ich; **she
lives in Glasgow — so do I** sie
wohnt in Glasgow — ich auch
4 (in tag questions) **you like him,
don't you?** du magst/Sie mögen
ihn doch, oder?
▷ vt **1** (carry out, perform etc) tun,
machen; **what are you doing
tonight?** was machst du/machen
Sie heute Abend?; **I've spent
nothing to do** ich habe nichts zu
tun; **to do one's hair/nails** sich
die Haare/Nägel machen
2 (car etc) fahren
▷ vi **1** (act, behave) **do as I do** mach
es wie ich
2 (get on, fare) **he's doing
well/badly at school** er ist
gut/schlecht in der Schule; **how
do you do?** guten Tag

3 (be suitable) gehen; (be sufficient)
reichen; **to make do (with)**
auskommen mit
do away with vt (kill)
umbringen; (abolish: law etc)
abschaffen
do up vt (laces, dress, buttons)
zumachen; (renovate: room, house)
renovieren
do with vt (need) brauchen; (be
connected) zu tun haben mit
do without vt, vi auskommen
ohne
do up vt (fasten) zumachen;
(parcel) verschnüren; (renovate)
wiederherrichten
do with vt (need) brauchen; **I
could ~ a drink** ich könnte einen
Drink gebrauchen
do without vt auskommen
ohne; **I can ~ your comments**
auf deine Kommentare kann ich
verzichten

dock [dɒk] n Dock nt; (Jur)
Anklagebank f; **docker** n
Hafenarbeiter m; **dockyard** n
Werft f

doctor ['dɒktə°] n Arzt m, Ärztin;
(in title, also academic) Doktor m

document ['dɒkjʊmənt] n
Dokument nt; **documentary**
[dɒkjʊ'mentərɪ] n Dokumentarfilm m; **documentation**
[dɒkjʊmen'teɪʃən] n Dokumen-
tation f

docusoap ['dɒkjʊsəʊp] n
Reality-Serie f, Dokusoap f

doddery ['dɒdərɪ] adj tatterig

dodgem ['dɒdʒəm] n Auto-
skooter m

dodgy ['dɒdʒɪ] adj nicht ganz in
Ordnung; (dishonest, unreliable)
zwielichtig; **he has a ~ stomach**
er hat sich den Magen verdorben

dog [dɒg] n Hund m; **dog food** n
Hundefutter nt; **doggie bag**

['dɒgɪˈbæg] n Tüte oder Box, in der
Essensreste aus dem Restaurant
mit nach Hause genommen werden
können

do-it-yourself ['duːɪtʃəˈself] n
Heimwerken nt, Do-it-yourself nt
▷ adj Heimwerker-;
do-it-yourselfer n Bastler(in)
m(f), Heimwerker(in) m(f)

doll [dɒl] n Puppe f

dollar ['dɒlə*] n Dollar m

dolphin ['dɒlfɪn] n Delphin m

domain n Domäne f; (Inform)
Domain f

dome [dəʊm] n Kuppel f

domestic [dəˈmestɪk] adj häuslich; (within country) Innen-,
Binnen-; **domestic animal** n
Haustier nt; **domesticated**
[dəˈmestɪkeɪtɪd] adj (person)
häuslich; (animal) zahm; **domestic
flight** n Inlandsflug m

domicile ['dɒmɪsaɪl] n (ständi-
ger) Wohnsitz

dominant ['dɒmɪnənt] adj
dominierend, vorherrschend;
dominate ['dɒmɪneɪt] vt
beherrschen

dominoes ['dɒmɪnəʊz] npl
Domino(spiel) nt

donate [dəʊˈneɪt] vt spenden;
donation n Spende f

done [dʌn] pp of **do** ▷ adj (cooked)
gar; **well ~** durchgebraten

doner (kebab) n ['dɒnəkəˈbæb] n
Döner (Kebab) m

dongle ['dɒŋgəl] n Dongle m

donkey ['dɒŋkɪ] n Esel m

donor ['dəʊnə] n Spender(in)
m(f)

don't [dəʊnt] contr of **do not**

doom [duːm] n Schicksal nt;
(downfall) Verderben nt

door [dɔː*] n Tür f; **doorbell** n
Türklingel f; **door handle** n
Türklinke f; **doorknob** n Türknauf
m; **doormat** n Fußabtreter m;

['dɒgɪˈbæg] n Tüte oder Box, in der

doorstep n Türstufe f; **right
on our ~** direkt vor unserer
Haustür

dope [dəʊp] (Sport) n (for athlete)
Aufputschmittel nt ▷ vt dopen

dormitory ['dɔːmɪtrɪ] n Schlafsaal m; (US) Studentenwohnheim
nt

dosage ['dəʊsɪdʒ] n Dosierung f;
dose [dəʊs] n Dosis f

dot [dɒt] n Punkt m; **on the ~** auf
die Minute genau, pünktlich

dotcom ['dɒtkɒm] n: ~ (**company**) Internetfirma f,
Dotcom-Unternehmen nt

dote on [dəʊt ɒn] vt abgöttisch
lieben

dotted line n punktierte Linie

double ['dʌbl] adj, adv doppelt;
~ the quantity die zweifache
Menge, doppelt so viel ▷ vt
verdoppeln ▷ n (person)
Doppelgänger(in) m(f); (Cine)
Double nt; **double bass** n
Kontrabass m; **double bed** n
Doppelbett nt; **double-click** vt
(Inform) doppelklicken; **double
cream** n Sahne mit hohem
Fettgehalt; **doubledecker** n
Doppeldecker m; **double glazing**
n Doppelverglasung f;
double-park vi in zweiter Reihe
parken; **double room** n
Doppelzimmer nt; **doubles** npl
(Sport: also match) Doppel nt

doubt [daʊt] n Zweifel m; **no
~** ohne Zweifel, zweifellos,
wahrscheinlich; **to have one's ~s**
Bedenken haben ▷ vt bezweifeln;
(statement, word) anzweifeln; **I ~ it**
das bezweifle ich; **doubtful** adj
zweifelhaft, zweifelnd; **it is
~ whether ...** es ist fraglich, ob ...;
doubtless adv ohne Zweifel,
sicherlich

dough [dəʊ] n Teig m; **doughnut**
n Donut m (rundes Hefegebäck)

dove [dʌv] n Taube f

down [daʊn] n Daunen pl; (fluff)
Flaum m ▷ adv unten; (motion)
nach unten; (towards speaker)
herunter; (away from speaker)
hinunter; **~ here/there** hier/dort
unten; (downstairs) **they came
~ for breakfast** sie kamen zum
Frühstück herunter; (southwards)
he came ~ from Scotland er kam
von Schottland herunter ▷ prep
(towards speaker) herunter; (away
from speaker) hinunter; **to drive
~ the hill/road** den Berg/die
Straße hinunter fahren; (along) **to
walk ~ the street** die Straße
entlang gehen; **he's ~ the pub**
(fam) er ist in der Kneipe ▷ vt
(fam: drink) runterkippen ▷ adj
niedergeschlagen, deprimiert

down-and-out adj
heruntergekommen ▷ n
Obdachlose(r) mf, Penner(in) m(f);
downcast adj niedergeschlagen;
downfall n Sturz m;
down-hearted adj entmutigt;
downhill adv bergab; **he's going
~** (fig) mit ihm geht es bergab

○ **DOWNING STREET**
○
○ **Downing Street** ist die Straße
○ in London, die von Whitehall
○ zum St James's Park führt, und
○ in der sich der offizielle
○ Wohnsitz des Premierministers
○ (Nr. 10) und des Finanzministers
○ (Nr. 11) befindet. Im weiteren
○ Sinne bezieht sich der Begriff
○ „Downing Street" auf die
○ britische Regierung.

download ['daʊnləʊd] vt
herunterladen; **downloadable** adj
(Inform) herunterladbar;
downmarket adj für den
Massenmarkt; **down payment** n

Anzahlung f; **downpour** n
Platzregen m; **downs** npl Hügel-
land nt; **downsize** vt verkleinern
▷ vi sich verkleinern

Down's syndrome
['daʊnz'sɪndrəʊm] n (Med)
Downsyndrom nt

downstairs [daʊn'steəz] adv
unten; (motion) nach unten;
downstream adv flussabwärts;
downtime n Ausfallzeit f;
downtown adv (be, work etc) in
der Innenstadt; (go) in die
Innenstadt ▷ adj (US) in der
Innenstadt; **~ Chicago** die
Innenstadt von Chicago; **down
under** adv (fam: in/to Australia)
in/nach Australien; (in/to New
Zealand) in/nach Neuseeland;
downwards adv, adj nach unten;
(movement, trend) Abwärts-

doze [dəʊz] vi dösen ▷ n
Nickerchen nt

dozen ['dʌzn] n Dutzend nt; **two
~ eggs** zwei Dutzend Eier; **~s of
times** x-mal

DP abbr = **data processing** DV f

drab [dræb] adj trist; (colour)
düster

draft [drɑːft] n (outline) Entwurf
m; (US Mil) Einberufung f

drag [dræg] vt schleppen ▷ n (fam)
to be a ~ (boring) stinklangweilig
sein; (laborious) ein ziemlicher
Schlauch sein; **drag on** vi sich in
die Länge ziehen

dragon ['drægən] n Drache m;
dragonfly n Libelle f

drain [dreɪn] n Abfluss m ▷ vt
(water, oil) ablassen; (vegetables etc)
abgießen; (land) entwässern,
trockenlegen ▷ vi (of water)
abfließen; **drainpipe** n
Abflussrohr nt

drama ['drɑːmə] n (a. fig) Drama
nt; **dramatic** [drə'mætɪk] adj
dramatisch

drank [dræŋk] pt of **drink**

drapes [dreips] npl (US) Vorhänge pl

drastic ['dræstik] adj drastisch

draught [dra:ft] n (Luft)zug m; **there's a ~** es zieht; **on ~** (beer) vom Fass; **draughts** nsing Damespiel nt; **draughty** adj zugig

draw [drɔ:] (**drew, drawn**) vt (pull) ziehen; (crowd) anlocken, anziehen; (picture) zeichnen ▷ vi (Sport) unentschieden spielen ▷ n (Sport) Unentschieden nt; (attraction) Attraktion f; (for lottery) Ziehung f; **draw out** vt herausziehen; (money) abheben; **draw up** vt (formulate) entwerfen; (list) erstellen ▷ vi (car) anhalten; **drawback** n Nachteil m; **drawbridge** n Zugbrücke f

drawer ['drɔ:ᵉ] n Schublade f

drawing ['drɔ:ɪŋ] n Zeichnung f; **drawing pin** n Reißzwecke f

drawn [drɔ:n] pp of **draw**

dread [dred] n Furcht f (of vor +dat) ▷ vt sich fürchten vor +dat; **dreadful** adj furchtbar; **dreadlocks** npl Rastalocken pl

dream [dri:m] (**dreamed** o **dreamt, dreamed** o **dreamt**) vt, vi träumen (about von) ▷ n Traum m; **dreamt** [dremt] pt, pp of **dream**

dreary ['drɪərɪ] adj (weather, place) trostlos; (book etc) langweilig

drench [drentʃ] vt durchnässen

dress [dres] n Kleidung f; (garment) Kleid nt ▷ vt anziehen; (Med: wound) verbinden; **to get ~ed** sich anziehen; **dress up** vi sich fein machen; (in costume) sich verkleiden (as als); **dress circle** n (Theat) erster Rang; **dresser** n Anrichte f; (US: dressing table) (Frisier)kommode f; **dressing** n (Gastr) Dressing nt, Soße f; (Med) Verband m; **dressing gown** n

Bademantel m; **dressing room** n (Theat) Künstlergarderobe f; **dressing table** n Frisierkommode f; **dress rehearsal** n (Theat) Generalprobe f

drew [dru:] pt of **draw**

dried [draid] adj getrocknet; (milk, flowers) Trocken-; **~ fruit** Dörrobst nt; **drier** ['draiᵉ] n see **dryer**

drift [drift] vi treiben ▷ n (of snow) Verwehung f; (fig) Tendenz f; **if you get my ~** wenn du mich richtig verstehst/wenn Sie mich richtig verstehen

drill [dril] n Bohrer m ▷ vt, vi bohren

drink [drɪŋk] (**drank, drunk**) vt, vi trinken ▷ n Getränk nt; (alcoholic) Drink m; **drink-driving** n (Brit) Trunkenheit f am Steuer; **drinking water** n Trinkwasser nt

drip [drip] n Tropfen m ▷ vi tropfen; **drip-dry** adj bügelfrei; **dripping** n Bratenfett nt ▷ adj: **~ (wet)** tropfnass

drive [draiv] (**drove, driven**) vt (car, person in car) fahren; (force: person, animal) treiben; (Tech) antreiben; **to ~ sb mad** jdn verrückt machen ▷ vi fahren ▷ n Fahrt f; (entrance) Einfahrt f, Auffahrt f; (Inform) Laufwerk nt; **to go for a ~** spazieren fahren; **drive away, drive off** vi wegfahren ▷ vt vertreiben

drive-in adj Drive-in-; **~ cinema** (US) Autokino nt

driven ['drɪvn] pp of **drive**

driver ['draivᵉ] n Fahrer(in) m(f); (of train) Treiber m; **~'s license** (US) Führerschein m; **~'s seat** Fahrersitz m; **driving** ['draiviŋ] n (Auto)fahren nt; **he likes ~** er fährt gern Auto; **driving lesson** n

Fahrstunde f; **driving licence** n (Brit) Führerschein m; **driving school** n Fahrschule f; **driving seat** n (Brit) Fahrersitz m; **to be in the ~** alles im Griff haben; **driving test** n Fahrprüfung f

drizzle ['drɪzl] n Nieselregen m ▷ vi nieseln

drop [drɒp] n (of liquid) Tropfen m; (fall in price etc) Rückgang m ▷ vt (a. fig: give up) fallen lassen ▷ vi (fall) herunterfallen; (figures, temperature) sinken, zurückgehen; **drop by, drop in** vi vorbeikommen; **drop off** vi (to sleep) einnicken; **drop out** vi (withdraw) aussteigen; (university) das Studium abbrechen; **dropout** n Aussteiger(in) m(f) .

drought [draʊt] n Dürre f

drove [drəʊv] pt of **drive**

drown [draʊn] vi ertrinken ▷ vt ertränken

drowsy ['draʊzɪ] adj schläfrig

drug [drʌg] n (Med) Medikament nt, Arznei f; (addictive) Droge f; (narcotic) Rauschgift nt; **to be on ~s** drogensüchtig sein ▷ vt (mit Medikamenten) betäuben; **drug addict** n Rauschgiftsüchtige(r) mf; **drug dealer** n Drogenhändler(in) m(f); **druggist** n (US) Drogist(in) m(f); **drugstore** n (US) Drogerie f

drum [drʌm] n Trommel f; **~s** pl Schlagzeug nt; **drummer** n Schlagzeuger(in) m(f)

drunk [drʌŋk] pp of **drink** ▷ adj betrunken; **to get ~** sich betrinken ▷ n Betrunkene(r) mf; (alcoholic) Trinker(in) m(f); **drunk-driving** n (US) Trunkenheit f am Steuer; **drunken** adj betrunken, besoffen

dry [draɪ] adj trocken ▷ vt trocknen; (dishes, oneself, one's hands etc) abtrocknen ▷ vi trocknen, trocken werden; **dry out**

vi trocknen; **dry up** vi austrocknen; **dry-clean** vt chemisch reinigen; **dry-cleaning** n chemische Reinigung; **dryer** n Trockner m; (for hair) Föhn m; (over head) Trockenhaube f

DTP abbr = **desktop publishing** DTP nt

dual ['djʊəl] adj doppelt; **~ carriageway** (Brit) zweispurige Schnellstraße f; **~ nationality** doppelte Staatsangehörigkeit

dubbed [dʌbd] adj (film) synchronisiert

dubious ['djuːbɪəs] adj zweifelhaft

duchess ['dʌtʃəs] n Herzogin f

duck [dʌk] n Ente f

dude [duːd] n (US fam) Typ m; **a cool ~** ein cooler Typ

due [djuː] adj (time) fällig; (fitting) angemessen; **in ~ course** zu gegebener Zeit; **~ to** infolge +gen, wegen +gen ▷ adv: **~ south/north** etc direkt nach Norden/Süden etc

dug [dʌg] pt, pp of **dig**

duke [djuːk] n Herzog m

dull [dʌl] adj (colour, light, weather) trübe; (boring) langweilig

duly ['djuːlɪ] adv ordnungsgemäß; (as expected) wie erwartet

dumb [dʌm] adj stumm; (fam: stupid) doof, blöde

dumb-bell [dʌmbel] n Hantel f

dummy ['dʌmɪ] n (sham) Attrappe f; (in game) Schaufensterpuppe f; (Brit: teat) Schnuller m; (fam: person) Dummkopf m ▷ adj unecht, Schein-; **~ run** Testlauf m

dump [dʌmp] n Abfallhaufen m; (fam: place) Kaff nt ▷ vt (lit, fig) abladen; (fam) **he ~ed her** er hat mir ihr Schluss gemacht

dumpling ['dʌmplɪŋ] n Kloß m, Knödel m

dune [djuːn] n Düne f

dung [dʌŋ] n (manure) Mist m
dungarees [dʌŋgə'riːz] npl
Latzhose f
dungeon ['dʌndʒən] n Kerker m
duplex ['djuːpleks] n
zweistöckige Wohnung; (US)
Doppelhaushälfte f
duplicate ['djuːplɪkɪt] n Dup-
likat nt ▷ ['djuːplɪkeɪt] vt (make
copies of) kopieren; (repeat)
wiederholen
durable ['djuərəbl] adj haltbar;
duration [djuə'reɪʃən] n Dauer f
during ['djuərɪŋ] prep (time)
während +gen
dusk [dʌsk] n Abenddämmerung f
dust [dʌst] n Staub m ▷ vt
abstauben; **dustbin** n (Brit)
Mülleimer m; **dustcart** n (Brit)
Müllwagen m; **duster** n
Staubtuch nt; **dust jacket** n
Schutzumschlag m; **dustman** n
(Brit) Müllmann m; **dustpan** n
Kehrschaufel f; **dusty** adj staubig
Dutch [dʌtʃ] adj holländisch ▷ n
(language) Holländisch nt; **to
speak/talk double ~** (fam)
Quatsch reden; **the ~** pl die
Holländer; **Dutchman** (pl **-men**)
n Holländer m; **Dutchwoman** (pl
-women) n Holländerin f
duty ['djuːtɪ] n Pflicht f; (task)
Aufgabe f; (tax) Zoll m; **on/off ~** im
Dienst/nicht im Dienst; **to be on
~** Dienst haben; **duty-free** adj
zollfrei; **~ shop** Dutyfreeshop m
duvet ['duːveɪ] n Federbett nt
DVD n abbr = **digital versatile
disk** DVD f; **DVD player** n
DVD-Player m; **DVD recorder** n
DVD-Rekorder m
dwelling ['dwelɪŋ] n Wohnung f
dwindle ['dwɪndl] vi schwinden
dye [daɪ] n Farbstoff m ▷ vt
färben
dynamic [daɪ'næmɪk] adj
dynamisch

dynamo ['daɪnəməʊ] n Dynamo m
dyslexia [dɪs'leksɪə] n Legasthenie
f; **dyslexic** adj legasthenisch; **to
be ~** Legastheniker(in) sein

e

E [iː] *abbr* = **east** (geo) O; *abbr* =
ecstasy (drug) Ecstasy *nt*

E111 form *n* ≈
Auslandskrankenschein *m*

each [iːtʃ] *adj* jeder/jede/jedes
▷ *pron* jeder/jede/jedes; **I'll have
one of ~** ich nehme von jedem
eins; **they ~ have a car** jeder von
ihnen hat ein Auto; **~ other**
einander, sich; **for/against
~ other** füreinander/
gegeneinander ▷ *adv* je; **they
cost 10 euros ~** sie kosten je 10
Euro, sie kosten 10 Euro das Stück

eager [ˈiːgə°] *adj* eifrig; **to be ~ to
do sth** darauf brennen, etw zu tun

eagle [ˈiːgl] *n* Adler *m*

ear [ɪə°] *n* Ohr *nt*; **earache** *n*
Ohrenschmerzen *pl*; **eardrum** *n*
Trommelfell *nt*

earl [ɜːl] *n* Graf *m*

early [ˈɜːlɪ] *adj, adv* früh; **to be 10
minutes ~** 10 Minuten zu früh
kommen; **at the earliest**
frühestens; **in ~ June/2008**
Anfang Juni/2008; **~ retirement**
vorzeitiger Ruhestand; **~ warning
system** Frühwarnsystem *nt*

earn [ɜːn] *vt* verdienen

earnest [ˈɜːnɪst] *adj* ernst; **in
~** im Ernst

earnings [ˈɜːnɪŋz] *npl* Verdienst
m, Einkommen *nt*

earplug *n* Ohrenstöpsel *m*,
Ohropax® *nt*; **earring** *n* Ohrring
m

earth [ɜːθ] *n* Erde *f*; **what on
~ ...?** was in aller Welt ...? ▷ *vt*
erden; **earthenware** *n* Tonwaren
pl; **earthquake** *n* Erdbeben *nt*

earwig [ˈɪəwɪg] *n* Ohrwurm *m*

ease [iːz] *vt* (pain) lindern;
(burden) erleichtern ▷ *n* (easiness)
Leichtigkeit *f*; **to feel at ~** sich
wohlfühlen; **to feel ill at ~** sich
nicht wohlfühlen; **easily** [ˈiːzɪlɪ]
adv leicht; **he is ~ the best** er ist
mit Abstand der Beste

east [iːst] *n* Osten *m*; **to the ~ of**
östlich von ▷ *adv* (go, face) nach
Osten ▷ *adj* Ost-, **~ wind** Ostwind
m; **eastbound** *adj* (in) Richtung
Osten

Easter [ˈiːstə°] *n* Ostern *nt*; **at
~** zu Ostern; **Easter egg** *n* Osterei
nt; **Easter Sunday** *n*
Ostersonntag *m*

eastern [ˈiːstən] *adj* Ost-,
östlich; **Eastern Europe** *n*
Osteuropa *nt*; **East Germany** *n*
Ostdeutschland *nt*; **former ~** die
ehemalige DDR, die neuen
Bundesländer; **eastwards**
[ˈiːstwədz] *adv* nach Osten

easy [ˈiːzɪ] *adj* leicht; (task,
solution) einfach; (life) bequem;
(manner) ungezwungen;
easy-going *adj* gelassen

eat [iːt] (**ate**, **eaten**) *vt* essen;
(animal) fressen; **eat out** *vi* zum

Essen ausgehen; **eat up** vt aufessen; (animal) auffressen

eaten ['iːtn] pp of **eat**

eavesdrop ['iːvzdrɒp] vi (heimlich) lauschen; **to ~ on sb** jdn belauschen

e-book ['iːbʊk] n **E-Book** nt

eccentric [ɪk'sentrɪk] adj exzentrisch

echo ['ekəʊ] (pl **-es**) n Echo nt ▷ vi widerhallen

ecological [iːkə'lɒdʒɪkl] adj ökologisch; **~ disaster** Umweltkatastrophe f; **ecology** [ɪ'kɒlədʒɪ] n Ökologie f

economic [iːkə'nɒmɪk] adj wirtschaftlich, Wirtschafts-; **~ aid** Wirtschaftshilfe f; **economical** adj wirtschaftlich; (person) sparsam; **economics** nsing or pl Wirtschaftswissenschaft f; **economist** [ɪ'kɒnəmɪst] n Wirtschaftswissenschaftler(in) m(f); **economize** [ɪ'kɒnəmaɪz] vi sparen (on an +dat); **economy** [ɪ'kɒnəmɪ] n (of state) Wirtschaft f; (thrift) Sparsamkeit f; **economy class** n (Aviat) Economyclass f

ecstasy ['ekstəsɪ] n Ekstase f; (drug) Ecstasy f

eczema ['eksɪmə] n Ekzem nt

edge [edʒ] n Rand m; (of knife) Schneide f; **on ~** nervös; **edgy** ['edʒɪ] adj nervös

edible ['edɪbl] adj essbar

Edinburgh ['edɪnbərə] n Edinburg nt

edit ['edɪt] vt (series, newspaper etc) herausgeben; (text) redigieren; (film) schneiden; (Inform) editieren; **edition** [ɪ'dɪʃən] n Ausgabe f; **editor** n Redakteur(in) m(f); (of series etc) Herausgeber(in) m(f); **editorial** [edɪ'tɔːrɪəl] adj Redaktions- ▷ n Leitartikel m

educate ['edjʊkeɪt] vt (child) erziehen; (at school, university)

ausbilden; (public) aufklären; **educated** adj gebildet; **education** [edjʊ'keɪʃən] n Erziehung f; (studies, training) Ausbildung f; (subject of study) Pädagogik f; (system) Schulwesen nt; (knowledge) Bildung f; **educational** adj pädagogisch; (instructive) lehrreich

eel [iːl] n Aal m

eerie ['ɪərɪ] adj unheimlich

effect [ɪ'fekt] n Wirkung f (on auf +akk); **to come into ~** in Kraft treten; **effective** adj wirksam, effektiv

effeminate [ɪ'femɪnət] adj (of man) tuntig

efficiency [ɪ'fɪʃənsɪ] n Leistungsfähigkeit f; (of method) Wirksamkeit f; **efficient** adj (Tech) leistungsfähig; (method) wirksam, effizient

effort ['efət] n Anstrengung f; (attempt) Versuch m; **to make an ~** sich anstrengen; **effortless** adj mühelos

e.g. abbr = exempli gratia (for example) z. B.

egg [eg] n Ei nt; **eggcup** n Eierbecher m; **eggplant** n (US) Aubergine f; **eggshell** n Eierschale f

ego ['iːgəʊ] (pl **-s**) n Ich nt; (self-esteem) Selbstbewusstsein nt; **ego(t)ist** ['egəʊ(t)ɪst] n Egozentriker(in) m(f)

Egypt ['iːdʒɪpt] n Ägypten nt; **Egyptian** [ɪ'dʒɪpʃən] adj ägyptisch ▷ n Ägypter(in) m(f)

eiderdown ['aɪdədaʊn] n Daunendecke f

eight [eɪt] num acht; **at the age of ~** im Alter von acht Jahren; **it's ~ (o'clock)** es ist acht Uhr ▷ n (a. bus etc) Acht f; (boat) Achter m; **eighteen** [eɪ'tiːn] num achtzehn ▷ n Achtzehn f; see also **eight**;

eighteenth adj achtzehnte(r, s);
see also **eighth**; **eighth** [eɪtθ] adj
achte(r, s); **the ~ of June** der achte
Juni ▷ n (fraction) Achtel nt; **an**
~ of a litre ein Achtelliter;
eightieth ['eɪtɪəθ] adj achtzig-
ste(r, s); see also **eighth**; **eighty**
['eɪtɪ] num achtzig ▷ n Achtzig f;
see also **eight**

Eire ['eərə] n die Republik Irland
either ['aɪðə°] conj: **~ ... or**
entweder ... oder ▷ pron: **~ of the**
two eine(r, s) von beiden ▷ adj:
on ~ side auf beiden Seiten ▷ adv:
I won't go ~ ich gehe auch nicht
eject [ɪ'dʒekt] vt ausstoßen;
(person) vertreiben
elaborate [ɪ'læbərət] adj (complex) kompliziert; (plan)
ausgeklügelt; (decoration)
kunstvoll ▷ vi [ɪ'læbəreɪt] **could**
you ~ on that? könntest
du/könnten Sie mehr darüber
sagen?
elastic [ɪ'læstɪk] adj elastisch;
~ band Gummiband nt
elbow ['elbəʊ] n Ellbogen m; **to**
give sb the ~ (fam) jdm den
Laufpass geben
elder ['eldə°] adj (of two) älter ▷ n
Ältere(r) mf; (Bot) Holunder m;
elderly adj ältere(r, s) ▷ n: **the**
~ die älteren Leute; **eldest**
['eldɪst] adj älteste(r, s)
elect [ɪ'lekt] vt wählen; **he was**
~ed chairman er wurde zum
Vorsitzenden gewählt; **election**
[ɪ'lekʃən] n Wahl f; **election**
campaign n Wahlkampf m;
electioneering [ɪlekʃə'nɪərɪŋ] n
Wahlpropaganda f; **electorate**
[ɪ'lektərɪt] n Wähler pl
electric [ɪ'lektrɪk] adj elektrisch;
(car, motor, razor etc) Elektro-;
~ blanket Heizdecke f; **~ cooker**
Elektroherd m; **~ current**
elektrischer Strom; **~ shock**

Stromschlag m; **electrical** adj
elektrisch; **~ goods/appliances**
Elektrogeräte; **electrician**
[ɪlek'trɪʃən] n Elektriker(in) m(f);
electricity [ɪlek'trɪsɪtɪ] n Elektrizität f; **electrocute**
[ɪ'lektrəʊkjuːt] vt durch einen
Stromschlag töten; **electronic**
[ɪlek'trɒnɪk] adj elektronisch

elegance ['elɪgəns] n Eleganz f;
elegant adj elegant
element ['elɪmənt] n Element
nt; **an ~ of truth** ein Körnchen
Wahrheit; **elementary**
[elɪ'mentərɪ] adj einfach; (basic)
grundlegend; **~ stage**
Anfangsstadium nt; **~ school** (US)
Grundschule f; **~ maths/French**
Grundkenntnisse in
Mathematik/Französisch
elephant ['elɪfənt] n Elefant m
elevator ['elɪveɪtə°] n (US)
Fahrstuhl m
eleven [ɪ'levn] num elf
▷ n (team, bus etc) Elf f see
eight; **eleventh** [ɪ'levnθ] adj
elfte(r, s) ▷ n (fraction) Elftel nt
see **eighth**
eligible ['elɪdʒəbl] adj infrage
kommend; (for grant etc)
berechtigt; **~ for a**
pension/competition
pensions-/teilnahmeberechtigt;
~ bachelor begehrter Junggeselle
eliminate [ɪ'lɪmɪneɪt] vt
ausschließen (from aus),
ausschalten; (problem etc)
beseitigen; **elimination** n
Ausschluss m (from aus); (of problem
etc) Beseitigung f
elm [elm] n Ulme f
elope [ɪ'ləʊp] vi durchbrennen
(with sb mit jdm)
eloquent ['eləkwənt] adj
redegewandt
else [els] adv: **anybody/any-**
thing ~ (in addition) sonst (noch)

jemand/etwas; *(other)* ein anderer/etwas anderes; **somebody** ~ jemand anders; **everyone** ~ alle anderen; **or** ~ sonst; **elsewhere** *adv* anderswo, woanders; *(direction)* woandershin

ELT *abbr* = **English Language Teaching**

email ['i:meɪl] *vi, vt* mailen *(sth to sb* jdm etw) ▷ *n* E-Mail *f;* **email address** *n* E-Mail-Adresse *f*

emancipated [ɪ'mænsɪpeɪtɪd] *adj* emanzipiert

embankment [ɪm'bæŋkmənt] *n* Böschung *f; (for railway)* Bahndamm *m*

embargo [ɪm'bɑːɡəʊ] *(pl* **-es**) *n* Embargo *nt*

embark [ɪm'bɑːk] *vi* an Bord gehen

embarrass [ɪm'bærəs] *vt* in Verlegenheit bringen; **embarrassed** *adj* verlegen; **embarrassing** *adj* peinlich

embassy ['embəsɪ] *n* Botschaft *f*

embrace [ɪm'breɪs] *vt* umarmen ▷ *n* Umarmung *f*

embroider [ɪm'brɔɪdə°] *vt* besticken; **embroidery** *n* Stickerei *f*

embryo ['embrɪəʊ] *(pl* **-s**) *n* Embryo *m*

emerald ['emərəld] *n* Smaragd *m*

emerge [ɪ'mɜːdʒ] *vi* auftauchen; **it ~d that ...** es stellte sich heraus, dass ...

emergency [ɪ'mɜːdʒənsɪ] *n* Notfall *m* ▷ *adj* Not-; **~ exit** Notausgang *m;* **~ landing** Notlandung *f;* **~ room** *(US)* Unfallstation *f;* **~ service** Notdienst *m;* **~ stop** Vollbremsung *f*

emigrate ['emɪɡreɪt] *vi* auswandern

emit [ɪ'mɪt] *vt* ausstoßen; *(heat)* abgeben

emoticon [ɪ'məʊtɪkən] *n (Inform)* Emoticon *nt*

emotion [ɪ'məʊʃən] *n* Emotion *f,* Gefühl *nt;* **emotional** *adj (person)* emotional; *(experience, moment, scene)* ergreifend

emperor ['empərə°] *n* Kaiser *m*

emphasis ['emfəsɪs] *n* Betonung *f;* **emphasize** ['emfəsaɪz] *vt* betonen; **emphatic;** **emphatically** [ɪm'fætɪk, -lɪ] *adj, adv* nachdrücklich

empire ['empaɪə°] *n* Reich *nt*

employ [ɪm'plɔɪ] *vt* beschäftigen; *(hire)* anstellen; *(use)* anwenden; **employee** [emplɔɪ'i:] *n* Angestellte(r) *mf;* **employer** *n* Arbeitgeber(in) *m(f);* **employment** *n* Beschäftigung *f; (position)* Stellung *f;* **employment agency** *n* Stellenvermittlung *f*

empress ['emprɪs] *n* Kaiserin *f*

empty ['emptɪ] *adj* leer ▷ *vt (contents)* leeren; *(container)* ausleeren

enable [ɪ'neɪbl] *vt:* **to ~ sb to do sth** es jdm ermöglichen, etw zu tun

enamel [ɪ'næməl] *n* Email *nt; (of teeth)* Zahnschmelz *m*

enchanting [ɪn'tʃɑːntɪŋ] *adj* bezaubernd

enclose [ɪn'kləʊz] *vt* einschließen; *(in letter)* beilegen *(in, with dat);* **enclosure** [ɪn'kləʊʒə°] *n (for animals)* Gehege *nt; (in letter)* Anlage *f*

encore ['ɒŋkɔː°] *n* Zugabe *f*

encounter [ɪn'kaʊntə°] *n* Begegnung *f* ▷ *vt (person)* begegnen *+dat; (difficulties)* stoßen auf *+akk*

encourage [ɪn'kʌrɪdʒ] *vt* ermutigen; **encouragement** *n* Ermutigung *f*

encyclopaedia
[ensaɪkləʊˈpiːdɪə] n Lexikon nt,
Enzyklopädie f

end [end] n Ende nt; (of film, play
etc) Schluss m; (purpose) Zweck m;
at the ~ of May Ende Mai; **in the
~** schließlich; **to come to an ~** zu
Ende gehen ▷ vt beenden ▷ vi
enden; **end up** vi enden

endanger [ɪnˈdeɪndʒə˚] vt
gefährden; **~ed species** vom
Aussterben bedrohte Art

endeavour [ɪnˈdevə˚] n Bemühung f ▷ vi sich bemühen
(to do sth etw zu tun)

ending [ˈendɪŋ] n (of book)
Ausgang m; (last part) Schluss m;
(of word) Endung f; **endless**
[ˈendlɪs] adj endlos; (possibilities)
unendlich

endurance [ɪnˈdjʊərəns] n
Ausdauer f; **endure** [ɪnˈdjʊə˚] vt
ertragen

enemy [ˈenɪmɪ] n Feind(in) m(f)
▷ adj feindlich

energetic [enəˈdʒetɪk] adj
energiegeladen; (active) aktiv;
energy [ˈenədʒɪ] n Energie f

enforce [ɪnˈfɔːs] vt durchsetzen;
(obedience) erzwingen

engage [ɪnˈgeɪdʒ] vt (employ)
einstellen; (singer, performer)
engagieren; **engaged** adj verlobt;
(toilet, telephone line) besetzt; **to
get ~** sich verloben (to mit);
engaged tone n (Brit Tel)
Belegtzeichen nt; **engagement** n
(to marry) Verlobung f; **~ ring**
Verlobungsring m; **engaging** adj
gewinnend

engine [ˈendʒɪn] n (Auto) Motor
m; (Rail) Lokomotive f; **~ failure**
(Auto) Motorschaden m; **~ trouble**
(Auto) Defekt m am Motor;
engineer [endʒɪˈnɪə˚] n In-
genieur(in) m(f); (US Rail)
Lokomotivführer(in) m(f);

engineering [endʒɪˈnɪərɪŋ] n
Technik f; (mechanical ~)
Maschinenbau m; (subject)
Ingenieurwesen nt; **engine
immobilizer** n (Auto)
Wegfahrsperre f

England [ˈɪŋglənd] n England
nt; **English** adj englisch; **he's ~**
ist Engländer; **the ~ Channel** der
Ärmelkanal ▷ n (language)
Englisch nt; **in ~** auf Englisch; **to
translate into ~** ins Englische
übersetzen; (people) **the ~** pl die
Engländer; **Englishman** (pl **-men**)
n Engländer m; **Englishwoman**
(pl **-women**) n Engländerin f

engrave [ɪnˈgreɪv] vt ein-
gravieren; **engraving** n Stich
m

engrossed [ɪnˈgrəʊst] adj
vertieft (in sth in etw akk)

enigma [ɪˈnɪgmə] n Rätsel nt

enjoy [ɪnˈdʒɔɪ] vt genießen; **I
~ reading** ich lese gern; **he ~s
teasing her** es macht ihm Spaß,
sie aufzuziehen; **did you ~ the
film?** hat dir der Film gefallen?;
enjoyable adj angenehm;
(entertaining) unterhaltsam;
enjoyment n Vergnügen nt;
(stronger) Freude f (of an +dat)

enlarge [ɪnˈlɑːdʒ] vt vergrößern;
(expand) erweitern; **enlargement**
n Vergrößerung f

enormous, enormously
[ɪˈnɔːməs, -lɪ] adj, adv riesig,
ungeheuer

enough [ɪˈnʌf] adj genug; **that's
~** das reicht!; (stop it) Schluss
damit!; **I've had ~** das hat mir
gereicht; (to eat) ich bin satt ▷ adv
genug, genügend

enquire [ɪnˈkwaɪə˚] vi sich
erkundigen (about nach); **enquiry**
[ɪnˈkwaɪərɪ] n (question) Anfrage
f; (for information) Erkundigung f
(about über +akk); (investigation)

Untersuchung f; **"Enquiries"** „Auskunft"

enrol [ɪnˈrəʊl] vi sich einschreiben; (for course, school) sich anmelden; **enrolment** n Einschreibung f, Anmeldung f

en suite [ɒnˈswiːt] adj, n: **~ room with ~ (bathroom)** Zimmer nt mit eigenem Bad

ensure [ɪnˈʃʊəˀ] vt sicherstellen

enter [ˈentəˀ] vt eintreten in +akk, betreten; (drive into) einfahren in +akk; (country) einreisen in +akk; (in list) eintragen; (Inform) eingeben; (race, contest) teilnehmen an +dat ▷ vi (towards speaker) hereinkommen; (away from speaker) hineingehen

enterprise [ˈentəpraɪz] n (Comm) Unternehmen nt

entertain [entəˈteɪn] vt (guest) bewirten; (amuse) unterhalten; **entertaining** adj unterhaltsam; **entertainment** n (amusement) Unterhaltung f

enthusiasm [ɪnˈθjuːzɪæzəm] n Begeisterung f; **enthusiastic** [ɪnθjuːzɪˈæstɪk] adj begeistert (about von)

entice [ɪnˈtaɪs] vt locken; (lead astray) verleiten

entire, entirely [ɪnˈtaɪəˀ, -lɪ] adj, adv ganz

entitle [ɪnˈtaɪtl] vt (qualify) berechtigen (to zu); (name) betiteln

entrance [ˈentrəns] n Eingang m; (for vehicles) Einfahrt f; (entering) Eintritt m; (Theat) Auftritt m; **entrance exam** n Aufnahmeprüfung f; **entrance fee** n Eintrittsgeld nt

entrust [ɪnˈtrʌst] vt: **to ~ sb with sth** jdm etw anvertrauen

entry [ˈentrɪ] n (way in) Eingang m; (entering) Eintritt m; (in vehicle) Einfahrt f; (into country) Einreise f; (admission) Zutritt m; (in diary, accounts) Eintrag m; **"no ~"** „Eintritt verboten"; (for vehicles) „Einfahrt verboten"; **entry phone** n Türsprechanlage f

E-number n (food additive) E-Nummer f

envelope [ˈenvələʊp] n (Brief)umschlag m

enviable [ˈenvɪəbl] adj beneidenswert; **envious** [ˈenvɪəs] adj neidisch

environment [ɪnˈvaɪərənmənt] n Umgebung f; (ecology) Umwelt f; **environmental** [ɪnvaɪərənˈmɛntəl] adj Umwelt-; **~ pollution** Umweltverschmutzung f; **environmentalist** n Umweltschützer(in) m(f)

envy [ˈenvɪ] n Neid m (of auf +akk) ▷ vt beneiden (sb sth jdn um etw)

epic [ˈepɪk] n Epos nt; (film) Monumentalfilm m

epidemic [epɪˈdemɪk] n Epidemie f

epilepsy [ˈepɪlepsɪ] n Epilepsie f; **epileptic** [epɪˈleptɪk] adj epileptisch

episode [ˈepɪsəʊd] n Episode f; (TV) Folge f

epoch [ˈiːpɒk] n Zeitalter nt, Epoche f

equal [ˈiːkwl] adj gleich (to +dat) ▷ n Gleichgestellte(r) mf ▷ vt gleichen; (match) gleichkommen +dat; **two times two ~s four** zwei mal zwei ist gleich vier; **equality** [ɪˈkwɒlɪtɪ] n Gleichheit f; (equal rights) Gleichberechtigung f; **equalize** vi (Sport) ausgleichen; **equalizer** n (Sport) Ausgleichstreffer m; **equally** adv gleich; (on the other hand) andererseits; **equation** [ɪˈkweɪʒən] n (Math) Gleichung f

equator [ɪˈkweɪtəˀ] n Äquator m

equilibrium [iːkwɪˈlɪbrɪəm] n
Gleichgewicht nt

equip [ɪˈkwɪp] vt ausrüsten;
(kitchen) ausstatten; **equipment** n
Ausrüstung f; (for kitchen)
Ausstattung f; **electrical
~** Elektrogeräte pl

equivalent [ɪˈkwɪvələnt] adj
gleichwertig (to dat);
(corresponding) entsprechend (to
dat) ▷ n Äquivalent nt; (amount)
gleiche Menge; (in money)
Gegenwert m

era [ˈɪərə] n Ära f, Zeitalter nt

erase [ɪˈreɪz] vt ausradieren;
(tape, disk) löschen; **eraser** n
Radiergummi m

e-reader [ˈiːriːdər] n E-Book-
Lesegerät nt

erect [ɪˈrekt] adj aufrecht ▷ vt
(building, monument) errichten;
(tent) aufstellen; **erection** n
Errichtung f; (Anat) Erektion f

erode [ɪˈrəʊd] vt zerfressen;
(land) auswaschen; (rights, power)
aushöhlen; **erosion** [ɪˈrəʊʒən] n
Erosion f

erotic [ɪˈrɒtɪk] adj erotisch

errand [ˈerənd] n Besorgung f

erratic [ɪˈrætɪk] adj (behaviour)
unberechenbar; (bus link etc)
unregelmäßig; (performance)
unbeständig

error [ˈerə°] n Fehler m; **in
~** irrtümlicherweise; **error
message** n (Inform)
Fehlermeldung f

erupt [ɪˈrʌpt] vi ausbrechen

escalator [ˈeskəleɪtə°] n Rolltreppe f

escalope [ˈeskələp] n Schnitzel
nt

escape [ɪˈskeɪp] n Flucht f; (from
prison etc) Ausbruch m; **to have a
narrow ~** gerade noch
davonkommen; **there's no ~** (fig)
es gibt keinen Ausweg ▷ vt

(pursuers) entkommen +dat;
(punishment etc) entgehen +dat ▷ vi
(from pursuers) entkommen (from
dat); (from prison etc) ausbrechen
(from dat); (leak: gas) ausströmen;
(water) auslaufen

escort [ˈeskɔːt] n (companion)
Begleiter(in) m(f); (guard) Eskorte f
▷ vt [ɪˈskɔːt] (lady) begleiten

especially [ɪˈspeʃəlɪ] adv
besonders

espionage [ˈespɪənɑːʒ] n Spio-
nage f

Esquire [ɪˈskwaɪə°] n (Brit: in
address): **J. Brown, Esq** Herrn J.
Brown

essay [ˈeseɪ] n Aufsatz m;
(literary) Essay m

essential [ɪˈsenʃəl] adj (necessary) unentbehrlich,
unverzichtbar; (basic) wesentlich
▷ n **the ~s** pl das Wesentliche;
essentially adv im Wesentlichen

establish [ɪˈstæblɪʃ] vt (set up)
gründen; (introduce) einführen;
(relations) aufnehmen; (prove)
nachweisen; **to ~ that ...**
feststellen, dass ...;
establishment n Institution f;
(business) Unternehmen nt

estate [ɪˈsteɪt] n Gut nt; (of
deceased) Nachlass m; (housing ~)
Siedlung f; (country house) Landsitz
m; **estate agent** n (Brit)
Grundstücksmakler(in) m(f),
Immobilienmakler(in) m(f); **estate
car** n (Brit) Kombiwagen m

estimate [ˈestɪmət] n Schätzung
f; (Comm: of price)
Kostenvoranschlag m ▷ [ˈestɪmeɪt]
vt schätzen

Estonia [eˈstəʊnɪə] n Estland nt;
Estonian [eˈstəʊnɪən] adj
estnisch; ▷ n (person) Este m;
Estin f; (language) Estnisch nt

estuary [ˈestjʊərɪ] n Mündung f

eternal, eternally [ɪˈtɜːnl, -nəlɪ]

adj, adv ewig; **eternity** *n* Ewigkeit *f*

ethical ['eθɪkəl] *adj* ethisch; **ethics** ['eθɪks] *npl* Ethik *f*

Ethiopia [iːθɪˈəʊpɪə] *n* Äthiopien *nt*

ethnic ['eθnɪk] *adj* ethnisch; *(clothes etc)* landesüblich; **~ minority** ethnische Minderheit

e-ticket ['iːtɪkɪt] *n* E-Ticket *nt*

EU *abbr* = **European Union** EU *f*

euphemism ['juːfɪmɪzəm] *n* Euphemismus *m*

euro ['jʊərəʊ] *(pl* **-s)** *n* *(Fin)* Euro *m*; **Eurocheque** ['jʊərəʊtʃek] *n* Euroscheck *m*; **Europe** ['jʊərəp] *n* Europa *nt*; **European** [jʊərəˈpiːən] *adj* europäisch; **~ Parliament** Europäisches Parlament; **~ Union** Europäische Union ▷ *n* Europäer(in) *m(f)*; **Eurosceptic** ['jʊərəʊskeptɪk] *n* Euroskeptiker(in) *m(f)*; **Eurotunnel** *n* Eurotunnel *m*

evacuate [ɪˈvækjʊeɪt] *vt* *(place)* räumen; *(people)* evakuieren

evade [ɪˈveɪd] *vt* ausweichen *+dat*; *(pursuers)* sich entziehen *+dat*

evaluate [ɪˈvæljʊeɪt] *vt* auswerten

evaporate [ɪˈvæpəreɪt] *vi* verdampfen; *(fig)* verschwinden; **~d milk** Kondensmilch *f*

even ['iːvən] *adj* *(flat)* eben; *(regular)* gleichmäßig; *(equal)* gleich; *(number)* gerade; **the score is ~** es steht unentschieden ▷ *adv* sogar; **~ you** selbst *(o* sogar) du/Sie; **~ if** selbst wenn, wenn auch; **~ though** obwohl; **not ~** nicht einmal; **~ better** noch besser; **even out** *vi* *(prices)* sich einpendeln

evening ['iːvnɪŋ] *n* Abend *m*; **in the ~** abends, am Abend; **this ~** heute Abend; **evening class** *n* Abendkurs *m*; **evening dress** *n*

(generally) Abendkleidung *f*; *(woman's)* Abendkleid *nt*

evenly ['iːvənlɪ] *adv* gleichmäßig

event [ɪˈvent] *n* Ereignis *nt*; *(organized)* Veranstaltung *f*; *(Sport: discipline)* Disziplin *f*; **in the ~ of** im Falle *+gen*; **~ful** *adj* ereignisreich

eventual [ɪˈventʃʊəl] *adj* *(final)* letztendlich; **eventually** [ɪˈventʃʊəlɪ] *adv* *(at last)* am Ende; *(given time)* schließlich

ever ['evə°] *adv* *(at any time)* je(mals); **don't ~ do that again** tu das ja nie wieder; **he's the best ~** er ist der Beste, den es je gegeben hat; **have you ~ been to the States?** bist du schon einmal in den Staaten gewesen?; **for ~** *(für)* immer; **for ~ and ~** auf immer und ewig; **so ...** *(fam)* äußerst ...; **~ so drunk** ganz schön betrunken

every ['evrɪ] *adj* jeder/jede/jedes; **~ day** jeden Tag; **~ other day** jeden zweiten Tag; **~ five days** alle fünf Tage; **I have ~ reason to believe that ...** ich habe allen Grund anzunehmen, dass ...; **everybody** *pron* jeder, alle *pl*; **everyday** *adj* *(commonplace)* alltäglich; *(clothes, language etc)* Alltags-; **everyone** *pron* jeder, alle *pl*; **everything** *pron* alles; **everywhere** *adv* überall; *(with direction)* überallhin

evidence ['evɪdəns] *n* Beweise *pl*; *(single piece)* Beweis *m*; *(testimony)* Aussage *f*; *(signs)* Spuren *pl*; **evident, evidently** *adj, adv* offensichtlich

evil ['iːvl] *adj* böse ▷ *n* Böse(s) *nt*; **an ~** ein Übel

evolution [iːvəˈluːʃən] *n* Entwicklung *f*; *(of life)* Evolution *f*; **evolve** [ɪˈvɒlv] *vi* sich entwickeln

ex- [eks] *pref* Ex-, ehemalig;

~boyfriend Exfreund m; **~wife** frühere Frau, Exfrau f; **ex** n (fam) Verflossene(r) mf, Ex mf

exact [ɪg'zækt] adj genau; **exactly** adv genau; **not ~ fast** nicht gerade schnell

exaggerate [ɪg'zædʒəreɪt] vt, vi übertreiben; **exaggerated** adj übertrieben; **exaggeration** n Übertreibung f

exam [ɪg'zæm] n Prüfung f; **examination** [ɪgzæmɪ'neɪʃən] n (Med etc) Untersuchung f, Prüfung f; (at university) Examen nt; (at customs etc) Kontrolle f; **examine** [ɪg'zæmɪn] vt untersuchen (for auf +akk); (check) kontrollieren, prüfen; **examiner** n Prüfer(in) m(f)

example [ɪg'zɑːmpl] n Beispiel nt (of für +akk); **for ~** zum Beispiel

excavation [ekskə'veɪʃən] n Ausgrabung f

exceed [ɪk'siːd] vt überschreiten, übertreffen; **exceedingly** adv äußerst

excel [ɪk'sel] vt übertreffen; **he ~led himself** er hat sich selbst übertroffen ▷ vi sich auszeichnen (in in +dat, at bei); **excellent, excellently** ['eksələnt, -lɪ] adj, adv ausgezeichnet

except [ɪk'sept] prep: **~ außer** +dat; **~ for** abgesehen von ▷ vt ausnehmen; **exception** [ɪk'sepʃən] n Ausnahme f; **exceptional, exceptionally** [ɪk'sepʃənl, -nəlɪ] adj, adv außergewöhnlich

excess [ek'ses] n Übermaß nt (of an +dat); **excess baggage** n Übergepäck nt; **excesses** npl Exzesse pl; (drink, sex) Ausschweifungen pl; **excessive, excessively** adj, adv übermäßig; **excess weight** n Übergewicht nt

exchange [ɪks'tʃeɪndʒ] n Austausch m (for gegen); (of bought items) Umtausch m (for gegen); (Fin) Wechsel m; (Tel) Vermittlung f, Zentrale f ▷ vt austauschen; (goods) tauschen; (bought items) umtauschen (for gegen); (money, blows) wechseln; **exchange rate** n Wechselkurs m

excite [ɪk'saɪt] vt erregen; **excited** adj aufgeregt; **to get ~** sich aufregen; **exciting** adj aufregend; (book, film) spannend

exclamation [eksklə'meɪʃən] n Ausruf m; **exclamation mark, exclamation point** (US) n Ausrufezeichen nt

exclude [ɪks'kluːd] vt ausschließen; **exclusion** [ɪks'kluːʒən] n Ausschluss m; **exclusive** [ɪks'kluːsɪv] adj (select) exklusiv; (sole) ausschließlich; **exclusively** adv ausschließlich

excrement ['ekskrɪmənt] n Kot m, Exkremente pl

excruciating [ɪks'kruːʃɪeɪtɪŋ] adj fürchterlich, entsetzlich

excursion [ɪks'kɜːʃən] n Ausflug m

excusable [ɪks'kjuːzəbl] adj entschuldbar; **excuse** [ɪks'kjuːz] vt entschuldigen; **~ me** Entschuldigung!; **to ~ sb for sth** jdm etw verzeihen; **to ~ sb from sth** jdn von etw befreien ▷ n [ɪks'kjuːs] n Entschuldigung f, Ausrede f

ex-directory [eksdaɪ'rektərɪ] adj: **to be ~** (Brit Tel) nicht im Telefonbuch stehen

execute ['eksɪkjuːt] vt (carry out) ausführen; (kill) hinrichten; **execution** n (killing) Hinrichtung f; (carrying out) Ausführung f; **executive** [ɪg'zekjʊtɪv] n (Comm) leitender Angestellter, leitende Angestellte

exemplary [ɪgˈzemplərɪ] adj beispielhaft

exempt [ɪgˈzempt] adj befreit (*from* von) ▷ vt befreien

exercise [ˈeksəsaɪz] n (*in school, sports*) Übung f; (*movement*) Bewegung f; **to get more ~** mehr Sport treiben; **exercise bike** n Heimtrainer m; **exercise book** n Heft nt

exert [ɪgˈzɜːt] vt (*influence*) ausüben

exhaust [ɪgˈzɔːst] n (*fumes*) Abgase pl; (*Auto*) **~ (pipe)** Auspuff m; **exhausted** adj erschöpft; **exhausting** adj anstrengend

exhibit [ɪgˈzɪbɪt] n (*in exhibition*) Ausstellungsstück nt; **exhibition** [eksɪˈbɪʃən] n Ausstellung f; **exhibitionist** [eksɪˈbɪʃənɪst] n Selbstdarsteller(in) m(f); **exhibitor** n Aussteller(in) m(f)

exhilarating [ɪgˈzɪləreɪtɪŋ] adj belebend, erregend

exile [ˈekzaɪl] n Exil nt; (*person*) Verbannte(r) mf ▷ vt verbannen

exist [ɪgˈzɪst] vi existieren; (*live*) leben (*on* von); **existence** n Existenz f; **to come into ~** entstehen; **existing** adj bestehend

exit [ˈeksɪt] n Ausgang m; (*for vehicles*) Ausfahrt f; **exit poll** n Umfrage direkt nach dem Wahlgang

exorbitant [ɪgˈzɔːbɪtənt] adj astronomisch

exotic [ɪgˈzɒtɪk] adj exotisch

expand [ɪksˈpænd] vt ausdehnen, erweitern ▷ vi sich ausdehnen; **expansion** [ɪksˈpænʃən] n Expansion f, Erweiterung f

expect [ɪkˈspekt] vt erwarten; (*suppose*) annehmen; **he ~s me to do it** er erwartet, dass ich es mache; **I ~ it'll rain** es wird wohl regnen; **I ~ so** ich denke schon

▷ vi: **she's ~ing** sie bekommt ein Kind

expedition [ekspɪˈdɪʃən] n Expedition f

expenditure [ɪkˈspendɪtʃəʳ] n Ausgaben pl

expense [ɪkˈspens] n Kosten pl; (*single cost*) Ausgabe f; (**business**) **~s** pl Spesen pl; **at sb's ~** auf jds Kosten; **expensive** [ɪkˈspensɪv] adj teuer

experience [ɪkˈspɪərɪəns] n Erfahrung f; (*particular incident*) Erlebnis nt; **by/from ~** aus Erfahrung ▷ vt erfahren, erleben; (*hardship*) durchmachen; **experienced** adj erfahren

experiment [ɪkˈsperɪmənt] n Versuch m, Experiment nt ▷ vi experimentieren

expert [ˈekspɜːt] n Experte m, Expertin f; (*professional*) Fachmann m, Fachfrau f; (*Jur*) Sachverständige(r) mf ▷ adj fachmännisch, Fach-; **expertise** [ekspəˈtiːz] n Sachkenntnis f

expire [ɪkˈspaɪəʳ] vi (*end*) ablaufen; **expiry date** [ɪkˈspaɪərdeɪt] n Verfallsdatum nt

explain [ɪkˈspleɪn] vt erklären (*sth to sb* jdm etw); **explanation** [ekspləˈneɪʃən] n Erklärung f

explicit [ɪkˈsplɪsɪt] adj ausdrücklich, eindeutig

explode [ɪkˈspləʊd] vi explodieren

exploit [ɪkˈsplɔɪt] vt ausbeuten

explore [ɪkˈsplɔːʳ] vt erforschen

explosion [ɪkˈspləʊʒən] n Explosion f; **explosive** [ɪkˈspləʊsɪv] adj explosiv ▷ n Sprengstoff m

export [ekˈspɔːt] vt, vi exportieren ▷ n [ˈekspɔːt] n Export m ▷ adj (*trade*) Export-

expose [ɪkˈspəʊz] vt (*to danger*

etc) aussetzen *(to dat)*; *(uncover)* freilegen; *(imposter)* entlarven; **exposed** *adj (position)* ungeschützt; **exposure** [ɪkˈspəʊʒə*] n (Med)* Unterkühlung *f*; *(Foto: time)* Belichtung(szeit) *f*; **24 ~s** 24 Aufnahmen

express [ɪkˈsprɛs] *adj (speedy)* Express-, Schnell-; **~ delivery** Eilzustellung *f* ▷ *n (Rail)* Schnellzug *m* ▷ *vt* ausdrücken ▷ *vr*: **to ~ oneself** sich ausdrücken; **expression** [ɪkˈsprɛʃən] *n (phrase)* Ausdruck *m*; *(look)* Gesichtsausdruck *m*; **expressive** *adj* ausdrucksvoll; **expressway** *n (US)* Schnellstraße *f*

extend [ɪkˈstɛnd] *vt (arms)* ausstrecken; *(lengthen)* verlängern; *(building)* vergrößern, ausbauen; *(business, limits)* erweitern; **extension** [ɪkˈstɛnʃən] *n (lengthening)* Verlängerung *f*; *(of building)* Anbau *m*; *(Tel)* Anschluss *m*; *(of business, limits)* Erweiterung *f*; **extensive** [ɪkˈstɛnsɪv] *adj (knowledge)* umfangreich; *(use)* häufig; **extent** [ɪkˈstɛnt] *n (length)* Länge *f*; *(size)* Ausdehnung *f*; *(scope)* Umfang *m*, Ausmaß *nt*; **to a certain/large ~** in gewissem/hohem Maße

exterior [ɛkˈstɪərɪə*] n* Äußere(s) *nt*

external [ɛkˈstɜːnl] *adj* äußere(r, s), Außen-; **externally** *adv* äußerlich

extinct [ɪkˈstɪŋkt] *adj (species)* ausgestorben

extinguish [ɪkˈstɪŋgwɪʃ] *vt* löschen; **extinguisher** *n* Löschgerät *nt*

extra [ˈɛkstrə] *adj* zusätzlich; **~ charge** Zuschlag *m*; **~ time** *(Sport)* Verlängerung *f* ▷ *adv*

besonders; **~ large** *(clothing)* übergroß ▷ *npl*: **~s** zusätzliche Kosten *pl*; *(food)* Beilagen *pl*; *(accessories)* Zubehör *nt*; *(for car etc)* Extras *pl*

extract [ɪkˈstrækt] *vt* herausziehen *(from aus)*; *(tooth)* ziehen ▷ [ˈɛkstrækt] *n (from book etc)* Auszug *m*

extraordinary [ɪkˈstrɔːdnrɪ] *adj* außerordentlich; *(unusual)* ungewöhnlich; *(amazing)* erstaunlich

extreme [ɪkˈstriːm] *adj* äußerste(r, s); *(drastic)* extrem ▷ *n* Extrem *nt*; **extremely** *adv* äußerst, höchst; **extreme sports** *npl* Extremsportarten *pl*; **extremist** [ɪkˈstriːmɪst] *adj* extremistisch ▷ *n* Extremist *m*

extricate [ˈɛkstrɪkeɪt] *vt* befreien *(from aus)*

extrovert [ˈɛkstrəʊvɜːt] *adj* extrovertiert

exuberance [ɪgˈzuːbərəns] *n* Überschwang *m*; **exuberant** *adj* überschwänglich

exultation [ɛgzʌlˈteɪʃən] *n* Jubel *m*

eye [aɪ] *n* Auge *nt*; **to keep an ~ on sb/sth** auf jdn/etw aufpassen *or* mustern; **eyebrow** *n* Augenbraue *f*; **eyelash** *n* Wimper *f*; **eyelid** *n* Augenlid *nt*; **eyeliner** *n* Eyeliner *m*; **eyeopener** *n*: **that was an ~** das hat mir die Augen geöffnet; **eyeshadow** *n* Lidschatten *m*; **eyesight** *n* Sehkraft *f*; **eyesore** *n* Schandfleck *m*; **eye witness** *n* Augenzeuge *m*, Augenzeugin *f*

f

fabric ['fæbrɪk] n Stoff m
fabulous ['fæbjʊləs] adj
sagenhaft
façade [fə'saːd] n (a. fig) Fassade
f
face [feɪs] n Gesicht nt; (of clock)
Zifferblatt nt; (of mountain) Wand f;
in the ~ of +gen; **to be ~ to
~ (people)** einander
gegenüberstehen ▷ vt, vi (person)
gegenüberstehen +dat; (at table)
gegenübersitzen +dat; **to ~ north
(room)** nach Norden gehen; **to be
~ (up to) the facts** den Tatsachen
ins Auge sehen; **to be ~d with sth**
mit etw konfrontiert sein; **face lift**
n Gesichtsstraffung f; (fig)
Verschönerung f; **face powder** n
Gesichtspuder m
facet ['fæsɪt] n (fig) Aspekt m
face value n Nennwert m
facial ['feɪʃəl] adj Gesichts- ▷ n
(fam) (kosmetische)
Gesichtsbehandlung

facilitate [fə'sɪlɪteɪt] vt
erleichtern
facility [fə'sɪlɪtɪ] n (building etc to
be used) Einrichtung f, Möglichkeit
f; (installation) Anlage f; (skill)
Gewandtheit f
fact [fækt] n Tatsache f; **as a
matter of ~, in ~** eigentlich,
tatsächlich
factor ['fæktə°] n Faktor m
factory ['fæktərɪ] n Fabrik f;
factory outlet n Fabrikverkauf m
factual ['fæktjʊəl] adj sachlich
faculty ['fækəltɪ] n Fähigkeit f;
(at university) Fakultät f; (US:
teaching staff) Lehrkörper m
fade [feɪd] vi (a. fig) verblassen;
faded adj verblasst, verblichen
faff about ['fæfəbaʊt] vi (Brit
fam) herumwursteln
fag [fæg] n (Brit fam: cigarette)
Kippe f; (US fam pej) Schwule(r) m
Fahrenheit ['færənhaɪt] n
Fahrenheit
fail [feɪl] vt (exam) nicht bestehen
▷ vi versagen; (plan, marriage)
scheitern; (student) durchfallen;
(eyesight) nachlassen; **words ~ me**
ich bin sprachlos; **failing** n
Schwäche f; **failure** ['feɪljə°] n
(person) Versager(in) m(f); (act, a.
Tech) Versagen nt; (of engine etc)
Ausfall m; (of plan, marriage)
Scheitern nt
faint [feɪnt] adj schwach; (sound)
leise; (idea) **I haven't the ~est
(idea)** ich habe keinen blassen
Schimmer ▷ vi ohnmächtig
werden (with vor +dat); **faintness**
n (Med) Schwächegefühl nt
fair [feə°] adj (hair) (dunkel)blond;
(skin) hell; (just) gerecht, fair;
(reasonable) ganz ordentlich; (in
school) befriedigend; (weather)
schön; (wind) günstig; **a
~ number/amount of** ziemlich
viele/viel ▷ adv: **to play ~ fair**

spielen; (fig) fair sein; **~ enough** in Ordnung! ▷ n (fun~) Jahrmarkt m; (Comm) Messe f; **fair-haired** adj (dunkel)blond; **fairly** adv (honestly) fair; (rather) ziemlich

fairy ['feərɪ] n Fee f; **fairy tale** n Märchen nt

faith [feɪθ] n (trust) Vertrauen nt (in sb zu jdm); (Rel) Glaube m; **faithful, faithfully** adj, adv treu; **Yours ~ly** Hochachtungsvoll

fake [feɪk] n (thing) Fälschung f ▷ adj vorgetäuscht ▷ vt fälschen

falcon ['fɔːlkən] n Falke m

fall [fɔːl] (**fell, fallen**) vi fallen; (from a height, badly) stürzen; **to ~ ill** krank werden; **to ~ asleep** einschlafen; **to ~ in love** sich verlieben ▷ n Fall m; (accident, fig: of regime) Sturz m; (decrease) Sinken nt (in +gen); (US: autumn) Herbst m; **fall apart** vi auseinanderfallen; **fall behind** vi zurückbleiben; (with work, rent) in Rückstand geraten; **fall down** vi (person) hinfallen; **fall off** vi herunterfallen; (decrease) zurückgehen; **fall out** vi (quarrel) sich streiten; **fall over** vi hinfallen; **fall through** vi (plan etc) ins Wasser fallen

fallen ['fɔːlən] pp of **fall**

fallout ['fɔːlaut] n radioaktiver Niederschlag, Fall-out m

false [fɔːls] adj falsch; (artificial) künstlich; **false alarm** n blinder Alarm; **false start** n (Sport) Fehlstart m; **false teeth** npl (künstliches) Gebiss

fame [feɪm] n Ruhm m

familiar [fə'mɪlɪə*] adj vertraut, bekannt; **to be ~ with** vertraut sein mit, gut kennen; **familiarity** [fəmɪlɪ'ærɪtɪ] n Vertrautheit f

family ['fæmɪlɪ] n Familie f; (including relations) Verwandtschaft

f; **family man** n Familienvater m; **family name** n Familienname m, Nachname m; **family practitioner** n (US) Allgemeinarzt m, Allgemeinärztin f

famine ['fæmɪn] n Hungersnot f; **famished** ['fæmɪʃt] adj ausgehungert

famous ['feɪməs] adj berühmt

fan [fæn] n (hand-held) Fächer m; (Elec) Ventilator m; (admirer) Fan m

fanatic [fə'nætɪk] n Fanatiker(in) m(f)

fancy ['fænsɪ] adj (elaborate) kunstvoll; (unusual) ausgefallen ▷ vt (like) gernhaben; **he fancies her** er steht auf sie; **~ that** stell dir vor!, so was!; **fancy dress** n Kostüm nt, Verkleidung f

fan heater ['fænhiːtə*] n Heizlüfter m; **fanlight** n Oberlicht nt

fan mail n Fanpost f

fantasise ['fæntəsaɪz] vi träumen (about von); **fantastic** [fæn'tæstɪk] adj (a. fam) fantastisch; **that's ~** (fam) das ist ja toll!; **fantasy** ['fæntəzɪ] n Fantasie f

far [fɑː*] (**further** o **farther, furthest** o **farthest**) adj weit; the **~ end of the room** das andere Ende des Zimmers; **the Far East** der Ferne Osten ▷ adv weit; **~ better** viel besser; **by ~ the best** bei weitem der/die/das Beste; **as ~ as ...** bis zum o zur ...; (with place name) bis nach ...; **as ~ as I'm concerned** was mich betrifft, von mir aus; **so ~** soweit, bisher; **faraway** [fɑːrə'weɪ] adj weit entfernt; (look) verträumt

fare [feə*] n Fahrpreis m; (money) Fahrgeld nt

farm [fɑːm] n Bauernhof m, Farm f; **farmer** n Bauer m, Bäuerin f, Landwirt(in) m(f); **farmhouse**

Bauernhaus nt; **farming** n Landwirtschaft f; **farmland** n Ackerland nt; **farmyard** n Hof m

far-reaching ['fɑːriːtʃɪŋ] adj weit reichend; **far-sighted** adj weitsichtig; (fig) weitblickend

fart [fɑːt] n (fam) Furz m; old ~ (fam: person) alter Sack ▷ vi (fam) furzen

farther ['fɑːðə°] adj, adv comparative of **far**; see **further**

farthest ['fɑːðɪst] adj, adv superlative of **far**; see **furthest**

fascinating ['fæsɪneɪtɪŋ] adj faszinierend; **fascination** n Faszination f

fascism ['fæʃɪzəm] n Faschismus m; **fascist** ['fæʃɪst] adj faschistisch ▷ Faschist(in) m(f)

fashion ['fæʃən] n (clothes) Mode f; (manner) Art (und Weise) f; **to be in** ~ (in) Mode sein; **out of** ~ unmodisch; **fashionable**, **fashionably** adj, adv (clothes, person) modisch; (author, pub etc) in Mode

fast [fɑːst] adj schnell; **to be** ~ (clock) vorgehen ▷ adv schnell; (firmly) fest; **to be** ~ **asleep** fest schlafen ▷ n Fasten nt ▷ vi fasten; **fastback** n (Auto) Fließheck nt

fasten ['fɑːsn] vt (attach) befestigen (to an +dat); (do up) zumachen; ~ **your seatbelts** bitte anschnallen; **fastener, fastening** n Verschluss m

fast food n Fast Food nt; **fast forward** n (for tape) Schnellvorlauf m; **fast lane** n Überholspur f

fat [fæt] adj dick; (meat) fett ▷ n Fett nt

fatal ['feɪtl] adj tödlich

fate [feɪt] n Schicksal nt

fat-free adj (food) fettfrei

father ['fɑːðə°] n Vater m; (priest)

Pfarrer m ▷ vt (child) zeugen; **Father Christmas** n der Weihnachtsmann; **father-in-law** (pl **fathers-in-law**) n Schwiegervater m

fatigue [fə'tiːg] n Ermüdung f

fattening ['fætnɪŋ] adj: **to be** ~ dick machen; **fatty** ['fætɪ] adj (food) fettig

faucet ['fɔːsɪt] n (US) Wasserhahn m

fault [fɔːlt] n Fehler m; (Tech) Defekt m; (Elec) Störung f; (blame) Schuld f; **it's your** ~ du bist daran schuld; **faulty** adj fehlerhaft; (Tech) defekt

favor (US), **favour** [ˈfeɪvəʳ] n (approval) Gunst f; (kindness) Gefallen m; **in** ~ **of** für; **I'm in** ~ **(of going)** ich bin dafür(, dass wir gehen); **to do sb a** ~ jdm einen Gefallen tun ▷ vt (prefer) vorziehen; **favourable** adj günstig (to, for für); **favourite** [ˈfeɪvərɪt] n Liebling m, Favorit(in) m(f) ▷ adj Lieblings-

fax [fæks] vt faxen ▷ n Fax nt; **fax number** n Faxnummer f

faze [feɪz] vt (fam) aus der Fassung bringen

FBI abbr = **Federal Bureau of Investigation** FBI nt

fear [fɪəʳ] n Angst f (of vor +dat) ▷ vt befürchten; **fearful** adj (timid) ängstlich, furchtsam; (terrible) fürchterlich; **fearless** adj furchtlos

feasible ['fiːzəbl] adj machbar

feast [fiːst] n Festessen nt

feather ['feðəʳ] n Feder f

feature ['fiːtʃəʳ] n (facial) (Gesichts)zug m; (characteristic) Merkmal n; (of car etc) Ausstattungsmerkmal nt; (in the press) (Cine) Feature nt ▷ vt bringen, (als Besonderheit)

zeigen; **feature film** n Spielfilm
m

February ['februəri] n Februar
m; see also **September**

fed [fed] pt, pp of **feed**

federal ['fedərəl] adj Bundes-;
**the Federal Republic of
Germany** die Bundesrepublik
Deutschland

fed-up [fed'ʌp] adj: **to be ~ with
sth** etw satthaben; **I'm ~** ich habe
die Nase voll

fee [fi:] n Gebühr f; (of doctor,
lawyer) Honorar nt

feeble ['fi:bl] adj schwach

feed [fi:d] (**fed, fed**) vt (sense)
animal) füttern; (support) ernähren
▷ n (for baby) Mahlzeit f; (for
animals) Futter nt; (Inform: paper ~)
Zufuhr f; **feed in** vt (information)
eingeben; **feedback** n
(information) Feed-back nt

feel [fi:l] (**felt, felt**) vt (sense)
fühlen; (pain) empfinden; (touch)
anfassen; (think) meinen ▷ vi
(person) sich fühlen; **I ~ cold** mir ist
kalt; **do you ~ like a walk?** hast du
Lust, spazieren zu gehen?; **feeling**
n Gefühl nt

feet [fi:t] pl of **foot**

fell [fel] pt of **fall** ▷ vt (tree) fällen

fellow ['feləʊ] n Kerl m, Typ m;
~ citizen Mitbürger(in) m(f);
~ countryman Landsmann m;
~ worker Mitarbeiter(in) m(f)

felt [felt] pt, pp of **feel** ▷ n Filz m;
felt tip, felt-tip pen n Filzstift m

female ['fi:meɪl] n (of animals)
Weibchen nt ▷ adj weiblich;
~ doctor Ärztin f; **feminine**
['femɪnɪn] adj weiblich; **feminist**
['femɪnɪst] n Feminist(in) m(f)
▷ adj feministisch

fence [fens] n Zaun m

fencing n (Sport) Fechten nt

fender ['fendə°] n (US Auto)
Kotflügel m

fennel ['fenl] n Fenchel m

fern [fɜ:n] n Farn m

ferocious [fə'rəʊʃəs] adj wild

ferry ['feri] n Fähre f ▷ vt
übersetzen

fertile ['fɜ:taɪl] adj fruchtbar;
fertility [fə'tɪlɪti] n Fruchtbarkeit
f; **fertilize** ['fɜ:tɪlaɪz] vt (Bio)
befruchten; (Agr: land) düngen;
fertilizer n Dünger m

festival ['festɪvəl] n (Rel) Fest nt;
(Art, Mus) Festspiele pl; (pop music)
Festival m; **festive** ['festɪv] adj
festlich; **festivities** [fe'stɪvɪtɪz] n
Feierlichkeiten pl

fetch [fetʃ] vt holen; (collect)
abholen; (in sale, money)
einbringen; **fetching** adj reizend

fetish ['fetɪʃ] n Fetisch m

fetus ['fi:təs] n (US) Fötus m

fever ['fi:və°] n Fieber nt;
feverish (Med) fiebrig; (fig)
fieberhaft

few [fju:] adj, pron pl wenige pl; **a
~** pl ein paar; **fewer** adj weniger;
fewest adj wenigste(r, s)

fiancé [fɪ'ɑ̃nseɪ] n Verlobte(r) m;
fiancée [fɪ'ɑ̃nseɪ] n Verlobte f

fiasco [fɪ'æskəʊ] (pl **-s** o US **-es**) n
Fiasko nt

fiber (US), **fibre** [faɪbə°] n
Faser f; (material) Faserstoff m

fickle ['fɪkl] adj unbeständig

fiction ['fɪkʃən] n (novels)
Prosaliteratur f; **fictional**,
fictitious [fɪk'tɪʃəs] adj erfunden

fiddle ['fɪdl] n Geige f; (trick)
Betrug m ▷ vt (accounts, results)
frisieren; **fiddle with** vt
herumfummeln an +dat; **fiddly**
adj knifflig

fidelity [fɪ'delɪti] n Treue f

fidget ['fɪdʒɪt] vi zappeln;
fidgety adj zappelig

field [fi:ld] n Feld nt;
(grass-covered) Wiese f; (fig: of work)
(Arbeits)gebiet nt

fierce [fɪəs] adj heftig; (animal, appearance) wild; (criticism, competition) scharf

fifteen [fɪftiːn] num fünfzehn ▷ n Fünfzehn f; see also **eight**; **fifteenth** adj fünfzehnte(r, s); see also **eighth**; **fifth** [fɪfθ] adj fünfte(r, s) ▷ n (fraction) Fünftel nt; see also **eighth**; **fifty** [fɪftɪ] num fünfzig ▷ n Fünfzig f; see also **eight**; **fiftieth** adj fünfzigste(r, s); see also **eighth**

fig [fɪg] n Feige f

fight [faɪt] (fought, fought) vi kämpfen (with, against gegen, for, over um) ▷ vt (person) kämpfen mit; (fig: disease, fire etc) bekämpfen ▷ n Kampf m; (brawl) Schlägerei f; (argument) Streit m; **fight back** vi zurückschlagen; **fight off** vt abwehren; **fighter** n Kämpfer(in) m(f)

figurative [fɪgərətɪv] adj übertragen

figure [fɪgə] n (person) Gestalt f; (of person) Figur f; (number) Zahl f, Ziffer f; (amount) Betrag m; **a four-figure sum** eine vierstellige Summe ▷ vt (US: think) glauben ▷ vi (appear) erscheinen; **figure out** vt (work out) herausbekommen; **I can't figure him out** ich werde aus ihm nicht schlau; **figure skating** n Eiskunstlauf m

file [faɪl] n (tool) Feile f; (dossier) Akte f; (Inform) Datei f; (folder) Aktenordner m; **on** ~ in den Akten ▷ vt (metal, nails) feilen; (papers) ablegen (under unter) ▷ vi: **to** ~ **in/out** hintereinander hereinkommen/hinausgehen; **filing cabinet** n Aktenschrank m

fill [fɪl] vt füllen; (tooth) plombieren; (post) besetzen; **fill in** vt (hole) auffüllen; (form) ausfüllen; (tell) informieren (on über); **fill out** vt (form) ausfüllen; **fill up** vi (Auto) volltanken

fillet [fɪlɪt] n Filet nt

filling [fɪlɪŋ] n (Gastr) Füllung f; (for tooth) Plombe f; **filling station** n Tankstelle f

film [fɪlm] n Film m ▷ vt (scene) filmen; **film star** n Filmstar m; **film studio** n Filmstudio nt

filter [fɪltə] n Filter m; (traffic lane) Abbiegespur f ▷ vt filtern

filth [fɪlθ] n Dreck m; **filthy** adj dreckig

fin [fɪn] n Flosse f

final [faɪnl] adj letzte(r, s); (stage, round) End-; (decision, version) endgültig; ~ **score** Schlussstand m ▷ n (Sport) Endspiel nt; (competition) Finale nt; ~**s** pl Abschlussexamen nt; **finalize** vt die endgültige Form geben +dat; **finally** adv (lastly) zuletzt; (eventually) schließlich, endlich

finance [faɪnæns] n Finanzwesen nt; ~**s** pl Finanzen pl ▷ vt finanzieren; **financial** [faɪnænʃl] adj finanziell; (adviser, crisis, policy etc) Finanz-

find [faɪnd] (found, found) vt finden; **he was found dead** er wurde tot aufgefunden; **I** ~ **myself in difficulties** ich befinde mich in Schwierigkeiten; **she** ~**s it difficult/easy** es fällt ihr schwer/leicht; **find out** vt herausfinden; **findings** npl (Jur) Ermittlungsergebnis nt; (of report, Med) Befund m

fine [faɪn] adj (thin) dünn, fein; (good) gut; (splendid) herrlich; (clothes) elegant; (weather) schön; **i'm** ~ es geht mir gut; **that's** ~ das ist OK ▷ adv (well) gut ▷ n (Jur) Geldstrafe f ▷ vt (Jur) mit einer Geldstrafe belegen; **fine arts** npl: **the** ~ die schönen Künste pl;

finely adv (cut) dünn; (ground) fein

finger ['fɪŋgə°] n Finger m ▷ vt herumfingern an +dat; **fingernail** n Fingernagel m; **fingerprint** n Fingerabdruck m; **fingertip** n Fingerspitze f

finicky ['fɪnɪkɪ] adj (person) pingelig; (work) knifflig

finish ['fɪnɪʃ] n Ende nt; (Sport) Finish nt; (line) Ziel nt; (of product) Verarbeitung f ▷ vt beenden; (book etc) zu Ende lesen; (food) aufessen; (drink) austrinken ▷ vi zu Ende gehen; (song, story) enden; (person) fertig sein; (stop) aufhören; **have you ~ed?** bist du fertig?; **to ~ first/second** (Sport) als erster/zweiter durchs Ziel gehen; **finishing line** n Ziellinie f

Finland ['fɪnlənd] n Finnland nt; **Finn** n Finne m, Finnin f; **Finnish** adj finnisch ▷ n (language) Finnisch nt

fir [fɜ:°] n Tanne f

fire [faɪə°] n Feuer nt; (house etc) Brand m; **to set ~ to** etw in Brand stecken; **to be on ~** brennen ▷ vt (bullets, rockets) abfeuern; (fam: dismiss) feuern ▷ vi (Auto: engine) zünden; **to ~ at sb** auf jdn schießen; **fire alarm** n Feuermelder m; **fire brigade** n Feuerwehr f; **fire engine** n Feuerwehrauto nt; **fire escape** n Feuerleiter f; **fire extinguisher** n Feuerlöscher m; **firefighter** n Feuerwehrmann m, Feuerwehrfrau f; **fireman** n Feuerwehrmann m; **fireplace** n (offener) Kamin; **fireproof** adj feuerfest; **fire station** n Feuerwache f; **firewood** n Brennholz nt; **fireworks** npl Feuerwerk nt

firm [fɜ:m] adj fest; (person) **to be ~** entschlossen auftreten ▷ n Firma f

first [fɜ:st] adj erste(r, s) ▷ adv (at first) zuerst; (firstly) erstens; (arrive, finish) als erste(r); (happen) zum ersten Mal; **~ of all** zuallererst ▷ n (person) Erste(r) mf; (Auto: gear) erster Gang; **at ~** zuerst, anfangs; **first aid** n erste Hilfe; **first-class** adj erstklassig; (compartment, ticket) erster Klasse; **~ mail** (Brit) bevorzugt beförderte Post ▷ adv (travel) erster Klasse; **first floor** n (Brit) erster Stock; (US) Erdgeschoss nt; **first lady** n (US) Frau f des Präsidenten; **firstly** adv erstens; **first name** n Vorname m; **first night** n (Theat) Premiere f; **first-rate** adj erstklassig

fir tree n Tannenbaum m

fish [fɪʃ] n Fisch m; **~ and chips** (Brit) frittierter Fisch mit Pommes frites ▷ vi fischen; (with rod) angeln; **to go ~ing** fischen/angeln gehen; **fishbone** n Gräte f; **fishcake** n Fischfrikadelle f; **fish farm** n Fischzucht f; **fish finger** n (Brit) Fischstäbchen nt; **fishing** ['fɪʃɪŋ] n Fischen nt; (with rod) Angeln nt; (as industry) Fischerei f; **fishing boat** n Fischerboot nt; **fishing line** n Angelschnur f; **fishing rod** n Angelrute f; **fishing village** n Fischerdorf nt; **fishmonger** ['fɪʃmʌŋgə°] n Fischhändler(in) m(f); **fish stick** n (US) Fischstäbchen nt; **fish tank** n Aquarium nt

fishy ['fɪʃɪ] adj (fam: suspicious) faul

fist [fɪst] n Faust f

fit [fɪt] adj (Med) gesund; (Sport) in Form, fit; (suitable) geeignet; **to keep ~** sich in Form halten ▷ vt passen +dat; (attach) anbringen (to an +dat); (install) einbauen (in in +akk) ▷ vi passen; (in space, gap) hineinpassen ▷ n (of clothes) Sitz m; (Med) Anfall m; **it's a good ~** es passt gut; **fit in** vt (accommodate) unterbringen; (find time for) einschieben ▷ vi (in space) hineinpassen; (plans, ideas) passen; **he doesn't ~ (here)** er passt nicht hierher; **to ~ with sb's plans** sich mit jds Plänen vereinbaren lassen; **fitness** n (Med) Gesundheit f; (Sport) Fitness f; **fitness trainer** n (Sport) Fitnesstrainer(in) m(f); **fitted carpet** n Teppichboden m; **fitted kitchen** n Einbauküche f; **fitting** adj passend ▷ n (of dress) Anprobe f; **~s** pl Ausstattung f

five [faɪv] num fünf ▷ n Fünf f; see also **eight**; **fiver** n (Brit fam) Fünfpfundschein m

fix [fɪks] vt (fasten) befestigen (to an +dat); (settle) festsetzen; (place, time) ausmachen; (repair) reparieren; **fixer** n (drug addict) Fixer(in) m(f); **fixture** ['fɪkstʃə'] n (Sport) Veranstaltung f; (match) Spiel nt; (in building) Installationsteil nt; **~s (and fittings)** pl Ausstattung f

fizzy ['fɪzɪ] adj sprudelnd; **~ drink** Limo f

flabbergasted ['flæbəgɑːstɪd] adj (fam) platt

flabby ['flæbɪ] adj (fat) wabbelig

flag [flæg] n Fahne f; **flagstone** n Steinplatte f

flake [fleɪk] n Flocke f ▷ vi: **to ~ (off)** abblättern

flamboyant [flæm'bɔɪənt] adj extravagant

flame [fleɪm] n Flamme f; (person) **an old ~** eine alte Liebe

flan [flæn] n (fruit ~) Obstkuchen m

flannel ['flænl] n Flanell m; (Brit: face ~) Waschlappen m; (fam: waffle) Geschwafel nt ▷ vi herumlabern

flap [flæp] n Klappe f; (fam) **to be in a ~** rotieren ▷ vt (wings) schlagen mit ▷ vi flattern

flared [fleəd] adj (trousers) mit Schlag; **flares** npl Schlaghose f

flash [flæʃ] n Blitz m; (news ~) Kurzmeldung f; (Foto) Blitzlicht nt; **in a ~** im Nu ▷ vt: **to ~ one's (head)lights** die Lichthupe betätigen ▷ vi aufblinken; (brightly) aufblitzen; **flashback** n Rückblende f, Flashback m; **flashlight** ['flæʃlaɪt] n (Photo) Blitzlicht nt; (US: torch) Taschenlampe f; **flashy** adj grell, schrill; (pej) protzig

flat [flæt] adj flach; (surface) eben; (drink) abgestanden; (tyre) platt; (battery) leer; (refusal) glatt ▷ n (Brit: rooms) Wohnung f; (Auto) Reifenpanne f; **flat screen** n (Inform) Flachbildschirm m; **flatten** vt platt machen, einebnen

flatter ['flætə'] vt schmeicheln +dat; **flattering** adj schmeichelhaft

flatware ['flætweə] n (US) Besteck nt

flavor (US), **flavour** ['fleɪvə'] n Geschmack m ▷ vt: Geschmack geben +dat; (with spices) würzen; **flavouring** n Aroma nt

flaw [flɔː] n Fehler m; **flawless** adj fehlerlos; (complexion) makellos

flea [fliː] n Floh m

fled [fled] pt, pp of **flee**

flee [fliː] (**fled, fled**) vi fliehen

fleece [fliːs] n (of sheep) Vlies nt; (soft material) Fleece m; (jacket) Fleecejacke f

fleet [fliːt] n Flotte f

Flemish ['flemɪʃ] adj flämisch ▷ n (language) Flämisch nt

flesh [fleʃ] n Fleisch nt

flew [fluː] pt of **fly**

flex [fleks] n (Brit Elec) Schnur f

flexibility [fleksɪ'bɪlɪtɪ] n Biegsamkeit f; (fig) Flexibilität f; **flexible** ['fleksɪbl] adj biegsam;

(plans, person) flexibel; **flexitime** n gleitende Arbeitszeit, Gleitzeit f

flicker ['flɪkə°] vi flackern; (TV) flimmern

flies [flaɪz] pl of **fly** ▷ n

flight [flaɪt] n Flug m; (escape) Flucht f; **~ of stairs** Treppe f; **flight attendant** n Flugbegleiter(in) m(f); **flight recorder** n Flugschreiber m

flimsy ['flɪmzɪ] adj leicht gebaut, nicht stabil; (thin) hauchdünn; (excuse) fadenscheinig

fling [flɪŋ] (**flung, flung**) vt schleudern ▷ n: **to have a ~** eine (kurze) Affäre haben

flip [flɪp] vt schnippen; **to ~ a coin** eine Münze werfen; **flip through** vt (book) durchblättern; **flipchart** n Flipchart m

flipper ['flɪpə°] n Flosse f

flirt [flɜːt] vi flirten

float [fləʊt] n (for fishing) Schwimmer m; (in procession) Festwagen m; (money) Wechselgeld nt ▷ vi schwimmen; (in air) schweben

flock [flɒk] n (of sheep) (Rel) Herde f; (of birds) Schwarm m; (of people) Schar f

flog [flɒg] vt auspeitschen; (Brit fam) verscheuern

flood [flʌd] n Hochwasser nt, Überschwemmung f; (fig) Flut f ▷ vt überschwemmen; **floodlight** n Flutlicht nt; **floodlit** adj (building) angestrahlt

floor [flɔː°] n Fußboden m; (storey) Stock m; **ground ~** (Brit), **first ~** (US) Erdgeschoss nt; **first ~** (Brit), **second ~** (US) erster Stock; **floorboard** n Diele f

flop [flɒp] n (fam: failure) Reinfall m, Flop m ▷ vi misslingen, floppen

floppy disk ['flɒpɪdɪsk] n Diskette f

Florence ['flɒrəns] n Florenz nt

florist ['flɒrɪst] n Blumenhändler(in) m(f); **florist's (shop)** ['flɒrɪsts] n Blumengeschäft m(f)

flounder ['flaʊndə°] n (fish) Flunder f

flour ['flaʊə°] n Mehl nt

flourish ['flʌrɪʃ] vi gedeihen; (business) gut laufen; (boom) florieren ▷ vt (wave about) schwenken; **flourishing** adj blühend

flow [fləʊ] n Fluss m; **to go with the ~** mit dem Strom schwimmen ▷ vi fließen

flower ['flaʊə°] n Blume f ▷ vi blühen; **flower bed** n Blumenbeet nt; **flowerpot** n Blumentopf m

flown [fləʊn] pp of **fly**

flu [fluː] n (fam) Grippe f

fluent ['fluːənt] adj (Italian etc) fließend; **to be ~ in German** fließend Deutsch sprechen

fluid ['fluːɪd] n Flüssigkeit f ▷ adj flüssig

flung [flʌŋ] pt, pp of **fling**

fluorescent [fluə'resnt] adj fluoreszierend, Leucht-

flush [flʌʃ] n (lavatory) Wasserspülung f; (blush) Röte f ▷ vi (lavatory) spülen

flute [fluːt] n Flöte f

fly [flaɪ] (**flew, flown**) vt, vi fliegen; **how time flies** wie die Zeit vergeht ▷ n (insect) Fliege f; **~/flies** (pl) (on trousers) Hosenschlitz m; **fly-drive** n Urlaub m mit Flug und Mietwagen; **flyover** n (Brit) Straßenüberführung f, Eisenbahnüberführung f; **flysheet** n Überzelt m

FM abbr = **frequency modulation** = UKW

FO abbr = **Foreign Office** = AA nt

foal [fəʊl] n Fohlen nt

foam [fəʊm] n Schaum m ▷ vi schäumen

fob off [fɒb ɒf] vt: **to fob sb off with sth** jdm etw andrehen

focus ['fəʊkəs] n Brennpunkt m; **in/out of ~** (photo) scharf/unscharf; (camera) scharf/unscharf eingestellt ▷ vt (camera) scharf stellen ▷ vi sich konzentrieren (on auf +akk)

foetus ['fiːtəs] n Fötus m

fog [fɒg] n Nebel m; **foggy** adj neblig; **fog light** n (Auto: at rear) Nebelschlussleuchte f

foil [fɔɪl] vt vereiteln ▷ n Folie f

fold [fəʊld] vt falten ▷ vi (fam: business) eingehen ▷ n Falte f; **fold up** vt (map etc) zusammenfalten; (chair etc) zusammenklappen ▷ vi (fam: business) eingehen; **folder** n (portfolio) Aktenmappe f; (pamphlet) Broschüre f; (Inform) Ordner m; **folding** adj zusammenklappbar; (bicycle, chair) Klapp-

folk [fəʊk] n Leute pl; (Mus) Folk m; **my ~s** pl (fam) meine Leute ▷ adj Volks-

follow ['fɒləʊ] vt folgen +dat; (pursue) verfolgen; (understand) folgen können +dat; (career, news etc) verfolgen; **as ~s** wie folgt ▷ vi folgen; (result) sich ergeben (from aus); **follow up** vt (request, rumour) nachgehen +dat, weiter verfolgen; **follower** n Anhänger(in) m(f); **following** adj folgend; **the ~ day** am (darauf)folgenden Tag ▷ prep nach; **follow up** n (event, book etc) Fortsetzung f

fond [fɒnd] adj: **to be ~ of** gernhaben; **fondly** adv (with love) liebevoll; **fondness** n Vorliebe f; (for people) Zuneigung f

fondue ['fɒnduː] n Fondue nt

font [fɒnt] n Taufbecken nt; (Typo) Schriftart f

food [fuːd] n Essen nt, Lebensmittel pl; (for animals) Futter nt; (groceries) Lebensmittel pl; **food poisoning** n Lebensmittelvergiftung f; **food processor** n Küchenmaschine f; **foodstuff** n Lebensmittel nt

fool [fuːl] n Idiot m, Narr m; **to make a ~ of oneself** sich blamieren ▷ vt (deceive) hereinlegen ▷ vi: **to ~ around** herumalbern; (waste time) herumtrödeln; **foolish** adj dumm; **foolproof** adj idiotensicher

foot [fʊt] n (pl **feet** [fiːt]) n Fuß m; (measure) Fuß m (30,48 cm); **on ~** zu Fuß ▷ vt (bill) bezahlen; **foot-and-mouth disease** n Maul- und Klauenseuche f; **football** n Fußball m; (US: American ~) Football m; **footballer** n Fußballspieler(in) m(f); **footbridge** n Fußgängerbrücke f; **footing** n (hold) Halt m; **footlights** npl Rampenlicht nt; **footnote** n Fußnote f; **footpath** n Fußweg m; **footprint** n Fußabdruck m; **footwear** n Schuhwerk nt

◯ KEYWORD

for [fɔː°] prep **1** für; **is this for me?** ist das für mich?; **the train for London** der Zug nach London; **he went for the paper** er ging die Zeitung holen; **give it to me — what for?** gib es mir — warum? **2** (because of) wegen; **for this reason** aus diesem Grunde **3** (referring to distance) **there are roadworks for 5 km** die Baustelle ist 5 km lang; **we walked for miles** wir sind meilenweit gegangen

4 *(referring to time)* seit; *(with future sense)* für; **he was away for 2 years** er war zwei Jahre lang weg **5** *(+infin clauses)* **it is not for me to decide** das kann ich nicht entscheiden; **for this to be possible ...** damit dies möglich wird/wurde ... **6** *(in spite of)* trotz +gen o *(inf)* dat; **for all his complaints** obwohl er sich ständig beschwert ▷ *conj* denn

forbade [fəˈbæd] *pt of* **forbid**

forbid [fəˈbɪd] **(forbade, forbidden)** *vt* verbieten

force [fɔːs] *n* Kraft *f*; *(compulsion)* Zwang *m*, Gewalt; **to come into ~** in Kraft treten; **the Forces** *pl* die Streitkräfte *pl* ▷ *vt* zwingen; **forced** *adj (smile)* gezwungen; **~ landing** Notlandung *f*; **forceful** *adj* kraftvoll

forceps [ˈfɔːseps] *npl* Zange *f*

forearm [ˈfɔːrɑːm] *n* Unterarm *m*

forecast [ˈfɔːkɑːst] *vt* voraussagen; *(weather)* vorhersagen ▷ *n* Vorhersage *f*

forefinger [ˈfɔːfɪŋɡəʳ] *n* Zeigefinger *m*

foreground [ˈfɔːɡraʊnd] *n* Vordergrund *m*

forehand [ˈfɔːhænd] *n (Sport)* Vorhand *f*

forehead [ˈfɔːhed, ˈfɒrɪd] *n* Stirn *f*

foreign [ˈfɒrən] *adj* ausländisch; **foreigner** *n* Ausländer(in) *m(f)*; **foreign exchange** *n* Devisen *pl*; **foreign language** *n* Fremdsprache *f*; **foreign minister** *n* Außenminister(in) *m(f)*; **Foreign Office** *n (Brit)* Außenministerium *nt*; **Foreign Secretary** *n (Brit)* Außenminister(in) *m(f)*; **foreign policy** *n* Außenpolitik *f*

foremost [ˈfɔːməʊst] *adj* erste(r, s); *(leading)* führend

forerunner [ˈfɔːrʌnəʳ] *n* Vorläufer(in) *m(f)*

foresee [fɔːˈsiː] *irr vt* vorhersehen; **foreseeable** *adj* absehbar

forest [ˈfɒrɪst] *n* Wald *m*; **forestry** [ˈfɒrɪstrɪ] *n* Forstwirtschaft *f*

forever [fəˈrevəʳ] *adv* für immer

forgave [fəˈɡeɪv] *pt of* **forgive**

forge [fɔːdʒ] *n* Schmiede *f* ▷ *vt* schmieden; *(fake)* fälschen; **forger** *n* Fälscher(in) *m(f)*; **forgery** *n* Fälschung *f*

forget [fəˈɡet] **(forgot, forgotten)** *vt, vi* vergessen; **to ~ about sth** etw vergessen; **forgetful** *adj* vergesslich; **forgetfulness** *n* Vergesslichkeit *f*; **forget-me-not** *n* Vergissmeinnicht *nt*

forgive [fəˈɡɪv] **(forgave, forgiven)** *irr vt* verzeihen; **to ~ sb for sth** jdm etw verzeihen

forgot [fəˈɡɒt] *pt of* **forget**

forgotten [fəˈɡɒtn] *pp of* **forget**

fork [fɔːk] *n* Gabel *f*; *(in road)* Gabelung *f* ▷ *vi (road)* sich gabeln

form [fɔːm] *n (shape)* Form *f*, Klasse *f*; *(document)* Formular *nt*; *(person)* **to be in (good) ~** in Form sein ▷ *vt* bilden

formal [ˈfɔːməl] *adj* förmlich, formell; **formality** [fɔːˈmælɪtɪ] *n* Formalität *f*

format [ˈfɔːmæt] *n* Format *m* ▷ *vt (Inform)* formatieren

former [ˈfɔːməʳ] *adj* frühere(r, s); *(opposite of latter)* erstere(r, s); **formerly** *adv* früher

formidable [ˈfɔːmɪdəbl] *adj* gewaltig; *(opponent)* stark

formula [ˈfɔːmjʊlə] *n* Formel *f*

formulate [ˈfɔːmjʊleɪt] *vt* formulieren

forth [fɔːθ] *adv*: **and so ~** und so weiter; **forthcoming** [fɔːθˈkʌmɪŋ] *adj* kommend, bevorstehend

fortieth [ˈfɔːtɪəθ] *adj* vierzigste(r, s); *see also* **eighth**

fortnight [ˈfɔːtnaɪt] *n* vierzehn Tage *pl*

fortress [ˈfɔːtrɪs] *n* Festung *f*

fortunate [ˈfɔːtʃənɪt] *adj* glücklich; **I was ~** ich hatte Glück; **fortunately** *adv* zum Glück; **fortune** [ˈfɔːtʃən] *n (money)* Vermögen *nt*; **good ~** Glück *nt*; **fortune-teller** *n* Wahrsager(in) *m(f)*

forty [ˈfɔːtɪ] *num* vierzig ⊳ *n* Vierzig *f*; *see also* **eight**

forward [ˈfɔːwəd] *adv* vorwärts ⊳ *n (Sport)* Stürmer(in) *m(f)* ⊳ *vt (send on)* nachsenden; *(Inform)* weiterleiten; **forwards** *adv* vorwärts

fossick [ˈfɒsɪk] *vi (Aust, NZ fam)* suchen *(for nach)*; **to ~ around** herumstöbern *(fam)*; **to ~ for gold** nach Gold graben

foster child [ˈfɒstətʃaɪld] *n* Pflegekind *nt*; **foster parents** *npl* Pflegeeltern *pl*

fought [fɔːt] *pt, pp of* **fight**

foul [faʊl] *adj (weather)* schlecht; *(smell)* übel ⊳ *n (Sport)* Foul *nt*

found [faʊnd] *pt, pp of* **find** ⊳ *vt (establish)* gründen; **foundations** [faʊnˈdeɪʃənz] *npl* Fundament *nt*

fountain [ˈfaʊntɪn] *n* Springbrunnen *m*; **fountain pen** *n* Füller *m*

four [fɔːʳ] *num* vier ⊳ *n* Vier *f*; *see also* **eight**; **fourteen** [ˈfɔːtiːn] *num* vierzehn ⊳ *n* Vierzehn *f*; *see also* **eight**; **fourteenth** *adj* vierzehnte(r, s); *see also* **eighth**; **fourth** [fɔːθ] *adj* vierte(r, s); *see also* **eighth**

four-wheel drive *n*

Allradantrieb *m*; *(car)* Geländewagen *m*

fowl [faʊl] *n* Geflügel *nt*

fox [fɒks] *n (a. fig)* Fuchs *m*

fraction [ˈfrækʃən] *n (Math)* Bruch *m*; *(part)* Bruchteil *m*

fracture [ˈfræktʃəʳ] *n (Med)* Bruch *m* ⊳ *vt* brechen

fragile [ˈfrædʒaɪl] *adj* zerbrechlich

fragment [ˈfrægmənt] *n* Bruchstück *nt*

fragrance [ˈfreɪgrəns] *n* Duft *m*

frail [freɪl] *adj* gebrechlich

frame [freɪm] *n* Rahmen *m*; *(of spectacles)* Gestell *nt*; **~ of mind** Verfassung *f* ⊳ *vt* einrahmen; **to ~ sb** *(incriminate)* jdm etwas anhängen; **framework** *n* Rahmen *m*, Struktur *f*

France [frɑːns] *n* Frankreich *nt*

frank [fræŋk] *adj* offen

frankfurter [ˈfræŋkfɜːtəʳ] *n* (Frankfurter) Würstchen *nt*

frankly [ˈfræŋklɪ] *adv* offen gesagt; **quite ~** ganz ehrlich

frantic [ˈfræntɪk] *adj (activity)* hektisch; *(effort)* verzweifelt; **~ with worry** außer sich vor Sorge

fraud [frɔːd] *n (trickery)* Betrug *m*; *(person)* Schwindler(in) *m(f)*

freak [friːk] *n* Anomalie *f*; *(animal, person)* Missgeburt *f*; *(fam: fan)* Fan *m*, Freak *m* ⊳ *adj (conditions)* außergewöhnlich, seltsam; **freak out** *vi (fam)* ausflippen

freckle [ˈfrekl] *n* Sommersprosse *f*

free [friː] *adj, adv* frei; *(without payment)* gratis, kostenlos; **for ~** umsonst ⊳ *vt* befreien; **freebie** [ˈfriːbɪ] *n (fam)* Werbegeschenk *nt*; **it was a ~** es war gratis; **freedom** [ˈfriːdəm] *n* Freiheit *f*; **freefone** [ˈfriːfəʊn] *adj*: **a ~ number** eine gebührenfreie

Nummer; **free kick** n (Sport) Freistoß m

freelance ['friːlɑːns] adj freiberuflich tätig; (artist) freischaffend ▷ n Freiberufler(in) m(f)

free-range ['friːreɪndʒ] adj frei laufend; **~ eggs** pl Freilandeier pl

freeway ['friːweɪ] n (US) (gebührenfreie) Autobahn

freeze [friːz] (froze, frozen) vi (feel cold) frieren; (of lake etc) zufrieren; (water etc) gefrieren ▷ vt einfrieren; **freezer** n Tiefkühltruhe f; (in fridge) Gefrierfach nt; **freezing** adj eiskalt; **I'm ~** mir ist eiskalt; **freezing point** n Gefrierpunkt m

freight [freɪt] n (goods) Fracht f; (money charged) Frachtgebühr f; **freight car** n (US) Güterwagen m; **freight train** n (US) Güterzug m

French [frentʃ] adj französisch ▷ n (language) Französisch nt; **the ~ pl** die Franzosen; **French bean** n grüne Bohne; **French bread** n Baguette f; **French dressing** n Vinaigrette f; **French fries** npl Pommes frites pl; **French kiss** n Zungenkuss m; **Frenchman** (pl **-men**) n Franzose m; **French toast** n (US) in Ei und Milch getunktes gebratenes Brot; **French window(s)** n(pl) Balkontür f, Terrassentür f; **Frenchwoman** (pl **-women**) n Französin f

frequency ['friːkwənsɪ] n Häufigkeit f; (Phys) Frequenz f; **frequent** ['friːkwənt] adj häufig; **frequently** adv häufig

fresco ['freskəʊ] (pl **-es**) n Fresko nt

fresh [freʃ] adj frisch; (new) neu; **freshen** vi: **to ~ (up)** (person) sich frisch machen; **fresher**, **freshman** (pl **-men**) n Erstsemester nt;

freshwater fish n Süßwasserfisch m

Fri abbr = **Friday** Fr

friction ['frɪkʃən] n (a. fig) Reibung f

Friday ['fraɪdeɪ] n Freitag m; see also **Tuesday**

fridge [frɪdʒ] n Kühlschrank m

fried [fraɪd] adj gebraten; **~ potatoes** Bratkartoffeln pl; **~ egg** Spiegelei nt; **~ rice** gebratener Reis

friend [frend] n Freund(in) m(f); (less close) Bekannte(r) mf; **to make ~s with sb** sich mit jdm anfreunden; **we're good ~s** wir sind gut befreundet; **friendly** adj freundlich; **to be ~ with sb** mit jdm befreundet sein ▷ n (Sport) Freundschaftsspiel nt; **friendship** ['frendʃɪp] n Freundschaft f

fright [fraɪt] n Schrecken m; **frighten** vt erschrecken; **to be ~ed** Angst haben; **frightening** adj beängstigend

frill [frɪl] n Rüsche f; **~s** (fam) Schnickschnack

fringe [frɪndʒ] n (edge) Rand m; (on shawl etc) Fransen pl; (hair) Pony m

frivolous ['frɪvələs] adj leichtsinnig; (remark) frivol

frizzy ['frɪzɪ] adj kraus

frog [frɒg] n Frosch m

KEYWORD

from [frɒm] prep **1** (indicating starting place) von; (indicating origin etc) aus +dat; **a letter/telephone call from my sister** ein Brief/Anruf von meiner Schwester; **where do you come from?** woher kommen Sie?; **to drink from the bottle** aus der Flasche trinken

2 (indicating time) von ... an; (past) seit; **from one o'clock to** o **until** o **till two** von ein Uhr bis zwei; **from January (on)** ab Januar

3 (indicating distance) von ... (entfernt)

4 (indicating price, number etc) ab +dat; **from £10** ab £10; **there were from 20 to 30 people there** es waren zwischen 20 und 30 Leute da

5 (indicating difference) **he can't tell red from green** er kann nicht zwischen Rot und Grün unterscheiden; **to be different from sb/sth** anders sein als jd/etw

6 (because of, based on) **from what he says** aus dem, was er sagt; **weak from hunger** schwach vor Hunger

front [frʌnt] n Vorderseite f; (of house) Fassade f; (in war, of weather) Front f; (at seaside) Promenade f; **in ~, at the ~** vorne; **in ~ of** vor; **up ~** (in advance) vorher, im Voraus ▷ adj vordere(r, s), Vorder-; (first) vorderste(r, s); **~ door** Haustür f; **~ page** Titelseite f; **~ seat** Vordersitz m; **~ wheel** Vorderrad m

frontier ['frʌntɪə'] n Grenze f

front-wheel drive n (Auto) Frontantrieb m

frost [frɒst] n Frost m; (white ~) Reif m; **frosting** n (US) Zuckerguss m; **frosty** adj frostig

froth [frɒθ] n Schaum m; **frothy** adj schaumig

frown [fraʊn] vi die Stirn runzeln

froze [frəʊz] pt of **freeze**

frozen ['frəʊzn] pp of **freeze** ▷ adj (food) tiefgekühlt, Tiefkühl-

fruit [fruːt] n (as collective, a. type) Obst nt; (single ~, a. fig) Frucht f;

fruit machine n Spielautomat m; **fruit salad** n Obstsalat m

frustrated [frʌ'streɪtɪd] adj frustriert; **frustratration** n Frustration f, Frust m

fry [fraɪ] vt braten; **frying pan** n Bratpfanne f

fuchsia ['fjuːʃə] n Fuchsie f

fuck [fʌk] vt (vulg) ficken; **~ off** verpiss dich!; **fucking** adj (vulg) Scheiß-

fudge [fʌdʒ] n weiche Karamellsüßigkeit

fuel [fjʊəl] n Kraftstoff m; (for heating) Brennstoff m; **fuel consumption** n Kraftstoffverbrauch m; **fuel gauge** n Benzinuhr f; **fuel oil** n Gasöl nt; **fuel rod** n Brennstab m; **fuel tank** n Tank m; (for oil) Öltank m

fugitive ['fjuːdʒɪtɪv] n Flüchtling m

fulfil [fʊl'fɪl] vt erfüllen

full [fʊl] adj voll; (person: satisfied) satt; (member, employment) Voll(zeit)-; (complete) vollständig; **~ of ...** voller ... gen; **full beam** n (Auto) Fernlicht nt; **full moon** n Vollmond m; **full stop** n Punkt m; **full-time** adj; **~ job** Ganztagsarbeit f; **fully** adv voll; (recover) voll und ganz; (discuss) ausführlich

fumble ['fʌmbl] vi herumfummeln (with, at an +dat)

fumes [fjuːmz] npl Dämpfe pl; (of car) Abgase pl

fun [fʌn] n Spaß m; **for ~** zum Spaß; **it's ~** es macht Spaß; **to make ~ of** sich lustig machen über +akk

function ['fʌŋkʃən] n Funktion f; (event) Feier f; (reception) Empfang m ▷ vi funktionieren; **function key** n (Inform) Funktionstaste f

fund [fʌnd] n Fonds m; **~s** pl Geldmittel pl

fundamental [fʌndə'mentl]
adj grundlegend; **fundamentally**
adv im Grunde

funding ['fʌndɪŋ] *n* finanzielle
Unterstützung

funeral ['fjuːnərəl] *n* Beerdigung *f*

funfair ['fʌnfeə°] *n* Jahrmarkt *m*

fungus ['fʌŋgəs] (*pl* **fungi** o
funguses) *n* Pilz *m*

funicular [fjuː'nɪkjʊlə°] *n* Seilbahn *f*

funnel ['fʌnl] *n* Trichter *m*; (*of
steamer*) Schornstein *m*

funny ['fʌnɪ] *adj* (*amusing*)
komisch, lustig; (*strange*) seltsam

fur [fɜː°] *n* Pelz *m*; (*of animal*) Fell
nt

furious ['fjʊərɪəs] *adj* wütend
(*with sb* auf jdn)

furnished ['fɜːnɪʃd] *adj* mög-
liert; **furniture** ['fɜːnɪtʃə°] *n*
Möbel *pl*; **piece of ~** Möbelstück *nt*

further ['fɜːðə°] *comparative of* **far**
▷ *adj* weitere(r, s); **~ education**
Weiterbildung *f*; **until ~ notice** bis
auf weiteres ▷ *adv* weiter;
furthest ['fɜːðɪst] *superlative of*
far ▷ *adj* am weitesten entfernt
▷ *adv* am weitesten

fury ['fjʊərɪ] *n* Wut *f*

fuse [fjuːz] *n* (*Elec*) Sicherung *f*
▷ *vi* (*Elec*) durchbrennen; **fuse box**
n Sicherungskasten *m*

fuss [fʌs] *n* Theater *nt*; **to make a
~** (ein) Theater machen; **fussy** *adj*
(*difficult*) schwierig, kompliziert;
(*attentive to detail*) pingelig

future ['fjuːtʃə°] *adj* künftig ▷ *n*
Zukunft *f*

fuze (*US*) *see* **fuse**

fuzzy ['fʌzɪ] *adj* (*indistinct*)
verschwommen; (*hair*) kraus

g

gable ['geɪbl] *n* Giebel *m*

gadget ['gædʒɪt] *n* Vorrichtung *f*,
Gerät *nt*

Gaelic ['geɪlɪk] *adj* gälisch ▷ *n*
(*language*) Gälisch *nt*

gain [geɪn] *vt* (*obtain, win*)
gewinnen; (*advantage, respect*) sich
verschaffen; (*wealth*) erwerben;
(*weight*) zunehmen ▷ *vi* (*improve*)
gewinnen (*in* an +*dat*); (*clock*)
vorgehen ▷ *n* Gewinn *m* (*in* an
+*dat*)

gale [geɪl] *n* Sturm *m*

gall bladder ['gɔːlblædə°] *n*
Gallenblase *f*

gallery ['gælərɪ] *n* Galerie *f*,
Museum *nt*

gallon ['gælən] *n* Gallone *f*; ((*Brit*)
4,546 *l*, (*US*) 3,79 *l*)

gallop ['gæləp] *n* Galopp *m* ▷ *vi*
galoppieren

gallstone ['gɔːlstəʊn] *n* Gallenstein *m*

Gambia ['gæmbɪə] n Gambia nt

gamble ['gæmbl] vi um Geld spielen, wetten ▷ n: **it's a ~** es ist riskant; **gambling** n Glücksspiel nt

game [geɪm] n Spiel nt; (animals) Wild nt; **a ~ of chess** eine Partie Schach; **~s** (in school) Sport m; **games console** n Spielkonsole f; **game show** n (TV) Gameshow f

gammon ['gæmən] n geräucherter Schinken

gang [gæŋ] n (of criminals, youths) Bande f, Gang f, Clique f ▷ vt: **to ~ up on** sich verschwören gegen

gangster ['gæŋstə°] n Gangster m

gangway ['gæŋweɪ] n (for ship) Gangway f; (Brit: aisle) Gang m, Gangway f

gap [gæp] n (hole) Lücke f; (in time) Pause f; (in age) Unterschied m

gap year n Jahr zwischen Schulabschluss und Studium, das oft zu Auslandsaufenthalten genutzt wird

garage ['gæra:ʒ] n Garage f; (for repair) (Auto)werkstatt f; (for fuel) Tankstelle f

garbage ['gɑ:bɪdʒ] n (US) Müll m; (fam: nonsense) Quatsch m; **garbage can** n (US) Mülleimer m; (outside) Mülltonne f; **garbage truck** n (US) Müllwagen m

garden ['gɑ:dn] n Garten m; (public) **~s** Park m; **garden centre** n Gartencenter nt; **gardener** n Gärtner(in) m(f); **gardening** n Gartenarbeit f

gargle ['gɑ:gl] vi gurgeln

gargoyle ['gɑ:gɔɪl] n Wasserspeier m

garlic ['gɑ:lɪk] n Knoblauch m; **garlic bread** n Knoblauchbrot nt; **garlic butter** n Knoblauchbutter f

gas [gæs] n Gas nt; (US: petrol)

Benzin nt; **to step on the ~** Gas geben; **gas cooker** n Gasherd m; **gas cylinder** n Gasflasche f; **gas fire** n Gasofen m

gasket ['gæskɪt] n Dichtung f

gas lighter n (for cigarettes) Gasfeuerzeug nt; **gas mask** n Gasmaske f; **gas meter** n Gaszähler m

gasoline ['gæsəli:n] n (US) Benzin nt

gasp [gɑ:sp] vi keuchen; (in surprise) nach Luft schnappen

gas pedal n (US) Gaspedal nt; **gas pump** n (US) Zapfsäule f; **gas station** n (US) Tankstelle f; **gas tank** n (US) Benzintank m

gastric ['gæstrɪk] adj Magen-; **~ flu** Magen-Darm-Grippe f; **~ ulcer** Magengeschwür nt

gasworks ['gæswɜ:ks] n Gaswerk nt

gate [geɪt] n Tor nt; (barrier) Schranke f; (Aviat) Gate nt, Flugsteig m

gateau ['gætəʊ] n (pl **gateaux**) Torte f

gateway n Tor nt

gather ['gæðə°] vt (collect) sammeln; **to ~ speed** beschleunigen ▷ vi (assemble) sich versammeln; (understand) schließen (from aus); **gathering** n Versammlung f

gauge [geɪdʒ] n Meßgerät nt

gauze [gɔ:z] n Gaze f; (for bandages) Mull m

gave [geɪv] pt of **give**

gay [geɪ] adj (homosexual) schwul; **~ village** (fam) Homoehe f

gaze [geɪz] n Blick m ▷ vi starren

GCSE abbr = **general certificate of secondary education** (school) Abschlussprüfung f der Sekundarstufe, ≈ mittlere Reife

gear [gɪə°] n (Auto) Gang m; (equipment) Ausrüstung f; (clothes)

Klamotten *pl*; **to change ~** schalten; **gearbox** *n* Getriebe *nt*; **gear change**, **gear shift** (US) *n* Gangschaltung *f*; **gear lever**, **gear stick** (US) *n* Schalthebel *m*

geese [giːs] *pl of* **goose**

gel [dʒel] *n* Gel *nt* ▷ *vi* gelieren; **they really ~led** sie verstanden sich auf Anhieb

gem [dʒem] *n* Edelstein *m*; (*fig*) Juwel *nt*

Gemini ['dʒeminiː] *nsing* (*Astr*) Zwillinge *pl*

gender ['dʒendə°] *n* Geschlecht *nt*

gene [dʒiːn] *n* Gen *nt*

general ['dʒenərəl] *adj* allgemein; **~ knowledge** Allgemeinbildung *f*; **~ election** Parlamentswahlen *pl*; **generalize** ['dʒenrəlaɪz] *vi* verallgemeinern; **generally** ['dʒenrəlɪ] *adv* im Allgemeinen

generation [dʒenə'reɪʃən] *n* Generation *f*; **generation gap** *n* Generationsunterschied *m*

generator ['dʒenəreɪtə°] *n* Generator *m*

generosity [dʒenə'rɒsɪtɪ] *n* Großzügigkeit *f*; **generous** ['dʒenərəs] *adj* großzügig; (*portion*) reichlich

genetic [dʒɪ'netɪk] *adj* genetisch; **~ research** Genforschung *f*; **~ technology** Gentechnik *f*; **genetically modified** *adj* gentechnisch verändert, genmanipuliert; *see also* **GM**

Geneva [dʒɪ'niːvə] *n* Genf *nt*; **Lake ~** der Genfer See

genitals ['dʒenɪtlz] *npl* Geschlechtsteile *pl*

genitive ['dʒenɪtɪv] *n* Genitiv *m*

genius ['dʒiːnɪəs] *n* (*Genie) nt*

gentle ['dʒentl] *adj* sanft; (*touch*) zart; **gentleman** (*pl* **-men**) *n*

Herr *m*; (*polite man*) Gentleman *m*

gents [dʒents] *n*: **"-"** (*lavatory*) „Herren"; **the ~** *pl* die Herrentoilette

genuine ['dʒenjʊɪn] *adj* echt

geographical [dʒɪə'græfɪkəl] *adj* geografisch; **geography** [dʒɪ'ɒgrəfɪ] *n* Geografie *f*; (*at school*) Erdkunde *f*

geological [dʒɪə'lɒdʒɪkəl] *adj* geologisch; **geology** [dʒɪ'ɒlədʒɪ] *n* Geologie *f*

geometry [dʒɪ'ɒmɪtrɪ] *n* Geometrie *f*

geranium [dʒɪ'reɪnɪəm] *n* Geranie *f*

gerbil ['dʒɜːbəl] *n* (*Zool*) Wüstenrennmaus *f*

germ [dʒɜːm] *n* Keim *m*; (*Med*) Bazillus *m*

German ['dʒɜːmən] *adj* deutsch; **she's ~** sie ist Deutsche; **~ shepherd** *n* (*person*) Schäferhund ▷ *n* (*dog*) Deutsche(r) *mf*; (*language*) Deutsch *nt*; **in ~** auf Deutsch; **German measles** *n sing* Röteln *pl*; **Germany** ['dʒɜːmənɪ] *n* Deutschland *nt*

gesture ['dʒestʃə°] *n* Geste *f*

KEYWORD

get [get] (*pt, pp* **got**, *pp* **gotten** (US)) *vi* **1** (*become, be*) werden; **to get old/tired** alt/müde werden; **to get married** heiraten
2 (*go*) (an)kommen, gehen
3 (*begin*) **to get to know sb** jdn kennenlernen; **let's get going** *o* **started!** fangen wir an!
4 (*modal vb aux*) **you've got to do it** du musst/Sie müssen es tun
▷ *vt* **1 to get sth done** (*do*) etw machen; (*have done*) etw machen lassen; **to get sth going** *o* **to go** etw in Gang bringen *o* bekommen;

to get sb to do sth jdn dazu bringen, etw zu tun **2** (*obtain: money, permission, results*) erhalten; (*find: job, flat*) finden; (*fetch: person, object*) holen; **to get sth for sb** jdm etw besorgen; **get me Mr Jones, please** (*Tel*) verbinde/verbinden Sie mich bitte mit Mr Jones; **get a life!** (*annoyed*) mach dich mal locker!, reg dich bloß ab!

3 (*receive: present, letter*) bekommen, kriegen; (*acquire: reputation etc*) erwerben **4** (*catch*) bekommen, kriegen; (*hit: target etc*) treffen, erwischen; **get him!** (*to dog*) fass! **5** (*take, move*) bekommen; **to get sth to sb** jdm etw bringen **6** (*understand*) (*hear*) mitbekommen; **I've got it!** ich hab's! **7** (*have, possess*) **to have got sth** etw haben

get about *vi* herumkommen, (*news*) sich verbreiten **get across** *vi*: **to get sth over etw** *akk* kommen; *vt*: **to get sth across** (*communicate*) etw klarmachen **get along** *vi* (*people*) (gut) zurecht-/auskommen (*with* mit); (*depart*) sich *akk* auf den Weg machen **get at** *vt* (*reach*) herankommen an +*akk*; (*facts*) herausbekommen; **what are you getting at?** worauf wollen Sie hinaus?, was meinst du damit?; **to get at sb** (*nag*) an jdm herumnörgeln **get away** *vi* (*leave*) sich *akk* davonmachen, weggehen (*escape*) **to get away from sth** von etw dat entkommen; **to get away with sth** mit etw davonkommen **get back** *vi* (*return*) zurückkommen; (*Tel*) **to get back**

to s.o. jdn zurückrufen
▷ *vt* zurückbekommen **get by** *vi* (*pass*) vorbeikommen; (*manage*) zurecht-/auskommen (*on*) mit **get down** *vi* (her)untergehen; **to get down to** in Angriff nehmen; (*find time to do*) kommen zu; ▷ *vt* (*depress*) fertigmachen; **it gets me down** (*fam*) es macht mich fertig; **to get sth down** (*write*) etw aufschreiben **get in** *vi* (*train*) ankommen; (*arrive home*) heimkommen **get into** *vt* (*enter*) hinein-/ hereinkommen in +*akk*; (*car, train etc*) einsteigen in +*akk*; (*clothes*) anziehen; (*rage, panic etc*) geraten in +*akk*; **to get into trouble** in Schwierigkeiten kommen **get off** *vi* (*from train etc*) aussteigen; (*from horse etc*) absteigen; (*fam: be enthusiastic*) **to get off on sth** auf etw abfahren; ▷ *vt* (*nail, sticker*) los-/abbekommen; (*clothes*) ausziehen **get on** *vi* (*progress*) vorankommen; (*be friends*) auskommen; (*age*) alt werden; (*onto horse etc*) einsteigen; (*onto horse etc*) aufsteigen ▷ *vt* etw +*akk* vorantreiben, mit etw *akk* losziehen **get out** *vi* (*of house*) herauskommen; (*of vehicle*) aussteigen; **get out!** raus! ▷ *vt* (*take out*) herausholen; (*stain, nail*) herausbekommen **get out of** *vi* (*duty etc*) herumkommen um **get over** *vi* (*illness*) sich *akk* erholen von; (*surprise*) verkraften; (*news*) fassen; (*loss*) sich abfinden mit **get round** *vi* herumkommen um; *vt* (*fig*) (*person*) herumkriegen

get through vi (Tel) durchkommen (to) zu

get together vi zusammenkommen

get up vi aufstehen ▷ vt hinaufbringen; (go up) hinaufgehen; (organize) auf die Beine stellen

get up to vi (reach) erreichen; (prank etc) anstellen

getaway n Flucht f;

get-together n Treffen nt

Ghana ['gɑːnə] n Ghana nt

gherkin ['gɜːkɪn] n Gewürzgurke f

ghetto ['gɛtəʊ] (pl -es) n Ghetto nt

ghost [gəʊst] n Gespenst nt; (of sb) Geist m

giant ['dʒaɪənt] n Riese m ▷ adj riesig

Gibraltar [dʒɪˈbrɔːltə*] n Gibraltar nt

giddy ['gɪdɪ] adj schwindlig

gift [gɪft] n Geschenk nt; (talent) Begabung f; **gifted** adj begabt; **giftwrap** vt als Geschenk verpacken

gig [gɪg] n (performance) Gig m; (gigabyte) Gigabyte f

gigantic [dʒaɪˈgæntɪk] adj riesig

giggle ['gɪgl] vi kichern ▷ n Gekicher nt

gill [gɪl] n (of fish) Kieme f

gimmick ['gɪmɪk] n (for sales, publicity) Gag m

gin [dʒɪn] n Gin m

ginger ['dʒɪndʒə*] n Ingwer m ▷ adj (colour) kupferrot; (cat) rötlichgelb; **ginger ale** n Gingerale nt; **ginger beer** n Ingwerlimonade f; **gingerbread** n Lebkuchen m (mit Ingwergeschmack); **ginger(-haired)** adj rotblond; **gingerly** adv (move) vorsichtig

gipsy ['dʒɪpsɪ] n Zigeuner(in) m(f)

giraffe [dʒɪˈrɑːf] n Giraffe f

girl [gɜːl] n Mädchen nt; **girlfriend** n (feste) Freundin f; **girl guide** n (Brit), **girl scout** (US) Pfadfinderin f

gist [dʒɪst] n: **to get the ~ (of it)** das Wesentliche verstehen

give [gɪv] (gave, given) vt geben; (as present) schenken (to sb jdm); (state: name etc) angeben; (speech) halten; (blood) spenden; **to ~ sb sth** jdm etw geben/schenken ▷ vi (yield) nachgeben; **give away** vt (give free) verschenken; (secret) verraten; **give back** vt zurückgeben; **give in** vi aufgeben; **give up** vt, vi aufgeben; **give way** vi (collapse, yield) nachgeben; (traffic) die Vorfahrt beachten

given ['gɪvn] pp of **give** ▷ adj (fixed) festgesetzt; (certain) bestimmt; **~ name** (US) Vorname m ▷ conj: **~ that ...** angesichts der Tatsache, dass ...

glacier ['glæsɪə*] n Gletscher m

glad [glæd] adj froh (about über); **I was ~ (to hear) that ...** es hat mich gefreut, dass ...; **gladly** ['glædlɪ] adv gerne

glance [glɑːns] n Blick m ▷ vi einen Blick werfen (at auf +akk)

gland [glænd] n Drüse f; **glandular fever** n Drüsenfieber nt

glare [glɛə*] n grelles Licht; (stare) stechender Blick ▷ vi (angrily) **to ~ at sb** jdn böse anstarren; **glaring** adj (mistake) krass

glass [glɑːs] n Glas nt; **~es** pl Brille f

glen [glɛn] n (Scot) (enges) Bergtal nt

glide [glaɪd] vi gleiten; (hover) schweben; **glider** n Segelflugzeug nt; **gliding** n Segelfliegen nt

glimmer ['glɪmə*] n (of hope) Schimmer m

glimpse [glɪmps] n flüchtiger Blick

glitter ['glɪtə*] vi glitzern; (eyes) funkeln

glitzy [glɪtsi] adj (fam) glanzvoll, Schickimicki-

global ['gləʊbəl] adj global, Welt-; ~ **warming** die Erwärmung der Erdatmosphäre; **globe** [gləʊb] n (sphere) Kugel f; (world) Erdball m; (map) Globus m

gloomily ['glu:mɪlɪ] , **gloomy** adv, adj düster

glorious ['glɔ:rɪəs] adj (victory, past) ruhmreich; (weather, day) herrlich; **glory** ['glɔ:rɪ] n Herrlichkeit f

gloss [glɒs] n (shine) Glanz m

glossary ['glɒsərɪ] n Glossar nt

glossy ['glɒsɪ] adj (surface) glänzend ▷ n (magazine) Hochglanzmagazin nt

glove [glʌv] n Handschuh m; **glove compartment** n Handschuhfach nt

glow [gləʊ] vi glühen

glucose ['glu:kəʊs] n Traubenzucker m

glue [glu:] n Klebstoff m ▷ vt kleben

glutton ['glʌtn] n Vielfraß m; **a ~ for punishment** (fam) Masochist m

GM abbr = **genetically modified** Gen-; ~ **foods** gentechnisch veränderte Lebensmittel

GMT abbr = **Greenwich Mean Time** WEZ f

go [gəʊ] (**went, gone**) vi gehen; (in vehicle, travel) fahren; (plane) fliegen; (road) führen (to nach); (depart: train, bus) (ab)fahren;

(person) (fort)gehen; (disappear) verschwinden; (time) vergehen; (function) gehen, funktionieren; (machine, engine) laufen; (fit, suit) passen (with zu); (fail) nachlassen; **I have to ~ to the doctor/to London** ich muss zum Arzt/nach London; **to ~ shopping** einkaufen gehen; **to ~ for a walk/swim** spazieren/schwimmen gehen; **has he gone yet?** ist er schon weg?; **the wine ~es in the cupboard** der Wein kommt in den Schrank; **to get sth ~ing** etw in Gang setzen; **to keep ~ing** weitermachen; (machine etc) weiterlaufen; **how's the job ~ing?** was macht der Job?; **his memory/eyesight is going** sein Gedächtnis lässt nach/seine Augen werden schwach; **to ~ deaf/mad/grey** taub/verrückt/grau werden ▷ vb aux: **to be ~ing to do sth** etw tun werden; **I was ~ing to do it** ich wollte es tun ▷ n (pl **-es**) (attempt) Versuch m; **can I have another ~?** darf ich noch mal (probieren)?; **it's my ~** ich bin dran; **in one ~** auf einen Schlag; (drink) in einem Zug; **go after** vt nachlaufen +dat; (in vehicle) nachfahren +dat; **go ahead** vi (in front) vorausgehen; (start) anfangen; **go away** vi weggehen; (on holiday, business) verreisen; **go back** vi (return) zurückgehen; **we ~ a long way** (fam) wir kennen uns schon ewig; **go by** vi vorbeigehen; (vehicle) vorbeifahren; (years, time) vergehen ▷ vt (judge by) gehen nach; **go down** vi (sun, ship) untergehen; (flood, temperature) zurückgehen; (price) sinken; **to ~ well/badly** gut/schlecht ankommen; **go in** vi hineingehen; **go into** vt (enter) hineingehen in +akk; (crash) fahren gegen, hineinfahren in +akk; to ~ **teaching/politics/the army** Lehrer werden/in die Politik gehen/zum Militär gehen; **go off** vi (depart) weggehen; (in vehicle) wegfahren; (lights) ausgehen; (milk etc) sauer werden; (gun, bomb, alarm) losgehen ▷ vt (dislike) nicht mehr mögen; **go on** vi (continue) weitergehen; (lights) angehen; to ~ **with** o doing sth etw weitermachen; **go out** vi (leave house) hinausgehen; (fire, light, person socially) ausgehen; to ~ **for a meal** essen gehen; **go up** vi (temperature, price) steigen; (lift) hochfahren; **go without** vt verzichten auf +akk; (food, sleep) auskommen ohne

go-ahead ['gəʊəhed] adj (progressive) fortschrittlich ▷ n grünes Licht

goal [gəʊl] n (aim) Ziel nt; (Sport) Tor nt; **goalie**, **goalkeeper** n Torwart m, Torfrau f; **goalpost** n Torpfosten m

goat [gəʊt] n Ziege f

gob [gɒb] n (Brit fam) Maul nt; **shut your ~** halt's Maul! ▷ vi spucken; **gobsmacked** (fam: surprised) platt

god [gɒd] n Gott m; **thank God** Gott sei Dank; **godchild** (pl -**children**) n Patenkind nt; **goddaughter** n Patentochter f; **goddess** ['gɒdes] n Göttin f; **godfather** n Pate m; **godmother** n Patin f; **godson** n Patensohn m

goggles npl Schutzbrille f; (for skiing) Skibrille f; (for diving) Taucherbrille f

going ['gəʊɪŋ] adj (rate) üblich; **goings-on** npl Vorgänge pl

go-kart ['gəʊkɑːt] n Gokart m

gold [gəʊld] n Gold nt; **golden** adj golden; **goldfish** n Goldfisch

m; **gold-plated** adj vergoldet

golf [gɒlf] n Golf nt; **golf ball** n Golfball m; **golf club** n Golfschläger m; (association) Golfklub m; **golf course** n Golfplatz m; **golfer** n Golfspieler(in) m(f)

gone [gɒn] pp of **go**; **he's ~** er ist weg ▷ prep: **just ~ three** kurz nach drei

good [gʊd] n (benefit) Wohl nt; (morally good things) Gute(s) nt; **for the ~ of** zum Wohle +gen; **it's for your own ~** es ist zu deinem/Ihrem Besten o Vorteil; **it's no ~** (doing sth) es hat keinen Sinn o Zweck; (thing) es taugt nichts; **for ~** für immer ▷ adj (better, best) gut; (suitable) passend; (thorough) gründlich; (well-behaved) brav; (kind) nett, lieb; **to be ~ at sport/maths** gut in Sport/Mathe sein; **to be no ~ at sport/maths** schlecht in Sport/Mathe sein; **it's ~ for you** es tut dir gut; **this is ~ for colds** das ist gut gegen Erkältungen; **too ~ to be true** zu schön, um wahr zu sein; **this is just not ~ enough** so geht das nicht; **a ~ three hours** gute drei Stunden; ~ **morning/evening** guten Morgen/Abend; ~ **night** gute Nacht; **to have a ~ time** sich gut amüsieren

goodbye [gʊd'baɪ] interj auf Wiedersehen

Good Friday n Karfreitag m

good-looking adj gut aussehend

goods [gʊdz] npl Waren pl, Güter pl; **goods train** n (Brit) Güterzug m

goodwill [gʊd'wɪl] n Wohlwollen nt

google ['guːgl] vt googeln

goose [guːs] n (pl **geese**) n Gans f

▷ vt (fam) **to ~ s.o.** jdn in den Arsch kneifen; **gooseberry** ['gʊzbərɪ] n Stachelbeere f; **goose bumps** n, **goose pimples** npl Gänsehaut f

gorge [gɔːdʒ] n Schlucht f

gorgeous ['gɔːdʒəs] adj wunderschön; **he's ~** er sieht toll aus

gorilla [gə'rɪlə] n Gorilla m

gossip ['gɒsɪp] n (talk) Klatsch m; (person) Klatschtante f ▷ vi klatschen, tratschen

got [gɒt] pt, pp of **get**

gotten ['gɒtn] (US) pp of **get**

govern ['gʌvən] vt regieren; (province etc) verwalten; **government** n Regierung f; **governor** n Gouverneur(in) m(f); **govt** abbr = **government** Regierung f

gown [gaʊn] n Abendkleid nt; (academic) Robe f

GP abbr = **General Practitioner** Allgemeinarzt, Allgemeinärztin

GPS n abbr = **global positioning system** GPS nt

grab [græb] vt packen; (person) schnappen

grace [greɪs] n Anmut f; (prayer) Tischgebet nt; **5 days' ~** 5 Tage Aufschub; **graceful** adj anmutig

grade [greɪd] n Niveau nt; (of goods) Güteklasse f; (mark) Note f; (US: year) Klasse f; **to make the ~** es schaffen; **grade crossing** n (US) Bahnübergang m; **grade school** n (US) Grundschule f

gradient ['greɪdɪənt] n (upward) Steigung f; (downward) Gefälle nt

gradual, gradually ['grædjʊəl, -lɪ] adj, adv allmählich

graduate ['grædjʊɪt] n Uniabsolvent(in) m(f), Hochschulabsolvent(in) m(f) ▷ ['grædjʊeɪt] vi einen akademischen Grad erwerben

grain [greɪn] n (cereals) Getreide nt; (of corn, sand) Korn nt; (in wood) Maserung f

gram [græm] n Gramm nt

grammar ['græmə°] n Grammatik f; **grammar school** n (Brit) ~ Gymnasium nt

gran [græn] n (fam) Oma f

grand [grænd] adj (pej) hochnäsig; (posh) vornehm ▷ n (fam) 1000 Pfund bzw. 1000 Dollar

grand(dad) n (fam) Opa m; **granddaughter** n Enkelin f; **grandfather** n Großvater m; **grandma** n (fam) Oma f; **grandmother** n Großmutter f; **grandpa** n (fam) Opa m; **grandparents** npl Großeltern pl; **grandson** n Enkel m

grandstand n (Sport) Tribüne f

granny ['grænɪ] n (fam) Oma f

grant [grɑːnt] vt gewähren (sb sth jdm etw); **to take sb/sth for ~ed** jdn/etw als selbstverständlich hinnehmen ▷ n Subvention f, finanzielle Unterstützung f; (for university) Stipendium nt

grape [greɪp] n Weintraube f; **grapefruit** n Grapefruit f; **grape juice** n Traubensaft m

graph [grɑːf] n Diagramm nt; **graphic** ['græfɪk] adj grafisch; (description) anschaulich

grasp [grɑːsp] vt ergreifen; (understand) begreifen

grass [grɑːs] n Gras nt; (lawn) Rasen m; **grasshopper** n Heuschrecke f

grate [greɪt] n Feuerrost m ▷ vi kratzen ▷ vt (cheese) reiben

grateful, gratefully ['greɪtfʊl, -fəlɪ] adj, adv dankbar

grater ['greɪtə°] n Reibe f

gratifying ['grætɪfaɪɪŋ] adj erfreulich

gratitude ['grætɪtjuːd] n Dankbarkeit f

9

grave [greɪv] n Grab nt ⊳ adj ernst; (mistake) schwer

gravel ['grævəl] n Kies m

graveyard ['greɪvjɑːd] n Friedhof m

gravity ['grævɪtɪ] n Schwerkraft f; (seriousness) Ernst m

gravy ['greɪvɪ] n Bratensoße f

gray [greɪ] adj (US) grau

graze [greɪz] vi (of animals) grasen ⊳ vt (touch) streifen; (Med) abschürfen ⊳ n (Med) Abschürfung f

grease [griːs] n (fat) Fett nt; (lubricant) Schmiere f ⊳ vt einfetten; (Tech) schmieren; **greasy** ['griːsɪ] adj fettig; (hands, tools) schmierig; (fam: person) schleimig

great [greɪt] adj groß; (fam: good) großartig, super; **a ~ deal of** viel; **Great Britain** ['greɪt'brɪtn] n Großbritannien nt; **great-grandfather** n Urgroßvater m; **great-grandmother** n Urgroßmutter f; **greatly** adv sehr; **~ disappointed** zutiefst enttäuscht

Greece [griːs] n Griechenland nt

greed [griːd] n Gier f (for nach); (for food) Gefräßigkeit f; **greedy** adj gierig; (for food) gefräßig

Greek [griːk] adj griechisch ⊳ n (person) Grieche m, Griechin f; (language) Griechisch nt; **it's all ~ to me** ich verstehe nur Bahnhof

green [griːn] adj grün; **~ with envy** grün/gelb vor Neid ⊳ n (colour; for golf) Grün nt; (village ~) Dorfwiese f; **~s** (vegetables) grünes Gemüse; **the Greens, the Green Party** (Pol) die Grünen; **green card** n (US: work permit) Arbeitserlaubnis f; (Brit: for car) grüne Versicherungskarte f

greengage n Reneklode f; **greengrocer** n Obst- und Gemüsehändler(in) m(f); **greenhouse** n Gewächshaus nt; **~ effect** Treibhauseffekt m; **Greenland** n Grönland nt; **green pepper** n grüner Paprika; **green salad** n grüner Salat

Greenwich Mean Time ['grenɪdʒ'miːntaɪm] n westeuropäische Zeit

greet [griːt] vt grüßen; **greeting** n Gruß m

grew [gruː] pt of **grow**

grey [greɪ] adj grau; **grey-haired** adj grauhaarig; **greyhound** n Windhund m

grid [grɪd] n Gitter nt; **gridlock** n Verkehrsinfarkt m; **gridlocked** adj (roads) völlig verstopft; (talks) festgefahren

grief [griːf] n Kummer m; (over loss) Trauer f

grievance ['griːvəns] n Beschwerde f

grieve [griːv] vi trauern (for um)

grill [grɪl] n (on cooker) Grill m ⊳ vt grillen

grim [grɪm] adj (face, humour) grimmig; (situation, prospects) trostlos

grin [grɪn] n Grinsen nt ⊳ vi grinsen

grind [graɪnd] (**ground, ground**) vt mahlen; (sharpen) schleifen; (US: meat) durchdrehen, hacken

grip [grɪp] n Griff m; **get a ~** nimm dich zusammen!; **to get to ~s with sth** etw in den Griff bekommen ⊳ vt packen; **gripping** adj (exciting) spannend

groan [grəʊn] vi stöhnen (with vor +dat)

grocer ['grəʊsə°] n Lebensmittelhändler(in) m(f); **groceries** npl Lebensmittel pl

groin [grɔɪn] n (Anat) Leiste f;

groin strain n (Med) Leistenbruch m
groom [gruːm] n Bräutigam m ▷ vt: **well ~ed** gepflegt
grope [grəʊp] vi tasten ▷ vt (sexually harrass) befummeln
gross [grəʊs] adj (coarse) derb; (extreme: negligence, error) grob; (disgusting) ekelhaft; (Comm) brutto; **~ national product** Bruttosozialprodukt nt; **~ salary** Bruttogehalt nt
grotty ['grɒtɪ] adj (fam) mies, vergammelt
ground [graʊnd] pt, pp of **grind** ▷ n Boden m, Erde f; (Sport) Platz m; **~s** pl (around house) (Garten)anlagen pl; (reasons) Gründe pl; (of coffee) Satz m; **on (the) ~s of** aufgrund von; **ground floor** n (Brit) Erdgeschoss nt; **ground meat** n (US) Hackfleisch nt
group [gruːp] n Gruppe f ▷ vt gruppieren
grouse [graʊs] (pl -) n (bird) Schottisches Moorhuhn; (complaint) Nörgelei f
grow [grəʊ] (**grew, grown**) vi wachsen; (increase) zunehmen (in an); (become) werden; **to ~ old** alt werden; **to ~ into ...** sich entwickeln zu ...; ▷ vt (crop, plant) ziehen; (commercially) anbauen; **I'm ~ing a beard** ich lasse mir einen Bart wachsen; **grow up** vi aufwachsen; (mature) erwachsen werden; **growing** adj wachsend; **a ~ number of people** immer mehr Leute
growl [graʊl] vi knurren
grown [grəʊn] pp of **grow**
grown-up [grəʊnˈʌp] adj erwachsen ▷ n Erwachsene(r) mf
growth [grəʊθ] n Wachstum nt; (increase) Zunahme f; (Med) Wucherung f

grubby ['grʌbɪ] adj schmuddelig
grudge [grʌdʒ] n Abneigung f (against gegen) ▷ vt: **to ~ sb sth** jdm etw nicht gönnen
gruelling ['gruəlɪŋ] adj aufreibend; (pace) mörderisch
gruesome ['gruːsəm] adj grausig
grumble ['grʌmbl] vi murren (about über +akk)
grumpy ['grʌmpɪ] adj (fam) mürrisch, grantig
grunt [grʌnt] vi grunzen
G-string ['dʒiːstrɪŋ] n String m, Stringtanga m
guarantee [gærənˈtiː] n Garantie f (of für); **it's still under ~** es ist noch Garantie darauf ▷ vt garantieren
guard [gɑːd] n (sentry) Wache f; (in prison) Wärter(in) m(f); (Brit Rail) Schaffner(in) m(f) ▷ vt bewachen; **a closely ~ed secret** ein streng gehütetes Geheimnis
guardian ['gɑːdɪən] n Vormund m; **~ angel** Schutzengel m
guess [ges] n Vermutung f; (estimate) Schätzung f; **have a ~ rate mal!** ▷ vt, vi raten; (estimate) schätzen; **I ~ you're right** du hast wohl recht; **I ~ so** ich glaube schon
guest [gest] n Gast m; **be my ~** nur zu!; **guest-house** n Pension f; **guest room** n Gästezimmer nt
guidance ['gaɪdəns] n (direction) Leitung f; (advice) Rat m; (counselling) Beratung f; **for your ~** zu Ihrer Orientierung; **guide** [gaɪd] n (person) Führer(in) m(f); (tour) Reiseleiter(in) m(f); (book) Führer m; (girl ~) Pfadfinderin f ▷ vt führen; **guidebook** n Reiseführer m; **guide dog** n Blindenhund m; **guided tour** n

Führung f (of durch); **guidelines**
npl Richtlinien pl

guilt [gɪlt] n Schuld f; **guilty** adj
schuldig (of gen); (look)
schuldbewusst; **to have a
~ conscience** ein schlechtes
Gewissen haben

guinea pig ['gɪnɪ pɪg] n
Meerschweinchen nt; (person)
Versuchskaninchen nt

guitar [gɪ'tɑː] n Gitarre f

gulf [gʌlf] n Golf m; (gap) Kluft f;
Gulf States npl Golfstaaten pl

gull [gʌl] n Möwe f

gullible ['gʌlɪbl] adj
leichtgläubig

gulp [gʌlp] n (kräftiger) Schluck
▷ vi schlucken

gum [gʌm] n (around teeth, usu pl)
Zahnfleisch nt; (chewing ~)
Kaugummi m

gun [gʌn] n Schusswaffe f; (rifle)
Gewehr nt; (pistol) Pistole f;
gunfire n Schüsse pl,
Geschützfeuer nt; **gunpowder** n
Schießpulver nt; **gunshot** n
Schuss m

gush [gʌʃ] vi (heraus)strömen
(from aus)

gut [gʌt] n Darm m; **~s** pl
(intestines) Eingeweide; (courage)
Mumm m

gutter ['gʌtə] n (for roof)
Dachrinne f; (in street) Rinnstein m,
Gosse f; **gutter press** n
Skandalpresse f

guy [gaɪ] n (man) Typ m, Kerl m; **~s**
pl (US) Leute pl

gym [dʒɪm] n Turnhalle f; (for
working out) Fitnesscenter nt;
gymnasium [dʒɪm'neɪzɪəm] n
Turnhalle f; **gymnastics**
[dʒɪm'næstɪks] nsing Turnen nt;
gym-toned adj durchtrainiert

gynaecologist [gaɪnɪ'kɒlədʒɪst]
n Frauenarzt m, Frauenärztin f,
Gynäkologe m, Gynäkologin f;

gynaecology n Gynäkologie f,
Frauenheilkunde f

gypsy ['dʒɪpsɪ] n Zigeuner(in)
m(f)

h

one's ~ cut sich dat die Haare schneiden lassen; **hairbrush** n Haarbürste f; **hair conditioner** n Haarspülung f; **haircut** n Haarschnitt m; **to have a ~** sich dat die Haare schneiden lassen; **hairdo** (pl **-s**) n Frisur f; **hairdresser** n Friseur m, Friseuse f; **hairdryer** n Haartrockner m; (hand-held) Fön® m; (over head) Trockenhaube f; **hairgel** n Haargel nt; **hairpin** n Haarnadel f; **hair remover** n Enthaarungsmittel nt; **hair spray** n Haarspray nt; **hair straighteners** npl Haarglätter m; **hair style** n Frisur f; **hairy** adj haarig, behaart; (fam: dangerous) brenzlig

haka ['hɑːkɑ] n (NZ) Haka m (Ritualtanz der Maori); dem Haka ähnlicher Tanz, der vor allem von neuseeländischen Rugby-Teams vor Spielbeginn aufgeführt wird

hake [heɪk] n Seehecht m

habit ['hæbɪt] n Gewohnheit f

hack [hæk] vt hacken; **hacker** n (Inform) Hacker(in) m(f)

had [hæd] pt, pp of **have**

haddock ['hædək] n Schellfisch m

hadn't ['hædnt] contr of **had not**

haemophiliac, **hemophiliac** (US) [hiːməʊˈfɪliæk] n Bluter(in) m(f); **haemorrhage**, **hemorrhage** (US) ['hemərɪdʒ] n Blutung f ▷ vi bluten; **haemorrhoids**, **hemorrhoids** (US) ['hemərɔɪdz] npl Hämorrhoiden pl

haggis ['hægɪs] n (Scot) mit gehackten Schafsinnereien und Haferschrot gefüllter Schafsmagen

Hague [heɪg] n: **the ~** Den Haag

hail [heɪl] n Hagel m ▷ vi hageln ▷ vt: **to ~ sb as sth** jdn als etw feiern; **hailstone** n Hagelkorn nt

hair [hɛə°] n Haar nt, Haare pl; **to do one's ~** sich frisieren; **to get**

half [hɑːf] (pl **halves**) n Hälfte f; (Sport: of game) Halbzeit f; **to cut in ~** halbieren ▷ adj halb; **three and a ~ pounds** dreieinhalb Pfund; **~ an hour, a ~ hour** eine halbe Stunde; **one and a ~** eineinhalb, anderthalb ▷ adv halb, zur Hälfte; **~ past three, ~ three** halb vier; **at ~ past** um halb; **~ asleep** fast eingeschlafen; **she's ~ German** sie ist zur Hälfte Deutsche; **as big (as)** halb so groß (wie); **half board** n Halbpension f; **half fare** n halber Fahrpreis; **half-hearted** adj halbherzig; **half-hour** n halbe Stunde; **half pint** n = Viertelliter m or nt; **half price** n: **(at) ~** zum halben Preis; **half-term** n (at school) Ferien pl in der Mitte des Trimesters; **half-time** n Halbzeit f; **halfway** adv auf halbem Wege

halibut ['hælɪbət] n Heilbutt m

hall [hɔːl] n (building) Halle f; (for

audience) Saal m; (entrance ~) Flur m; (large) Diele f; ~ of residence (Brit) Studentenwohnheim nt

hallmark ['hɔ:lmɑ:k] n Stempel m; (fig) Kennzeichen nt

hallo [hʌ'ləʊ] interj hallo

Hallowe'en [hæləʊ'i:n] n Halloween nt (Tag vor Allerheiligen, an dem sich Kinder verkleiden und von Tür zu Tür gehen)

● **HALLOWE'EN**
●
● **Hallowe'en** ist der 31. Oktober,
● der Vorabend von Allerheiligen,
● und nach altem Glauben der
● Abend, an dem man Geister und
● Hexen anrufen kann. In
● Großbritannien und vor allem in
● den USA feiern die Leute
● Hallowe'en, indem sie sich
● verkleiden und mit selbst
● gemachten Laternen aus
● Kürbissen von Tür zu Tür
● ziehen.

halo ['heɪləʊ] (pl -es) n (of saint) Heiligenschein m

halt [hɔ:lt] n Pause f, Halt m; **to come to a ~** zum Stillstand kommen ▷ vt, vi anhalten

halve [hɑ:v] vt halbieren

ham [hæm] n Schinken m; **~ and eggs** Schinken mit Spiegelei

hamburger ['hæmbɜ:gə] n (Gastr) Hamburger m

hammer ['hæmə] n Hammer m ▷ vt, vi hämmern

hammock ['hæmək] n Hängematte f

hamper ['hæmpə] vt behindern ▷ n (as gift) Geschenkkorb m; (for picnic) Picknickkkorb m

hamster ['hæmstə] n Hamster m

hand [hænd] n Hand f; (of clock, instrument) Zeiger m; (in card game) Blatt nt; **to be made by**

~ Handarbeit sein; **~s up!** Hände hoch!; (at school) meldet euch!; **~s off!** Finger weg!; **on the one ~ ...**, **on the other ~ ...** einerseits ..., andererseits ...; **to give sb a ~** jdm helfen (with bei); **it's in his ~s** er hat es in der Hand; **to be in good ~s** gut aufgehoben sein; **to get out of ~** außer Kontrolle geraten ▷ vt (pass) reichen (to sb jdm); **hand down** vt (tradition) überliefern; (heirloom) vererben; **hand in** vt einreichen; (at school, university etc) abgeben; **hand out** vt verteilen; **hand over** vt übergeben

handbag n Handtasche f; **handbook** n Handbuch nt; **handbrake** n (Brit) Handbremse f; **handcuffs** npl Handschellen pl; **handful** n Handvoll f; **handheld PC** n Handheld m

handicap ['hændɪkæp] n Behinderung f, Handikap nt ▷ vt benachteiligen; **handicapped** adj behindert; **the ~** die Behinderten

handicraft ['hændɪkrɑ:ft] n Kunsthandwerk nt

handkerchief ['hæŋkətʃɪf] n Taschentuch nt

handle ['hændl] n Griff m; (of door) Klinke f; (of cup etc) Henkel m; (for winding) Kurbel f ▷ vt (touch) anfassen; (deal with: matter) sich befassen mit; (people, machine etc) umgehen mit; (situation, problem) fertig werden mit; **handlebars** npl Lenkstange f

hand luggage ['hændlʌgɪdʒ] n Handgepäck nt; **handmade** adj handgefertigt; **to be ~** Handarbeit sein; **handout** n (sheet) Handout nt, Thesenpapier nt; **handset** n Hörer m; **please replace the ~** bitte legen Sie auf; **hands-free phone** n Freisprechanlage f; **handshake** n Händedruck m

handsome ['hænsəm] *adj (man)* gut aussehend

hands-on [hændz'ɒn] *adj* praxisorientiert; **~ experience** praktische Erfahrung

handwriting ['hændraɪtɪŋ] *n* Handschrift *f*

handy ['hændɪ] *adj (useful)* praktisch

hang [hæŋ] **(hung, hung)** *vt (auf)hängen; (execute: hanged, hanged)* hängen; **to ~ sth on sth** etw an etw *akk* hängen ▷ *vi* hängen ▷ *n:* **he's got the ~ of it** er hat den Dreh raus; **hang about** *vi* herumtreiben, rumhängen; **hang on** *vi* sich festhalten *(to* an *+dat); (fam: wait)* warten; **to ~ on to sth** etw behalten; **hang up** *vi (Tel)* auflegen ▷ *vt* aufhängen

hangar ['hæŋəˀ] *n* Flugzeughalle *f*

hanger ['hæŋəˀ] *n* Kleiderbügel *m*

hang glider ['hæŋglaɪdəˀ] *n (Flug)drachen m; (person)* Drachenflieger(in) *m(f)*;
hang-gliding *n* Drachenfliegen *nt*

hangover ['hæŋəʊvəˀ] *n (bad head)* Kater *m; (relic)* Überbleibsel *nt*

hankie ['hæŋkɪ] *n (fam)* Taschentuch *nt*

happen ['hæpən] *vi* geschehen; *(sth strange, unpleasant)* passieren; **if anything should ~ to me** wenn mir etwas passieren sollte; **it won't ~ again** es wird nicht wieder vorkommen; **I ~ed to be passing** ich kam zufällig vorbei; **happening** *n* Ereignis *nt,* Happening *nt*

happily ['hæpɪlɪ] *adv* fröhlich, glücklich; *(luckily)* glücklicherweise; **happiness** ['hæpɪnəs] *n* Glück *nt;* **happy** ['hæpɪ] *adj* glücklich; *(satisfied)*

~ with sth mit etw zufrieden; *(willing)* **to be ~ to do sth** etw gerne tun; **Happy Christmas** fröhliche Weihnachten!; **Happy New Year** ein glückliches Neues Jahr!; **Happy Birthday** herzlichen Glückwunsch zum Geburtstag!; **happy hour** *n* Happy Hour *f (Zeit, in der man in Bars Getränke zu günstigeren Preisen bekommt)*

harass ['hærəs] *vt (ständig)* belästigen; **harassment** *n* Belästigung *f; (at work)* Mobbing *nt;* **sexual ~** sexuelle Belästigung

harbor (US), **harbour** ['hɑːbəˀ] *n* Hafen *m*

hard [hɑːd] *adj* hart; *(difficult)* schwer, schwierig; *(harsh)* hart(herzig); **don't be ~ on him** sei nicht zu streng zu ihm; **it's ~ to believe** es ist kaum zu glauben ▷ *adv (work)* schwer; *(run)* schnell; *(rain, snow)* stark; **to try ~/-er** sich *dat* große/mehr Mühe geben; **hardback** *n* gebundene Ausgabe; **hard-boiled** *adj (egg)* hart gekocht; **hard copy** *n (Inform)* Ausdruck *m;* **hard disk** *n (Inform)* Festplatte *f;* **harden** *vt* härten ▷ *vi* hart werden; **hardened** *adj (person)* abgehärtet *(to* gegen); **hard-hearted** *adj* hartherzig; **hardliner** *n* Hardliner(in) *m(f);* **hardly** ['hɑːdlɪ] *adv* kaum; **~ ever** fast nie; **hardship** ['hɑːdʃɪp] *n* Not *f;* **hard shoulder** *n (Brit)* Standspur *f;* **hardware** *n (Inform)* Hardware *f,* Haushalts- und Eisenwaren *pl;* **hard-working** *adj* fleißig, tüchtig

hare [heəˀ] *n* Hase *m*

harm [hɑːm] *n* Schaden *m; (bodily)* Verletzung *f;* **it wouldn't do any ~** es würde nicht schaden ▷ *vt* schaden *+dat; (person)* verletzen; **harmful** *adj* schädlich; **harmless** *adj* harmlos

harp [hɑːp] *n* Harfe *f*

harsh [hɑːʃ] *adj* (*climate, voice*) rau; (*light, sound*) grell; (*severe*) hart, streng

harvest ['hɑːvɪst] *n* Ernte *f*; (*time*) Erntezeit *f* ▷ *vt* ernten

has [hæz] *pres of* **have**

hash [hæʃ] *n* (*Gastr*) Haschee *nt*; (*fam: hashish*) Haschisch *nt*; **to make a ~ of sth** etw vermasseln; **hash browns** *npl* (*US*) ≈ Kartoffelpuffer/Rösti mit Zwiebeln *pl*

hassle ['hæsl] *n* Ärger *m*; (*fuss*) Theater *nt*; **no ~** kein Problem ▷ *vt* bedrängen

hasn't ['hæznt] *contr of* **has not**

haste [heɪst] *n* Eile *f*; **hasty** *adv, adj* hastig; (*rash*) vorschnell

hat [hæt] *n* Hut *m*

hatch [hætʃ] *n* (*Naut*) Luke *f*; (*in house*) Durchreiche *f*; **hatchback** ['hætʃbæk] *n* (*car*) Wagen *m* mit Hecktür

hate [heɪt] *vt* hassen; **I ~ doing this** ich mache das sehr ungern ▷ *n* Hass *m* (*of auf +akk*)

haul [hɔːl] *vt* ziehen, schleppen ▷ *n* (*booty*) Beute *f*; **haulage** ['hɔːlɪdʒ] *n* Transport *m*; (*trade*) Spedition *f*; **haunted** *adj*: **a ~ house** ein Haus, in dem es spukt

◯ **KEYWORD**

have [hæv] (*pt, pp* **had**) *vb aux* **1** haben; (*esp with vbs of motion*) sein; **to have arrived/slept** angekommen sein/geschlafen haben; **to have been** gewesen sein; **having eaten** *o* **when he had eaten, he left** nachdem er gegessen hatte, ging er

2 (*in tag questions*) **you've done it, haven't you?** du hast/Sie haben es doch gemacht, oder nicht?

3 (*in short answers and questions*) **you've made a mistake — so I have/no I haven't** du hast/Sie haben einen Fehler gemacht — ja, stimmt/nein; **we haven't paid — yes we have!** wir haben nicht bezahlt — doch!; **I've been there before, have you?** ich war schon einmal da, du/Sie auch?

▷ *modal vb aux* (*be obliged*): **to have (got) to do sth** etw tun müssen; **you haven't to tell her** du darfst es ihr nicht erzählen

▷ *vt* **1** (*possess*) haben; **he has (got) blue eyes** er hat blaue Augen; **I have (got) an idea** ich habe eine Idee

2 (*referring to meals etc*) **to have breakfast/a cigarette** frühstücken/eine Zigarette rauchen

3 (*receive, obtain etc*) haben; **may I have your address?** kann ich deine/Ihre Adresse haben?; **to have a baby** ein Kind bekommen

4 (*maintain, allow*) **he will have it that he is right** er besteht darauf, dass er recht hat; **I won't have it** das lasse ich mir nicht bieten

5 to have sth done etw machen lassen; **to have sb do sth** jdn etw machen lassen; **he soon had them all laughing** er brachte sie alle zum Lachen

6 (*experience, suffer*) **she had her bag stolen** man hat ihr die Tasche gestohlen; **he had his arm broken** er hat sich den Arm gebrochen

7 (*+noun: take, hold etc*) **to have a walk/rest** spazieren gehen/sich ausruhen; **to have a meeting/party** eine Besprechung/Party haben;

have on *vt* (*be wearing*) anhaben; (*have arranged*) vorhaben; (*Brit*) **you're having me on** du verarschst mich doch;

have out vt: **to have it out with sb** (settle problem) etw mit jdm bereden

Hawaii [hə'waɪiː] n Hawaii nt
hawk [hɔːk] n Habicht m
hay [heɪ] n Heu nt; **hay fever** n Heuschnupfen m
hazard ['hæzəd] n Gefahr f; (risk) Risiko nt; **hazardous** adj gefährlich; **~ waste** Sondermüll m; **hazard warning lights** npl Warnblinkanlage f
haze [heɪz] n Dunst m
hazelnut ['heɪzlnʌt] n Haselnuss f
hazy ['heɪzɪ] adj (misty) dunstig; (vague) verschwommen
he [hiː] pron er
head [hed] n Kopf m; (leader) Leiter(in) m(f); (at school) Schulleiter(in) m(f); (of state) Staatsoberhaupt nt; **at the ~ of** an der Spitze von; (tossing coin) **~s or tails?** Kopf oder Zahl? ▷ adj (leading) Ober-; **~ boy** Schulsprecher m; **~ girl** Schulsprecherin f ▷ vt anführen; (organization) leiten; **head for** vt zusteuern auf +akk; **he's heading for trouble** er wird Ärger bekommen
headache ['hedeɪk] n Kopfschmerzen pl, Kopfweh nt; **header** n (football) Kopfball m; (dive) Kopfsprung m; **headfirst** adj kopfüber; **headhunt** vt (Comm) abwerben; **heading** n Überschrift f; **headlamp**, **headlight** n Scheinwerfer m; **headline** n Schlagzeile f; **headmaster** n Schulleiter m; **headmistress** n Schulleiterin f; **head-on collision** adj Frontalzusammenstoß m; **headphones** npl Kopfhörer m; **headquarters** npl (of firm) Zentrale f; **headrest**, **head**

restraint n Kopfstütze f; **headscarf** (pl **-scarves**) n Kopftuch nt; **head teacher** n Schulleiter(in) m(f)
heal [hiːl] vt, vi heilen
health [helθ] n Gesundheit f; **good/bad for one's ~** gesund/ungesund; **your ~!** zum Wohl!; **~ and beauty** Wellness; **health centre** n Ärztezentrum nt; **health club** n Fitnesscenter nt; **health food** n Reformkost f; **~ shop**, **~ store** Bioladen m; **health insurance** n Krankenversicherung f; **health service** n Gesundheitswesen nt; **healthy** adj gesund
heap [hiːp] n Haufen m; **~s of** (fam) jede Menge ▷ vt, vi häufen
hear [hɪə*] (**heard**, **heard**) vt, vi hören; **to ~ about sth** von etw erfahren; **I've ~d of it/him** ich habe schon davon/von ihm gehört; **hearing** n Gehör nt; (Jur) Verhandlung f; **hearing aid** n Hörgerät nt; **hearsay** n: **from ~** vom Hörensagen
heart [hɑːt] n Herz nt; **to lose/take ~** den Mut verlieren/Mut fassen; **to learn by ~** auswendig lernen; (cards) **~s** Herz nt; **queen of ~s** Herzdame f; **heart attack** n Herzanfall m; **heartbeat** n Herzschlag m; **heartbreaking** adj herzzerreißend; **heartbroken** adj todunglücklich, untröstlich; **heartburn** n Sodbrennen nt; **heart failure** n Herzversagen nt; **heartfelt** adj tief empfunden; **heartless** adj herzlos; **heart-throb** n (fam) Schwarm m; **heart-to-heart** n offene Aussprache; **hearty** ['hɑːtɪ] adj (meal, appetite) herzhaft; (welcome) herzlich
heat [hiːt] n Hitze f; (pleasant) Wärme f; (temperature) Temperatur

f; (Sport) Vorlauf m ▷ vt (house,
room) heizen; **heat up** vi warm
werden ▷ vt aufwärmen; **heated**
adj beheizt; (fig) hitzig; **heater** n
Heizofen m; (Auto) Heizung f

heath [hiːθ] n (Brit) Heide f;
heather ['hɛðə°] n Heidekraut
nt

heating ['hiːtɪŋ] n Heizung f;
heat resistant adj
hitzebeständig; **heatwave** n
Hitzewelle f

heaven ['hɛvn] n Himmel m;
heavenly adj himmlisch

heavily ['hɛvɪlɪ] adv (rain, drink
etc) stark; **heavy** ['hɛvɪ] adj
schwer; (rain, traffic, smoker etc)
stark; **heavy goods vehicle** n
Lastkraftwagen m

Hebrew ['hiːbruː] adj hebräisch
▷ n (language) Hebräisch nt

hectic ['hɛktɪk] adj hektisch

he'd [hiːd] contr of **he had**; **he
would**

hedge [hɛdʒ] n Hecke f

hedgehog ['hɛdʒhɒg] n Igel
m

heel [hiːl] n (Anat) Ferse f; (of
shoe) Absatz m

hefty ['hɛftɪ] adj schwer; (person)
stämmig; (fine, amount) saftig

height [haɪt] n Höhe f; (of person)
Größe f

heir [ɛə°] n Erbe m; **heiress**
['ɛərɪs] n Erbin f

held [hɛld] pt, pp of **hold**

helicopter ['hɛlɪkɒptə°] n
Hubschrauber m; **heliport**
['hɛlɪpɔːt] n Hubschrauber-
landeplatz m

hell [hɛl] n Hölle f; **go to ~** scher
dich zum Teufel ▷ interj
verdammt; **that's a ~ of a lot of
money** das ist verdammt viel Geld

he'll [hiːl] contr of **he will**; **he
shall**

hello [hʌ'ləʊ] interj hallo

helmet ['hɛlmɪt] n Helm m

help [hɛlp] n Hilfe f ▷ vt, vi
helfen +dat (with bei); **to ~ sb (to)
do sth** jdm helfen, etw zu tun; **can
I ~?** kann ich (Ihnen) behilflich
sein?; **I couldn't ~ laughing** ich
musste einfach lachen; **I can't ~ it**
ich kann nichts dafür; **~ yourself**
bedienen Sie sich; **helpful** adj
(person) hilfsbereit; (useful)
nützlich; **helping** n Portion f;
helpless adj hilflos

hem [hɛm] n Saum m

hemophiliac [hiːməʊ'fɪlɪæk] n
(US) Bluter m; **hemorrhage**
['hɛmərɪdʒ] n (US) Blutung f;
hemorrhoids ['hɛmərɔɪdz] npl
(US) Hämorrhoiden pl

hen [hɛn] n Henne f

hen night n (Brit)
Junggesellinnenabschied m

hence [hɛns] adv (reason) daher

henpecked ['hɛnpɛkt] adj: **to
be ~** unter dem Pantoffel stehen

hepatitis [hɛpə'taɪtɪs] n Hepatitis f

her [hɜː°] adj ihr; **she's hurt - leg**
sie hat sich dat das Bein verletzt
▷ pron (direct object) sie; (indirect
object) ihr; **do you know ~?** kennst
du sie?; **can you help ~?** kannst du
ihr helfen?; **it's ~** sie ist's

herb [hɜːb] n Kraut nt

herbal medicine ['hɜːbəl–] n
Pflanzenheilkunde f; **herbal tea** n
Kräutertee m

herd [hɜːd] n Herde f; **herd
instinct** n Herdentrieb m

here [hɪə°] adv hier; (to this place)
hierher; **come ~** komm her; **I
won't be ~ for lunch** ich bin zum
Mittagessen nicht da; **~ and there**
hier und da, da und dort

hereditary [hɪ'rɛdɪtərɪ] adj
erblich; **hereditary disease** n
Erbkrankheit f; **heritage**
['hɛrɪtɪdʒ] n Erbe nt

hernia ['hɜːnɪə] n Leistenbruch m, Eingeweidebruch m

hero ['hɪərəʊ] (pl -es) n Held m

heroin ['herəʊɪn] n Heroin nt

heroine ['herəʊɪn] n Heldin f; **heroism** ['herəʊɪzəm] n Heldentum nt

herring ['herɪŋ] n Hering m

hers [hɜːz] pron ihre(r, s); **this is ~** das gehört ihr; **a friend of ~** ein Freund von ihr

herself [hɜːˈself] pron (reflexive) sich; **she's bought ~ a flat** sie hat sich eine Wohnung gekauft; **she needs it for ~** sie braucht es für sich (selbst); (emphatic) **she did it ~** sie hat es selbst gemacht; **(all) by ~** allein

he's [hiːz] contr of **he is**; **he has**

hesitant ['hezɪtənt] adj zögernd; **hesitate** ['hezɪteɪt] vi zögern; **don't ~ to ask** fragen Sie ruhig; **hesitation** n Zögern nt; **without ~** ohne zu zögern

heterosexual [hetərəʊˈsekʃʊəl] adj heterosexuell ▷ n Heterosexuelle(r) mf

HGV abbr = **heavy goods vehicle** LKW m

hi [haɪ] interj hi, hallo

hiccup ['hɪkʌp] n Schluckauf m; (minor problem) Problemchen nt; **to have (the) ~s** Schluckauf haben

hid [hɪd] pt of **hide**

hidden ['hɪdn] pp of **hide**

hide [haɪd] (hid, hidden) vt verstecken (from vor +dat); (feelings, truth) verbergen; (cover) verdecken ▷ vi sich verstecken (from vor +dat)

hideous ['hɪdɪəs] adj scheußlich

hiding ['haɪdɪŋ] n (beating) Tracht f Prügel; (concealment) **to be in ~** sich versteckt halten; **hiding place** n Versteck nt

hi-fi ['haɪfaɪ] n Hi-Fi nt; (system) Hi-Fi-Anlage f

high [haɪ] adj hoch; (wind) stark; (living) im großen Stil; (on drugs) high ▷ adv hoch ▷ n (Meteo) Hoch nt; **highchair** n Hochstuhl m; **higher** adj höher; **higher education** n Hochschulbildung f; **high flier** n Hochbegabte(r) f(m)f; **high heels** npl Stöckelschuhe pl; **high jump** n Hochsprung m; **Highlands** npl (schottisches) Hochland nt; **highlight** n (in hair) Strähnchen nt; (fig) Höhepunkt m ▷ vt (with pen) hervorheben; **highlighter** n Textmarker m; **highly** adj hoch, sehr; **~ paid** hoch bezahlt; **I think ~ of him** ich habe eine hohe Meinung von ihm; **high-performance** adj Hochleistungs-; **high school** n (US) Highschool f, ≈ Gymnasium nt; **high-speed** adj Schnell-; **~ train** Hochgeschwindigkeitszug m; **high street** n Hauptstraße f; **high tech** adj Hightech- ▷ n Hightech nt; **high tide** n Flut f; **highway** n (US) = Autobahn f; (Brit) Landstraße f

hijack ['haɪdʒæk] vt entführen, hijacken; **hijacker** n Entführer(in) m(f), Hijacker m

hike [haɪk] vi wandern ▷ n Wanderung f; **hiker** n Wanderer m, Wanderin f; **hiking** n Wandern nt

hilarious [hɪˈlɛərɪəs] adj zum Schreien komisch

hill [hɪl] n Hügel m; (higher) Berg m; **hilly** adj hügelig

him [hɪm] pron (direct object) ihn; (indirect object) ihm; **do you know ~?** kennst du ihn?; **can you help ~?** kannst du ihm helfen?; **it's ~** er ist's; **~ too** er auch

himself [hɪmˈself] pron (reflexive) sich; **he's bought ~ a flat** er hat sich eine Wohnung gekauft; **he needs it for ~** er braucht es für sich (selbst); (emphatic) **he did it**

~ er hat es selbst gemacht; **(all) by ~** allein

hinder ['hɪndə°] vt behindern; **hindrance** ['hɪndrəns] n Behinderung f

Hindu ['hɪndu:] adj hinduistisch ▷ n Hindu m; **Hinduism** ['hɪndu:ɪzəm] n Hinduismus m

hinge [hɪndʒ] n Scharnier nt; (on door) Angel f

hint [hɪnt] n Wink m, Andeutung f; (trace) Spur f ▷ vi andeuten (at akk)

hip [hɪp] n Hüfte f

hippopotamus [hɪpə'pɒtəməs] n Nilpferd nt

hire ['haɪə°] vt (worker) anstellen; (car, bike etc) mieten ▷ n Miete f; **for ~** (taxi) frei; **hire car** n Mietwagen m; **hire charge** n Benutzungsgebühr f; **hire purchase** n Ratenkauf m

his [hɪz] adj sein; **he's hurt ~ leg** er hat sich dat das Bein verletzt ▷ pron seine(r, s); **it's ~** es gehört ihm; **a friend of ~** ein Freund von ihm

historic [hɪ'stɒrɪk] adj (significant) historisch; **historical** adj (monument etc) historisch; (studies etc) geschichtlich; **history** ['hɪstərɪ] n Geschichte f

hit [hɪt] n (blow) Schlag m; (on target) Treffer m; (successful film, CD etc) Hit m ▷ vt (**hit, hit**) schlagen; (bullet, stone etc) treffen; **the car ~ the tree** das Auto fuhr gegen einen Baum; **to ~ one's head on sth** sich dat den Kopf an etw dat stoßen; **hit (up)on** vt stoßen auf +akk; **hit-and-run** adj: **~ accident** Unfall m mit Fahrerflucht

hitch [hɪtʃ] vt (also: **~ up**) hochziehen ▷ n Schwierigkeit f; **without a ~** reibungslos

hitch-hike ['hɪtʃhaɪk] vi trampen; **hitch-hiker** n Tramper(in)

m(f); **hitchhiking** n Trampen

HIV abbr = **human immunodeficiency virus** HIV nt; **~ positive/negative** HIV-positiv/negativ

hive [haɪv] n Bienenstock m

HM abbr = **His/Her Majesty**

HMS abbr = **His/Her Majesty's Ship**

hoarse [hɔːs] adj heiser

hoax [həʊks] n Streich m, Jux m; (false alarm) blinder Alarm

hob [hɒb] n (of cooker) Kochfeld nt

hobble ['hɒbl] vi humpeln

hobby ['hɒbɪ] n Hobby nt

hobo ['həʊbəʊ] (pl **-es**) n (US) Penner(in) m(f)

hockey ['hɒkɪ] n Hockey nt

hold [həʊld] (**held, held**) vt halten; (contain) enthalten; (be able to contain) fassen; (post, office) innehaben; (value) behalten; (meeting) abhalten; (person as prisoner) gefangen halten; **to ~ one's breath** den Atem anhalten; **to ~ hands** Händchen halten; **~ the line** (Tel) bleiben Sie am Apparat ▷ vi halten; (weather) sich halten ▷ n (grasp) Halt m; (of ship, aircraft) Laderaum m; **hold back** vt zurückhalten; (keep secret) verheimlichen; **hold on** vi sich festhalten; (wait) warten; (Tel) dranbleiben; **to ~ to sth** etw festhalten; **hold out** vt ausstrecken; (offer) hinhalten; (offer) bieten ▷ vi durchhalten; **hold up** vt hochhalten; (support) stützen; (delay) aufhalten; **holdall** n Reisetasche f; **holder** n (person) Inhaber(in) m(f); **holdup** n (in traffic) Stau m; (robbery) Überfall m

hole [həʊl] n Loch nt; (of fox, rabbit) Bau m; **~ in the wall** (cash dispenser) Geldautomat m

holiday ['hɒlɪdeɪ] n (day off)
freier Tag; (public ~) Feiertag m;
(vacation) Urlaub m; (at school)
Ferien pl; **on ~** im Urlaub; **to go on
~** Urlaub machen; **holiday camp**
n Ferienlager nt; **holiday home** n
Ferienhaus nt; (flat)
Ferienwohnung f; **holidaymaker**
n Urlauber(in) m(f); **holiday
resort** n Ferienort m

Holland ['hɒlənd] n Holland nt

hollow ['hɒləʊ] adj hohl; (words)
leer ▷ n Vertiefung f

holly ['hɒlɪ] n Stechpalme f

holy ['həʊlɪ] adj heilig; **Holy
Week** n Karwoche f

home [həʊm] n Zuhause nt;
(area, country) Heimat f; (institution)
Heim nt; **at ~** zu Hause; **to make
oneself at ~** es sich dat bequem
machen; **away from ~** verreist
▷ adv: **to go ~** nach Hause
gehen/fahren; **home address** n
Heimatadresse f; **home country**
n Heimatland nt; **home game** n
(Sport) Heimspiel nt; **homeless** adj
obdachlos; **homely** adj häuslich;
(US: ugly) unscheinbar;
home-made adj selbst gemacht;
home movie n Amateurfilm m;
Home Office n (Brit)
Innenministerium nt

homeopathic adj (US) see
homeopathic

home page ['həʊmpeɪdʒ] n
(Inform) Homepage f; **Home
Secretary** n (Brit)
Innenminister(in) m(f); **homesick**
adj: **to be ~** Heimweh haben;
home town n Heimatstadt f;
homework n Hausaufgaben pl

homicide ['hɒmɪsaɪd] n (US)
Totschlag m

homoeopathic
[həʊmɪəʊ'pæθɪk] adj
homöopathisch

homosexual [hɒməʊ'seksjʊəl]

adj homosexuell ▷ n Homosex-
uelle(r) mf

Honduras [hɒn'djʊərəs] n
Honduras nt

honest ['ɒnɪst] adj ehrlich;
honesty n Ehrlichkeit f

honey ['hʌnɪ] n Honig m;
honeycomb n Honigwabe f;
honeydew melon n
Honigmelone f; **honeymoon** n
Flitterwochen pl

Hong Kong [hɒŋ 'kɒŋ] n
Hongkong nt

honor (US) see **honour**; **honorary**
['ɒnərərɪ] adj (member, title etc)
Ehren-, ehrenamtlich; **honour**
['ɒnə] vt ehren; (cheque) einlösen;
(contract) einhalten ▷ n Ehre f; **in
~ of** zu Ehren von; **honourable** adj
ehrenhaft; **honours degree** n
akademischer Grad mit Prüfung im
Spezialfach

hood [hʊd] n Kapuze f; (Auto)
Verdeck nt; (US Auto) Kühlerhaube
f

hoof [hu:f] (pl hooves) n Huf
m

hook [hʊk] n Haken m; **hooked**
adj (keen) besessen (on von);
(drugs) abhängig sein (on von)

hooligan ['hu:lɪgən] n Hooligan
m

hoot [hu:t] vi (Auto) hupen

Hoover® ['hu:və] n Staubsauger
m; **hoover** vi, vt staubsaugen

hop [hɒp] vi hüpfen ▷ n (Bot)
Hopfen m

hope [həʊp] vi, vt hoffen (for auf
+akk); **I ~ so/~ not**
hoffentlich/hoffentlich nicht; **I
~ (that) we'll meet** ich hoffe, dass
wir uns sehen werden ▷ n
Hoffnung f; **there's no ~** es ist
aussichtslos; **hopeful** adj
hoffnungsvoll; **hopefully** adv (full
of hope) hoffnungsvoll; (I hope so)
hoffentlich; **hopeless** adj

hoffnungslos; (*incompetent*)
miserabel

horizon [həˈraɪzn] n Horizont m;
horizontal [hɒrɪˈzɒntl] adj
horizontal

hormone [ˈhɔːməʊn] n Hormon
nt

horn [hɔːn] n Horn nt; (*Auto*)
Hupe f

hornet [ˈhɔːnɪt] n Hornisse f

horny [ˈhɔːnɪ] adj (*fam*) geil

horoscope [ˈhɒrəskəʊp] n
Horoskop nt

horrible, horribly [ˈhɒrɪbl, -blɪ]
adj, adv schrecklich; **horrid,
horridly** [ˈhɒrɪd, -lɪ] adj, adv
abscheulich; **horrify** [ˈhɒrɪfaɪ] vt
entsetzen; **horror** [ˈhɒrə°] n
Entsetzen nt; **~s** (*things*) Schrecken
pl

hors d'oeuvre [ɔːˈdɜːvr] n
Vorspeise f

horse [hɔːs] n Pferd nt; **horse
chestnut** n Rosskastanie f;
horsepower n Pferdestärke f, PS
nt; **horse racing** n Pferderennen
nt; **horseradish** n Meerrettich m;
horse riding n Reiten nt;
horseshoe n Hufeisen nt

horticulture [ˈhɔːtɪkʌltʃə°] n
Gartenbau m

hose, hosepipe [həʊz, ˈhəʊzpaɪp]
n Schlauch m

hospitable [hɒˈspɪtəbl] adj
gastfreundlich

hospital [ˈhɒspɪtl] n Krankenhaus nt

hospitality [hɒspɪˈtælɪtɪ] n
Gastfreundschaft f

host [həʊst] n Gastgeber m; (*TV:
of show*) Moderator(in) m(f),
Talkmaster(in) m(f) ▷ vt
(*party*) geben; (*TV: TV show*)
moderieren

hostage [ˈhɒstɪdʒ] n Geisel f

hostel [ˈhɒstəl] n Wohnheim nt;
(*youth ~*) Jugendherberge f

hostess [ˈhəʊstɪs] n (*of a party*)
Gastgeberin f

hostile [ˈhɒstaɪl] adj feindlich;
hostility [hɒsˈtɪlɪtɪ] n Feind-
seligkeit f

hot [hɒt] adj heiß; (*drink, food,
water*) warm; (*spiced*) scharf; **I'm
(feeling)** ~ mir ist heiß; **hot cross
bun** n Rosinenbrötchen mit einem
Kreuz darauf, hauptsächlich zu
Ostern gegessen; **hot dog** n
Hotdog m

hotel [həʊˈtel] n Hotel nt; **hotel
room** n Hotelzimmer nt

hothouse n Treibhaus nt;
hotline n Hotline f; **hotplate** n
Kochplatte f; **hotspot** n
(*Inform*) Hotspot m; **hot-water
bottle** n Wärmflasche f

hour [ˈaʊə°] n Stunde f; **to wait
for ~s** stundenlang warten; **~s** pl
(*of shops etc*) Geschäftszeiten pl;
hourly adj stündlich

house [haʊs] (*pl* **houses**) n Haus
nt; **at my** ~ bei mir (zu Hause); **to
my** ~ zu mir (nach Hause); **on the
~** auf Kosten des Hauses; **the
House of Commons/Lords** das
britische Unterhaus/Oberhaus; **the
Houses of Parliament** das
britische Parlamentsgebäude
▷ [haʊz] vt unterbringen;
houseboat n Hausboot nt;
household n Haushalt m;
~ appliance n Haushaltsgerät nt;
house-husband n Hausmann m;
housekeeping n Haushaltung f;
(*money*) Haushaltsgeld nt;
house-trained adj stubenrein;
house-warming (party) n
Einzugsparty f; **housewife** (*pl
-wives*) n Hausfrau f; **house wine**
n Hauswein m; **housework** n
Hausarbeit f

housing [ˈhaʊzɪŋ] n (*houses*)
Wohnungen pl; (*house building*)
Wohnungsbau m; **housing**

benefit n Wohngeld nt; **housing development, housing estate** (Brit) n Wohnsiedlung f

hover ['hɒvə°] vi schweben; **hovercraft** n Luftkissenboot nt

how [haʊ] adv wie; **~ many** wie viele; **~ much** wie viel; **~ are you?** wie geht es Ihnen?; **~ are things?** wie geht's?; **~'s work?** was macht die Arbeit?; **~ about ...?** wie wäre es mit ...?; **however** [haʊˈevə°] conj jedoch, aber ▷ adv (no matter how) wie ... auch; **~ much it costs** wie viel es auch kostet; **~ you do it** wie man es auch macht

howl [haʊl] vi heulen; **howler** ['haʊlə°] n (fam) grober Schnitzer

HP, hp n (Brit) abbr = **hire purchase** Ratenkauf m ▷ abbr = **horsepower** PS

HQ abbr = **headquarters**

hubcap ['hʌbkæp] n Radkappe f

hug [hʌg] vt umarmen ▷ n Umarmung f

huge [hjuːdʒ] adj riesig

hum [hʌm] vi, vt summen

human ['hjuːmən] adj menschlich; **~ rights** Menschenrechte pl ▷ n: **~ (being)** Mensch m; **humanitarian** [hjuːmænɪˈteərɪən] adj humanitär; **humanity** [hjuːˈmænɪtɪ] n Menschheit f; (kindliness) Menschlichkeit f; **humanities** Geisteswissenschaften pl

humble ['hʌmbl] adj demütig; (modest) bescheiden

humid ['hjuːmɪd] adj feucht; **humidity** [hjuːˈmɪdɪtɪ] n (Luft)feuchtigkeit f

humiliate [hjuːˈmɪlɪeɪt] vt demütigen; **humiliation** [hjuːmɪlɪˈeɪʃn] n Erniedrigung f, Demütigung f

humor (US) see **humour**;

humorous ['hjuːmərəs] adj humorvoll; (story) lustig, witzig; **humour** ['hjuːmə°] n Humor m; **sense of ~** Sinn m für Humor

hump [hʌmp] n Buckel m

hunch [hʌntʃ] n Gefühl nt, Ahnung f ▷ vt (back) krümmen; **hunchback** n Bucklige(r) mf

hundred ['hʌndrəd] num: **one ~, a ~** (ein)hundert; **a ~ and one** hundert(und)eins; **two ~** zweihundert; **hundredth** adj hundertste(r, s) ▷ n (fraction) Hundertstel nt; **hundredweight** n Zentner m (50,8 kg)

hung [hʌŋ] pt, pp of **hang**

Hungarian [hʌŋˈgeərɪən] adj ungarisch ▷ n (person) Ungar(in) m(f); (language) Ungarisch nt; **Hungary** ['hʌŋgərɪ] n Ungarn nt

hunger ['hʌŋgə°] n Hunger m; **hungry** ['hʌŋgrɪ] adj hungrig; **to be ~** Hunger haben

hunk [hʌŋk] n (fam) gut gebauter Mann; **hunky** ['hʌŋkɪ] adj (fam) gut gebaut

hunt [hʌnt] n Jagd f; (search) Suche f (for nach) ▷ vt, vi jagen; (search) suchen (for nach); **hunting** n Jagen nt, Jagd f

hurdle ['hɜːdl] n (a. fig) Hürde f; **the 400m-~s** der 400m-Hürdenlauf

hurl [hɜːl] vt schleudern

hurricane ['hʌrɪkən] n Orkan m

hurried ['hʌrɪd] adj eilig; **hurry** ['hʌrɪ] n Eile f; **to be in a ~** es eilig haben; **there's no ~** es eilt nicht ▷ vi sich beeilen; **~ (up)** mach schnell! ▷ vt antreiben

hurt [hɜːt] (**hurt, hurt**) vt wehtun +dat; (wound: person, feelings) verletzen; **I've ~ my arm** ich habe mir am Arm wehgetan ▷ vi wehtun; **my arm ~s** mir tut der Arm weh

husband [ˈhʌzbənd] n Ehemann m

husky [ˈhʌskɪ] adj rau ▷ n Schlittenhund m

hut [hʌt] n Hütte f

hyacinth [ˈhaɪəsɪnθ] n Hyazinthe f

hybrid [ˈhaɪbrɪd] n Kreuzung f; ~ **car** Hybridauto nt

hydroelectric [ˈhaɪdrəʊˈlektrɪk] adj; ~ **power station** Wasserkraftwerk nt

hydrofoil [ˈhaɪdrəʊfɔɪl] n Tragflächenboot nt

hydrogen [ˈhaɪdrədʒən] n Wasserstoff m

hygiene [ˈhaɪdʒiːn] n Hygiene f; **hygienic** [haɪˈdʒiːnɪk] adj hygienisch

hymn [hɪm] n Kirchenlied nt

hyperlink [ˈhaɪpəlɪŋk] n Hyperlink m; **hypermarket** n Großmarkt m; **hypersensitive** adj überempfindlich

hyphen [ˈhaɪfən] n Bindestrich m

hypnosis [hɪpˈnəʊsɪs] n Hypnose f; **hypnotize** [ˈhɪpnətaɪz] vt hypnotisieren

hypochondriac [haɪpəʊˈkɒndrɪæk] n eingebildete(r) Kranke(r), eingebildete Kranke

hypocrisy [hɪˈpɒkrəsɪ] n Heuchelei f; **hypocrite** [ˈhɪpəkrɪt] n Heuchler(in) m(f)

hypodermic [haɪpəˈdɜːmɪk] adj, n: ~ (**needle**) Spritze f

hypothetical [haɪpəʊˈθetɪkəl] adj hypothetisch

hysteria [hɪˈstɪərɪə] n Hysterie f; **hysterical** [hɪˈsterɪkəl] adj hysterisch; (amusing) zum Totlachen

◆

I [aɪ] pron ich

ice [aɪs] n Eis nt ▷ vt (cake) glasieren; **iceberg** n Eisberg m; **iceberg lettuce** n Eisbergsalat m; **icebox** n (US) Kühlschrank m; **icecold** adj eiskalt; **ice cream** n Eis nt; **ice cube** n Eiswürfel m; **iced** adj eisgekühlt; (coffee, tea) Eis-; (cake) glasiert; **ice hockey** n Eishockey nt

Iceland [ˈaɪslənd] n Island nt; **Icelander** n Isländer(in) m(f); **Icelandic** [aɪsˈlændɪk] adj isländisch ▷ n (language) Isländisch nt

ice lolly [ˈaɪslɒlɪ] n (Brit) Eis nt am Stiel; **ice rink** n Kunsteisbahn f; **ice skating** n Schlittschuhlaufen nt

icing [ˈaɪsɪŋ] n (on cake) Zuckerguss m

icon [ˈaɪkɒn] n Ikone f; (Inform) Icon nt, Programmsymbol nt

icy ['aɪsɪ] *adj* (slippery) vereist; (cold) eisig
I'd [aɪd] *contr of* **I would; I had**
ID *abbr* = **identification** Ausweis *m*
idea [aɪ'dɪə] *n* Idee *f*; (**I've**) **no ~** (ich habe) keine Ahnung; **that's my ~ of ...** vor
ideal [aɪ'dɪəl] *n* Ideal *nt* ▷ *adj* ideal; **ideally** *adv* ideal; (before statement) idealerweise
identical [aɪ'dentɪkl] *adj* identisch; **~ twins** eineiige Zwillinge
identify [aɪ'dentɪfaɪ] *vt* identifizieren; **identity** [aɪ'dentɪtɪ] *n* Identität *f*; **identity card** *n* Personalausweis *m*
idiom ['ɪdɪəm] *n* Redewendung *f*; **idiomatic** [ɪdɪ'mætɪk] *adj* idiomatisch
idiot ['ɪdɪət] *n* Idiot(in) *m(f)*
idle ['aɪdl] *adj* (doing nothing) untätig; (worker) unbeschäftigt; (machines) außer Betrieb; (lazy) faul; (promise, threat) leer
idol ['aɪdl] *n* Idol *nt*; **idolize** ['aɪdəlaɪz] *vt* vergöttern
idyllic [ɪ'dɪlɪk] *adj* idyllisch
i.e. *abbr* = **id est** d.h.

O **KEYWORD**

if [ɪf] *conj* **1** wenn; (in case also) falls; **if I were you** wenn ich Sie wäre
2 (although) (**even**) **if** (selbst *o* auch) wenn
3 (whether) ob
4 **if so/not** wenn ja/nicht; **if only ...** wenn ... doch nur ...; **if only I could** wenn ich doch nur könnte; *see also* **as**

ignition [ɪg'nɪʃən] *n* Zündung *f*; **ignition key** *n* (Auto) Zündschlüssel *m*
ignorance ['ɪgnərəns] *n* Unwissenheit *f*; **ignorant** *adj*

unwissend; **ignore** [ɪg'nɔ:°] *vt* ignorieren, nicht beachten
I'll [aɪl] *contr of* **I will; I shall**
ill [ɪl] *adj* krank; **~ at ease** unbehaglich
illegal [ɪ'li:gəl] *adj* illegal
illegitimate [ɪlɪ'dʒɪtɪmət] *adj* unzulässig; (child) unehelich
illiterate [ɪ'lɪtərət] *adj*: **to be ~** Analphabet(in) sein
illness ['ɪlnəs] *n* Krankheit *f*
illuminate [ɪ'lu:mɪneɪt] *vt* beleuchten; **illuminating** *adj* (remark) aufschlussreich
illusion [ɪ'lu:ʒən] *n* Illusion *f*; **to be under the ~ that ...** sich einbilden, dass ...
illustrate ['ɪləstreɪt] *vt* illustrieren; **illustration** *n* Abbildung *f*, Bild *nt*
I'm [aɪm] *contr of* **I am**
image ['ɪmɪdʒ] *n* Bild *nt*; (public ~) Image *nt*; **imaginable** [ɪ'mædʒɪnəbl] *adj* denkbar; **imaginary** [ɪ'mædʒɪnərɪ] *adj* eingebildet; **~ world** Fantasiewelt *f*; **imagination** [ɪmædʒɪ'neɪʃən] *n* Fantasie *f*; (mistaken) Einbildung *f*; **imaginative** [ɪ'mædʒɪnətɪv] *adj* fantasievoll; **imagine** [ɪ'mædʒɪn] *vt* sich vorstellen; (wrongly) sich einbilden; **~!** stell dir vor!
imbecile ['ɪmbəsi:l] *n* Trottel *m*
imitate ['ɪmɪteɪt] *vt* nachahmen, nachmachen; **imitation** *n* Nachahmung *f* ▷ *adj* imitiert, Kunst-
immaculate [ɪ'mækjʊlɪt] *adj* tadellos; (spotless) makellos
immature [ɪmə'tjʊə°] *adj* unreif
immediate [ɪ'mi:dɪət] *adj* unmittelbar; (instant) sofortig; (reply) umgehend; **immediately** *adv* sofort
immense, immensely [ɪ'mens, -lɪ] *adj, adv* riesig, enorm

immersion heater [ɪ'mɜːʃn
hiːtə] n Boiler m

immigrant ['ɪmɪgrənt] n Einwanderer m, Einwanderin f;
immigration [ɪmɪ'greɪʃən] n
Einwanderung f; (facility)
Einwanderungskontrolle f

immobilize [ɪ'məubɪlaɪz] vt
lähmen; **immobilizer** n (Auto)
Wegfahrsperre f

immoral [ɪ'mɒrəl] adj
unmoralisch

immortal [ɪ'mɔːtl] adj
unsterblich

immune [ɪ'mjuːn] adj (Med)
immun (from, to gegen); **immune
system** n Immunsystem nt

impact ['ɪmpækt] n Aufprall m;
(effect) Auswirkung f (on auf +akk)

impatience [ɪm'peɪʃəns] n
Ungeduld f; **impatient**,
impatiently adj, adv ungeduldig

impeccable [ɪm'pekəbl] adj
tadellos

impede [ɪm'piːd] vt behindern

imperative [ɪm'perətɪv] adj
unbedingt erforderlich ▷ n (Ling)
Imperativ m

imperfect [ɪm'pɜːfɪkt] adj
unvollkommen; (goods) fehlerhaft
▷ n (Ling) Imperfekt nt;
imperfection [ɪmpə'fekʃən] n
Unvollkommenheit f; (fault) Fehler
m

imperial [ɪm'pɪərɪəl] adj kaiserlich, Reichs-; **imperialism** n
Imperialismus m

impertinence [ɪm'pɜːtɪnəns] n
Unverschämtheit f, Zumutung f;
impertinent adj unverschämt

implant ['ɪmplaːnt] n (Med)
Implantat nt

implausible [ɪm'plɔːzəbl] adj
unglaubwürdig

implement ['ɪmplɪmənt] n
Werkzeug nt, Gerät nt
▷ [ɪmplɪ'ment] vt durchführen

implication [ɪmplɪ'keɪʃən] n
Folge f, Auswirkung f; (logical)
Schlussfolgerung f; **implicit**
[ɪm'plɪsɪt] adj implizit,
unausgesprochen; **imply**
[ɪm'plaɪ] vt (indicate) andeuten;
(mean) bedeuten; **are you ~ing
that ...** wollen Sie damit sagen,
dass ...

impolite [ɪmpə'laɪt] adj
unhöflich

import [ɪm'pɔːt] vt einführen,
importieren ▷ n ['ɪmpɔːt] Einfuhr f, Import m

importance [ɪm'pɔːtəns] n
Bedeutung f; **of no ~** unwichtig;
important adj wichtig (to sb für
jdn); (significant) bedeutend;
(influential) einflussreich

import duty ['ɪmpɔːt djuːtɪ] n
Einfuhrzoll m; **import licence** n
Einfuhrgenehmigung f

impose [ɪm'pəuz] vt (conditions)
auferlegen (on dat); (penalty,
sanctions) verhängen (on gegen);
imposing [ɪm'pəuzɪŋ] adj eindrucksvoll, imposant

impossible [ɪm'pɒsəbl] adj
unmöglich

impotence ['ɪmpətəns] n
Machtlosigkeit f; (sexual)
Impotenz f; **impotent** adj
machtlos; (sexually) impotent

impractical [ɪm'præktɪkəl] adj
unpraktisch; (plan)
undurchführbar

impress [ɪm'pres] vt beeindrucken; **impression** [ɪm'preʃən]
n Eindruck m; **impressive** adj
eindrucksvoll

imprison [ɪm'prɪzn] vt inhaftieren; **imprisonment** n
Inhaftierung f

improbability [ɪmprɒbə'bɪlɪtɪ]
n Unwahrscheinlichkeit f;
improbable [ɪm'prɒbəbl] adj
unwahrscheinlich

improper [ɪmˈprɔpə°] adj
(indecent) unanständig; (use)
unsachgemäß

improve [ɪmˈpruːv] vt
verbessern ▷ vi sich verbessern,
besser werden; (patient)
Fortschritte machen;
improvement n Verbesserung f
(in +gen; on gegenüber); (in
appearance) Verschönerung f

improvise [ˈɪmprəvaɪz] vt, vi
improvisieren

impulse [ˈɪmpʌls] n Impuls m;
impulsive [ɪmˈpʌlsɪv] adj
impulsiv

○ **KEYWORD**

in [ɪn] prep 1 (indicating place,
position) in +dat; (with motion) in
+akk: **in here/there** hier/dort; **in
London** in London; **in the United
States** in den Vereinigten Staaten
2 (indicating time: during) in +dat: **in
summer** im Sommer; **in 1988** (im
Jahre) 1988; **in the afternoon**
nachmittags, am Nachmittag
3 (indicating time: in the space of)
innerhalb von; **I'll see you in 2
weeks** o **in 2 weeks' time** ich sehe
dich/Sie in zwei Wochen
4 (indicating manner, circumstances,
state etc) in +dat; **in the sun/rain**
in der Sonne/im Regen; **in
English/French** auf
Englisch/Französisch; **in a
loud/soft voice** mit lauter/leiser
Stimme
5 (with ratios, numbers) **1 in 10** jeder
Zehnte; **20 pence in the pound** 20
Pence pro Pfund; **they lined up in
twos** sie stellten sich in
Zweierreihe auf
6 (referring to people, works) **the
disease is common in children**
die Krankheit ist bei Kindern
häufig; **in Dickens** bei Dickens;

we have a loyal friend in him er
ist uns ein treuer Freund
7 (indicating profession etc) **to be in
teaching/the army** Lehrer,
Lehrerin/beim Militär sein; **to be
in publishing** im Verlagswesen
arbeiten
8 (with present participle) **in saying
this, I ...** wenn ich das sage, ... ich;
in accepting this view, he ... weil
er diese Meinung akzeptierte, ...
er
▷ adv: **to be in** (person: at home,
work) da sein; (train, ship, plane)
angekommen sein; (in fashion) in
sein; **to ask sb in** jdn hereinbitten;
to run/limp etc in
hereingerannt/gehumpelt etc
kommen
▷ n: **the ins and outs** (of proposal,
situation etc) die Feinheiten

inability [ɪnəˈbɪlɪtɪ] n Unfähig-
keit f

inaccessible [ɪnækˈsesəbl] adj
(a. fig) unzugänglich

inaccurate [ɪnˈækjʊrɪt] adj
ungenau

inadequate [ɪnˈædɪkwət] adj
unzulänglich

inapplicable [ɪnəˈplɪkəbl] adj
unzutreffend

inappropriate [ɪnəˈprəʊprɪət]
adj unpassend; (clothing)
ungeeignet; (remark)
unangebracht

inborn [ˈɪnˈbɔːn] adj angeboren

incapable [ɪnˈkeɪpəbl] adj
unfähig (of zu); **to be ~ of doing
sth** nicht imstande sein, etw zu
tun

incense [ˈɪnsens] n Weihrauch
m

incentive [ɪnˈsentɪv] n Anreiz m

incessant [ɪnˈsesnt], **incessantly** [ɪnˈsesnt,
-lɪ] adj, adv unaufhörlich

incest [ˈɪnsest] n Inzest m

inch [ɪntʃ] n Zoll m (2,54 cm)
incident ['ɪnsɪdənt] n Vorfall m;
(disturbance) Zwischenfall m;
incidentally [ɪnsɪ'dentlɪ]
adv nebenbei bemerkt,
übrigens
inclination [ɪnklɪ'neɪʃən] n
Neigung f; **inclined** ['ɪnklaɪnd]
adj: **to be ~ to do sth** dazu neigen,
etw zu tun
include [ɪn'klu:d] vt einschließen; (on list, in group)
aufnehmen; **including** prep
einschließlich (+gen); **not
~ service** Bedienung nicht
inbegriffen; **inclusive** [ɪn'klu:sɪv]
adj einschließlich (of +gen); (price)
Pauschal-
incoherent [ɪnkəʊ'hɪərənt] adj
zusammenhanglos
income ['ɪnkʌm] n Einkommen
nt; (from business) Einkünfte pl;
income tax n Einkommensteuer
f; (on wages, salary) Lohnsteuer f;
incoming ['ɪnkʌmɪŋ] adj an-
kommend; (mail) eingehend
incompatible [ɪnkəm'pætəbl]
adj unvereinbar; (people)
unverträglich; (Inform) nicht
kompatibel
incompetent [ɪn'kɒmpɪtənt]
adj unfähig
incomplete [ɪnkəm'pli:t] adj
unvollständig
incomprehensible
[ɪnkɒmprɪ'hensəbl] adj
unverständlich
inconceivable [ɪnkən'si:vəbl]
adj unvorstellbar
inconsiderate [ɪnkən'sɪdərət]
adj rücksichtslos
inconsistency [ɪnkən'sɪstənsɪ]
n Inkonsequenz f; (contradictory)
Widersprüchlichkeit f;
inconsistent adj inkonsequent;
(contradictory) widersprüchlich;
(work) unbeständig

inconvenience [ɪnkən'vi:nɪəns]
n Unannehmlichkeit f; (trouble)
Umstände pl; **inconvenient** adj
ungünstig, unbequem; (time) **it's
~ for me** es kommt mir
ungelegen; **if it's not too ~ for
you** wenn es dir/Ihnen passt
incorporate [ɪn'kɔ:pəreɪt] vt
aufnehmen (into in +akk); (include)
enthalten
incorrect ['ɪnkərekt] adj falsch;
(improper) inkorrekt
increase ['ɪnkri:s] n Zunahme f
(in an +dat); (in amount, speed)
Erhöhung f (in +gen) ▷ [ɪn'kri:s] vt
(price, taxes, salary, speed etc)
erhöhen; (wealth) vermehren;
(number) vergrößern; (business)
erweitern ▷ vi zunehmen (in an
+dat); (prices) steigen; (in size)
größer werden; (in number) sich
vermehren; **increasingly**
[ɪn'kri:sɪŋlɪ] adv zunehmend
incredible, incredibly
[ɪn'kredəbl, -blɪ] adj, adv
unglaublich; (very good)
fantastisch
incredulous [ɪn'kredjʊləs] adj
ungläubig, skeptisch
incriminate [ɪn'krɪmɪneɪt] vt
belasten
incubator ['ɪnkjʊbeɪtə°] n
Brutkasten m
incurable [ɪn'kjʊərəbl] adj
unheilbar
indecent [ɪn'di:snt] adj
unanständig
indecisive [ɪndɪ'saɪsɪv] adj
(person) unentschlossen; (result)
nicht entscheidend
indeed [ɪn'di:d] adv tatsächlich;
(as answer) allerdings; **very hot
~** wirklich sehr heiß
indefinite [ɪn'defɪnɪt] adj
unbestimmt; **indefinitely** adv
endlos; (postpone) auf
unbestimmte Zeit

independence [ɪndɪˈpɛndəns]
n Unabhängigkeit *f*

● **INDEPENDENCE DAY**
●
● Der **Independence Day**, der 4.
● Juli, ist in den USA ein
● gesetzlicher Feiertag zum
● Gedenken an die
● Unabhängigkeitserklärung am
● 4. Juli 1776, mit der die 13
● amerikanischen Kolonien ihre
● Freiheit und Unabhängigkeit
● von Großbritannien erklärten.

independent [ɪndɪˈpɛndənt]
adj unabhängig (*of* von); (*person*)
selbstständig

indescribable [ɪndɪˈskraɪbəbl]
adj unbeschreiblich

index [ˈɪndɛks] *n* Index *m*,
Verzeichnis *nt*; **index finger** *n*
Zeigefinger *m*

India [ˈɪndɪə] *n* Indien *nt*; **Indian**
[ˈɪndɪən] *adj* indisch; (*Native
American*) indianisch ▷ *n* Inder(in)
m(f); (*Native American*) Indianer(in)
m(f); **Indian Ocean** *n* Indischer
Ozean; **Indian summer** *n* Spät-
sommer *m*, Altweibersommer *m*

indicate [ˈɪndɪkeɪt] *vt* (*show*)
zeigen; (*instrument*) anzeigen;
(*suggest*) hinweisen auf +*akk* ▷ *vi*
(*Auto*) blinken; **indication**
[ɪndɪˈkeɪʃn] *n* (*sign*) Anzeichen *nt*
(*of* für); **indicator** [ˈɪndɪkeɪtə°] *n*
(*Auto*) Blinker *m*

indifferent [ɪnˈdɪfrənt] *adj* (*not
caring*) gleichgültig (*to, towards*
gegenüber); (*mediocre*)
mittelmäßig

indigestible [ɪndɪˈdʒɛstəbl] *adj*
unverdaulich; **indigestion**
[ɪndɪˈdʒɛstʃən] *n* Verdau-
ungsstörung *f*

indignity [ɪnˈdɪgnɪtɪ] *n* Demütigung *f*

indirect, **indirectly** [ɪndɪˈrɛkt, -lɪ]
adj, *adv* indirekt

indiscreet [ɪndɪˈskriːt] *adj*
indiskret

indispensable [ɪndɪˈspɛnsəbl]
adj unentbehrlich

indisposed [ɪndɪˈspəʊzd] *adj*
unwohl

indisputable [ɪndɪˈspjuːtəbl]
adj unbestreitbar; (*evidence*)
unanfechtbar

individual [ɪndɪˈvɪdjʊəl] *n*
Einzelne(r) *mf* ▷ *adj* einzeln;
(*distinctive*) eigen, individuell;
~ case Einzelfall *m*; **individually**
adv (*separately*) einzeln

Indonesia [ɪndəʊˈniːzjə] *n*
Indonesien *n*

indoor [ˈɪndɔː°] *adj* (*shoes*)
Haus-; (*plant, games*) Zimmer-;
(*Sport: football, championship, record
etc*) Hallen-; **indoors** *adv* drinnen,
im Haus

indulge [ɪnˈdʌldʒ] *vi*: **to ~ in sth**
sich *dat* etw gönnen; **indulgence**
n Nachsicht *f*; (*enjoyment*)
(übermäßiger) Genuss; (*luxury*)
Luxus *m*; **indulgent** *adj*
nachsichtig (*with* gegenüber)

industrial [ɪnˈdʌstrɪəl] *adj*
Industrie-, industriell; **~ estate**
n Industriegebiet *nt*; **industry**
[ˈɪndəstrɪ] *n* Industrie *f*

inedible [ɪnˈɛdɪbl] *adj* nicht
essbar, ungenießbar

ineffective [ɪnɪˈfɛktɪv] *adj*
unwirksam, wirkungslos;
inefficient *adj* unwirksam; (*use,
machine*) unwirtschaftlich; (*method
etc*) unrationell

ineligible [ɪnˈɛlɪdʒəbl] *adj* nicht
berechtigt (*for* zu)

inequality [ɪnɪˈkwɒlɪtɪ] *n*
Ungleichheit *f*

inevitable [ɪnˈɛvɪtəbl] *adj*
unvermeidlich; **inevitably** *adv*
zwangsläufig

inexcusable [ɪnɪks'kju:zəbl]
adj unverzeihlich; **that's ~** das
kann man nicht verzeihen
inexpensive [ɪnɪks'pensɪv] adj
preisgünstig
inexperience [ɪnɪks'pɪərɪəns]
n Unerfahrenheit f;
inexperienced adj unerfahren
inexplicable [ɪnɪks'plɪkəbl] adj
unerklärlich
infallible [ɪn'fæləbl] adj
unfehlbar
infamous ['ɪnfəməs] adj (person)
berüchtigt (for wegen); (deed)
niederträchtig
infancy ['ɪnfənsɪ] n frühe
Kindheit; **infant** ['ɪnfənt] n
Säugling m; (small child)
Kleinkind nt; **infant school** n
Vorschule f
infatuated [ɪn'fætjʊeɪtɪd] adj
vernarrt (with in +akk), verknallt
(with in +akk)
infect [ɪn'fekt] vt (person)
anstecken; (wound) infizieren;
infection [ɪn'fekʃən] n Infektion
f; **infectious** [ɪn'fekʃəs] adj
ansteckend
inferior [ɪn'fɪərɪəʳ] adj (in quality)
minderwertig; (in rank)
untergeordnet; **inferiority**
[ɪnfɪərɪ'brɪtɪ] n Minderwertigkeit
f; **~ complex** Minderwertigkeitskomplex m
infertile [ɪn'fɜ:taɪl] adj
unfruchtbar
infidelity [ɪnfɪ'delɪtɪ] n Untreue
f
infinite ['ɪnfɪnɪt] adj unendlich
infinitive [ɪn'fɪnɪtɪv] n (Ling)
Infinitiv m
infinity [ɪn'fɪnɪtɪ] n Unend-
lichkeit f
infirmary [ɪn'fɜ:mərɪ] n
Krankenhaus nt
inflame [ɪn'fleɪm] vt (Med)
entzünden; **inflammation**

[ɪnflə'meɪʃən] n (Med)
Entzündung f
inflatable [ɪn'fleɪtəbl] adj auf-
blasbar; **~ dinghy** Schlauchboot
nt; **inflate** [ɪn'fleɪt] vt
aufpumpen; (by blowing)
aufblasen; (prices) hochtreiben
inflation [ɪn'fleɪʃən] n Inflation
f
inflexible [ɪn'fleksəbl] adj
unflexibel
inflict [ɪn'flɪkt] vt: **to ~ sth on sb**
jdm etw zufügen; (punishment)
jdm etw auferlegen; (wound) jdm
etw beibringen
in-flight [ɪn'flaɪt] adj (catering,
magazine) Bord-; **~ entertainment**
Bordprogramm nt
influence ['ɪnflʊəns] n Einfluss
m (on auf +akk) ▷ vt beeinflussen;
influential [ɪnflʊ'enʃəl] adj
einflussreich
influenza [ɪnflʊ'enzə] n Grippe
f
inform [ɪn'fɔ:m] vt informieren
(of, about über +akk); **to keep sb
~ed** jdn auf dem Laufenden halten
informal [ɪn'fɔ:məl] adj zwanglos, ungezwungen
information [ɪnfə'meɪʃən] n
Auskunft f, Informationen pl; **for
your ~** zu deiner/Ihrer
Information; **further ~** weitere
Informationen, Weiteres;
information desk n
Auskunftsschalter m; **information
technology** n Informations-
technik f; **informative**
[ɪn'fɔ:mətɪv] adj aufschlussreich
infra-red ['ɪnfrə'red] adj infrarot
infrastructure n Infrastruktur
f
infuriate [ɪn'fjʊərɪeɪt] vt wütend
machen; **infuriating** adj äußerst
ärgerlich
infusion [ɪn'fju:ʒən] n (herbal
tea) Aufguss m; (Med) Infusion f

ingenious [ɪnˈdʒiːnɪəs] adj (person) erfinderisch; (device) raffiniert; (idea) genial
ingredient [ɪnˈɡriːdɪənt] n (Gastr) Zutat f
inhabit [ɪnˈhæbɪt] vt bewohnen; **inhabitant** n Einwohner(in) m(f)
inhale [ɪnˈheɪl] vt einatmen; (cigarettes, Med) inhalieren; **inhaler** n Inhalationsgerät nt
inherit [ɪnˈherɪt] vt erben; **inheritance** n Erbe nt.
inhibited [ɪnˈhɪbɪtɪd] adj gehemmt; **inhibition** [ɪnhɪˈbɪʃən] n Hemmung f.
in-house ['ɪnhaʊs] adj intern
inhuman [ɪnˈhjuːmən] adj unmenschlich
initial [ɪˈnɪʃəl] adj anfänglich; ~ **stage** Anfangsstadium nt ▷ vt mit Initialen unterschreiben; **initially** adv anfangs; **initials** npl Initialen pl
initiative [ɪˈnɪʃətɪv] n Initiative f.
inject [ɪnˈdʒekt] vt (drug etc) einspritzen; **to ~ sb with sth** jdm etw (ein)spritzen; **injection** n Spritze f, Injektion f
in-joke ['ɪndʒəʊk] n Insiderwitz m
injure ['ɪndʒə'] vt verletzen; **to ~ one's leg** sich dat das Bein verletzen; **injury** ['ɪndʒərɪ] n Verletzung f
injustice [ɪnˈdʒʌstɪs] n Ungerechtigkeit f
ink [ɪŋk] n Tinte f; **ink-jet printer** n Tintenstrahldrucker m
inland ['ɪnlənd] adj Binnen- ▷ adv landeinwärts; **inland revenue** n (Brit) Finanzamt nt
in-laws ['ɪnlɔːz] npl (fam) Schwiegereltern pl
inline skates ['ɪnlaɪnskeɪts] npl Inlineskates pl, Inliner pl
inmate ['ɪnmeɪt] n Insasse m
inn [ɪn] n Gasthaus nt

innate [ɪˈneɪt] adj angeboren
inner ['ɪnə'] adj innere(r, s); ~ **city** Innenstadt f
innocence ['ɪnəsns] n Unschuld f; **innocent** adj unschuldig
innovation [ɪnəʊˈveɪʃən] n Neuerung f
innumerable [ɪˈnjuːmərəbl] adj unzählig
inoculate [ɪˈnɒkjʊleɪt] vt impfen (against gegen); **inoculation** [ɪnɒkjʊˈleɪʃən] n Impfung f
in-patient ['ɪnpeɪʃənt] n stationärer Patient, stationäre Patientin
input ['ɪnpʊt] n (contribution) Beitrag m; (Inform) Eingabe f
inquest ['ɪnkwest] n gerichtliche Untersuchung (einer Todesursache)
inquire [ɪnˈkwaɪə'] see enquire; **inquiry** [ɪnˈkwaɪərɪ] see enquiry
insane [ɪnˈseɪn] adj wahnsinnig; (Med) geisteskrank; **insanity** [ɪnˈsænɪtɪ] n Wahnsinn m
insatiable [ɪnˈseɪʃəbl] adj unersättlich
inscription [ɪnˈskrɪpʃən] n (on stone etc) Inschrift f
insect ['ɪnsekt] n Insekt nt; **insecticide** [ɪnˈsektɪsaɪd] n Insektenbekämpfungsmittel nt; **insect repellent** n Insektenschutzmittel nt
insecure [ɪnsɪˈkjʊə'] adj (person) unsicher; (shelves) instabil
insensitive [ɪnˈsensɪtɪv] adj unempfindlich (to gegen); (unfeeling) gefühllos; **insensitivity** [ɪnsensɪˈtɪvɪtɪ] n Unempfindlichkeit f (to gegen); (unfeeling nature) Gefühllosigkeit f
inseparable [ɪnˈsepərəbl] adj unzertrennlich
insert [ɪnˈsɜːt] vt einfügen; (coin) einwerfen; (key etc) hineinstecken

▷ *n* (*in magazine*) Beilage *f*;
insertion *n* (*in text*) Einfügen *nt*

inside ['ɪn'saɪd] *n*: **the ~** das
Innere; (*surface*) die Innenseite;
from the ~ von innen ▷ *adj*
innere(r, s), Innen-; **~ lane** (*Auto*)
Innenspur *f*; (*Sport*) Innenbahn *f*
▷ *adv* (*place*) innen; (*direction*)
hinein; **to go ~** hineingehen
▷ *prep* (*place*) in +*dat*; (*into*) in +*akk*
... hinein; (*time, within*) innerhalb
+*gen*; **inside out** *adv* verkehrt
herum; (*know*) in- und auswendig;
insider *n* Eingeweihte(r) *mf*,
Insider(in) *m(f)*

insight ['ɪnsaɪt] *n* Einblick *m*
(*into* in +*akk*)

insignificant [ɪnsɪg'nɪfɪkənt]
adj unbedeutend

insincere [ɪnsɪn'sɪə°] *adj* un-
aufrichtig, falsch

insinuate [ɪn'sɪnjueɪt] *vt*
andeuten; **insinuation**
[ɪnsɪnju'eɪʃən] *n* Andeutung *f*

insist [ɪn'sɪst] *vi* darauf bestehen;
to ~ on sth auf etw *dat* bestehen;
insistent *adj* hartnäckig

insoluble [ɪn'sɒljʊbl] *adj*
unlöslich

insomnia [ɪn'sɒmnɪə] *n* Schlaf-
losigkeit *f*

inspect [ɪn'spekt] *vt* prüfen,
kontrollieren; **inspection** *n*
Prüfung *f*; (*check*) Kontrolle *f*;
inspector (*police ~*)
Inspektor(in) *m(f)*; (*senior*)
Kommissar(in) *m(f)*; (*on bus etc*)
Kontrolleur(in) *m(f)*

inspiration [ɪnspɪ'reɪʃən] *n*
Inspiration *f*; **inspire** [ɪn'spaɪə°]
vt einflößen (*respect*) in *dat*;
(*person*) inspirieren

install [ɪn'stɔːl] *vt* (*software*)
installieren; (*furnishings*) einbauen

installment, instalment
[ɪn'stɔːlmənt] *n* Rate *f*; (*of story*)
Folge *f*; **to pay in ~s** auf Raten

zahlen; **installment plan** *n* (US)
Ratenkauf *m*

instance ['ɪnstəns] *n* (*of*
discrimination) Fall *m*; (*example*)
Beispiel *nt* (*of* für +*akk*); **for ~** zum
Beispiel

instant ['ɪnstənt] *n* Augenblick
m ▷ *adj* sofortig; **instant coffee**
n löslicher Kaffee *m*; **instantly** *adv*
sofort

instead [ɪn'sted] *adv* stattdes-
sen; **instead of** *prep* (an)statt
+*gen*; **~ of me** an meiner Stelle;
~ of going (an)statt zu gehen

instinct ['ɪnstɪŋkt] *n* Instinkt *m*;
instinctive, instinctively
[ɪn'stɪŋktɪv, -lɪ] *adj, adv*
instinktiv

institute ['ɪnstɪtjuːt] *n* Institut
nt; **institution** [ɪnstɪ'tjuːʃən] *n*
(*organisation*) Institution *f*,
Einrichtung *f*; (*home*) Anstalt *f*

instruct [ɪn'strʌkt] *vt* anweisen;
instruction [ɪn'strʌkʃən] *n*
(*teaching*) Unterricht *m*; (*command*)
Anweisung *f*; **~s for use**
Gebrauchsanweisung *f*;
instructor *n* Lehrer(in) *m(f)*; (US)
Dozent(in) *m(f)*

instrument ['ɪnstrəmənt] *n*
Instrument *nt*; **instrument panel**
n Armaturenbrett *nt*

insufficient [ɪnsə'fɪʃənt] *adj*
ungenügend

insulate ['ɪnsjʊleɪt] *vt* (*Elec*)
isolieren; **insulating tape** *n*
Isolierband *nt*; **insulation**
[ɪnsjʊ'leɪʃən] *n* Isolierung *f*

insulin ['ɪnsjʊlɪn] *n* Insulin *nt*

insult ['ɪnsʌlt] *n* Beleidigung *f*
▷ [ɪn'sʌlt] *vt* beleidigen;
insulting [ɪn'sʌltɪŋ] *adj*
beleidigend

insurance [ɪn'ʃʊərəns] *n* Versicherung *f*; **~ company**
Versicherungsgesellschaft *f*;
~ policy Versicherungspolice *f*;

insure [ɪnˈʃʊə°] vt versichern (against gegen)
intact [ɪnˈtækt] adj intakt
intake [ˈɪnteɪk] n Aufnahme f
integrate [ˈɪntɪˈgreɪt] vt integrieren (into in +akk); **integration** n Integration f
integrity [ɪnˈtegrɪtɪ] n Integrität f, Ehrlichkeit f
intellect [ˈɪntɪlekt] n Intellekt m; **intellectual** [ɪntɪˈlektjʊəl] adj intellektuell; (interests etc) geistig
intelligence [ɪnˈtelɪdʒəns] n (understanding) Intelligenz f; **intelligent** adj intelligent
intend [ɪnˈtend] vt beabsichtigen; **to ~ to do sth** vorhaben, etw zu tun
intense [ɪnˈtens] adj intensiv; (pressure) enorm; (competition) heftig; **intensity** n Intensität f; **intensive** adj intensiv; **intensive care unit** n Intensivstation f; **intensive course** n Intensivkurs m
intent [ɪnˈtent] adj: **to be ~ on doing sth** fest entschlossen sein, etw zu tun; **intention** [ɪnˈtenʃən] n Absicht f; **intentional, intentionally** adj, adv absichtlich
interact [ɪntərˈækt] vi aufeinander einwirken; **interaction** n Interaktion f, Wechselwirkung f; **interactive** adj interaktiv
interchange [ˈɪntətʃeɪndʒ] n (of motorways) Autobahnkreuz nt; **interchangeable** [ɪntəˈtʃeɪndʒəbl] adj austauschbar
intercity [ɪntəˈsɪtɪ] n Intercityzug m, IC m
intercom [ˈɪntəkɒm] n (Gegen)sprechanlage f
intercourse [ˈɪntəkɔːs] n (sexual) Geschlechtsverkehr m
interest [ˈɪntrɪst] n Interesse nt;

(Fin: on money) Zinsen pl; (Comm: share) Anteil m; **to be ~ of** von Interesse sein (to für) ▷ vt interessieren; **interested** adj interessiert (in an +dat); **to be ~ed in** sich interessieren für; **are you ~ in coming?** hast du Lust, mitzukommen?; **interest-free** adj zinsfrei; **interesting** adj interessant; **interest rate** n Zinssatz m
interface [ˈɪntəfeɪs] n (Inform) Schnittstelle f
interfere [ɪntəˈfɪə°] vi (meddle) sich einmischen (with, in in +akk); **interference** n Einmischung f; (TV, Radio) Störung f
interior [ɪnˈtɪərɪə°] adj Innen- ▷ n Innere(s) nt; (of car) Innenraum m; (of house) Innenausstattung f
intermediate [ɪntəˈmiːdɪət] adj Zwischen-; **~ stage** n Zwischenstadium nt
intermission [ɪntəˈmɪʃən] n Pause f
intern [ɪnˈtɜːn] n Assistent(in) m(f)
internal [ɪnˈtɜːnl] adj innere(r, s); (flight) Inlands-; **~ revenue** (US) Finanzamt nt; **internally** adv innen; (in body) innerlich
international [ɪntəˈnæʃnəl] adj international; **~ match** n Länderspiel nt; **~ flight** n Auslandsflug m ▷ n (Sport: player) Nationalspieler(in) m(f)
Internet [ˈɪntənet] n (Inform) Internet nt; **Internet access** n Internetzugang m; **Internet auction** n Internetauktion f; **Internet banking** n Onlinebanking nt; **Internet café** n Internetcafé nt; **Internet connection** n Internetanschluss m; **Internet provider** n Internetprovider m
interpret [ɪnˈtɜːprɪt] vi, vt

(*translate*) dolmetschen; (*explain*) interpretieren; **interpretation** [ɪntɜːprɪˈteɪʃən] *n* Interpretation *f*; **interpreter** [ɪnˈtɜːprɪtə*] *n* Dolmetscher(in) *m(f)*

interrogate [ɪnˈterəgeɪt] *vt* verhören; **interrogation** *n* Verhör *nt*

interrupt [ɪntəˈrʌpt] *vt* unterbrechen; **interruption** [ɪntəˈrʌpʃən] *n* Unterbrechung *f*

intersection [ɪntəˈsekʃən] *n* (*of roads*) Kreuzung *f*

interstate [ˈɪntəsteɪt] *n* (US) zwischenstaatlich; **~ highway** = Bundesautobahn *f*

interval [ˈɪntəvəl] *n* (*space, time*) Abstand *m*; (*theatre etc*) Pause *f*

intervene [ɪntəˈviːn] *vi* eingreifen (*in in*); **intervention** [ɪntəˈvenʃən] *n* Eingreifen *nt*; (*Pol*) Intervention *f*

interview [ˈɪntəvjuː] *n* Interview *nt*; (*for job*) Vorstellungsgespräch *nt* ▷ *vt* interviewen; (*job applicant*) ein Vorstellungsgespräch führen mit; **interviewer** *n* Interviewer(in) *m(f)*

intestine [ɪnˈtestɪn] *n* Darm *m*; **~s** *pl* Eingeweide *pl*

intimate [ˈɪntɪmət] *adj* (*friends*) vertraut, eng; (*atmosphere*) gemütlich; (*sexually*) intim

intimidate [ɪnˈtɪmɪdeɪt] *vt* einschüchtern; **intimidation** *n* Einschüchterung *f*

into [ˈɪntʊ] *prep in +akk*; (*crash*) gegen; **to change ~ sth** (*turn ~*) zu etw werden; (*put on*) sich *dat* etw anziehen; **to translate ~ French** ins Französische übersetzen; **to be ~ sth** (*fam*) auf etw akk stehen

intolerable [ɪnˈtɒlərəbl] *adj* unerträglich

intolerant [ɪnˈtɒlərənt] *adj* intolerant

intoxicated [ɪnˈtɒksɪkeɪtɪd] *adj* betrunken; (*fig*) berauscht

intricate [ˈɪntrɪkət] *adj* kompliziert

intrigue [ɪnˈtriːg] *vt* faszinieren; **intriguing** *adj* faszinierend, fesselnd

introduce [ɪntrəˈdjuːs] *vt* (*person*) vorstellen (*to sb jdm*); (*sth new*) einführen (*to in +akk*); **introduction** [ɪntrəˈdʌkʃən] *n* Einführung *f* (*to in +akk*); (*to book*) Einleitung *f* (*to zu*); (*to person*) Vorstellung *f*

introvert [ˈɪntrəvɜːt] *n* Introvertierte(r) *mf*

intuition [ɪntjuːˈɪʃn] *n* Intuition *f*

invade [ɪnˈveɪd] *vt* einfallen in *+akk*

invalid [ˈɪnvəlɪd] *n* Kranke(r) *mf*; (*disabled*) Invalide *m* ▷ *adj* [ɪnˈvælɪd] (*not valid*) ungültig

invaluable [ɪnˈvæljʊəbl] *adj* äußerst wertvoll, unschätzbar

invariably [ɪnˈvɛərɪəblɪ] *adv* ständig; (*every time*) jedes Mal, ohne Ausnahme

invasion [ɪnˈveɪʒən] *n* Invasion *f* (*of in +akk*), Einfall *m* (*of in +akk*)

invent [ɪnˈvent] *vt* erfinden; **invention** [ɪnˈvenʃən] *n* Erfindung *f*; **inventor** *n* Erfinder(in) *m(f)*

inverted commas [ɪnˈvɜːtɪd ˈkɒməz] *npl* Anführungszeichen *pl*

invest [ɪnˈvest] *vt, vi* investieren (*in in +akk*)

investigate [ɪnˈvestɪgeɪt] *vt* untersuchen; **investigation** [ɪnvestɪˈgeɪʃən] *n* Untersuchung *f* (*into +gen*)

investment [ɪnˈvestmənt] *n* Investition *f*; **it's a good ~** es ist eine gute Anlage; (*it'll be useful*) es macht sich bezahlt

invigorating [ɪnˈvɪgəreɪtɪŋ] adj
erfrischend, belebend; (tonic)
stärkend
invisible [ɪnˈvɪzəbl] adj
unsichtbar
invitation [ɪnvɪˈteɪʃən] n Einladung f; **invite** [ɪnˈvaɪt] vt
einladen
invoice [ˈɪnvɔɪs] n (bill)
Rechnung f
involuntary [ɪnˈvɒləntərɪ] adj
unbeabsichtigt
involve [ɪnˈvɒlv] vt verwickeln
(in sth in etw akk); (entail) zur Folge
haben; **to be ~d in sth** (participate
in) an etw dat beteiligt sein; **I'm
not ~d** (affected) ich bin nicht
betroffen
inward [ˈɪnwəd] adj innere(r, s);
inwardly adv innerlich; **inwards**
adv nach innen
iodine [ˈaɪədiːn] n Jod nt
IOU [aɪəʊˈjuː] abbr = **I owe you**
Schuldschein m
iPod® [ˈaɪpɒd] n iPod® m
IQ abbr = **intelligence quotient** IQ
m
Iran [ɪˈrɑːn] n der Iran
Iraq [ɪˈrɑːk] n der Irak
Ireland [ˈaɪələnd] n Irland nt
iris [ˈaɪrɪs] n (flower) Schwertlilie
f; (of eye) Iris f
Irish [ˈaɪrɪʃ] adj irisch; **~ coffee**
Irish Coffee m; **~ Sea** die Irische
See ▷ n (language) Irisch nt; **the
~ pl** die Iren; **Irishman** (pl **-men**)
n Ire m; **Irishwoman** (pl **-women**)
n Irin f
iron [ˈaɪən] n Eisen nt; (for ironing)
Bügeleisen nt ▷ adj eisern ▷ vt
bügeln
ironic(al) [aɪˈrɒnɪk(əl)] adj
ironisch
ironing board n Bügelbrett nt
irony [ˈaɪrənɪ] n Ironie f
irrational [ɪˈræʃənl] adj
irrational

irregular [ɪˈregjʊlə*] adj
unregelmäßig; (shape)
ungleichmäßig
irrelevant [ɪˈreləvənt] adj
belanglos, irrelevant
irreplaceable [ɪrɪˈpleɪsəbl] adj
unersetzlich
irresistible [ɪrɪˈzɪstəbl] adj
unwiderstehlich
irrespective of [ɪrɪˈspektɪv ɒv]
prep ungeachtet +gen
irresponsible [ɪrɪˈspɒnsəbl] adj
verantwortungslos
irretrievable [ɪrɪˈtriːvəbl] adv
unwiederbringlich; (loss)
unersetzlich
irritable [ˈɪrɪtəbl] adj reizbar;
irritate [ˈɪrɪteɪt] vt (annoy)
ärgern; (deliberately) reizen;
irritation [ɪrɪˈteɪʃən] n (anger)
Ärger m; (Med) Reizung f
IRS abbr = **Internal Revenue
Service** (US) Finanzamt nt
is [ɪz] present of **be** ist
Islam [ˈɪzlɑːm] n Islam m; **Islamic**
[ɪzˈlæmɪk] adj islamisch
island [ˈaɪlənd] n Insel f; **Isle**
[aɪl] N (in names) **the ~ of Man** die
Insel Man; **the ~ of Wight** die Insel
Wight; **the British ~s** die
Britischen Inseln
isn't [ˈɪznt] contr of **is not**
isolate [ˈaɪsəleɪt] vt isolieren;
isolated adj (remote) abgelegen;
(cut off) abgeschnitten (from von);
an ~ case ein Einzelfall; **isolation**
[aɪsəˈleɪʃən] n Isolierung f
Israel [ˈɪzreɪl] n Israel nt; **Israeli**
[ɪzˈreɪlɪ] adj israelisch ▷ n Israeli
m of
issue [ˈɪʃuː] n (matter) Frage f;
(problem) Problem nt; (subject)
Thema nt; (of newspaper etc)
Ausgabe f; **that's not the ~** darum
geht es nicht ▷ vt ausgeben;
(document) ausstellen; (orders)
erteilen; (book) herausgeben

it [ɪt] *pron* **1** *(specific: subject)*
er/sie/es; *(direct object)* ihn/sie/es;
(indirect object) ihm/ihr/ihm;
about/from/in/of it
darüber/davon/darin/davon
2 *(impers)* es; **it's raining** es regnet;
it's Friday tomorrow morgen ist
Freitag; **who is it? — it's me** wer ist
da? — ich (bin's)

IT *abbr* = **information technology**
IT *f*

Italian [ɪ'tæljən] *adj* italienisch
▷ *n* Italiener(in) *m(f)*; *(language)*
Italienisch *nt*

italic [ɪ'tælɪk] *adj* kursiv ▷ *npl*: **in
~s** kursiv

Italy ['ɪtəlɪ] *n* Italien *nt*

itch [ɪtʃ] *n* Juckreiz *m*; **I have an
~** mich juckt es ▷ *vi* jucken; **he is
~ing to ...** es juckt ihn, zu ...; **itchy**
adj juckend

it'd ['ɪtd] *contr of* **it would**; **it had**

item ['aɪtəm] *n (article)*
Gegenstand *m*; *(in catalogue)*
Artikel *m*; *(on list, in accounts)*
Posten *m*; *(on agenda)* Punkt *m*; *(in
show programme)* Nummer *f*; *(in
news)* Bericht *m*; *(TV, radio)*
Meldung *f*

itinerary [aɪ'tɪnərərɪ] *n* Reiseroute *f*

it'll ['ɪtl] *contr of* **it will**; **it shall**

its [ɪts] *pron* sein; *(feminine form)*
ihr

it's [ɪts] *contr of* **it is**; **it has**

itself [ɪt'self] *pron (reflexive)* sich;
(emphatic) **the house** ~ das Haus
selbst *o* an sich; **by** ~ allein; **the
door closes (by)** ~ die Tür schließt
sich von selbst

I've [aɪv] *contr of* **I have**

ivory ['aɪvərɪ] *n* Elfenbein *nt*

ivy ['aɪvɪ] *n* Efeu *m*

jab [dʒæb] *vt (needle, knife)*
stechen *(into in +akk)* ▷ *n (fam)*
Spritze *f*

jack [dʒæk] *n (Auto)* Wagenheber
m; *(Cards)* Bube *m*; **jack in** *vt (fam)*
aufgeben, hinschmeißen; **jack up**
vt (car etc) aufbocken

jacket ['dʒækɪt] *n (man's suit)* Jacke *f*; *(of
man's suit)* Jackett *nt*; *(of book)*
Schutzumschlag *m*; **jacket potato**
(pl **-es)** *n* (in der Schale)
gebackene Kartoffel

jack-knife ['dʒæknaɪf] *(pl*
jack-knives) *n* Klappmesser *nt*
▷ *vi (truck)* sich quer stellen

jackpot ['dʒækpɒt] *n* Jackpot *m*

jacuzzi® [dʒə'ku:zɪ] *n (bath)*
Whirlpool® *m*

jail [dʒeɪl] *n* Gefängnis *nt* ▷ *vt*
einsperren

jam [dʒæm] *n* Konfitüre *f*,
Marmelade *f*; *(traffic ~)* Stau *m* ▷ *vt*
(street) verstopfen; *(machine)*

blockieren; **to be ~med** (*stuck*) klemmen; **to ~ on the brakes** eine Vollbremsung machen

Jamaica [dʒəˈmeɪkə] n Jamaika nt

jam-packed adj proppenvoll

janitor [ˈdʒænɪtəʳ] n (US) Hausmeister(in) m(f)

Jan abbr = **January** Jan

January [ˈdʒænjʊərɪ] n Januar m

Japan [dʒəˈpæn] n Japan nt; **Japanese** [dʒæpəˈniːz] adj japanisch ▷ n (person) Japaner(in) m(f); (language) Japanisch nt

jar [dʒɑːʳ] n Glas nt

jaundice [ˈdʒɔːndɪs] n Gelbsucht f

javelin [ˈdʒævlɪn] n Speer m; (Sport) Speerwerfen nt

jaw [dʒɔː] n Kiefer m

jazz [dʒæz] n Jazz m

jealous [ˈdʒeləs] adj eifersüchtig (of auf +akk); **don't make me ~** mach mich nicht neidisch; **jealousy** n Eifersucht f

jeans [dʒiːnz] npl Jeans pl

jeep® [dʒiːp] n Jeep® m

jelly [ˈdʒelɪ] n Gelee nt; (dessert) Götterspeise f; Gallert nt; (US: jam) Marmelade f; **jelly baby** n (sweet) Gummibärchen nt; **jellyfish** n Qualle f

jeopardize [ˈdʒepədaɪz] vt gefährden

jerk [dʒɜːk] n Ruck m; (fam: idiot) Trottel m ▷ vt ruckartig bewegen ▷ vi (rope) rucken; (muscles) zucken

Jerusalem [dʒəˈruːsələm] n Jerusalem nt

jet [dʒet] n (of water etc) Strahl m; (nozzle) Düse f; (aircraft) Düsenflugzeug nt; **jet foil** n Tragflächenboot nt; **jetlag** n Jetlag m (Müdigkeit nach langem Flug)

Jew [dʒuː] n Jude m, Jüdin f

jewel [ˈdʒuːəl] n Edelstein m; (esp fig) Juwel nt; **jeweller, jeweler** (US) n Juwelier(in) m(f); **jewellery, jewelry** (US) n Schmuck m

Jewish [ˈdʒuːɪʃ] adj jüdisch; **she's ~** sie ist Jüdin

jigsaw (puzzle) [ˈdʒɪgsɔː(ˌpʌzl)] n Puzzle nt

jilt [dʒɪlt] vt den Laufpass geben +dat

jingle [ˈdʒɪŋgl] n (advert) Jingle m; (verse) Reim m

jitters [ˈdʒɪtəz] npl (fam) **to have the ~** Bammel haben; **jittery** adj (fam) ganz nervös

job [dʒɒb] n (piece of work) Arbeit f; (task) Aufgabe f; (occupation) Stellung f, Job m; **what's your ~?** was machen Sie beruflich?; **it's a good ~ you did that** gut, dass du das gemacht hast; **jobcentre** n Arbeitsvermittlungsstelle f, Arbeitsamt nt; **job-hunting** n: **to go ~** auf Arbeitssuche gehen; **jobless** adj arbeitslos; **job seeker** n Arbeitssuchende(r) mf; **jobseeker's allowance** n Arbeitslosengeld nt; **job-sharing** n Arbeitsplatzteilung f

jockey [ˈdʒɒkɪ] n Jockey m

jog [dʒɒg] vt (person) anstoßen ▷ vi (run) joggen; **jogging** n Jogging nt; **to go ~** joggen gehen

john [dʒɒn] n (US fam) Klo nt

join [dʒɔɪn] vt (put together) verbinden (to mit); (club etc) beitreten +dat; **to ~ sb** sich anschließen; (sit with) sich zu jdm setzen ▷ vi (unite) sich vereinigen; (rivers) zusammenfließen ▷ n Verbindungsstelle f; (seam) Naht f; **join in** vi mitmachen (sth bei etw)

joint [dʒɔɪnt] n (of bones) Gelenk nt; (in pipe etc) Verbindungsstelle f; (of meat) Braten m; (of marijuana)

Joint *m* ▷ *adj* gemeinsam; **joint account** *n* Gemeinschaftskonto *nt*; **jointly** *adv* gemeinsam

joke [dʒəʊk] *n* Witz *m*; (*prank*) Streich *m*; **for a ~** zum Spaß; **it's no ~** das ist nicht zum Lachen ▷ *vi* Witze machen; **you must be joking** das ist ja wohl nicht dein Ernst!

jolly ['dʒɒlɪ] *adj* lustig, vergnügt

Jordan ['dʒɔːdən] *n* (*country*) Jordanien *nt*; (*river*) Jordan *m*

jot down [dʒɒt daʊn] *vt* sich notieren; **jotter** *n* Notizbuch *nt*

journal ['dʒɜːnl] *n* (*diary*) Tagebuch *nt*; (*magazine*) Zeitschrift *f*; **journalism** *n* Journalismus *m*; **journalist** *n* Journalist(in) *m(f)*

journey ['dʒɜːnɪ] *n* Reise *f*; (*esp on stage, by car, train*) Fahrt *f*

joy [dʒɔɪ] *n* Freude *f* (*at* über +*akk*); **joystick** (*Inform*) Joystick *m*; (*Aviat*) Steuerknüppel *m*

judge [dʒʌdʒ] *n* Richter(in) *m(f)*; (*Sport*) Punktrichter(in) *m(f)* ▷ *vt* beurteilen (*by* nach); **as far as I can ~** meinem Urteil nach ▷ *vi* urteilen (*by* nach); **judg(e)ment** *n* (*Jur*) Urteil *nt*; (*opinion*) Ansicht *f*; **an error of ~** Fehleinschätzung *f*

judo ['dʒuːdəʊ] *n* Judo *nt*

jug [dʒʌg] *n* Krug *m*

juggle ['dʒʌgl] *vi* (*lit, fig*) jonglieren (*with* mit)

juice [dʒuːs] *n* Saft *m*; **juicy** *adj* saftig; (*story, scandal*) pikant

July [dʒuˈlaɪ] *n* Juli *m*; *see also* **September**

jumble ['dʒʌmbl] *n* Durcheinander *nt* ▷ *vt*: **to ~ (up)** durcheinanderwerfen; (*facts*) durcheinanderbringen; **jumble sale** *n* (*for charity*) Flohmarkt *m*, Wohltätigkeitsbasar *m*

jumbo ['dʒʌmbəʊ] *adj* (*sausage etc*) Riesen-; **jumbo jet** *n* Jumbojet *m*

jump [dʒʌmp] *vi* springen; (*nervously*) zusammenzucken; **to ~ to conclusions** voreilige Schlüsse ziehen; **to ~ from one thing to another** dauernd das Thema wechseln ▷ *vt* (*a. fig: omit*) überspringen; **to ~ the lights** bei Rot über die Kreuzung fahren; **to ~ the queue** sich vordrängen ▷ *n* Sprung *m*; (*for horses*) Hindernis *nt*; **jumper** *n* Pullover *m*; (*US: dress*) Trägerkleid *nt*; (*person, horse*) Springer(in) *m(f)*; **jumper cable** *n* (*US*), **jump lead** *n* (*Brit Auto*) Starthilfekabel *nt*

junction ['dʒʌŋkʃən] *n* (*of roads*) Kreuzung *f*; (*Rail*) Knotenpunkt *m*

June [dʒuːn] *n* Juni *m*; *see also* **September**

jungle ['dʒʌŋgl] *n* Dschungel *m*

junior ['dʒuːnɪə] *adj* (*younger*) jünger; (*lower position*) untergeordnet (*to* jdm) ▷ *n*: **she's two years my ~** sie ist zwei Jahre jünger als ich; **junior high (school)** *n* (*US*) = Mittelschule *f*; **junior school** *n* (*Brit*) Grundschule *f*

junk [dʒʌŋk] *n* (*trash*) Plunder *m*; **junk food** *n* Nahrungsmittel *pl* mit geringem Nährwert, Junkfood *nt*; **junkie** *n* (*fam*) Junkie *m*, Fixer(in) *m(f)*; (*fig: fan*) Freak *m*; **junk mail** *n* Reklame *f*; (*Inform*) Junkmail *f*; **junk shop** *n* Trödelladen *m*

jury ['dʒʊərɪ] *n* Geschworene *pl*; (*in competition*) Jury *f*

just [dʒʌst] *adj* gerecht ▷ *adv* (*recently*) gerade; (*exactly*) genau; **~ as expected** genau wie erwartet; **~ as nice** genauso nett; (*barely*) **~ in time** gerade noch rechtzeitig; (*immediately*) **~ before/after ...** gleich vor/ nach ...; (*small distance*) **~ round the corner** gleich um die Ecke; (*a little*)

~ over an hour etwas mehr als eine Stunde; (only) **~ the two of us** nur wir beide; **~ a moment** Moment mal; (absolutely, simply) **it was ~ fantastic** es war einfach klasse; **~ about** so etwa; (more or less) mehr oder weniger; **~ about ready** fast fertig

justice [ˈdʒʌstɪs] n Gerechtigkeit f; **justifiable** [dʒʌstɪˈfaɪəbl] adj berechtigt; **justifiably** adv zu Recht; **justify** [ˈdʒʌstɪfaɪ] vt rechtfertigen

jut [dʒʌt] vi: **to ~ (out)** herausragen

juvenile [ˈdʒuːvənaɪl] n adj Jugend-, jugendlich ▷ n Jugendliche(r) mf

k abbr = **thousand**; **15k** 15 000
K abbr = **kilobyte** KB
kangaroo [kæŋɡəˈruː] n Känguru nt
karaoke [kærɪˈəʊkɪ] n Karaoke nt
karate [kəˈrɑːtɪ] n Karate nt
kart [kɑːt] n Gokart m
kayak [ˈkaɪæk] n Kajak m o nt; **kayaking** [ˈkaɪækɪŋ] n Kajak-fahren nt
Kazakhstan [kæzækˈstɑːn] n Kasachstan nt
kebab [kəˈbæb] n (shish ~) Schaschlik nt o m; (doner ~) Kebab m
keel [kiːl] n (Naut) Kiel m; **keel over** vi (boat) kentern; (person) umkippen
keen [kiːn] adj begeistert (on von); (hardworking) eifrig; (mind, wind) scharf; (interest, feeling) stark; **to be ~ on sb** von jdm angetan sein; **she's ~ on riding** sie reitet

gern; **to be ~ to do sth** darauf erpicht sein, etw zu tun

keep [ki:p] **(kept, kept)** vt (retain) behalten; (secret) für sich behalten; (observe) einhalten; (promise) halten; (run: shop, diary, accounts) führen; (animals) halten; (support, family etc) unterhalten, versorgen; (store) aufbewahren; **to ~ sb waiting** jdn warten lassen; **to ~ sb from doing sth** jdn davon abhalten, etw zu tun; **to ~ sth clean/secret** etw sauber/geheim halten; **"~ clear"** „(bitte) frei halten"; **~ this to yourself** behalten Sie das für sich ▷ vi (food) sich halten; (remain, with adj) bleiben; **~ quiet** sei ruhig!; **~ left** links fahren; **to ~ doing sth** (repeatedly) etw immer wieder tun; **~ it up** mach weiter so!; **it ~s happening** es passiert immer wieder ▷ n (livelihood) Unterhalt m; **keep back** vi zurückbleiben ▷ vt zurückhalten; (information) verschweigen (from sb jdm); **keep off** vt (person, animal) fernhalten; **"~ off the grass"** „Betreten des Rasens verboten"; **keep on** vi weitermachen; (walking) weitergehen; (in car) weiterfahren; **to ~ doing sth** (persistently) etw immer wieder tun ▷ vt (coat etc) anbehalten; **keep out** vt nicht hereinlassen ▷ vi draußen bleiben; **~** (on sign) Eintritt verboten; **keep to** vt (road, path) bleiben auf +dat; (plan etc) sich halten an +akk; **to ~ the point** bei der Sache bleiben; **keep up** vi Schritt halten (with mit) ▷ vt (maintain) aufrechterhalten; (speed) halten; **to ~ appearances** den Schein wahren; **keep it up!** (fam) weiter so!

keeper n (museum etc) Aufseher(in) m(f); (goal~) Torwart

m; (zoo ~) Tierpfleger(in) m(f); **keep-fit** n Fitnesstraining nt; **~ exercises** Gymnastik f

kennel ['kenl] n Hundehütte f; **kennels** n Hundepension f

Kenya ['kenjə] n Kenia nt

kept [kept] pt, pp of **keep**

kerb [kɜ:b] n Randstein m

kerosene ['kerəsi:n] n (US) Petroleum nt

ketchup ['ketʃʌp] n Ketchup nt o m

kettle ['ketl] n Kessel m

key [ki:] n Schlüssel m; (of piano, computer) Taste f; (Mus) Tonart f; (for map etc) Zeichenerklärung f ▷ vt: **to ~ (in)** (Inform) eingeben ▷ adj entscheidend; **keyboard** n (piano, computer) Tastatur f; **keyhole** n Schlüsselloch nt; **keypad** n (Inform) Nummernblock m; **keyring** n Schlüsselring m

kick [kɪk] n Tritt m; (Sport) Stoß m; **I get a ~ out of it** (fam) es turnt mich an ▷ vt, vi treten; **kick out** vt (fam) rausschmeißen (of jdn); **kick-off** n (Sport) Anstoß m

kid [kɪd] n (child) Kind nt ▷ vt (tease) auf den Arm nehmen ▷ vi Witze machen; **you're ~ding** das ist doch nicht dein Ernst!; **no ~ding** aber echt!

kidnap ['kɪdnæp] vt entführen; **kidnapper** n Entführer(in) m(f); **kidnapping** n Entführung f

kidney ['kɪdnɪ] n Niere f; **kidney machine** n künstliche Niere

kill [kɪl] vt töten; (esp intentionally) umbringen; (weeds) vernichten; **killer** n Mörder(in) m(f)

kilo ['ki:ləʊ] (pl **-s**) n Kilo nt; **kilobyte** n Kilobyte nt; **kilogramme**, **kilogram** (US), **kilometre** n Kilometer m; **~s per hour**

Stundenkilometer pl; **kilowatt** n
Kilowatt nt

kilt [kɪlt] n Schottenrock m
kind [kaɪnd] adj nett, freundlich
(to zu) ▷ n Art f; (of coffee, cheese
etc) Sorte f; **what ~ of ...?** was für
ein(e) ...?; **this ~ of ...** so eine(e) ...;
~ of (+ adj) irgendwie
kindergarten ['kɪndəgɑːtn] n
Kindergarten m
kindly ['kaɪndlɪ] adj nett,
freundlich ▷ adv liebenswürdi-
gerweise; **kindness** ['kaɪndnəs]
n Freundlichkeit f
king [kɪŋ] n König m; **kingdom** n
Königreich nt; **kingfisher** n
Eisvogel m; **king-size** adj im
Großformat; (bed) extra groß
kipper ['kɪpə°] n Räucherhering
m
kiss [kɪs] n Kuss m; **~ of life**
Mund-zu-Mund-Beatmung f ▷ vt
küssen
kit [kɪt] n (equipment) Ausrüstung
f; (fam) Sachen pl; (sports ~)
Sportsachen pl; (belongings, clothes)
Sachen pl; (for building sth) Bausatz
m
kitchen ['kɪtʃɪn] n Küche f;
kitchen foil n Alufolie f; **kitchen
scales** n Küchenwaage f; **kitchen
unit** n Küchenschrank m;
kitchenware n Küchengeschirr
nt
kite [kaɪt] n Drachen m
kitten ['kɪtn] n Kätzchen nt
kiwi ['kiːwiː] n (fruit) Kiwi f
km abbr = **kilometres** km
knack [næk] n Dreh m, Trick m; **to
get/have got the ~** den Dreh
herauskriegen/heraushaben;
knackered ['nækəd] adj (Brit fam)
fix und fertig, kaputt
knee [niː] n Knie nt; **kneecap** n
Kniescheibe f; **knee-jerk** adj
(reaction) reflexartig; **kneel** [niːl]
(**knelt** o **kneeled**, **knelt** o **kneeled**)

vi knien; (action, ~ down) sich
hinknien
knelt [nelt] pt, pp of **kneel**
knew [njuː] pt of **know**
knickers ['nɪkəz] npl (Brit fam)
Schlüpfer m
knife [naɪf] (pl **knives**) n Messer
nt
knight [naɪt] n Ritter m; (in
chess) Pferd nt, Springer m
knit [nɪt] vt, vi stricken; **knitting**
n (piece of work) Strickarbeit f;
(activity) Stricken nt; **knitting
needle** n Stricknadel f; **knitwear**
n Strickwaren pl
knob [nɒb] n (on door) Knauf m;
(on radio etc) Knopf m
knock [nɒk] vt (with hammer etc)
schlagen; (accidentally) stoßen; **to
~ one's head** sich dat den Kopf
anschlagen ▷ vi klopfen (on, at an
+akk) ▷ n (blow) Schlag m; (on door)
Klopfen nt; **there was a ~ (at the
door)** es hat geklopft; **knock
down** vt (object) umstoßen;
(person) niederschlagen; (with car)
anfahren; (building) abreißen;
knock out vt (stun) bewusstlos
schlagen; (boxer) k.o. schlagen;
knock over vt umstoßen; (with
car) anfahren; **knocker** n
Türklopfer m; **knockout** n
Knockout m, K.o. m
knot [nɒt] n Knoten m
know [nəʊ] (**knew, known**) vt, vi
wissen; (be acquainted with: people,
places) kennen; (recognize)
erkennen; (language) können; **I'll
let you ~** ich sage ihr Bescheid; **I
~ some French** ich kann etwas
Französisch; **to get to ~ sb** jdn
kennenlernen; **to be ~n as**
bekannt sein als; **know about** vt
Bescheid wissen über +akk;
(subject) sich auskennen in +dat;
(cars, horses etc) sich auskennen
mit; **know of** vt kennen; **not that**

I ~ nicht dass ich wüsste;
know-all n (fam) Klugscheißer m;
know-how n Kenntnis f,
Know-how nt; **knowing** adj
wissend; (look, smile) vielsagend;
knowledge ['nɒlɪdʒ] n Wissen
nt; (of a subject) Kenntnisse pl; **to
(the best of) my ~** meines
Wissens

known [nəʊn] pp of know
knuckle ['nʌkl] n (Finger)knöchel m; (Gastr) Hachse f;
knuckle down vi sich an die
Arbeit machen

Koran [kʊ'rɑːn] n Koran m
Korea [kə'rɪə] n Korea nt
Kosovo ['kɒsɒvəʊ] n der Kosovo
kph abbr = **kilometres per hour**
km/h
Kremlin ['kremlɪn] n: **the ~** der
Kreml
Kurd [kɛːd] n Kurde m, Kurdin f;
Kurdish adj kurdisch
Kuwait [kʊ'weɪt] n Kuwait nt

L abbr (Brit Auto) = **learner**
LA abbr = **Los Angeles**
lab [læb] n (fam) Labor nt
label ['leɪbl] n Etikett nt; (tied)
Anhänger m; (adhesive) Aufkleber
m; (record ~) Label nt ▷ vt
etikettieren; (pej) abstempeln
laboratory [lə'bɒrətərɪ] n Labor
nt

● **LABOR DAY**
●
● Der **Labor Day** ist in den USA
● und Kanada der Name für den
● Tag der Arbeit. Er wird dort als
● gesetzlicher Feiertag am ersten
● Montag im September
● begangen.

laborious [lə'bɔːrɪəs] adj
mühsam; **labor** (US), **labour**
['leɪbə*] n Arbeit f; (Med) Wehen
pl; **to be in ~** Wehen haben ▷ adj

(Pol) Labour-; **~ Party** Labour Party f; **labor union** n (US) Gewerkschaft f; **labourer** n Arbeiter(in) m(f)

lace [leɪs] n (fabric) Spitze f; (of shoe) Schnürsenkel m ▷ vt: **to ~ (up)** zuschnüren

lack [læk] vt, vi: **to be ~ing** fehlen; **sb ~s** o **is ~ing in sth** es fehlt jdm an etw dat; **we ~ the time** uns fehlt die Zeit ▷ n Mangel m (of an +dat)

lacquer ['lækə°] n Lack m; (Brit: hair ~) Haarspray nt

lad [læd] n Junge m

ladder ['lædə°] n Leiter f; (in tight) Laufmasche f

laddish ['lædɪʃ] adj (Brit) machohaft

laden ['leɪdn] adj beladen (with mit)

ladies ['leɪdɪz], **ladies' room** n Damentoilette f

lad mag n Männerzeitschrift f

lady ['leɪdɪ] n Dame f; (as title) Lady f; **ladybird, ladybug** (US) n Marienkäfer m; **Ladyshave®** n Epiliergerät nt

lag [læg] vi: **to ~ (behind)** zurückliegen ▷ vt (pipes) isolieren

lager ['lɑːgə°] n helles Bier; **~ lout** betrunkener Rowdy

lagging ['lægɪŋ] n Isolierung f

laid [leɪd] pt, pp of **lay**; **laid-back** adj (fam) cool, gelassen

lain [leɪn] pp of **lie**

lake [leɪk] n See m; **the Lake District** Seengebiet im Nordwesten Englands

lamb [læm] n Lamm nt; (meat) Lammfleisch nt; **lamb chop** n Lammkotelett nt

lame [leɪm] adj lahm; (excuse) faul; (argument) schwach

lament [lə'ment] n Klage f ▷ vt beklagen

laminated ['læmɪneɪtɪd] adj beschichtet

lamp [læmp] n Lampe f; (in street) Laterne f; (of car) Licht nt, Scheinwerfer m; **lamppost** n Laternenpfahl m; **lampshade** n Lampenschirm m

land [lænd] n Land nt ▷ vi (from ship) an Land gehen; (Aviat) landen ▷ vt (passengers) absetzen; (goods) abladen; (plane) landen; **landing** n Landung f; (on stairs) Treppenabsatz m; **landing stage** n Landesteg m; **landing strip** n Landebahn f

landlady n Hauswirtin f, Vermieterin f; **landline** n Festnetz nt; **landlord** n (of house) Hauswirt m, Vermieter m; (of pub) Gastwirt m; **landmark** n Wahrzeichen nt; (event) Meilenstein m; **landowner** n Grundbesitzer(in) m(f); **landscape** n Landschaft f; (format) Querformat nt; **landslide** n (Geo) Erdrutsch m

lane [leɪn] n (in country) enge Landstraße, Weg m; (in town) Gasse f; (of motorway) Spur f; (Sport) Bahn f; **to get in ~** (in car) sich einordnen

language ['læŋgwɪdʒ] n Sprache f; (style) Ausdrucksweise f

lantern ['læntən] n Laterne f

lap [læp] n Schoß m; (in race) Runde f ▷ vt (in race) überholen

lapse [læps] n (mistake) Irrtum m; (moral) Fehltritt m ▷ vi ablaufen

laptop ['læptɒp] n Laptop m

large [lɑːdʒ] adj groß; **by and ~ im Großen und Ganzen; **largely** adv zum größten Teil; **large-scale** adj groß angelegt, Groß-

lark [lɑːk] n (bird) Lerche f

laryngitis [lærɪn'dʒaɪtɪs] n Kehlkopfentzündung f; **larynx** ['lærɪŋks] n Kehlkopf m

laser ['leɪzə°] n Laser m; **laser printer** n Laserdrucker m

lash [læʃ] vt peitschen; **lash out** vi (with fists) um sich schlagen; (spend money) sich in Unkosten stürzen (on mit)

lass [læs] n Mädchen nt

last [lɑːst] adj letzte(r, s); **the ~ but one** der/die/das vorletzte; **~ night** gestern Abend; **~ but not least** nicht zuletzt ▷ adv zuletzt; (last time) das letzte Mal; **at ~** endlich ▷ n (person) Letzte(r) mf; (thing) Letzte(s) nt; **he was the ~ to leave** er ging als Letzter ▷ vi (continue) dauern; (remain in good condition) durchhalten; (remain good) sich halten; (money) ausreichen; **lasting** adj dauerhaft; (impression) nachhaltig; **lastly** adv schließlich; **last-minute** adj in letzter Minute; **last name** n Nachname m

late [leɪt] adj spät; (after proper time) zu spät; (train etc) verspätet; (dead) verstorben; **to be ~** zu spät kommen; (train etc) Verspätung haben ▷ adv spät; (after proper time) zu spät; **late availibility flight** n Last-Minute-Flug m; **lately** adv in letzter Zeit; **late opening** n verlängerte Öffnungszeiten pl; **later** [ˈleɪtə] adj, adv später; **see you ~** bis später; **latest** [ˈleɪtɪst] adj späteste(r, s); (most recent) neueste(r, s) ▷ n: **the ~** (news) das Neueste; **at the ~** spätestens

Latin [ˈlætɪn] n Latein nt ▷ adj lateinisch; **Latin America** n Lateinamerika nt; **Latin-American** adj lateinamerikanisch ▷ n Lateinamerikaner(in) m(f)

latter [ˈlætə] adj (second of two) letztere(r, s); (last: part, years) letzte(r, s), später

Latvia [ˈlætviə] n Lettland nt;

Latvian [ˈlætviən] ▷ adj lettisch; ▷ n (person) Lette m; Lettin f; (language) Lettisch nt

laugh [lɑːf] n Lachen nt; **for a ~** aus Spaß ▷ vi lachen (at, about über +akk); **to ~ at sb** sich über jdn lustig machen; **it's no ~ing matter** es ist nicht zum Lachen; **laughter** [ˈlɑːftə] n Gelächter nt

launch [lɔːntʃ] n (launching of ship) Stapellauf m; (of rocket) Abschuss m; (of product) Markteinführung f; (with hype) Lancierung f; (event) Eröffnungsfeier f ▷ vt (ship) vom Stapel lassen; (rocket) abschießen; (product) einführen; (with hype) lancieren; (project) in Gang setzen

launder [ˈlɔːndə] vt waschen und bügeln; (fig: money) waschen; **launderette** [lɔːnˈdret] n (Brit), **laundromat** [ˈlɔːndrəmæt] n (US) Waschsalon m; **laundry** [ˈlɔːndrɪ] n (place) Wäscherei f; (clothes) Wäsche f

lavatory [ˈlævətrɪ] n Toilette f

lavender [ˈlævɪndə] n Lavendel m

lavish [ˈlævɪʃ] adj verschwenderisch; (furnishings etc) üppig; (gift) großzügig

law [lɔː] n Gesetz nt; (system) Recht nt; (for study) Jura; (of sport) Regel f; **against the ~** gesetzwidrig; **law-abiding** adj gesetzestreu; **law court** n Gerichtshof m; **lawful** adj rechtmäßig

lawn [lɔːn] n Rasen m; **lawnmower** n Rasenmäher m

lawsuit [ˈlɔːsuːt] n Prozess m; **lawyer** [ˈlɔːjə] n Rechtsanwalt m, Rechtsanwältin f

laxative [ˈlæksətɪv] n Abführmittel nt

lay [leɪ] pt of **lie** ▷ vt (**laid**, **laid**) legen; (table) decken; (vulg) poppen, bumsen; (egg) legen ▷ adj Laien-; **lay down** vt hinlegen; **lay off** vt (workers) (vorübergehend) entlassen; (stop attacking) in Ruhe lassen; **lay on** vt (provide) anbieten; (organize) veranstalten, bereitstellen; **lay out** vt (spread out) auslegen; (money) ausgeben; **lay-by** n Parkbucht f; (bigger) Parkplatz m

layer ['leɪə'] n Schicht f

layman ['leɪmən] n Laie m

layout ['leɪaʊt] n Gestaltung f; (of book etc) Lay-out nt

laze [leɪz] vi faulenzen; **laziness** ['leɪzɪnɪs] n Faulheit f; **lazy** ['leɪzɪ] adj faul; (day, time) gemütlich

lb abbr = **pound** Pfd.

lead [led] n Blei nt ▷ vt, vi [li:d] (**led**, **led**) führen; (group etc) leiten; **to ~ the way** vorangehen; **this is ~ing us nowhere** das bringt uns nicht weiter ▷ [li:d] n (race) Führung f; (distance, time ahead) Vorsprung m (over vor +dat); (of police) Spur f; (Theat) Hauptrolle f; (dog's) Leine f; (Elec: flex) Leitung f; **lead astray** vt irreführen; **lead away** vt wegführen; **lead back** vi zurückführen; **lead on** vi anführen; **lead to** vt (street) hinführen nach; (result) führen zu; **lead up to** vt (drive) führen zu

leaded ['ledɪd] adj (petrol) verbleit

leader ['li:də'] n Führer(in) m(f); (of party) Vorsitzende(r) mf; (of project, expedition) Leiter(in) m(f); (Sport: in race) der/die Erste; (in league) Tabellenführer m; **leadership** ['li:dəʃɪp] n Führung f

lead-free ['led'fri:] adj (petrol) bleifrei

leading ['li:dɪŋ] adj führend, wichtig

leaf [li:f] (pl **leaves**) n Blatt nt;

leaflet ['li:flɪt] n Prospekt m; (pamphlet) Flugblatt nt; (with instructions) Merkblatt nt

league [li:g] n Bund m; (Sport) Liga f

leak [li:k] n (gap) undichte Stelle; (escape) Leck nt; **to take a ~** (fam) pinkeln gehen ▷ vi (pipe etc) undicht sein; (liquid etc) auslaufen; **leaky** adj undicht

lean [li:n] adj (meat) mager; (face) schmal; (person) drahtig ▷ vi (**leant** o **leaned**, **leant** o **leaned**) (not vertical) sich neigen; (rest) **to ~ against sth** sich an etw akk lehnen; (support oneself) **to ~ on sth** sich auf etw akk stützen ▷ vt lehnen (on, against an +akk); **lean back** vi sich zurücklehnen; **lean forward** vi sich vorbeugen; **lean over** vi sich hinüberbeugen; **lean towards** vt tendieren zu

leant [lent] pt, pp of **lean**

leap [li:p] n Sprung m ▷ vi (**leapt** o **leaped**, **leapt** o **leaped**) springen; **leapt** [lept] pt, pp of **leap**; **leap year** n Schaltjahr nt

learn [lɜ:n] (**learnt** o **learned**, **learnt** o **learned**) vt, vi lernen; (find out) erfahren; **to ~ (how) to swim** schwimmen lernen; **learned** ['lɜ:nɪd] adj gelehrt; **learner** n Anfänger(in) m(f); (Brit: driver) Fahrschüler(in) m(f)

learnt [lɜ:nt] pt, pp of **learn**

lease [li:s] n (of land, premises etc) Pacht f; (contract) Pachtvertrag m; (of house, car etc) Miete f; (contract) Mietvertrag m ▷ vt pachten; (house, car etc) mieten; **lease out** vt vermieten; **leasing** ['li:sɪŋ] n Leasing f

least [li:st] adj wenigste(r, s); (slightest) geringste(r, s) ▷ adv am wenigsten; **~ expensive** billigste(r, s) ▷ n: **the ~** das Mindeste; **not in the ~** nicht im geringsten; **at ~** wenigstens; (*with number*) mindestens

leather ['leðəʳ] n Leder nt ⊳ adj ledern, Leder-

leave [liːv] n (*time off*) Urlaub m; **on ~** auf Urlaub; **to take one's ~** Abschied nehmen (*of* von) ⊳ vt (**left, left**) (*place, person*) verlassen; (*not remove, not change*) lassen; (*~ behind: message, scar etc*) hinterlassen; (*forget*) hinter sich lassen; (*after death*) hinterlassen (*to sb* jdm); (*entrust*) überlassen (*to sb* jdm); **to be left** (*remain*) übrig bleiben; **~ me alone** lass mich in Ruhe!; **don't ~ it to the last minute** warte nicht bis zur letzten Minute ⊳ vi (*weg*)gehen, (*weg*)fahren; (*on journey*) abreisen; (*bus, train*) abfahren (*for* nach); **leave behind** vt zurücklassen; (*scar etc*) hinterlassen; (*forget*) hinter sich lassen; **leave out** vt auslassen; (*person*) ausschließen (*of* von)

leaves [liːvz] pl of **leaf**

leaving do [liːvɪŋ duː] n Abschiedsfeier f

Lebanon ['lebənən] n: **the ~** der Libanon

lecture ['lektʃəʳ] n Vortrag m; (*at university*) Vorlesung f; **to give a ~** einen Vortrag/eine Vorlesung halten; **lecturer** n Dozent(in) m(f); **lecture theatre** n Hörsaal m

led [led] pt, pp of **lead**

LED abbr = **light-emitting diode** Leuchtdiode f

ledge [ledʒ] n Leiste f; (*window ~*) Sims m or nt

leek [liːk] n Lauch m

left [left] pt, pp of **leave** ⊳ adj linke(r, s) ⊳ adv (*position*) links; (*movement*) nach links; n (*side*) linke Seite; **the Left** (*Pol*) die Linke; **on/to the ~** links (*of* von); **move/fall to the ~** nach links

rücken/fallen; **left-hand** adj linke(r, s); **~ bend** Linkskurve f; **~ drive** Linkssteuerung f; **left-handed** adj linkshändig; **left-hand side** n linke Seite

left-luggage locker n Gepäckschließfach nt; **left-luggage office** n Gepäckaufbewahrung f

leftovers npl Reste pl

left wing n linker Flügel; **left-wing** adj (*Pol*) linksgerichtet

leg [leg] n Bein nt; (*of meat*) Keule f

legacy ['legəsɪ] n Erbe nt, Erbschaft f

legal ['liːgl] adj Rechts-, rechtlich; (*allowed*) legal; (*limit, age*) gesetzlich; **~ aid** Rechtshilfe f; **legalize** vt legalisieren; **legally** adv legal

legend ['ledʒənd] n Legende f

legible, legibly ['ledʒəbl, -blɪ] adj, adv leserlich

legislation [ledʒɪs'leɪʃn] n Gesetze pl

legitimate [lɪ'dʒɪtɪmət] adj rechtmäßig, legitim

legroom ['legrʊm] n Beinfreiheit f

leisure ['leʒəʳ] n (*time*) Freizeit f ⊳ adj Freizeit-; **~ centre** Freizeitzentrum nt; **leisurely** ['leʒəlɪ] adj gemächlich

lemon ['lemən] n Zitrone f; **lemonade** [lemə'neɪd] n Limonade f; **lemon curd** n Brotaufstrich aus Zitronen, Butter, Eiern und Zucker; **lemon juice** n Zitronensaft m; **lemon sole** n Seezunge f

lend [lend] (**lent, lent**) vt leihen; **to ~ sb sth** jdm etw leihen; **to (sb) ~ a hand** (jdm) behilflich sein; **lending library** n Leihbücherei f

length [leŋθ] n Länge f; **4 metres in ~** = 4 Meter lang; **what**

~ is it? wie lange ist es?; **for any ~ of time** für längere Zeit; **at ~** (lengthily) ausführlich; **lengthen** ['leŋθən] vt verlängern; **lengthy** adj sehr lange; (dragging) langwierig

lenient ['li:niənt] adj nachsichtig

lens [lenz] n Linse f; (Foto) Objektiv nt

lent [lent] pt, pp of **lend**

Lent [lent] n Fastenzeit f

lentil ['lentl] n (Bot) Linse f

Leo ['li:əu] (pl -s) n (Astr) Löwe m

leopard ['lepəd] n Leopard m

lesbian ['lezbiən] adj lesbisch ▷ n Lesbe f

less [les] adj, adv, n weniger; **~ and ~** immer weniger; (~ often) immer seltener; **lessen** ['lesn] vi abnehmen, nachlassen ▷ vt verringern; (pain) lindern; **lesser** ['lesə°] adj geringer; (amount) kleiner

lesson ['lesn] n (at school) Stunde f; (unit of study) Lektion f; (fig) Lehre f; (Rel) Lesung f; **~s start at 9** der Unterricht beginnt um 9

let [let] (let, let) vt lassen; (lease) vermieten; **to ~ sb have sth** jdm etw geben; **~'s go** gehen wir; **to ~ go (of sth)** (etw) loslassen; **let down** vt herunterlassen; (fail to help) im Stich lassen; (disappoint) enttäuschen; **let in** vt hereinlassen; **let off** vt (bomb) hochgehen lassen; (person) laufen lassen; **let out** vt hinauslassen; (secret) verraten; (scream etc) ausstoßen; **let up** vi nachlassen; (stop) aufhören

lethal ['li:θəl] adj tödlich

let's contr = **let us**

letter ['letə°] n (of alphabet) Buchstabe m; (message) Brief m; (official ~) Schreiben nt; **letter bomb** n Briefbombe f; **letterbox** n Briefkasten m

lettuce ['letis] n Kopfsalat m

leukaemia, leukemia (US) [lu:'ki:miə] n Leukämie f

level ['levl] adj (horizontal) waagerecht; (ground) eben; (two things, two runners) auf selber Höhe; **to be ~ with sb/sth** mit jdm/etw auf gleicher Höhe sein; **~ on points** punktgleich ▷ adv (run etc) auf gleicher Höhe, gleich auf; **to draw ~** (in race) gleichziehen (with mit); (in game) ausgleichen ▷ n (altitude) Höhe f; (standard) Niveau nt; (amount, degree) Grad m; **to be on a ~ with** auf gleicher Höhe sein mit ▷ vt (ground) einebnen; **level crossing** n (Brit) (schienengleicher) Bahnübergang m; **level-headed** adj vernünftig

lever ['li:və°, (US) 'levə°] n Hebel m; (fig) Druckmittel nt; **lever up** vt hochstemmen

liability [laiə'biliti] n Haftung f; (burden) Belastung f; (obligation) Verpflichtung f; **liable** ['laiəbl] adj: **to be ~ for sth** (responsible) für etw haften; **~ for tax** steuerpflichtig

liar ['laiə°] n Lügner(in) m(f)

Lib Dem [lib'dem] abbr = **Liberal Democrat**

liberal ['libərəl] adj (generous) großzügig; (broad-minded) liberal; **Liberal Democrat** n (Brit Pol) Liberaldemokrat(in) m(f) ▷ adj liberaldemokratisch

liberate ['libəreit] vt befreien; **liberation** [libə'reifn] n Befreiung f

Liberia [lai'biəriə] n Liberia nt

liberty ['libəti] n Freiheit f

Libra ['li:brə] n (Astr) Waage f

library ['laibrəri] n Bibliothek f; (lending ~) Bücherei f

Libya ['lɪbɪə] n Libyen nt
lice [laɪs] pl of **louse**
licence ['laɪsəns] n (permit)
Genehmigung f; (Comm) Lizenz f;
(driving ~) Führerschein m; **license**
['laɪsəns] n (US) see **licence** ▷ vt
genehmigen; **licensed** adj
(restaurant etc) mit
Schankerlaubnis; **license plate** n
(US Auto) Nummernschild nt;
licensing hours npl
Ausschankzeiten pl
lick [lɪk] vt lecken ▷ n Lecken nt
licorice ['lɪkərɪs] n Lakritze f
lid [lɪd] n Deckel m; (eye~) Lid nt
lie [laɪ] n Lüge f; **~ detector**
Lügendetektor m ▷ vi lügen; (also
~ to sb jdn belügen ▷ vi (**lay, lain**)
(rest, be situated) liegen; (~ down)
sich legen; (snow) liegen bleiben;
to be lying third an dritter Stelle
liegen; **lie about** vi herumliegen;
lie down vi sich hinlegen
Liechtenstein ['lɪktənstaɪn] n
Liechtenstein nt
lie in [laɪ'ɪn] n: **to have a**
~ ausschlafen
life [laɪf] (pl **lives**) n Leben nt; **to**
get ~ lebenslänglich bekommen;
there isn't much ~ here hier ist
nicht viel los; **how many lives**
were lost? wie viele sind ums
Leben gekommen?; **life assurance**
n Lebensversicherung f; **lifebelt** n
Rettungsring m; **lifeboat** n
Rettungsboot nt; **lifeguard** n
Bademeister(in) m(f),
Rettungsschwimmer(in) m(f); **life**
insurance n Lebensversicherung
f; **life jacket** n Schwimmweste f;
lifeless adj (dead) leblos; **lifelong**
adj lebenslang; **life preserver** n
(US) Rettungsring m; **life-saving**
adj lebensrettend; **life-size(d)** adj
in Lebensgröße; **life span** n
Lebensspanne f; **life style** n

Lebensstil m; **lifetime** n
Lebenszeit f
lift [lɪft] vt (hoch)heben; (ban)
aufheben ▷ n (Brit: elevator)
Aufzug m, Lift m; **to give sb a ~**
im Auto mitnehmen; **lift up** vt
hochheben; **lift-off** n Start m
ligament ['lɪgəmənt] n Band nt
light [laɪt] o **lighted, lit** o
lighted) vt beleuchten; (fire,
cigarette) anzünden ▷ n Licht nt;
(lamp) Lampe f; **~s** pl (Auto)
Beleuchtung f; (traffic ~s) Ampel f;
in the ~ of angesichts +gen ▷ adj
(bright) hell; (not heavy, easy) leicht;
(punishment) milde; (taxes) niedrig;
~ blue/green hellblau/hellgrün;
light up vi (illuminate) beleuchten
▷ vt (a. eyes) aufleuchten
light bulb n Glühbirne f
lighten ['laɪtn] vi hell werden
▷ vt (give light to) erhellen; (make
less heavy) leichter machen; (fig)
erleichtern
lighter ['laɪtə*] n (cigarette ~)
Feuerzeug nt
light-hearted adj unbeschwert;
lighthouse n Leuchtturm m;
lighting n Beleuchtung f; **lightly**
adv leicht; **light meter** n (Foto)
Belichtungsmesser m
lightning ['laɪtnɪŋ] n Blitz m
lightweight adj leicht
like [laɪk] vt mögen, gernhaben;
he ~s swimming er schwimmt
gern; **would you ~ ...?** möchten
du/hätten Sie gern ...?; **I'd ~ to go**
home ich möchte nach Hause
(gehen); **I don't ~ the film** der
Film gefällt mir nicht ▷ prep wie;
what's it/he ~? wie ist es/er?; **he**
looks ~ you er sieht dir/Ihnen
ähnlich; **~ that** so; **likeable**
['laɪkəbl] adj sympathisch
likelihood ['laɪklɪhʊd] n Wahrscheinlichkeit f; **likely** ['laɪklɪ]
adj wahrscheinlich; **the bus is**

~ to be late der Bus wird wahrscheinlich Verspätung haben; **he's not (at all) ~ to come** (höchst)wahrscheinlich kommt er nicht

like-minded [laɪkˈmaɪndɪd] *adj* gleich gesinnt

likewise [ˈlaɪkwaɪz] *adv* ebenfalls; **to do ~** das Gleiche tun

liking [ˈlaɪkɪŋ] *n* (for person) Zuneigung *f*; (for type, things) Vorliebe *f* (for für)

lilac [ˈlaɪlək] *n* Flieder *m* ▷ *adj* fliederfarben

lily [ˈlɪlɪ] *n* Lilie *f*; **~ of the valley** Maiglöckchen *nt*

limb [lɪm] *n* Glied *nt*

limbo [ˈlɪmbəʊ] *n*: **in ~** (plans) auf Eis gelegt

lime [laɪm] *n* (tree) Linde *f*; (fruit) Limone *f*; (substance) Kalk *m*; **lime juice** *n* Limonensaft *m*; **limelight** *n* (fig) Rampenlicht *nt*

limerick [ˈlɪmərɪk] *n* Limerick *m* (fünfzeiliges komisches Gedicht)

limestone [ˈlaɪmstəʊn] *n* Kalkstein *m*

limit [ˈlɪmɪt] *n* Grenze *f*; (for pollution etc) Grenzwert *m*; **there's a ~ to that** dem sind Grenzen gesetzt; **to be over the ~** (speed) das Tempolimit überschreiten; (alcohol consumption) fahrtüchtig sein; **that's the ~** jetzt reicht's!, das ist die Höhe! ▷ *vt* beschränken (to auf +akk); (freedom, spending) einschränken

limitation [lɪmɪˈteɪʃən] *n* Beschränkung *f*; (of freedom, spending) Einschränkung *f*;

limited *adj* begrenzt; **~ liability company** Gesellschaft *f* mit beschränkter Haftung, GmbH *f*; **public ~ company** Aktiengesellschaft *f*

limousine [ˈlɪməziːn] *n* Limousine *f*

limp [lɪmp] *vi* hinken ▷ *adj* schlaff

line [laɪn] *n* Linie *f*; (written) Zeile *f*; (rope) Leine *f*; (on face) Falte *f*; (row) Reihe *f*; (US: queue) Schlange *f*; (Rail) Bahnlinie *f*; (between A and B) Strecke *f*; (Tel) Leitung *f*; (range of items) Kollektion *f*; **hold the ~** bleiben Sie am Apparat; **to stand in ~** Schlange stehen; **in ~ with** in Übereinstimmung mit; **something along those ~s** etwas in dieser Art; **drop me a ~** schreib mir ein paar Zeilen; **~s** (Theat) Text *m* ▷ *vt* (clothes) füttern; (streets) säumen; **lined** *adj* (paper) liniert; (face) faltig; **line up** *vi* sich aufstellen; (US: form queue) sich anstellen

linen [ˈlɪnɪn] *n* Leinen *nt*; (sheets etc) Wäsche *f*

liner [ˈlaɪnə] *n* Überseedampfer *m*, Passagierschiff *nt*

linger [ˈlɪŋɡə] *vi* verweilen; (smell) nicht weggehen

lingerie [ˈlænʒərɪ] *n* Damenunterwäsche *f*

lining [ˈlaɪnɪŋ] *n* (of clothes) Futter *nt*; (brake) Bremsbelag *m*

link [lɪŋk] *n* (connection) Verbindung *f*; (of chain) Glied *nt*; (relationship) Beziehung *f* (with zu); (between events) Zusammenhang *m*; (Internet) Link *m* ▷ *vt* verbinden

lion [ˈlaɪən] *n* Löwe *m*; **lioness** *n* Löwin *f*

lip [lɪp] *n* Lippe *f*; **lipstick** *n* Lippenstift *m*

liqueur [lɪˈkjʊə] *n* Likör *m*

liquid [ˈlɪkwɪd] *n* Flüssigkeit *f* ▷ *adj* flüssig

liquidate [ˈlɪkwɪdeɪt] *vt* liquidieren

liquidizer [ˈlɪkwɪdaɪzə] *n* Mixer *m*

liquor [ˈlɪkə] *n* Spirituosen *pl*

liquorice ['lɪkərɪs] n Lakritze f
Lisbon ['lɪzbən] n Lissabon nt
lisp [lɪsp] vt, vi lispeln
list [lɪst] n Liste f ▷ vi (ship)
Schlagseite haben ▷ vt auflisten,
aufzählen; **~ed building** unter
Denkmalschutz stehendes
Gebäude
listen ['lɪsn] vi zuhören, horchen
(for sth auf etw akk); **listen to** vt
(person) zuhören +dat; (radio)
hören; (advice) hören auf; **listener**
n Zuhörer(in) m(f); (to radio)
Hörer(in) m(f)
lit [lɪt] pt, pp of **light**
liter ['liːtə°] n (US) Liter m
literacy ['lɪtərəsɪ] n Fähigkeit f
zu lesen und zu schreiben; **literal**
['lɪtərəl] adj (translation, meaning)
wörtlich; (actual) buchstäblich;
literally adv (translate, take sth)
wörtlich; (really) buchstäblich,
wirklich; **literary** ['lɪtərərɪ] adj
literarisch; (critic, journal etc)
Literatur-; (language) gehoben;
literature ['lɪtrətʃə°] n Literatur
f; (brochures etc)
Informationsmaterial nt
Lithuania [lɪθjuː'eɪnjə] n Litauen
nt; **Lithuanian** [lɪθjuː'eɪnjən]
▷ adj litauisch; ▷ n (person)
Litauer(in) m(f); (language)
Litauisch nt
litre ['liːtə°] n Liter m
litter ['lɪtə°] n Abfälle pl; (of
animals) Wurf m ▷ vt to be **~ed
with** übersät sein mit; **litter bin** n
Abfalleimer m
little ['lɪtl] adj (smaller,
smallest) klein; (in quantity)
wenig; **a ~ while ago** vor kurzer
Zeit ▷ adv, n (fewer, fewest)
wenig; **a ~** ein bisschen, ein
wenig; **as ~ as possible** so wenig
wie möglich; **for as ~ as £5** um 5
Pfund; **I see very ~ of them** ich
sehe sie sehr selten; **~ by ~** nach

und nach; **little finger** n kleiner
Finger
live [laɪv] adj lebendig; (Elec)
geladen, unter Strom; (TV, Radio:
event) live; **~ broadcast**
Direktübertragung f ▷ [lɪv] vi
leben; (not die) überleben; (dwell)
wohnen; **you ~ and learn** man
lernt nie aus ▷ vt (life) führen; **to
~ a life of luxury** im Luxus leben;
live on vi weiterleben ▷ vt: **to
~ sth** von etw leben; (feed) sich von
etw ernähren; **to earn enough to
~** genug verdienen, um davon zu
leben; **live together** vi
zusammenleben; **live up to** vt
(reputation) gerecht werden +dat;
(expectations) entsprechen +dat;
live with vt (parents etc) wohnen
bei; (partner) zusammenleben mit;
(difficulty) **you'll just have to ~ it**
du musst dich/Sie müssen sich
eben damit abfinden
liveliness ['laɪvlɪnɪs] n Lebhaf-
tigkeit f; **lively** ['laɪvlɪ] adj
lebhaft
liver ['lɪvə°] n Leber f
lives [laɪvz] pl of **life**
livestock ['laɪvstɒk] n Vieh nt
living ['lɪvɪŋ] n Lebensunterhalt
m; **what do you do for a ~?** was
machen Sie beruflich? ▷ adj
lebend; **living room** n
Wohnzimmer nt
lizard ['lɪzəd] n Eidechse f
llama ['lɑːmə] n (Zool) Lama nt
load [ləʊd] n Last f; (cargo)
Ladung f; (Tech, fig) Belastung f; **~s
of** (fam) massenhaft; **it was a ~ of
rubbish** (fam) es war
grottenschlecht ▷ vt (vehicle)
beladen; (Inform) laden; (film)
einlegen
loaf [ləʊf] (pl loaves) n: **a ~ of
bread** ein (Laib) Brot (m)nt
loan [ləʊn] n (item leant)
Leihgabe f; (Fin) Darlehen nt; **on**

~ geliehen ▷ vt leihen (to sb jdm)

loathe [ləʊð] vt verabscheuen

loaves [ləʊvz] pl of **loaf**

lobby ['lɒbɪ] n Vorhalle f; (Pol) Lobby f

lobster ['lɒbstə°] n Hummer m

local ['ləʊkəl] adj (traffic, time etc) Orts-; (radio, news, paper) Lokal-; (government, authority) Kommunal-; (anaesthetic) örtlich; ~ **call** (Tel) Ortsgespräch nt; ~ **elections** Kommunalwahlen pl; ~ **time** Ortszeit f; ~ **train** Nahverkehrszug m; **the ~ shops** die Geschäfte am Ort ▷ n (pub) Stammlokal nt; **the ~s** pl die Ortsansässigen pl; **locally** adv örtlich, am Ort

locate [ləʊ'keɪt] vt (find) ausfindig machen; (position) legen; (establish) errichten; **to be ~d** sich befinden (in, at in +dat); **location** [ləʊ'keɪʃən] n (position) Lage f; (Cine) Drehort m

loch [lɒx] n (Scot) See m

lock [lɒk] n Schloss nt; (Naut) Schleuse f; (of hair) Locke f ▷ vt (door etc) abschließen ▷ vi (door etc) sich abschließen lassen; (wheels) blockieren; **lock in** vt einschließen, einsperren; **lock out** vt aussperren; **lock up** vt (house) abschließen; (person) einsperren

locker ['lɒkə°] n Schließfach nt; **locker room** n (US) Umkleideraum m

locksmith ['lɒksmɪθ] n Schlosser(in) m(f)

locust ['ləʊkəst] n Heuschrecke f

lodge [lɒdʒ] n (small house) Pförtnerhaus nt; (porter's ~) Pförtnerloge f ▷ vi in Untermiete wohnen (with bei); (get stuck) stecken bleiben; **lodger** n Untermieter(in) m(f); **lodging** n Unterkunft f

loft [lɒft] n Dachboden m

log [lɒg] n Klotz m; (Naut) Log nt; **to keep a ~ of sth** über etw Buch führen; **log in, log on** vi (Inform) sich einloggen; **log off, log out** vi (Inform) sich ausloggen

logic ['lɒdʒɪk] n Logik f; **logical** adj logisch

login ['lɒgɪn] n (Inform) Log-in nt, Anmeldung f

logo ['lɒgəʊ] (pl ~s) n Logo nt

loin [lɔɪn] n Lende f

loiter ['lɔɪtə°] vi sich herumtreiben

lollipop ['lɒlɪpɒp] n Lutscher m; ~ **man/lady** (Brit) Schülerlotse m, Schülerlotsin f

lolly ['lɒlɪ] n Lutscher m

London ['lʌndən] n London nt; **Londoner** n Londoner(in) m(f)

loneliness ['ləʊnlɪnɪs] n Einsamkeit f; **lonely** ['ləʊnlɪ], (esp US) **lonesome** ['ləʊnsəm] adj einsam

long [lɒŋ] adj lang; (distance) weit; **it's a ~ way** es ist weit (to nach); **for a ~ time** lange; **how ~ is the film?** wie lange dauert der Film?; **in the ~ run** auf die Dauer ▷ adv lange; **not for ~** nicht lange; ~ **ago** vor langer Zeit; **before ~** bald; **all day** ~ den ganzen Tag; **no ~er** nicht mehr; **as ~ as** solange ▷ vi sich sehnen (for nach); (be waiting) sehnsüchtig warten (for auf); **long-distance call** n Ferngespräch nt; **long drink** n Longdrink m; **long-haul flight** n Langstreckenflug m; **longing** n Sehnsucht f (for nach); **longingly** adv sehnsüchtig; **longitude** ['lɒŋgɪtjuːd] n Länge f; **long jump** n Weitsprung m; **long-life milk** n H-Milch f; **long-range** adj Langstrecken-, Fern-; ~ **missile** Langstreckenrakete f; **long-sighted** adj weitsichtig; **long-standing** adj alt, langjährig; **long-term** adj

langfristig; (car park, effect etc)
Langzeit-; **~ unemployment**
Langzeitarbeitslosigkeit f; **long
wave** n Langwelle f

loo [luː] n (Brit fam) Klo nt

look [lʊk] n Blick m; (appearance)
~(s) pl Aussehen nt; **I'll have a
~** ich schau mal nach; **to have a
~ at** sth sich dat etw ansehen; **can
I have a ~?** darf ich mal sehen?
▷ vi schauen, gucken; (with prep)
sehen; (search) nachsehen; (appear)
aussehen; **(I'm) just ~ing** ich
schaue nur; **it ~s like rain** es sieht
nach Regen aus ▷ vt: **~ what
you've done** sieh dir mal an, was
du da angestellt hast; (appear) **he
~s his age** man sieht ihm sein Alter
an; **to ~ one's best** sehr vorteilhaft
aussehen; **look after** vt (care for)
sorgen für; (keep an eye on) aufpassen auf +akk; **look at** vt
ansehen, anschauen; **look back** vi
sich umsehen; (fig) zurückblicken;
look down on vt (fig) herabsehen
auf +akk; **look for** vt suchen; **look
forward to** vt sich freuen auf +akk;
look into vt (investigate) untersuchen; **look out** vi hinaussehen
(of the window zum Fenster); (watch
out) Ausschau halten (for nach); (be
careful) aufpassen, Acht geben (for
auf +akk); **~!** Vorsicht!; **look up** vt
aufsehen ▷ vt (word etc)
nachschlagen; **look up to** vt
aufsehen zu

loony ['luːnɪ] adj (fam) bekloppt

loop [luːp] n Schleife f

loose [luːs] adj locker; (knot,
button) lose; **loosen** vt lockern;
(knot) lösen

loot [luːt] n Beute f

lop-sided ['lɒp'saɪdɪd] adj schief

lord [lɔːd] n (ruler) Herr m; (Brit:
title) Lord m; **the Lord** (God) Gott
der Herr; **the (House of) Lords**
(Brit) das Oberhaus

lorry ['lɒrɪ] n (Brit) Lastwagen m

lose [luːz] vt (lost, lost) vt
verlieren; (chance) verpassen; **to
~ weight** abnehmen; **to ~ one's
life** umkommen ▷ vi verlieren;
(clock, watch) nachgehen; **loser** n
Verlierer(in) m(f); **loss** [lɒs] n
Verlust m; **lost** [lɒst] pt, pp of **lose**;
we're ~ wir haben uns verlaufen
▷ adj verloren; **lost-and-found**
(US), **lost property (office)** n
Fundbüro nt

lot [lɒt] n (fam: batch) Menge f,
Haufen m, Stoß m; **this is the first
~** das ist die erste Ladung; **a
~** viel(e); **a ~ of money** viel Geld;
~s of people viele Leute; **the
(whole) ~** alles; (people) alle

lotion ['ləʊʃən] n Lotion f

lottery ['lɒtərɪ] n Lotterie f

loud [laʊd] adj laut; (colour)
schreiend; **loudspeaker** n
Lautsprecher m; (of stereo) Box f

lounge [laʊndʒ] n Wohnzimmer
nt; (in hotel) Aufenthaltsraum m;
(at airport) Warteraum m ▷ vi sich
herumlümmeln

louse [laʊs] (pl **lice**) n Laus f;
lousy ['laʊzɪ] adj (fam) lausig

lout [laʊt] n Rüpel m

lovable ['lʌvəbl] adj liebenswert

love [lʌv] n Liebe f (of zu); (person,
address) Liebling m, Schatz m;
(Sport) null; **to be in ~** verliebt sein
(with sb in jdn); **to fall in ~** sich
verlieben (with sb in jdn); **to make
~** (sexually) sich lieben; **to make
~ to** (o with) sb mit jdm schlafen;
(in letter) **he sends his ~** er lässt
grüßen; **give her my ~** grüße sie
von mir; **~, Tom** liebe Grüße, Tom
▷ vt (person) lieben; (activity) sehr
gerne mögen; **to ~ to do sth** etw
für sein Leben gerne tun; **I'd ~ a
cup of tea** ich hätte liebend gern
eine Tasse Tee; **love affair** n
(Liebes)verhältnis nt; **love letter** n

Liebesbrief m; **love life** n Liebesleben nt; **lovely** ['lʌvlɪ] adj schön, wunderschön; (charming) reizend; **we had a ~ time** es war sehr schön; **lover** ['lʌvə] n Liebhaber(in) m(f); **loving** adj liebevoll

low [ləʊ] adj niedrig; (rank) niedere(r, s); (level, note, neckline) tief; (intelligence, density) gering; (quality, standard) schlecht; (not loud) leise; (depressed) niedergeschlagen; **we're ~ on petrol** wir haben kaum noch Benzin ▷ n (Meteo) Tief nt; **low-calorie** adj kalorienarm; **lowcut** adj (dress) tief ausgeschnitten; **low-emission** adj schadstoffarm; **lower** ['ləʊə°] adj niedriger; (storey, class etc) untere(r, s) ▷ vt herunterlassen; (eyes, price) senken; (pressure) verringern; **low-fat** adj fettarm; **low tide** [ləʊˈtaɪd] n Ebbe f

loyal ['lɔɪəl] adj treu; **loyalty** n Treue f

lozenge ['lɒzɪndʒ] n Pastille f

Ltd abbr = **limited** ≈ GmBH f

lubricant ['luːbrɪkənt] n Schmiermittel nt, Gleitmittel nt

luck [lʌk] n Glück nt; **bad ~** Pech

nt; **luckily** adv glücklicherweise, zum Glück; **lucky** adj (number, day etc) Glücks-; **to be ~** Glück haben

ludicrous ['luːdɪkrəs] adj grotesk

luggage ['lʌgɪdʒ] n Gepäck nt; **luggage compartment** n Gepäckraum m; **luggage rack** n Gepäcknetz n

lukewarm ['luːkwɔːm] adj lauwarm

lullaby ['lʌləbaɪ] n Schlaflied nt

lumbago [lʌmˈbeɪgəʊ] n Hexenschuss m

luminous ['luːmɪnəs] adj leuchtend

lump [lʌmp] n Klumpen m; (Med) Schwellung f; (in breast) Knoten m; (of sugar) Stück nt; **lump sum** n Pauschalsumme f; **lumpy** adj klumpig

lunacy ['luːnəsɪ] n Wahnsinn m; **lunatic** ['luːnətɪk] adj wahnsinnig ▷ n Wahnsinnige(r) mf

lunch, luncheon [lʌntʃ, -ən] n Mittagessen nt; **to have ~** zu Mittag essen; **lunch break, lunch hour** n Mittagspause f; **lunchtime** n Mittagszeit f

lung [lʌŋ] n Lunge f

lurch [lɜːtʃ] n: **to leave sb in the ~** jdn im Stich lassen

lurid ['ljʊərɪd] adj (colour) grell; (details) widerlich

lurk [lɜːk] vi lauern

lust [lʌst] n (sinnliche) Begierde f (for nach)

Luxembourg ['lʌksəmbɜːg] n Luxemburg nt; **Luxembourger** [lʌksəmˈbɜːgə°] n Luxemburger(in) m(f)

luxurious [lʌgˈʒʊərɪəs] adj luxuriös, Luxus-; **luxury** ['lʌkʃərɪ] n (a. luxuries pl) Luxus m; **~ goods** Luxusgüter pl

lynx [lɪŋks] n Luchs m

lyrics ['lɪrɪks] npl Liedtext m

m

m *abbr* = **metre** m

M *abbr* (*street*) = **Motorway** A; (*size*) = **medium** M

MA *abbr* = **Master of Arts** Magister Artium m

ma [mɑː] *n* (*fam*) Mutti f

mac [mæk] *n* (*Brit fam*) Regenmantel m

macaroon [mækəˈruːn] *n* Makrone f

Macedonia [mæsɪˈdəʊnɪə] *n* Mazedonien nt

machine [məˈʃiːn] *n* Maschine f; **machine gun** Maschinengewehr nt; **machinery** [məˈʃiːnərɪ] *n* Maschinen pl; (*fig*) Apparat m; **machine washable** *adj* waschmaschinenfest

mackerel [ˈmækrəl] *n* Makrele f

macro [ˈmækrəʊ] (*pl* **-s**) *n* (*Inform*) Makro nt

mad [mæd] *adj* wahnsinnig, verrückt; (*dog*) tollwütig; (*angry*)

wütend, sauer (*at* auf +akk); (*fam*) **~ about** (*fond of*) verrückt nach; **to work like ~** wie verrückt arbeiten; **are you ~?** spinnst du/spinnen Sie?

madam [ˈmædəm] *n* gnädige Frau

mad cow disease [mædˈkaʊdɪziːz] *n* Rinderwahnsinn m; (*fig*) Wahnsinn m

made [meɪd] *pt, pp of* **make**

made-to-measure [ˈmeɪdtəˈmeʒə*] *adj* nach Maß; **~ suit** Maßanzug m

madly [ˈmædlɪ] *adv* wie verrückt; (*with adj*) wahnsinnig; **madman** [ˈmædmən] (*pl* **-men**) *n* Verrückte(r) m; **madwoman** [ˈmædwʊmən] (*pl* **-women**) *n* Verrückte f; **madness** [ˈmædnɪs] *n* Wahnsinn m

magazine [mægəˈziːn] *n* Zeitschrift f

maggot [ˈmægət] *n* Made f

magic [ˈmædʒɪk] *n* Magie f; (*activity*) Zauberei f; (*fig*: *effect*) Zauber m; **as if by ~** wie durch Zauberei ▷ *adj* Zauber-; (*powers*) magisch; **magician** [məˈdʒɪʃən] *n* Zauberer m, Zaub(r)erin f

magnet [ˈmægnɪt] *n* Magnet m; **magnetic** [mægˈnetɪk] *adj* magnetisch; **magnetism** [ˈmægnɪtɪzəm] *n* (*fig*) Anziehungskraft f

magnificent, magnificently [mægˈnɪfɪsənt, -lɪ] *adj, adv* herrlich, großartig

magnify [ˈmægnɪfaɪ] *vt* vergrößern; **magnifying glass** *n* Vergrößerungsglas nt, Lupe f

magpie [ˈmægpaɪ] *n* Elster f

maid [meɪd] *n* Dienstmädchen nt; **maiden name** *n* Mädchenname m; **maiden voyage** *n* Jungfernfahrt f

mail [meɪl] n Post f; (e-mail) Mail f ▷ vt (post) aufgeben; (send) mit der Post schicken (to an +akk); **mailbox** n (US) Briefkasten m; (Inform) Mailbox f; **mailing list** n Adressenliste f; **mailman** n (pl -men) (US) Briefträger m; **mail order** n Bestellung f per Post; **mail order firm** n Versandhaus nt; **mailshot** n Mailing nt

main [meɪn] adj Haupt-; ~ **course** Hauptgericht nt; **the ~ thing** die Hauptsache f ▷ n (pipe) Hauptleitung f; **mainframe** n Großrechner m; **mainland** n Festland nt; **mainly** adv hauptsächlich; **main road** n Hauptverkehrsstraße f; **main street** n (US) Hauptstraße f

maintain [meɪn'teɪn] vt (keep up) aufrechterhalten; (machine, roads) instand halten; (service) warten; (claim) behaupten; **maintenance** ['meɪntənəns] n Instandhaltung f; (Tech) Wartung f

maize [meɪz] n Mais m

majestic [mə'dʒestɪk] adj majestätisch; **majesty** ['mædʒɪstɪ] n Majestät f; **Your/His/Her Majesty** Eure/Seine/Ihre Majestät

major ['meɪdʒə*] adj (bigger) größer; (important) bedeutend; ~ **part** Großteil m; (role) wichtige Rolle; ~ **road** Hauptverkehrsstraße f; (Mus) **A** ~ A-Dur nt ▷ vi (US) **to ~ in sth** etw als Hauptfach studieren

Majorca [mə'jɔːkə] n Mallorca nt

majority [mə'dʒɒrɪtɪ] n Mehrheit f; **to be in the ~** in der Mehrzahl sein

make [meɪk] n Marke f ▷ vt (made, made) machen; (manufacture) herstellen; (clothes) anfertigen; (dress) nähen; (soup) zubereiten; (bread, cake) backen; (tea, coffee) kochen; (speech) halten; (earn) verdienen; (decision) treffen; **it's made of gold** es ist aus Gold; **to ~ sb do sth** jdn dazu bringen, etw zu tun; (force) jdn zwingen, etw zu tun; **she made us wait** sie ließ uns warten; **what ~s you think that?** wie kommen Sie darauf; **it ~s the room look smaller** es lässt den Raum kleiner wirken; **to ~ (it to) the airport** (reach) den Flughafen erreichen; (in time) es zum Flughafen schaffen; **he never really made it** er hat es nie zu etwas gebracht; **she didn't ~ it through the night** sie hat die Nacht nicht überlebt; (calculate) **I ~ it £5/a quarter to six** nach meiner Rechnung kommt es auf 5 Pfund/nach meiner Uhr ist es dreiviertel sechs; **he's just made for this job** er ist für diese Arbeit wie geschaffen; **make for** vt zusteuern auf +akk; **make of** vt (think of) halten von; **I couldn't ~ anything of it** ich wurde daraus nicht schlau; **make off** vi sich davonmachen (with mit); **make out** vi zurechtkommen ▷ vt (cheque) ausstellen; (list) aufstellen; (understand) verstehen; (discern) ausmachen; **to ~ (that) ...** es so hinstellen, als ob ...; **make up** vt (team etc) bilden; (face) schminken; (invent: story etc) erfinden; **to ~ one's mind** sich entscheiden; **to make (it) up with sb** sich mit jdm aussöhnen ▷ vi sich versöhnen; **make up for** vt ausgleichen; (time) aufholen

make-believe adj Fantasie-; **makeover** n gründliche Veränderung, Verschönerung f; **maker** n (Comm) Hersteller(in) m(f); **makeshift** adj behelfsmäßig; **make-up** n

Make-up nt, Schminke f; **making** ['meɪkɪŋ] n Herstellung f

maladjusted [mælə'dʒʌstɪd] adj verhaltensgestört

malaria [mə'lɛərɪə] n Malaria f

Malaysia [mə'leɪzɪə] n Malaysia nt

male [meɪl] n Mann m; (animal) Männchen nt ▷ adj männlich; **~ chauvinist** Chauvi m, Macho m; **~ nurse** Krankenpfleger m

malfunction [mæl'fʌŋkʃən] vi nicht richtig funktionieren ▷ n Defekt m

malice ['mælɪs] n Bosheit f;

malicious [mə'lɪʃəs] adj boshaft; (behaviour, action) böswillig; (damage) mutwillig

malignant [mə'lɪgnənt] adj bösartig

mall [mɔːl] n (US) Einkaufszentrum nt

malnutrition [mælnjʊ'trɪʃən] n Unterernährung f

malt [mɔːlt] n Malz nt

Malta ['mɔːltə] n Malta nt; **Maltese** [mɔːl'tiːz] adj maltesisch ▷ n (person) Malteser(in) m(f); (language) Maltesisch nt

maltreat [mæl'triːt] vt schlecht behandeln; (violently) misshandeln

mammal ['mæməl] n Säugetier nt

mammoth ['mæməθ] adj Mammut-, Riesen-

man [mæn] (pl **men**) n (male) Mann m; (human race) der Mensch, die Menschen pl; (in chess) Figur f ▷ vt besetzen

manage ['mænɪdʒ] vi zurechtkommen; **can you ~?** schaffst du es?; **to ~ without sth** ohne etw auskommen, auf etw verzichten können ▷ vt (control) leiten; (musician, sportsman) managen; (cope with) fertig werden mit; (task,

portion, climb etc) schaffen; **to ~ to do sth** es schaffen, etw zu tun;

manageable adj (object) handlich; (task) zu bewältigen;

management n Leitung f; (directors) Direktion f; (subject) Management nt, Betriebswirtschaft f;

management consultant n Unternehmensberater(in) m(f);

manager n Geschäftsführer(in) m(f); (departmental ~) Abteilungsleiter(in) m(f); (of branch, bank) Filialleiter(in) m(f); (of musician, sportsman) Manager(in) m(f); **managing director** n Geschäftsführer(in) m(f)

mane [meɪn] n Mähne f

maneuver (US) see **manoeuvre**

mango ['mæŋgəʊ] (pl **-es**) n Mango f

man-hour n Arbeitsstunde f

manhunt n Fahndung f

mania ['meɪnɪə] n Manie f; **maniac** ['meɪnɪæk] n Wahnsinnige(r) mf; (fan) Fanatiker(in) m(f)

manicure ['mænɪkjʊə°] n Maniküre f

manipulate [mə'nɪpjʊleɪt] vt manipulieren

mankind [mæn'kaɪnd] n Menschheit f

manly ['mænlɪ] adj männlich

man-made ['mænmeɪd] adj (product) künstlich

manner ['mænə°] n Art f; **in this ~** auf diese Art und Weise; **~s** pl Manieren pl

manoeuvre [mə'nuːvə°] n Manöver nt ▷ vt, vi manövrieren

manor ['mænə°] n: **~ (house)** Herrenhaus nt

manpower ['mænpaʊə°] n Arbeitskräfte pl

mansion ['mænʃən] n Villa f; (of old family) Herrenhaus nt

manslaughter ['mænslɔːtə°] n
Totschlag m

mantelpiece ['mæntlpiːs] n
Kaminsims m

manual ['mænjʊəl] adj manuell,
Hand- ▷ n Handbuch nt

manufacture [mænjʊ'fæktʃə°]
vt herstellen ▷ n Herstellung f;
manufacturer n Hersteller m

manure [mə'njʊə°] n Dung m;
(esp artificial) Dünger m

many ['menɪ] (**more, most**) adj,
pron viele; ~ **times** oft; **not**
~ **people** nicht viele Leute; **too**
~ **problems** zu viele Probleme

map [mæp] n Landkarte f; (of
town) Stadtplan m

maple ['meɪpl] n Ahorn m

marathon ['mærəθən] n Marathon m

marble ['mɑːbl] n Marmor m; (for
playing) Murmel f

march [mɑːtʃ] vi marschieren
▷ n Marsch m; (protest)
Demonstration f

March [mɑːtʃ] n März m; see also
September

mare [meə°] n Stute f

margarine [mɑːdʒə'riːn] n
Margarine f

margin ['mɑːdʒɪn] n Rand m;
(extra amount) Spielraum m;
(Comm) Gewinnspanne f;
marginal adj (difference etc)
geringfügig

marijuana [mærjʊ'ɑːnə] n
Marihuana nt

marine [mə'riːn] adj Meeres-

marital ['mærɪtl] adj ehelich;
~ **status** Familienstand m

maritime ['mærɪtaɪm] adj See-

marjoram ['mɑːdʒərəm] n
Majoran m

mark [mɑːk] n (spot) Fleck m; (at
school) Note f; (sign) Zeichen nt
▷ vt (make ~) Flecken machen auf
+akk; (indicate) markieren;

(schoolwork) benoten, korrigieren,
Flecken machen auf +akk;
markedly ['mɑːkɪdlɪ] adv merk-
lich; (with comp adj) wesentlich;
marker n (in book) Lesezeichen nt;
(pen) Marker m

market ['mɑːkɪt] n Markt m;
(stock ~) Börse f ▷ vt (Comm: new
product) auf den Markt bringen;
(goods) vertreiben; **marketing** n
Marketing nt; **market leader** n
Marktführer m; **market place** n
Marktplatz m; **market research** n
Marktforschung f

marmalade ['mɑːməleɪd] n
Orangenmarmelade f

maroon [mə'ruːn] adj rötlich
braun

marquee [mɑː'kiː] n großes Zelt

marriage ['mærɪdʒ] n Ehe f;
(wedding) Heirat f (to mit);
married ['mærɪd] adj (person)
verheiratet

marrow ['mærəʊ] n (bone~)
Knochenmark nt; (vegetable) Kürbis
m

marry ['mærɪ] vt heiraten; (join)
trauen; (take as husband, wife)
heiraten ▷ vi: **to ~ / to get**
married heiraten

marsh [mɑːʃ] n Marsch f, Sumpf
m

marshal ['mɑːʃəl] n (at rally etc)
Ordner m; (US: police)
Bezirkspolizeichef m

martial arts ['mɑːʃəl'ɑːts] npl
Kampfsportarten pl

martyr ['mɑːtə°] n Märtyrer(in)
m(f)

marvel ['mɑːvəl] n Wunder nt
▷ vi staunen (at über +akk);
marvellous, marvelous (US) adj
wunderbar

marzipan [mɑːzɪ'pæn] n Marzipan nt o m

mascara [mæ'skɑːrə] n Wimperntusche f

mascot ['mæskɒt] n Maskottchen nt

masculine ['mæskjʊlɪn] adj männlich

mashed [mæʃt] adj ~ **potatoes** pl Kartoffelbrei m, Kartoffelpüree nt

mask [mɑːsk] n (a. Inform) Maske f ▷ vt (feelings) verbergen

masochist ['mæsəʊkɪst] n Masochist(in) m(f)

mason ['meɪsn] n (stone~) Steinmetz(in) m(f); **masonry** n Mauerwerk nt

mass [mæs] n Masse f; (of people) Menge f; (Rel) Messe f; **~es of** massenhaft

massacre ['mæsəkə°] n Blutbad nt

massage ['mæsɑːʒ] n Massage f ▷ vt massieren

massive ['mæsɪv] adj (powerful) gewaltig; (very large) riesig

mass media ['mæs'miːdɪə] npl Massenmedien pl; **mass-produce** vt in Massenproduktion herstellen; **mass production** n Massenproduktion f

master ['mɑːstə°] n Herr m; (of dog) Besitzer m, Herrchen nt; (teacher) Lehrer m; (artist) Meister m ▷ vt meistern; (language etc) beherrschen; **masterly** adj meisterhaft; **masterpiece** n Meisterwerk nt

masturbate ['mæstəbeɪt] vi masturbieren

mat [mæt] n Matte f; (for table) Untersetzer m

match [mætʃ] n Streichholz nt; (Sport) Wettkampf m; (ball games) Spiel nt; (tennis) Match nt ▷ vt (be like, suit) passen zu; (equal) gleichkommen +dat ▷ vi zusammenpassen; **matchbox** n Streichholzschachtel f; **matching** adj (one item)

passend; (two items) zusammenpassend

mate [meɪt] n (companion) Kumpel m; (of animal) Weibchen nt/Männchen nt ▷ vi sich paaren

material [mə'tɪərɪəl] n Material nt; (for book etc, cloth) Stoff m; **materialistic** [mətɪərɪə'lɪstɪk] adj materialistisch; **materialize** [mə'tɪərɪəlaɪz] vi zustande kommen; (hope) wahr werden

maternal [mə'tɜːnl] adj mütterlich; **maternity** [mə'tɜːnɪtɪ] adj; **~ dress** Umstandskleid nt; **~ leave** Elternzeit f (der Mutter); **~ ward** Entbindungsstation f

math [mæθ] n (US fam) Mathe f; **mathematical** [mæθə'mætɪkəl] adj mathematisch; **mathematics** [mæθə'mætɪks] nsing Mathematik f; **maths** [mæθs] nsing (Brit fam) Mathe f

matinée ['mætɪneɪ] n Nachmittagsvorstellung f

matter ['mætə°] n (substance) Materie f; (affair) Sache f; a **personal ~** eine persönliche Angelegenheit; **~ of taste** eine Frage des Geschmacks; **no ~ how/what** egal wie/was; **what's the ~?** was ist los?; **as a ~ of fact** eigentlich; **a ~ of time** eine Frage der Zeit ▷ vi darauf ankommen, wichtig sein; **it doesn't ~** es macht nichts; **matter-of-fact** adj sachlich, nüchtern

mattress ['mætrəs] n Matratze f

mature [mə'tjʊə°] adj reif ▷ vi reif werden; **maturity** [mə'tjʊərɪtɪ] n Reife f

maximum ['mæksɪməm] adj Höchst-, höchste(r, s); **~ speed** Höchstgeschwindigkeit f ▷ n Maximum nt

may [meɪ] (**might**) vb aux (be

possible) können; *(have permission)* dürfen; **it ~ rain** es könnte regnen; **~ I smoke?** darf ich rauchen?; **it ~ not happen** es passiert vielleicht gar nicht; **we ~ as well go** wir können ruhig gehen

May [meɪ] *n* Mai *m; see also* **September**

maybe ['meɪbiː] *adv* vielleicht

May Day ['meɪdeɪ] *n* der erste Mai

mayo ['meɪəʊ] *(US fam)*, **mayonnaise** [meɪə'neɪz] *n* Mayo *f*, Mayonnaise *f*, Majonäse *f*

mayor [mɛəʳ] *n* Bürgermeister *m*

maze [meɪz] *n* Irrgarten *m*; *(fig)* Wirrwarr *nt*

MB *abbr* = **megabyte** MB *nt*

⊙ **KEYWORD**

me [miː] *pron* **1** *(direct)* mich; **it's me** ich bin's
2 *(indirect)* mir; **give them to me** gib sie mir
3 *(after prep)* (+*akk*) mich; (+*dat*) mir; **with/without me** mit mir/ohne mich

meadow ['medəʊ] *n* Wiese *f*

meal [miːl] *n* Essen *nt*, Mahlzeit *f*; **to go out for a ~** essen gehen; **meal pack** *n (US)* tiefgekühltes Fertiggericht; **meal time** *n* Essenszeit *f*

mean [miːn] *(meant, meant) vt (signify)* bedeuten; *(have in mind)* meinen; *(intend)* vorhaben; **what do you ~ (by that)?** was willst du damit sagen?; **to ~ to do sth** etw tun wollen; **it was ~t for you** es war für dich bestimmt *(o gedacht)*; **it was ~t to be a joke** es sollte ein Witz sein ▷ *vi*: **he ~s well** er

meint es gut ▷ *adj (stingy)* geizig; *(spiteful)* gemein *(to zu)*; **meaning** ['miːnɪŋ] *n* Bedeutung *f*; *(of life, poem)* Sinn *m*; **meaningful** *adj* sinnvoll; **meaningless** *adj (text)* ohne Sinn

means [miːnz] *(pl* **means**) *n* Mittel *nt*; *(pl: funds)* Mittel *pl*; **by ~ of** durch, mittels; **by all ~** selbstverständlich; **by no ~** keineswegs; **~ of transport** Beförderungsmittel

meant [ment] *pt, pp of* **mean**

meantime [miːn'taɪm] *adv*: **in the ~** inzwischen; **meanwhile** [miːn'waɪl] *adv* inzwischen

measles ['miːzlz] *nsing* Masern *pl*; **German ~** Röteln *pl*

measure ['meʒəʳ] *vt, vi* messen ▷ *n (unit, device for measuring)* Maß *nt*; *(step)* Maßnahme *f*; **to take ~s** Maßnahmen ergreifen; **measurement** *n (amount measured)* Maß *nt*

meat [miːt] *n* Fleisch *nt*; **meatball** *n* Fleischbällchen *nt*

mechanic [mɪ'kænɪk] *n* Mechaniker(in) *m(f)*; **mechanical** *adj* mechanisch; **mechanics** *nsing* Mechanik *f*; **mechanism** ['mekənɪzəm] *n* Mechanismus *m*

medal ['medl] *n* Medaille *f*; *(decoration)* Orden *m*; **medalist** *(US)*, **medallist** ['medəlɪst] *n* Medaillengewinner(in) *m(f)*

media ['miːdɪə] *npl* Medien *pl*

median strip ['miːdɪən strɪp] *n (US)* Mittelstreifen *m*

mediate ['miːdɪeɪt] *vi* vermitteln

medical ['medɪkəl] *adj* medizinisch; *(treatment etc)* ärztlich; **~ student** Medizinstudent(in) *m(f)* ▷ *n* Untersuchung *f*; **Medicare** ['medɪkɛəʳ] *n (US)* Krankenkasse *f* für ältere Leute; **medication**

[medɪˈkeɪʃən] n Medikamente pl;
to be on ~ Medikamente nehmen;
medicinal [meˈdɪsɪnl] adj Heil-;
medicine [ˈmedsɪn] n Arznei f;
(science) Medizin f
medieval [medɪˈiːvəl] adj
mittelalterlich
mediocre [miːdɪˈəʊkəʳ] adj
mittelmäßig
meditate [ˈmedɪteɪt] vi meditieren; (fig) nachdenken (on über
+akk)
Mediterranean
[medɪtəˈreɪnɪən] n (sea)
Mittelmeer nt; (region)
Mittelmeerraum m
medium [ˈmiːdɪəm] adj (quality,
size) mittlere(r, s); (steak)
halbdurch; **~ (dry)** (wine)
halbtrocken; **~ sized** mittelgroß;
~ wave Mittelwelle f ▷ n (pl
media) Medium nt; (means) Mittel
nt
meet [miːt] (**met, met**) vt
treffen; (by arrangement) sich
treffen mit; (difficulties) stoßen auf
+akk; (get to know) kennenlernen;
(requirement, demand) gerecht
werden +dat; (deadline) einhalten;
pleased to ~ you sehr angenehm!;
to ~ sb at the station jdn vom
Bahnhof abholen ▷ vi sich
treffen; (become acquainted) sich
kennenlernen; **we've met
(before)** wir kennen uns schon;
meet up vt sich treffen (with
mit); **meet with** vt (group)
zusammenkommen mit;
(difficulties, resistance etc) stoßen
auf +akk; **meeting** n Treffen nt;
(business ~) Besprechung f; (of
committee) Sitzung f; (assembly)
Versammlung f; **meeting place,
meeting point** n Treffpunkt m
megabyte [ˈmegəbaɪt] n
Megabyte nt
melody [ˈmelədɪ] n Melodie f

melon [ˈmelən] n Melone f
melt [melt] vt, vi schmelzen
member [ˈmembəʳ] n Mitglied
nt; (of tribe, species) Angehörige(r)
mf; **Member of Parliament**
Parlamentsabgeordnete(r) mf;
membership n Mitgliedschaft f;
membership card n
Mitgliedskarte f
memento [məˈmentəʊ] (pl -es)
n Andenken nt (of an +akk)
memo [ˈmeməʊ] (pl -s) n
Mitteilung f, Memo nt; **memo pad**
n Notizblock m
memorable [ˈmemərəbl] adj
unvergesslich; **memorial**
[mɪˈmɔːrɪəl] n Denkmal nt (to
für); **memorize** [ˈmeməraɪz] vt
sich einprägen, auswendig lernen;
memory [ˈmeməri] n Gedächtnis nt; (Inform: of computer)
Speicher m; (sth recalled)
Erinnerung f; **in ~ of** zur
Erinnerung an +akk; **memory card**
n Speicherkarte f; **memory stick**
n (Inform) Memorystick® m
men [men] pl of **man**
menace [ˈmenɪs] n Bedrohung f;
(danger) Gefahr f
mend [mend] vt reparieren;
(clothes) flicken ▷ n: **on the ~** auf
dem Wege der Besserung
meningitis [menɪnˈdʒaɪtɪs] n
Hirnhautentzündung f
menopause [ˈmenəʊpɔːz] n
Wechseljahre pl
mental [ˈmentl] adj geistig;
mentality [menˈtælɪtɪ] n Mentalität f; **mentally** [ˈmentlɪ] adv
geistig; **~ handicapped** geistig
behindert; **~ ill** geisteskrank
mention [ˈmenʃən] n Erwäh-
nung f ▷ vt erwähnen (to sb jdm
gegenüber); **don't ~ it** bitte sehr,
gern geschehen
menu [ˈmenjuː] n Speisekarte f;
(Inform) Menü nt

merchandise ['mɜːtʃəndaɪz] n
Handelsware f; **merchant**
['mɜːtʃənt] adj Handels-

merciful ['mɜːsɪfʊl] adj gnädig;
mercifully adv glücklicherweise

mercury ['mɜːkjʊrɪ] n Quecksilber nt

mercy ['mɜːsɪ] n Gnade f

mere [mɪə°] adj Verdienst nt;
['mɪəlɪ] adv bloß, lediglich

merge [mɜːdʒ] vi verschmelzen;
(Auto) sich einfädeln; (Comm)
fusionieren; **merger** n (Comm)
Fusion f

meringue [mə'ræŋ] n Baiser nt

merit ['merɪt] n Verdienst nt;
(advantage) Vorzug m

merry ['merɪ] adj fröhlich; (fam:
tipsy) angeheitert; **Merry**
Christmas Fröhliche
Weihnachten!; **merry-go-round** n
Karussell nt

mess [mes] n Unordnung f;
(muddle) Durcheinander nt; (dirty)
Schweinerei f;
Schwierigkeiten pl; **in a**
~ (muddled) durcheinander; (untidy)
unordentlich; (fig: person) in der
Klemme; **to make a ~ of sth** etw
verpfuschen; **to look a**
~ unmöglich aussehen; **mess**
about vi (tinker with)
herummurksen (with an +dat);
(play the fool) herumalbern; (do
nothing in particular)
herumgammeln; **mess up** vt
verpfuschen; (make untidy) in
Unordnung bringen; (dirty)
schmutzig machen

message ['mesɪdʒ] n Mitteilung
f, Nachricht f; (meaning) Botschaft
f; **can I give him a ~?** kann ich
ihm etwas ausrichten?; **please**
leave a ~ (on answerphones)
bitte hinterlassen Sie eine
Nachricht; **I get the ~** ich hab's
verstanden

messenger ['mesɪndʒə°] n Bote
m

messy ['mesɪ] adj (untidy)
unordentlich; (situation etc)
verfahren

met [met] pt, pp of **meet**

metal ['metl] n Metall nt;
metallic [mɪ'tælɪk] adj
metallisch

meteorology [miːtɪə'rɒlədʒɪ] n
Meteorologie f

meter ['miːtə°] n Zähler m;
(parking meter) Parkuhr f; (US) see
metre

method ['meθəd] n Methode f;
methodical [mɪ'θɒdɪkəl] adj
methodisch

meticulous [mɪ'tɪkjʊləs] adj
(peinlich) genau

metre ['miːtə°] n Meter m o nt;
metric ['metrɪk] adj metrisch;
~ system Dezimalsystem nt

Mexico ['meksɪkəʊ] n Mexiko nt

mice [maɪs] pl of **mouse**

mickey ['mɪkɪ] n: **to take the**
~ (out of sb) (fam) (jdn) auf den
Arm nehmen

microchip ['maɪkrəʊtʃɪp] n
(Inform) Mikrochip m; **microphone**
n Mikrofon nt; **microscope**
n Mikroskop nt; **microwave (oven)**
n Mikrowelle(nherd) f(m)

mid [mɪd] adj: **in ~ January**
Mitte Januar; **he's in his ~ forties**
er ist Mitte vierzig

midday ['mɪd'deɪ] n Mittag m;
at ~ mittags

middle ['mɪdl] n Mitte f; (waist)
Taille f; **in the ~ of** mitten in +dat;
to be in the ~ of doing sth gerade
dabei sein, etw zu tun ▷ adj
mittlere(r, s), Mittel-; **the ~ one**
der/die/das Mittlere;
middle-aged adj mittleren
Alters; **Middle Ages** npl: **the**
~ das Mittelalter; **middle-class**
adj mittelständisch; (bourgeois)

bürgerlich; **middle classes** *npl*:
the ~ der Mittelstand; **Middle
East** *n*: the ~ der Nahe Osten;
middle name *n* zweiter
Vorname

Midlands ['mɪdləndz] *npl*: the
~ Mittelengland *nt*

midnight ['mɪdnaɪt] *n* Mitternacht *f*

midst [mɪdst] *n*: in the ~ of
mitten in +*dat*

midsummer ['mɪdsʌmə°] *n*
Hochsommer *m*; **Midsummer's
Day** Sommersonnenwende *f*

midway [mɪd'weɪ] *adv* auf
halbem Wege; ~ through the film
nach der Hälfte des Films;
midweek [mɪd'wiːk] *adj, adv* in
der Mitte der Woche

midwife ['mɪdwaɪf] (*pl* -**wives**) *n*
Hebamme *f*

midwinter [mɪd'wɪntə°] *n*
tiefster Winter

might [maɪt] *pt of* **may**:
(*possibility*) könnte; (*permission*)
dürfte; (*would*) würde; **they** ~ **still
come** sie könnten noch kommen;
he ~ have let me know er hätte
mir doch Bescheid sagen können;
I thought she ~ change her mind
ich dachte schon, sie würde sich
anders entscheiden ▷ *n* Macht *f*,
Kraft *f*

mighty ['maɪtɪ] *adj* gewaltig,
(*powerful*) mächtig

migraine ['miːgreɪn] *n* Migräne
f

migrant ['maɪgrənt] *n* (*bird*)
Zugvogel *m*; ~ **worker**
Gastarbeiter(in) *m(f)*; Migrant(in)
m(f); **migrate** ['maɪ'greɪt] *vi*
abwandern; (*birds*) nach Süden
ziehen

mike [maɪk] *n* (*fam*) Mikro *nt*

Milan [mɪ'læn] *n* Mailand *nt*

mild [maɪld] *adj* mild; (*person*)
sanft; **mildly** *adv*: to put it

~ gelinde gesagt; **mildness** *n*
Milde *f*

mile [maɪl] *n* Meile *f* (=1,609 km);
for ~s (and ~s) = kilometerweit; **~s
per hour** Meilen pro Stunde; **~s
better than** hundertmal besser
als; **mileage** ⇒ Meilen *pl*,
Meilenzahl *f*; **mileometer**
[maɪ'lɒmɪtə°] *n* =
Kilometerzähler *m*; **milestone** *n*
(*a. fig*) Meilenstein *m*

militant ['mɪlɪtənt] *adj* militant;
military ['mɪlɪtərɪ] *adj* Militär-,
militärisch

milk [mɪlk] *n* Milch *f* ▷ *vt*
melken; **milk chocolate** *n*
Vollmilchschokolade *f*; **milkman**
(*pl* -**men**) *n* Milchmann *m*; **milk
shake** *n* Milchshake *m*,
Milchmixgetränk *nt*

mill [mɪl] *n* Mühle *f*; (*factory*)
Fabrik *f*

millennium [mɪ'lenɪəm] *n*
Jahrtausend *nt*

milligramme ['mɪlɪgræm] *n*
Milligramm *nt*; **milliliter** (US),
millilitre *n* Milliliter *m*;
millimeter (US), **millimetre** *n*
Millimeter *m*

million ['mɪljən] *n* Million *f*; **five
~** fünf Millionen; **~s of people**
Millionen von Menschen;
millionaire [mɪljə'neə°] *n* Mil-
lionär(in) *m(f)*

mime [maɪm] *n* Pantomime *f*
▷ *vt, vi* mimen; **mimic** ['mɪmɪk]
n Imitator(in) *m(f)* ▷ *vt, vi*
nachahmen; **mimicry** ['mɪmɪkrɪ]
n Nachahmung *f*

mince [mɪns] *vt* (zer)hacken
▷ *n* (*meat*) Hackfleisch *nt*;
mincemeat *n* süße Gebäckfüllung
aus Rosinen, Äpfeln, Zucker, Gewürzen
und Talg; **mince pie** *n* mit
'mincemeat' gefülltes süßes
Weihnachtsgebäck

mind [maɪnd] *n* (*intellect*)

Verstand m; *(also person)* Geist m; **out of sight, out of ~** aus den Augen, aus dem Sinn; **he is out of his ~** er ist nicht bei Verstand; **to keep sth in ~** etw im Auge behalten; **do you have sth in ~?** denken Sie an etwas Besonderes?; **I've a lot on my ~** mich beschäftigt so vieles im Moment; **to change one's ~** es sich *dat* anders überlegen ▷ vt *(look after)* aufpassen auf +akk; *(object to)* etwas haben gegen ...; **~ you,** ... allerdings ...; **I wouldn't ~ ...** ich hätte nichts gegen ...; **"~ the step"** „Vorsicht Stufe!" ▷ vi etwas dagegen haben; **do you ~ if I ...** macht es Ihnen etwas aus, wenn ich ...; **I don't ~** es ist mir egal, meinetwegen; **never ~** macht nichts

mine [maɪn] *pron* meine(r, s); **this is ~** das gehört mir; **a friend of ~** ein Freund von mir ▷ n *(coalmine)* Bergwerk nt; *(Mil)* Mine f; **miner** n Bergarbeiter(in) m(f)

mineral ['mɪnərəl] n Mineral nt; **mineral water** n Mineralwasser nt

mingle ['mɪŋgl] vi sich mischen *(with* unter +akk)

miniature ['mɪnɪtʃə°] adj Miniatur-

minibar ['mɪnɪbɑːʳ] n Minibar f; **minibus** n Kleinbus m; **minicab** n Kleintaxi nt

minimal ['mɪnɪml] adj minimal; **minimize** ['mɪnɪmaɪz] vt auf ein Minimum reduzieren; **minimum** ['mɪnɪməm] n Minimum nt ▷ adj Mindest-

mining ['maɪnɪŋ] n Bergbau m

miniskirt n Minirock m

minister ['mɪnɪstəʳ] n *(Pol)* Minister(in) m(f); *(Rel)* Pastor(in) m(f), Pfarrer(in) m(f); **ministry** ['mɪnɪstrɪ] n *(Pol)* Ministerium nt

minor ['maɪnəʳ] adj kleiner; *(insignificant)* unbedeutend; *(operation, offence)* harmlos; **~ road** Nebenstraße f; *(Mus)* **A ~** a-Moll nt ▷ n *(Brit: under 18)* Minderjährige(r) mf; **minority** [maɪ'nɒrɪtɪ] n Minderheit f

mint [mɪnt] n Minze f; *(sweet)* Pfefferminz(bonbon) nt; **mint sauce** n Minzsoße f

minus ['maɪnəs] prep minus; *(without)* ohne

minute [maɪ'njuːt] adj winzig; **in ~ detail** genauestens ▷ ['mɪnɪt] n Minute f; **just a ~** Moment mal!; **any ~** jeden Augenblick; **~s** pl *(of meeting)* Protokoll nt

miracle ['mɪrəkl] n Wunder nt; **miraculous** [mɪ'rækjʊləs] adj unglaublich

mirage ['mɪrɑːʒ] n Fata Morgana f, Luftspiegelung f

mirror ['mɪrəʳ] n Spiegel m

misbehave [mɪsbɪ'heɪv] vi sich schlecht benehmen

miscalculation ['mɪskælkjʊ'leɪʃən] n Fehlkalkulation f; *(misjudgement)* Fehleinschätzung f

miscarriage [mɪs'kærɪdʒ] n *(Med)* Fehlgeburt f

miscellaneous [mɪsɪ'leɪnɪəs] adj verschieden

mischief ['mɪstʃɪf] n Unfug m; **mischievous** ['mɪstʃɪvəs] adj *(person)* durchtrieben; *(glance)* verschmitzt

misconception [mɪskən'sepʃən] n falsche Vorstellung

misconduct [mɪs'kɒndʌkt] n Vergehen nt

miser ['maɪzəʳ] n Geizhals m

miserable ['mɪzərəbl] adj *(person)* todunglücklich; *(conditions, life)* elend; *(pay, weather)* miserabel

miserly ['maɪzəlɪ] adj geizig

misery ['mɪzərɪ] n Elend nt; (suffering) Qualen pl

misfit ['mɪsfɪt] n Außenseiter(in) m(f)

misfortune [mɪs'fɔːtʃən] n Pech nt

misguided [mɪs'gaɪdɪd] adj irrig; (optimism) unangebracht

misinform [mɪsɪn'fɔːm] vt falsch informieren

misinterpret [mɪsɪn'tɜːprɪt] vt falsch auslegen

misjudge [mɪs'dʒʌdʒ] vt falsch beurteilen

mislay [mɪs'leɪ] irr vt verlegen

mislead [mɪs'liːd] irr vt irreführen; **misleading** adj irreführend

misprint ['mɪsprɪnt] n Druckfehler m

mispronounce [mɪsprə'naʊns] vt falsch aussprechen

miss [mɪs] vt (fail to hit, catch) verfehlen; (not notice, hear) nicht mitbekommen; (be too late for) verpassen; (chance) versäumen; (regret the absence of) vermissen; **I ~ you** du fehlst mir ▷ vi nicht treffen; (shooting) danebenschießen; (ball, shot etc) danebengehen; **miss out** vt auslassen ▷ vi: **to ~ on sth** etw verpassen

Miss [mɪs] n (unmarried woman) Fräulein nt

missile ['mɪsaɪl] n Geschoss nt; (rocket) Rakete f

missing ['mɪsɪŋ] adj (person) vermisst; (thing) fehlend; **to be/go ~** vermisst werden, fehlen

mission ['mɪʃən] n (Pol, Mil, Rel) Auftrag m, Mission f; **missionary** ['mɪʃənrɪ] n Missionar(in) m(f)

mist [mɪst] n (feiner) Nebel m; (haze) Dunst m; **mist over, mist up** vi sich beschlagen

mistake [mɪ'steɪk] n Fehler m; **by ~** aus Versehen ▷ irr vt

(mistook, mistaken) (misunderstand) falsch verstehen; (mix up) verwechseln (for mit); **there's no mistaking ...** ... ist unverkennbar; (meaning) ... ist unmissverständlich; **mistaken** adj (idea, identity) falsch; **to be ~** sich irren, falschliegen

mistletoe ['mɪsltəʊ] n Mistel f

mistreat [mɪs'triːt] vt schlecht behandeln

mistress ['mɪstrɪs] n (lover) Geliebte f

mistrust [mɪs'trʌst] n Misstrauen nt (of gegen) ▷ vt misstrauen +dat

misty ['mɪstɪ] adj neblig; (hazy) dunstig

misunderstand [mɪsʌndə'stænd] irr vt, vi falsch verstehen; **misunderstanding** n Missverständnis nt; (disagreement) Differenz f

mitten ['mɪtn] n Fausthandschuh m

mix [mɪks] n (mixture) Mischung f ▷ vt mischen; (blend) vermischen (with mit); (drinks, music) mixen; **to ~ business with pleasure** das Angenehme mit dem Nützlichen verbinden ▷ vi (liquids) sich vermischen lassen; **mix up** vt (mix) zusammenmischen; (confuse) verwechseln (with mit); **mixed** adj gemischt; **a ~ bunch** eine bunt gemischte Truppe; **~ grill** Mixed Grill m; **~ vegetables** Mischgemüse nt; **mixer** n (for food) Mixer m; **mixture** ['mɪkstʃə²] n Mischung f; (Med) Saft m; **mix-up** n Durcheinander nt, Missverständnis nt

ml abbr = **millilitre** ml

mm abbr = **millimetre** mm

moan [məʊn] n Stöhnen nt; (complaint) Gejammer nt ▷ vi

stöhnen; (complain) jammern, meckern (about über +akk)

mobile ['məʊbaɪl] adj beweglich; (on wheels) fahrbar ▷ n (phone) Handy nt; **mobile phone** n Mobiltelefon nt, Handy nt; **mobile-phone mast** Handymast m

mobility [məʊ'bɪlɪtɪ] n Beweglichkeit f

mock [mɒk] vt verspotten ▷ adj Schein-; **mockery** n Spott m

mod cons ['mɒd'kɒnz] abbr = **modern conveniences** (moderner) Komfort

mode [məʊd] n Art f; (Inform) Modus m

model ['mɒdl] n Modell nt; (example) Vorbild nt; (fashion ~) Model nt ▷ adj (miniature) Modell-; (perfect) Muster- ▷ vt (make) formen ▷ vi: **she ~s for Versace** sie arbeitet als Model bei Versace

modem ['məʊdem] n Modem nt

moderate ['mɒdərət] adj mäßig; (views, politics) gemäßigt; (income, success) mittelmäßig ▷ n (Pol) Gemäßigte(r) mf ▷ ['mɒdəreɪt] vt mäßigen; **moderation** [mɒdə'reɪʃən] n Mäßigung f; **in ~** mit Maßen

modern ['mɒdən] adj modern; **~ history** neuere Geschichte; **~ Greek** Neugriechisch nt; **modernize** ['mɒdənaɪz] vt modernisieren

modest ['mɒdɪst] adj bescheiden; **modesty** n Bescheidenheit f

modification [mɒdɪfɪ'keɪʃən] n Abänderung f; **modify** ['mɒdɪfaɪ] vt abändern

moist [mɔɪst] adj feucht; **moisten** ['mɔɪsn] vt befeuchten; **moisture** n Feuchtigkeit f; **moisturizer** n Feuchtigkeitscreme f

molar ['məʊləʳ] n Backenzahn m

mold (US) see **mould**

mole [məʊl] n (spot) Leberfleck m; (animal) Maulwurf m

molecule ['mɒlɪkju:l] n Molekül nt

molest [məʊ'lest] vt belästigen

molt (US) see **moult**

molten ['məʊltən] adj geschmolzen

mom [mɒm] n (US) Mutti f

moment ['məʊmənt] n Moment m, Augenblick m; **just a ~** Moment mal; **at** (o for) **the ~** im Augenblick; **in a ~** gleich

momentous [məʊ'mentəs] adj bedeutsam

Monaco ['mɒnəkəʊ] n Monaco nt

monarch ['mɒnək] n Monarchie f

monastery ['mɒnəstrɪ] n (for monks) Kloster nt

Monday ['mʌndeɪ] n Montag m; see also **Tuesday**

monetary ['mʌnɪtərɪ] adj (reform, policy, union) Währungs-; **~ unit** Geldeinheit f

money ['mʌnɪ] n Geld nt; **to get one's ~'s worth** auf seine Kosten kommen; **money order** n Postanweisung f

mongrel ['mʌŋgrəl] n Promenadenmischung f

monitor ['mɒnɪtəʳ] n (screen) Monitor m ▷ vt (progress etc) überwachen; (broadcasts) abhören

monk [mʌŋk] n Mönch m

monkey ['mʌŋkɪ] n Affe m; **~ business** Unfug m

monopolize [mə'nɒpəlaɪz] vt monopolisieren; (fig: person, thing) in Beschlag nehmen; **monopoly** [mə'nɒpəlɪ] n Monopol nt

monotonous [mə'nɒtənəs] adj eintönig, monoton

monsoon [mɒn'su:n] n Monsun m

monster ['mɒnstəʳ] n (animal,

m

thing) Monstrum nt ▷ *adj* Riesen-;
monstrosity [mɒnˈstrɒsɪtɪ] *n*
Monstrosität *f*; *(thing)* Ungetüm
nt
Montenegro [mɒntɪˈniːɡrəʊ] *n*
Montenegro *nt*
month [mʌnθ] *n* Monat *m*;
monthly *adj* monatlich; *(ticket,
salary)* Monats- ▷ *adv* monatlich
▷ *n (magazine)* Monatsschrift *f*
monty [ˈmɒntɪ] *n*: **to go the full
~** *(fam: strip)* alle Hüllen fallen
lassen; *(go the whole hog)* aufs
Ganze gehen
monument [ˈmɒnjʊmənt] *n*
Denkmal *nt* (to für); **monumental**
[mɒnjʊˈmentl] *adj (huge)*
gewaltig
mood [muːd] *n (of person)*
Laune *f*; *(a. general)* Stimmung *f*;
**to be in a good/bad
~** gute/schlechte Laune haben;
to be in the ~ for sth zu etw
aufgelegt sein; **I'm not in the
~** ich fühle mich nicht danach;
moody *adj* launisch
moon [muːn] *n* Mond *m*; **to be
over the ~** *(fam)* überglücklich
sein; **moonlight** *n* Mondlicht *nt*
▷ *vi* schwarzarbeiten; **moonlit**
adj (night, landscape) mondhell
moor [mɔːˀ] *n* Moor *nt* ▷ *vt, vi*
festmachen; **moorings** *npl*
Liegeplatz *m*; **moorland** *n*
Moorland *nt*, Heideland *nt*
moose [muːs] *(pl -)* *n* Elch *m*
mop [mɒp] *n* Mopp *m*; **mop up**
vt aufwischen
mope [məʊp] *vi* Trübsal blasen
moped [ˈməʊped] *n (Brit)* Moped
nt
moral [ˈmɒrəl] *adj* moralisch;
(values) sittlich ▷ *n* Moral *f*; **-s** *pl*
Moral *f*; **morale** [mɒˈrɑːl] *n*
Stimmung *f*, Moral *f*; **morality**
[məˈrælɪtɪ] *n* Moral *f*, Ethik *f*
morbid [ˈmɔːbɪd] *adj* krankhaft

KEYWORD

more [mɔːˀ] *adj (greater in number
etc)* mehr; *(additional)* noch mehr;
do you want (some) more tea?
möchtest du/möchten Sie noch
etwas Tee?; **I have no** *o* **I don't
have any more money** ich habe
kein Geld mehr
▷ *pron (greater amount)* mehr;
(further o additional amount) noch
mehr; **is there any more?** gibt es
noch mehr?; *(left over)* ist noch
etwas da?; **there's no more** es ist
nichts mehr da
▷ *adv* mehr; **more
dangerous/easily etc (than)**
gefährlicher/einfacher *etc* (als);
more and more immer mehr;
more and more excited immer
aufgeregter; **more or less** mehr
oder weniger; **more than ever**
mehr denn je; **more beautiful
than ever** schöner denn je

moreish *adj (food)* **these
crisps are really ~** ich kann mit
diesen Chips einfach nicht
aufhören; **moreover** *adv*
außerdem
morgue [mɔːg] *n* Leichen-
schauhaus *nt*
morning [ˈmɔːnɪŋ] *n* Morgen *m*;
in the ~ am Morgen, morgens;
(tomorrow) morgen früh; **this
~** heute morgen; *adj* Morgen-;
(early) Früh-; *(walk etc)*
morgendlich; **morning after pill**
n die Pille danach; **morning
sickness** *n* Schwangerschafts-
übelkeit *f*
Morocco [məˈrɒkəʊ] *n* Marokko
nt
moron [ˈmɔːrɒn] *n* Idiot(in) *m(f)*
morphine [ˈmɔːfiːn] *n* Morphium *nt*

morsel ['mɔːsl] n Bissen m

mortal ['mɔːtl] adj sterblich; (wound) tödlich ▷ n Sterbliche(r) mf; **mortality** [mɔːˈtælɪtɪ] n (death rate) Sterblichkeitsziffer f; **mortally** adv tödlich

mortgage ['mɔːgɪdʒ] n Hypothek f ▷ vt mit einer Hypothek belasten

mortified ['mɔːtɪfaɪd] adj: **I was ~** es war mir schrecklich peinlich

mortuary ['mɔːtjʊərɪ] n Leichenhalle f

mosaic [məʊˈzeɪɪk] n Mosaik nt

Moscow ['mɒskəʊ] n Moskau nt

Moslem ['mɒzləm] adj, n see **Muslim**

mosque [mɒsk] n Moschee f

mosquito [mɒsˈkiːtəʊ] (pl **-es**) n (Stech)mücke f; (tropical) Moskito m; **~ net** Moskitonetz nt

moss [mɒs] n Moos nt

most [məʊst] adj meiste pl, die meisten; **in ~ cases** in den meisten Fällen ▷ adv (with verbs) am meisten; (with adj) ...ste; (with adv) am ...sten; (very) äußerst, höchst; **he ate the (the) ~** er hat am meisten gegessen; **the ~ beautiful/interesting** der/die/das schönste/interessanteste; **~ interesting** hochinteressant! ▷ n das meiste, der größte Teil; (people) die meisten; **~ of the money/players** das meiste Geld/die meisten Spieler; **for the ~ part** zum größten Teil; **five at the ~** höchstens fünf; **to make the ~ of sth** etw voll ausnützen; **mostly** adv (most of the time) meistens; (mainly) hauptsächlich; (for the most part) größtenteils

MOT abbr = Ministry of Transport; **~ (test)** ≈ TÜV m

motel [məʊˈtel] n Motel nt

moth [mɒθ] n Nachtfalter m;

(wool-eating) Motte f; **mothball** n Mottenkugel f

mother ['mʌðəʳ] n Mutter f ▷ vt bemuttern; **mother-in-law** (pl **mothers-in-law**) n Schwiegermutter f; **mother-to-be** (pl **mothers-to-be**) n werdende Mutter

motif [məʊˈtiːf] n Motiv nt

motion ['məʊʃən] n Bewegung f; (in meeting) Antrag m; **motionless** adj bewegungslos

motivate ['məʊtɪveɪt] vt motivieren; **motive** ['məʊtɪv] n Motiv nt

motor ['məʊtəʳ] n Motor m; (fam: car) Auto nt ▷ adj Motor-; **Motorail train®** n (Brit) Autoreisezug m; **motorbike** n Motorrad nt; **motorboat** n Motorboot nt; **motorcycle** n Motorrad nt; **motor industry** n Automobilindustrie f; **motoring** ['məʊtərɪŋ] n Autofahren nt; **~ organization** Automobilklub m; **motorist** ['məʊtərɪst] n Autofahrer(in) m(f); **motor oil** n Motorenöl nt; **motor racing** n Autorennsport m; **motor scooter** n Motorroller m; **motor show** n Automobilausstellung f; **motor vehicle** n Kraftfahrzeug nt; **motorway** n (Brit) Autobahn f

motto ['mɒtəʊ] (pl **-es**) n Motto nt

mould [məʊld] n Form f; (mildew) Schimmel m ▷ vt (a. fig) formen; **mouldy** ['məʊldɪ] adj schimmelig

moult [məʊlt] vi sich mausern, haaren

mount [maʊnt] vt (horse) steigen auf +akk; (exhibition etc) organisieren; (painting) mit einem Passepartout versehen ▷ vi: **to ~ (up)** (an)steigen ▷ n Passepartout nt

mountain ['maʊntɪn] n Berg m;
mountain bike n Mountainbike
nt; **mountaineer** [maʊntɪ'nɪə']
n Bergsteiger(in) m(f);
mountaineering [maʊntɪ'nɪərɪŋ]
n Bergsteigen nt; **mountainous**
adj bergig; **mountainside** n
Berghang m

mourn [mɔːn] vt betrauern ▷ vi
trauern (for um); **mourner** n
Trauernde(r) mf; **mournful** adj
trauervoll; **mourning** n Trauer f;
to be in ~ trauern (for um)

mouse [maʊs] (pl **mice**) n (a.
Inform) Maus f; **mouse mat**,
mouse pad (US) n Mauspad nt;
mouse trap n Mausefalle f

mousse [muːs] n (Gastr) Creme f;
(styling ~) Schaumfestiger m

moustache [mə'stɑːʃ] n
Schnurrbart m

mouth [maʊθ] n Mund m; (of
animal) Maul nt; (of cave) Eingang
m; (of bottle etc) Öffnung f; (of river)
Mündung f; **to keep one's ~ shut**
(fam) den Mund halten; **mouthful**
n (of drink) Schluck m; (of food)
Bissen m; **mouth organ** n
Mundharmonika f; **mouthwash** n
Mundwasser nt; **mouthwatering**
adj appetitlich, lecker

move [muːv] n (movement)
Bewegung f; (in game) Zug m; (step)
Schritt m; (moving house) Umzug m;
to make a ~ (in game) ziehen;
(leave) sich auf den Weg machen;
to get a ~ on (with sth) sich (mit
etw) beeilen ▷ vt bewegen;
(object) rücken; (car) wegfahren;
(transport: goods) befördern;
(people) transportieren; (in job)
versetzen; (emotionally) bewegen,
rühren; **I can't ~ it** (stuck, too heavy)
ich bringe es nicht von der Stelle;
to ~ (house) umziehen ▷ vi sich
bewegen; (change place) gehen;
(vehicle, ship) fahren; (move house,

town etc) umziehen; (in game)
ziehen; **move about** vi sich
bewegen; (travel) unterwegs sein;
move away vi weggehen; (move
town) wegziehen; **move in** vi (to
house) einziehen; **move off** vi
losfahren; **move on** vi
weitergehen; (vehicle)
weiterfahren; **move out** vi
ausziehen; **move up** vi (in queue
etc) aufrücken; **movement** n
Bewegung f

movie ['muːvɪ] n Film m; **the ~s**
(the cinema) das Kino; **movie
theatre** n (US) Kino nt

moving ['muːvɪŋ] adj (emotionally) ergreifend, berührend

mow [maʊ] (**mowed**, **mown** o
mowed) vt mähen; **mower** n
(lawn~) Rasenmäher m

mown [maʊn] pp of **mow**

Mozambique [maʊzæm'biːk] n
Mosambik nt

MP abbr = **Member of Parliament**
Parlamentsabgeordnete(r) mf

mph abbr = **miles per hour** Meilen
pro Stunde

MPV abbr = **multi-purpose
vehicle** Mehrzweckfahrzeug nt

MP3 player [empiː'θriː 'pleɪə']
n MP3-Player m

Mr ['mɪstə'] n (written form of
address) Herr

Mrs ['mɪsɪz] n (written form of
address) Frau

Ms [mɪz] n (written form of address
for any woman, married or unmarried)
Frau

MS n abbr = **multiple sclerosis** MS
f

Mt abbr = **Mount** Berg m

much [mʌtʃ] (**more**, **most**) adj
viel; **we haven't got ~ time** wir
haben nicht viel Zeit; **how
~ money?** wie viel Geld? ▷ adv
viel; (with verb) sehr; **~ better** viel
besser; **I like it very ~** es gefällt

mir sehr gut; **I don't like it ~** ich mag es nicht besonders; **thank you very ~** danke sehr; **I thought as ~** das habe ich mir gedacht; **~ as I like him** so sehr ich ihn mag; **we don't see them ~** wir sehen sie nicht sehr oft; **~ the same** fast gleich ▷ n viel; **as ~ as you want** so viel du willst; **he's not ~ of a cook** er ist kein großer Koch

muck [mʌk] n (fam) Dreck m; **muck about** vi (fam) herumalbern; **muck up** vt (fam) dreckig machen; (spoil) vermasseln; **mucky** adj dreckig

mucus ['mjuːkəs] n Schleim m

mud [mʌd] n Schlamm m

muddle ['mʌdl] n Durcheinander nt; **to be in a ~** ganz durcheinander sein ▷ vt: **to ~ (up)** durcheinanderbringen; **muddled** adj konfus

muddy ['mʌdɪ] adj schlammig; (shoes) schmutzig; **mudguard** ['mʌdɡɑːd] n Schutzblech nt

muesli ['muːzlɪ] n Müsli nt

muffin ['mʌfɪn] n Muffin m; (Brit) weiches, flaches Milchbrötchen aus Hefeteig, das meist getoastet und mit Butter gegessen wird

muffle ['mʌfl] vt (sound) dämpfen; **muffler** n (US) Schalldämpfer m

mug [mʌɡ] n (cup) Becher m; (fam: fool) Trottel m ▷ vt (attack and rob) überfallen; **mugging** n Raubüberfall m

muggy ['mʌɡɪ] adj (weather) schwül

mule [mjuːl] n Maulesel m

mull over [mʌl 'əʊvə*] vt nachdenken über +akk

mulled [mʌld] adj: **~ wine** Glühwein m

multicolored, multicoloured ['mʌltɪ'kʌləd] adj bunt; **multicultural** adj

multikulturell; **multi-grade** adj: **~ oil** Mehrbereichsöl nt; **multilingual** adj mehrsprachig; **multinational** n (company) Multi m

multiple ['mʌltɪpl] n Vielfache(s) nt ▷ adj mehrfach; (several) mehrere; **multiple-choice (method)** n Multiple-Choice-Verfahren nt; **multiple sclerosis** [mʌltɪplskle'rəʊsɪs] n Multiple Sklerose f

multiplex ['mʌltɪpleks] adj, n: **~ (cinema)** Multiplexkino nt

multiplication [mʌltɪplɪ'keɪʃən] n Multiplikation f; **multiply** ['mʌltɪplaɪ] vt multiplizieren (by mit) ▷ vi sich vermehren

multi-purpose ['mʌltɪ'pɜːpəs]- adj Mehrzweck-; **multistorey (car park)** n Parkhaus nt; **multitasking** n (Inform) Multitasking nt

mum [mʌm] n (fam: mother) Mutti f, Mami f

mumble ['mʌmbl] vt, vi murmeln

mummy ['mʌmɪ] n (dead body) Mumie f; (fam: mother) Mutti f, Mami f

mumps [mʌmps] nsing Mumps m

munch [mʌntʃ] vt, vi mampfen

Munich ['mjuːnɪk] n München nt

municipal [mjuː'nɪsɪpəl] adj städtisch

mural ['mjʊərəl] n Wandgemälde nt

murder ['mɜːdə*] n Mord m; **the traffic was ~** der Verkehr war die Hölle ▷ vt ermorden; **murderer** n Mörder(in) m(f)

murky ['mɜːkɪ] adj düster; (water) trüb

murmur ['mɜːmə*] vt, vi murmeln

muscle ['mʌsl] n Muskel m;
muscular ['mʌskjʊlə°] adj (strong)
muskulös; (cramp, pain etc) Muskel-
museum [mju:'zɪəm] n Museum
nt

mushroom ['mʌʃrʊm] n (ess-
barer) Pilz; (button ~) Champignon
m ▷ vi (fig) emporschießen

mushy ['mʌʃɪ] adj breiig; ~ **peas**
Erbsenmus nt

music ['mju:zɪk] n Musik f;
(printed) Noten pl; **musical** adj
(sound) melodisch; (person)
musikalisch; ~ **instrument**
Musikinstrument nt ▷ n (show)
Musical nt; **musically** adv
musikalisch; **musician**
[mju:'zɪʃən] n Musiker(in) m(f)

Muslim ['mʊzlɪm] adj
moslemisch ▷ n Moslem m,
Muslime f

mussel ['mʌsl] n Miesmuschel f

must [mʌst] (**had to, had to**) vb
aux (need to) müssen; (in negation)
dürfen; **I ~n't forget that** ich darf
das nicht vergessen; (certainty) **he
~ be there by now** er ist
inzwischen bestimmt schon da;
(assumption) **I ~ have lost it** ich
habe es wohl verloren; ~ **you?**
muss das sein? ▷ n Muss nt

mustache ['mʌstæʃ] n (US)
Schnurrbart m

mustard ['mʌstəd] n Senf m; **to
cut the ~** es bringen

mustn't ['mʌsnt] contr of **must
not**

mute [mju:t] adj stumm

mutter ['mʌtə°] vt, vi murmeln

mutton ['mʌtn] n Ham-
melfleisch nt

mutual ['mju:tjʊəl] adj gegenseitig; **by ~ consent** in
gegenseitigem Einvernehmen

my [maɪ] adj mein; **I've hurt
~ leg** ich habe mir das Bein
verletzt

Myanmar ['maɪænmɑ:] n
Myanmar nt

myself [maɪ'self] pron (reflexive)
mich akk, mir dat; **I've hurt ~** ich
habe mich verletzt; **I've bought
~ a flat** ich habe mir eine
Wohnung gekauft; **I need it for
~** ich brauche es für mich (selbst);
(emphatic) **I did it ~** ich habe es
selbst gemacht; (all) **by ~** allein

mysterious [mɪ'stɪərɪəs] adj
geheimnisvoll, mysteriös;
(inexplicable) rätselhaft; **mystery**
['mɪstərɪ] n Geheimnis nt; (puzzle)
Rätsel nt; **it's a ~ to me** es ist mir
schleierhaft; **mystify** ['mɪstɪfaɪ]
vt verblüffen

myth [mɪθ] n Mythos m; (fig:
untrue story) Märchen nt; **mythical**
adj mythisch; (fig: untrue)
erfunden; **mythology**
[mɪ'θɒlədʒɪ] n Mythologie f

n

N *abbr* = **north** N

nag [næg] *vt, vi* herumnörgeln (*sb* an jdm); **nagging** *n* Nörgelei *f*

nail [neɪl] *n* Nagel *m* ▷ *vt* nageln (to an); **nail down** *vt* festnageln; **nailbrush** *n* Nagelbürste *f*; **nail clippers** *npl* Nagelknipser *m*; **nailfile** *n* Nagelfeile *f*; **nail polish** *n* Nagellack *m*; **nail polish remover** *n* Nagellackentferner *m*; **nail scissors** *npl* Nagelschere *f*; **nail varnish** *n* Nagellack *m*

naïve [naɪˈiːv] *adj* naiv

naked [ˈneɪkɪd] *adj* nackt

name [neɪm] *n* Name *m*; **his ~ is ...** er heißt ...; **what's your ~?** wie heißen Sie?; (*reputation*) **to have a good/bad ~** einen guten/schlechten Ruf haben ▷ *vt* nennen (*after nach*); (*sth new*) benennen; (*nominate*) ernennen (*as als/zu*); **a boy ~d ...** ein Junge

namens ...; **namely** *adv* nämlich; **name plate** *n* Namensschild *nt*

nan bread [ˈnɑːnˈbred] *n* (*warm serviertes*) *indisches Fladenbrot*

nanny [ˈnænɪ] *n* Kindermädchen *nt*

nap [næp] *n*: **to have/take a ~** ein Nickerchen machen

napkin [ˈnæpkɪn] *n* (*at table*) Serviette *f*

Naples [ˈneɪplz] *n* Neapel *nt*

nappy [ˈnæpɪ] *n* (*Brit*) Windel *f*

narcotic [nɑːˈkɒtɪk] *n* Rauschgift *nt*

narrate [nəˈreɪt] *vt* erzählen; **narration** [nəˈreɪʃən] , **narrative** [ˈnærətɪv] *n* Erzählung *f*; **narrator** [nəˈreɪtə°] *n* Erzähler(in) *m(f)*

narrow [ˈnærəʊ] *adj* eng, schmal; (*victory, majority*) knapp; **to have a ~ escape** mit knapper Not davonkommen ▷ *vi* sich verengen; **narrow down** *vt* einschränken (to sth auf etw *akk*); **narrow-minded** *adj* engstirnig

nasty [ˈnɑːstɪ] *adj* ekelhaft; (*person*) fies; (*remark*) gehässig; (*accident, wound etc*) schlimm

nation [ˈneɪʃən] *n* Nation *f*; **national** [ˈnæʃənl] *adj* national; **~ anthem** Nationalhymne *f*; **National Health Service** (*Brit*) staatlicher Gesundheitsdienst; **~ insurance** (*Brit*) Sozialversicherung *f*; **~ park** Nationalpark *m*; **~ service** Wehrdienst *m*; **~ socialism** (*Hist*) Nationalsozialismus *m* ▷ *n* Staatsbürger(in) *m(f)*

○ **NATIONAL TRUST**

○ Der **National Trust** ist ein 1895
○ gegründeter Natur- und
○ Denkmalschutzverband in
○ Großbritannien, der Gebäude
○ und Gelände von besonderem

● historischen oder ästhetischen
● Interesse erhält und der
● Öffentlichkeit zugänglich
● macht.

nationality [næʃ'nælɪtɪ] n
Staatsangehörigkeit f,
Nationalität f; **nationalize**
['næʃnəlaɪz] vt verstaatlichen;
nationwide adj, adv landesweit
native ['neɪtɪv] adj einheimisch;
(inborn) angeboren, natürlich;
Native American Indianer(in)
m(f); **~ country** Heimatland nt; **a
~ German** ein gebürtiger
Deutscher, eine gebürtige
Deutsche; **~ language**
Muttersprache f; **~ speaker**
Muttersprachler(in) m(f) ▷ n
Einheimische(r) mf; (in colonial
context) Eingeborene(r) mf
nativity play [nə'tɪvətɪpleɪ] n
Krippenspiel nt
NATO ['neɪtəʊ] acr = **North
Atlantic Treaty Organization**
Nato f
natural ['nætʃrəl] adj natürlich;
(law, science, forces etc) Natur-;
(inborn) angeboren; **~ gas** Erdgas
nt; **~ resources** Bodenschätze pl;
naturally adv natürlich; (by
nature) von Natur aus; **it comes
~ to her** es fällt ihr leicht
nature ['neɪtʃə'] n Natur f;
(type) Art f; **it is not in my ~** es
entspricht nicht meiner Art;
by ~ von Natur aus; **nature
reserve** n Naturschutzgebiet nt
naughty ['nɔːtɪ] adj (child)
ungezogen; (cheeky) frech
nausea ['nɔːsɪə] n Übelkeit f
nautical ['nɔːtɪkəl] adj nautisch;
~ mile Seemeile f
nave [neɪv] n Hauptschiff nt
navel ['neɪvəl] n Nabel m
navigate ['nævɪgeɪt] vi navi-
gieren; (in car) lotsen, dirigieren;

navigation [nævɪ'geɪʃən] n
Navigation f; (in car) Lotsen nt
navy ['neɪvɪ] n Marine f; **~ blue**
Marineblau nt
Nazi ['nɑːtsɪ] n Nazi m
NB abbr = **nota bene** NB
NE abbr = **northeast** NO
near [nɪə'] adj nahe; **in the
~ future** in nächster Zukunft; **that
was a ~ miss** (o thing) das war
knapp; (with price) ... **or ~est offer**
Verhandlungsbasis ... ▷ adv in der
Nähe; **so ~** so nahe; **come ~er**
näher kommen; (event) näher
rücken ▷ prep: **~ (to)** (space) nahe
an +dat; (vicinity) in der Nähe +gen;
~ the sea nahe am Meer; **~ the
station** in der Nähe des Bahnhofs,
in Bahnhofsnähe; **nearby** adj
nahe gelegen ▷ adv in der Nähe;
nearly adv fast; **nearside** n
(Auto) Beifahrerseite f;
near-sighted adj kurzsichtig
neat [niːt] adj ordentlich; (work,
writing) sauber; (undiluted) pur
necessarily [nesə'serəli] adv
notwendigerweise; **not ~** nicht
unbedingt; **necessary** ['nesəsəri]
adj notwendig, nötig; **it's ~ to ...**
man muss ...; **it's not ~ for him to
come** er braucht nicht
mitzukommen; **necessity**
[nɪ'sesɪtɪ] n Notwendigkeit f; **the
bare necessities** das absolut
Notwendigste; **there is no ~ to ...**
man braucht nicht (zu) ..., man
muss nicht ...
neck [nek] n Hals m; (size)
Halsweite f; **back of the ~** Nacken
m; **necklace** ['neklɪs] n
Halskette f; **necktie** n (US)
Krawatte f
nectarine ['nektərɪn] n Nektarine f
née [neɪ] adj geborene
need [niːd] n (requirement)
Bedürfnis nt (for für); (necessity)

Notwendigkeit f; (poverty) Not f; **to be in ~ of sth** etw brauchen; **if ~(s) be** wenn nötig; **there is no ~ to ...** man braucht nicht (zu) ..., man muss nicht ... ▷ vt brauchen; **I ~ to speak to you** ich muss mit dir reden; **you ~n't go** du brauchst nicht (zu) gehen, du musst nicht gehen

needle ['niːdl] n Nadel f

needless, needlessly ['niːdlɪs, -lɪ] adj, adv unnötig; **~ to say** selbstverständlich

needy ['niːdɪ] adj bedürftig

negative ['nɛɡətɪv] n (Ling) Verneinung f; (Foto) Negativ nt ▷ adj negativ; (answer) verneinend

neglect [nɪ'glɛkt] n Vernachlässigung f ▷ vt vernachlässigen; **to ~ to do sth** es versäumen, etw zu tun; **negligence** ['nɛɡlɪdʒəns] n Nachlässigkeit f; **negligent** adj nachlässig

negligible ['nɛɡlɪdʒəbl] adj unbedeutend; (amount) geringfügig

negotiate [nɪ'ɡəʊʃɪeɪt] vi verhandeln; **negotiation** [nɪɡəʊʃɪ'eɪʃən] n Verhandlung f

neigh [neɪ] vi (horse) wiehern

neighbour (US), **neighbor** ['neɪbə°] n Nachbar(in) m(f); **neighbo(u)rhood** n Nachbarschaft f; **neighbo(u)ring** adj benachbart

neither ['naɪðə°] adj, pron keine(r, s) von beiden; **~ of you/us** keiner von euch/uns beiden ▷ adv: **~ ... nor ...** weder ... noch ... ▷ conj: **I'm not going - ~ am I** ich gehe nicht - ich auch nicht

neon ['niːɒn] n Neon nt; **~ sign** (advertisement) Leuchtreklame f

nephew ['nɛfjuː] n Neffe m

nerd [nɜːv] n (fam) Schwachkopf m; **he's a real computer ~** er ist ein totaler Computerfreak

nerve [nɜːv] n Nerv m; **he gets on my ~s** er geht mir auf die Nerven; (courage) **to keep/lose one's ~** die Nerven behalten/verlieren; (cheek) **to have the ~ to do sth** die Frechheit besitzen, etw zu tun; **nerve-racking** adj nervenaufreibend; **nervous** ['nɜːvəs] adj (apprehensive) ängstlich; (on edge) nervös; **nervous breakdown** n Nervenzusammenbruch m

nest [nɛst] n Nest nt ▷ vi nisten

net [nɛt] n Netz nt; **the Net** (Internet) das Internet; **on the ~** im Netz ▷ adj (price, weight) Netto-; **~ profit** Reingewinn m; **netball** n Netzball m

Netherlands ['nɛðələndz] npl: **the ~** die Niederlande pl

nettle ['nɛtl] n Nessel f

network ['nɛtwɜːk] n Netz nt; (TV, Radio) Sendenetz nt; (Inform) Netzwerk nt; **networking** n Networking nt (das Knüpfen und Pflegen von Kontakten, die dem beruflichen Fortkommen dienen)

neurosis [njʊə'rəʊsɪs] n Neurose f; **neurotic** [njʊə'rɒtɪk] adj neurotisch

neuter ['njuːtə°] adj (Bio) geschlechtslos; (Ling) sächlich

neutral ['njuːtrəl] adj neutral ▷ n (gear in car) Leerlauf m

never ['nɛvə°] adv nie(mals); **~ before** noch nie; **~ mind** macht nichts!; **never-ending** adj endlos; **nevertheless** [nɛvəðə'lɛs] adv trotzdem

new [njuː] adj neu; **this is all ~ to me** das ist für mich noch ungewohnt; **newcomer** n Neuankömmling m; (in job, subject) Neuling m

New England [njuː'ɪŋglənd] n Neuengland nt

Newfoundland ['nju:fəndlənd]
n Neufundland *nt*

newly ['nju:lɪ] *adv* neu; ~ **made**
(*cake*) frisch gebacken;
newly-weds *npl* Frischvermählte
pl; **new moon** *n* Neumond *m*

news [nju:z] *nsing* (*item of* ~)
Nachricht *f*; (*Radio, TV*)
Nachrichten *pl*; **good** ~ **ein**
erfreuliche Nachricht; **what's the**
~? was gibt's Neues?; **have you**
heard the ~? hast du das Neueste
gehört?; **that's** ~ **to me** das ist mir
neu; **newsagent**, **news dealer**
(*US*) *n* Zeitungshändler(in) *m(f)*;
news bulletin *n*
Nachrichtensendung *f*; **news flash**
n Kurzmeldung *f*; **newsgroup** *n*
(*Inform*) Diskussionsforum *nt*,
Newsgroup *f*; **newsletter** *n*
Mitteilungsblatt *nt*; **newspaper**
['nju:speɪpə] *n* Zeitung *f*

New Year ['nju:'jɪə] *n* das
neue Jahr; **Happy** ~ (ein) frohes
Neues Jahr!; (*toast*) Prosit
Neujahr!; ~'s **Day** Neujahr *nt*,
Neujahrstag *m*; ~'s **Eve**
Silvesterabend *m*; ~'s **resolution**
guter Vorsatz fürs neue Jahr

New York [nju:'jɔ:k] *n* New
York *nt*

New Zealand [nju:'zi:lənd] *n*
Neuseeland *nt* ▷ *adj*
neuseeländisch; **New Zealander**
n Neuseeländer(in) *m(f)*

next [nekst] *adj* nächste(r, s);
the week after ~ übernächste
Woche; ~ **time I see him** wenn ich
ihn das nächste Mal sehe; **you're**
~ du bist jetzt dran ▷ *adv* als
Nächstes; (*then*) dann, darauf; ~ **to**
neben +*dat*; ~ **to last** vorletzte(r,
s); ~ **to impossible** nahezu
unmöglich; **the** ~ **best thing** das
Nächstbeste; ~ **door** nebenan
NHS *abbr* = **National Health**
Service

Niagara Falls [naɪ'ægrə'fɔ:lz]
npl Niagarafälle *pl*

nibble ['nɪbl] *vt* knabbern an
+*dat*; **nibbles** *npl* Knabberzeug *nt*

Nicaragua [nɪkə'rægjʊə] *n*
Nicaragua *nt*

nice [naɪs] *adj* nett, sympathisch;
(*taste, food, drink*) gut; (*weather*)
schön; ~ **and ...** schön ...; **be** ~ **to**
him sei nett zu ihm; **have a** ~ **day**
(*US*) schönen Tag noch!; **nicely** *adv*
nett; (*well*) gut; **that'll do** ~ das
genügt vollauf

nick [nɪk] *vt* (*fam: steal*) klauen;
(*capture*) schnappen

nickel ['nɪkl] *n* (*Chem*) Nickel *nt*;
(*US: coin*) Nickel *m*

nickname ['nɪkneɪm] *n*
Spitzname *m*

nicotine ['nɪkəti:n] *n* Nikotin *nt*;
nicotine patch *n* Nikotinpflaster
nt

niece [ni:s] *n* Nichte *f*

Nigeria [naɪ'dʒɪərɪə] *n* Nigeria
nt

night [naɪt] *n* Nacht *f*; (*before bed*)
Abend *m*; **good** ~ gute Nacht!; **at**
(*o by*) ~ nachts; **to have an early**
~ früh schlafen gehen; **nightcap** *n*
Schlummertrunk *m*; **nightclub** *n*
Nachtklub *m*; **nightdress** *n*
Nachthemd *nt*; **nightie** ['naɪtɪ] *n*
(*fam*) Nachthemd *nt*

nightingale ['naɪtɪŋgeɪl] *n*
Nachtigall *f*

night life ['naɪtlaɪf] *n*
Nachtleben *nt*; **nightly** *adv* (*every*
evening) jeden Abend; (*every night*)
jede Nacht; **nightmare**
['naɪtmeə] *n* Albtraum *m*;
nighttime *n* Nacht *f*; **at** ~ nachts

nil [nɪl] *n* (*Sport*) null

Nile [naɪl] *n* Nil *m*

nine [naɪn] *num* neun; ~ **times**
out of ten so gut wie immer ▷ *n*
(*a. bus etc*) Neun *f*; *see also* **eight**;
nineteen [naɪn'ti:n] *num*

neunzehn ▷ n (a. bus etc)
Neunzehn f; see also **eight**;
nineteenth adj neunzehnte(r, s);
see also **eighth**; **ninetieth**
['naɪntɪəθ] adj neunzigste(r, s);
see also **eighth**; **ninety** ['naɪntɪ]
num neunzig ▷ n Neunzig f; see
also **eight**; **ninth** [naɪnθ] adj
neunte(r, s) ▷ n (fraction) Neuntel
nt; see also **eighth**
nipple ['nɪpl] n Brustwarze f
nitrogen ['naɪtrədʒən] n Stick-
stoff m

◯ KEYWORD

no [nəʊ] (pl noes) adv (opposite of
yes) nein; **to answer no** (to
question) mit Nein antworten; (to
request) Nein o nein sagen; **no
thank you** nein, danke
▷ adj (not any) kein(e); **I have no
money/time** ich habe kein
Geld/keine Zeit; **"no smoking"**
„Rauchen verboten"
▷ n Nein nt; (no vote) Neinstimme f

nobility [nəʊ'bɪlɪtɪ] n Adel m;
noble ['nəʊbl] adj (rank) adlig;
(quality) edel ▷ n Adlige(r)
m/f
nobody ['nəʊbədɪ] pron niemand; (emphatic) keiner; ~ **knows**
keiner weiß es; ~ **else** sonst
niemand, kein anderer ▷ n
Niemand m
no-claims bonus
[nəʊ'kleɪmzbəʊnəs] n Schadenfreiheitsrabatt m
nod [nɒd] vi, vt nicken; **nod off** vi
einnicken
noise [nɔɪz] n (loud) Lärm m;
(sound) Geräusch nt; **noisy** adj
laut; (crowd) lärmend
nominate ['nɒmɪneɪt] vt (in
election) aufstellen; (appoint)
ernennen

nominative ['nɒmɪnətɪv] n
(Ling) Nominativ m
nominee [nɒmɪ'niː] n Kandi-
dat(in) m(f)
non- [nɒn] pref Nicht-; (with adj)
nicht-, un-; **non-alcoholic** adj
alkoholfrei
none [nʌn] pron keine(r, s); ~ **of
them** keiner von ihnen; ~ **of it is
any use** nichts davon ist
brauchbar; **there are ~ left** es sind
keine mehr da; (with comparative)
to be ~ the wiser auch nicht
schlauer sein; **I was ~ the worse
for it** es hat mir nichts geschadet
nonentity [nɒ'nentɪtɪ] n Null
f
nonetheless [nʌnðə'les] adv
nichtsdestoweniger, dennoch
non-event n Reinfall m;
non-existent adj nicht
vorhanden; **non-fiction** n
Sachbücher pl; **non-iron** adj
bügelfrei; **non-polluting** adj
schadstofffrei; **non-resident** n:
"open to ~s" „auch für
Nichthotelgäste"; **non-returnable**
adj: ~ **bottle** Einwegflasche f
nonsense ['nɒnsəns] n Unsinn
m; **don't talk ~** red keinen Unsinn
non-smoker [nɒn'sməʊkəʳ] n
Nichtraucher(in) m(f);
non-smoking adj Nichtraucher-;
~ **area** Nichtraucherbereich m;
nonstop adj (train) durchgehend;
(flight) Nonstop- ▷ adv (talk)
ununterbrochen; (travel) ohne
Unterbrechung; (fly) ohne
Zwischenlandung; **non-violent**
adj gewaltfrei
noodles ['nuːdlz] npl Nudeln pl
noon [nuːn] n Mittag m; **at ~** um
12 Uhr mittags
no one ['nəʊwʌn] pron
niemand; (emphatic) keiner; ~ **else**
sonst niemand, kein anderer
nor [nɔː] conj: **neither ... ~ ...**

weder ... noch ...; **I don't smoke,
~ does he** ich rauche nicht, er
auch nicht

norm [nɔːm] n Norm f

normal ['nɔːməl] adj normal; **to
get back to ~** sich wieder
normalisieren; **normally** adv
(usually) normalerweise

north [nɔːθ] n Norden m; **to the
~ of** nördlich von ▷ adv (go, face)
nach Norden ▷ adj Nord-; **~ wind**
Nordwind m; **North America** n
Nordamerika nt; **northbound** adj
(in) Richtung Norden; **northeast**
n Nordosten m; **to the ~ of**
nordöstlich von ▷ adv (go, face)
nach Nordosten ▷ adj Nordost-;
northern ['nɔːðən] adj nördlich;
~ France Nordfrankreich m;
Northern Ireland n Nordirland
nt; **North Pole** n Nordpol m;
North Sea n Nordsee f;
northwards adv nach Norden;
northwest n Nordwesten m; **to
the ~ of** nordwestlich von ▷ adv
(go, face) nach Nordwesten ▷ adj
Nordwest-

Norway ['nɔːweɪ] n Norwegen
nt; **Norwegian** [nɔːˈwiːdʒən] adj
norwegisch ▷ n (person)
Norweger(in) m(f); (language)
Norwegisch nt

nos. abbr = **numbers** Nr.

nose [nəʊz] n Nase f; **nose
around** vi herumschnüffeln;
nosebleed n Nasenbluten nt;
nose-dive n Sturzflug m; **to take
a ~** abstürzen

nosey ['nəʊzɪ] see **nosy**

nostalgia [nɒˈstældʒɪə] n Nos-
talgie f (for nach); **nostalgic** adj
nostalgisch

nostril ['nɒstrɪl] n Nasenloch nt

nosy ['nəʊzɪ] adj neugierig

not [nɒt] adv nicht; **~ a** kein;
~ one of them kein einziger von
ihnen; **he is ~ an expert** er ist kein

Experte; **I told him ~ to** (**do it**) ich
sagte ihm, er solle es nicht tun;
~ at all überhaupt nicht,
keineswegs; (don't mention it) gern
geschehen; **~ yet** noch nicht

notable ['nəʊtəbl] adj bemerkenswert; **note** [nəʊt] n (written)
Notiz f; (short letter) paar Zeilen pl;
(on scrap of paper) Zettel m;
(comment in book etc) Anmerkung f;
(bank-) Schein m; (Mus: sign) Note
f; (sound) Ton m; **to make a ~ of
sth** sich dat etw notieren; **~s** (of
lecture etc) Aufzeichnungen pl; **to
take ~s** sich dat Notizen machen
(of über +akk) ▷ vt (notice)
bemerken (that dass); (write down)
notieren; **notebook** n Notizbuch
nt; (Inform) Notebook nt; **notepad**
n Notizblock m; **notepaper** n
Briefpapier nt

nothing ['nʌθɪŋ] n nichts; **~
but ...** lauter ...; for umsonst; **he
thinks ~ of it** er macht sich nichts
daraus

notice ['nəʊtɪs] n (announcement)
Bekanntmachung f; (on ~ board)
Anschlag m; (attention) Beachtung
f; (advance warning) Ankündigung f;
(to leave job, flat etc) Kündigung f;
at short ~ kurzfristig; **until
further ~** bis auf weiteres; **to give
sb ~** jdm kündigen; **to hand in
one's ~** kündigen; **to take** (**no)
~ of** (**sth**) etw (nicht) beachten;
take no ~ kümmere dich nicht
darum! ▷ vt bemerken; **noticeable**
adj erkennbar; (visible) sichtbar; **to be ~** auffallen;
notice board n Anschlagtafel f

notification [nəʊtɪfɪˈkeɪʃən] n
Benachrichtigung f (of von); **notify**
['nəʊtɪfaɪ] vt benachrichtigen (of
von)

notion ['nəʊʃən] n Idee f

notorious [nəʊˈtɔːrɪəs] adj
berüchtigt

nought [nɔːt] n Null f
noun [naʊn] n Substantiv nt
nourish ['nʌrɪʃ] vt nähren;
nourishing adj nahrhaft;
nourishment n Nahrung f
novel ['nɒvəl] n Roman m ▷ adj
neuartig; **novelist** n
Schriftsteller(in) m(f); **novelty** n
Neuheit f
November [nəʊ'vembə°] n
November m; see also **September**
novice ['nɒvɪs] n Neuling m
now [naʊ] adv (at the moment)
jetzt; (introductory phrase) also;
right ~ jetzt gleich; **just ~** gerade;
by ~ inzwischen; **from ~ on** ab
jetzt; **~ and again** (o then) ab und
zu; **nowadays** adv heutzutage
nowhere ['nəʊweə°] adv nirgends; **we're getting ~** wir
kommen nicht weiter; **~ near**
noch lange nicht
nozzle ['nɒzl] n Düse f
nuclear ['njuːklɪə°] adj (energy
etc) Kern-; **~ power station**
Kernkraftwerk nt; **nuclear waste**
n Atommüll m
nude [njuːd] adj nackt ▷ n (person) Nackte(r) mf; (painting etc) Akt
m
nudge [nʌdʒ] vt stupsen; **nudist**
['njuːdɪst] n Nudist(in) m(f),
FKK-Anhänger(in) m(f); **nudist
beach** n FKK-Strand m
nuisance ['njuːsns] n Ärgernis
nt; (person) Plage f; **what a ~** wie
ärgerlich!
nuke [njuːk] (US fam) n (bomb)
Atombombe f ▷ vt eine
Atombombe werfen auf +akk
numb [nʌm] adj taub, gefühllos
▷ vt betäuben
number ['nʌmbə°] n Nummer f;
(Math) Zahl f; (quantity) (An)zahl f;
in small/large ~s in
kleinen/großen Mengen; **a ~ of
times** mehrmals ▷ vt (give a

number to) nummerieren; (count)
zählen (among zu); **his days are
~ed** seine Tage sind gezählt;
number plate n (Brit Auto)
Nummernschild nt
numeral ['njuːmərəl] n Ziffer f;
numerical [njuː'merɪkəl] adj
numerisch; (superiority)
zahlenmäßig; **numerous**
['njuːmərəs] adj zahlreich
nun [nʌn] n Nonne f
Nuremberg ['njuərembɜːg] n
Nürnberg nt
nurse [nɜːs] n Krankenschwester
f; (male ~) Krankenpfleger m ▷ vt
(patient) pflegen; (baby) stillen;
nursery n Kinderzimmer nt; (for
plants) Gärtnerei f; (tree)
Baumschule f; **nursery rhyme** n
Kinderreim m; **nursery school** n
Kindergarten m; **~ teacher**
Kindergärtner(in) m(f),
Erzieher(in) m(f); **nursing** n
(profession) Krankenpflege f;
~ home Privatklinik f
nut [nʌt] n Nuss f; (Tech: for bolt)
Mutter f; **nutcase** n (fam)
Spinner(in) m(f); **nutcracker** n,
nutcrackers npl Nussknacker m
nutmeg ['nʌtmeg] n Muskat m,
Muskatnuss f
nutrient ['njuːtrɪənt] n Nährstoff
m
nutrition [njuː'trɪʃn] n Ernährung f; **nutritious** [njuː'trɪʃəs]
adj nahrhaft
nuts [nʌts] (fam) adj verrückt; **to
be ~ about sth** nach etw verrückt
sein ▷ npl (testicles) Eier pl
nutshell ['nʌtʃel] n Nussschale f;
in a ~ kurz gesagt
nutter ['nʌtə°] n (fam)
Spinner(in) m(f); **nutty** ['nʌtɪ]
adj (fam) verrückt
NW abbr = **northwest** NW
nylon® ['naɪlɒn] n Nylon® nt
▷ adj Nylon-

O

O [əʊ] n (Tel) Null f
oak [əʊk] n Eiche f ▷ adj Eichen-
OAP abbr = **old-age pensioner**
Rentner(in) m(f)
oar [ɔːʳ] n Ruder nt
oasis [əʊˈeɪsɪs] n (pl **oases**) n Oase f
oatcake [ˈəʊtkeɪk] n Haferkeks m
oath [əʊθ] n (statement) Eid m
oats [əʊts] npl Hafer m; (Gastr) Haferflocken pl
obedience [əˈbiːdɪəns] n Gehorsam m; **obedient** adj gehorsam; **obey** [əˈbeɪ] vt, vi gehorchen +dat
object [ˈɒbdʒekt] n Gegenstand m; (abstract) Objekt nt; (purpose) Ziel nt ▷ [əbˈdʒekt] vi dagegen sein; (raise objection) Einwände erheben (to gegen); (morally) Anstoß nehmen (to an +dat); **do you ~ to my smoking?** haben Sie etwas dagegen, wenn ich rauche?; **objection** [əbˈdʒekʃən] n Einwand m
objective [əbˈdʒektɪv] n Ziel nt ▷ adj objektiv; **objectivity** [ɒbdʒekˈtɪvɪtɪ] n Objektivität f
obligation [ɒblɪˈɡeɪʃən] n (duty) Pflicht f; (commitment) Verpflichtung f; **no ~** unverbindlich; **obligatory** [əˈblɪɡətərɪ] adj obligatorisch; **oblige** [əˈblaɪdʒ] vt: **to ~ sb to do sth** jdn (dazu) zwingen, etw zu tun; **he felt ~d to accept the offer** er fühlte sich verpflichtet, das Angebot anzunehmen
oblique [əˈbliːk] adj schräg; (angle) schief
oboe [ˈəʊbəʊ] n Oboe f
obscene [əbˈsiːn] adj obszön
obscure [əbˈskjʊəʳ] adj unklar; (unknown) unbekannt
observant [əbˈzɜːvənt] adj aufmerksam; **observation** [ɒbzəˈveɪʃən] n (watching) Beobachtung f; (remark) Bemerkung f; **observe** [əbˈzɜːv] vt (notice) bemerken; (watch) beobachten; (customs) einhalten
obsessed [əbˈsest] adj besessen (with an idea etc von einem Gedanken etc); **obsession** [əbˈseʃən] n Manie f
obsolete [ˈɒbsəliːt] adj veraltet
obstacle [ˈɒbstəkl] n Hindernis nt (to für); **to be an ~ to sth** einer Sache im Weg stehen
obstinate [ˈɒbstɪnət] adj hartnäckig
obstruct [əbˈstrʌkt] vt versperren; (pipe) verstopfen; (hinder) behindern, aufhalten; **obstruction** [əbˈstrʌkʃən] n Blockierung f; (of pipe) Verstopfung f; (obstacle) Hindernis nt
obtain [əbˈteɪn] vt erhalten; **obtainable** adj erhältlich

obvious ['ɒbvɪəs] *adj*
offensichtlich; **it was ~ to me
that ...** es war mir klar, dass ...;
obviously *adj* offensichtlich

occasion [ə'keɪʒən] *n* Gelegenheit *f*; (*special event*) (großes)
Ereignis; **on the ~ of** anlässlich
+*gen*; **special ~** besonderer Anlass;
occasional, occasionally *adj, adv*
gelegentlich

occupant ['ɒkjʊpənt] *n* (*of
house*) Bewohner(in) *m(f)*; (*of
vehicle*) Insasse *m*, Insassin *f*;
occupation [ɒkjʊ'peɪʃən] *n*
Beruf *m*; (*pastime*) Beschäftigung *f*;
(*of country etc*) Besetzung *f*;
occupied *adj* (*country, seat, toilet*)
besetzt; (*person*) beschäftigt; **to
keep sb/oneself ~** jdn/sich
beschäftigen; **occupy** ['ɒkjʊpaɪ]
vt (*country*) besetzen; (*time*)
beanspruchen; (*mind, person*)
beschäftigen

occur [ə'kɜː] *vi* vorkommen;
~ to sb jdm einfallen; **occurrence**
[ə'kʌrəns] *n* (*event*) Ereignis *nt*;
(*presence*) Vorkommen *nt*

ocean ['əʊʃən] *n* Ozean *m*; (*US:
sea*) das Meer *nt*

o'clock [ə'klɒk] *adv* **5 ~** 5 Uhr; **at
10 ~** um 10 Uhr

octagon ['ɒktəgən] *n* Achteck
nt

October [ɒk'təʊbə] *n* Oktober
m; *see also* **September**

octopus ['ɒktəpəs] *n* Tintenfisch *m*

odd [ɒd] *adj* (*strange*) sonderbar;
(*not even*) ungerade; (*one missing*)
einzeln; **to be the ~ one out** nicht
dazugehören; **~ jobs**
Gelegenheitsarbeiten *pl*; **odds** *npl*
Chancen *pl*; **against all
~** entgegen allen Erwartungen;
~ and ends (*fam*) Kleinkram *f*

odometer [əʊ'dɒmɪtə] *n* (*US
Auto*) Meilenzähler *m*

odor (*US*), **odour** ['əʊdə] *n*
Geruch *m*

KEYWORD

of [ɒv, əv] *prep* **1** von +*dat* = use of
gen; **the history of Germany** die
Geschichte Deutschlands; **a friend
of ours** ein Freund von uns; **a boy
of 10** ein 10-jähriger Junge;
that was kind of you das war
sehr freundlich von Ihnen
2 (*expressing quantity, amount,
dates etc*) **a kilo of flour** ein Kilo
Mehl; **how much of this do you
need?** wie viel brauchen Sie
(davon)?; **there were 3 of them**
(*people*) sie waren zu dritt; (*objects*)
es gab 3 (davon); **a cup of
tea/vase of flowers** eine
Tasse Tee/Vase mit Blumen;
the 5th of July der 5. Juli
3 (*from, out of*) aus; **a bridge made
of wood** eine Holzbrücke, eine
Brücke aus Holz

off [ɒf] *adv* (*away*) weg, fort; (*free*)
frei; (*switch*) ausgeschaltet; (*milk*)
sauer; **a mile ~** eine Meile
entfernt; **I'll be ~ now** ich gehe
jetzt; **to have the day/Monday
~** heute/Montag freihaben; **the
lights are ~** die Lichter sind aus;
the concert is ~ das Konzert fällt
aus; **I got 10 % ~** ich habe 10 %
Nachlass bekommen ▷ *prep* (*away
from*) von; **to jump/fall ~ the roof**
vom Dach springen/fallen; **to get
~ the bus** aus dem Bus
aussteigen; **he's ~ work/school** er
hat frei/schulfrei; **to take £20
~ the price** den Preis um 20 Pfund
herabsetzen

offence [ə'fens] *n* (*crime*)
Straftat *f*; (*minor*) Vergehen *nt*; (*to
feelings*) Kränkung *f*; **to
cause/take ~** Anstoß

erregen/nehmen; **offend** [ə'fɛnd]
vt kränken; (eye, ear) beleidigen;
offender n Straffällige(r) mf;
offense (US) see **offence**.
offensive [ə'fɛnsɪv] adj anstößig;
(insulting) beleidigend; (smell) übel,
abstoßend ▷ n (Mil) Offensive f
offer ['ɒfə°] n Angebot nt; **on**
~ (Comm) im Angebot ▷ vt
anbieten (to sb jdm); (money, a
chance etc) bieten
offhand [ɒf'hænd] adj lässig
▷ adv (say) auf Anhieb
office ['ɒfɪs] n Büro nt; (position)
Amt nt; **doctor's ~** (US) Arztpraxis
f; **office block** n Bürogebäude nt;
office hours npl Dienstzeit f;
(notice) Geschäftszeiten pl; **officer**
['ɒfɪsə°] n (Mil) Offizier(in) m(f);
(official) Polizeibeamte(r) m,
Polizeibeamtin f; **office worker**
['ɒfɪswɜːkə°] n Büroangestellte(r)
mf; **official** [ə'fɪʃəl] adj offiziell;
(report etc) amtlich; **~ language**
n Amtssprache f ▷ n Beamte(r) m,
Beamtin f, Repräsentant(in)
m(f)
off-licence ['ɒflaɪsəns] n (Brit)
Wein- und Spirituosenhandlung f;
off-line adj (Inform) offline;
off-peak adj außerhalb der
Stoßzeiten; (rate, ticket) verbilligt;
off-putting [ɒf] adj abstoßend,
entmutigend, irritierend;
off-season adj außerhalb der
Saison
offshore ['ɒfʃɔː°] adj küstennah,
Küsten-; (oil rig) im Meer; **offside**
['ɒf'saɪd] n (Auto) Fahrerseite f;
(Sport) Abseits nt
often ['ɒfn] adv oft; **every so**
~ von Zeit zu Zeit
oil [ɔɪl] n Öl nt ▷ vt ölen; **oil level**
n Ölstand m; **oil painting** n
Ölgemälde nt; **oil-rig** n
(Öl)bohrinsel f; **oil slick** n
Ölteppich m; **oil tanker** n

Öltanker m; (truck) Tankwagen m;
oily adj ölig; (skin, hair) fettig
ointment ['ɔɪntmənt] n Salbe f
OK, okay [əu'keɪ] adj (fam) okay,
in Ordnung; **that's ~ by** (o **with**)
me das ist mir recht
old [əuld] adj alt; **old age** n Alter
nt; **~ pension** Rente f; **~ pensioner**
Rentner(in) m(f); **old-fashioned**
adj altmodisch; **old people's**
home n Altersheim nt
olive ['ɒlɪv] n Olive f; **olive oil** n
Olivenöl nt
Olympic [əu'lɪmpɪk] adj olympisch; **the ~ Games, the ~s** pl die
Olympischen Spiele pl, die
Olympiade
omelette ['ɒmlət] n Omelett nt
omission [əu'mɪʃən] n Auslas-
sung f; **omit** [əu'mɪt] vt
auslassen

O KEYWORD

on [ɒn] prep **1** (indicating position)
auf +dat; (with vb of motion) auf
+akk; (on vertical surface, part of
body) an +dat/akk; **it's on the table**
es ist auf dem Tisch; **she put the**
book on the table sie legte das
Buch auf den Tisch; **on the left**
links
2 (indicating means, method,
condition etc) **on foot** (go, be) zu
Fuß; **on the train/plane** (go) mit
dem Zug/Flugzeug; (be) im
Zug/Flugzeug; **on the**
telephone/television am
Telefon/im Fernsehen; **to be on**
drugs Drogen nehmen; **to be on**
holiday/business im Urlaub/auf
Geschäftsreise sein
3 (referring to time) **on Friday** (am)
Freitag; **on Fridays** freitags; **on**
June 20th am 20. Juni; **a week on**
Friday Freitag in einer Woche; **on**
arrival he ... als er ankam, ... er ...

4 (about, concerning) über +akk
▷ adv **1** (referring to dress) an; **she put her boots/hat on** sie zog ihre Stiefel an/setzte ihren Hut auf **2** (further, continuously) weiter; **to walk on** weitergehen
▷ adj **1** (functioning, in operation: machine, TV, light) an; (tap) aufgedreht; (brakes) angezogen; **is the meeting still on?** findet die Versammlung noch statt?; **there's a good film on** es läuft ein guter Film
2 that's not on! (inf) (of behaviour) das ist nicht drin!

once [wʌns] adv (one time, in the past) einmal; **at ~** sofort; (at the same time) gleichzeitig; **~ more** noch einmal; **for ~** ausnahmsweise (einmal); **~ in a while** ab und zu mal ▷ conj wenn ... einmal; **~ you've got used to it** sobald Sie sich daran gewöhnt haben

oncoming ['ɒnkʌmɪŋ] adj entgegenkommend; **~ traffic** Gegenverkehr m

○ **KEYWORD**

one [wʌn] num eins; (with noun, referring back to noun) ein/eine/ein; **it is one (o'clock)** es ist eins, es ist ein Uhr; **one hundred and fifty** einhundertfünfzig
▷ adj **1** (sole) einzige(r, s); **the one book which** das einzige Buch, welches
2 (same) derselbe/dieselbe/dasselbe; **they came in the one car** sie kamen alle in dem einen Auto
3 (indef) **one day I discovered ...** eines Tages bemerkte ich ...
▷ pron **1** eine(r, s); **do you have a red one?** haben Sie einen

roten/eine rote/ein rotes?; **this one** diese(r, s); **that one** der/die/das; **which one?** welche(r, s)?; **one by one** einzeln
2 one another einander; **do you two ever see one another?** seht ihr beide euch manchmal?
3 (impers) man; **one never knows** man kann nie wissen; **to cut one's finger** sich in den Finger schneiden

one-off adj einmalig ▷ n: **a ~** etwas Einmaliges; **one-parent family** n Einelternfamilie f; **one-piece** adj einteilig; **oneself** pron (reflexive) sich; **one-way** adj: **~ street** Einbahnstraße f; **~ ticket** (US) einfache Fahrkarte

onion ['ʌnjən] n Zwiebel f

on-line ['ɒnlaɪn] adj (Inform) online; **~ banking** Homebanking nt

only ['əʊnlɪ] adv nur; (with time) erst; **~ yesterday** erst gestern; **he's ~ four** er ist erst vier; **~ just arrived** gerade erst angekommen ▷ adj einzige(r, s); **~ child** Einzelkind nt

o.n.o. abbr = **or nearest offer** VB

onside ['ɒn'saɪd] adv (Sport) nicht im Abseits

onto ['ɒntʊ] prep auf +akk; (vertical surface) an +akk; **to be ~ sb** jdm auf die Schliche gekommen sein

onwards ['ɒnwədz] adv voran, vorwärts; **from today ~** von heute an, ab heute

open ['əʊpən] adj offen; **in the ~ air** im Freien; **~ to the public** für die Öffentlichkeit zugänglich; **the shop is ~ all day** das Geschäft ist den ganzen Tag offen ▷ vt öffnen, aufmachen; (meeting, account, new building) eröffnen; (road) dem Verkehr übergeben ▷ vi (door, window etc) aufgehen, sich öffnen; (shop, bank) öffnen, aufmachen; (begin) anfangen (with mit); **open-air** adj Freiluft-; **open day** n Tag m der offenen Tür; **opening** n Öffnung f; (beginning) Anfang m; (official, of exhibition etc) Eröffnung f; (opportunity) Möglichkeit f; **~ hours** (o times) Öffnungszeiten pl; **openly** adv offen; **open-minded** adj aufgeschlossen; **open-plan** adj: **~ office** Großraumbüro nt

opera ['ɔpərə] n Oper f; **opera glasses** npl Opernglas nt; **opera house** n Oper f, Opernhaus nt; **opera singer** n Opernsänger(in) m(f)

operate ['ɔpəreɪt] vt (machine) bedienen; (brakes, lights) betätigen ▷ vi (machine) laufen; (bus etc) verkehren (between zwischen); **to ~ on sb** (Med) (jdn) operieren; **operating theatre** n Operationssaal m; **operation** [ɔpə'reɪʃən] n (of machine) Bedienung f; (functioning) Funktionieren nt; (Med) Operation f (on an +dat); (undertaking) Unternehmen nt; **in ~** (machine) in Betrieb; **to have an ~** operiert werden (for wegen); **operator** ['ɔpəreɪtə] n: **to phone the ~** die Vermittlung anrufen

opinion [ə'pɪnjən] n Meinung f (on zu); **in my ~** meiner Meinung nach

opponent [ə'pəʊnənt] n Gegner(in) m(f)

opportunity [ɔpə'tjuːnɪtɪ] n Gelegenheit f

oppose [ə'pəʊz] vt sich widersetzen +dat; (idea) ablehnen; **opposed** adj: **to be ~ to sth** gegen etw sein; **as ~ to** im

Gegensatz zu; **opposing** adj (team) gegnerisch; (points of view) entgegengesetzt

opposite ['ɔpəzɪt] adj (house) gegenüberliegend; (direction) entgegengesetzt; **the ~ sex** das andere Geschlecht ▷ adv gegenüber ▷ prep gegenüber +dat; **~ me** mir gegenüber ▷ n Gegenteil nt

opposition [ɔpə'zɪʃən] n Widerstand m (to gegen); (Pol) Opposition f

oppress [ə'pres] vt unterdrücken; **oppressive** adj (heat) drückend

opt [ɔpt] vi: **to ~ for sth** sich für etw entscheiden; **to ~ to do sth** sich entscheiden, etw zu tun

optician [ɔp'tɪʃən] n Optiker(in) m(f)

optimist ['ɔptɪmɪst] n Optimist(in) m(f); **optimistic** [ɔptɪ'mɪstɪk] adj optimistisch

option ['ɔpʃən] n Möglichkeit f; (Comm) Option f; **to have no ~** keine Wahl haben; **optional** adj freiwillig; **~ extras** (Auto) Extras pl

or [ɔː] conj oder; (otherwise) sonst; (after neg) noch; **hurry up, ~** (else) **we'll be late** beeil dich, sonst kommen wir zu spät

oral ['ɔːrəl] adj mündlich; **~ sex** Oralverkehr m ▷ n (exam) Mündliche(s) nt; **oral surgeon** n Kieferchirurg(in) m(f)

orange ['ɔrɪndʒ] n Orange f ▷ adj orangefarben; **orange juice** n Orangensaft m

orbit ['ɔːbɪt] n Umlaufbahn f; **to be out of ~** (fam) nicht zu erreichen sein ▷ vt umkreisen

orchard ['ɔːtʃəd] n Obstgarten m

orchestra ['ɔːkɪstrə] n Orchester nt; (US Theat) Parkett nt

orchid ['ɔːkɪd] n Orchidee f

ordeal [ɔːˈdiːl] n Tortur f; (emotional) Qual f

order [ˈɔːdəᵉ] n (sequence) Reihenfolge f; (good arrangement) Ordnung f; (command) Befehl m; (Jur) Anordnung f; (condition) Zustand m; (Comm) Bestellung f; **out of ~** (not functioning) außer Betrieb; (unsuitable) nicht angebracht; **in ~** (items) richtig geordnet; (all right) in Ordnung; **in ~ to do sth** um etw zu tun ▷ vt (arrange) ordnen; (command) befehlen; **to ~ sb to do sth** jdm befehlen, etw zu tun; (food, product) bestellen; **order form** n Bestellschein m

ordinary [ˈɔːdɪnrɪ] adj gewöhnlich, normal; (average) durchschnittlich

ore [ɔːᵉ] n Erz nt

organ [ˈɔːgən] n (Mus) Orgel f; (Anat) Organ nt

organic [ɔːˈgænɪk] adj organisch; (farming, vegetables) Bio-, Öko-; **~ farmer** Biobauer m, Biobäuerin f; **~ food** Biokost f

organization [ɔːgənaɪˈzeɪʃən] n Organisation f; (arrangement) Ordnung f; **organize** [ˈɔːgənaɪz] vt organisieren; **organizer** n (elektronisches) Notizbuch

orgasm [ˈɔːgæzəm] n Orgasmus m

orgy [ˈɔːdʒɪ] n Orgie f

oriental [ɔːrɪˈentəl] adj orientalisch

orientation [ˌɔːrɪenˈteɪʃən] n Orientierung f

origin [ˈɒrɪdʒɪn] n Ursprung m; (of person) Herkunft f; **original** [əˈrɪdʒɪnl] adj (first) ursprünglich; (painting) original; (idea) originell ▷ n Original nt; **originality** [ərɪdʒɪˈnælɪtɪ] n Originalität f; **originally** adv ursprünglich

Orkneys [ˈɔːknɪz] npl, **Orkney Islands** npl Orkneyinseln pl

ornament [ˈɔːnəmənt] n Schmuckgegenstand m; **ornamental** [ɔːnəˈmentl] adj dekorativ

orphan [ˈɔːfən] n Waise f, Waisenkind nt; **orphanage** [ˈɔːfənɪdʒ] n Waisenhaus nt

orthodox [ˈɔːθədɒks] adj orthodox

orthopaedic, orthopedic (US) [ɔːθəʊˈpiːdɪk] adj orthopädisch

ostentatious [ɒstenˈteɪʃəs] adj protzig

ostrich [ˈɒstrɪtʃ] n (Zool) Strauß m

other [ˈʌðəᵉ] adj, pron andere(r, s); **any ~ questions?** sonst noch Fragen?; **the ~ day** neulich; **every ~ day** jeden zweiten Tag; **any person ~ than him** alle außer ihm; **someone/something or ~** irgendjemand/irgendetwas; **otherwise** adv sonst; (differently) anders

OTT adj abbr = **over the top** übertrieben

otter [ˈɒtəᵉ] n Otter m

ought [ɔːt] vb aux (obligation) sollte; (probability) dürfte; (stronger) müsste; **you ~ to do that** du solltest/Sie sollten das tun; **he ~ to win** er müsste gewinnen; **that ~ to do** das müsste reichen

ounce [aʊns] n Unze f (28,35 g)

our [aʊəᵉ] adj unser; **ours** pron unsere(r, s); **this is ~** das gehört uns; **a friend of ~** ein Freund von uns; **ourselves** pron (reflexive) uns; **we enjoyed ~** wir haben uns amüsiert; **we've got the house to ~** wir haben das Haus für uns; (emphatic) **we did it ~** wir haben es selbst gemacht; **(all) by ~** allein

out [aʊt] adv hinaus/heraus; (not

indoors) draußen; (*not at home*)
nicht zu Hause; (*not alight*) aus;
(*unconscious*) bewusstlos;
(*published*) herausgekommen;
(*results*) bekannt gegeben; **have
you been ~ yet?** warst du/waren
Sie schon draußen?; **I was ~ when
they called** ich war nicht da, als
sie vorbeikamen; **to be ~ and
about** unterwegs sein; **the sun is
~** die Sonne scheint; **the fire is
~** das Feuer ist ausgegangen;
(*wrong*) **the calculation is (way)
~** die Kalkulation stimmt (ganz
und gar) nicht; **they're ~ to get
him** sie sind hinter ihm her ▷ *vt*
(*fam*) outen

outback ['aʊtbæk] *n* (*in Australia*)
the ~ das Hinterland
outboard ['aʊtbɔːd] *adj*: **~ motor**
Außenbordmotor *m*
outbreak ['aʊtbreɪk] *n* Ausbruch *m*
outburst ['aʊtbɜːst] *n* Ausbruch *m*
outcome ['aʊtkʌm] *n* Ergebnis
nt
outcry ['aʊtkraɪ] *n* (*public protest*)
Protestwelle *f* (*against* gegen)
outdo [aʊt'duː] *irr vt* übertreffen
outdoor ['aʊtdɔː°] *adj* Außen-;
(*Sport*) im Freien; **~ swimming
pool** Freibad *nt*; **outdoors**
[aʊt'dɔːz] *adv* draußen, im Freien
outer ['aʊtə°] *adj* äußere(r, s);
outer space *n* Weltraum *m*
outfit ['aʊtfɪt] *n* Ausrüstung *f*;
(*clothes*) Kleidung *f*
outgoing [aʊt'gəʊɪŋ] *adj*
kontaktfreudig
outgrow [aʊt'grəʊ] *irr vt*
(*clothes*) herauswachsen aus
outing ['aʊtɪŋ] *n* Ausflug *m*
outlet ['aʊtlet] *n* Auslass *m*,
Abfluss *m*; (*US*) Steckdose *f*; (*shop*)
Verkaufsstelle *f*
outline ['aʊtlaɪn] *n* Umriss *m*;
(*summary*) Abriss *m*

outlive [aʊt'lɪv] *vt* überleben
outlook ['aʊtlʊk] *n* Aussicht(en)
f(pl); (*prospects*) Aussichten *pl*;
(*attitude*) Einstellung *f*
(*on zu*)
outnumber [aʊt'nʌmbə°] *vt*
zahlenmäßig überlegen sein +*dat*;
~ed zahlenmäßig unterlegen
out of ['aʊtəv] *prep* (*motion,
motive, origin*) aus; (*position, away
from*) außerhalb +*gen*;
~ danger/sight/breath außer
Gefahr/Sicht/Atem; **made ~ wood**
aus Holz gemacht; **we are ~ bread**
wir haben kein Brot mehr;
out-of-date *adj* veraltet;
out-of-the-way *adj* abgelegen
outpatient ['aʊtpeɪʃənt] *n*
ambulanter Patient, ambulante
Patientin
output ['aʊtpʊt] *n* Produktion *f*;
(*of engine*) Leistung *f*; (*Inform*)
Ausgabe *f*
outrage ['aʊtreɪdʒ] *n* (*great
anger*) Empörung *f* (*at* über);
(*wicked deed*) Schandtat *f*; (*crime*)
Verbrechen *nt*; (*indecency*) Skandal
m; **outrageous** [aʊt'reɪdʒəs] *adj*
unerhört; (*clothes, behaviour etc*)
unmöglich, schrill
outright ['aʊtraɪt] *adv* (*killed*)
sofort ▷ *adj* total; (*denial*) völlig;
(*winner*) unbestritten
outside [aʊt'saɪd] *n* Außenseite
f; **on the ~** außen ▷ *adj* äuße-
re(r, s), Außen-; (*chance*) sehr
gering ▷ *adv* außen; **to go ~** nach
draußen gehen ▷ *prep* außerhalb
+*gen*; **outsider** *n* Außenseiter(in)
m(f)
outskirts ['aʊtskɜːts] *npl* (*of
town*) Stadtrand *m*
outstanding [aʊt'stændɪŋ] *adj*
hervorragend; (*debts etc*)
ausstehend
outward ['aʊtwəd] *adj* äuße-
re(r, s); **~ journey** Hinfahrt *f*;

outwardly adv nach außen hin;
outwards adv nach außen
oval ['əʊvəl] adj oval
ovary ['əʊvərɪ] n Eierstock m
ovation [əʊ'veɪʃən] n Ovation f,
Applaus m
oven ['ʌvn] n Backofen m; **oven
glove** n Topfhandschuh m;
ovenproof adj feuerfest;
oven-ready adj bratfertig
over ['əʊvə°] prep (position) über
+dat; (motion) über +akk; **they
spent a long time ~ it** sie haben
lange dazu gebraucht; **from all
~ England** aus ganz England;
~ £20 mehr als 20 Pfund; **~ the
phone/radio** am Telefon/im
Radio; **to talk ~ a glass of wine**
sich bei einem Glas Wein
unterhalten; **~ and above** über
das hinaus; **~ the summer**
während des Sommers ▷ adv
(across) hinüber/herüber; (finished)
vorbei; (match, play etc) zu Ende;
(left) übrig; (more) mehr;
~ there/in America da
drüben/drüben in Amerika; **~ to
you** du bist/Sie sind dran; **it's (all)
~ between us** es ist aus zwischen
uns; **~ and ~ again** immer wieder;
to start (all) ~ again noch einmal
von vorn anfangen; **children of 8
and ~** Kinder ab 8 Jahren
over- ['əʊvə°] pref über-
overall ['əʊvərɔːl] n (Brit) Kittel
m ▷ adj (situation) allgemein;
(length) Gesamt-; **~ majority**
absolute Mehrheit ▷ adv
insgesamt; **overalls** npl Overall
m
overboard ['əʊvəbɔːd] adv über
Bord
overbooked [əʊvə'bʊkt] adj
überbucht; **overbooking** n
Überbuchung f
overcharge [əʊvə'tʃɑːdʒ] vt zu
viel verlangen von

overcoat ['əʊvəkəʊt] n Wintermantel m
overcome [əʊvə'kʌm] irr vt
überwinden; **~ by sleep/emotion**
von Schlaf/Rührung übermannt;
we shall ~ wir werden siegen
overcooked [əʊvə'kʊkt] adj
verkocht; (meat) zu lange gebraten
overcrowded [əʊvə'kraʊdɪd]
adj überfüllt
overdo [əʊvə'duː] irr vt übertreiben; **overdone** adj
übertrieben; (food) zu lange
gekocht; (meat) zu lange gebraten
overdose ['əʊvədəʊs] n Über-
dosis f
overdraft ['əʊvədrɑːft] n Kon-
toüberziehung f; **overdrawn**
[əʊvə'drɔːn] adj überzogen
overdue [əʊvə'djuː] adj
überfällig
overestimate [əʊvər'estɪmeɪt]
vt überschätzen
overexpose [əʊvərɪks'pəʊz] vt (Foto)
überbelichten
overflow [əʊvə'fləʊ] vi
überlaufen
overhead ['əʊvəhed] adj (Aviat)
~ locker Gepäckfach nt;
~ projector Overheadprojektor m;
~ railway Hochbahn f
▷ [əʊvə'hed] adv oben;
overhead, (Brit) **overheads** n
(Comm) allgemeine
Geschäftskosten pl
overhear [əʊvə'hɪə°] irr vt zufällig
mit anhören
overheat [əʊvə'hiːt] vi (engine)
heiß laufen
overjoyed [əʊvə'dʒɔɪd] adj
überglücklich (at über)
overland ['əʊvəlænd] adj Über-
land- ▷ [əʊvə'lænd] adv (travel)
über Land
overlap [əʊvə'læp] vi (dates etc)
sich überschneiden; (objects) sich
teilweise decken

overload [əʊvə'ləʊd] vt
überladen

overlook [əʊvə'lʊk] vt (view from
above) überblicken; (not notice)
übersehen; (pardon) hinwegsehen
über +akk

overnight [əʊvə'naɪt] adj (jour-
ney, train) Nacht-; ~ **bag**
Reisetasche f; ~ **stay**
Übernachtung f ▷ adv über Nacht

overpass ['əʊvəpɑːs] n
Überführung f

overpay [əʊvə'peɪ] vt
überbezahlen

overrule [əʊvə'ruːl] vt verwerfen; (decision) aufheben

overseas [əʊvə'siːz] adj Über-
see-; ausländisch; (fam) Auslands-
▷ adv (go) nach Übersee; (live,
work) in Übersee

oversee [əʊvə'siː] irr vt
beaufsichtigen

overshadow [əʊvə'ʃædəʊ] vt
überschatten

overshoot [əʊvə'ʃuːt] irr vt
(runway) hinausschießen über
+akk; (turning) vorbeifahren
+dat

oversight ['əʊvəsaɪt] n Versehen nt

oversimplify [əʊvə'sɪmplɪfaɪ]
vt zu sehr vereinfachen

oversleep [əʊvə'sliːp] irr vi
verschlafen

overtake [əʊvə'teɪk] irr vt, vi
überholen

overtime ['əʊvətaɪm] n Überstunden pl

overturn [əʊvə'tɜːn] vt, vi
umkippen

overweight [əʊvə'weɪt] adj: **to
be** ~ Übergewicht haben

overwhelm [əʊvə'welm] vt
überwältigen; **overwhelming** adj
überwältigend

overwork [əʊvə'wɜːk] n
Überarbeitung f ▷ vi sich

überarbeiten; **overworked** adj
überarbeitet

owe [əʊ] vt schulden; **to ~ sth to
sb** (money) jdm etw schulden;
(favour etc) jdm etw verdanken;
how much do I ~ you? was bin ich
dir/Ihnen schuldig?; **owing to**
prep wegen +gen

owl [aʊl] n Eule f

own [əʊn] vt besitzen ▷ adj eigen;
on one's ~ allein; **he has a flat of
his ~** er hat eine eigene Wohnung;
own up vi: **to ~ to sth** etw
zugeben; **owner** n Besitzer(in)
m(f); (of business) Inhaber(in) m(f);
ownership n Besitz m; **under
new ~** unter neuer Leitung

ox [ɒks] (pl **oxen**) n Ochse m;
oxtail ['ɒksteɪl] n Ochsen-
schwanz m; ~ **soup**
Ochsenschwanzsuppe f

oxygen ['ɒksɪdʒən] n Sauerstoff
m

oyster ['ɔɪstə] n Auster f

oz abbr = **ounces** Unzen pl

Oz ['ɒz] n (fam) Australien nt

ozone ['əʊzəʊn] n Ozon nt;
~ **layer** Ozonschicht f

p

p *abbr* = **page** S.; *abbr* = **penny, pence**

p.a. *abbr* = **per annum**

pace [peɪs] *n* (speed) Tempo *nt*; (step) Schritt *m*; **pacemaker** *n* (Med) Schrittmacher *m*

Pacific [pəˈsɪfɪk] *n*: **the ~ (Ocean)** der Pazifik; **Pacific Standard Time** *n* pazifische Zeit

pacifier [ˈpæsɪfaɪə] *n* (US: for baby) Schnuller *m*

pack [pæk] *n* (of cards) Spiel *nt*; (esp US: of cigarettes) Schachtel *f*; (gang) Bande *f*; (US: backpack) Rucksack *m* ▷ *vt* (case) packen; (clothes) einpacken ▷ *vi* (for holiday) packen; **pack in** *vt* (Brit fam: job) hinschmeißen; **package** [ˈpækɪdʒ] *n* (a. Inform, fig) Paket *nt*; **package deal** *n* Pauschalangebot *nt*; **package holiday, package tour** *n* Pauschalreise *f*; **packaging** *n*

(material) Verpackung *f*; **packed lunch** *n* (Brit) Lunchpaket *nt*; **packet** *n* Päckchen *nt*; (of cigarettes) Schachtel *f*

pad [pæd] *n* (of paper) Schreibblock *m*; (padding) Polster *nt*; **padded envelope** *n* wattierter Umschlag; **padding** *n* (material) Polsterung *f*

paddle [ˈpædl] *n* (for boat) Paddel *nt* ▷ *vi* (in boat) paddeln; **paddling pool** *n* (Brit) Planschbecken *nt*

padlock [ˈpædlɒk] *n* Vorhängeschloss *nt*

page [peɪdʒ] *n* (of book etc) Seite *f*

pager [ˈpeɪdʒə] *n* Piepser *m*

paid [peɪd] *pt, pp of* **pay** ▷ *adj* bezahlt

pain [peɪn] *n* Schmerz *m*; **to be in ~** Schmerzen haben; **she's a (real) ~** sie nervt; **painful** *adj* (physically) schmerzhaft; (embarrassing) peinlich; **painkiller** *n* schmerzstillendes Mittel

painstaking *adj* sorgfältig

paint [peɪnt] *n* Farbe *f* ▷ *vt* anstreichen; (picture) malen; **paintbrush** *n* Pinsel *m*; **painter** *n* Maler(in) *m(f)*; **painting** *n* (picture) Bild *nt*, Gemälde *nt*

pair [peə⁰] *n* Paar *nt*; **a ~ of shoes** ein Paar Schuhe; **a ~ of scissors** eine Schere; **a ~ of trousers** eine Hose

pajamas [pəˈdʒɑːməz] *npl* (US) Schlafanzug *m*

Pakistan [pɑːkɪˈstɑːn] *n* Pakistan *nt*

pal [pæl] *n* (fam) Kumpel *m*

palace [ˈpælɪs] *n* Palast *m*

pale [peɪl] *adj* (face) blass, bleich; (colour) hell

palm [pɑːm] *n* (of hand) Handfläche *f*; **~ (tree)** Palme *f*; **palmtop (computer)** *n* Palmtop(computer) *m*

pamper ['pæmpə°] vt
verhätscheln

pan [pæn] n (saucepan) Topf m;
(frying pan) Pfanne f; **pancake**
['pænkeɪk] n Pfannkuchen m;
Pancake Day n (Brit)
Fastnachtsdienstag m

pandemic [pæn'demɪk] n Pandemie f

panel ['pænl] n (of wood) Tafel f;
(in discussion) Diskussionsteil-
nehmer m; (in jury) Jurymitglieder
pl

panic ['pænɪk] n Panik f ▷ vi in
Panik geraten; **panicky** ['pænɪkɪ]
adj panisch

pansy ['pænzɪ] n (flower)
Stiefmütterchen nt

panties ['pæntɪz] npl (Damen-)
slip m

pantomime ['pæntəmaɪm] n
(Brit) um die Weihnachtszeit
aufgeführte Märchenkomödie

pants [pænts] npl Unterhose f;
(esp US: trousers) Hose f

pantyhose ['pæntɪhəʊz] npl
(US) Strumpfhose f; **panty-liner** n
Slipeinlage f

paper ['peɪpə°] n Papier nt;
(newspaper) Zeitung f; (exam)
Klausur f; (for reading at conference)
Referat nt; ~s pl (identity papers)
Papiere pl; ~ **bag** Papiertüte f;
~ **cup** Pappbecher m ▷ vt (wall)
tapezieren; **paperback** n
Taschenbuch nt; **paper clip** n
Büroklammer f; **paper feed** n (of
printer) Papiereinzug m; **paper
round** n: **to do a ~** Zeitungen
austragen; **paperwork** n
Schreibarbeit f

parachute ['pærəʃuːt] n Fallschirm m ▷ vi abspringen

paracetamol [pærə'siːtəmɒl] n
(tablet) Paracetamoltablette f

parade [pə'reɪd] n (procession)

Umzug m; (Mil) Parade f ▷ vi
vorbeimarschieren

paradise ['pærədaɪs] n Paradies
nt

paragliding ['pærəglaɪdɪŋ] n
Gleitschirmfliegen nt

paragraph ['pærəgrɑːf] n Absatz
m

parallel ['pærəlel] adj parallel
▷ n (Math, fig) Parallele f

paralyze ['pærəlaɪz] vt lähmen;
(fig) lahmlegen

paranoid ['pærənɔɪd] adj
paranoid

paraphrase ['pærəfreɪz] vt
umschreiben; (sth spoken) anders
ausdrücken

parasailing ['pærəseɪlɪŋ] n
Parasailing n

parasol ['pærəsɒl] n Sonnenschirm m

parcel ['pɑːsl] n Paket nt

pardon ['pɑːdn] n (Jur)
Begnadigung f; ~ **me/I beg your
~** verzeih/verzeihen Sie bitte;
(objection) aber ich bitte dich/Sie; **I
beg your ~?/~ me?** wie bitte?

parent ['peərənt] n Elternteil m;
~**s** pl Eltern pl; ~**s-in-law** pl
Schwiegereltern pl; **parental**
[pə'rentl] adj elterlich, Eltern-

parish ['pærɪʃ] n Gemeinde f

park [pɑːk] n Park m ▷ vt, vi
parken; **parking** n Parken nt; **"no
~"** "Parken verboten"; **parking
brake** n (US) Handbremse f;
parking disc n Parkscheibe f;
parking fine n Geldbuße f für
falsches Parken; **parking lights**
npl (US) Standlicht nt; **parking lot**
n (US) Parkplatz m; **parking meter**
n Parkuhr f; **parking place**,
parking space n Parkplatz m;
parking ticket n Strafzettel m

parliament ['pɑːləmənt] n Parlament nt

parrot ['pærət] n Papagei m

parsley ['pɑːslɪ] n Petersilie f

parsnip ['pɑːsnɪp] n Pastinake f (längliches, weißes Wurzelgemüse)

part [pɑːt] n Teil m; (of machine) Teil nt; (Theat) Rolle f; (US: in hair) Scheitel m; **to take ~** teilnehmen (in an +dat); **for the most ~** zum größten Teil ▷ adj Teil- ▷ vt (separate) trennen; (hair) scheiteln ▷ vi (people) sich trennen

partial ['pɑːʃəl] adj (incomplete) teilweise, Teil-

participant [pɑːˈtɪsɪpənt] n Teilnehmer(in) m(f); **participate** [pɑːˈtɪsɪpeɪt] vi teilnehmen (in an +dat)

particular [pəˈtɪkjʊləˈ] adj (specific) bestimmt; (exact) genau; (fussy) eigen; **in ~** insbesondere ▷ n **~s** pl (details) Einzelheiten pl; (about person) Personalien pl; **particularly** adv besonders

parting ['pɑːtɪŋ] n (farewell) Abschied m; (Brit: in hair) Scheitel m

partly ['pɑːtlɪ] adv teilweise

partner ['pɑːtnəˈ] n Partner(in) m(f); **partnership** n Partnerschaft f

partridge ['pɑːtrɪdʒ] n Rebhuhn nt

part-time ['pɑːtˈtaɪm] adj Teilzeit- ▷ adv: **to work ~** Teilzeit arbeiten

party ['pɑːtɪ] n (celebration) Party f; (Pol, Jur) Partei f; (group) Gruppe f ▷ vi feiern

pass [pɑːs] vt (on foot) vorbeigehen an +dat; (in car etc) vorbeifahren an +dat; (time) verbringen; (exam) bestehen; (law) verabschieden; **to ~ sth to sb**, **to ~ sb sth** jdm etw reichen; **to ~ the ball to sb** jdm den Ball zuspielen ▷ vi (on foot) vorbeigehen; (in car etc) vorbeifahren; (years) vergehen; (in exam) bestehen ▷ n (document) Ausweis m; (Sport) Pass m; **pass**

away vi (die) verscheiden; **pass by** vi (on foot) vorbeigehen; (in car etc) vorbeifahren ▷ vt (on foot) vorbeigehen an +dat; (in car etc) vorbeifahren an +dat; **pass on** vt weitergeben (to an +akk); (disease) übertragen (to auf +akk); **pass out** vi (faint) ohnmächtig werden; **pass round** vt herumreichen

passage ['pæsɪdʒ] n (corridor) Gang m; (in book, music) Passage f; **passageway** n Durchgang m

passenger ['pæsɪndʒəˈ] n Passagier(in) m(f); (on bus) Fahrgast m; (on train) Reisende(r) mf; (in car) Mitfahrer(in) m(f)

passer-by ['pɑːsəˈbaɪ] (pl **passers-by**) n Passant(in) m(f)

passion ['pæʃən] n Leidenschaft f; **passionate** ['pæʃənɪt] adj leidenschaftlich; **passion fruit** n Passionsfrucht f

passive ['pæsɪv] adj passiv; **~ smoking** Passivrauchen nt ▷ n: **~ (voice)** (Ling) Passiv nt

passport ['pɑːspɔːt] n (Reise)pass m; **passport control** n Passkontrolle f

password ['pɑːswɜːd] n (Inform) Passwort nt

past [pɑːst] n Vergangenheit f ▷ adv (by) vorbei; **it's five ~** es ist fünf nach ▷ adj (years) vergangen; (president etc) ehemalig; **in the ~ two months** in den letzten zwei Monaten ▷ prep (telling time) nach; **half ~ 10** halb 11; **to go ~ sth** an etw dat vorbeigehen/-fahren

pasta ['pæstə] n Nudeln pl

paste [peɪst] vt (stick) kleben; (Inform) einfügen ▷ n (glue) Kleister m

pastime ['pɑːstaɪm] n Zeitvertreib m

pastry ['peɪstrɪ] n Teig m; (cake) Stückchen nt

pasty ['pæstɪ] n (Brit) Pastete f

patch [pætʃ] n (area) Fleck m; (for mending) Flicken ▷ vt flicken; **patchy** adj (uneven) ungleichmäßig

pâté ['pæteɪ] n Pastete f

paternal [pə'tɜ:nl] adj väterlich; **~ grandmother** Großmutter f väterlicherseits; **paternity leave** [pə'tɜ:nɪtɪli:v] n Elternzeit f (des Vaters)

path [pɑ:θ] n (a. Inform) Pfad m; (a. fig) Weg m

pathetic [pə'θetɪk] adj (bad) kläglich, erbärmlich; **it's ~** es ist zum Heulen

patience ['peɪʃəns] n Geduld f; (Brit Cards) Patience f; **patient** adj geduldig ▷ n Patient(in) m(f)

patio ['pætɪəʊ] n Terrasse f

patriotic [pætrɪ'ɒtɪk] adj patriotisch

patrol car [pə'trəʊlkɑ:ʳ] n Streifenwagen m; **patrolman** (pl **-men**) n (US) Streifenpolizist m

patron ['peɪtrən] n (sponsor) Förderer m, Förderin f; (in shop) Kunde m, Kundin f

patronize ['pætrənaɪz] vt (treat condescendingly) von oben herab behandeln; **patronizing** adj (attitude) herablassend

pattern ['pætən] n Muster nt

pause [pɔ:z] n Pause f ▷ vi (speaker) innehalten

pavement n (Brit) Bürgersteig m; (US) Pflaster nt

pay [peɪ] (**paid, paid**) vt bezahlen; **he paid (me) £20 for it** er hat (mir) 20 Pfund dafür gezahlt; **to ~ attention** Acht geben (to auf +akk); **to ~ sb a visit** jdn besuchen ▷ vi zahlen; (be profitable) sich bezahlt machen; **to ~ for sth** etw bezahlen ▷ n Bezahlung f, Lohn m; **pay back** vt (money) zurückzahlen; **pay in** vt (into account) einzahlen; **payable**

adj zahlbar; (due) fällig; **payday** n Zahltag m; **payee** [peɪ'i:] n Zahlungsempfänger(in) m(f); **payment** n Bezahlung f; (money) Zahlung f **pay-per-view** adj Pay-per-View-; **pay phone** n Münzfernsprecher m; **pay TV** nt Pay-TV nt

PC abbr = **personal computer** PC m; abbr = **politically correct** politisch korrekt

PDA abbr = **personal digital assistant** PDA m

PE abbr = **physical education** (school) Sport m

pea [pi:] n Erbse f

peace [pi:s] n Frieden m; **peaceful** adj friedlich

peach [pi:tʃ] n Pfirsich m

peacock ['pi:kɒk] n Pfau m

peak [pi:k] n (of mountain) Gipfel m; (fig) Höhepunkt m; **peak period** n Stoßzeit f; (season) Hochsaison

peanut [pi:nʌt] n Erdnuss f; **peanut butter** n Erdnussbutter f

pear [peəʳ] n Birne f

pearl [pɜ:l] n Perle f

pebble ['pebl] n Kiesel m

pecan [pɪ'kæn] n Pekannuss f

peck [pek] vt, vi picken; **peckish** adj (Brit fam) ein bisschen hungrig

peculiar [pɪ'kju:lɪəʳ] adj (odd) seltsam; **~ to** charakteristisch für; **peculiarity** [pɪkjʊlɪ'ærɪtɪ] n (singular quality) Besonderheit f; (strangeness) Eigenartigkeit f

pedal ['pedl] n Pedal nt

pedestrian [pɪ'destrɪən] n Fußgänger(in) m(f); **pedestrian crossing** n Fußgängerüberweg m

pee [pi:] vi (fam) pinkeln

peel [pi:l] n Schale f ▷ vt schälen ▷ vi (paint etc) abblättern; (skin etc) sich schälen

peer [pɪəʳ] n Gleichaltrige(r) mf ▷ vi starren

peg [peg] n (for coat etc) Haken m; (for tent) Hering m; **(clothes)** ~ (Wäsche)klammer f

pelvis ['pelvis] n Becken nt

pen [pen] n (ball-point) Kuli m, Kugelschreiber; (fountain~) Füller m

penalize ['pi:nəlaiz] vt (punish) bestrafen; **penalty** ['penlti] n (punishment) Strafe f; (in football) Elfmeter m

pence [pens] pl of **penny**

pencil ['pensl] n Bleistift m; **pencil sharpener** n (Bleistift)spitzer m

penetrate ['penitreit] vt durchdringen; (enter into) eindringen in +akk

penfriend ['penfrend] n Brieffreund(in) m(f)

penguin ['peŋgwin] n Pinguin m

penicillin [peni'silin] n Penizillin nt

peninsula [pi'ninsjulə] n Halbinsel f

penis ['pi:nis] n Penis m

penknife ['pennaif] n (pl **penknives**) n Taschenmesser nt

penny ['peni] (pl **pence** o **pennies**) n (Brit) Penny m; (US) Centstück nt

pension ['penʃən] n Rente f; (for civil servants, executives etc) Pension f; **pensioner** n Rentner(in) m(f); **pension plan, pension scheme** n Rentenversicherung f

penultimate [pi'nʌltimət] adj vorletzte(r, s)

people ['pi:pl] npl (persons) Leute pl; (von Staat) Volk nt; (inhabitants) Bevölkerung f; **people carrier** n Minivan m

pepper ['pepə°] n Pfeffer m; (vegetable) Paprika m; **peppermint** n (sweet) Pfefferminz nt

per [pɜ:°] prep pro; ~ **annum** pro Jahr; ~ **cent** Prozent nt

percentage [pə'sentidʒ] n Prozentsatz m

perceptible [pə'septəbl] adj wahrnehmbar

percolator ['pɜ:kəleitə°] n Kaffeemaschine f

percussion [pɜ:'kʌʃən] n (Mus) Schlagzeug nt

perfect ['pɜ:fikt] adj perfekt; (utter) völlig ▷ [pə'fekt] vt vervollkommnen; **perfectly** adv perfekt; (utterly) völlig

perform [pə'fɔ:m] vt (task) ausführen; (play) aufführen; (Med: operation) durchführen ▷ vi (Theat) auftreten; **performance** n (show) Vorstellung f; (efficiency) Leistung f

perfume ['pɜ:fju:m] n Duft m; (substance) Parfüm nt

perhaps [pə'hæps] adv vielleicht

period ['piəriəd] n (length of time) Zeit f; (in history) Zeitalter nt; (school) Stunde f; (Med) Periode f; (US: full stop) Punkt m; **for a ~ of three years** für einen Zeitraum von drei Jahren; **periodical** [piəri'ɒdikəl] n Zeitschrift f

peripheral [pə'rifərəl] n (Inform) Peripheriegerät nt

perjury ['pɜ:dʒəri] n Meineid m

perm [pɜ:m] n Dauerwelle f

permanent, permanently ['pɜ:mənənt, -li] adj, adv ständig

permission [pə'miʃən] n Erlaubnis f; **permit** ['pɜ:mit] n Genehmigung f ▷ [pə'mit] vt erlauben, zulassen; **to ~ sb to do sth** jdm erlauben, etw zu tun

persecute ['pɜ:sikju:t] vt verfolgen

perseverance [pɜ:si'viərəns] n Ausdauer f

persist [pə'sist] vi (in belief etc) bleiben (in bei); (rain, smell) andauern; **persistent** adj beharrlich

p

person ['pɜːsn] n Mensch m; (in official context) Person f; **in ~** persönlich; **personal** adj persönlich; (private) privat; **personality** [pɜːsə'nælətɪ] n Persönlichkeit f; **personal organizer** n Organizer m; **personal stereo** (pl **-s**) n Walkman® m; **personnel** [pɜːsə'nel] n Personal nt

perspective [pə'spektɪv] n Perspektive f

persuade [pə'sweɪd] vt überreden; (convince) überzeugen; **persuasive** [pə'sweɪsɪv] adj überzeugend

perverse [pə'vɜːs] adj eigensinnig; abwegig; **pervert** ['pɜːvɜːt] n Perverse(r) mf ▷ [pə'vɜːt] vt (morally) verderben; **perverted** [pə'vɜːtɪd] adj pervers

pessimist ['pesɪmɪst] n Pessimist(in) m(f); **pessimistic** [pesɪ'mɪstɪk] adj pessimistisch

pest [pest] n (insect) Schädling m; (fig: person) Nervensäge f; (thing) Plage f; **pester** ['pestə°] vt plagen; **pesticide** ['pestɪsaɪd] n Schädlingsbekämpfungsmittel nt

pet [pet] n (animal) Haustier nt; (person) Liebling m

petal ['petl] n Blütenblatt nt

petition [pə'tɪʃən] n Petition f

petrol ['petrəl] n (Brit) Benzin nt; **petrol pump** n (at garage) Zapfsäule f; **petrol station** n Tankstelle f; **petrol tank** n Benzintank m

pharmacy ['fɑːməsɪ] n (shop) Apotheke f; (science) Pharmazie f

phase [feɪz] n Phase f

PhD abbr = **Doctor of Philosophy** Dr. phil; (dissertation) Doktorarbeit f; **to do one's ~** promovieren

pheasant ['feznt] n Fasan m

phenomenon [fɪ'nɒmɪnən] n (pl **phenomena**) n Phänomen nt

Philippines ['fɪlɪpiːnz] npl Philippinen pl

philosophical [fɪlə'sɒfɪkəl] adj philosophisch; (fig) gelassen; **philosophy** [fɪ'lɒsəfɪ] n Philosophie f

phone [fəʊn] n Telefon nt ▷ vt, vi anrufen; **phone book** n Telefonbuch nt; **phone bill** n Telefonrechnung f; **phone booth**, **phone box** (Brit) n Telefonzelle f; **phonecall** n Telefonanruf m; **phonecard** n Telefonkarte f; **phone-in** n Rundfunkprogramm, bei dem Hörer anrufen können; **phone number** n Telefonnummer f

photo ['fəʊtəʊ] (pl **-s**) n Foto nt; **photo booth** n Fotoautomat m; **photocopier** ['fəʊtəʊkɒpɪə°] n Kopiergerät nt; **photocopy** ['fəʊtəʊkɒpɪ] n Fotokopie f ▷ vt fotokopieren; **photograph** ['fəʊtəɡrɑːf] n Fotografie f, Aufnahme f ▷ vt fotografieren; **photographer** [fə'tɒɡrəfə°] n Fotograf(in) m(f); **photography** [fə'tɒɡrəfɪ] n Fotografie f

phrase [freɪz] n (expression) Redewendung f, Ausdruck m; **phrase book** n Sprachführer m

physical ['fɪzɪkəl] adj (bodily) körperlich, physisch ▷ n ärztliche Untersuchung; **physically** adv (bodily) körperlich, physisch; **~ handicapped** körperbehindert

physics ['fɪzɪks] nsing Physik f

physiotherapy [fɪzɪə'θerəpɪ] n Physiotherapie f

physique [fɪ'ziːk] n Körperbau m

piano ['pjɑːnəʊ] (pl **-s**) n Klavier nt

pick [pɪk] vt (flowers, fruit) pflücken; (choose) auswählen; (team) aufstellen; **pick out** vt auswählen; **pick up** vt (lift up) aufheben; (collect) abholen; (learn) lernen

pickle ['pɪkl] n (food) (Mixed) Pickles pl ▷ vt einlegen

pickpocket ['pɪkpɒkɪt] n Taschendieb(in) m(f)

picnic ['pɪknɪk] n Picknick nt

picture ['pɪktʃə°] n Bild nt; **to go to the ~s** (Brit) ins Kino gehen ▷ vt (visualize) sich vorstellen; **picture book** n Bilderbuch nt; **picturesque** [pɪktʃə'resk] adj malerisch

pie [paɪ] n (meat) Pastete f; (fruit) Kuchen m

piece [piːs] n Stück nt; (part) Teil nt; (in chess) Figur f; (in draughts) Stein m; **a ~ of cake** ein Stück Kuchen; **to fall to ~s** auseinanderfallen

pier [pɪə°] n Pier m

pierce [pɪəs] vt durchstechen, durchbohren; (cold, sound) durchdringen; **pierced** adj (part of body) gepierct; **piercing** adj durchdringend

pig [pɪg] n Schwein nt

pigeon ['pɪdʒən] n Taube f; **pigeonhole** n (compartment) Ablegefach nt

piggy ['pɪgɪ] adj (fam) verfressen; **pigheaded** ['pɪg'hedɪd] adj dickköpfig; **piglet** ['pɪglət] n Ferkel nt; **pigsty** ['pɪgstaɪ] n Schweinestall m; **pigtail** ['pɪgteɪl] n Zopf m

pile [paɪl] n (heap) Haufen m; (one on top of another) Stapel m; **pile up** vi (accumulate) sich anhäufen

piles [paɪlz] npl Hämorr(ho)iden pl

pile-up ['paɪlʌp] n (Aut) Massenkarambolage f

pilgrim ['pɪlgrɪm] n Pilger(in) m(f)

pill [pɪl] n Tablette f; **the ~** die (Antibaby)pille; **to be on the ~** die Pille nehmen

pillar ['pɪlə°] n Pfeiler m

pillow ['pɪləʊ] n (Kopf)kissen nt; **pillowcase** n (Kopf)kissenbezug m

pilot ['paɪlət] n (Aviat) Pilot(in) m(f)

pimple ['pɪmpl] n Pickel m

pin [pɪn] n (for fixing) Nadel f; (in sewing) Stecknadel f; (Tech) Stift m; **I've got ~s and needles in my leg** mein Bein ist mir eingeschlafen ▷ vt (fix with ~) heften (to an +akk)

PIN [pɪn] acr = **personal identification number** **~ (number)** PIN f, Geheimzahl f

pinch [pɪntʃ] n (of salt) Prise f ▷ vt zwicken; (fam: steal) klauen ▷ vi (shoe) drücken

pine [paɪn] n Kiefer f

pineapple ['paɪnæpl] n Ananas f

pink [pɪŋk] adj rosa

pinstripe(d) ['pɪnstraɪp(d)] adj Nadelstreifen-

pint [paɪnt] n Pint nt (Brit: 0,57 l, US: 0,473l); (Brit: glass of beer) Bier nt

pious ['paɪəs] adj fromm

pip [pɪp] n (of fruit) Kern m

pipe [paɪp] n (for smoking) Pfeife f; (for water, gas) Rohrleitung f

pirate ['paɪərɪt] n Pirat(in) m(f); **pirated copy** n Raubkopie f

Pisces ['paɪsiːz] nsing (Astr) Fische pl; **she's a ~** sie ist Fisch

piss [pɪs] n (vulg) pissen ▷ n (vulg) Pisse f; **to take the ~ out of sb** jdn verarschen; **piss off** vi (vulg) sich verpissen; **~!** verpiss dich!; **pissed** adj (Brit fam: drunk) sturzbesoffen; (US fam: annoyed) stocksauer

pistachio [pɪ'stɑːʃɪəʊ] (pl **-s**) n Pistazie f

piste [piːst] n (Ski) Piste f

pistol ['pɪstl] n Pistole f

pit [pɪt] n (hole) Grube f; (coalmine) Zeche f; **the ~s** (motor racing) die Box; **to be the ~s** grottenschlecht sein

pitch [pɪtʃ] n (Sport) Spielfeld nt; (Mus: of instrument) Tonlage f; (of voice) Stimmlage f ▷ vt (tent)

aufschlagen; (throw) werfen;
pitch-black adj pechschwarz

pitcher ['pɪtʃə*] n (US: jug) Krug m

pitiful ['pɪtɪful] adj (contemptible)
jämmerlich

pitta bread ['pɪtə] n Pittabrot nt

pity ['pɪtɪ] n Mitleid nt; **what a
~** wie schade; **it's a ~** es ist schade
▷ vt Mitleid haben mit

pizza ['piːtsə] n Pizza f

place [pleɪs] n m (spot, in text)
Stelle f; (town etc) Ort; (house) Haus
nt; (position, seat, on course) Platz m;
~ of birth Geburtsort m; **at my
~** bei mir; **in third ~** auf dem dritten
Platz; **to three decimal ~s** bis auf
drei Stellen nach dem Komma; **out
of ~** nicht an der richtigen Stelle;
(fig: remark) unangebracht; **in ~ of**
anstelle von; **in the first ~** (firstly)
erstens; (immediately) gleich; (in any
case) überhaupt ▷ vt (put) stellen,
setzen; (lay flat) legen; (advertisement) setzen (in in +akk); (Comm:
order) aufgeben; **place mat** n Set nt

plague [pleɪg] n Pest f

plaice [pleɪs] n Scholle f

plain [pleɪn] adj (clear) klar,
deutlich; (simple) einfach; (not
beautiful) unattraktiv; (yoghurt)
Natur-; (Brit: chocolate)
(Zart)bitter- ▷ n Ebene f; **plainly**
adv (frankly) offen; (simply) einfach;
(obviously) eindeutig

plait [plæt] n Zopf m ▷ vt
flechten

plan [plæn] n Plan m; (for essay
etc) Konzept nt ▷ vt planen; **to
~ to do sth, to ~ on doing sth**
vorhaben, etw zu tun ▷ vi planen

plane [pleɪn] n (aircraft)
Flugzeug nt; (tool) Hobel m

planet ['plænɪt] n Planet m

plank [plæŋk] n Brett nt

plant [plɑːnt] n Pflanze f;
(equipment) Maschinen pl; (factory)
Werk nt ▷ vt (tree etc) pflanzen;

plantation [plæn'teɪʃən] n Planta-
ge f

plaque [plæk] n Gedenktafel f;
(on teeth) Zahnbelag m

plaster ['plɑːstə*] n (Brit Med:
sticking ~) Pflaster nt; (on wall)
Verputz m; **to have one's arm in
~** den Arm in Gips haben

plastered ['plɑːstəd] adj (fam)
besoffen; **to get (absolutely)
~** sich besaufen

plastic ['plæstɪk] n Kunststoff m;
to pay with ~ mit Kreditkarte
bezahlen ▷ adj Plastik-; **plastic
bag** n Plastiktüte f; **plastic
surgery** n plastische Chirurgie f

plate [pleɪt] n (for food) Teller m;
(flat sheet) Platte f; (plaque) Schild
nt

platform ['plætfɔːm] n (Rail)
Bahnsteig m; (at meeting) Podium
nt

platinum ['plætɪnəm] n Platin nt

play [pleɪ] n Spiel m; (Theat)
(Theater)stück nt ▷ vt spielen;
(another player or team) spielen
gegen; **to ~ the piano** Klavier
spielen; **to ~ a part in** (fig) eine
Rolle spielen bei ▷ vi spielen;
play at vt: **what are you ~ing at?**
was soll das?; **play back** vt
abspielen; **play down** vt
herunterspielen

playacting n Schauspielerei f;
playback n Wiedergabe f; **player**
n Spieler(in) m(f); **playful** adj
(person) verspielt; (remark)
scherzhaft; **playground** n
Spielplatz m; (in school) Schulhof m;
playgroup n Spielgruppe f;
playing card n Spielkarte f;
playing field n Sportplatz m;
playmate n Spielkamerad(in)
m(f); **playwright** n
Dramatiker(in) m(f)

plc abbr = **public limited company**
AG f

plea [pli:] n Bitte f (for um)
plead [pli:d] vi dringend bitten (with sb jdn); (Jur) **to ~ guilty** sich schuldig bekennen
pleasant, **pleasantly** ['pleznt, -lı] adj, adv angenehm
please [pli:z] adv bitte; **more tea? - yes, ~** noch Tee? - ja, bitte ▷ vt (be agreeable to) gefallen +dat; **~ yourself** wie du willst/Sie wollen; **pleased** adj zufrieden; (glad) erfreut; **~ to meet you** freut mich, angenehm; **pleasing** adj erfreulich; **pleasure** ['pleʒə°] n Vergnügen nt, Freude f; **it's a ~** gern geschehen
pledge [pledʒ] n Versprechen nt ▷ vt versprechen
plenty ['plentı] n: **~ of** eine Menge, viel(e); **to be ~** genug sein, reichen; **I've got ~** ich habe mehr als genug ▷ adv (US fam) ganz schön
pliable ['plaıəbl] adj biegsam
pliers ['plaıəz] npl (Kombi)zange f
plimsoll ['plımsəl] n (Brit) Turnschuh m
plonk [plɒŋk] n (Brit fam: wine) billiger Wein ▷ vt: **to ~ sth (down)** etw hinknallen
plot [plɒt] n (of story) Handlung f; (conspiracy) Komplott nt; (of land) Stück nt Land, Grundstück nt ▷ vi ein Komplott schmieden
plough, plow (US) [plaʊ] n Pflug m ▷ vt, vi (Agr) pflügen; **ploughman's lunch** n (Brit) in einer Kneipe serviertes Gericht aus Käse, Brot, Mixed Pickles etc
pluck [plʌk] vt (eyebrows, guitar) zupfen; (chicken) rupfen; **pluck up** vt: **to ~ (one's) courage** Mut aufbringen
plug [plʌg] n (for sink, bath) Stöpsel m; (Elec) Stecker m; (Auto) (Zünd)kerze f; (fam: publicity)

Schleichwerbung f ▷ vt (fam: advertise) Reklame machen für; **plug in** vt anschließen
plum [plʌm] n Pflaume f ▷ adj (fam: job etc) Super-
plumber ['plʌmə°] n Klempner(in) m(f); **plumbing** ['plʌmıŋ] n (fittings) Leitungen pl; (craft) Installieren nt
plump [plʌmp] adj rundlich
plunge [plʌndʒ] vt (knife) stoßen; (into water) tauchen ▷ vi stürzen; (into water) tauchen
plural ['plʊərəl] n Plural m
plus [plʌs] prep plus; (as well as) und ▷ adj Plus-; **20 ~** mehr als 20 ▷ n adj (fig) Plus nt
plywood ['plaıwʊd] n Sperrholz nt
pm abbr = **post meridiem**; **at 3 ~** um 3 Uhr nachmittags; **at 8 ~** um 8 Uhr abends
pneumonia [nju:'məʊnıə] n Lungenentzündung f
poached [pəʊtʃt] adj (egg) pochiert, verloren
PO Box abbr = **post office box** Postfach m
pocket ['pɒkıt] n Tasche f ▷ vt (put in ~) einstecken; **pocketbook** n (US: wallet) Brieftasche f; **pocket calculator** n Taschenrechner m; **pocket money** n Taschengeld nt
podcast ['pɒdka:st] n Podcast m
poem ['pəʊəm] n Gedicht nt; **poet** ['pəʊıt] n Dichter(in) m(f); **poetic** [pəʊ'etık] adj poetisch; **poetry** ['pəʊıtrı] n (art) Dichtung f; (poems) Gedichte pl
point [pɔınt] n (spot) Stelle f; (sharp tip) Spitze f; (moment) Zeitpunkt m; (purpose) Zweck m; (idea) Argument nt; (decimal) Dezimalstelle f; **~s** pl (Rail) Weiche f; **~ of view** Standpunkt m; **three ~ two** drei Komma zwei; **at some ~** irgendwann (mal); **to get**

to the ~ zur Sache kommen;
there's no ~ es hat keinen Sinn; **I
was on the ~ of leaving** ich wollte
gerade gehen ▷ vt (gun etc)
richten (at at +akk); to ~ one's
finger at mit dem Finger zeigen
auf +akk ▷ vi (with finger etc)
zeigen (at, to auf +akk); **point out**
vt (indicate) aufzeigen; (mention)
hinweisen auf +akk; **pointed** adj
spitz; (question) gezielt; **pointer** n
(on dial) Zeiger m; (tip) Hinweis m;
pointless adj sinnlos

poison ['pɔɪzn] n Gift nt ▷ vt
vergiften; **poisonous** adj giftig

poke [pəʊk] vt (with stick, finger)
stoßen, stupsen; (put) stecken

Poland ['pəʊlənd] n Polen nt

polar ['pəʊlə] adj Polar-, polar;
~ bear Eisbär m

pole [pəʊl] n Stange f; (Geo, Elec)
Pol m

Pole [pəʊl] n Pole m, Polin f

pole vault n Stabhochsprung m

police [pə'liːs] n Polizei f; **police
car** n Polizeiwagen m; **policeman**
(pl **-men**) n Polizist m; **police
station** n (Polizei)wache f;
policewoman (pl **-women**) n
Polizistin f

policy ['pɒlɪsɪ] n (plan) Politik f;
(principle) Grundsatz m; (insurance
~) (Versicherungs)police f

polio ['pəʊlɪəʊ] n Kinderlähmung f

polish ['pɒlɪʃ] n (for furniture)
Politur f; (for floor) Wachs nt; (for
shoes) Creme f; (shine) Glanz m;
(fig) Schliff m ▷ vt polieren;
(shoes) putzen; (fig) den letzten
Schliff geben +dat

Polish ['pəʊlɪʃ] adj polnisch ▷ n
Polnisch nt

polite [pə'laɪt] adj höflich;
politeness n Höflichkeit f

political, politically [pə'lɪtɪkəl, -ɪ]
adj, adv politisch; **~ly correct**
politisch korrekt; **politician**

n Politiker(in) m(f);
politics ['pɒlɪtɪks] nsing o pl
Politik f

poll [pəʊl] n (election) Wahl f;
(opinion ~) Umfrage f

pollen ['pɒlən] n Pollen m,
Blütenstaub m; **pollen count** n
Pollenflug m

polling station ['pəʊlɪŋsteɪʃən]
n Wahllokal nt

pollute [pə'luːt] vt verschmut-
zen; **pollution** [pə'luːʃən] n
Verschmutzung f

pompous ['pɒmpəs] adj aufge-
blasen; (language) geschwollen

pond [pɒnd] n Teich m

pony ['pəʊnɪ] n Pony nt;
ponytail n Pferdeschwanz m

poodle ['puːdl] n Pudel m

pool [puːl] n (swimming ~)
Schwimmbad nt; (private)
Swimmingpool m; (of spilt liquid,
blood) Lache f; (game) Poolbillard
nt ▷ vt (money etc)
zusammenlegen

poor [pɔː] adj arm; (not good)
schlecht ▷ npl: **the ~** die Armen
pl; **poorly** adv (badly) schlecht
▷ adj (Brit) krank

pop [pɒp] n (music) Pop m; (noise)
Knall m ▷ vt (put) stecken;
(balloon) platzen lassen ▷ vi
(balloon) platzen; (cork) knallen; **to
~ in** (person) vorbeischauen; **pop
concert** n Popkonzert nt;
popcorn n Popcorn nt

Pope [pəʊp] n Papst m

pop group ['pɒpgruːp] n
Popgruppe f; **pop music** n
Popmusik f

poppy ['pɒpɪ] n Mohn m

Popsicle® ['pɒpsɪkl] n (US) Eis
nt am Stiel

pop star ['pɒpstɑː] n Popstar m

popular ['pɒpjʊlə] adj (well-
liked) beliebt (with bei);
(widespread) weit verbreitet

population [pɒpjʊ'leɪʃən] n
Bevölkerung f; (of town) Einwohner
pl

porcelain ['pɔːslɪn] n Porzellan nt

porch [pɔːtʃ] n Vorbau m; (US:
verandah) Veranda f

porcupine ['pɔːkjʊpaɪn] n
Stachelschwein nt

pork [pɔːk] n Schweinefleisch nt;
pork chop n Schweinekotelett;
pork pie n Schweinefleischpastete
f

porn [pɔːn] n Porno m;
pornographic [pɔːnə'græfɪk] adj
pornografisch; **pornography**
[pɔː'nɒgrəfɪ] n Pornografie f

porridge ['pɒrɪdʒ] n Haferbrei m

port [pɔːt] n (harbour) Hafen m;
(town) Hafenstadt f; (Naut: left side)
Backbord nt; (wine) Portwein m;
(Inform) Anschluss m

portable ['pɔːtəbl] adj tragbar;
(radio) Koffer-

portal ['pɔːtl] n (Inform) Portal n

porter ['pɔːtə*] n Pförtner(in)
m(f); (for luggage) Gepäckträger m

porthole ['pɔːthəʊl] n Bullauge
nt

portion ['pɔːʃən] n Teil m; (of
food) Portion f

portrait ['pɔːtrɪt] n Porträt nt

portray [pɔː'treɪ] vt darstellen

Portugal ['pɔːtʃʊgl] n Portugal
nt; **Portuguese** [pɔːtʃʊ'giːz] adj
portugiesisch ▷ n Portugiese m,
Portugiesin f; (language)
Portugiesisch nt

pose [pəʊz] n Haltung f ▷ vi
posieren ▷ vt (threat, problem)
darstellen

posh [pɒʃ] adj (fam) piekfein

position [pə'zɪʃən] n Stellung f;
(place) Position f, Lage f; (job) Stelle
f; (opinion) Standpunkt m; **to be in
a ~ to do sth** in der Lage sein, etw
zu tun; **in third ~** auf dem dritten
Platz ▷ vt aufstellen; (Inform:

cursor) positionieren

positive ['pɒzɪtɪv] adj positiv;
(convinced) sicher

possess [pə'zes] vt besitzen;
possession [pə'zeʃən] n **~(s** pl)
Besitz m; **possessive** adj (person)
besitzergreifend

possibility [pɒsə'bɪlɪtɪ] n
Möglichkeit f; **possible** ['pɒsəbl]
adj möglich; **if ~** wenn möglich; **as
big/soon as ~** so groß/bald wie
möglich; **possibly** adv (perhaps)
vielleicht; **I've done all I ~ can** ich
habe ein Möglichstes getan

post [pəʊst] n (mail) Post f; (pole)
Pfosten m; (job) Stelle f ▷ vt
(letters) aufgeben; (on website)
posten; **to keep sb ~ed** jdn auf
dem Laufenden halten; **postage**
['pəʊstɪdʒ] n Porto nt; **~ and
packing** Porto und Verpackung;
postal adj Post-; (Brit) **~ order**
Postanweisung f; **postbox** n
Briefkasten m; **postcard** n
Postkarte f; **postcode** n (Brit)
Postleitzahl f

poster ['pəʊstə*] n Plakat nt,
Poster nt

postgraduate [pəʊst'grædjuɪt]
n jmd, der seine Studien nach dem
ersten akademischen Grad weiterführt

postman ['pəʊstmən] (pl -men)
n Briefträger m; **postmark** n
Poststempel m

postmortem [pəʊst'mɔːtəm] n
Autopsie f

post office ['pəʊstɒfɪs] n Post® f

postpone [pə'spəʊn] vt verschieben (till aud +akk)

posture ['pɒstʃə*] n Haltung f

pot [pɒt] n Topf m; (tea-, coffee ~)
Kanne f; (fam: marijuana) Pot nt
▷ vt (plant) eintopfen

potato [pə'teɪtəʊ] (pl -es) n
Kartoffel f; **potato chips** (US) npl
Kartoffelchips pl; **potato peeler** n
Kartoffelschäler m

potent ['pəʊtənt] adj stark

potential [pəʊ'tenʃəl] adj potenziell ▷ n Potenzial nt; **potentially** adv potenziell

pothole ['pɒthəʊl] n Höhle f; (in road) Schlagloch nt

potter about ['pɒtərəbaʊt] vi herumhantieren

pottery ['pɒtərɪ] n (objects) Töpferwaren pl

potty ['pɒtɪ] adj (Brit fam) verrückt ▷ n Töpfchen nt

poultry ['pəʊltrɪ] n Geflügel nt

pounce [paʊns] vi: **to ~ on** sich stürzen auf +akk

pound [paʊnd] n (money) Pfund nt; (weight) Pfund nt (0,454 kg); **a ~ of cherries** ein Pfund Kirschen; **ten-~ note** Zehnpfundschein m

pour [pɔː°] vt (liquid) gießen; (rice, sugar etc) schütten; **to ~ sb sth** (drink) jdm etw eingießen; **pouring** adj (rain) strömend

poverty ['pɒvətɪ] n Armut f

powder ['paʊdə°] n Pulver nt; (cosmetic) Puder m; **powdered milk** n Milchpulver nt; **powder room** n Damentoilette f

power ['paʊə°] n Macht f; (ability) Fähigkeit f; (strength) Stärke f; (Elec) Strom m; **to be in ~** an der Macht sein ▷ vt betreiben, antreiben;

power-assisted steering n Servolenkung f; **power cut** n Stromausfall m; **powerful** adj (politician etc) mächtig; (engine, government) stark; (argument) durchschlagend; **powerless** adj machtlos; **power station** n Kraftwerk nt

p&p abbr = **postage and packing**

PR abbr = **public relations** ▷ abbr = **proportional representation**

practical, practically ['præktɪkəl,

-l] adj, adv praktisch; **practice** ['præktɪs] n (training) Übung f; (custom) Gewohnheit f; (doctor's, lawyer's) Praxis f; **in ~** (in reality) in der Praxis; **out of ~** außer Übung; **to put sth into ~** etw in die Praxis umsetzen ▷ vt, vi (US) see

practise, practise ['præktɪs] vt (instrument, movement) üben; (profession) ausüben ▷ vi üben; (doctor, lawyer) praktizieren

Prague [prɑːg] n Prag nt

praise [preɪz] n Lob nt ▷ vt loben

pram [præm] n (Brit) Kinderwagen m

prawn [prɔːn] n Garnele f, Krabbe f; **prawn crackers** npl Krabbenchips pl

pray [preɪ] vi beten; **to ~ for sth** (fig) stark auf etw akk hoffen; **prayer** ['preə°] n Gebet nt

pre- [priː] pref vor-, prä-

preach [priːtʃ] vi predigen

prearrange [priːə'reɪndʒ] vt im Voraus vereinbaren

precaution [prɪ'kɔːʃən] n Vorsichtsmaßnahme f

precede [prɪ'siːd] vt vorausgehen +dat; **preceding** adj vorhergehend

precinct ['priːsɪŋkt] n (Brit: pedestrian ~) Fußgängerzone f; (Brit: shopping ~) Einkaufsviertel nt; (US: district) Bezirk m

precious ['preʃəs] adj kostbar; **~ stone** Edelstein m

précis ['preɪsiː] n Zusammenfassung f

precise, precisely [prɪ'saɪs, -lɪ] adj, adv genau

precondition [priːkən'dɪʃən] n Vorbedingung f

predecessor ['priːdɪsesə°] n Vorgänger(in) m(f)

predicament [prɪ'dɪkəmənt] n missliche Lage

predict [prɪˈdɪkt] vt voraussagen; **predictable** adj vorhersehbar; (*person*) berechenbar

predominant [prɪˈdɒmɪnənt] adj vorherrschend; **predominantly** adv überwiegend

preface [ˈprefɪs] n Vorwort nt

prefer [prɪˈfɜːʳ] vt vorziehen (to dat), lieber mögen (to als); **to ~ to do sth** etw lieber tun; **preferably** [ˈprefrəblɪ] adv vorzugsweise, am liebsten; **preference** [ˈprefərəns] n (*liking*) Vorliebe f; **preferential** [prefəˈrenʃəl] adj: **to get ~ treatment** bevorzugt behandelt werden

prefix [ˈpriːfɪks] n (*US Tel*) Vorwahl f

pregnancy [ˈpregnənsɪ] n Schwangerschaft f; **pregnant** [ˈpregnənt] adj schwanger; **two months ~** im zweiten Monat schwanger

prejudice [ˈpredʒudɪs] n Vorurteil nt; **prejudiced** adj (*person*) voreingenommen

preliminary [prɪˈlɪmɪnərɪ] adj (*measures*) vorbereitend; (*results*) vorläufig; (*remarks*) einleitend

premature [ˈpremətʃʊəʳ] adj vorzeitig; (*hasty*) voreilig

premiere [ˈpremɪeəʳ] n Premiere f

premises [ˈpremɪsɪz] npl (*offices*) Räumlichkeiten pl; (*of factory, school*) Gelände nt

premium-rate [ˈpriːmɪəmreɪt] adj (*Tel*) zum Höchsttarif

preoccupied [priːˈɒkjupaɪd] adj: **to be ~ with sth** mit etw sehr beschäftigt sein

prepaid [priːˈpeɪd] adj vorausbezahlt; (*envelope*) frankiert

preparation [prepəˈreɪʃən] n Vorbereitung f; **prepare** [prɪˈpeəʳ] vt vorbereiten (*for* auf +akk); (*food*) zubereiten; **to be ~d to do sth** bereit sein, etw zu tun ▷ vi sich vorbereiten (*for* auf +akk)

prerequisite [priːˈrekwɪzɪt] n Voraussetzung f

prescribe [prɪˈskraɪb] vt vorschreiben; (*Med*) verschreiben; **prescription** [prɪˈskrɪpʃən] n Rezept nt

presence [ˈprezns] n Gegenwart f; **present** [ˈpreznt] adj (*in attendance*) anwesend (*at* bei); (*current*) gegenwärtig; **~ tense** Gegenwart f, Präsens nt ▷ n (*liking*) Gegenwart f, Präsens nt; (*gift*) Geschenk nt; **at ~** zurzeit ▷ [prɪˈzent] vt (*TV, Radio*) präsentieren; (*problem*) darstellen; (*report etc*) vorlegen; **to ~ sb with sth** jdm etw überreichen; **present-day** adj heutig; **presently** adv bald; (*at present*) zurzeit

preservative [prɪˈzɜːvətɪv] n Konservierungsmittel nt; **preserve** [prɪˈzɜːv] vt erhalten; (*food*) einmachen, konservieren

president [ˈprezɪdənt] n Präsident(in) m(f); **presidential** [prezɪˈdenʃəl] adj Präsidenten-; (*election*) Präsidentschafts-

press [pres] n (*newspapers, machine*) Presse f ▷ vt (*push*) drücken; **to ~ a button** auf einen Knopf drücken ▷ vi (*push*) drücken; **pressing** adj dringend; **press-stud** n Druckknopf m; **press-up** n (*Brit*) Liegestütz m; **pressure** [ˈpreʃəʳ] n Druck m; **to be under ~** unter Druck stehen; **to put ~ on sb** jdn unter Druck setzen; **pressure cooker** n Schnellkochtopf m; **pressurize** [ˈpreʃəraɪz] vt (*person*) unter Druck setzen

presumably [prɪˈzjuːməblɪ] adv vermutlich; **presume** [prɪˈzjuːm] vt, vi annehmen

presumptuous [pri'zʌmptʃʊəs]
adj anmaßend

presuppose [pri:sə'pəuz] vt
voraussetzen

pretend [pri'tend] vt: **to ~ that**
so tun als ob; **to ~ to do sth**
vorgeben, etw zu tun ▷ vi: **she's
~ing** sie tut nur so

pretentious [pri'tenʃəs] adj
anmaßend; (person)
wichtigtuerisch

pretty ['priti] adj hübsch ▷ adv
ziemlich

prevent [pri'vent] vt verhindern;
to ~ sb from doing sth jdn daran
hindern, etw zu tun

preview ['pri:vju:] n (Cine) Vor-
aufführung f; (trailer) Vorschau f

previous , **previously** ['pri:viəs,
-li] adj, adv früher

prey [prei] n Beute f

price [prais] n Preis m ▷ vt: **it's ~d
at £10** es ist mit 10 Pfund ausgezeichnet; **priceless** adj unbezahl-
bar; **price list** n Preisliste f; **price
tag** n Preisschild nt

prick [prik] n Stich m; (vulg: penis)
Schwanz m; (vulg: person) Arsch m
▷ vt stechen in +akk; **to ~ one's
finger** sich dat in den Finger
stechen; **prickly** ['prikli] adj
stachelig

pride [praid] n Stolz m; (arro-
gance) Hochmut m ▷ vt: **to ~ oneself on sth** auf etw akk stolz sein

priest [pri:st] n Priester m

primarily ['praimərili] adv
vorwiegend; **primary** ['praiməri]
adj Haupt-; **~ education**
Grundschulausbildung f; **~ school**
Grundschule f

prime [praim] adj Haupt-;
(excellent) erstklassig ▷ n: **in one's
~** in den besten Jahren; **prime
minister** n Premierminister(in)
m(f); **prime time** n (TV)
Hauptsendezeit f

primitive ['primitiv] adj
primitiv

primrose ['primrəuz] n
Schlüsselblume f

prince [prins] n Prinz m; (ruler)
Fürst m; **princess** [prin'ses] n
Prinzessin f; Fürstin f

principal ['prinsipəl] adj
Haupt-, wichtigste(r, s) ▷ n
(school) Rektor(in) m(f)

principle ['prinsəpl] n Prinzip nt;
in ~ im Prinzip; **on ~** aus Prinzip

print [print] n (picture) Druck m;
(Foto) Abzug m; (made by feet,
fingers) Abdruck m; **out of
~** vergriffen ▷ vt drucken; (photo)
abziehen; (write in block letters) in
Druckschrift schreiben; **print out**
vt (Inform) ausdrucken; **printed
matter** n Drucksache f; **printer** n
Drucker m; **printout** n (Inform)
Ausdruck m

prior ['praiə°] adj früher; **a
~ engagement** eine vorher
getroffene Verabredung; **~ to sth**
vor etw dat; **~ to going abroad,
she had ...** bevor sie ins Ausland
ging, hatte sie ...

priority [prai'ɒriti] n (thing
having precedence) Priorität f

prison ['prizn] n Gefängnis nt;
prisoner n Gefangene(r) mf; **~ of
war** Kriegsgefangene(r) mf

privacy ['privəsi] n Privatleben
nt; **private** ['praivit] adj privat;
(confidential) vertraulich ▷ n
einfacher Soldat; **in ~** privat;
privately adv privat;
(confidentially) vertraulich;
privatize ['praivətaiz] vt
privatisieren

privilege ['privilidʒ] n Privileg
nt; **privileged** adj privilegiert

prize [praiz] n Preis m; **prize
money** n Preisgeld nt;
prizewinner n Gewinner(in) m(f);
prizewinning adj preisgekrönt

pro [prəʊ] (pl **-s**) n (professional) Profi m; **the ~s and cons** pl das Für und Wider

pro- [prəʊ] pref pro-

probability [prɒbə'bɪlətɪ] n Wahrscheinlichkeit f; **probable**, **probably** ['prɒbəbl, -blɪ] adj, adv wahrscheinlich

probation [prə'beɪʃən] n Probezeit f; (Jur) Bewährung f

probe [prəʊb] n (investigation) Untersuchung f ▷ vt untersuchen

problem ['prɒbləm] n Problem nt; **no ~** kein Problem!

procedure [prə'siːdʒə°] n Verfahren nt

proceed [prə'siːd] vi (continue) fortfahren; (set about sth) vorgehen ▷ vt: **to ~ to do sth** anfangen, etw zu tun; **proceedings** npl (Jur) Verfahren nt; **proceeds** ['prəʊsiːdz] npl Erlös m

process ['prəʊsɛs] n Prozess m, Vorgang m; (method) Verfahren nt ▷ vt (application etc) bearbeiten; (food, data) verarbeiten; (film) entwickeln

procession [prə'sɛʃən] n Umzug m

processor ['prəʊsɛsə°] n (Inform) Prozessor m; (Gastr) Küchenmaschine f

produce n ['prɒdjuːs] n (Agr) Produkte pl, Erzeugnisse pl ▷ vt [prə'djuːs] vt (manufacture) herstellen, produzieren; (on farm) erzeugen; (film, play, record) produzieren; (cause) hervorrufen; (evidence, results) liefern; **producer** n (manufacturer) Hersteller(in) m(f); (of film, play, record) Produzent(in) m(f); **product** ['prɒdʌkt] n Produkt nt, Erzeugnis nt; **production** [prə'dʌkʃən] n Produktion f; (Theat) Inszenierung f; **productive** [prə'dʌktɪv] adj produktiv; (land) ertragreich

prof [prɒf] n (fam) Prof m

profession [prə'fɛʃən] n Beruf m; **professional** [prə'fɛʃənl] n Profi m ▷ adj beruflich; (expert) fachlich; (sportsman, actor etc) Berufs-

professor [prə'fɛsə°] n Professor(in) m(f); (US: lecturer) Dozent(in) m(f)

proficient [prə'fɪʃənt] adj kompetent (in in +dat)

profile ['prəʊfaɪl] n Profil nt; **to keep a low ~** sich rarmachen

profit ['prɒfɪt] n Gewinn m ▷ vi profitieren (by, from von); **profitable** adj rentabel

profound [prə'faʊnd] adj tief; (idea, thinker) tiefgründig; (knowledge) profund

program ['prəʊɡræm] n (Inform) Programm nt; (US) see **programme** ▷ vt programmieren; (US) see **programme**

programme ['prəʊɡræm] n Programm nt; (TV, Radio) Sendung f ▷ vt programmieren; **programmer** n Programmierer(in) m(f); **programming** n (Inform) Programmieren nt; **~ language** Programmiersprache f

progress n ['prəʊɡrɛs] n Fortschritt m; **to make ~** Fortschritte machen ▷ [prə'ɡrɛs] vi (work, illness etc) fortschreiten; (improve) Fortschritte machen; **progressive** [prə'ɡrɛsɪv] adj (person, policy) fortschrittlich; **progressively** [prə'ɡrɛsɪvlɪ] adv zunehmend

prohibit [prə'hɪbɪt] vt verbieten

project ['prɒdʒɛkt] n Projekt nt

projector [prə'dʒɛktə°] n Projektor m

prolong [prə'lɒŋ] vt verlängern

prom [prɒm] n (at seaside) Promenade f; (Brit: concert) Konzert nt (bei dem ein Großteil des Publikums im Parkett Stehplätze hat); (US:

dance) Ball für die Schüler und Studenten von Highschools oder Colleges

prominent ['prɒminənt] adj (politician, actor etc) prominent; (easily seen) auffallend

promiscuous [prə'miskjuəs] adj promisk

promise ['prɒmis] n Versprechen nt ▷ vt versprechen; to ~ sb sth jdm etw versprechen; to ~ to do sth versprechen, etw zu tun ▷ vi versprechen; **promising** adj vielversprechend

promote [prə'məut] vt (in rank) befördern; (help on) fördern; (Comm) werben für; **promotion** [prə'məuʃən] n (in rank) Beförderung f; (Comm) Werbung f (of für)

prompt [prɒmpt] adj prompt; (punctual) pünktlich ▷ adv: at two o'clock ~ Punkt zwei Uhr ▷ vt (Theat: actor) souffllieren +dat

prone [prəun] adj: to be ~ to sth zu etw neigen

pronounce [prə'nauns] vt (word) aussprechen; **pronounced** adj ausgeprägt; **pronunciation** [prənʌnsɪ'eɪʃən] n Aussprache f

proof [pru:f] n Beweis m; (of alcohol) Alkoholgehalt m

prop [prɒp] n Stütze f; (Theat) Requisit nt ▷ vt: to ~ sth against sth etw gegen etw lehnen; **prop up** vt stützen; (fig) unterstützen

proper ['prɒpə°] adj richtig; (morally correct) anständig

property ['prɒpətɪ] n (possession) Eigentum nt; (house) Haus nt; (land) Grundbesitz m; (characteristic) Eigenschaft f

proportion [prə'pɔːʃən] n Verhältnis nt; (share) Teil m; ~s pl (size) Proportionen pl; **in ~ to** im Verhältnis zu; **proportional** adj

proportional; ~ **representation** Verhältniswahlrecht nt

proposal [prə'pəuzl] n Vorschlag m; ~ (of marriage) (Heirats)antrag m; **propose** [prə'pəuz] vt vorschlagen ▷ vi (offer marriage) einen Heiratsantrag machen (to sb jdm)

proprietor [prə'praɪətə°] n Besitzer(in) m(f); (of pub, hotel) Inhaber(in) m(f)

prose [prəuz] n Prosa f

prosecute ['prɒsɪkjuːt] vt verfolgen (for wegen)

prospect ['prɒspekt] n Aussicht f

prosperity [prɒ'sperɪtɪ] n Wohlstand m; **prosperous** adj wohlhabend; (business) gut gehend

prostitute ['prɒstɪtjuːt] n Prostituierte(r) mf

protect [prə'tekt] vt schützen (from, against vor +dat, gegen); **protection** [prə'tekʃən] n Schutz m (from, against vor +dat, gegen); **protective** adj schützend; (clothing etc) Schutz-

protein ['prəutiːn] n Protein nt

protest ['prəutest] n Protest m; (demonstration) Protestkundgebung f ▷ [prə'test] vi protestieren (against gegen); (demonstrate) demonstrieren

Protestant ['prɒtəstənt] adj protestantisch ▷ n Protestant(in) m(f)

proud [praud] adj, **proudly** [praud, -lɪ] adj, adv stolz (of auf +akk)

prove [pruːv] vt beweisen; (turn out to be) sich erweisen als

proverb ['prɒvɜːb] n Sprichwort nt

provide [prə'vaɪd] vt zur Verfügung stellen; (drinks, music etc) sorgen für; (person) versorgen (with mit); **provide for** vt (family

etc) sorgen für; **provided** *conj:*
~ **(that)** vorausgesetzt, dass;
provider *n* (*Inform*) Provider *m*

provision [prə'vɪʒən] *n* (*condition*) Bestimmung *f*; **~s** *pl* (*food*) Proviant *m*

provisional, provisionally
[prə'vɪʒənl, -lɪ] *adj, adv*
provisorisch

provoke [prə'vəʊk] *vt*
provozieren; (*cause*) hervorrufen

proximity [prɒk'sɪmɪtɪ] *n* Nähe *f*

prudent ['pruːdənt] *adj* klug;
(*person*) umsichtig

prudish ['pruːdɪʃ] *adj* prüde

prune [pruːn] *n* Backpflaume *f*
▷ *vt* (*tree etc*) zurechtstutzen

PS *abbr* = **postscript** PS *nt*

psalm [sɑːm] *n* Psalm *m*

pseudo ['sjuːdəʊ] *adj* pseudo-,
Pseudo-; **pseudonym** ['sjuːdə-
nɪm] *n* Pseudonym *nt*

PST *abbr* = **Pacific Standard Time**

psychiatric [saɪkɪ'ætrɪk] *adj*
psychiatrisch; (*illness*) psychisch;
psychiatrist [saɪ'kaɪətrɪst] *n*
Psychiater(in) *m(f)*; **psychiatry**
[saɪ'kaɪətrɪ] *n* Psychiatrie *f*;
psychic ['saɪkɪk] *adj* über-
sinnlich; **I'm not ~** ich kann keine
Gedanken lesen; **psychoanalysis**
[saɪkəʊə'næləsɪs] *n* Psychoanalyse *f*; **psychoanalyst**
[saɪkəʊ'ænəlɪst] *n* Psychoanaly-
tiker(in) *m(f)*; **psychological** [saɪ-
kə'lɒdʒɪkəl] *adj* psychologisch;
psychology [saɪ'kɒlədʒɪ] *n* Psychologie *f*; **psychopath** ['saɪkəʊ-
pæθ] *n* Psychopath(in) *m(f)*

pt *abbr* = **pint**

pto *abbr* = **please turn over** b.w.

pub [pʌb] *n* (*Brit*) Kneipe *f*

● PUB

● Ein **pub** ist ein Gasthaus mit
● einer Lizenz zum Ausschank von

● alkoholischen Getränken. Ein
● „Pub" besteht meist aus
● verschiedenen gemütlichen
● (**lounge, snug**) oder
● einfacheren (**public bar**)
● Räumen, in denen oft auch
● Spiele wie Darts, Domino und
● Poolbillard zur Verfügung
● stehen. In „Pubs" werden vor
● allem mittags auch Mahlzeiten
● angeboten (**pub lunch**). Die
● Sperrstunde wurde 2005
● aufgehoben. Dennoch sind
● „Pubs" oft nur von 11 bis 23 Uhr
● geöffnet. Nachmittags bleiben
● sie häufig geschlossen.

puberty ['pjuːbətɪ] *n* Pubertät
f

public ['pʌblɪk] *n:* **the** (*general*)
~ die (breite) Öffentlichkeit; **in**
~ in der Öffentlichkeit ▷ *adj*
öffentlich; (*relating to the State*)
Staats-; ~ **convenience** (*Brit*)
öffentliche Toilette; ~ **holiday**
gesetzlicher Feiertag; ~ **opinion**
die öffentliche Meinung;
~ **relations** *pl*
Öffentlichkeitsarbeit *f*, Public
Relations *pl*; ~ **school** (*Brit*)
Privatschule *f*; **publication**
[pʌblɪ'keɪʃən] *n* Veröffentlichung
f; **publicity** [pʌb'lɪsɪtɪ] *n*
Publicity *f*; (*advertisements*)
Werbung *f*; **publish** ['pʌblɪʃ] *vt*
veröffentlichen; **publisher** *n*
Verleger(in) *m(f)*; (*company*) Verlag
m; **publishing** *n* Verlagswesen *nt*

pub lunch ['pʌb'lʌntʃ] *n* (*oft
einfacheres*) Mittagessen in einer
Kneipe

pudding ['pʊdɪŋ] *n* (*course*)
Nachtisch *m*

puddle ['pʌdl] *n* Pfütze *f*

puff [pʌf] *vi* (*pant*) schnaufen

puffin ['pʌfɪn] *n* Papageien-
taucher *m*

puff paste (US), **puff pastry**
['pʌf peɪstrɪ] n Blätterteig m
pull [pʊl] n Ziehen nt; **to give sth
a ~** an etw dat ziehen ▷ vt (cart,
tooth) ziehen; (rope, handle) ziehen
an +dat; (fam: date) abschleppen;
to ~ a muscle sich dat einen
Muskel zerren; **to ~ sb's leg** jdn
auf den Arm nehmen ▷ vi ziehen;
pull apart vt (separate)
auseinanderziehen; **pull down** vt
(blind) herunterziehen; (house)
abreißen; **pull in** vi hineinfahren;
(stop) anhalten; **pull off** vt (deal
etc) zuwege bringen; (clothes)
ausziehen; **pull on** vt (clothes)
anziehen; **pull out** vi (car from
lane) ausscheren; (train) abfahren;
(withdraw) aussteigen (of aus) ▷ vt
herausziehen; (tooth) ziehen;
(troops) abziehen; **pull round**, **pull
through** vi durchkommen; **pull
up** vt (raise) hochziehen; (chair)
heranziehen ▷ vi anhalten
pullover ['pʊləʊvə*] n Pullover m
pulp [pʌlp] n Brei m; (of fruit)
Fruchtfleisch nt
pulpit ['pʊlpɪt] n Kanzel f
pulse [pʌls] n Puls m
pump [pʌmp] n Pumpe f; (in
petrol station) Zapfsäule f; **pump up**
vt (tyre etc) aufpumpen
pumpkin ['pʌmpkɪn] n Kürbis m
pun [pʌn] n Wortspiel nt
punch [pʌntʃ] n (blow)
(Faust)schlag m; (tool) Locher m;
(hot drink) Punsch m; (cold drink)
Bowle f ▷ vt (strike) schlagen;
(ticket, paper) lochen
punctual, **punctually**
['pʌŋktjʊəl, -ɪ] adj, adv
pünktlich
punctuation [pʌŋktjʊˈeɪʃən] n
Interpunktion f; **punctuation
mark** n Satzzeichen nt
puncture ['pʌŋktʃə*] n (flat tyre)
Reifenpanne f

punish ['pʌnɪʃ] vt bestrafen;
punishment n Strafe f; (action)
Bestrafung f
pupil ['pjuːpl] n (school)
Schüler(in) m(f)
puppet ['pʌpɪt] n Marionette f
puppy ['pʌpɪ] n junger Hund
purchase ['pɜːtʃɪs] n Kauf m ▷ vt
kaufen
pure [pjʊə*] adj rein; (clean)
sauber; (utter) pur; **purely**
['pjʊəlɪ] adv rein; **purify**
['pjʊərɪfaɪ] vt reinigen; **purity**
['pjʊərɪtɪ] n Reinheit f
purple ['pɜːpl] adj violett
purpose ['pɜːpəs] n Zweck m; (of
person) Absicht f; **on ~** absichtlich
purr [pɜː*] vi (cat) schnurren
purse [pɜːs] n Geldbeutel m; (US:
handbag) Handtasche f
pursue [pəˈsjuː] vt (person, car)
verfolgen; (hobby, studies)
nachgehen +dat; **pursuit**
[pəˈsjuːt] n (chase) Verfolgung f;
(occupation) Beschäftigung f;
(hobby) Hobby nt
pus [pʌs] n Eiter m
push [pʊʃ] n Stoß m ▷ vt (person)
stoßen; (car, chair etc) schieben;
(button) drücken; (drugs) dealen
▷ vi (in crowd) drängeln; **push in** vi
(in queue) sich vordrängeln; **push
off** vi (fam: leave) abhauen; **push
on** vi (with job) weitermachen;
push up vt (prices) hochtreiben;
pushchair n (Brit)
Sport(kinder)wagen m; **pusher** n
(of drugs) Dealer(in) m(f); **push-up**
n (US) Liegestütz m; **pushy** adj
(fam) aufdringlich, penetrant
put [pʊt] (pt, put) vt tun;
(upright) stellen; (flat) legen;
(express) ausdrücken; (write)
schreiben; **he ~ his hand in his
pocket** er steckte die Hand in die
Tasche; **he ~ his hand on her
shoulder** er legte ihr die Hand auf

die Schulter; **to ~ money into one's account** Geld auf sein Konto einzahlen; **put aside** vt (tidy away) wegräumen; **put back** vt zurücklegen; (clock) zurückstellen; **put down** vt (in writing) aufschreiben; (Brit: animal) einschläfern; (rebellion) niederschlagen; **to put the phone down** (den Hörer) auflegen; **to put one's name down for sth** sich für etw eintragen; **put forward** vt (idea) vorbringen; (name) vorschlagen; (clock) vorstellen; **put in** vt (install) einbauen; (submit) einreichen; **put off** vt (switch off) ausschalten; (postpone) verschieben; **to put sb off doing sth** jdn davon abbringen, etw zu tun; **put on** vt (switch on) anmachen; (clothes) anziehen; (hat, glasses) aufsetzen; (make-up, CD) auflegen; (play) aufführen; **to put the kettle on** Wasser aufsetzen; **to put weight on** zunehmen; **put out** vt (hand, foot) ausstrecken; (light, cigarette) ausmachen; **put up** vt (hand) hochheben; (picture) aufhängen; (tent) aufstellen; (building) errichten; (price) erhöhen; (person) unterbringen; **to ~ with** sich abfinden mit; **I won't ~ with it** das lasse ich mir nicht gefallen

putt [pʌt] vt, vi (Sport) putten

puzzle [ˈpʌzl] n Rätsel nt; (toy) Geduldsspiel nt; (jigsaw) ~ Puzzle nt ▷ vt vor ein Rätsel stellen; **it ~s me** es ist mir ein Rätsel; **puzzling** adj rätselhaft

pyjamas [pɪˈdʒɑːməz] npl Schlafanzug m

pylon [ˈpaɪlən] n Mast m

pyramid [ˈpɪrəmɪd] n Pyramide f

q

quack [kwæk] vi quaken

quaint [kweɪnt] adj (idea, tradition) kurios; (picturesque) malerisch

qualification [kwɒlɪfɪˈkeɪʃən] n (for job) Qualifikation f; (from school, university) Abschluss m; **qualified** [ˈkwɒlɪfaɪd] adj (for job) qualifiziert; **qualify** vt (limit) einschränken; **to be qualified to do sth** berechtigt sein, etw zu tun ▷ vi (finish training) seine Ausbildung abschließen; (contest etc) sich qualifizieren

quality [ˈkwɒlɪtɪ] n Qualität f; (characteristic) Eigenschaft f

quantity [ˈkwɒntɪtɪ] n Menge f, Quantität f

quarantine [ˈkwɒrəntiːn] n Quarantäne f

quarrel [ˈkwɒrəl] n Streit m ▷ vi sich streiten

quarter [ˈkwɔːtə°] n Viertel nt;

(of year) Vierteljahr nt; (US: coin) Vierteldollar m; **a ~ of an hour** eine Viertelstunde; **~ to/past** (Brit) (o **~ of/after** (US)) **three** Viertel vor/nach drei ▷ vt vierteln; **quarter final** n Viertelfinale nt; **quarters** npl (Mil) Quartier nt

quartet [kwɔːˈtet] n Quartett nt

quay [kiː] n Kai m

queasy ['kwiːzɪ] adj: **I feel ~** mir ist übel

queen [kwiːn] n Königin f; (in cards, chess) Dame f

queer [kwɪə] adj (strange) seltsam, sonderbar; (pej: homosexual) schwul ▷ n (pej) Schwule(r) m

quench [kwentʃ] vt (thirst) löschen

query ['kwɪərɪ] n Frage f ▷ vt infrage stellen; (bill) reklamieren

question ['kwestʃən] n Frage f; **that's out of the ~** das kommt nicht infrage ▷ vt (person) befragen; (suspect) verhören; (express doubt about) bezweifeln; **questionable** adj zweifelhaft; (improper) fragwürdig; **question mark** n Fragezeichen nt; **questionnaire** [kwestʃəˈnɛə] n Fragebogen m

queue [kjuː] n (Brit) Schlange f; **to jump the ~** sich vordrängeln ▷ vi: **to ~ (up)** Schlange stehen

quibble ['kwɪbl] vi kleinlich sein; (argue) streiten

quiche [kiːʃ] n Quiche

quick [kwɪk] adj schnell; (short) kurz; **be ~** mach schnell!; **quickly** adv schnell

quid [kwɪd] (pl **quid**) n (Brit fam) Pfund nt; **20 ~** 20 Pfund

quiet ['kwaɪət] adj (not noisy) leise; (peaceful, calm) still, ruhig; **be ~** sei still!; **to keep ~ about sth** über etw akk nichts sagen ▷ n

Stille f, Ruhe f; **quiet down** (US), **quieten down** ['kwaɪətənˈdaʊn] vi sich beruhigen ▷ vt beruhigen; **quietly** adv leise; (calmly) ruhig

quilt [kwɪlt] n (Stepp)decke f

quit [kwɪt] (**quit** o **quitted**, **quit** o **quitted**) vt (leave) verlassen; (job) aufgeben; **to ~ doing sth** aufhören, etw zu tun ▷ vi aufhören; (resign) kündigen

quite [kwaɪt] adv (fairly) ziemlich; (completely) ganz, völlig; **I don't ~ understand** ich verstehe das nicht ganz; **~ a few** ziemlich viele; **~ so!** richtig!

quits [kwɪts] adj: **to be ~ with sb** mit jdm quitt sein

quiver ['kwɪvə] vi zittern

quiz [kwɪz] n (competition) Quiz nt

quota ['kwəʊtə] n Anteil m; (Comm, Pol) Quote f

quotation [kwəʊˈteɪʃən] n Zitat nt; (price) Kostenvoranschlag m; **quotation marks** npl Anführungszeichen pl; **quote** [kwəʊt] vt (text, author) zitieren; (price) nennen ▷ n Zitat nt; (price) Kostenvoranschlag m; **in ~s** in Anführungszeichen

r

rabbi ['ræbaɪ] n Rabbiner m
rabbit ['ræbɪt] n Kaninchen nt
rabies ['reɪbiːz] nsing Tollwut f
raccoon [rə'kuːn] n Waschbär m
race [reɪs] n (competition) Rennen nt; (people) Rasse f ⊳ vt um die Wette laufen/fahren ⊳ vi (rush) rennen; **racecourse** n Rennbahn f; **racehorse** n Rennpferd nt; **racetrack** n Rennbahn f
racial ['reɪʃəl] adj Rassen-; ~ **discrimination** Rassendiskriminierung f
racing ['reɪsɪŋ] n: (horse) ~ Pferderennen nt; (motor) ~ Autorennen nt; **racing car** n Rennwagen m
racism ['reɪsɪzəm] n Rassismus m; **racist** ['reɪsɪst] n Rassist(in) m(f) ⊳ adj rassistisch
rack [ræk] n Ständer m, Gestell n ⊳ vt: **to ~ one's brains** sich dat den Kopf zerbrechen

racket ['rækɪt] n (Sport) Schläger m; (noise) Krach m
radar ['reɪdɑː°] n Radar nt o m; **radar trap** n Radarfalle f
radiation [reɪdɪ'eɪʃən] n (radioactive) Strahlung f
radiator ['reɪdɪeɪtə°] n Heizkörper m; (Auto) Kühler m
radical ['rædɪkəl] adj radikal
radio ['reɪdɪəʊ] (pl -s) n Rundfunk m, Radio nt
radioactivity [reɪdɪəʊæk'tɪvɪtɪ] n Radioaktivität f
radio alarm ['reɪdɪəʊə'lɑːm] n Radiowecker m; **radio station** n Rundfunkstation f
radiotherapy [reɪdɪəʊ'θerəpɪ] n Strahlenbehandlung f
radish ['rædɪʃ] n Radieschen nt
radius ['reɪdɪəs] n Radius m; **within a five-mile ~** im Umkreis von fünf Meilen (of um)
raffle ['ræfl] n Tombola f; **raffle ticket** n Los nt
raft [rɑːft] n Floß nt
rag [ræg] n Lumpen m; (for cleaning) Lappen m
rage [reɪdʒ] n Wut f; **to be all the ~** der letzte Schrei sein ⊳ vi (noise; (disease) wüten
raid [reɪd] n Überfall m (on auf +akk); (by police) Razzia f (on gegen) ⊳ vt (bank etc) überfallen; (by police) eine Razzia machen in +dat
rail [reɪl] n (on stairs, balcony etc) Geländer nt; (of ship) Reling f; (Rail) Schiene f; **railcard** n (Brit) = Bahncard® f; **railing** n Geländer nt; **-s** pl (fence) Zaun m; **railroad** n (US) Eisenbahn f; **railroad station** n (US) Bahnhof m; **railway** n (Brit) Eisenbahn f; **railway line** n Bahnlinie f; (track) Gleis m; **railway station** n Bahnhof m
rain [reɪn] n Regen m ⊳ vi regnen; **it's ~ing** es regnet; **rainbow** n Regenbogen m;

raincoat n Regenmantel m;
rainfall n Niederschlag m;
rainforest n Regenwald m; **rainy** adj regnerisch

raise [reɪz] n (US: of wages/salary) Gehalts-/Lohnerhöhung f ▷ vt (lift) hochheben; (increase) erhöhen; (family) großziehen; (livestock) züchten; (money) aufbringen; (objection) erheben; **to ~ one's voice** laut werden

raisin ['reɪzən] n Rosine f

rally ['rælɪ] n (Pol) Kundgebung f; (Aut) Rallye f; (Tennis) Ballwechsel m

RAM [ræm] acr = **random access memory** RAM m

ramble ['ræmbl] n Wanderung f ▷ vi (walk) wandern; (talk) schwafeln

ramp [ræmp] n Rampe f

ran [ræn] pt of **run**

ranch [rɑːntʃ] n Ranch f

rancid ['rænsɪd] adj ranzig

random ['rændəm] adj willkürlich ▷ n: **at ~** (choose) willkürlich; (fire) ziellos

rang [ræŋ] pt of **ring**

range [reɪndʒ] n (selection) Auswahl f (of an +dat); (Comm) Sortiment nt (of an +dat); (of missile, telescope) Reichweite f; (of mountains) Kette f; **in this price ~** in dieser Preisklasse ▷ vi: **to ~ from ... to ...** gehen von ... bis ...; (temperature, sizes, prices) liegen zwischen ... und ...

rank [ræŋk] n (Mil) Rang m; (social position) Stand m ▷ vt einstufen

ransom ['rænsəm] n Lösegeld nt

rap [ræp] n (Mus) Rap m

rape [reɪp] n Vergewaltigung f ▷ vt vergewaltigen

rapid, rapidly ['ræpɪd, -lɪ] adj, adv schnell

rapist ['reɪpɪst] n Vergewaltiger m

rare [rɛə°] adj selten, rar; (especially good) vortrefflich; (steak) blutig; **rarely** adv selten; **rarity** ['rɛərɪtɪ] n Seltenheit f

rash [ræʃ] adj unbesonnen ▷ n (Med) (Haut)ausschlag m

rasher ['ræʃə°] n: **~ (of bacon)** (Speck)scheibe f

raspberry ['rɑːzbərɪ] n Himbeere f

rat [ræt] n Ratte f; (pej: person) Schwein nt

rate [reɪt] n (proportion, frequency) Rate f; (speed) Tempo nt; **~ (of exchange)** (Wechsel)kurs m; **~ of inflation** Inflationsrate f; **~ of interest** Zinssatz m; **at any ~** auf jeden Fall ▷ vt (evaluate) einschätzen (as als)

rather ['rɑːðə°] adv (in preference) lieber; (fairly) ziemlich; **I'd ~ stay here** ich würde lieber hierbleiben; **I'd ~ not** lieber nicht; **or ~** (more accurately) vielmehr

ratio ['reɪʃɪəʊ] (pl **-s**) n Verhältnis nt

rational ['ræʃənl] adj rational; **rationalize** ['ræʃnəlaɪz] vt rationalisieren

rattle ['rætl] n (toy) Rassel f ▷ vt (keys, coins) klimpern mit; (person) durcheinanderbringen ▷ vi (window) klappern; (bottles) klirren; **rattle off** vt herunterrasseln; **rattlesnake** f Klapperschlange f

rave [reɪv] vi (talk wildly) fantasieren; (rage) toben; (enthuse) schwärmen (about von) ▷ n (Brit: event) Raveparty f

raven ['reɪvn] n Rabe m

raving ['reɪvɪŋ] adv: **~ mad** total verrückt

ravishing ['rævɪʃɪŋ] adj hinreißend

raw [rɔː] adj (food) roh; (skin) wund; (climate) rau

ray [reɪ] n (of light) Strahl m; ~ of
hope Hoffnungsschimmer m
razor ['reɪzə'] n Rasierapparat
m; **razor blade** n Rasierklinge f
Rd abbr = **road** Str.
re [riː] prep (Comm) betreffs +gen
RE abbr = **religious education**
reach [riːtʃ] n: within/out of
(sb's) ~ in/außer (jds) Reichweite;
within easy ~ of the shops nicht
weit von den Geschäften ▷ vt
(arrive at, contact) erreichen ▷ vi
(come down/up as far as) reichen bis zu;
(contact) **can you ~ it?** kommst
du/kommen Sie dran?; **reach for**
vt greifen nach; **reach out** vi die
Hand ausstrecken; **to ~ for** greifen
nach
react [riːˈækt] vi reagieren (to auf
+akk); **reaction** [riːˈækʃən] n
Reaktion f (to auf +akk); **reactor**
[riːˈæktə'] n Reaktor m
read [riːd] (read, read) vt lesen;
(meter) ablesen; **to ~ to sb** jdm
etw vorlesen ▷ vi lesen; **to ~ to sb**
jdm vorlesen; **it ~s well** es liest
sich gut; **it ~s as follows** es lautet
folgendermaßen; **read out** vt
vorlesen; **read through** vt
durchlesen; **read up on** vt
nachlesen über +akk; **readable** adj
(book) lesenswert; (handwriting)
lesbar; **reader** n Leser(in) m(f);
readership n Leserschaft f
readily ['redɪlɪ] adv (willingly)
bereitwillig; **~ available** leicht
erhältlich
reading ['riːdɪŋ] n (action) Lesen
nt; (from meter) Zählerstand m;
reading glasses npl Lesebrille f;
reading lamp n Leselampe f;
reading list n Leseliste f; **reading
matter** n Lektüre f
readjust [riːəˈdʒʌst] vt (mechanism etc) neu einstellen ▷ vi sich
wieder anpassen (to an +akk)
ready ['redɪ] adj fertig, bereit; **to**

be ~ to do sth (willing) bereit sein,
etw zu tun; **are you ~ to go?** bist
du so weit?; **to get sth ~** etw
fertig machen; **to get (oneself)**
~ sich fertig machen; **ready cash**
n Bargeld nt; **ready-made** adj
(product) Fertig-; (clothes)
Konfektions-; **~ meal**
Fertiggericht nt
real [rɪəl] adj wirklich; (actual)
eigentlich; (genuine) echt; (idiot etc)
richtig ▷ adv (fam, esp US) echt;
for ~ echt; **this time it's for**
~ diesmal ist es ernst; **get ~** sei
realistisch!; **real ale** n Ale nt; **real
estate** n Immobilien pl
realistic, realistically [rɪəˈlɪstɪk,
-əlɪ] adj, adv realistisch; **reality**
[riːˈælɪtɪ] n Wirklichkeit f; **in ~** in
Wirklichkeit; **reality TV** n
Reality-TV nt; **realization**
[rɪəlaɪˈzeɪʃən] n (awareness)
Erkenntnis f; **realize** ['rɪəlaɪz] vt
(understand) begreifen; (plan, idea)
realisieren; **I ~d (that)** ... mir
wurde klar, dass ...
really ['rɪəlɪ] adv wirklich
real time [rɪəlˈtaɪm] n (Inform)
in ~ in Echtzeit
realtor ['rɪəltə'] n (US)
Grundstücksmakler(in) m(f)
reappear [rɪəˈpɪə'] vi wieder
erscheinen
rear [rɪə'] adj hintere(r, s),
Hinter- ▷ n (of building, vehicle)
hinterer Teil; **at the ~ of** hinter
+dat; (inside) hinten in +dat; **rear
light** n (Auto) Rücklicht nt
rearm [riːˈɑːm] vi wieder
aufrüsten
rearrange [riːəˈreɪndʒ] vt (furniture, system) umstellen; (meeting)
verlegen (for auf +akk)
rear-view mirror
['rɪəvjuːˈmɪrə'] n Rückspiegel m;
rear window n (Auto)
Heckscheibe f

reason ['riːzn] n (cause) Grund m (for für); (ability to think) Verstand m; (common sense) Vernunft f; **for some ~** aus irgendeinem Grund ⊳ vi: **to ~ with sb** mit jdm vernünftig reden; **reasonable** adj (person, price) vernünftig; (offer) akzeptabel; (chance) reell; (food, weather) ganz gut; **reasonably** adv (fairly) ziemlich

reassure [riːə'ʃʊə°] vt beruhigen; **she ~d me that ...** sie versicherte mir, dass ...

rebel ['rebl] n Rebell(in) m(f) ⊳ [ri'bel] vi rebellieren; **rebellion** [ri'beliən] n Aufstand m

reboot [riː'buːt] vt, vi (Inform) rebooten

rebound [ri'baʊnd] vi (ball etc) zurückprallen

rebuild [riː'bild] irr vt wieder aufbauen

recall [ri'kɔːl] vt (remember) sich erinnern an +akk; (call back) zurückrufen

recap ['riːkæp] vt, vi rekapitulieren

receipt [ri'siːt] n (document) Quittung f; (receiving) Empfang m; **~s** pl (money) Einnahmen pl

receive [ri'siːv] vt (news etc) erhalten, bekommen; (visitor) empfangen; **receiver** n (Tel) Hörer m; (Radio) Empfänger m

recent ['riːsnt] adj (event) vor Kurzem stattgefunden; (photo) neueste(r,s); (invention) neu; **in ~ years** in den letzten Jahren; **recently** adv vor Kurzem; (in the last few days or weeks) in letzter Zeit

reception [ri'sepʃən] n Empfang m; **receptionist** n (in hotel) Empfangschef m, Empfangsdame f; (woman in firm) Empfangsdame f; (Med) Sprechstundenhilfe f

recess [ri'ses] n (in wall) Nische f; (US: in school) Pause f

recession [ri'seʃən] n Rezession f

recharge [riː'tʃɑːdʒ] vt (battery) aufladen; **rechargeable** [riː'tʃɑːdʒəbl] adj wiederaufladbar

recipe ['resipi] n Rezept nt (for für)

recipient [ri'sipiənt] n Empfänger(in) m(f)

reciprocal [ri'siprəkəl] adj gegenseitig

recite [ri'saɪt] vt vortragen; (details) aufzählen

reckless ['rekləs] adj leichtsinnig; (driving) gefährlich

reckon ['rekən] vt (calculate) schätzen; (think) glauben ⊳ vi: **to ~ with/on** rechnen mit

reclaim [ri'kleɪm] vt (baggage) abholen; (expenses, tax) zurückverlangen

recline [ri'klaɪn] vi (person) sich zurücklehnen; **reclining seat** n Liegesitz m

recognition [rekəg'niʃən] n (acknowledgement) Anerkennung f; **in ~ of** in Anerkennung +gen; **recognize** ['rekəgnaɪz] vt erkennen; (approve officially) anerkennen

recommend [rekə'mend] vt empfehlen; **recommendation** [rekəmen'deiʃən] n Empfehlung f

reconfirm [riːkən'fɜːm] vt (flight etc) rückbestätigen

reconsider [riːkən'sɪdə°] vt noch einmal überdenken ⊳ vi es sich dat noch einmal überlegen

reconstruct [riːkən'strʌkt] vt wieder aufbauen; (crime) rekonstruieren

record ['rekɔːd] n (Mus) (Schall)platte f; (best performance) Rekord m; **~s** pl (files) Akten pl; **to keep a ~ of** Buch führen über +akk ⊳ adj (time etc) Rekord- ⊳ [ri'kɔːd] vt (write down) aufzeichnen; (on *tape etc*) aufnehmen; **~ed message** Ansage *f*; **recorded delivery** *n* (*Brit*) **by ~** per Einschreiben

recorder [rɪˈkɔːdəʳ] *n* (*Mus*) Blockflöte *f*; (**cassette**) ~ (Kassetten)rekorder *m*;

recording [rɪˈkɔːdɪŋ] *n* (*on tape etc*) Aufnahme *f*; **record player** [ˈrekɔːdpleɪəʳ] *n* Plattenspieler *m*

recover [rɪˈkʌvəʳ] *vt* (*money, item*) zurückbekommen; (*appetite, strength*) wiedergewinnen ▷ *vi* sich erholen

recreation [rekrɪˈeɪʃən] *n* Erholung *f*; **recreational** *adj* Freizeit-; **~ vehicle** (*US*) Wohnmobil *nt*

recruit [rɪˈkruːt] *n* (*Mil*) Rekrut(in) *m(f)*; (*in firm, organization*) neues Mitglied ▷ *vt* (*Mil*) rekrutieren; (*members*) anwerben; (*staff*) einstellen; **recruitment agency** *n* Personalagentur *f*

rectangle [ˈrektæŋgl] *n* Rechteck *nt*; **rectangular** [rekˈtæŋgjuləʳ] *adj* rechteckig

rectify [ˈrektɪfaɪ] *vt* berichtigen

recuperate [rɪˈkuːpəreɪt] *vi* sich erholen

recyclable [riːˈsaɪkləbl] *adj* recycelbar, wiederverwertbar; **recycle** [riːˈsaɪkl] *vt* recyceln, wiederverwerten; **~d paper** Recyclingpapier *nt*; **recycling** *n* Recycling *nt*, Wiederverwertung *f*

red [red] *adj* rot ▷ *n*: **in the ~** in den roten Zahlen; **Red Cross** *n* Rotes Kreuz; **red cabbage** *n* Rotkohl *m*; **redcurrant** *n* (rote) Johannisbeere

redeem [rɪˈdiːm] *vt* (*Comm*) einlösen

red-handed [redˈhændɪd] *adj*: **to catch sb ~** jdn auf frischer Tat ertappen; **redhead** *n* Rothaarige(r) *mf*

redial [riːˈdaɪəl] *vt, vi* nochmals wählen

redirect [riːdaɪˈrekt] *vt* (*traffic*) umleiten; (*forward*) nachsenden

red light [redˈlaɪt] *n* (*traffic signal*) rotes Licht; **to go through the ~** bei Rot über die Ampel fahren; **red meat** *n* Rind-, Lamm-, Rehfleisch

redo [riːˈduː] *irr vt* nochmals machen

reduce [rɪˈdjuːs] *vt* reduzieren (*to* auf +*akk*, *by* um); **reduction** [rɪˈdʌkʃən] *n* Reduzierung *f*; (*in price*) Ermäßigung *f*

redundant [rɪˈdʌndənt] *adj* überflüssig; **to be made ~** entlassen werden

red wine [redˈwaɪn] *n* Rotwein *m*

reef [riːf] *n* Riff *nt*

reel [riːl] *n* Spule *f*; (*on fishing rod*) Rolle *f*; **reel off** *vt* herunterrasseln

ref [ref] *n* (*fam: referee*) Schiri *m*

refectory [rɪˈfektərɪ] *n* (*at college*) Mensa *f*

refer [rɪˈfɜːʳ] *vt*: **to ~ sb to sb/sth** jdn an jdn/etw verweisen; **to ~ sth to sb** (*query, problem*) etw an jdn weiterleiten ▷ *vi*: **to ~ to** (*mention, allude to*) sich beziehen auf +*akk*; (*book*) nachschlagen in +*dat*

referee [refəˈriː] *n* Schiedsrichter(in) *m(f)*; (*in boxing*) Ringrichter *m*; (*Brit: for job*) Referenz *f*

reference [ˈrefrəns] *n* (*allusion*) Anspielung *f* (*to* auf +*akk*); (*for job*) Referenz *f*; (*in book*) Verweis *m*; **~ (number)** (*in document*) Aktenzeichen *nt*; **with ~ to** mit Bezug auf +*akk*; **reference book** *n* Nachschlagewerk *nt*

referendum [refəˈrendəm] *n* (*pl* **referenda**) *n* Referendum *nt*

refill [ˈriːfɪl] *vt* [riːˈfɪl] nachfüllen ▷ *n* (*for ballpoint pen*) Ersatzmine *f*

refine [rɪ'faɪn] vt (purify)
raffinieren; (improve) verfeinern;
refined adj (genteel) fein

reflect [rɪ'flekt] vt reflektieren;
(fig) widerspiegeln ▷ vi
nachdenken (on über +akk);
reflection [rɪ'flekʃən] n (image)
Spiegelbild nt; (thought)
Überlegung f; **on ~** nach reiflicher
Überlegung

reflex ['riːfleks] n Reflex m

reform [rɪ'fɔːm] n Reform f ▷ vt
reformieren; (person) bessern

refrain [rɪ'freɪn] vi: **to ~ from
doing sth** es unterlassen, etw zu
tun

refresh [rɪ'freʃ] vt erfrischen;
refresher course n
Auffrischungskurs m; **refreshing**
adj erfrischend; **refreshments** npl
Erfrischungen pl

refrigerator [rɪ'frɪdʒəreɪtə°] n
Kühlschrank m

refuel [riː'fjʊəl] vt, vi auftanken

refugee [refjʊ'dʒiː] n Flüchtling
m

refund ['riːfʌnd] n (of money)
Rückerstattung f; **to get a ~ (on
sth)** sein Geld (für etw)
zurückbekommen ▷ [rɪ'fʌnd] vt
zurückerstatten

refusal [rɪ'fjuːzəl] n (to do sth)
Weigerung f; **refuse** ['refjuːs] n
Müll m, Abfall m ▷ [rɪ'fjuːz] vt
ablehnen; **to ~ sb sth** jdm etw
verweigern; **to ~ to do sth** sich
weigern, etw zu tun ▷ vi sich
weigern

regain [rɪ'geɪn] vt wiedergewinnen, wiedererlangen; **to
~ consciousness** wieder zu
Bewusstsein kommen

regard [rɪ'gɑːd] n: **with ~ to** in
Bezug auf +akk; **in this ~** in dieser
Hinsicht; **~s** (at end of letter) mit
freundlichen Grüßen; **give my ~s
to ...** viele Grüße an ... +akk ▷ vt:

to ~ sb/sth as sth jdn/etw als etw
betrachten; **as ~s ...** was ...
betrifft; **regarding** prep bezüglich
+gen; **regardless** adj: **~ of** ohne
Rücksicht auf +akk ▷ adv
trotzdem; **to carry on ~** einfach
weitermachen

regime [reɪ'ʒiːm] n (Pol) Regime
nt

region ['riːdʒən] n (of country)
Region f, Gebiet nt; **in the ~ of**
(about) ungefähr; **regional** adj
regional

register ['redʒɪstə°] n Register
nt; (school) Namensliste f ▷ vt
(with an authority) registrieren
lassen; (birth, death, vehicle)
anmelden ▷ vi (at hotel, for course)
sich anmelden; (at university) sich
einschreiben; **registered** adj
eingetragen; (letter)
eingeschrieben; **by ~ post** per
Einschreiben; **registration**
[redʒɪ'streɪʃən] n (for course)
Anmeldung f; (at university)
Einschreibung f; (Auto: number)
(polizeiliches) Kennzeichen;
registration form n
Anmeldeformular nt; **registration
number** n (Auto) (polizeiliches)
Kennzeichen; **registry office**
['redʒɪstrɒfɪs] n Standesamt nt

regret [rɪ'gret] n Bedauern f
▷ vt bedauern; **regrettable** adj
bedauerlich

regular ['regjʊlə°] adj regelmäßig; (size) normal ▷ n (client)
Stammkunde m, Stammkundin f;
(in bar) Stammgast m; (petrol)
Normalbenzin nt; **regularly** adv
regelmäßig

regulate ['regjʊleɪt] vt
regulieren; (using rules) regeln;
regulation [regjʊ'leɪʃən] n (rule)
Vorschrift f

rehabilitation [riːəbɪlɪ'teɪʃən]
n Rehabilitation f

rehearsal [rɪ'hɜːsəl] n Probe f; **rehearse** vt, vi proben

reign [reɪn] n Herrschaft f ▷ vi herrschen (over über +akk)

reimburse [riːɪm'bɜːs] vt (person) entschädigen; (expenses) zurückerstatten

reindeer ['reɪndɪə*] n Rentier nt

reinforce [riːɪn'fɔːs] vt verstärken

reinstate [riːɪn'steɪt] vt (employee) wieder einstellen; (passage in text) wieder aufnehmen

reject [rɪ'dʒekt] n (Comm) Ausschussartikel m ▷ ['riːdʒekt] vt ablehnen; **rejection** [rɪ'dʒekʃən] n Ablehnung f

relapse [rɪ'læps] n Rückfall m

relate [rɪ'leɪt] vt (story) erzählen; (connect) in Verbindung bringen (to mit) ▷ vi: **to ~ to** (refer) sich beziehen auf +akk; **related** adj verwandt (to mit); **relation** [rɪ'leɪʃən] n (relative) Verwandte(r) mf; (connection) Beziehung f; **~s** pl (dealings) Beziehungen pl; **relationship** n (connection) Beziehung f; (between people) Verhältnis m

relative ['relətɪv] n Verwandte(r) mf ▷ adj relativ; **relatively** adv relativ, verhältnismäßig

relax [rɪ'læks] vi sich entspannen; **~!** reg dich nicht auf! ▷ vt (grip, conditions) lockern; **relaxation** [riːlæk'seɪʃən] n (rest) Entspannung f; **relaxed** adj entspannt; **relaxing** adj entspannend

release [rɪ'liːs] n (from prison) Entlassung f; **new/recent ~** (film, CD) Neuerscheinung f ▷ vt (animal, hostage) freilassen; (prisoner) entlassen; (handbrake) lösen; (news) veröffentlichen; (film, CD) herausbringen

relent [rɪ'lent] vi nachgeben; **relentless, relentlessly** adj, adv (merciless) erbarmungslos; (neverending) unaufhörlich

relevance ['relvəns] n Relevanz f (to für); **relevant** adj relevant (to für)

reliable, reliably [rɪ'laɪəbl, -blɪ] adj, adv zuverlässig; **reliant** [rɪ'laɪənt] adj: **~ on** abhängig von

relic ['relɪk] n (from past) Relikt nt

relief [rɪ'liːf] n (from anxiety, pain) Erleichterung f; (assistance) Hilfe f; **relieve** [rɪ'liːv] vt (pain) lindern; (boredom) überwinden; (take over from) ablösen; **I'm ~d** ich bin erleichtert

religion [rɪ'lɪdʒən] n Religion f; **religious** [rɪ'lɪdʒəs] adj religiös

relish ['relɪʃ] n (for food) würzige Soße f ▷ vt (enjoy) genießen; **I don't ~ the thought of it** der Gedanke behagt mir gar nicht

reluctant [rɪ'lʌktənt] adj widerwillig; **to be ~ to do sth** etw nur ungern tun; **reluctantly** adv widerwillig

rely on [rɪ'laɪ ɒn] vt sich verlassen auf +akk; (depend on) abhängig sein von

remain [rɪ'meɪn] vi bleiben; (be left over) übrig bleiben; **remainder** n (a Math) Rest m; **remaining** adj übrig; **remains** npl Überreste pl

remark [rɪ'mɑːk] n Bemerkung f ▷ vt: **to ~ that** bemerken, dass ▷ vi: **to ~ on sth** über etw akk eine Bemerkung machen; **remarkable, remarkably** adj, adv bemerkenswert

remarry [riː'mærɪ] vi wieder heiraten

remedy ['remədɪ] n Mittel nt (for gegen) ▷ vt abhelfen +dat

remember [rɪ'membə*] vt sich erinnern an +akk; **to ~ to do sth** daran denken, etw zu tun; **I ~ seeing her** ich erinnere mich daran, sie gesehen zu haben; **I must ~ that** das muss ich mir merken ▷ vi sich erinnern

Remembrance Day [rɪ'membrəns'deɪ] n (Brit) = Volkstrauertag m

● **REMEMBRANCE DAY**
●
● **Remembrance Sunday/Day** ist
● der britische Gedenktag für die
● Gefallenen der beiden
● Weltkriege und anderer Kriege.
● Er fällt auf einen Sonntag vor
● oder nach dem 11. November
● (am 11.11.1918 endete der Erste
● Weltkrieg) und wird mit einer
● Schweigeminute,
● Kranzniederlegungen an
● Kriegerdenkmälern und dem
● Tragen von Anstecknadeln in
● Form einer Mohnblume
● begangen.

remind [rɪ'maɪnd] vt: **to ~ sb of/about sb/sth** jdn an jdn/etw erinnern; **to ~ sb to do sth** jdn daran erinnern, etw zu tun; **that ~s me** dabei fällt mir ein ...; **reminder** n (to pay) Mahnung f

reminisce [remɪ'nɪs] vi in Erinnerungen schwelgen (about an +akk); **reminiscent** [remɪ'nɪsənt] adj: **to be ~ of** erinnern an +akk

remittance n Überweisung f (to an +akk)

remnant ['remnənt] n Rest m

remote [rɪ'məʊt] adj (place) abgelegen; (slight) gering ▷ n (TV) Fernbedienung f; **remote control** n Fernsteuerung f; (device) Fernbedienung f

removal [rɪ'muːvəl] n Entfernung f; (Brit: move from house) Umzug m; **removal firm** n (Brit) Spedition f; **remove** [rɪ'muːv] vt entfernen; (lid) abnehmen;

(clothes) ausziehen; (doubt, suspicion) zerstreuen

rename [riː'neɪm] vt umbenennen

renew [rɪ'njuː] vt erneuern; (licence, passport, library book) verlängern lassen; **renewable** adj (energy) erneuerbar

renounce [rɪ'naʊns] vt verzichten auf +akk; (faith, opinion) abschwören +dat

renovate ['renəveɪt] vt renovieren

renowned [rɪ'naʊnd] adj berühmt (for für)

rent [rent] n Miete f; **for ~** (US) zu vermieten ▷ vt (as hirer, tenant) mieten; (as owner) vermieten; **~ed car** Mietwagen m; **rent out** vt vermieten; **rental** n Miete f; (for car, TV etc) Leihgebühr f ▷ adj Miet-

reorganize [riː'ɔːgənaɪz] vt umorganisieren

rep [rep] n Vertreter(in) m(f)

repair [rɪ'peəʳ] n Reparatur f ▷ vt reparieren; (damage) wiedergutmachen; **repair kit** n Flickzeug nt

repay [riː'peɪ] irr vt (money) zurückzahlen; **to ~ sb for sth** (fig) sich bei jdm für etw revanchieren

repeat [rɪ'piːt] n (Radio, TV) Wiederholung f ▷ vt wiederholen; **repetition** [repə'tɪʃən] n Wiederholung f; **repetitive** [rɪ'petɪtɪv] adj sich wiederholend

rephrase [riː'freɪz] vt anders formulieren

replace [rɪ'pleɪs] vt ersetzen (with durch); (put back) zurückstellen, zurücklegen; **replacement** n (thing, person) Ersatz m; (temporarily in job) Vertretung f; **replacement part** n Ersatzteil nt

replay ['riːpleɪ] n: (action)

~ Wiederholung f ⊳ ['ri:'pleɪ] vt (game) wiederholen

replica ['replɪkə] n Kopie f

reply [rɪ'plaɪ] n Antwort f ⊳ vi antworten; **to ~ to sb/sth** jdm/auf etw akk antworten ⊳ vt: **to ~ that** antworten, dass

report [rɪ'pɔ:t] n Bericht m; (school) Zeugnis nt ⊳ vt (tell) berichten; (give information against) melden; (to police) anzeigen ⊳ vi (present oneself) sich melden; **to ~ sick** sich krankmelden; **report card** n (US: school) Zeugnis nt; **reporter** n Reporter(in) m(f);

represent [reprɪ'zent] vt darstellen; (speak for) vertreten; **representation** [reprɪzen'teɪʃən] n (picture etc) Darstellung f; **representative** [reprɪ'zentətɪv] n Vertreter(in) m(f); (US Pol) Abgeordnete(r) mf ⊳ adj repräsentativ (of für)

reprimand ['reprɪmɑ:nd] n Tadel m ⊳ vt tadeln

reprint ['ri:prɪnt] n Nachdruck m

reproduce [ri:prə'dju:s] vt (copy) reproduzieren ⊳ vi (Bio) sich fortpflanzen; **reproduction** [ri:prə'dʌkʃən] n (copy) Reproduktion f; (Bio) Fortpflanzung f

reptile ['reptaɪl] n Reptil nt

republic [rɪ'pʌblɪk] n Republik f; **republican** adj republikanisch ⊳ n Republikaner(in) m(f)

repulsive [rɪ'pʌlsɪv] adj abstoßend

reputable ['repjʊtəbl] adj seriös

reputation [repjʊ'teɪʃən] n Ruf m; **he has a ~ for being difficult** er hat den Ruf, schwierig zu sein

request [rɪ'kwest] n Bitte f (for um); **on ~** auf Wunsch ⊳ vt bitten um; **to ~ sb to do sth** jdn bitten, etw zu tun

require [rɪ'kwaɪə'] vt (need)

brauchen; (desire) verlangen; **what qualifications are ~d?** welche Qualifikationen sind erforderlich?; **required** adj erforderlich; **requirement** n (condition) Anforderung f; (need) Bedingung f

rerun ['ri:rʌn] n Wiederholung f

rescue ['reskju:] n Rettung f; **to come to sb's ~** jdm zu Hilfe kommen ⊳ vt retten; **rescue party** n Rettungsmannschaft f

research [rɪ'sɜ:tʃ] n Forschung f ⊳ vi forschen (into über +akk) ⊳ vt erforschen; **researcher** n Forscher(in) m(f)

resemblance [rɪ'zembləns] n Ähnlichkeit f (to mit); **resemble** [rɪ'zembl] vt ähneln +dat

resent [rɪ'zent] vt übel nehmen

reservation [rezə'veɪʃən] n (booking) Reservierung f; (doubt) Vorbehalt m; **I have a ~** (in hotel, restaurant) ich habe reserviert; **reserve** [rɪ'zɜ:v] n (store) Vorrat m (of an +dat); (manner) Zurückhaltung f; (Sport) Reservespieler(in) m(f); (game ~) Naturschutzgebiet nt ⊳ vt (book in advance) reservieren; **reserved** adj reserviert

reservoir ['rezəvwɑ:'] n (for water) Reservoir nt

reside [rɪ'zaɪd] vi wohnen; **residence** ['rezɪdəns] n Wohnsitz m; (living) Aufenthalt m; **~ permit** Aufenthaltsgenehmigung f; **~ hall** Studentenwohnheim nt; **resident** ['rezɪdənt] n (in house) Bewohner(in) m(f); (in town, area) Einwohner(in) m(f)

resign [rɪ'zaɪn] vt (post) zurücktreten von; (job) kündigen ⊳ vi (from post) zurücktreten; (from job) kündigen; **resignation** [rezɪg'neɪʃən] n (from post)

Rücktritt m; *(from job)* Kündigung f; **resigned** adj resigniert; **he is ~ to it** er hat sich damit abgefunden

resist [rɪˈzɪst] vt widerstehen +dat; **resistance** n Widerstand m *(to* gegen)

resit [riːˈsɪt] *(Brit)* irr vt wiederholen ▷ [ˈriːsɪt] n Wiederholungsprüfung f

resolution [rezəˈluːʃən] n *(intention)* Vorsatz m; *(decision)* Beschluss m

resolve [rɪˈzɒlv] vt *(problem)* lösen

resort [rɪˈzɔːt] n *(holiday ~)* Urlaubsort m; *(health ~)* Kurort m; **as a last ~** als letzter Ausweg ▷ vi: **to ~ to** greifen zu; *(violence)* anwenden

resources [rɪˈsɔːsɪz] npl *(money)* (Geld)mittel pl; *(mineral ~)* Bodenschätze pl

respect [rɪˈspekt] n Respekt m *(for* vor +dat); *(consideration)* Rücksicht f *(for* auf +akk); **with ~ to** in Bezug auf +akk; **in this ~** in dieser Hinsicht; **with all due ~** bei allem Respekt ▷ vt respektieren; **respectable** [rɪˈspektəbl] adj *(person, family)* angesehen; *(district)* anständig; *(achievement, result)* beachtlich; **respected** [rɪˈspektɪd] adj angesehen

respective [rɪˈspektɪv] adj jeweilig; **respectively** adv: **5 % and 10 %** = 5 % beziehungsweise 10 %

respiratory [rɪˈspɪrətərɪ] adj: **~ problems** *(o* trouble) Atembeschwerden pl

respond [rɪˈspɒnd] vi antworten *(to* auf +akk); *(react)* reagieren *(to* auf +akk); *(to treatment)* ansprechen *(to* auf +akk); **response** [rɪˈspɒns] n Antwort f; *(reaction)* Reaktion f; **in ~ to** als Antwort auf +akk

responsibility [rɪspɒnsəˈbɪlɪtɪ] n Verantwortung f; **that's her ~** dafür ist sie verantwortlich; **responsible** [rɪˈspɒnsəbl] adj verantwortlich *(for* für); *(trustworthy)* verantwortungsbewusst; *(job)* verantwortungsvoll

rest [rest] n *(relaxation)* Ruhe f; *(break)* Pause f; *(remainder)* Rest m; **to have (o take) a ~** sich ausruhen; *(break)* Pause machen; **the ~ of the wine/the people** der Rest des Weins/der Leute ▷ vi *(relax)* sich ausruhen; *(lean)* lehnen *(on, against* an +dat, gegen)

restaurant [ˈrestərɒnt] n Restaurant nt; **restaurant car** n *(Brit)* Speisewagen m

restful [ˈrestfʊl] adj *(holiday etc)* erholsam, ruhig; **restless** [ˈrestləs] adj unruhig

restore [rɪˈstɔːˀ] vt *(painting, building)* restaurieren; *(order)* wiederherstellen; *(give back)* zurückgeben

restrain [rɪˈstreɪn] vt *(person, feelings)* zurückhalten; **to ~ oneself** sich beherrschen

restrict [rɪˈstrɪkt] vt beschränken *(to* auf +akk); **restricted** adj beschränkt; **restriction** [rɪˈstrɪkʃən] n Einschränkung f *(on* +gen)

rest room [ˈrestruːm] n *(US)* Toilette f

result [rɪˈzʌlt] n Ergebnis nt; *(consequence)* Folge f; **as a ~ of** infolge +gen ▷ vi: **to ~ in** führen zu; **to ~ from** sich ergeben aus

resume [rɪˈzjuːm] vt *(work, negotiations)* wieder aufnehmen; *(journey)* fortsetzen

résumé [ˈrezjʊmeɪ] n Zusammenfassung f; *(US: curriculum vitae)* Lebenslauf m

resuscitate [rɪˈsʌsɪteɪt] *vt* wiederbeleben

retail [ˈriːteɪl] *adv* im Einzelhandel; **retailer** *n* Einzelhändler(in) *m(f)*

retain [rɪˈteɪn] *vt* behalten; *(heat)* halten

rethink [riːˈθɪŋk] *irr vt* noch einmal überdenken

retire [rɪˈtaɪəʳ] *vi (from work)* in den Ruhestand treten; *(withdraw)* sich zurückziehen; **retired** *adj (person)* pensioniert; **retirement** *n (time of life)* Ruhestand *m*; **retirement age** *n* Rentenalter *nt*

retrace [rɪˈtreɪs] *vt* zurückverfolgen

retrain [riːˈtreɪn] *vi* sich umschulen lassen

retreat [rɪˈtriːt] *n (Mil)* Rückzug *m (from aus)*; *(refuge)* Zufluchtsort *m* ▷ *vi (Mil)* sich zurückziehen; *(step back)* zurückweichen

retrieve [rɪˈtriːv] *vt (recover)* wiederbekommen; *(rescue)* retten; *(data)* abrufen

retrospect [ˈretrəʊspekt] *n*: **in ~** rückblickend; **retrospective** [retrəʊˈspektɪv] *adj* rückblickend; *(pay rise)* rückwirkend

return [rɪˈtɜːn] *n (going back)* Rückkehr *f*; *(giving back)* Rückgabe *f*; *(profit)* Gewinn *m*; *(Brit: ~ ticket)* Rückfahrkarte *f*; *(plane ticket)* Rückflugticket *nt*; *(Tennis)*, Return *m*; **in ~** als Gegenleistung *(for* für*)*; **many happy ~s (of the day)** herzlichen Glückwunsch zum Geburtstag! ▷ *vi (person)* zurückkehren; *(doubts, symptoms)* wieder auftreten; **to ~ to school/work** wieder in die Schule/die Arbeit gehen ▷ *vt (give back)* zurückgeben; **I ~ed his call** ich habe ihn zurückgerufen; **returnable** *adj (bottle)* Pfand-;

return flight *n (Brit)* Rückflug *m*; *(both ways)* Hin- und Rückflug *m*; **return key** *n (Inform)* Eingabetaste *f*; **return ticket** *n (Brit)* Rückfahrkarte *f*; *(for plane)* Rückflugticket *nt*

reunification [riːjuːnɪfɪˈkeɪʃən] *n* Wiedervereinigung *f*

reunion [riːˈjuːnjən] *n (party)* Treffen *nt*; **reunite** [riːjuːˈnaɪt] *vt* wieder vereinigen

reusable [riːˈjuːzəbl] *adj* wiederverwendbar

reveal [rɪˈviːl] *vt (make known)* enthüllen; *(secret)* verraten; *(show)* zeigen; **revealing** *adj* aufschlussreich; *(dress)* freizügig

revenge [rɪˈvendʒ] *n* Rache *f*; *(in game)* Revanche *f*; **to take ~ on sb (for sth)** sich an jdm (für etw) rächen

revenue [ˈrevənjuː] *n* Einnahmen *pl*

reverse [rɪˈvɜːs] *n (back)* Rückseite *f*; *(opposite)* Gegenteil *nt*; *(Auto)* **~ (gear)** Rückwärtsgang *m* ▷ *adj*: **in ~ order** in umgekehrter Reihenfolge ▷ *vt (order)* umkehren; *(decision)* umstoßen; *(car)* zurücksetzen; **to ~ the charges** *(Brit)* ein R-Gespräch führen ▷ *vi (Auto)* rückwärtsfahren

review [rɪˈvjuː] *n (of book, film etc)* Rezension *f*, Kritik *f*; **to be under ~** überprüft werden ▷ *vt (book, film etc)* rezensieren; *(re-examine)* überprüfen

revise [rɪˈvaɪz] *vt* revidieren; *(text)* überarbeiten; *(Brit: in school)* wiederholen ▷ *vi (Brit, in school)* (für eine Prüfung) lernen; **revision** [rɪˈvɪʒən] *n (of text)* Überarbeitung *f*; *(Brit, in school)* Wiederholung *f*

revitalize [riːˈvaɪtəlaɪz] *vt* neu beleben

revive [rɪ'vaɪv] vt (person)
wiederbeleben; (tradition, interest)
wieder aufleben lassen ▷ vi
(regain consciousness) wieder zu
sich kommen

revolt [rɪ'vəʊlt] n Aufstand m;
revolting adj widerlich

revolution [revə'lu:ʃən] n (Pol,
fig) Revolution f; (turn)
Umdrehung f; **revolutionary** adj
revolutionär ▷ n Revolutionär(in)
m(f)

revolve [rɪ'vɒlv] vi sich drehen
(around um); **revolver** n Revolver
m; **revolving door** n Drehtür f

reward [rɪ'wɔːd] n Belohnung f
▷ vt belohnen; **rewarding** adj
lohnend

rewind [riː'waɪnd] irr vt (tape)
zurückspulen

rewritable [riː'raɪtəbl] adj (CD,
DVD) wiederbeschreibbar; **rewrite**
irr vt (write again; recast)
umschreiben

rheumatism ['ruːmətɪzəm] n
Rheuma nt

Rhine [raɪn] n Rhein m

rhinoceros [raɪ'nɒsərəs] n
Nashorn nt

Rhodes [rəʊdz] n Rhodos nt

rhubarb ['ruːbɑːb] n Rhabarber m

rhyme [raɪm] n Reim m ▷ vi
sich reimen (with auf +akk)

rhythm ['rɪðəm] n Rhythmus m

rib [rɪb] n Rippe f

ribbon ['rɪbən] n Band nt

rice [raɪs] n Reis m; **rice pudding**
n Milchreis m

rich [rɪtʃ] adj reich; (food) schwer
▷ npl: **the ~** die Reichen pl

rickety ['rɪkɪtɪ] adj wackelig

rid [rɪd] (**rid, rid**) vt: **to get ~ of
sb/sth** jdn/etw loswerden

ridden ['rɪdn] pp of **ride**

riddle ['rɪdl] n Rätsel nt

ride [raɪd] (**rode, ridden**) vt
(horse) reiten; (bicycle) fahren ▷ vi

(on horse) reiten; (on bike) fahren
▷ n (in vehicle, on bike) Fahrt f; (on
horse) (Aus)ritt m; **to go for a ~** (in
car, on bike) spazieren fahren; (on
horse) reiten gehen; **to take sb for
a ~** (fam) jdn verarschen; **rider** n
(on horse) Reiter(in) m(f); (on bike)
Fahrer(in) m(f)

ridiculous [rɪ'dɪkjʊləs] adj
lächerlich; **don't be ~** red keinen
Unsinn!

riding ['raɪdɪŋ] n Reiten nt; **to go
~ reiten gehen ▷ adj** Reit-

rifle ['raɪfl] n Gewehr nt

rig [rɪg] n: **oil ~** Bohrinsel f ▷ vt
(election etc) manipulieren

right [raɪt] adj (correct, just)
richtig; (opposite of left) rechte(r, s);
(clothes, job etc) passend; **to be
~** (person) recht haben; (clock)
richtig gehen; **that's ~** das
stimmt! ▷ n Recht nt (to auf +akk);
(side) rechte Seite; **the Right** (Pol)
die Rechte; **to take a ~** (Auto)
rechts abbiegen; **on the ~** rechts
(of von); **to the ~** nach rechts; (on
the ~) rechts (of von) ▷ adv
(towards the ~) nach rechts;
(directly) direkt; (exactly) genau; **to
turn ~** (Auto) rechts abbiegen;
~ away sofort; **~ now** im
Moment; (immediately) sofort;
right angle n rechter Winkel;
right-hand drive n
Rechtssteuerung f ▷ adj
rechtsgesteuert; **right-handed**
adj: **he is ~** er ist Rechtshänder;
right-hand side n rechte Seite;
on the ~ auf der rechten Seite;
rightly adv zu Recht; **right of
way** n: **to have ~** (Auto) Vorfahrt
haben; **right wing** n (Pol, Sport)
rechter Flügel; **right-wing** adj
Rechts-; **~ extremist**
Rechtsradikale(r) mf

rigid ['rɪdʒɪd] adj (stiff) starr;
(strict) streng

rigorous, rigorously [ˈrɪgərəs, -lɪ] *adj, adv* streng

rim [rɪm] *n (of cup etc)* Rand *m; (of wheel)* Felge *f*

rind [raɪnd] *n (of cheese)* Rinde *f; (of bacon)* Schwarte *f; (of fruit)* Schale *f*

ring [rɪŋ] **(rang, rung)** *vt, vi (bell)* läuten; *(Tel)* anrufen ▷ *n (on finger, in boxing)* Ring *m; (circle)* Kreis *m; (at circus)* Manege *f;* **to give sb a ~** *(Tel)* jdn anrufen; **ring back** *vt, vi* zurückrufen; **ring up** *vt, vi* anrufen

ring binder *n* Ringbuch *nt*

ringleader *n* Anführer(in) *m(f)*

ring road *n (Brit)* Umgehungsstraße *f*

ringtone *n* Klingelton *m*

rink [rɪŋk] *n (ice-)* Eisbahn *f; (for roller-skating)* Rollschuhbahn *f*

rinse [rɪns] *vt* spülen

riot [ˈraɪət] *n* Aufruhr *m*

rip [rɪp] *n* Riss *m* ▷ *vt* zerreißen; **to ~ sth open** etw aufreißen ▷ *vi* reißen; **rip off** *vt (fam: person)* übers Ohr hauen; **rip up** *vt* zerreißen

ripe [raɪp] *adj (fruit)* reif; **ripen** *vi* reifen

rip-off [ˈrɪpɒf] *n:* **that's a ~** *(fam: too expensive)* das ist Wucher

rise [raɪz] **(rose, risen)** *vi (from sitting, lying)* aufstehen; *(sun)* aufgehen; *(prices, temperature)* steigen; *(ground)* ansteigen; *(in revolt)* sich erheben ▷ *n (increase)* Anstieg *m (in +gen); (pay-)* Gehaltserhöhung *f; (to power, fame)* Aufstieg *m (to zu); (slope)* Steigung *f;* **risen** [ˈrɪzn] *pp of* **rise**

risk [rɪsk] *n* Risiko *nt* ▷ *vt* riskieren; **to ~ doing sth** es riskieren, etw zu tun; **risky** *adj* riskant

risotto [rɪˈzɒtəʊ] *(pl -s) n* Risotto *nt*

ritual [ˈrɪtjʊəl] *n* Ritual *nt* ▷ *adj* rituell

rival [ˈraɪvəl] *n* Rivale *m,* Rivalin *f (for um); (Comm)* Konkurrent(in) *m(f); (Sport)* Konkurrenz *f;* **rivalry** *n* Rivalität *f; (Comm, Sport)* Konkurrenz *f*

river [ˈrɪvər] *n* Fluss *m;* **the River Thames** *(Brit),* **the Thames River** *(US)* die Themse; **riverside** *n* Flussufer *nt* ▷ *adj* am Flussufer

road [rəʊd] *n* Straße *f; (fig)* Weg *m;* **on the ~** *(travelling)* unterwegs, mit dem Auto/Bus *etc* fahren; **roadblock** *n* Straßensperre *f;* **roadmap** *n* Straßenkarte *f;* **road rage** *n* aggressives Verhalten im Straßenverkehr; **roadside** *n:* **at** *(o* **by)** **the ~** am Straßenrand; **roadsign** *n* Verkehrsschild *nt;* **road tax** *n* Kraftfahrzeugssteuer *f;* **roadworks** *npl* Bauarbeiten *pl;* **roadworthy** *adj* fahrtüchtig

roar [rɔːʳ] *n (of person, lion)* Brüllen *nt; (von Verkehr)* Donnern *nt* ▷ *vi (person, lion)* brüllen *(with vor +dat)*

roast [rəʊst] *n* Braten *m* ▷ *adj:* **~ beef** Rinderbraten *m;* **~ chicken** Brathähnchen *nt;* **~ pork** Schweinebraten *m;* **~ potatoes** *pl* im Backofen gebratene Kartoffeln ▷ *vt (meat)* braten

rob [rɒb] *vt* bestehlen; *(bank, shop)* ausrauben; **robber** *n* Räuber(in) *m(f);* **robbery** *n* Raub *m*

robe [rəʊb] *n (US: dressing gown)* Morgenrock *m; (of judge, priest etc)* Robe *f,* Talar *m*

robin [ˈrɒbɪn] *n* Rotkehlchen *nt*

robot [ˈrəʊbɒt] *n* Roboter *m*

robust [rəʊˈbʌst] *adj* robust; *(defence)* stark

rock [rɒk] *n (substance)* Stein *m; (boulder)* Felsbrocken *m; (Mus)* Rock *m;* **stick of ~** *(Brit)* Zuckerstange *f;* **on the ~s** *(drink)*

mit Eis; *(marriage)* gescheitert
▷ *vt, vi (swing)* schaukeln; *(dance)*
rocken; **rock climbing** n Klettern
nt; **to go ~** klettern gehen
rocket ['rɒkɪt] n Rakete f; *(in salad)* Rucola f
rocking chair ['rɒkɪŋtʃeə⁎] n
Schaukelstuhl m
rocky ['rɒkɪ] adj *(landscape)* felsig;
(path) steinig
rod [rɒd] n *(bar)* Stange f; *(fishing ~)* Rute f
rode [rəʊd] pt of **ride**
rogue [rəʊg] n Schurke m,
Gauner m
role [rəʊl] n Rolle f; **role model** n
Vorbild nt
roll [rəʊl] n *(of film, paper etc)*
Rolle f; *(bread ~)* Brötchen nt ▷ vt
(move by ~ing) rollen; *(cigarette)*
drehen ▷ vi *(move by ~ing)* rollen;
(ship) schlingern; *(camera)* laufen;
roll out vt *(pastry)* ausrollen; **roll
over** vi *(person)* sich umdrehen;
roll up vi *(fam: arrive)* antanzen
▷ vt *(carpet)* aufrollen; **to roll
one's sleeves up** die Ärmel
hochkrempeln
roller n *(hair ~)* (Locken)wickler m;
Rollerblades® npl Inlineskates
pl; **rollerblading** n Inlineskaten
nt; **roller coaster** n Achterbahn f;
roller skates npl Rollschuhe pl;
roller-skating n Rollschuhlaufen
nt; **rolling pin** n Nudelholz nt;
roll-on (deodorant) n Deoroller
m
ROM [rɒm] acr = **read only
memory** ROM m
Roman ['rəʊmən] adj römisch
▷ n Römer(in) m(f); **Roman
Catholic** adj römisch-katholisch
▷ n Katholik(in) m(f)
romance [rəʊ'mæns] n Romantik f; *(love affair)* Romanze f
Romania [rəʊ'meɪnɪə] n
Rumänien nt; **Romanian** adj

rumänisch ▷ n Rumäne m,
Rumänin f; *(language)* Rumänisch
nt
romantic [rəʊ'mæntɪk] adj
romantisch
roof [ru:f] n Dach nt; **roof rack** n
Dachgepäckträger m
rook [rʊk] n *(in chess)* Turm m
room [ru:m] n Zimmer nt, Raum
m; *(large, for gatherings etc)* Saal m;
(space) Platz m; *(fig)* Spielraum m;
to make ~ for Platz machen für;
roommate n Zimmergenosse m,
Zimmergenossin f;
Mitbewohner(in) m(f); **room
service** n Zimmerservice m;
roomy adj geräumig; *(garment)*
weit
root [ru:t] n Wurzel f; **root out** vt
(eradicate) ausrotten; **root
vegetable** n Wurzelgemüse nt
rope [rəʊp] n Seil nt; **to know
the ~s** *(fam)* sich auskennen
rort [rɔ:t] n *(Aust, NZ fam)* n
Betrugsschema nt, Abzocke f *(fam)*
▷ vt austricksen *(fam)*; *(money)*
abschöpfen
rose [rəʊz] pt of **rise** ▷ n Rose f
rosé ['rəʊzeɪ] n Rosé(wein) m
rot [rɒt] vi verfaulen
rota ['rəʊtə] n *(Brit)* Dienstplan m
rotate [rəʊ'teɪt] vt *(turn)* rotieren
lassen ▷ vi rotieren
rotten ['rɒtn] adj *(decayed)* faul;
(mean) gemein; *(unpleasant)*
scheußlich; *(ill)* elend
rough [rʌf] adj *(not smooth)* rau;
(path) uneben; *(coarse, violent)*
grob; *(crossing)* stürmisch; *(without
comforts)* hart; *(unfinished,
makeshift)* grob; *(approximate)*
ungefähr; **~ draft** Rohentwurf m; **I
have a ~ idea** ich habe eine
ungefähre Vorstellung ▷ adv: **to
sleep ~** im Freien schlafen; **to
~ it** primitiv leben; **roughly** adv
grob; *(approximately)* ungefähr

round [raʊnd] *adj* rund ▷ *adv*: **all ~ (on all sides)** rundherum; **the long way ~** der längere Weg; **I'll be ~ at 8** ich werde um acht Uhr da sein; **the other way ~** umgekehrt ▷ *prep (surrounding)* um (... herum); **~ (about)** *(approximately)* ungefähr; **~ the corner** um die Ecke; **to go ~ the world** um die Welt reisen; **she lives ~ here** sie wohnt hier in der Gegend ▷ *n* Runde *f; (of bread, toast)* Scheibe *f; (of drinks)* die Runde geht auf mich ▷ *vt (corner)* biegen um; **round off** *vt* abrunden; **round up** *vt (number, price)* aufrunden

roundabout *n (Brit Auto)* Kreisverkehr *m; (Brit: merry-go-round)* Karussell *nt* ▷ *adj* umständlich; **round-the-clock** *adj* rund um die Uhr; **round trip** *n* Rundreise *f;* **round-trip ticket** *n (US)* Rückfahrkarte *f; (for plane)* Rückflugticket *nt*

rouse [raʊz] *vt (from sleep)* wecken

route [ruːt] *n* Route *f; (bus, plane etc service)* Linie *f; (fig)* Weg *m*

routine [ruːˈtiːn] *n* Routine *f* ▷ *adj* Routine-

row¹ [rəʊ] *n (line)* Reihe *f;* **three times in a ~** dreimal hintereinander ▷ *vt, vi (boat)* rudern ▷ [raʊ] *n (noise)* Krach *m; (dispute)* Streit *m*

rowboat ['rəʊbəʊt] *n (US)* Ruderboot *nt*

row house ['rəʊhaʊs] *n (US)* Reihenhaus *nt*

rowing ['rəʊɪŋ] *n* Rudern *nt;* **rowing boat** *n (Brit)* Ruderboot *nt;* **rowing machine** *n* Rudergerät *nt*

royal ['rɔɪəl] *adj* königlich; **royalty** *n (family)* Mitglied *pl* der königlichen Familie; **royalties** *pl (from book, music)* Tantiemen *pl*

RSPCA *abbr* = **Royal Society for the Prevention of Cruelty to Animals** britischer Tierschutzverein

RSPCC *abbr* = **Royal Society for the Prevention of Cruelty to Children** britischer Kinderschutzverein

RSVP *abbr* = **répondez s'il vous plaît** u. A. w. g.

rub [rʌb] *vt* reiben; **rub in** *vt* einmassieren; **rub out** *vt (with eraser)* ausradieren

rubber ['rʌbə*] *n* Gummi *m; (Brit: eraser)* Radiergummi *m; (US fam: contraceptive)* Gummi *m;* **rubber band** *n* Gummiband *nt;* **rubber stamp** *n* Stempel *m*

rubbish ['rʌbɪʃ] *n* Abfall *m; (nonsense)* Quatsch *m; (poor-quality thing)* Mist *m;* **don't talk ~** red keinen Unsinn!; **rubbish bin** *n* Mülleimer *m;* **rubbish dump** *n* Müllablageplatz *m*

rubble ['rʌbl] *n* Schutt *m*

ruby ['ruːbɪ] *n (stone)* Rubin *m*

rucksack ['rʌksæk] *n* Rucksack *m*

rude [ruːd] *adj (impolite)* unhöflich; *(indecent)* unanständig

rug [rʌg] *n* Teppich *m; (next to bed)* Bettvorleger *m; (for knees)* Wolldecke *f*

rugby ['rʌgbɪ] *n* Rugby *nt*

rugged ['rʌgɪd] *adj (coastline)* zerklüftet; *(features)* markant

ruin ['ruːɪn] *n* Ruine *f; (financial, social)* Ruin *m* ▷ *vt* ruinieren

rule [ruːl] *n* Regel *f; (governing)* Herrschaft *f;* **as a ~** in der Regel ▷ *vt, vi (govern)* regieren; *(decide)* entscheiden; **ruler** *n* Lineal *nt; (person)* Herrscher(in) *m(f)*

rum [rʌm] *n* Rum *m*

rumble ['rʌmbl] *vi (stomach)* knurren; *(train, truck)* rumpeln

rummage ['rʌmɪdʒ] *vi:* **~ (around)** herumstöbern

rumor (US), **rumour** ['ru:mə°] n
Gerücht nt

run [rʌn] (**ran, run**) vt (race,
distance) laufen; (machine, engine,
computer program, water) laufen
lassen; (manage) leiten, führen;
(car) unterhalten; **I ran her home**
ich habe sie nach Hause gefahren
▷ vi laufen; (move quickly) rennen;
(bus, train) fahren; (pitch etc)
verlaufen; (machine, engine,
computer program) laufen; (flow)
fließen; (colours, make-up)
verlaufen; **to ~ for President** für
die Präsidentschaft kandidieren;
to be ~ning low knapp werden;
my nose is ~ning mir läuft die
Nase; **it ~s in the family** es liegt in
der Familie ▷ n (on foot) Lauf m;
(in car) Spazierfahrt f; (series) Reihe
f; (sudden demand) Ansturm m (on
auf +akk); (in tights) Laufmasche f;
(in cricket, baseball) Lauf m; **to go
for a ~** laufen gehen; (in car) eine
Spazierfahrt machen; **in the long
~** auf die Dauer; **on the ~** auf der
Flucht (from vor +dat); **run about**
vi herumlaufen; **run away** vi
weglaufen; **run down** vt (with car)
umfahren; (criticize)
heruntermachen; **to be ~** (tired)
abgespannt sein; **run into** vt
(meet) zufällig treffen; (problem)
stoßen auf +akk; **run off** vi
weglaufen; **run out** vi (person)
hinausrennen; (liquid) auslaufen;
(lease, time) ablaufen; (money,
supplies) ausgehen; **he ran ~ of
money** ihm ging das Geld aus; **run
over** vt (with car) überfahren; **run
up** vt (debt, bill) machen

rung [rʌŋ] pp of **ring**

runner ['rʌnə°] n (athlete)
Läufer(in) m(f); **to do a ~** (fam)
wegrennen; **runner bean** n (Brit)
Stangenbohne f

running ['rʌnɪŋ] n (Sport) Laufen

nt; (management) Leitung f,
Führung f ▷ adj (water) fließend;
~ costs Betriebskosten pl; (for car)
Unterhaltskosten pl; **3 days ~** 3
Tage hintereinander

runny ['rʌnɪ] adj (food) flüssig;
(nose) laufend

runway ['rʌnweɪ] n Start- und
Landebahn f

rural ['rʊərəl] adj ländlich

rush [rʌʃ] n Eile f; (for tickets etc)
Ansturm m (for auf +akk); **to be in
a ~** es eilig haben; **there's no ~** es
eilt nicht ▷ vt (do too quickly)
hastig machen; (meal) hastig
essen; **to ~ sb to hospital** jdn auf
dem schnellsten Weg ins
Krankenhaus bringen; **don't ~ me**
dräng mich nicht ▷ vi (hurry)
eilen; **don't ~** lass dir Zeit; **rush
hour** n Hauptverkehrszeit f

rusk [rʌsk] n Zwieback m

Russia ['rʌʃə] n Russland nt;
Russian adj russisch ▷ n Russe
m, Russin f; (language) Russisch nt

rust [rʌst] n Rost m ▷ vi rosten;
rustproof ['rʌstpru:f] adj rostfrei; **rusty** ['rʌstɪ] adj rostig

ruthless ['ru:θləs] adj rücksichtslos; (treatment, criticism)
schonungslos

rye [raɪ] n Roggen m; **rye bread**
n Roggenbrot nt

S

S *abbr* = **south** S

sabotage ['sæbətɑːʒ] *vt* sabotieren

sachet ['sæʃeɪ] *n* Päckchen *nt*

sack [sæk] *n* (bag) Sack *m*; **to get the ~** (fam) rausgeschmissen werden ▷ *vt* (fam) rausschmeißen

sacred ['seɪkrɪd] *adj* heilig

sacrifice ['sækrɪfaɪs] *n* Opfer *nt* ▷ *vt* opfern

sad [sæd] *adj* traurig

saddle ['sædl] *n* Sattel *m*

sadistic [sə'dɪstɪk] *adj* sadistisch

sadly ['sædlɪ] *adv* (unfortunately) leider

safari [sə'fɑːrɪ] *n* Safari *f*

safe [seɪf] *adj* (free from danger) sicher; (out of danger) in Sicherheit; (careful) vorsichtig; **have a ~ journey** gute Fahrt! ▷ *n* Safe *m*; **safeguard** *n* Schutz *m* ▷ *vt* schützen (against vor +dat); **safely** *adv* sicher; (arrive) wohlbehalten;

(drive) vorsichtig; **safety** *n* Sicherheit *f*; **safety belt** *n* Sicherheitsgurt *m*; **safety pin** *n* Sicherheitsnadel *f*

Sagittarius [sædʒɪ'tɛərɪəs] *n* (Astr) Schütze *m*

Sahara [sə'hɑːrə] *n*: **the ~** (Desert) die (Wüste) Sahara

said [sed] *pt, pp of* **say**

sail [seɪl] *n* Segel *nt*; **to set ~** losfahren (for nach) ▷ *vi* (in yacht) segeln; (on ship) mit dem Schiff fahren; (ship) auslaufen (for nach) ▷ *vt* (yacht) segeln mit; (ship) steuern; **sailboat** *n* (US) Segelboot *nt*; **sailing** *n*: **to go ~** segeln gehen; **sailing boat** *n* (Brit) Segelboot *nt*; **sailor** *n* Seemann *m*; (in navy) Matrose *m*

saint [seɪnt] *n* Heilige(r) *mf*

sake [seɪk] *n*: **for the ~ of** um +gen ... willen; **for your ~** deinetwegen, dir zuliebe

salad ['sæləd] *n* Salat *m*; **salad cream** *n* (Brit) majonäseartige Salatsoße; **salad dressing** *n* Salatsoße *f*

salary ['sælərɪ] *n* Gehalt *nt*

sale [seɪl] *n* Verkauf *m*; (at reduced prices) Ausverkauf *m*; **the ~s** *pl* (in summer, winter) der Schlussverkauf; **for ~** zu verkaufen; **sales clerk** *n* (US) Verkäufer(in) *m(f)*; **salesman** (pl **-men**) *n* Verkäufer *m*; (rep) Vertreter *m*; **sales rep** *n* Vertreter(in) *m(f)*; **sales tax** *n* (US) Verkaufssteuer *f*; **saleswoman** (pl **-women**) *n* Verkäuferin *f*; (rep) Vertreterin *f*

salmon ['sæmən] *n* Lachs *m*

saloon [sə'luːn] *n* (ship's lounge) Salon *m*; (US: bar) Kneipe *f*

salt [sɔːlt] *n* Salz *nt* ▷ *vt* (flavour) salzen; (roads) mit Salz streuen; **salt cellar**, **salt shaker** (US) *n* Salzstreuer *m*; **salty** *adj* salzig

salvage ['sælvɪdʒ] vt bergen (from aus); (fig) retten

same [seɪm] adj: **the ~** (similar) der/die/das gleiche, die gleichen pl; (identical) der-/die-/dasselbe, dieselben pl; **they live in the ~ house** sie wohnen im selben Haus ▷ pron: **the ~** (similar) der/die/das Gleiche, die Gleichen pl; (identical) der-/die-/dasselbe, dieselben pl; **all the ~** trotzdem; **the ~ to you** gleichfalls; **it's all the ~ to me** es ist mir egal ▷ adv: **the ~** gleich; **they look the ~** sie sehen gleich aus

sample ['sɑːmpl] n Probe f; (of fabric) Muster nt ▷ vt probieren

sanctions ['sæŋkʃənz] npl (Pol) Sanktionen pl

sanctuary ['sæŋktjʊərɪ] n (refuge) Zuflucht f; (for animals) Schutzgebiet n

sand [sænd] n Sand m

sandal ['sændl] n Sandale f

sandpaper n Sandpapier nt ▷ vt schmirgeln

sandwich ['sænwɪdʒ] n Sandwich nt

sandy ['sændɪ] adj (full of sand) sandig; **~ beach** Sandstrand m

sane [seɪn] adj geistig gesund, normal; (sensible) vernünftig

sang [sæŋ] pt of **sing**

sanitary ['sænɪtərɪ] adj hygienisch; **sanitary napkin** (US), **sanitary towel** n Damenbinde f

sank [sæŋk] pt of **sink**

Santa (Claus) ['sæntə'klɔːz)] n der Weihnachtsmann

sarcastic [sɑːˈkæstɪk] adj sarkastisch

sardine [sɑːˈdiːn] n Sardine f

Sardinia [sɑːˈdɪnɪə] n Sardinien nt

sari [ˈsɑːrɪ] n Sari m (von indischen Frauen getragenes Gewand)

sat [sæt] pt, pp of **sit**

Sat abbr = **Saturday** Sa.

satellite ['sætəlaɪt] n Satellit m; **satellite dish** n Satellitenschüssel f; **satellite TV** n Satellitenfernsehen nt

satin ['sætɪn] n Satin m

satisfaction [sætɪsˈfækʃən] n (contentment) Zufriedenheit f; **is that to your ~?** bist du/sind Sie damit zufrieden?; **satisfactory** [sætɪsˈfæktərɪ] adj zufriedenstellend; **satisfied** ['sætɪsfaɪd] adj zufrieden (with mit); **satisfy** ['sætɪsfaɪ] vt zufriedenstellen; (convince) überzeugen; (conditions) erfüllen; (need, demand) befriedigen; **satisfying** adj befriedigend

Saturday ['sætədeɪ] n Samstag m, Sonnabend m; see also **Tuesday**

sauce [sɔːs] n Soße f; **saucepan** n Kochtopf m; **saucer** n Untertasse f

saucy ['sɔːsɪ] adj frech

Saudi Arabia ['saʊdɪəˈreɪbɪə] n Saudi-Arabien n

sauna ['sɔːnə] n Sauna f

sausage ['sɒsɪdʒ] n Wurst f; **sausage roll** n mit Wurst gefülltes Blätterteigröllchen

savage ['sævɪdʒ] adj (person, attack) brutal; (animal) wild

save [seɪv] vt (rescue) retten (from vor +dat); (money, time, electricity etc) sparen; (strength) schonen; (Inform) speichern; **to ~ sb's life** jdm das Leben retten ▷ vi sparen ▷ n (in football) Parade f; **save up** vi sparen (for auf +akk); **saving** n (of money) Sparen nt; **~s pl** Ersparnisse pl; **~s account** Sparkonto nt

savory (US), **savoury** ['seɪvərɪ] adj (not sweet) pikant

saw [sɔː] (**sawed**, **sawn**) vt, vi sägen ▷ n (tool) Säge f ▷ pt of **see**; **sawdust** n Sägemehl nt

saxophone ['sæksəfəʊn] n Saxophon nt

say [seɪ] (**said, said**) vt sagen (to sb jdm); (prayer) sprechen; **what does the letter ~?** was steht im Brief!; **the rules ~ that ...** in den Regeln heißt es, dass ...; **he's said to be rich** er soll reich sein ▷ n: **to have a ~ in sth** bei etw ein Mitspracherecht haben ▷ adv zum Beispiel; **saying** nt Sprichwort nt

scab [skæb] n (on cut) Schorf m

scaffolding ['skæfəʊldɪŋ] n (Bau)gerüst nt

scale [skeɪl] n (of map etc) Maßstab m; (on thermometer etc) Skala f; (of pay) Tarifsystem nt; (Mus) Tonleiter f; (of fish, snake) Schuppe f; **to ~** maßstabsgerecht; **on a large/small ~** in großem/kleinem Umfang; **scales** npl (for weighing) Waage f

scalp [skælp] n Kopfhaut f

scan [skæn] vt (examine) genau prüfen; (read quickly) überfliegen; (Inform) scannen ▷ n (Med) Ultraschall m; **scan in** vt (Inform) einscannen

scandal ['skændl] n Skandal m; **scandalous** adj skandalös

Scandinavia [skændɪ'neɪvɪə] n Skandinavien nt; **Scandinavian** adj skandinavisch ▷ n Skandinavier(in) m(f)

scanner ['skænə*] n Scanner m

scapegoat ['skeɪpgəʊt] n Sündenbock m

scar [skɑ:*] n Narbe f

scarce ['skeəs] adj selten; (in short supply) knapp; **scarcely** adv kaum

scare ['skeə*] n (general alarm) Panik f ▷ vt erschrecken; **to be ~d** Angst haben (of vor +dat)

scarf [skɑ:f] (pl **-scarves**) n Schal m; (on head) Kopftuch nt

scarlet ['skɑ:lət] adj scharlachrot; **scarlet fever** n Scharlach m

scary ['skeərɪ] adj (film, story) gruselig

scatter ['skætə*] vt verstreuen; (seed, gravel) streuen; (disperse) auseinandertreiben

scene [si:n] n (location) Ort m; (division of play) (Theat) Szene f; (view) Anblick m; **to make a ~** eine Szene machen; **scenery** ['si:nərɪ] n (landscape) Landschaft f; (Theat) Kulissen pl; **scenic** ['si:nɪk] adj (landscape) malerisch; **~ route** landschaftlich schöne Strecke

scent [sent] n (perfume) Parfüm nt; (smell) Duft m

sceptical ['skeptɪkəl] adj (Brit) skeptisch

schedule ['fedju:l, 'skedʒʊəl] n (plan) Programm nt; (of work) Zeitplan m; (list) Liste f; (US: of trains, buses, air traffic) Fahr-, Flugplan m; **on ~** planmäßig; **to be behind ~ with** sth mit etw in Verzug sein ▷ vt: **the meeting is ~d for next Monday** die Besprechung ist für nächsten Montag angesetzt; **scheduled** adj (departure, arrival) planmäßig; **~ flight** Linienflug m

scheme [ski:m] n (plan) Plan m; (project) Projekt nt; (dishonest) Intrige f ▷ vi intrigieren

schizophrenic [skɪtsə'frenɪk] adj schizophren

scholar ['skɒlə*] n Gelehrte(r) mf; **scholarship** n (grant) Stipendium nt

school [sku:l] n Schule f; (university department) Fachbereich m; (US: university) Universität f; **school bag** n Schultasche f; **schoolbook** n Schulbuch nt; **schoolboy** n Schüler m; **school bus** n Schulbus m; **schoolgirl** n

Schülerin f; **schoolteacher** n
Lehrer(in) m(f); **schoolwork** n
Schularbeiten pl

sciatica [saɪˈætɪkə] n Ischias m

science [ˈsaɪəns] n Wissenschaft
f; (natural ~) Naturwissenschaft f;
science fiction n Sciencefiction
f; **scientific** [saɪənˈtɪfɪk] adj
wissenschaftlich; **scientist**
[ˈsaɪəntɪst] n Wissenschaftler(in)
m(f); (in natural sciences)
Naturwissenschaftler(in) m(f)

scissors [ˈsɪzəz] npl Schere f

scone [skɒn] n (scratch)
Hefebrötchen mit oder ohne Rosinen,
das mit Butter oder Dickrahm und
Marmelade gegessen wird

scoop [skuːp] n (exclusive story)
Exklusivbericht m; **a ~ of
ice-cream** eine Kugel Eis ▷ vt: to
~ (up) schaufeln

scooter [ˈskuːtə*] n (Motor)-
roller m; (toy) (Tret)roller m

scope [skəʊp] n Umfang m;
(opportunity) Möglichkeit f

score [skɔː*] n (Sport) Spielstand
m; (final result) Spielergebnis nt; (in
quiz etc) Punktestand m; (Mus)
Partitur f; **to keep (the)
~** mitzählen ▷ vt (goal) schießen;
(points) punkten ▷ vi (keep ~)
mitzählen; **scoreboard** n
Anzeigetafel f

scorn [skɔːn] n Verachtung f;
scornful adj verächtlich

Scorpio [ˈskɔːpɪəʊ] (pl **-s**) n (Astr)
Skorpion m

scorpion [ˈskɔːpɪən] n Skorpion
m

Scot [skɒt] n Schotte m, Schottin
f; **Scotch** [skɒtʃ] n (whisky)
schottischer Whisky, Scotch m

Scotch tape® n (US) Tesafilm®
m

Scotland [ˈskɒtlənd] n Schottland nt; **Scotsman** (pl **-men**) n
Schotte m; **Scotswoman** (pl

-women) n Schottin f; **Scottish**
adj schottisch

scout [skaʊt] n (boy ~) Pfadfinder
m

scowl [skaʊl] vi finster blicken

scrambled eggs npl Rührei nt

scrap [skræp] n (bit) Stückchen
nt, Fetzen m; (metal) Schrott m ▷ vt
(car) verschrotten; (plan)
verwerfen; **scrapbook** n
Sammelalbum nt

scrape [skreɪp] n (scratch)
Kratzer m ▷ vt (car) schrammen;
(wall) streifen; **to ~ one's knee**
sich das Knie schürfen; **scrape
through** n (exam) mit knapper
Not bestehen

scrap heap [ˈskræphiːp] n
Schrotthaufen m; **scrap metal** n
Schrott m; **scrap paper** n
Schmierpapier nt

scratch [skrætʃ] n (mark) Kratzer
m; **to start from ~** von vorne
anfangen ▷ vt kratzen; (car)
zerkratzen; **to ~ one's arm** sich
am Arm kratzen ▷ vi kratzen;
(~ oneself) sich kratzen

scream [skriːm] n Schrei m ▷ vi
schreien (with vor +dat); **to ~ at sb**
jdn anschreien

screen [skriːn] n (TV, Inform)
Bildschirm m; (Cine) Leinwand f
▷ vt (protect) abschirmen; (hide)
verdecken; (film) zeigen;
(applicants, luggage) überprüfen;
screenplay n Drehbuch nt;
screensaver n (Inform)
Bildschirmschoner m

screw [skruː] n Schraube f ▷ vt
(vulg: have sex with) ficken; **to ~ sth
to sth** etw an etw akk schrauben;
to ~ off/on (lid)
ab-/aufschrauben; **screw up** vt
(paper) zusammenknüllen; (make a
mess of) vermasseln; **screwdriver**
n Schraubenzieher m; **screw top**
n Schraubverschluss m

scribble ['skrɪbl] vt, vi kritzeln

script [skrɪpt] n (of play) Text m; (of film) Drehbuch nt; (style of writing) Schrift f

scroll down ['skrəʊl'daʊn] vi (Inform) runterscrollen; **scroll up** vi (Inform) raufscrollen; **scroll bar** n (Inform) Scrollbar f

scrub [skrʌb] vt schrubben; **scrubbing brush**, **scrub brush** (US) n Scheuerbürste f

scruffy ['skrʌfɪ] adj vergammelt

scrupulous, **scrupulously** ['skru:pjʊləs, -lɪ] adj, adv gewissenhaft; (painstaking) peinlich genau

scuba-diving ['sku:bədaɪvɪŋ] n Sporttauchen nt

sculptor ['skʌlptə°] n Bildhauer(in) m(f); **sculpture** ['skʌlptʃə°] n (Art) Bildhauerei f; (statue) Skulptur f

sea [si:] n Meer nt, See f; **seafood** n Meeresfrüchte pl; **sea front** n Strandpromenade f; **seagull** n Möwe f

seal [si:l] n (animal) Robbe f; (stamp, impression) Siegel nt; (Tech) Verschluss m; (ring etc) Dichtung f ⊳ vt versiegeln; (envelope) zukleben

seam [si:m] n Naht f

search [sɜ:tʃ] n Suche f (for nach); **to do a ~ for** (Inform) suchen nach; **in ~ of** auf der Suche nach ⊳ vi suchen (for nach) ⊳ vt durchsuchen; **search engine** n (Inform) Suchmaschine f

seashell ['si:ʃel] n Muschel f; **seashore** n Strand m; **seasick** adj seekrank; **seaside** n: **at the ~** am Meer; **to go to the ~** ans Meer fahren; **seaside resort** n Seebad nt

season ['si:zn] n Jahreszeit f; (Comm) Saison f; **high/low**

~ Hoch-/Nebensaison f ⊳ vt (flavour) würzen

seasoning n Gewürz nt

season ticket n (Rail) Zeitkarte f; (Theat) Abonnement nt; (Sport) Dauerkarte f

seat [si:t] n (place) Platz m; (chair) Sitz m; **take a ~** setzen Sie sich ⊳ vt: **the hall ~s 300** der Saal m hat 300 Sitzplätze; **please be ~ed** bitte setzen Sie sich; **to remain ~ed** sitzen bleiben; **seat belt** n Sicherheitsgurt m

sea view ['si:vju:] n Seeblick m; **seaweed** n Seetang m

secluded [sɪ'klu:dɪd] adj abgelegen

second ['sekənd] adj zweite(r, s); **the ~ of June** der zweite Juni ⊳ adv (in ~ position) an zweiter Stelle; (secondly) zweitens; **he came ~** er ist Zweiter geworden ⊳ n (of time) Sekunde f; (moment) Augenblick m; **~ (gear)** der zweite Gang; (~ helping) zweite Portion; **just a ~** (einen) Augenblick!; **secondary** adj (less important) zweitrangig; **~ education** höhere Schulbildung f; **~ school** weiterführende Schule; **second-class** adj (ticket) zweiter Klasse; **~ stamp** Briefmarke für nicht bevorzugt beförderte Sendungen ⊳ adv (travel) zweiter Klasse; **second-hand** adj, adv gebraucht; (information) aus zweiter Hand; **secondly** adv zweitens; **second-rate** adj (pej) zweitklassig

secret ['si:krət] n Geheimnis nt ⊳ adj geheim; (admirer) heimlich

secretary ['sekrətrɪ] n Sekretär(in) m(f); (minister) Minister(in) m(f); **Secretary of State** n (US) Außenminister(in) m(f); **secretary's office** n Sekretariat nt

secretive ['siːkrətɪv] *adj* (person) geheimnistuerisch; **secretly** ['siːkrətlɪ] *adv* heimlich

sect [sekt] *n* Sekte *f*

section ['sekʃən] *n* (part) Teil *m*; (of document) Abschnitt *m*; (department) Abteilung *f*

secure [sɪ'kjʊə*] *adj* (safe) sicher (from vor +dat); (firmly fixed) fest ▷ *vt* (make firm) befestigen; (window, door) fest verschließen; **securely** *adv* (safely) sicher; **security** [sɪ'kjʊərɪtɪ] *n* Sicherheit *f*

sedative ['sedətɪv] *n* Beruhigungsmittel *nt*

seduce [sɪ'djuːs] *vt* verführen; **seductive** [sɪ'dʌktɪv] *adj* verführerisch; (offer) verlockend

see [siː] (saw, seen) *vt* sehen; (understand) verstehen; (check) nachsehen; (accompany) bringen; (visit) besuchen; (talk to) sprechen; **to ~ the doctor** zum Arzt gehen; **to ~ sb home** jdn nach Hause begleiten; **I saw him swimming** ich habe ihn schwimmen sehen; **~ you** tschüs!; **~ you on Friday** bis Freitag! ▷ *vi* sehen; (understand) verstehen; (check) nachsehen; **(you) ~** siehst du!; **we'll ~** mal sehen; **see about** *vt* (attend to) sich kümmern um; **see off** *vt* (say goodbye to) verabschieden; **see out** *vt* (show out) zur Tür bringen; **see through** *vt* **to see sth through** etw zu Ende bringen; **to ~ sb/sth** jdn/etw durchschauen; **see to** *vt* sich kümmern um; **~ it that ...** sieh zu, dass ...

seed [siːd] *n* (of plant) Samen *m*; (in fruit) Kern *m*; **seedless** *adj* kernlos

seedy ['siːdɪ] *adj* zwielichtig

seek [siːk] (sought, sought) *vt* suchen; (fame) streben nach; **to ~ sb's advice** jdn um Rat fragen

seem [siːm] *vi* scheinen; **he ~s (to be) honest** er scheint ehrlich zu sein; **it ~s to me that ... es** scheint mir, dass ...

seen [siːn] *pp of* **see**

seesaw ['siːsɔː] *n* Wippe *f*

see-through *adj* durchsichtig

segment ['segmənt] *n* Teil *m*

seize [siːz] *vt* packen; (confiscate) beschlagnahmen; (opportunity, power) ergreifen

seldom ['seldəm] *adv* selten

select [sɪ'lekt] *adj* (exclusive) exklusiv ▷ *vt* auswählen; **selection** [sɪ'lekʃən] *n* Auswahl *f* (of an +dat); **selective** *adj* (choosy) wählerisch

self [self] (pl selves) *n* Selbst *nt*, Ich *nt*; **he's his old ~ again** er ist wieder ganz der Alte; **self-adhesive** *adj* selbstklebend; **self-assured** *adj* selbstsicher; **self-catering** *adj* für Selbstversorger; **self-centred** *adj* egozentrisch; **self-confidence** *n* Selbstbewusstsein *nt*; **self-confident** *adj* selbstbewusst; **self-conscious** *adj* befangen, verklemmt; **self-contained** *adj* (flat) separat; **self-control** *n* Selbstbeherrschung *f*; **self-defence** *n* Selbstverteidigung *f*; **self-employed** *adj* selbstständig; **self-evident** *adj* offensichtlich

selfish ['selfɪʃ], **selfishly**, **-lɪ] *adj*, *adv* egoistisch; selbstsüchtig; **selfless**, **selflessly** *adj*, *adv* selbstlos

self-pity [self'pɪtɪ] *n* Selbstmitleid *nt*; **self-portrait** *n* Selbstporträt *nt*; **self-respect** *n* Selbstachtung *f*; **self-service** *n* Selbstbedienung *f* ▷ *adj* Selbstbedienungs-

sell [sel] (sold, sold) *vt* verkaufen; **to ~ sb sth**, **to ~ sth to**

sb jdm etw verkaufen; **do you ~ postcards?** haben Sie Postkarten? ▷ vi (product) sich verkaufen; **sell out** vt: **to be sold ~** ausverkauft sein; **sell-by date** n Haltbarkeitsdatum nt

Sellotape® ['seləteɪp] n (Brit) Tesafilm® m

semester [sɪ'mestə°] n Semester nt

semi ['semɪ] n (Brit: house) Doppelhaushälfte f; **semicircle** n Halbkreis m; **semicolon** n Semikolon nt; **semidetached (house)** n (Brit) Doppelhaushälfte f; **semifinal** n Halbfinale nt

seminar ['semɪnɑː°] n Seminar nt

semiskimmed milk ['semɪskɪmd'mɪlk] n Halbfettmilch f

senate ['senət] n Senat m; **senator** n Senator(in) m(f)

send [send] (**sent, sent**) vt schicken; **to ~ sb sth, to ~ sth to sb** jdm etw schicken; **~ her my best wishes** grüße sie von mir; **send away** vt wegschicken ▷ vi: **to ~ for** anfordern; **send back** vt zurückschicken; **send for** vt (person) holen lassen; (by post) anfordern; **send off** vt (by post) abschicken; **send out** vt (invitations etc) verschicken ▷ vi: **to ~ for sth** etw holen lassen

sender ['sendə°] n Absender(in) m(f)

senior ['siːnɪə°] adj (older) älter; (high-ranking) höher; (pupils) älter; **he is ~ to me** er ist mir übergeordnet ▷ n: **he's eight years my ~** er ist acht Jahre älter als ich; **senior citizen** n Senior(in) m(f)

sensation [sen'seɪʃən] n Gefühl nt; (excitement, person, thing)

Sensation f; **sensational** adj sensationell

sense [sens] n (faculty, meaning) Sinn m; (feeling) Gefühl nt; (understanding) Verstand m; **~ of smell/taste** Geruchs-/Geschmackssinn m; **to have a ~ of humour** Humor haben; **to make ~** (sentence etc) einen Sinn ergeben; (be sensible) Sinn machen; **in a ~** gewissermaßen ▷ vt spüren; **senseless** adj (stupid) sinnlos

sensible, sensibly ['sensbl, -blɪ] adj, adv vernünftig

sensitive ['sensɪtɪv] adj empfindlich (to gegen); (easily hurt) sensibel; (subject) heikel

sensual ['sensjʊəl] adj sinnlich

sensuous ['sensjʊəs] adj sinnlich

sent [sent] pt, pp of **send**

sentence ['sentəns] n (Ling) Satz m; (Jur) Strafe f ▷ vt verurteilen (to zu)

sentiment ['sentɪmənt] n (sentimentality) Sentimentalität f; (opinion) Ansicht f; **sentimental** [sentɪ'mentl] adj sentimental

separate ['seprət] adj getrennt, separat; (individual) einzeln ▷ ['sepəreɪt] vt trennen (from von); **they are ~d** (couple) sie leben getrennt ▷ vi sich trennen; **separately** adv getrennt; (singly) einzeln

September [sep'tembə°] n September m; **in ~** im September; **on the 2nd of ~** am 2. September; **at the beginning/in the middle/at the end of ~** Anfang/Mitte/Ende September; **last/next ~** letzten/nächsten September

septic ['septɪk] adj vereitert

sequel ['siːkwəl] n (to film, book) Fortsetzung f (to von)

sequence ['si:kwəns] n (order) Reihenfolge f

Serbia ['sɜ:bjə] n Serbien nt

sergeant ['sɑ:dʒənt] n Polizeimeister(in) m(f); (Mil) Feldwebel(in) m(f)

serial ['sɪərɪəl] n (TV) Serie f; (in newspaper etc) Fortsetzungsroman m ▷ adj (Inform) seriell; **~ number** Seriennummer f

series ['sɪərɪz] nsing Reihe f; (TV, Radio) Serie f

serious ['sɪərɪəs] adj ernst; (injury, illness, mistake) schwer; (discussion) ernsthaft; **are you ~?** ist das dein Ernst?; **seriously** adv ernsthaft; (hurt) schwer; **~?** im Ernst?; **to take sb ~** jdn ernst nehmen

sermon ['sɜ:mən] n (Rel) Predigt f

servant ['sɜ:vənt] n Diener(in) m(f); **serve** [sɜ:v] vt (customer) bedienen; (food) servieren; (one's country etc) dienen +dat; (sentence) verbüßen; **I'm being ~d** ich werde schon bedient; **it ~s him right** es geschieht ihm recht ▷ vi dienen (as als), aufschlagen ▷ n Aufschlag m

server n (Inform) Server m

service ['sɜ:vɪs] n (in shop, hotel) Bedienung f; (activity, amenity) Dienstleistung f; (set of dishes) Service nt; (Auto) Inspektion f; (Tech) Wartung f; (Rel) Gottesdienst m; Aufschlag m; **train/bus ~** Zug-/Busverbindung f; **"~ not included"** „Bedienung nicht inbegriffen" ▷ vt (Auto, Tech) warten; **service area** n (on motorway) Raststätte f (mit Tankstelle); **service charge** n Bedienung f; **service provider** n (Inform) Provider m; **service station** n Tankstelle f

session ['seʃən] n (of court, assembly) Sitzung f

set [set] (**set, set**) vt (place) stellen; (lay flat) legen; (arrange) anordnen; (table) decken; (trap, record) aufstellen; (time, price) festsetzen; (alarm, alarm) stellen (for auf +akk); **to ~ sb a task** jdm eine Aufgabe stellen; **to ~ free** freilassen; **to ~ a good example** ein gutes Beispiel geben; **the novel is ~ in London** der Roman spielt in London ▷ vi (sun) untergehen; (become hard) fest werden; (bone) zusammenwachsen ▷ n (collection of things) Satz m; (of cutlery, furniture) Garnitur f; (group of people) Kreis m; (Radio, TV) Apparat m, Satz m; (Theat) Bühnenbild nt; (Cine) (Film)kulisse f ▷ adj (agreed, prescribed) festgelegt; (ready) bereit; **~ meal** Menü nt; **set aside** vt (money) beiseitelegen; (time) einplanen; **set off** vi aufbrechen (for nach) ▷ vt (alarm) auslösen; (enhance) hervorheben; **set out** vi aufbrechen (for nach) ▷ vt (chairs, chesspieces etc) aufstellen; (state) darlegen; **to ~ to do sth** (intend) beabsichtigen, etw zu tun; **set up** vt (firm, organization) gründen; (stall, tent, camera) aufbauen; (meeting) vereinbaren ▷ vi: **to ~ as a doctor** sich als Arzt niederlassen

setback n Rückschlag m

settee [se'ti:] n Sofa nt, Couch f

setting ['setɪŋ] n (of novel, film) Schauplatz m; (surroundings) Umgebung f

settle ['setl] vt (bill, debt) begleichen; (dispute) beilegen; (question) klären; (stomach) beruhigen ▷ vi: **to ~ (down)** (feel at home) sich einleben; (calm down) sich beruhigen; **settle in** vi (in place) sich einleben; (in job) sich eingewöhnen; **settle up** vi (be)zahlen; **to ~ with sb** mit jdm abrechnen; **settlement** n (of bill, debt) Begleichung f; (colony) Siedlung f; **to reach a ~** sich einigen

setup ['setʌp] n (organization) Organisation f; (situation) Situation f

seven ['sevn] num sieben ▷ n Sieben f; see also **eight**; **seventeen** ['sevn'ti:n] num siebzehn ▷ n Siebzehn f; see also **eight**; **seventeenth** adj siebzehnte(r, s); see also **eighth**; **seventh** ['sevnθ] adj siebte(r, s) ▷ n (fraction) Siebtel nt; see also **eighth**; **seventieth** ['sevntɪɪθ] adj siebzigste(r, s); see also **eighth**; **seventy** ['sevntɪ] num siebzig; **~-one** einundsiebzig ▷ n Siebzig f; **to be in one's seventies** in den Siebzigern sein; see also **eighty**

several ['sevrəl] adj, pron mehrere

severe [sɪ'vɪəʳ] adj (strict) streng; (serious) schwer; (pain) stark; (winter) hart; **severely** adv (harshly) hart; (seriously) schwer

sew [səʊ] (**sewed, sewn**) vt, vi nähen

sewage ['su:ɪdʒ] n Abwasser nt; **sewer** ['suəʳ] n Abwasserkanal m

sewing ['səʊɪŋ] n Nähen nt; **sewing machine** n Nähmaschine f

sewn [səʊn] pp of **sew**

sex [seks] n Sex m; (gender) Geschlecht nt; **to have ~** Sex haben (with mit); **sexism** ['seksɪzəm] n Sexismus m; **sexist** ['seksɪst] adj sexistisch ▷ n Sexist(in) m(f); **sex life** n Sex(ual)leben nt

sexual ['seksjʊəl] adj sexuell; **~ discrimination/harassment** sexuelle Diskriminierung/ Belästigung; **~ intercourse** Geschlechtsverkehr m; **sexuality**

[seksjʊ'ælɪtɪ] n Sexualität f; **sexually** adv sexuell

sexy ['seksɪ] adj sexy, geil

Seychelles ['seɪʃelz] npl Seychellen pl

shabby ['ʃæbɪ] adj schäbig

shack [ʃæk] n Hütte f

shade [ʃeɪd] n (shadow) Schatten m; (for lamp) (Lampen)schirm m; (colour) Farbton m; **~s** (US: sunglasses) Sonnenbrille f ▷ vt (from sun) abschirmen; (in drawing) schattieren

shadow ['ʃædəʊ] n Schatten m

shady ['ʃeɪdɪ] adj schattig; (fig) zwielichtig

shake [ʃeɪk] (**shook, shaken**) vt schütteln; (bottle) schütteln; **to ~ hands with sb** jdm die Hand geben; **to ~ one's head** den Kopf schütteln ▷ vi (tremble) zittern; (building, ground) schwanken; **shake off** vt abschütteln; **shaken** ['ʃeɪkn] pp of **shake**; **shaky** ['ʃeɪkɪ] adj (trembling) zittrig; (table, chair, position) wackelig; (weak) unsicher

shall [ʃæl] (**should**) vb aux werden; (in questions) sollen; **I ~ do my best** ich werde mein Bestes tun; **~ I come too?** soll ich mitkommen?; **where ~ we go?** wo gehen wir hin?

shallow ['ʃæləʊ] adj (a. fig) seicht; (person) oberflächlich

shame [ʃeɪm] n (feeling of ~) Scham f; (disgrace) Schande f; **what a ~!** wie schade!; **~ on you!** schäm dich/schämen Sie sich!; **it's a ~ that ...** schade, dass ...

shampoo [ʃæm'pu:] n Shampoo nt; **to have a ~ and set** sich die Haare waschen und legen lassen ▷ vt (hair) waschen; (carpet) schamponieren

shandy ['ʃændɪ] n Radler m, Alsterwasser nt

shan't [ʃɑːnt] contr of **shall not**

shape [ʃeɪp] n Form f;
(unidentified figure) Gestalt f; **in
the ~ of** in Form +gen; **to be in
good ~** (healthwise) in guter
Verfassung sein; **to take ~** (plan,
idea) Gestalt annehmen ▷ vt (clay,
person) formen; **-shaped** [ʃeɪpt]
suf -förmig; **shapeless** adj
formlos

share [ʃeə°] n Anteil +dat (in, of an
m); (Fin) Aktie f ▷ vt, vi teilen;
shareholder n Aktionär(in) m(f)

shark [ʃɑːk] n (Zool) Haifisch m

sharp [ʃɑːp] adj scharf; (pin) spitz;
(person) scharfsinnig; (pain) heftig;
(increase, fall) abrupt; **C/F ~** (Mus)
Cis/Dis nt ▷ adv: **at 2 o'clock
~** Punkt 2 Uhr; **sharpen** vt (knife)
schärfen; (pencil) spitzen;
sharpener n (pencil ~) Spitzer m

shatter [ˈʃætə°] vt zerschmet-
tern; (fig) zerstören ▷ vi
zerspringen; **shattered** adj
(exhausted) kaputt

shave [ʃeɪv] (shaved, shaved o
shaven) vt rasieren ▷ vi sich
rasieren ▷ n Rasur f; **that was a
close ~** (fig) das war knapp; **shave
off** vt: **to shave one's beard off**
sich den Bart abrasieren; **shaven**
[ˈʃeɪvn] pp of shave ▷ adj (head)
kahl geschoren; **shaver** n (Elec)
Rasierapparat m; **shaving brush**
n Rasierpinsel m; **shaving foam** n
Rasierschaum m; **shaving tackle**
n Rasierzeug nt

shawl [ʃɔːl] n Tuch nt

she [ʃiː] pron sie

shed [ʃed] (shed, shed) n
Schuppen m ▷ vt (tears, blood)
vergießen; (hair, leaves) verlieren

she'd [ʃiːd] contr of she had; she
would

sheep [ʃiːp] (pl -) n Schaf nt;
sheepdog n Schäferhund m;
sheepskin n Schaffell nt

sheer [ʃɪə°] adj (madness) rein;

(steep) steil; **by ~ chance** rein
zufällig

sheet [ʃiːt] n (on bed) Betttuch nt;
(of paper) Blatt nt; (of metal) Platte f;
(of glass) Scheibe f; **a ~ of paper**
ein Blatt Papier

shelf [ʃelf] (pl shelves) n
Bücherbord nt, Regal nt; **shelves** pl
(item of furniture) Regal nt

she'll [ʃiːl] contr of she will; she
shall

shell [ʃel] n (of egg, nut) Schale f;
(sea-) Muschel f ▷ vt (peas, nuts)
schälen; **shellfish** n (as food)
Meeresfrüchte pl

shelter [ˈʃeltə°] n (protection)
Schutz m; (accommodation)
Unterkunft f; (bus ~)
Wartehäuschen nt ▷ vt schützen
(from vor +dat) ▷ vi sich
unterstellen; **sheltered** adj (spot)
geschützt; (life) behütet

shelve [ʃelv] vt (fig) aufschieben;
shelves pl of shelf

shepherd [ˈʃepəd] n Schäfer m;
shepherd's pie n
Hackfleischauflauf mit Decke aus
Kartoffelpüree

sherry [ˈʃerɪ] n Sherry m

she's [ʃiːz] contr of she is; she has

shield [ʃiːld] n Schild m; (fig)
Schutz m ▷ vt schützen (from vor
+dat)

shift [ʃɪft] n (change)
Veränderung f; (period at work,
workers) Schicht f; (on keyboard)
Umschalttaste f ▷ vt (furniture etc)
verrücken; (stain) entfernen; **to
~ gear(s)** (US Auto) schalten ▷ vi
(move) sich bewegen; (move up)
rutschen; **shift key** n
Umschalttaste f

shin [ʃɪn] n Schienbein nt

shine [ʃaɪn] (shone, shone) vi
(be shiny) glänzen; (sun) scheinen;
(lamp) leuchten ▷ vt (polish)
polieren ▷ n Glanz m

shingles ['ʃɪŋglz] nsing (Med) Gürtelrose f

shiny ['ʃaɪnɪ] adj glänzend

ship [ʃɪp] n Schiff nt ▷ vt (send) versenden; (by ship) verschiffen; **shipment** n (goods) Sendung f; (sent by ship) Ladung f; **shipwreck** n Schiffbruch m; **shipyard** n Werft f

shirt [ʃɜːt] n Hemd nt

shit [ʃɪt] n (vulg) Scheiße f; (person) Arschloch nt; **~!** Scheiße!; **shitty** ['ʃɪtɪ] adj (fam) beschissen

shiver ['ʃɪvə°] vi zittern (with vor +dat)

shock [ʃɒk] n (mental, emotional) Schock m; **to be in ~** unter Schock stehen; **to get a ~** (Elec) einen Schlag bekommen ▷ vt schockieren; **shock absorber** n Stoßdämpfer m; **shocked** adj schockiert (by über +akk); **shocking** adj schockierend; (awful) furchtbar

shoe [ʃuː] n (mental, emotional) Schuh m; **shoelace** n Schnürsenkel m; **shoe polish** n Schuhcreme f

shone [ʃɒn] pt, pp of **shine**

shonky ['ʃɒŋkɪ] adj (Aust, NZ fam) schäbig; (work) stümperhaft

shook [ʃʊk] pt of **shake**

shoot [ʃuːt] (shot, shot) vt (wound) anschießen; (kill) erschießen; (Cine) drehen; (fam: heroin) drücken ▷ vi (with gun, move quickly) schießen; **to ~ at sb** auf jdn schießen ▷ n (of plant) Trieb m; **shooting** n (exchange of gunfire) Schießerei f; (killing) Erschießung f

shop [ʃɒp] n Geschäft nt, Laden m ▷ vi einkaufen; **shop assistant** n Verkäufer(in) m(f); **shopkeeper** n Geschäftsinhaber(in) m(f); **shoplifting** n Ladendiebstahl m; **shopper** n Käufer(in) m(f); **shopping** n (activity) Einkaufen nt; (goods) Einkäufe pl; **to do the ~** einkaufen; **to go ~** einkaufen gehen; **shopping bag** n Einkaufstasche f; **shopping cart** n (US) Einkaufswagen m; **shopping center** (US), **shopping centre** n Einkaufszentrum nt; **shopping list** n Einkaufszettel m; **shopping trolley** n (Brit) Einkaufswagen m; **shop window** n Schaufenster nt

shore [ʃɔː°] n Ufer nt; **on ~** an Land

short [ʃɔːt] adj kurz; (person) klein; **to be ~ of money** knapp bei Kasse sein; **to be ~ of time** wenig Zeit haben; **~ of breath** kurzatmig; **to cut ~** (holiday) abbrechen; **we are two ~** wir haben zwei zu wenig; **it's ~ for ...** das ist die Kurzform von ... ▷ n (drink, Elec) Kurze(r) m; **shortage** n Knappheit f (of an +dat); **shortbread** n Buttergebäck nt; **short circuit** n Kurzschluss m; **shortcut** n (quicker route) Abkürzung f; (Inform) Shortcut m; **shorten** vt kürzen; (in time) verkürzen; **shorthand** n Stenografie f; **shortlist** n: **to be on the ~** in der engeren Wahl sein; **short-lived** adj kurzlebig; **shortly** adv bald; **shorts** npl Shorts pl; **short-sighted** adj (a. fig) kurzsichtig; **short-sleeved** adj kurzärmelig; **short-stay car park** n Kurzzeitparkplatz m; **short story** n Kurzgeschichte f; **short-term** adj kurzfristig; **short wave** n Kurzwelle f

shot [ʃɒt] pt, pp of **shoot** ▷ n (from gun, in football) Schuss m; (Foto, Cine) Aufnahme f; (injection) Spritze f; (of alcohol) Schluss m

should [ʃʊd] pt of **shall** ▷ vb aux: **I ~ go now** ich sollte jetzt gehen; **what ~ I do?** was soll ich tun?; **you ~n't have said that** das hättest du/hätten Sie nicht sagen sollen; **that ~ be enough** das müsste reichen

shoulder [ˈʃəʊldəˢ] n Schulter f

shouldn't [ˈʃʊdnt] contr of **should not**

should've [ˈʃʊdəv] contr of **should have**

shout [ʃaʊt] n Schrei m; (call) Ruf m ▷ vt rufen; (order) brüllen ▷ vi schreien; **to ~ at** anschreien; **to ~ for help** um Hilfe rufen

shove [ʃʌv] vt (person) schubsen; (car, table etc) schieben ▷ vi (in crowd) drängeln

shovel [ˈʃʌvl] n Schaufel f ▷ vt schaufeln

show [ʃəʊ] (**showed, shown**) vt zeigen; **to ~ sb sth, to ~ sth to sb** jdm etw zeigen; **to ~ sb in** jdn hereinführen; **to ~ sb out** jdn zur Tür bringen ▷ vi (Cine, Theat) Vorstellung f; (TV) Show f; (exhibition) Ausstellung f; **show off** vi (pej) angeben; **show round** vt herumführen; **to show sb round the house/the town** jdm das Haus/die Stadt zeigen; **show up** vi (arrive) auftauchen

shower [ˈʃaʊəˢ] n Dusche f; (rain) Schauer m; **to have** (o **take**) **a ~** duschen ▷ vi (wash) duschen; **shower gel** n Duschgel nt

showing [ˈʃəʊɪŋ] n (Cine) Vorstellung f

shown [ʃəʊn] pp of **show**

showroom [ˈʃəʊruːm] n Ausstellungsraum m

shrank [ʃræŋk] pt of **shrink**

shred [ʃred] n (of paper, fabric) Fetzen m ▷ vt (in shredder) (im Reißwolf) zerkleinern; **shredder** n (for paper) Reißwolf m

shrimp [ʃrɪmp] n Garnele f

shrink [ʃrɪŋk] (**shrank, shrunk**) vi schrumpfen; (clothes) eingehen ▷ vt schrumpfen lassen

shrivel [ˈʃrɪvl] vi: **to ~ (up)**

schrumpfen; (skin) runzlig werden; (plant) welken

Shrove Tuesday [ˈʃrəʊvtjuːzdeɪ] n Fastnachtsdienstag m

shrub [ʃrʌb] n Busch m, Strauch m

shrug [ʃrʌg] vt, vi: **to ~ (one's shoulders)** die Achseln zucken

shrunk [ʃrʌŋk] pp of **shrink**

shudder [ˈʃʌdəˢ] vi schaudern; (ground, building) beben

shuffle [ˈʃʌfl] vt, vi mischen

shut [ʃʌt] (**shut, shut**) vt zumachen, schließen; **~ your face!** (fam) halt den Mund! ▷ vi schließen ▷ adj geschlossen; **we're ~** wir haben geschlossen; **shut down** vt schließen; (computer) ausschalten ▷ vi schließen; (computer) sich ausschalten; **shut in** vt einschließen; **shut out** vt (lock out) aussperren; **to shut oneself out** sich aussperren; **shut up** vt (lock up) abschließen; (silence) zum Schweigen bringen ▷ vi (keep quiet) den Mund halten; **~!** halt den Mund!; **shutter** n (on window) (Fenster)laden m; **shutter release** n Auslöser m; **shutter speed** n Belichtungszeit f

shuttle bus [ˈʃʌtlbʌs] n Shuttlebus m

shuttlecock [ˈʃʌtlkɒk] n Federball m

shuttle service [ˈʃʌtlsɜːvɪs] n Pendelverkehr m

shy [ʃaɪ] adj schüchtern; (animal) scheu

Siberia [saɪˈbɪərɪə] n Sibirien nt

Sicily [ˈsɪsɪlɪ] n Sizilien nt

sick [sɪk] adj krank; (joke) makaber; **to be ~** (Brit: vomit) sich übergeben; **to be off ~** wegen Krankheit fehlen; **I feel ~** mir ist schlecht; **to be ~ of sb/sth** jdn/etw satthaben; **it makes me**

~ (fig) es ekelt mich an; **sickbag** n
Spucktüte f; **sick leave** n: **to be
on ~** krankgeschrieben sein;
sickness n Krankheit f; (Brit:
nausea) Übelkeit f; **sickness
benefit** n (Brit) Krankengeld nt
side [saɪd] n Seite f; (of road) Rand
m; (of mountain) Hang m; (Sport)
Mannschaft f; **by my ~** neben mir;
~ by ~ nebeneinander ▷ adj (door)
Seiten-; **sideboard** n Anrichte f;
sideburns npl Koteletten pl; **side
dish** n Beilage f; **side effect** n
Nebenwirkung f; **sidelight** n (Brit
Auto) Parklicht nt; **side order** n
Beilage f; **side road** n Nebenstraße f; **side street** n Seitenstraße
f; **sidewalk** n (US) Bürgersteig m;
sideways adv seitwärts
sieve [sɪv] n Sieb nt
sift [sɪft] vt (flour etc) sieben
sigh [saɪ] vi seufzen
sight [saɪt] n (power of seeing)
Sehvermögen nt; (view, thing seen)
Anblick m; **~s** pl (of city) Sehenswürdigkeiten pl; **to have
bad ~** schlecht sehen; **to lose ~ of**
aus den Augen verlieren; **out of
~** außer Sicht; **sightseeing** n: **to
go ~** Sehenswürdigkeiten
besichtigen; **~ tour** Rundfahrt f
sign [saɪn] n Zeichen nt; (notice,
road ~) Schild nt ▷ vt
unterschreiben ▷ vi unterschreiben; **to ~ for sth** den
Empfang einer Sache gen
bestätigen; **to ~ in/out** sich
ein-/austragen; **sign on** vi (Brit:
register as unemployed) sich
arbeitslos melden; **sign up** vi (for
course) sich einschreiben; (Mil) sich
verpflichten
signal ['sɪɡnl] n Signal nt ▷ vi
(car driver) blinken
signature ['sɪɡnətʃə] n Unter-
schrift f
significant [sɪɡ'nɪfɪkənt] adj

(important) bedeutend, wichtig;
(meaning sth) bedeutsam;
significantly adv (considerably)
bedeutend
sign language ['saɪnlæŋɡwɪdʒ]
n Zeichensprache f; **signpost** n
Wegweiser m
silence ['saɪləns] n Stille f; (of
person) Schweigen nt; **~!** Ruhe! ▷ vt
zum Schweigen bringen; **silent**
adj still; (taciturn) schweigsam;
she remained ~ sie schwieg
silk [sɪlk] n Seide f ▷ adj Seiden-
silly ['sɪlɪ] adj dumm, albern;
don't do anything ~ mach keine
Dummheiten; **the ~ season** das
Sommerloch
silver ['sɪlvə] n Silber nt; (coins)
Silbermünzen pl ▷ adj
Silber-, silbern; **silver-plated** adj
versilbert; **silver wedding** n
silberne Hochzeit
SIM card ['sɪm-] n (Tel) SIM-Karte f
similar ['sɪmɪlə] adj ähnlich (to
dat); **similarity** [sɪmɪ'lærɪti] n
Ähnlichkeit f (to mit); **similarly**
adv (equally) ebenso
simple ['sɪmpl] adj einfach;
(unsophisticated) einfach; **simplify**
['sɪmplɪfaɪ] vt vereinfachen;
simply adv einfach; (merely) bloß;
(dress) schlicht
simulate ['sɪmjʊleɪt] vt
simulieren
simultaneous, simultaneously
[sɪməl'teɪnɪəs, -lɪ] adj, adv
gleichzeitig
sin [sɪn] n Sünde f ▷ vi sündigen
since [sɪns] adv seitdem; (in the
meantime) inzwischen ▷ prep seit
+dat; **ever ~ 1995** schon seit 1995
▷ conj (time) seit, seitdem;
(because) da, weil; **ever ~ I've
known her** seit ich sie kenne; **it's
ages ~ I've seen him** ich habe
ihn seit Langem nicht mehr
gesehen

sincere [sɪn'sɪə°] adj aufrichtig;
sincerely adv aufrichtig;
Yours ~ mit freundlichen
Grüßen

sing [sɪŋ] (**sang, sung**) vt, vi
singen

Singapore [sɪŋgə'pɔː°] n Singapur nt

singer ['sɪŋə°] n Sänger(in) m(f)

single ['sɪŋgl] adj (one only)
einzig; (not double) einfach; (bed,
room) Einzel-; (unmarried) ledig;
(Brit: ticket) einfach ▷ n (Brit:
ticket) einfache Fahrkarte; (Mus)
Single f; **a ~ to London, please**
(Brit Rail) einfach nach London,
bitte; **single out** vt (choose)
auswählen; **single-handed,
single-handedly** adv im
Alleingang; **single parent** n
Alleinerziehende(r) mf; **single
supplement** n (for hotel room)
Einzelzimmerzuschlag m

singular ['sɪŋgjʊlə°] n Singular m

sinister ['sɪnɪstə°] adj
unheimlich

sink [sɪŋk] (**sank, sunk**) vt (ship)
versenken ▷ vi sinken ▷ n
Spülbecken nt; (in bathroom)
Waschbecken nt

sip [sɪp] vt nippen an +dat

sir [sɜː°] n: **yes, ~** ja(, mein Herr);
can I help you, ~? kann ich Ihnen
helfen?; **Sir James** (title) Sir James

sister ['sɪstə°] n Schwester f;
(Brit: nurse) Oberschwester f;
sister-in-law (pl **sisters-in-law**) n
Schwägerin f

sit [sɪt] (**sat, sat**) vi (be sitting)
sitzen; (~ down) sich setzen;
(committee, court) tagen ▷ vt (Brit:
exam) machen; **sit down** vi sich
hinsetzen; **sit up** vi (from lying
position) sich aufsetzen

sitcom ['sɪtkɒm] n Situ-
ationskomödie f

site [saɪt] n Platz m; (building ~)
Baustelle f; (web~) Site f

sitting ['sɪtɪŋ] n (meeting, for
portrait) Sitzung f; **sitting room** n
Wohnzimmer nt

situated ['sɪtjʊeɪtɪd] adj: **to be
~** liegen

situation [sɪtjʊ'eɪʃən] n (circum-
stances) Situation f, Lage f; (job)
Stelle f; **"~s vacant/wanted"** (Brit)
"Stellenangebote/Stellengesuche"

six [sɪks] num sechs ▷ n Sechs f;
see also **eight**; **sixpack** n (of beer
etc) Sechserpack nt; **sixteen**
['sɪks'tiːn] num sechzehn ▷ n
Sechzehn f; see also **eight**;
sixteenth adj sechzehnte(r, s); see
also **eighth**; **sixth** [sɪksθ] adj
sechste(r, s); **~ form** (Brit) ~
Oberstufe f ▷ n (fraction) Sechstel
nt; see also **eighth**; **sixtieth**
['sɪkstɪɪθ] adj sechzigste(r, s); see
also **eighth**; **sixty** ['sɪkstɪ] num
sechzig; **~-one** einundsechzig ▷ n
Sechzig f; **to be in one's sixties** in
den Sechzigern sein; see also **eight**

size [saɪz] n Größe f; **what ~ are
you?** welche Größe hast du/haben
Sie?; **a ~ too big** eine Nummer zu
groß

sizzle ['sɪzl] vi (Gastr) brutzeln

skate [skeɪt] n Schlittschuh m;
(roller~) Rollschuh m ▷ vi
Schlittschuh laufen; (roller~)
Rollschuh laufen; **skateboard** n
Skateboard nt; **skating** n Eislauf
m; (roller-~) Rollschuhlauf m;
skating rink n Eisbahn f; (for
roller-skating) Rollschuhbahn f

skeleton ['skelɪtn] n (a. fig)
Skelett nt

skeptical n (US) see **sceptical**

sketch [sketʃ] n Skizze f; (Theat)
Sketch m ▷ vt skizzieren;
sketchbook n Skizzenbuch nt

ski [skiː] n Ski m ▷ vi Ski laufen;
ski boot n Skistiefel m

skid [skɪd] vi (Auto) schleudern

skier ['skiːə°] n Skiläufer(in) m(f);
skiing n Skilaufen nt; **to go ~** Ski
laufen gehen; **~ holiday** Skiurlaub
m; **skiing instructor** n
Skilehrer(in) m(f)

skilful, skilfully ['skɪlful, -fəlɪ]
adj, adv geschickt

ski-lift ['skiːlɪft] n Skilift m

skill [skɪl] n Geschick nt; (acquired
technique) Fertigkeit f; **skilled** adj
geschickt (at, in in +dat); (worker)
Fach-; (work) fachmännisch

skim [skɪm] vt: **to ~ (off)** (fat etc)
abschöpfen; **to ~ (through)** (read)
überfliegen; **skimmed milk** n
Magermilch f

skin [skɪn] n Haut f; (fur) Fell nt;
(peel) Schale f; **skin diving** n
Sporttauchen nt; **skinny** adj dünn

skip [skɪp] vi hüpfen; (with rope)
seilspringen ▷ vt (miss out)
überspringen; (meal) ausfallen
lassen; (school, lesson) schwänzen

ski pants ['skiːpænts] npl
Skihose f; **ski pass** n Skipass m;
ski pole n Skistock m; **ski resort**
n Skiort m

skirt [skɜːt] n Rock m

ski run ['skiːrʌn] n (Ski)abfahrt
f; **ski stick** n Skistock m; **ski tow**
n Schlepplift m

skittle ['skɪtl] n Kegel m; **~s**
(game) Kegeln nt

skive [skaɪv] vi: **to ~ (off)** (Brit)
(from school) schwänzen; (from
work) blaumachen

skull [skʌl] n Schädel m

sky [skaɪ] n Himmel m;
skydiving n Fallschirmspringen
nt; **skylight** n Dachfenster nt;
skyscraper n Wolkenkratzer m

slam [slæm] vt (door) zuschlagen;
slam on vt: **to slam the brakes
on** voll auf die Bremse treten

slander ['slɑːndə°] n Verleumdung f ▷ vt verleumden

slang [slæŋ] n Slang m

slap [slæp] n Klaps m; (across face)
Ohrfeige f ▷ vt schlagen; **to ~ sb's
face** jdn ohrfeigen

slash [slæʃ] n (punctuation mark)
Schrägstrich m ▷ vt (face, tyre)
aufschlitzen; (prices) stark
herabsetzen

slate [sleɪt] n (rock) Schiefer m;
(roof ~) Schieferplatte f

slaughter ['slɔːtə°] vt (animals)
schlachten; (people) abschlachten

Slav [slɑːv] adj slawisch ▷ n
Slawe m, Slawin f

slave [sleɪv] n Sklave m, Sklavin f;
slave away vi schuften;
slave-driver n (fam)
Sklaventreiber(in) m(f); **slavery**
['sleɪvərɪ] n Sklaverei f

sleaze [sliːz] n (corruption)
Korruption f; **sleazy** adj (bar,
district) zwielichtig

sledge ['sledʒ] n Schlitten m

sleep [sliːp] (slept, slept) vi
schlafen; **to ~ with sb** mit jdm
schlafen ▷ n Schlaf m; **to put to
~** (animal) einschläfern; **sleep in** vi
(lie in) ausschlafen; **sleeper** n
(Rail: train) Schlafwagenzug m;
(carriage) Schlafwagen m; **sleeping
bag** n Schlafsack m; **sleeping car**
n Schlafwagen m; **sleeping pill** n
Schlaftablette f; **sleepless** adj
schlaflos; **sleepover** n Übernachtung f (bei Freunden etc); **sleepy**
adj schläfrig; (place) verschlafen

sleet [sliːt] n Schneeregen m

sleeve [sliːv] n Ärmel m;
sleeveless adj ärmellos

sleigh [sleɪ] n (Pferde)schlitten m

slender ['slendə°] adj schlank;
(fig) gering

slept [slept] pt, pp of **sleep**

slice [slaɪs] n Scheibe f; (of cake,
tart, pizza) Stück nt ▷ vt: **to ~ (up)**
in Scheiben schneiden; **sliced
bread** n geschnittenes Brot

slid [slɪd] pt, pp of **slide**

slide [slaɪd] (**slid, slid**) vt gleiten lassen; (push) schieben ▷ vi gleiten; (slip) rutschen ▷ n (Foto) Dia nt; (in playground) Rutschbahn f; (Brit: for hair) Spange f

slight [slaɪt] adj leicht; (problem, difference) klein; **not in the ~est** nicht im Geringsten; **slightly** adv etwas; (injured) leicht

slim [slɪm] adj (person) schlank; (book) dünn; (chance, hope) gering ▷ vi abnehmen

slime [slaɪm] n Schleim m; **slimy** adj schleimig

sling [slɪŋ] (**slung, slung**) vt werfen ▷ n (for arm) Schlinge f

slip [slɪp] n (mistake) Flüchtigkeitsfehler m; **~ of paper** Zettel m ▷ vt (put) stecken; **to ~ on/off** (garment) an-/ausziehen; **it ~ped my mind** ich habe es vergessen ▷ vi (lose balance) (aus)rutschen; **slip away** vi (leave) sich wegstehlen; **slipper** n Hausschuh m; **slippery** adj (path, road) glatt; (soap, fish) glitschig; **slip-road** n (Brit: onto motorway) Auffahrt f; (off motorway) Ausfahrt f

slit [slɪt] (**slit, slit**) vt aufschlitzen ▷ n Schlitz m

slope [sləʊp] n Neigung f; (side of hill) Hang m ▷ vi (be sloping) schräg sein; **sloping** adj (floor, roof) schräg

sloppy [ˈslɒpɪ] adj (careless) schlampig; (sentimental) rührselig

slot [slɒt] n (opening) Schlitz m; (Inform) Steckplatz m; **we have a ~ free at 2** (free time) um 2 ist noch ein Termin frei; **slot machine** n Automat m; (for gambling) Spielautomat m

Slovak [ˈsləʊvæk] adj slowakisch ▷ n (person) Slowake m, Slowakin f; (language) Slowakisch nt; **Slovakia** [sləʊˈvækɪə] n Slowakei f

Slovene [ˈsləʊviːn], **Slovenian** [sləʊˈviːnɪən] adj slowenisch ▷ n (person) Slowene m, Slowenin f; (language) Slowenisch nt; **Slovenia** [sləʊˈviːnɪə] n Slowenien nt

slow [sləʊ] adj langsam; (business) flau; **to be ~** (clock) nachgehen; (stupid) begriffsstutzig sein; **slow down** vi langsamer werden; (when driving/walking) langsamer fahren/gehen; **slowly** adv langsam; **slow motion** n: **in ~** in Zeitlupe

slug [slʌg] n (Zool) Nacktschnecke f

slum [slʌm] n Slum m

slump [slʌmp] n Rückgang m (in an +dat) ▷ vi (onto chair etc) sich fallen lassen; (prices) stürzen

slung [slʌŋ] pt, pp of **sling**

slur [slɜːʳ] n (insult) Verleumdung f; **slurred** [slɜːd] adj undeutlich

slush [slʌʃ] n (snow) Schneematsch m

slut [slʌt] n (pej) Schlampe f

smack [smæk] n Klaps m ▷ vt: **to ~ sb** jdm einen Klaps geben ▷ vi: **to ~ of** riechen nach

small [smɔːl] adj klein; **small ads** npl (Brit) Kleinanzeigen pl; **small change** n Kleingeld nt; **small letters** npl: **in ~** in Kleinbuchstaben; **smallpox** n Pocken pl; **small print** n: **the ~** das Kleingedruckte; **small-scale** adj (map) in kleinem Maßstab; **small talk** n Konversation f, Smalltalk m

smart [smɑːt] adj (elegant) schick; (clever) clever; **smartarse**, **smartass** (US) n (fam) Klugscheißer (in) m(f); **smart card** n Chipkarte f; **smartly** adv (dressed) schick; **smartphone** n (Tel) Smartphone f

smash [smæʃ] n (car crash) Zusammenstoß m, Schmetterball *m* ▷ *vt* (*break*) zerschlagen; (*fig: record*) brechen, deutlich übertreffen ▷ *vi* (*break*) zerbrechen; **to ~ into** (*car*) krachen gegen

smear [smɪə°] *n* (*mark*) Fleck *m*; (*Med*) Abstrich *m*; (*fig*) Verleumdung *f* ▷ *vt* (*spread*) schmieren; (*make dirty*) beschmieren; (*fig*) verleumden

smell [smɛl] (**smelt** *o* **smelled, smelt** *o* **smelled**) *vt* riechen ▷ *vi* riechen (*of* nach); (*unpleasantly*) stinken ▷ *n* Geruch *m*; (*unpleasant*) Gestank *m*; **smelly** *adj* übel riechend; **smelt** [smɛlt] *pt, pp of* **smell**

smile [smaɪl] *n* Lächeln *nt* ▷ *vi* lächeln; **to ~ at sb** jdn anlächeln

smock [smɒk] *n* Kittel *m*

smog [smɒɡ] *n* Smog *m*

smoke [sməʊk] *n* Rauch *m* ▷ *vt* rauchen; (*food*) räuchern ▷ *vi* rauchen; **smoke alarm** *n* Rauchmelder *m*; **smoked** *adj* (*food*) geräuchert; **smoke-free** *adj* (*zone, building*) rauchfrei; **smoker** *n* Raucher(in) *m(f)*; **smoking** *n* Rauchen *nt*; **"no ~"** „Rauchen verboten"

smooth [smuːð] *adj* glatt; (*flight, crossing*) ruhig; (*movement*) geschmeidig; (*without problems*) reibungslos; (*pej: person*) aalglatt ▷ *vt* (*hair, dress*) glatt streichen; (*surface*) glätten; **smoothly** *adv* reibungslos; **to run ~** (*engine*) ruhig laufen

smudge [smʌdʒ] *vt* (*writing, lipstick*) verschmieren

smug [smʌɡ] *adj* selbstgefällig

smuggle [ˈsmʌɡl] *vt* schmuggeln; **to ~ in/out** herein-/herausschmuggeln

smutty [ˈsmʌtɪ] *adj* (*obscene*) schmutzig

snack [snæk] *n* Imbiss *m*; **to have**

a ~ eine Kleinigkeit essen; **snack bar** *n* Imbissstube *f*

snail [sneɪl] *n* Schnecke *f*; **snail mail** *n* (*fam*) Schneckenpost *f*

snake [sneɪk] *n* Schlange *f*

snap [snæp] *n* (*photo*) Schnappschuss *m* ▷ *adj* (*decision*) spontan ▷ *vt* (*break*) zerbrechen; (*rope*) zerreißen ▷ *vi* (*break*) brechen; (*rope*) reißen; (*bite*) schnappen (*at* nach); **snap off** *vt* (*break*) abbrechen; **snap fastener** *n* (*US*) Druckknopf *m*; **snapshot** *n* Schnappschuss *m*

snatch [snætʃ] *vt* (*grab*) schnappen

sneak [sniːk] *vi* (*move*) schleichen; **sneakers** *npl* (*US*) Turnschuhe *pl*

sneeze [sniːz] *vi* niesen

sniff [snɪf] *vi* schniefen; (*smell*) schnüffeln (*at* an +*dat*) ▷ *vt* schnuppern an +*dat*; (*glue*) schnüffeln

snob [snɒb] *n* Snob *m*; **snobbish** *adj* versnobt

snog [snɒɡ] *vi, vt* knutschen

snooker [ˈsnuːkə°] *n* Snooker *nt*

snoop [snuːp] *vi*: **to ~ (around)** (herum)schnüffeln

snooze [snuːz] *n, vi*: **to (have a) ~** ein Nickerchen machen

snore [snɔː°] *vi* schnarchen

snorkel [ˈsnɔːkl] *n* Schnorchel *m*; **snorkelling** *n* Schnorcheln *nt*; **to go ~** schnorcheln gehen

snout [snaʊt] *n* Schnauze *f*

snow [snəʊ] *n* Schnee *m* ▷ *vi* schneien; **snowball** *n* Schneeball *m*; **snowboard** *n* Snowboard *nt*; **snowboarding** *n* Snowboarding *nt*; **snowdrift** *n* Schneewehe *f*; **snowdrop** *n* Schneeglöckchen *nt*; **snowflake** *n* Schneeflocke *f*; **snowman** (*pl* -**men**) *n* Schneemann *m*; **snowplough**,

snowplow (US) n Schneepflug m;
snowstorm n Schneesturm m;
snowy adj (region) schneereich;
(landscape) verschneit
snug [snʌg] adj (person, place)
gemütlich
snuggle up ['snʌgl'ʌp] vi:
~ **to sb** sich an jdn ankuscheln

○ **KEYWORD**

so [səʊ] adv 1 (thus) so; (likewise)
auch; **so saying he walked away**
indem er das sagte, ging er; **if so**
wenn ja; **I didn't do it — you did
so!** ich hab das nicht gemacht —
hast du wohl!; **so do I, so am I** etc
ich auch; **so it is!** tatsächlich!; **I
hope/think so** hoffentlich/ich
glaube schon; **so far** bis jetzt
2 (in comparisons etc: to such a
degree) so; **so quickly/big (that)**
so schnell/groß, dass; **I'm so glad
to see you** ich freue mich so,
dich/Sie zu sehen
3 **so many** so viele; **so much work**
so viel Arbeit; **I love you so much**
ich liebe dich so sehr
4 (phrases) **10 or so** etwa 10; **so
long!** (inf) (goodbye) tschüss!
▷ conj 1 (expressing purpose) **so as to**
um ... zu; **so (that)** damit
2 (expressing result) also; **so I was
right after all** ich hatte also doch
recht; **so you see ...** wie du
siehst/Sie sehen ...

soak [səʊk] vt durchnässen;
(leave in liquid) einweichen; **I ~ed**
ich bin klatschnass; **soaking** adj:
~ **(wet)** klatschnass
soap [səʊp] n Seife f; **soap
(opera)** n Seifenoper f; **soap
powder** n Waschpulver nt
sob [sɒb] vi schluchzen
sober ['səʊbə°] adj nüchtern;
sober up vi nüchtern werden

so-called ['səʊ'kɔːld] adj
sogenannt
soccer ['sɒkə°] n Fußball m
sociable ['səʊʃəbl] adj gesellig
social ['səʊʃəl] adj sozial;
(sociable) gesellig; **socialist** adj
sozialistisch ▷ n Sozialist(in)
m(f); **socialize** vi unter die Leute
gehen; **social networking** n
Netzwerken nt; **social security** n
(Brit) Sozialhilfe f; (US)
Sozialversicherung f
society [sə'saɪətɪ] n Gesellschaft
f; (club) Verein m
sock [sɒk] n Socke f
socket ['sɒkɪt] n (Elec) Steckdose
f
soda ['səʊdə] n (~ water) Soda f;
(US: pop) Limo f; **soda water** n
Sodawasser nt
sofa ['səʊfə] n Sofa nt; **sofa bed**
n Schlafcouch f
soft [sɒft] adj weich; (quiet) leise;
(lighting) gedämpft; (kind)
gutmütig; (weak) nachgiebig;
~ **drink** alkoholfreies Getränk;
softly adv sanft; (quietly) leise;
software n (Inform) Software f
soil [sɔɪl] n Erde f; (ground) Boden
m
solar ['səʊlə°] adj Sonnen-, Solar-
solarium [sə'lɛərɪəm] n
Solarium nt
sold [səʊld] pt, pp of **sell**
soldier ['səʊldʒə°] n Soldat(in)
m(f)
sole [səʊl] n Sohle f; (fish)
Seezunge f ▷ vt besohlen ▷ adj
einzig; (owner, responsibility)
alleinig; **solely** adv nur
solemn ['sɒləm] adj feierlich;
(person) ernst
solicitor [sə'lɪsɪtə°] n (Brit)
Rechtsanwalt m, Rechtsanwältin f
solid ['sɒlɪd] adj (hard) fest; (gold,
oak etc) massiv; (~ly built) solide;
(meal) kräftig

solitary ['sɒlɪtərɪ] adj einsam; (single) einzeln; **solitude** ['sɒlɪtjuːd] n Einsamkeit f

solo ['səʊləʊ] n (Mus) Solo nt

soluble ['sɒljʊbl] adj löslich; **solution** [sə'luːʃən] n Lösung f (to +gen); **solve** [sɒlv] vt lösen

somber (US), **sombre** ['sɒmbə°] adj düster

KEYWORD

some [sʌm] adj 1 (a certain amount o number of) einige; (a few) ein paar; (with singular nouns) etwas; **some tea/biscuits** etwas Tee/ein paar Kekse; **I've got some money, but not much** ich habe ein bisschen Geld, aber nicht viel

2 (certain: in contrasts) manche(r, s); **some people say that ...** manche Leute sagen, dass ...

3 (unspecified) irgendein(e); **some woman was asking for you** da hat eine Frau nach dir/Ihnen gefragt; **some day** eines Tages; **some day next week** irgendwann nächste Woche

▷ pron 1 (a certain number) einige; **have you got some?** hast du/haben Sie welche?

2 (a certain amount) etwas; **I've read some of the book** ich habe das Buch teilweise gelesen

▷ adv: **some 10 people** etwa 10 Leute

somebody pron jemand; ~ (or other) irgendjemand; ~ else jemand anders; **someday** adv irgendwann; **somehow** adv irgendwie; **someone** pron see **somebody**; **someplace** adv (US) see **somewhere**; **something** ['sʌmθɪŋ] pron etwas; ~ (or other) irgendetwas; ~ else etwas anderes; ~ nice etwas Nettes;

would you like ~ to drink? möchtest du/möchten Sie etwas trinken? ▷ adv: ~ **like 20** ungefähr 20; **sometime** adv irgendwann; **sometimes** adv manchmal; **somewhat** adv ein wenig; **somewhere** adv irgendwo; (to a place) irgendwohin; ~ **else** irgendwo anders; (to another place) irgendwo anders hin

son [sʌn] n Sohn m

song [sɒŋ] n Lied nt; Song m

son-in-law ['sʌnɪnlɔː] n (pl **sons-in-law**) n Schwiegersohn m

soon [suːn] adv bald; (early) früh; **too** ~ zu früh; **as** ~ **as I ...** sobald ich ...; **as** ~ **as possible** so bald wie möglich; **sooner** adv (time) früher; (for preference) lieber

soot [sʊt] n Ruß m

soothe [suːð] vt beruhigen; (pain) lindern

sophisticated [sə'fɪstɪkeɪtɪd] adj (person) kultiviert; (machine) hoch entwickelt; (plan) ausgeklügelt

sophomore ['sɒfəmɔː°] n (US) College-Student(in) m(f) im zweiten Jahr

soppy ['sɒpɪ] adj (fam) rührselig

soprano [sə'prɑːnəʊ] n Sopran m

sore [sɔː°] adj: **to be** ~ wehtun; **to have a** ~ **throat** Halsschmerzen haben ▷ n wunde Stelle

sorrow ['sɒrəʊ] n Kummer m

sorry ['sɒrɪ] adj (sight, figure) traurig; (I'm) ~ (excusing) Entschuldigung!; **I'm** ~ (regretful) es tut mir leid; ~? wie bitte?; **I feel** ~ **for him** er tut mir leid

sort [sɔːt] n Art f; **what** ~ **of film is it?** was für ein Film ist das?; **a** ~ **of** eine Art +gen; **all** ~**s of things** alles Mögliche f; ~ **of** (fam) irgendwie ▷ vt sortieren; **everything's ~ed** (dealt with) alles ist geregelt; **sort out** vt (classify etc) sortieren; (problems) lösen

sought [sɔːt] pt, pp of **seek**

soul [səʊl] n Seele f; (music) Soul m

sound [saʊnd] adj (healthy) gesund; (safe) sicher; (sensible) vernünftig; (theory) stichhaltig; (thrashing) tüchtig ▷ n (noise) Geräusch nt; (Mus) Klang m; (TV) Ton m ▷ vt: **to ~ the alarm** Alarm schlagen; **to ~ one's horn** hupen ▷ vi (seem) klingen (like wie); **soundcard** n (Inform) Soundkarte f; **sound effects** npl Klangeffekte pl; **soundproof** adj schalldicht; **soundtrack** n (of film) Filmmusik f, Soundtrack m

soup [suːp] n Suppe f

sour ['saʊəʳ] adj sauer; (fig) mürrisch

source [sɔːs] n Quelle f; (fig) Ursprung m

sour cream [saʊə'kriːm] n saure Sahne

south [saʊθ] n Süden m; **to the ~ of** südlich von ▷ adv (go, face) nach Süden ▷ adj Süd-; **South Africa** n Südafrika nt; **South African** adj südafrikanisch ▷ n Südafrikaner(in) m(f); **South America** n Südamerika nt; **South American** adj südamerikanisch ▷ n Südamerikaner(in) m(f); **southbound** n (in) Richtung Süden; **southern** ['sʌðən] adj Süd-, südlich; **~ Europe** Südeuropa nt; **southwards** ['saʊθwədz] adv nach Süden

souvenir [suːvə'nɪəʳ] n Andenken nt (of an +akk)

sow [səʊ] (sowed, sown o sowed) vt (a. fig) säen; (field) besäen ▷ [saʊ] n (pig) Sau f

soya bean ['sɔɪə'biːn] n Sojabohne f

soy sauce ['sɔɪ'sɔːs] n Sojasoße f

spa [spɑː] n (place) Kurort m

space [speɪs] n (room) Platz m, Raum m; (outer ~) Weltraum m; (gap) Zwischenraum m; (for parking) Lücke f; **space bar** n Leertaste f; **spacecraft** (pl ~) n Raumschiff nt; **space ship** n Raumschiff nt; **space shuttle** n Raumfähre f

spacing ['speɪsɪŋ] n (in text) Zeilenabstand m; **double ~** zweizeiliger Abstand

spacious ['speɪʃəs] adj geräumig

spade [speɪd] n Spaten m; **~s** Pik nt

spaghetti [spə'getɪ] nsing Spaghetti pl

Spain [speɪn] n Spanien nt

spam [spæm] n (Inform) Spam m

Spaniard ['spænɪəd] n Spanier(in) m(f); **Spanish** ['spænɪʃ] adj spanisch ▷ n (language) Spanisch nt

spanner ['spænəʳ] n (Brit) Schraubenschlüssel m

spare [speəʳ] adj (as replacement) Ersatz-; **~ part** Ersatzteil nt; **~ room** Gästezimmer nt; **~ time** Freizeit f; **~ tyre** Ersatzreifen m ▷ n (~ part) Ersatzteil nt ▷ vt (lives, feelings) verschonen; **can you ~ (me) a moment?** hättest du/hätten Sie einen Moment Zeit?

spark [spɑːk] n Funke m; **sparkle** ['spɑːkl] vi funkeln; **sparkling wine** n Schaumwein m, Sekt m; **spark plug** n Zündkerze f

sparrow ['spærəʊ] n Spatz m

sparse [spɑːs] adj spärlich; **sparsely** adv: **~ populated** dünn besiedelt

spasm ['spæzəm] n Krampf m

spat [spæt] pt, pp of **spit**

speak [spiːk] (spoke, spoken) vt sprechen; **can you ~ French?** sprechen Sie Französisch?; **to**

~ one's mind seine Meinung sagen ▷ vi sprechen (to mit, zu); (make speech) reden; **~ing** (Tel) am Apparat; **so to ~** sozusagen; **~ for yourself** das meinst auch nur du!; **speak up** vi (louder) lauter sprechen; **speaker** n Sprecher(in) m(f); (public ~) Redner(in) m(f); (loud~) Lautsprecher m, Box f

special ['speʃəl] adj besondere(r, s), speziell ▷ n (on menu) Tagesgericht nt; (TV, Radio) Sondersendung f; **special delivery** n Eilzustellung f; **special effects** npl Spezialeffekte pl; **specialist** n Spezialist(in) m(f); (Tech) Fachmann m, Fachfrau f; (Med) Facharzt m, Fachärztin f; **speciality** [speʃɪ'ælɪtɪ] n Spezialität f; **specialize** vi sich spezialisieren (in auf +akk); **specially** adv besonders; (specifically) extra; **special offer** n Sonderangebot nt; **specialty** n (US) see **speciality**

species ['spiːʃiːz] nsing Art f

specific [spə'sɪfɪk] adj spezifisch; (precise) genau; **specify** ['spesɪfaɪ] vt genau angeben

specimen ['spesɪmən] n (sample) Probe f; (example) Exemplar n

specs [speks] npl (fam) Brille f

spectacle ['spektəkl] n Schauspiel nt

spectacles npl Brille f

spectacular [spek'tækjʊlə°] adj spektakulär

spectator [spek'teɪtə°] n Zuschauer(in) m(f)

sped [sped] pt, pp of **speed**

speech [spiːtʃ] n (address) Rede f; (faculty) Sprache f; **to make a ~** eine Rede halten; **speechless** adj sprachlos (with vor +dat)

speed [spiːd] n (sped o speeded, sped o speeded) vi rasen; (exceed

~ limit) zu schnell fahren ▷ n Geschwindigkeit f; (of film) Lichtempfindlichkeit f; **speed up** vt beschleunigen ▷ vi schneller werden/fahren; (drive faster) schneller fahren; **speedboat** n Rennboot nt; **speed bump** n Bodenschwelle f; **speed camera** n Blitzgerät nt; **speed limit** n Geschwindigkeitsbegrenzung f; **speedometer** [spɪ'dɒmɪtə°] n Tachometer m; **speed trap** n Radarfalle f; **speedy** adj schnell

spell [spel] (spelt o spelled, spelt o spelled) vt buchstabieren; **how do you ~ ...?** wie schreibt man ...? ▷ n (period) Weile f; (enchantment) Zauber m; **a cold/hot ~** (weather) ein Kälteeinbruch/eine Hitzewelle; **spellchecker** n (Inform) Rechtschreibprüfung f; **spelling** n Rechtschreibung f; (of a word) Schreibweise f; **~ mistake** Schreibfehler m

spelt [spelt] pt, pp of **spell**

spend [spend] (spent, spent) vt (money) ausgeben (on für); (time) verbringen; **spending money** n Taschengeld nt

spent [spent] pt, pp of **spend**

sperm [spɜːm] n Sperma nt

sphere [sfɪə°] n (globe) Kugel f; (fig) Sphäre f

spice [spaɪs] n Gewürz nt; (fig) Würze f ▷ vt würzen; **spicy** ['spaɪsɪ] adj würzig; (fig) pikant

spider ['spaɪdə°] n Spinne f

spike [spaɪk] n (on railing etc) Spitze f; (on shoe, tyre) Spike m

spill [spɪl] (spilt o spilled, spilt o spilled) vt verschütten

spin [spɪn] (spun, spun) vi (turn) sich drehen; (washing) schleudern; **my head is ~ning** mir dreht sich alles ▷ vt (turn) drehen; (coin) hochwerfen ▷ n (turn) Drehung f

spinach ['spɪnɪtʃ] n Spinat m

spin doctor n Spindoktor m
(Verantwortlicher für die
schönrednerische Öffentlichkeitsarbeit
besonders von Politikern)

spin-drier ['spɪndraɪə°] n
Wäscheschleuder f; **spin-dry** vt
schleudern

spine [spaɪn] n Rückgrat nt; (of
animal, plant) Stachel m; (of book)
Rücken m

spiral ['spaɪrəl] n Spirale f ▷ adj
spiralförmig; **spiral staircase** n
Wendeltreppe f

spire ['spaɪə°] n Turmspitze f

spirit ['spɪrɪt] n (essence, soul)
Geist m; (humour, mood) Stimmung
f; (courage) Mut m; (verve) Elan m;
~s pl (drinks) Spirituosen pl

spiritual ['spɪrɪtjʊəl] adj geistig;
(Rel) geistlich

spit [spɪt] (**spat, spat**) vi
spucken ▷ n (for roasting)
(Brat)spieß m; (saliva) Spucke f;
spit out vt ausspucken

spite [spaɪt] n Boshaftigkeit f; **in
~ of** trotz +gen; **spiteful** adj
boshaft

spitting image ['spɪtɪŋ'ɪmɪdʒ]
n: **he's the ~ of you** er ist
dir/Ihnen wie aus dem Gesicht
geschnitten

splash [splæʃ] vt (person, object)
bespritzen ▷ vi (liquid) spritzen;
(play in water) planschen

splendid ['splendɪd] adj herrlich

splinter ['splɪntə°] n Splitter
m

split [splɪt] (**split, split**) vt (stone,
wood) spalten; (share) teilen ▷ vi
(stone, wood) sich spalten; (seam)
platzen ▷ n (in stone, wood) Spalt
m; (in clothing) Riss m; (fig)
Spaltung f; **split up** vi (couple) sich
trennen ▷ vt (divide up) aufteilen;
split ends npl (Haar)spliss m;
splitting adj (headache) rasend

spoil [spɔɪl] (**spoiled** o **spoilt,**

spoiled o **spoilt**) vt verderben;
(child) verwöhnen ▷ vi (food)
verderben

spoilt [spɔɪlt] pt, pp of **spoil**

spoke [spəʊk] pt of **speak** ▷ n
Speiche f

spoken ['spəʊkən] pp of **speak**

spokesperson ['spəʊkspɜːsən]
(pl **-people**) n Sprecher(in) m(f)

sponge [spʌndʒ] n (for washing)
Schwamm m; **sponge bag** n
Kulturbeutel m; **sponge cake** n
Biskuitkuchen m

sponsor ['spɒnsə°] n (of event,
programme) Sponsor(in) m(f) ▷ vt
unterstützen; (event, programme)
sponsern

spontaneous, spontaneously
[spɒn'teɪnɪəs, -lɪ] adj, adv
spontan

spool [spuːl] n Spule f

spoon [spuːn] n Löffel m

sport [spɔːt] n Sport m; **sports
car** n Sportwagen m; **sports
centre** n Sportzentrum nt;
sports club n Sportverein m;
sportsman (pl **-men**) n Sportler
m; **sportswear** n Sportkleidung f;
sportswoman (pl **-women**) n
Sportlerin f; **sporty** adj sportlich

spot [spɒt] n (dot) Punkt m; (of
paint, blood etc) Fleck m; (place)
Stelle f; (pimple) Pickel m; **on the
~ vor Ort**; (at once) auf der Stelle
▷ vt (notice) entdecken; (difference)
erkennen; **spotless** adj (clean)
blitzsauber; **spotlight** n (lamp)
Scheinwerfer m; **spotty** adj
(pimply) pickelig

spouse [spaʊs] n Gatte m,
Gattin f

spout [spaʊt] n Schnabel m

sprain [spreɪn] n Verstauchung
f ▷ vt: **to ~ one's ankle** sich den
Knöchel verstauchen

sprang [spræŋ] pt of **spring**

spray [spreɪ] n (liquid in can)

Spray nt o m; (~ (can)) Spraydose f
▷ vt (plant, insects) besprühen;
(car) spritzen

spread [sprɛd] (**spread, spread**)
vt (open out) ausbreiten; (news,
disease) verbreiten; (butter, jam)
streichen; (bread, surface)
bestreichen ▷ vi (news, disease,
fire) sich verbreiten ▷ n (of disease,
religion etc) Verbreitung f; (for bread)
Aufstrich m; **spreadsheet** n
(Inform) Tabellenkalkulation f

spring [sprɪŋ] (**sprang, sprung**)
vi (leap) springen ▷ n (season)
Frühling m; (coil) Feder f; (water)
Quelle f; **springboard** n
Sprungbrett nt; **spring onion** n
(Brit) Frühlingszwiebel f; **spring
roll** n (Brit) Frühlingsrolle f;
springy adj (mattress) federnd

sprinkle ['sprɪŋkl] vt streuen;
(liquid) (be)träufeln; **to ~ sth with
sth** etw mit etw bestreuen; (with
liquid) etw mit etw besprengen;
sprinkler n (for lawn)
Rasensprenger m; (for fire)
Sprinkler m

sprint [sprɪnt] vi rennen; (Sport)
sprinten

sprout [spraʊt] n (of plant) Trieb
m; (from seed) Keim m; (**Brussels)
~s** pl Rosenkohl m ▷ vi sprießen

sprung [sprʌŋ] pp of **spring**

spun [spʌn] pt, pp of **spin**

spy [spaɪ] n Spion(in) m(f) ▷ vi
spionieren; **to ~ on sb** jdm
nachspionieren ▷ vt erspähen

squad [skwɒd] n (Sport) Kader m;
(police ~) Kommando nt

square [skwɛə°] n (shape)
Quadrat nt; (open space) Platz m;
(on chessboard etc) Feld nt ▷ adj (in
shape) quadratisch; **2 ~ metres** 2
Quadratmeter; **2 metres ~** 2 Meter
im Quadrat ▷ vt: **3 ~d** 3 hoch 2;
square root n Quadratwurzel f

squash [skwɒʃ] n (drink)

Fruchtsaftgetränk nt; (Sport)
Squash nt; (US: vegetable) Kürbis m
▷ vt zerquetschen

squat [skwɒt] vi (be crouching)
hocken; **to ~ (down)** sich
(hin)hocken

squeak [skwiːk] vi (door, shoes
etc) quietschen; (animal) quieken

squeal [skwiːl] vi (person)
kreischen (with vor +dat)

squeeze [skwiːz] vt drücken;
(orange) auspressen ▷ vi: **to ~ into
the car** sich in den Wagen
hineinzwängen; **squeeze up** vi
(on bench etc) zusammenrücken

squid [skwɪd] n Tintenfisch m

squint [skwɪnt] vi schielen; (in
bright light) blinzeln

squirrel ['skwɪrəl] n Eichhörnchen nt

squirt [skwɜːt] vt, vi (liquid)
spritzen

Sri Lanka [sriː'læŋkə] n Sri
Lanka nt

st abbr = **stone** Gewichtseinheit (6,35
kg)

St abbr = **saint** St.; abbr = **street** Str.

stab [stæb] vt (person) einstechen
auf +akk; (to death) erstechen;
stabbing adj (pain) stechend

stabilize ['steɪbəlaɪz] vt
stabilisieren ▷ vi sich
stabilisieren

stable ['steɪbl] n Stall m ▷ adj
stabil

stack [stæk] n (pile) Stapel m
▷ vt: **to ~ (up)** (auf)stapeln

stadium ['steɪdɪəm] n Stadion
nt

staff [stɑːf] n (personnel) Personal
nt, Lehrkräfte pl

stag [stæg] n Hirsch m

stag night n (Brit)
Junggesellenabschied m

stage [steɪdʒ] n (Theat) Bühne f;
(of project, life etc) Stadium nt; (of
journey) Etappe f; **at this ~** zu

diesem Zeitpunkt ⊳ vt (*Theat*) aufführen, inszenieren; (*demonstration*) veranstalten

stagger ['stægə°] vi wanken ⊳ vt (*amaze*) verblüffen; **staggering** *adj* (*amazing*) umwerfend; (*amount, price*) schwindelerregend

stagnate [stæg'neɪt] vi (*fig*) stagnieren

stain [steɪn] n Fleck m; **stained-glass window** n Buntglasfenster nt; **stainless steel** n rostfreier Stahl; **stain remover** n Fleck(en)entferner m

stair [steə°] n (Treppen)stufe f; **~s** pl Treppe f; **staircase** n Treppe f

stake [steɪk] n (*post*) Pfahl m; (*in betting*) Einsatz m; (*Fin*) Anteil m (in an +*dat*); **to be at ~** auf dem Spiel stehen

stale [steɪl] *adj* (*bread*) alt; (*beer*) schal

stalk [stɔːk] n Stiel m ⊳ vt (*wild animal*) sich anpirschen an +*akk*; (*person*) nachstellen +*dat*

stall [stɔːl] n (*in market*) (Verkaufs)stand m; (*in stable*) Box f; **~s** pl (*Theat*) Parkett nt ⊳ vt (*engine*) abwürgen ⊳ vi (*driver*) den Motor abwürgen; (*car*) stehen bleiben; (*delay*) Zeit schinden

stamina ['stæmɪnə] n Durchhaltevermögen nt

stammer ['stæmə°] vi, vt stottern

stamp [stæmp] n (*postage ~*) Briefmarke f; (*for document*) Stempel m ⊳ vt (*passport etc*) stempeln; (*mail*) frankieren; **stamped addressed envelope** n frankierter Rückumschlag

stand [stænd] (**stood, stood**) n stehen; (*as candidate*) kandidieren ⊳ vt (*place*) stellen; (*endure*) aushalten; **I can't ~ her** ich kann sie nicht ausstehen ⊳ n (*stall*)

Stand m; (*seats in stadium*) Tribüne f; (*for coats, bicycles*) Ständer m; (*for small objects*) Gestell nt; **stand around** vi herumstehen; **stand by** vi (*be ready*) sich bereithalten; (*be inactive*) danebenstehen ⊳ vt (*fig: person*) halten zu; (*decision, promise*) stehen zu; **stand for** vt (*represent*) stehen für; (*tolerate*) hinnehmen; **stand in for** vt einspringen für; **stand out** vi (*be noticeable*) auffallen; **stand up** vi (*get up*) aufstehen ⊳ vt (*girlfriend, boyfriend*) versetzen; **stand up for** vt sich einsetzen für; **stand up to** vt: **to ~ sb** jdm die Stirn bieten

standard ['stændəd] n (*norm*) Norm f ⊳ ~ **of living** Lebensstandard m ⊳ *adj* Standard-

standardize ['stændədaɪz] vt vereinheitlichen

stand-by ['stændbaɪ] n (*thing in reserve*) Reserve f; **on ~** in Bereitschaft ⊳ *adj* (*flight, ticket*) Stand-by-; **standing order** n (*at bank*) Dauerauftrag m; **standpoint** ['stændpɔɪnt] n Standpunkt m; **standstill** ['stændstɪl] n Stillstand m; **to come to a ~** stehen bleiben; (*fig*) zum Erliegen kommen

stank [stæŋk] *pt of* **stink**

staple ['steɪpl] n (*for paper*) Heftklammer f ⊳ vt heften (*to* an +*akk*); **stapler** n Hefter m

star [stɑː°] n Stern m; (*person*) Star m ⊳ vt: **the film ~s Hugh Grant** der Film zeigt Hugh Grant in der Hauptrolle ⊳ vi die Hauptrolle spielen

starch [stɑːtʃ] n Stärke f

stare [steə°] vi starren; **to ~ at** anstarren

starfish ['stɑːfɪʃ] n Seestern m

star sign ['stɑːsaɪn] n Sternzeichen nt

start [stɑːt] n (beginning) Anfang m, Beginn m; (Sport) Start m; (lead) Vorsprung m; **from the ~** von Anfang an ▷ vt anfangen; (car, engine) starten; (business, family) gründen; **to ~ to do sth, to ~ doing sth** anfangen, etw zu tun ▷ vi (begin) anfangen; (car) anspringen; (on journey) aufbrechen; (Sport) starten; (jump) zusammenfahren; **~ing from Monday** ab Montag; **start off** vt (discussion, process etc) anfangen, beginnen ▷ vi (begin) anfangen, beginnen; (on journey) aufbrechen; **start over** vi (US) wieder anfangen; **start up** vi (in business) anfangen ▷ vt (car, engine) starten; (business) gründen; **starter** n (Brit: first course) Vorspeise f; (Auto) Anlasser m; **starting point** n (a. fig) Ausgangspunkt m

startle ['stɑːtl] vt erschrecken; **startling** adj überraschend

starve [stɑːv] vi hungern; (to death) verhungern; **I'm starving** ich habe einen Riesenhunger

state [steɪt] n (condition) Zustand m; (Pol) Staat m; **the (United) States** die (Vereinigten) Staaten ▷ adj Staats-; (control, education) staatlich ▷ vt erklären; (facts, name etc) angeben; **stated** adj (fixed) festgesetzt

statement ['steɪtmənt] n (official declaration) Erklärung f; (to police) Aussage f; (from bank) Kontoauszug m

state-of-the-art [steɪtəvði:'ɑːt] adj hochmodern, auf dem neuesten Stand der Technik

static ['stætɪk] adj (unchanging) konstant

station ['steɪʃən] n (for trains, buses) Bahnhof m; (underground ~) Station f; (police ~, fire ~) Wache f; (TV, Radio) Sender m ▷ vt (Mil) stationieren

stationer's ['steɪʃənəz] n: **~ (shop)** Schreibwarengeschäft nt; **stationery** n Schreibwaren pl

station wagon ['steɪʃənwægən] n (US) Kombiwagen m

statistics [stə'tɪstɪks] nsing (science) Statistik f; (figures) Statistiken pl

statue ['stætjuː] n Statue f

status ['steɪtəs] n Status m; (prestige) Ansehen nt; **status bar** n (inform) Statuszeile f

stay [steɪ] n Aufenthalt m ▷ vi bleiben; (with friends, in hotel) wohnen (with being); **to ~ the night** übernachten; **stay away** vi wegbleiben; **to ~ from sb** sich von jdm fernhalten; **stay behind** vi zurückbleiben; (at work) länger bleiben; **stay in** vi (at home) zu Hause bleiben; **stay out** vi (not come home) wegbleiben; **stay up** vi (at night) aufbleiben

steady ['stedɪ] adj (speed) gleichmäßig; (progress, increase) stetig; (job, income, girlfriend) fest; (worker) zuverlässig; (hand) ruhig; **they've been going ~ for two years** sie sind seit zwei Jahren fest zusammen ▷ vt (nerves) beruhigen; **to ~ oneself** Halt finden

steak [steɪk] n Steak nt; (of fish) Filet nt

steal [stiːl] (stole, stolen) vt stehlen; **to ~ sth from sb** jdm etw stehlen

steam [stiːm] n Dampf m ▷ vt (Gastr) dämpfen; **steam up** vi (window) beschlagen; **steamer** n (Gastr) Dampfkochtopf m; (ship) Dampfer m; **steam iron** n Dampfbügeleisen m

steel [stiːl] n Stahl m ▷ adj Stahl-

steep [stiːp] adj steil

steeple ['stiːpl] n Kirchturm m

steer [stɪəʳ] vt, vi steuern; (car, bike etc) lenken; **steering** n (Auto) Lenkung f; **steering wheel** n Steuer nt, Lenkrad nt

stem [stem] n (of plant, glass) Stiel m

step [step] n Schritt m; (stair) Stufe f; (measure) Maßnahme f; **~ by** Schritt für Schritt ▷ vi treten; **~ this way, please** hier entlang, bitte; **step down** vi (resign) zurücktreten

stepbrother n Stiefbruder m; **stepchild** (pl **-children**) n Stiefkind nt; **stepfather** n Stiefvater m

stepladder n Trittleiter f

stepmother n Stiefmutter f; **stepsister** n Stiefschwester f

stereo ['stɪərɪəʊ] (pl **-s**) n; **~ system** Stereoanlage f

sterile ['sterail] adj steril; **sterilize** ['sterilaiz] vt sterilisieren

sterling ['stɜːlɪŋ] n (Fin) das Pfund Sterling

stew [stjuː] n Eintopf m

steward ['stjuːəd] n (on plane, ship) Steward m; **stewardess** n Stewardess f

stick [stɪk] (**stuck, stuck**) vt (with glue etc) kleben; (pin etc) stecken; (fam: put) tun ▷ vi (get jammed) klemmen; (hold fast) haften ▷ n Stock m; (hockey ~) Schläger m; (of chalk) Stück nt; (of celery, rhubarb) Stange f; **stick out** vt: **to stick one's tongue out (at sb)** (jdm) die Zunge herausstrecken ▷ vi (protrude) vorstehen; (ears) abstehen; (be noticeable) auffallen; **stick to** vt (rules, plan etc) sich halten an +akk; **sticker** ['stɪkəʳ] n Aufkleber m; **sticky** ['stɪkɪ] adj klebrig;

(weather) schwül; **~ label** Aufkleber m; **~ tape** Klebeband nt

stiff [stɪf] adj steif

stifle ['staɪfl] vt (yawn etc, opposition) unterdrücken; **stifling** adj drückend

still [stɪl] adj still; (drink) ohne Kohlensäure ▷ adv (yet, even now) (immer) noch; (all the same) immerhin; (sit, stand) still; **he ~ doesn't believe me** er glaubt mir immer noch nicht; **keep ~** halt still; **bigger/better** ~ noch größer/besser

still life (pl **still lives**) n Stillleben nt

stimulate ['stɪmjʊleɪt] vt anregen, stimulieren; **stimulating** adj anregend

sting [stɪŋ] (**stung, stung**) vt (wound with ~) stechen ▷ vi (eyes, ointment etc) brennen ▷ n (insect wound) Stich m

stingy ['stɪndʒɪ] adj (fam) geizig

stink [stɪŋk] (**stank, stunk**) vi stinken (of nach) ▷ n Gestank m

stir [stɜːʳ] vt (mix) (um)rühren; **stir up** vt (mob) aufhetzen; (memories) wachrufen; **to ~ trouble** Unruhe stiften; **stir-fry** vt (unter Rühren) kurz anbraten

stitch [stɪtʃ] n (in sewing) Stich m; (in knitting) Masche f; **to have a ~ (pain)** Seitenstechen haben; **he had to have ~es** er musste genäht werden; **she had her ~es out** ihr wurden die Fäden gezogen; **to be in ~es** (fam) sich kaputtlachen ▷ vt nähen; **stitch up** vt (hole, wound) nähen

stock [stɒk] n (supply) Vorrat m (of an +dat); (of shop) Bestand m; (for soup etc) Brühe f; **~s and shares** pl Aktien und Wertpapiere pl; **to be in/out of ~** vorrätig/nicht vorrätig sein; **to**

take ~ Inventur machen; (fig)
Bilanz ziehen ▷ vt (keep in shop)
führen; **stock up** vi sich
eindecken (on, with mit)
stockbroker n Börsenmakler(in)
m(f)
stock cube n Brühwürfel m
stock exchange n Börse f
stocking ['stɒkɪŋ] n Strumpf m
stock market ['stɒkmɑːkɪt] n
Börse f
stole [stəʊl] pt of **steal**; **stolen**
['stəʊlən] pp of **steal**
stomach ['stʌmək] n Magen m;
(belly) Bauch m; **on an empty ~** auf
leeren Magen; **stomach-ache** n
Magenschmerzen pl; **stomach
upset** n Magenverstimmung f
stone [stəʊn] n Stein m; (seed)
Kern m, Stein m; (weight) britische
Gewichtseinheit (6,35 kg) ▷ adj
Stein-, aus Stein; **stony** adj
(ground) steinig
stood [stʊd] pt, pp of **stand**
stool [stuːl] n Hocker m
stop [stɒp] n Halt m; (for bus,
tram, train) Haltestelle f; **to come
to a ~** anhalten ▷ vt (vehicle,
passer-by) anhalten; (put an end to)
ein Ende machen +dat; (cease)
aufhören mit; (prevent from
happening) verhindern; (bleeding)
stillen; (engine, machine) abstellen;
(payments) einstellen; (cheque)
sperren; **to ~ doing sth** aufhören,
etw zu tun; **to ~ sb (from) doing
sth** jdn daran hindern, etw zu tun;
~ it hör auf (damit)! ▷ vi (vehicle)
anhalten; (during journey) Halt
machen; (pedestrian, clock, heart)
stehen bleiben; (rain, noise)
aufhören; (stay) bleiben; **stop by**
vi vorbeischauen; **stop over** vi
Halt machen; (overnight)
übernachten; **stopgap** n
Provisorium nt, Zwischenlösung f;
stopover n (on journey)

Zwischenstation f; **stopper** n
Stöpsel m; **stop sign** n
Stoppschild nt; **stopwatch** n
Stoppuhr f
storage ['stɔːrɪdʒ] n Lagerung f;
store [stɔː°] n (supply) Vorrat m
(of an +dat); (place for storage) Lager
nt; (large shop) Kaufhaus nt; (US:
shop) Geschäft nt ▷ vt lagern;
(Inform) speichern; **storecard** n
Kundenkreditkarte f; **storeroom**
n Lagerraum m
storey ['stɔːrɪ] n (Brit) Stock m,
Stockwerk nt
storm [stɔːm] n Sturm m;
(thunder~) Gewitter nt ▷ vt, vi
(with movement) stürmen; **stormy**
adj stürmisch
story ['stɔːrɪ] n Geschichte f;
(plot) Handlung f; (US: of building)
Stock m, Stockwerk nt
stout [staʊt] adj (fat) korpulent
stove [stəʊv] n Herd m; (for
heating) Ofen m
stow [stəʊ] vt verstauen;
stowaway n blinder Passagier
straight [streɪt] adj (not curved)
gerade; (hair) glatt; (honest) ehrlich
(with zu); (fam: heterosexual) hetero
▷ adv (directly) direkt; (immediately)
sofort; (drink) pur; (think) klar;
~ ahead geradeaus; **to go ~ on**
geradeaus weitergehen/
weiterfahren; **straightaway** adv
sofort; **straightforward** adj
einfach; (person) aufrichtig,
unkompliziert
strain [streɪn] n Belastung f ▷ vt
(eyes) überanstrengen; (rope,
relationship) belasten; (vegetables)
abgießen; **to ~ a muscle** sich
einen Muskel zerren; **strained** adj
(laugh, smile) gezwungen;
(relations) gespannt; **~ muscle**
Muskelzerrung f; **strainer** n Sieb
nt
strand [strænd] n (of wool) Faden

m; *(of hair)* Strähne *f* ▷ *vt*: **to be (left) ~ed** *(person)* festsitzen

strange [streɪndʒ] *adj* seltsam; *(unfamiliar)* fremd; **strangely** *adv* seltsam; **~ enough** seltsamerweise; **stranger** *n* Fremde(r) *mf*; **I'm a ~ here** ich bin hier fremd

strangle ['stræŋgl] *vt (kill)* erdrosseln

strap [stræp] *n* Riemen *m*; *(on dress etc)* Träger *m*; *(on watch)* Band *nt* ▷ *vt (fasten)* festschnallen (to an +*dat*); **strapless** *adj* trägerlos

strategy ['strætɪdʒɪ] *n* Strategie *f*

straw [strɔ:] *n* Stroh *nt*; *(drinking ~)* Strohhalm *m*

strawberry *n* Erdbeere *f*

stray [streɪ] *n* streunendes Tier ▷ *adj (cat, dog)* streunend ▷ *vi* streunen

streak ['stri:k] *n (of colour, dirt)* Streifen *m*; *(in hair)* Strähne *f*; *(in character)* Zug *m*

stream [stri:m] *n (flow of liquid)* Strom *m*; *(brook)* Bach *m* ▷ *vi* strömen; **streamer** *n (of paper)* Luftschlange *f*

street [stri:t] *n* Straße *f*; **streetcar** *n (US)* Straßenbahn *f*; **street lamp**, **street light** *n* Straßenlaterne *f*; **street map** *n* Stadtplan *m*

strength [streŋθ] *n* Kraft *f*, Stärke *f*; **strengthen** *vt* verstärken; *(fig)* stärken

strenuous ['strenjʊəs] *adj* anstrengend

stress [stres] *n* Stress *m*; *(on word)* Betonung *f*; **to be under ~** im Stress sein ▷ *vt* betonen; *(put under ~)* stressen; **stressed** *adj*: **~ (out)** gestresst

stretch [stretʃ] *n (of land)* Stück *nt*; *(of road)* Strecke *f* ▷ *vt (material, shoes)* dehnen; *(rope, canvas)*

spannen; *(person in job etc)* fordern; **to ~ one's legs** *(walk)* sich die Beine vertreten ▷ *vi (person)* sich strecken; *(area)* sich erstrecken (to bis zu); **stretch out** *vt*: **to stretch one's hand/legs out** die Hand/die Beine ausstrecken, ausstrecken ▷ *vi (reach)* sich strecken; *(lie down)* sich ausstrecken; **stretcher** *n* Tragbahre *f*

strict, **strictly** [strɪkt, -lɪ] *adj, adv (severe(ly))* streng; *(exact(ly))* genau; **~ speaking** genauer gesagt

strike [straɪk] **(struck, struck)** *vt (match)* anzünden; *(hit)* schlagen; *(find)* finden; **it struck me as strange** es kam mir seltsam vor ▷ *vi (stop work)* streiken; *(attack)* zuschlagen; *(clock)* schlagen ▷ *n (by workers)* Streik *m*; **to be on ~** streiken; **strike up** *vt (conversation)* anfangen; *(friendship)* schließen; **striking** *adj* auffallend

string [strɪŋ] *n (for tying)* Schnur *f*; *(Mus, Tennis)* Saite *f*; **the ~s** *pl (section of orchestra)* die Streicher *pl*

strip [strɪp] *n* Streifen *m*; *(Brit: of footballer etc)* Trikot *nt* ▷ *vi (undress)* sich ausziehen, strippen

stripe [straɪp] *n* Streifen *m*; **striped** *adj* gestreift

stripper ['strɪpə°] *n* Stripper(in) *m(f)*; *(paint ~)* Farbentferner *m*

strip-search ['strɪpsз:tʃ] *n* Leibesvisitation *f (bei der man sich ausziehen muss)*

striptease ['strɪpti:z] *n* Striptease *m*

stroke [strəʊk] *n (Med, Tennis etc)* Schlag *m*; *(of pen, brush)* Strich *m* ▷ *vt* streicheln

stroll [strəʊl] *n* Spaziergang *m* ▷ *vi* spazieren; **stroller** *n (US: for baby)* Buggy *m*

strong [strɒŋ] *adj* stark; *(healthy)*

robust; (wall, table) stabil; (shoes)
fest; (influence, chance) groß;
strongly adv stark; (believe) fest;
(constructed) stabil
struck [strʌk] pt, pp of **strike**
structural, structurally
['strʌktʃərəl, -lı] adj strukturell;
structure ['strʌktʃə⁺] n Struktur
f; (building, bridge) Konstruktion f,
Bau m
struggle ['strʌgl] n Kampf m (for
um) ▷ vi (fight) kämpfen (for um);
(do sth with difficulty) sich
abmühen; **to ~ to do sth** sich
abmühen, etw zu tun
stub [stʌb] n (of cigarette) Kippe f;
(of ticket, cheque) Abschnitt m ▷ vt:
to ~ one's toe sich dat den Zeh
stoßen (on an +dat)
stubble ['stʌbl] n Stoppelbart m;
(field) Stoppeln pl
stubborn ['stʌbən] adj (person)
stur
stuck [stʌk] pt, pp of **stick** ▷ adj:
to be ~ (jammed) klemmen; (at a
loss) nicht mehr weiterwissen; **to
get ~** (car in snow etc) stecken
bleiben
student ['stju:dənt] n Stu-
dent(in) m(f), Schüler(in) m(f)
studio ['stju:dıəʊ] (pl **-s**) n
Studio nt
studious ['stju:dıəs] adj fleißig
study ['stʌdı] n (investigation)
Untersuchung f; (room)
Arbeitszimmer nt ▷ vt, vi
studieren
stuff [stʌf] n Zeug nt, Sachen pl
▷ vt (push) stopfen; (Gastr)
füllen; **to ~ oneself** (fam) sich
vollstopfen; **stuffing** n (Gastr)
Füllung f
stuffy ['stʌfı] adj (room) stickig;
(person) spießig
stumble ['stʌmbl] vi stolpern;
(when speaking) stocken
stun [stʌn] vt (shock) fassungslos

machen; **I was ~ned** ich war
fassungslos (o völlig überrascht)
stung [stʌŋ] pt, pp of **sting**
stunk [stʌŋk] pp of **stink**
stunning ['stʌnıŋ] adj (marvellous) fantastisch; (beautiful)
atemberaubend; (very surprising,
shocking) überwältigend;
unfassbar
stunt [stʌnt] n (Cine) Stunt m
stupid ['stju:pıd] adj dumm;
stupidity [stju:'pıdıtı] n
Dummheit f
sturdy ['stɜ:dı] adj robust;
(building, car) stabil
stutter ['stʌtə⁺] vi, vt stottern
stye [staı] n (Med) Gerstenkorn nt
style [staıl] n Stil m ▷ vt (hair)
stylen; **styling mousse** n
Schaumfestiger m; **stylish**
['staılıʃ] adj elegant, schick
subconscious [sʌb'kɒnʃəs] adj
unterbewusst ▷ n: **the ~** das
Unterbewusstsein
subdivide [sʌbdı'vaıd] vt
unterteilen
subject ['sʌbdʒıkt] n (topic)
Thema nt; (in school) Fach nt;
(citizen) Staatsangehörige(r) mf; (of
kingdom) Untertan(in) m(f); (Ling)
Subjekt nt; **to change the ~** das
Thema wechseln ▷ adj [səb'dʒekt]
to be ~ to (dependent on) abhängen
von; (under control of) unterworfen
sein +dat
subjective [səb'dʒektıv] adj
subjektiv
sublet [sʌb'let] irr vt unterver-
mieten (to an +akk)
submarine [sʌbmə'ri:n] n
U-Boot nt
submerge [səb'mɜ:dʒ] vt (put in
water) eintauchen ▷ vi tauchen
submit [səb'mıt] vt (application,
claim) einreichen ▷ vi (surrender)
sich ergeben
subordinate [sə'bɔ:dınət] adj

untergeordnet (to +dat) ▷ n Untergebene(r) mf

subscribe [səb'skraɪb] vi: **to ~ to** (magazine etc) abonnieren; **subscription** [səb'skrɪpʃən] n (to magazine etc) Abonnement nt; (to club etc) (Mitglieds)beitrag m

subsequent ['sʌbsɪkwənt] adj nach(folgend); **subsequently** adv später, anschließend

subside [səb'saɪd] vi (floods) zurückgehen; (storm) sich legen; (building) sich senken

substance ['sʌbstəns] n Substanz f

substantial [səb'stænʃəl] adj beträchtlich; (improvement) wesentlich; (meal) reichhaltig; (furniture) solide

substitute ['sʌbstɪtjuːt] n Ersatz m; (Sport) Ersatzspieler(in) m(f) ▷ vt: **to ~ A for B** B durch A ersetzen

subtitle ['sʌbtaɪtl] n Untertitel m

subtle ['sʌtl] adj (difference, taste) fein; (plan) raffiniert

subtotal ['sʌbtəʊtl] n Zwischensumme f

subtract [səb'trækt] vt abziehen (from von)

suburb ['sʌbɜːb] n Vorort m; **in the ~s** am Stadtrand; **suburban** [sə'bɜːbən] adj vorstädtisch, Vorstadt-

subway ['sʌbweɪ] n (Brit) Unterführung f; (US Rail) U-Bahn f

succeed [sək'siːd] vi erfolgreich sein; **he ~ed (in doing it)** es gelang ihm(, es zu tun) ▷ vt nachfolgen +dat; **succeeding** adj nachfolgend; **success** [sək'ses] n Erfolg m; **successful, successfully** adj, adv erfolgreich

successive [sək'sesɪv] adj aufeinanderfolgend; **successor** n Nachfolger(in) m(f)

succulent ['sʌkjʊlənt] adj saftig

succumb [sə'kʌm] vi erliegen (to +dat)

such [sʌtʃ] adj solche(r, s); **~ a book** so ein Buch, ein solches Buch; **it was ~ a success that ...** es war solch ein Erfolg, dass ...; **~ as** wie ▷ adv so; **~ a hot day** so ein heißer Tag ▷ pron: **as ~** als solche(r, s)

suck [sʌk] vt (toffee etc) lutschen; (liquid) saugen; **it ~s** (fam) das ist beschissen

Sudan [suː'dɑːn] n: **(the) ~** der Sudan

sudden ['sʌdn] adj plötzlich; **all of a ~** ganz plötzlich; **suddenly** adv plötzlich

sudoku [suː'dəʊkuː] n Sudoku nt

sue [suː] vt verklagen

suede [sweɪd] n Wildleder nt

suffer ['sʌfəʳ] vt erleiden ▷ vi leiden; **to ~ from** (Med) leiden an +dat

sufficient, sufficiently [sə'fɪʃənt, -lɪ] adj, adv ausreichend

suffocate ['sʌfəkeɪt] vt, vi ersticken

sugar ['ʃʊgəʳ] n Zucker m ▷ vt zuckern; **sugar bowl** n Zuckerdose f; **sugary** adj (sweet) süß

suggest [sə'dʒest] vt vorschlagen; (imply) andeuten; **I ~ saying nothing** ich schlage vor, nichts zu sagen; **suggestion** n (proposal) Vorschlag m; **suggestive** adj vielsagend; (sexually) anzüglich

suicide ['sʊɪsaɪd] n (act) Selbstmord m; **suicide bomber** n Selbstmordattentäter(in) m(f); **suicide bombing** n Selbstmordattentat nt

suit [suːt] n (man's clothes) Anzug m; (lady's clothes) Kostüm nt; (Cards) Farbe f ▷ vt (be convenient for) passen +dat; (clothes, colour) stehen +dat; (climate, food) bekommen +dat; **suitable** adj geeignet (for für); **suitcase** n Koffer m

suite [swi:t] n (of rooms) Suite f; (sofa and chairs) Sitzgarnitur f

sulk [sʌlk] vi schmollen; **sulky** adj eingeschnappt

sultana [sʌl'tɑːnə] n (raisin) Sultanine f

sum [sʌm] n Summe f; (money a.) Betrag m; (calculation) Rechenaufgabe f; **sum up** vt, vi (summarize) zusammenfassen

summarize ['sʌməraɪz] vt, vi zusammenfassen; **summary** n Zusammenfassung f

summer ['sʌmə*] n Sommer m; **summer camp** n (US) Ferienlager nt; **summer holidays** pl; **summertime** n: **in (the) ~** im Sommer

summit ['sʌmɪt] n (a. Pol) Gipfel m

summon ['sʌmən] vt (doctor, fire brigade etc) rufen; (to one's office) zitieren; **summon up** vt (courage, strength) zusammennehmen

summons ['sʌmənz] nsing (Jur) Vorladung f

sumptuous ['sʌmptjuəs] adj luxuriös; (meal) üppig

sun [sʌn] n Sonne f ▷ vt: **to ~ oneself** sich sonnen

Sun abbr = **Sunday** So.

sunbathe vi sich sonnen; **sunbathing** n Sonnenbaden nt; **sunbed** n Sonnenbank f; **sunblock** n Sunblocker m; **sunburn** n Sonnenbrand m; **sunburnt** adj: **to be/get ~** einen Sonnenbrand haben/bekommen

sundae ['sʌndeɪ] n Eisbecher m

Sunday ['sʌndɪ] n Sonntag m; see also **Tuesday**

sung [sʌŋ] pp of **sing**

sunglasses ['sʌnɡlɑːsɪz] npl

Sonnenbrille f; **sunhat** n Sonnenhut m

sunk [sʌŋk] pp of **sink**

sunlamp ['sʌnlæmp] n Höhensonne f; **sunlight** n Sonnenlicht nt; **sunny** ['sʌnɪ] adj sonnig; **sun protection factor** n Lichtschutzfaktor m; **sunrise** n Sonnenaufgang m; **sunroof** n (Auto) Schiebedach nt; **sunscreen** n Sonnenschutzmittel nt; **sunset** n Sonnenuntergang m; **sunshade** n Sonnenschirm m; **sunshine** n Sonnenschein m; **sunstroke** n Sonnenstich m; **suntan** n (Sonnen)bräune f; **to get/have a ~** braun werden/sein; **~ lotion** (o oil) Sonnenöl nt

super ['su:pə*] adj (fam) toll

superb, **superbly** [su:'pɜːb, -lɪ] adj, adv ausgezeichnet

superficial, **superficially** [su:pə'fɪʃəl, -ɪ] adj, adv oberflächlich

superfluous [su'pɜːfluəs] adj überflüssig

superglue ['su:pəglu:] n Sekundenkleber m

superior [su'pɪərɪə*] adj (better) besser (to als); (higher in rank) höhergestellt (to als), höher ▷ n (in rank) Vorgesetzte(r) mf

supermarket ['su:pəmɑːkɪt] n Supermarkt m

supersede [su:pə'si:d] vt ablösen

supersonic [su:pə'sɒnɪk] adj Überschall-

superstition [su:pə'stɪʃən] n Aberglaube m; **superstitious** [su:pə'stɪʃəs] adj abergläubisch

superstore ['su:pəstɔː*] n Verbrauchermarkt m

supervise ['su:pəvaɪz] vt beaufsichtigen; **supervisor** ['su:pəvaɪzə] n Aufsicht f; (at university) Doktorvater m

supper ['sʌpə*] n Abendessen nt; (late-night snack) Imbiss

supplement ['sʌplɪmənt] n (extra payment) Zuschlag m; (of newspaper) Beilage f ▷ vt ergänzen; **supplementary** [sʌplɪ'mentərɪ] adj zusätzlich

supplier [sə'plaɪə*] n Lieferant(in) m(f); **supply** [sə'plaɪ] vt (deliver) liefern; (drinks, music etc) sorgen für; to ~ sb with sth (provide) jdn mit etw versorgen ▷ n (stock) Vorrat m (of an +dat)

support [sə'pɔːt] n Unterstützung f; (Tech) Stütze f ▷ vt (hold up) tragen, stützen; (provide for) ernähren, unterhalten; (speak in favour of) unterstützen; **he ~s Manchester United** er ist Manchester-United-Fan

suppose [sə'pəʊz] vt (assume) annehmen; **I ~ so** ich denke schon; **I ~ not** wahrscheinlich nicht; **you're not ~d to smoke here** du darfst/Sie dürfen hier nicht rauchen; **supposedly** [sə'pəʊzɪdlɪ] adv angeblich; **supposing** conj angenommen

suppress [sə'pres] vt unterdrücken

surcharge ['sɜːtʃɑːdʒ] n Zuschlag m

sure [ʃʊə*] adj sicher; **I'm (not)** ~ ich bin mir (nicht) sicher; **make** ~ **you lock up** vergiss/vergessen Sie nicht abzuschließen ▷ adv: ~! klar!; ~ **enough** tatsächlich; **surely** adv: ~ **you don't mean it?** das ist nicht dein/Ihr Ernst, oder?

surf [sɜːf] n Brandung f ▷ vt (Sport) surfen ▷ vt: to ~ **the net** im Internet surfen

surface ['sɜːfɪs] n Oberfläche f ▷ vi auftauchen; **surface mail** n: **by** ~ auf dem Land-/Seeweg

surfboard ['sɜːfbɔːd] n Surfbrett nt; **surfer** n Surfer(in) m(f);

surfing n Surfen nt; **to go** ~ surfen gehen

surgeon ['sɜːdʒən] n Chirurg(in) m(f); **surgery** ['sɜːdʒərɪ] n (operation) Operation f; (room) Praxis f, Sprechzimmer nt; (consulting time) Sprechstunde f; **to have** ~ operiert werden

surname ['sɜːneɪm] n Nachname m

surpass [sɜː'pɑːs] vt übertreffen

surplus ['sɜːpləs] n Überschuss m (of an +dat)

surprise [sə'praɪz] n Überraschung f ▷ vt überraschen; **surprising** adj überraschend; **surprisingly** adv überraschenderweise, erstaunlicherweise

surrender [sə'rendə*] vi sich ergeben (to +dat) ▷ vt (weapon, passport) abgeben

surround [sə'raʊnd] vt umgeben; (stand all round) umringen; **surrounding** adj (countryside) umliegend ▷ n ~s pl Umgebung f

survey ['sɜːveɪ] n (opinion poll) Umfrage f; (of literature etc) Überblick m (of über +akk); (of land) Vermessung f ▷ [sɜː'veɪ] vt (look out over) überblicken; (land) vermessen

survive [sə'vaɪv] vt, vi überleben

susceptible [sə'septəbl] adj empfänglich (to für); (Med) anfällig (to für)

sushi ['suːʃɪ] n Sushi nt

suspect ['sʌspekt] n Verdächtige(r) mf ▷ adj verdächtig ▷ [sə'spekt] vt verdächtigen (of +gen); (think likely) vermuten

suspend [sə'spend] vt (from work) suspendieren; (payment) vorübergehend einstellen; (player) sperren; (hang up) aufhängen; **suspender** n (Brit) Strumpfhalter m; **~s** pl (US: for trousers) Hosenträger pl

suspense [səˈspɛns] n Spannung f

suspicious [səˈspɪʃəs] adj misstrauisch (of sb/sth jdm/etw gegenüber); (causing suspicion) verdächtig

SUV abbr = **sport utility vehicle** SUV m, Geländewagen m

swallow [ˈswɒləʊ] n (bird) Schwalbe f ▷ vt, vi schlucken

swam [swæm] pt of **swim**

swamp [swɒmp] n Sumpf m

swan [swɒn] n Schwan m

swap [swɒp] vt, vi tauschen; **to ~ sth for sth** etw gegen etw eintauschen

sway [sweɪ] vi schwanken

swear [swɛəʳ] (**swore**, **sworn**) vi (promise) schwören; (curse) fluchen; **to ~ at sb** jdn beschimpfen; **swear by** vt (have faith in) schwören auf +akk; **swearword** n Fluch m

sweat [swɛt] n Schweiß m ▷ vi schwitzen; **sweatband** n Schweißband n; **sweater** n Pullover m; **sweatshirt** n Sweatshirt n; **sweaty** adj verschwitzt

swede [swiːd] n Steckrübe f

Swede [swiːd] n Schwede m, Schwedin f; **Sweden** n Schweden nt; **Swedish** adj schwedisch ▷ n (language) Schwedisch nt

sweep [swiːp] (**swept**, **swept**) vt, vi (with brush) kehren, fegen; **sweep up** vt (dirt etc) zusammenkehren, zusammenfegen

sweet [swiːt] n (Brit: candy) Bonbon nt; (dessert) Nachtisch m ▷ adj süß; (kind) lieb; **sweet-and-sour** adj süßsauer; **sweetcorn** n Mais m; **sweeten** vt (tea etc) süßen; **sweetener** n (substance) Süßstoff m; **sweet**

potato n Süßkartoffel f

swell [swɛl] (**swelled**, **swollen** o **swelled**) vi: **to ~ (up)** (an)schwellen ▷ adj (US fam) toll; **swelling** n (Med) Schwellung f

sweltering [ˈswɛltərɪŋ] adj (heat) drückend

swept [swɛpt] pt, pp of **sweep**

swift [swɪft] adj schnell

swig [swɪg] n (fam) Schluck m

swim [swɪm] (**swam**, **swum**) vi schwimmen ▷ n: **to go for a ~** schwimmen gehen; **swimmer** n Schwimmer(in) m(f); **swimming** n Schwimmen nt; **to go ~** schwimmen gehen; **swimming cap** n (Brit) Badekappe f; **swimming costume** n (Brit) Badeanzug m; **swimming pool** n Schwimmbad nt; (private, in hotel) Swimmingpool m; **swimming trunks** npl (Brit) Badehose f; **swimsuit** n Badeanzug m

swindle [ˈswɪndl] vt betrügen (out of um)

swine [swaɪn] n (person) Schwein nt; **swine flu** n Schweinegrippe f

swing [swɪŋ] (**swung**, **swung**) vt, vi (object) schwingen ▷ n (for child) Schaukel f

swipe [swaɪp] vt (credit card etc) durchziehen; (fam: steal) klauen; **swipe card** n Magnetkarte f

Swiss [swɪs] adj schweizerisch ▷ n Schweizer(in) m(f)

switch [swɪtʃ] n (Elec) Schalter m ▷ vi (change) wechseln (to zu); **switch off** vt abschalten, ausschalten; **switch on** vt anschalten, einschalten; **switchboard** n (Tel) Vermittlung f

Switzerland [ˈswɪtsələnd] n die Schweiz

swivel [ˈswɪvl] vi sich drehen ▷ vt drehen

swollen [ˈswəʊlən] pp of **swell**

▷ *adj* (*Med*) geschwollen; (*stomach*) aufgebläht

swop [swɒp] *see* **swap**

sword [sɔːd] *n* Schwert *nt*

swore [swɔːʳ] *pt of* **swear**

sworn [swɔːn] *pp of* **swear**

swot [swɒt] *vi* (*Brit fam*) büffeln (*for* für)

swum [swʌm] *pp of* **swim**

swung [swʌŋ] *pt*, *pp of* **swing**

syllable ['sɪləbl] *n* Silbe *f*

syllabus ['sɪləbəs] *n* Lehrplan *m*

symbol ['sɪmbəl] *n* Symbol *nt*; **symbolic** [sɪm'bɒlɪk] *adj* symbolisch; **symbolize** *vt* symbolisieren

symmetrical [sɪ'metrɪkəl] *adj* symmetrisch

sympathetic [sɪmpə'θetɪk] *adj* mitfühlend; (*understanding*) verständnisvoll; **sympathize** ['sɪmpəθaɪz] *vi* mitfühlen (*with sb* mit jdm); **sympathy** ['sɪmpəθɪ] *n* Mitleid *nt*; (*after death*) Beileid *nt*; (*understanding*) Verständnis *nt*

symphony ['sɪmfənɪ] *n* Sinfonie *f*

symptom ['sɪmptəm] *n* (*a. fig*) Symptom *nt*

synagogue ['sɪnəgɒg] *n* Synagoge *f*

synonym ['sɪnənɪm] *n* Synonym *nt*; **synonymous** [sɪ'nɒnɪməs] *adj* synonym (*with* mit)

synthetic [sɪn'θetɪk] *adj* (*material*) synthetisch

syphilis ['sɪfɪlɪs] *n* Syphilis *f*

Syria ['sɪrɪə] *n* Syrien *nt*

syringe [sɪ'rɪndʒ] *n* Spritze *f*

system ['sɪstəm] *n* System *nt*; **systematic** [sɪstə'mætɪk] *adj* systematisch; **system disk** *n* (*Inform*) Systemdiskette *f*; **system(s) software** *n* (*Inform*) Systemsoftware *f*

t

tab [tæb] *n* (*for hanging up coat etc*) Aufhänger *m*; (*Inform*) Tabulator *m*; **to pick up the ~** (*fam*) die Rechnung übernehmen

table ['teɪbl] *n* Tisch *m*; (*list*) Tabelle *f*; **~ of contents** Inhaltsverzeichnis *nt*; **tablecloth** *n* Tischdecke *f*; **tablelamp** *n* Tischlampe *f*; **tablemat** *n* Set *nt*; **tablespoon** *n* Servierlöffel *m*; (*in recipes*) Esslöffel *m*

tablet ['tæblət] *n* (*Med*) Tablette *f*

table tennis ['teɪbltɛnɪs] *n* Tischtennis *nt*; **table wine** *n* Tafelwein *m*

tabloid ['tæblɔɪd] *n* Boulevardzeitung *f*

taboo [tə'buː] *n* Tabu *nt* ▷ *adj* tabu

tacit, tacitly ['tæsɪt, -lɪ] *adj, adv* stillschweigend

tack [tæk] *n* (*small nail*) Stift *m*; (*US: thumb~*) Reißzwecke *f*

tackle ['tækl] n (Sport) Angriff m; (equipment) Ausrüstung f ▷ vt (deal with) in Angriff nehmen; (Sport) angreifen; (verbally) zur Rede stellen (about wegen)

tacky ['tækɪ] adj trashig, heruntergekommen

tact [tækt] n Takt m; **tactful, tactfully** adj, adv taktvoll; **tactic(s)** ['tæktɪk(s)] n(pl) Taktik f; **tactless, tactlessly** ['tæktləs, -lɪ] adj, adv taktlos

tag [tæg] n (label) Schild nt; (with maker's name) Etikett nt

Tahiti [tɑːˈhiːtɪ] n Tahiti nt

tail [teɪl] n Schwanz m; **heads or ~s?** Kopf oder Zahl?; **tailback** n (Brit) Rückstau m; **taillight** n (Auto) Rücklicht nt

tailor ['teɪləʳ] n Schneider(in) m(f)

tailpipe ['teɪlpaɪp] n (US Auto) Auspuffrohr nt

tainted ['teɪntɪd] adj (US: food) verdorben

Taiwan [taɪˈwæn] n Taiwan nt

take [teɪk] (**took, taken**) vt nehmen; (~ along with one) mitnehmen; (~ to a place) bringen; (subtract) abziehen (from von); (capture: person) fassen; (gain, obtain) bekommen; (Fin, Comm) einnehmen; (train, taxi) nehmen, fahren mit; (trip, walk, holiday, exam, course, photo) machen; (bath) nehmen; (phone call) entgegennehmen; (decision, precautions) treffen; (risk) eingehen; (advice, job) annehmen; (consume) zu sich nehmen; (tablets) nehmen; (heat, pain) ertragen; (react to) aufnehmen; (have room for) Platz haben für; **I'll ~ it** (item in shop) ich nehme es; **how long does it ~?** wie lange dauert es?; **it ~s 4 hours** man braucht 4 Stunden; **do you ~ sugar?** nimmst

du/nehmen Sie Zucker?; **I ~ it that** ... ich nehme an, dass ...; **to ~ part in** teilnehmen an; **to ~ place** stattfinden; **take after** vt nachschlagen +dat; **take along** vt mitnehmen; **take apart** vt auseinandernehmen; **take away** vt (remove) wegnehmen (from sb jdm); (subtract) abziehen (from von); **take back** vt (return) zurückbringen; (retract) zurücknehmen; (remind) zurückversetzen (to in +akk); **take down** vt (picture, curtains) abnehmen; (write down) aufschreiben; **take in** vt (understand) begreifen; (give accommodation to) aufnehmen; (deceive) hereinlegen; (include) einschließen; (show, film etc) mitnehmen; **take off** vi (plane) starten ▷ vt (clothing) ausziehen; (hat, lid) abnehmen; (deduct) abziehen; (Brit: imitate) nachmachen; **to take a day off** sich einen Tag freinehmen; **take on** vt (undertake) übernehmen; (employ) einstellen; (Sport) antreten gegen; **take out** vt (wallet etc) herausnehmen; (person, dog) ausführen; (insurance) abschließen; (money from bank) abheben; (book from library) ausleihen; **take over** vt übernehmen ▷ vi: **he took over (from me)** er hat mich abgelöst; **take to** vt: **I've taken to her/it** ich mag sie/es; **to ~ doing sth** (begin) anfangen, etw zu tun; **take up** vt (carpet) hochnehmen; (space) in Anspruch nehmen; (time) in Anspruch nehmen; (hobby) anfangen mit; (new job) antreten; (offer) annehmen

takeaway n (Brit: meal) Essen nt zum Mitnehmen

taken ['teɪkn] pp of **take** ▷ adj

(seat) besetzt; **to be ~ with** angetan sein von

takeoff ['teɪkɒf] n (Aviat) Start m; (imitation) Nachahmung f; **takeout** (US) see **takeaway**; **takeover** n (Comm) Übernahme f

takings ['teɪkɪŋz] npl Einnahmen pl

tale [teɪl] n Geschichte f

talent ['tælənt] n Talent nt; **talented** adj begabt

talk [tɔːk] n (conversation) Gespräch nt; (rumour) Gerede nt; (to audience) Vortrag m ▷ vi sprechen, reden; (have conversation) sich unterhalten; **to ~ to** (o **with**) sb (**about sth**) mit jdm (über etw akk) sprechen ▷ vt (language) sprechen; (nonsense) reden; (politics, business) reden über +akk; **to ~ sb into doing/out of doing sth** jdn überreden/jdm ausreden, etw zu tun; **talk over** vt besprechen

talkative adj gesprächig; **talk show** n Talkshow f

tall [tɔːl] adj groß; (building, tree) hoch; **he is 6ft ~** er ist 1,80m groß

tame [teɪm] adj zahm; (joke, story) fade ▷ vt (animal) zähmen

tampon ['tæmpɒn] n Tampon m

tan [tæn] n (on skin) (Sonnen)bräune f; **to get/have a ~** braun werden/sein ▷ vi braun werden

tangerine [tændʒə'riːn] n Mandarine f

tango ['tæŋgəʊ] n Tango m

tank [tæŋk] n Tank m; (for fish) Aquarium nt; (Mil) Panzer m

tanker ['tæŋkə*] n (ship) Tanker m; (vehicle) Tankwagen m

tanned [tænd] adj (by sun) braun

tantalizing ['tæntəlaɪzɪŋ] adj verlockend

Tanzania [tænzə'nɪə] n Tansania nt

tap [tæp] n (for water) Hahn m ▷ vt, vi (strike) klopfen; **to ~ sb on the shoulder** jdm auf die Schulter klopfen; **tap-dance** vi steppen

tape [teɪp] n (adhesive ~) Klebeband nt; (for tape recorder) Tonband nt; (cassette) Kassette f; (video) Video nt ▷ vt (record) aufnehmen; **tape up** vt (parcel) zukleben; **tape measure** n Maßband nt; **tape recorder** n Tonbandgerät nt

tapestry ['tæpɪstrɪ] n Wandteppich m

tap water ['tæpwɔːtə*] n Leitungswasser nt

target ['tɑːgɪt] n Ziel nt; (board) Zielscheibe f; **target group** n Zielgruppe f

tariff ['tærɪf] n (price list) Preisliste f; (tax) Zoll m

tarmac ['tɑːmæk] n (Aviat) Rollfeld nt

tart [tɑːt] n (fruit ~) (Obst)kuchen m; (small) (Obst)törtchen nt; (fam, pej: prostitute) Nutte f; (fam: promiscuous person) Schlampe f

tartan ['tɑːtən] n Schottenkaro nt; (material) Schottenstoff m

tartar(e) sauce ['tɑːtə'sɔːs] n Remouladensoße f

task [tɑːsk] n Aufgabe f; (duty) Pflicht f; **taskbar** n (Inform) Taskbar f

Tasmania [tæz'meɪnɪə] n Tasmanien nt

taste [teɪst] n Geschmack m; (sense of ~) Geschmackssinn m; (small quantity) Kostprobe f; **it has a strange ~** es schmeckt komisch ▷ vt schmecken; (try) probieren ▷ vi (food) schmecken (of nach); **to ~ good/strange** gut/komisch schmecken; **tasteful, tastefully** adj, adv geschmackvoll; **tasteless, tastelessly** adj, adv geschmacklos; **tasty** adj lecker

tattered ['tætəd] adj (clothes) zerlumpt; (fam: person) angespannt; **I'm absolutely ~** ich bin mit den Nerven am Ende

tattoo [tə'tu:] n, pp of **teach**

Taurus ['tɔ:rəs] n (Astr) Stier m

tax [tæks] n Steuer f (on auf +akk) ▷ vt besteuern; **taxable** adj steuerpflichtig; **taxation** [tæk'seɪʃən] n Besteuerung f; **tax bracket** n Steuerklasse f; **tax disc** n (Brit Auto) Steuermarke f; **tax-free** adj steuerfrei

taxi ['tæksɪ] n Taxi nt ▷ vi (plane) rollen; **taxi driver** n Taxifahrer(in) m(f); **taxi rank** (Brit), **taxi stand** n Taxistand m

tax return ['tæksrɪ'tɜ:n] n Steuererklärung f

tea [ti:] n Tee m; (afternoon ~) ≈ Kaffee und Kuchen; (meal) frühes Abendessen; **teabag** n Teebeutel m; **tea break** n (Tee)pause f

teach [ti:tʃ] (**taught**, **taught**) vt (person, subject) unterrichten; **to ~ sb (how) to dance** jdm das Tanzen beibringen ▷ vi unterrichten; **teacher** n Lehrer(in) m(f); **teaching** n (activity) Unterrichten nt; (profession) Lehrberuf m

teacup ['ti:kʌp] n Teetasse f

team [ti:m] n (Sport) Mannschaft f, Team nt; **teamwork** n Teamarbeit f

teapot ['ti:pɒt] n Teekanne f

tear [tɪə*] n (in eye) Träne f

tear [tɛə*] n (tore, torn) vt zerreißen; **to ~ a muscle** sich einen Muskel zerren ▷ vi (material etc) Riss m; **tear down** vt (building) abreißen; **tear up** vt (paper) zerreißen

tearoom ['ti:rum] n Teestube f,

Café, in dem in erster Linie Tee serviert wird

tease [ti:z] vt (person) necken (about wegen)

tea set n Teeservice nt; **teashop** n Teestube f; **teaspoon** n Teelöffel m; **tea towel** n Geschirrtuch nt

technical ['teknɪkəl] adj technisch; (knowledge, term, dictionary) Fach-; **technically** adv technisch; **technique** [tek'ni:k] n Technik f

techno ['teknəʊ] n Techno f

technological [teknə'lɒdʒɪkəl] adj technologisch; **technology** [tek'nɒlədʒɪ] n Technologie f, Technik f

tedious ['ti:dɪəs] adj langweilig

teen(age) ['ti:n(eɪdʒ)] adj (fashions etc) Teenager-; **teenager** n Teenager m; **teens** [ti:nz] npl: **in one's ~** im Teenageralter

teeth [ti:θ] pl of **tooth**

teetotal ['ti:təʊtl] adj abstinent

telegraph pole ['telɪgrɑ:fpəʊl] n (Brit) Telegrafenmast m

telephone ['telɪfəʊn] n Telefon nt ▷ vi telefonieren ▷ vt anrufen; **telephone banking** n Telefonbanking nt; **telephone book** n Telefonbuch nt; **telephone booth, telephone box** (Brit) n Telefonzelle f; **telephone call** n Telefonanruf m; **telephone directory** n Telefonbuch nt; **telephone number** n Telefonnummer f

telephoto lens ['telɪfəʊtəʊ'lenz] n Teleobjektiv nt

telescope ['telɪskəʊp] n Teleskop nt

televise ['telɪvaɪz] vt im Fernsehen übertragen; **television** ['telɪvɪʒən] n Fernsehen nt; **television programme** n Fernsehsendung f; **television (set)** n Fernseher m

teleworking ['teliwɜːkiŋ] n
Telearbeit f

tell [tel] n (told, told) vt (say,
inform) sagen (sb sth jdm etw);
(story) erzählen; (truth) sagen;
(difference) erkennen; (reveal secret)
verraten; **to ~ sb about sth** jdm
von etw erzählen; **to ~ sth from
sth** etw von etw unterscheiden
▷ vi (be sure) wissen; **tell apart** vt
unterscheiden; **tell off** vt
schimpfen

telling adj aufschlussreich

telly ['teli] n (Brit fam) Glotze f; **on
(the) ~** in der Glotze

temp [temp] n Aushilfskraft f
▷ vi als Aushilfskraft arbeiten

temper ['tempə°] n (anger) Wut f;
(mood) Laune f; **to lose one's ~** die
Beherrschung verlieren; **to have a
bad ~** jähzornig sein;
temperamental
[tempərə'mentl] adj (moody)
launisch

temperature ['temprɪtʃə°] n
Temperatur f; (Med: high ~) Fieber
nt; **to have a ~** Fieber haben

temple ['templ] n Tempel m;
(Anat) Schläfe f

temporarily ['tempərərɪlɪ] adv
vorübergehend; **temporary**
['tempərərɪ] adj vorübergehend;
(road, building) provisorisch

tempt [tempt] vt in Versuchung
führen; **I'm ~ed to accept** ich bin
versucht anzunehmen;
temptation [temp'teɪʃən] n
Versuchung f; **tempting** adj
verlockend

ten [ten] num zehn ▷ n Zehn f;
see also **eight**

tenant ['tenənt] n Mieter(in)
m(f); (of land) Pächter(in) m(f)

tend [tend] vi: **to ~ to do sth**
(person) dazu neigen, etw zu tun;
to ~ towards neigen zu;
tendency ['tendənsɪ] n Tendenz

f; **to have a ~ to do sth** (person)
dazu neigen, etw zu tun

tender ['tendə°] adj (loving)
zärtlich; (sore) empfindlich; (meat)
zart

tendon ['tendən] n Sehne f

Tenerife [tenə'riːf] n Teneriffa nt

tenner ['tenə°] n (Brit fam: note)
Zehnpfundschein m; (amount) zehn
Pfund

tennis ['tenɪs] n Tennis nt;
tennis ball n Tennisball m; **tennis
court** n Tennisplatz m; **tennis
racket** n Tennisschläger m

tenor ['tenə°] n Tenor m

tenpin bowling, **tenpins** (US)
['tenpɪn'bəʊlɪŋ, 'tenpɪnz] n
Bowling nt

tense [tens] adj angespannt;
(stretched tight) gespannt; **tension**
['tenʃən] n Spannung f; (strain)
Anspannung f

tent [tent] n Zelt nt

tenth [tenθ] adj zehnte(r, s) ▷ n
(fraction) Zehntel nt; see also **eighth**

tent peg ['tentpeg] n Hering m;
tent pole n Zeltstange f

term [tɜːm] n (in school, at
university) Trimester nt; (expression)
Ausdruck m; **~s** pl (conditions)
Bedingungen pl; **to be on good ~s
with sb** mit jdm gut auskommen;
to come to ~s with sth sich mit
etw abfinden; **in the long/short
~** langfristig/kurzfristig; **in ~s
of ...** was ... betrifft

terminal ['tɜːmɪnl] n (bus ~ etc)
Endstation f; (Aviat) Terminal m;
(Inform) Terminal nt; (Elec) Pol m
▷ adj (Med) unheilbar; **terminally**
adv (ill) unheilbar

terminate ['tɜːmɪneɪt] vt (contract) lösen; (pregnancy) abbrechen
▷ vi (train, bus) enden

terminology [tɜːmɪ'nɒlədʒɪ] n
Terminologie f

terrace ['terəs] n (of houses)

Häuserreihe f; (in garden etc)
Terrasse f; **terraced** adj (garden)
terrassenförmig angelegt;
terraced house n (Brit)
Reihenhaus nt
terrible ['terəbl] adj schrecklich
terrific [tə'rɪfɪk] adj (very good)
fantastisch
terrify ['terɪfaɪ] vt erschrecken;
to be terrified schreckliche Angst
haben (of vor +dat)
territory ['terɪtərɪ] n Gebiet nt
terror ['terə°] n Schrecken m;
(Pol) Terror m; **terrorism** n
Terrorismus m; **terrorist** n
Terrorist(in) m(f)
test [test] n Test m, Klassenarbeit
f; (driving ~) Prüfung f; **to put to
the ~** auf die Probe stellen ▷ vt
testen, prüfen; (patience, courage
etc) auf die Probe stellen
Testament ['testəmənt] n: **the
Old/New ~** das Alte/Neue
Testament
test-drive ['testdraɪv] vt Probe
fahren
testicle ['testɪkl] n Hoden m
testify ['testɪfaɪ] vi (Jur)
aussagen
test tube ['testtju:b] n
Reagenzglas nt
tetanus ['tetənəs] n Tetanus m
text [tekst] n Text m; (of
document) Wortlaut m; (sent by
mobile phone) SMS f ▷ vt (message)
simsen, SMSen; **to ~ sb**
simsen, jdm eine SMS schicken;
I'll ~ it to you ich schicke es dir per
SMS
textbook n Lehrbuch nt
texting ['tekstɪŋ] n SMS-
Messaging nt; **text message** n
SMS f; **text messaging** n
SMS-Messaging nt
texture ['tekstʃə°] n
Beschaffenheit f
Thailand ['taɪlænd] n Thailand nt

Thames [temz] n Themse f
than [ðæn] prep, conj als;
bigger/faster ~ me
größer/schneller als ich; **I'd rather
walk ~ drive** ich gehe lieber zu
Fuß als mit dem Auto
thank [θæŋk] vt danken +dat;
~ you danke; **~ you very much**
vielen Dank; **thankful** adj
dankbar; **thankfully** adv (luckily)
zum Glück; **thankless** adj
undankbar; **thanks** npl Dank m;
~ dankel; **~ to dank +gen

● **THANKSGIVING DAY**
●
● **Thanksgiving (Day)** ist ein
● Feiertag in den USA, der auf den
● vierten Donnerstag im
● November fällt. Er soll daran
● erinnern, wie die Pilgerväter die
● gute Ernte im Jahre 1621
● feierten. In Kanada gibt es einen
● ähnlichen Erntedanktag (der
● aber nichts mit den Pilgervätern
● zu tun hat) am zweiten Montag
● im Oktober.

○ **KEYWORD**

that [ðæt, ðət] adj (demonstrative)
(pl those) der/die/das, jene(r, s);
that one das da
▷ pron 1 (demonstrative) (pl those)
das; **who's/what's that?** wer ist
da/was ist das?; **is that you?** bist
du/sind Sie das?; **that's what he
said** genau das hat er gesagt;
what happened after that? was
passierte danach?; **that is** das
heißt
2 (relative) (subj) der/die/das, die;
(direct obj) den/die/das, die;
(indirect obj) dem/der/dem, denen;
all (that) I have alles, was ich
habe
3 (relative) (of time); **the day (that)**

an dem Tag, als; **the winter (that) he came** in dem Winter, in dem er kam
▷ *conj* dass; **he thought that I was ill** er dachte, dass ich krank sei, er dachte, ich sei krank
▷ *adv* (*demonstrative*) so; **I can't work that much** ich kann nicht so viel arbeiten

that's [ðæts] *contr of* **that is; that has**

thaw [θɔː] *vi* tauen; (*frozen food*) auftauen ▷ *vt* auftauen lassen

 KEYWORD

the [ðə, ði:] *def art* 1 der/die/das; **to play the piano/violin** Klavier/Geige spielen; **I'm going to the butcher's/the cinema** ich gehe zum Fleischer/ins Kino; **Elizabeth the First** Elisabeth die Erste
2 (+*adj to form noun*) das, die; **the rich and the poor** die Reichen und die Armen
3 (*in comparisons*) **the more he works the more he earns** je mehr er arbeitet, desto mehr verdient er

theater (*US*), **theatre** ['θɪətə°] *n* Theater *nt*; (*for lectures etc*) Saal *m*

theft [θeft] *n* Diebstahl *m*

their [ðeə°] *adj* ihr; (*unidentified person*) sein; **they cleaned ~ teeth** sie putzten sich die Zähne; **someone has left ~ umbrella here** jemand hat seinen Schirm hier vergessen; **theirs** *pron* ihre(r, s); (*unidentified person*) seine(r, s); **it's ~** es gehört ihnen; **a friend of ~** ein Freund von ihnen; **someone has left ~ here** jemand hat seins hier liegen lassen

them [ðem, ðəm] *pron* (*direct object*) sie; (*indirect object*) ihnen;

(*unidentified person*) ihn/ihm, sie/ihr; **do you know ~?** kennst du/kennen Sie sie?; **can you help ~?** kannst du/können Sie ihnen helfen?; **it's ~** sie sind's; **if anyone has a problem you should help ~** wenn jemand ein Problem hat, solltest du/sollten Sie ihm helfen

theme [θiːm] *n* Thema *nt*; (*Mus*) Motiv *nt*; **~ park** Themenpark *m*; **~ song** Titelmusik *f*

themselves [ðəm'selvz] *pron* sich; **they hurt ~** sie haben sich verletzt; **they ~ were not there** sie selbst waren nicht da; **they did it ~** sie haben es selbst gemacht; **they are not dangerous in ~** an sich sind sie nicht gefährlich; (**all**) **by ~** allein

then [ðen] *adv* (*at that time*) damals; (*next*) dann; (*therefore*) also; (*furthermore*) ferner; **from ~ on** von da an; **by ~** bis dahin ▷ *adj* damalig

theoretical, **theoretically** [θɪə'retɪkəl, -l] *adj*, *adv* theoretisch

theory ['θɪərɪ] *n* Theorie *f*; **in ~** theoretisch

therapy ['θerəpɪ] *n* Therapie *f*

 KEYWORD

there [ðeə°] *adv* 1 **there is/there are** es o da ist/sind; (*there exists/exist also*) es gibt; **there are 3 of them** (*people, things*) es gibt 3 davon; **there has been an accident** da war ein Unfall
2 (*place*) da, dort; (*direction*) dahin, dorthin; **put it in/on there** leg es so dahinein/dorthinauf
3 **there, there** (*esp to child*) na, na

thereabouts *adv* (*approximately*) so ungefähr; **therefore** *adv* daher, deshalb

thermometer [θə'mɒmɪtə*] n
Thermometer nt

Thermos® ['θɜːməs] n: ~ (**flask**)
Thermosflasche® f

these [ðiːz] pron, adj diese; **I
don't like ~ apples** ich mag diese
Äpfel nicht; ~ **are not my books**
das sind nicht meine Bücher

thesis ['θiːsɪs] (pl **theses**) n (for
PhD) Doktorarbeit f

they [ðeɪ] pron pl sie; (people in
general) man; (unidentified person)
er/sie; ~ **are rich** sie sind reich;
~ **say that ...** man sagt, dass ...; **if
anyone looks at this, ~ will see
that ...** wenn sich jemand dies
ansieht, wird er erkennen, dass ...

they'd [ðeɪd] contr of **they had**;
they would

they'll [ðeɪl] contr of **they will**;
they shall

they've [ðeɪv] contr of **they have**

thick [θɪk] adj dick; (fog) dicht;
(liquid) dickflüssig; (fam: stupid)
dumm; **thicken** vi (fog) dichter
werden; (sauce) dick werden ▷ vt
(sauce) eindicken

thief [θiːf] (pl **thieves**) n
Dieb(in) m(f)

thigh [θaɪ] n Oberschenkel m

thimble ['θɪmbl] n Fingerhut m

thin [θɪn] adj dünn

thing [θɪŋ] n Ding nt; (affair)
Sache f; **my ~s** pl meine Sachen pl;
how are ~s? wie geht's?; **I can't
see a ~** ich kann nichts sehen; **he
knows a ~ or two about cars** er
kennt sich mit Autos aus

think [θɪŋk] (**thought, thought**)
vt, vi denken; (believe) meinen; **I
~ so** ich denke schon; **I don't ~ so**
ich glaube nicht; **think about** vt
denken an +akk; (reflect on)
nachdenken über +akk; (have
opinion of) halten von; **think of** vt
denken an +akk; (devise) sich
ausdenken; (have opinion of) halten

von; (remember) sich erinnern an
+akk; **think over** vt überdenken;
think up vt sich ausdenken

third [θɜːd] adj dritte(r, s); **the
Third World** die Dritte Welt ▷ n
(fraction) Drittel nt; **in ~ (gear)** im
dritten Gang; see also **eighth**;
thirdly adv drittens; **third-party
insurance** n Haftpflichtversicherung f

thirst [θɜːst] n Durst m (for nach);
thirsty adj: **to be ~** Durst haben

thirteen ['θɜː'tiːn] num dreizehn
▷ n Dreizehn f; see also **eight**;
thirteenth adj dreizehnte(r, s);
see also **eighth**; **thirtieth** ['θɜːtɪɪθ]
adj dreißigste(r, s); see also **eighth**;
thirty ['θɜːtɪ] num dreißig;
~-one einunddreißig ▷ n Dreißig
f; **to be in one's thirties** in den
Dreißigern sein; see also **eight**

KEYWORD

this [ðɪs] adj (demonstrative) (pl
these) diese(r, s); **this evening**
heute Abend; **this one** diese(r, s)
(da)
▷ pron (demonstrative) (pl these)
dies, das; **who/what is this?**
wer/was ist das?; **this is where I
live** hier wohne ich; **this is what
he said** das hat er gesagt; **this is
Mr Brown** dies ist Mr Brown; (on
telephone) hier ist Mr Brown
▷ adv (demonstrative) **this
high/long** etc so groß/lang etc

thistle ['θɪsl] n Distel f

thong [θɒŋ] n String m

thorn [θɔːn] n Dorn m, Stachel m

thorough ['θʌrə] adj gründlich;
thoroughly adv gründlich; (agree
etc) völlig

those [ðəʊz] pron die da, jene;
~ **who** diejenigen, die ▷ adj die,
jene

though [ðəʊ] *conj* obwohl; **as ~** als ob ▷ *adv* aber

thought [θɔːt] *pt, pp of* **think** ▷ *n* Gedanke *m*; *(thinking)* Überlegung *f*; **thoughtful** *adj (kind)* rücksichtsvoll; *(attentive)* aufmerksam; *(in Gedanken versunken)* nachdenklich; **thoughtless** *adj (unkind)* rücksichtslos, gedankenlos

thousand ['θaʊzənd] *num:* **(one) ~, a ~** tausend; **five ~** fünftausend; **~s of** Tausende von

thrash [θræʃ] *vt (hit)* verprügeln; *(defeat)* vernichtend schlagen

thread [θred] *n* Faden *m* ▷ *vt (needle)* einfädeln; *(beads)* auffädeln

threat [θret] *n* Drohung *f*; *(danger)* Bedrohung *f (to für)*; **threaten** *vt* bedrohen; **threatening** *adj* bedrohlich

three [θriː] *num* drei ▷ *n* Drei *f*; *see also* **eight**; **three-dimensional** *adj* dreidimensional; **three-piece suit** *n* Anzug *m* mit Weste; **three-quarters** *npl* drei Viertel *pl*

threshold ['θreʃhəʊld] *n* Schwelle *f*

threw [θruː] *pt of* **throw**

thrifty ['θrɪftɪ] *adj* sparsam

thrilled [θrɪld] *adj:* **to be ~ (with sth)** sich (über etw *akk*) riesig freuen; **thriller** *n* Thriller *m*; **thrilling** *adj* aufregend

thrive [θraɪv] *vi* gedeihen *(on* bei*)*; *(fig, business)* florieren

throat [θrəʊt] *n* Hals *m*, Kehle *f*

throbbing ['θrɒbɪŋ] *adj (pain, headache)* pochend

thrombosis [θrɒm'bəʊsɪs] *n* Thrombose *f*; **deep vein ~** tiefe Venenthrombose *f*

throne [θrəʊn] *n* Thron *m*

through [θruː] *prep (place)* durch; *(time)* während +*gen*; *(because of)* aus, durch; *(US: up to and including)* bis;

arranged ~ him durch ihn arrangiert ▷ *adv* durch; **to put sb ~** *(Tel)* jdn verbinden *(to* mit*)* ▷ *adj (ticket, train)* durchgehend; **~ flight** Direktflug *m*; **to be ~ with sb/sth** mit jdm/etw fertig sein;

throughout [θruː'aʊt] *prep (place)* überall in +*dat*; *(time)* während +*gen*; **~ the night** die ganze Nacht hindurch ▷ *adv* überall; *(time)* die ganze Zeit

throw [θrəʊ] *(threw, thrown) vt* werfen; *(rider)* abwerfen; *(party)* geben; **to ~ sth to sb, to ~ sb sth** jdm etw zuwerfen; **I was ~n by his question** seine Frage hat mich aus dem Konzept gebracht ▷ *n* Wurf *m*; **throw away** *vt* wegwerfen; **throw in** *vt (include)* dazugeben; **throw out** *vt (unwanted object)* wegwerfen; *(person)* hinauswerfen *(of* aus*)*; **throw up** *vt, vi (fam: vomit)* übergeben; **throw-in** *n* Einwurf *m*

thrown [θrəʊn] *pp of* **throw**

thru (US) *see* **through**

thrush [θrʌʃ] *n* Drossel *f*

thrust [θrʌst] *(thrust, thrust) vt, vi (push)* stoßen

thruway ['θruːweɪ] *n (US)* Schnellstraße *f*

thumb [θʌm] *n* Daumen *m* ▷ *vt:* **to ~ a lift** per Anhalter fahren; **thumbtack** *n (US)* Reißzwecke *f*

thunder ['θʌndə'] *n* Donner *m* ▷ *vi* donnern; **thunderstorm** *n* Gewitter *nt*

Thur(s) *abbr* = **Thursday** Do.

Thursday ['θɜːzdɪ] *n* Donnerstag *m*; *see also* **Tuesday**

thus [ðʌs] *adv (in this way)* so; *(therefore)* somit, also

thyme [taɪm] *n* Thymian *m*

Tibet [tɪ'bet] *n* Tibet *nt*

tick [tɪk] *n (Brit: mark)* Häkchen *nt* ▷ *vt (name)* abhaken; *(box, answer)* ankreuzen ▷ *vi (clock)* ticken

ticket ['tɪkɪt] n (for train, bus) (Fahr)karte f; (plane ~) Flugschein m, Ticket nt; (for theatre, match, museum etc) (Eintritts)karte f; (price ~) (Preis)schild nt; (raffle ~) Los nt; (for car park) Parkschein m; (for traffic offence) Strafzettel m; **ticket collector, ticket inspector** (Brit) n Fahrkartenkontrolleur(in) m(f); **ticket machine** n (for public transport) Fahrscheinautomat m; (in car park) Parkscheinautomat m; **ticket office** n (Rail) Fahrkartenschalter m; (Theat) Kasse f

tickle ['tɪkl] vt kitzeln; **ticklish** ['tɪklɪʃ] adj kitzlig

tide [taɪd] n Gezeiten pl; **the ~ is in/out** es ist Flut/Ebbe

tidy ['taɪdɪ] adj ordentlich ▷ vt aufräumen; **tidy up** vt, vi aufräumen

tie [taɪ] n (neck~) Krawatte f; (Sport) Unentschieden nt; (bond) Bindung f ▷ vt (attach, do up) binden (to an +akk); (~ together) zusammenbinden; (knot) machen ▷ vi (Sport) unentschieden spielen; **tie down** vt festbinden (to an +dat); (fig) binden; **tie up** vt (dog) anbinden; (parcel) verschnüren; (shoelace) binden; (boat) festmachen; **I'm tied up** (fig) ich bin beschäftigt

tiger ['taɪgə] n Tiger m

tight [taɪt] adj (clothes) eng; (knot) fest; (screw, lid) fest sitzend; (control, security measures) streng; (timewise) knapp; (schedule) eng ▷ adv (shut) fest; (pull) stramm; **hold ~** festhalten!; **sleep ~** schlaf gut!; **tighten** vt (knot, rope, screw) anziehen; (belt) enger machen; (restrictions, control) verschärfen; **tights** npl (Brit) Strumpfhose f

tile [taɪl] n (on roof) Dachziegel m; (on wall, floor) Fliese f; **tiled** adj (roof) Ziegel-; (floor, wall) gefliest

till [tɪl] n Kasse f ▷ prep, conj see **until**

tilt [tɪlt] vt kippen; (head) neigen ▷ vi sich neigen

time [taɪm] n Zeit f; (occasion) Mal nt; (Mus) Takt m; **local ~** Ortszeit; **what ~ is it?, what's the ~?** wie spät ist es?, wie viel Uhr ist es?; **to take one's ~** (over sth) sich (bei etw) Zeit lassen; **to have a good ~** Spaß haben; **in two weeks' ~** in zwei Wochen; **at ~s** manchmal; **at the same ~** gleichzeitig; **all the ~** die ganze Zeit; **by the ~ he ...** bis er ...; (in past) als er ...; **for the ~ being** vorläufig; **in ~** (not late) rechtzeitig; **on ~** pünktlich; **the first ~** das erste Mal; **this ~** diesmal; **five ~s** fünfmal; **five ~s six** fünf mal sechs; **four ~s a year** viermal im Jahr; **three at a ~** drei auf einmal ▷ vt (with stopwatch) stoppen; **you ~d that well** das hast du/haben Sie gut getimt; **time difference** n Zeitunterschied m; **time limit** n Frist f; **timer** n Timer m; (switch) Schaltuhr f; **time-saving** adj zeitsparend; **time switch** n Schaltuhr f; **timetable** n (for public transport) Fahrplan m; (school) Stundenplan m; **time zone** n Zeitzone f

timid ['tɪmɪd] adj ängstlich

timing ['taɪmɪŋ] n (coordination) Timing nt, zeitliche Abstimmung

tin [tɪn] n (metal) Blech nt; (Brit: can) Dose f; **tinfoil** n Alufolie f; **tinned** [tɪnd] adj (Brit) aus der Dose; **tin opener** n (Brit) Dosenöffner m

tinsel ['tɪnsəl] n ~ Lametta nt

tint [tɪnt] n (Farb)ton m; (in hair) Tönung f; **tinted** adj getönt

tiny ['taɪnɪ] *adj* winzig

tip [tɪp] *n* (*money*) Trinkgeld *nt*; (*hint*) Tipp *m*; (*end*) Spitze *f*; (*of cigarette*) Filter *m*; (*Brit: rubbish ~*) Müllkippe *f* ▷ *vt* (*waiter*) Trinkgeld geben +*dat*; **tip over** *vt, vi* (*overturn*) umkippen

tipsy ['tɪpsɪ] *adj* beschwipst

tiptoe ['tɪptəʊ] *n*: **on ~** auf Zehenspitzen

tire ['taɪə] *n* (US) *see* **tyre** ▷ *vt* müde machen ▷ *vi* müde werden; **tired** *adj* müde; **to be ~ of sb/sth** jdn/etw satthaben; **to be ~ of doing sth** es satthaben, etw zu tun; **tireless, tirelessly** *adv* unermüdlich; **tiresome** *adj* lästig; **tiring** *adj* ermüdend

Tirol [tɪ'rəʊl] *see* **Tyrol**

tissue ['tɪʃuː] *n* (*Anat*) Gewebe *nt*; (*paper handkerchief*) Tempotaschentuch® *nt*, Papier(taschen)tuch *nt*; **tissue paper** *n* Seidenpapier *nt*

tit [tɪt] *n* (*bird*) Meise *f*; (*fam: breast*) Titte *f*

title ['taɪtl] *n* Titel *m*

titter ['tɪtə] *vi* kichern

 KEYWORD

to [tuː, tə] *prep* **1** (*direction*) zu, nach; **I go to France/school** ich gehe nach Frankreich/zur Schule; **to the left** nach links

2 (*as far as*) bis

3 (*with expressions of time*) vor; **a quarter to 5** Viertel vor 5

4 (*for, of*) für; **secretary to the director** Sekretärin des Direktors

5 (*expressing indirect object*) **to give sth to sb** jdm etw geben; **to talk to sb** mit jdm sprechen; **I sold it to a friend** ich habe es einem Freund verkauft

6 (*in relation to*) zu; **30 miles to the gallon** 30 Meilen pro Gallone

7 (*purpose, result*) zu; **to my surprise** zu meiner Überraschung ▷ *with vb* **1** (*infin*) **to go/eat** gehen/essen; **to want to do sth** etw tun wollen; **to try/start to do sth** versuchen/anfangen, etw zu tun; **he has a lot to lose** er hat viel zu verlieren

2 (*with vb omitted*) **I don't want to** ich will (es) nicht

3 (*purpose, result*) um; **I did it to help you** ich tat es, um dir/Ihnen zu helfen

4 (*after adj etc*) **ready to use** gebrauchsfertig; **too old/young to ...** zu alt/jung, um ... zu ... ▷ *adv*: **push/pull the door to** die Tür zuschieben/zuziehen

toad [təʊd] *n* Kröte *f*; **toadstool** *n* Giftpilz *m*

toast [təʊst] *n* (*bread, drink*) Toast *m*; **a piece** (*o* **slice**) **of ~** eine Scheibe Toast; **to propose a ~ to sb** einen Toast auf jdn ausbringen ▷ *vt* (*bread*) toasten; (*person*) trinken auf +*akk*; **toaster** *n* Toaster *m*

tobacco [tə'bækəʊ] (*pl* **-es**) *n* Tabak *m*; **tobacconist's** [tə'bækənɪsts] *n*: **~ (shop)** Tabakladen *m*

toboggan [tə'bɒgən] *n* Schlitten *m*

today [tə'deɪ] *adv* heute; **a week ~** heute in einer Woche; **~'s newspaper** die Zeitung von heute

toddler ['tɒdlə] *n* Kleinkind *nt*

toe [təʊ] *n* Zehe *f*, Zeh *m*; **toenail** *n* Zehennagel *m*

toffee ['tɒfɪ] *n* (*sweet*) Karamellbonbon *nt*; **toffee apple** *n* kandierter Apfel; **toffee-nosed** *adj* hochnäsig

tofu ['təʊfuː] *n* Tofu *m*

together [tə'geðə] *adv*

zusammen; **I tied them ~** ich habe sie zusammengebunden

toilet ['tɔɪlət] n Toilette f; **to go to the ~** auf die Toilette gehen; **toilet bag** n Kulturbeutel m; **toilet paper** n Toilettenpapier nt; **toiletries** ['tɔɪlətrɪz] npl Toilettenartikel pl; **toilet roll** n Rolle f Toilettenpapier

token ['təukən] n Marke f; (in casino) Spielmarke f; (voucher, gift ~) Gutschein m; (sign) Zeichen nt

Tokyo ['təukɪəu] n Tokio nt

told [təuld] pt, pp of **tell**

tolerant ['tɒlərənt] adj tolerant (of gegenüber); **tolerate** ['tɒləreɪt] vt tolerieren; (noise, pain, heat) ertragen

toll [təul] n (charge) Gebühr f; **the death ~** die Zahl der Toten; **toll-free** adj, adv (US Tel) gebührenfrei; **toll road** n gebührenpflichtige Straße

tomato [tə'mɑːtəu] (pl **-es**) n Tomate f; **tomato juice** n Tomatensaft m; **tomato ketchup** n Tomatenketchup m o nt; **tomato sauce** n Tomatensoße f; (Brit: ketchup) Tomatenketchup m o nt

tomb [tuːm] n Grabmal nt; **tombstone** n Grabstein m

tomorrow [tə'mɒrəu] adv morgen; **~ morning** morgen früh; **~ evening** morgen Abend; **the day after ~** übermorgen; **a week (from) ~/~ week** morgen in einer Woche

ton [tʌn] n (Brit) Tonne f (1016 kg); (US) Tonne f (907 kg); **~s of books** (fam) eine Menge Bücher

tone [təun] n Ton m; **tone down** vt mäßigen; **toner** ['təunə*] n (for printer) Toner m; **toner cartridge** n Tonerpatrone f

tongs [tɒŋz] npl Zange f; (curling ~) Lockenstab m

tongue [tʌŋ] n Zunge f

tonic ['tɒnɪk] n (Med) Stärkungsmittel nt; **~ (water)** Tonic nt; **gin and ~** Gin m Tonic

tonight [tə'naɪt] adv heute Abend; (during night) heute Nacht

tonsils ['tɒnslz] n Mandeln pl; **tonsillitis** [tɒnsɪ'laɪtɪs] n Mandelentzündung f

too [tuː] adv zu; (also) auch; **~ fast** zu schnell; **~ much/many** zu viel/viele; **me ~** ich auch; **she liked it ~** ihr gefiel es auch

took [tuk] pt of **take**

tool [tuːl] n Werkzeug nt; **toolbar** n (Inform) Symbolleiste f; **toolbox** n Werkzeugkasten m

tooth [tuːθ] (pl **teeth**) n Zahn m; **toothache** n Zahnschmerzen pl; **toothbrush** n Zahnbürste f; **toothpaste** n Zahnpasta f; **toothpick** n Zahnstocher m

top [tɒp] n (of tower, class, company etc) Spitze f; (of mountain) Gipfel m; (of tree) Krone f; (of street) oberes Ende; (of tube, pen) Kappe f; (of box) Deckel m; (of bikini) Oberteil nt; (sleeveless) Top nt; **at the ~ of the page** oben auf der Seite; **at the ~ of the league** an der Spitze der Liga; **on ~** oben; **on ~ of** auf +dat; (in addition to) zusätzlich zu; **in ~ (gear)** im höchsten Gang; **over the ~** übertrieben ▷ adj (floor, shelf) oberste(r, s); (price, note) höchste(r, s); (best) Spitzen-; (pupil, school) beste(r, s) ▷ vt (exceed) übersteigen; (be better than) übertreffen; (league) an erster Stelle liegen in +dat; **~ped with cream** mit Sahne obendrauf; **top up** vt auffüllen; **can I top you up?** darf ich Ihr nachschenken?

topic ['tɒpɪk] n Thema nt; **topical** adj aktuell

topless ['tɒpləs] *adj, adv* oben ohne

topping ['tɒpɪŋ] *n* (on top of pizza, ice-cream etc) Belag *m*, Garnierung *f*

top-secret ['tɒp'si:krət] *adj* streng geheim

torch [tɔ:tʃ] *n* (Brit) Taschenlampe *f*

tore [tɔ:ʳ] *pt of* **tear**

torment ['tɔ:ment] *vt* quälen

torn [tɔ:n] *pp of* **tear**

tornado [tɔ:'neɪdəʊ] (*pl* **-es**) *n* Tornado *m*

torrential [tə'renʃəl] *adj* (rain) sintflutartig

tortoise ['tɔ:təs] *n* Schildkröte *f*

torture ['tɔ:tʃə'] *n* Folter *f*; (fig) Qual *f* ▷ *vt* foltern

Tory ['tɔ:rɪ] (Brit) *n* Tory *m*, Konservative(r) *mf* ▷ *adj* Tory-

toss [tɒs] *vt* (throw) werfen; (salad) anmachen; **to ~ a coin** eine Münze werfen ▷ *n*: **I don't give a ~** (fam) es ist mir scheißegal

total ['təʊtl] *n* (of figures, money) Gesamtsumme *f*; **a ~ of 30** insgesamt 30; **in ~** insgesamt ▷ *adj* total; (sum etc) Gesamt- ▷ *vt* (amount to) sich belaufen auf +*akk*; **totally** *adv* total

touch [tʌtʃ] *n* (act of ~ing) Berührung *f*; (sense of ~) Tastsinn *m*; (trace) Spur *f*; **to be/keep in ~ with sb** mit jdm in Verbindung stehen/bleiben; **to get in ~ with sb** sich mit jdm in Verbindung setzen; **to lose ~ with sb** den Kontakt zu jdm verlieren ▷ *vt* (feel) berühren; (emotionally) bewegen; **touch on** *vt* (topic) berühren; **touchdown** *n* (Aviat) Landung *f*; (Sport) Touchdown *m*; **touching** *adj* (moving) rührend; **touch screen** *n* Touchscreen *m*, Berührungsbildschirm *m*; **touchy** *adj* empfindlich, zickig

tough [tʌf] *adj* hart; (meat) zäh; (material) robust; (meat) zäh

tour [tʊə'] *n* Tour *f* (of durch); (of town, building) Rundgang *m* (of durch); (of pop group etc) Tournee *f* ▷ *vt* eine Tour/einen Rundgang/eine Tournee machen durch ▷ *vi* (on holiday) umherreisen; **tour guide** *n* Reiseleiter(in) *m(f)*

tourism ['tʊərɪzəm] *n* Tourismus *m*, Fremdenverkehr *m*; **tourist** *n* Tourist(in) *m(f)*; **tourist class** *n* Touristenklasse *f*; **tourist guide** *n* (book) Reiseführer *m*; (person) Fremdenführer(in) *m(f)*; **tourist office** *n* Fremdenverkehrsamt *nt*

tournament ['tʊənəmənt] *n* Turnier *nt*

tour operator ['tʊərɒpəreɪtə'] *n* Reiseveranstalter *m*

tow [təʊ] *vt* abschleppen; (caravan, trailer) ziehen; **tow away** *vt* abschleppen

towards [tə'wɔ:dz] *prep*: **~ me** mir entgegen, auf mich zu; **we walked ~ the station** wir gingen in Richtung Bahnhof; **my feelings ~ him** meine Gefühle ihm gegenüber; **she was kind ~ me** sie war nett zu mir

towel ['taʊəl] *n* Handtuch *nt*

tower ['taʊə'] *n* Turm *m*; **tower block** *n* (Brit) Hochhaus *nt*

town [taʊn] *n* Stadt *f*; **town center** (US), **town centre** *n* Stadtmitte *f*, Stadtzentrum *nt*; **town hall** *n* Rathaus *nt*

towrope ['təʊrəʊp] *n* Abschleppseil *nt*; **tow truck** *n* (US) Abschleppwagen *m*

toxic ['tɒksɪk] *adj* giftig, Gift-

toy [tɔɪ] *n* Spielzeug *nt*; **toy with** *vt* spielen mit; **toyshop** *n* Spielwarengeschäft *nt*

trace [treɪs] *n* Spur *f*; **without**

~ spurlos ▷ vt (find) ausfindig machen; **tracing paper** n Pauspapier nt
track [træk] n (mark) Spur f; (path) Weg m; (Rail) Gleis nt; (on CD, record) Stück nt; **to keep/lose ~ of sb/sth** jdn/etw im Auge behalten/aus den Augen verlieren; **track down** vt ausfindig machen; **trackball** n (Inform) Trackball m; **tracksuit** n Trainingsanzug m
tractor ['træktə⁰] n Traktor m
trade [treid] n (commerce) Handel m; (business) Geschäft nt; (skilled job) Handwerk nt ▷ vi handeln (in mit) ▷ vt (exchange) tauschen (for gegen); **trademark** n Warenzeichen nt; **tradesman** (pl **-men**) n (shopkeeper) Geschäftsmann m; (workman) Handwerker m; **trade(s) union** n (Brit) Gewerkschaft f
tradition [trə'dɪʃən] n Tradition f; **traditional, traditionally** adj, adv traditionell
traffic ['træfɪk] n Verkehr m; (pej: trading) Handel m (in mit); **traffic circle** n (US) Kreisverkehr m; **traffic island** n Verkehrsinsel f; **traffic jam** n Stau m; **traffic lights** npl Verkehrsampel f; **traffic warden** n (Brit) ≈ Politesse f
tragedy ['trædʒədɪ] n Tragödie f; **tragic** ['trædʒɪk] adj tragisch
trail [treil] n Spur f; (path) Weg m ▷ vt (follow) verfolgen; (drag) schleppen; (drag behind) hinter sich herziehen; (Sport) zurückliegen hinter +dat ▷ vi (hang loosely) schleifen; (Sport) weit zurückliegen; **trailer** n Anhänger m; (US: caravan) Wohnwagen m; (Cine) Trailer m
train [trein] n (Rail) Zug m ▷ vt (teach) ausbilden; (Sport) trainieren

▷ vi (Sport) trainieren; **to ~ as** (o to be) **a teacher** eine Ausbildung als Lehrer machen; **trained** adj (person, voice) ausgebildet; **trainee** n Auszubildende(r) mf; (academic, practical) Praktikant(in) m(f); **traineeship** n Praktikum nt; **trainer** n (Sport) Trainer(in) m(f); **~s** (Brit: shoes) Turnschuhe pl; **training** n Ausbildung f; (Sport) Training nt; **train station** n Bahnhof m
tram ['træm] n (Brit) Straßenbahn f
tramp [træmp] n Landstreicher(in) m(f) ▷ vi trotten
tranquillizer ['træŋkwɪlaɪzə⁰] n Beruhigungsmittel nt
transaction n (piece of business) Geschäft nt
transatlantic ['trænzət'læntɪk] adj transatlantisch; **~ flight** Transatlantikflug m
transfer ['trænsfə⁰] n (of money) Überweisung f; (US: ticket) Umsteigekarte f ▷ [træns'fɜː⁰] vt (money) überweisen (to sb an jdn); (patient) verlegen; (employee) versetzen; (player) transferieren ▷ vi (on journey) umsteigen; **transferable** [træns'fɜːrəbl] adj übertragbar
transform [træns'fɔːm] vt umwandeln; **transformation** [trænsfə'meɪʃən] n Umwandlung f
transfusion [træns'fjuːʒən] n Transfusion f
transistor [træn'zɪstə⁰] n Transistor m; **~ (radio)** Transistorradio nt
transition [træn'zɪʃən] n Übergang m (from ... to von ... zu)
transit lounge ['trænzɪtlaʊndʒ] n Transitraum m; **transit passenger** n Transitreisende(r) mf

translate [trænz'leɪt] vt, vi
übersetzen; **translation**
[trænz'leɪʃən] n Übersetzung f;
translator [trænz'leɪtə°] n
Übersetzer(in) m(f)
transmission [trænz'mɪʃən] n
(Auto) Getriebe nt
transparent [træns'pærənt] adj
durchsichtig; (fig) offenkundig
transplant [træns'plɑ:nt] (Med)
vt transplantieren ▷ ['trænsplɑ:nt]
n (operation) Transplantation f
transport ['trænspɔ:t] n (of
goods, people) Beförderung f; **public
~** öffentliche Verkehrsmittel pl
▷ [træns'pɔ:t] vt befördern,
transportieren; **transportation**
[trænspɔ:'teɪʃən] n see transport
trap [træp] n Falle f ▷ vt: **to be
~ped** (in snow, job etc) festsitzen
trash [træʃ] n (book, film etc)
Schund m; (US: refuse) Abfall m;
trash can n (US) Abfalleimer m;
trashy adj niveaulos; (novel)
Schund-
traumatic [trɔ:'mætɪk] adj
traumatisch
travel ['trævl] n Reisen pl ▷ vi
(journey) reisen ▷ vt (distance)
zurücklegen; (country) bereisen;
travel agency, travel agent n
(company) Reisebüro nt; **traveler**
(US) see **traveller**; **traveler's
check** (US) see **traveller's cheque**;
travel insurance n
Reiseversicherung f; **traveller** n
Reisende(r) mf; **traveller's cheque**
n (Brit) Reisescheck m; **travelsick**
n reisekrank
tray [treɪ] n Tablett nt; (for mail
etc) Ablage f; (of printer, photocopier)
Fach nt
tread [tred] n (on tyre) Profil nt;
tread on [tred] (trod, trodden) vt
treten auf +akk
treasure ['treʒə°] n Schatz m
▷ vt schätzen

treat [tri:t] n besondere Freude;
it's my ~ das geht auf meine
Kosten ▷ vt behandeln; **to ~ sb
(to sth)** jdn (zu etw) einladen; **to
~ oneself to sth** sich etw leisten;
treatment ['tri:tmənt] n
Behandlung f
treaty ['tri:tɪ] n Vertrag m
tree [tri:] n Baum m
tremble ['trembl] vi zittern
tremendous [trə'mendəs] adj
gewaltig; (fam: very good) toll
trench [trentʃ] n Graben m
trend [trend] n Tendenz f;
(fashion) Mode f, Trend m; **trendy**
adj trendig
trespass ['trespas] vi: **"no ~ing"**
"Betreten verboten"
trial ['traɪəl] n (Jur) Prozess m;
(test) Versuch m; **by ~ and error**
durch Ausprobieren; **trial period**
n (for employee) Probezeit f
triangle ['traɪæŋgl] n Dreieck nt;
(Mus) Triangel m; **triangular**
[traɪ'æŋgjʊlə°] adj dreieckig
tribe [traɪb] n Stamm m
trick [trɪk] n Trick m; (mischief)
Streich m ▷ vt hereinlegen
tricky ['trɪkɪ] adj (difficult)
schwierig, heikel; (situation)
verzwickt
trifle ['traɪfl] n Kleinigkeit f; (Brit
Gastr) Trifle nt (Nachspeise aus
Biskuit, Wackelpudding, Obst,
Vanillesoße und Sahne)
trigger ['trɪgə°] n (of gun) Abzug
m ▷ vt: **to ~ (off)** auslösen
trim [trɪm] adj (hair, beard)
nachschneiden; (nails) schneiden;
(hedge) stutzen ▷ n: **just a ~,
please** nur etwas nachschneiden,
bitte; **trimmings** npl (decorations)
Verzierungen pl; (extras) Zubehör
nt; (Gastr) Beilagen pl
trip [trɪp] n Reise f; (outing)
Ausflug m ▷ vi stolpern (over über
+akk)

triple ['trɪpl] adj dreifach ▷ adv:
~ **the price** dreimal so teuer ▷ vi
sich verdreifachen; **triplet**
['trɪplɪt] n Drilling m

tripod ['traɪpɒd] n (Foto) Stativ
nt

trite [traɪt] adj banal

triumph ['traɪʌmf] n Triumph m

trivial ['trɪvɪəl] adj trivial

trod [trɒd] pt of **tread**

trodden pp of **tread**

trolley ['trɒlɪ] n (Brit: in shop)
Einkaufswagen m; (for luggage)
Kofferkuli m; (serving ~) Teewagen
m

trombone [trɒm'bəʊn] n
Posaune f

troops [tru:ps] npl (Mil) Truppen
pl

trophy ['trəʊfɪ] n Trophäe f

tropical ['trɒpɪkl] adj tropisch

trouble ['trʌbl] n (problems)
Schwierigkeiten pl; (worry) Sorgen
pl; (effort) Mühe f; (unrest) Unruhen
pl; (Med) Beschwerden pl; **to be in**
~ in Schwierigkeiten sein; **to get
into** ~ (with authority) Ärger
bekommen; **to make**
~ Schwierigkeiten machen ▷ vt
(worry) beunruhigen; (disturb)
stören; **my back's troubling me**
mein Rücken macht mir zu
schaffen; **sorry to ~ you** ich muss
dich/Sie leider kurz stören;
troubled adj (worried)
beunruhigt; **trouble-free** adj
problemlos; **troublemaker** n
Unruhestifter(in) m(f);
troublesome adj lästig

trousers ['traʊzəz] npl Hose f

trout [traʊt] n Forelle f

truck [trʌk] n Lastwagen m; (Brit
Rail) Güterwagen m; **trucker** n
(US: driver) Lastwagenfahrer(in)
m(f)

true [tru:] adj (factually correct)
wahr; (genuine) echt; **to come**

~ **wahr werden**

truly ['tru:lɪ] adv wirklich; **Yours
~** (in letter) mit freundlichen
Grüßen

trumpet ['trʌmpɪt] n Trompete
f

trunk [trʌŋk] n (of tree) Stamm
m; (Anat) Rumpf m; (of elephant)
Rüssel m; (piece of luggage)
Überseekoffer m; (US Auto)
Kofferraum m; **trunks** npl:
(swimming) ~ Badehose f

trust [trʌst] n (confidence)
Vertrauen nt (in zu) ▷ vt vertrauen
+dat; **trusting** adj vertrauensvoll;
trustworthy adj
vertrauenswürdig

truth [tru:θ] n Wahrheit f;
truthful adj ehrlich; (statement)
wahrheitsgemäß

try [traɪ] n Versuch m ▷ vt
(attempt) versuchen; (~ out)
ausprobieren; (sample) probieren;
(Jur: person) vor Gericht stellen;
(courage, patience) auf die Probe
stellen ▷ vi versuchen; (make
effort) sich bemühen; **~ and come**
versuch zu kommen; **try on** vt
(clothes) anprobieren; **try out** vt
ausprobieren

T-shirt ['ti:ʃɜ:t] n T-Shirt nt

tub [tʌb] n (for ice-cream,
margarine) Becher m

tube [tju:b] n (pipe) Rohr nt; (of
rubber, plastic) Schlauch m; (for
toothpaste, glue etc) Tube f; **the
Tube** (in London) die U-Bahn;
tube station ['tju:bsteɪʃən] n
U-Bahn-Station f

tuck [tʌk] vt (put) stecken; **tuck
in** vt (shirt) in die Hose stecken;
(blanket) feststecken; (person)
zudecken ▷ vi (eat) zulangen

tucker ['tʌkə] n (Aust, NZ fam)
Essen nt, Fressalien pl (fam)

Tue(s) abbr = **Tuesday** Di.

Tuesday ['tju:zdɪ] n Dienstag m;

on ~ (am) Dienstag; **on ~s**
dienstags; **this/last/next**
~ diesen/letzten/nächsten
Dienstag; **(on) ~ morning/**
afternoon/evening (am)
Dienstagmorgen/-nachmittag/
-abend; **every** ~ jeden
Dienstag; **a week on ~/~ week**
Dienstag in einer Woche

tug [tʌg] vt ziehen; **she ~ged his**
sleeve sie zog an seinem Ärmel
▷ vi ziehen (at an +dat)

tuition [tjuːˈɪʃən] n Unterricht m;
(US: fees) Studiengebühren pl;
~ **fees** pl Studiengebühren pl

tulip [ˈtjuːlɪp] n Tulpe f

tumble [ˈtʌmbl] vi (person, prices)
fallen; **tumble dryer** n
Wäschetrockner m; **tumbler** n
(glass) (Becher)glas nt

tummy [ˈtʌmɪ] n (fam) Bauch m;
tummyache n (fam) Bauchweh nt

tumor (US), **tumour** [ˈtjuːməʳ]
n Tumor m

tuna [ˈtjuːnə] n Thunfisch m

tune [tjuːn] n Melodie f; **to be**
in/out of ~ (instrument)
gestimmt/verstimmt sein; (singer)
richtig/falsch singen ▷ vt
(instrument) stimmen; (radio)
einstellen (to auf +akk); **tuner** n
(in stereo system) Tuner m

Tunisia [tjuːˈnɪzɪə] n Tunesien
nt

tunnel [ˈtʌnl] n Tunnel m;
(under road, railway) Unterführung
f

turban [ˈtɜːbən] n Turban m

turbulence [ˈtɜːbjʊləns] n
(Aviat) Turbulenzen pl; **turbulent**
adj stürmisch

Turk [tɜːk] n Türke m, Türkin f

turkey [ˈtɜːkɪ] n Truthahn m

Turkey [ˈtɜːkɪ] n die Türkei;
Turkish adj türkisch ▷ n (language) Türkisch nt

turmoil [ˈtɜːmɔɪl] n Aufruhr m

turn [tɜːn] n (rotation) Drehung f;
(performance) Nummer f; **to make**
a left ~ nach links abbiegen; **at**
the ~ of the century um die
Jahrhundertwende; **it's your** ~ du
bist/Sie sind dran; **in ~, by ~s**
abwechselnd; **to take ~s** sich
abwechseln ▷ vt (wheel, key, screw)
drehen; (to face other way)
umdrehen; (corner) biegen um;
(page) umblättern; (transform)
verwandeln (into in +akk) ▷ vi
(rotate) sich drehen; (to face other
way) sich umdrehen; (change
direction: driver, car) abbiegen;
(become) werden; (weather)
umschlagen; **to ~ into sth**
(become) sich in etw akk
verwandeln; **to ~ cold/green**
kalt/grün werden; **to ~ left/right**
links/rechts abbiegen; **turn away**
vt (person) abweisen; **turn back** vt
(person) zurückweisen ▷ vi (go
back) umkehren; **turn down** vt
(refuse) ablehnen; (radio, TV) leiser
stellen; (heating) kleiner stellen;
turn off vi abbiegen ▷ vt (switch
off) ausschalten; (tap) zudrehen;
(engine, electricity) abstellen; **turn**
on vt (switch on) einschalten; (tap)
aufdrehen; (engine, electricity)
anstellen; (fam: person) anmachen,
antörnen; **turn out** vt (light)
ausmachen; (pockets) leeren ▷ vi
(develop) sich entwickeln; **as it**
turned out wie sich herausstellte;
turn over vi umdrehen ▷ vt (page)
umblättern ▷ vi (person) sich
umdrehen; (car) sich
überschlagen; (TV) umschalten (to
auf +akk); **turn round** vt (to face
other way) umdrehen ▷ vi (person)
sich umdrehen; (go back)
umkehren; **turn to** vi sich
zuwenden +dat; **turn up** vi
(person, lost object) auftauchen ▷ vt
(radio, TV) lauter stellen; (heating)

höher stellen; **turning** n (in road)
Abzweigung f; **turning point** n
Wendepunkt m

turnip ['tɜːnɪp] n Rübe f

turnover ['tɜːnəʊvə*] n (Fin)
Umsatz m

turnpike ['tɜːnpaɪk] n (US)
gebührenpflichtige Autobahn

turntable ['tɜːnteɪbl] n (on
record player) Plattenteller m

turn-up ['tɜːnʌp] n (Brit: on
trousers) Aufschlag m

turquoise ['tɜːkwɔɪz] adj türkis

turtle ['tɜːtl] n (Brit)
Wasserschildkröte f; (US)
Schildkröte f

tutor ['tjuːtə*] n (private)
Privatlehrer(in) m(f); (Brit: at
university) Tutor(in) m(f)

tux [tʌks] , **tuxedo** [tʌk'siːdəʊ]
(pl -s) n (US) Smoking m

TV ['tiː'viː] n Fernsehen nt; (~ set)
Fernseher m; **to watch
~** fernsehen; **on ~** im Fernsehen
▷ adj Fernseh-; **~ programme** n
Fernsehsendung f

tweed [twiːd] n Tweed m

tweet [twiːt] vi (on Twitter)
twittern

tweezers ['twiːzəz] npl Pinzette
f

twelfth [twelfθ] adj zwölfte(r, s);
see also **eighth**; **twelve** [twelv]
num zwölf ▷ n Zwölf f; see also
eight

twentieth ['twentɪɪθ] adj
zwanzigste(r, s); see also **eighth**;
twenty ['twentɪ] num zwanzig;
~-one einundzwanzig ▷ n
Zwanzig f; **to be in one's twenties**
in den Zwanzigern sein; see also
eight

twice [twaɪs] adv zweimal; **~ as
much/many** doppelt so viel/viele

twig [twɪg] n Zweig m

twilight ['twaɪlaɪt] n (in evening)
Dämmerung f

twin [twɪn] n Zwilling m ▷ adj
(brother etc) Zwillings-; **~ beds** zwei
Einzelbetten ▷ vt: **York is ~ned
with Münster** York ist eine
Partnerstadt von Münster

twinge [twɪndʒ] n (pain)
stechender Schmerz

twinkle ['twɪŋkl] vi funkeln

twin room n
Zweibettzimmer nt; **twin town** n
Partnerstadt f

twist [twɪst] vt (turn) drehen,
winden; (distort) verdrehen; **I've
~ed my ankle** ich bin mit dem Fuß
umgeknickt

two [tuː] num zwei; **to break sth
in ~** etw in zwei Teile brechen ▷ n
Zwei f; **the ~ of them** die beiden;
see also **eight**; **two-dimensional**
adj zweidimensional; (fig)
oberflächlich; **two-faced** adj
falsch, heuchlerisch; **two-piece**
adj zweiteilig; **two-way** adj:
~ traffic Gegenverkehr

type [taɪp] n (sort) Art f; (typeface)
Schrift(art) f; **what ~ of car is it?**
was für ein Auto ist das?; **he's not
my ~** er ist nicht mein Typ;
typeface n Schrift(art) f;
typewriter n Schreibmaschine f

typhoid ['taɪfɔɪd] n Typhus m

typhoon [taɪ'fuːn] n Taifun m

typical ['tɪpɪkl] adj typisch (of
für)

typing error ['taɪpɪŋerə*] n
Tippfehler m

tyre [taɪə*] n (Brit) Reifen m; **tyre
pressure** n Reifendruck m

Tyrol [tɪ'rəʊl] n: **the ~** Tirol nt

u

UFO [ˈjuːfəʊ] *acr* = **unidentified flying object** Ufo *nt*

Uganda [juːˈgændə] *n* Uganda *nt*

ugly [ˈʌglɪ] *adj* hässlich

UHT *adj abbr* = **ultra-heat treated** ~ **milk** H-Milch *f*

UK *abbr* = **United Kingdom**

Ukraine [juːˈkreɪn] *n*: **the** ~ die Ukraine

ulcer [ˈʌlsə°] *n* Geschwür *nt*

ulterior [ʌlˈtɪərɪə°] *adj*: ~ **motive** Hintergedanke *m*

ultimate [ˈʌltɪmət] *adj* (*final*) letzte(r, s); (*authority*) höchste(r, s); **ultimately** *adv* letzten Endes; (*eventually*) schließlich; **ultimatum** [ʌltɪˈmeɪtəm] *n* Ultimatum *nt*

ultra- [ˈʌltrə] *pref* ultra-

ultrasound [ˈʌltrəsaʊnd] *n* (*Med*) Ultraschall *m*

umbrella [ʌmˈbrelə] *n* Schirm *m*

umpire [ˈʌmpaɪə°] *n* Schieds-richter(in) *m(f)*

umpteen [ˈʌmptiːn] *num* (*fam*) zig; ~ **times** zigmal

un- [ʌn] *pref* un-

UN *nsing abbr* = **United Nations** VN, Vereinte Nationen *pl*

unable [ʌnˈeɪbl] *adj*: **to be** ~ **to do sth** etw nicht tun können

unacceptable [ʌnəˈkseptəbl] *adj* unannehmbar

unaccountably [ʌnəˈkaʊntəblɪ] *adv* unerklärlicherweise

unaccustomed [ʌnəˈkʌstəmd] *adj*: **to be** ~ **to sth** etw nicht gewohnt sein

unanimous, unanimously [juːˈnænɪməs, -lɪ] *adj, adv* einmütig

unattached [ʌnəˈtætʃt] *adj* (*without partner*) ungebunden

unattended [ʌnəˈtendɪd] *adj* (*luggage, car*) unbeaufsichtigt

unauthorized [ʌnˈɔːθəraɪzd] *adj* unbefugt

unavailable [ʌnəˈveɪləbl] *adj* nicht erhältlich; (*person*) nicht erreichbar

unavoidable [ʌnəˈvɔɪdəbl] *adj* unvermeidlich

unaware [ʌnəˈweə°] *adj*: **to be** ~ **of sth** sich einer Sache *dat* nicht bewusst sein; **I was** ~ **that ...** ich wusste nicht, dass ...

unbalanced [ʌnˈbælənst] *adj* unausgewogen; (*mentally*) gestört

unbearable [ʌnˈbeərəbl] *adj* unerträglich

unbeatable [ʌnˈbiːtəbl] *adj* unschlagbar

unbelievable [ʌnbɪˈliːvəbl] *adj* unglaublich

unblock [ʌnˈblɒk] *vt* (*pipe*) frei machen

unbutton [ʌnˈbʌtn] *vt* aufknöpfen

uncertain [ʌnˈsɜːtən] adj
unsicher

uncle [ˈʌŋkl] n Onkel m

uncomfortable [ʌnˈkʌmfətəbl]
adj unbequem

unconditional [ʌnkənˈdɪʃənl]
adj bedingungslos

unconscious [ʌnˈkɒnʃəs] adj
(Med) bewusstlos; **to be ~ of sth**
sich einer Sache dat nicht bewusst
sein; **unconsciously** adv
unbewusst

uncork [ʌnˈkɔːk] vt entkorken

uncover [ʌnˈkʌvə°] vt
aufdecken

undecided [ʌndɪˈsaɪdɪd] adj
unschlüssig

undeniable [ʌndɪˈnaɪəbl] adj
unbestreitbar

under [ˈʌndə°] prep (beneath)
unter +dat; (with motion) unter
+akk; **children ~ eight** Kinder
unter acht; **~ an hour** weniger als
eine Stunde ▷ adv (beneath)
unten; (with motion) darunter;
children aged eight and ~ Kinder
bis zu acht Jahren; **under-age** adj
minderjährig

undercarriage [ˈʌndəkærɪdʒ] n
Fahrgestell nt

underdog [ˈʌndədɒg] n (outsider)
Außenseiter(in) m(f)

underdone [ʌndəˈdʌn] adj
(Gastr) nicht gar, durch;
(deliberately) nicht durchgebraten

underestimate [ʌndərˈestɪmeɪt] vt unterschätzen

underexposed [ʌndərɪksˈpəʊzd]
adj (Foto) unterbelichtet

undergo [ʌndəˈgəʊ] irr vt
(experience) durchmachen;
(operation, test) sich unterziehen
+dat

undergraduate [ʌndəˈgrædjʊət]
n Student(in) m(f)

underground [ˈʌndəgraʊnd]
unterirdisch ▷ n (Brit Rail) U-Bahn
f; **underground station** n
U-Bahn-Station f

underlie [ʌndəˈlaɪ] irr vt
zugrunde liegen +dat

underline [ʌndəˈlaɪn] vt
unterstreichen

underlying [ʌndəˈlaɪɪŋ] adj
zugrunde liegend

underneath [ʌndəˈniːθ] prep
unter; (with motion) unter +akk
▷ adv darunter

underpants [ˈʌndəpænts] npl
Unterhose f; **undershirt**
[ˈʌndəʃɜːt] n (US) Unterhemd nt;
undershorts [ˈʌndəʃɔːts] npl (US)
Unterhose f

understand [ʌndəˈstænd] irr vt,
vi verstehen; **I ~ that …** (been told)
ich habe gehört, dass …;
(sympathize) ich habe Verständnis
dafür, dass …; **to make oneself
understood** sich verständlich
machen; **understandable** adj
verständlich; **understanding** adj
verständnisvoll

undertake [ʌndəˈteɪk] irr vt
(task) übernehmen; **to ~ to do sth**
sich verpflichten, etw zu tun;
undertaker n Leichenbestat-
ter(in) m(f); **~'s** (firm)
Bestattungsinstitut nt

underwater [ʌndəˈwɔːtə°] adv
unter Wasser ▷ adj Unterwasser-

underwear [ˈʌndəweə°] n
Unterwäsche f

undesirable [ʌndɪˈzaɪərəbl] adj
unerwünscht

undo [ʌnˈduː] irr vt (unfasten)
aufmachen; (work)
zunichtemachen; (Inform)
rückgängig machen

undoubtedly [ʌnˈdaʊtɪdlɪ] adv
zweifellos

undress [ʌnˈdres] vt ausziehen;
to get ~ed sich ausziehen ▷ vi
sich ausziehen

undue [ʌnˈdjuː] adj übermäßig

u

unduly [ʌnˈdjuːlɪ] adv
übermäßig

unearth [ʌnˈɜːθ] vt (dig up)
ausgraben; (find) aufstöbern

unease [ʌnˈiːz] n Unbehagen nt;
uneasy adj (person) unbehaglich;
I'm ~ about it mir ist nicht wohl
dabei

unemployed [ʌnɪmˈplɔɪd] adj
arbeitslos ▷ ▷ npl: **the ~ die**
Arbeitslosen pl; **unemployment**
[ʌnɪmˈplɔɪmənt] n Arbeitslosigkeit f; **unemployment**
benefit n Arbeitslosengeld nt

unequal [ʌnˈiːkwəl] adj
ungleich

uneven [ʌnˈiːvən] adj (surface,
road) uneben; (contest) ungleich

unexpected [ʌnɪkˈspɛktɪd] adj
unerwartet

unfair [ʌnˈfɛəʳ] adj unfair

unfamiliar [ʌnfəˈmɪljəʳ] adj: **to**
be ~ with sb/sth jdn/etw nicht
kennen

unfasten [ʌnˈfɑːsn] vt
aufmachen

unfit [ʌnˈfɪt] adj ungeeignet (for
für); (in bad health) nicht fit

unforeseen [ʌnfɔːˈsiːn] adj
unvorhergesehen

unforgettable [ʌnfəˈɡɛtəbl] adj
unvergesslich

unforgivable [ʌnfəˈɡɪvəbl] adj
unverzeihlich

unfortunate [ʌnˈfɔːtʃnət] adj
(unlucky) unglücklich; **it is ~**
that ... es ist bedauerlich, dass ...;
unfortunately adv leider

unfounded [ʌnˈfaʊndɪd] adj
unbegründet

unhappy [ʌnˈhæpɪ] adj (sad)
unglücklich, unzufrieden; **to be**
~ with sth mit etw unzufrieden
sein

unhealthy [ʌnˈhɛlθɪ] adj
ungesund

unheard-of [ʌnˈhɜːdɒv] adj

(unknown) gänzlich unbekannt;
(outrageous) unerhört

unhelpful [ʌnˈhelpfʊl] adj nicht
hilfreich

unhitch [ʌnˈhɪtʃ] vt (caravan,
trailer) abkoppeln

unhurt [ʌnˈhɜːt] adj unverletzt

uniform [ˈjuːnɪfɔːm] n Uniform
f ▷ adj einheitlich

unify [ˈjuːnɪfaɪ] vt vereinigen

unimportant [ʌnɪmˈpɔːtənt]-
adj unwichtig

uninhabited [ʌnɪnˈhæbɪtɪd] adj
unbewohnt

uninstall [ʌnɪnˈstɔːl] vt (Inform)
deinstallieren

unintentional [ʌnɪnˈtenʃənl]
adj unabsichtlich

union [ˈjuːnjən] n (uniting)
Vereinigung f; (alliance) Union f;
Union Jack n Union Jack m
(britische Nationalflagge)

unique [juːˈniːk] adj einzigartig

unit [ˈjuːnɪt] n Einheit f; (of
system, machine) Teil nt; (in school)
Lektion f

unite [juːˈnaɪt] vt vereinigen;
the United Kingdom das
Vereinigte Königreich; **the United**
Nations pl die Vereinten Nationen
pl; **the United States (of**
America) pl die Vereinigten
Staaten (von Amerika) pl ▷ vi sich
vereinigen

universe [ˈjuːnɪvɜːs] n Univer-
sum nt

university [juːnɪˈvɜːsɪtɪ] n
Universität f

unkind [ʌnˈkaɪnd] adj unfreundlich (to zu)

unknown [ʌnˈnəʊn] adj
unbekannt (to +dat)

unleaded [ʌnˈledɪd] adj bleifrei

unless [ənˈles] conj es sei denn,
wenn ... nicht; **don't do it - I tell**
you to mach das nicht, es sei
denn, ich sage es dir; **~ I'm**

mistaken ... wenn ich mich nicht irre ...

unlicensed [ʌnˈlaɪsənst] *adj* (to sell alcohol) ohne Lizenz

unlike [ʌnˈlaɪk] *prep* (in contrast to) im Gegensatz zu; **it's ~ her to be late** es sieht ihr gar nicht ähnlich, zu spät zu kommen; **unlikely** [ʌnˈlaɪklɪ] *adj* unwahrscheinlich

unload [ʌnˈləʊd] *vt* ausladen

unlock [ʌnˈlɒk] *vt* aufschließen

unlucky [ʌnˈlʌkɪ] *adj* unglücklich; **to be ~** Pech haben

unmistakable [ʌnmɪˈsteɪkəbl] *adj* unverkennbar

unnecessary [ʌnˈnesəsərɪ] *adj* unnötig

unobtainable [ʌnəbˈteɪnəbl] *adj* nicht erhältlich

unoccupied [ʌnˈɒkjʊpaɪd] *adj* (seat) frei; (building, room) leer stehend

unpack [ʌnˈpæk] *vt, vi* auspacken

unpleasant [ʌnˈpleznt] *adj* unangenehm

unplug [ʌnˈplʌg] *vt*: **to ~ sth** den Stecker von etw herausziehen

unprecedented [ʌnˈpresɪdəntɪd] *adj* beispiellos

unpredictable [ʌnprɪˈdɪktəbl] *adj* (person, weather) unberechenbar

unreasonable [ʌnˈriːznəbl] *adj* unvernünftig; (demand) übertrieben

unreliable [ʌnrɪˈlaɪəbl] *adj* unzuverlässig

unsafe [ʌnˈseɪf] *adj* nicht sicher; (dangerous) gefährlich

unscrew [ʌnˈskruː] *vt* abschrauben

unsightly [ʌnˈsaɪtlɪ] *adj* unansehnlich

unskilled [ʌnˈskɪld] *adj* (worker) ungelernt

unsuccessful [ʌnsəkˈsesfʊl] *adj* erfolglos

unsuitable [ʌnˈsuːtəbl] *adj* ungeeignet (for für)

until [ənˈtɪl] *prep* bis; **not ~** erst; **from Monday ~ Friday** von Montag bis Freitag; **he didn't come home ~ midnight** er kam erst um Mitternacht nach Hause; **~ then** bis dahin ▷ *conj* bis; **she won't come ~ you invite her** sie kommt erst, wenn du sie einlädst/wenn Sie sie einladen

unusual, unusually [ʌnˈjuːʒʊəl, -ɪ] *adj, adv* ungewöhnlich

unwanted [ʌnˈwɒntɪd] *adj* unerwünscht, ungewollt

unwell [ʌnˈwel] *adj* krank; **to feel ~** sich nicht wohlfühlen

unwilling [ʌnˈwɪlɪŋ] *adj*: **to be ~ to do sth** nicht bereit sein, etw zu tun

unwind [ʌnˈwaɪnd] *irr vt* abwickeln ▷ *vi* (relax) sich entspannen

unwrap [ʌnˈræp] *vt* auspacken

unzip [ʌnˈzɪp] *vt* den Reißverschluss aufmachen an +*dat*; (Inform) entzippen

KEYWORD

up [ʌp] *prep*: **to be up sth** oben auf etw dat sein; **to go up sth** (auf) etw *akk* hinaufgehen; **go up that road** gehen Sie die Straße hinauf

▷ *adv* **1** (upwards, higher) oben; **put it up a bit higher** stell es etwas weiter nach oben; **up there** da oben, dort oben; **up above** hoch oben

2 to be up (out of bed) auf sein; (prices, level) gestiegen sein; (building, tent) stehen

3 up to (as far as) bis; **up to now** bis jetzt

4 to be up to (depending on): **it's up to you** das hängt von dir ab; (equal to): **he's not up to it** (job, task etc) er ist dem nicht gewachsen; (inf: be doing) (showing disappoint, suspicion) **what is he up to?** was führt er im Schilde?; **his work is not up to the required standard** seine Arbeit entspricht nicht dem geforderten Niveau
▷ n: **ups and downs** (in life, career) Höhen und Tiefen pl

upbringing ['ʌpbrɪŋɪŋ] n Erziehung f

update [ʌp'deɪt] n (list etc) Aktualisierung f; (software) Update nt ▷ vt (list etc, person) auf den neuesten Stand bringen, aktualisieren

upgrade [ʌp'greɪd] vt (computer) aufrüsten; **we were ~d** das Hotel hat uns ein besseres Zimmer gegeben

upheaval [ʌp'hiːvəl] n Aufruhr m; (Pol) Umbruch m

uphill [ʌp'hɪl] adv bergauf

upload [ʌp'ləʊd] vt hochladen

upon [ə'pɒn] prep see on

upper ['ʌpəʳ] adj obere(r, s); (arm, deck) Ober-

upright ['ʌpraɪt] adj, adv aufrecht

uprising ['ʌpraɪzɪŋ] n Aufstand m

upset [ʌp'set] irr vt (overturn) umkippen; (disturb) aufregen; (sadden) bestürzen; (offend) kränken; (plans) durcheinanderbringen ▷ adj (disturbed) aufgeregt; (sad) bestürzt; (offended) gekränkt; **~ stomach** ['ʌpset] Magenverstimmung f

upside down [ʌpsaɪd'daʊn] adv verkehrt herum; (fig) drunter und drüber; **to turn sth ~** (box etc) etw umdrehen/durchwühlen

upstairs [ʌp'steəz] adv oben; (go, take) nach oben

up-to-date ['ʌptə'deɪt] adj modern; (fashion, information) aktuell; **to keep sb ~** jdn auf dem Laufenden halten

upwards ['ʌpwədz] adv nach oben

urban ['ɜːbən] adj städtisch, Stadt-

urge [ɜːdʒ] n Drang m ▷ vt: **to ~ sb to do sth** jdn drängen, etw zu tun; **urgent, urgently** ['ɜːdʒənt, -lɪ] adj, adv dringend

urine ['juərɪn] n Urin m

URL abbr = **uniform resource locator** (Inform) URL-Adresse f

us [ʌs] pron uns; **do they know ~?** kennen sie uns?; **can he help ~?** kann er uns helfen?; **it's ~** wir sind's; **both of ~** wir beide

US, USA nsing abbr = **United States (of America)** USA pl

USB stick [juːes'biːstɪk] n USB-Stick m

use [juːs] n (using) Gebrauch m; (for specific purpose) Benutzung f; **to make ~ of** Gebrauch machen von; **in/out of ~** in/außer Gebrauch; **it's no ~ (doing that)** es hat keinen Zweck(, das zu tun); **it's (of) no ~ to me** das kann ich nicht brauchen ▷ [juːz] vt benutzen, gebrauchen; (for specific purpose) verwenden; (method) anwenden; **use up** vt aufbrauchen

used [juːzd] adj (secondhand) gebraucht ▷ vb aux: **to be ~d to sb/sth** an jdn/etw gewöhnt sein; **to get ~d to sb/sth** sich an jdn/etw gewöhnen; **she ~d to live here** sie hat früher mal hier gewohnt; **useful** adj nützlich; **useless** adj nutzlos; (unusable) unbrauchbar; (pointless) zwecklos; **user** ['juːzəʳ] n Benutzer(in) m(f);

user-friendly adj
benutzerfreundlich; **username** n
Benutzername

usual ['juːʒʊəl] adj üblich,
gewöhnlich; **as ~** wie üblich;
usually adv normalerweise

ute ['juːt] n (Aust, NZ fam)
Kleintransporter m

utensil [juːˈtensl] n Gerät nt

uterus ['juːtərəs] n Gebärmutter
f

utilize ['juːtɪlaɪz] vt verwenden

utmost ['ʌtməʊst] adj äußerst;
to do one's ~ sein Möglichstes
tun

utter ['ʌtə°] adj völlig ▷ vt von
sich geben; **utterly** adv völlig

U-turn ['juːtɜːn] n (Auto) Wende
f; **to do a ~** wenden; (fig) eine
Kehrtwendung machen

V

vacancy ['veɪkənsɪ] n (job)
offene Stelle; (room) freies Zimmer;
vacant ['veɪkənt] adj (room,
toilet) frei; (post) offen; (building)
leer stehend; **vacate** [vəˈkeɪt] vt
(room, building) räumen; (seat) frei
machen

vacation [vəˈkeɪʃən] n (US)
Ferien pl, Urlaub m; (at university)
(Semester)ferien pl; **to go on ~** in
Urlaub fahren; **~ course**
Ferienkurs m

vaccinate ['væksɪneɪt] vt
impfen; **vaccination**
[væksɪˈneɪʃən] n Impfung f; **~ card**
Impfpass m

vacuum ['vækjʊm] n Vakuum nt
▷ vt, vi (staub)saugen; **vacuum
(cleaner)** n Staubsauger m

vagina [vəˈdʒaɪnə] n Scheide f

vague [veɪɡ] adj (imprecise) vage;
(resemblance) entfernt; **vaguely**
adv in etwa, irgendwie

vain [veɪn] adj (attempt)
vergeblich; (conceited) eitel; **in
~** vergeblich, umsonst; **vainly** adv
(in vain) vergeblich

valentine (card)
['vælantaɪn(kɑ:d)] n Valentins-
karte f; **Valentine's Day** n
Valentinstag m

valid ['vælɪd] adj (ticket, passport
etc) gültig; (argument) stichhaltig;
(claim) berechtigt

valley ['vælɪ] n Tal nt

valuable ['væljʊəbl] adj wertvoll;
(time) kostbar; **valuables** npl
Wertsachen pl

value ['vælju:] n Wert m ▷ vt
(appreciate) schätzen; **value added
tax** n Mehrwertsteuer f

valve [vælv] n Ventil nt

van [væn] n (Auto) Lieferwagen m

vanilla [vəˈnɪlə] n Vanille f

vanish ['vænɪʃ] vi verschwinden

vanity ['vænɪtɪ] n Eitelkeit f;
vanity case n Schminkkoffer m

vapor (US), **vapour** ['veɪpə°] n
(mist) Dunst m; (steam) Dampf
m

variable ['veərɪəbl] adj (weather,
mood) unbeständig; (quality)
unterschiedlich; (speed, height)
regulierbar; **varied** ['veərɪd] adj
(interests, selection) vielseitig;
(career) bewegt; (work, diet)
abwechslungsreich; **variety**
[vəˈraɪətɪ] n (diversity)
Abwechslung f; (assortment)
Vielfalt f (of an +dat); (type) Art f;
various ['veərɪəs] adj
verschieden

varnish ['vɑːnɪʃ] n Lack m ▷ vt
lackieren

vary ['veərɪ] vt (alter) verändern
▷ vi (be different) unterschiedlich
sein; (fluctuate) sich verändern;
(prices) schwanken

vase [vɑːz, ?? veɪz] (US) n Vase f

vast [vɑːst] adj riesig; (area) weit

VAT [væt] abbr = **value added tax**
Mehrwertsteuer f, MwSt.

Vatican ['vætɪkən] n: **the ~** der
Vatikan

VCR [vi:si:'ɑ:°] abbr = **video
cassette recorder** Videorekorder
m

VD [vi:'di:] abbr = **venereal
disease** Geschlechtskrankheit f

VDU [vi:di:'ju:] abbr = **visual
display unit**

veal [vi:l] n Kalbfleisch nt

vegan ['vi:gən] n Veganer(in)
m(f)

vegetable ['vedʒtəbl] n Gemüse
nt

vegetarian [vedʒɪ'teərɪən] n
Vegetarier(in) m(f) ▷ adj
vegetarisch

veggie ['vedʒɪ] n (fam)
Vegetarier(in) m(f); Gemüse nt
▷ adj vegetarisch; **veggieburger**
n Veggieburger m, Gemüseburger
m

vehicle ['vi:ɪkl] n Fahrzeug nt

veil [veɪl] n Schleier m

vein [veɪn] n Ader f

Velcro® ['velkrəʊ] n Klettband
nt

velvet ['velvɪt] n Samt m

vending machine
['vendɪŋməʃi:n] n Automat m

venetian blind [vɪ'ni:ʃən'blaɪnd]
n Jalousie f

Venezuela [vene'zweɪlə] n
Venezuela nt

Venice ['venɪs] n Venedig nt

venison ['venɪsn] n Rehfleisch
nt

vent [vent] n Öffnung f

ventilate ['ventɪleɪt] vt lüften;
ventilation [ventɪ'leɪʃən] n
Belüftung f; **ventilator**
['ventɪleɪtə°] n (in room)
Ventilator m; **to be on a ~** (Med)
künstlich beatmet werden

venture ['ventʃə°] n (project)

Unternehmung f; (Comm)
Unternehmen nt ▷ vi (go) (sich)
wagen

venue ['venju:] n (for concert etc)
Veranstaltungsort m; (Sport)
Austragungsort m

verb [vɜ:b] n Verb nt; **verbal** adj
(agreement) mündlich; (skills)
sprachlich; **verbally** adv
mündlich

verdict ['vɜ:dɪkt] n Urteil nt

verge [vɜ:dʒ] n (of road)
(Straßen)rand m; **to be on the ~ of
doing sth** im Begriff sein, etw zu
tun ▷ vi: **to ~ on** grenzen an +akk

verification [verɪfɪ'keɪʃən] n
(confirmation) Bestätigung f;
(check) Überprüfung f; **verify**
['verɪfaɪ] vt (confirm) bestätigen;
(check) überprüfen

vermin ['vɜ:mɪn] npl Schädlinge
pl; (insects) Ungeziefer nt

verruca [ve'ru:kə] n Warze f

versatile ['vɜ:sətaɪl] adj
vielseitig

verse [vɜ:s] n (poetry) Poesie f;
(stanza) Strophe f

version ['vɜ:ʃən] n Version f

versus ['vɜ:səs] prep gegen

vertical ['vɜ:tɪkəl] adj senkrecht,
vertikal

very ['verɪ] adv sehr; **~ much** sehr
▷ adj: **the ~ book I need** genau
das Buch, das ich brauche; **at that
~ moment** gerade in dem
Augenblick; **at the ~ top** ganz
oben; **the ~ best** der/die/das
Allerbeste

vest [vest] n (Brit) Unterhemd nt;
(US: waistcoat) Weste f

vet [vet] n Tierarzt m, Tierärztin f

veto ['vi:təʊ] (pl -es) n Veto nt
▷ vt sein Veto einlegen gegen

VHF abbr = **very high frequency**
UKW

via ['vaɪə] prep über +akk

viable ['vaɪəbl] adj (plan)

realisierbar; (company) rentabel

vibrate [vaɪ'breɪt] vi vibrieren;
vibration [vaɪ'breɪʃən] n
Vibration f

vicar ['vɪkə*] n Pfarrer(in) m(f)

vice [vaɪs] n (evil) Laster nt; (Tech)
Schraubstock m ▷ pref Vize-;
~chairman stellvertretender
Vorsitzender; **~president**
Vizepräsident(in) m(f)

vice versa ['vaɪs'vɜ:sə] adv
umgekehrt

vicinity [vɪ'sɪnɪtɪ] n: **in the ~** in
der Nähe (of +gen)

vicious ['vɪʃəs] adj (violent)
brutal; (malicious) gemein; **vicious
circle** n Teufelskreis m

victim ['vɪktɪm] n Opfer nt

Victorian [vɪk'tɔ:rɪən] adj
viktorianisch

victory ['vɪktərɪ] n Sieg m

video ['vɪdɪəʊ] (pl -s) adj Video-
▷ n Video nt; (recorder)
Videorekorder m ▷ vt (auf Video)
aufnehmen; **video camera** n
Videokamera f; **video cassette** n
Videokassette f; **video clip** n
Videoclip m; **video game** n
Videospiel nt; **videophone** n
Bildtelefon nt; **video recorder** n
Videorekorder m; **video shop** n
Videothek f; **videotape** n
Videoband nt ▷ vt (auf Video)
aufnehmen

Vienna [vɪ'enə] n Wien nt

Vietnam [vjet'næm] n Vietnam
nt

view [vju:] n (sight) Blick m (of auf
+akk); (vista) Aussicht f; (opinion)
Ansicht f, Meinung f; **in ~ of**
angesichts +gen ▷ vt (situation,
event) betrachten; (house)
besichtigen; **viewer** n (for slides)
Diabetrachter m; (TV)
Zuschauer(in) m(f); **viewpoint** n
(fig) Standpunkt m

vigilant ['vɪdʒɪlənt] adj wachsam

vile [vaɪl] adj abscheulich; (weather, food) scheußlich

village ['vɪlɪdʒ] n Dorf nt; **villager** n Dorfbewohner(in) m(f)

villain ['vɪlən] n Schurke m; (in film, story) Bösewicht m

vine [vaɪn] n (Wein)rebe f

vinegar ['vɪnɪgə*] n Essig m

vineyard ['vɪnjəd] n (of wine) Weinberg m

vintage ['vɪntɪdʒ] n (of wine) Jahrgang m; **vintage wine** n edler Wein

vinyl ['vaɪnɪl] n Vinyl nt

viola [vɪ'əʊlə] n Bratsche f

violate ['vaɪəleɪt] vt (treaty) brechen; (rights, rule) verletzen

violence ['vaɪələns] n (brutality) Gewalt f; (of person) Gewalttätigkeit f; **violent** adj (brutal) brutal; (death) gewaltsam

violet ['vaɪələt] n Veilchen nt

violin [vaɪə'lɪn] n Geige f, Violine f

VIP abbr = **very important person** VIP mf

virgin ['vɜ:dʒɪn] n Jungfrau f

Virgo ['vɜ:gəʊ] n (Astr) Jungfrau f

virile ['vɪraɪl] adj (man) männlich

virtual ['vɜ:tjʊəl] adj (Inform) virtuell; **virtually** adv praktisch; **virtual reality** n virtuelle Realität

virtue ['vɜ:tju:] n Tugend f; **by ~ of** aufgrund +gen; **virtuous** ['vɜ:tjʊəs] adj tugendhaft

virus ['vaɪrəs] n (Med, Inform) Virus m

visa ['vi:zə] n Visum nt

visibility [vɪzɪ'bɪlɪtɪ] n (Meteo) Sichtweite f; **good/poor ~** gute/schlechte Sicht; **visible** ['vɪzəbl] adj sichtbar; (evident) sichtlich; **visibly** adv sichtlich

vision ['vɪʒən] n (power of sight) Sehvermögen nt; (foresight) Weitblick m; (dream, image) Vision f

visit ['vɪzɪt] n Besuch m; (stay) Aufenthalt m ▷ vt besuchen; **visiting hours** npl Besuchszeiten pl; **visitor** n Besucher(in) m(f); **-'s book** Gästebuch nt; **visitor centre** n Informationszentrum nt

visor ['vaɪzə*] n (on helmet) Visier nt; (Auto) Blende f

visual ['vɪzjʊəl] adj Seh-; (image, joke) visuell; **~ aid** n Anschauungsmaterial nt; **~ display unit** Monitor m; **visualize** vt sich vorstellen; **visually** adv visuell; **~ impaired** sehbehindert

vital ['vaɪtl] adj (essential) unerlässlich, wesentlich; (argument, moment) entscheidend; **vitality** [vaɪ'tælɪtɪ] n Vitalität f; **vitally** adv äußerst

vitamin ['vɪtəmɪn] n Vitamin nt

vivacious [vɪ'veɪʃəs] adj lebhaft

vivid ['vɪvɪd] adj (description) anschaulich; (memory) lebhaft; (colour) leuchtend

V-neck ['vi:nek] n V-Ausschnitt m

vocabulary [vəʊ'kæbjʊlərɪ] n Wortschatz m, Vokabular nt

vocal ['vəʊkəl] adj (of the voice) Stimm-; (group) Gesangs-; (protest, person) lautstark

vocation [vəʊ'keɪʃən] n Berufung f; **vocational** adj Berufs-

vodka ['vɒdkə] n Wodka m

voice [vɔɪs] n Stimme f ▷ vt äußern; **voice mail** n Voicemail f

void [vɔɪd] n Leere f ▷ adj (Jur) ungültig; **~ of** (ganz) ohne

volcano [vɒl'keɪnəʊ] n (pl **-es**) Vulkan m

volley ['vɒlɪ] n (Tennis) Volley m; **volleyball** n Volleyball m

volt [vəʊlt] n Volt nt; **voltage** n Spannung f

volume ['vɒlju:m] n (of sound) Lautstärke f; (space occupied by sth)

Volumen nt; (size, amount) Umfang m; (book) Band m; **volume control** n Lautstärkeregler m
voluntary, voluntarily ['vɒləntəri, -li] adj, adv freiwillig; (unpaid) ehrenamtlich; **volunteer** [vɒlən'tɪə°] n Freiwillige(r) mf ▷ vi sich freiwillig melden ▷ vt: **to ~ to do sth** sich anbieten, etw zu tun
voluptuous [və'lʌptjʊəs] adj sinnlich
vomit ['vɒmɪt] vi sich übergeben
vote [vəʊt] n Stimme f; (ballot) Wahl f; (result) Abstimmungsergebnis nt; (right to vote) Wahlrecht nt ▷ vt (elect) wählen; **they ~d him chairman** sie wählten ihn zum Vorsitzenden ▷ vi wählen; **to ~ for/against sth** für/gegen etw stimmen; **voter** n Wähler(in) m(f)
voucher ['vaʊtʃə°] n Gutschein m
vow [vaʊ] n Gelöbnis nt ▷ vt: **to ~ to do sth** geloben, etw zu tun
vowel ['vaʊəl] n Vokal m
voyage ['vɔɪɪdʒ] n Reise f
vulgar ['vʌlgə°] adj vulgär, ordinär
vulnerable ['vʌlnərəbl] adj verwundbar; (sensitive) verletzlich
vulture ['vʌltʃə°] n Geier m

W

W abbr = **west** W
wade [weɪd] vi (in water) waten
wafer ['weɪfə°] n Waffel f; (Rel) Hostie f; **wafer-thin** adj hauchdünn
waffle ['wɒfl] n Waffel f; (Brit fam: empty talk) Geschwafel nt ▷ vi (Brit fam) schwafeln
wag [wæg] vt (tail) wedeln mit
wage [weɪdʒ] n Lohn m
waggon (Brit), **wagon** ['wægən] n (horse-drawn) Fuhrwerk nt; (Brit Rail) Waggon m; (US Auto) Wagen m
waist [weɪst] n Taille f; **waistcoat** n (Brit) Weste f; **waistline** n Taille f
wait [weɪt] n Wartezeit f ▷ vi warten (for auf +akk); **to ~ and see** abwarten; **~ a minute** Moment mal!; **wait up** vi aufbleiben
waiter n Kellner m; **~!** Herr Ober!
waiting n: **"no ~"** „Halteverbot";

waiting list n Warteliste f;
waiting room n (Med)
Wartezimmer nt; (Rail) Wartesaal
m

waitress n Kellnerin f

wake [weɪk] (**woke** o **waked**,
woken o **waked**) vt wecken ▷ vi
aufwachen; **wake up** vt
aufwecken ▷ vi aufwachen;
wake-up call n (Tel) Weckruf m

Wales [weɪlz] n Wales nt

walk [wɔːk] n Spaziergang m;
(ramble) Wanderung f; (route) Weg
m; **to go for a ~** spazieren gehen;
it's only a five-minute ~ es sind
nur fünf Minuten zu Fuß ▷ vi
gehen; (stroll) spazieren gehen;
(ramble) wandern ▷ vt (dog)
ausführen; **walking** n: **to go
~** wandern; **walking shoes** npl
Wanderschuhe pl; **walking stick** n
Spazierstock m

Walkman® (pl **-s**) n Walkman®
m

wall [wɔːl] n (inside) Wand f;
(outside) Mauer f

wallet [ˈwɒlɪt] n Brieftasche
f

wallpaper [ˈwɔːlpeɪpə] n
Tapete f; (Inform)
Bildschirmhintergrund m ▷ vt
tapezieren

walnut [ˈwɔːlnʌt] n (nut)
Walnuss f

waltz [wɔːlts] n Walzer m

wander [ˈwɒndə] vi (person)
herumwandern

want [wɒnt] n (lack) Mangel m
(of an +dat); (need) Bedürfnis nt; **for
~ of** aus Mangel an +dat ▷ vt
(desire) wollen; (need) brauchen; **I
~ to stay here** ich will hier
bleiben; **he doesn't ~ to** er will
nicht

WAP phone [ˈwæpfəʊn] n
WAP-Handy nt

war [wɔːʳ] n Krieg m

ward [wɔːd] n (in hospital)
Station f; (child) Mündel nt

warden [ˈwɔːdən] n Aufseher(in)
m(f); (in youth hostel) Herbergsvater
m, Herbergsmutter f

wardrobe [ˈwɔːdrəʊb] n
Kleiderschrank m

warehouse [ˈwɛəhaʊs] n
Lagerhaus nt

warfare [ˈwɔːfɛəʳ] n Krieg m;
(techniques) Kriegsführung f

warm [wɔːm] adj warm;
(welcome) herzlich; **I'm ~** mir ist
warm ▷ vt wärmen; (food)
aufwärmen; **warm over** vt (US:
food) aufwärmen; **warm up** vt
(food) aufwärmen; (room)
erwärmen ▷ vi (food, room) warm
werden; (Sport) sich aufwärmen;
warmly adv warm; (welcome)
herzlich; **warmth** n Wärme f; (of
welcome) Herzlichkeit f

warn [wɔːn] vt warnen (of,
against vor +dat); **to ~ sb not to do
sth** jdn davor warnen, etw zu tun;
warning n Warnung f; **warning
light** n Warnlicht nt; **warning
triangle** n (Auto) Warndreieck nt

warranty [ˈwɒrəntɪ] n Garantie
f

wart [wɔːt] n Warze f

wary [ˈwɛərɪ] adj vorsichtig;
(suspicious) misstrauisch

was [wɒz, wəz] pt of **be**

wash [wɒʃ] n: **to have a ~** sich
waschen; **it's in the ~** es ist in der
Wäsche ▷ vt waschen; (plates,
glasses etc) abwaschen; **to ~ one's
hands** sich auf die Hände
waschen; **to ~ the dishes** (das
Geschirr) abwaschen ▷ vi (clean
oneself) sich waschen; **wash off** vt
abwaschen; **wash up** vi (Brit:
wash dishes) abwaschen; (US: clean
oneself) sich waschen; **washable**
adj waschbar; **washbag** n (US)
Kulturbeutel m; **washbasin** n

Waschbecken nt; **washcloth** n
(US) Waschlappen m; **washer** n
(Tech) Dichtungsring m; (washing
machine) Waschmaschine f;
washing n (laundry) Wäsche f;
washing machine n
Waschmaschine f; **washing
powder** n Waschpulver nt;
washing-up n (Brit) Abwasch m;
to do the ~ abwaschen;
washing-up liquid n (Brit)
Spülmittel nt; **washroom** n (US)
Toilette f

wasn't ['wɒznt] contr of **was not**

wasp [wɒsp] n Wespe f

waste [weist] n (materials) Abfall
m; (wasting) Verschwendung f; **it's
a ~ of time** das ist
Zeitverschwendung ▷ adj
(superfluous) überschüssig ▷ vt
verschwenden (on an +akk);
(opportunity) vertun; **waste bin** n
Abfalleimer m; **wastepaper
basket** n Papierkorb m

watch [wɒtʃ] n (timepiece)
(Armband)uhr f ▷ vt (observe)
beobachten; (guard) aufpassen auf
+akk; (film, play, programme) sich
dat ansehen; **to ~ TV** fernsehen
▷ vi zusehen; (guard) Wache
halten; **to ~ for sb/sth** nach
jdm/etw Ausschau halten; **~ out**
pass auf!; **watchdog** n
Wachhund m; (fig)
Aufsichtsbehörde f; **watchful** adj
wachsam

water ['wɔːtə] n Wasser nt ▷ vt
(plant) gießen ▷ vi (eye) tränen;
my mouth is ~ing mir läuft das
Wasser im Mund zusammen;
water down vt verdünnen;
watercolor (US), **watercolour** n
(painting) Aquarell nt; (paint)
Wasserfarbe f; **watercress** n
(Brunnen)kresse f; **waterfall** n
Wasserfall m; **watering can** n
Gießkanne f; **water level** n

Wasserstand m; **watermelon** n
Wassermelone f; **waterproof** adj
wasserdicht; **water-skiing** n
Wasserskilaufen nt; **water sports**
npl Wassersport m; **watertight**
adj wasserdicht; **water wings** npl
Schwimmflügel pl; **watery** adj
wässerig

wave [weiv] n Welle f ▷ vt (move
to and fro) schwenken; (hand, flag)
winken mit ▷ vi (person) winken;
(flag) wehen; **wavelength** n
Wellenlänge f; **to be on the same
~** (fig) die gleiche Wellenlänge
haben; **wavy** ['weivi] adj wellig

wax [wæks] n Wachs nt; (in ear)
Ohrenschmalz nt

way [wei] n Weg m; (direction)
Richtung f; (manner) Art f; **can you
tell me the ~ to ... ?** wie komme
ich (am besten) zu ... ?; **we went
the wrong ~** wir sind in die
falsche Richtung
gefahren/gegangen; **to lose one's
~** sich verirren; **to make ~ for
sb/sth** jdm/etw Platz machen; **to
get one's own ~** seinen Willen
durchsetzen; **"give ~"** (Auto)
"Vorfahrt achten"; **the other
~ round** andersherum; **one ~ or
another** irgendwie; **in a ~** in
gewisser Weise; **in the ~** im Weg;
by the ~ übrigens; **"~ in"**
"Eingang"; **"~ out"** "Ausgang"; **no
~** (fam) kommt nicht infrage!

we [wiː] pron wir

weak [wiːk] adj schwach;
weaken vt schwächen ▷ vi
schwächer werden

wealth [welθ] n Reichtum m;
wealthy adj reich

weapon ['wepən] n Waffe f

wear [weə] (wore, worn) vt
(have on) tragen; **what shall I ~?**
was soll ich anziehen? ▷ vi
(become worn) sich abnutzen ▷ n:
~ (and tear) Abnutzung f; **wear**

off vi (diminish) nachlassen; **wear
out** vt abnutzen; (person)
erschöpfen ▷ vi sich
abnutzen

weather ['weðə'] n Wetter nt;
I'm feeling under the ~ ich fühle
mich nicht ganz wohl; **weather
forecast** n Wettervorhersage
f

weave [wi:v] (wove o weaved,
woven o weaved) vt (cloth)
weben; (basket etc) flechten

web [web] n (a. fig) Netz nt; **the
Web** das Web, das Internet;
webcam ['webkæm] n Webcam
f; **web page** n Webseite f;
website n Website f

we'd [wi:d] contr of **we had; we
would**

Wed abbr = **Wednesday**

wedding ['wedɪŋ] n Hochzeit f;
wedding anniversary n
Hochzeitstag m; **wedding dress** n
Hochzeitskleid nt; **wedding ring**
n Ehering m

wedding shower n (US) Party für
die zukünftige Braut

wedge [wedʒ] n (under door etc)
Keil m; (of cheese etc) Stück nt, Ecke
f

Wednesday ['wenzdeɪ] n
Mittwoch m; see also **Tuesday**

wee [wi:] adj klein ▷ vi (fam)
Pipi machen

weed [wi:d] n Unkraut nt ▷ vt
jäten

week [wi:k] n Woche f; **twice a
~** zweimal in der Woche; **a ~ on
Friday/Friday** ~ Freitag in einer
Woche; **a ~ last Friday** letzten
Freitag vor einer Woche; **in two
~s' time, in two ~s** in zwei
Wochen; **for ~s** wochenlang;
weekday n Wochentag m;
weekend n Wochenende nt;
weekend break n
Wochenendurlaub m; **weekly** adj,

adv wöchentlich; (magazine)
Wochen-

weep [wi:p] (wept, wept) vi
weinen

weigh [weɪ] vt, vi wiegen; **it ~s
20 kilos** es wiegt 20 Kilo; **weigh
up** vt abwägen; (person)
einschätzen; **weight** [weɪt] n
Gewicht nt; **to lose/put on
~** abnehmen/zunehmen;
weightlifting n Gewichtheben
nt; **weight training** n
Krafttraining nt; **weighty** adj
(important) schwerwiegend

weird [wɪəd] adj seltsam; **weirdo**
['wɪədəʊ] n Spinner(in) m(f)

welcome ['welkəm] n Empfang
m ▷ adj willkommen; (news)
angenehm; **~ to London**
willkommen in London! ▷ vt
begrüßen; (approve) begrüßen;
freundlich

welfare ['welfeə'] n Wohl nt; (US:
social security) Sozialhilfe f; **welfare
state** n Wohlfahrtsstaat m

well [wel] n Brunnen m ▷ adj (in
good health) gesund; **are you ~?**
geht es dir/Ihnen gut?; **to feel
~** sich wohlfühlen; **get ~ soon**
gute Besserung! ▷ interj nun; **~, I
don't know** nun, ich weiß nicht
▷ adv gut; **~ done** gut gemacht!; **it
may ~ be** das kann wohl sein; **as
~** (in addition) auch; **~ over 60** weit
über 60

we'll [wi:l] contr of **we will; we
shall**

well-behaved [welbɪ'heɪvd]
adj brav; **well-being** n Wohl nt;
well-built adj (person) gut gebaut;
well-done adj (steak)
durchgebraten; **well-earned** adj
wohlverdient

wellingtons ['welɪŋtənz] npl
Gummistiefel pl

well-known [wel'nəʊn] adj
bekannt; **well-off** adj (wealthy)

wohlhabend; **well-paid** adj gut bezahlt

Welsh [welʃ] adj walisisch ▷ n (language) Walisisch nt; **the ~** pl die Waliser pl; **Welshman** (pl **-men**) n Waliser m; **Welshwoman** (pl **-women**) n Waliserin f

went [went] pt of **go**

wept [wept] pt, pp of **weep**

were [wɜː] pt of **be**

we're [wɪə*] contr of **we are**

weren't [wɜːnt] contr of **were not**

west [west] n Westen m; **the West** (Pol) der Westen ▷ adv (go, face) nach Westen ▷ adj West-; **westbound** adj (in) Richtung Westen; **western** adj West-, westlich; **Western Europe** Westeuropa nt ▷ n (Cine) Western m; **West Germany** n: **(the former) ~** (das ehemalige) Westdeutschland, Westdeutschland n; **westwards** ['westwədz] adv nach Westen

wet [wet] (**wet, wet**) adj vt: to **~ oneself** in die Hose machen ▷ adj nass, feucht; **"~ paint"** „frisch gestrichen"; **wet suit** n Taucheranzug m

we've [wiːv] contr of **we have**

whale [weɪl] n Wal m

wharf [wɔːf] (pl **-s** o **wharves**) n Kai m

○ **KEYWORD**

what [wɒt] adj 1 (in questions) welche(r, s) was für ein(e); **what size is it?** welche Größe ist das?

2 (in exclamations) was für ein(e); **what a mess!** was für ein Durcheinander!

▷ pron (interrogative/relative) was; **what are you doing?** was machst du/machen Sie gerade?; **what are you talking about?** wovon redest

du/reden Sie?; **what's your name?** wie heißt du/heißen Sie?; **what is it called?** wie heißt das?; **what about ...?** wie wär's mit ...?; **I saw what you did** ich habe gesehen, was du gemacht hast/Sie gemacht haben

▷ excl (disbelieving) wie, was; **what, no coffee!** wie, kein Kaffee!; **I've crashed the car — what!** ich hatte einen Autounfall — was!

whatever pron: **I'll do ~ you want** ich tue alles, was du willst/Sie wollen; **~ he says** egal, was er sagt

what's [wɒts] contr of **what is; what has**

wheat [wiːt] n Weizen m

wheel [wiːl] n Rad nt; (steering wheel) Lenkrad nt ▷ vt (bicycle, trolley) schieben; **wheelbarrow** n Schubkarren m; **wheelchair** n Rollstuhl m; **wheel clamp** n Parkkralle f

○ **KEYWORD**

when [wen] adv wann ▷ conj 1 (at, during, after the time that) wenn; (in past) als; **she was reading when I came in** sie las, als ich hereinkam; **be careful when you cross the road** sei vorsichtig, wenn du über die Straße gehst/seien Sie vorsichtig, wenn Sie über die Straße gehen

2 (on, at which) als; **on the day when I met him** an dem Tag, an dem ich ihn traf

3 (whereas) wo ... doch

whenever adv (every time) immer wenn; **come ~ you like** komm, wann immer du willst/kommen Sie, wann immer sie wollen

w

where [wɛə⁰] *adv* wo; **~ are you going?** wohin gehst du/gehen Sie?; **~ are you from?** woher kommst du/kommen Sie? ▷ *conj* wo; **that's ~ I used to live** da habe ich früher gewohnt; **whereabouts** [wɛərə'baʊts] *adv* wo ▷ *npl* ['wɛərəbaʊts] Aufenthaltsort *m*; **whereas** [wɛər'æz] *conj* während, wohingegen; **whereby** *adv* wodurch; **wherever** [wɛər'evə⁰] *conj* wo immer; **~ that may be** wo immer das sein mag; **~ I go** überall, wohin ich gehe

whether ['wɛðə⁰] *conj* ob

○ **KEYWORD**

which [wɪtʃ] *adj* **1** (*interrogative*) (*direct, indirect*) welche(r, s); **which one?** welche(r, s)?
2 in which case zu diesem Fall; **by which time** zu dieser Zeit
▷ *pron* **1** (*interrogative*) welche(r, s); (*of people also*) wer
2 (*relative*) der/die/das; (*referring to people*) was; **the apple which you ate/which is on the table** der Apfel, den du gegessen hast/der auf dem Tisch liegt; **he said he saw her, which is true** er sagte, er habe sie gesehen, was auch stimmt

whichever *adj, pron* welche(r, s) auch immer

while [waɪl] *n*: **a ~** eine Weile; **for a ~** eine Zeit lang; **a short ~ ago** vor Kurzem ▷ *conj* während; (*although*) obwohl

whine [waɪn] *vi* (*person*) jammern

whip [wɪp] *n* Peitsche *f* ▷ *vt* (*beat*) peitschen; **~ped cream** Schlagsahne *f*

whirl [wɜːl] *vt, vi* herumwirbeln;

whirlpool *n* (*in river, sea*) Strudel *m*; (*pool*) Whirlpool *m*

whisk [wɪsk] *n* Schneebesen *m* ▷ *vt* (*cream etc*) schlagen

whisker ['wɪskə⁰] *n* (*of animal*) Schnurrhaar *nt*; **~s** *pl* (*of man*) Backenbart *m*

whisk(e)y ['wɪskɪ] *n* Whisky *m*

whisper ['wɪspə⁰] *vi, vt* flüstern; **to ~ sth to sb** jdm etw zuflüstern

whistle ['wɪsl] *n* Pfiff *m*; (*instrument*) Pfeife *f* ▷ *vt, vi* pfeifen

white [waɪt] *n* (*of egg*) Eiweiß *nt*; (*of eye*) Weiße *nt* ▷ *adj* weiß; (*with fear*) blass; (*coffee*) mit Milch/Sahne; **White House** *n*: **the ~** das Weiße Haus; **white lie** *n* Notlüge *f*; **white meat** *n* helles Fleisch; **white sauce** *n* weiße Soße; **white water rafting** *n* Rafting *nt*; **white wine** *n* Weißwein *m*

Whitsun ['wɪtsn] *n* Pfingsten *nt*

○ **KEYWORD**

who [huː] *pron* **1** (*interrogative*) wer; (*akk*) wen; (*dat*) wem; **who is it?, who's there?** wer ist da?
2 (*relative*) der/die/das; **the woman/man who spoke to me** die Frau/der Mann, die/der mit mir sprach

whoever [huː'evə⁰] *pron* wer auch immer; **~ you choose** wen auch immer du wählst/Sie wählen

whole [həʊl] *adj* ganz ▷ *n* Ganze(s) *nt*; **the ~ of my family** meine ganze Familie; **on the ~** im Großen und Ganzen; **wholefood** *n* (*Brit*) Vollwertkost *f*; **~ store** Bioladen *m*; **wholeheartedly** *adv* voll und ganz; **wholemeal** *adj* (*Brit*) Vollkorn-; **wholesale** *adv* (*buy, sell*) im Großhandel; **wholesome**

adj gesund; **whole wheat** *adj* Vollkorn-; **wholly** ['həʊlɪ] *adv* völlig

○ **KEYWORD**

whom [huːm] *pron* **1** (*interrogative*) (*akk*) wen; (*dat*) wem; **whom did you see?** wen hast du/haben Sie gesehen?; **to whom did you give it?** wem hast du/haben Sie es gegeben? **2** (*relative*) (*akk*) den/die/das; (*dat*) dem/der/dem; **the man whom I saw/to whom I spoke** der Mann, den ich sah/mit dem ich sprach

whooping cough ['huːpɪŋkɒf] *n* Keuchhusten *m*

whose [huːz] *adj* (*in questions*) wessen; (*in relative clauses*) dessen/deren/dessen, deren *pl*; **~ bike is that?** wessen Fahrrad ist das? ▷ *pron* (*in questions*) wessen; **~ is this?** wem gehört das?

○ **KEYWORD**

why [waɪ] *adv* warum, weshalb ▷ *conj* warum, weshalb; **that's not why I'm here** ich bin nicht deswegen hier; **that's the reason why** deshalb ▷ *excl* (*expressing surprise, shock*) na so was; (*explaining*) also dann; **why, it's you!** na so was, du bist/Sie sind es!

wicked ['wɪkɪd] *adj* böse; (*fam: great*) geil
wide [waɪd] *adj* breit; (*skirt, trousers*) weit; (*difference*) groß ▷ *adv* weit; **wide-angle lens** *n* Weitwinkelobjektiv *nt*; **wide-awake** *adj* hellwach; **widely** *adv* weit; **~ known**

allgemein bekannt; **widen** *vt* verbreitern; (*fig*) erweitern; **wide-open** *adj* weit offen; **widescreen TV** *n* Breitbildfernseher *m*; **widespread** *adj* weit verbreitet
widow ['wɪdəʊ] *n* Witwe *f*; **widowed** *adj* verwitwet; **widower** *n* Witwer *m*
width [wɪdθ] *n* Breite *f*
wife [waɪf] (*pl* **wives**) *n* (Ehe)frau *f*
Wi-Fi ['waɪfaɪ] *n* Wi-Fi *nt*
wig [wɪg] *n* Perücke *f*
wiggle ['wɪgl] *vt* wackeln mit
wild [waɪld] *adj* wild; (*violent*) heftig; (*plan, idea*) verrückt ▷ *n*: **in the ~** in freier Wildbahn; **wildlife** *n* Tier- und Pflanzenwelt *f*; **wildly** *adv* wild; (*exaggerated*) maßlos

○ **KEYWORD**

will [wɪl] *vb aux* **1** (*forms future tense*) werden; **I will finish it tomorrow** ich mache es morgen zu Ende **2** (*in conjectures, predictions*) **he will** o **he'll be there by now** er dürfte jetzt da sein; **that will be the postman** das wird der Postbote sein **3** (*in commands, requests, offers*) **will you be quiet!** sei/seien Sie endlich still!; **will you help me?** hilfst du/helfen Sie mir?; **will you have a cup of tea?** trinkst du/trinken Sie eine Tasse Tee?; **I won't put up with it!** das lasse ich mir nicht gefallen! ▷ *vt* wollen ▷ *n* Wille *m*; (*jur*) Testament *nt*

willing *adj* bereitwillig; **to be ~ to do sth** bereit sein, etw zu tun; **willingly** *adv* gern(e)
willow ['wɪləʊ] *n* Weide *f*

w

willpower ['wɪlpauə⁰] n Willenskraft f

wimp [wɪmp] n Weichei nt

win [wɪn] (**won, won**) vt, vi gewinnen ▷ n Sieg m; **win over**, **win round** vt für sich gewinnen

wind [waɪnd] (**wound, wound**) vt (rope, bandage) wickeln; **wind down** vt (car window) herunterkurbeln; **wind up** vt (clock) aufziehen; (car window) hochkurbeln; (meeting, speech) abschließen; (person) aufziehen, ärgern

wind [wɪnd] n Wind m; (Med) Blähungen pl; **wind farm** n Windpark m; **wind instrument** n Blasinstrument nt; **windmill** n Windmühle f

window ['wɪndəʊ] n Fenster nt; (counter) Schalter m; **~ of opportunity** Chance f, Gelegenheit f; **window box** n Blumenkasten m; **windowpane** n Fensterscheibe f; **window-shopping** n **to go ~** einen Schaufensterbummel machen; **windowsill** n Fensterbrett nt

windpipe ['wɪndpaɪp] n Luftröhre f; **windscreen** n (Brit) Windschutzscheibe f; **windscreen wiper** n (Brit) Scheibenwischer m; **windshield** n (US) Windschutzscheibe f; **windshield wiper** n (US) Scheibenwischer m; **windsurfer** n Windsurfer(in) m(f); (board) Surfbrett nt; **windsurfing** n Windsurfen nt; **wind turbine** n Windturbine f

windy ['wɪndɪ] adj windig

wine [waɪn] n Wein m; **wine bar** n Weinlokal nt; **wineglass** n Weinglas nt; **wine list** n Weinkarte f; **wine tasting** n (event) Weinprobe f

wing [wɪŋ] n Flügel m; (Brit Auto) Kotflügel m; **~s** pl (Theat) Kulissen pl

wink [wɪŋk] vi zwinkern; **to ~ at sb** jdm zuwinkern

winner ['wɪnə⁰] n Gewinner(in) m(f); (Sport) Sieger(in) m(f); **winning** adj (team, horse etc) siegreich; **~ number** Gewinnzahl f ▷ n **~s** pl Gewinn m

winter ['wɪntə⁰] n Winter m; **winter sports** npl Wintersport m; **wint(e)ry** ['wɪntrɪ] adj winterlich

wipe [waɪp] vt abwischen; **to ~ one's nose** sich dat die Nase putzen; **to ~ one's feet** (on mat) sich dat die Schuhe abtreten; **wipe off** vt abwischen; **wipe out** vt (destroy) vernichten; (data, debt) löschen; (epidemic etc) ausrotten

wire ['waɪə⁰] n Draht m; (Elec) Leitung f; (US: telegram) Telegramm nt ▷ vt (plug in) anschließen; (US Tel) telegrafieren (sb sth jdm etw); **wireless** ['waɪələs] adj drahtlos

wisdom ['wɪzdəm] n Weisheit f; **wisdom tooth** n Weisheitszahn m

wise, wisely [waɪz, -lɪ] adj, adv weise

wish [wɪʃ] n Wunsch m (for nach); **with best ~es** (in letter) herzliche Grüße ▷ vt wünschen, wollen; **to ~ sb good luck/Merry Christmas** jdm viel Glück/frohe Weihnachten wünschen; **I ~ I'd never seen him** ich wünschte, ich hätte ihn nie gesehen

witch [wɪtʃ] n Hexe f

 KEYWORD

with [wɪð] prep 1 (accompanying, in the company of) mit; **we stayed with friends** wir übernachteten bei Freunden; **I'll be with you in a minute** einen Augenblick, ich bin sofort da; **I'm not with you** (I don't understand) das verstehe ich nicht; **to be with it** (inf) (up-to-date) auf dem Laufenden sein; (alert) (voll) da sein inf

2 (descriptive, indicating manner etc) mit; **the man with the grey hat** der Mann mit dem grauen Hut; **red with anger** rot vor Wut

withdraw [wɪθˈdrɔː] irr vt zurückziehen; (money) abheben; (comment) zurücknehmen ▷ vi sich zurückziehen

wither [ˈwɪðəʳ] vi (plant) verwelken

withhold [wɪθˈhəʊld] irr vt vorenthalten (from sb jdm)

within [wɪðˈɪn] prep innerhalb +gen; **~ walking distance** zu Fuß erreichbar

without [wɪðˈaʊt] prep ohne; **~ asking** ohne zu fragen

withstand [wɪðˈstænd] irr vt standhalten +dat

witness [ˈwɪtnəs] n Zeuge m, Zeugin f ▷ vt Zeuge sein; **witness box, witness stand** (US) n Zeugenstand m

witty [ˈwɪtɪ] adj geistreich

wives [waɪvz] pl of **wife**

WMD abbr = **weapon of mass destruction** Massenvernichtungswaffe

wobble [ˈwɒbl] vi wackeln; **wobbly** adj wackelig

wok [wɒk] n Wok m

woke [wəʊk] pt of **wake**

woken [ˈwəʊkn] pp of **wake**

wolf [wʊlf] (pl **wolves**) n Wolf m

woman [ˈwʊmən] (pl **women**) n Frau f

womb [wuːm] n Gebärmutter f

women [ˈwɪmɪn] pl of **woman**

won [wʌn] pt, pp of **win**

wonder [ˈwʌndəʳ] n (marvel) Wunder nt; (surprise) Staunen nt ▷ vt, vi (speculate) sich fragen; **I ~ what/if ...** ich frage mich, was/ob ...; **wonderful** adj; **wonderfully** adj, adv wunderbar

won't [wəʊnt] contr of **will not**

wood [wʊd] n Holz nt; **~s** Wald m; **wooden** adj Holz-; (fig) hölzern; **woodpecker** n Specht m; **woodwork** n (wooden parts) Holzteile pl; (in school) Werken nt

wool [wʊl] n Wolle f; **woollen, woolen** (US) adj Woll-

word [wɜːd] n Wort nt; (promise) Ehrenwort nt; **~s** pl (of song) Text m; **to have a ~ with sb** mit jdm sprechen; **in other ~s** mit anderen Worten ▷ vt formulieren; **wording** n Wortlaut m, Formulierung f; **word processing** n Textverarbeitung f; **word processor** n (program) Textverarbeitungsprogramm nt

wore [wɔːʳ] pt of **wear**

work [wɜːk] n Arbeit f; (of art, literature) Werk nt; **~ of art** Kunstwerk nt; **he's at ~** er ist in/auf der Arbeit; **out of ~** arbeitslos ▷ vi arbeiten (at, on an +dat); (machine, plan) funktionieren; (medicine) wirken; (succeed) klappen ▷ vt (machine) bedienen; **work out** vi (plan) klappen; (sum) aufgehen; (person) trainieren ▷ vt (price, speed etc) ausrechnen; (plan) ausarbeiten; **work up** vt: **to get worked up** sich aufregen; **workaholic** [wɜːkəˈhɒlɪk] n Arbeitstier nt; **worker** n Arbeiter(in) m(f); **working class** n Arbeiterklasse f; **workman** (pl **-men**) n Handwerker m; **workout** n (Sport) Fitnesstraining nt, Konditionstraining nt; **work permit** n Arbeitserlaubnis f;

w

workplace n Arbeitsplatz m;
workshop n Werkstatt f;
(meeting) Workshop m; **work
station** n (Inform) Workstation
f

world [wɜːld] n Welt f; **world
championship** n Weltmeisterschaft f; **World War** n: **~ I/II, the
First/Second** ~ der Erste/Zweite
Weltkrieg; **world-wide** adj, adv
weltweit; **World Wide Web** n
World Wide Web nt

worm [wɜːm] n Wurm m

worn [wɔːn] pp of **wear** ▷ adj
(clothes) abgetragen; (tyre)
abgefahren; **worn-out** adj
abgenutzt; (person) erschöpft

worried [wʌrɪd] adj besorgt; **be
~ about** sich dat Sorgen machen
um; **worry** [wʌrɪ] n Sorge f ▷ vt
Sorgen machen +dat ▷ vi sich
Sorgen machen (about um); **don't
~!** keine Sorge!; **worrying** adj
beunruhigend

worse [wɜːs] adj comparative of
bad; schlechter; (pain, mistake etc)
schlimmer ▷ adv comparative of
badly; schlechter; **worsen** vt
verschlechtern ▷ vi sich
verschlechtern

worship [wɜːʃɪp] vt anbeten,
anhimmeln

worst [wɜːst] adj superlative of
bad; schlechteste(r, s); (pain,
mistake etc) schlimmste(r, s) ▷ adv
superlative of **badly**; am
schlechtesten ▷ n: **the ~ is over**
das Schlimmste ist vorbei; **at (the)
~** schlimmstenfalls

worth [wɜːθ] n Wert m; **£10 ~ of
food** Essen für 10 Pfund ▷ adj: **it is
~ £50** es ist 50 Pfund wert;
~ seeing sehenswert; **it's ~ it**
(rewarding) es lohnt sich;
worthless adj wertlos;
worthwhile adj lohnend,
lohnenswert; **worthy** [wɜːðɪ]

adj (deserving respect) würdig; **to
be ~ of sth** etw verdienen

KEYWORD

would [wʊd] vb aux **1** (conditional
tense) **if you asked him he would
do it** wenn du ihn fragtest/Sie ihn
fragten, würde er es tun; **if you
had asked him he would have
done it** wenn du ihn gefragt
hättest/Sie ihn gefragt hätten,
hätte er es getan
2 (in offers, invitations, requests)
would you like a biscuit?
möchtest du/möchten Sie einen
Keks?; **would you ask him to
come in?** würdest du/würden Sie
ihn bitte hereinbitten?
3 (in indirect speech) **I said I would
do it** ich sagte, ich würde es tun
4 (emphatic) **it WOULD have to
snow today!** es musste ja
ausgerechnet heute schneien!
5 (insistence) **she wouldn't behave**
sie wollte sich partout nicht
anständig benehmen
6 (conjecture) **it would have been
midnight** es mag ungefähr
Mitternacht gewesen sein; **it
would seem so** so sieht wohl so
aus
7 (indicating habit) **he would go
there on Mondays** er ging jeden
Montag dorthin

wouldn't [wʊdnt] contr of
would not

would've [wʊdəv] contr of
would have

wound [wuːnd] n Wunde f ▷ vt
verwunden; (fig) verletzen
▷ [waʊnd] pt, pp of **wind**

wove [wəʊv] pt of **weave**

woven [wəʊvn] pp of **weave**

wrap [ræp] vt (parcel, present)
einwickeln; **to ~ sth round sth**

etw um etw wickeln; **wrap up** vt (parcel, present) einwickeln ▷ vi (dress warmly) sich warm anziehen; **wrapper** n (of sweet) Papier nt; **wrapping paper** n Packpapier nt; (giftwrap) Geschenkpapier nt

wreath [riːθ] n Kranz m

wreck [rek] n (ship, plane, car) Wrack nt; **a nervous ~** ein Nervenbündel m ▷ vt (car) zu Schrott fahren; (fig) zerstören; **wreckage** ['rekɪdʒ] n Trümmer pl

wrench [rentʃ] n (tool) Schraubenschlüssel m

wrestling ['resliŋ] n Ringen nt

wring out ['rɪŋ'aʊt] (**wrung, wrung**) vt auswringen

wrinkle ['rɪŋkl] n Falte f

wrist [rɪst] n Handgelenk nt; **wristwatch** n Armbanduhr f

write [raɪt] (**wrote, written**) vt schreiben; (cheque) ausstellen ▷ vi schreiben; **to ~ to sb** jdm schreiben; **write down** vt aufschreiben; **write off** vt (debt, person) abschreiben; (car) zu Schrott fahren ▷ vi: **to ~ off for sth** etw anfordern; **write out** vt (name etc) ausschreiben; (cheque) ausstellen; **write-protected** adj (Inform) schreibgeschützt; **writer** n Verfasser(in) m(f); (author) Schriftsteller(in) m(f); **writing** n Schrift f; (profession) Schreiben nt; **in ~** schriftlich; **writing paper** n Schreibpapier nt

written ['rɪtən] pp of **write**

wrong [rɒŋ] adj (incorrect) falsch; (morally) unrecht; **you're ~** du hast/Sie haben unrecht; **what's ~ with your leg?** was ist mit deinem/Ihrem Bein los?; **you've got the ~ number** du bist/Sie sind falsch verbunden; **I dialled the ~ number** ich habe mich verwählt; **don't get me ~** versteh/verstehen Sie mich

nicht falsch; **to go ~** (plan) schiefgehen; **wrongly** adv falsch; (unjustly) zu Unrecht

wrote [rəʊt] pt of **write**

WWW abbr = **World Wide Web** WWW

xenophobia [zenə'fəʊbɪə] n
Ausländerfeindlichkeit f
XL abbr = **extra large** XL, übergroß
Xmas ['krɪsməs] n Weihnachten
nt
X-ray ['eksreɪ] n (picture)
Röntgenaufnahme f ▷ vt röntgen
xylophone ['zaɪləfəʊn] n Xylo

yacht [jɒt] n Jacht f; **yachting** n
Segeln nt; **to go** ~ segeln gehen
yam [jæm] n (US) Süßkartoffel
f
yard [jɑːd] n Hof m; (US: garden)
Garten m; (measure) Yard nt (0,91 m)
yawn [jɔːn] vi gähnen
yd abbr = **yard(s)**
year ['jɪə°] n Jahr nt; **this/last/
next** ~ dieses/letztes/nächstes
Jahr; **he is 28 ~s old** er ist 28 Jahre
alt; **~s ago** vor Jahren; **a
five-year-old** ein(e)
Fünfjährige(r); **yearly** adj, adv
jährlich
yearn [jɜːn] vi sich sehnen (for
nach +dat); **to** ~ **to do sth** sich
danach sehnen, etw zu tun
yeast [jiːst] n Hefe f
yell [jel] vi, vt schreien; **to** ~ **at sb**
jdn anschreien
yellow ['jeləʊ] adj gelb; ~ **card**

(Sport) gelbe Karte; **~ fever** Gelbfieber nt; **~ line** (Brit) = Halteverbot nt; **double ~ line** (Brit) = absolutes Halteverbot; **the Yellow Pages®** pl die Gelben Seiten pl

yes [jes] adv ja; (answering negative question) doch; **to say ~ to sth** ja zu etw sagen ▷ n Ja nt

yesterday ['jestədeɪ] adv gestern; **~ morning/evening** gestern Morgen/Abend; **the day before ~** vorgestern; **~'s newspaper** die Zeitung von gestern

yet [jet] adv (still) noch; (up to now) bis jetzt; (in a question: already) schon; **he hasn't arrived ~** er ist noch nicht gekommen; **have you finished ~?** bist du/sind Sie schon fertig?; **~ again** schon wieder; **as ~** bis jetzt ▷ conj doch

yield [jiːld] n Ertrag m ▷ vt (result, crop) hervorbringen; (profit, interest) bringen ▷ vi nachgeben (to +dat); (Mil) sich ergeben (to +dat); **"~"** (US Auto) „Vorfahrt beachten"

yoga ['jəʊɡə] n Yoga nt

yog(h)urt ['jɒɡət] n Jog(h)urt m

yolk [jəʊk] n Eigelb nt

Yorkshire pudding ['jɔːkʃə'pʊdɪŋ] n gebackener Eierteig, der meist zum Roastbeef gegessen wird

○ **KEYWORD**

you [juː] pron **1** (subj, in comparisons) (familiar form) (sg) du; (pl) ihr; (in letters) Du, Ihr; (polite form) Sie; **you Germans** ihr Deutschen; **she's younger than you** sie ist jünger als du/ihr/Sie **2** (direct object, after prep +akk) (familiar form) (sg) dich; (pl) euch; (in letters) Dich, Euch; (polite form)

Sie; **I know you** ich kenne dich/euch/Sie **3** (indirect object, after prep +dat) (familiar form) (sg) dir; (pl) euch; (in letters) Dir, Euch; (polite form) Ihnen; **I gave it to you** ich gab es dir/euch/Ihnen **4** (impers) (one) (subj) man; (direct object) einen; (indirect object) einem; **fresh air does you good** frische Luft tut (einem) gut

you'd [juːd] contr of **you had; you would; ~ better leave** du solltest/Sie sollten gehen

you'll [juːl] contr of **you will; you shall**

young [jʌŋ] adj jung ▷ n **the ~ pl** (~ people) die jungen Leute pl; (animals) die Jungen pl; **youngster** ['jʌŋstə°] n Jugendliche(r) mf

your ['jɔː°] adj sing dein; polite form Ihr; pl euer; polite form Ihr; **have you hurt ~ leg?** hast du dir/haben Sie sich das Bein verletzt?

you're ['jʊə°] contr of **you are**

yours ['jɔːz] pron sing deine(r, s); polite form Ihre(r, s); pl eure(r, s); polite form Ihre(r, s); **is this ~?** gehört das dir/Ihnen?; **a friend of ~** ein Freund von dir/Ihnen

yourself [jɔː'sɛlf] pron sing dich; polite form sich; **have you hurt ~?** hast du dich/haben Sie sich verletzt?; **did you do it ~?** hast du/haben Sie es selbst gemacht?; **(all) by ~** allein; **yourselves** pron pl euch; polite form sich; **have you hurt ~?** habt ihr euch/haben Sie sich verletzt?; **did you do it ~?** habt ihr/haben Sie es selbst gemacht?; **(all) by ~** allein

youth [juːθ] n (period) Jugend f; (young man) junger Mann; (young people) Jugend f; **youth group** n

Jugendgruppe f; **youth hostel** n
Jugendherberge f
you've [juːv] *contr of* **you have**
yucky [ˈjʌkɪ] *adj. (fam)* eklig
yummy [ˈjʌmɪ] *adj (fam)* lecker
yuppie, yuppy [ˈjʌpɪ] n Yuppie
m

Z

zap [zæp] *vt (Inform)* löschen; *(in
computer game)* abknallen ▷ *vi (TV)*
zappen; **zapper** n *(TV)*
Fernbedienung f; **zapping** n *(TV)*
ständiges Umschalten, Zapping *nt*
zebra [ˈzebrə, ?? ˈziːbrə] *(US)* n
Zebra *nt*; **zebra crossing** n *(Brit)*
Zebrastreifen m
zero [ˈzɪərəʊ] *(pl* **-es)** n Null f; **10
degrees below ~** 10 Grad unter
null
zest [zest] n *(enthusiasm)*
Begeisterung f
zigzag [ˈzɪgzæg] n Zickzack m
▷ *vi (person, vehicle)* im Zickzack
gehen/fahren; *(path)* im Zickzack
verlaufen
zinc [zɪŋk] n Zink *nt*
zip [zɪp] n *(Brit)* Reißverschluss m
▷ *vt:* **to ~ (up)** den Reißverschluss
zumachen; *(Inform)* zippen; **zip
code** n *(US)* Postleitzahl f; **Zip
disk®** n *(Inform)* ZIP-Diskette® f;

Zip drive® n (*Inform*)
ZIP-Laufwerk® nt; **Zip file®** n
(*Inform*) ZIP-Datei® f; **zipper** n
(*US*) Reißverschluss m

zit [zɪt] n (*fam*) Pickel m

zodiac ['zəʊdɪæk] n Tierkreis m;
sign of the ~ Tierkreiszeichen
nt

zone [zəʊn] n Zone f; (*area*)
Gebiet nt; (*in town*) Bezirk m

zoo [zuː] n Zoo m

zoom [zuːm] vi (*move fast*)
brausen, sausen ▷ n: **~ (lens)**
Zoomobjektiv nt; **zoom in** vi
(*Foto*) heranzoomen (*on* an +*akk*)

zucchini [zuːˈkiːnɪ] (*pl* **-(s)**) n
(*US*) Zucchini f

2